The Rough Guide to

Andalucía

D0168491

There are more than one hundred and fifty Rough Guide titles
covering destinations from Amsterdam to Zimbabwe

Forthcoming titles include

Argentina • Croatia • Ecuador • Southeast Asia

Rough Guide Reference Series

Classical Music • Country Music • Drum 'n' Bass • English Football
European Football • House • The Internet • Jazz • Music USA • Opera
Reggae • Rock Music • Techno • Unexplained Phenomena • World Music

Rough Guide Phrasebooks

Czech • Dutch • Egyptian Arabic • European Languages • French • German
Greek • Hindi & Urdu • Hungarian • Indonesian • Italian • Japanese
Mandarin Chinese • Mexican Spanish • Polish • Portuguese • Russian
Spanish • Swahili • Thai • Turkish • Vietnamese

Rough Guides on the Internet

www.roughguides.com

ROUGH GUIDE CREDITS

Text editor: Lisa Nellis
Series editor: Mark Ellingham
Editorial: Martin Dunford, Jonathan Buckley, Jo Mead, Kate Berens, Amanda Tomlin, Ann-Marie Shaw, Paul Gray, Helena Smith, Judith Bamber, Orla Duane, Olivia Eccleshall, Ruth Blackmore, Geoff Howard, Claire Saunders, Gavin Thomas, Alexander Mark Rogers, Polly Thomas, Joe Staines, Andrew Tomičić, Richard Lim, Duncan Clark, Peter Buckley (UK); Andrew Rosenberg, Mary Beth Maioli, Don Bapst, Stephen Timblin (US)
Production: Susanne Hillen, Andy Hilliard, Link Hall, Helen Ostick, Julia Bovis, Michelle Draycott,

Katie Pringle, Robert Evers, Niamh Hatton, Mike Hancock, Robert McKinlay
Cartography: Melissa Baker, Maxine Repath, Nichola Goodliffe, Ed Wright
Picture research: Louise Boulton, Sharon Martins
Online editors: Kelly Cross (US)
Finance: John Fisher, Gary Singh, Edward Downey, Mark Hall, Tim Bill
Marketing & Publicity: Richard Trillo, Niki Smith, David Wearn, Jemima Broadbridge (UK); Jean-Marie Kelly, Myra Campolo, Simon Carloss (US)
Administration: Tania Hummel, Demelza Dallow, Julie Sanderson

ACKNOWLEDGEMENTS

On our third edition grateful **thanks** must go to Josep Vergés and Angela García for more invaluable information and hospitality in Almería, to Pau for tremendous work in Sevilla and Huelva as well as to Claire Hunt in Málaga and Antonia Secchi in Granada. A big thank you also goes to Han for priceless help and support (especially when the battery went flat) along the highways and byways. Valuable assistance on the ground for this edition was also rendered by Josefina and Andreas del Castillo in Alcaudique, Pepe Morales in Punta Umbria, Manuel Carlos Viñuelas in Sevilla, Mª. Angeles Rodríguez Ruiz in Antequera, Gina de los Santos in Sevilla, Jean & Christine Hofer in El Chorro, Maddy Conway in Ronda, James Stuart in Vejer, Vicente Sierra in Aracena, Adam and Teresa Page in Gaucín, Vanessa Reyes in Marbella, Rafael Calzado Reca in Andujar, Mercedes Galvez in Jaén, Pasqual Rovira in Rute, Elma Thompson in Nerja and Kiki Didden in Granada.

Special thanks are also due to Hugh Broughton for architectural suggestions, Tony Wailey for Civil War background, Huw Morgan for information on birdspotting and Pilar Ortuño Anaya for her comments on modern politics. We would also like to thank Inma Felip and the staff of the Spanish National Tourist Office in London for their help with numerous queries, and the staff of the Sherry Institute in London.

Last but by no means least a big thank you to all involved at Rough Guides for a great editorial and production job; we'd like to single out our editors Lisa Nellis and Paul Gray, US and Australasian Basics researchers Robert Mackey, Stephen Townshend and Alistair McDermott, Robert McKinlay for typesetting, Nichola Goodliffe for cartography, Matthew Teller for proofreading and Sharon Martins for picture research.

PUBLISHING INFORMATION

This third edition published August 2000 by Rough Guides Ltd, 62–70 Shorts Gardens, London, WC2H 9AH.
Distributed by the Penguin Group:
Penguin Books Ltd, 27 Wrights Lane, London W8 5TZ.
Penguin Putnam, Inc. 375 Hudson Street, NY 10014, USA.
Penguin Books Australia Ltd, 487 Maroondah Highway, PO Box 257, Ringwood, Victoria 3134, Australia.
Penguin Books Canada Ltd, 10 Alcorn Avenue, Toronto, Ontario, Canada M4V 1E4.
Penguin Books (NZ) Ltd, 182–190 Wairau Road, Auckland 10, New Zealand.
Typeset in Linotron Univers and Century Old Style to an original design by Andrew Oliver.
Printed in England by Clays Ltd, St Ives PLC.
Illustrations in Part One and Part Three by Edward Briant.

The Rough Guide to

Andalucía

written and researched by

Geoff Garvey and Mark Ellingham

with additional contributions by

Pau Sandham and Chris Stewart

ROUGH
GUIDES

We set out to do something different when the first Rough Guide was published in 1982. Mark Ellingham, just out of university, was travelling in Greece. He brought along the popular guides of the day, but found they were all lacking in some way. They were either strong on ruins and museums but went on for pages without mentioning a beach or taverna. Or they were so conscious of the need to save money that they lost sight of Greece's cultural and historical significance. Also, none of the books told him anything about Greece's contemporary life – its politics, its culture, its people, and how they lived.

So with no job in prospect, Mark decided to write his own guidebook, one which aimed to provide practical information that was second to none, detailing the best beaches and the hottest clubs and restaurants, while also giving hard-hitting accounts of every sight, both famous and obscure, and providing up-to-the-minute information on contemporary culture. It was a guide that encouraged independent travellers to find the best of Greece, and was a great success, getting shortlisted for the Thomas Cook travel guide award, and encouraging Mark, along with three friends, to expand the series.

The Rough Guide list grew rapidly and the letters flooded in, indicating a much broader readership than had been anticipated, but one which uniformly appreciated the Rough Guide mix of practical detail and humour, irreverence and enthusiasm. Things haven't changed. The same four friends who began the series are still the caretakers of the Rough Guide mission today: to provide the most reliable, up-to-date and entertaining information to independent-minded travellers of all ages, on all budgets.

We now publish more than 150 titles and have offices in London and New York. The travel guides are written and researched by a dedicated team of more than 100 authors, based in Britain, Europe, the USA and Australia. We have also created a unique series of phrasebooks to accompany the travel series, along with an acclaimed series of music guides, and a best-selling pocket guide to the Internet and World Wide Web. We also publish comprehensive travel information on our web site:

www.roughguides.com

HELP US UPDATE

We've gone to a lot of effort to ensure that the third edition of *The Rough Guide to Andalucía* is accurate and up-to-date. However, things change – places get "discovered", opening hours are notoriously fickle, restaurants and rooms raise prices or lower standards. If you feel we've got it wrong or left something out, we'd like to know, and if you can remember the address, the price, the time, the phone number, so much the better.

We'll credit all contributions, and send a copy of the next edition (or any other Rough Guide if you prefer) for the best letters. Please mark letters: "Rough Guide Andalucía Update" and send to:

Rough Guides, 62–70 Shorts Gardens, London WC2H 9AH, or Rough Guides, 4th Floor, 345 Hudson St, New York, NY 10014.

Or send email to: mail@roughguides.co.uk
Online updates about this book can be found on Rough Guides' Web site at www.roughguides.com

We'd like to thank the readers of previous editions who took the time to write in with comments, corrections and suggestions. For this edition we were considerably helped by letters, faxes or emails from:

John & Carol Johnson, Ditteke Mensink, Ann Manley, Eddy le Couvreur, Stan Roberts, Robert Shore, Lucia Sanou, Jürgen Paeger, Stephen Hayward, Alan Lambert, Margaret Glover, Roger Walker, Tony Gamble, Susan Bostock, Karen Granat, Christine & Eamonn Malone, Marian de Schipper, Peter R Wenban, Martyn & Margaret Mitchell, Sam Deasy, Marion Seymour, Miriam Toblowsky, Simon Cleaver, Miriam Zukas, Thijs Boel, Andrew & Helen Evans, Joan Ratcliffe, Brian Catlos, David Thomas, Peter Johnson, Geoffrey Vaughan, David Hook, Claudio González Carrasco, Juan José Caballero Grimaldi, Katie Ward, John Taylor, Lourdes Isasa López, Tarall Lundevall, Di Bligh, Jon & Jan Hilary, Jo Kewley, James Heron, Gail Johnson, Clive Jones & Sue Massie, Susan Bostock, Vanessa Conte & Dr Andrew Hogg, Sally Ashbrook, R J Jones, Terry Croft, Adrienne Byrne, Geme Rodríguez, Michael James Sproat, Tony Silver, Martin McGarry, Pete Martin, Andrew Gouldstone & Bronwyn Pugh, Danny Bethell, Alice Kildsgaard, Andy & Petra Chapman Gibbs, Sara Anstey, Mark Godber, Mrs J Young, Kay Burtenshaw, Joseph L Costello, Magnus Schoeman, Dr Gordon Watson, Mick McGrath, Jeremy Grant, Samantha Barton, Donna Fleming, Diane Davies, Nicholas Watson, Tim Mangan, R M M Rowe, Patrick Hughes, Rachel Silcock & Dean Smith, Roger Lushington, Darryn Snell, Jill Rose, Pauline Salamon & David Morgan, Rebecca Grimshaw & Alan Rigby, Mary Whelan, Mark Booth, Mr & Mrs D Widdup, Ton Langenhuyzen, Allegra Mostyn Owen & Daniel Jeffreys, Yasmin Ajmal, N J Parker, Sara Callender, Mike Wilson, H Sutcliffe, J W Klomp, Tony & Jane Keith, Lucia Alvarez de Toledo, Susan Ogden, Margaret A Twentyman, Jannie Pedersen, Alexandra Pemberton, Anne Kühn, David Chadwick, Susan Fisk & Miguel Giménez, Margaretha Schön, Elisabeth Stokke, Jon Miles, Mike Ramsey, Simon Edwards, Truusja Kofflard, Andrew Sloan, Paul & Elspeth Rowson, Leslie and Dawn Walker, Ian Howe, David Sheridan, K & M O'Mahoney, Frank Sierowski, Janet Ford, Rev David Jacks, Phil Brew, Sarah Woolston, Anna White, Edwin Jansen & Gemmie Hermens, Ellen Anne Teigen, David White, Pella Bergquist, Angela Peebles, Carmen Jaldo, Manuel Sordo, Marja Dullaart, Sheila MacDonald, Tom Patton, Gabriella Vergés, Richard Brady, Stewart Horrocks, Monica Cornelis, Anthony Leavis, Maureen & Brian Blain, Jo O'Rourke, Loli Cervantes, Ken Porter, Barnaby Rogerson, Loretta Chilcoat, Michael Baker. Harriet Lloyd, Andrew & Karen Bevans, Julia Fiehn, J Keeling, A Farrimond, Carmen Ladron de Guevara, David Cramp, D A Simmons, Mary Thomas, Dan Posner, Laura Smith Spark, Alastair Douglas, Iain Campbell Aird, Ian Maunders & Nicola Green, Lawrence Hansen, R J & E A Cripps, Jackie Downes & Michael Cupit, Rosalind, Juliet & Richard Evans, May Shortland, Frederik Saxborn, Hamish M Brown, Gabriele B Dahms, Anne Cartwright, Ann Sargent, Helen Willson, Clare West, K C Simpkins, Susan Davison, Peter Holland, Robert Campbell, Ian Nicol, J Elisa Bayley, Björn Svensson, D L & D C Baker, Richard R Rowe, Edwin A J Truman, Robert Walker, Graham Perkins, Mark Ottaway, Chris Pajdowski, Phil Wood, E A Lawson, Stewart Smith, Paul de Zylva, J A Groves, Eusebio García, Jenny & Jay Close, Rev John A R Methuen, Judith Flanagan, Steven Ashton, Daniel Britten, José Antonio Roldán Caro, David & Wera Hougham, Ruth N Cohen, Gavin McNaughton, I A Monroe, Helen Clarke, John & Jeanette Spooner, Ulver Fallon, Bjorg Bjerkreim, Irene López Martínez, Trevor & Lynne Meacock, H Massey, G B Wilkins, H T Taylor, Bas Hillebrand, T R W Mundy, Francis Chantree, Torkel Røstad, Rob Wightman, Elaine Jennings, M A Jones, Charles Stuart, Joy Fisher & Geoffrey Taylor, Paul Hughes, Robert Alcock, Deirdre Maultside, I M Frampton, Nic & Tom Cusack, Robert & Lin Coleman, Mike Ford, Tony Lancelott, Judge Nicholas Philpot, Peter Roberts, Jane & Tony Keith, R H & P R Mahy, Jack Fortune, Fritz & Susanne Woldt, Adrien Hardels, Peg Aurand, Sylvia Morris, Peter Spiegel, Phoebe & John Nichols, D Winter, Chris Whiteman, Matthew Lonsdale, Michael Wilks & Sue Hogg, Pedro Tejada Rusillo, John F Watkins, Tina Scopa, Francis Chantree, Martien Behrens, Tarald Lundevall, Celia Gould, Juliet Gore, D C Bryant, Fred Spee & Sonja Nunnink, Alderman John Kelleher, Liz Wood, Alan R W Flowerday & Ann Daly, Sheila Cornett & Robin Dixon, John & Jan Hilary, A Quinn, Jeanne Marrazzo, J F E Paxton, Susan Murray, Bob & Jill Bewley, Alison Macdonald, Alfonso García Teno, Margaret Poethig, Bruce Little, Alvaro García-Manzano Salazar, Michael Graubart, Eileen Andel, Fiona Reeve & Cliff Speed, Harry Browne. L Reynolds. Z Bhanji, Simon Muth, Bob Scurr, Robin Palmer, Sue Berridge, Mary Cashin, Christopher Fitz-Simon, Peter & Carol Armon, Andrea Bruschini, Jean Hathaway, S Green, Jenny Holmes, Harvey Bell, Michael L Johnson, Peter Ratzer, D G Barnes, Trudi C Johnson, Bill & Carolyn Thomas, P S Heelis, R A & V J Hazelwood, N M Sackwood, Elena Posa, T G Bennett, Peter Bennett, Athene Reiss, Harry Mount, Ben Reiss, John McLaughlin, Rosario Acacio, Ellen Schot, Alan & Pauline Bourne, Beverly Kemp, Helen Farvis, Torben Retbøll, Wendy Anton, Barbara Hauck. L A Taylor, Clare Jennings, David Roberts, John Harper, Neil Adams, Jim Fletcher, Hazel Humphreys, George & Emily Cassedy, John Main, Dorothy Van Puyvelde, Sandra Milne, Pauline M Vann, Isabel Church & Peter White, and apologies to quite a few others whose names we were unable to decipher.

THE AUTHORS

Mark Ellingham started Rough Guides in 1981 – and co-wrote Spain, the second title in the series, the following year. He has spent time in Andalucía most years since then, both writing and researching, and doing nothing – a state he achieves most easily on a small farm in Las Alpujarras, south of Granada.

Geoff Garvey first experienced the lure of Iberia as an impoverished student when he hiked over the Spanish border at the fag-end of the Franco years and into a confrontation with the Guardia Civil, who seized a number of "seditious" volumes in his backpack. Undaunted, he pressed on to be captivated by the character of the people, the drama of the big sierras and the infinite variety of the customs and cultures. He currently writes on Spain from a North London base, but escapes whenever possible to the hills of the Sierra Morena and the bars of Sevilla.

CONTENTS

Introduction ix

LIST OF MAPS

MAP SYMBOLS

▬▬▬	Motorway	◆	Point of interest
═══	Major road	∴	Ruin/Archeological site
━━━	Minor road	🏛	Monastery
────	Track	✡	Synagogue
ⅢⅢⅢ	Steps	🅿	Parking
───────	Wall	⛷	Skiing
━ ━━ ━	Railway	⊠—⊠	Gates
●–·–·–·	Cable car	⚠	Campsite
── ──	Ferry route	ⓘ	Tourist information
∼∼∼∼	River	⊠	Post office
━ ━ ━	National boundary	◷	Phone office
▬▬ ··	Provincial boundary	◉	Hotel
━ ━ · ━	Chapter boundary	▮	Building
▲	Mountain peak	┿	Church/cathedral
◠	Caves	▒	Built-up area
☽	Dunes	░	Park
⋏	View point	▨	National Park
犬	Lighthouse	▱	Forest
✈	Airport	⸬	Beach

INTRODUCTION

Andalucía is the southernmost territory of Spain and the part of the Iberian peninsula that is most quintessentially Spanish. The popular image of Spain as a land of bullfights, flamenco, sherry and ruined castles derives from this spectacularly beautiful region. The influences that have washed over Andalucía since the first paintings were etched on cave walls here more than twenty-five thousand years ago are many – Phoenicians, Carthaginians, Greeks, Romans, Visigoths and Vandals all came and left their mark. And the most influential invaders of all, **the Moors**, who ruled the region for seven centuries and named it *al-Andalus*, have left an enduring imprint on Andalucian culture and customs.

The sight and sound of **flamenco**, when the guitar laments and heels stamp the boards, or *cante jondo*, Andalucía's blues, as it mournfully pierces the smoke-laden gloom of a backstreet café, also tell you there's something unique about the people here. The Muslim influence on speech and vocabulary, a stoical fatalism in the face of adversity, and an obsession with the drama of death are all facets of the modern Andalucian character. Contrastingly, the *andaluces* also love nothing more than a party and the colour and sheer energy of the region's countless and legendary **fiestas** – always in traditional flamenco costume worn with pride – make them among the most exciting in the world. The **romerías**, wild and semi-religious pilgrimages to honour local saints at country shrines are yet another excuse for a jamboree. And in quieter moments there are few greater pleasures than to join the drinkers at a local bar winding down over a glass of traditional *fino* (dry sherry from Jerez), while nibbling *tapas* – Andalucia's great titbit invention.

Few places in the world can boast such a wealth of **natural wonders** in so compact an area. The mighty Guadalquivir river which crosses and irrigates the region from its source in the Cazorla mountains of Jaén in the northeast, reaches the sea 400 kilometres away at the dune-fringed beaches and *marismas* of the **Coto Doñana National Park**, Europe's largest and most important wildlife sanctuary. To the east and towering above Granada, the peaks of the **Sierra Nevada** include the Spanish peninsula's highest mountain, snowcapped for most of the year, while thirty kilometres away and close to the sweltering beaches, sugar cane thrives. This crop was another contribution to Europe by the Moors, along with oranges, almonds, aubergines, saffron and most of the spices now used to flavour the region's cooking which features an astonishing variety of **seafood**. Nestling in the folds of the same mountains are the valleys of the Alpujarras, a wildly picturesque region dotted with dozens of mountain villages, many of them little changed since Moorish times. Further east again come the gulch-ridden badlands and lunar landscapes of Almería's deserts, sought out by film-makers and astronomers for the clearest skies in Europe.

On **the coast** it's easy to despair. Extending to the west of **Málaga** is the **Costa del Sol**, Europe's most developed resort area, with its beaches hidden behind a remorseless density of concrete hotels and apartment complexes. But even here the real Andalucía is still to be found if you're prepared to seek it out: go merely a few kilometres inland and you'll encounter the timeless Spain of white villages and wholehearted country fiestas. Travel further, both east and west, along the coast and you'll find some of the best beaches in all Spain, along the **Costa de la Luz**, near Cádiz, or the **Costa de Almería**.

Andalucía's sunshine image – projected across the world in advertising campaigns – belies the fact that this is also Spain's poorest region where an economy rooted in near-feudal land ownership (two per cent of the landowners possess fifty per cent of the land

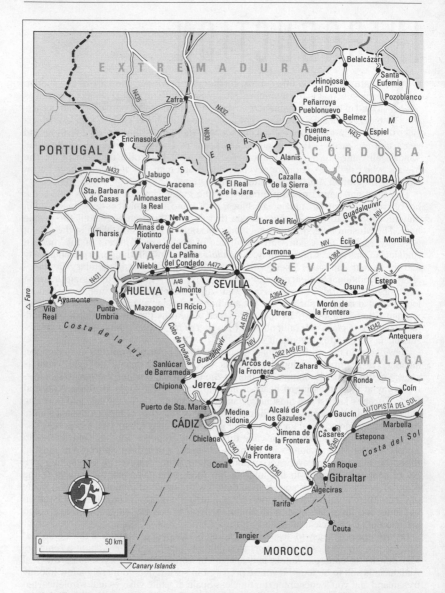

area) stifles investment and is the cause of desperate poverty. Rural life is bleak; you soon begin to notice the appalling **economic structure** of vast absentee-landlord estates, and landless peasants. The *andaluz* villages saw little economic aid or change during the Franco years, or indeed since, even though the former governing Socialist party has its principal power base here. Tourism in coastal areas has brought some respite to the alarmingly high levels of unemployment, and Spain's growing importance

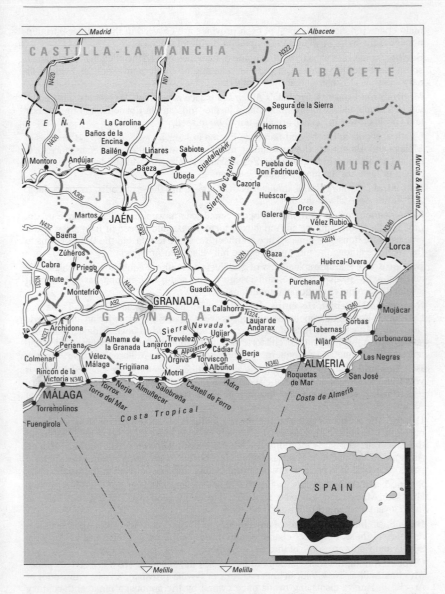

as a member of the European Union promises to speed up progress, but there is still a mighty long way to go.

Where to go: some highlights

Andalucía's manageable size makes it easy to take in something of each of its elements – inland cities, extensive coastline and mountaineous sierras – even on a brief visit. The main characteristics and appeal of each province are covered in the chapter introductions, but the more obvious and compelling highlights include:

Sevilla. Andalucía's capital city, the home of flamenco and all the clichés of the Spanish south has beautiful quarters, major Christian and Moorish monuments and extraordinary festivals at Easter and at the April *feria*.

Moorish monuments. Granada's Alhambra palace is perhaps the most sensual building in Europe; the exquisite Mezquita, a former mosque, in Córdoba, and the Alcázar and Giralda tower in Sevilla, are also not to be missed.

Castles. Niebla in Huelva and Baños de Encina in Jaén, as well as those in the cities of Málaga and Almería are the outstanding Moorish examples; the best Renaissance forts are at La Calahorra in Granada and Vélez Blanco in Almería, whilst hilltop Segura de la Sierra in Jaén has the most dramatic location.

Cathedrals. Sevilla's Gothic monster is the biggest, but those of Cádiz, Granada, Jaén, and Almería are all worthy of a visit.

Renaissance towns and hill villages. Small-scale towns and villages, once grand, now hardly significant, are an Andalucian forte. Baeza and Úbeda in Jaén are remarkable treasure-houses of Renaissance architecture, while Ronda and the White Towns to the west are among the most picturesque hill villages in Andalucía.

Baroque. The Baroque splendours of Andalucía are without equal; towns such as Écija and Osuna in Sevilla province, and Priego to the south of Córdoba have clusters of stunning Baroque churches and mansions.

Roman and prehistoric ruins. Itálica near Sevilla, Baelo Claudia near Tarifa and Carmona's Roman necropolis are all impressive Roman sites, while for an atmospheric "lost city" Mulva, in the hills of the Sierra Morena, is hard to beat. Andalucía also has some of the most important prehistoric sites in Europe, including a group of third millennium BC dolmens at Antequera, and the remarkable Los Millares site near Almería.

Beaches and resorts. For brashness and nightlife it has to be the Costa del Sol, but you'll find that the more authentic resorts such as Nerja, Almuñecar and Mojácar are less frenzied. The region's best beaches lie along the Atlantic coast and to the east of Almería.

Hiking. The Sierra Nevada and the nearby foothills of Las Alpujarras in Granada are excellent places for hiking, as are the densely wooded hills of the Sierra de Cazorla and the Sierra de Morena – including the latter's less well-known offshoot, the Sierra de Aracena, in the north of Huelva. Andalucía's dozen or so *parques naturales* (natural parks) are located in areas of great natural beauty, and are detailed in the Guide.

Seafood. This is Andalucía's speciality and is excellent all along the coast but particularly so in Málaga and seafood-crazy Cádiz. The many good places to try it are listed in the relevant chapters throughout the Guide.

Bars. Spain has the most bars of any country in Europe, and Andalucía has more than its share of these. For sheer character and diversity, the bars of the cities of Córdoba, Sevilla and Cádiz are some of the best anywhere.

Offbeat. Among the more curious things to see in Andalucía are a self-styled "pope" who has built a "New Vatican" near Utrera in Sevilla province; a rosary museum at Aroche in Huelva displaying beads once owned by the famous; a nineteenth-century English-designed housing estate in the middle of the city of Huelva; a mini-Hollywood in Almería which preserves the film-set of famous "paella westerns"; still-functioning nineteenth-century sulphur baths used by Lord Byron at Carratraca in Málaga; a Communist village run on Utopian principles at Marinaleda in Sevilla; the spectacular mines of Río Tinto in Huelva; and Andalucía's oldest inn, complete with highwayman's cell, at Alfarnate, in the rugged Axarquía district of Málaga.

When to go

In terms of **climate** the question is mainly one of how much heat you can take. During the **summer** months of July and August temperatures of over 40°C (104°F) on the coast are normal and inland they rise even higher in cities such as Sevilla, generally reckoned to be the hottest in Spain. The solution here is to follow the natives and get about in the relative cool of the mornings and late afternoons, finding somewhere shady to rest up as the city roasts in the midday furnace. The major resorts are busy in July and packed in August (the Spanish holiday month) when prices also are at their highest.

Better times to visit are the **spring** months of April, May and early June when lower temperatures combine with a greener landscape awash with wild flowers. The **autumn** is good, too, although by this time much of the coastal landscape looks parched and the resorts have begun to wind down; in hilly areas, however, such as the sierras of Cazorla and Aracena and the high valleys of Las Alpujarras the splendours of autumn can be especially scenic. The **winter** months – particularly December and January – can often be dismal and wet as well as cold at altitude, although Almería sees only one day of rain a year on average and in winter has many days of perfect crystal visibility.

AVERAGE DAILY TEMPERATURES (°C)		Feb	April	June	Aug	Oct	Dec
Almería	av. max temp	16	20	26	29	23	17
	av. min temp	8	12	18	22	16	9
Cádiz	av. max temp	16	21	27	30	23	16
	av. min temp	9	12	18	20	16	9
Córdoba	av. max temp	16	23	32	36	24	14
	av. min temp	5	10	17	20	13	5
Granada	av. max temp	14	20	30	34	22	12
	av. min temp	2	7	14	17	9	2
Huelva	av. max temp	18	22	29	32	25	17
	av. min temp	7	11	16	18	14	7
Jaén	av. max temp	14	20	30	34	22	12
	av. min temp	5	10	17	21	13	5
Málaga	av. max temp	17	21	28	30	24	17
	av. min temp	8	11	17	20	15	9
Sevilla	av. max temp	17	23	32	36	26	16
	av. min temp	6	11	17	20	14	7
Tarifa	av. max temp	17	20	24	27	23	17
	av. min temp	11	13	17	20	17	1

To convert °C to °F, multiply by 9/5 and add 32

PART ONE

THE

BASICS

GETTING THERE FROM BRITAIN

BY AIR

There's a vast number of **flights** from Britain to Andalucía throughout the year, mostly serving the Costa del Sol. Out of season, or if you're prepared to book at the last minute, they can be very good value indeed – often as little as £80–100 return to Málaga, though more likely £150–230 in the height of summer.

No-frills operators such as EasyJet and Go (see box p.4) are also a good source for very cheap deals. If you want to shop around and have access to the Internet, you could check out sites such as *www.cheapflights.co.uk/Destination. html* which gives a comprehensive list of discount flights worldwide.

CHARTER FLIGHTS

Charters are usually block-booked by package holiday firms, but even in the middle of August they're rarely completely full and spare seats are often sold off at discounts. For an idea of current prices and availability, contact any high street travel agent, or a specialist agency or operator. The widest selection of ads for London departures is invariably found in the classified pages of the London listings magazine *Time Out*, the *Evening Standard* or *TNT*. For departures **from other British airports** check the local evening papers and *The Sunday Times* and *Observer*. The agents and operators listed on p.4–5 make a good start.

The independent travel specialists, STA Travel, offer a range of special discount flights, most

frequently on the Madrid and Barcelona routes, while **students** – and anyone else **under 26** – can also try Usit Campus; they offer return flights to Málaga for £135–165. Student union travel bureaus can usually fix you up with flights through one of these operators, and they're both worth calling for charters, whether you're a student or not.

The major disadvantage of charter flights is the fixed return date – a maximum of four weeks from the outward journey. Some return charters are good value even if you use only half, but for more flexibility you'll probably want to buy a ticket for a scheduled flight.

SCHEDULED FLIGHTS

Spain's national airline, Iberia, and British Airways have the widest range of **scheduled flights**, including regular services to Sevilla and Málaga. British Airways also link many regional airports to its London flights to southern Spain.

Scheduled flights are rarely the cheapest option but some of their special offers can be highly competitive, especially if you need the greater **flexibility** of a scheduled airline. They offer, for example, open-jaw flights (fly in to one airport, back from another); fly-drive deals; and inexpensive connections from most regional UK airports. The cheapest tickets with Iberia or BA go by various names at different times of the year, but they are usually valid for one month only, require you to stay at least one Saturday night, and don't allow for change or cancellation. Consequently there's no great difference

SAMPLE SCHEDULED FLIGHT PRICES TO SPAIN		
	Low	High
From **London** to:		
Madrid	£140	£240
Málaga	£150	£270
Sevilla	£150	£270
Gibraltar	£145	£270
From **Manchester** to:		
Madrid	£160	£260
Málaga	£254	£345
Sevilla	£254	£345
Gibraltar	£190	£280

AIRLINES, AGENTS AND OPERATORS

AIRLINES

British Airways 156 Regent St, London W1R 5TA (☎0845/773 3377; www.british-airways.com). From Heathrow and Gatwick to Málaga, Sevilla and Gibraltar.

Buzz, Endeavour House, Stansted Airport, Essex CM24 1RS (☎0870/240 7070; www.buzzaway.com). Cheap weekly flights to Jerez on Saturdays from March to October; service frequency may increase if demand is sufficient.

EasyJet (☎0870/600 0000; www.easyjet.com) Daily low cost flights to Málaga from Luton and Liverpool.

Go Enterprise House, Stansted Airport, Essex CM2 1SB (☎0845/605 4321; www.go-fly.com). Cheap daily flights from Stansted to Málaga.

Iberia 29 Glasshouse St, London W1R 5TA (☎0870/534 1341; www.iberia.com). Direct flights from London Heathrow to Málaga and Sevilla, and from Manchester via Barcelona. Connections (via Mádrid) to Jerez, Almería and Granada.

Monarch Airlines Luton Airport, Luton, Bedfordshire LU2 9NU (☎08700/40 50 40; www.monarch/airlines.com). Competitively priced airline flying from Luton to Málaga and Gibraltar daily in summer, and five times weekly in winter; also daily summer flights from Manchester to Málaga.

AGENTS AND OPERATORS

Andalucian Adventures Washpool, Horsley, Gloucestershire GL6 OPP (☎ & fax 01453/834 137; www.andalucian-adventures.co.uk). Painting and walking holidays in Córdoba province and Las Alpujarras.

APA Travel 138 Eversholt St, London NW1 (☎020/7387 5337). Spanish flight specialists.

AVRO plc Vantage House, 1 Weir Road, Wimbledon, London SW19 8UX (☎020/8715 0000). Specialists in charter and scheduled flights.

B&B Abroad 5 World's End Lane, Green Street Green, Orpington, Kent BR6 6AA (☎01689/857 838). Operator with a wide range of bed and breakfast accommodation – from rustic farmhouses to luxurious country manors. Also has hotel accommodation.

Cox and Kings 4th Floor, Gordon House, Greencoat Place, London SW1P 1PH (☎020/7873 5000; www.coxandkings.co.uk). Nature tours of Andalucía; staying in farmhouses.

Dance Holiday Company 12 Chapel St, North, Colchester, Essex CO2 7AT (☎01206/577000). Flamenco, salsa and Argentinian tango holiday courses in Málaga, Granada and Jerez.

Discover Adventure 5 Netherhampton Cottages, Netherhampton Road, Salisbury, Wiltshire SP2 8PX (☎01722/741123; www.discoveradventure.com). Mountain bike trips across the Sierra Nevada with your own bike or theirs, plus guided walking holidays in Las Alpujarras.

Exodus Expeditions 9 Weir Rd, London SW12 OLT (☎020/8675 5550). Walking and cycling in Andalucía.

Explore Worldwide 1 Frederick St, Aldershot, Hants GU11 (☎01252/760333). Walking in Andalucía, Sierra Nevada and Picos de Europa.

between these and a charter ticket but prices are competitive: fares start from around £210 return from London to Málaga in low season up to £280 in July and August; it's worth shopping around the various operators as there can sometimes be significant differences in their fares for the same destination. For a more flexible ticket, such as BA's "Excursion" fare – which is valid for six months, can be upgraded and is fully refundable – you're looking at paying around £440 from London to Málaga (£475 from Manchester) and £440 from London to Sevilla (£475 from Manchester); off-peak deals can slash these fares by up to £300, so it may be worth your while enquiring.

PACKAGES AND CITY BREAKS

Package holiday deals, too, can be worth looking at. Certainly if you book late – or out of season – you'll often find incredible prices. While these may seem to restrict you to some of the worst parts of the coast, remember that there's no

Gourmet Birds Windrush, Coles Lane, Brasted, Westerham, Kent TN16 1NN (☎01959/563627). *One-week horse-riding and birdwatching holidays in the countryside around Ronda.*

Headwater Holidays 146 London Rd, Northwich, Cheshire CW9 5HH (☎01606/813333). *Trekking holidays in the Alpujarras and Sierra de Aracena.*

Individual Travellers Bignor, Pulborough, West Sussex RH20 1QD (☎01798/869461). *Farmhouses, cottages and village houses all over Spain.*

Keytel International 402 Edgware Rd, London W2 1ED (☎020/7402 8182). *Official UK agents for the paradores in Spain.*

Kirker Travel 3 New Concordia Wharf, Mill Street, London SE1 (☎020/7231 3333). *Tours of the Coto de Doñana National Park led by wildlife experts.*

Lupus Travel 11 Vale Rd, Tunbridge Wells, Kent TN1 1BS (☎01892/553500). *Cheap charter flights to Spain; also does scheduled flight deals and packages.*

Magic of Spain 227 Shepherd's Bush Rd, London W6 7AS (☎020/8741 4440). *High-quality, out-of-the-way hotels, paradores and villas.*

Mundi Color 276 Vauxhall Bridge Rd, London SW1 (☎020/7828 6021). *Spanish specialists for flights, packages, city breaks and paradores.*

Peng Travel (☎01708/471832). *Naturist holidays in Almería province.*

Ramblers Holidays Box 43, Welwyn Garden City, AL8 6PQ (☎01707/331133). *Walking and hiking holidays throughout Spain, including Andalucía.*

Rustic Blue Barrio de Ermita, 18412 Bubión, Granada, Spain (☎958 76 33 81, fax 958 76 31 34; *www.rusticblue.com*). *Alpujarras-based company specializing in rural and activity holidays (rambling and horse trekking) and renting traditional village houses.*

Sherpa Expeditions 131a Heston Rd, Hounslow, Middlesex TW5 0RD (☎020/8577 2717). *Trekking in the Sierra Nevada and the Alpujarras.*

Spain at Heart Watley Farm, Watley, Frome, Somerset BA11 3LA (☎01373/836070). *Tutored painting and drawing holidays in the Axarquía region of Málaga province.*

STA Travel (*www.statravel.co.uk*) 86 Old Brompton Rd, London SW7 (☎020/7361 6161); 117 Euston Rd, London NW1 (☎020/7361 6161); 25 Queen's Rd, Bristol BS8 1QE (☎0117/929 4399); 38 Sidney St, Cambridge CB2 3HX (☎01223/366966); 36 George St, Oxford OX1 2OJ (☎01865/792 800); 75 Deansgate, Manchester M3 2BW (☎0161/834 0668). *Independent travel specialists offering discounted flights.*

Time Off 1 Elmfield Park, Bromley, Kent BR1 1LU (☎0845/733 6622). *City breaks to Granada and Sevilla.*

Travellers Way Hewell Lane, Tardebigge, Bromsgrove, Worcs B60 1LP (☎01527/836791). *Tailor-made holidays and city breaks in Andalucía.*

Usit Campus 52 Grosvenor Gdns, London SW1 (☎0870/240 1010; *www.usitcampus.co.uk*); 541 Bristol Rd, Selly Oak, Birmingham (☎021/414 1848); 39 Queen's Rd, Clifton, Bristol (☎0117/929 2494); 5 Emmanuel St, Cambridge (☎01223/324283); 53 Forest Rd, Edinburgh (☎0131/225 6111); 166 Deansgate, Manchester (☎0161/833 2046); 13 High St, Oxford (☎01865/242067). Also in YHA shops and on university campuses throughout Britain. *Youth/student specialist.*

Waymark Holidays 44 Windsor Rd, Slough SL1 2EJ (☎01753/516477). *Walking holidays in Andalucía.*

Wine Trails Greenways, Vann Lake, Ockley, Dorking (☎01306/712111). *Wine-based tours of Andalucía.*

---

compulsion to stick around your hotel. Get a good enough deal and it can be worth it simply for the flight, with transfer to a reasonably comfortable hotel laid on for a night or two at each end. Bargains can be found at virtually any high street travel agent – look for Skytours' brochure which offers most of the Costa del Sol resorts. Prices for two weeks in a self-catering apartment on the Costa del Sol (based on four people sharing), including flights, start at around £300 per person (low season) and rise to around £450 in July and

August. Fly-drive deals are well worth considering as a combined air ticket and car rental arrangement can be excellent value. Considerable discounts (up to £200) are often to be had on these prices by booking early or ringing around at the last minute.

City breaks are available to several Spanish cities, with Sevilla and Granada the most popular destinations in Andalucía. Flying from London or Manchester, prices start at around £280 for three days (two nights) for both destinations;

adding extra nights or upgrading your hotel is possible, too, at a reasonable cost. The prices always include return flights and bed and breakfast in a centrally located one-, two- or three-star hotel. Again, ask your travel agent for the best deal, and check the addresses in the "Agents" box.

BY TRAIN

You've got the choice between making the Channel crossing by boat or taking the Eurostar as far as Paris. Both options involve changing trains in **Paris** (and stations, from Nord to Austerlitz via Metro line #5), and again at the Spanish border. The standard rail and boat journey is around 27 to 29 hours, from London to Barcelona or Madrid; with the Eurostar, it's around 20 to 21 hours. If you're prepared to pay a good deal extra, you can take a sleeper on the Trenhotel from Paris to Madrid or Barcelona direct, which reduces the journey by 2–3 hours.

Current departures are at 9.30am from Charing Cross if you're crossing to France by boat, or 4.23pm from Waterloo if you're taking the Eurostar. Either way, you pick up your connection in Paris around 9.30–11pm, change trains at Portbou or Irún the next morning at around 8.15 or 9.15am, and arrive in Barcelona at around 12.30pm, and in Madrid at around 3pm. To get to Málaga from Barcelona will take you another 9 hours. The journey to Málaga from Madrid takes between 4hr 30min to 6 hours, depending on the type of train.

TICKETS AND PASSES

A **standard rail ticket** from London to Málaga, Sevilla or Granada will currently cost you around £209 return for travelling by Eurostar to Paris (going by non-Eurostar services takes longer and costs almost the same). Reservation charges from Paris, which can be reserved before travelling, are £3–4 for a seat or £10–15 for a couchette. Details and tickets are available through some travel agents, Usit Campus, Wasteels or Rail Europe (see box below) and it's currently cheaper – especially if you're a student – to buy your Eurostar tickets from such agents as they offer special combined Eurostar/SNCF ticket deals.

If you're under 26, or if you plan to use Spanish trains extensively, there are better-value options than simply buying a return ticket. The best-known

TRAIN AND BUS INFORMATION

Eurolines National Express, 164 Buckingham Palace Road, London SW1 (☎0870/514 3219; *www.gobycoach.com*)

Eurostar Waterloo Station, London SE1 (☎0870/518 6186; *www.eurostar.com*)

Rail Europe Victoria Station, London SW1 (☎0870/584 8848; *www.raileurope.co.uk*)

Wasteels Victoria Station, London SW1 (☎020/7834 7066; *www.greyro.com/ wasteels-tickets.html*)

is to buy an **InterRail pass** from Rail Europe or a travel agent; the only restriction is that you must have been resident in Europe for at least six months. The pass comes in two forms: either an InterRail Global pass, valid for one month's unlimited travel in 26 European countries including Spain (£349/259 for under-26s), or an InterRail Zonal pass, whereby the 26 countries are split into seven zones and you choose which countries you want the pass to be valid for – Spain is grouped with Portugal and Morocco. A 22-day pass for any one zone costs £229/159; any two zones, valid for one month, costs £279/209; any three, also for one month, £309/229. In addition, all InterRail passes offer discounts on rail travel in the UK, Channel ferries, and ferries from Spain to the Balearics and Morocco. Since Spain has an extensive rail network this is basically a bargain, though be prepared to pay various and unpredictable supplements (see p.31) on some of the Spanish services, and be aware that they are not valid on AVE or EuroMed trains, or on one or two private lines.

BY BUS

Travelling by **bus** to Andalucía works out to be more expensive than the cheapest charter flights. The main **bus routes** from Britain to Spain are from London to Barcelona (5 weekly in summer, 3 weekly out of season; 24hr), Alicante (3 weekly; 32hr) and San Sebastián (3 weekly; 21hr). There are also two buses a week to Algeciras via Paris (39hr), Madrid (26hr; more buses run this far in season), Málaga and the Costa del Sol (33hr). Expect to pay around £80 one way and £140 return to reach any destination in Andalucía. All these routes are operated by Eurolines in Britain and by Iberbus/Linebus and Julia in Spain. In both Britain and Spain tickets are bookable through most major travel agents; Eurolines sells tickets and through-transport to London at all British National Express bus terminals.

To the Spanish border the journey is long but quite bearable – just make sure you take along enough to eat, drink and read, and a small amount of French and Spanish currency for coffee and the like. The final ten hours are a bit of an ordeal and you may reach your destination seat-sore and road-weary, wondering why you didn't fly in the first place. There are stops for around twenty minutes every four to five hours and the routine is also broken by the Dover–Calais ferry (which is included in the cost of the ticket), if you choose not to travel by the Eurostar.

BY CAR, FERRY AND EUROTUNNEL

The bus routes follow the most direct road routes from London to southern Spain: if you plan to **drive** them yourself, unless you're into non-stop rally motoring, you'll need roughly to double their times. There are now two **direct ferry sailings** to **Bilbao** and **Santander** from Britain which are worth considering as a way of cutting down on fatigue and avoiding expensive autoroute tolls crossing France. See the box on p.8 for ferry company addresses, or contact your local travel agent for the latest ticket and sailing details; alternatively you can check out the ferries' Web site at *www.seaview.co.uk*

EUROTUNNEL AND CROSS-CHANNEL SERVICES

The **Eurotunnel** service through the Channel Tunnel doesn't significantly affect travel times for

drivers to Spain, though it does of course speed up the cross-Channel section of the journey. Eurotunnel operates trains 24 hours a day carrying cars, motorcycles, buses and their passengers, taking 35 minutes between Folkestone and Calais. At peak times, services operate every twenty minutes and during the night there are one to two trains hourly, which makes advance booking unnecessary, although if you have a motorcycle, caravan or motorised caravan it would be advisable. A return ticket currently costs around £149–199 per vehicle (passengers included).

The alternative cross-Channel options for travellers heading to Andalucía via Barcelona are the conventional **ferry** or **hovercraft** links from Dover or Folkestone to Calais or Boulogne. With more time you might want to consider one of the ferries to Caen, Le Havre, Cherbourg or St Malo (from Portsmouth) or even Roscoff (from Plymouth). Any of these cuts out the trek round or through Paris, and opens up some interesting detours around Brittany and the French Atlantic coast. Ferry **prices** vary according to the time of year and, for motorists, according to the size of your car. The Dover–Calais/Boulogne runs, for example, start at about £60–90 one-way (£125–155 open return) for a car, two adults and two kids, but this figure doubles in high season. Foot passengers should be able to cross for about £10–25 one-way or £25–50 open return.

TO SANTANDER AND BILBAO

The direct car and passenger **ferry services** from England to Spain are convenient but expensive.

The ferry from **Plymouth to Santander** is operated by Brittany Ferries, takes 24 hours and runs on Mondays and Wednesdays during the summer (April to mid-Sept) and Wednesdays and Sundays the rest of the year. Ticket prices vary enormously according to the season, the number of passengers carried and the length of time you want the ticket to be valid for; a return ticket for a small car and two adults costs around £197–359 in low season, £312–569 in mid-season, and £352–644 in high season. Foot passengers pay around £50–80 one-way (depending on season), and everyone has to book some form of accommodation; cheapest is a pullman seat (£4–6). A berth (£19–24), and two- and four-berth cabins (£54–96) are other options. Tickets are best booked in advance, through any major travel agent.

MOTORAIL

SNCF operates the very useful **Motorail** service. Cars or motorbikes are loaded onto the special daily train at Paris – which departs Paris 10.50pm and arrives in Madrid at 8.05am the next day. From here you can drive to Córdoba and Málaga in about three to four hours. For a small car (such as a Fiat Uno) the single fare is FF1200 (£120), plus FF809 per adult (FF647 for under-26s, although prices rise around fifty percent in July and August. Information and bookings can be made only by contacting SNCF direct in France on their Motorail service (☎0033/8.36.35.35.39; *www.sncf.fr*), they have English-speaking operators and accept most credit cards.

FERRY COMPANIES AND EUROTUNNEL

Brittany Ferries Millbay Docks, Plymouth; Wharf Rd, Portsmouth; New Harbour Rd, Poole (☎0870/5360 360; *www.brittany-ferries.com*). *Ferries to Santander, St Malo, Roscoff, Cherbourg and Caen.*

Eurotunnel Customer Services Centre (☎0870/535 3535; *www.eurotunnel.com*).

Hoverspeed International Hoverport, Dover, Kent (☎0870/5240 241; *www.hoverspeed.co.uk*). *Hovercraft to Boulogne and Calais.*

P&O Portsmouth Peninsular House, Wharf Road, Portsmouth (☎0870/24 24 999; *www.poportsmouth.com*). *Ferries to Cherbourg, Le Havre and Bilbao. Bookings can be made on their Web site.*

P&O Stena Line Ferries Channel House, Channel View Road, Dover (☎0870/600 0600; *www.posl.com*). *Ferries to Calais.*

Seafrance Eastern Docks, Dover, Kent (☎0870/571 1711; *www.seafrance.co.uk*). *To Calais, Cherbourg, Le Havre & Bilbao.*

P&O operates a twice-weekly ferry service from **Portsmouth to Bilbao**. The journey takes approximately 33–34 hours and leaves Portsmouth on Saturdays and Tuesdays. Typical mid-season fares for a car and two people work out at around £425–665 (according to season), with foot passengers paying £161–304. Cabins are included in these prices. Note that this sailing is significantly cheaper for motorcyclists than for cars, especially if you can find one of the frequent discounts from motorcycling publications.

HITCHING

Hitching on major French routes – and Spanish ones too – can be dire, and stopping people in cafés and asking directly for lifts is about the only technique that works. At all events don't try to hitch from the Channel ports to Paris (organize a lift while you're still on the ferry) nor (worse still) out of Paris itself. If you can afford it, perhaps the best approach is to buy a train ticket to somewhere south of Paris and set out from there. Orléans is reasonably well placed for Barcelona, and Tours or Chartres for San Sebastián.

GETTING THERE FROM IRELAND

Summer charter flights to the Costa del Sol and Costa Brava are easy to pick up from either Dublin or Belfast, while year-round scheduled services operate to Madrid and Barcelona. However, other package holi-days or city breaks are often routed via London, with an add-on fare from Ireland for the connection. Students, and anyone under the age of 31, should contact Usit, which generally has the best discount deals on flights and train tickets (for InterRail details, see p.6).

Iberia has non-stop **scheduled flights** from Dublin to Barcelona costing from IR£229 return in the low season (January to February) to IR£289 in high season (July and August), as well as scheduled flights from Dublin to Madrid, via Barcelona, costing from IR£215–255. A flight connection to Andalucía will add about IR£95 to these prices. These cheapest fares have several restrictions – you must stay at least one Saturday night, and can stay for a maximum of only one month – and departure and return flight dates are fixed. Aer Lingus also operate flights, although these run from April to late-October only, and are routed through London.

There are direct once-a-week summer (late June to early September) **charter flights** to the Costa del Sol (Málaga) from Belfast (around £270–300 return) and Dublin (IR£240–270), with

USEFUL ADDRESSES IN IRELAND

AIRLINES

Aer Lingus (☎01/844 4747; *www.aerlingus.ie*) 41 Upper O'Connell St, Dublin 1; 2 Academy St, Cork; 136 O'Connell St, Limerick; 46 Castle St, Belfast BT1 1HB.

British Airways (*www.british-airways.com*) 9 Fountain Centre, College St, Belfast (☎0845/773 3377); Dublin reservations (☎1800/626 747). They don't have a Dublin office; Aer Lingus acts as their agent.

British Midland Belfast International Airport (Aldergrover) (☎02890/240530; *www. iflybritishmidland.com*).

Iberia 54 Dawson St, Dublin 2 (☎01/677 9846; *www.iberia.com*).

Ryanair Phoenix House, Coyningham Road, Dublin 8 (☎01/609 7800; *www.ryanair.ie*).

AGENTS AND OPERATORS

Joe Walsh Tours 8–11 Lower Baggot St, Dublin (☎01/678 9555). *General budget fares agent.*

Thomas Cook (*www.thomascook.co.uk*) 118 Grafton St, Dublin (☎01/677 1721); 11 Donegall Place, Belfast BT1 5AJ (☎028/9055 4455). *Package holiday and flight agent, with occasional discount offers.*

Usit (*www.usit.ie*) O'Connell Bridge, 19–21 Aston Quay, Dublin 2 (☎01/602 1600); 10–11 Market Parade, Patrick St, Cork (☎021/270900); 31a Queen St, Belfast BT1 6ET (☎028/9024 2562). *Student and youth specialist for flights and surface travel.*

prices at their highest during August and dropping a little in the months either side. If you're prepared to book at the last minute, you'll often get much better deals than this (as little as £99 from Belfast), though obviously you can't guarantee the departure date you want in advance.

For a two-week **package** to the Costa del Sol (based on four people sharing a self-catering apartment), you can expect to pay from around £260 (low season) to £370 (high) from Belfast;

and from IR£260 (low) to IR£445 (high) from Dublin.

If you're really trying to get to Andalucía in the cheapest possible way, you might find that budget flights from Dublin or Belfast to London, plus a last-minute London charter flight, will save you a few pounds, but don't count on it. Buying a Eurotrain ticket (from Usit) from Dublin to London will slightly undercut the plane's price, but by this time you're starting to talk about a journey of days and not hours.

GETTING THERE FROM NORTH AMERICA

There is a fair variety of scheduled and charter flights from most parts of the US to Madrid, with connections on to Sevilla and Málaga – Andalucía's main airports. Occasionally, however – and especially if you're travelling from Canada – you'll still find it cheaper to route via London, picking up an inexpensive onward flight from there (see "Getting there from Britain", p.3 for all the details). If Spain is part of a longer European trip, you'll also want to check out details of the Eurail pass, which must be purchased in advance of your arrival and can get you by train from anywhere in Europe to Spain.

SHOPPING FOR TICKETS

Leaving aside discounted tickets, the cheapest way to travel is with an **Apex** (Advance Purchase

Excursion) ticket, although these carry certain restrictions: you have to book your seat – and pay for it – at least 21 days before departure, spend at least seven days abroad (maximum stay three months), and you tend to get penalized if you change your schedule. There are winter **Super Apex** tickets, sometimes known as "Eurosavers" – slightly cheaper than an ordinary Apex, but limiting your stay to between 7 and 21 days. Some airlines also issue **Special Apex** tickets to those under 24, often extending the maximum stay to a year.

However, discount outlets can usually do better than any Apex fare. They come in several forms. **Consolidators** buy up large blocks of tickets that airlines don't think they'll be able to sell at their published fares, and sell them at a discount. Besides being cheap, consolidators normally don't impose advance purchase requirements (although in busy times you'll want to book ahead just to be sure of getting a ticket), but they do often charge very stiff fees for date changes. Also, these companies' margins are pretty tiny, so they make their money by dealing in volume – don't expect them to entertain lots of questions. **Discount agents** – such as STA, Council Travel, Nouvelles Frontières, or others listed on p.12 – also wheel and deal in blocks of tickets offloaded by the airlines, but they typically offer a range of other travel-related services such as travel insurance, rail passes, youth and student ID cards, car rentals, tours and the like. These agencies tend to be most worthwhile to students and under-26s, who can often benefit from special fares and deals. You should bear in mind, however, that discount agents tend to concentrate on high-volume routes to major cities; they'll give you a good deal on Madrid, but they won't be able to help you with any of the lesser destinations in Andalucía. **Travel clubs** are another option for those who travel a lot – most charge an annual membership fee, which may be worth it for discounts on air tickets and car rental for example. You should also check the travel section in the Sunday *New York Times*, or your own major local newspaper, for current bargains, and consult a good travel agent.

Regardless of where you buy your ticket, the fare you pay will depend on season. Fares to Spain (like the rest of Europe) are highest from around early June to the end of August, when everyone wants to travel; they drop during the "shoulder" seasons, September–October and April–May, and you'll get the best deals during the low season, November through March (excluding Christmas). Note that flying on weekends ordinarily adds $50 to the round-trip fare; price ranges quoted here assume midweek travel and exclude tax.

FROM THE US

Obviously Madrid is the main air destination in Spain, and the best fares are usually found on flights into the capital – but don't assume this always to be the case. In the summer many airlines will throw in a connecting flight to **Sevilla** or **Málaga** on Iberia for free; during the winter, these add-ons will cost an extra $150–175 round-trip, which still isn't bad. A third possibility in Andalucía is **Almería**, a more obscure destination that will add $50–200 to the Madrid fare, depending on the season.

Iberia flies direct to Madrid from New York, Miami and Chicago, and to Barcelona from New York. It is also possible to connect to these flights from other US cities through Iberia's partnership with American Airlines. High-season **Apex** fares to Madrid from JFK or Los Angeles start at $820; low-season prices are considerably less – as low as $298 from New York or $448 from LA. One advantage of Iberia is that it offers connecting flights to almost anywhere in Spain, often very good value if booked with your transatlantic flight.

Several US airlines also fly direct from the East Coast to Madrid and Barcelona. Continental flies from Newark to Madrid at much the same prices as Iberia; Delta flies from its Atlanta hub to Madrid and Barcelona, costing somewhat more. American Airlines flies non-stop from Miami to Madrid and offers very good low-season fares (about $350), with high-season rates comparable to the other airlines.

Coming from anywhere else in the US, a connecting flight on the same airline should add only $50–200 from Midwest cities, $150–200 from the West Coast (a connecting flight with a different carrier may run $300–500).

AIRLINES IN NORTH AMERICA

Air France (☎1-800/237-2747; in Canada, ☎1-800/667-2747, *www.airfrance.fr*). Flies from many cities to Paris and then on to Madrid, Barcelona, Málaga and Sevilla.

American Airlines (☎1-800/433-7300; *www.aa.com*). Direct from Miami to Madrid, with connections from many other US cities.

British Airways (☎1-800/247-9297; in Canada, ☎1-800/668-1059; *www.britishairways.com*). Flies from many cities to London, with connections to Madrid, Barcelona, Bilbao and Málaga.

Continental Airlines (☎1-800/231-0856; *www.flycontinental.com*). Newark to Madrid.

Delta Airlines (☎1-800/241-4141; *www.delta-air.com*). Atlanta to Madrid non-stop and Barcelona via Madrid.

Iberia (☎1-800/772-4642; *www.iberia.com*). Flies direct from New York, Miami and Chicago to Madrid and Barcelona, with connections to Málaga and Sevilla, and in partnership with American Airlines from other US cities, such as LA.

KLM/Northwest (☎1-800/447-4747; in Canada, ☎1-800/361-5073; *www.klm.com*). Numerous flights, via Amsterdam, to Madrid and Barcelona.

Lufthansa (☎1-800/645-3880; in Canada, ☎1-800/563-5954; *www.lufthansa.com*). Flights from many cities to Madrid, Barcelona, Valencia, Málaga, Bilbao and Palma, all via Frankfurt.

Sabena (☎1-800/955-2000; *www.sabena-usa.com*). Flights from East Coast cities to Brussels and on to Madrid, Barcelona, Málaga and Bilbao.

TAP Air Portugal (☎1-800/221-7370; *www.tap-airportugal.pt*). New York and Newark to Madrid, via Lisbon.

DISCOUNT AGENTS, CONSOLIDATORS AND TRAVEL CLUBS IN NORTH AMERICA

Airhitch 2641 Broadway, New York, NY 10025 (☎1-800/326-2009 or ☎212/864-2000; *www.airhitch.org*). *Standby-seat broker who, for a set price, guarantee to get you on a flight as close to your preferred destination as possible, within a week.*

Council Travel Head Office: 205 E 42nd St, New York, NY 10017 (☎1-800/226-8624; *www.counciltravel.com*). *Nationwide US student travel organization with branches in San Francisco, Washington DC, Boston, Austin, Seattle, Chicago and Minneapolis, among others.*

Encore Travel Club 4501 Forbes Blvd, Lanham, MD 20706 (☎1-800/444-9800; *www. emitravel.com*). *East Coast travel club – $69 membership fee.*

Interworld Travel 800 Douglass Rd, Suite 140, Miami, FL 33134 (☎1-800/468-3796 or ☎305/443-4929; *www.interworldtravel.com*). *Southeastern US consolidator.*

New Frontiers/Nouvelles Frontières 12 E 33rd St, New York, NY 10016 (☎1-800/366-6387 or ☎212/779-0600; *www.nouvelles-frontieres.com*); 1180 Drummond, Suite 330, Montréal, H3G 2R7 (☎514/871-3060); and other branches in LA, San Francisco and Québec City. *French discount travel firm.*

Now Voyager 74 Varick St, Suite 307, New York, NY 10013 (☎212/431-1616; *www. nowvoyagertravel.com*). *Courier flight broker and consolidator.*

STA Travel (☎1-800/777-0112; *www. sta-travel.com*). Offices across the country, including: Boston (☎212/627-3111); Chicago (☎312/786-9050); Los Angeles (☎323/934-8722); Minneapolis (☎612/615-1800); New York (☎212/627-3111); Philadelphia (☎215/382-2928); and San Francisco (☎415/391-8407). *Worldwide specialist in independent travel.*

Stand Buys 311 W Superior St, Chicago, IL 60610 (☎1-800/255-0200). *Midwestern travel club.*

Travac 989 Sixth Ave, New York, NY 10018 (☎1-800/872-8800 or ☎212/563-3303; *www. thetravelsite.com*). *Consolidator and charter broker. They will fax current fares from their fax line – toll-free 1-888/872-8327.*

Travel Cuts Head Office: 187 College St, Toronto, ON M5T 1P7 (☎416/979-2406; *www.travelcuts.com*). Others include: MacEwan Hall Student Centre, University of Calgary, Calgary, AL T2N 1N4 (☎403/282-7687); 10127 124th St, Edmonton, AL T5N 1P5 (☎780/488-8487); 6139 South St, Halifax, NS B3H 4J2 (☎902/494-7027); 1613 rue St Denis, Montréal, PQ H2X 3K3 (☎514/843-8511); 222 Laurie Ave East, Ottawa, ON K1N 6P2 (☎613/238-8222); 100–2383 Ch St Foy, St Foy, G1V 1T1 (☎418/654-0224); Place Riel Campus Centre, University of Saskatchewan, Saskatoon, SK S7N 5A3 (☎306/975-3722); 5728 University Blvd, Vancouver, BC V6B 1P2 (☎604/659-2830); University Centre, University of Manitoba, Winnipeg, MB R3T 2N2 (☎204/269-9530). *Canadian student travel organization, specializing in student fares, IDs and other travel services.*

Travelers Advantage 3033 S Parker Rd, Suite 1000, Aurora, CO 80014 (☎1-800/548-1116; *www.travelersadvantage.com*). *Discount travel club – annual membership of $59.95.*

Travelocity (*www.travelocity.com*). *Online consolidator.*

Unitravel 11737 Administration Dr, Suite 120, St Louis, MO 63146 (☎1-800/325-2222 or ☎314/569-2501; *www.flightsforless.com*). *US consolidator.*

Worldwide Discount Travel Club 1674 Meridian Ave, Miami Beach, FL 33139 (☎305/534-2082). *Discount travel club.*

Discount travel agents might have cheaper deals on routings to Madrid **via other major European cities** with the airlines of those countries: Air France via Paris, KLM via Amsterdam, Lufthansa via Frankfurt, TAP via Lisbon, British Airways via London, or Sabena via Brussels. Competition is intense, so look out for bargains, especially out of season. TAP also has flights from Lisbon to Málaga (usually with a stop in Madrid).

FROM CANADA

Since Iberia no longer flies from Canada to Spain, you may have to find a charter flight if you want to avoid going through a third country.

Discount travel agents deal mainly in flights **via London** (usually using a combination of airlines) or **via Lisbon** (on TAP Air Portugal). British Airways, for example, will fly you from Vancouver to London and continue on to Madrid or another Spanish city for about CDN\$1240 low season or about CDN\$1470 high season. There are several other possibilities using other European national airlines via their respective capitals (see box). Another alternative is obviously to fly via a US city such as Seattle, Chicago, or New York.

Travel Cuts is the most reliable student/youth agency, with some deals for non-students, too; or check the travel ads in your local newspaper and consult a good travel agent.

PACKAGE TOURS

Package tours may not sound like your kind of travel, but don't dismiss the idea out of hand. It's true that tours arranged in North America tend to be of the everybody-on-the-bus group variety, but many agents can put together very flexible deals, sometimes amounting to no more than a flight plus car or rail pass and accommodation; if you're planning to travel in moderate or luxury style, and especially if your trip is geared around special interests, such packages can work out cheaper than the same arrangements made on arrival. A package can also be great for your peace of mind, if only just to ensure a worry-free first week while you're finding your feet on a longer tour (of course, you can jump off the itinerary any time you like). Most companies will expect you to book through a local travel agent, and since it costs the same you might as well. A number of American outfits offer tours that focus on Andalucía. For the most part they boil down to two basic formulas: escorted **historic city tours**, making a circuit of Granada, Córdoba and Sevilla; and accommodation-only packages on the **Costa del Sol**. Some operators allow you to build your own itinerary with a few nights in each of various cities. Any way you slice it, though, going with a tour company will land you in fairly expensive hotels, in the neighbourhood of \$100 a night per person — even more if you're staying in paradores. In

---

TOUR OPERATORS IN NORTH AMERICA

Abercrombie & Kent 1520 Kensington Rd, Oak Brook, IL 60521 (☎1-800/323-7308; *www. abercrombiekent.com*). *Offer several packages, including "Walking in Southern Spain," a six-day tour starting in Sevilla, with an average jaunt of ten kilometres per day.*

Backroads 816 Cedar St, Berkeley, CA 94710 (☎1-800/462-2848; *www.backroads.com*). *Biking or hiking and biking tours of Andalucía. Also offer combined Spain/Portugal cycling tours.*

Contiki Holidays 300 Plaza Alicante, Suite 900, Garden Grove, CA (☎1-800/266-8454; *www. contiki.com*). *Spain and Portugal coach tours for 18 to 35 year olds, with stops in Sevilla and Gibraltar.*

Discover Spain Vacations 120 Sylvan Ave, Englewood Cliffs, NJ 07632 (☎1-800/227-5858; *www.book.centralh.com*). *Costa del Sol packages and parador tours.*

EC Tours 12500 Riverside Drive, Valley Village, CA 91607 (☎1-800/388-0877; *www.ectours.com*). *Offers a variety of tours including pilgrimages, historic city, and wine and gourmet tours.*

Elderhostel 75 Federal St, Boston, MA 02110 (☎1-877/426-8056; *www.elderhostel.com*). *Specialists in educational and activity pro-grammes, cruises and homestays for senior trav-ellers. A tour starting in Barcelona and going to* the Canary Islands includes stops in Granada and Sevilla.

Escapade Tours 630 Third Ave, 4th Floor, New York, NY 10017 (☎1-800/356-2405; *www. escapadetours.com*). *Independent travel and package tours.*

Globus and Cosmos 5301 South Federal Circle, Littleton, CO 80123 (☎1-800/221-0090; *www. cosmostours.com*). *Offers coach sightseeing tours, with stops in Andalucía as part of larger trips of Spain or tours combining Spain and Portugal, or Spain, Portugal and Morocco. Bookable through travel agents only.*

Holidaze Ski Tours 810 Belmar Plaza, Belmar, NJ 07719 (☎1-800/526-2827). *Skiing holidays in the Sierra Nevada.*

MI Travel 450 7th Ave, Suite 1805, New York, NY (☎1-800/848-2314 or ☎212/967-6565; *www.mitravel-melia.com*). *Historic tours and packages.*

Petrabax 19710 Ventura Blvd, Suite 210, Woodland Hills, CA 91364 (☎1-800/634-1188; *www.petrabax.com*). *Bus tours.*

Sun Holidays 1650 Avenue Road, Toronto ON M5M 3Y1 (☎1-800/387-0571 or ☎416/789-1010; *www.sunholidays.ca*). *City packages and parador tours.*

addition, a few American companies organize biking and **trekking** trips in Andalucía, which cost at least as much as city tours due to all the logistics involved.

RAIL PASSES

The **Eurail pass**, which allows unlimited first-class travel almost anywhere in Europe for a specified period, isn't an economical way to see Spain, though if you're planning a longer European trip it may prove useful, since it allows for travel in sixteen other countries. The pass costs US$554 for 15 days of unlimited rail travel; $718 for 21 days; $890 for one month; $1260 for two months, and $1558 for three months. If you're under 26, you can save money with a **Eurail Youthpass**, which is valid for second-class travel and is available in 15-day ($388); 21-day ($499); one-month ($623); two-month ($882) and three-month ($1089) increments. If you're travelling with one to four companions, of any age, the joint **Eurail Saverpass** is available in 15-day ($470 per person), 21-day ($610), one-month ($756), two-month ($1072), and three-month ($1324) increments.

You might stand a better chance of getting your money's worth out of a **Eurail Flexipass**, which is good for a certain number of travel days in a two-month period. This, too, comes in first-class and second-class (under-26) versions: 10 days cost $654/$458, and 15 days, $862/$599. Once again parties of two to five can save fifteen percent with the **Eurail Saver Flexipass**.

A scaled-down version of the Flexipass, the **Europass** allows first-class travel in France, Germany, Italy, Spain and Switzerland for any 5 days in 2 months ($348); 6 days ($368); 8 days ($448); 10 days ($528); or 15 days ($728). Up to four "associate" countries or regions (Austria and Hungary, Benelux, Greece or Portugal) can be included for an additional fare. The **Europass Saverpass** is a version of the Europass for people travelling in groups of two or more and offers savings of 15 percent per person on the regular fare. The **Europass Youth** for under-26s, costs $233 for any 5 days of second-class travel in 2 months; $253 for 6 days; $313 for 8 days; $363 for 10 days; and $513 for 15 days.

Other alternatives for travel within Spain, include the **Spain Flexipass** (see p.31), and **Rail 'n' Drive** pass (see p.31).

All of these passes can be reserved through Rail Europe, 226 Westchester Ave, White Plains, NY 10604 (☎1-800/438-7245; *www.raileurope.com*), or through travel agents.

GETTING THERE FROM AUSTRALIA & NEW ZEALAND

There are no direct flights to Spain from Australia or New Zealand, but by combining services some airlines – Singapore Airlines, Thai Airways and JAL providing the most direct routings – now offer travel to Madrid (and sometimes Barcelona) in conjunction with a stopover in Europe. While this means around 24 hours in the air – not counting the hours spent waiting for connections – this is a good way to see places on the way, if you're not rushed for time.

As destinations in Europe are "common rated" – you pay the same fare whatever your destination – some airlines offer free flight coupons, car rental or accommodation if you book a flight with them. Choose carefully, though, as such perks are impossible to alter later. Alternatively, you could buy the cheapest possible flight to anywhere in Europe and make your way to Spain using standby flights, trains or buses, but this would rarely work out as cheaply as buying a discounted flight that will take you all the way.

Fares change according to the time of year you travel. Mid-December to mid-January are high season; early October through to mid-November the low season; and the rest of the year the shoulder season. The current lowest standard return fares to Madrid (low/high season) are around A$1550/2050 from eastern Australia; A$1770/2270 from Perth, and NZ$2140/2760 from Auckland.

Otherwise, discount agents can usually provide prices ranging from as low as A$1000/NZ$1300 for last-minute specials, although they do charge heavily for cancellations or alterations. Full-time students, and those under 26 or over 60, can also make big savings through specialist agents (see the box on p.16). The travel sections of the major Saturday papers usually provide a good source of agents.

For more extended trips, **round-the-world (RTW)** tickets that are valid for one year are a good option – especially from New Zealand, where airlines tend to offer fewer bonuses to fly with them. Among them is the BA/Qantas "Explorer Plus" which costs, for low and high season departures, A$2099/A$2749 or NZ$2623/3432. These also allow five free stopovers, which includes London, and you can buy additional stopovers. Thai Airways in conjunction with Air New Zealand and Varig offer the "Star Alliance" ticket, that includes up to fifteen stopovers – except within the US and Canada – which are worked out by the miles you travel. Fares start at A$2699/NZ$3370 for 29,000 miles and go to A$3699/NZ$4620 for 39,000 miles.

RAIL PASSES

Eurail passes, which can only be purchased before leaving home, are generally a good idea if Spain is part of a longer European trip. The **Eurail** pass allows unlimited travel for practically anywhere in Europe, and includes sixteen countries as well as Spain. The pass is for first-class travel for people 26 and over and costs A$880/NZ$1100 for the 15-day option, and A$2475/NZ$3055 for three months. Under-26s can save by purchasing the **Eurail Youthpass**, with 15 days second-class travel costing A$615/NZ$768, and three months A$1730/NZ$2135.

You'll probably find a **Eurail Flexipass** better value as it's are valid for a certain number of travel days within a two-month period; and also comes in youth/first-class versions: 10 days cost A$725/1040 or NZ$900/1285; and 15 days, A$950/1370 or NZ$1175/1700.

A scaled-down version of the Flexipass, the **Europass** allows travel in France, Germany, Italy, Spain and Switzerland for (youth/first-class) A$370/550 or NZ$460/675 for five days in two months, on up to A$815/1155 or NZ$1020/1435 for 15 days in two month. Up to four "associate" countries or regions (Austria and Hungary, Benelux, Greece or Portugal) can be included for an additional fare.

AIRLINES IN AUSTRALIA AND NEW ZEALAND

Alitalia-KLM (*www.alitalia.it; www.klm.com*) Level 13, 115 Pitt St, Sydney (☎1-300/303-747); Level 2, Salvation Army Building, 369 Queen St, Auckland (☎09/309-1782). *Six connections a week to Madrid or Barcelona from Sydney and Melbourne, via Milan or Amsterdam. There is a code-share arrangement with a partner airline, Ansett, to get you from New Zealand to Sydney.*

British Airways (*www.british-airways.com*) Level 19, AAP Centre, 259 George St, Sydney (☎02/9258-3200); 154 Queen St, Auckland (☎09/356-8690). *Daily to Madrid or Barcelona, via London, from all major Australian cities. There is a code-share arrangement with a partner airline, Qantas, to get you from New Zealand to Sydney.*

JAL (*www.jal.co.jp*) Level 14, Darling Park, 201 Sussex St, Sydney (☎02/9272-1100); Level 12, Westpac Trust, 120 Albert St, Auckland (☎09/379-3202). *Daily from Sydney and Melbourne to Madrid, via Tokyo and Amsterdam. Three times a week from Auckland to Barcelona, via Tokyo.*

Qantas (*www.qantas.com.au*) Chifley Square, 70 Hunter St, Sydney (☎02/9691-3636); 191 Queen St, Auckland (☎09/357-8900). *Daily from Sydney and Melbourne to London linking with other carriers such as British Airways on to Spain. Daily from Auckland, via Sydney or Melbourne, to London. Qantas is an extremely flexible carrier and can arrange daily flights from most major cities if you don't mind stopovers.*

Singapore Airlines (*www.singaporeair.com*) 17 Bridge St, Sydney (☎02/9350-0130); cnr Albert St & Fanshawe St, Auckland (☎09/303-2129 or ☎0800/808-909). *Daily from Sydney, Melbourne and Auckland to Madrid, via Singapore. Note that most flights are designed to connect so you avoid undue waiting times.*

Thai Airways (*www.thaiair.com*) 75–77 Pitt St, Sydney (☎02/9844-0999); Level 1, Kensington Swan Building, 22 Fanshawe St, Auckland (☎09/377-3886). *Three connections weekly to Madrid from Sydney and Melbourne, via Bangkok. From Auckland, flights link to Bangkok, via Sydney.*

There's also a **Eurail Saverpass**, **Saver Flexipass** and **Euro Saverpass**. These are first class passes, valid for between 2 and 5 people who must be travelling together on all journeys. The cost is slightly less than the full 1st class passes.

Other alternatives include the more specific **Spain Flexipass** (see p.31). These passes can be bought from CIT, Level 2, 263 Clarence Street, Sydney (☎02/9267-1255; *www.cittravel.com.au*), or at their branches in Melbourne, Adelaide, Brisbane and Perth – there is no NZ office and enquiries and reservations must go via Australian offices – and from many regular travel agents, especially youth and student specialists (see box below).

AUSTRALIAN & NEW ZEALAND DISCOUNT AGENTS

Accent on Travel 545 Queen St, Brisbane (☎07/3832-1777).

Anywhere Travel 345 Anzac Parade, Kingsford, Sydney (☎02/9663-0411; *anywhere@ ozemail.com.au*).

Budget Travel 16 Fort St, Auckland (☎09/366-0061 or ☎0800/808-040).

Destinations Unlimited Level 7, FAI Building, 220 Queen St, Auckland (☎09/373-4033).

Flight Centres (*www.flightcentre.com*) Gateway Quayside, 1 Macquarie Place, Sydney (☎02/9241-2422); 19 Bourke St, Melbourne (☎03/9650-2899); plus other branches nationwide (☎13-1600); National Bank Towers, 205–225 Queen St, Auckland (☎0800/354-448 or ☎09/309-6171); and other branches countrywide.

Harvey World Travel 631 Princes Highway, Kogarah, Sydney (☎02/9567-6099); branches nationwide.

Northern Gateway 22 Cavenagh St, Darwin (☎08/8941-1394; *oztravel@norgate.com.au*).

Passport Travel Suite 11a/401 St Kilda Rd, Melbourne (☎03/9867-3888; *www. travelcentre.com.au*).

STA Travel (*www.statravel.com.au*) 855 George St, Sydney (☎02/9212-1255); 208 Swanston St, Melbourne (☎03/9639-0599); other offices in state capitals and major universities (☎13-1776; fastfare telesales ☎1-300/360 960); Travellers' Centre, 10 High St, Auckland (☎09/309-0458, fastfare telesales ☎09/366-6673, toll-free ☎0800/874-773), plus branches in Wellington, Christchurch, Dunedin, Palmerston North, Hamilton and at major universities.

Thomas Cook (*www.thomascook.com.au*) 175 Pitt St, Sydney (☎02/9231-2877); 257 Collins St, Melbourne (☎03/9282-0222); branches in other state capitals (☎13-1771 or toll-free ☎1-800/063-913); 191 Queen St, Auckland (☎09/379-3920).

Topdeck Travel, 65 Grenfell St, Adelaide (☎08/8232-7222).

Travel Direct Pty Ltd, Level 3, 349 Queen Street, Brisbane (☎07/3221-4933).

Travel Shop, Suite 13, 890 Canning Highway, Perth (☎08/9316-3888 or ☎1-800/108-108).

Tymtro Travel, Level 3, 355 Bulwara Rd, Sydney (☎1-300/652-969).

SPECIALIST TOUR OPERATORS

IB Tours Level 1, 47 New Canterbury Road, Petersham, Sydney (☎02/9560-6722). *Good variety of Andalucian tours ranging from 3-day packages from Madrid combining Sevilla and the Costa del Sol (A$690), to 9 days departing Madrid visiting Merida, Córdoba, Sevilla and the Costa del Sol (A$1350). Prices are per person, twin share, and include accommodation, some meals and excursions, but exclude airfares.*

Ibertours Level 1, 84 William St, Melbourne (☎03/9670-8388 or ☎1-800/500-016; *www.users.bigpond.com/ibertours*). *Spend 5 days on an Andalucian "Fiesta" package encompassing Madrid, Merida, Córdoba, Sevilla,* *Granada and Toledo (A$685), or 9 days touring Andalucía and the Mediterranean coast (A$1015). Prices are per person twin share and include accommodation, some meals and excursions; airfares are excluded.*

Spanish Tourism Promotions Level 1, 178 Collins St, Melbourne (☎03/9650-7377). *Operates a variety of tours including a 4-day Andalucían package that takes in Madrid and Sevilla among other destinations, with three-star accommodation and some meals (A$540). Another option is a 14-day luxury all-inclusive Spain and Andalucía tour, with first-class accommodation, meals, transport and excursions (A$2290). Both prices exclude airfares.*

RED TAPE AND VISAS

Citizens of most EU countries (and of Norway and Iceland) need only a valid national identity card to enter Spain for up to ninety days. Since Britain has no identity card system, however, British citizens have to take a passport. US, Canadian and New Zealand citizens do not need a visa for stays of up to ninety days. Australians do not need a visa for stays of up to thirty days, but for a longer visit (up to ninety days), will need to obtain one before arrival. Visa requirements do change and it is always advisable to check the current situation before leaving home.

To **stay longer**, EU nationals (and citizens of Norway and Iceland) can apply for a *permiso de residencia* (residence permit) once in Spain. A temporary residence permit is valid for up to a year, and you'll need a permanent one after that. Applications need to be made at the police station nearest to where you'll be taking up residency, or at the relevant provincial police station. You'll have to produce proof that you have sufficient funds, officially 5000ptas a day, to be able to support yourself without working – easiest done by keeping bank exchange forms every time you change money. Otherwise you'll need to get a contract of employment (*contrato de trabajo*), or to become self-employed (as a teacher for example), which involves registering at the tax office. Other nationalities are obliged to get a special visa from a Spanish consulate before departure (see below for addresses), or to apply – usually at any police station – for a ninety-day extension, showing proof of funds.

SPANISH EMBASSIES AND CONSULATES

Australia PO Box 76, Deakin, ACT 2600 (☎02/6273-3555); Level 4, 540 Elizabeth St, Melbourne, VIC 3000 (☎03/9347-1966); Level 24, St Martin's Tower, 31 Market St, Sydney, NSW 2000 (☎02/9261-2433).

Canada 74 Stanley Ave, Ottawa, ON K1M 1P4 (☎613/747-2252); 1 Westmount #1456, Montréal, PQ H3Z 2P9 (☎514/935-5235); Simcoe Place, 200 Front St #2401, PO Box 15, Toronto, ON M5V 3K2 (☎416/977-1661).

Ireland 17a Merlyn Park, Ballsbridge, Dublin 4 (☎01/269 1640).

UK 20 Draycott Place, London SW3 2RZ (☎020/7581 5921); Suite 1a, Brook House, 70 Spring Gardens, Manchester M22 2BQ (☎0161/236 1233).

USA 545 Boylston St #803, Boston, MA 02116 (☎617/536-2506); 180 N Michigan Ave #1500, Chicago, IL 60601 (☎312/782-4588); 1800 Berins Drive #660, Houston, TX 77057 (☎713/783-6200); 5055 Wilshire Blvd #960, Los Angeles, CA 90036 (☎213/938-0158); 2655 Lejeune Rd #203, Coral Gables, Miami, FL 33134 (☎305/446-5511); 2102 World Trade Center, 2 Canal St, New Orleans, LA 70130 (☎504/525-4951); 150 E 58th St, New York, NY 10155 (☎212/355-4090); 1405 Sutter St, San Francisco, CA 94109 (☎415/922-2995); 2375 Pennsylvania Ave NW, Washington DC 20009 (☎202/728-2330).

INSURANCE

As an EU country, Spain has free reciprocal health agreements with other member states. To take advantage, British and other EU citizens will need form E111, available over the counter from main post offices. For details of what to do and where to go in a medical emergency, see the following section on "Health".

A typical **travel insurance** policy usually provides cover for the loss of baggage, tickets and – up to a certain limit – cash or cheques, as well as cancellation or curtailment of your journey. Most of them exclude so-called dangerous sports unless an extra premium is paid: in Andalucía this can mean horse riding, windsurfing, skiing, trekking and mountaineering. Read the small print

and benefits tables of prospective policies carefully; coverage can vary wildly for roughly similar premiums. Many policies can be chopped and changed to exclude coverage you don't need – for example, sickness and accident benefits can often be excluded or included at will. If you do take medical coverage, ascertain whether benefits will be paid as treatment proceeds or only after returning home, and whether there is a 24-hour medical emergency number. When securing baggage cover, make sure that the per-article limit – typically under £500 equivalent – will cover your most valuable possession. If you need to make a claim, you should keep receipts for medicines and medical treatment, and in the event you have anything stolen, you must obtain an official statement from the police. Bank and credit cards often have certain levels of medical or other insurance included and you may automatically get travel insurance if you use a major credit card to pay for your trip.

Even with an E111, **British** and **Irish** travellers would do well to take out an insurance policy before departing to cover against theft, loss and illness or injury. Travel agents and tour operators are likely to require some sort of insurance when you book a package holiday, though according to UK law they can't make you buy their own (other than a £1 premium for "schedule airline failure"). If you have a good all-risks home insurance policy it *may* cover your possessions against loss or

ROUGH GUIDES TRAVEL INSURANCE

Rough Guides now offer their own travel insurance, customized for our readers by a leading UK broker and backed by a Lloyds underwriter. It's available for anyone, of any nationality, travelling anywhere in the world, and we are convinced that this is the best-value scheme you'll find.

There are two main Rough Guide insurance plans: Essential, for effective, no-frills cover, starting at £11.75 for 2 weeks; and Premier – more expensive but with more generous and extensive benefits. Each offer European or Worldwide cover, and can be supplemented with a "Hazardous Activities Premium" if you plan to

indulge in sports considered dangerous, such as skiing, scuba-diving or trekking. Unlike many policies, the Rough Guides schemes are calculated by the day, so if you're travelling for 27 days rather than a month, that's all you pay for. You can alternatively take out annual multi-trip insurance, which covers you for all your travel throughout the year (with a maximum of 60 days for any one trip).

For a policy quote, call the Rough Guides Insurance Line on UK freefone ☎0800/015 0906, or, if you're calling from outside Britain on (☎+44) 1243 621046. Alternatively, get an online quote at *www.roughguides.com/insurance*.

theft even when overseas. Many private medical schemes such as BUPA or PPP also offer coverage plans for abroad, including baggage loss, cancellation or curtailment and cash replacement as well as sickness or accident.

Americans and **Canadians** should also check that they're not already covered. Canadian provincial health plans usually provide partial cover for medical mishaps overseas. Holders of official student/teacher/youth cards are entitled to meagre accident coverage and hospital in-patient benefits. Students will often find that their student health coverage extends during the vacations and for one term beyond the date of last enrollment. Homeowners' or renters' insurance often covers theft or loss of documents, money and valuables while overseas, though conditions and maximum amounts vary from company to company.

HEALTH

No inoculations are required for Spain, though if you plan on continuing to North Africa, typhoid and polio boosters are highly recommended. The worst that's likely to happen to you is that you might fall victim to an upset stomach. To be safe, wash fruit and avoid *tapas* dishes that look like they were cooked last week.

If you fall ill, it's easiest to go to a **farmacia** – found in almost every village and town – for minor complaints; see the phone book for major towns. Pharmacists are highly trained, will give advice (often in English), and can dispense many drugs which would be available only on prescription in most other countries. They keep usual shop hours (9am–1pm & 4–8pm), but some open late and at weekends, and a rota system keeps at least one open 24 hours. The rota is displayed in the window of every pharmacy, or in local newspapers under *Farmacias de guardia*.

In more serious cases you can get the address of an English-speaking **doctor** from the nearest relevant consulate, or, with luck, from a *farmacia*, the local police or Turismo. In emergencies dial ☎091 for the *Servicios de Urgencia* (Emergency Services), or ☎061 for an ambulance, or look up the *Cruz Roja Española* (Red Cross), which runs a national ambulance service. Treatment at **hospitals** for EU citizens in possession of form E111 is free (see p.18); otherwise you'll be charged at private hospital rates, which can be as much as 14,000ptas per visit.

EMERGENCY TELEPHONE NUMBER

Dial ☎091 in an emergency for the *Servicios de Urgencia*.

TRAVELLERS WITH DISABILITIES

Spain is not exactly at the forefront of providing facilities for travellers with disabilities. That said, things are steadily improving and there are accessible hotels in each of the major cities and resorts. By law, all new public buildings are required to be fully accessible. The staging of the 1992 Paralympic Games in Barcelona did a great deal towards helping attitudes and facilities there; and there are also a number of active and forceful groups of disabled people: *ONCE*, the Spanish organization for the blind, is particularly active, its huge lottery bringing with it considerable power.

TRANSPORT

The main problem is still **transport**, since buses are virtually impossible for wheelchairs – although some of the newer buses now allow wheelchair access – and trains are only slightly better (though there are wheelchairs at major stations and wheelchair spaces in some carriages, especially on the more modern trains such as the AVE between Madrid and Sevilla). Taxi drivers in most towns are usually helpful. The Brittany Ferries crossing from Plymouth to Santander offers good facilities if you're **driving to Spain** (as do most cross-Channel ferries).

CONTACTS FOR TRAVELLERS WITH DISABILITIES

SPAIN

Spanish National Tourist Office (See p.22 for addresses). *Publishes a fact sheet, listing a variety of useful addresses and some accessible accommodation.*

PIMS c/Manuel Villalobos 41, 41009 Sevilla (☎95 435 87 89). *Advice centre which can provide information on Sevilla and on Andalucía generally. They also publish a leaflet (in Spanish): Guía de Turismo Accesible.*

Organización Nacional de Ciegos de España (*ONCE*) c/de Prado 24, Madrid (☎91 589 46 00); c/Calabria 66–76, 08015 Barcelona (☎93 325 92 00). *Sells Braille maps and can arrange trips for blind people; write for details.*

ECOM (Federation of Spanish private organizations for the disabled) Gran Vía de las Corts Catalanes 562 principal, 2ª, 08011 Barcelona (☎93 451 69 04). *Information on holidays and facilities throughout Spain.*

BRITAIN

Holiday Care Service 2nd floor, Imperial Building, Victoria Rd, Horley, Surrey RH6 9HW (☎01293/774535). *Information on all aspects of travel.*

Mobility International Rue de Manchester 25, B-1070 Brussels (☎00322/201 5711, fax 201 5763). *Information, access guides, tours and exchange programmes for British disabled travellers.*

RADAR 12 City Forum, 250 City Road, London EC1V 8AF (☎020/7250 3222). *A good source of advice on holidays and travel abroad.*

IRELAND

Disability Action Group 2 Annadale Ave, Belfast BT7 3JH (☎028/9049 1011). *Information on access for disabled travellers abroad.*

Irish Wheelchair Association Blackheath Drive, Clontarf, Dublin 3 (☎01/833 8241). *Source of information on access for disabled travellers abroad.*

NORTH AMERICA

Directions Unlimited 123 Green Lane, Bedford Hills, NY 10507 (☎1-800/533-5343 or ☎914/241-1700; *cruisesusa@aol.com*). *Tour operator specializing in custom tours, packages and cruises for people with disabilities.*

Disabled **facilities** at cafés, petrol stations and restaurants along the major roads and *autovías* are improving, particularly in coastal areas, but once out of the cities and away from the coast, the difficulties increase. Road surfaces in the mountain regions can be rough, and toilet facilities for disabled travellers are a rare sight.

ACCOMMODATION

On the **accommodation** front wheelchair access is improving, and in major towns you'll have no problem finding places with facilities within all price brackets; outside the major conurbations things tend to be less easy, although the more stars awarded to a place, the more likely it is to have been converted to accommodate disabled visitors. Many places which optimistically claim to be accessible, however, still retain obstacles such

as flights of steps at the entrance. An invaluable information source is the *Guía de Hoteles y Pensiones de Andalucía*, published by the Junta de Andalucía. It costs 900ptas and is available from all Turismo offices or from the head office in Marbella (☎95 283 87 85; *www.andalucia.org*). Updated annually, the guide identifies every hotel and *hostal* in the region which has accessible accommodation with a wheelchair symbol. All bar one of Andalucía's *Albergues Juveniles* or **youth hostels** are equipped with disabled accommodation ranging from El Bosque's three en-suite rooms to Jerez's 28. If you can afford them, *paradores* are one answer to the problem of unsuitable accommodation. In Andalucía all except three are wheelchair accessible, and even though most are converted castles and monasteries they still have plenty of room inside to manoeuvre a wheelchair.

Jewish Rehabilitation Hospital 3205 Place Alton Goldbloom, Montréal, PQ H7V 1R2 (☎450/688-9550, ext 226). *Guidebooks and travel information.*

Mobility International USA PO Box 10767, Eugene, OR 97440 (Voice and TDD ☎541/343-1284; *www.miusa.org*). *Information and referral services, access guides, tours and exchange programs. Annual membership $35 (includes quarterly newsletter).*

Society for the Advancement of Travel for the Handicapped (SATH) 347 5th Ave, New York, NY 10016 (☎212/447-7284; *www.sath.org*). *Non-profit travel industry referral service that passes queries on to its members as appropriate; allow plenty of time for a response.*

Travel Information Service Moss Rehabilitation Hospital, 1200 West Tabor Rd, Philadelphia, PA 19141 (☎215/456-9603). *Telephone information and referral service.*

Twin Peaks Press Box 129, Vancouver, WA 98666 (☎360/694-2462 or ☎1-800/637-2256). *Publisher of the "Directory of Travel Agencies for the Disabled" ($19.95), listing more than 370 agencies worldwide; "Travel for the Disabled"*

($19.95); the "Directory of Accessible Van Rentals" ($9.95), and "Wheelchair Vagabond" ($14.95) – all loaded with personal tips.

Wheels Up! (☎1-888/389-4335; *www.wheelsup.com*). *Provides discounted tour and cruise prices and airfares for disabled travellers; also publishes a free monthly newsletter and has a comprehensive Web site.*

AUSTRALIA

Australian Council for the Rehabilitation of the Disabled (ACROD), PO Box 60, Curtin, ACT 2605 (☎02/6282-4333); 24 Cabarita Rd, Cabarita NSW 2137 (☎02/9743-2699). *Good repository of information on travel agencies and tour operators for people with disabilities.*

NEW ZEALAND

Disability Resource Centre, 60 Bennett St, Palmerston North (☎06/952-0011). *Comprehensive resource covering everything from legislation to travel, complete listing of organizations and tour operators, also publishes mobility maps and access guides.*

INFORMATION AND MAPS

The Spanish National Tourist Office (SNTO) produces and gives away an impressive variety of maps, pamphlets and special interest leaflets. Visit one of their offices before you leave and stock up, especially on city plans, as well as lists of hotels, *hostales* and campsites.

INFORMATION OFFICES

Throughout Andalucía you'll find Junta de Andalucía (regional government) tourist offices –

called **Turismo** – in virtually every major town (addresses are detailed in the *Guide*) and from these you can usually get more specific local information and useful maps (now sold by most at a nominal charge). They vary enormously in quality of service, but while generally extremely useful for local information, they cannot be trusted to know anything about what goes on outside their patch. Turismo hours are usually Mon–Fri 9am–1pm and 3.30–6pm, Sat 9am–1pm – but there are wide variations across the region and you can't always rely on the official hours, especially in more out-of-the-way places, where offices are known to close without notice or (especially around holiday periods) not open at all. On the other hand, the major coastal resorts often have enthusiastic offices staying open until nine at night and even later in season.

MAPS

In addition to the various free leaflets, the one extra you'll probably want is a reasonable **road map**. This is best bought in Spain, where you'll find a good selection in most bookshops (*librerías*) and at street kiosks or petrol stations. Among the best are those published by Editorial Almax, which also produces reliable indexed street plans of Sevilla and Granada. The best **single map** for

SNTO OFFICES ABROAD

For Internet enquiries of a national nature go to *www.tourspain.org*, and for Andalucía only consult *www.andalucia.org*.

Australia and New Zealand: There is no official SNTO office in either country. The best resources are in Australia at the Spanish Chamber of Commerce, Suite 205, Edgcliff Centre, 203 New South Head Road, Sydney (☎02/9362-3168), and Spanish Tourism Promotions, Level 1, 178 Collins St, Melbourne (☎03/9650-7377).

Belgium 21–22 Ave des Arts, 1040 Bruxelles (☎02/280 1926, fax 02/280 2147).

Canada 2 Bloor St West, 34th Floor, Toronto, Ontario M4W 3E2 (☎416/961-3131, fax 961-1992).

Netherlands Laan Van Meerdervoor 8a, 2517 AJ Den Haag (☎070/346 59 00, fax 364 98 59).

Sweden Stureplan 6, 1TR, 114-35 Stockholm (☎08/611 41 36, fax 611 44 07).

UK 22–23 Manchester Square, London W1M 5AP (☎020/7486 8077, premium rate brochure line ☎09001/66 99 20, fax 020/7486 8034; *buzon. oficial@londres.oet.mcx.es*). *The telephone number is invariably engaged so write, fax, e-mail or visit.*

USA (*www.okspain.org*) 8383 Wilshire Boulevard, Suite 960, Beverly Hills, CA 90211 (☎323/658-7188); Water Tower Place, Suite 915 East, 845 North Michigan Ave, Chicago, IL 60611 (☎312/642-1992); 1211 Brickell Ave #1850, Miami, FL 33131 (☎305/358-1992); 666 Fifth Ave, New York, NY 10103 (☎212/265-8822).

MAP OUTLETS

UK

Glasgow John Smith and Sons, 57–61 St Vincent St (☎0141/221 7472).

London National Map Centre, 22–24 Caxton St, SW1 (☎020/7222 2466); Stanfords, 12–14 Long Acre, WC2 (☎020/7836 1321); The Travel Bookshop, 13–15 Blenheim Crescent, W11

(☎020/7229 5260; *www.thetravelbookshop. co.uk*),

Note: maps by **mail or phone order** are available from Stanfords (☎020/7836 1321, fax 020/7836 0189; *sales@stanfords.co.uk*; *www.stanfords.com*).

IRELAND

Belfast Waterstones, Queen's Bldg, 8 Royal Ave (☎028/9024 7355).

Dublin Easons Bookshop, 40 O'Connell St (☎01/873 3811); Fred Hanna's Bookshop, 27–29

Nassau St (☎01/677 1255); Hodges Figgis Bookshop, 56–58 Dawson St (☎01/677 4754); Waterstones, 7 Dawson St (☎01/679 1415).

NORTH AMERICA

Chicago Rand McNally, 444 N Michigan Ave, IL 60611 (☎312/321-1751; *www. randmcnally.com*).

Montréal Ulysses Travel Bookshop, 4176 St-Denis (☎514/843-9447; *www.ulysses.ca*).

New York The Complete Traveler Bookstore, 199 Madison Ave, NY 10016 (☎212/685-9007); Rand McNally, 150 E 52nd St, NY 10022 (☎212/758-7488); The Travel Shop, 551 Fifth Ave, NY 10176 (☎212/490-6688); Traveler's Choice Bookstore, 22 W 52nd St, NY 10019 (☎212/941-1535; *tvlchoice@aol.com*).

San Francisco The Complete Traveler Bookstore, 3207 Fillmore St, CA 94123 (☎415/923-1511); Rand McNally, 595 Market St, CA 94105 (☎415/777-3131).

Santa Barbara Map Link Inc, 30 S La Petera Lane, Unit #5, CA 93117 (☎805/692-6777; *www.maplink.com*).

Seattle Elliot Bay Book Company, 101 S Main St, WA 98104 (☎206/624-6600; *www. elliottbaybook.com*).

Toronto Open Air Books and Maps, 25 Toronto St, ON, M5R 2C1 (☎416/363-0719).

Vancouver World Wide Books and Maps, 552 Seymour Street, Vancouver, BC V6B 3J5 (☎604/687-3320; *www.itmb.com*).

Note: Rand McNally now has 24 stores across the US; call ☎1-800/333-0136 (ext 2111) for the address of your nearest store, or for **direct mail** maps, alternatively consult their Web site at *www.randmcnally.com*.

AUSTRALIA AND NEW ZEALAND

Adelaide The Map Shop, 6 Peel St (☎08/8231-2033).

Auckland Auckland Specialty Maps, 58 Albert St (☎09/307-2217).

Brisbane Brisbane Worldwide Maps and Guides, 187 George St (☎07/3221-4330).

Christchurch Mapworld, 173 Gloucester St (☎03/374-5399; *www.mapworld.co.nz*).

Melbourne Foreign Language Bookshop, 259 Collins St (☎03/9654-2883; *www.languages. com.au*); Mapland, 372 Little Bourke St (☎03/9670-4383; *www.mapland.com.au*).

Perth Perth Map Centre, 884 Hay St (☎08/9322-5733; *www.perthmap.com.au*).

Sydney Travel Bookshop, 175 Liverpool St (☎02/9261-8200).

Andalucía is the annually updated *Michelin Andalucía* (1:400,000), which includes a plan to get you in and out of Sevilla, the region's only serious traffic headache. Good alternatives, especially if you're shopping before arrival, are the 1:300,000 RV (Reise und Verkehrsverlag) *Andalucía*, distributed in the UK by Roger

Lascelles and by Plaza y Janés in Spain, as well as the less detailed Firestone and Rand McNally. The most comprehensive **city street plans** are the somewhat unwieldy *Plano Callejeros* by Editorial Everest, which cover all the major towns in Andalucía and have street indexes; they are obtainable from most *librerías*, but outside Sevilla the free maps handed out by most tourist offices serve just as well. For Sevilla, the best street plan is the pocketable *La Guía Verde*, generally available from city bookshops; the fold-out *Falkplan Sevilla* is also good.

Serious **hikers** can get more detailed maps from the offices and stores listed in the city Listings sections of the *Guide*. All the provincial capitals have a **CNIG** (National Geographical Information Centre), which stocks the full range of **topographical maps** issued by two government agencies: the IGN (Instituto Geográfico Nacional) and the SGE (Servicio Geográfico del Ejército). The maps are available at scales of 1:200,000, 1:100,000, 1:50,000, and even occasionally 1:25,000. The various SGE series are considered to be more up-to-date and accurate by those in the know, although no Spanish maps are up to the standards that British or North American hikers are used to. The relevant CNIG offices, or their commercial equivalents where IGN and SGE maps can be bought, are listed in the Sevilla, Córdoba, Granada and Málaga Listings sections at the end of each city account; the local Turismo will provide addresses for the others should you need them. If you are likely to be passing through Madrid, La Tienda Verde, c/Maudes 38 (☎91 534 32 57, fax 91 533 64 54) has all the maps mentioned above and many more, and is willing to do business by post.

A Catalunya-based company, Editorial Alpina, produces 1:40,000 or 1:25,000 map **booklets** for most of the mountain and foothill areas of interest, including a new three-part guide to the Sierra de · Cazorla (see p.394) in Jaén. Penthalon is another publisher with a range of guides in Spanish covering many of Andalucía's major walking areas. These are on sale in many bookshops. Other guidebooks dealing with hikes in specific areas (mostly in Spanish) are noted in the text where appropriate.

ANDALUCIA ON THE INTERNET

Spain and Andalucía are represented pretty strongly on the Internet, with Web sites in both English and Spanish offering information on most conceivable subjects. Andalucía's provincial capitals all have their own Web sites and many small towns and villages are starting them up too; all are fairly easy to find. In addition many major tourist attractions such as the Alhambra in Granada have sites, and these are listed in the relevant sections of the *Guide*. The Web sites detailed below are useful starting points, and most contain numerous links to more detailed areas.

The *soc.culture.spain* **newsgroup** is also highly recommended if you want to ask questions on any cultural matters.

Andalucía Online
www.andalucia.com
This site promises links across the province and all kinds of information, though it's early days yet.

Andalucía There's Only One
www.andalucia.org/ing/homepage.html
The official tourism site of the Junta de Andalucía.

Andalunet
www.andalunet.com
Extensive Sevilla site with lots of useful information including the Semana Santa procession routes.

City.Net: Spain
www.city.net/countries/spain
City.Net's Web indexes are a superb resource, arranged in clear categories including travel and sightseeing, news media and food and drink, and with a constant weather update as you log in. The main Andalucían cities are featured in some detail, and you can use links to explore beyond.

Costa del Sol Online
www.costasol.com
Another site which aims to draw together the Costa's commercial sites, along with a directory of property listings.

Dónde
donde.uji.es
Search engine for Spanish-language Web sites.

El País Digital
www.elpais.es
Digital version of Spain's major newspaper. And a most impressive production it is, too.

Flamenco
www.flamencoworld.com
Commercial flamenco site that nevertheless has good background info on history and new developments, besides trying to sell you discs and videos.

Gournet Spain
www.winwork.es/gournet-spain/
Searchable restaurant database that – at present
– promises more than it delivers.

Grupos Españoles en la Teleraña
www.get.es
Collective site for a number of Spanish rock
bands. Also details rock festivals.

Interbook
www.disbumad.es
Major Spanish online bookstore, offering more
than a million titles.

Parques Naturales Andaluces
www.cma.caan.es/parques/idxparques.htm
Details – with maps – of locations and facilities
at all the natural parks throughout the region.

Sherry
www.sherry.org
The story of Andalucía's great wine with explana-
tions of how it's made, the different styles, and
bodegas to visit.

Si Spain/
www.DocuWeb.ca/SiSpain
Posted by the Spanish Embassy in Ottawa, this is
the largest – and best – Spain-oriented English-
language site on the Web, bringing together
reams of information on all aspects of Spanish
culture, politics, history and tourist information,
as well as directing you to a host of specialist
sites. A particularly neat feature is the searchable
Fiesta Directory. Tokyo's embassy site is also
good: *www.spaintour.com*

Semana Santa
www.andal.es/guiaSemanaSanta
Good wide-ranging Spanish site with lots of background and links on the history and customs connected to Andalucía's major religious festival.

Sevilla
www.sol.com
Sevilla's Web site has details of accommodation,
restaurants, sights, weather and lots more.

Sevilla Tapas
www.acraba.com/tapeandoporsevilla
A guide to Sevilla's *tapas* bars and what they

serve up. Limited to only a score of bars so far but
should improve as it grows.

Sierra Nevada Ski Information
www.cetursa.es
Details of weather conditions, snow type and
real-time images from the slopes near Granada
(in Spanish but easy to follow).

Spain Online
www.spacelab.net/~spain/index.html
This looks set to be a useful bookmark, embracing
a range of sites, including the *Páginas Amarillas*
(Spanish Web Yellow Pages), Yahoo-Reuter daily
news about Spain (in English), and InterMedia's
summaries of the Spanish press and magazines
(in Spanish).

Spanish Tourist Office
www.turspain.es
General information board for the whole of Spain
with useful links.

Spatour
www.spatour.com
This site lists hotels, restaurants, campsites,
events and other tourist information for the whole
of Spain. Excellent site, but unfortunately only
available in Spanish at present.

Sur in English
www.surinenglish.com
The Web site of Málaga's main daily newspaper
covers the latest stories taken from its Spanish
edition plus lots of other background gen.

Todo Sobre España
www.red2000.com/spain/1index.html
Extensive site with details on all aspects of Spain
from bullfights, bars and beaches to fiestas, food
and flamenco.

Train timetables and fares
www.renfe.es
Renfe's online schedules include full route details,
times, and fares.

Yahoo! Spain
www.yahoo.com/r/es
The Spain section from this fine Web directory
always provides good leads.

COSTS, MONEY AND BANKS

Although many people still think of Spain as a budget destination, hotel prices have increased considerably over recent years, and if you're spending a lot of your time in the cities of Andalucía you can expect to spend easily as much as you would at home, if not more. However, there are still few places where you'll get a better deal on the cost of budget accommodation or simple meals and drink.

On average, if you're prepared to buy your own picnic lunch, stay in inexpensive *hostales* and hotels or youth hostels, and stick to local restaurants and bars, you could just get by on £15–20/US$24–32 a day per person sharing accommodation, but we're talking absolute basics here. If you intend to upgrade your accommodation, experience the city nightlife and eat fancier meals then you'll need more like £40/$64 a day. On £50–60/$75–90 a day and upwards you'll be limited only by your energy reserves – though of course if you're planning to stay in four- and five-star hotels or any of Andalucía's magnificent *paradores*, this figure won't even cover your room.

Room prices vary considerably according to season. In the summer you'll find that for rooms without en-suite bath there's little below 1500ptas (£6/$9.50) single, 2500ptas (£10/$16) double, and 2000ptas single (£8/$12), 3000ptas double (£12/$18) might be a more realistic average, but in popular coastal areas prices can be much higher. Campsites start at around 400ptas

(£1.60/$2.40) a night per person (more like 600–700ptas in some of the major resorts), plus a similar charge for a tent and any vehicle.

The cost of **eating** can vary wildly, but in most towns there'll be restaurants offering a basic three-course meal for somewhere between 750 and 1500ptas (£3–6/$4.50–9.50). As often as not, though, you'll end up wandering from one bar to the next sampling *tapas* without getting round to a real sit-down meal – this is certainly tastier though rarely any cheaper (see "Eating and drinking"). Drink, and wine in particular, costs ridiculously little: £3/$5 will see you through a night's very substantial intake of the local vintage, though again, cruising some of the swankier city and coastal bars could easily treble this.

Most of the **journeys** you'll be making inside Andalucía will rarely be longer than 250km (the distance between Sevilla and Granada) and unless you plan to travel daily your **transport** budget should not prove a major expense. Sevilla to Granada, for example, on the cheapest regional train currently costs around 2400ptas one-way (£9.50/$14.50), 4800ptas for a return (£19/$29), or 2350ptas one-way and 4700ptas return by bus. Although things are improving, trains on average still tend to be slower than buses on all routes bar those linking Cádiz, Sevilla and Córdoba. Urban transport almost always operates on a flat fare of 150–250ptas (60p–£1/$1–1.60).

All of the above, inevitably, is affected by where you are and when. The larger cities such as Sevilla and Granada, as well as the tourist resorts, are invariably more expensive than remoter areas; and prices are hiked up, too, to take advantage of special events like *Semana Santa*. Despite official controls, you'd be lucky to find a room in Sevilla during Easter week or the April *feria*, which follows on its heels, at less than a third above the usual rate. As always, if you're travelling alone you'll end up spending much more than you would in a group of two or more – sharing rooms saves greatly. An ISIC **student card** is worth having – it'll get you free or reduced entry to many museums and sites as well as occasional other discounts – and a FIYTO youth card (available to anyone under 26) is almost as good.

One thing to look out for on prices is the addition of sales tax – **IVA** (pronounced "iba") –

THE EURO

Spain is one of the eleven member nations of the European Union who on January 1, 1999 entered into economic and monetary union (EMU) and started using a single currency, the **Euro**, with one Euro permanently fixed at 166.386ptas. Until the start of 2002, however, it will only be possible to make paper transactions in the new currency (if you have, for example Euro travellers' cheques or a Euro bank or credit-card account), and the peseta will remain until then the normal unit of currency in Spain. **Euro notes and coins** will be issued from **January 2002** and will then circulate with Spanish pesetas in tandem for a six-month period following this. From July 1, 2002, the Euro will replace the peseta entirely and will be the only legal tender. For at least six months before and after the changeover hotels, *hostales* and restaurants as well as train and bus companies will display their prices in both currencies, and the same will apply on bills and receipts. The Euro is a decimal currency comprised of 100 centimos (cents).

EURO CONVERTER

25ptas = €0.15	1000ptas = €6.01
50ptas = €0.30	5000ptas = €30.05
100ptas = €0.60	10,000ptas = €60.10
500ptas = €3.01	20,000ptas = €120.20

which may come as an unexpected and irritating extra when you pay the bill for food or accommodation (currently seven percent), especially in more expensive establishments. Normally restaurants will include this in the price but hotels and *hostales* often leave out the tax (especially in phone or fax bookings) to make the price seem more attractive. "*¿Está incluido el IVA?*" (Is sales tax included?) is what you should ask.

MONEY AND THE EXCHANGE RATE

Until July 1, 2002 when the Euro will be the only legal tender in Spain (see above), the official Spanish currency continues to be the **peseta**, indicated in this book as "ptas". **Coins** come in denominations of 1, 5, 10, 25 (with a hole), 50 (indented), 100, 200 and 500 pesetas; **notes** as 1000, 2000, 5000 and 10,000 pesetas. The only oddity is that in a shop when paying for something, you'll often be asked for a duro (5ptas) or cinco duros (25ptas), and even, in country districts, quince (fifteen) or veinte (twenty) duros – which can test your mental arithmetic.

The **exchange rate** for the Spanish peseta is currently around 250 to the pound sterling (around €1.60 to the pound), and 150 to the US dollar (with €1.00 to the dollar). You can take in as much money as you want (in any form), although amounts over one million pesetas must be declared; and you can take out up to 500,000 pesetas, unless you can prove that you brought more than this with you in the first place. Not that this is likely to prove a major holiday worry.

TRAVELLERS' CHEQUES AND CREDIT CARDS

Probably the safest and easiest way to carry your funds is in **travellers' cheques** – though watch out for occasional outrageous commissions; 500–600ptas per transaction isn't unusual. It's worth noting a deal between American Express and the nationwide Banco Central Hispano bank whose branches will cash Amexco cheques commission-free – a substantial saving. Any American Express office in Spain also provides the same service.

Most **cards** including Visa, Mastercard (Access) or British automatic bank cards, and US cards in the Cirrus or Plus systems, can also be used for **withdrawing cash from ATMs** in Spain: even Andalucía's smaller villages are getting them now and they can be very useful especially at night, weekends or on the frequent public holidays when banks can sometimes close down for days at a time. Using cards also cuts out waiting in time-consuming queues – something that happens often in the more popular destinations. Check with your bank to find out about these reciprocal arrangements – the system is highly sophisticated and all Spanish machines now give instructions in a variety of languages.

Leading **credit and charge cards** are recognized, too, and are useful for such extra expenses as car rental and buying petrol, as well as for cash advances at banks. All upmarket hotels and restaurants will also accept this method of payment, and quite a few budget places are starting to do so now as well. American Express and Visa, which has an arrangement with the Banco de Bilbao, are the most useful; Mastercard is less widely accepted.

CHANGING MONEY

Spanish **banks** and *cajas de ahorros* (equivalent to a building society) have branches in all but the smallest towns, and most of them should be prepared to change travellers' cheques (albeit occasionally with reluctance for certain brands, and almost always with hefty commissions). Banco Central Hispano, Banco Bilbao Vizcaya and La Caixa are three of the most efficient, with numerous branches; all change most brands of travellers' cheques, and give cash advances on credit cards; commissions at La Caixa and Banco Central Hispano are generally the lowest, but you

should aim never to pay more than 500ptas. Elsewhere you may have to queue up at two or three windows, a twenty- to thirty-minute process.

Banking hours are generally Mon–Fri 9am–2pm, Sat 9am–1pm (except from May to September when banks close on Saturday). Outside these times, it's usually possible to change cash at larger hotels (generally bad rates, but low commission) or with travel agents, who may initially grumble but will eventually give a rate with the commission built in – useful for small amounts in a hurry.

In tourist areas you'll also find specialist *casas de cambio*, with more convenient hours (though the rates vary), and most branches of El Corte Inglés, a major department store found throughout Spain, have efficient exchange facilities open throughout store hours (until late evening) and offering competitive rates and generally a much lower commission than the banks, though they're worse for cash. American Express offices, which don't charge any commission on their own travellers' cheques, can also be useful, especially in Málaga, Sevilla and Granada.

GETTING AROUND

Most of Andalucía is well covered by both bus and rail networks and for most journeys between major towns – excepting Cádiz, Sevilla and Córdoba where lines have been upgraded – buses tend to be faster than trains. On shorter or less obvious routes buses also tend to be quicker and will normally take you closer to your destination; some train stations are several miles from the town or village they serve and you've no guarantee of a connecting bus – these instances are noted throughout the *Guide*. Approximate journey times and frequencies can be found in the "Travel details" at the end of each chapter, and local peculiarities are also pointed out in the text of the *Guide*. Car rental may also be worth considering, with costs among the lowest in Europe.

BUSES AND TAXIS

Unless you're travelling on a rail pass, **buses** will probably meet most of your transport needs; many smaller villages are accessible only by bus, almost always leaving from the capital of their province. Service varies in quality, but on the whole the buses are fast, reliable and comfortable enough, with prices pretty standard at around 850ptas per 100km. The only real problem involved is that many towns still have no main bus station, and buses may leave from a variety of places (even if they're heading in the same direction, since some destinations are served by more than one company). Where a new terminal has been built, it's often on the outer fringes of town. As far as possible, departure points are detailed in the *Guide*. One thing to bear in mind when comparing a long-distance journey by train or bus is the latter's pervasive video culture. Movies

start rolling as you leave the bus station and a surreal audio backdrop of Wild West gunfights, war battles or screaming police sirens may not ideally complement the scenic delights outside the window; many of the bigger bus companies are now installing headphone systems similar to those used by airlines.

One important point to remember is that all public transport, and the bus service especially, is drastically reduced on **Sundays and holidays** – it's best not even to consider travelling to out-of-the-way places on these days. The words to look out for on timetables are *diario* (daily), *laborables* (workdays, including Saturday), and *domingos y festivos* (Sundays and holidays).

Taxis in city areas are incredibly good value and are certainly the safest way to travel late at night. Make full use of them, particularly in Sevilla, Málaga and Granada.

TRAINS

RENFE, the Spanish rail company, operates a horrendously complicated variety of train services divided into three main sections. **Cercanías** are local commuter trains in and around the major cities. **Regionales**, roughly equivalent to buses in speed and cost, run locally between cities, although Regional exprés and Delta trains can cover longer distances. **Largo Recorridos** are long distance express trains, which have a bewildering number of names; in ascending order of speed and luxury, they are known as Diurno, Intercity (IC), Estrella (often just signified by a star), Talgo, Talgo P(endular), Talgo 200 (T200) and Trenhotel. Anything above Intercity can cost more than twice as much as standard second class. A growing number of super-high-speed trains from Madrid such as the impressive **AVE** (*tren alta velocidad*) run on a dedicated track connecting the capital with Córdoba and Sevilla. Costing just under double the normal second class fare, these trains have cut travelling times dramatically for those who can afford it. RENFE is so confident of its performance that if arrival is more than five minutes later than scheduled you get your money back. Andalucía's train system varies dramatically in its efficiency and operation and whilst lines and services such as those running between Cádiz, Sevilla and Córdoba have recently been

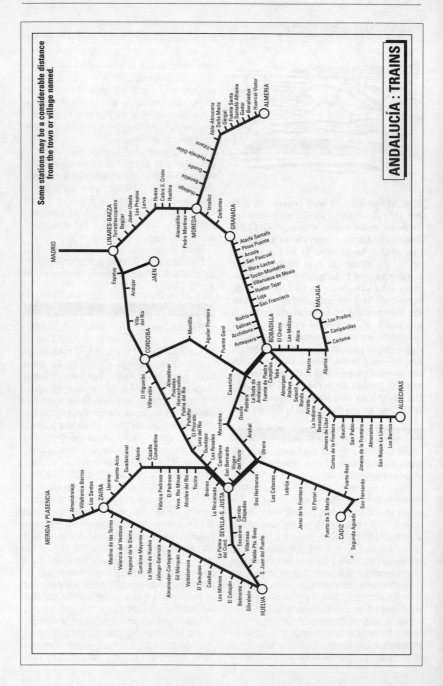

Some stations may be a considerable distance from the town or village named.

ANDALUCÍA : TRAINS

upgraded to modern European standards and faster **TRD** (*Trenes Regionales Diésel*) trains have been introduced on journeys between Sevilla, Málaga, Córdoba, Granada and Almería, services in other areas lag a long way behind and can be tortuously time-consuming; worth bearing in mind especially when planning longer journeys.

In recent years many bona fide train services have been phased out in favour of buses operated jointly by RENFE and a private bus company. This is particularly the case when the connection is indirect or when the train departure is at an inconvenient time. On some routes the **rail buses** outnumber the conventional departures by a ratio of four to one. Prices are the same as on the trains, and these services usually leave from and arrive at the bus stations/stops of the towns concerned.

RAIL PASSES

InterRail (see p.6) and **Eurail** (p.14 and p.15) passes are valid on most RENFE services (not on AVE and other dedicated high-speed lines), though it may be necessary to pay a supplement for travelling on the faster and more luxurious trains. The apparently random nature of these **surcharges** – which seem to depend on the individual train guard – can be a source of considerable irritation. It's better to know what you're letting yourself in for by reserving a seat in advance, something you'll be obliged to do in any case on some trains. For 600ptas, you'll get a large, computer-printed ticket which will satisfy even the most unreasonable of guards.

If using the trains extensively in Spain, but not outside the country, and you are under 26, you might consider a **RENFE Tarjeta Explorerail**, accepted on all services except some high-speed lines – and currently the only pass available within Spain itself (although it can also be purchased before arrival from selected travel agents). You can buy passes for seven-, fifteen- or thirty-day periods; a second-class seven-day pass costs 19,000ptas; a fifteen-day pass costs 23,000ptas; and a thirty-day pass costs 30,000ptas.

British and Irish residents might also consider purchasing the **Spanish EuroDomino Pass** from Rail Europe (see p.6), Usit Campus or some travel agents before arrival, allowing three, five or ten days' travel in one calendar month within Spain. Prices for under-26s are for three days £69, five days £106, ten days £182; over-26 prices are three days £89, five days £132 and ten days £227.

The North American and Australian **Spain Flexipass** (see p.31 and p.16) can be purchased before arrival in both first- and second-class versions, and allows three days' unlimited travel in a two month period for US$196/154 (first-/second-class), with the option of buying up to seven additional rail days at US$40/32 per day. North Americans considering a combination of rail and car travel might also be interested in the **Spain Rail 'n' Drive** pass, valid for three or more days' rail travel and two or more days' car hire in a two-month period. Prices vary according to the number of travel days, style of car, and number of adults sharing it. See p.14 for details of where to buy the Spain Flexipass and Rail 'n' Drive Pass.

Note that with all these passes you may also be stung for surcharges.

TICKETS AND FARES

RENFE offers a whole range of **discount fares** of 25–40 percent for those over sixty, the disabled, children aged four to twelve years and groups of more than ten. Return fares are also discounted by ten per cent on *regionales* (valid for fifteen days) and twenty per cent on *largo recorridos* (valid for sixty days).

Tickets can be bought at stations between sixty days and fifteen minutes before the train leaves, from the *venta anticipada* window, or in the final two hours from the *venta inmediata* window. Don't leave it to the last minute, however, as there are usually long lines. There may also be separate windows for *largo recorrido* (long-distance) trains and *regionales* or *cercanías* (locals). If you board the train without a ticket the conductor may charge you up to double the normal fare; if you don't have the cash, they'll call the police. If you do get on a train without a ticket it's always best to find the conductor first and explain, rather than wait to have them find you.

Most larger towns have a much more convenient RENFE office in the town centre as well, which sells **tickets in advance** and has schedule pamphlets – many of these are listed in the *Guide* under the relevant towns. The same offices also stock the free *Horarios de Trenes Regionales* leaflet (make sure it's the current edition) detailing all major services throughout Andalucía, or you can buy the *Guía RENFE* timetable here too (and at major stations) – useful if you plan to travel extensively in Spain by train. You can also buy tickets at travel agents which display the RENFE sign – they should have a sophisticated computer system that can also make seat reservations (the cost is the same as at the station); if they are not linked up by computer don't bother, as the alternative — booking by fax — can be more trouble than it's worth. For long journeys, a reserved seat is a good idea, as many trains are very crowded.

You can **change the departure date** of an electronically issued, reserved-seat, long-distance (*largo recorrido*) ticket up to one hour before your originally scheduled departure with a penalty of 200ptas. If you want to cancel the same sort of ticket you'll be entitled to an 85 percent refund of the ticket price, provided you do so at least half an hour before departure.

DRIVING AND VEHICLE RENTAL

Whilst getting around on public transport is easy enough, you'll obviously have a great deal more freedom if you have your **own car**. Major roads are generally good, and traffic, while a little hectic in Sevilla, is generally well behaved — though Spain does have one of the highest incidences of traffic accidents in Europe. But you'll be spending more, even with a full car; petrol prices are only marginally lower than in Britain (almost double US prices), and in the larger cities you'll probably want to pay extra for the security of a hotel with parking, or be forced to stay on the outskirts.

Also, **vehicle crime** is rampant — never leave anything visible in the car, and in major cities such as Sevilla and Málaga empty it if the car is to be left on the street overnight. A useful tip for rental-car drivers is to get your vehicle as dirty as possible as soon as possible and leave it that way; a shiny new car spells "tourist" to the car thieves, who even know which models are used by the major rental companies. Needless to say, remove any visible stickers bearing the rental company's name or logo and check that all locks are fully functioning when you take delivery. Another hazard to be aware of is break-ins when parking at out-of-the-way beauty spots or isolated attractions such as caves. If a quick perusal of the road or car park reveals evidence of broken window glass it's a sure sign that thieves are frequent visitors and you'll need to park elsewhere or take appropriate action. That said, most of the people you'll meet in Andalucía will be shiningly honest, and although car crime is bad in cities such as Sevilla and Málaga, it is rarely accompanied by physical violence against the person.

Tow-cranes or *gruas* are now big business in most Spanish towns and cities, as the municipal-ities attempt to control **illegal parking**. In all cities check carefully where you park, for if you return to find your car gone it will usually be in the pound and the only way to retrieve it is by paying a stiff fine (currently around 15,000ptas or £60/$90); no excuses will be accepted and without payment in cash you won't get your vehicle back. When parking, look out for the tow-crane symbol on street signs and study the time regulations carefully; if in doubt ask a local. It is also a towable offence to park on a taxi-rank. You're more likely to find a parking space in summer if you plan to arrive in the larger towns and cities during the siesta period (roughly 2–5pm) when many inner city workers vacate their parking spaces to drive home.

Most foreign **driver's licences** are honoured in Spain — including all EU, US and Canadian ones — but an International Driver's Permit (particularly if your UK licence is pre-1986) is available in Britain from the AA or RAC for £4.00 and is an easy way to set your mind at rest. If you're bringing your own car, you must have a green card from your insurers, and a bail bond or extra coverage for legal costs is also worth having, since if you do have an accident it'll very likely be your fault, as a foreigner, regardless of the circumstances. Without a bail bond both you and the car could be locked up pending investigation.

Spanish **road signs** are often badly sited — either too near or too far from the junctions and other potential hazards they indicate; the signing of the new Costa del Sol motorway (the *Autopista del Sol*) seems purposely intended to entice confused drivers onto this toll highway resulting in vehicles then having to pay the toll to get off it. Away from main roads you yield to vehicles approaching from the right, but rules are not too strictly observed anywhere. **Speed limits** are posted — maximum on urban roads is 50kph (30mph), other roads 90kph (55mph), motorways 120kph (75mph) — and (on the main highways at least) speed traps are common. If you're stopped for any violation, the Spanish police have the power to levy stiff on-the-spot fines. The Policía Local (urban police) are fairly lenient in applying the law, especially when it comes to such offences as not wearing a crash helmet on a motorcycle. The Guardia Civil traffic police who have responsibilty for the main national routes (*carreteras nacionales*) and autovías (semi-motorways) are a very different matter, however, and

CAR RENTAL AGENCIES

AUSTRALIA
Avis	☎1-800/225-533
Budget	☎1-300/362-848
Dollar	☎02/9223 1444
Hertz	☎1-800/550-067
Thrifty	☎1-300/367-227

NEW ZEALAND
Avis	☎09/525-1982 or 0800/655-111
Budget	☎09/238-5758 or 0800/652-227
Dollar	☎0800/486-677
Hertz	☎09/256-8692 or 0800/655-955
Thrifty	☎09/275-6666

NORTH AMERICA
Auto Europe	☎1-800/223-5555;
	www.autoeurope.com
Avis	☎1-800/331-1084;
	www.avis.com
Budget	☎1-800/527-0700;
	www.budget.com
Dollar	☎1-800/800-4000;
	www.europcar.com

Europe by Car	☎1-800/223-1516 or 212/581 3040; *www.europebycar.com*
Hertz	☎1-800/654-3001; *www.hertz.com*
Holiday Autos	☎1-800/442-7737; *www.kemwel.com*
National Car Rental	☎1-800/CAR-RENT; *www.nationalcar.com*

REPUBLIC OF IRELAND
Avis	☎01/874 5844
Budget	☎0800/973159
Europcar	☎01/874 5844
Hertz	☎01/676 7476

UK
Avis	☎0870/606 0100
Budget	☎0800/181181
Europcar	☎0870/607 5000
Hertz	☎0870/599 6699
Holiday Autos	☎0870/530 0400
Sun Cars	☎0870/500 5566

have a mean reputation. For traffic infringements they will usually levy an on-the-spot fine, which can range from 50,000 to 100,000ptas, before letting you go on your way, especially since as a foreigner you're unlikely to want, or be able, to appear in court. If you are cautioned, polite acceptance is the best policy, as antagonizing them can lead to other offences being tacked on to the original infringement (such as not carrying a warning triangle or lacking a first-aid kit). If you wish to contest the fine write the words *garantía, no es pago y no está conformé* on the citation in the space provided and sign it. This leaves the way open to contest the ticket later – but if you decide to do so you'd be wise to seek legal advice. However, you'll still need to pay up on the spot (foreigners get a 20 percent reduction for this "prompt payment") and failure to do so can mean the impounding of your vehicle and documents until you do. If you haven't got the cash on you the police will obligingly accompany you to the nearest bank or *cajero automático* (cash machine).

Andalucía still has a great number of manned **garages** where, when buying petrol (*gasolina*), you'll need to know the terms Super (four star leaded), *gasoil* (diesel) and *sin plomo* (unleaded). Credit cards are accepted by most stations.

VEHICLE RENTAL

Renting a car lets you out of many of the hassles, and Andalucía is one of the cheapest places in Europe to do this. There's usually a choice of companies in any major town or city, with the biggest ones – Hertz, Avis and Europcar – represented at the airports as well as in town centres. You'll need to be 21 (and have been driving for at least a year), and many companies levy a surcharge (around 500ptas per day) on drivers under 25. You're looking at a cost starting at around 5000ptas per day for a small car (less by the week; special rates at the weekend). **Fly-drive deals** with Iberia and other operators can be good value if you know in advance that you'll want to rent a car. The big companies all offer schemes, but you'll often get a better deal through someone who deals with local agents. Sun Cars and Holiday Autos are among the best, substantially undercutting the large companies. If you're going in high season, it's best to try and book well in advance.

MOTORBIKES, MOPEDS AND SCOOTERS

Seeing Andalucía on two wheels is an attractive proposition, especially away from the coast, and most of the major tourist resorts have companies where you can rent **motorbikes, mopeds and scooters**. The smaller bikes and mopeds are ideal for pottering around for a day or two, but don't regard them as serious transport. Inland Andalucía is very mountainous and mopeds simply won't go up some of the steeper hills, even with only one person aboard. For serious touring or exploration you'll need at least 100cc to cope and probably 150cc and more if you're going to be carrying baggage or a passenger.

To **rent a motorbike** (3000–4000ptas a day, cheaper by the week) you have to be 14 to ride a machine under 75cc, 18 for one over 75cc, and crash helmets are compulsory; there's a stiff on-the-spot fine if you're caught not wearing one. Note that mopeds and motorbikes are often rented out with insurance that doesn't include theft – always check with the company first. You will generally be asked to produce a driving licence as a deposit. When renting, check the bike thoroughly before riding off as many are only cosmetically repaired and if you break down it's often your responsibility to return the machine. It's wise to get a phone number from the rental company in case it does collapse miles from anywhere, or you lose your ignition key! Bike repairs after a spill could leave you with a massive bill so make sure that you are adequately insured, both in the rental agreement and by your own travel insurance – many of these schemes specifically exclude injuries sustained while riding motorcycles. Turarche, c/Roger de Flor 1 (at the Málaga bus station; ☎95 231 80 69, fax 95 231 63 42), are a reliable company who rent out a range of bikes (and cars) and will deliver to the airport to meet your plane.

CYCLING

There's no great popularity for **cycling** in Andalucía, not surprisingly, perhaps, in view of the terrain and fierce summer heat, but the saddle of a bike offers an incomparable view of the region and guarantees contact with locals the average visitor could never meet. Do remember, though, that peninsular Spain is one of the most mountainous countries in Europe and that Andalucía contains its two highest peaks, so you'll need to be a hardy hill-climber. In searing high summer temperatures, attempting to scale the hills becomes an endurance test: seasoned cycle tourists advise starting out at dawn and covering the main part of the day's schedule by mid-morn-

ing, before the temperature peaks. That leaves the rest of the day for sightseeing, picnicking around riverbanks or dipping in the often pleasant village pools, before covering a few more kilometres in the cooler hours before sunset.

The Spanish are keen cycle fans – though their interest is mainly in racing, and active cycling is largely restricted to racing club members – which means that you'll be well received and find reasonable facilities. There are bike shops in the larger towns and parts can often be found at auto repair shops or garages – look for Michelin signs. Cars tend to hoot before they pass, which can be alarming at first but is useful once you're used to it. Cycle-touring guides to the better areas can be found in good bookshops – in Spanish, of course.

Taking your own bike can be an inexpensive and flexible way of getting around and transporting your bike there should present few problems. Most airlines are happy to take them as ordinary baggage provided they come within your allowance (though it's sensible to check first to avoid any nasty surcharge surprises at the check-in desk; crowded charters may be less obliging). Deflate the tyres to avoid explosions in the unpressurized hold.

Spanish long-distance **trains** are also reasonably accessible, though bikes can only go on a train with a guard's van (*furgón*) and must be registered – go to the *Equipajes* or *Paquexpres* desk at the station. If you are not travelling with the bike you can either send it as a package or buy an undated ticket and use the method above; be aware, though, that this can often mean a few days' wait if (as often happens) the bike gets delayed en route. For travel inside Andalucía the *cercanías* (local trains) will often allow you to take your bike on board outside the rush hours, but this is at the discretion of the guard. Buses have no set policy on carrying cycles and again it will usually depend on your powers of persuasion with the driver and how full the bus is.

In many of the coastal resorts you'll find basic pedal bikes for **rent**; they're reasonably cheap for a few hours' exploration and child seats are sometimes available too. Some of these outlets are also starting to rent out mountain bikes for more serious jaunts, and these are detailed in the *Guide*. Most *hostales* and hotels have somewhere safe for overnight storage and you should not leave your bike on the street overnight in either Málaga or Sevilla; elsewhere there should be no problem, but take a strong lock or chain.

HITCHING

As for most other countries today, we do not recommend **hitching** in Spain as a safe method of getting around. If you are determined to hitch in Andalucía, be warned that away from the main roads things can become very tedious, often involving long, hot waits. Always carry water with you and some kind of hat or cap – lifts all too often dry up at some shadeless junction in the middle of nowhere. On the other hand, thumbing on back roads in areas such as Las Alpujarras can be surprisingly productive; the fewer cars there are, the more likely they are to stop.

FLYING

Both Iberia and the smaller, slightly cheaper Aviaco operate an extensive network of **internal flights**. While these are quite reasonable by international standards, they still work out very pricey, and are only really worth considering if you're in an extraordinary hurry and need to cross the entire peninsula.

COMMUNICATIONS: POST, PHONES AND MEDIA

Post offices (*Correos*) are generally found near the centre of towns and are open Monday to Friday from 8am to noon and again from 5 to 7.30pm (some also open on Saturday mornings), though big branches in large cities may have considerably longer hours and do not usually close at midday. Except in the cities there's only one post office in each town, and queues can be long: stamps (*sellos*) are also sold at tobacconists (look for the brown and yellow *Tabac* sign).

You can have letters sent **poste restante** to any Spanish post office: they should be addressed (preferably with surname underlined and in capitals) to *Lista de Correos*, followed by the name of the town and province. To collect, take your passport and, if you're expecting mail, ask the clerk to check under all of your names – letters are often to be found filed under first or middle names.

American Express in Málaga, Sevilla and Granada will hold mail for at least a month for customers, and have windows for mail pickup.

Outbound mail is reasonably reliable, with letters or cards taking around five days to a week to the UK, a week to ten days to North America.

PHONES

Spanish public **phones** work well and have instructions in English (obtained by pressing the language button). If you can't find one, many bars also have pay phones you can use. Cabins take 5-, 25-, or 100-ptas coins, or phone cards (*tarjeta telefonica*) of 1000ptas or 2000ptas, which you can buy in tobacconists (*Tabac* or *estanco*): in old-style phones, rest the coins in the groove at the top and they'll drop when someone answers; in the newer cabins follow the instructions automatically displayed. In 2002 this will all change, of course, with the arrival of the **Euro** (see p.27). Spanish provincial (and some overseas) dialling codes are listed in the cabins. The **ringing tone** is long, **engaged** is shorter and rapid; the standard Spanish response is "*Dígame*" (speak to me) often abbreviated to *diga*.

For **international calls**, you can use almost any street cabin (marked *teléfono internacional*) or go to a **Telefónica** office where you pay afterwards. International and domestic rates are slightly cheaper after 10pm, and after 2pm on Saturday and all day Sunday. If you're using a cabin to call abroad, you're best off putting at least 200ptas in to ensure a connection, and make sure you have a good stock of 100-peseta pieces. **Locutorios** – often privately owned – offer a similar service to Telefonica offices and are found in many larger towns and cities.

If you want to make a **reverse-charge call** (*cobro revertido*), you'll have to go to a *Telefónica*, where you can expect queues at cheap-rate times. Some hotels will arrange reverse-charge calls for you, but as with all phone calls from hotels you'll be stung for an outrageous surcharge.

THE PRESS

British newspapers and the *International Herald Tribune* are on sale in most large cities and resorts. The main resort areas have their own English-language publications catering to the vast army of (largely elderly) expats. The glossy monthly *Lookout* is one of the best, often with travel articles and background on Spanish affairs. Along the Costa del Sol, *Sur in English* is a free Friday publication by the Málaga daily, *Sur*, cashing in on the same market; the Spanish edition's small ads section can be good for picking up odd jobs such as bar work and it carries details of local events and entertainment.

Andalucians, in line with the Spanish generally, are not great devourers of newsprint and none of the **Spanish national papers** has a circulation above 400,000. The best of these is *El País* – liberal-left, and the only one with much serious analysis or foreign news coverage; its daily Andalucía supplement is also a good source of information on the region. In the last decade, the appearance of the centre-right *El Mundo* has provided competition for *El País* as a serious centrist newspaper and made a big play of hounding the socialist government of Felipe González during the scandals enveloping it in the years leading up to its defeat in 1996. The rest are mostly well to the right, notably the dated-format *ABC*, solidly old-order with a hard moral line against divorce and abortion, and the Catholic *Ya*. *Diario 16* and Barcelona's *La Vanguardia* (available in Andalucía) are both centrist and solid.

However, with a smattering of Spanish by far the most entertaining breakfast read are **Andalucía's regional papers**. Here the scandals and stories from around the parish pump can give the outsider fascinating and often amusing insights into the communities encountered,

besides providing handy information on festivals and entertainment. There's always something of interest in most of the local papers but if you're in or around Cádiz the *Diario de Cádiz* – in keeping with the province's liberal traditions – has one of the liveliest readers' letters pages in the region, whilst *El Diario de Sevilla* does a similar job of monitoring Sevilla's pulse. Córdoba's *Diario*, Málaga's *Sur* and Granada's *Ideal* are others to look out for. Best for keeping up with **sport** (including foreign soccer results) are the Madrid sports papers *As* and *Marca* and the Catalan *El Mundo Deportivo*, all widely available in Andalucía, which has a phenomenal number of supporters of the Madrid and Barcelona teams.

TV AND RADIO

You'll inadvertently catch more **TV** than you expect sitting in bars and restaurants as only the snootiest places seem to be able to function without the blaring box – usually not being watched or listened to by anybody. On the whole the output is a fairly entertaining mixture of ghastly game and chat shows, foreign-language films and TV series dubbed into Spanish. Soaps are a particular speciality, either South American *telenovelas*, which take up most of the daytime programming, or well-travelled British, US and Australian exports. Throughout most of the summer TV carries live bullfights in the early evening and no one expresses the slightest quiver of concern that children may be looking on. News programmes, particularly on the state channels, are comprehensive, with wide coverage given to foreign news and the arts. There are two state channels, *TVE1* and *TVE2*, plus the private *Antena 3* and *Telecinco*. Andalucía also has its own *Canal Sur*. *Canal Plus* is a cable company showing mainly films and sport. Most of Andalucía's upmarket hotels are now equipped with satellite TV giving access to channels such as *BBC World*, *CNN* and *Sky*. **Sports** fans are well catered for, with regular live coverage of football and basketball matches – in the football season, you can watch two or more live matches a week in most bars, or hotel rooms. Since the death of Franco the reaction against any form of censorship has meant that satellite hard-core pornography channels proliferate; in stark contrast to places such as the UK and Ireland the general Spanish attitude is blasé, so don't be surprised to find it on one of your hotel's TV channels.

If you're going to be getting around by car, twiddling the dial on the **radio** will soon give you

TELEPHONE CODES

Since 1998 all Spanish regional prefixes have become an integral part of telephone numbers and it is now necessary to dial these digits even when calling from within the city or province. Whilst all the numbers in this guide conform to the new system you should be aware that on many business cards, letterheads and other publicity these preliminary digits may not appear, and people may not always include them when giving out a number.

PHONING SPAIN FROM ABROAD

From Australia: dial ☎0011 + 34 + number (including regional prefix).

From Britain: dial ☎00 + 34 + number (including regional prefix).

From Ireland: dial ☎00 + 34 + number (including regional prefix).

From New Zealand: dial ☎00 + 34 + number (including regional prefix).

From North America: dial ☎011 + 34 + number (including regional prefix).

PHONING ABROAD FROM SPAIN

To Australia: dial ☎00 then 61 + area code minus first 0 + number.

To Britain: dial ☎00 then 44 + area code minus first 0 + number.

To Ireland: dial ☎00 then 353 + area code minus first 0 + number.

To New Zealand: dial ☎00 then 64 + area code minus first 0 + number.

To North America: dial ☎00 then 1 + area code + number.

USEFUL TELEPHONE NUMBERS

Alarm Call	☎096	International Operator (Europe)	☎1008
Directory Enquiries	☎1003	International Operator (rest of the world)	☎1005
		Weather	☎906 365365

an idea of what's available on the Spanish broadcasting system, where many Spaniards pick up their daily fix of current affairs, especially on the early-morning and late-evening news programmes. Stations to listen out for are the state-owned *Radio Nacional* (AM) whilst *Onda Cero* (FM) and *Cadena Cuarenta* (FM) are pop stations with big followings. There are a number of English language stations along the Costa del Sol such as *Central* (FM) and *Coastline Radio* (FM) with similar middle-of-the-road music and talk formats, and *Radio Gibraltar* (FM) puts out English news bulletins. If you have a radio which picks up short-wave you can tune in to the *BBC World Service*, broadcasting in English for most of the day on frequencies between 12MHz (24m) and 4MHz (75m). You may also be able to receive *Voice of America* and American Forces' stations.

ACCOMMODATION

Reasonably priced rooms are still very widely available in Andalucía, and in almost any town you'll be able to get a simple double for around 2500–3500ptas (£10–15/$16–24), a single for 1500–2500ptas (£6–10/$10–16). Rooms with en-suite bath or shower start at just above these prices. Only in major resorts and a handful of "tourist cities" (such as Granada or Sevilla) need you pay more.

We've detailed where to find **places to stay** in most of the destinations listed in the *Guide*, and given a price range for each (see box on the following page), from the most basic rooms to luxury hotels. As a general rule, all you have to do is head for the cathedral or main square of any town, invariably surrounded by an old quarter full of accommodation possibilities. In Spain, unlike most countries, you don't seem to pay any more for a central location (this goes for bars and cafés, too), though you do tend to get a comparatively bad deal if you're travelling on your own as there are relatively few single rooms. Much of the time you'll have to negotiate a reduction on the price of a double.

It's always worth **bargaining** over room prices in fact, since although they're officially regulated this doesn't necessarily mean much. In high season you're unlikely to have much luck (although many places do have rooms at different prices, and tend to offer the more expensive ones first) but at quiet times you may get quite

a discount. If there are more than two of you, most places have rooms with three or four beds at not a great deal more than the double room price – a bargain, especially if you have children.

FONDAS, PENSIONES, HOSTALES AND HOTELES

The one thing all travellers need to master is the elaborate variety of types and places to stay. Least expensive of all – and most basic – are **fondas** (mostly identifiable by a square blue sign with a white **F** on it, and often positioned above a bar), closely followed by **casas de huéspedes** (**CH** on a similar sign), **pensiones** (**P**) and, less commonly, **hospedajes**. Distinctions between all of these are rather blurred, but in general you'll often find food served at both *fondas* and *pensiones* (some of which may offer rooms only on a meals-inclusive basis). *Casas de huéspedes* – literally "guest houses" – were traditionally for longer stays; and to some extent, particularly in the older family seaside resorts, they still are. A variation on these are *casas particulares*, or unlicensed guesthouses, where the householder decides to let the odd room. Particularly common in holiday resorts where they soak up the overflow in high season, they are often a welcome option if things get tight.

Slightly more expensive but far more common are **hostales** (marked **Hs**) and **hostal-residencias** (**HsR**). These are categorized from one to three stars, but even so prices vary enormously according to location – in general the more remote, the less expensive. Most *hostales* offer good functional rooms, usually with private shower, and, for doubles at least, they can be excellent value. The *residencia* designation means that no meals other than perhaps breakfast are served.

Moving up the scale you finally reach **hoteles** (**H**), again star-graded by the authorities (from one to five). One-star hotels cost no more than three-star *hostales* – sometimes they're actually less expensive – but at three stars you pay a lot more, and at four or five you're in the luxury class with prices to match. Near the top end of this scale

ACCOMMODATION PRICE CODES

All the establishments listed in this book have been price-graded according to the following scale. The prices quoted are for the **cheapest available double room in high season**; effectively this means that anything in the ①, and most places in the ② range will be without private bath, though there's usually a washbasin in the room. In the ③ category and above you will probably be getting private bath facilities (except in major tourist cities such as Sevilla and Granada where prices are higher). Remember, though, that many of the budget places will also have more expensive rooms including en-suite facilities. Youth hostels are graded under ① as the price per person is less than the category's upper limit.

Note that in the more upmarket hostales and pensiones, and in anything calling itself a hotel, you'll pay a **tax** (IVA) of seven percent on top of the room price. Approximate Euro rates (operative from January 1, 2002) are also given for each category.

① Under 2000ptas/ Under €12
② 2000–3000ptas/€12–18
③ 3000–4500ptas/€18–27

④ 4500–6000ptas/€27–37
⑤ 6000–8000ptas/€37–49
⑥ 8000–10,000ptas/€49–60

⑦ 10,000–15,000ptas/€60–90
⑧ 15,000–20,000ptas/€90–120
⑨ Over 20,000ptas/Over €120

---

there are also luxury hotel chains as well as the state-run **paradores**: beautiful places (although there are modern exceptions), often converted from castles, monasteries and other minor Spanish monuments. If you can afford them, these are almost all wonderful (the best ones in Andalucía are detailed in the *Guide*), despite a reputation amongst Spanish critics for offhand service. Even if you can't afford to stay, the buildings are often worth a look in their own right, and usually have pleasantly classy bars and cafés, open to non-residents.

Outside all of these categories you will sometimes see **camas** (beds) and **habitaciones** (rooms) advertised in private houses or above bars, often with the phrase *camas y comidas* ("beds and meals"). If you're travelling on a very tight budget these can be worth looking out for – particularly if you're offered one at a bus station and the owner is prepared to bargain with you.

If you have any **problems** with Spanish rooms – overcharging, most obviously – you can usually produce an immediate resolution by asking for the *libro de reclamaciones* (official complaints book). By law all establishments must keep one and bring it out for regular inspection by the authorities. Although little is ever written in them they are worth using and, as the pages are numbered, difficult to tamper with. Add your home address, too, as you are entitled to be informed of any action taken, including – but don't count on it – compensation.

Consult the "Language" section (p.541) for how to ask for accommodation and specify your needs.

RURAL TOURISM AND *VILLAS TURISTICAS*

There has been a significant growth in **rural tourism** over recent years, encouraged by the *Junta de Andalucía*, in an attempt to spread the wealth of tourism away from the coast and into the less prosperous hinterland. As well as working out cheaper than staying on the coast or in the cities, this can be a great way to discover the most beautiful and unspoilt tracts of Andalucía.

There are several **Spanish guides** to rural accommodation in farmhouses and villages, among which are the *Anuario de Turismo Rural* (Ediciones Susaeta, Madrid) and the *Guía de Alojamiento Rural* (El País/Águilar), which are both easily comprehensible with photos of each property. Both are available from most Spanish bookshops. A **central organization** for Andalucía, the *Red Andaluza de Alojamientos Rurales*, Apartado 2035, 04080 Almería (☎950 26 50 18, fax 950 27 04 31; *www.raar.es*; English spoken), takes bookings and produces a free brochure with photos and descriptions of rural properties for rent. They also have details of rooms at farmhouses and village *casas particulares* (guesthouses). Many of these places encourage longer lets, but out of high season you can often get away with a single night (or perhaps two). The *Asociación de Hoteles Rurales de*

Andalucía, c/José Zorrilla 5, 14008 Córdoba (☎ & fax 957 49 04 18; English spoken), does a similar job for small rural hotels and also has a free brochure.

Villas turísticas are new hotels or groups of free-standing dwellings set up and run by the regional government. Built in scenic locations, they often use the vernacular architecture of the region. Technically they are self-catering apartments but usually they have all the facilities, including reception, restaurant and room service, that you'd find in a four-star hotel. They would normally be in category ⑤–⑦ of our price code. Some *villas turísticas* are mentioned in the *Guide* but for a complete list contact *Centro Internacional de Turismo de Andalucía*, 29600 Marbella (☎95 283 87 85, fax 95 283 63 69; *www.andalucia.org*; English spoken).

There are also **casas rurales** (rural houses), a scheme established along the lines of the French gîtes. Accommodation at these can vary from bed and breakfast at a farmhouse to a rental cottage. Local Turismos have details.

YOUTH HOSTELS AND REFUGES

Albergues Juveniles (youth hostels) are a possible option, especially in Andalucía's major towns, and we've detailed the most useful of these in the *Guide*. Most have been extensively refurbished and now stay open all year – the rest operate just for the summer (or spring and sum-mer) in temporary premises – although in towns they can be inconveniently located. Andalucía's nineteen year-round hostels are affiliated to **Inturjoven**, the region's official youth hostel organisation, and a leaflet with details of the locations of these, their facilities and tariffs can be obtained from any *albergue* or the Inturjoven office, c/Miño 24, 41011 Sevilla (☎95 427 70 87, or central reservations ☎902 50 50 50, fax 955 03 58 48; *www.inturjoven.com*). While Andalucía's hostels are pretty lenient when it comes to annoyances such as curfews, be warned that the most popular places are often block-reserved by school groups, or by hostellers who have booked months ahead, and also demand production of a YHA card (though this is generally available on the spot if you haven't already bought one from your national organization). At 1000–1800ptas per person (depending on your age and the season – under 26s get the cheaper rates), you can quite easily pay more than you would sharing a cheap double room in a *hostal*. That said, many of the newer youth hostels such as those in Málaga, Córdoba and Granada, are almost like hotels (with double rooms and en-suite bath or shower), and make for a pleasant stopover.

In isolated **mountain areas** the *Federación Andaluza de Montañismo*, Camino de Ronda 101, 18003 Granada (☎ & fax 958 29 13 40), runs a number of *refugios*: simple, cheap dormitory-huts for climbers and hikers, generally equipped only with bunks and a very basic kitchen.

YOUTH HOSTEL ASSOCIATIONS

Australia: Australian Youth Hostel Association, Level 3, 10 Mallet St, Camperdown, NSW 2050 (☎02/9565-1699; *www.yha.org.au*).

Canada Canadian Hostelling Association, Room 400, 205 Catherine St, Ottawa, ON K2P 1C3 (☎613/237-7884 or 1-800/663-5777; *www.hostellingintl.ca*).

England and Wales Youth Hostel Association (YHA), Trevelyan House, 8 St Stephen's Hill, St Albans, Herts AL1 2DY (☎01727/845047; *www.yha.org.uk*). London shop & information office: 14 Southampton St, London WC2 (☎020/7836 1036).

Ireland An Oige, 61 Mountjoy St, Dublin 7 (☎01/830 4555; *www.irelandyha.org*).

New Zealand: Youth Hostel Association of New Zealand, PO Box 436, Christchurch (☎03/379-9970; *www.yha.org.nz*).

Northern Ireland Youth Hostel Association of Northern Ireland (YHANI), 22–32 Donegall Rd, Belfast, BT12 5JN (☎028/9032 4733; *www.hini.org.uk*).

Scotland Scottish Youth Hostel Association (SYHA), 7 Glebe Crescent, Stirling, FK8 2JA (☎01786/891400; *www.syha.org.uk*).

USA Hostelling International/American Youth Hostels (HI/AYH), Suite 840, 733 15th St NW, PO Box 37613, Washington, DC 20005 (☎202/783-6161; *www.hiayh.org*).

CAMPING

There are some 130 authorized **campsites** in Andalucía, predominantly on the coast. Graded into three classes according to facilities, they usually work out at around 500ptas (£2/$3) per person per night. You'll also pay the same again for a tent and a similar amount for each car or caravan, perhaps twice as much for a van. Only a few of the most popular coastal sites are significantly more expensive. Again we've detailed the most useful in the text, but if you plan to camp extensively then pick up the free *Guía de Camping* published by the Junta de Andalucía, which details virtually all of them in map format; it's available from most Turismos, and in advance from Spanish National Tourist Offices abroad. A complete nationwide *Guía de Campings*, listing full prices, facilities and exact locations, is available from most Spanish bookshops. The *Club de Camping y Caravanning de Andalucía*, c/Francisco Carrión Mejías 13, 41003 Sevilla (☎95 422 77 66), also provides information on campsites and their facilities throughout the region.

Camping outside campsites is legal – but with certain restrictions. You're not allowed to camp "in urban areas, areas prohibited for military or touristic reasons, or within 1km of an official campsite". What this means in practice is that you can't camp on tourist beaches (though you can, discreetly, nearby) but with a little sensitivity you can set up a tent for a short period almost anywhere in the countryside. However, it's common courtesy to respect local sensibilities and whenever possible you should ask first – if there is a problem with your proposed site, somewhere nearby will, more often than not, be recommended.

If you're planning to spend a lot of your time camping, an *international camping carnet* is a good investment, available from home motoring organizations, or from one of the following: in Britain, the Camping and Caravan Club, Greenfields House, Westwood Way, Coventry CV4 8JH (☎024/7669 4995, fax 7669 4886); in the US and Canada, Family Campers and RVers, 4804 Transit Rd, Building 2, Depew, NY 14043 (☎1-800/245-9755). The carnet serves as useful identification and covers you for third-party insurance when camping.

EATING AND DRINKING

There are two ways to eat out in Andalucía: you can go to a *restaurante* or *comedor* (dining room) and have a full meal, or you can have a succession of *tapas* (small snacks) or *raciones* (larger ones) at one or more bars. At the bottom line a *comedor* – where you'll get a basic, filling, three-course meal with a drink, the *menú del día* – is nearly always the cheapest option, but they're often tricky to find, and rather drab. Nowadays most restaurants also offer a *menú del día* too, often very good value. Bars tend to be a lot more interesting, allowing you to do the rounds and sample local (often house) specialities.

BREAKFAST, SNACKS AND SANDWICHES

For breakfast you're best off in a bar or café, though some *hostales* and *fondas* will serve the "Continental" basics. Traditionally in Andalucía, it's *churros con chocolate* – long, tubular doughnuts (not for the weak of stomach) with thick drinking chocolate. But most places also serve *tostadas* (toasted rolls) with oil (*con aceite*) or butter (*con mantequilla*) – and jam (*y mermelada*), or egg dishes (*huevos fritos* are fried eggs). Croissants (*cruasán*) are now widely available in most town bars and *cafeterías* as is the French *pain au chocolat* which transmutes into a *napolitana* on this side of the border. Cold tortilla with a slice of toast (*pan tostada*) also makes an excel-

lent breakfast. Many of the more modern breakfast bars now offer wholemeal bread (*pan integral*) as an option.

Coffee and pastries (*pastas* or *pasteles*) or doughnuts are available at most cafés, too, though for a wider selection of cakes you should head for one of the many excellent *pastelerías* or *confiterías*. In larger towns, there will often be a *panadería* or *croissantería* serving quite an array of appetizing baked goods besides the obvious bread, croissants and pizza. For the different ways of ordering coffee see p.50.

Some bars specialize in sandwiches (*bocadillos*), and as they're usually outsize affairs in French bread, they'll do for breakfast or lunch. In a bar with *tapas* (see below), you can have most of what's on offer put in a sandwich, and you can often get them prepared (or buy the materials to do so) at grocery shops. Incidentally, a *sandwich* is a toasted cheese and ham sandwich, usually on sad processed bread.

TAPAS AND RACIONES

Andalucía has more *tapas* bars than anywhere else in Spain, and Sevilla seems to have one on every street corner. One of the advantages of eating in bars is that you are able to experiment. Many places have food laid out on the counter, so you can see what's available and order by pointing without necessarily knowing the names; others have blackboards (see the lists opposite). Tapas are small portions, three or four small chunks of fish or meat, or a dollop of salad, which traditionally used to be served up free with a drink. These days you have to pay for anything more than a few olives (although many country districts and not a few city bars – especially in Andalucía's four eastern provinces of Córdoba, Granada, Jaén and Almería – retain this generous custom); in most of the city-centre places where you do get free food now, it will often be called a *pincho*, or morsel; *pinchos morunos* (small kebabs) are often also available. A single *tapa* helping rarely costs more than 200–400ptas unless you're somewhere very flashy or you choose one of the expensive kinds of *jamón serrano* (cured ham). *Raciones* are simply bigger plates of the same, and can be enough in them-

TAPAS AND OTHER SNACKS

The most usual **fillings for *bocadillos*** are *lomo* (loin of pork), *tortilla* and *calamares* (all of which may be served hot), *jamón* (*York* or, much better, *serrano*), *chorizo*, *salchichón* (and various other regional sausages – such as the small, spicy Catalan *butifarras*), *queso* (cheese), or *atún* (tuna – probably canned). **Standard *tapas* and *raciones*** might include:

Aceitunas	Olives	*Hígado*	Liver
Albóndigas	Meatballs, usually in sauce	*Huevo cocido*	Hard-boiled egg
Anchoas	Anchovies	*Jamón serrano*	Mountain cured ham
Berberechos	Cockles	*Jamón York*	Regular ham
Boquerones	Fresh anchovies	*Judias*	Beans
Calamares a la romana	Squid, deep fried in rings	*Mejillones*	Mussels (either steamed, or served with diced tomatoes and onion)
Calamares en su tinta	Squid in ink		
Callos	Tripe	*Morcilla*	Blood sausage, or black pudding
Caracoles	Snails, often served in a spicy/curry sauce	*Navajas*	Razor clams
		Pan con tomate	Bread, rubbed with tomato and oil
Carne en salsa	Meat in tomato sauce		
Champiñones	Mushrooms, usually fried in garlic	*Patatas alioli*	Potatoes in mayonnaise
		Patatas bravas	Fried potato cubes topped with spicy sauce and mayonnaise
Chipirones	Whole baby squid		
Chorizo	Spicy sausage		
Cocido	Stew	*Pimientos*	Peppers
Croqueta	Fish or chicken croquette	*Pincho moruno*	Kebab
Empanadilla	Fish/meat pasty	*Pulpo*	Octopus
Ensaladilla	Russian salad (diced vegetables in mayonnaise)	*Riñones al Jerez*	Kidneys in sherry
		Salchichón	Cured sausage
Escalibada	Aubergine (eggplant) and pepper salad	*Sardinas*	Sardines
		Sepia	Cuttlefish
Gambas	Shrimps	*Tortilla española*	Potato omelette
Habas con jamón	Broad beans with ham	*Tortilla francesa*	Plain omelette

selves for a light meal. Make sure you make it clear whether you want a *racion* or just a *tapa*. The more people you're with, of course, the better; half a dozen *tapas* or *pinchos* and three *raciones* can make a varied and quite filling meal for three or four people.

Tascas, **bodegas**, **cervecerías** and **tabernas** are all types of bar where you'll find *tapas* and *raciones*. Most of them have different sets of prices depending on whether you stand at the bar to eat (the basic charge) or sit at tables (up to 50 percent more expensive – and even more if you sit out on a terrace). **Casinos** are essentially places to drink and relax – quieter and more comfortable than most of the bars – and serve as a kind of club, with locals paying a nominal monthly membership charge. Most small towns have one, and tourists and visitors are always welcome to use the facilities free of charge – worth doing

since the membership rule means everybody drinks at reduced prices.

MEALS AND RESTAURANTS

This category is where Spain and Andalucía come into their own; there's simply nowhere else in Europe where you can get a quality three-course meal with wine for what a bowl of soup or a dessert would cost you in an average restaurant in London or New York. This comes from the roadhouse or *venta* tradition along the major highways, where fierce competition for customers has shaved prices whilst upholding standards; and these places – many in business for a couple of centuries – still turn out bargain *menús del día* for amazingly little.

Once again here, there's a multitude of distinctions. You can sit down and have a full meal in a

SPANISH FOOD AND DRINK TERMS

Andaluz cuisine reflects its history and climate: many of the spices used, like cumin, coriander and saffron, were introduced by the Moors, and the variety of cold dishes such as gazpacho are intended to cool you down as much as to nourish. The list below should cover most of your needs, and local specialities are mentioned in the body of the Guide. Other things you'll simply see people eating. *Quisiera uno asi* (I'd like one like that) can be an amazingly useful phrase.

BASICS

Aceite	Oil	*Huevos*	Eggs	*Sal*	Salt
Ajo	Garlic	*Mantequilla*	Butter	*Verduras/*	
Arroz	Rice	*Pan*	Bread	*Legumbres*	Vegetables
Azúcar	Sugar	*Pimienta*	Pepper	*Vinagre*	Vinegar
Fruta	Fruit	*Queso*	Cheese		

IN THE RESTAURANT

Almuerzo	Lunch	*Cuchara*	Spoon	*Mesa*	Table
Botella	Bottle	*Cuchillo*	Knife	*Tenedor*	Fork
La carta	Menu	*La cuenta*	The bill	*Vaso*	Glass
Cena	Dinner	*Desayuno*	Breakfast		

SOUPS (*SOPAS*)

Ajo blanco	Creamy gazpacho with garlic and almonds	*Sopa de picadillo*	A type of gazpacho with garnish
Caldillo	Clear fish soup	*Sopa de cocido*	Meat soup
Caldo verde or gallego	Thick, cabbage-based broth	*Sopa de gallina*	Chicken soup
		Sopa de mariscos	Seafood soup
Gazpacho	Cold tomato and cucumber soup	*Sopa de pasta (fideos)*	Noodle soup
		Sopa de pescado	Fish soup

SALAD (*ENSALADA*) AND STARTERS

Arroz a la cubana	Rice with fried egg and homemade tomato sauce	*Pimientos rellenos*	Stuffed peppers
Ensalada (mixta/ verde)	(Mixed/green) salad	*Verduras con patatas*	Boiled potatoes with greens

FISH (*PESCADOS*)

Anchoas	Anchovies (tinned)	*Merluza*	Hake
Anguila	Eel	*Mero*	Grouper
Angulas	Elvers (baby eel)	*Mojama*	Salted blue-fin tuna
Atún	Tuna	*Pez espada*	Swordfish
Bacalao	Cod (often salt)	*Rape*	Monkfish
Besugo/Dorada	Sea bream	*Rodaballo*	Turbot
Bonito	Tuna	*Salmón*	Salmon
Boquerones	Anchovies (fresh)	*Salmonete*	Mullet
Chanquetes	Whitebait	*Sardinas*	Sardines
Lenguado	Sole	*Trucha*	Trout
Lubina/Baila	Bass	*Urta*	Member of the bream family

SEAFOOD (*MARISCOS*)

Almejas	Clam	*Mejillones*	Mussels
Calamares	Squid	*Ostras*	Oysters
Cangrejo	Crab	*Percebes*	Goose-barnacles
Centollo	Spider-crab	*Pescadilla*	Small whiting
Chipirones	Small squid	*Pulpo*	Octopus
Cigalas	King prawns	*Puntillitas*	Baby squid
Conchas finas	Large scallops	*Sepia*	Cuttlefish
Gambas	Prawns/shrimps	*Vieiras/Conchas*	Scallops
Langosta	Lobster	*Zamburiñas*	Baby clams
Langostinos	Giant king prawns		

MEAT (*CARNE*) AND POULTRY (*AVES*)

Albóndigas	Meatballs	*Cordero*	Lamb	*Perdiz*	Partridge
Callos	Tripe	*Escalopa*	Escalope	*Pollo*	Chicken
Cabra	Goat	*Faisán*	Pheasant	*Pato*	Duck
Carne de vaca	Beef	*Hamburguesa*	Hamburger	*Pavo*	Turkey
Cerdo	Pork	*Hígado*	Liver	*Riñones*	Kidneys
Chorizo	Spicy sausage	*Jabalí*	Boar	*Salchicha*	Sausage
Chuletas	Chops	*Lengua*	Tongue	*Salchichón*	Cured salami-type sausage
Cochinillo	Suckling pig	*Lomo*	Loin (of pork)		
Conejo	Rabbit	*Mollejas*	Sweetbreads	*Sesos*	Brains
Codorniz	Quail	*Morcilla*	Blood sausage	*Ternera*	Veal

SOME TERMS

al ajillo	in garlic	*alioli*	with mayonnaise
asado	roast	*cazuela, cocido*	stew
a la Navarra	stuffed with ham	*en salsa*	in (usually tomato) sauce
a la parilla/plancha	grilled	*frito*	fried
a la romana	fried in batter	*guisado*	casserole
al horno	baked	*rehogado*	baked

VEGETABLES (*LEGUMBRES*)

Aguacate	Avocado	*Judías verdes, rojas, negras*	Green, red, black beans
Alcachofas	Artichokes	*Lechuga*	Lettuce
Berenjenas	Aubergine/eggplant	*Nabos*	Turnips
Champiñones/Setas	Mushrooms	*Palmitos*	Palm hearts
Coliflor	Cauliflower	*Patatas (fritas)*	Potatoes (chips/french fries)
Cebollas	Onions	*Pepino*	Cucumber
Espárragos	Asparagus	*Pimientos*	Peppers
Espinacas	Spinach	*Puerros*	Leeks
Garbanzos	Chickpeas	*Repollo*	Cabbage
Guisantes	Peas	*Tomate*	Tomato
Habas	Broad beans	*Zanahoria*	Carrot
Judías blancas	Haricot beans		

Continued over. . .

RICE DISHES

Arroz negro	"Black rice", cooked with squid ink	Paella a la catalana	Mixed meat and seafood sometimes distinguished from a seafood paella by being called Paella a la valenciana
Arroz a banda	Rice with seafood, the rice served separately		
Arroz a la marinera	Paella: rice with seafood and saffron		

DESSERTS (*POSTRES*)

Alfajores	Honey and almond pastries	Natillas	Custard
Arroz con leche	Rice pudding	Pestiños	Anís or wine fritters
Flan	Crème caramel	Polvorones	Almond cakes
Helados	Ice cream	Tocino de cielo	Andalucía's rich crème caramel
Melocotón en almíbar	Peaches in syrup	Yemas	Egg-yolk cakes
Miel	Honey	Yogur	Yogurt
Nata	Whipped cream (topping)		

FRUIT (*FRUTAS*)

Albaricoques	Apricots	Limón	Lemon	Piña	Pineapple
Chirimoyas	Custard apples	Manzanas	Apples	Plátanos	Bananas
Cerezas	Cherries	Melocotónes	Peaches	Pomelo	Grapefruit
Ciruelas	Plums, prunes	Melón	Melon	Sandía	Watermelon
Dátiles	Dates	Naranjas	Oranges	Uvas	Grapes
Fresas	Strawberries	Nectarinas	Nectarines		
Higos	Figs	Peras	Pears		

comedor, a cafetería, a restaurante, a mesón or a marisquería – all in addition to the more food-oriented bars. **Comedores** are the places to seek out if your main criteria are price and quantity. Sometimes you will see them attached to a bar (often in a room behind), or as the dining room of a hostal or fonda, but as often as not they're virtually unmarked and discovered only if you pass an open door. Since they're essentially workers' cafés they tend to serve more substantial meals at lunchtime than in the evenings (when they may be closed altogether). When you can find them – the tradition, with its family-run business and marginal wages, is on the way out – you'll probably pay around 700–1300ptas for a **menú del día** or **menú de la casa**, a complete meal of three courses, usually with wine.

Replacing comedores to some extent are **cafeterías**, which the local authorities now grade from one to three cups (the ratings, as with restaurants, seem to be based on facilities offered rather than the quality of the food). These can be good value, too, especially the self-service places, but their emphasis is more northern European and the light snack-meals served tend to be dull. Food here often comes in the form of a **plato combinado** – literally a combined plate – which will be something like egg and chips or calamares and salad (or occasionally a weird combination like steak and a piece of fish), sometimes with bread and a drink included. This will generally cost in the region of 700–1000ptas. Cafeterías often serve some kind of menú del día as well. You may prefer to get your plato combinado at a bar, which in small towns with no comedores may be the only way to eat inexpensively. Moving up the scale there are **restaurantes** (designated by one to five forks – which relate to price, not quality), **mesones** (inns) and **marisquerías**. Of the latter two, a mesón formerly offered both food and lodging but today they tend to serve traditional local cuisine, whilst *marisquerías* specialize exclusively in fish and seafood and are the most popular places to eat out in Andalucía. *Restaurantes* which are at the bottom of the scale are often not much different in price from *comedores*, and will also generally have *platos combinados* available. A fixed-price *menú del día*, *menú de la casa* or occasionally *cubierto* (all of which mean the same and which are referred to as a **menú** throughout the *Guide*) is often better value: two or three courses plus wine and bread for around 600–1500ptas. Do note, however, that some restaurants only offer their *menú del día* at lunchtimes and in tourist areas many establishments tend not to publicize theirs, hoping you'll select from the more expensive à-la-carte; it's always worth asking "*hay un menú del dia?*" Sunday lunchtime – the day when *andaluz* families traditionally go out for lunch – is another time when the *menú del día* is largely unavailable. If you move above two forks on the *restaurantes* scale, or find yourself in one of the more fancy *marisquerías* (as opposed to a basic seafront fish-fry place), prices can escalate rapidly. However, even here most of the top restaurants offer an upmarket *menú* called a **menú de degustación** (a sampler meal, often including wine) which are often excellent value and allow you to try out some of the region's finest cooking for between 3000–5000ptas. To avoid receiving confused stares from waiters in restaurants, you should always ask for **la carta** when you want a menu; *menú* in Spanish refers only to a fixed-price meal.

In addition, in all but the most rock-bottom establishments it is customary to leave a small **tip** (*propina*). Andalucians (and Spaniards generally) are judicious tippers, so only do so if the service merits it: the amount is up to you, though 5 to 10 percent of the bill in a restaurant is quite sufficient and ten or fifteen pesetas in a bar. Service is normally included in a *menú del día*. The other thing to take account of in medium- and top-price restaurants is the addition of **IVA**, a 7 percent tax on your bill. It should say on the menu if you have to pay this.

In most restaurants your visit will usually be wholly satisfactory, but if you do feel you are being short-changed in terms of quality or service, or if you wish to dispute the bill, a good last resort is to request the **libro de reclamaciones** (complaints book), which every hotel and restaurant is required to have by law. The act of requesting this item can often result in a remarkable transforma-tion in attitude. Should you go on to make an entry – English is perfectly okay, but write clearly and simply – then you will get a copy, and as all the pages are numbered, when government inspectors come to do their periodic checks there could be some awkward questions for the proprietor. If you enclose your address you are in theory entitled to be informed of the outcome of your complaint, but don't count on this.

You'll find numerous recommendations, in all price ranges, in the main body of the *Guide*. Spaniards generally **eat very late** and Andalucians eat later still, so most places serve food from around 1pm until 4 or 5pm (though no one considers lunch until at least 2pm) and from 8pm to midnight and later (but, again, no one eats before 10pm). Many restaurants close on Sunday evening. If you insist on dining at more familiar hours you'll often be eating alone, with the waiters looking on. The best thing is to try and adjust to the southern style, and in between do what the locals do – keep going on *tapas*.

WHAT TO EAT

Our food glossary should give you an idea of what's on offer and help you cope when faced with a restaurant menu. Local specialities are highlighted in the *Guide*, too. It's possible to make a few generalizations about Spanish food. If you like **fish and seafood** you'll be in heaven in Andalucía as this forms the basis of a vast variety of *tapas* and is fresh and excellent everywhere. It's not cheap, unfortunately, so rarely forms part of the lowest priced *menús* (though you may get the most common fish – cod, often salted, and hake – or squid) but you really should make the most of what's on offer. Fish stews (*zarzuelas*) and rice-based paellas (which also contain meat, usually rabbit or chicken) are often memorable in seafood restaurants. Paella comes originally from Valencia and is still best there, but you'll find *arroz marinero*, the Andalucian version, just as good. The coastal strip's obsession with seafood is detailed in the main body of the *Guide*, although Cádiz and the nearby "sherry triangle" of Sanlúcar, El Puerto de Santa María and Jerez deserve top spot for sheer volume and variety. Be aware when **ordering fish** in restaurants that often the price quoted is per kilo or per 100g, and an average white-fish portion will be around 200–300g.

Meat is most often grilled and served with a few fried potatoes and a couple of salad leaves, or cured or dried and served as a starter or in sandwiches. **Jamón serrano**, the Spanish version of Parma ham, is superb, and a passion in Andalucía. The best varieties, though, from Jabugo in the Sierra de Aracena (see p.315) and Trevélez in the Sierra Nevada, are extremely expensive. If you're tempted, they are best appreciated with a glass of **fino** (see p.49). More meat is eaten in inland provinces than on the coast and Córdoba's *rabo de toro* (stewed bull's tail) is renowned. The Sierra de Aracena is also a good place for cooked pork dishes, with *solomillo de cerdo* (pork sirloin) usually outstanding. In country areas bordering the slopes of the Sierra Morena and in the province of Jaén, game is very much a speciality – venison, partridge, hare and wild boar all feature on menus in these parts, as well as fresh trout.

Vegetables rarely amount to more than a few fries or boiled potatoes with the main dish (but you can often order a side dish à la carte). The provinces of Córdoba and Jaén are again the exceptions, and the latter's *pipirrana jaenera* (salad with green peppers and hard-boiled eggs) is only one of a number of hearty vegetable-based dishes to be found in these parts. It's more usual, though, to start your meal with a simple salad or with Andalucía's most famous dish, *gazpacho*; regional variations include Córdoba's *salmorejo* (with more body), Málaga's *ajo blanco* (with almonds and grapes) or Cádiz's *sopa de picadillo* (garnished with jamón and hard-boiled eggs).

Dessert (*postre*) in Andalucía tends to be sweet and sticky – another hangover from the region's long period under Moorish dominion. The cheaper places will usually offer little variety: nearly always fresh fruit or flan, the Spanish *crème caramel*, often replaced on Andalucian menus by the similar *tocino de cielo* ("heavenly lard") or *natillas* (custard). Keep an eye out in more upmarket places for delicious regional specialities such as *peras al vino* (pears baked in wine with cinnamon) from Málaga, *piononos* (liqueur-soaked cakes) from Granada and *crema de Jerez* (sherry pudding) from Cádiz, as well as *brazo de gitano* (rolled pastry filled with cream), an Andalucía-wide dessert.

Cheese (*queso*) is always eaten as a *tapa* rather than after a meal in Andalucía. The cheeses of the region don't usually travel beyond their immediate area of production, which offers you the chance to make some interesting discoveries, especially in areas such as Las Alpujarras. The best-known brand region-wide is Córdoba Province's sheep's-milk cheese from Pedroches, although the hard, salty *Manchego* from neighbouring La Mancha is also widespread.

VEGETARIANS

Vegetarians have a fairly hard time of it in Andalucía and Spain generally: there's always something to eat, but you may get weary of eggs and omelettes (*tortilla francesa* is a plain omelette, *con champiñones* with mushrooms). In the big cities you'll find vegetarian restaurants and ethnic places which serve vegetable dishes, and these are referred to in the *Guide*. Otherwise, superb fresh produce is always available in the markets and shops, and cheese, fruit and eggs are available everywhere. In restaurants you're faced with the extra problem that pieces of meat – especially ham, which the Spanish don't seem to regard as real meat – are often added to vegetable dishes to "spice them up".

The phrase to get to know is "*Soy vegetariano. Hay algo sin carne?*" (I'm a vegetarian. Is there anything without meat?); you may have to add *y sin mariscos* (and without seafood) *y sin jamón* (and without ham) to be really safe.

If you're a vegan, you're either going to have to compromise or accept weight loss if you're away for any length of time. Some salads and vegetable dishes are strictly vegan, but they're few and far between. Fruit and nuts are widely available, though, nuts being sold by street vendors everywhere.

ALCOHOLIC DRINKS

Vino (wine), either *tinto* (red), *blanco* (white) or *rosado/clarete* (rosé), is the invariable accompaniment to every meal and is, as a rule, extremely inexpensive. Andalucía's wine-making genius lies elsewhere (see below) and so most table wines are imported from outside the region. The most common bottled variety is Valdepeñas, a good standard wine from the central plains of New Castile (Los Llanos, Viña Albali and Señorío de Guadianeja are good labels). Rioja, from the area round Logroño in the north, is one of Spain's classic wines but a lot more expensive (Cune, Faustino I & V, Berberana, Viña Ardanza). Another top-drawer, and currently fashionable, region is Ribera del Duero in Castilla-León which produces Spain's most expensive wine, Vega Sicilia,

DRINKS AND BEVERAGES					
Hot drinks		chocolate	*Chocolate*	Tiger nut drink	*Horchata*
Coffee	*Café*	**Soft drinks**		**Alcohol**	
Espresso coffee	*Café solo*	Water	*Agua*	Beer	*Cerveza*
White coffee	*Café con*	Mineral water	*Agua mineral*	Champagne	*Champán*
leche		... (sparkling)	*...(con gas)*	Wine	*Vino*
Decaff	*Descafeinado*	... (still)	*...(sin gas)*	Sherry	*Fino*
Tea	*Té*	Milk	*Leche*		
Drinking		Juice	*Zumo*		

besides other outstanding reds (Pesquera, Viña Pedrosa, Ribeño and Señorio de Nava are names to look out for). There are also scores of other excellent wines to try from regions such as Catalunya (Bach, Raimat, Torres) which also produces the champagne-like Cava (Codorníu, Freixenet); Galicia (Fefiñanes and San Trocado); Navarra (Gran Feudo, Señorio de Sarría, Ochoa), and Valencia (Murviedro, Gandía) are others, and even the once unpromising La Mancha (Señorio de Guadianeja, Estola) is now making a name for itself as a producer of quality wines. Andalucía's solitary table-wine area of any volume is the Condado de Huelva zone, which turns out reasonably dry whites. An interesting new development near Ronda is the foundation of a vineyard geared to the production of quality red wine – something previously thought to be impossible in this climate, and the early vintages seem promising (see p.150). There are also many local wines made in the country districts, such as the *costa* wine of the eastern and the Laujar de Andarax wines of the western Alpujarras, and these are always worth trying.

Outside the larger towns and cities you'll rarely be given any choice apart from whatever dusty old bottles the proprietor can dig up. Busy *ventas* and restaurants with a healthy reputation, however, usually have well-stocked cellars. Otherwise it's whatever comes out of the barrel, or the house-bottled special (ask for *caserío* or *de la casa*). This can be great, it can be lousy, but at least it will be distinctively local. In a bar, a small glass of wine will generally cost around 50–100ptas; in a restaurant, if wine is not included in the *menú*, prices start at around 300–400ptas a bottle. If it is included, you'll usually get a whole bottle for two people, a *media botella* (a third to a half of a litre) for one. Be on your guard for the odd skinflint establishment which may try to get away with serving you a sin-

gle glass to comply with the "including wine" offer, thus obliging you to buy a bottle on top. A polite but firm word with the waiter is usually enough to secure your rights.

The classic Andalucian wine is **sherry** – *vino de jerez* – which is excellent, widely available and consumed with gusto by *andaluzes*. Served chilled or at bodega temperature – a perfect drink to wash down *tapas* – like everything Spanish, it comes in a perplexing variety of forms. The main distinctions are between *fino* or *jerez seco* (dry sherry), *amontillado* (medium), and *oloroso* (full-bodied) or *jerez dulce* (sweet), and these are the terms you should use to order. Similar in the way they are made – though not identical in flavour – are *montilla* and *manzanilla*, which are not fortified with alcohol as is the case with other *finos*. The first of these dry, sherry-like wines comes from the province of Córdoba, and the latter from Sanlúcar de Barrameda, part of the "sherry triangle" along with Jerez and El Puerto de Santa María. More information about these wines is given in the *Guide* under each production centre.

Cerveza, lager-type beer, is generally pretty good, though more expensive than wine. It comes in 200ml (*botellines*) or 330ml (*tercios*) bottles or, for about the same price, on tap – a *caña* of draught beer is a small glass, a *caña doble* larger. Many bartenders will assume you want a *doble* (especially in tourist areas), so if you don't, say so. Simply asking for *un tubo* (roughly half a pint) avoids these complications. Andalucía's main brand is Cruz Campo, produced in Sevilla and now part of the Heineken group, which is also the best beer in Spain, easily surpassing the heavily marketed San Miguel. Cruz Campo is served on draught just about everywhere, although "foreign" brands such as the Castilian Mahou and Aguila or the ubiquitously produced Estrella Dorada are making inroads. Granada's Alhambra beer is another one to look out for.

Equally refreshing, though often deceptively strong, is ***sangría***, a wine-and-fruit punch which you'll come across at fiestas and in tourist bars; *tinto de verano* is basically the same red wine and soda or lemonade combination.

In mid-afternoon – or even at breakfast – many Spaniards take a *copa* of **liqueur** with their coffee (for that matter many Spaniards drink wine and beer at breakfast, too). One of the best is *anís* (like Pernod) – in its respectable guise – whose coarser brother appears at romerías and fiestas as the often lethally potent *aguardiente* firewater. Slightly more palatable perhaps is *pacharán*, which, as well as being highly popular across the peninsula, is a favourite pre- or post-meal liqueur in Andalucía. *Pacharán* is best taken "on the rocks", is red in hue, and is made from sloes and *anís*; Zoco is the leading brand. *Coñac* (also "brandy" in Spanish) is another excellent choice and Andalucía is the main centre of production for Spain's leading brands. Produced by the sherry bodegas, the distinctive flavour is imparted by its maturation in old sherry casks. Try Magno, Soberano or Carlos III ("*tercero*") to get an idea of the variety, and Carlos I ("*primero*"), Lepanto and Gran Duque de Alba for a measure of the quality. One "imported" brandy worth looking out for is Mascaró, produced in Catalunya and resembling an armagnac. Most spirits are ordered by brand name, since there are generally less expensive Spanish equivalents for standard imports. Larios gin from Málaga, for instance, is about half the price of Gordon's gin. Specify "nacional" to avoid getting an expensive foreign brand. The measures of spirits are generous and usually glugged from the bottle into the glass in front of you with deft skill. Mixed drinks are universally known as *Cuba libre* or *Cubata*, though strictly speaking this is rum and Coke. Juice is *zumo*; orange, *naranja*; lemon, *limón*; tonic is *tónica*.

SOFT DRINKS AND HOT DRINKS

Soft drinks are much the same as anywhere in the world, but try in particular *granizado* (slush) or *horchata* (a milky drink made from tiger nuts or almonds) from one of the street stalls that spring up everywhere in summer. You can also get these drinks from *horchaterías* and from *heladerías* (ice cream – *helado* – parlours). Although you can drink the **water** almost everywhere it usually tastes better out of the bottle – inexpensive *agua mineral* comes either sparkling (*con gas*) or still (*sin gas*); Lanjarón from Las Alpujarras is Andalucía's main brand.

Coffee – served in cafés, *heladerías* and bars – is invariably espresso, slightly bitter and, unless you specify otherwise, served black (*café solo*). If you want it white ask for *café cortado* (a small cup with a drop of milk) or *café con leche* (made with lots of hot milk). For a large cup ask for a *doble* or *grande*. Coffee is also frequently mixed with brandy, cognac or whisky, all such concoctions being called *carajillo*. Decaffeinated coffee (*descafeinado*) is increasingly available in many city bars, though in villages and towns you'll only find it in undistinguished sachet form or spooned from a jar at the back of the bar. A great summer refresher is *café helado*: a cup of coffee accompanied by a glass of ice cubes. Pour the coffee onto the cubes – it cools instantly.

Tea (*té*) is also available at most bars, although Spaniards usually drink it black. If you want milk it's safest to ask afterwards, since ordering *té con leche* might well get you a glass of milk with a tea bag floating on top. *Manzanilla* (camomile, not to be confused with the sherry of the same name) is a popular herbal infusion served in most bars; *poleomenta* (mint tea), *tila* (lime) and *hierba luisa* (lemon verbena) are other refreshing herbal possibilities.

OPENING HOURS AND PUBLIC HOLIDAYS

Almost everything in Spain – shops, museums, churches, tourist offices – closes for a siesta of at least two hours in the hottest part of the day. There's a lot of variation (and the siesta tends to be longer in the south) but basic summer working hours are 9.30am–1.30pm and 4.30–7.30pm. Certain shops (such as El Corte Inglés) do now stay open all day, and there is a move towards "normal" working hours. Nevertheless, you'll get far less aggravated if you accept that the early afternoon is best spent asleep, or in a bar, or both.

Museums, with very few exceptions, follow the rule above, with a break between 1 and 4 in the afternoon. Their summer schedules are listed in the *Guide*; watch out for Sundays (most open mornings only) and Mondays (most closed all day). Admission charges vary, but there's usually a big reduction or free entrance if you show an ISIC or FIYTO card. Anywhere run by the Patrimonio Nacional, the national organization which preserves monuments, is free to EU citizens on Wednesday – you'll need your passport to prove your nationality. Most of the sites and museums administered by the Junta de Andalucía are free to EU citizens on production of an identity card (or passport for UK visitors).

Getting into **churches** can present more of a problem. The really important ones, including most cathedrals, operate in much the same way as museums and almost always have some entry charge to see their most valued treasures and paintings, or their cloisters. Other churches, though, are usually kept locked, opening only for worship in the early morning and/or the evening (between around 6–9pm). So you'll either have to try at these times, or find someone with a key. This is time-consuming but rarely difficult, since a sacristán or custodian almost always lives nearby and most people will know where to direct you. You're expected to give a small tip, or donation.

For all churches "decorous" dress is required, ie no garish beach shorts, bare shoulders, etc.

NATIONAL HOLIDAYS

Official **national holidays** can disrupt your plans. There are fifteen national holidays, listed in the box, and scores of local festivals (different in every town and village, usually marking the local saint's day); any of them will mean that everything except bars (and *hostales*, etc) locks its doors. In addition, **August** is Spain's own holiday month, when many of the larger cities are semi-deserted, and shops and restaurants, occasionally museums, may close. In contrast, it can prove nearly impossible to find a free bed in the more popular coastal and mountain resorts at these times; similarly, seats on planes, trains, and buses should be booked in advance.

SPANISH NATIONAL HOLIDAYS

January 1, *Año Nuevo*, New Year's Day
January 6, *Epifanía*, Epiphany
Good Friday, *Viernes Santo*
Easter Sunday, *Domingo de la Resurrección*
Easter Monday, *Lunes de Pascua*
May 1, *Fiesta de Trabajo*, Labour Day
Corpus Christi (early or mid-June)
June 24, *Día de San Juan*, the king's name-saint
July 25, *Día de Santiago*, Spain's patron saint
August 15, *La Asunción*, Assumption of the Virgin
October 12, *Día de la Hispanidad*, National Day
November 1, *Todos Santos*, All Saints' Day
December 6, *Día de la Constitución*, Constitution Day
December 8, *La Inmaculada Concepción*, Immaculate Conception.
December 25, *Navidad*, Christmas Day.

FIESTAS, THE BULLFIGHT AND FOOTBALL

It's hard to beat the experience of arriving in some small village, expecting no more than a bed for the night, to discover the streets decked out with flags and streamers, spectacular fireworks lighting up the sky, a band playing in the plaza and the entire population out celebrating the local fiesta. Everywhere in Andalucía, from the tiniest hamlet to the great cities, will take at least one day off a year to devote to partying. Usually it's the local saint's day, but there are celebrations, too, of harvests, of deliverance from the Moors, of safe return from the sea – any excuse will do.

Each festival is different. In Andalucía horses, flamenco, fireworks and the guitar are essential parts of any celebration, usually accompanied by the downing of oceans of fino – which is probably why the sherry companies seem to provide most of the bunting. And along with the music there is always dancing, usually *sevillanas*, in traditional flamenco costume, and an immense spirit of enjoyment. The main event of most fiestas is a parade, either behind a revered holy image, or a more celebratory affair with fancy costumes and *gigantones*, grotesque giant carnival figures which terrorize children.

Although these festivals take place throughout the year – and it is often the obscure and unexpected event which proves to be most fun – there are certain occasions which stand out. **Easter Week (Semana Santa)** and **Corpus Christi** (in early June) are celebrated all over the country with magnificent religious processions. Easter, particularly, is worth trying to coincide with – head for Sevilla, Málaga, Granada or Córdoba, where huge *pasos*, floats of wildly theatrical religious scenes, are carried down the streets, accompanied by weirdly hooded penitents atoning for the year's misdeeds. And just as moving in their own more intimate way are the countless small town and village observances of *Semana Santa* with smaller processions, traditional customs and sometimes a Passion play.

Among the biggest and best-known of Andalucía's other **popular festivals** are: the Cádiz *Carnaval* (mid-February); Sevilla's enormous April *Feria* (a week at the end of the month); Jerez's *Feria del Caballo* (Horse Fair, April/May); the *Romería del Rocío*, an extraordinary pilgrimage to El Roció near Huelva (arriving there on Whit Sunday) and Málaga's boisterous and good-humoured *Feria* (mid-August).

The list is potentially endless, and although you'll find more major events detailed in the accompanying box, we can't pretend that this is exhaustive. The Junta de Andalucía publishes an annual *Ferias y Fiestas de Andalucía* guide, available from local tourist offices. Outsiders are always welcome at these festivals, the one problem being that during any of the most popular you'll find it difficult and expensive to find a bed. If you're planning to coincide with a festival, try and book your accommodation well in advance.

THE BULLFIGHT

Bullfights are an integral part of many Spanish festivals. In Andalucía, especially, any village that can afford it will put on a *corrida* for an afternoon, while in big cities like Madrid or Sevilla, the main festivals are accompanied by a week-long (or more) season of prestige fights.

Los Toros (or La Lidia), as Spaniards refer to bullfighting, are big business. Each year an estimated 24,000 bulls are killed before a live audience of over thirty million (with many more watching on television). It is said that 150,000 people are involved, in some way, in the industry, and the top performers, the *matadores*, are major earners, on a par with the country's biggest pop stars. There is some opposition to the activity from animal welfare groups but it is not widespread: if Spaniards tell you that bullfighting is controversial, they are likely to be referring to practices in the trade. In recent years, bullfighting critics (whom you will find on the arts pages of the newspapers) have been expressing their perennial outrage at the widespread but illegal shaving of bulls' horns prior to the *corrida*. Bulls' horns are as sensitive as fingernails, and shaving just a few millimetres deters the animal from charging; they affect the creature's balance, too, reducing the danger for the matador still further.

Notwithstanding such abuse (and there is plenty more), *Los Toros* maintain their aficionados throughout the country. Indeed, in some areas they are on the rise, with the elaborate language of the *corrida* quite a cult among the young, as the days of Franco's patronage of bullfighting are forgotten, and TV stations pay big money for major events. To aficionados (a word that implies more knowledge and appreciation than "fan"), the bulls are a culture and a ritual – one in which the emphasis is on the way man and bull "perform" together – in which the art is at issue rather than the cruelty. If pressed on the issue of the slaughter of an animal, they generally fail to understand. Fighting bulls are, they will tell you, bred for the industry; they live a reasonable life before they are killed; and, if the bullfight went, so too would the bulls.

Whether you attend a *corrida*, obviously, is down to your own feelings and ethics. If you spend any time at all in Spain during the season (which runs from March to October), you will encounter *Los Toros*, at least on a bar TV, and that will as likely as not make up your mind. If you decide to go, try to see the biggest and most prestigious that is on, in a major city, where star performers are likely to despatch the bulls with "art" and a successful, "clean" kill. This happens much less frequently than many aficionados would have you believe and the beginners' fights, or *novilladas*, are often little more than a gruesome repetition of botched jobs. And even in the senior *corridas*, there are few sights worse than a *matador* making a prolonged and messy kill, while the audience whistles its disgust. Established and popular **matadores** include Enrique Ponce, César Rincón, Vicente Barrera, Espartaco, Finito de Córdoba, the teenage sensation El Juli and, at the opposite end of the age range, Curro Romero, still wielding the *capote* (cape) at the ripe age of 66. Two recent stars in the headlines are El Cordobés

– a young pretender of spectacular technique who claims to be his legendary namesake's illegitimate son – and Cristina Sánchez, the first woman *torero* to make it into the top flight for some time. Although there have been women *matadores* since the eighteenth century, she is the first woman to have been carried shoulder high through the *puerta grande* of the Madrid ring – a distinction awarded to few of her male peers. Sánchez's telling comment later was that fighting bulls is easy compared to fighting the macho sexist prejudice she has encountered throughout the whole business, and many leading *matadores* such as Jesulín de Ubrique ("It is unnatural for women to fight, they should be in the kitchen") and Enrique Ponce refuse to appear on the same bill as a woman. This prejudice led to Sánchez retiring in disgust in 1999 at the age of 27, when she found it increasingly difficult to get high-status fights due to the continuing refusal of many big names to share a ring with her.

Perhaps the most exciting and skilful performances of all are by mounted *matadores*, or **rejoneadores** as they are known (from *rejón*, "lance"); this is the oldest form of corrida, developed at Ronda in the seventeenth century. However, they still dismount to despatch the bull.

THE CORRIDA

The corrida begins with a **procession**, to the accompaniment of a *paso doble* by the band. Leading the procession are two *alguacilillos* or "constables", on horseback and in traditional costume, followed by the three matadores, who will each fight two bulls, and their *cuadrillas*, their personal "team", each comprising two mounted *picadores* and three *banderilleros*. At the back are the mule teams who will drag off the dead bulls.

Once the ring is empty, the *alguacilillo* opens the *toril* (the bulls' enclosure) and the first bull appears – a moment of great physical beauty – to be "tested" by the matador or his *banderilleros* using pink and gold capes. These preliminaries conducted (and they can be short, if the bull is ferocious), the **suerte de picar** ensues, in which the *picadores* ride out and take up position at opposite sides of the ring, while the bull is distracted by other *toreros*. Once they are in place, the bull is made to charge one of the horses, at which moment the *picador* drives his short-pointed lance into the bull's neck, while it tries to toss his padded and blindfolded (on the right eye) mount. The whole purpose here is to tire and

FIESTAS

Listed below are some of Andalucía's main **fiestas**, all worth trying to get to if you're going to be in the area around the time; more are listed under locations covered in the *Guide*. Note that saints' day festivals – indeed all Spanish celebrations – can vary in date, and are often observed over the weekend closest to the dates given.

JANUARY

1–2 *La Toma* – celebration of the entry of the *Reyes Católicos* into the city – at Granada.

5 *Cabalgata de los Reyes Magos* – Epiphany parade at Málaga.

6 *Romería de la Virgen del Mar* – pilgrimage procession from Almería.

17 *Romería del Ermita del Santo* – similar event at Guadix.

FEBRUARY

1 *San Cecilio* – fiesta in Granada's traditionally gypsy quarter of Sacromonte.

Mid-month: *Carnaval* is an extravagant week-long event (leading up to Lent) in all the Andalucían cities. Cádiz, above all, celebrates with fancy dress, flamenco, spectacular parades and street-singers' competitions.

MARCH

5–15 El Puerto de Santa María (Cádiz) celebrates its *carnaval*.

Holy Week (*Semana Santa*), following Palm Sunday, has its most elaborate and dramatic celebrations in Andalucía. You'll find moving and memorable processions of floats and penitents at (in descending order of importance) Sevilla, Málaga, Granada and Córdoba, and to a lesser extent in smaller towns such as Jerez, Arcos, Baeza and Úbeda. All culminate with the full drama of the Passion on **Good Friday**, with **Easter Day** itself more of a family occasion.

APRIL

Last week (2 weeks after Easter, usually in April, occasionally May, but check with the tourist office) Week-long *Feria de Abril* at Sevilla: the largest fair in Spain, a little refined in the way of the city, but an extraordinary event nonetheless. A small April fair – featuring bull-running – is held in Vejer.

Last Sunday Three-day *Romería de Nuestra Señora de la Cabeza* at Andujar (Jaén) culminates in a huge procession to the sanctuary of the Virgin in the Sierra Morena.

MAY

1–2 *Romería de Nuestra Señora de la Estrella* at Navas de San Juan – Jaén Province's most important pilgrimage.

3 "Moors and Christians" carnival at Pampaneira (Alpujarras).

First week *Cruces de Mayo* (Festival of the Patios) in Córdoba – celebrates the Holy Cross and includes a competition for the prettiest patio and numerous events and concerts organized by the local city council.

Early May (usually the week after Sevilla's fair) Somewhat aristocratic Horse Fair at Jerez de la Frontera.

17 *San Isidro Romería* at Setenil (Cádiz).

Pentecost (7 weeks after Easter) *Romería del Rocío* – Spain's biggest: a million often inebriated pilgrims in horse-drawn carriages and processions converge on El Rocío (Huelva) from all over the south.

Corpus Christi (variable – Thursday after Trinity). Bullfights and festivities at Granada, Sevilla, Ronda, Vejer and Zahara de la Sierra. At Sevilla, *Los Seises* (six choirboys) perform a dance before the altar of the cathedral.

Third weekend *Romería de Santa Eulalia* at Almonaster La Real in the Sierra de Aracena – pilgrimage, fireworks, parades and *fandangos* in honour of the village's patron saint.

Last week *Feria de la Manzanilla*, Sanlúcar de Barrameda. Prolonged binge to celebrate the town's major product which is used to wash down huge quantities of seafood whilst watching flamenco and sporting events from beachfront *casetas*.

JUNE

Second week *Feria de San Bernabé* at Marbella – often spectacular since this is the richest town in Andalucía.

13–14 *Fiestas Patronales de San Antonio* at Trevélez (Alpujarras) – includes mock battles between Moors and Christians.

23–24 *Candelas de San Juan* – bonfires and effigies at Vejer and elsewhere.

23–26 *Feria* of Alhaurin de la Torre (Málaga) – processions, giants and an important flamenco competition.

30 Conil (Cádiz) *feria*.

End June/early July International Festival of Music and Dance: major dance groups, chamber orchestras and flamenco artistes perform in Granada's Alhambra palace, Generalife and Carlos V palace.

JULY

Early July International Guitar Festival at Córdoba – brings together top international acts from classical, flamenco and Latin American music.

9–14 Around feast of *San Francisco Solano* Montilla (Córdoba) celebrates its annual *feria*.

End of month Almería's *Virgen del Mar* summer fiesta – parades, horse-riding events and usually a handful of major jazz and rock concerts in its Plaza Vieja.

AUGUST

3 *Colombinas* at Huelva celebrate Columbus's voyages of discovery with a fiesta.

First week Berja (Almería) holds its annual fiesta in honour of the Virgin of Gádor.

5 Trevélez (Granadan Alpujarras) observes a midnight *romería* to Mulhacén.

13–21 *Feria de Málaga* – one of Andalucía's most enjoyable fiestas for visitors, who are heartily welcomed by the ebullient *malagueños*.

15 Ascension of the Virgin – fair with *casetas* (dance tents) at Vejer and throughout Andalucía.

15 *Noche del Vino* at Competa (Málaga) – a riotous wine festival with dancing, singing and endless drinking.

17–20 The first cycle of horse races along Sanlúcar de Barrameda's beach, with heavy official and unofficial betting; the second tournament takes place exactly a week later.

19–21 *Vendimia* – grape harvest fiesta at Montilla (Córdoba).

Third week The Algeciras fair and fiesta, another major event of the south.

Third weekend *Fiesta de San Mamés* at Aroche (Huelva) in the extremities of the Sierra de Aracena – unpretentious and great fun, everything a village fiesta should be.

22–25 *Feria de Grazalema* (Cádiz).

23–25 *Guadalquivir festival* at Sanlúcar de Barrameda – bullfights and an important flamenco competition.

25–30 *Fiestas Patronales* in honour of San Agustín at Mojácar (Almería).

SEPTEMBER

7 *Romería del Cristo de la Yedra* at Baeza (Jaén) – singing and dancing in the streets.

7–14 *Feria de la Moscatel/Feria de Nuestra Señora de Regla* at Chipiona (Cádiz). Includes bull-running, flamenco tournaments and much wine-swilling to acclaim the sweet sherry grape grown hereabouts.

8 *Romería de Nuestra Señora de los Ángeles* at Alajar (Huelva) – lots of colour and horse races to the peak sanctuary of Arias Montano.

8–9 *Fiesta de la Virgen de la Cabeza* at Almuñecar (Granada).

First/second week *Vendimia* (celebration of the vintage) at Jerez – starts with the blessing of the new grapes, after which everyone gets sozzled on the old.

6–13 Celebration of the *Virgen de la Luz* in Tarifa – street processions and horseback riding.

First two weeks Ronda bursts into life with a *feria*, flamenco contests and the *Corrida Goyesca*, bullfights in eighteenth-century dress.

24–25 *Día del Señor* (Lord's Day) at Orgiva (Granada) – celebrated with impressive fireworks and processions.

28–October 4 Úbeda's (Jaén) *Fiesta de San Miguel* with a fair and *casetas*.

OCTOBER

1 *Fiesta de San Miguel* in Granada's Albaicín quarter and dozens of other towns, even at Torremolinos.

6–12 Fuengirola's *Feria del Rosario* – horse-riding events and flamenco.

15–23 *Feria de San Lucas* – Jaén's major fiesta, dating back to the fifteenth century.

DECEMBER

28 *Fiesta de los Verdiales/Santos Innocentes* Various towns and villages of Málaga's mountain districts celebrate Spain's equivalent of April Fool's Day with dances, Moorish-inspired music and outlandish headdress. Good places to see it include Comares, Almogía and Casabermeja.

If you want to know more about the **international opposition to bullfighting**, contact the World Society for the Protection of Animals, 2 Langley Lane, London SW8 1TJ (☎020/7793 0540); PO Box 190, Boston, MA 02130 (☎617/522-7000); 44 Victoria St, Suite 1310, Toronto (☎416/369-0044). Andalucía's anti-bullfighting pressure group is ASANDA (Asociación Andaluza para la Defensa de los Animales), Apartado de Correos 4365, 41080 Sevilla (☎95 456 10 58). Spain's national opposition to bullfighting is coordinated by ADDA (Associación para la Defensar de los Derechos de Animal), c/Bailén 164, Local 2, Interior EO8037, Barcelona (*www.intercom.es/adda*).

weaken the bull's powerful neck and back muscles, thus forcing him to lower his head – without which (as was discovered at the very outset of the *corrida*) it would be impossibly dangerous to fight and kill on foot. This is repeated up to three times, until the horn sounds for the *picadores* to leave. For most neutral spectators, it is the least acceptable and most squalid stage of the proceedings, and it is clearly not a pleasant experience for the horses, their ears stuffed with rags to shut out the noise of the bull and spectators, and their vocal cords cut to prevent any terrified cries from alarming the crowd.

The next stage, the **suerte de banderillas**, involves the placing of three sets of *banderillas* (barbed darts mounted on coloured shafts) into the bull's shoulders. Each of the three *banderilleros* delivers these in turn, attracting the bull's attention with the movement of his own body rather than a cape, and deftly placing the *banderillas* whilst both he and the bull are running towards each other. He then runs to safety out of the bull's vision, sometimes with the assistance of his colleagues, but occasionally a canny animal will set off in pursuit of his tormentor, often resulting in an undignified leap over the *barrera* to escape the charging horns.

Once the *banderillas* have been placed, the **suerte de matar** begins, and the matador enters the ring alone, having exchanged his pink and gold cape for the red muleta. He (or she) salutes the president and then dedicates the bull either to an individual, to whom he gives his hat, or to the audience, by placing his hat in the centre of the ring. It is in this part of the *corrida* that judgements are made and the performance is focused,

as the *matador* displays his skills on the (by now exhausted) bull. He uses the movements of the cape to attract the bull, while his body remains still. If he does well, the band will start to play, while the crowd *olé* each pass. This stage lasts around ten minutes and ends with the kill. The *matador* attempts to get the bull into a position where he can drive a sword between its shoulders and through to the heart for a coup de grâce. In practice, they rarely succeed in this, instead taking a second sword, the *descabello*, crossed at the end, to cut the bull's spinal cord; this causes instant death. If things get really bad and he can't finish the job with this, then he will instruct one of his *cuadrilla* to end the business with a *puntilla*, a dagger stabbed into the base of the beast's skull. By this time the crowd will be whistling their derision whilst "the whole spectacle of theatre, courage and art is reduced to the level of a knacker's yard", as one commentator vividly described it.

Alternatively, if the audience are impressed by the *matador*'s performance, they will wave their handkerchiefs and shout for an award to be made by the president. He can award one or both ears, and a tail – the better the display, the more pieces the matador gets – while if he has excelled himself, he will be carried shoulder high out of the ring by the crowd, through the *puerta grande*, the main door, which is normally kept locked. The bull, too, may be applauded for its performance, as it is dragged out by the mule team.

Tickets for *corridas* start at 3000ptas, rising to 15,000ptas for the prime seats at prestigious fights in rings such as Sevilla's Maestranza. The cheapest seats are *gradas*, the highest rows at the back, from where you can see everything that happens without too much of the detail; the front rows are known as the *barreras*. Seats are also divided into *sol* (sun), *sombra* (shade), and *sol y sombra* (shaded after a while), though these distinctions have become less relevant as more bullfights start later in the day, at 6 or 7pm, rather than the traditional 5pm. The *sombra* seats are more expensive – not so much for the spectators' personal comfort but because most of the action takes place in the shade. Tickets for *novilladas* (novice fights with young bulls) are much cheaper, costing 1500–6500ptas, and are often given away by bars or agents outside the bullring prior to the corrida if there hasn't been much demand (which often happens).

On the way in, you can rent **cushions** – two hours sitting on concrete is not much fun. They also count as something to toss in the ring when there's an especially awful performance – as frequently happens. Beer and soft drinks are sold inside.

FOOTBALL

To foreigners, the bullfight is easily the most celebrated of Spain's spectacles. In terms of popular support in modern Spain, however, it ranks far below **fútbol**. If you want the excitement of a genuinely Spanish afternoon out, a football stadium will usually have more passion than anything you'll find in the Plaza de Toros.

For many years, the country's two dominant teams have been **Real Madrid** and **F.C. Barcelona**, and these have shared the League and Cup honours more often than is healthy. Recently though, the big two have faced a bit more opposition than usual from clubs like Atletico de Madrid, Real Zaragoza, Valencia, and new forces Deportivo La Coruña and Celta Vigo (both from Galicia) along with Madrid's "unknown" club, Rayo Vallecano and Barcelona's second string, Espanyol.

Sevilla are the main team in Andalucía, but have only recently returned to the top flight following an ignominious three seasons in the Second Division. The only other Andalucian sides with any pretensions are **Real Betis**, Sevilla's

other club who have been outperforming their fierce rival in recent seasons, and **Málaga** who returned to the First Division in 1999 after a decade away. The region's highest placed teams outside the first division are currently **Córdoba** and **Recreativo Huelva** – Spain's oldest club – both playing in Division 2. Andalucía's other major teams (Cádiz, Granada, Jaén and Poledeportivo Almería) are currently playing in Section B of the Second Division (effectively the third division). See the "Listings" section of each provincial capital for details and grounds of the major teams.

With the exception of a few important games – such as when either of the big two plays Sevilla or the two Sevilla teams play their derbys – **tickets** are pretty easy to get; they start at around 2500ptas for average First Division games but get close to double this when *Real* or *Barça* are in town. Trouble is very rare: English fans, in particular, will be amazed at the easy-going family atmosphere and mixed sex crowds. And August is a surprisingly good time to catch games since there's a glut of warm-up matches for the new season, often involving top foreign clubs.

If you don't go to a game, the atmosphere can be pretty good watching on **TV** in a local bar, especially in a city whose team is playing away. Many bars advertise the matches they screen, which, if they have Canal 5, can include Sunday afternoon English League and Cup games.

MUSIC

Andalucía is the home of much Spanish traditional music and you should try to catch all that is going on. At the numerous fiestas and *romerías* (see pp.54–55) you can see many of Andalucía's best performers; other likely venues are listed in the body of the *Guide*.

MUSIC

Traditional **flamenco** (see Contexts, p.513), Spain's most famous sound, is best witnessed in its native Andalucía, and particularly at one of the major fiestas. There are also some specifically flamenco festivals in the summer, most notably at Córdoba, Jerez and around Granada. Clubs and bars which feature flamenco performers tend on the whole to be expensive and tourist-oriented, while the traditional **peñas** (clubs) are often members-only affairs. However, it is possible to find accessible places which cater for aficionados, and in Andalucía itself almost any flamenco guitarist you come across is likely to be extremely good – just watch the cost of the drinks. In recent years, there has been an exciting development in the shape of new flamenco bands, some

of which have attempted to introduce jazz, rock and African elements into their music. Names to watch out for are the Maghreb-influenced Radio Tarifa as well as Ketama and Pata Negra, two bands featured on the recommended Hannibal Records compilation *Los Jovenes Flamencos*.

If you're anywhere in Andalucía between about December 18 and January 3, look out for performances in local churches of **villancicos**. These are Christmas carols in local style – they can be flamenco, waltz or polyphonic – and are sung by fairly large *coral/rondalla* groups of instrumentalists and vocalists. When they're good they're an extremely beautiful spectacle.

Rock music in Spain may tend to follow British and American trends, but the scene is considerably livelier – and less slavishly derivative – than in almost any other West European country, at its best drawing from a broad range of influences in which traditional Spanish and Latin American rhythms play a major part. There are some excellent home-grown bands and regular gigs in most of the big cities.

Thanks to Spain's relatively large expatriate populations, there are also good places to hear **Latin American and African music** – again, keep your eye out for posters and check the club and dance-hall listings in the local papers. **Jazz** also has a considerable following, with most of Andalucía's venues located in the cities, although they tend to close down in August; one summer jazz festival of note is that of Almuñecar, held in July and often featuring international big names. Worth checking out, too, is the **International Festival of Guitar** in Córdoba (early July), where most of the great classical guitarists put in an appearance along with exponents of Latin American and flamenco styles. Among its more adventurous practitioners – merging flamenco (to the outrage of purists) with modern jazz – look out especially for the brilliant *córdobes*, Paco de Lucía.

TROUBLE, THE POLICE AND SEXUAL HARASSMENT

While you're unlikely to encounter any trouble during the course of a normal visit, it's worth remembering that the Spanish police, polite enough in the usual course of events, can be extremely unpleasant if you get on the wrong side of them.

AVOIDING TROUBLE

Almost all the problems tourists encounter are to do with **petty crime** – pickpocketing and bag-snatching – rather than more serious physical confrontations, so it's as well to be on your guard and know where your possessions are at all times. Sensible **precautions** include: carrying bags slung across your neck, not over your shoulder; not carrying anything in zipped pockets facing the street; having photocopies of your passport and leaving passport and air tickets in the hotel safe; noting down travellers' cheque and credit card numbers; and carrying as little cash and as few valuables as possible – preferably concealed on your person – especially at night in areas such as Granada's Albaicín or the less frequented parts of any city. There are also several ploys to be aware of and situations to avoid as you do the rounds of the city.

Thieves often work in pairs, so watch out for people standing unusually close if you're studying postcards or papers at stalls; keep an eye on your wallet if it appears you're being distracted. Ploys (by some very sophisticated operators) include: the "helpful" person pointing out birdshit (shaving cream or something similar) on your jacket while someone relieves you of your money; the card or paper you're invited to read on the street to distract your attention; the move by someone in a café for your drink with one hand (the other hand's in your bag as you react to save your drink).

If you have a **car** don't leave anything in view when you park it; if possible take the radio with you. When parked overnight in large towns and cities you'd be wise to remove everything, making sure that a hatchback's boot area is left uncovered. Vehicles are rarely stolen, but luggage and valuables left in cars do make a tempting target and rental cars are easy to spot; see also p.32.

Looking for **hotel rooms**, don't leave any bags unattended anywhere. This applies especially to blocks where the hotel or *hostal* is on the higher floors and you're tempted to leave baggage in the hallway or ground-floor lobby. And check, if you leave your room windows open while you're out, that there's no possibility of "fishing-rod" crime. This is a new phenomenon where thieves go fishing through even barred windows to "hook" any valuables in sight.

WHAT TO DO IF YOU'RE ROBBED

If you're robbed, you need to **go to the police** to report it, not least because your insurance company will require a police report. Don't expect a great deal of concern if your loss is relatively small – and expect the process of completing forms and formalities to take ages.

In the unlikely event that you're **mugged**, or otherwise threatened, never resist; hand over what's wanted and run straight to the police, who will be more sympathetic on these occasions. There's also a police office – Centro Atencíon Policial – specifically designed to help tourists, with English-speaking officers, legal and medical advice, and practical help if you've lost your money and credit cards.

If you have your passport stolen or lose all your money, you can contact your **consulate** (see p.62) which is required to assist you to some degree.

THE POLICE

There are three basic types of **police**: the Guardia Civil, the Policía Municipal and the Policía Nacional, all of them armed.

The **Guardia Civil**, in green uniforms, are the most officious and the ones to avoid. Though their role has been cut back since they operated as Franco's right hand, they remain a reactionary force (it was a Guardia Civil colonel, Tejero, who held the Cortes hostage in the February 1981 failed coup).

If you do need the police – and above all if you're reporting a serious crime such as rape – you should always go to the more sympathetic **Policía Municipal**, who wear blue-and-white uniforms with red trim. In the countryside there may be only the Guardia Civil; though they're usually helpful, they are inclined to resent the suggestion that any crime exists on their turf and you may end up feeling as if you are the one who stands accused.

The brown-uniformed **Policía Nacional** are mainly seen in cities, armed with submachine guns and guarding key installations such as embassies, stations, post offices and their own barracks. They are also the force used to control crowds and demonstrations.

OFFENCES

There are a few offences you may possibly commit unwittingly that it's as well to be aware of.

In theory you're supposed to carry some kind of **identification** at all times, and the police can stop you in the streets and demand it. In practice they're rarely bothered if you're clearly a foreigner.

Nude bathing or **unauthorized camping** are activities more likely to bring you into contact with officialdom, though a warning to cover up or move on is a more probable result than any real confrontation. Topless tanning is now commonplace at all the trendier resorts, but in country areas, where attitudes are still very traditional, you should take care not to upset local sensibilities.

If you have an **accident while driving**, try not to make a statement to anyone who doesn't speak English. The SNTO in your home country can provide a list of the most important rules of the road in Spain; and see p.32.

Spanish **drug laws** are in a somewhat bizarre state at present. After the socialists came to power in 1983, cannabis use (possession of up to 8 grammes of what the Spanish call *chocolate*) was decriminalized. Subsequent pressures, and an influx of harder drugs in recent years, have changed that policy and – in theory at least – any drug use is now forbidden. You'll see signs in some bars saying "*no porros*" (no joints), which

you should heed. However, in practice the police are not too worried about personal use. Larger quantities (and any other drugs) are a very different matter.

Should you be **arrested** on any charge you have the right to contact your **consulate** (see p.62). If you've been detained for a drugs offence though, don't expect any sympathy or help from consular officials.

SEXUAL HARASSMENT

Spain's macho image has faded dramatically in the post-Franco years and these days there are relatively few parts of the country where foreign women, travelling alone, are likely to feel threatened, intimidated, or noteworthy.

Inevitably, the **big cities** – like any others in Europe – have their no-go areas, where street crime and especially drug-related hassles are on the rise, but there is little of the pestering and propositions that you have to contend with in, say, the larger French or Italian cities. The outdoor culture of terrazas (terrace bars) and the tendency of Spaniards to move around in large, mixed crowds, filling central bars, clubs and streets late into the night, help to make you feel less exposed. If you are in any doubt, there are always taxis – plentiful and reasonably priced.

The major coastal **resorts** have their own artificial holiday culture. The Spaniards who hang around in discos here or at fiesta fairgrounds pose no greater or lesser threat than similar operators at home. The language barrier simply makes it harder to know whom to trust. "*Déjame en paz*" (leave me in peace) is a fairly standard rebuff and the more potent "*¡vete a (la mierda!)*" (piss off) should work on those hard of hearing.

Predictably, it is in **more isolated regions**, separated by less than a generation from desperate poverty (or still starkly poor), that most serious problems can occur. We have had two reports over the last ten years of women being followed and attacked in remote parts of Andalucía but these are extremely isolated, if worrying, incidents and the overwhelming majority of people you meet will display the dignity and courtesy innate to the region. However, and particularly if you're alone, you do need to know a bit about the land you're travelling around.

In some areas you can walk for hours without coming across an inhabited farm or house, and you still come upon shepherds working for nothing but the wine they take to their pastures. It's rare that this poses a threat – help and hospitality are much more the norm – but you are certainly more vulnerable. That said, **trekking** is becoming more popular in Spain as a whole and in Andalucía many women happily tramp the footpaths of the Sierra Nevada, Las Alpujarras and the Sierra Morena. In the south, especially, though, it is worth finding rooms in the larger villages, or, if you camp out, asking permission to do so on private land, rather than striking out alone.

WORK

Andalucía has Spain's highest level of unemployment and unless you've applied for a job advertised in your home country, such as au pair work, the only real chance of long-term work here is in language schools. If you intend to stay in Spain longer than three months, you'll need a permiso de residencia – see "Red Tape and Visas" (p.17). A word of warning: police are cracking down on people without these and may ask for either your passport or residence papers, or both, on the spot, especially out of the tourist season.

European Union citizens may find the EU's Web site for those planning to live or work abroad within the EU a useful resource; it can be found at *http://citizens.EU.int/*.

TEACHING AND TRANSLATION WORK

Finding a **teaching job** is mainly a question of pacing the streets, stopping in at every language school around and asking about vacancies. For the addresses of schools look in the Yellow Pages under *Academias de Idiomas*. There is now much less work about than in the boom years of the 1980s; although more schools are beginning to open they tend to be computer-based operations employing very few teachers, so you'll need to persevere if you're to come up with a rewarding position. You'll need a TEFL (Teaching English as a Foreign Language) or ESL (English as a Second Language) certificate to give yourself any kind of chance.

You could also try advertising **private lessons** (better paid at 1500–2500ptas an hour, but harder to make a living at) on the noticeboards of university faculties, British consulates, shop windows, bars and in the small ads magazine *Cambalache* (available from most newsstands), in which advertisements are free.

Another possibility, so long as you speak and write excellent Spanish, is **translation work**, most of which will be business correspondence – look in the Yellow Pages under *Traductores*. If you intend doing agency work, you'll usually need access to a fax and a PC with e-mail. Agency work does not pay well (around 7ptas per word) and you'll get more (approximately double) if you work freelance, although then you'll need to pay for a *licencia fiscal* (around 20,000ptas annually) and make monthly social security payments to work legally.

TEMPORARY WORK

If you're looking for **temporary work** the best chances are in the **bars, restaurants, shops and hotels** of the big resorts. This may help you have a good time but it's unlikely to bring in very much money; pay (often from British bar owners) will reflect your lack of official status or work permit. If you turn up in spring and are willing to stay through the season you might get a better deal – also true if you're offering some special skill such as wind-surfing (there are "schools" sprouting up all along the coast). Quite often there are jobs at **yacht marinas**, too, scrubbing down and repainting the boats of the rich; just turn up and ask around, especially from March until June. As a foreigner you've got little hope of work on the grape or olive harvests – these are jealously guarded seasonal jobs for the region's largely unemployed (for the rest of the year) male population.

DIRECTORY

ADDRESSES are written as: c/Picasso 2, 4° izda. – which means Picasso street (calle) no. 2, 4th floor, left-hand (izquierda) flat or office; dcha. (derecha) is right; cto. (centro) centre; s/n (sin número) means the building has no number.

AIRPORT TAX You can happily spend your last pesetas – there's no departure tax.

BIRTHDAYS A Spaniard gets two birthdays a year – one is the anniversary of the actual birth whilst the other (and more important one) celebrates the *día del santo* or feast day of the saint he or she is named after; it is unusual for anyone in Spain not to be named after a saint.

CONSULATES Practically every nation has an embassy in Madrid: there are also British consulates at Málaga (Edificio Eurocom, Block Sur, c/Mauricio Moro Pareto 2; ☎95 221 75 71), Sevilla (Plaza Nueva 8; ☎95 422 88 75), and of course Gibraltar (65 Irish Town; ☎350/78305). US consulates are based in Fuengirola (Centro Comercial Las Rampas, Fase 2, Planta 1, Locales 12-G7; ☎95 247 48 91) and Sevilla (Paseo de las Delicias 7; ☎95 423 18 85). Among others are

Ireland (Galerías Santa Mónica, Avda. Boliches 15, Fuengirola ☎95 247 51 08); Australia (c/Federico Rubio 14, Sevilla; ☎95 422 09 71); Canada (Edificio Horizonte, Plaza Malagueta 3, Málaga; ☎95 222 33 46); and the Netherlands (Alameda de Colon 3, Málaga; ☎95 270 07 20).

CONTRACEPTIVES Condoms (*condones* or *preservativos*) are available from *farmacias*, supermarkets and slot machines in some bars. Most brands of the pill (*la píldora*) you should be able to buy over the counter at any *farmacia*; if you encounter difficulties the pharmacist will usually be able to recommend a doctor nearby who will be able to advise. If you take along your E111 form (see p.18) you won't need to pay for the consultation. Another useful source of help is a private women's clinic which is usually fast and will cost around 3000ptas for a consultation (see under *Planificación Familiar* in Yellow Pages).

ELECTRICITY Current in most of Spain is 220 volts AC (just occasionally it's still 110V and such sockets should be labelled): most European appliances should work as long as you have an adaptor for European-style two-pin plugs. North Americans will need this plus a transformer.

FISHING Fortnightly permits are easily and cheaply obtained from any ICONA office – there's one in every big town (addresses from the local Turismo). For information on the whereabouts of the best trout streams and other wrinkles contact the Spanish Fishing Federation, Navas de Tolosa 3, 28013 Madrid (☎91 225 59 85).

GAY LIFE The largest gay communities in Andalucía are in Cádiz, Sevilla and Torremolinos, and attitudes in all three places, as well as other major cities and resorts, are fairly relaxed. Sevilla and Cádiz in particular have large permanent gay communities and a thriving scene. The age of consent is eighteen. Two guides to the Spanish scene worth getting hold of are *Spartacus*

España, available in the UK and US, and *Guía Gay Visado*, a regularly updated Spanish guide to gay and lesbian activities and entertainment across Spain. NOS (Asociación Andaluza de Lesbianas y Gais), c/Lavadero de las Tablas 15, Granada (☎958 20 06 02; *www.lander.es/~chema/*), operates the Teléfono Andaluz de Información Homosexual.

KIDS/BABIES don't pose great travel problems. *Hostales, pensiones* and *restaurantes* generally welcome them and offer rooms with three or four beds; RENFE allows children under four to travel free on trains, with forty per cent discount for those between four and twelve years; and some cities and resorts – the Costa del Sol is particularly good – have long lists or special pamphlets on kids' attractions. As far as babies go, food seems to work out quite well (*hostales* often prepare food specially – or will let you use the kitchen to do so), though you might want to bring powdered milk: babies, like most Spaniards, are pretty contemptuous of the UHT (ultra heat-treated) stuff generally available. If you're likely to be travelling out of season, however, bear in mind that cheaper *hostales* (as opposed to more expensive hotels) often don't have any heating systems – and it can get cold. Disposable nappies and other standard needs are very widely available. Many *hostales* will be prepared to baby-sit, or at least to listen out for trouble. This is more likely if you're staying in an old-fashioned family-run place than in the fancier hotels.

LANGUAGE COURSES are offered at most Spanish universities, and in a growing number of special language schools for foreigners. For details overseas and a complete list write to a branch of the Spanish Institute: the London one is at 102 Eaton Square, London SW1 (☎020/7235 1484) – other addresses from the nearest tourist office in your respective country. Many American universities have their own courses based in Spain – or try the Education Office of Spain, 150 Fifth Ave #600, Suite 918, New York, NY 10011 (☎212/741-5144).

LAUNDRIES You'll find a few self-service launderettes (*lavanderías automáticas*) in the major cities and some are quoted in the relevant city "Listings" sections in the *Guide*, but generally they're rare – you normally have to leave your clothes for the full (and somewhat expensive) works. Note that you're not allowed by law to leave laundry hanging out of windows over a street. A dry cleaner is a *tintorería*.

LUGGAGE After a long period of absence following terrorist actions in the late 1970s, self-service *consignas* are back at most important Spanish train stations. You'll find lockers large enough to hold most backpacks, plus a smaller bag, which cost about 400–600ptas a day; put the coins in to free the key. These are not a good idea for long-term storage, however, as they're periodically emptied by station staff. Bus terminals have staffed *consignas* where you present a claim stub to get your gear back; cost is about the same.

SKIING Andalucía's main ski centre is the Solynieve resort in the Sierra Nevada, detailed in the "Granada" chapter or covered on the Sierra Nevada's Ski Information Web site (*www.cetursa.es/*). The SNTO's Skiing in Spain pamphlet is also useful. If you want to arrange a weekend or more while you're in Spain, Viajes Ecuador (Spain's biggest travel firm, with branches in most cities) is good for inexpensive, all-inclusive trips. Get the address of the nearest branch from any Turismo.

SURNAMES Spaniards use of double-barrelled surnames is a source of constant confusion to foreigners. Women on getting married do not adopt their husband's surnames but continue to use their own name which means that children, when born, are given their father's first surname first followed by that of their mother. Thus Miguel Cervantes Saavedra would use only his father's name (Cervantes) in most situations but his legal name remains the full one.

SWIMMING POOLS Most Andalucian towns – and even quite small villages – have a *piscina municipal*, a lifesaver in the summer and yet another reason not to keep exclusively to the coast. They're often landscaped with a garden, quite a few have cafés and there's usually no problem if you want to bring food in. Many of these, along with river swimming spots, are detailed throughout the *Guide*.

TIME Spain is one hour ahead of the UK, six hours ahead of Eastern Standard Time, nine hours ahead of Pacific Standard Time, except for brief periods during the changeovers to and from daylight saving. In Spain the clocks go forward in the last week of March and back again in the last week of October.

TOILETS Public ones are averagely clean but rarely have any paper (best to carry your own).

The old-fashioned squat-style WCs are now — thankfully — a rarity. The most common euphemisms are *baño* (literally "bathroom"), *aseos*, *servicios* (the most used), *retretes* or *sanitarios*. *Señoras* (Ladies) and *Caballeros* (Gentlemen) or the initials "S" or "C" are the usual signs, though you may also see *Damas* used for women's conveniences and the potentially hazardous combination of *Señoras* (Ladies) and *Señores* (Men).

PART TWO

THE

GUIDE

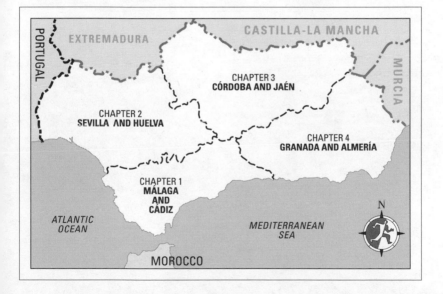

> "The Andalucian sun starts singing a fire song, and
> all creation trembles at the sound."
>
> Federico García Lorca

CHAPTER ONE

MÁLAGA AND CÁDIZ

The smallest of Andalucía's eight provinces, **Málaga** is also its most populous, swelling to bursting point with the sheer weight of visitors in high summer. Although primarily known as the gateway to the Costa del Sol and its unashamedly commercial resorts such as **Torremolinos** and **Marbella**, the province has much more to offer than just its coastline. To most incoming tourists the provincial capital **Málaga** is merely "the place by the airport", but it is also a vibrant city in its own right, with a population of half a million people. Away from the beaches, in the west of Málaga's provincial heartland, lies the **Serranía de Ronda** – a series of small mountain ranges sprinkled with gleaming villages hugging the peaks beneath ancient Moorish castles. Andalucía is dotted with these small, brilliantly whitewashed settlements – the **pueblos blancos** or "white towns", all of which look great from a distance, though many are rather less interesting on arrival. **Ronda**, located astride a stunningly beautiful *tajo*, or gorge, is justly the most famous of these *pueblos blancos*.

To the north lies the appealing market town of **Antequera** with its remarkable prehistoric dolmens and sumptuous Baroque churches, and from here it's just a quick hop south to the natural wonders of **El Torcal**, where vast limestone outcrops have been eroded into a landscape of weird natural sculptures. Another possible trip from Antequera is to the spectacular **El Chorro Gorge**, which, along with the Guadalhorce lake, has become a major climbing and camping centre. Nearby, the saline **Laguna de Fuente de Piedra** is Europe's only inland breeding ground for the greater flamingo, whose flying flocks make a spectacular sight in summer.

Northeast of the city of Málaga is the largely unknown and little-visited **Axarquía** region, an area of rugged natural beauty and once the haunt of mountain bandits. Now the domain of the *cabra hispanica*, a distinctive Iberian long-horned goat, the area's magnificent scenery and earthy villages contrast starkly with the crowded **beaches** to the south.

With a two-hundred-kilometre coastline fronting both the Atlantic and the Mediterranean **Cádiz** is the most southerly province of Andalucía. The sea has played

---

ACCOMMODATION PRICE CODES

Throughout this guide, accommodation is graded on a scale from ① to ⑨. These show the cost per night of the cheapest double room in each establishment in high season, though remember that many of the cheap places will have more expensive rooms with en-suite facilities. See p.39 for more details. Approximate Euro rates (operative from January 2002) are given for each category:

① Under 2000ptas/
Under €12

② 2000–3000ptas/
€12–18

③ 3000–4500ptas/
€18–27

④ 4500–6000ptas/
€27–37

⑤ 6000–8000ptas/
€37–49

⑥ 8000–10,000ptas/
€49–60

⑦ 10,000–15,000ptas/
€60–90

⑧ 15,000–20,000ptas/
€90–120

⑨ Over 20,000ptas/
Over €120

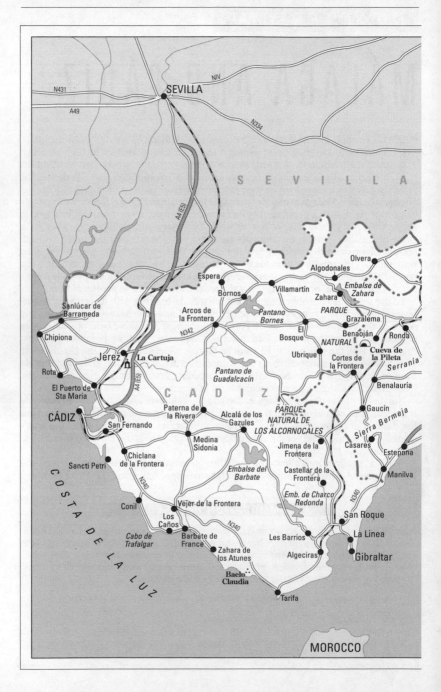

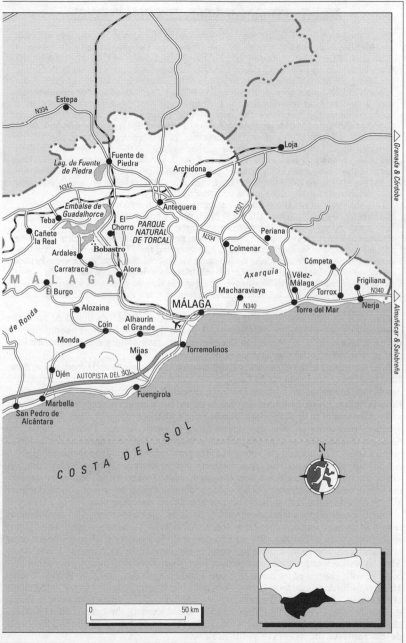

ANDALUCÍA'S MOROCCAN ENCLAVES

Across the straits from Gibraltar on the north coast of Morocco lie the enclaves of **Ceuta** and **Melilla**, both Spanish territories and officially part of the autonomous region of Andalucía. When they celebrated in 1997 the quincentenary of their founding by the Catholic monarchs FERNANDO and ISABEL, neither King Juan Carlos nor the prime minister José María Aznar saw fit to join in the deliberately low-key festivities – the Spanish establishment acceded to the wishes of Morocco, with which for economic reasons it desires good relations, for minimal observation of the event. This is because Morocco views the territories as China viewed Hong Kong – and as Spain views Gibraltar. Ceuta and Melilla are the remnants of a string of Spanish fortresses built along the coast of North Africa after Andalucía had been reconquered from the Moors. Intended to protect the peninsula from further incursions, they survived into modern times as an anachronism – the United Nations does not even list them as colonies because they were settled long before Morocco existed in its present shape. Their combined populations of 138,000 citizens have the same rights as those on Spain's mainland and vociferously oppose any plans to cede the territories to Morocco.

The inhabitants of Ceuta and Melilla have found a new champion in Jesus Gil, the Mayor of Marbella (see p.121), whose GIL party has built up a power base here, winning seats on both towns' ruling councils. This has further complicated matters for Madrid who see the enclaves as burning up vast amounts of money in grants and subsidies as well as providing an easy entry point for illegal immigrants into Spain and the EU. In line with what is happening in the former Spanish Sahara, Ceuta and Melilla could eventually gain some form of autonomy within Morocco – but so far the inhabitants are unconvinced and the tug of war between Spain and its North African neighbour seems likely to continue for some time yet.

a large part in the history of the province, and most of Cádiz's dozen or so major conurbations are within easy distance of a beach. Founded by the Phoenicians, the city of **Cádiz** itself makes up for in sheer elegance, atmosphere and sea-girthed location what it lacks in the way of irresistible sights.

After the tumult of the Costa del Sol, the bracing Atlantic winds and broad, white, dune-lined beaches of the **Costa de la Luz** – great stretches of which have so far survived the developers' attentions and which are often deserted – can come as a welcome relief. Resorts such as **Conil**, **Chipiona** and **Sanlúcar de Barrameda** possess a low-key charm, while at the southern tip of the coast, **Tarifa** – also with miles of fine beaches – has become a major windsurfing centre. The entire thirty-kilometre stretch between Tarifa and Algeciras (Andalucía's main port for sailings to Morocco) has been designated a "potential military zone". This sounds off-putting – and in parts, marked by *"Paso Prohibido"* signs, it is – but the ruling has also had happier effects, placing strict controls on Spanish developments and preventing foreigners from buying up land. Flanked by La Linea and Algeciras, the British colony of **Gibraltar** sits beneath its daunting mountain of rock, regarded uneasily by Spaniards and a strange, hybrid curiosity to almost everyone else.

Inland, Cádiz offers a fascinating variety of landscapes and towns. The mountainous region in its northeastern corner, which it shares with Málaga, is dotted with hill-top white towns such as **Zahara**, **Olvera** and **Arcos de la Frontera**, while the green oasis of **Grazalema**, the wettest point in Spain, is surrounded by its **Natural Park**, a paradise for walkers and naturalists. South of here sharp contours give way to rolling hills covered with clumps of walnut trees, pines and Spanish firs, and the ranches around **Medina Sidonia** where *toros bravos* – ominous black fighting bulls – graze in the shade of cork oaks. To the west, the hills are left behind and the vines take over, covering thousands of acres of dazzling white chalk soil, and forming the famous **sherry triangle** between **Jerez**, a fine town in its own right, **Puerto de Santa María** and **Sanlúcar de Barrameda**, the oldest vineyards in Europe.

Málaga

First impressions of **MÁLAGA** are not encouraging. A large and bustling seaport with a population passing half a million, it's the second city of Andalucía (after Sevilla) and also one of the poorest: official unemployment figures for the area estimate the jobless at one in four of the workforce. Yet, though many visitors get no further than the train or bus stations, put off by the grim clusters of highrises on the fringes, if you penetrate beyond these you will find yourself in one of the most atmospheric and historic cities in Spain. Lorca described Málaga as his favourite town and given a chance it can be a surprisingly attractive place, an impression boosted by the ebullient and big-hearted *malagueños*, among the friendliest people in Andalucía.

There are many intriguing corners to explore, such as the Moorish-inspired alley-ways circling the market, and the bleakly-lit old cafés where wizened characters sip *fino* or coffee beneath hanging cured ham shanks. Around the old fishing villages of **El Palo** and **Pedregalejo**, now absorbed into the suburbs, is a series of small beaches and a *paseo* lined with some of the best fish and seafood cafés in the province. Overlooking the town and port, the Moorish citadels of the **Alcazaba** and **Gibralfaro** give excellent introductions to what you can expect at Córdoba and Granada, and while *sevillanos* loudly proclaim that there is only one *Semana Santa* worthy of the name, *malagueños* furiously disagree. The processions are celebrated here with great fervour and with much larger *pasos* (floats, actually called *tronos* or "thrones" here) than those of Sevilla, carried by up to 200 sober-suited males. In mid-August at the peak of the tourist season the town lets rip in its **Feria de Málaga** – one of the wildest and most spectacular fiestas in Andalucía.

Incidentally, **Picasso** was born in Málaga, and although the artist moved away in his early years, you can still visit his birthplace and – opening in 2001 – a new **museum** housing some of his major works.

Some history

The **Phoenicians** founded the settlement they called *Malaka* in the eighth century BC, building a fortress on the summit of the hill today dominated by the Alcazaba. Later incorporated into the Roman province of Baetica in the wake of Rome's victory over Carthage, Málaga prospered as a **trading port** exporting iron, copper and lead from mines in the hills near Ronda, as well as olive oil, wine and *garum*, a relish made from pickled fish to which the Romans were particularly partial. When the city fell into the hands of the **Moors** early in the eighth century Málaga was soon flourishing again as the main port for the city of Granada. Although in the fourteenth century the ruler Yusuf I constructed the Gibralfaro as defence, in 1487 Málaga was taken by Christian forces following a bitter siege, after which the large Moorish population was persecuted and its property confiscated on a grand scale; the city's main mosque was also transformed into a cathedral, and another twenty into churches. Málaga entered into a decline only exacerbated by a revolt of the Moors in 1568 which resulted in their complete expulsion.

It was not until the nineteenth century that real prosperity returned – and then only briefly. Middle-class families arriving from the north invested in textile factories, sugar refineries and shipyards, and gave their names to city streets such as Larios and Heredia, while Málaga **dessert wine** became the favourite tipple of Victorian ladies. Then, in the early part of this century, the bottom fell out of the boom as the new industries succumbed to foreign competition and the phylloxera bug got to work wiping out the vines. A number of radical revolts leading up to the Civil War also brought the city an unhealthy reputation.

Given its volatile nature it was inevitable that Málaga would be staunchly Republican during the **Civil War**. In six years of struggle, churches and convents were burned while Italian planes bombed the city, destroying much of its ancient central core, and mass executions of "reds and anarchists" by the conquering Franco forces were to leave enduring emotional scars.

The 1960s finally brought an economic lifeline in the form of **mass tourism** and the exploitation of the Costa del Sol. Coastal nightmares, however, barely touch the heart of Málaga. The airport lies west of the city, with the result that most of the millions of visitors attracted to the beach resorts are hardly aware of the existence of a vibrant metropolis nearby. All that may be about to change, however, as plans are afoot to transform the beaches on the town's eastern flank as far as El Palo into a full-blown resort, with promenade, upmarket hotels and bars. It is to be hoped that all this doesn't impact too adversely on the city's unique character.

Arrival and information

From the **airport** (☎95 224 88 04), the **electric train** provides the easiest, and cheapest, approach into town (every 30min, 7am–11.45pm; 135ptas). From the arrivals hall, go up one floor to the *Salidas* or departures hall, take any exit and then turn right to reach a pedestrian overpass at the end of the airport building. Follow the *Ferrocarril* signs and cross the overpass (baggage trolleys allowed) to the unstaffed station; the sweet kiosk, if open, sells tickets or you can buy one on the train. Make sure that you're on the Málaga platform (the one farthest away and reached by an underpass) and stay on the train right to the end of the line – the **Centro-Alameda** stop (a 12min ride). From here, you can cross the bridge over the Río Guadalmedina riverbed to the western end of the tree-lined Alameda, effectively the town centre. The stop before this is RENFE, Malagá's main **train station**, from where it's a slightly longer walk into the heart of town (bus #3 runs from here to the centre approximately every 10min). **Buses** from the airport to the centre depart from a stop outside the arrivals hall (half-hourly; 6.30am–11.30pm), and call at the main train and bus stations en route. The same journey by **taxi** from the centre of town costs about 1200ptas and takes roughly 15min. Going back **out to the airport**, the electric train leaves the Centro/Alameda station on the hour and half-hour (daily 5.45am–10.30pm). Remember that there are two airport stops: first Carga (cargo), then Aeropuerto (international and domestic departures).

All buses from and to destinations outside Málaga (run by a number of different companies) operate from the one **bus station** (☎95 287 26 57), a little northwest of the RENFE station on Paseo de los Tilos.

Arriving in Málaga **by car** you'll face the serious problem of **parking**; one good-value on-street car park (about 200ptas per day; free at nightime) is located along the east bank of the Río Guadalmedina (Avda. Comandante Benitez), below the Alameda. As **theft from cars** is rampant in Málaga, be careful to remove all valuables before leaving it on the street overnight, or use a hotel with a garage or one of the many multi-storey guarded car parks that are clearly signed around the centre. You should also remove any visible stickers bearing a car rental company's name or logo as these make the car a magnet for thieves.

Information

The helpful **Turismo**, Pasaje de Chinitas 4 (Mon–Fri 9.30am–1.30pm & 4–6pm, Sat 9.30am–2pm; ☎95 221 34 45) can provide full accommodation lists and a larger, more detailed map of the city than the one printed here; they also have lots of information on the Costa del Sol. They stock the monthly *¿Que Hacer?* which covers events and entertainments happening throughout Andalucía as well as the weekly *Sur* (in English), published by Malaga's main daily, which has a useful listings section on entertainment in the city. A simple **Turismo Municipal** (Mon–Fri 8am–2.30pm & 4.30–7.30pm, Sat 9.30am–1.30pm; ☎95 260 44 10) is located in the Casa del Jardinero, Avenida Cervantes 1, on the north side of the Paseo del Parque close to the old customs house; it also operates a kiosk (summer only) in Plaza Merced as well as two other branches in the arrivals hall at the airport and at the bus station.

Accommodation

Málaga boasts dozens of **fondas** and **hostales**, so budget rooms are rarely hard to come by, and there are some real bargains in winter. Numerous possibilities are to be found in the grid of streets just north and south of the Alameda, which is probably the best place to start looking. The cheapest option is the **youth hostel**, though this isn't particularly convenient for the centre, as it lies out in the western suburbs. For those who want a little more luxury, we've listed a couple of places further out. Málaga's **campsite** has closed with no plans to re-open, which means the nearest campsites along the coast are at: Torremolinos heading west (see p.117), and Torre del Mar (see p.99) to the east.

South of the Alameda

Hostal Alameda, c/Casas de Campos 3 (☎95 222 20 99). Friendly place, with good-value rooms, some with bath. ③.

Hostal Avenida, Alameda Principal 5 (☎95 221 77 29). Right on the Alameda but not too noisy. Some rooms with bath. ③.

Hostal El Cenachero, c/Barroso 5 (☎95 222 40 88). Clean, quiet, third-floor *hostal* with friendly proprietors and all rooms en-suite; in a quiet street just off the seafront end of c/Córdoba. ④.

Hotel Lis, c/Córdoba 7 (☎95 222 73 00, fax 95 222 73 09). Good-quality hotel offering rooms with bath, TV and balcony. ⑤.

Hotel Sur, c/Trinidad Grund 13 (☎95 222 48 03, fax 95 221 24 16). Quiet, efficient hotel with garage; all rooms have bath and TV. ⑤.

Hotel Venecia, Alameda Principal 9 (☎95 221 36 36). Central, new hotel with all facilities, balconies overlooking the Alameda, and satellite TV. ⑤.

North of the Alameda

Hostal Aurora II, c/Cisneros 5 (☎95 222 40 04). Spacious, ensuite rooms in renovated house. Same owners also run the slightly cheaper *Aurora I* around the corner in c/Muro Puerta Nueva offering rooms without bath. ④.

Hostal Buenos Aires, c/la Bolsa 12 (☎95 221 89 35). Clean, light rooms on a reasonably quiet street near the cathedral. ③.

Hotel Carlos V, c/Cister 10 (☎95 221 51 20, fax 95 221 51 29), close to the cathedral. Good-value, mid-range hotel; ensuite rooms and own garage. ⑤.

Hostal Cisneros, c/Cisneros 7, west of Plaza Constitución (☎95 221 26 33). Pleasant rooms with bath and friendly proprietors. ④.

Hostal Córdoba, c/Bolsa 9–11, near the cathedral (☎95 221 44 69). Inexpensive, simple rooms in family-run establishment. ②.

Hostal Derby, c/San Juan de Dios 1 (☎95 222 13 01). Very friendly and excellent-value fourth-floor establishment, on a tiny street north of the Plaza de la Marina, with some rooms overlooking the harbour. ③.

Pensión Juanita, c/Alarcón Luján 8 (☎95 221 35 86). Basic, central and friendly *pensión* on the fourth floor with lift. ③.

Hostal La Palma, c/Martínez 7 (☎95 222 67 72). Pleasant *hostal* run by a friendly couple. Sometimes willing to give discounts. ③.

Hostal Ramos, c/Martínez 8, just above the Alameda (☎95 222 72 68). Clean, basic rooms without bath. ②.

Hostal Victoria, c/Sancha de Lara 3 (☎95 222 42 23). Smart *hostal* with good ensuite doubles and singles. ④.

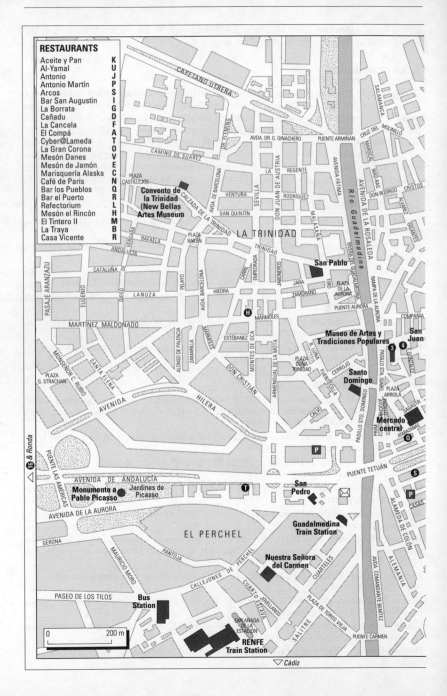

RESTAURANTS

Aceite y Pan	K
Al-Yamal	U
Antonio	J
Antonio Martín	P
Arcos	S
Bar San Augustin	I
La Borrata	G
Cañadu	D
La Cancela	F
El Compá	A
Cyber@Lameda	T
La Gran Corona	O
Mesón Danes	V
Mesón de Jamón	E
Marisquería Alaska	C
Café de Paris	N
Bar los Pueblos	Q
Bar el Puerto	R
Refectorium	L
Mesón el Rincón	H
El Tintero II	M
La Traya	B
Casa Vicente	R

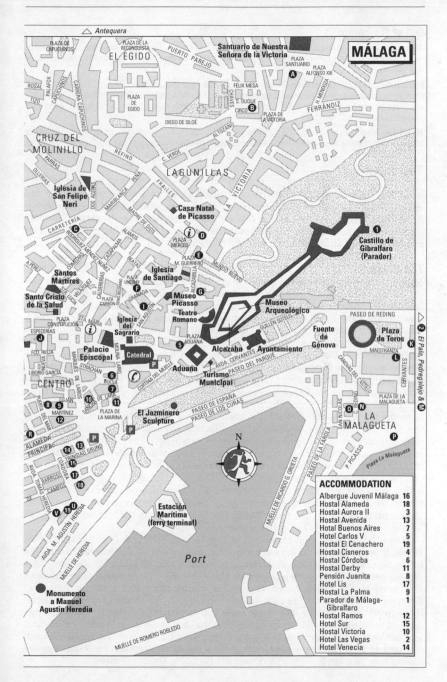

△ Antequera

MÁLAGA

EL EGIDO

Santuario de Nuestra
Señora de la Victoria

PLAZA DE CAPUCHINOS
PLAZA DE LA RECONQUISTA
PUERTO PAREJO
PLAZA SANTUARIO
PLAZA ALFONSO XIII

ROSAL
PALAFOX
TIZO
CAPUCHINOS
CARRERA CAPUCHINOS
PLAZA DE EGIDO
DIEGO DE SILOÉ
FÉLIX MESA
CHAVES
S. DUQUE
CIRCO
PLAZA DE LA VICTORIA
H. MENDOZA
FERRÁNDIZ

Ⓐ

Ⓑ

CRUZ DEL MOLINILLO

PARRAS
OLLERIAS
REFINO
C. VERDE
ALTOZANO

LAGUNILLAS

LA VICTORIA

Iglesia de
San Felipe
Neri

Casa Natal
de Picasso

CARRETERÍA
Ⓒ
RODRÍGUEZ MÉNDEZ NÚÑEZ
A. PÉREZ
COMEDIAS
CASAPALMA
BEATAS
ALAMOS
MADRE DE DIOS
DOS ACERAS
MARIBLANCA
PEÑA
FRAILES
CASABERMEJA

PLAZA MERCED
Ⓘ Ⓓ

Castillo de
Gibralfaro
(Parador)

❶

Santos
Mártires

Santo Cristo
de la Salud

PLAZA M. GUERRERO
Ⓔ
MUNDO NUEVO

Iglesia
de Santiago

Museo
Picasso

PLAZA UNCIBAY
GRANADA
PLAZA CARBÓN
ALCAZABILLA

Ⓖ

Museo
Arqueológico

Teatro
Romano

Iglesia
del
Sagrario

PLAZA CONSTITUCIÓN
Ⓘ

Ⓕ

SAN AGUSTÍN
STA. MARÍA
MOLINA LARIO

PLAZA ADUANA

GUILLEN SOTELO

Fuente
de
Génova

PASEO DE REDING

Plaza
de Toros

△ ❷ El Palo, Pedregalejo & Ⓜ

ESPECERÍAS
Ⓙ
FCO. RICIJA
Ⓘ
MARQUÉS DE LARIOS

Palacio
Episcopal

Catedral
Ⓟ

Aduana

Ⓤ
❺

Alcazaba

Ayuntamiento

AVDA. CERVANTES

Turismo
Municipal

PASEO DEL PARQUE

CÁNOVAS DE CASTILLO
MAESTRANZA

Ⓚ
CERVANTES
Ⓛ

CENTRO

Ⓡ
LIBORIO GARCÍA
STRACHAN
BOLSA
DE LARA
SALITRE
PLAZA DE LA MARINA
Ⓤ
LUJÁN
MARTÍNEZ

Ⓤ
Ⓐ Ⓤ

❾
❿
Ⓤ
Ⓤ
❶❶
Ⓤ
⓬

El Jazminero
Sculpture

PASEO DE ESPAÑA
PASEO DE LOS CURAS

SAN NICOLÁS
REDING
PLAZA DE LA MALAGUETA
SAN NICOLÁS
Ⓝ
LA
MALAGUETA

ALAMEDA PRINCIPAL
PUERTA DEL MAR
Ⓡ
⓮ ⓭
Ⓟ
TRINIDAD GRUND
⓯
BARROSO
⓱
CÓRDOBA
⓲
CAMPOS
Ⓤ
⓳ Ⓤ
AVDA. TOMÁS HEREDIA
AVDA. M. AGUSTÍN HEREDIA

Ⓟ

PASEO DE LA FAROLA
P. PICASSO

Playa La Malagueta

Ⓟ

Estación
Marítima
(ferry terminal)

MUELLE DE RICARDO G. ORUETA

N

Port

Monumento
a Manuel
Agustín Heredia

MUELLE DE HEREDIA

MUELLE DE ROMERO ROBLEDO

ACCOMMODATION

Albergue Juvenil Málaga	16
Hostal Alameda	18
Hostal Aurora II	3
Hostal Avenida	13
Hotal Buenos Aires	7
Hotel Carlos V	5
Hostal El Cenachero	19
Hostal Cisneros	4
Hostal Córdoba	6
Hostal Derby	11
Pensión Juanita	8
Hotel Lis	17
Hostal La Palma	9
Parador de Málaga-Gibralfaro	1
Hostal Ramos	12
Hotel Sur	15
Hostal Victoria	10
Hotel Las Vegas	2
Hotel Venecia	14

Out of the centre

Albergue Juvenil Málaga, Plaza de Pío XII 6 (☎95 230 85 00). Pleasantly modern double rooms, complete with sun-terrace. The #18 bus (heading east across the river) from the Alameda will drop you nearby. ①.

Parador de Málaga–Gibralfaro, Monte de Gibralfaro (☎95 222 19 02, fax 222 19 04). You won't get a better panoramic view of the coast than from this eagle's nest on top of the Gibralfaro hill; it's quite small for a *parador*, although it does have a pool. Well worth calling in for a drink or a meal (see under "Eating" p.82). ⑧.

Hotel Las Vegas, Paseo de Sancha 22 (☎95 221 77 12, fax 95 222 48 89). Smartish hotel, east of the bullring and close to the beach with sea view balcony rooms; own swimming pool and car park. ⑥.

The Town

Málaga is bisected by the seasonal Guadalmedina torrent, which was recently and unsuccessfully landscaped at colossal cost with dismal walkways and reluctant grass. All the major sights lie to the east of this and below the **Alcazaba**. From the **Alameda**, the city's main thoroughfare, the **cathedral**, new **Museo Picasso** and a clutch of interesting **churches** all lie within a few minutes' walk.

The Alcazaba

Málaga's magnificent **Alcazaba** (daily except Tues 9.30am–6.30pm; free) is an exuberant contrast to the dour fortresses of Castile. At its entrance stands a **Roman theatre**, accidentally unearthed in 1951 during the construction of the Casa de Cultura, which was recently demolished to allow restoration of its ancient predecessor. The theatre is now used as an auditorium for various outdoor entertainments. From here a path winds upwards, lined by the cypresses and flower-encircled arbours so loved by the sybaritic Moors. The citadel too, is Roman, and interspersed among the Moorish brick of the double- and triple-arched gateways are recycled blocks and columns of classical marble.

Although the main structures were begun by the Moors in the 700s, the palace higher up the hill dates from the early decades of the eleventh century. It was the residence of the Arab Emirs of Málaga, who carved out an independent kingdom for themselves upon the break-up of the Western Caliphate. Their independence lasted a mere thirty years, but for a while the kingdom grew to include Granada, Carmona and Jaén. The palace, restored as an **archeological museum**, is scattered chaotically with fragments of statuary and mosaics, and is not always easy to make sense of. And although the prehistoric, Phoenician and Roman artefacts testify to the city's antique pedigree, the simple truth is that they are not very inspiring. The Moorish section is altogether better, with some striking examples of the ceramics for which Málaga was renowned during the thirteenth and fourteenth centuries, particularly its gilded work exemplified by the **Barco plate**. Note, too, the more recent fine stucco work in the museum, and 1920s Moorish-style ceilings (a big vogue at that time in Spain).

Above the Alcazaba, and connected to it by a long double wall, is the **Gibralfaro castle** (free access). By far the most appealing approach is to take the road to the right of the Alcazaba, then a path up through gardens, a ramble of towers, bougainvillea-draped ramparts and sentry-box-shaped Moorish wells (the approach from the town side, used by the tourist buses, is a rather unattractive walk). Built by Yusuf I of Granada in the fourteenth century and last used in 1936 during the Civil War, the heavily restored castle, with its formidable walls and turrets, affords terrific views over the city and the complex fortifications of the Alcazaba. A pleasant place to take refreshment is at the nearby **parador** with its terrace overlooking the city (see "Accommodation"). It's reached by following the road leading out of the castle's car park for 500m. If you're feeling lazy, take bus #35 from the Paseo del Parque in the city centre.

The Cathedral and the Museo Picasso

Dominating the views from the Gibralfaro is Málaga's peculiar, unfinished **Catedral** (Mon–Sat 10am–6.45pm; 200ptas). It lacks a tower on the west front, the result of a radical *malagueño* bishop having donated the earmarked money to the American War of Independence against the British. Despite this curiosity, which has resulted in the building's popular nickname *La Manquita* ("the one-armed lady"), the cathedral lacks much else of interest. The interior is distinguished only by an intricately carved and naturalistic seventeenth-century *sillería* (choir stall) with outstanding sculptural work – in particular *St Francis* and *John the Baptist* – by Pedro de Mena. However, the **Iglesia del Sagrario** (same ticket and times as cathedral, also open during services), on the cathedral's northern flank, is worth a look, if only for its fine Gothic **portal**, dating from an earlier, uncompleted Isabelline church. Inside, a newly restored and magnificent gilded **Plateresque retablo**, which is brilliantly illuminated during services, is the work of Juan Balmaseda. Just along the street (c/Cister) from here, you could take a look at the exterior of the house where **Pedro de Mena** – often described as Andalucía's Michelangelo – lived during his years in Málaga; a crumbling place marked by a plaque, it's in a small cul-de-sac named c/Afligidos.

The former Museo de Bellas Artes has now been transformed into the new **Museo Picasso** (due to open in 2001; check with the Turismo, or consult *www.andalucia.org*) honouring Málaga's most famous son. The collection's core will consist of 182 major works purchased at a bargain price from Picasso's daughter-in-law Christine Ruíz-Picasso, who felt that her inheritance should go to the artist's birthplace. Located just round the corner from the cathedral on c/San Agustín, the museum is housed in an impressive sixteenth-century mansion – the former residence of the Counts of Buenavista – with an elegant patio. The **Bellas Artes collection** – including works by Murillo and Zurbarán – will move to the Convento de la Trinidad (also opening in 2001), c/Calzada de Trinidad s/n, across the river, which is being restored to house it. In the meantime a selection from the collection is on display in the old Aduana building on the Paseo del Parque (Tues 3–8pm, Wed–Fri 9am–8pm, Sat & Sun 9am–3pm; free).

Casa Natal de Picasso

Picasso's birthplace and family home during his early years, the **Casa Natal de Picasso**, Plaza de la Merced 15, is now the headquarters of the Picasso Foundation (Mon–Sat 10am–2pm & 5–8pm, Sun 11am–2pm; free) whose friendly staff are pleased to allow you in to look around. It was during his formative years in Málaga that Picasso's prodigious talent for drawing was first noticed – "When I was a child I could draw like Raphael," he later wrote. "It took me all my life to learn to draw like a child." It was in the cafés around the square that the boy saw the first solid shape that he wanted to commit to paper: *churros*, those oil-steeped fritters that Spaniards dip into their breakfast chocolate. Although there is a ground floor exhibition space (for guest shows) this is more academic institute than museum, containing only some photos of his life, a couple of notebooks with some early sketches and a few lithographs and ceramic works by the master – most visitors are scholars and art historians who come here to research.

Pasaje de Chinitas and the Jardines de Picasso

Tucked behind the Plaza de la Constitución is one of Málaga's most evocative corners, the **Pasaje de Chinitas**. In the last century, when Málaga was a thriving industrial town, this narrow white-walled street was filled with *tascas*, or bars, where businessmen would meet to discuss deals over fine wines before slinking off to the *Café de Chinitas* to hear some of the best flamenco in town. In the 1920s and 1930s the fame of this flamenco shrine, now a mundane textile store, grew as it became a noted meeting place of artists and writers, bullfighters and singers. Lorca loved the place and composed a poem in its honour, part of which appears on a plaque fixed to the former café, at the junction with c/Sánchez Pastor:

In the Café de Chinitas
Said Paquiro to his brother:
"I'm more valiant than you,
more brave and more gitano.*"*

West of here stands the modern garden, **Jardines de Picasso**, at the end of the Avda. de Andalucía 100m or so beyond the El Corte Inglés department store. In 1978 the country's first monument to the artist was erected here, a curiously restrained abstract work by Ramón Calderón. Second thoughts were in a much more monumental vein and Ortiz Berrocal was commissioned to produce something of the size required: a wonderfully intestinal bronze, flanked by two magnificent dragon trees which are fairly remarkable sculptures in their own right. Don't hang around here at dusk or after dark, however, as the area has a dubious reputation.

Museo de Artes y Tradiciones Populares

Housed in a seventeenth-century inn, the entertaining **Museo de Artes y Tradiciones Populares**, c/Pasillo Santa Isabel 10 (Mon–Fri 10am–1.30pm & 4–7pm, Sat 10am–1.30pm; 200ptas) uses the former stables and stores on the lower floor as well as the lodging rooms above to mount displays of arts, crafts and furniture from previous eras. These include a collection of *barros malagueños* – typical painted clay figurines – as well as boats, carriages, farming and wine-making implements and rooms furnished in period style.

Mercado Atarazanas

Lying at the heart of an area that bustles with life, the nineteenth-century wrought-iron, Mudéjar-style **Mercado Atarazanas**, just north of the Alameda on c/Atarazanas, incorporates a little-known gem of which the thousands of shoppers who pass beneath it daily, looking for all kinds of produce, are hardly aware. The remarkable **fourteenth-century Moorish arch** on its southern facade was built for Yusuf I of Granada – the ruler also responsible for that other great gateway, the Puerta de la Justicia in the Alhambra – when Málaga was part of the Nasrid kingdom. In those days it formed the entrance to the Moorish arsenal, and the original building's purpose is preserved in the market's present name: Atarazanas in Arabic translates as "the house that guards the arsenal". Note the two coats of arms in the upper corners inscribed in Arabic with the confident proclamation, "There is no Conqueror but Allah. All Praise to Him."

Paseo del Parque

An ideal place for a stroll, especially on summer evenings when the air has cooled, the **Paseo del Parque** is an elegant, palm-shaded avenue laid out at the turn of the century on land reclaimed from the sea as a result of the construction of the Cánovas Harbour. Along its length are a number of architectural delights as well as a **botanical garden** containing hundreds of exotic plants and flowers and many varieties of fig, bamboo, jacaranda and yucca trees. Discreet plaques placed at intervals along the esplanade identify the different species. Among the buildings of note are the Neoclassical **Aduana** (the former Customs house) started in 1788, with an austerely impressive patio, further along, **El Correo**, or the old post office. The Aduana will temporarily house a selection from the Bellas Artes museum until 2001 (see p.77 for further details). Don't miss the

Paseo's star turn a little further on, the exuberant **Ayuntamiento**, a delightful cream and brown Art Nouveau pile, constructed to coincide with the opening of the esplanade. Almost opposite the Correo in the gardens stands the first of Pimentel's twin evocative bronzes which are two of Málaga's best-loved sculptures: **El Jazminero** (the jasmine seller) celebrates the men who once sold their trays of blooms throughout the city. At the Paseo's eastern end you'll come to the **Fuente Genovesa**, or Genoa fountain, now encircled by traffic and difficult to appreciate. An Italian Renaissance work, it was captured during the reign of Carlos V by pirates while being transported to its Spanish buyer; when it was finally retrieved, the king awarded it to the city by royal edict. Finally, just south of here at the entrance to the port, is Pimentel's twin work to the one above, **El Cenachero** (the fish seller) who, with their baskets of fish dangling from a yoke, used to be a common sight on the city's streets.

The English Cemetery

Flanked by carved stone rampant lions, the **English Cemetery**, 150m east of the bull-ring (Mon–Fri 9am–5pm, Sat & Sun 9–11am; free) dates from an era when gunboats flying Union Jacks held the world in awe. This did not, however, disturb the Spanish authorities from their post-*reconquista* custom of denying Christian burial to all "infidels" unlucky enough to die on Iberian turf. British Protestants – who were included in this grouping – suffered the indignity after death of burial upright in the sand below the tide line to their necks. Málaga's expatriate population, which increased during the early nineteenth century, was, understandably, not amused when some of these "shore burials" were washed up on the beach or even seen bobbing on the waves. Thus in 1830 the British consul, William Mark, finally persuaded the authorities to let him found the English Cemetery. In the early days, and to get the place established, it seems that Mark pursued corpses with the zeal of a body-snatcher, hardly waiting for the deceased to expire before carting them off to the new graveyard. Traveller Richard Ford, whose wife's frailty was his original reason for coming to Spain, became alarmed when Mark began to make overtures. "Hearing of my wife's ill health, he tried all in his power to get me to Málaga to have a pretty female specimen in his sepulchral museum," he wrote to a friend.

The cemetery itself, once an isolated site overlooking the sea but now enveloped by urban sprawl, is still nevertheless a leafy and tranquil oasis. Follow the path from the Paseo de Reding up to the modest red stone **church of St George** where, just before it, stands the sepulchre of William Mark. Behind Mark's tomb an obelisk denotes the grave of Robert Boyd, an idealistic young British army officer and friend of Tennyson and Carlyle, who donated his inherited fortune to the revolutionary cause and left for Spain to fight against the tyrannical rule of Fernando VII. After taking part in an uprising at Málaga, led by General Torrijos, which was betrayed to the authorities, he was executed by firing squad. His tombstone records that he died "in the sacred cause of liberty, 11th December 1831, aged 26 years."

Further up the hill you'll see the original **walled cemetery** containing the oldest graves, among them a number studded with seashells (an ancient symbol of immortality), marking the passing of child victims of fever and consumption, the scourge of that age. Alongside the old cemetery's eastern wall the tombstone of Gamel Woolsey, poet and wife of Gerald Brenan, is inscribed with a poignant message from Shakespeare's *Cymbeline*: "Fear no more the heat o' the sun." Many of the other tombstones with their dedications to wives, loyal servants and men of military zeal, most of them in English, make fascinating reading.

The cemetery's plants and flowers have been tended by gardener "Pepe" José Quevedo for over half a century, and you'll no doubt encounter him and his faithful dog as you look around.

Nuestra Señora de la Victoria and Málaga's other churches

Sited on the spot where Fernando and Isabel pitched their tent during the 1487 siege of Málaga, **Nuestra Señora de la Victoria**, at the north end of c/La Victoria, is, after the cathedral, Málaga's most prestigious church, where the city's Virgin patron is venerated. The fifteenth-century building was substantially rebuilt in the seventeenth century by the Count of Buenavista, whose remains, along with those of his descendants, lie in an eerie **crypt** decorated with symbolic stucco skeletons and skulls. Above, the main altar's centrepiece is an image of the Virgin in a *camerín* attributed to Pedro de Mena (see p.77). Legend has it that the *reja*, or altar screen, was wrought from the chains wrested off the liberated Christian slaves after the city was taken from the Moors.

Other churches with interesting features are the **Iglesia de Santiago**, c/Granada, with an original fifteenth-century Mudéjar tower – note the intricate *sebka* brickwork reminiscent of the Giralda in Sevilla – and the **Iglesia de San Juan**, c/San Juan 3, founded in 1487, with the addition of a curious Baroque tower-portal. The heavily restored interior contains a fine seventeenth-century sculpture of *San Juan* by Francisco Ortiz. Finally, to the north of San Juan, the sixteenth-century **Iglesia de los Santos Mártires**, in the street of the same name, underwent a flamboyant Rococo remodelling a century after construction and is the home church of many of the *cofradías* (brotherhoods) who march in the *Semana Santa* processions bearing many of the fine **images of Christ and the Virgin** to be seen in the side chapels.

The Jardín Botánico La Concepción and El Retiro

There are a couple of pleasant trips out of town if you want to escape the centre for a few hours. The remarkable new **botanical gardens** (guided visits, daily except Mon: June–Sept 10am–9pm; Oct–May 10am–5.30pm; last visit 1hr 30min before closing; 435ptas), 3km out of Málaga at La Concepción, are among the finest in Spain. Originally designed in the 1850s by Amalia Loring, granddaughter of the British consul, the gardens were purchased in 1990 by Málaga city council, and converted into the present tropical gardens. Beneath the thirty species of soaring palms, waving pines and lofty eucalyptus, you'll find yellow-flowering acacia, violet-blooming jacaranda and all kinds of exotic blooms trying to steal the show. There are trees of all shapes and continents, such as the Australian banyan with its serpentine aerial roots, giant sequoias, and a variety of bamboos, all to be seen on any one of the five guided itineraries. To get there by car, take the N331 north out of Málaga, turning off at Km 166, and follow signs to the Pantano del Agujero reservoir. You will eventually meet signs for the "Jardín Botánico". Departing from the north side of the Alameda **bus** #2 will drop you at the gates on Saturday, Sunday and public holidays, but on weekdays it will drop you at its terminus, leaving a ten minute walk. A **taxi** ride out here will cost about 750ptas one-way from the centre. It's worth noting that the garden has no restaurant or bar but makes an ideal location for a discreet picnic.

The **El Retiro Jardín Botánico** (daily: April–Sept 9am–8pm; Oct–March 9am–6pm; 1250ptas) lies just west of the airport in Churriana and would make an excellent place to kill time while waiting for a flight home. Founded by an eighteenth century bishop of Málaga the tranquil gardens studded with fountains, lakes and sculptures contain more than 800 species of plants and trees. The gardens also hold Andalucia's largest **aviary** where more than a thousand exotic birds can be viewed in depressingly cramped cages. El Retiro has a **restaurant** and **bar** but is not well served by public transport; to get there with your own vehicle take the N340 out of Málaga towards the airport leaving at the Coín-Churriana exit just beyond the airport turnoff. The garden is signposted on the right a little beyond Churriana village some 4km from the *autovía*. To go by public transport take an Alhaurín de la Torre bound bus from the main bus station which will drop you in Churriana.

Eating

Málaga has a justified reputation for its splendid **fried fish**, served everywhere and acknowledged as among the best in Spain. You'll find many fish restaurants grouped around the Alameda, although for the very best you need to head out to the suburbs of Pedregalejo and El Palo, served by bus #11 from the Paseo del Parque. On the seafront *paseo* at **Pedregalejo**, almost all of the cafés and restaurants serves terrific fish – though you should check the prices on the menu before you enter. Further on, as the *paseo* trails away, you find yourself amid fishing shacks and smaller, sometimes quite ramshackle, cafés. This is **El Palo**, an even better place to eat, with a beach and fishing huts. Málaga's non-seafood restaurants are hardly in the same league, but we've listed some places where the food is well above average for the price.

To stock up on food for trips or **picnics**, your best bet is the *mercado Atarazanas* (see also p.78), and for a sweet treat, the nuns at the Abadia (Abbey) of Santa Clara, c/Cister 11 (between the cathedral and the Alcazaba), sell their *dulces* (see box below) between 9am and 1pm. Specialities are coconut and quince cakes. The *Convento de las Clarisas* does the same at c/Zumaya 1, across the river.

Fish restaurants and marisquerías

Marisquería Alaska, Plaza San Pedro de Alcántara, off c/Carretería. Good and cheap seafood served at tables under the trees in a charming *plazuela*.

Antonio Martín, Paseo Marítimo 16. One of Málaga's most celebrated fish restaurants, a century old and the traditional haunt of *matadores* celebrating their successes in the nearby bullring. Expensive, but probably the best in town. Has a new seaview terrace to sit out on and a *menú* for 4000ptas.

La Traya, c/Circo 1, just above Plaza de la Victoria at the end of c/Victoria. Good neighbourhood fish bar that's inexpensive and very popular. Ask for directions from Plaza Victoria as it's not easy to find. Closed Thurs.

Aceite y Pan, c/Cervantes 5. Facing the eastern wall of the Plaza de Toros, this place serves up a wide variety of seafood. When you've chosen your fish from the chilled display you can eat inside or, more atmospherically, at tables on the pavement. Closed Mon.

Bar El Puerto, c/Comisario. Another good *marisquería* a mere shrimp shell's throw away from the *Casa Vicente* (see p.82).

Refectorium, c/Cervantes 8, close to *Aceite y Pan* (see above). Stylish, medium-priced, mainly fish restaurant where the *fritura malagueña*, *urta* (sea bream) and *pez espada* (swordfish) are mouthwateringly tasty. A small bar also serves outstanding *tapas*.

CONVENT DULCES

Many convents throughout Andalucía and Spain are in the business of supporting their orders by making "**convent dulces**": cakes and pastries which they can sell to the community. Many recipes date back to the Arabs, who used rich combinations of eggs, almonds, sugar and honey to concoct their Moorish goodies. Each convent guards its recipes jealously, and many are so good that they supply local restaurants. The **sherry manufacturers** also had an influence on the development of *convent dulces*, for they traditionally used egg whites to clarify their wines and donated the leftover yolks to the nuns. This is the origin of many egg yolk-based creations such as *tocino de cielo* (Andalucía's richest flan) and *yemas* (sweet cakes), two of the region's most popular pastries.

In most convents you pay your money and are served with the sweets of your choice through a *torno* – a kind of revolving dumb waiter – which means you never see the nun who serves you.

Mesón El Rincón, junction of c/Mármoles and c/Armengual de la Mota. Neighbourhood restaurant well worth seeking out across Río Guadalmedina in the old *gitano* quarter of El Perchel. A real *malagueño* fish place, it may seem like two establishments, but one is a bar with outdoor tables (for *tapas* and *raciones*) while the other (under the same ownership) is a great restaurant. Take care in this area at night as it's slightly off the tourist beat.

El Tintero II, El Palo. Right at the far end of the seafront, just before the *Club Náutico* (stay on bus #11 and ask for "Tintero Dos"), this is a huge beach restaurant where the waiters charge round with plates of fish (all costing the same for a plate) and you shout for, or grab, anything you like. It's not *haute cuisine*, but among the more worthy choices are *mero* (grouper), *rosada* (rockfish), along with Andalucían regulars such as *boquerones* (fresh anchovies), *gambas* (shrimp), *calamares*, *jibia* (squid) and *chopos* and *sepia* (both cuttlefish).

Casa Vicente, c/Comisario. Lively *marisquería* in a narrow alley on the northern side of the Alameda.

Non-fish restaurants

Al-Yamal, c/Blasco de Garay 3. Good Arab restaurant serving up pricey, but authentic meat in spicy sauces, *couscous* and other typical dishes.

Antonio, Fernando Lesseps 7. Popular small restaurant serving well prepared *malagueño* dishes with an outdoor terrace in an atmospheric cul-de-sac off the north end of c/Nueva; *menú* for around 1500ptas.

Restaurante Arcos, Alameda 31. Efficient central place behind a garish neon exterior on the south side of the Alameda, towards the Tetuán bridge. Recommended for its all-day *platos combinados* and late-night meals – for breakfast they serve *pan tostada* with wholemeal bread, *pan integral*.

La Borrata, c/Alcazabilla, just north of the Roman Theatre. Good dining place serving up the cheapest *menú* in town for a remarkable 800ptas (including wine).

Cafe de Paris, c/Vélez Málaga 8. Close to the Plaza de Toros, this is one of Málaga's top restaurants for sampling *la cocina malagueña* at its very best. Dining *à la carte* doesn't come cheap but there's a *menú de degustación* for about 3500ptas. Has no terrace so perhaps is a better low season option.

Cañadu, Plaza de la Merced 21. A rare vegetarian option serving a good selection of salad and pasta-based dishes accompanied by organic wines and beers. Operates as a teahouse outside dining periods with a wide range of herbal teas.

La Cancela, c/Denis Belgrano 3, off c/Granada. A *malagueño* institution with an economical *menú* and outdoor tables in a pleasant pedestrian street – *ajo blanco* (cold soup with garlic, grapes and almonds) is a must. Next door there's *Gambrinus*, a good stand-up *tapas* bar.

El Compá, c/Compás de la Victoria 24. Pleasant small *mesón* fronting the church of Nuestra Señora de la Victoria, which offers a good value *menú* for under 1000ptas.

Cyber@lameda, Avda. Andalucía 13. This internet bar (see "Listings") does a great value *menú* for just 800ptas (including wine).

Mesón Danes, c/Barroso 5. Just up the street from the *Al-Yamal*, this long-established Danish restaurant does an interesting combination of Spanish and Scandinavian dishes, served on traditional Nordic red tablecloths.

Mesón de Jamón, Plaza María Guerrero 5. Good-value *menú* and a tasty selection of *jamón* and cheese *tapas*.

Parador de Málaga–Gibralfaro, Monte de Gibralfaro (☎95 222 19 02). Superior terrace dining with spectacular views over the coast and town. Specializing in malagueño fish and meat dishes. Definitely worth a splurge, or try the *menú* (around 3500ptas) for excellent value. If you can't face the climb, bus #35 heading east along the Paseo del Parque will take you there. Book ahead if you want a front line view. (See also p.76 for accommodation.)

La Gran Corona, c/Reding 8. This is a new restaurant, with a terrace, which serves *malagueño* standards and offers a good-value 1000ptas *menú*.

Bar Los Pueblos, c/Atarazanas, opposite the *mercado*. Simple and economical workers' place, serving satisfying food all day – bean soups and *estofados* are their speciality; *gazpacho* is served in half-pint glasses.

Bar San Agustín, c/San Agustín 11. A central place for *tapas* and *raciones*, near the cathedral, and especially good for lunch.

Drinking

Málaga has a variety of places to **drink**, from bustling breakfast cafés for *churros* and morning coffee to atmospheric bars where you can while away an evening. The best of the breakfast places are clustered around the Atarazanas market, where the daily bustle starts at dawn. **Bars** for more serious drinking – usually with *tapas* thrown in – are concentrated north of the Alameda and around the cathedral. A number of traditional bars serve the sweet **Málaga wine**, made from muscatel grapes and dispensed from huge barrels; other options include the new, incredibly sweet wine, *Pedriot*, and the much more palatable *Seco Añejo*, which has matured for a year.

Cafés

Casa Aranda, c/Herrería del Rey just east of the market. One of the best of the market cafés, renowned for its excellent *churros*, served at outside tables. There are actually two bars here, one each side of the alley, but owned by the same family and operating as one.

Bar Central, east side of Plaza de la Constitución. Cavernous old institution in the centre of town, one of the city's favourite meeting places for generations. Serves *tapas* and also has an enticing *pastelería* counter.

El Jardín, c/Canon s/n, directly behind the cathedral. Nice place for breakfast *café* and *pasteles*, with a fountain, garden and cathedral view fronting outdoor tables. Also does *platos combinados* later in the day.

Mayra, Plaza de la Malagueta opposite the Antonio Martín restaurant (see p.81). Diminutive ice-cream bar with a difference, serving them *sin azucar* (without sugar).

Casa Mira, c/Larios, 5. This is the place where *malagueños* flock on summer nights for the best *helados* (ices) in town.

Nuestra Señora de la Victoria Hospital Cafetería, Plaza Santuario, adjoining the church of the same name. This café is one of Málaga's best kept secrets and where – for the price of a coffee – you can enjoy a table on a delightful seventeenth-century patio complete with fountain.

Bar la Nueva Cubana, Puerta del Mar 3, a block east of the market. Stylish place with outdoor tables for breakfast coffee and fresh *cruasanes* (croissants) or tea and tempting *pasteles* later in the day. There's another branch at c/Caldería 6, off c/Granada.

Tetería Alcazaba, c/San Agustín 21. Cosy Moroccan tearoom almost opposite the Museo Picasso serving a wide range of herbal and oriental teas. The nearby *La Tetería* at number 9 is similar and also good.

Bars

Antigua Casa Guardia, corner of c/Pastora, on the Alameda. Great old nineteenth-century spit-and-sawdust bar. Picasso was a devotee of their wines, and a photo on the wall shows him toting one of the bar's *jarras*. Try the house mussels with Málaga wine.

Cafetería Axarquía, Alameda Principal 36. Stylish *tapas* bar near the Guadalmedina bridge with a wide *tapas* selection and good *fino*. Also does breakfast *chocolate y churros*.

La Dehesa, Alameda Principal 11. Good little *tapas* bar at the eastern end of the Alameda tucked behind a shop which sells *quesos* and *jamones* (cheeses and hams).

Mesón Las Garrafas, c/Mendez Núñez 5, off Plaza de Uncibay. Fine old bar with tiled walls, wooden beams, stacked barrels and good *fino*.

Mesón Juan y Mariano, c/Granados s/n, off Plaza de Uncibay. Another excellent *tapas* stop with a tiny restaurant. Try their *ensaladilla malagueño* with potatoes, oranges and cod.

Bar Lo Güeno, c/Marín García 9, off c/Larios. Smartish haunt with a wide range of *tapas*; try their *pincho* (spicy shrimp) or *habas* (broad beans with black sausage).

La Manchega, c/Marín García 4. Another fine old drinking den; *jibias guisadas* (stewed cuttlefish) is a speciality.

Bar Orellana, Moreno Monroy, 5. Down a small side street off the east side of c/Marques de Larios close to Plaza Constitución, this is one of Málaga's very best and friendliest *tapas* bars. House specials include a mouthwatering *palometa* (Ray's Bream).

Rincón de Oliva, c/Don Cristián 1. Typical neighbourhood *tapas* bar round the back of El Corte Inglés with tasty *jamón serrano*.

Rincón de Mata, c/Esparteros 8. One of Málaga's oldest *tapas* bars, located in a tiny alley to the west of c/Larios, and decorated with wine bottles. The recommended *tapas* here are *ensalada tropical* and *calamares rellenos* (stuffed squid).

Sibarita, c/Cervantes 12, near the Plaza de Toros. Excellent and atmospheric neighbourhood *tapas* bar with outdoor tables. The adjacent *El Cantillo* is also good.

Siete de Julio, Avda. Canovas del Castillo 12, near the Plaza de Toros. Great Basque-run *tapas* bar, with restaurant upstairs, taking its name from the start-date of the great festival of San Fermín in Pamplona – celebrated with a vengeance here.

Bar la Tosca, c/Marín García 12. Popular, city-centre bar with a wide *tapas* selection and excellent *jamón serrano*.

Nightlife

You'll find most of Málaga's nightlife northeast of the cathedral along and around **calles Granada** and **Beatas** as well as the streets circling **Plaza Uncibay** and in **Malagueta**, south of the bullring. At weekends and holidays dozens of youth-oriented disco-bars fill the crowded streets in these areas with a cacophony of sound, and over the summer – though it's dead out of season – the scene spreads out along the seafront to the suburb of **Pedregalejo**. Here the streets just behind the beach host most of the action, and dozens of discos and smaller music bars lie along and off the main street, Juan Sebastián Elcano. Málaga's daily paper, *El Sur*, is good for local entertainment listings and there's a weekly English edition.

Flamenco

Genuine **flamenco** is, as always, hard to come by and the few shows there are in Málaga aren't up to much. Many of the *peñas* where it is performed are private, but you could try the places below for something approaching the real thing.

Doña Pepa c/Vélez-Málaga 6, two blocks south of the Plaza de Toros. This *bar-restaurante* has a flamenco show at weekends in its main room. Turn up after 10pm.

La Lecheria, Paseo de Sancha 25, east of the bullring, with live flamenco on Wed evenings.

Peña Flamenca Juan Breva, c/Picador 2, off c/Beatas (☎95 221 08 76). Authentic flamenco *peña* (club) which has frequent performances and welcomes visitors with a genuine interest. Phone first.

Nightclubs and music bars

Anden, Plaza de Uncibay. Disco-bar with a wild crowd that's open till very late.

Anubis, c/Juan Sebastián Elcano s/n, Pedregalejo. Big, brash, overdecorated disco with clientele to match.

Barsovia, c/Belgrano 3. Low-key music bar open till late.

Bolivia, c/Bolivia s/n. Cocktails and music for the style brigade.

La Botellita, adjacent to *Luna Rubia*, Pasaje Mitjana, slightly west of Plaza Uncibay. A change of scene, with Spanish music and a wide range of drinks at non-club prices, open till late.

Café Teatro, c/Afligidos 5, near the cathedral. Stylish bar at the bottom of a cul-de-sac with unobtrusive live music most nights.

La Chancla, the beach, Pedregalejo. One of a recent rash of bars on the beach; bursts forth at midnight and continues until 3am or later.

Cervecería Brow Beer, c/Ángel 3 off c/Granada. Bar specialising in a wide variety of world beers. Serious drinkers at midday, youthful revellers at night. Also serves *tapas*.

El Pimpi, c/Granada 62. Cavernous night spot with flashing TV screens and wide selection of sounds.

Ragtime, c/Reding 12, Malagueta. Specializing in jazz, blues and rock, often with live performers.

Luna Rubia, Pasaje Mitjana 4, slightly west of Plaza Uncibay. Wide range of international sounds in a place that's open till dawn.

Siempre Asi, c/Convalecientes 5, north of Plaza Uncibay. Another late bar opening 11pm–3.30am playing Spanish rock and techno.

Salsa, at the top of c/Denis Belgrano, off c/Granada. Salsa and karaoke at weekends, samba and mambo on weekday nights. Next door to the *Barsovia*. It also gives dance tuition.

Listings

Banks Numerous places with ATMs/cash machines along c/Larios and on the Plaza de la Constitución. El Corte Inglés (see below) will also change currency free of charge.

Books and music El Corte Inglés department store (Avda. Andalucía 4) stocks most foreign newspapers and periodicals. Librerías Prometeo y Proteo (c/Puerta Buenaventura 3, at the eastern end of c/Carretería), is the city's biggest and best bookshop with an excellent selection of flamenco and folk on CD, and English-speaking staff. Candilejas (c/Sta. Lucía 9, north of Plaza Constitución) is another good outlet which also has cassettes. Librería de Ocasión, c/Salinas 7, has a selection of English second-hand books as do Librería Malagueña, c/Mártires 5; Biblos, c/Dos Aceros 11; and Librería Prometeo, c/Carretería 101.

Car, scooter and motorbike rental Reliable and inexpensive deals are available from Turarche, c/Roger de Flor 1, at the side of the bus station (☎95 231 80 69, fax 95 231 63 42; *www.turarche.es*). The same company also rents out a variety of outboard dinghies, boats and trailer-tents.

Consulates Britain, c/Duquesa Parcent 8 (☎ 95 221 75 71); USA, Centro las Rampas 1, Fuengirola (☎95 247 48 91); Ireland, Avda. Los Boliches s/n, Fuengirola (☎95 247 51 08); Netherlands, Alameda de Colon 3 (☎95 270 07 20).

Ferries Daily sailings (except Sunday) to the Spanish enclave of Melilla in Morocco, generally leaving around 1pm; the crossing takes 7hr. Tickets from Transmediterranea, Estación Maritima (☎95 222 43 91), south of Plaza de la Marina.

Football The city threw a three-day fiesta when C.F. Málaga won the second division title in June 1999, launching themselves back into the top flight after a decade away. Games are at La Rosaleda stadium, Paseo de Martiricos s/n, at the northern end of the Río Guadalmedina (☎95 261 42 10). Tickets can be purchased from the stadium.

Hospital Cruz Roja, Avda. José Silvela 64 (☎95 225 04 50).

Internet Málaga's two internet cafés are close to each other on the south side of Avda. Andalucía, near El Corte Inglés. *Cyber@lameda* (☎ & fax 95 234 45 58) at no. 13 charges 800ptas per hour (minimum of 1hr) and has a good bar (see "Eating") whilst *Ciber Málaga Café* (☎95 204 03 03) at no. 11 will let you check your email for 250ptas for 15min.

Left luggage There are lockers at the train station (daily 7am–10.45pm), and also at the bus station (daily 6.30am–11pm).

Outdoor pursuits Equipment and advice available from two excellent shops in c/Carretería (north of Plaza de la Constitucíon): El Campista (no. 71; ☎95 222 93 23) and La Trucha (no. 100; ☎95 221 22 03), who also sell top brand Spanish walking and climbing boots at bargain prices and provide information on a variety of courses for rock climbing, hang-gliding, canoeing, caving etc. Colonel Tapioca, c/Antonio Baena Gómez 3, off c/Larios, sells a similar range. IGN walking maps, as well as 1:50,000 Mapas Cartografía Militar (military maps), are sold by Atlante Mapas, c/Alamos 5, off Plaza de la Merced (☎95 260 27 65). The boss, Joaquín Almagro, will also make you good photocopies from the unpublished *Junta de Andalucía* master map at 1:25,000 or 1:10,000 – the only map that accurately marks walking routes and rights of way.

Police The Policía Local are at Avda. La Rosaleda 19 (☎95 260 00 92); in emergencies dial ☎092 (local police) or ☎091(national).

Post office Avda. de Andalucía 1, on the left across the bridge at the end of the Alameda (Mon–Fri 8.30am–8.30pm, Sat 9.30am–2pm).

Telephones Locutorio at c/Molina Larios 11, near the cathedral (Mon–Sat 9am–9pm; Sun 10am–1pm). However, most international calls are more easily made from cardphone street kiosks. Cards can be purchased from any *estanco* (state tobacco outlet).

El Chorro Gorge and around

Inland, some 50km north of Málaga, the **Garganta del Chorro** (El Chorro Gorge) is an amazing place. Located to the south of the Embalse del Guadalhorce it's impressive in itself – an immense cleft cut through a vast limestone massif by the Río Guadalhorce – with daunting walls of rock as high as 400m along its 3km length. But the real attraction is a **concrete catwalk**, *El Camino del Rey*, which threads the length of the gorge hanging precipitously halfway up its side. Built in the 1920s as part of a burgeoning hydroelectric scheme and opened by King Alfonso XIII who walked its whole length and gave it its name, it used to figure in all the guidebooks as one of the wonders of Spain; today it's largely fallen into disrepair, though a deal has recently been struck between the Madrid central government and Málaga provincial government to fund renovation works due to start in 2000. At present, despite a few wobbly – and decidedly dangerous – sections (one tourist fell to her death in 1998), with random holes in the concrete through which you can see the gorge hundreds of feet below, it's still possible to walk much of its length. You will, however, need a head for heights (see box opposite), and at least a full day starting from Málaga. If you've neither, it's possible to get a glimpse of both gorge and *camino* from any of the trains going north from Málaga – the line, slipping in and out of tunnels, follows the river for quite a distance along the gorge, before plunging into a last long tunnel just before its head.

If you want to explore the gorge, head for **EL CHORRO**, served by two daily direct trains from Málaga (for eight persons or more any northbound train will make a special stop which you arrange by calling RENFE on ☎95 212 80 52); there are no bus services. The village is rapidly becoming a centre of outdoor activities for the gorge, particularly rock climbing, and if you want to **stay** there are a number of options. The village has an excellent shady **campsite** (☎95 211 26 96) with pool, reached by heading downhill to your right for 400m after getting off the train. *Bar-Restaurante Garganta del Chorro* (☎95 249 72 19; ④), at the southern end of the station platform, offers spacious and reasonably priced apartments inside a converted mill, has a pool and serves **food** in its restaurant. At the other end of the station platform there's a grocery shop and a couple of bars, including *Bar Isabel*, which also has a couple of basic rooms (☎95 249 50 04; ③). For a more tranquil option though, follow the signs from the station along a track for 2km to the *Finca La Campana* (☎ & fax 95 211 20 19; *www.malaganet.com/lacampana*), a farmhouse set in rural surroundings, run by friendly Swiss climber Jean Hofer and his wife Christine, who can put you up in an economical bunkhouse (①), or en-suite cottages with kitchen and two or four beds (③). The farm has a small shop where you can hire out climbing equipment and mountain bikes, and Jean offers climbing and caving courses as well as guided tours along the *Camino del Rey*. He'll also pick you up from the station at Álora which has ten daily trains from Málaga.

WALKING EL CHORRO GORGE

Walking the **Camino del Rey** catwalk is a risky proposition whichever way you decide to do it and should not be attempted by anyone of a nervous disposition or without a very good head for heights. Due to the obvious dangers involved, the safest way to do the Camino is on an **organized trip** with expert climber Jean Hofer at *La Campana* (see opposite) who uses ropes to ensure maximum safety.

The majority of **independent hikers** walk through the rail tunnel from El Chorro train station – which is not recommended. It's far safer to leave the station and follow the road along the east side of the reservoir for 800m passing the campsite to your right. You will pass two railway viaducts (the first made of stone, the second of steel); after the second viaduct (above a hydro electric plant) you can walk up a track into railway tunnel 9 (which has three separate sections) – keep to the right hand (wider) side of the tunnel to avoid passing trains and **do not walk along the line**. Go through tunnels 8 and 7 beyond which, to the left, you will see a narrow concrete footbridge across the gaping gorge – without handrails or parapets – leading to the *Camino*. If you lose track of which tunnel you are in always make sure that you can see light at the far end – if not, you have gone too far and should turn back. Once on the *Camino*, the catwalk can then be followed for about 1.5km – the handrail is missing in parts and there are holes in the floor – to a track leading down to the *Mirador* restaurant (see below), from where you can walk back by road to El Chorro.

A slightly safer way to experience the *Camino* on your own is to follow the road from the train station, signposted *Pantano de Guadalhorce*, reached by crossing over the dam and turning right, then following the road north along the lake towards the hydroelectric plant. After 8km turn right at a junction to reach – after 2km – the bar-restaurant *El Mirador*, poised above a road tunnel and overlooking the various lakes and reservoirs of the Guadalhorce scheme. From the bar (where you should leave any transport) a dirt track on the right covers the 2km to an abandoned power plant at the mouth of the gorge. The footpath to the left of this will take you into the chasm and to the beginning of *El Camino*. Although it is marked "No Entry" you'll probably come upon a number of young Spaniards exploring the catwalk. The first section, at least, seems reasonably safe – despite places where it is only a metre wide and where parts of the handrail are missing – and this is in fact the most dramatic part of the canyon. Towards the end, where the passageway gets really dangerous, the gorge widens and it's possible to climb down and follow the riverbank or have a swim. You can then walk back to the *Mirador*.

From the station it's about 12km to some nice lakes and reservoirs for swimming, such as the **Embalse del Guadalhorce**. Recent years of prolonged drought have dramatically lowered the water levels, making this area a great deal less attractive than in the past, but the lakes are often swimmable. You can camp along the rocky shores; alternatively, the tiny village of **Ardales** (see p.89), 4km beyond the lake, has shops, bars, a lone *hostal* on the main square and two daily buses to and from Ronda. The walk is beautiful, and hitching is also feasible with quite a few cars passing along here in summer.

Bobastro

A few kilometres beyond El Chorro, amid some of the wildest scenery in the whole peninsula, lies **BOBASTRO**, the mountain-top remains of a Mozarabic (Arabized Christian) fortified settlement. Famous as the isolated eyrie of colourful ninth-century rebel Ibn Hafsun (see box overleaf), the castle was said to be the most impregnable in all Andalucía, but only a ruined church, carved into an enormous boulder, remains of the once-great fortress.

Situated outside the original fortified area, and below some cave dwellings of uncertain date, the **church** is typically Mozarabic in style, its nave and two aisles separated

IBN HAFSUN

Born near Ronda around 860 **Ibn Hafsun** was a *muwallad* (that is, of mixed Christian-Arab parentage) who, after killing a man, fell out with the Umayyad caliphate at Córdoba and resorted to a life of brigandage. Gathering around him a formidable army, he built his stronghold at Bobastro, and during the years 880–917 scored a number of spectacular victories over the many Umayyad forces sent to defeat him. At the height of his power Hafsun controlled an area between the straits of Gibraltar in the west and Jaén in the east. His defence of the poor against excessive Umayyad taxation and forced labour further served to increase the popularity of this Robin Hood-style figure, especially among his fellow *muwalladin* who believed they were getting a raw deal from their pure-blooded Arab rulers. After he converted to Christianity in 899, the church at Bobastro was constructed to receive his remains, which were duly interred there upon his death in 917. When Abd ar-Rahman III finally conquered Bobastro in 927 he exhumed the body of Hafsun and hung it on a gibbet outside the Alcázar in Córdoba as a "salutory warning to imitators and a pleasant spectacle to believers (true Muslims)".

by horseshoe-arched arcades. The transept, and a deep apse chapel flanked by two side chapels, can clearly be seen making the edifice one of the few identifiable traces of building from the period.

Nearby and to the west is the **Cueva de Doña Trinidad** with Paleolithic cave paintings; to see them you'll need to get a key from the *Ayuntamiento* at Ardales (see p.89). You can **get to Bobastro** from El Chorro by crossing the dam from the train station and turning right along the road to *El Mirador* (see box on "Walking El Chorro Gorge"). After a couple of kilometres a signed turn-off for the *Mesas de Villaverde* restaurant (on the left and easy to miss) indicates a twisting 2km route to another sign (marked "Iglesia Mozárabe") pointing to a slope with steps on the left. Leave any transport here and follow the path for 400m through the pine woods to the site. Back on the main road and continuing west to just beyond the *El Mirador* restaurant will allow you to view the impressive **dam** at the junction of the two great reservoirs, with the marble table and throne where Alfonso XIII signed the completion of the work on May 21, 1921.

Álora

Located by the road to Antequera, 12km south of El Chorro, and seen from afar **ÁLORA** is a sparkling cluster of white-walled dwellings nestling between three rocky spurs topped by the ruins of a Moorish *alcazaba*. On closer acquaintance it's a rather dusty market town with a traffic problem and many narrow, cobbled streets that are tricky to negotiate – which you'll need to do to get a look at the eighteenth-century church of **La Encarnación** on the main square or to climb up to the impressive **castle**, now the town graveyard. Monday is market day, when the village becomes a lively mass of stallholders and shoppers. **Places to stay** include the elegant *Hostal Durán*, c/La Parra 9 (☎95 249 66 42; ③), with ensuite rooms. Álora also has a municipal **swimming pool** on the road towards El Chorro, which you may be glad of if the drought-stricken waters of the nearby lakes are too low for bathing.

On to Carratraca

Some 2km out of Álora, heading towards Ardales, the scenic MA441 passes the eighteenth-century Baroque **Convento de las Flores**, raised over the site of an earlier *ermita* left behind by Ferdinand and Isabel in thanksgiving after the town fell to Christian forces in 1484. The small convent **church** is a delight, with restrained frescoes and *retablo*. The road corkscrews onwards through the hills and some excellent **hiking country** to reach **CARRATRACA**, 5km southeast of Ardales. The town is famous for its **sulphur spa**, which has recently re-opened after a long closure and in summer the village fills up with visitors taking the waters, which you may wish to do yourself.

Although the baths date back to the days of the Greeks and Romans, it wasn't until the nineteenth century that Carratraca became one of the foremost spas in Europe, and a gathering point for the continent's aristocracy. During its heyday the *balneario* attracted kings, princesses and literary bigwigs such as Lord Byron, Alexandre Dumas and Rainer Maria Rilke. The three casinos, where these socialites used to while away their time between plunges in the stinking, sulphurous waters which gush from the rocks, are long gone. However, vestiges of the past can be seen throughout; the bath used by Empress Eugénie of France (wife of Napoleon III) is preserved "in perpetuity", the bathrooms are marked with their original signs, and you can visit an "injections room" containing a frightening collection of antique instruments used for propelling the waters into various bodily orifices. A visit to the baths (June–Sept daily 8am–1pm & 5–7pm) is an adventure in itself – the hot baths (1000ptas) are reputedly more beneficial than the cold plunge (500ptas), although the latter are taken in wonderful eighteenth-century, open-air pools surrounded by classical Tuscan columns.

Carratraca's other sights include a Regency-style **Ayuntamiento**, whose tower is now a **Turismo** (Mon–Fri 9.30am–1pm; ☎95 245 80 16) on the edge of the village, formerly the residence of Doña Trinidad Grund, a local benefactor who donated funds for the excavation of the cave near Bobastro which bears her name. She also provided funds for the curious **bullring** nearby, hacked out of solid rock and the scene of the village passion play during *Semana Santa*.

PRACTICALITIES

Carratraca has one of the most exotic **hostales** in Andalucía: a royal palace built by the tyrannical King Fernando VII early in the last century to accommodate himself and his retinue while visiting the spa (although he probably never used it). The *Hostal El Príncipe*, c/Antonio Rioboó 9 (☎95 245 80 20, fax 95 245 81 01), is a wonderful old place, with an imposing portal and facade oozing faded grandeur. Currently undergoing renovation it is scheduled to reopen in the year 2000, probably with rates well above its former budget category. From the *hostal* there's easy access to the *balneario* behind. Just along from the baths, *Casa Pepa* (☎95 245 80 49; ②) also offers simple rooms and meals. Other places **to eat and drink** include *Venta El Trillo*, on the main road as you enter from Álora with *Bar Venta Martillo* and *Venta El Punto* nearby, all of which serve decent *menús*. *Terraza La Cueva*, downhill from the *Hostal El Príncipe*, is a pleasant bar which is built into a cave and surrounded by gardens and fountains.

Ardales

At the southern point of the third of the lakes that comprise the Guadalteba–Guadalhorce reservoir, **ARDALES** tumbles down the hill below La Peña, a rocky outcrop topped by remains of the Iberian settlement of Turóbriga as well as a Roman fort and ruined Moorish alcázar. On the way up to the summit, look out for the fifteenth-century Mudéjar **Iglesia de la Virgen de los Remedios** with its distinctive, partly tiled, tower. When you reach the top, it becomes clear that the tower was the minaret of the former mosque. The interior also has Moorish arches dividing the nave and side aisles, the right of which has the mosque's original *mihrab* oriented towards Mecca. To see the church, call at the house of sprightly octogenarian Sra. Asunción Martín, Plaza de la Iglesia 1, opposite, who will effortlessly sprint up the church steps to let you in. A new **Museo Municipal** facing the bridge as you enter the village (Tues–Sun 10.30am–2pm & 5–8pm; 200ptas) has Roman and Moorish archeological finds, sections dealing with local traditions and history as well as copies of the rock paintings in the nearby paleolithic Cueva de Doña Trinidad; the curator can also provide information on visits to see them.

Activity in Ardales revolves around a wide and animated central plaza, where you'll find the *Ayuntamiento* (which can also advise on visits to the Cueva de Doña Trinidad), as well as comfortable simple **rooms** at the friendly *Hostal Bobastro*, La Plaza 13 (☎95 245 80 81; ③). While there's a lively **bar** scene for *tapas* and *raciones* on the main plaza – *Bar El Mellizo* is the meeting place for the village's characters but *Bar El Casino* has the best *tapas* – to **eat** more substantially you'll have to cross the bridge at the bottom of the village to the *Hostal-Restaurante El Cruce*, which serves a good-value *menú* and has some en-suite rooms (☎95 245 90 12; ③). *Casa Marcos*, just along the tree-lined main street at c/San Isidro 31, is renowned for its tasty *roscos de almendras* (almond cakes). There's even a bit of a **nightlife** scene here and *Terraza & Copas* at the end of the main street is an atmospheric music bar with a pleasant terrace and live rock and rumba at weekends.

Six kilometres east of Ardales along the MA444 lies the village's scenic lakeside **campsite** (actually next to a reservoir), *Camping Parque Ardales* (☎ & fax 95 211 24 01) which has a small **museum** (daily 11am–2pm & 5–7pm; 200ptas) devoted to local flora and fauna. There's no bus to the campsite but a taxi from Ardales will cost about 1000ptas.

El Burgo

A partly paved road leaves Ardales for the tiny settlement of **EL BURGO**, 20km southwest. It's a beautifully scenic drive – and a fine three- to four-hour **walk** – through the rugged valley of the Río Turón which gurgles beneath the heights of the Sierra de Ortegicar. There's plenty of birdlife, and, halfway along the route, a deserted village with a ruined mill to explore. Until relatively recently, this was bandit country, where travellers needed to be constantly on their guard against robbers and kidnappers. One particularly ruthless *bandolero* named Pasos Largos (Big Steps) worked this stretch in the 1930s and ended his days in a shoot-out with the Guardia Civil – his memory is still fresh around El Burgo where he was born. El Burgo, when you finally reach it, is a pleasant enough place with another ruined Moorish fort, and makes a good stopover.

The best **place to stay** is *Posada del Canónigo*, c/Mesones 24 (☎95 216 01 85; ④), in a beautifully restored mansion, with friendly owners who can provide you with maps, and organize walks and horse riding in the surrounding hill country (and little-known Natural Park) of the Sierra de las Nieves. Budget rooms are available at a simple *fonda*, the *Berrocal*, c/Heredia 5 (☎95 287 29 45; ②). Places to **eat** and **drink** include the central *Bar El Porra* and *Restaurante Sierra de las Nieves* which also has rooms (☎95 216 00 17; ③) as well the *Venta Yoni*, slightly out of the village on the Yunquera road.

You can also get rooms at **YUNQUERA**, 7km to the south, where there's another good *hostal*: the *Asencio*, c/Mesones 1 (☎95 248 27 16; ③). A small **Turismo** on c/Pozo 17 (June–Sept daily 10am–1.30pm; ☎95 248 25 01) has an informative leaflet in Spanish on the sights around the village and walking in the Parque Natural. The village is noted for its local *mosto* wine (very tasty unfermented grape juice), which is best sampled at the delightfully rustic *Bar Antonio Lopez*, c/Antonio 26.

The paved A366 from El Burgo meanders through the valley of the Río Turón and more ruggedly picturesque and uninhabited terrain, eventually climbing to the Puerto del Viento at 1190m. The descent from here crosses valley plains shared by wheatfields and grazing cattle overlooked by brooding, rocky heights until, after 20km, it reaches the suburbs of Ronda (see p.142) passing on the way a well-preserved stretch of **Roman aqueduct**.

Teba

About 15km north of Ardales, the village of **TEBA** spreads itself below a hill crowned by a striking ruined **Moorish castle** built on Roman foundations. There's a well-preserved dungeon in the castle, but you'll need a torch to find your way around. The castle battlements give wonderful **views** over the surrounding countryside; you can also glimpse the tempting municipal **swimming pool**, close by.

On the plain below the castle, a battle against the Moors took place in 1331 when the forces of Alfonso XI recovered Teba for Christian Spain. In this battle fought Sir James Douglas, who had been commissioned by a dying **Robert Bruce** to carry the Scottish king's heart to the Holy Land "to be carried in battle against the enemies of Christ". Douglas took the long way round, via Spain, and ended up getting involved at the siege of Teba. He wore the royal heart in a silver case around his neck and – at a critical moment in the battle – to spur on his men he threw it into the fray and charged after it to his death. The well-travelled heart was then recovered and taken back to Scotland to be buried in Melrose Abbey, where it was rediscovered in 1996. Near the centre of the village, in the Plaza de España, a block of Scottish granite has been set up to mark Teba's illustrious connection with Robert Bruce and the exploits of Douglas; it was unveiled by one of Douglas's descendants in 1989.

Teba's other main sight is **Santa Cruz Real**, an eighteenth-century Baroque church at the western end of c/San Francisco, which quite a few surprises. The enormous triple naved interior is divided by lofty Tuscan columns of red marble. Among the church's many treasures, there's a sixteenth-century **gold plated cross** near the main altar which was given to the castle's church by Ferdinand and Isabel and is one of only two in the whole of Spain. When the castle was destroyed, the church's valuables were moved here. The **tesoro** (the church's treasure and valuables) contains some beautiful early sixteenth-century vestments embroidered in gold thread also donated (and probably partly made) by Isabel, who was an accomplished seamstress. To see the church, call (preferably between 5–6pm) at the adjoining house of the *cura* who will open it up.

You'll find **places to stay** on and around the main thoroughfare c/San Francisco where, at no. 26, the *Hostal Sevillano* (☎95 274 80 11; ③) has clean rooms above a **restaurant** with a good-value *menú*. The same street and the nearby Plaza de Andalucía have more places for eating and drinking.

About 3km to the east of the village lies the small but picturesque Garganta de Teba or **Teba Gorge**, where the oleander-fringed Río la Venta cuts through the limestone hills to join the reservoir. A haven for all kinds of butterflies, there's also plenty of birdlife along the river banks and the gorge is a nesting site for the Egyptian vulture and Bonelli's eagle, along with plenty of other varieties such as black kites and choughs. To reach the gorge, descend the track which leaves the roadside by the bridge over the Río la Venta on the edge of the reservoir.

Antequera

Sitting on two low hills in the valley of the Río Guadalhorce, **ANTEQUERA** is an attractive market town with some important ancient monuments and a clutch of fine churches. On the main train line to Granada and at the junction of roads heading inland to Córdoba, Granada and Sevilla, it's easy to get to, and makes a good **day trip from Málaga**, which lies 40km to the south. Travelling from Málaga, the bus takes you along the fastest (but least interesting) route, the recently constructed N331 which follows the Guadalmedina river valley. If you're hitching or driving, however, it's far nicer to take the older, more picturesque road that meanders through **Almogía**, a small hill town with tortuously narrow streets. It's a sleepy place, except on Friday –

market day – when the whole place spills over with shoppers. From here the road climbs on through hills of baked red earth dotted with wild olives to **Villanueva de la Concepcíon**. Nearing Antequera you pass a turning to **Parque Natural El Torcal** (see p.96), which is quickly followed by a spectacular view over the sea plain to the south.

Arrival, information and accommodation

Antequera's RENFE station c/Divina Pastora 8 (☎95 287 16 73), is rather out of the way, a one-kilometre walk to the centre of town (the bus service has been suspended). If you don't want to take a taxi (about 500ptas), cross the car park outside the station and head straight uphill following the yellow signs for the centre, a ten-minute walk. The bus from Málaga brings you closer in, disembarking at the **bus station** (☎95 284 35 73) near the bullring. For information on the town, or help with finding a room, head for the helpful **Turismo** (Mon–Sat 10am–2pm & 5–8pm, Sun 10am–2pm; ☎ 95 270 25 05) on Plaza San Sebastián alongside the church of the same name. They can also provide information on Torcal and have details on horse-riding and mountain bike rental inside the park.

You shouldn't have a problem finding a **place to stay**, as demand is low. Good choices include *Hostal Reyes*, c/Tercia 4 (☎95 284 10 28; ③–④), for rooms with or without bath, and the friendly *Pensión-Bar Madrona*, near the market at c/Calzada 25 (☎95 284 00 14; ③) for neat ensuite rooms. On the opposite side of the market, Plaza de Abastos, the tranquil *Pensión Toril*, c/Toril 3 (☎95 284 31 84; ②–③), has rooms with and without bath arranged around a leafy patio. Slightly west of here, *Número Uno*, c/Lucena 40 (☎95 284 31 34; ③) is a new *hostal* with pleasant ensuite rooms and a roof terrace. Two places to try near the Turismo are *Hostal Manzanito* (☎95 284 10 23; ③) with en-suite rooms above a bar facing the church of San Sebastián, and around the corner the simpler *Camas El Gallo*, c/Nueva 2 (☎95 284 21 04; ②). The central *Hotel Colón*, c/Infante Don Fernando 31 (☎95 284 00 10, fax 95 284 11 64; ④), has extra creature comforts such as air conditioning and TV. Antequera's modern *parador*, to the north of the Plaza de Toros, at c/García del Olmo s/n (☎95 284 02 61, fax 95 284 13 12; ⑦), has pleasant gardens and a pool, but the service often lacks a smile. The nearest **campsite** is at El Torcal (see p.97).

The Town

A bustling agricultural centre where farmers from the surrounding *vega* come to stock up on everything from tractor tyres to seeding attachments, Antequera has a modern appearance that belies its history. In Roman times *Anticaria* ("ancient city") seems to have had a substantial population; much later, in 1410, the town was the first in Andalucía to fall to the Christian forces, who in this battle introduced gunpowder to Spanish warfare for the first time.

Antequera divides into two zones: a **monumental quarter** situated at the foot of the hill dominated by the Alcazaba, and the mainly nineteenth-century **commercial sector** concentrated around the Alameda de Andalucía. This end of town is where modern Antequera works and plays, and there's not much in the way of sights, though the nineteenth-century bullring is worth a look. Probably the most famous sights, however, are the prehistoric **dolmen caves**, on the northern edge of town.

Antequera's annual **feria** happens during the third week in August, a harvest fiesta (*recolección*) with *corridas*, dancing and parades.

The Museo Municipal

At the heart of the monumental quarter, the **Museo Municipal**, c/Coso Viejo s/n (Tues–Fri 10am–1.30pm & 4–6pm, Sat & Sun 11am–1.30pm; hourly guided tours; 200ptas), is located in a striking eighteenth-century ducal palace. It's just as well that the palace is worth visiting for itself, because the exhibits do little justice to the setting, despite the efforts of a guide who tries his best to enliven the proceedings with a few time-worn jokes. Largely a hotchpotch of church vestments, silver plate and indifferent paintings, the collection is, however, distinguished by two works of sculpture: a fine first-century AD **Roman bronze** of a youth known as the "Efebo de Antequera", and an eerily lifelike carving in wood of **St Francis of Assisi** by the seventeenth-century Andalucian sculptor Pedro de Mena. More fragments of ancient statuary and tombstones are dotted around the courtyard, and a room on the ground floor devotes itself to the art works of a modern painter born in Antequera, Cristóbal Toral.

Just to the east of the museum, on the way to the Alcazaba, the eighteenth-century **Carmelite nunnery of San José** on Plaza de las Descalzas has a good selection of *dulces*. The entrance is behind the small fountain. Inside, the sweets are sold via a *torno* – asking for a *surtido* (sampler) gets you a bit of everything. You won't see the nun who serves you, but, in a sign of changing times, she may ask you to pay first.

Nuestra Señora del Carmen

The nearby Cuesta de los Rojas climbs steeply to the Postigo de la Estrella, an old postern gate. To the east of this – and not to be missed – lies the seventeenth-century Mudéjar church of **Nuestra Señora del Carmen** (Mon 10.30am–2pm, Tues–Sun 10am–2pm, Sat also 4–7pm; 200ptas), whose plain facade little prepares you for the eighteenth-century interior, recently and painstakingly restored to its former glory. The main altar's sensational 13-metre-high **retablo** – one of the finest of its kind in Andalucía – is a masterly late-Baroque extravaganza of carved wood by Antonio Primo and Diego Márquez, its centrepiece a Virgin in a *camarín* flanked by a bevy of polychromed saints and soaring angels.

The Alcazaba

Further up Cuesta de los Rojas lies the ruined medieval **Alcazaba**, with its thirteenth-century Islamic fortification, the **Torre del Homenaje** (Tues–Sun 10am–2pm; free). The first fortress to fall to the Christians during the Reconquest of the kingdom of Granada, the ruined Alcazaba now encloses a municipal garden, giving fine views over the town towards the curiously anthropoid **Peña de las Enamorados** ("Lovers' Rock") resembling the profiled head of a sleeping giant. The outcrop acquired its name from two lovers (a Christian girl and a Muslim youth) during the Moorish period, who are said to have thrown themselves from the top when their parents forbade their marriage.

Adjoining the Alcazaba, the sixteenth-century **Arco de los Gigantes** preserves stones and inscriptions embedded in its walls which were rescued by antiquaries from the destruction of the Roman town in the same period. Large parts of the town were still standing – including a fine theatre – until used for the construction of many churches in the seventeenth and eighteenth centuries.

East of the castle, in the spacious Plaza Alta, the sixteenth-century collegiate church of **Santa María** (Tues–Sun 10am–2pm) boasts a great Plateresque facade inspired by a Roman triumphal arch. Inside the church – which now serves as a concert hall – you'll also see a superb Mudéjar coffered ceiling.

Antequera's other churches

Walking from the Alcazaba back into the town centre you'll pass a number of **churches**. The seventeenth-century **San Sebastián** (daily 9.30am–7pm), in the elegant plaza of the same name, possesses a striking brick steeple that dominates the town. Note the carved angels and the tower's weather vane, *El Angelote*, which has the remains of Antequera's patron saint, Santa Euphemia, in a reliquary hung around its neck. This church also has some beautifully carved choir stalls, as does the nearby eighteenth-century **San Agustín**, at the start of c/Infante Fernando. At the western end of this street and close to the Palacio Consistorial – a stylish seventeenth-century mansion now functioning as the *Ayuntamiento* (access to view patio during working hours) – lies the Renaissance church of **San Juan de Dios** (Tues–Sat 5–7pm, Sun 11.30am–1pm), constructed almost entirely with stone taken from the demolition of a perfectly preserved Roman theatre. Slightly further away up a steep climb at the southern end of the town, the Plaza del Portichuelo has the flamboyant Baroque-Mudéjar **Capilla de la Virgen del Socorro** with a double tier of triple arches built to house Antequera's most revered image, Nuestra Señora del Socorro (Our Lady of Succour). The nearby white-walled Baroque chapel of **Santa María de Jesús**, with storks nests in its belfry, is also worth a look. From a *mirador* behind the churches there are great views towards the Alcazaba and the surrounding hills.

The Plaza de Toros

The western end of town has little in the way of sights, though the nineteenth-century **Plaza de Toros** (museum hours Sat 5–8pm; Sun 10am–1pm & 5–8pm), on the

Alameda de Andalucía, is well worth a look – access is usually available to the ring when the restaurant (see "Eating and drinking") is open. This bullring staged its first *corrida* on August 20, 1848, and whatever your view about the morality of this "sport", it's difficult not to pick up on the atmosphere that the old place generates, especially when you view the amphitheatre from the *matador*'s position in the centre of the burning sand.

The dolmen caves

On the town's northern outskirts – an easy one-kilometre walk along the Granada road – lie a group of **prehistoric dolmens** (Tues 3–5.30pm, Wed–Sat 10am–2pm & 3–5.30pm, Sun 10am–2pm; free), which rank among the most important in Spain. The grandest of these megalithic monuments is the **Cueva de Menga**, its roof formed by massive stone slabs, among them a 180-ton monolith. Dating from around 2500 BC, the columned gallery leading to an oval burial chamber was probably the final resting place of an important chieftain. On the last stone slab of the left wall you'll see some engraved – and probably symbolic – forms; the star, however, is a more recent addition. If you stand just inside the entrance to the Menga dolmen you will be able to see the Lovers' Rock, precisely framed in the portal – something that cannot have been accidental and suggests that the rock may have had some religious or ritual significance. This is underlined by the fact that the sun rises behind the "head" of the rock at the summer solstice and penetrates into the burial chamber, much as happens in the New Grange passage grave in Ireland.

The **Cueva de Viera**, dating from a century later, has better-cut stones, forming a long, narrow tunnel leading to a smaller burial chamber. To the west of here it is possible to make out the quarry on the peak of a nearby hill (topped by a rather incongruous school) from where the stone used to construct the dolmens was hewn before being hauled across the intervening valley. The cave guardian will point it out on request.

The third dolmen, **El Romeral**, is a further 2km down the road on the left behind a sugar factory (easily identified by its chimney). Once you've crossed the train line, the road to it is signed on the left; if it's locked you'll have to return to the Cueva de Menga for the key. Built more than half a millennium later than the other two dolmens and containing dual chambers roofed with splendid corbel vaulting, El Romeral has something of an eastern Mediterranean feel, and bears an uncanny resemblance to the tholos tombs constructed in Crete at around the same time.

Should you turn up outside the official opening hours, pause outside the garage beside the main entrance; you may be approached by a couple of rum old characters who have spare keys and will allow you to see the dolmens for a consideration.

Eating and drinking

Antequera, unlike its neighbours on the coast to the south, has little in the way of exciting food or entertainment options. You'll trail past a variety of fast-food places, bars and *heladerías* along the Alameda, but a far better bet, during the day at least, is to head for the many **places to eat** around the market on Plaza Abastos, catering for the traders and customers who flock in from miles around. Among numerous good *tapas* bars here, there's the *Pensión-Bar Madrona*, c/Calzada 25, which serves a hearty and inexpensive *menú* and even has rooms (see p.93).

Nearer the centre, *El Angelote*, c/Encarnación s/n near the museum, is probably the town's best **restaurant** and although mid-priced has a *menú* for under 1500ptas; there's a pleasant terrace too. The *Mesón Noelía*, Alameda 12, serves medium-priced *platos combinados* and a good-value *menú*, and has pavement tables – only really feasible once the traffic has died down. A quieter location to sit out is at the **Plaza de**

Toros. The bullring's very own restaurant, *La Espuela* ("the spur") offers a medium-priced *menú*, as well as more expensive meals – the bar here is also a good place to stop for lunchtime *tapas*. More places for **tapas** are *Bar Infante*, c/Infante Don Fernando, *Bar Manzanito*, Plaza San Sebastián and *Bar Lo Güeno*, c/Avisos just east of the Plaza de Abastos. *Bienmesabe*, Plaza de las Descalzas in the monumental quarter, is another good *tapas* venue, and stages **flamenco** at midnight on Friday and Saturday nights. Finally, a good **breakfast bar** is *Café del Centro* at c/Cantareros 3, slightly north of the main street, where the walls are decorated with photos from Antequera's past.

Around Antequera

Within easy distance of Antequera are trips to the vast natural park of **El Torcal** with its marvellous weathered limestone rock formations, and the important flamingo breeding grounds of **Fuente de Piedra**.

Parque Natural El Torcal

EL TORCAL, 13km south of Antequera, and 32km north of Málaga, is the most geologically arresting of Andalucía's natural parks. A massive high plateau of glaciated limestone, tempered by a lush growth of hawthorn, ivy, wild rose and thirty species of orchid, it's quite easily explored using the **walking routes** that radiate from the centre of the park where the road ends. A **Centro de Recepción** here (Mon–Sat 9.30am–1.30pm & 4–7pm, Sun 10am–2pm; ☎95 203 13 89) gives out maps and general information on the park and its walks, and has audio-visual presentations covering geology, flora and fauna. Try to leave your explorations until the more peaceful late afternoon, when the setting sun throws the natural sculptures into sharp relief.

The best designed and most exciting **trails** are the yellow and red routes, the former climaxing with suitable drama on a cliff edge with magnificent views over a valley. The latter gives fantastic vantage points of the looming limestone outcrops, eroded into vast, surreal sculptures. However, because of the need to protect flora and fauna these are now in a restricted zone and can only be visited with a **guide** (ring ahead or arrange a guide when you arrive). The green route (waymarked) is the only one for which you don't need a guide, and is also the shortest at 1.5km (about 40min if you don't dawdle). In early summer you may find yourself competing with gangs of schoolkids who arrive en masse on vaguely educational trips, excitedly trying to spot "La Copa" (the wineglass), "El Lagarto" (the lizard) and "La Loba" (the she-wolf) as well as other celebrated rock sculptures. Keep an eye on the skies while you're here, for Griffon vultures are frequent visitors and, with their huge wingspans, often make a spectacular sight as they glide overhead.

Park practicalities

No buses link El Torcal to Antequera, and it's an arduous hike in high summer; take the C3310 road to Villanueva de la Concepción and head down the second signed turning on the right to El Torcal. You've got good chances of hitching a lift, especially on weekends, when it may possible to persuade one of the school buses to take you back. Failing this, you might consider a **taxi** (about 1500ptas one-way) or the daily buses which run Mon–Fri from Antequera to Villanueva de la Concepcíon (1pm & 6.30pm) – ask the driver to drop you at the road for El Torcal from where it's a 4km uphill slog to the visitor centre. The return bus should pass the same turn-off at 7.45am and 4pm, which is not much use unless you plan to stay overnight. If you can afford it, the most convenient way to visit, however, is to take the **taxi turistico**, a new innovation which can be arranged through the Turismo at Antequera; for 2700ptas a taxi will drop you off at the Centro de Recepción and wait until you have completed the green route before returning you to Antequera. Torcal has a **campsite**, *Camping Torcal* (☎95 270 35 82) just off the A3310 6km south of Antequera, which also has a restaurant, supermarket and pool – very welcome in high summer. Camping rough is not allowed inside the park.

Laguna de Fuente de Piedra

About 20km northwest of Antequera lies **Laguna de Fuente de Piedra**, the largest natural lake in Andalucía and a celebrated site for observing birdlife. The shallow water-level and high saline content of the lake, and the crustaceans that these conditions encourage, attract a glorious flock of **greater flamingo** each spring, making this Europe's only inland breeding ground for the species. Unfortunately the droughts of recent years and the demands for more water by local farmers, who have cashed in on an asparagus boom in the nearby Sierra de Yeguas, have led to the lake almost drying up completely in the summer months, thus placing many of the young flamingo in peril. This resulted in rescue missions being mounted by teams from the Coto Doñana (see p.291) who transferred many young birds back to the wetlands of Huelva. Andalucía's environmental agency, the *Agencia del Medio Ambiente*, is working on a system to prevent this happening again.

Besides supporting a variety of waders at all times of the year, in winter the lake is often a haven for cranes, and the surrounding marshes provide a habitat for numerous amphibians and reptiles. Remember that because this is a sanctuary, the beaches are strictly out of bounds (ruling out swimming) and because many sections are privately owned, limiting access, it's not possible to make a complete circuit of the lake. You're also at a distinct advantage with your own transport as species such as flamingo often gather at the far end of the lake, up to 7km away.

Easy to get to, the village of Fuente de Piedra is on the train route from Málaga to Córdoba, while the lake itself lies a ten-minute walk east of the station. There are four daily buses from Antequera or, with your own transport, take the A354 (direction Sevilla) north, to join the A92 *autovía*, and continue along this for 14km until the signed turn-off. Over the bridge beyond the train station the lakeside **Centro de Visitantes** (daily 9am–2pm & 4–7pm; ☎95 211 10 50) has displays of the flora and fauna of the lake, and rents out binoculars.

For **rooms**, the *Hostal–Hotel La Laguna* (☎95 273 52 92; ③) close to the village, overlooks the lake and has rooms with bath. It also has a decent **restaurant** with an economical *menú* and a **swimming pool.** The grounds are occupied by its **campsite**, and bungalow-apartments which can sleep up to four (④) are available for longer stays.

East from Málaga: the coast to Torre del Mar

The dreary eastern stretch of the **Costa del Sol** – the beaches within easy distance of Málaga – is a largely unbroken landscape of urbanization and unlovely holiday towns, packed to the gunnels in summer with day-tripping *malagueños*. There are enough places of interest, however, to warrant stopping off en route, before arriving at the unremarkable resort of **Torre del Mar**.

With your own transport it's possible to avoid the Málaga suburbs by using the N331 *circunvalación* – picked up on the northern edge of town – which comes out just beyond Rincón de la Victoria (see over). Otherwise, heading out of Málaga the N340 traverses the suburbs of Pedragalejo and El Palo where for most of the summer the beaches are covered with a forest of parasols.

Cueva del Tesoro and Rincón de la Victoria

Just beyond Cala del Moral, a signed road on the left indicates the **CUEVA DEL TESORO** (daily 10am–2pm & 4–8pm; 500ptas), a spectacular network of underground caves less commercialized than those at Nerja (see p.105). A series of seven chambers, spiked with stalagmites and stalactites, leads to the eighth, the **sala de los lagos**, a Gaudí-esque rock cathedral with natural underground pools. Paleolithic cave paintings were discovered here in 1918 (presently not on view) as well as other prehistoric remains indicating almost continual human habitation. The cave's name (*tesoro* means treasure) derives from the legend that five fleeing Moorish kings took refuge in its depths and stashed a large quantity of gold. The gold is long gone but the cave retains its name.

Two kilometres further on, **RINCÓN DE LA VICTORIA** is a no-nonsense, scruffy sort of place, and another local resort for *malagueño* families. It's a functional spot to swim if you have a day to fill before catching a plane home, but nothing more. A seafood speciality in the *marisquerías* here are *coquinas*, tasty small clams.

Macharaviaya and around

To break the monotony along this strip you could follow a small road north at the featureless suburb of Torre de Benagalbón which winds up into the hills and approaches the hamlet of **MACHARAVIAYA.** Surrounded by slopes covered with olive and almond trees, the village was built in the eighteenth century by the Galvéz family, one of Andalucía's great imperial dynasties. Count Bernardo de Galvéz became governor general of Spanish North America and gave his name to Galveston in Texas after laying siege to the town during the American War of Independence in 1777. Today, even taking into account its impressive Baroque church (a Galvéz construction), it's hard to believe that this tiny, cobble-paved village was once known as "little Madrid". It was a wealthy place, benefiting from the extensive Galvéz family vineyards as well as a playing-card factory which had a monopoly for supplying cards to the Americas. This was all to end, however, when the phylloxera plague of the 1870s wiped out the vines, the card monopoly lapsed and the Galvéz line died out. The family title died with them, and the last Visconte de Galveston is buried in the church crypt among the tombs.

At the entrance to the village is a rather proprietorial whitewashed brick temple erected by the family in 1786 and, at its centre, the once crumbling exterior of the **Church of San Jacinto** now over-restored as part of the *Expo 92* celebrations. To enter you'll need to get two keys from the mayor's house, up a ramp beside the *Ayuntamiento* – as it's a private house, avoid calling in at siesta time. Inside the single nave church, altars dedicated to various Galvéz family members are decorated with fine marble, and inscriptions express the ultimately vain hope that Mass would be said on certain days for their souls *in perpetuum*. Don't miss the eerie crypt behind the church, where a remarkable collection of sombre **alabaster family busts** face each other around an alcove and seem about to start up a gloomy conversation. The great marble tomb of Don José Galvéz, Marquis of Sonora and Minister for the Indias during the eighteenth-century reign of Carlos III, stands nearby.

Facing the church is the old playing-card factory, now converted into dwellings, and including the *Bar Sonora*. Should this be closed and you need refreshment, follow signs to the simple *Taberna El Candil* around the corner, which will serve you *tapas* if pushed.

Torre del Mar

Back on the main coast road, the chain of localities with "torre" in their names refers to the numerous *atalayas* or watch towers which have been used to guard this coast since Roman and Moorish times, many strikingly visible on the headlands. There is little to detain you between Torre de Benagalbón and Almayate – though the latter has a reasonable **campsite**, *Almayate-Costa* (☎95 255 62 89) with limited shade – from where it's only a couple of kilometres to **TORRE DEL MAR**. A line of concrete tower blocks on a grey, pebble beach, this is Torremolinos without the money or fun. Nevertheless, it's fairly peaceful, and recent improvements include a paved promenade area, El Copo, in an attempt to swoop the place upmarket. Over the summer months the numerous **restaurants and bars** here fill up in the evenings, but it never really takes off.

If you want to **stay**, head for the central and friendly *Hostal Generalife*, c/Patrón Veneno 22 (☎95 254 33 09; ④), a *pensión* just 30m from the beach. Like everywhere else around here, though, rooms are at a premium in high season, when your best hope will probably be the basic **campsite** *Torre del Mar* (☎95 254 02 24) on the Paseo Marítimo. Otherwise the helpful **Turismo**, Avda. de Andalucía 120, opposite the public library (☎95 254 11 04), may be able to advise. Walkers and readers may want to look up a useful **bookshop**, Pasa Tiempo, c/Infantes 30 facing Plaza de la Paz, where a Yorkshire couple – both enthusiastic walkers – keep a wide range of maps including the SGE military maps for the south.

The Axarquía

If you have your own transport, a trip up into the often spectacularly beautiful region of **Axarquía** makes a refreshing change from the sun-bed culture of the Costa del Sol. Bounded by the coast, the Sierra de Tejeda to the north and, on its eastern flank, the mountainous edge of the province of Granada, this rugged, ham-shaped wedge of territory offers excellent walking country and abundant wildlife, as well as a host of attractive mountain villages that make easy-going stopoffs. Long a breeding ground for *bandoleros* who preyed on traders carrying produce from the coast to Granada, during the Civil War Axarquía was also a notorious guerrilla encampment whose members fought on against Franco's Guardia Civil until the early 1950s: it is only in relatively recent times that the area has become safe for travellers. For Spanish speakers the hiker's guide *Sendas y Caminos de la Axarquía* from *Interguias Clave* (available from most bookshops) details walking routes, refuges and campsites throughout the region.

Vélez-Málaga

Frequent buses head the 4km inland from Torre del Mar to **VÉLEZ-MÁLAGA**, a bustling market town, supply centre for the region's farmers and capital of Axarquía. In the fertile valley of the Río Vélez, Vélez-Málaga (often simply referred to as Vélez) was important in both Roman times – under the name of *Menoba* – and Moorish, when as *Ballix-Malaca* ("Fortress of Málaga") it had an important role in subduing what has always been a turbulent zone. A number of Phoenician cemeteries and tombs discovered nearby testify to an older pedigree still. When Ferdinand conquered the town in 1487, the Christian flag was raised on the castle's battlements as the Moors were ejected. This victory, which drove a wedge through the kingdom of Granada dividing it in two, paved the way for the fall of the Nasrid city five years later.

The town climbs up a slope from the main street, **Avenida Vivar Téllez** – where you'll arrive whether you're travelling by bus or car – towards the **castillo**, as good a place as any to start a tour of the sights. What's left of it clings to a rocky outcrop, which from its dominant position above the white-walled *barrio* of San Sebastián gives good views out over the coast. The castle suffered badly during the War of the Spanish Succession when the English lost to the French here after a bitter struggle in 1704. Visible from the castle is the sixteenth-century Mudéjar church of **Santa María la Mayor** whose beautiful sectioned tower still holds the minaret of the mosque that

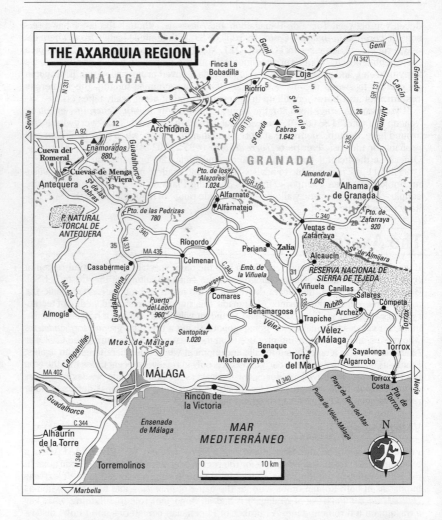

preceded it. Inside, Moorish arches separate a triple nave, and there's a fine Mudéjar ceiling. Immediately below the castle another church, **Nuestra Señora de la Encarnación**, has a history reflecting that of Andalucía itself. Beginning life as a Visigoth bishopric, the building was transformed into a mosque during the Moorish period, and back into a church again following the *reconquista*. The late-Gothic **San Juan Bautista**, on Plaza de España, is also worth a look, featuring an elegant tower and, inside, a superbly naturalistic sculpture, *Cristo Crucificado* by Pedro de Mena.

The recently restored **Palacio del Marqués de Beniel**, Plaza Palacio 1, is an elegant sixteenth-century mansion – formerly the town hall – which now hosts the International Summer School of the Axarquía covering all aspects of culture, including poetry and theatre as well as flamenco and classical guitar. A prestigious annual **guitar**

competition is held here every July, with free concerts taking place on the *palacio*'s delightful patio. The reception desk can provide details of a varied programme of cultural activities throughout the summer, and the *Ayuntamiento* can also give information in Spanish (☎95 250 01 00).

Less attractively, Vélez is also one of the last bastions of **cock-fighting** in Europe, and the Sunday fights held in the town in winter pull in crowds of aficionados from miles around to bet on the outcome as the feathers fly.

Practicalities

Vélez-Málaga's **bus station** is on Avda. Vivar Téllez, the main street leading out of town towards the sea. **Finding a place to stay** isn't usually a problem, except possibly at the end of July when every *hostal* bedroom seems to be twanging furiously as the young competitors go through their exercises in preparation for the guitar competition. Best of the bunch for simple rooms is the friendly *Casa Los Martínez*, c/Cristo 58, on the main crossroad as you approach the centre from Avda. Vivar Téllez (☎95 250 42 87; ③); they also have a good **restaurant**. Just across the road, the more expensive *Hotel Dila*, Avda. Vivar Téllez 11 (☎95 250 39 00; ⑤), has air-conditioned rooms with bath, while the local **campsite**, *Valle Niza* on the edge of town on Avda. Vivar Téllez (☎95 251 31 81), is a more pleasant option than the one down in Torre del Mar (see p.99).

Many places to **eat and drink** line the Avda. Vivar Tellez, including the excellent medium-priced *Mesón Los Migueles* at no. 83, serving a variety of fish and meat dishes and a good-value *menú*.

North to Alfarnate

A number of good **driving routes** around Axarquía begin at **Trapiche**, about 3km north of Vélez. One possibility is to veer northwest towards **BENAMARGOSA**, a village surrounded by citrus orchards and olive groves. You could take a look at its sixteenth-century Gothic-style church of **La Encarnación** before moving on to La Zubía, where a road left climbs to **COMARES**, a white town spectacularly clinging to the peak of its conical hill. At the highest point of all, beside a charming cemetery, a ruined Moorish fort – built on Roman foundations – was one of the strongholds, along with Bobastro (see p.88), of rebel leader Ibn Hafsun. In the village is yet another church of **Nuestra Señora de la Encarnación**, this time a sixteenth-century Mudéjar building with a picturesque tower. A **mirador** in the nearby Plaza del Ayuntamiento gives fine views over the Axarquía. There are **rooms** at the *Hotel Atalaya*, c/Encinilla s/n (☎95 250 92 08; ④).

Continuing north out of La Zubía the road follows the course of the Río Cueva, finally ascending to **RIOGORDO**, a village with Phoenician and Roman origins that was a fortified stronghold during the Moorish period. After the *reconquista* the Moors were replaced by settlers from Castile, the ancestors of the modern inhabitants. The *Semana Santa* celebrated here is a particularly vivid affair, when local people – dressed for the part – act out the scenes from the Passion with often bloodcurdling gusto. The village also boasts an attractive municipal swimming pool, a great place to splash around in the summer heat.

From Riogordo, you have a choice of routes: head east to Alfarnate or west, following a stiff climb, to **COLMENAR**, another brilliant white hill town and the Axarquía's most westerly outpost. A centre of honey production thanks to the rich variety of flowering plants and shrubs growing in the surrounding hills, the village takes its name from *colmena*, the Spanish for "beehive". The route from here – via the Puerto del Léon – down to Málaga, twisting through forests of cork oaks and pines, is wonderful, offering during its latter stages great views over the Costa del Sol.

Alcaucín and Zálía

The second route out of Vélez forks right at Trapiche and follows the old coach route from Málaga to Granada. VIÑUELA, 7km beyond the fork, was originally a *venta* stop and the atmospheric old inn here, *La Viña* – dating from the eighteenth century – still stands opposite the fountain in the narrow main street. A spit-and-sawdust place today, it's usually jammed full on midsummer afternoons with old men arguing around the domino tables and farmhands sheltering from the burning sun. Just down the street, the simple sixteenth-century **Iglesia de San José** (key from neighbour opposite) has a finely worked sculpture of the *Pietà*. For **rooms** on the shores of the nearby Embalse de Viñuela reservoir try the *Hotel Viñuela* (☎95 253 62 22; ⑤) which also has its own restaurant.

At the Puente de Don Manuel, 3km further on, a road cuts off on the right and ascends to the village of **ALCAUCÍN**. On the way up keep an eye to your left where, across a valley, you will be able to make out the ruins of the deserted medieval village of Zalía (see below) and, beyond, the Puerto de Zafaraya, a great U-shaped cleavage in the Sierra de Alhama through which passes the ancient route to Granada. Alcaucín itself, perched on the slopes of the Sierra de Tejeda, is a beautiful little village with wrought-iron balconies ablaze with flowering geraniums and a web of narrow white-walled streets reflecting its Moorish origins. As befits a mountain village there are numerous spring-fed fountains, among which the five-spouted Fuente San Sebastián has been restored very much in the Moorish style, complete with *azulejos*.

Continuing north from the Puente de Don Manuel, the A335 takes you to the dauntingly impressive **Zafaraya Pass**, where 30,000-year-old remains found in a nearby cave in 1983 have now been confirmed as the latest-known site in Europe inhabited by Neanderthal man. On the way, the route passes the ruins of the fort and the deserted medieval village of **ZALÍA**. Local legend has it that the Moorish village was attacked by a plague of vipers after Patricio, a *malagueño* church minister, arrived in an attempt to convert the inhabitants to Christianity and they spurned him. The more likely explanation is that the population of the village was put to the sword during the uprisings following the *reconquista*. Throughout most of the Moorish period Zalía's fortress, together with those at Comares and Bentomiz (near Arenas to the south), formed a defensive triangle to control this central sector of the Axarquía region. From here it is possible to continue to Granada via the Puerto de Zafaraya and Alhama de Granada (see p.437).

Periana, Alfarnatejo and Alfarnate

Pressing on along the C340, joined a short distance beyond the Alcaucín turnoff (see above), leads to **PERIANA**, a noted centre of peach-growing and *anís* production and now the location for a brand new and good-value **Villa Turística** (☎ & fax 95 253 62 22; ⑤ inc. breakfast) where traditionally styled chalet accommodation surrounds a pool and terrace with fine views towards the coast. There's a restaurant and bar, horses can be hired from their own stables and mountain biking and tennis are on offer as well. Heading on into the Axarquía's more remote extremities, about 3km beyond Periana you'll reach a fork; if you don't want to face a tortuous switchback secondary road which is unsealed for the last few kilometres, ignore the sign for "Alfarnate 15km" and continue along the road signed to Riogordo and Colmenar. A further 4km will bring you to a right turn and an easier route to the village of **ALFARNATEJO** and, a little beyond this, the Axarquía's most northerly outpost, **ALFARNATE**. Although they lie a mere couple of kilometres apart, it would be difficult to find two places in Andalucía with less in common. Alfarnatejo, the smaller of the two, is staunchly rightwing, while Alfarnate has always been on the left, and, unable to agree or cooperate on anything, they have built up a strong mutual animosity, which even discourages marriages between the two communities. In truth, neither village would win any beauty prizes, though Alfarnate, set on a plain covered with wheatfields is worth a visit for its attractive church, **Santa Ana**, a sixteenth-century edifice with a graceful Mudéjar tower.

However, Alfarnate's real claim to fame is the thirteenth-century **Venta de Alfarnate** (☎95 275 93 88) on the village's western edge, which maintains – with some justification – that it is the **oldest inn in Andalucía**. Situated in an isolated spot in the midst of brooding hills, it's not hard to see what attracted the various brigands and highwaymen to the place. Indeed, the interior, as well as being a bar-restaurant, is also a **museum** dedicated to keeping alive the memory of such outlaws as Luís Candelas, who spent a night in the *venta*'s well-preserved prison cell en route to justice in Málaga. By far the most terrifying *bandolero* of all, however, was El Tempranillo, who arrived unannounced one hot day in the 1820s, and, when there were no spoons for him to eat with, ordered the dining clients to eat their wooden ones at gunpoint, cracking their teeth in the process. The place is more civilized these days and serves a hearty mountain speciality, *huevos a lo bestia* (fried eggs with local sausage, ham and black pudding). The proprietors have recently restored the *venta*'s accommodation, and **rooms** (④) are available providing a great base to explore the wonderful walking country nearby. Alternatives include a fully equipped house (⑤) available for rent in the village or the stunning *cortijo* 4km outside capable of sleeping eight (☎95 275 92 05 or 95 233 61 99 for both). Keep your eyes peeled in this area for the amazingly agile *cabra hispanica*, the rare Spanish goat; the long-horned male is a spectacular sight as he effortlessly scales almost vertical cliff faces.

East from Torre del Mar: the coast to Nerja

The coast east from Torre del Mar is a nondescript stretch of faceless towns and the occasional concrete resort, dotted with more ancient *atalayas* or watch towers. Inland lie more tempting villages in the **eastern Axarquía** but along the coast the first town of any real interest is **Nerja**, with some fine beaches and a relatively slow pace. Further east, **Almuñécar**, and even better **Salobreña**, are the city of Granada's Mediterranean playgrounds, flanked by numerous coves and inlets where for most of the year you can have a beach all to yourself.

Cómpeta

Beyond Torre del Mar the coast road climbs slightly to Algarrobo-Costa, an unappealing highrise beach resort. With your own transport it's worth ignoring this – and the bleak stretch of coast that follows – to head inland for some delightful villages in the eastern Axarquía, finally rejoining the coastal road 10km east at Torrox Costa.

From Algarrobo-Costa the MA103 climbs inland for a stretch towards the village of Algarrobo proper. Look out for for some well-conserved **Phoenician tombs** (signposted on the right) dating from the eighth century BC. Originally these tombs formed part of an extensive cemetery, built of stone blocks and roofed in wood – the main tomb produced rich finds now in the Alcazaba museum at Málaga (see p.76).

Passing through the village of Algarrobo the road toils on upwards as the fruit orchards of the coastal strip give way to the olive groves and vineyards of the higher slopes. The road then passes **Sayalonga** 5km further on, a pretty village nestling in the valley of the Río Algarrobo and then ascends again, twisting and turning for a further 8km until it reaches **CÓMPETA**, a huddle of brilliant white boxes tumbling down a hillside, and surrounded by vineyards. A Moorish settlement in origin, and now discovered by migrants from northern Europe, Cómpeta retains a relaxed atmosphere, and the easy-going villagers don't seem too worried about being swamped by foreigners. The sweet – and potent – wine made from the area's Moscatel grapes is renowned as the best in the whole province. You can try it for yourself at the *Bar Buena Uva* or the *Museo del Vino* on Avda. de la Constitución, both close to the charming main square, Plaza de la Almijara. Beneath the lofty bell tower (a later addition) of the sixteenth-century church of La Asunción each year on August 15, Cómpeta rolls out the barrels – hundreds of them – during its annual fiesta, the *Noche del Vino*, when the square is filled with revellers determined to sink as much of the free *vino* as they can hold. Above the plaza to the left, c/San Antonio leads to a shrine with a superb **view** over the valley to the west and the sea beyond.

Practicalities

Maps and information can be obtained from the **Turismo** on c/La Rampa just below the main square (Mon–Sat 10am–2pm; ☎95 255 33 01); they also have information on renting houses. If you decide **to stay**, the only budget option is *Hostal Albardini* (☎95 251 62 41; ③) offering rooms with a view 1km out of the village on the Torrox road. The upmarket *Hotel Balcón de Cómpeta*, c/San Antonio s/n, south-west of the main square (☎95 255 35 35, fax 95 255 35 10; ⑥) with comfortable balcony rooms and a pool, is the only central option.

The best place **to eat** is the excellent *Restaurante Perico* on the Plaza Almijara, where the house *menú* often includes the zone's *sopa de berza*, a tasty cabbage and *morcilla* soup; in summer they use the square as their terrace. Slightly south-west of the main square *El Pilón*, c/Laberinto s/n, offers more eclectic international cuisine. *Bar Franquelo*, at the top of c/José Antonio just off the main square, is a good place for **tapas** and the nearby *Bar Laura* in Plaza Pantaleon Romero is also good for cheap meals. *Casa Rustico*, Avda. Torrox on the edge of the village towards Torrox, does very good local dishes and is followed by a string of *ventas* which dot the road towards the coast and make for pleasant lunch stops.

An English bookshop, Marco Polo, at c/José Antonio 3 just off the main square, stocks walking maps and copies of *25 Walks in and Around Competa and Canillas* by A. & D. Kraaijenzank, which will enable a more detailed exploration of this area. They also distribute a local magazine, *Market Place*, which includes a useful map of the village (and many other towns and resorts along this coast), leaving copies on their doorstep when closed.

Archez

To push on further into the Axarquía from Competa you'll need to double back for 2km to the turning north to Archez. Nestling in the foothills of the Sierra Almijara, **ARCHEZ**, when you reach it, is an attractive village with strong Moorish roots. This influence is vividly in evidence at the church of **Nuestra Señora de La Encarnación** whose remarkable fourteenth-century tower is the minaret of an earlier mosque. It is one of the best examples from this period, and the *sebka* brickwork and blind arches above are particularly fine.

Salares and Sedella

The road climbs for another 5km to the brilliant white village of **SALARES**, a centre of olive and wine production and one of the most picturesque villages of the Axarquía. Its charms are enhanced by the banning of traffic from its narrow streets, where colourful potted geraniums line the walls and dogs lie prostrate in the afternoon heat. There's a car park at the edge of the village; from here, head downhill to the friendly

Ayuntamiento (Mon–Fri 9am–2pm), where you can pick up a small map. Next door, the church of **Santa Ana** should be your first stop. Just as the church at Archez, this one conserves a fine **minaret** of the mosque it replaced. Inside, a simple interior holds the image of Santa Ana, *patrona* of the village.

The road climbs on to **SEDELLA** 4km away, perched beneath a massive hill terraced with orchards and vegetable gardens. Looming up behind, the Sierra de Almijara is laced with numerous streams and springs that provide necessary irrigation. Apart from winding, narrow streets daubed with liberal amounts of whitewash, there are few sights, though the **Casa Torreón**, an ancient *Ayuntamiento* with a fine Mudéjar tower topped off by paired arches, is mildly interesting. On the village's northern edge there is a delightful and economical **place to stay**, *Hostal Casa Pinta* (☎95 250 88 77; ③), offering rooms with bath, fine views, a terrace with swimming pool and a good restaurant with a remarkably cheap *menú*.

Canillas and Torrox

Beyond Sedella the road allows fine views over the Vélez and Rubite river valleys to the west and, after 6km, there's a summer **campsite** signed on the right; to reach it you'll need to leave any transport at the car park below and climb through the woods to the site. A little beyond here, surrounded by slopes of almonds, vines and the olives from which it takes its name, is the large and prosperous village of **CANILLAS DE ACEITUNO**. Gathered below its sixteenth-century church of **Nuestra Señora del Rosario**, Canillas is a relaxing place with plenty of thirst-quenching bars serving tapas, dotted along the narrow streets circling the church – *Bar Sociedad* is one to try. If you want to **stay**, the central *Pensión Canillas* (☎95 251 81 02; ②) has clean and simple rooms.

To get back to the coast you'll need to retrace your tracks to Cómpeta, and then follow the MA137 as it descends to Torrox and the coast. **TORROX** is a sizeable village some 4km inland from its coastal offshoot, and not without charm. Historically, Torrox reached the height of its prosperity during the Moorish period due to its pivotal role in the silk trade between Granada and Near Eastern cities such as Baghdad and Damascus. Now a permanent haven for colonies of expat Germans and Scandinavians, it has a pretty enough centre, with brilliant white-walled houses clinging to the steep slope on which the town is built.

Back on the coast, **Torrox Costa** is a depressing concrete corral again favoured largely by German and Scandinavian visitors. In high season – when there's little chance of finding a room or a place for your towel on the overcrowded beach – your best bet is to take a quick look at the remains of a **Roman necropolis and villa** immediately west of the lighthouse, before moving straight on to Nerja.

Nerja

Although **NERJA**, 8km along the coast from Torrox, cannot claim to have been bypassed by the tidal wave of post-1960s tourist development, this attractive resort has, nevertheless, held out against Torremolinos-type tower blocks, and its mainly villa and *urbanizaciones* construction has been more in keeping with its origins. Its setting, too, is spectacular, nestling among the foothills of the Almijara range and with a striking belvedere flanked by some attractive **beaches**.

Arrival and information

The main **bus station** (actually a stand) lies at the north end of the town slightly northwest of Plaza Cantarero; buses also leave from here for the hill village of Frigiliana and the Nerja Caves (see p.109). It's a five-minute walk south from the station to the beach and centre, or old town. From the bus station locate the nearby **Plaza Cantarero**, slightly east, and then follow c/Pintada south towards the sea. This street will eventually bring you to the helpful **Turismo**, c/Puerta del Mar 2 (summer daily 10am–2pm & 5.30–8.30pm; ☎95 252 15 31), just to the east of the Balcón de Europa. There's an English bookshop, W. H. Smiffs, in the small shopping arcade next to the **post office** on c/Cristo (aka c/Puerta del Mar); they also have a notice board which often lists job vacancies should you be looking for employment. Incidentally, Nerja boasts one of the best second-hand bookshops on the coast, **The Book Centre**, at c/Granada 30. It's a huge place, and well worth a visit, especially for rare and out-of-print paperbacks in many languages.

If you'd like to do some **walking** in the area, the Turismo has its own leaflets and at Libreria Idiomas almost opposite you can buy copies of the excellent *Twelve Walks around Nerja, Frigiliana and Maro* by Elma and Denis Thompson. Elma is a chirpy Mancunian who – when not struggling with the authorities to keep footpaths open and make them easier to use – offers guided walks from November to May (call for details; ☎95 253 07 82). Club Nautico de Nerja (☎95 252 46 54), Avda. Castilla Pérez 2 west of

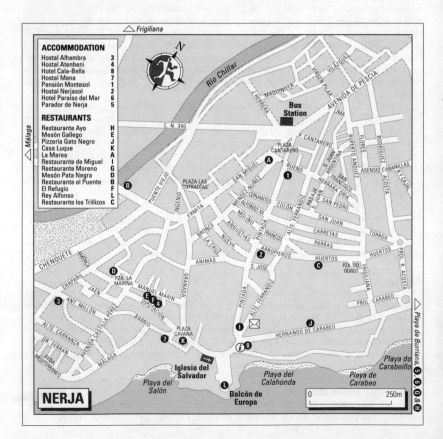

the centre, rents out **mopeds** as well as bikes and offers horse riding and diving tuition and excursions. Nerja's friendly **internet café** *Cibernet* at c/Antonio Millón 1 (10min for 100ptas) has, tucked away in a backroom, wonderful Scalextric racing car circuits should you wish to kill time between emails.

Accommodation

There is usually no problem finding **rooms** in Nerja except in August, when you should book in advance if you want to avoid the desperate twilight scramble for what's left. The lowest-priced possibilities are in the streets south of the bus station heading towards the sea. If everything's full, one solution is to stay inland at Frigiliana (see p.109) or you could try renting an apartment – which may even be a more economical bet for a group in high season. The Turismo can help with information on apartments, and many of the *hostales* listed below have arrangements with *casas particulares* to soak up the overflow. There's a **campsite** (☎95 252 97 14) with good shade, pool, bar and restaurant 4km east of the town close to Maro (p.110) and just beyond the turn-off for the caves on the left-hand side.

Hostal Alhambra, c/Antonio Millón s/n, on the junction with c/Chaparil (☎95 252 21 74). Immaculate rooms with bath, some with sea-facing balcony, in this pleasant *hostal* a little west of the centre. ④.

Hostal Atenbeni, c/Diputación 12 (☎95 252 13 41). Friendly and tidy place offering rooms with bath; close to the Turismo. ④.

Hotel Cala-Bella, c/Puerta del Mar 10 (☎95 252 07 00). Excellent hotel almost on the Turismo's doorstep; ask for a room with a sea view. Guests get reductions in the restaurant, also overlooking the Calahonda beach. Book ahead in high season. ④.

Hostal Mena, c/El Barrio 15 (☎95 252 05 41, fax 95 252 17 64). Rooms with bath and sea view and a delightful garden at the rear. ④.

Pensión Montesol, c/Pintada 130 (☎95 252 00 14). Friendly hostal with en-suite rooms which is more impressive inside than its exterior suggests. ④.

Hostal Nerjasol, c/Arropieros 4 (☎95 252 21 21). On a quiet street, with sparkling en-suite rooms and a roof patio; this *pensión* can direct you to a *casa particular* if it's full. ④.

Parador de Nerja, c/Almuñecar 8 (☎95 252 00 50, fax 95 252 19 97). Modern *parador* which, despite an exterior resembling an open prison, has a pleasant, plant-filled garden and patio, and a small park with a bar (worth a visit) overlooking the sea, plus an elevator down the cliff to Burriana, one of Nerja's most popular beaches. The restaurant serves a good-value *menú*. ⑧.

Hotel Paraíso del Mar, c/Prolongación de Carabeo 22, next door to the *Parador* (☎95 252 16 21, fax 95 252 23 09). Some rooms have a sea-view balcony and jacuzzi. There's also a pool, gardens, a sauna dug out of the cliff face and access to the beach. ⑦.

The Town

Nerja's **old town** fans out to the north of the **Balcón de Europa**, a natural palm-lined belvedere which offers magnificent views over the rocky coastline. The tangle of pretty, narrow streets is crowded with visitors all summer long, but the brash shops which service them have yet to suffocate the town's easy-going tranquillity. Nerja's obvious charm has attracted the inevitable colony of migrants – in this case the English – who make their presence felt in the numerous foreign-owned shops and bars. Sights, as such, are few, and once you have strolled along the Balcón and taken a look at the nearby seventeenth-century whitewashed **El Salvador** church – which has a fine *Dolorosa* – you should head for the beach or make a short excursion out of town. Nerja's best **beach** is Burriana, to the east of the centre. There's also a series of coves within walking distance if you want to escape the crowds.

An entertaining **market** takes place on Tuesday mornings and spreads along the streets surrounding c/Ruperto Anduez, to the east of the centre.

Eating

Restaurant prices in the old town tend to be high and standards indifferent; you'll do better to head further out for good, reasonably priced places. On the western side of town, there are many authentic Spanish restaurants concentrated around Plaza Marina. For **tapas**, four of the best are *Marisquería La Marina* on the plaza of the same name; *Marisquería La Familia*, c/Diputacíon 17; *Las 4 Esquinas*, on c/Pintada; and *El Chispa*, c/San Pedro 12, which specializes in fried fish.

Ayo, Burriana beach. Their giant open-air paella fry up on Sunday lunchtimes (big plate for 750ptas) is a Burriana institution.

Cala-Bella, c/Puerto del Mar 10. One of the best restaurants in town, inside the hotel of the same name, with balcony dining and a great sea view.

Mesón Gallego, c/Manuel Marín 12. Galician restaurant near Plaza Marina serving an economical *menú* as well as specialities such as *pulpo a la gallega* (octopus in a paprika sauce).

Casa Luque, Plaza Cavana 2. Good but expensive nouvelle cuisine served up in stylish, if rather pretentious surroundings, with panoramic terrace at rear.

La Marea, Plaza Cantarero s/n. Good and modestly priced fish restaurant with terrace.

Restaurante de Miguel, c/Pintada 2. Stylish if bland restaurant near the Turismo, with outdoor tables and an international menu.

Restaurante Moreno, Burriana beach. Nicest out of a cluster of eating places at the back of the beach; one chef cooks barbecue-style (in an old boat) outside on the terrace. The fried *sardinas* and paella are excellent.

Mesón Pata Negra, Plaza La Marina. Authentic regional dishes, a little more expensive than the other restaurants on the square.

Pizzería Gato Negro, c/Hernando de Carabeo 13. The town's best pizzeria, extremely popular with locals as well as visitors.

Bar-Restaurante El Puente, c/Carretera 4. On the town's western flank – walk to the bridge on the main road into town from Málaga. Decent restaurant with terrace, serving an inexpensive *menú*.

El Refugio, c/Diputación 12. Excellent choice of fish, mariscos and regional dishes in a friendly rustic setting with a reasonable *menú*. The street becomes their terrace in the evening.

Rey Alfonso, below the tip of the Balcón de Europa. Best sea-view in town, though it can get a bit too briny in hot weather.

Bar-Restaurante Los Trillizos, c/Los Huertos 38. Budget restaurant offering well-prepared standards with an attractive terrace at the back.

Bars and nightlife

Most of Nerja's **bars** and **discos** are almost carbon copies of places you'd find in England. You'll find them concentrated east of the centre around Plaza Tutti Frutti and especially along the nearby c/Antonio Millón. There are also numerous bars and restaurants with **live music**, including flamenco. The **flamenco** shows at *Triana* (c/Chaparil s/n) and *El Rincón de Paloma* (c/Antonio Millón 7) are fun, but for more authentic renderings head for *Peña Nerjeña de Chaparil* or *Peña de Flamenco Solea* (see below). The *Guía del Ocio* lists nightlife venues and special events, and is available from the Turismo.

Bar Cavana, Plaza Cavana. One of Nerja's traditional old bars, behind the Iglesia El Salvador; a tranquil place serving food and great for leisurely breakfasts.

Restaurante Bar-El Colono, c/Granada 6, just north of Plaza Cavana. Entertaining, free flamenco show for diners and people just here for a drink.

Peña Nerjeña de Chaparil, c/Chaparil, almost next door to the *Hostal Alhambra* (see map). Officially a flamenco club for members only; the surroundings may be too intimate for outsiders on regular nights, but it's well worth finding out when there are concerts and fiestas.

Peña de Flamenco Solea, c/Antonio Millon s/n next to *Discoteca Jimmy*. Nerja's most authentic flamenco club which welcomes visitors to their *espectaculos* providing they have a genuine interest.

Around Nerja

A popular excursion from Nerja is the six-kilometre-trip north to **FRIGILIANA**, a pretty Moorish hill village clinging to the lower slopes of Monte El Fuerte. After the *reconquista*, Frigiliana became a Morisco settlement where only those Moors who had converted to Christianity were allowed to live. Although a little of the atmosphere of this period survives in the steep, narrow streets, the place is prettified today by the addition of geranium pots and historical plaques.

In keeping with the village's status as a tourist draw, some of the restaurants and bars here tend to be overpriced, but if you want to **stay over**, the hospitable *Hotel Las Chinas*, Plaza Capitán Cortés 14 (☎95 253 30 73; ④), is a good bet for balcony rooms with bath, and may be able to supply a village map. They also have a good restaurant, and the proprietor, Miguel Castillo, can advise (in Spanish) on walking in the area. Other good **eating places** are *La Bodeguilla*, an excellent family-run restaurant in the upper village, the nearby *Restaurante Jaime* and the *Aserradero Ingenio*, an old sawmill converted into a bar with pleasant terrace. Six **buses** per day leave for Frigiliana from the bus station in Nerja, the earliest of which give you enough time to take a walk in the surrounding hills and get back before the last bus returns at 7.30pm.

Cynics might find the "accidental" discovery in 1957 of the **CUEVAS DE NERJA** (daily 10am–2pm & 4–8pm; 650ptas) – neatly coinciding with the arrival of mass tourism – a little suspect. Immediately they were revealed, the series of enormous caverns, scattered with Paleolithic and Neolithic tools, pottery and cave paintings stretching back 30,000 years, became a local, then national, sensation. Nowadays, however, the fairy lights, piped muzak, and a cave theatre – which hosts various shows from rock to ballet and flamenco – can't help but detract from the appreciation of a spectacular natural wonder, and the cave paintings are currently not on public view and possibly never

WALKS AROUND FRIGILIANA

One easy walk (roughly 3–4hr) is to follow the 15km dirt track through the foothills of the **Almijara range**, leading from Frigiliana, via the hamlet of Venta del Jaro, to the Axarquía village of Cómpeta (see p.103), which has good facilities and accommodation.

Another circular 8km walk covers the **hill country** to the northwest of Frigiliana. Follow the road north out of the village towards the pleasant refreshment stop of *Venta de Frigiliana* (summer daily 11am–4pm) which you'll reach after 3km. Turn left down the dirt track just beyond the entrance, which leads down the ridge, passing some old cottages and villas. Ten minutes or so further on you'll pass the gates of the *Peñones* and the *Cortijo del Peñon* farmhouses on the right. Continue down this track between pine woods and crags until you reach a crossroads, with a walled villa on the far side. Fork sharply left at this point, passing some more old cottages on the right. One of these has a single palm tree, the ancient Moorish sign of welcome. At the first fork, below a large villa, continue left, uphill. The road winds round the villa wall, swings right and crosses the lower Pedregal valley, from where it climbs up the hill to the col on the Loma de la Cruz. Just below the crest of the ridge, where a *carril* (track) comes up from the right, keep straight on up, passing a villa. In front of this villa, a water-cover stamped "SAT no. 7196 Monte Ariza" will confirm that you're on the right road. At the col, go straight across at the cross-tracks marked with red paint and follow the track down and round, keeping left of the fork on the next ridge. This will bring you down past the *Casa del Valle*, on the left. A little further on, round the bend, you'll see some tumbledown houses on the right; the first of these contains an old olive or wine press which is worth a look. The *carril* now passes through open country, then through *huertas*, rejoining the Torrox road at *Casa Fernando*. A right and then a left turn will take you to the upper car park on the edge of Frigiliana.

will be. However, you might want to seek out the world's longest known **stalactite** – all 63m of it and verified by the *Guinness Book of Records* – whilst you're probing the depths. The **restaurant** at the cave entrance serves an economical buffet, but can resemble a train station in the busy high season. A far better place to eat is the *Hostal al Andalus*, down the hill, which serves an excellent-value *menú* often featuring paella and delicious *peras al vino* (pears in wine); there's a terrace here, too. From Nerja the caves are an easy three-kilometre-walk east along the main coast road; there's also a bus service running approximately hourly from the Nerja bus station.

Further east of Nerja, the coastal road zigzags around the foothills of the Sierra Almijara, climbing above a number of tiny coves. The first settlement, the coastal hamlet of **MARO**, is a sparkling cluster of white-walled houses set above an attractive cove beach. Lying close to the ancient Roman settlement of *Detunda*, the town was revitalized in the eighteenth century by the construction of a sugar factory, now a ruin behind the simple church of Nuestra Señora de las Maravillas, which dates from the same period. There are three **places to stay**. *Hotel Playa Maro* (☎95 252 95 82, fax 95 252 96 22; ⑦) is a formal hotel at the entrance to the village but *Casa Maro* (☎95 252 96 90, fax 95 252 95 52; ⑥), a German-run apartment hotel with sea-view balconies and parrots in their garden, is much the better option; they also have special deals for students. Slightly cheaper studios – sleeping up to four people – are on offer from *Balcón de Maro*, Plaza de Maravillas (☎95 252 95 23, fax 95 252 26 08; ⑨), near the church.

The Costa Tropical (west)

The **Costa Tropical** is the name given to Granada Province's 60km of coastline, much of it refreshingly tranquil after the concrete sprawls along the Costa del Sol; its western stretch, including the attractive towns of **Almuñecar** and **Salobreña**, is most conveniently reached from Nerja.

Beyond Nerja, the N340 passes tracks leading down to inviting coves with quiet **beaches**, a few of which have welcoming bars. One, the Torre Caleta, lies just below the bridge which marks the border of Málaga and Granada provinces. Entering Granada Province, the N340 launches into one of the most panoramic stretches along the whole coast, climbing and twisting inland before running along sheer cliffs high above the jagged coast. Eventually it surfaces at **LA HERRADURA**, a fishing village-resort suburb of Almuñécar, and for anyone with their own transport a good place to stop off and swim. **Rooms**, however, don't come cheap here – *Hostal Peña Parda*, Peña Parda Playa (☎958 64 00 66; ④) at the western end of the seafront, is the most reasonable, although there's also a summer **campsite**, *La Herradura* (☎958 64 00 56) which gets overloaded in high season. Good *raciones* are to be had at *El Tinao*, a friendly little **bar** on the Paseo Marítimo seafront. The next headland, the Punta de la Mona, gives way to a fine view of the spur of Almuñécar, crowned by its castle.

Almuñécar

ALMUÑÉCAR is Granada's flagship seaside resort and although marred by a number of towering holiday apartments, has made admirable attempts to preserve its Andalucian character. Founded early in the first millennium BC by the Phoenicians – believe it or not – as *Sexi*, it possesses ruins both from this and its later Roman and Moorish periods. The town's pebble beaches, it has to be said, are rather cramped and not improved by the greyish sand, but the esplanade, **Paseo Puerta del Mar** (aka Paseo del Altillo), behind them, with palm-roofed bars (many offering free *tapas*) and restaurants, is fun, and the *casco antiguo*, or old town, is attractive.

Arrival and information

The **bus station** – with frequent connections to Granada and Málaga – is at the junction of Avda. Juan Carlos I and Avda. Fenicia, northeast of the centre. Inconveniently, the **Turismo**, Avda. Europa s/n, one block in from the Playa San Cristóbal (Mon–Sat 10am–2pm & 6–9pm; ☎958 63 11 25, fax 958 63 50 07), is at the opposite end of town (a good ten-minute walk away), near the sea. It is, however, located in a striking nineteenth-century neo-Moorish mansion and is well worth a look. The Turismo also has information on Almuñécar's annual **jazz festival** – now one of the most important in Spain – held in July and often attracting big names. Following Avda. de Andalucía from the bus station through the old town will take you to many of the town's *hostales* and *fondas*.

Accommodation

The pressure on **accommodation** in Almuñécar is not quite as acute as back at Nerja. Half a dozen good-value *fondas* and *hostales* encircle the central Plaza de la Rosa in the old town, as well as, just east of here, in the streets off the Avda. de Andalucía. Almuñécar's beachfront **campsite**, the misnamed *El Paraíso* (☎958 63 23 70) on the eastern edge of town, is a claustrophobic hell-hole with cars and tents jammed in like sardines during high-season. The resort's other campsite, *Carambalo* (☎958 63 03 22) is some way inland off the N340 heading east; La Herradura (see opposite) is perhaps a better bet for camping.

Hotel Casablanca, Plaza San Cristóbal 4 (aka Plaza Abderramán) (☎958 63 55 75). Excellent family-run establishment with flamboyant neo-Moorish facade, and balcony ensuite rooms with sea view. In slack times you can often (amicably) haggle the price down a bit. ⑥.

Hotel Epsylon, Paseo de la China 5 (☎ & fax 958 63 42 02) at the extreme western end of the seafront. Giant hotel offering bargain-priced rooms with bath and sea view balcony. ④.

Hotel Helios, Paseo San Cristóbal s/n (☎958 63 44 59, fax 958 63 44 69). Almuñécar's leading hotel on the seafront is functional and offers comfortable rooms and a pool. ⑦.

Hostal Plaza Damasco, c/Cerrajeros 8 (☎958 63 01 65). Cosy and recently renovated *hostal* just off the plaza it's named after. ③.

Hostal Rocamar, c/Córdoba 3 (☎958 63 00 23). Pleasant French-owned place near the bus station, offering rooms with bath. ③.

Hostal Tropical, Avda. Europa s/n (☎958 63 34 58). Near the beach, with comfortable en-suite rooms. A good deal, considering its position. ④.

Hostal Victoria, Plaza de la Victoria 6, off Avda. de Andalucía (☎958 63 00 22). Impersonal, hostel-style place owned by the more expensive hotel (also good) of the same name a few doors away. Budget rooms with bath are clean and most have balconies overlooking the square. ③.

The Town

Almuñécar's impressive **Castillo de San Miguel** (Tues–Sat 10am–12.30pm & 7–10pm, Sun 10am–12.30pm; 300ptas), sitting atop a headland which bisects the resort's two bays, replaced the Moorish Alcazaba – itself built on top of an earlier Roman fort – in the time of Carlos V. Distinctive for its massive tower known as *La Mazmorra* ("the dungeon") this is where, in the Nasrid period, Granada's rulers imprisoned out-of-favour ministers or overweening military commanders whom they saw as a threat. During the *reconquista* it was taken by FERNANDO and Isabel in 1489, three years before the fall of Granada itself, and given the name of Almuñécar's patron saint. Held by the French in the War of Independence, in 1808 it was bombarded by the English navy and largely ruined, after which it served as the the town's graveyard. This was recently dug up – bones, coffins and all – and relocated in a new cemetery on the outskirts of town, and the castle restored. The interior now houses the town's interesting **museum** containing artefacts and information documenting Almuñécar's distinguished three-thousand-year history.

RETURN TO CASTILLO OF THE SUGAR CANES

After being trapped in Spain during the Civil War, in the 1950s Laurie Lee revisited some of the places he knew well, one of which was Castillo (a pseudonym for Almuñécar). He describes the pain of this experience in *A Rose for Winter*:

"Everything now was as it had been before – though perhaps a little more ignoble, more ground in dust. As I walked through the town time past hung heavy on my feet. The face of a generation had disappeared completely. A few old women recognized me, throwing up their hands with an exclamation, then came running towards me with lowered voices as though we shared a secret. But of the men I had known there was little news, and such as there was, confused. Most of them, it seemed, were either dead or fled. The old women peered up at me with red-rimmed, clouded eyes, and each tale they told was different. My ex-boss, the hotel keeper, who used to pray for Franco in his office, had been shot as a red spy; he had died of pneumonia in prison; he had escaped to France. Lalo, the hotel porter, had been killed on the barricades in Málaga; he ran a bar in Lyon; he was a barber in Jaén. Young Paco, the blond dynamiter of enemy tanks, was still a local fisherman – you could run into him at any time; no, he had blown himself up; he had married and gone to Mallorca. Luíz, the carpenter, had betrayed his comrades and been stoned to death; he lived in Vélez Málaga; he sold chickens in Granada. ... In the end I gave up. There was no point in making any further inquiries. Nobody lied deliberately, but nobody wished to seem certain of the truth. For the truth, in itself, was unendurable."

Below the castle, to the west in the Parque Botanico El Majuelo, a remarkable **Factoría de Salazones** or Roman fish-curing factory has been excavated. The tanks in which the famous *garum*, a sort of "Gentleman's Relish" (see p.169), was prepared are well-preserved, and the quality of the *garum sexitanus* is recorded in the writings of Pliny the Elder. The surrounding botanical garden is extremely peaceful with fine views towards the castillo and walls (open at all times).

Nearby to the south, the **Parque Ornitológico** (July–Sept daily 11am–2pm & 6–9pm; Oct–March daily 11am–2pm & 4–6pm; 400ptas) is an aviary filled with a squawking collection of 1500 birds representing 120 international species.

In town, it's well worth stopping off at the small **Museo Arqueológico** (Tues–Sat 10am–12.30pm & 7–10pm, Sun 10am–12.30pm; 300ptas), located above and south of the elegant Plaza Ayuntamiento (officially the Plaza de la Constitución, a name nobody uses) in the Cueva de los Siete Palacios or "Cave of the Seven Palaces" – an ancient structure that may well have been a water reservoir. The museum exhibits finds – mostly discovered locally – from the Phoenician, Roman and Moorish periods, including an inscribed seventeenth-century BC **Egyptian vase** which carries not only the oldest piece of written text discovered on the Iberian peninsula, but also the only known reference to the early sixteenth-century BC Pharaoh Apophis I, a ruler during Egypt's hazy Hyksos period when foreign usurpers grasped the throne.

More ancient remains are visible about 1km out of town along the Río Seco, where there's a first-century two-level **Roman aqueduct** that until recently was part of the town's water supply. With your own transport, you could visit another aqueduct opposite the church in the village of Torrecuevas, which you can reach by following the road north towards Otívar for 3km. Three far more spectacular stretches of aqueduct, however, can be seen by turning left up a road signed *"Casa Minerva"* opposite the Venta Luciano on the same village's southern edge. When you reach the Río Seco turn left – the dry river bed is driveable – and after 500m beyond orchards on the left you will see three wonderfully preserved spans including one which is double tiered. This visit could be combined with a trip to the restaurant in Otívar (see below).

Eating and drinking

There are countless **places to eat** lined along the Paseo Puerta del Mar, many of them offering cheap if unspectacular *menús*. But the town's more interesting possibilities lie away from the seafront hurly-burly in the *casco antiguo*. One kilometre out of town is the *Jacquy Cotobro*, an unmissable restaurant worth making the effort to get to and paying the extra for. For **breakfast**, head for the cafés around the Plaza Ayuntamiento in the old town.

Antonio, Paseo Marítimo 12. Great seafront (and not exclusively) fish restaurant and *tapas* bar with an excellent *menú* for about 2500ptas. Try their *aguacate con gambas* (avocado stuffed with prawns).

Restaurante El Capricho, Otívar, 13km north of town (☎958 64 50 75). Great little country restaurant on the north edge of this hill village which is famed for its *pollo a la manzana* (chicken with apples) and *cordero asado* (roast lamb). You'll need to give them at least three hours, notice that you're coming (open lunch and dinner); there's a daily bus from Almuñécar at 2pm and 8.30pm, and they have cheap rooms should you want to stay (②).

Bar-Taberna El Cortijillo, Plaza Kelibia 4. Lively *tapas* bar popular with young locals in an attractive square – one of the few in town with an outdoor terrace.

Jacquy Cotobro, Playa Cotobro. Located in a delightful *cala* (bay) 1km west of the centre and easily reached by following the Paseo San Cristóbal to its end, this is without doubt one of the best restaurants in Andalucía. Belgian chef Jacques Vanhoren has married the best of his native and Spanish cuisines and the result guarantees a memorable dining experience. The best doesn't come cheap, but the *menú gastronómico* at 3500ptas is worth every peseta.

Bar-Restaurante Cuchi, c/Alta del Mar 10, near Plaza de la Rosa. Friendly small restaurant with an 875ptas *menú* which includes wine and a *licor* on the house to round it off.

Los Geranios, Plaza de la Rosa 4. Good-value restaurant in the heart of the old quarter.

Horno de Candida, c/Orovia 3, south-west of Plaza Ayuntamiento. The restaurant of Almuñécar's hotel school is located in an elegant mansion which itself incorporates a Moorish bakery (*horno*). The food – prepared under the supervision of top chefs – is outstanding and reasonably priced and there's a delightful roof terrace as well.

Restaurante La Muralla, c/Ángel Gamay s/n. East of Plaza Ayuntamiento, this is an excellent *bodega* serving a range of cheap *tapas* and *comidas*, in a tiny alley off c/San José.

La Trastienda, Plaza Damasco s/n. Decent bar serving excellent *roscos* (doughnuts).

La Última Ola, Paseo Puerto del Mar 4. Pleasant seafront fish restaurant also serving *tapas*.

Nightlife

Almuñécar's **nightlife** moves at a leisurely pace and centres around the bars and discos circling Plaza Rosa and behind the Playa Puerta del Mar.

Agua Tropic, Paseo Velilla s/n at the eastern end of the seafront. Open-air disco with an eclectic taste in sounds, but just the thing on sultry summer nights.

Bodega Francisco, c/Real 15, north of Plaza Rosa. Wonderful old bar with barrels stacked up to the ceiling behind the counter, and walls covered with ageing *corrida* posters and mounted boars' heads. The *fino* and *montilla* are both excellent, and the bar offers a wide range of *tapas* and *platos combinados*. Impromptu flamenco often gets going here.

Kings, Avda. Juan Carlos 23, behind the Playa Puerta del Mar. One of a number of clubs in this zone that pack them in to dance to flamenco-rock and *bakalao* (techno). The nearby *Fantasy* is another popular place.

Salobreña

The road east from Almuñécar crosses the Río Verde and slowly makes its way upwards, past slopes dotted with almond and *chirimoya* (custard apple) trees until, 13km later, a spectacular vista opens up to reveal **SALOBREÑA**, a white town tumbling down a hill topped by the shell of its Moorish castle and surrounded by a sea of sugarcane fields. Comparatively undeveloped, the town is set back a two-kilometre hike from the sea (although there are hourly buses), and is thus less marketable for mass tourism, making it a far more relaxed destination than Almuñécar. Beginning life as a Phoenician city dedicated to Salambo (the Syrian name for the goddess of love), the town retained some importance in Moorish times – as is evidenced by the much restored Alcázar – but then languished in poverty until rescued by more recent prosperity generated, in part, by its new trickles of tourism.

On the eastern side of town, the **Alcázar** (daily 9.45am–2pm & 3.30–10pm; 300ptas) is worth a look, not least for the fine views from its crenellated towers. Below this, down at the foot of the hill, the sixteenth-century church of **Nuestra Señora del Rosario** stands on the site previously occupied by a Moorish mosque. A stone's throw away, the old *Ayuntamiento* houses the town **museum** (same hours and ticket as the Alcázar) which has artefacts from all periods of Salobreña's history. There's also an animated **market** each Monday to Saturday morning in the central Plaza del Mercado, but that's about as far as sightseeing goes.

Practicalities

Buses arrive and leave from the Plaza de Goya, close to the **Turismo**, Plaza de Goya s/n (Tues–Sun 10am–1.30pm & 5–8pm; ☎958 61 03 14), whose town map will help you find your way around; they also do guided visits to the old town on Fridays at 6.30pm. There's usually no problem in finding **accommodation** in Salobreña, even in high season, and the lack of demand is reflected in the low prices. Most of the budget places are on the western side of town. Close to c/de Hortensia, the main avenue winding down from the town to the beach, worthy options include the *Pensión Arnedo*, c/Nueva 21 (☎958 61 02 27; ②), which has terraces in some rooms, and delightful seaviews. Over the road, at no. 21, the *Pensión Mari Carmen* (☎958 61 09 06; ②) is equally nice, with fans in the rooms. Around the corner from here, the family-run *Palomares*, c/Fábrica Nueva 44 (☎958 61 01 81; ②), offers simple rooms (some with bath) above a restaurant and garden.

Places to eat are limited, and the best-quality place to eat in town is probably *El Patio de Rosa*, c/Antequera 4, off Paseo de las Flores near the Alcázar which has a pleasant terrace with fine views. *Mesón de la Villa*, Plaza F. Ramirez de Madrid, not far from the Turismo, is another fine place. *Pensión Palomares* (see above) serves a cheap menú. Otherwise, your best bet is one of the many *chiringuitos* lining the seafront, among which *El Peñon*, on the promontory from which it takes its name, is extremely popular, good value and serves up great paella. When *salobreñanos* want to eat in style they usually head for *Hotel Salambina*, Ctra. de Málaga s/n (☎958 61 00 37; ④), perched on the head to the west of the town, where the dining room has a balcony view overlooking the Peñon de Salobreña. For **tapas** the old quarter has *Bar-Restaurante Pesetas*, c/Boveda s/n, and Mesón *Rincon Yusuf*, c/Agrela 4, both close to the church of Nuestra Señora del Rosario. At the south end of town, *Rincón de Miguel*, c/Guadalfeo 3, is another option.

The Costa del Sol

West of Málaga – or more correctly, west of Málaga airport – the real **Costa del Sol** gets going. If you've never seen this level of touristic development before, it's going to come as quite a shock, not least when you see how grit-grey the sands are; you have to keep going, around the corner to Tarifa, before you reach the golden sands of the tourist brochures. With their faceless 1960s' and 1970s' concrete tower blocks, these are certainly not the kind of resorts you find in Greece or even Portugal. Since the 1980s' boom in time-share apartments and leisure complexes, it's estimated that 300,000 foreigners live on the Costa del Sol, the majority of them retired and British.

THE CARRETERA NACIONAL N340

A special note of warning has to be made about the **Costa del Sol's main highway**, which is one of the most dangerous roads in Europe. Nominally a national highway, it's really a 100-kilometre-long city street, passing through the middle of towns and *urbanizaciones*. Drivers treat it like a motorway, yet pedestrians have to get across, and cars are constantly turning off or into the road – hence the terrifying number of accidents, with, on average, over a hundred fatalities a year. A large number of casualties are inebriated British package tourists who are unfamiliar with left-hand-drive vehicles and traffic patterns. The first few kilometres, between the airport with its various car rental offices and Torremolinos, are among the most treacherous, but worse still is the stretch heading west from Marbella: around thirty accidents a year occur on each kilometre between Marbella and San Pedro.

A new full-scale, four-lane toll motorway to replace it – the **Autopista del Sol** – linking Málaga with Estepona in the west and Nerja in the east is now nearing completion, and the first stretch as far as Marbella is already open. Charges to use the road are steep (high-season tolls cost between 450–750ptas for relatively short stretches of road and around 1300ptas for the whole Málaga – Estapona journey; low-season rates are roughly half this) and due to misleading road signs it is easy to end up paying the toll without intending to. At the time of writing most locals seem to have given the new road (and its high charges) the thumbs down and the N340 – whose congestion the motorway was intended to relieve – is as bad as ever, leaving the new *autopista* often devoid of traffic, which may be a perfect reason for you to use it.

Meanwhile, if you're using the old N340 don't make dangerous (and illegal) left turns from the fast lane – use the *"Cambio de Sentido"* junctions which allow you to reverse direction. Also be particularly careful after a heavy rain, when the hot, oily road surface sends you easily into a skid. **Pedestrians** should cross at traffic lights, a bridge or an underpass if possible.

On the other hand, the cheap package tour industry – largely responsible for the transformation of the string of poverty-stricken fishing villages that dotted this coast until the 1950s – no longer brings in the numbers it once did, placing the future of purpose-built resorts such as Torremolinos in peril.

Approached in the right kind of spirit, it *is* possible to have fun in **Torremolinos**, and, at a price, in **Marbella**. The sea, at least, is reasonably clean around here, after a lot of work on the sewerage systems. But if you've come to Andalucía to discover the real Spain, or even just to forget what inner-city housing looks like, put on your shades and keep going at least until you reach **Estepona**.

Torremolinos

The approach to **TORREMOLINOS** – easiest on the electric railway from Málaga or the airport – is a depressing trawl through a drab, soulless landscape of kitchenette apartments and half-finished developments. The town itself, rechristened "Torrie" by English package tourists, it has to be said is certainly an experience: a vast, grotesque parody of a seaside resort with its own kitschy fascination. This bizarre place, lined with sweeping (but crowded) beaches and infinite shopping arcades, crammed with Irish pubs and real-estate agents, has a large permanent expat population of Britons, Germans and Scandinavians. It's a weird mix, which, in addition to thousands of retired people, has attracted – due to a previous lack of extradition arrangements between Britain and Spain – a notorious concentration of British Jack-the-lad crooks. Torremolinos's social scene is also bizarre, including a thriving transvestite scene among the middle-of-the-road family discos.

In recent years a dynamic town council has been moving heaven and earth to rid the resort of its "Terrible Torrie" image, and whilst they've stopped short of flattening the concrete monsters overlooking the beach they have made a few commendable improvements. The new seafront promenade which runs all the way to La Carihuela can be quite scenic in parts and the maze of alleys in the old town – now largely cleared of their tawdry boutiques and tacky stalls – also have some charm.

Torremolinos will never be Marbella; its whole purpose is geared to giving people a roaring good time, and if that's what you're looking for, there are few places on the coast with as many bars and discos. Throughout the summer the municipality puts on an infinite variety of free events, including festivals of music, dance and jazz, as well as beach volleyball and football competitions and children's theatre.

Arrival and information

The **train** from Málaga drops you right in the centre of the action, on Paseo de la Nogalera (☎95 236 02 02), a couple of blocks west of the town's main artery, c/San Miguel. The **bus station** (☎95 238 24 19) is a five-minute walk away on c/Hoyo, to the east. The main **Turismo** at Plaza Pablo Picasso, a little to the north of Plaza Costa del

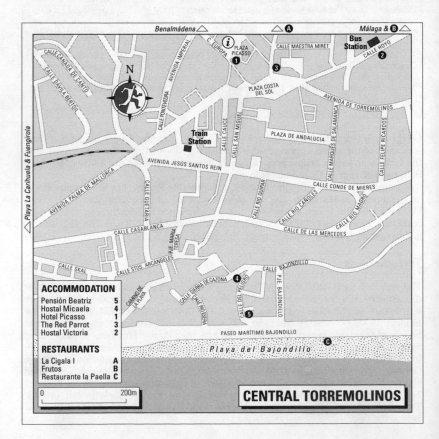

CENTRAL TORREMOLINOS

ACCOMMODATION
Pensión Beatriz	5
Hostal Micaela	4
Hotel Picasso	1
The Red Parrot	3
Hostal Victoria	2

RESTAURANTS
La Cigala I	A
Frutos	B
Restaurante la Paella	C

0   200m

Sol (Mon–Fri 9.30am–1.30pm; ☎95 237 95 12), is supported by a number of other **sub offices** which open longer hours; the most convenient are located on the seafront at Plaza del Lido (daily 10am–2pm & 5–8pm) southeast of the centre, and in the small fishing village of **La Carihuela** (1km west of the town centre) at Plaza Borbollón (daily 10am–2pm & 5–8pm).

Accommodation

It's usually easy enough to find a **place to stay** in Torremolinos, with plenty of economical *hostales* sandwiched between the highrise horrors, and a couple of very pleasant places a little further out. You'll find a **campsite** (☎95 238 26 02) 3km east of the centre on the main Málaga–Cádiz highway, 500m from the sea. To get there, take the *cercanía* train (get off at Los Alamos) or go by bus (Línea B) from outside the central Plaza Costa del Sol. The campsite is near *Hotel Los Alamos*, in the *urbanización* of the same name.

Apartamentos Alegría, c/Carmen 23, La Carihuela (☎95 238 06 38, fax 95 237 27 35). Pleasant, two-person seafront serviced apartments with kitchen and bath available for minimum stays of three days. ⑤.

Pensión Beatriz, c/del Peligro 4, Playa Bajondillo (☎95 238 51 10). Small and good-value *hostal* which has rooms with bath and sea view. ③.

Hostal Flor Blanco, Paseo de la Carihuela 4 (☎95 238 20 71). Clean rooms with bath, and some with sea view, 50m from the beach in La Carihuela. ④.

La Fonda Benalmádena, c/Santo Domingo 7, Benalmádena Pueblo (☎ & fax 95 256 82 73). A tranquil oasis sited in the inland hill village of Benalmádena 4km west of Torremolinos. This charming hotel has fine views, a pool, and pleasant rooms – including breakfast – which are often available in high season; they also have some apartments in the village for the same price. ⑥

Hotel Miami, c/Aladino 14, west of the centre in La Carihuela (☎95 238 52 55). One of the most charming hotels on the whole Costa del Sol, this enchanting villa was built by a cousin of Picasso and contains many of the original designer furnishings. Behind its walls is a garden filled with palms and oleanders and a swimming pool. ⑤.

Hostal Micaela, c/Bajondillo 4 (☎95 238 33 10, fax 95 267 68 42). Serviceable rooms with bath, close to the beach. ④.

Hotel Picasso, Plaza Independencia s/n, to the north of Plaza Costa del Sol (☎95 238 76 00, fax 95 238 78 23). Upmarket hotel in a quiet plaza. ⑦.

The Red Parrot, Avda. Los Manantiales 4 (☎95 237 54 45). Bang in the centre, all rooms with balcony and bath. ⑤.

Hotel Tiburón, c/Los Nidos 7, La Carihuela (☎95 238 13 20). Small but decent hotel with pool. All rooms have bath and TV and some have sea views. ⑤.

Hostal Victoria, c/Los Naranjos 103, opposite the bus station (☎95 238 10 47). Well-located *hostal*, offering rooms with bath. Try bargaining for a reduction out of August. ④.

The Town

To get the flavour of Torremolinos, take a stroll along Calle San Miguel, the main pedestrian mall east of the train station. Cutting through the old quarter (which even has a fourteenth-century Moorish tower), the street is lined with garish illuminated signs, tatty amusement arcades and boutiques, and even tattier restaurants serving steak and kidney pie and all its variations. It's an intriguing blend of the smart and the squalid, bargains and rip-offs. One haven of tranquillity is George's Secondhand Bookshop, on the first floor at no. 26; an excellent source of used paperbacks.

Unlike the street itself, the maze of alleys around c/San Miguel give you a flavour of the old town prior to the tourist invasion and are dotted with bars used by locals. The new seafront promenade is quite scenic in parts, and runs east all the way to the village of La Carihuela, the more elegant (and slightly saner) part of the resort, with a decent beach and a number of good fish restaurants on the seafront.

To the west Torremolinos merges imperceptibly into **Benalmádena Costa**, which is the fairly forgettable coastal offspring of the pleasant inland hill village of the same name. Besides being noted for Tivoli World, the Costa del Sol's biggest **amusement park** at Arroyo de Miel (daily 6pm–3am; 600ptas; ☎95 244 28 48), the resort is not as frenetic as its brash neighbour and the beach is usually less crowded.

Eating, drinking and nightlife

Hidden away among the many culinary disasters of Torremolinos are a surprising number of excellent **bars** and **restaurants** offering good value for money. At the cheaper end of the scale the sheer competition between outlets is so intense that if you're prepared to walk round, checking a few prices, you can have a decent night out for remarkably little money. For **afternoon tea** or an after-dinner coffee with scrumptious *pasteles* (cakes), head for *Pastelería Lepanto*, c/San Miguel 52 or the equally good *Goyesca* on the same street at No. 42.

La Bodega, c/San Miguel 40, near the town end. Good central *tapas* bar with small *comedor*. Specials include *boquerones en vinagre* (anchovies) and *ensalada de pulpo* (octopus).

La Cigala I, Avda. Los Manantiales 23, north of Plaza Costa del Sol and opposite Supermercado Supersol. Lively *marisquería* with fine fish and a bargain lunchtime *menú* for 750ptas.

Frutos, Avda. Riviera 80, Los Alamos, near the *Los Alamos Hotel* on the east side of town. Medium-priced, high-quality fish and meat restaurant with a terrace. Closed Sun eve.

Casa Guaquin, c/Carmen 37, La Carihuela. Excellent fish restaurant on the seafront, with a terrace and a great *tapas* bar. As well as pricey à la carte specialities, including *rape a la marinera* (monkfish) and *dorada a la sal* (sea bream), there's a good-value *menú*. Closed Thurs.

Restaurante La Huerta, c/Decano Higueras del Castillo 1, La Carihuela, near the *Hotel Miami*. Great little mid-priced restaurant festooned with plants and vines outside, serving up tasty fish and meat dishes. Closed Wed.

El Mesón de la Bodega, c/Conde de Mieres 11, near Plaza de Andalucía. Quality *tapas* haunt run by the same proprietors as *La Bodega* (above). Specials include *revuelto de ajetes* (young garlic shoots with scrambled eggs) and *morcilla* (blood sausage). There's also a *comedor* for diners.

Restaurante La Paella, Paseo Marítimo Bajondillo. One of the better central seafront fish restaurants, with moderate prices.

Bodega Quitapeñas, c/San Miguel s/n. Delicious *tapas* and *raciones* served in a bustling bar with small terrace by the steps at the beach end of c/San Miguel.

Restaurante El Roqueo, c/Carmen 35, La Carihuela. Very good mid-priced fish restaurant on the seafront, with terrace. Specialities include *fritura malagueña*. Superb *tapas* at the bar. Closed Tues.

Nightlife

When night falls, Torremolinos comes into its own, with a vibrant **nightlife** lifting off in high summer at about 10pm and continuing well beyond dawn. Some of Europe's biggest and brashest discos can be found here, mostly clustered around the **Avda. Palma de Mallorca**, to the west of the Plaza Costa del Sol. The resort also has a fairly decent **flamenco** scene, and while it's hardly *flamenco puro*, if you take it on its own terms you'll have fun.

Atrevete, Avda. Salvador Allende s/n, opposite the *Hotel Pez Espada* in La Carihuela. Salsa venue with two dance floors and a real party atmosphere.

New Pipers Disco, Avda. de Palma Mallorca s/n. With eight dance floors, go-go girls and stage performers, this claims to be the biggest club in Europe. They've also managed to squeeze in a World War II fighter plane suspended from one ceiling. *Metropolis* and *Paladium* are similar places nearby.

Voltage, Pasaje Emilio Estebán, just off the north end of Avda. Palma de Mallorca. The main *bakalao* joint where a youthful crowd go mental to deafening techno rhythms.

El Carrete Pasaje Decano, near the *Hotel Pez Espada* in La Carihuela. Flamenco venue, and the most authentic you'll get in Torremolinos. Free entry, but you'll have to fork out 1000ptas for your first drink. Turn up after 10pm.

Fuengirola

FUENGIROLA, a thirty-minute train journey from Torremolinos, or a rapid 21km along the old N340 or the new toll *autopista*, is very slightly less developed and infinitely more staid, middle-aged and family-oriented than "Torrie". Fuengirola's two sights are easily located: on the road west out of town there's the restored but impressive **castillo**, a tenth-century fortress built by Abd ar-Rahman III of Córdoba, as well as the scanty remains of a **Roman temple** at the eastern end of the Paseo Marítimo. Further in, the rather dull Plaza de la Constitución is officially Fuengirola's centre, but most people are here for the **beach**; a huge, long strand divided into restaurant-beach strips, each renting out lounge chairs and pedal-boats. At the far end is a windsurfing school.

Practicalities

Fuengirola's helpful **Turismo** (Mon–Fri 9.30am–2pm & 4.30–7pm, Sat 10am–1pm; ☎95 246 74 57) can supply a town map and is located at Avda. Jesús S. Rein 6, close to the train (☎95 247 85 40) and bus (☎95 247 50 66) stations. Fuengirola's **internet café**, *Daytona*, is located at Edificio Solplaya 6 in c/Martinez Catena, a couple of blocks south-west of the Turismo. **Accommodation** is only a problem in August when you'll struggle to find anything at all. The friendly *Hostal Italia*, c/de la Cruz 1 (☎95 247 41 93; ⑤) is the nicest option around the Plaza de la Constitución or, continuing along c/Capitan would bring you to *Hostal Cuevas*, c/Capitan 7 (☎95 246 06 06; ④) which also has pleasant rooms with bath. Off the opposite (west) side of the Plaza Constitución *Hostal Marbella*, c/Marbella 34 (☎95 247 58 02; ④) is a slightly cheaper and more basic option. There's a **campsite** (☎95 247 41 08) 2km to the east of the centre (bus Línea Roja from Avda. Ramón y Cajal) on the main Marbella road.

The streets to the south of the main square are lined with **restaurants** of a rather depressing similarity. Three exceptions are *Restaurante Romy*, c/Moncayo 10, serving fish at fair prices with a cheap menú; the excellent *Restaurante Moreno*, nearby in the same street, which also specializes in fish with a 1200ptas menú; and *Mesón Don Pé*, c/de la Cruz s/n, for mid-price meat dishes (evening only). Plaza Constitución has the pleasant *La Plaza*, a good breakfast and *tapas* bar with a terrace. A charming enclosed square Plaza Yates, just to the west of here, is also worth a look and is a focus for numerous **tapas bars** in the surrounding streets. A little-known gem is *Sol y Sombra*, near the start of c/Maestro Aspiazu, slightly northwest of the Turismo, which serves wholesome food and is located in a workers' quarter. For something a bit more refined, *Bar La Paz Garrido* on the Avda. de Mijas just north of the Plaza de la Constitución serves some of the best seafood in town – the *gazpacho* and *cazón* (shark) here are recommended. On the seafront, *Restaurante Portofino*, Paseo Marítimo Rey de España 29, is a medium-priced place serving classy Italian and international dishes to a high standard. At the other extreme, a couple of seafront "as much as you can eat" places are good value if you're on a tight budget: *Versalles,* Paseo Marítimo 3, and *Las Palmeras* at Paseo Marítimo s/n, nearer the harbour, both charge around 850ptas to gorge yourself. A rare **vegetarian restaurant** *Vegetalia*, has opened at the junction of calles Santa Ana and Santa Isabel, to the east of the Turismo off Avda. Santos Rein, serving up a variety of salads and bean-based dishes.

Nightlife is centred around the bars and discos to the west of Plaza Constitución in the streets circling Plaza Yates and to the north of the harbour where, sharing space with some good *chiringuitos* on the seafront, a fair number of expat singalong bars boom out after sunset with tuneless bellowing in English and Dutch. A **flamenco** bar, *La Bamba*, c/Cervantes 7, south of Plaza Constitución, puts on a decent show on Tuesdays and Wednesdays at 10.30pm, but get your tickets in advance.

Mijas

Often grouped with the more famous white towns further north (see p.139), the once tranquil hill town of **MIJAS**, a winding eight-kilometre climb into the hills above Fuengirola from where it is served by frequent **buses**, is sited a little too close to the Costa del Sol for its own good, making it an obvious target for bus tours in search of the "typical" Andalucian village. However, despite a host of tacky gift shops and the numbered *burro* (donkey) taxis which transport visitors around the main square, the village retains some of its original character, and there are fine views towards the coast. The ancient Plaza de Toros which claims – wrongly – to be Andalucía's only rectangular bullring, is worth a look. Above the square, the ludicrous *Carromato de Max* (daily 10am–9pm), a wagon full of junk, claims to house "the smallest curiosities in the world". If items such as Churchill's head sculpted from a stick of chalk, a copy of Leonardo's *Last Supper* painted on a grain of rice, or the shrunken head of a white man retrieved from South American indians and "certified genuine by the FBI" grab you, then it's well worth the 500ptas entry fee.

After dusk, when the day-trippers have gone, the village is far more peaceful. Should you fancy **staying overnight**, the excellent value *Pensión Romana*, c/Coín 47 (☎95 248 53 10; ②), has apartment-style rooms including fridge and stove. To get there, find your way to Plaza de la Constitución, a small square below the bullring, and ask for directions, as the house itself has no sign.

For **food**, *Bar-Restaurante Alarcón*, c/Lasta 1, near the centre of the village, is good-value and has a pleasant roof terrace with fine views. Another good, if pricier, bet is the Belgian-French *Finca La Capucine*, roughly halfway along the road between Fuengirola and Mijas, serving up mouthwatering dishes such as *cordonices flambeadas* (quail) and equally tasty desserts.

Marbella

Undisputedly the "quality resort" of the Costa del Sol, **MARBELLA** stands in considerable contrast to most of what's come before. Sheltered from the winds by the hills of the Sierra Blanca, it has a couple of excellent **beaches** which first brought it to the attention of the 1960s' smart set. However, don't strain your eyes for celebrities nowadays; the only time the mega-rich descend from their villas in the hills is to attend a private club or put in an appearance at glitzy places like the *Puente Romano Hotel* on the way to San Pedro, where a beluga caviare starter in the restaurant will cost you the price of a good hotel room. Marbella's image took a nose dive in the 1970s when British crooks and drug barons began setting up home here, bringing their feuds and rivalries with them. A series of brutal gangland killings – usually carried out at luxury mansions rather than on the streets – led one police chief to describe the town as "Spain's Marseille". Recently the police are even more exercised by the arrival of Russian and Italian mafia bosses who control their empires from luxury villas and yachts harboured in nearby Puerto Banus. In an ironic twist of history, there's also been a massive return of Arabs to the area, especially since King Fahd of Saudi Arabia built a White House lookalike, complete with adjacent mosque, on the town's outskirts.

Arrival and information

The bus will drop you at the new bus station which is a twenty-minute walk north from the centre, at the end of c/Trapiche (☎95 276 44 00). Buses from Estepona and San Pedro de Alcántara (heading east) and Fuengirola (heading west) still make stops in the centre. Otherwise you are best advised to take buses #2 or #7 from the bus station which will drop you near to the centre of the old town, the *casco antiguo*. The **Turismo**

THE MAYOR OF MARBELLA

Marbella's notoriety in the rest of Spain today springs not from its glitterati or gangsters but from the activities of its over-the-top mayor, **Jesús Gil y Gil**, a wildly eccentric businessman whose property development schemes landed him in jail after one of his buildings collapsed in 1969, killing over fifty people (he was subsequently pardoned by General Franco). Mayor of Marbella since 1991, Gil's extreme right-wing ideas win him landslide victories and despite frequent stunts – such as marching through the Puerto Deportivo flanked by police and yelling abuse at the "drunkards, dissolutes and drug addicts" in the open-air bars and cafés – still the vote from the silent majority holds up. His boundless megalomania projected him on to the national stage when he became chairman of leading football team Atlético de Madrid, but an anti-corruption prosecutor recently suspended the whole Atlético board along with Gil and froze the club's accounts pending investigation of serious "financial irregularities" involving the chairman. Scandal and Gil are inseparable and recently Marbella's top judge (and close friend of Gil) Pilar Ramírez, has been sacked and removed from the bench for tampering with cases brought before her court involving the mayor and his business partners who include, it seems, senior members of the Sicilian Mafia. If found guilty of corruption charges Gil faces 34 years in jail and – despite continuing to run the town after being re-elected in 1999 – is currently on bail. A slippery customer when it comes to avoiding the wrath of the authorities, he hatched a plan to stand as a candidate for parliament in a Madrid constituency in the general elections of March 2000 because, as a *diputado* or MP, he could only be tried by the Supreme Court, a cumbersome and time-consuming process. This plan fell through, however, when he was soundly defeated.

These minor irritations have done little to curb Gil's grandiose schemes forMarbella, the latest of which proposes to build a vast offshore island casino complex where the rich can park up their yachts and head straight into the gambling action. His political aspirations are as rampant as his ego and you may notice the huge billboards at the entrance to the town proclaiming "Bienvenidos a Marbella, G.I.L." referring to the national political party he founded and continues to lead, *Grupo Independiente Liberal*, whose acronym says it all.

on the north side of Plaza de los Naranjos (Mon–Fri 9am–9pm, Sat 10am–2pm; ☎95 282 35 50), has excellent street-indexed maps, and produces a leaflet, *Verano Cultural*, detailing the many events held in the town throughout the summer which often star big names. To explore the surrounding hill country or merely cruise the coast you can rent **mountain bikes**, Velosolexes (French motorised cycles), scooters and larger machines from *Rainbow*, Avda. Severa Ochoa 9 (☎95 277 16 99), on the main road that enters the town from the east.

Accommodation

All Marbella's budget **accommodation** is in the old town, on or around c/Luna or, a couple of blocks west, along the pretty c/San Cristóbal, the street of a thousand plants carefully tended by its residents – not without recognition since it has won Marbella's annual "best street" competition more than once. There's also a very good **youth hostel**, c/Trapiche 2 (☎95 277 14 91; ①), with double rooms (some with bath), pool and plenty of activities.

Hostal Berlin, c/San Ramón 21 (☎95 282 13 10, fax 95 282 66 77). Sparkling and friendly German-run *hostal*; all rooms with bath, air conditioning and satellite TV. ⑤.

Castillo de Monda, 14km north of Marbella in the village of the same name (☎95 245 71 42, fax 95 245 73 36). Stunning hill-top castle converted into a palatial hotel with restaurant and pool. ⑦.

Hostal Enriqueta, c/Los Caballeros 18 (☎95 282 75 52). Quiet, comfortable *hostal* in elegant reja-fronted building above the Plaza de los Naranjos. ④.

Hostal La Estrella, c/San Cristóbal 36 (☎95 277 94 72). Nicely located in a pleasant street, offering rooms with bath, and some with balcony. ④.

Hostal Guerra, Llanos de San Ramón 2 (☎95 277 42 20). Clean and simple rooms with bath and some with balcony, near the beach. ④.

Hostal Juan, c/Luna 18 (☎95 277 94 75). One of the nicest and best-value places on this popular street, with clean, ensuite rooms and a friendly atmosphere. ③.

Refugio de Juanar, 12km north of Marbella and signed off the A355 (☎95 288 10 00, fax 95 288 10 01). Tucked away in the pine forests of the Sierra Blanca, this is a luxurious 3-star hotel complete with attractive pool and restaurant. A more tranquil place would be difficult to imagine. Make sure to do the 3km walk to the *Mirador de Juanar* with spectacular views over the coast. ⑦.

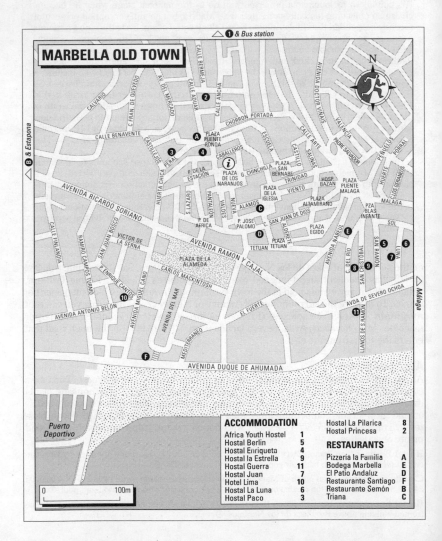

MARBELLA OLD TOWN

ACCOMMODATION		Hostal La Pilarica	8
Africa Youth Hostel	1	Hostal Princesa	2
Hostal Berlin	5	**RESTAURANTS**	
Hostal Enriqueta	4		
Hostal la Estrella	9	Pizzería la Familia	A
Hostal Guerra	11	Bodega Marbella	E
Hostal Juan	7	El Patio Andaluz	D
Hotel Lima	10	Restaurante Santiago	F
Hostal La Luna	6	Restaurante Semón	B
Hostal Paco	3	Triana	C

Hotel Lima, Avda. Antonio Belón 2 (☎95 277 05 00, fax 95 286 30 91). Efficient hotel near the harbour with high balcony rooms offering sea views. ⑦.

Hostal La Luna, c/Luna 7 (☎95 282 57 78). Delightful, spotless *pensión* with balconied rooms around a renovated old patio at the rear; all rooms with bath and fridge. ④.

Hostal Paco, c/Peral 16 (☎95 277 12 00, fax 95 282 22 65). Central *hostal*, all rooms with bath. ④.

Hostal La Pilarica, c/San Cristóbal 31 (☎95 277 42 52). Pretty and good-value *hostal* in lovely location. Rooms with and without bath. ④.

Hostal Princesa, c/Princesa s/n (☎95 282 00 49). Close to the Plaza Puente de Ronda, this friendly *hostal* offers clean, simple rooms. ②.

Hostal El Solar, c/Córdoba 2, Ojen, 7km north of Marbella and served by regular buses (☎95 288 11 49). The *pensión* of this charming hill village makes a pleasant alternative to the hurly burly of staying in town. The village has plenty of places to eat, the best of which is *Restaurante El Patio* on the square. ③.

The Town

Spared the worst excesses of concrete architecture which have been inflicted upon Torremolinos, Marbella itself is decidedly tasteful, retaining the greater part of its old town or **casco antiguo**. Slowly, this original quarter is being bought up and turned over to "quaint" clothes boutiques and restaurants, but you can still sit in an ordinary bar in a small old square and look up beyond the whitewashed alleyways to the mountains of Ronda.

The *casco antiguo*, partially walled, is set back from the sea and hidden from the main road. Here the main sights are clustered in the web of streets surrounding the picturesque **Plaza de los Naranjos**, whose delights are somewhat marred by the invasive terraces of the surrounding restaurants which use it as an open-air dining room. On the plaza (next to the Turismo), the striking sixteenth-century **Ayuntamiento** has fine coffered ceilings. Nearby, in Plaza de la Iglesia, is the church of **Nuestra Señora de la Encarnación**. Built in the sixteenth century, it was later remodelled in the Baroque style and has a fine tower as well as, inside, a striking *retablo*. The **Museo Arqueológico** with Neolithic and Roman finds from the surrounding area – including the Roman villa at Río Verde (see p.125) – is currently closed while a new site is found for it; there is talk of housing a small display in the *Ayuntamiento*; ask at the Turismo for information. In the meantime its former home – a fine Renaissance hospital founded by Alonso Bazán, then mayor of Marbella – now hosts a mildly interesting **Museo del Grabado Contemporáneo**, c/Hospital Bazán s/n (Mon–Fri 10am–2pm & 6–9pm; 300ptas), an engraving museum with works by Miró and Picasso. Northeast of the Plaza de los Naranjos you'll find Spain's one and only Bonsai tree museum, the **Museo Bonsai**, Arroyo de la Represa s/n (daily 10am–1.30pm & 4–8pm; 400ptas) with 150 examples of this arboraceous curiosity.

Eating and drinking

When it comes to **food and drink** you're better off heading for Marbella's numerous and excellent tapas bars, rather than the touristy and overpriced restaurants around the Plaza de los Naranjos. There are, however, a fair number of good-value eating places within a five-minute walk of the square, and following the Avenida del Mar – now lined with Dali bronzes – towards the sea will lead you to the Puerto Deportivo and another zone filled with bars and restaurants.

RESTAURANTS

Bodega Marbella, c/del Río 16, east of the centre. Excellent little bar-restaurant with bags of character, serving a good selection of seafood dishes; the paella is recommended.

El Patio Andaluz, c/San Juan de Dios 4, off Plaza Palomo. Surprisingly inexpensive – and tasty – meat and fish dishes served at tables in the charming patio of a medieval town house.

Pizzería La Familia, c/Cruz 5, off the Plaza Puente de Ronda. Marbella's best pizzas served up in a pleasant atrium dining room.

Restaurante Santiago, Avda. Duque de Ahumada s/n, near the Puerto Deportivo. One of Marbella's swankiest restaurants, attracting many of the town's smart set to its terrace. The food matches the hype, and their 4500ptas *menú* is a bargain. Also has an equally outstanding *tapas* bar.

Restaurante Semón, c/Gregorio Marañón s/n, at the west end of town. Top-notch medium-priced Catalan restaurant behind a delicatessen selling mouthwatering Cátalan comestibles; closes at 4pm (shop open until 9pm), also offers a good-value lunchtime *menú*.

Triana, c/Gloria 11, just south of Plaza de la Iglesia. Superb mid-priced fish restaurant occupying an old *casa señorial* and specializing in *arroz a banda*, a two-course Valencian fish and rice dish, and *gazpacho*; also has a good *tapas* bar.

TAPAS BARS

Bar Altamirano, Plaza de Altamirano 4, south east of Plaza Naranjos. Great place for *tapas* and *raciones*, with tables spread across a small square.

Asador Puerta del Príncipe, Plaza Victoria s/n, west of Plaza de los Naranjos. Despite the touristy ambience, this is a fine *tapas* bar. House specials include *mollejitas* (sweetbreads) and *pimientos* (peppers).

Bar California, junction c/Málaga & c/Severo Ochoa, east of the *casco antiguo*. Excellent *marisco* and *pescado frito* bar, where the *fino* (as proclaimed above the entrance) is as good as the seafood *tapas* and *raciones*. *Casa de los Martinez*, nearby at c/Málaga 7, is another good *tapas* venue.

Bar Guerra, Avda. Ramón y Cajal 5. Just south of the old quarter, with delicious *boquerones fritos al limón* (fresh anchovies) and a wide variety of other seafood *tapas*.

Los Mellizos, Plaza del Marqués del Turia 9. East of the centre and well off the tourist beat, this is a great seafood *tapas* emporium, with a shaded terrace on a multi-levelled plaza. Other places in this area, including *El Tajo* and *Mesón de los Ángeles*, are also good and the *Sala Rociera La Carreta* over the road hosts late-night flamenco.

Marisquería La Pesquera, Plaza de la Victoria s/n, west of Plaza de los Naranjos. A town favourite for *tapas* (although its restaurant is overpriced), with first-class *tapas* and *fino*. House specials include *cigalitas cocidas* (Dublin Bay prawns) and *almejas marinera* (clams in wine).

Cervecería Simon, Avda. Arias Maldonado 1, west of the old town. Fine *tapas* served here at low prices; also has a pleasant terrace. Specials include *chopitos fritas* (cuttlefish) and *patatas bravas*.

CAFÉS AND DRINKING BARS

Café de Africa, c/Buitrago s/n, near Plaza de Africa. Pleasant café-bar which keeps late hours and plays recorded jazz. Both this street and the parallel c/Pantaleón have more late-night music bars.

Atrium, c/Gregorio Marañón 11, west of the centre. One of several fashionable outdoor bars in this area frequented by Marbella's well-heeled for early-evening and late-night drinks.

Kashmir, c/Rafina 6, north of Plaza Puente de Ronda. Blues and jazz bar with a Sixties feel.

Lepanto, Avda. Puerta del Mar s/n, southeast corner of the Alameda. Stylish café just south of the old quarter, which excels in chocolate confectionery creations.

Cafetería Marbella, Alameda Gardens, Avda. Ramón y Cajal. Lovely place to come for breakfast, overlooking the main drag with two shady terraces.

La Notte, Camino de la Cruz s/n, near Plaza Puente de Ronda. Summer terrace inside the *Restaurante Meridiana* much favoured by Marbella's "in crowd".

Nightlife

Marbella has one of the liveliest **nightlife** scenes on the coast, with action centred around Plaza Puente de Ronda, c/Pantaleón, and Plaza Africa, all in the old town. The main street cutting through the centre, Avda. Ramon y Cajal, and the Puerto Deportivo, the seafront yacht harbour, also pulse with life, the latter particularly so in summer when youthful *marbellíes* arrive in their thousands to fill the frenzied discos and music bars beneath the lighthouse until the crack of dawn and beyond. Not surprisingly Mayor Gil regards this zone as a den of iniquity and has tried on numerous occasions to close the whole Puerto scene down. Massive demonstrations and protests by its aficionados have so far prevented him.

San Pedro de Alcántara

The road west of Marbella (providing you don't take the toll-charged Autopista del Sol) soon passes – after 7km – the marina and casino complex of **PUERTO BANUS**, where the jetset park up their yachts. In summer the place presents a bizarre spectacle as crowds of Costa del Sol gawpers come to celebrity-spot, while the bronzed plutocrats attempt to steer their Rolls Royces and Ferraris through the crush to their vessels.

Six kilometres further, and about the only place on the Costa del Sol which isn't purely a holiday *urbanización* is the small town of **SAN PEDRO DE ALCÁNTARA**, a none too inspiring resort striving to go the way of its neighbour but hindered by the fact that its centre is set back over a kilometre from the sea. The seafront area has recently been landscaped with the almost obligatory palm-lined promenade, but this has done little to raise San Pedro's profile. What little activity there is centres on the tranquil, palm-fringed Plaza de la Iglesia in the town proper – at its most lively during the Thursday morning flea market – but there's not much else to disturb the calm. However, there are three remarkable **ancient ruins** in the area (see below) which are definitely worth going out of your way to see. A **Turismo** (daily 10am–midnight; ☎95 278 13 60) located beneath the huge arch over the main N340 to the west of the town can arrange visits to the three (locked) sites mentioned below on either Tuesdays, Thursdays or Saturdays at noon. You will need your own transport and a guide will accompany you to open the sites. This service and entry to the sites is free and although there is no need to book in advance it might be a good idea to ring the day before and let them know you are coming.

The **San Pedro Turismo**, Avda. Marques del Duero 69 – the main street you turn in to when leaving the N340 (Mon–Fri 9am–9pm, Sat 10am–2pm; ☎95 278 90 90) – can supply information on renting apartments for longer stays as well as a map of the town. Should you require **accommodation**, *Pensión Avenida*, c/Las Margaritas 19 (☎95 278 31 92; ④), north of the Plaza de la Iglesia has decent rooms with bath, whilst other possiblities include the basic *Pensión Armando*, just to the south-east of the same square on c/19 Octubre 53 (☎95 278 11 90; ③), and the equally basic *Pensión Marta*, c/Lagasca 24 (☎95 278 33 36; ③), a couple of streets away. For **food** *Alfredos*, Avda. Andalucía 8, west of the main junction with the N340, does good meat and fish *raciones* and the nearby *Restaurante Andalucía*, Avda. Andalucía 4, has an economical *menú* and offers *cocina andaluza* specialities.

Around San Pedro

Four kilometres back along the road east to Marbella is a second-century **Roman villa** at Río Verde. To get there from San Pedro, pass the turn-off for Puerto Banús and, after crossing the river, take a right before the *Puente Romano Hotel* and follow the signs. Constructed in the late first or early second century, the rooms are decorated with an unusual series of black and white **mosaics** depicting not classical themes or intricate designs as elsewhere, but everyday kitchen equipment. The kitchen utensils are a delight, and the shoes portrayed by the door are evidence of the Roman custom of leaving one's footwear outside the *triclinium*, or dining room. One of the amphoras displayed is so accurately portrayed that its style has helped to date the villa almost precisely. Note also the hanging fowl and fish, ready for the pot. The mosaic's theme leads you to wonder who may have been the villa's occupant; perhaps a grand gourmet, or even a wealthy restaurateur (Río Verde was a prosperous area in

Roman times) made rich from catering to the ancient predecessors of nearby Puerto Banús.

The sixth-century **Visigothic Christian basilica** of Vega del Mar lies close to the sea at the bottom of the Avda. del Mediterráneo, the main road out of San Pedro towards the coast. Take the last road on the right before the beach and you'll come to the railed-off site in the midst of a stand of eucalyptus trees. It is one of the most important Visigothic monuments on the peninsula; the remains enable you to make out clearly a rectangular basilica with a double-apse, unique in Spain. Large boulders cemented with lime-mortar were used in its construction along with still-visible brickwork at the corners. A wonderful **baptismal font** is especially well preserved and was deep enough for total immersion, the custom of the time. In and around the basilica is a cemetery of some two hundred tombs (which yielded a wealth of artefacts now in the Marbella and Madrid museums) most with the head to the north, the orientation of the church. Note the graves lined with marble, evidence of social stratification even in death.

The third site, the **Roman bath-house** of Las Bovedas, lies a little way west of here, almost on the beach. Leave any transport at the beach edge *chiringuito* and walk the fifty metres along the beach to the site. The substantial remains belong to an octagonal third-century Roman baths. Seven chambers, which would have served as a series of heated "steam" rooms, surround the well-preserved central bath (parts of the under-floor hypocaust system are visible). Above the central pool was a skylight surrounded by a roof terrace. Because the complex was constructed with a special lime – which, when mixed with sand and pebbles from the beach, set to a granite-like hardness – the building has defied the elements impressively.

Estepona

West of San Pedro the coast road is littered with more depressing *urbanizaciones* bearing names such as *Picasso* or – taking irony to the limit – *Paraíso* (paradise), each served by its *centro comercial*. Should you feel an irresistible urge to stop, **ESTEPONA** 17km beyond San Pedro, is about the only good bet, a more or less Spanish resort with much of its identity still intact. Lacking the enclosed hills that give Marbella character, it is at least developed on a human scale; the hotel and apartment blocks which sprawl along the front are restrained in size, and there's a pleasant EU blue-flagged beach in town, as well as the Costa del Sol's oldest nudist beach to the west.

One of the best, and busiest, times to visit Estepona is during the first week of July, when the *Fiesta y Feria* week brings out whole families in flamenco-style finery and the town is transformed into a riot of colour.

Arrival, information and accommodation

Estepona's **bus station**, on Avda. de España, lies west of the centre behind the seafront. Two hundred metres east of here at the foot of Avda. Juan Carlos I, an efficient **Turismo**, Avda. San Lorenzo 1 (Mon–Fri 9.30am–9pm, Sat & Sun 9.30am–1.30pm; ☎95 280 09 13), will supply town maps and can help you find a room. Outside August you should have no problem finding a **place to stay** in Estepona. The nearest **campsite**, *Chullera III* (☎95 289 03 20), lies 8km south of town, just beyond the village of San Luís de Sabanillas.

Hotel Buenavista, Paseo Marítimo 180 (☎95 280 01 37). Good-value hotel with sea view balcony rooms with bath and TV. ⑤.

Pensión La Malagueña, c/Castillo s/n (☎95 280 00 11). Comfortable and reliable pensión, offering rooms with bath, around the corner from the Plaza Las Flores. ④.

Hotel Mediterráneo, Avda. de España 68, on the seafront to the east of c/Terraza (☎95 279 33 93). Functional but good-value seafront hotel, where rooms have bath, TV and sea views. ⑤.

Hostal El Pilar, Plaza Las Flores (☎95 280 00 18). Friendly *hostal* on a charming plaza; some rooms with bath. ④.

Pensión San Miguel, c/Terraza 16 (☎95 280 26 16). Friendly establishment with its own bar, a little west of the Plaza Las Flores. Some rooms are ensuite. ③.

Pensión Vista al Mar, c/Real 154 (☎95 280 32 47). Barely squeezes in a sea view, thus justifying its name. Simple rooms at the western end of the central zone. ③.

The Town

Estepona is the last stop on the Costa del Sol and one of the most pleasant. By no means as picturesque as Marbella, it makes up in enthusiasm and warmth what it lacks in architecture. The seafront is attractive, with a promenade studded with flowers and palms, and behind this, the older part of the town has some charming corners with cobbled alleyways and two delightful squares, the **Plaza Las Flores** and **Plaza Arce**. Calle Terraza bisects the centre and around this are to be found most of the eating and drinking options, especially along the recently pedestrianised **c/Real**, behind the seafront, which has become the focus for a lively *marcha nocturna*. The **Puerto Deportivo** to the west of town beyond the lighthouse and near the bullring is a daintier version of Marbella's nightspot, with the few bars and discos becoming really animated only at weekends.

The nearby **fish market** is also worth seeing: Estepona has the biggest fishing fleet west of Málaga, and the daily dawn ritual in the port at the western end of the promenade, where the returning fleets auction off the fish they've just caught, is worth getting up early for – be there at 6am, since by 7am it's all over. Afterwards you can head for the animated covered **market**, on c/Castillo, also at its best in the morning. Estepona's **nudist beach**, the Costa Natura, is located a short bus ride away, 4km west of town. From May onward, the town's **bullfighting** season gets underway in a modern bullring reminiscent of a Henry Moore sculpture.

Eating and drinking

Among Estepona's many **places to eat** is a bunch of excellent *freidurías* and *marisquerías*. Worth trying are *El Chanquete* at c/Terraza 86 and the nearby *La Gamba*. *El Barquito*, just off here in c/Reyes, is another good bet, as is *Simonito*, on Avda. San Lorenzo near the Turismo. *La Rada*, Avda. España 4, at the extreme eastern end of the seafront, is a lively *marisquería* popular with locals. **Restaurants** are generally less distinguished, although *Bar La Trocha* on c/Terraza serves good *platos combinados*. For more upmarket eating, head for *La Hierbabuena*, c/Caridad 48, or *Sabor Andaluz*, c/Caridad 44. Good pizzas are on offer at *Sur*, Plazoleta Ortiz 11, which spreads its tables on this leafy square off the eastern end of the promenade.

Of the Estepona **tapas bars**, *Mesón Genaro*, c/Lozano 15 (off c/Terraza), and *La Jerezana* in c/Estremadura nearby, are two of the best. Another good choice, with a distinctly *andaluz* flavour, is *Casa Típico Andaluz*, c/Caridad 55 to the east of c/Terraza, which serves outstanding *jamón* and *queso tapas* and *raciones*; its special, called a *plaza de toros*, gets you a little of everything on one plate for around 1000ptas. For an after-dinner **ice-cream**, *Heladería Vitin* in Plaza Las Flores has the edge, if only for location. The bars in the same plaza – who spread their tables around the central fountain – are also good places for **breakfast**, or try the excellent *churrería* towards the southern end of c/del Mar (one block back from, and parallel to, the promenade) – get there before 11am as they sell out early. For **picnic supplies**, there's a daily market; if you're self-catering, you could try the fish market.

When it comes to **nightlife**, Estepona has a range of possibilities. There are the usual **flamenco** burlesques around which are best avoided, but *Peña Flamenca* in c/Fuerzas Armadas in the north of town puts on the genuine stuff on Saturday nights at 10pm.

Nearer the centre, most action takes place along and in the streets around c/Real where terrace bars, music places and clubs compete for the custom of a mainly – and gratifyingly – local clientele. **Discos** proper are mostly grouped around the **Puerto Deportivo**, a more sedate version of Marbella's, or in town there's *Niagara,* Avda. Juan Carlos, 1300m beyond the Turismo on the left.

Casares

The greyish coast west of Estepona is punctuated with watch towers used by peoples as diverse as Phoenicians, Romans and Arabs to protect themselves from pirate attacks. There's little reason to stop along here but one worthwhile detour is to head to **CASARES**, 18km inland from Estepona. One of the lesser known of Andalucía's white towns, it's a beautiful place, clinging tenaciously – and spectacularly – to a steep hillside below a castle, and attracting its fair share of arty types and expatriates. The village is reputed to take its name from Julius Caesar, who is said to have used the still-functioning **sulphurous springs** at nearby Manilva to cure a liver complaint. More concrete historical evidence attributes the impressive Alcázar (built on Roman foundations) to the Moorish period, from the ruins of which there are spectacular **views** as far as Gibraltar on clear days. There's little else in the way of sights, but it's satisfying enough simply to wander around, losing yourself in the twisting and narrow, white-walled streets – another vestige of the Arab period. Flanked by an eighteenth-century church, the central plaza is a good place to sit and have a drink, cooled by breezes off the sierra. The surrounding hill country, richly wooded with cork oaks and pine as well as stands of *pinsapo,* the rare Spanish fir, offers a verdant contrast with the arid plains below and is fine **walking terrain** with plenty of *caminos* or dirt-tracks to follow winding through the folds of the Sierra Bermeja. With your own vehicle you could return to the N340 by way of Manilva, reached by continuing through Casares and turning left (and south) along the A377 towards Manilva. Alternatively, turning right here would allow you to make a 16km detour to Gaucín (p.141).

Practicalities

Only three **buses** a day (except Sun) leave for Casares from Estepona (11am, 1.30pm & 7pm; return 8.15am 12.45pm & 4pm; 45min) meaning, if you're without transport, a very brief visit, a difficult hitch back on a quiet road, or an **overnight stay**. Should you opt for the latter, head for the central Plaza España, where *Hostal Plaza* (☎95 289 40 30; ②) has good value ensuite rooms above a bar. There are more bars than restaurants in Casares, but decent **places to eat** include *La Terraza,* a restaurant just outside the village on the Estepona road which has great views from its terrace. A small **Turismo,** c/Fuente 91 (Mon–Fri 9am–2pm; ☎95 289 41 26), can provide information about activities such as walking and horse-riding and has a list of *casas rurales* to rent for longer stays.

On to Gibraltar

Beyond Estepona the scenery takes on a wilder and greener aspect as the Sierra Bermeja yields to the Sierra Almenara. Once across the Río Guadiaro, the road turns inland, offering, as it climbs, distant views of the Rock of Gibraltar, its monumental silhouette often girdled with a halo of cloud. The views of the urban sprawl and towers of the Bay of Algeciras's oil refineries signal that this is also a major industrial zone.

San Roque

SAN ROQUE, 35km south of Estepona in Cádiz Province, was founded in 1704 by the people of Gibraltar fleeing the British, who had captured the Rock and looted their homes and churches. They expected to return within months, since the troops had taken the garrison in the name of the Archduke Carlos of Austria, whose rights Britain had been promoting in the War of the Spanish Succession. But it was the British flag that was raised on the conquered territory – and so it has remained. There are few sights, but c/San Felipe, which leads up from the main square to the *mirador*, has some fine *reja*-fronted houses. From the **mirador** you can see the Rock of Gibraltar and the hazy coast of Africa beyond – you'll have to ignore the ugly oil refinery. Nearby, the *Ayuntamiento* displays a banner given to the earlier Spanish Gibraltar by Ferdinand and Isabel, while the eighteenth-century church of **Santa María Coronada** – built over the ancient hermitage of San Roque – has a fine image of the Virgin also rescued from the Rock in the flight from the British invaders. Don't miss taking a look at San Roque's dilapidated **bullring**. Built in the middle of the last century it's now a crumbling pile, with still-inhabited dwellings built into its outer walls reminiscent of the Middle Ages. Surprisingly, it still stages *corridas* during the town's summer *feria*.

Practicalities

San Roque's **campsite**, *Camping San Roque* (☎956 78 00 31), is on the N340 highway just east of the town. Far better, though, if you want to stay is **LOS BARRIOS**, 10km to the west, an atmospheric, tranquil place away from the depressing nature of this industrial zone. There's a good-value *hostal* here on the palm-lined main street, *El Semáforo*, c/Alhóndiga 5 (☎956 62 01 29; ②), the slightly plusher *Hotel Real*, Avda. Pablo Picasso 7 (☎956 62 00 24; ④), and plenty of places to eat and drink. At the other end of the scale, you could stay in palatial luxury at *Monte de la Torre* (☎956 66 00 00, fax 956 63 48 63; ⑨), an Edwardian mansion in its own grounds, with views to Gibraltar and Morocco. To get there, turn left at the end of the palm-lined avenue in Los Barrios and keep going for 3km. The drive leading to the house is signed on the right.

La Línea

Obscured by San Roque's huge oil refinery, the **Spanish-British frontier** is 8km south of San Roque at **LA LÍNEA** ("the line"). When Franco closed the frontier in 1969, it was La Línea that suffered most as workers lost their jobs on the Rock overnight and the town's population dropped by 35 percent. After sixteen years of Spanish-imposed isolation, the gates were re-opened in February 1985, and crossing between here and Gibraltar is now routine – except for the odd flare-up when petulant disputes impose long delays on those waiting to cross. La Línea remains in a depressed state, a fact which has pushed many of its people into assisting the Rock's smugglers by warehousing contraband tobacco prior to its distribution throughout Spain. There are no sights as such; it's just a fishing village which has exploded in size due to the employment opportunities in Gibraltar and the industrialized zone around the Bay of Algeciras.

Practicalities

The **bus station** and **Turismo** (Mon–Fri 8am–3pm, Sat 9am–1pm; ☎956 76 99 50) are both on Avda. 20 Abril, to the south of the main **Plaza de la Constitución**, a large modern square at the heart of La Línea. Their leaflet *Campo de Gibraltar* (100ptas) has street maps of both La Linea and Algeciras and they also give out a free *Ruta del Tapeo* (*tapas* route). The closest main-line train station is San Roque–La Línea, 11km west of town from where you can pick up a train to **Ronda** and beyond.

Although La Línea's greater number of hotels make it a better overnight bet than Gibraltar, many of its **hostales** are depressingly grim and not cheap – with the exception of the ones listed here. Accommodation is concentrated around the Plaza de la Constitución. The friendly *La Campana*, c/Carboneras 3, (☎956 17 30 59; ④), is clean, and has ensuite rooms with TV. Almost opposite, *Hostal-Restaurante Carlos*, c/Carboneras 6 (☎956 76 21 35; ④), is also good value for rooms with bath and TV. Slightly north of here, *Hostal Florida*, c/Sol 37 (☎956 17 13 00; ③), offers more rooms with bath and has a decent restaurant. Cheaper rooms are available at *Pensión La Perla*, c/Clavel 10 (☎956 76 95 13; ②), off the north side of Plaza de la Constitución.

For **eating and drinking**, the *hostales* Campana and Carlos (see above) both have good and economical restaurants. To eat in a more vibrant atmosphere, however, make your way to Plaza Cruz de Herrera, through an arch off the east side of the Plaza de la Constitución. Of the various *tapas* bars and fast-food outlets here, *La Nueva Mesón Jerezana* does good *fino* and *jamón*. C/Real, the main pedestrianized shopping street offers plenty of reasonably priced bars and cafés – good for breakfast pastries – as well as restaurants. *La Venta*, c/Dr Villar 19, just off the north side of the same street, does a good-value *menú* and an excellent paella. *Bar El Choni*, on Plaza Iglesia at the end of c/Real is unmissable and serves a wide range of reasonably priced *tapas* on an animated terrace facing the church. Two of La Linea's best fish restaurants are *La Marina*, Paseo Marítimo s/n, and *Linares*, c/Pavia 4, both north east of the centre and close to the sea. For picnic supplies, head for the market, north of c/Real.

Gibraltar

GIBRALTAR's interest is essentially its novelty: the genuine appeal of the strange, looming physical presence of its rock, and the increasingly dubious one of its preservation as one of Britain's last remaining colonies. This enormous hunk of limestone, five kilometres long, two kilometres wide and 450 metres high – a land area smaller than the city of Algeciras across the water – has fascinated and attracted the people of the Mediterranean basin since Neanderthal times, confirmed by the finds of skulls and artefacts in a number of the Rock's many caves.

The Rock is a curious place to visit, not least to witness the bizarre process of its opening to mass tourism from the Costa del Sol. Ironically, this threatens both to destroy Gibraltar's highly individual society and at the same time to make it much more British, after the fashion of the expat communities and huge resorts up the coast. The frontier opening has benefited most people: locals can buy cheaper goods in Spain, while expats living on the Costas can pick up from stores like Safeway, Tesco and Marks & Spencer such familiar essentials as baked beans, sliced bread and women's underwear. In recent years the economic boom Gibraltar enjoyed throughout the Eighties, following the reopening of the border with Spain, has started to wane. The colony has reached yet another crossroads in its tortuous history and the likely future – whether its population agrees to this or not – is almost certain to involve closer ties with Spain.

Some history

Recent discoveries in a cave on the southeast tip of the Rock – flint tools and evidence of camp-fires and cooked meals – are regarded as one of the most important **prehistoric** finds in modern times. The cave appears to have been inhabited both by Neanderthals and homo sapiens. It's hoped that further excavations here may provide vital evidence as to the extinction or amalgamation of our species with the earlier race.

The **Phoenicians** called the Rock *Calpe* and had a fortified naval base here, barring the way to jealously guarded Atlantic trading destinations such as Tartessus. In **Greek** mythology this was the northernmost of the two pillars erected by Heracles. Following

Nerja, Costa del Sol

RONDA

Barbershop, Ronda

Puerto Banús, Marbella

Arcos de la Frontera

Fiestas del Toro, Grazalema

Seafront and Catedral Nueva, Cádiz

Olvera, Cádiz

Carnival, Cádiz

Domecq Bodega, Jerez de la Frontera

PETER WILSON

Landscape near Olvera, Cádiz

PETER WILSON

El Rocío, Huelva

the demise of the Roman Empire, the Rock became the bridgehead for a **Berber** assault on the Visigothic domains of southern Spain. In 711 Tariq ibn Ziryab, governor of Tangier, crossed the straits at the head of an army, defeated the Visigoths and named the Rock "Jabal Tariq" or the Mountain of Tariq, the name – albeit garbled – it still has today.

Gibraltar remained in Moorish hands until taken in 1309 by Guzmán el Bueno, but it was not long before it was recovered. The end finally came when another Guzmán, the Duke of Medina Sidonia, claimed it for Spain in 1462. Apart from the raids of Barbarossa, which caused Carlos V to fortify the Rock, Spanish possession was undisturbed until the **War of the Spanish Succession**, when Britain sided with Spain against the French. The outcome of this was the seizure of the Rock in 1704 by the **British** forces whose admiral, Sir George Rooke, gave the inhabitants the choice of swearing allegiance to the Habsburg claimant to the throne – Archduke Charles of Austria – or getting out. Those that left to found San Roque (see p.129) thought their absence would be temporary. But in 1715 the British contrived to have Gibraltar ceded to them "in perpetuity" in the Treaty of Utrecht, no doubt having calculated the military advantages of such a strategic bastion. Despite military and diplomatic attempts by Spain to recover the Rock since, however, the British have maintained their grip, and Gibraltar played an important strategic role in both World Wars. General **Franco** mounted persistent campaigns to get it back and closed the access link with Spain in 1969, which re-opened only in 1985, a period of enforced isolation that is indelibly etched into the Gibraltarian collective consciousness.

The Rock, it seems, is destined to be a recurring cause of friction between the two nations; in 1988 three **IRA suspects** were gunned down by British agents near the petrol station at the entrance to the town and close to the frontier. The British government – which went to enormous lengths to obscure the facts of the case – produced a version of events much at odds with that of the Spanish police and once more the issue of a "foreign power on Spanish soil" sparked a national debate. For more on the history of Gibraltar, see *Contexts*.

PHONING GIBRALTAR

From Spain (except Cádiz province) dial 956-7 + number
From Cádiz province dial 7 + number
From UK dial 00 + 350 + number
From North America dial 011 + 350 + number

Arrival and information

If you have a car, don't attempt to bring it to Gibraltar – the queues at the border are always atrocious, and parking on the Rock is a nightmare, due to lack of space. Use the underground car parks in La Línea – there's one beneath the central Plaza de la Constitución – instead (it's worth paying for the extra security) and **walk across**. From the frontier, where passport checking is a formality, it's a short **bus ride** (buses 10min past or 20min to the hour) or about a ten-minute walk across part of the airport's runway to **Main Street** (La Calle Real), which runs for most of the town's length a couple of blocks back from the port. Most of the shops – cheap, duty-free whisky is a major attraction – are clustered in and around Main Street, along with nearly all of the British-style pubs and hotels.

For information, the main **tourist office** is housed in Duke of Kent House on Cathedral Square (Mon–Fri 9am–5.30pm, Sat 10am–2pm; ☎74950). There are sub-branches in The Piazza on Main Street (Mon–Fri 9am–5.30pm, Sat 10am–2pm; ☎74982), and in the customs and immigration building at the border. The John

GIBRALTAR

LA LINEA
DE LA
CONCEPCIÓN

Catalan
Bay

CATALAN BAY ROAD

SIR HERBERT

Water
Catchments

The
Galleries

SIGNAL STATION ROAD

Cable Car

CHARLES V ROAD

QUEEN'S ROAD
OLD QUEEN'S ROAD

GREEN LANE

WINSTON CHURCHILL AV

DEVIL'S TOWER ROAD

Airport

Police &
Customs

The Moorish
Castle

See Inset

MAIN STREET

ROSIA

A

Marina
Bay

QUEENSWAY

QUEENSWAY

Bahia
de
Gibraltar

Tangier Ferry
& Hydrofoil

Puerto
de Gibraltar

North
Mole

N

RESTAURANTS

Buddies Pasta	**B**
The Clipper	**E**
Corks Wine Bar	**D**
Market Café	**A**
Ministers Restaurant	**C**
Penny Farthing	**F**

Detached
Mole

0   200m

Mackintosh Hall (Mon–Fri 9.30am–10.30pm), at the south end of Main Street, is also a useful resource – it's the cultural centre, with exhibitions and a library. The Gibraltar Bookshop, 300 Main Street, is a good source for stocking up on holiday reading and has a good selection of books on the Rock's history. Much of Gibraltar, with the exception of the cheap booze shops, closes down on Saturday afternoon, but the tourist sights remain open, and this can often be a quiet time to visit. Virtually everything closes on Sunday.

Gibraltar is a good place to **change money**, since the exchange rate is slightly higher than in Spain and there's no commission charged. The currency used here is the Gibraltar pound (the same value as the British pound, but different notes and coins); if you pay in pesetas, you generally fork out about five percent more. Gibraltar pounds can be hard to change in Spain or anywhere else.

A word of warning **when leaving Gibraltar**: if approached by locals do not carry any packages for strangers across the border back into Spain. What may seen like a simple carton of cigarettes could contain drugs and – if searched – you, and not they, will suffer the consequences.

ACCOMMODATION	
Hotel Bristol	4
Cannon Hotel	2
Queen's Hotel	1
Seruya's Guesthouse	3
Toc H Hostel	5
Youth Hostel	6

Accommodation

Shortage of space on the Rock means that **accommodation** is at a premium, especially in summer, and most of it is not overly inviting. It's really not worth your while searching out a good place to stay unless you have to: your best bet is to visit on day-trips from Algeciras (buses on the hour and half-hour, journey time 30min) or La Línea.

The only budget accommodation is at the friendly *Toc H Hostel* on Line Wall Rd (☎73431; about £5 a person) – though rooms here are none too comfortable and almost always occupied by long-term residents – or the tiny, eccentric *Seruya's Guest House* at 92 Irish Town, a street west of and running parallel to, Main St (☎73220; about £15 a double). The new *Hotel Cannon*, 9 Cannon Lane near the cathedral (☎51711; about £35 a double including breakfast), is another possiblity. Otherwise, you're going to have to pay standard British hotel prices: the cheapest are the *Queen's Hotel* on Boyd Street (☎74000), and the *Hotel Bristol* in Cathedral Square (☎76800), each charging over £40 for a double room. At Gibraltar's *Emile Youth Hostel*, Montagu Bastion, Line Wall Rd (☎51106, fax 78581), expect to pay £10 a night for a dormitory bed (breakfast included)

GIBRALTAR'S SOVEREIGNTY

Sovereignty over the Rock will doubtless eventually return to Spain, but at present neither side is in much of a hurry. For Britain it's a question of precedent – Gibraltar is in too similar a situation to the Falklands/Malvinas, a conflict which pushed the Spanish into postponing an initial frontier-opening date in 1982. For Spain, too, there are unsettling parallels with the *presidios* (Spanish enclaves) on the Moroccan coast at Ceuta and Melilla – both at present part of Andalucía. Nonetheless, the British presence is in practice waning, and the British foreign office clearly wants to steer Gibraltar towards a new, harmonious relationship with Spain. To this end they are running down the significance of the military base, and now only a token force of less than a hundred remains – most of these working in a top-secret hi-tech bunker buried deep inside the Rock from where the Royal Navy monitors the sea traffic through the straits (accounting for a quarter of the world movement of all shipping). In financial terms this has cut the British government's contribution to Gibraltar's GDP from 65 percent in the early 1980s to five percent today, and the figure is still falling.

The Gibraltarians see all these issues as irrelevant in light of their firmly stated opposition to a return to **Spanish control**. In 1967, just before Franco closed the border in the hope of forcing a quick agreement, the colony voted on the issue – rejecting it by 12,138 votes to 44 (a poll which was not recognised, incidentally, by the UN). Most people would probably sympathize with that vote – against a Spain that was then still a dictatorship – but more than thirty years have gone by, Spanish democracy is now secure, and the arguments are becoming increasingly tenuous. Despite its impressive claims to law and order, Gibraltar is no model society either; its dirty jobs, for instance, are nearly all done by Moroccans, who were recruited en masse to replace Spanish workers after the border between Gibraltar and Spain was closed by Franco, and who have always been treated as second-class citizens. This was underlined in the late 1990s by tough new immigration laws stripping them of residence, pension and health care rights, which were upheld by the colony's supreme court, despite accusations of "ethnic cleansing".

May 1996 saw a change in the trend of internal politics with the **defeat of the Socialist government** of Joe Bossano (following two previous landslide victories). Voters, apparently concerned that Bossano's pugnacious anti-Spanish posture jeopardized a viable economic future for the colony in which Spain realistically must play a role, elected a **Social Democrat administration**, led by **Peter Caruana**. However, whilst Caruana talked of opening up a more constructive dialogue with Spain during the election campaign, once in control he soon began to voice the traditional Gibraltarian paranoia. His stance caused some dismay in Madrid and London, who were both behind Spain's offer in 1997 to give the colony the status of an autonomous region inside the Spanish state similar to that of the Basques or Catalans. The proposal was rejected out of hand by Caruana who has since ruled out any deals and in 1999 made a speech at the UN castigating Spain's intransi-

---

or £25 for a double room. No **camping** is allowed on the peninsula, and if you're caught sleeping rough or inhabiting abandoned bunkers, you're likely to be arrested and fined. This law is enforced by Gibraltar and British Ministry of Defence police, and raids of the beaches are regular.

Around the Rock

Be on your guard for touting taxi drivers who offer "tours of the Rock" – they're generally overpriced and very rushed. Near the end of Main Street you can hop on a reassuringly Swiss-built **cable car** (Mon–Sat 9.30am–6pm, last trip down 5.45pm; £4.90 return) which will carry you up to the summit – the **Top of the Rock** as it's logically gence, claiming the right of Gibraltar to exercise "self-determination". After calling a snap **election** in February 2000, the Caruana government was returned for another four-year term with an increased majority. Caruana has regularly been urged by Britain (under pressure from Spain) to crack down on the smuggling of contraband tobacco over the Spanish border and to curb the activities of the Rock's 75,000 "offshore" financial institutions which have mushroomed over the last decade. Many of these companies, Spain claims, are guilty of drugs money-laundering besides providing a refuge for Russian mafia money, accusations given some credibilty by the EU's decision to start legal proceedings against a number of them in 1999.

The Spanish prohibit access to the Rock's airport by non-British aircraft thus denying an expansion of tourism, and Gibraltar's seaport is not permitted direct communications with any port in Spain. The latest cause of rancour between the two administrations is the refusal by Spain to integrate Gibraltar's mobile phone system into their own – with the result that the Rock's mobiles work all over Europe, except in Spain. The political stalemate seems set to continue for as long as Britain uses the wishes of the Gibraltarians as a pretext for blocking any change in the colony's status – a policy that infuriates the Spanish government whose foreign minister, Abel Matutes, recently stated that the wishes of the residents "did not apply in the case of Hong Kong".

What most outsiders don't realise about the political situation is that the Gibraltarians feel very vulnerable, caught between the interests of two big states; they are well aware that both governments' concerns have nothing to do with their own personal wishes. Until very recently people were sent over from Britain to fill all the top civil service and Ministry of Defence jobs, a practice which, to a lesser degree, still continues – the present Governor is Richard Luce, a former British cabinet minister. Large parts of the Rock are no-go areas for "natives"; the South District in particular being taken up by military facilities. The withdrawal of British forces has somewhat improved the chronic housing shortage: there's a huge new development in the reclaimed land of the port, and much former army housing been handed over to the local government.

Locals – particularly on the Spanish side of the border – also vigorously protest about the Royal Navy nuclear-powered submarines which dock regularly at the naval base, and secrecy surrounds the issue of whether nuclear warheads and/or chemical and biological weapons are stored in the arsenal, probably deep inside the Rock itself. Yet Gibraltarians – sounding at times eerily similar to Ulster Unionists in Ireland – stubbornly cling to British status, and all their institutions are modelled on English lines. Contrary to popular belief, they are of neither mainly Spanish nor British blood, but an ethnic mix descended from Genoese, Portuguese, Spanish, Menorcan, Jewish, Maltese and British forebears. English is the official language, but more commonly spoken is what sounds to an outsider like perfect Andalucian Spanish. It is, in fact, *llanito*, an Andalucian dialect with borrowed words which reflect its diverse origins – only a Spaniard from the south can tell a Gibraltarian from an Andalucian.

known – via **Apes' Den** halfway up, a fairly reliable viewing point to see the tailless monkeys (Barbary apes) and hear the guides explain their legend. The story goes that the British will keep the rock only so long as the apes remain too; Winston Churchill was superstitious enough to augment their numbers during World War II when they started to decline. The Top gives good views over to the Atlas Mountains and down to the town, its elaborate water catchment system cut into the side of the rock.

From the Top of the Rock it's an easy walk south along St Michael's Road passing one of the apes' dens. Keep a tight grip on your belongings; the unruly primates are prone to stealing tourists' bags and sometimes their cameras – often tossing the items on to rocks a couple of hundred metres below.

Passing through the so-called "Nature Reserve", the leafy path leads to **Saint Michael's Cave** (daily 9.30am–7pm; free entry with cable car ticket), an immense natural cavern which led ancient people to believe the rock was hollow and gave rise to its old name of *Mons Calpe* (Hollow Mountain). Used during the last war as a bomb-proof military hospital, the cave nowadays hosts occasional concerts at a theatre constructed within. You can arrange at the tourist office for a guided visit to **Lower Saint Michael's Cave**, a series of chambers going deeper down and ending in an underground lake.

Although it is possible to be lazy and take the cable car both ways, you might instead continue up Queen's Road to visit the fourteenth-century **Tower of Homage**. This is the most visible survivor from the fourteenth-century Moorish castle, today filled with wax dummies of British soldiers hacking at the stone and doing battle with the Spanish. Further up you'll find the **Upper Galleries** (aka the Great Siege Tunnels), blasted out of the rock during the Great Siege of 1779–1782 in order to point guns down at the Spanish lines.

To walk down from the Top of the Rock, you can take the **Mediterranean Steps** at the end of O'Hara's Road – but they're not very well signposted and you have to climb over O'Hara's Battery, a big gun emplacement with a very steep descent most of the way down the east side, turning the southern corner of the Rock. You'll pass through the Jews' Gate into Engineer Road. From here, return to town through the Alameda Gardens and the **Trafalgar Cemetery** with graves of the Battle of Trafalgar dead; overgrown and evocative, it has a good line in epitaphs.

Back in town, incorporated into the **Gibraltar Museum** (Mon–Fri 10am–6pm, Sat 10am–2pm; £2), are two well-preserved, beautiful fourteenth-century **Moorish Baths**. Resembling the ancient Roman model, the baths had a cold room and hot rooms heated by a hypocaust. Note the star-shaped skylights, and the pillars used in the construction: one Roman, two Visigothic and four Moorish. Otherwise, the museum's **collection** is an odd assortment including an incongruous Egyptian mummy washed up in the bay, a natural history display of stuffed birds in glass cases, and a rather dreary military section documenting how the British came to rule the roost here. The museum's star exhibit should be a female skull, dating from around 100,000 years ago and unearthed in 1848 on the Rock's north face. Ironically, because the find was then stored away, it was the later discovery of a skull in Germany's Neander Valley that gave its name to the era we know as Neanderthal, which could just as easily have been termed "Gibraltarian". The museum now retains only a copy, the original having been removed to the research collection of the Natural History Museum in London.

Other sites include **Nelson's Anchorage** (Mon–Sat 9.30am–5.15pm; free) on Rosia Road, to the south of the harbour, where a 100-ton Victorian gun marks the site where Nelson's body was brought ashore – preserved in a rum barrel – from HMS Victory after the Battle of Trafalgar in 1805. Dolphin-spotting **boat trips** leave the Queensway Quay daily (☎74958; £15–18) but you should ring first to book a place or ask the Tourist Office to do it for you. The best **beach** is at the tiny fishing village at **Catalan Bay**, whose inhabitants like to think of themselves as distinct from the townies on the other side of the Rock. There's a bus service from Line Wall Road (every 15min) to the eastern beaches.

Eating and drinking

Eating is a bit of a sad affair in Gibraltar, and relatively expensive by Spanish standards. Pub snacks or fish and chips are the norm. Main Street is crowded with dismal touristy places and fast food outlets, although *Smiths Fish & Chip Shop*, 295 Main Street, is worth a try. Other choices are *Penny Farthing* at 9 King Street, off Cathedral Square, a Lilliputian restaurant with an English menu, while to the east, decent pasta in all its varieties is served up at *Buddies Pasta Casa*, 15 Cannon Lane, by the cathedral. *Corks Wine*

ONWARD TRAVEL

One of the functional attractions of Gibraltar is its role as a **port for Morocco**. The *Estrella* sails to Tangier on Mondays & Wednesdays at 8.15am and Fridays at 6.30pm, taking two hours. The return trip from Tangier is on Sundays & Tuesdays at 3pm and Fridays at 9pm. Tickets cost £18 one way and £30 return for a foot passenger, and £40 single and £80 return for a car. Tickets and updated timetables are available from Tourafrica, Unit G10, International Commercial Centre, 2a Main St (☎77666, fax 76754). A new daily **catamaran** service to Tangier, the *Mons Calpe*, leaves daily at 9.30am with additional sailings on Mondays and Fridays at 7pm. The crossing takes 1hr 15min and tickets cost £30 for a period return or £25 for a day-trip. Bookings and confirmation of times should be made through Bland Travel, Cloister Building, Irish Town (☎79200, fax 76189). Bland Travel can also assist with – albeit expensive – daily flights to Casablanca and Marrakesh with GB Airways and Monarch Airlines, and guided day-trips to Tangier.

If you're looking for other exotic destinations, at the end of summer the yacht marina fills up with boats heading for the **Canaries**, **Madeira** and the **West Indies** – many take on crew to work in exchange for passage.

Bar, 79 Irish Town, is a tranquil venue for light meals, and nearby at no. 78 *The Clipper* serves pub grub in a varnished lounge. The *Market Café*, Market Place at the north end of town beyond Casemates Square, serves up traditional "English breakfasts" all day long. Slightly more tempting is *Ministers Restaurant*, 310 Main Street (southern end) with a pleasant terrace and Spanish-style *menú* for around £7. *Saccarello's Coffee House* at 57 Irish Town is a local institution and a great place for tea and homemade confectionery. Further afield, at Marina Bay, try *Biancas*, for reasonably priced seafood, or *Da Paolo* which serves good Italian fare. At Catalan Bay the *Seawave Bar* does decent shellfish *raciones* – try the *gambas a la plancha* – and good seafood.

Gibraltarian **pubs** mimic traditional English styles (and prices), but are often rowdy, full of soldiers and visiting sailors. Unlike in Spain, there's hardly anywhere to sit outdoors, which often means drinking beer in the equivalent of a sauna during high summer. For pub food, the *Royal Calpe*, 176 Main Street; *Calpe Hounds* on Cornwall's Lane; *Gibraltar Arms*, 14 Main St; and *The Horseshoe*, 193 Main Street, are among the best, all offering hearty meals. These pubs all have some outdoor seating. For a quieter drink try the *Cannon Bar* in Cannon Lane beside the cathedral, or the *Piccadilly Gardens Bar*, 3 Rosia Rd, just beyond the Referendum Gates.

Algeciras

ALGECIRAS occupies the far side of the bay from Gibraltar, spewing out smoke and pollution in its direction. The last town of the Spanish Mediterranean, it was once an elegant resort; today it's unabashedly a port and industrial centre, its suburbs sprawling out on all sides. When Franco closed the border with Gibraltar at La Línea it was Algeciras that he decided to develop to absorb the Spanish workers formerly employed in the British naval dockyards, thus breaking the area's dependence on the Rock.

Most travellers are scathing about the city's ugliness, and unless you're waiting for a bus or train, or heading for Morocco, there's admittedly little reason to stop. However, Algeciras has a real port atmosphere, and even if you're just passing through it's hard to resist the urge to get on a boat south. This is the main port for Moroccan migrant workers, who drive home every year during their holidays from the factories, farms and mines of Northern Europe. In summer, the port bustles with groups of Moroccans in transit, dressed in flowing *djelabas* and yellow slippers, and lugging unbelievable amounts of possessions. Half-a-million cross Spain each year, often becoming victims of all levels of racial discrimination, from being ripped off to being violently attacked.

Once you start to explore, you'll also discover that the old town has some very attractive corners which seem barely to have changed in fifty years, especially around the **Plaza Alta**. This leafy square, arguably the town's only sight of any note, lies a five-minute walk from the bus station/port area and if you're killing time provides a much more pleasant place to sit out than around the port. On the square, the eighteenth-century church of **Nuestra Señora de la Palma** and the Baroque chapel of **Nuestra Señora de Europa** – with a fine facade – are worth a look.

Nearer the port, the romantic *Hotel Reina Cristina*, Paseo de la Conferencia s/n, south of the harbour (☎956 60 26 22, fax 956 60 33 23; ⑨), set in a park and built in the nineteenth century in British colonial style, is a wonderful throwback to the days of the Grand Tour and steam trains. Call in for a drink in their terrace bar and take a look at the plaques behind the reception desk bearing the signatures of famous guests, such as Sir Arthur Conan Doyle, W.B. Yeats, Cole Porter and Federico García Lorca.

Practicalities

The main **bus station** is in c/San Bernardo, 250m or so behind the port, beside the *Hotel Octavio* and just short of the **train station**. If you need any information about the town, or want to pick up an accommodation list or map, make for the **Turismo**, c/Juan de la Cierva, on the south side of the train track (official hours Mon–Fri 9am–2pm, but frequently fails to open; ☎956 57 26 36). Room rates tend to go up dramatically in mid-season, but Algeciras has plenty of low-priced **hostales** and **pensiones** in the grid of streets between the port and the train station, and lots of simple *casas de huéspedes* clustered round the market. There are several possibilities in c/Duque de Almodóvar, including *Levante* at no. 21 (☎956 65 15 05; ②) which has rooms with and without bath; along nearby c/José Santacana there's the more comfortable *González* at no. 7 (☎956 65 28 43; ③) or the diminutive but pleasant *Nuestra Señora del Carmen* (☎956 65 63 01; ③) at no. 14, also with ensuite rooms. On Plaza Palma, the market square, there's the surprisingly spruce *Hostal Nuestra Señora de la Palma* (☎956 63 24 81; ③) for rooms with bath; *Casa Sánchez* (see below; ☎956 69 65 57; ②) also has basic rooms. A pleasant hotel close to the waterfront is the *Marina Victoria*, Avda. de la Marina 7 (☎956 65 01 11, fax 956 63 28 65; ④), whose high, air-conditioned balcony rooms overlook the bay. Algeciras's luxurious **youth hostel**, Ctra. Nacional 340 (☎956 67 90 60, fax 956 67 90 17; ①) which has a pool, tennis courts and double rooms with bath, lies 8km west of town on the Tarifa road. Buses heading for Tarifa will drop you outside on request (ask for the "*Albergue Juvenil*").

The huge number of people passing through the town also guarantees endless possibilities for **food and drink**, especially around the port/harbour area. Among them, across the railway line from the Turismo and invariably crowded, is the good-value *Casa Gil* at c/Sigismundo Moret 2, and 50m along the same street, *Casa Sánchez*, which has an inexpensive *menú*. A little north of the bus station, *Restaurante Montes*, c/Juan Morrison 27, is more upmarket, with a cheaper and excellent **tapas** bar lower down the hill on the same street, at the junction with c/Emilio Castelar. Tasty *tapas* are also on offer at *Bar Castro*, c/Castillo 14, just north of the market and en route to the Plaza Alta, where there are more bars, cafés and *heladerías*. The daily **markets** are useful places to buy food, as well as vibrant and fascinating to visit; the main one, on Plaza Palma down by the port, is a riot of colour on Saturday mornings.

Onward travel

At Algeciras the **train line** begins again, heading north to Ronda and the Bobadilla junction where there are connections to Sevilla, Málaga, Córdoba and Granada. The stunningly scenic route to Ronda is one of the best journeys in Andalucía; there are four

Morocco is easily enough visited from Algeciras: in summer there are at least eighteen **crossings to Tangier** (daily; 2hr), and at least the same number to the Spanish *presidio* of **Ceuta** (daily; 1hr 30min), little more than a Spanish Gibraltar with a brisk business in duty-free goods, but a relatively painless way to enter Morocco. Alternatively you can go by **hydrofoil** to Tangier (1 daily; 1hr) or Ceuta (1 daily; 30min). **Tickets** cost around 3200ptas one-way to Tangier or Ceuta, with an additional 500ptas for hydrofoils, and are sold at the scores of travel agents along the waterfront and on most approach roads; they all cost the same, though some places may give you a better rate of exchange than others if you want to pay in foreign currency. Viajes Transafric, Avda. Marina 4 (☎956 65 43 11) near the port, are reliable and will provide up-to-date information on timetable changes. They also do a daily all-inclusive **day-trip to Tangier** by hydrofoil which includes a guided tour, lunch and time for shopping for about 7000ptas. Wait till Tangier – or Tetouan if you're going via Ceuta – before buying any Moroccan currency; rates in the embarkation building kiosks are very poor. Check the date and time on your ferry ticket, and beware the ticket sellers who congregate near the dock entrance wearing official Ceuta/Tangier badges: they add a whopping "commission" charge. InterRail/Eurail card holders should note that they're entitled to a twenty percent discount on the standard ferry price: if you have trouble getting this, go to the official sales desk in the embarkation building.

departures a day. For Málaga, hourly **buses** leave from Empresa Portillo, Avda. Virgen del Carmen 15 on the waterfront (☎956 65 10 55); from here too, less frequently, are direct connections to Granada and Almería. For Tarifa, Cádiz, Sevilla and most other destinations you'll need the **main bus station** on c/San Bernardo. The bus to La Línea also goes every thirty minutes from here.

Ronda and the White Towns

Though Andalucía boasts many pretty *pueblos blancos*, the best known are the "**White Towns**" – unfeasibly picturesque places, each with its own plaza, church and tavern – set in the roughly triangular area between Málaga, Algeciras and Sevilla. At their centre, in a region of wild mountainous beauty, is spectacular **Ronda**, very much the transportation hub and a great attraction in its own right. From Ronda, almost any route north or west is rewarding, taking you past a whole series of lovely little villages, among cherry orchards and vines, many of them fortified since the days of the Reconquest – hence the mass of "de la Frontera" suffixes. Of these, **Arcos de la Frontera**, a truly spectacular white town perched on a high limestone spur, comes close to Ronda as the best place to spend a few days in the region.

Described here, after the Ronda account, are two of the major White Town routes – the first roughly northeast from Ronda (p.153) and the second veering southwest towards Cádiz (p.157).

To Ronda from the coast

Of several possible approaches to Ronda from the coast, the route up from Algeciras is the most rewarding – and worth going out of your way to experience. From Málaga most of the buses to Ronda follow the coastal highway to San Pedro de Alcántara before turning into the mountains: dramatic enough, but rather a bleak route, with no villages and only limited views of the dark rock face of the Serranía. The train ride up from

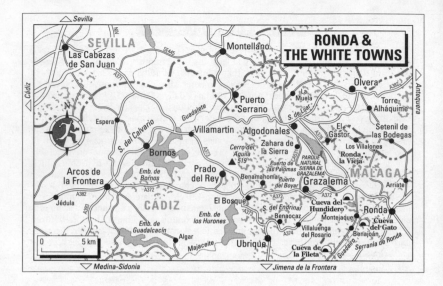

Málaga is better, with three connecting services daily, the last currently running at 6.05pm.

You can follow the **Algeciras route** – via Gaucín – by either bus or train, or, if you've time and energy, on a four- or five-day walk. En route, you're always within reach of a river and there's a series of hill towns, each one visible from the next, to provide targets for the day; Casares (see p.128) is almost on the route, but more easily reached from Estepona.

Castellar de la Frontera

Heading **north out of Algeciras** along the A369, after 8km (and just before the turnoff for Castellar below) a turning on the left signed "Casa Convento" leads through expansive woodlands to the enchanting *Convento La Almoraima* hotel (☎956 69 30 02, fax 956 69 32 14; ⑦), which is located inside a rehabilitated seventeenth-century convent with a fine Florentine tower and a restaurant in the former cloister. It's surrounded by vast tracts of wooded walking country in the Parque Natural de los Alcornocales (see below), all making it hard to imagine a more serene stopover.

The next turning, about 2km further on, leads to the first white town on the route proper, **CASTELLAR DE LA FRONTERA**, a bizarre hill village within a thirteenth-century Moorish castle, whose population, in accord with some grandiose scheme, was moved downriver in 1971 to a "new" town on the edge of nearby La Almoraima. The relocation was subsequently dropped and a few villagers moved back to their old houses, but many of the dwellings were taken over by retired hippies (mainly affluent Germans). Perhaps not surprisingly, the result wasn't totally successful, and the two groups didn't gel – reflecting this tension, the place today has a brooding, claustrophobic atmosphere. The situation was worsened by a scandal some years back when the artificial lake below the village was drained, revealing the corpses of two Germans joined together by a rope. Agitation to clean out what local graffiti called "drug-addicted swine" started up and there is presently only an uneasy truce between the two sides. Recent plans to rebuild the castle as a tourist centre – complete with *parador* – appear to have ground to a halt and the Germans remain, their cars and vans parked on the approach roads to the village. At the start of the village there's a venta as well as a bar near the entrance to the castle, but not a lot more to detain you. There are two main **accommodation** options: the *Posada Antigua*, inside the castle walls (☎956 23 61 01; ③), with two en-suite rooms, or *Hostal El Pilar*, c/León Esquivel 4 (☎956 69 30 22; ③), which lies below in the new town.

Jimena de la Frontera

JIMENA DE LA FRONTERA, 20km north along the A369, lacks the traumas of Castellar; again, it's a hill town but it's far larger and more open, rising to a grand if ruined **Moorish castle** with a triple-gateway entrance. In recent years it has become home to a considerable contingent of British expats who probably feel the need to be within working and shopping distance of Gibraltar. Jimena is also a gateway to the **Parque Natural de los Alcornocales**, a vast expanse of verdant hill country stretching south to the sea and north to El Bosque and covered with cork oaks (*alcornocales*); a haven for large numbers of birds and insects, it's also a paradise for walkers.

In town are several bars, and a beautiful old **fonda** which has no sign and isn't easy to find – ask for the *Casa María* (c/Sevilla 36; ①). There's also the plusher *Hostal El Anon*, c/Consuelo 34 (☎956 64 01 13, fax 956 64 11 10; ⑤), a series of tastefully renovated houses and stables with patio, bar, restaurant and rooftop pool. They can also arrange horse riding in the scenic surrounding countryside. A little way out at the train station, *Los Arcos* (☎956 64 03 28; ④) is another slightly cheaper *hostal* for rooms with bath. Places to **eat** include the simple *La Parra*, c/Sevilla 18, and the excellent *Restaurante Bar Cuenca*, Avda. de los Deportes on the way into town, which also serves *tapas* and has a pretty terrace patio at the rear.

Gaucín

Beyond Jimena the A369 climbs for 23km through woods of cork oak and olive groves to reach Gaucín, and along the way there are bars at San Pablo, a hamlet about 7km out. Just beyond the Málaga border, **GAUCÍN**, almost a mountain village and perched on a ridge below yet another Moorish fort, commands tremendous views and makes a fine place to stopover. The village has a prosperous air somewhat sustained by a longstanding international community comprised of British and other European emigrants.

Gaucín's charming and historical *fonda*, the *Nacional*, c/San Juan de Dios 8, sadly no longer takes lodgers, but serves **food** at its quaintly austere restaurant (the paella is recommended). The bonus of eating here is to read the amazing visitors' books from the past century and a quarter. Gaucín's only other attraction is the **Castillo del Aguila** (daily 11am–1pm & 4–6pm; free), a Moorish castle reached by a track at the eastern end of the village. From the battlements there are great views across terrain studded with olive, oak and chestnut trees to Gibraltar and even the Moroccan coast beyond on a very clear day. Easter Sunday is always celebrated here with a fiesta and **encierro** (bull run) when beefy fighting bulls career through the streets looking for partying inebriates to get their horns into.

There's a small **Turismo** (daily 11am–1pm & 4–6pm; ☎952 15 16 00) in the centre between the *farmacía* and the post office. If you want to **stay**, *Hostal Moncada* is a good bet (☎95 215 13 24; ③) next to the *gasolinera* as you come into the village from Jimena; get a room at the back for a view of the Serranía de Ronda, otherwise you'll be contemplating the petrol station. The more upmarket *Hotel Casablanca*, Teodora de Molina 12 (☎952 15 10 19; ⑥), near the main square, is very comfortable. The Turismo has a list of village houses (⑥) which are often available to rent at short notice. For longer stays you can rent one of the expats' houses from Adam Page, c/Lorenzo García 98

(☎952 15 10 93, fax 952 15 16 01). He may also be able to put you in touch with some delightful *casas particulares* and is a friendly source of local information. **Food** is available at the *Moncada*'s terrace restaurant, or *Venta Pilar*, down some steps over the road opposite, flanking the swimming pool. Near the centre of the village, *La Fructuosa* offers delicious traditional dishes whilst the *Venta Socorro*, on the main Ronda road, is another worthy choice and serves up a wide selection of *tapas*. Excellent *tapas* are also to be had at *Bar Pepe-Paco* on c/San Juan de Dios, near the *Nacional*.

You can reach Gaucín by **bus**, but perhaps more rewarding is the 13-kilometre walk from its **train station**, not served by buses. Although it's known as Gaucín, the station is actually at El Colmenar, on the fringes of the Cortés nature reserve. Should you need to rest up before the hike (getting on for 3hr, mostly uphill) there are simple rooms and meals at *Bar-Restaurante Las Flores* (☎952 15 30 26; ②) as well as several bars. *Las Flores* can also arrange a taxi (about 2000ptas) should you chicken out.

Ronda

Rising amid a ring of dark, angular mountains, the full natural drama of **RONDA** is best appreciated as you enter the town. Built on an isolated ridge of the sierra, it's split in half by a gaping river gorge (*El Tajo*, though the river itself is the Guadalévin) that drops sheer for 130m on three sides. Still more spectacular, the gorge is spanned by a stupendous eighteenth-century arched bridge, while tall whitewashed houses lean perilously from its precipitous edges.

Not surprisingly, this dramatic and dominant location attracted not only the early Celts, who named it *Arunda*, but Phoenicians and Greeks as well. Under Rome it became an important military bastion referred to by Pliny the Elder as *Arunda Laus* ("the glorious"). When the later Moors came to rule the roost here, *Medina Runda* was transformed and enlarged into the provincial capital of the Tarakuna district. Embellished with lavish mosques and palaces, it ruled an independent and isolated **Moorish kingdom** until 1485, when it was taken by Ferdinand and Isabel.

Ronda is also notable for having been the birthplace of the Maestranza, an order of knights who laid down the rules for early bullfights performed on horseback. During the nineteenth century the town became an increasingly popular destination for Romantic travellers, and still today much of Ronda's attraction lies in its extraordinary **setting**, or in simply walking down by the river, following one of the donkey tracks through the rich green valley. Bird-watchers should look out for the lesser kestrels, rare in northern Europe, nesting in and launching themselves from the cliffs beneath the Alameda park. Lower down you can spot crag martins. But the town itself is of equal interest and has sacrificed little of its enchanting character to the flow of day-trippers from the Costa del Sol.

Arrival, information and orientation

The **bus station** is in the north of the Mercadillo quarter on Plaza Redondo (☎95 287 26 25), while **trains** pull in a couple of blocks east on Avda. Andalucía (☎95 287 16 73). There's a RENFE office for tickets and timetables at c/Infante 20, near the Plaza del Socorro. Coming in by **car** you will soon be aware of Ronda's chronic parking problem. The town has a crazy plan to dig a gigantic underground car park beneath the bullring but until then your best bet is to park as far out as possible (near the train station is usually feasible) and walk to the centre, or head straight for one of the pay car parks (clearly signed). At the northern end of the Plaza de España, Ronda's helpful and enthusiastic **Turismo** (Mon–Fri 9am–7pm, Sat & Sun 10am–2pm; ☎95 287 12 72) has maps and walking information on the Serranía de Ronda (see p.152) plus details of organisations offering guided walks, horse trekking and horse and mountain bike hire. A **Turismo Municipal** opens the same hours in theory, inside the Palacio de Mondragón (see below) on the Plaza de Mondragón. Just north and west of the Plaza de España is the **Carrera Espinal**, Ronda's main pedestrianized thoroughfare and shopping area. It can be confusing walking around Ronda as many of the streets have **multiple names**: if in doubt, refer to as many maps as possible.

The main **telephone office** is located in c/Sevilla, and the **post office** is at Virgen de la Paz 20, near the Plaza de Toros. A variety of **foreign newspapers** are available from c/Mariano Souviron 5 (above the Plaza del Socorro), who also have fax machines and international phones. One block north of here again, Cervecería Zaidin, c/Pozo 11, has **internet access**. *Ronda Semanal* is the town's weekly paper and useful for local news and entertainment. Hiking **maps** of the Sierras de Ronda and Grazalema are available from *Librería Hispania*, c/Espinel 15.

Accommodation

The best **places to stay** in Ronda are in the heart of the Mercadillo quarter, and to the east of the Plaza del Socorro off c/Borrego and its continuations, c/Cristo and then c/Almendra. The most upmarket options are to be found near the Plaza de Toros.

Ronda's **campsite**, *Camping El Sur* (☎95 287 59 39) with swimming pool, bar and restaurant, lies 2km out of town along the road to Algeciras. You can rent **bungalows** here, too. It's not served by bus, so if you don't fancy the walk (especially from the train and bus stations which adds an extra kilometre), take a taxi (approximately 1000ptas).

Hostal Águilar, c/Naranja 28 (☎95 287 19 94). Clean, friendly, family-run *hostal* off c/Cristo. ②.

Hostal Andalucía, c/Martínez Astein 19 (☎95 287 54 50). Pleasant rooms in leafy surroundings opposite the train station, all rooms en suite. ③.

Hotel La Española, c/José Aparicio 3, near the Turismo (☎95 287 10 52, fax 95 287 80 01). Beloved old *fonda* refurbished and reborn as a spanking new hotel. Amazing views from some rooms (towards the Serranía de Ronda). ⑥.

Hotel Don Miguel, c/Villanueva 8 (☎95 287 77 22, fax 95 287 83 77). New hotel with comfortable rooms overlooking the *Tajo*, and a highly recommended restaurant (see p.148). Garage. ⑥.

Hostal Morales, c/Sevilla 51 (☎95 287 15 38). Good budget option for clean and simple rooms. ②.

Parador de Ronda, Plaza de España (☎95 287 75 00, fax 95 287 81 88). This imposing new *parador* teetering on the edge of the *Tajo* has now become Ronda's flagship hotel with a superb and tasteful building, luxurious accommodation, pool, terrace bar and garage. ⑧.

Hotel Polo, c/Mariano Soubiron (c/Benitez on some maps) 8 (☎95 287 24 47, fax 95 287 24 49). Swish hotel; good value for the price with off-season deals. Garage. ⑥.

Pensión La Purísima, c/Sevilla 10 (☎95 287 10 50). Family-run *pensión* with basic but comfortable rooms, behind the Plaza del Socorro. ②.

Hotel Reina Victoria, c/Jerez 25 (☎95 287 12 40, fax 95 287 10 75). Nineteenth-century retreat for British military visitors from Gibraltar – although recently refurbished, the air of decaying grandeur lingers; ask for one of the corner rooms with a spectacular view over the Serranía de Ronda. With pool, gardens and parking. ⑧.

Hostal Ronda Sol, c/Cristo 11, near the intersection with c/Sevilla (☎95 287 44 97). Good budget *hostal*, although some of the interior rooms are a bit claustrophobic. ②.

Hotel Royal, c/Virgen de la Paz 42 (☎95 287 11 41, fax 95 287 81 32). Comfortable en suite rooms, air conditioning and TV, in an ugly modern building opposite the Alameda. ④.

Hostal San Francisco, c/María Cabrera (c/Prim on some maps) 18 (☎95 287 32 99). Excellent value and friendly place, where all rooms come with bath. ③.

Hotel San Gabriel, c/José Holgado 19, La Ciudad (☎95 219 03 92, fax 95 219 01 17; *sangabriel@ronda.net*). Stunning restoration of an eighteenth-century mansion with beautifully furnished air-conditioned rooms and friendly proprietors. This is the only hotel in La Ciudad. ⑥.

Hotel El Tajo, c/Cruz Verde 7, off c/Almendra (☎95 287 40 40, fax 95 287 50 99). Pleasant traditional hotel with its own economical restaurant. Garage. ④.

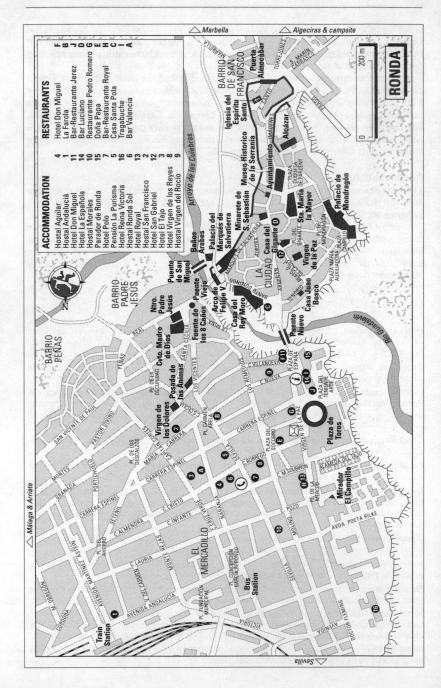

RONDA

200 m

△ Marbella   △ Algeciras & campsite

△ Málaga & Arriate

▷ Sevilla

RESTAURANTS

Hotel Don Miguel	4
La Farola	1
Bar-Restaurante Jerez	11
Bar Luciano	14
Restaurante Pedro Romero	10
Doña Pepa	15
Bar-Restaurante Royal	7
Casa Santa Pola	5
Tragabuche	16
Bar Valencia	13

F
B
J
D
G
H
C
I
A

ACCOMMODATION

Hostal Aguilar	
Hostal Andalucía	
Hotel Don Miguel	
Hotel La Española	
Hostal Morales	
Parador de Ronda	
Hotel Polo	
Pensión La Purisma	
Hotel Reina Victoria	
Hostal Ronda Sol	
Hotel Royal	
Hotel San Gabriel	
Hotel El Tajo	
Hotel Virgen de los Reyes	
Hostal Virgen del Rocío	

Hotel Virgen de los Reyes, c/Borrego 13 (☎95 287 11 40). Congenial hotel offering good-value ensuite rooms with TV. ④.

Hostal Virgen del Rocío, c/Nueva 18 (☎95 287 74 25). Refurbished *hostal* for rooms with bath; one street off the eastern side of the Plaza de España. ④.

The Town

Ronda divides into three parts: on the northwest side of the gorge is the largely modern **Mercadillo** quarter, while across the bridge is the old Moorish town – the **Ciudad** – and its **San Francisco** suburb. The Ciudad is so intricate a maze that you can do little else but wander at random. However, at some stage, make your way across the eighteenth-century **Puente Nuevo** bridge, peering down the walls of limestone rock into the yawning *Tajo* which claimed the bridge's architect, Martín de Aldehuela, as he clambered over the parapet to inspect his finished work: clutching for his hat in the wind, he fell to his death. Hemingway, in *For Whom the Bell Tolls*, recorded how prisoners were thrown alive into the gorge. These days, Ronda remains a major military garrison post and houses much of the Spanish Africa Legion, Franco's old crack regiment, who can often be seen wandering around town in their tropical green coats and *chapiri* forage caps, resembling tasselled fezes. They have a mean reputation.

CASA DEL REY AND BAÑOS ÁRABES

The somewhat arbitrarily named **Casa del Rey Moro** ("House of the Moorish King"; daily 10am–7pm; 600ptas), an early eighteenth-century mansion built on Moorish foundations, stands on c/Marqués de Parada (aka c/Santo Domingo). Local legend has it that this was the palace of the Moorish emir Badis, an Arabian Bluebeard, who was reputed to drink his wine from the skulls of the victims he beheaded. From the house a remarkable underground stairway (the *Mina*) descends to the river at the foot of the *Tajo*; these 365 steps, guaranteeing a water supply in times of siege, were cut by Christian slaves in the fourteenth century. There's a viewing balcony at the bottom where you can admire the towering walls of rock and the gorge's birdlife but the long climb back up will probably make you wonder if it was worth the stiff entry fee.

Further down the same street is the **Palacio del Marqués de Salvatierra** (Mon–Wed, Fri & Sat 11am–2pm & 4–7pm, Thurs & Sun 11am–2pm; 300ptas), a splendid Renaissance mansion with an oddly primitive, half-grotesque frieze of Adam and Eve on its portal together with the colonial images of four Peruvian Indians; the house is still used by the family but can be visited on mildly interesting guided tours. Just down the hill you reach the two old town bridges – the **Puente Viejo** of 1616 and the single-span Moorish **Puente de San Miguel** – and nearby, on the southeast bank of the river, are the distinctive hump-shaped cupolas and bizarre glass roof-windows of the newly refurbished **Baños Árabes** (Tues 3–5.30pm, Wed–Sat 10am–2pm & 3–5.30pm, Sun 10am–2pm; free). Dating from the thirteenth century and wonderfully preserved, these are truly remarkable structures, with star-shaped windows set in a barrel-vaulted ceiling and beautiful octagonal brick columns supporting horseshoe arches. A channel from the nearby river fed the water into this bath-house complex which was formerly surrounded by plant-filled gardens.

IGLESIA DE SANTA MARÍA AND PALACIO DE MONDRAGÓN

At the centre of the Ciudad quarter in Ronda's most picturesque square stands the cathedral church of **Santa María La Mayor** (daily 10am–7pm; 200ptas), originally the Moorish town's Friday mosque. Externally it's a graceful combination of Moorish, Gothic and Renaissance styles with the belfry built on top of the old minaret. Inside, the church itself is sombre and dull but you can see an arch covered with Arabic calligraphy, and just in front of the current street door a part of the old Arab *mihrab*, or prayer niche, has been exposed. Just east of the church along the Callejón de los Tramposos stands the **Minarete de San Sebastián**, a tower that survives from a fourteenth-century mosque. In the opposite direction and a short distance west from Santa María La Mayor is the most important of Ronda's palaces, the fourteenth-century **Palacio de Mondragón** (Mon–Fri 10am–6pm, Sat & Sun 10am–3pm; 250ptas) on the plaza of the same name. Probably the real *"palace of the Moorish kings"*, following the *reconquista* it was much altered in order to accommodate Ferdinand and Isabel who lodged here when they visited Ronda. Inside, three of the patios preserve original stucco work and mosaics and there's a magnificent carved wood ceiling; the palace also houses a **museum** covering local archeology and aspects of Moorish Ronda, in particular burial practices relating to the recently discovered cemetery outside the walls (see below). From a restored Mudéjar courtyard there's a fine **view** over the *Tajo* towards the Serranía de Ronda.

Just north of here at **Casa Juan Bosco** (daily 9am–6pm; 100ptas), c/Tenorio 20, you can visit a nineteenth-century mansion stuffed full of heavy mahogany furniture. The house itself is dull and oppressive, but the reconstructed Mudéjar gardens with fountain and mosaics are a delight, offering more great views over the *Tajo*. Heading south on c/Armiñan which bisects La Ciudad, on the left at no. 65 you'll find the new **Museo Historico de La Serranía** (daily 10am–7pm; 200ptas), largely devoted to celebrating the Serranía's illustrious, mainly nineteenth-century bandits including displays of their weapons as well as tableaux and audiovisual presentations. Further along the same street, near the southern end of the Ciudad to the right are the ruins of the **Alcázar**, razed by the French in 1809 and now partially occupied by a school. Once it was virtually impregnable – now it's full of litter and the occasional stray sheep.

Continuing downhill along c/Armiñán you'll pass the sixteenth-century **Iglesia del Espíritu Santo** (daily 10am–6pm; 75ptas) with a fine interior, en route to the town's principal Moorish gate, the magnificent **Puerta de Almocabar**. Deriving from the Arabic *al maqabir* (cemetery) it would have led to the recently discovered burial grounds which – following the Roman practice – were always located outside the walls. In 1485, the Christian conquerors, led by Ferdinand, passed through this gate to claim the town. The adjoining arch of **Puerta de Carlos V** was constructed during the reign of Ferdinand's successor, the Habsburg emperor.

THE MERCADILLO QUARTER AND THE PLAZA DE TOROS

When Ronda was retaken from the Moors in 1485, the impoverished governors imposed such heavy taxes on all goods and foodstuffs entering it that the merchants set up their own quarter outside the Ciudad to avoid paying them. This area, the **Mercadillo**, has effectively become the centre of the modern town, and is currently undergoing a face-lift after years of neglect. Many buildings in and around the focal Plaza de España have undergone renovation, among which is a stylish new *parador* – the former *Ayuntamiento* – overlooking the *Tajo*. A newly constructed path, the **Paseo Blas Infante** at the rear of the *parador*, can be followed along the edge of the *Tajo* northwards to the Alameda and *Hotel Reina Victoria* and offers fine **views** towards the Serranía de Ronda. The *barrio's* major monument has to be the **Plaza de Toros**, to the north of the Plaza de España (daily 10am–7pm; 400ptas), the oldest, one of the largest and certainly the most venerated bullring in Spain. Opened in 1785, it became the stage upon which the father of the modern bullfight, Pedro Romero, laid down and demonstrated the rules of fighting bulls on foot (see box). Once you've passed through the elaborate Baroque doorway, it's possible to wander around the arena with its unusual stone barriers and an elegant double tier of seats supported by stone columns. The **museum** gives an illuminating history of the *corrida* or bullfight; besides posters advertising the first *corrida* held here on May 19, 1785, and Pedro Romero's *traje de luces* ("suit of lights"), there are photos of Hemingway and Orson Welles, two regular visitors. Welles's last wish was to have his ashes buried in Ronda and they are now

PEDRO ROMERO: FATHER OF THE *CORRIDA*

Born in Ronda in 1754, Pedro Romero is the father of the modern **bullfight**; previously bulls had been killed only on horseback with a *rejón* or spear, as a patrician pastime. However, Romero was not the first to fight bulls on foot: legend has it that this accolade goes to his grandfather Francisco Romero, who leapt into the ring when an aristocrat had been dismounted by a bull and began to distract it with his hat, delighting the crowd in the process. The hat was changed for the red *muleta*, or cape, and the bullfight was born. Once the *corrida* had been created however, it was Pedro Romero who laid down the pattern for all future contests with his passes and moves, many still in use today, along with the invention of the almost mystical *arte* – the union of animal and man in a form of ballet. In the newly constructed Ronda ring, Romero killed over 5000 bulls and fought into his eighties, passing on to his students his soberly classical Ronda style, which is markedly different from the more flamboyant styles of Sevilla and Córdoba. A statue honouring Romero stands in the Alameda del Tajo.

interred on the nearby estate of his friend and one of Spain's greatest *toreros*, the *rondeño* Antonio Ordóñez, whose bronze statue (alongside that of his father) stands near the bullring's Puerta Grande. The artist Goya made a number of paintings here of the *matadores* in action, and each September in a tribute to Goya and Romero the *corrida goyesca* is staged (supervised by Ordóñez), with fighters in eighteenth-century-style gear similar to those in the paintings.

Along the pedestrianized c/Espinel, the *barrio*'s main thoroughfare, are a number of interesting señorial mansions including, at no. 4, a particularly elegant one now irreverently transformed into a mundane electrical shop. A little way down the same street, the picturesque **Plaza del Socorro** opens to the left. Recently pedestrianized it has become a favourite spot with *rondeños*, especially on summer nights, when they gather to chat on the terraces of numerous bars and restaurants. The northern end is overlooked by the **Círculo de Artistas**, a fine eighteenth-century *señorial* mansion and now superbly restored as the town's casino. The doorman will usually not object to you stepping inside to view the building's delightful patio.

AROUND THE ALAMEDA DEL TAJO

To the north of the bullring lies the **Alameda del Tajo**, a pleasant park completed in the early nineteenth century with views towards the Serranía de Ronda. The garden is said to have been laid out at no cost to the local council, the funds raised by fines on those using "obscene language in public, thereby causing a scandal". Continuing in the same direction will bring you to the Carmelite **Convent** on the Plaza de la Merced, its doors flanked by two great palms. Inside, the nuns sell their *dulces* – after 5pm.

You could continue along Avenida Fleming (aka c/Jerez) to the **Hotel Reina Victoria**, built by an English company in the first decade of the century to house British visitors, many of whom came from the military base at Gibraltar. The Austrian poet Rainer Maria Rilke put up here in 1913, and his room (no. 208) – complete with his fascinating framed hotel bill – has been preserved as a museum which the management will allow you to view on request. The hotel's **bar** has a terrace with stunning views down the Guadiaro river valley to the distant Serranía. Finally, a couple of blocks in from the Plaza de España is the remarkably preserved inn where Miguel Cervantes once slept, the sixteenth-century **Posada de las Ánimas** ("Inn of Souls") on c/Cecilia. Today, although this is officially the town's *Hogar del Pensionista*, or old people's home, the building looks every bit the ancient inn, with a skull and crossbones carved in the keystone above the door, which may have something to do with the building's name. The elderly residents are only too happy to let you see inside. Nearby, the eighteenth-century **Virgen de los Dolores** in the street of the same name is a chapel with a curious porch projecting into the street. Carved on the porch's pillars are some weird, bird-like creatures, as well as others that are part beast, part human with ropes fastened around their necks. The site of the church was formerly a gallows for condemned prisoners and this strange imagery may be connected with the representation of these unfortunates.

Eating and drinking

A great many of Ronda's best **eating and drinking** options are on or around the recently pedestrianized Plaza del Socorro. There are numerous good places for breakfast along c/Espinel, and a couple of good restaurants in Ciudad, but few of the touristy restaurants along the c/Virgen de la Paz fronting the bullring are worth bothering with. For **tapas** aficionados there are plenty of quality places to try out.

RESTAURANTS

La Farola, Plaza Carmen Abela 9. Friendly and economical *raciones* and *platos combinados* place, which is open till late.

Bar-Restaurante Jerez, Plaza del Teniente Arce. Terraced restaurant, flanking the bullring, serving good *raciones* and *platos combinados*.

Bar Luciano, c/Armiñan 42, La Ciudad. Pleasant new bar-restaurant with a good-value *menú* for 1200ptas.

Don Miguel, *Hotel Don Miguel*, Plaza de España. One of the best restaurants around here, with *rondeño* specialities such as *perdiz estofado* (partridge stew) and *arroz con conejo* (rabbit with rice), as well as a medium-priced *menú*. The main attraction, though, is the terrace, offering a marvellous view of the *Tajo*.

Parador de Ronda, Plaza de Espana. The parador's restaurant has an excellent choice of local and regional dishes such as *conejo del monte* (rabbit) and *rabo de toro* (oxtail), many of them appearing on a *menú* for around 4000ptas.

Doña Pepa, Plaza del Socorro. Decent, family-run restaurant with, on the opposite side of the intervening Pasaje Correos, a separate café-bar serving *bocadillos* and freshly squeezed orange juice.

Restaurante Pedro Romero, Virgen de la Paz 18. Excellent, mid-priced restaurant opposite the bullring's Puerta Grande through which the *matadores* are carried shoulder high after a spectacular performance. A favourite with locals; in winter they dine in the interior rooms surrounded by bullfighting memorabilia. There's also an economical *menú*.

Bar-Restaurante Royal, c/Virgen de la Paz 42 opposite the Alameda. Good-value *tapas* bar and restaurant with a 900ptas *menú*. Some terrace tables front the park.

Casa Santa Pola, c/Santo Domingo 3, La Ciudad. Impressive restaurant in a former *casa señorial* containing bits of the ninth-century house which preceded it. On three floors with views over the *Tajo*, a wide range of local dishes are on offer and there are *menús del dia* for 1500ptas and 2000ptas.

Tragabuche, José Aparicio 1, near Plaza de España. Ronda's most stylish restaurant with an adventurous menu designed by noted chef Sergio López. Minimalist decor and slightly formal, but worth the extra for this standard of dining.

Bar Valencia, c/Naranja 6. Good *platos combinados* in an earthy and authentic atmosphere with an unbelievably cheap *menú* for 600ptas.

TAPAS BARS

Bodega La Giralda, c/Nueva 19, off Plaza de España. Hugely popular bar serving up good *fino* and excellent *tapas* in a great setting. It's a traditional place, so you may have trouble finding somewhere to sit.

Marisquería Cervecería Paco, Plaza del Socorro 8. Best place in this area; the seafood is fresh and the *tapas* and *raciones* – washed down with a beer at outdoor tables – are excellent.

Patatín Patatán, c/Borrego 7, off the east side of Plaza del Socorro. Popular *tapas* bar with a buzzing ambiente and a wide range of specials including *conejo en salsa* (rabbit) and *habas a la rondería* (broad beans). *Bar Rosalejo*, next door, is also good.

El Portón, c/Pedro Romero 7, off the west side of Plaza del Socorro. Favourite haunt of bullfighting aficionados; does good *jamón* and *cazón* (shark) *tapas* and serves an economical *menú* at terrace tables.

Casa Romero, c/Ríos Rosas 16, south of Plaza del Socorro. Popular *tapas* and *raciones* bar which also serves *platos combinados*. House specials include *gambas al pil pil* (shrimps with garlic) and *pulpo* (octopus).

CAFETERÍAS, BREAKFAST BARS AND HELADERÍAS

Café Alba, c/Espinel 44. Piping hot *churros* and delicious breakfast coffee. If this popular place is too packed, the nearby *Cafetería La Ibense* is a good alternative.

El Molino, Plaza del Socorro 6. Housed in the corner of the casino with a pleasant terrace, this is a good place for breakfast croissants and snacks. They have similar outlets at c/Molino 6 just to the north, and c/Los Remedios 1, just to the south of the same plaza.

Rico, c/Espinel 42, south side of the Plaza del Socorro. Nicest *heladería* in town – also good for afternoon tea and, in winter, steaming cups of hot chocolate.

Salon de Té Al-Zahra, c/Las Tiendas 19, slightly west of Plaza Carmen Abela. Pleasant Moroccan-style tea room offering over a hundred different teas and tasty *pasteles* to go with them. Try the *Tunecino* Arab tea or the *Marroqui*. Open 4pm till late.

Nightlife

Ronda's **nightlife** tends to be provincial and low key. However, with a little persistence and luck you may catch some memorable flamenco.

Pub Baco, c/Borrego at the north corner of Plaza del Socorro. Lively music bar popular with a younger crowd. *Rilke*, c/Cabrera Prim, and *Feu*, c/Naranja, are similar places nearby.

Disco-Pub La Barraca, north of the bus station on the Sevilla road. Ronda's only disco (check for an almost annual name change though); it opens at 10pm and stages live flamenco shows on Fri and Sat. Closed Mon.

Las Bridas, c/Remedios s/n south of Plaza del Socorro. Music bar which often puts on live shows and *flamenco moderna*.

Peña Flamenco Tobalo, Plaza los Descalzos, east of Plaza Carmen Abela (☎95 287 60 94). Housed in the *Bar la Plazuela*, the *peña* puts on live flamenco most Friday nights and welcomes visitors. Ring the night before if possible to save yourself a wasted journey.

Around Ronda

Ronda makes an excellent base for exploring the superb countryside in the immediate vicinity or for visiting more of the White Towns; one of the most unusual is **Setenil**, 15km away with curious cave-like streets. In the vicinity lies **Arriate**, famous for its bell ringers, and the **Cortijo de Las Monjas**, the only vineyard in Andalucía producing top-drawer red wines. If you're attracted by ancient ruins and awesome caves then you shouldn't miss Ronda's Roman predecessor **Ronda La Vieja** or the **Cueva de la Pileta** whose remarkable Stone Age cave paintings are unique on the peninsula. To the west are the temptingly scenic villages of **Benaoján** and **Montejaque**, ringed by rugged limestone heights that hold numerous caves such as the Cueva del Gato, a magnet for cavers.

Arriate and the Cortijo de las Monjas

Eight kilometres from the northern end of Ronda, across a plain of olive groves, the pleasant village of **ARRIATE** is reached by turning off the A367 to Campillos. Its fame stems from the Campaneros de la Aurora ("bell-ringers of the dawn"), who rise at dawn every Saturday and tour the streets until 7am singing hymns to the accompaniment of bells, guitars and cymbals. Pausing at the doors of houses who have "pre-booked" numbers from the repertoire, their *salves,* which last ten minutes, cost the most, or they offer a quick cheap blast called a *Pater Noster.* You can get ensuite **rooms** at *Pensión El Chozo,* Avda. Andalucía s/n (☎95 216 53 44; ③). Two daily **trains** to Ronda leave from the station on the southern edge of the village.

Three kilometres beyond Arriate along the Setenil road (CA4211), a dirt track signed on the right leads to the unique **Cortijo de las Monjas** (Mon–Fri 8am–7pm; ☎95 211 41 24), a vineyard producing something long believed to be impossible in this climate: a red wine worthy of comparison with the great wines of the north. The vineyard was founded in 1990 by Costa del Sol socialite Prince Alonso Hohenlohe, and French experts were hired to advise on the planting of Gallic vines in the Serranía de Ronda which, with its cold winters and temperate summers, was judged the ideal terrain. The first vintages were favourably received by Spain's wine pundits and the 1995 was so good that it was snapped up within weeks of going on sale. The *bodega* tour ends with a tasting and the chance to buy some of the other vintages. If you can't get to the vineyard the wines are on sale in Ronda at Super Marquez, c/Espinel 13, and are served in many restaurants.

Setenil de las Bodegas

Seven kilometres north beyond the vineyard turn, **SETENIL DE LAS BODEGAS** is the strangest of all the White Towns, its cave-like streets formed from the overhanging ledge of a gorge carved through the tufa rock by the Río Trejo. Many of the houses – sometimes two or three storeys high – have natural roofs in the rock which, in places, block out the sky completely. This was once a major wine-producing centre, since the caves made good wine cellars; thus the town's name. The phylloxera plague of the last century destroyed the vines, however, and brought economic ruin in its wake, from which Setenil has only recently recovered.

Sights in Setenil are limited, but if you can get into the church of **La Encarnación** (ask the neighbours) – a sixteenth-century Gothic structure – you'll see a fine, twelve-panelled Flemish painting that survived Civil War devestation. The ruins of the nearby Moorish **castillo** are worth a look, too, and below the church, the **Ayuntamiento** has a superb Mudéjar *artesonado* ceiling. There are a couple of **bars** – *Las Flores,* near the river at the opposite end of the town from the church, has nice views – and a decent **hotel**, *El Almendral* (☎956 13 40 29; ⑤), on the road just outside town, with an excellent **restaurant** downstairs.

Don't take the train from Ronda to Setenil station, which is a good 8km from Setenil village itself. If public transport lets you down – there are infrequent buses from Ronda – the roads around here are pleasant for walking or **hitching**, and rides aren't usually hard to come by. Take care when **driving** in Setenil however, as many visitors end up getting completely stuck in the narrow, hilly streets – much to the amusement of the locals. From Setenil it's possible to **walk** the 8km to the ruins of Ronda La Vieja (see below) via the hamlets of Campiña and Venta de Leche.

Ronda La Vieja

Some 12km northwest of Ronda are the ruins of **RONDA LA VIEJA**, the first-century Roman town of Acinipo, set in the midst of beautiful hill country. The ruins (Tues–Sat 11am–5pm, Sun 11am–3pm) are reached by turning right (along the MA449) 6km down the main road to Arcos/Sevilla, and following the signs to a farmhouse where the friendly farmer will present you with a plan (in Spanish only) and record your nationality for statistical purposes. Entry to the site, which sprawls away up the hill to the west, is free.

Based on Neolithic foundations, and also an outpost of the Phoenicians, Acinipo reached its zenith in the first century AD as a Roman town. The piles of stones interspersed with small fragments of glittering marble strewn across the hillside once constituted the forum, baths, temples and other edifices of this prosperous agricultural centre, which also had access to iron ore, marble, good building stone and fine potters' clay in close proximity.

Today only a **Roman theatre** – of which just the stage backdrop and some seating survives – alludes to the importance of Acinipo; inscriptions found here tell of crowds flocking to see the chariot races. Immediately west of the theatre, the ground falls away in a startlingly steep escarpment and from here there are fine **views** all around, taking in also the hill village of Olvera to the north (see p.156). For reasons not entirely clear, Acinipo declined in the third century and, in the fourth, ceded its power in the area to nearby Arunda (modern Ronda). On your way out take a look at the foundations of some recently discovered prehistoric stone huts beside the farmhouse. From here a track leads off towards the strange "cave village" of Setenil de las Bodegas.

Cueva de la Pileta

Probably the most interesting trip out from Ronda is to the prehistoric **Cueva de la Pileta** (daily 10am–1pm & 4–6pm; the final group tours leave at 1pm & 6pm; 800ptas), set in a deep valley and surrounded by a spectacular wall of white rock. These fabulous caverns, with their remarkable **Paleolithic paintings** of animals, fish and what are apparently magic symbols, were discovered by a local farmer in 1905 when hunting for guano fertilizer for his fields, and are still supervised by the same family, the Bullóns, one of whom will be your guide. After the usual jokes, as various "cauliflowers", "castles", and a "Venus de Milo" are pointed out among the stalactites and stalagmites en route, the paintings in the depths of the caves, when you reach them, are genuinely awe-inspiring, particularly those in the central chamber.

These etchings – in charcoal, and red and yellow ochres – depict an abundance of wildlife including fish, the *cabra hispanica* and a pregnant mare, all painted on walls which bear the scorch marks of ancient fires. Other abstract signs and symbols have been interpreted as having some magical or ritual purpose. The occupation of the caves, and the earliest red paintings, date from about 25,000 BC, thus predating the more famous caves at Altamira near Santander, down to the end of the Bronze Age. The section of the caves (and paintings) open to view is but a small part of a more massive subterranean labyrinth, and archeologists will be kept busy for many years to come documenting this Paleolithic art gallery. Tours last one hour on average, but can be longer (endlessly so if you haven't brought a pullover to keep warm), and are in Spanish – though the guide may speak a little English. There are hundreds of bats in the cave, and no artificial lighting (a torch is useful), so visitors carry lanterns with them, only adding to the sense of adventure and privilege at being able to view something so stupendously old.

To **reach the caves** with your own transport, take the A376 Arcos/Sevilla road northwest from Ronda, turning left after 14km along the MA505 to Montejaque; the caves are a further 12km from the turn-off, beyond Benaoján. By **public transport**, take an Algeciras-bound local train (4 daily; 20min) to the Estación Benaoján-Montejaque; or a bus, which drops you a little closer, in Benaoján. There's a bar at the train station where you can stock up on drink before the hour-and-a-half long (6km) walk to the caves. Follow the farm track from the right bank of the river until you reach the farmhouse (approximately 30min). From here a track goes straight uphill to the main road just before the signposted turning for the caves. Upon arrival you should wait at the cave entrance; a strict **maximum of 25 persons** is allowed on each tour and larger groups should book ahead (☎95 216 73 43). No photography is allowed inside the cave and if you leave your vehicle at the car park, make sure to remove any valuables not locked in a secure boot.

THE SERRANÍA DE RONDA

Some of the best walking terrain in this stretch of Andalucía lies to the south of Ronda among the ruggedly scenic mountain *pueblos* vividly described by Alastair Boyd in his book *The Sierras of the South*. One of the most starkly beautiful areas of Andalucía, **the Serranía de Ronda** is a region of great natural diversity where wooded ravines, awesome crags and vast forests of cork oaks provide abundant habitats for a rich variety of flora and fauna. The remote hamlets are reachable by road, albeit often with difficulty, but the ideal way to travel this region is with a backpack and compass, from which perspective the landscape – with whitewashed villages set among cherry orchards and vines, each with its own plaza, church and taverna (and sometimes a bed) – becomes an enchanting adventure. The Ronda Turismo should have details on the villages and limited accommodation available.

One good jumping-off point for the Serranía is **Cartajima**, 15km south of Ronda, where a **Refugio** (☎952 18 08 34) has thirty dormitory places and can advise on many fine treks in the area; ring the warden Manuel (who speaks some English) to book a place – they also rent out mountain bikes and offer climbing courses. The Refugio can be reached from Ronda by *Autobuses Lara* (Mon–Fri 2.45pm, returning at 7am). There's also a very pleasant five-hour walking route to Cartajima; again, the Ronda Turismo can provide details. Should you feel like renting a house, the *Centro de Iniciativas Turísticas de la Serranía de Ronda*, c/Pozo 6, north of the Plaza de Toros (Mon–Fri 10am–1pm; ☎952 87 07 39, fax 952 87 90 33), has a list of *casas rurales* to rent throughout the Serranía.

The best maps covering the Serranía are the 1:200,000 *IGN Mapa Provincial de Málaga*, complemented by the 1:50,000 IGN sheet, number 1.065. For Spanish readers, the best book on the region is *Rutas por la Serranía de Ronda* by *Interguías Clave* which clearly describes fifty walks – ranging between 5km and 40km – and has accommodation and background information; it's widely available from bookshops.

An organized half-day **guided tour** for small groups by Land Rover from Ronda (Turismo Alternativo, c/Dr Fleming 56; ☎95 287 55 56; 3000ptas per person) also takes in the caves.

Benaoján, Montejaque and the Cueva del Gato

The nearby villages of **BENAOJÁN** and **MONTEJAQUE**, 3km apart, are both worth a visit. The former has a sixteenth-century church built on the site of an earlier mosque (this was a Moorish stronghold well into Christian times) and a couple of **places to stay**: at c/Ronda 8 the friendly *Hostal Pepita* (☎95 216 72 46; ②) has basic but clean rooms, or there's the upmarket *Molino del Santo*, Bda. Estación (☎95 216 71 51; ⑦), a British-run haven with gardens and pool. **Food** is available here, or *Bar Tajillas* (near the hostal) can provide tasty *tapas* and *raciones*.

Montejaque, cradled between two rocky crags, has a great, typically Spanish square – with its own sparkling white church – fringed with bars, any of which will rustle you up *raciones* if asked. The friendly *Bar Alemán*, in the opposite corner to the church tower, is the best. **Places to stay** include *Palacete de Mañara*, Plaza Constitución 2 (☎95 216 72 52; ⑥) a charming new hotel in a converted *palacio antiguo* with restaurant and mini-pool; they can arrange horse riding, caving and ballooning excursions. A budget choice is the rustic, family-run *Bar La Cabaña*, Avda. Europa s/n, near the entrance to the village (☎95 216 71 58; ②) with simple rooms above a bar where you'll be endlessly entertained by the household's comings and goings. Otherwise *Casitas de la Sierra* (☎95 216 73 92, fax 95 216 72 99; ⑥) rents out fully equipped village houses for longer stays and will often agree to a couple of nights' stopover if there are places free (which also allows you use of a pool). The office lies off the main square, and their nearby restaurant has an economical *menú*.

Returning to Ronda along the direct road from Benaoján (MA555), after 2km you'll pass on the left the *Venta Cueva del Gato* – serving a superb *conejo casero* (rabbit) – behind which a short track leads to the **Cueva del Gato**, a cave fronted by a lagoon. To reach this popular bathing spot, take a track descending to the right of the *venta* which brings you to a wobbly log footbridge over the Río Guadiaro. Once across, turn right along the railway track; after about 100m you'll see the cave and lagoon to the left. The cave mouth high in the rock above the oleander-fringed lagoon must have been occupied by early man, but no paintings have so far been discovered. The cave is open but to penetrate much further than 50m you'll need ropes, lights and some expertise; it's an isolated place and a well-equipped caver perished here in 1999, so don't take chances. Caver and climber Jean Hofer at El Chorro (see p.86) leads fully equipped explorations of the cave and its dramatic subterranean lakes.

Grazalema, El Bosque and northeast to Cañete

Looping through the rocky contours of the last foothills of the Cordillera Subbética mountain range, much of which is covered in pine forest, this route travels first west from Ronda through the verdantly spectacular **Sierra de Grazalema Natural Park** before exploring yet more picturesque hill villages to the north and east of Ronda.

Grazalema

The A376 winds away from Ronda into the Sierra de Sanguijuela, and forking left after about 16km, along the A372, takes you across the provincial border into Cádiz. Another 17km from the turning, the road arrives at **GRAZALEMA**, the central point of the Sierra de Grazalema, now a **Natural Park**. A pretty white village beneath the craggy peak of San Cristóbal, with lots of sloping narrow streets and window boxes full of blooms in summer, it makes an ideal base for delving into the park. This is also the spot with the country's highest rainfall – and there's quite a bit of snow in winter too – which explains the lush vegetation covering the surrounding park, home to a spectacular variety of flora and fauna. Quite apart from the attractions of the park the village has its own charm, its simple main square – adorned with a *pinsapo* fir tree – overlooked by the eighteenth-century church of **Nuestra Señora de la Aurora**.

Grazalema's **Turismo** on the main square, Plaza de España (Tues–Sun 10am–2pm & 5–8pm; ☎956 13 22 25), can give you information about the park and activities such as **horse riding** as well as the surprisingly limited **accommodation** available here. If you're considering a longer stay – and it's certainly worth taking time to enjoy the spectacular countryside hereabouts – ask the Turismo about renting *casas de labranza* (farm cottages). Otherwise your only choice is between the rather sterile *Hotel Grazalema*, 500m along the Ronda road (☎956 13 21 36, fax 956 13 22 13; ⑥), which also has some detached self-catering apartments which sleep four to eight people (⑦), or the pleasant *Casa de las Piedras*, c/Las Piedras 32 (☎956 13 20 14; ②–④), above the main square, which has rooms with and without bath. Both places have restaurants. There's a **campsite**, Tajo Rodillo (☎956 13 20 63), located above the village at the end of c/Las Piedras, whose office has literature on the Natural Park and will provide information about walks and horse-treks in the Sierra; they also rent out mountain bikes. The **bars** and **restaurants** on the square are reasonably priced for *raciones* and *menús*; two places worth singling out for value are *Cádiz El Chico*, on Plaza de España and *Torreón*, c/Agua 44, just north of it. The village's **nightlife** centres around *Disco Chorrito* on c/Chorrito, and the bars along c/Agua get pretty lively, too, when hikers and climbers gather. If the weather's warm enough, you may feel inclined to try out the village **swimming pool** which is spectacularly sited below the village.

PARQUE NATURAL SIERRA DE GRAZALEMA

Bounded by the towns of Grazalema, Ubrique, El Bosque and Zahara, the **Parque Natural Sierra de Grazalema** is an important mountain wilderness, unique to Andalucía. The limestone mass of the Sierra was formed in the Jurassic and Triassic periods and the close proximity of the range to the sea – which traps many of the clouds drifting in from the Atlantic – has produced a microclimate where numerous botanical species dating from before the Ice Age have survived. The most famous of these is the rare **pinsapo**, or Spanish fir, native only to this area of Europe, which grows at an altitude of between 1000m and 1700m. The high rainfall here, plus the wet, cool summers, are essential to its survival. The Sierra also supports a wealth of birdlife: eagles (Bonelli's, booted, and golden), vultures (griffon and Egyptian), as well as various owls and woodpeckers are all common. The streams and riverbanks are the domain of water voles and otters, the latter not popular with a number of fish farms in the area. On the Sierra's higher reaches the magnificent Spanish ibex has been re-introduced to a craggy habitat where its numbers are increasing.

The best way to appreciate the park is by walking, but to protect wildlife and nesting birds access is restricted to different sections at certain times, and in July and August many routes are closed due to the high fire risk. The park's main **information office** is at El Bosque, Avda. de la Diputación s/n (daily 10am–2pm & Wed–Sun 6–8pm; ☎956 72 70 29), and there's a smaller branch in Grazalema, c/Las Piedras 11 (Tues–Sun 10.30am–2pm & 5–6pm; ☎956 13 22 30). Both provide access *permisos* (permits; free), as well as maps with walking routes – the *Itinerario del Pinsapar* (guided only) takes you through the major stands of the *pinsapo* Spanish fir. In Zahara de la Sierra, at c/San Juan 1, the *Turismo Rural de Bocaleones* (☎ & fax 956 12 31 14), organizes **outdoor activities** in the park, including horse-trekking, mountain bike tours, guided walks and Land Rover trips – as well as rugged stuff such as parascending, potholing, climbing and canoeing. They also conduct a variety of wildlife and bird-watching excursions and can even arrange accommodation for you.

El Bosque

Located on the Natural Park's western flank, the village of **EL BOSQUE**, surrounded by slopes of planted pine, is easily reached from Grazalema via a delightfully wooded drive along the A372 which bisects the park. When travel writer Richard Ford passed through here in the 1830s he described it as a "robbers' lair" and counted "fifteen monumental crosses in the space of fifty yards" – victims of the ruthless bandits who preyed on travellers. He advised his readers to make sure they carried a watch to buy off these brigands, preferably one with a gaudy gilt chain, "the lack of which the bandit considered an unjustifiable attempt to defraud him of his right." Today it's a far more peaceful place, although the tranquillity is interrupted in August, when nearby summer camps increase the 2000-odd population threefold.

El Bosque provides an alternative to Grazalema as a base for visiting the Natural Park: there's usually space at *Hostal Enrique Carillo*, Avda. Diputación 5 (☎956 71 61 05; ③) in the centre. Close by, the aptly named *Hotel Las Truchas*, Avda. Diputacíon 1 (☎956 71 60 61; ⑤), has a **restaurant** where fresh trout features strongly on the menu, often with a slice of *jamón serrano* tucked inside; El Bosque has the most southerly trout river in Europe, the nearby Río Majaceite. At the splendid *Albergue-Campamento* – a **youth hostel** and **campsite** tucked away in the woods (☎956 71 62 12, fax 956 71 62 58; ①–③), you can get double and triple rooms with bath, or rent a tent complete with camp beds. There's a great pool and a mind-boggling list of activities on offer, including climbing and hang-gliding courses as well as trekking, horse riding and bungee-jumping. To get there, follow the road which bends up behind the *Hotel Las Truchas*.

The village has plenty of places to **eat**, with trout much in evidence. For a great-value meal, head for the trout farm Piscifactoría Acuario, hidden in the woods just beyond the *Albergue-Campamento*; the Mesón Majaceite opposite does the freshest trout you can get as part of a 900ptas *menú*. In the village proper the friendly *Venta Julian* also has a good *menú*.

One scenic **walk** along the Río El Bosque is best started from Benamahoma, 4km east: the steep descent is easier this way. Starting from the *El Bujio* bar (a taxi will drop you there if you don't fancy the walk), make for some green gates at the end of the car park. Step through a small stand of eucalyptus to the right of the gates and keep ahead along the left bank of the river. As you follow the river back to El Bosque, there are plenty of opportunities for bird-spotting and picnicking. Incidentally, Benamahoma also has a cheap and cheerful *hostal*, *Pensión Milagros*, c/Real 37 (☎956 71 60 84; ①), should you wish to extend your stay.

Zahara de la Sierra and Algodonales

It's worth going back to Grazalema to take the spectacular CA531 road which climbs to the Puerto de las Palomas (Pass of the Doves, at 1350m the second-highest pass in Andalucía). A little before the pass you'll see on the left an entrance to the forest of the *pinsapo* Spanish fir – this is the start of the *Itinerario del Pinsapar* walking route (see the previous box). Once through the pass the road embarks on a dramatic descent to **ZAHARA DE LA SIERRA** (or *de los Membrillos* – "of the Quinces"), today surrounded by olive groves. This is perhaps the most perfect of Andalucía's fortified hill *pueblos*, a landmark for miles around, its red-tiled houses huddled round a church beneath a ruined castle on a stark outcrop of rock. It was once an important Moorish town, and its capture by the Christians in 1483 opened the way for the conquest of Ronda – and ultimately Granada. The heart of the village, which was declared a national monument in 1983, is a cobbled main street which connects the church of **San Juan** and the eighteenth-century Baroque church of **Santa María de la Mesa**, which has a fine *retablo* with a sixteenth-century image of the Virgin. The surviving tower of the twelfth-century **Moorish castle** (always open with fine views) – constructed over a previous Roman one – looms over the village and incorporates the remains of an early church.

Along the main street, c/San Juan, are a couple of **places to stay** – the homely *Pensión Gonzalo* (☎956 12 32 17; ②) at no. 9 (no sign), with rooms overlooking the church, is maintained in spotless condition by the charming Señora Contrera Gil. A little further along, *Hotel Marqués de Zahara* (☎956 12 30 61; ④) has balcony rooms, shady patio, a restaurant serving local specialities and information on renting out *casas rurales* for longer stays.

On the road to the castle the stylish, good-value *Hotel Arco de la Villa* (☎956 30 56 11, fax 956 30 55 59; ⑤) has rooms with spectacular views over the nearby *embalse*, but unfortunately, no balconies. Towards the swimming pool on the edge of the village, the renovated *Hostal Los Estribos*, c/Fuerte 3 (☎956 13 74 45; ③), is another option for rooms with bath and views. For **meals**, *Restaurante Tadeos*, Paseo de la Fuente s/n (☎956 12 30 86), is a good bet; in summer it decamps to the swimming pool where it offers a budget *menú* and terrace view; there are a few simple rooms here too (③). Zahara's **campsite** lies 3km out of the village on the old Ronda road ("*carretera vieja*") and can be reached by taxi from the village for around 500ptas one way; here you can rent a tent complete with camp beds.

Enclosed by the folds of the Sierra de Líjar, **ALGODONALES**, 6km north, is a pleasant enough place with a long, central plaza dominated by the lofty tower of the eighteenth-century Neoclassical church of **Santa Ana**. Should you wish to stay the night, there are ensuite **rooms** at the welcoming *Hostal Sierra de Líjar*, c/Ronda 5 (☎956 13 70 65; ③), just below the square, which also has a restaurant with a great-value *menú*.

Olvera

OLVERA, 18km beyond Algodonales in an area thick with olives (from which the town's name may derive), couldn't look more dramatic – a great splash of whitewashed houses tumbling down a hill below the twin towers of its church and a fine Moorish castle. You can ascend the hill along the town's long main street. The church, **La Encarnación**, is disappointing when you get up close, as it's actually a nineteenth-century version of an earlier, fifteenth-century edifice. More interesting is the twelfth-century **Moorish castle** (Tues–Sun 10am–2pm & 5.30–8.30pm; voluntary donations) which formed part of Nasrid Granada's line of defence against the Christian lands; entry is gained through a gate to the side of no. 3 on the plaza (Plaza de la Iglesia) facing the church. There are great **views** from here over the town and to the surrounding hill villages.

Should you want to **stay** and explore the region with its river, olive groves and stark backdrop of the Sierra de Líjar, options include the excellent-value *Hostal Maqueda*, c/Calvario 35 (☎956 13 07 33; ②), and the plusher *Hotel Sierra y Cal*, Avda. Ntra. Sra. de los Remedios 2 (☎956 13 05 03; ⑤), both near the centre. On the way into town, on the Antequera road, the new *Hotel Fuente del Pino* (☎ & fax 956 13 03 09; ④) is a tempting alternative with air-conditioned rooms, restaurant and an excellent pool. For **food**, *Bar Pepe* on the small square below the church does good tapas in air-conditioned comfort, and you'll find superb *tapas*, *fino* and a budget *menú* at the friendly *Bar Manolo* in Plaza Andalucía at the foot of the main street; the restaurant of the *Sierra y Cal* hotel also offers a good-value *menú*.

Cañete La Real

Some 20km east of Olvera lies **CAÑETE LA REAL** (the 2pm bus from Ronda to Almargen passes through), famed around these parts for a monumental century-old feud with its enemy Olvera over the custody of the **sacred image of the Virgen de los Cañosantos**. The result has been a bitter Andalucian compromise: Cañete grabbed the work's head and arms and quickly locked them up in the town's impressive Baroque church – no doubt to thwart any sneaky sorties from Olvera. To see the revered fragments you'll need to raise the priest, who lives in the house behind the church and can be a little deaf. Should you not succeed, there's always the medieval castle to divert you, and a municipal swimming pool (close to the entrance to the town before the main square). For *accommodation* the *Hotel Restaurante Piedras* on the Almargen road at the edge of the village (☎952 18 31 38; ③) has ensuite rooms above a restaurant with a good-value 700ptas *menú*.

From Ronda to Cádiz

One truly spectacular White Town route is **from Ronda to Cádiz** via the appealing villages of Ubrique, Alcalá de los Gazules and Medina Sidonia, cutting its way across the Sierra de Grazalema and Los Alcornocales Natural Parks, and winding through rocky hills, deep gorges and dense cork oak forests.

Villaluenga del Rosario

Perching about 10km northeast of Ubrique on a winding secondary road, the tiny village of **VILLALUENGA DEL ROSARIO** is the highest in Cádiz Province. Tucked beneath a great crag, it's a simple place, with narrow streets, flower-filled balconies and pan-tiled roofs, frequently enveloped by mountain mists. When the Córdoban Caliphate fell, the village was taken by forces under the Duke of Arcos and repopulated with settlers from Arcos and Villamartín. Its curious **Plaza de Toros**, partly hacked out of the rock, is worth a look and sees action once a year on October 7, when the feast of the Virgen Del Rosario is celebrated with a *corrida*. The friendly *Hostal Villaluenga* (☎956 46 19 12; ③) has comfortable **rooms**.

Benaocaz

From Villaluenga the road continues through the Manga Pass, an area which has yielded many prehistoric artefacts and dolmens, to the farming settlement of **BENAOCAZ**, another ancient village founded by the Moors in the eighth century. There's little to see apart from a Baroque **church** built over the former mosque, which used part of its minaret to make its tower, and a small **museum** documenting the life of the Sierra. The *Ayuntamiento* on the main square, Plaza de la Libertades 1 (☎956 46 14 91), gives **tourist information**.

If you want to stretch your legs, a four-kilometre **walk** to the northwest along the Río Tavizna brings you to the ruined Moorish castle of the same name, one of a string of defensive bastions that once gave protection to these isolated hamlets. There's a good chance of seeing choughs, booted eagles and griffon vultures patrolling the crags here. You can get **rooms** – and apartments for a longer stay – at *Hotel San Antón*, Plaza de San Antón 5 (☎956 12 55 77; ⑥); there's also a **campsite**, *Camping Tavizna* (☎956 46 30 11) near the entrance to the village, with a restaurant.

Ubrique

From Benaocaz the road corkscrews down from the mountainous sierra until the snow-white vista of **UBRIQUE** comes into view below, spreading along the valley of the Río Ubrique with the daunting knife-edged crag of the Cruz de Tajo rearing up behind. Despite this stunning first appearance, on closer contact it's a rather large and disappointingly dull industrial centre, but there are enough features to divert you for a while.

A place which has always bred tenacious guerrilla fighters and which fought dourly against the French in the War of Independence (actually defeating a contingent of the Imperial Guard near Gaucín), Ubrique is a natural mountain fortress which was one of the last Republican strongholds in the Civil War. Today, it's a relatively prosperous if unexciting town, surviving largely on its medieval guild craft of **leather-making**, the products of which are sold in shops along the main street, where most of the bars and restaurants are also gathered. There's only one **place to stay** – *Hostal Ocurris*, Avda. Solis Pascual 49 (☎956 46 39 39; ⑤), which has ensuite rooms with TV.

Alcalá de los Gazules

The A375 road from Ubrique towards Alcalá, 44km to the southwest, runs through the **Parque Natural de Los Alcornocales** with magnificently rugged but sparsely populated mountain scenery and, in parts, densely wooded forests of cork oak and pine. Close to the Sierra de Aljibe to the south, the road skirts the frontier with Málaga and at the junction with the CA503 at the Puerto de Galis the solitary but excellent *Venta del Puerto de Galis* is a hunters' favourite and often has game on its menu. Beyond here the road joins the valley of the Río Barbate for the final descent into the White Town of **ALCALÁ DE LOS GAZULES**, the geographical centre of the province of Cádiz. When the Romans were conquering this area early in the second century BC, they tried to divide and rule the Iberian tribes by granting the status of *colonia* to selected settlements – a crucial first step on the way to full Roman citizenship and all the privileges such status could bestow. One such settlement was the Iberian *Turris Lascutana*, as Alcalá then was, and this was an attempt to win its allegiance away from the Turditanian tribal capital at Hasta Regia near Jerez. A surviving bronze plaque (in the archeological museum in Madrid) records the decree of the Roman governor, Lucius Aemelius Paullus in 189 BC, which granted Turris possession of the fields and town which they had formerly held as a fief of Hasta. Apart from the winding, narrow streets, little remains of the later Moorish settlement founded by the Berber family the Gazules, who gave their name to the town in the twelfth century when this was a *taifa* state of the kingdom of Granada.

A cascade of white dwellings gathered beneath its ruined Alcázar, Alcalá is a sleepy little place. In the Plaza Alta in the upper town there's the fifteenth-century Gothic church of **San Jorge**, with an imposing tower, beautifully carved choir and an effigy attributed to Martínez Montañes, but not much else. In the lower town the **Plaza de Toros** has been turned into a disco, somewhat blasphemously given the surrounding bull-breeding country). Just over the road from the bullring-disco on the c/Paseo de la Playa is *Restaurante Pizarro*, a decent mid-priced **restaurant** with a good-value *menú*. A little further along, the same proprietors run the comfortable *Hostal Pizarro* (☎956 42 01 03; ③) with ensuite rooms; resist attempts to place you in their more expensive hotel.

Tajo de las Figuras and El Cuervo Monastery

An alternative route to Medina Sidonia from Alcalá takes you 17km southwest to **BENALUP DE SIDONIA** where the **Tajo de las Figuras** caves have important Neolithic cave paintings. The caves, 7km south of Benalup along the CA212, are signed on the left and the *abrigos*, or rock shelters, can be seen from the road. Enquire about current visiting arrangements first at the *Ayuntamiento* in Benalup, c/Cantera s/n (☎956 42 41 29), to save yourself a wasted journey.

Roughly 6km further east on the same road is the start of a delightfully picturesque walk to the **abandoned monastery of El Cuervo**. The monastery was founded in the eighteenth century by the Carmelite order, occupied by the French troops during the War of Independence, and abandoned in 1835. The tranquillity of the spot and the poignant sight of the ruined monastery buildings makes the hour-long walk to reach it more than worthwhile. Due to the land having been privately purchased, access is currently possible only on guided visits (every Wed and the last Sat of the month; not July or Aug) starting at 9.30am from the Medina Sidonia Turismo (☎956 41 24 04), returning at 2.30pm (200ptas). More access may be allowed in the near future and the same Turismo will advise.

La Ruta del Toro

Heading towards Medina Sidonia by the direct C440 route, you'll join, beyond Alcalá, what is known as **La Ruta del Toro** ("route of the bull"), passing many of the ranches that breed the mean, black *toros bravos*, or fighting bulls used in the *corridas*. These mighty beasts, grazing on pastures shaded by olives and holm oaks, are tended by mounted *vaqueros* who guard them while noting their potential for valour. This will eventually be tested in the *tienta* or trial ring, an important first step in deciding whether the bull will die in the *corrida* or the abattoir.

About 4km east of Medina Sidonia, a turn-off on the right leads to another White Town, the tiny **PATERNA DE LA RIVERA**. Set among rolling hills, and famous for its *ganaderías* (cattle ranches) and horse breeding studs, it's also celebrated among gourmets for the quality of its asparagus and its snails. Nearby, the **Castillo de la Gigonza**, an ancient Moorish fort, lies a walkable 4km to the northeast. Take care, however, not to cross the paths of any bulls – it may be safer to follow the circuitous route via the hamlet of La Parrilla. Returning from here via the minor road east will bring you to the main A381 road from Jerez to Medina Sidonia where, at the crossroads, the *Ventorillo de Carbón* has excellent **tapas** and makes an ideal lunch stop.

Medina Sidonia

Following its reconquest by Alfonso X in 1264, **MEDINA SIDONIA**, another ancient hill-top town, was to become one of Spain's most prestigious ducal seats; it supplied the admiral who led the Armada against England. The title of Duque de Medina Sidonia was bestowed upon the family of Guzmán El Bueno for his valiant role in taking the town, a line which continues and is currently led by the firebrand socialist Duchess of Medina Sidonia (see p.196), whose actions and pronouncements probably have some of her ancestors spinning in the family vault.

Not unlike the ducal house, the town, depopulated and now somewhat ramshackle, has seen better days. Nevertheless, the tidy narrow cobbled streets with their rows of reja-fronted houses, still offer glimpses of bygone grandeur. A good place to begin a look around is the elegant Plaza de Espana dominated by the wonderful Renaissance facade of the seventeenth-century *Ayuntamiento*. The **Turismo** (Mon–Fri 10am–1.30pm & 5–8pm; ☎956 41 00 05), which has town maps, lies at the top of the steep main street, fronting a charming square, Plaza Iglesia Mayor. The same square contains the church after which it is named, **Santa María la Coronada** (daily 10.30am–2.30pm & 5–9pm; 250ptas), built over an earlier mosque. Inside, an enormous and exquisite **retablo** – 15m high – depicting scenes from the life of Christ, is a stunning work of craftsmanship in polychromed wood. There's also a fine sculpted image of *Cristo del Perdón* attributed to Luisa Roldán ("La Roldana"). The guardian will also point out on request some sixteenth-century benches used by the Inquisition. Medina's importance in Roman times, when it was known as *Asido Caesarina*, is evidenced by some remarkable **Roman sewers** (entry at c/Espíritu Santo 3; Tues–Sun 10am–1.30pm & 6–8pm; free) which are buried beneath the town's eastern flank. Dating from the first century AD, the extensive stone-built sewers stand over two metres in height, and are a tribute to Roman engineering skills. Medina Sidonia also boasts three **Moorish gates** of which the Arco de la Pastora, close to the Jerez road, is the best preserved.

The town is unused to tourists and rooms tend to be spartan but clean. At *Pensión Amalia*, Plaza de España 6 near the *Ayuntamiento* (☎956 41 00 35; ②), you'll be greeted with a glass of local *fino*, or there's *Casa Napoleón* nearby at c/San Juan 21 (☎956 41 01 83; ②), a spotless *pensión* which puts up *matadores* who come to train at the local bull-breeding ranches. Photos of famous past guests – dressed to kill in their *corrida* finery – line the walls. Both places have a few rooms with bath. *Hotel El*

Molino, Avda. Andalus 1 on the east side of town (☎956 41 03 00; ④), has better en suite rooms above a restaurant, but is not so central. For **food** and **drink** head for the main square, Plaza de España; *Restaurante Cádiz* serves very good regional dishes, has a *menú* and does *tapas*, while *Mesón Machín*, Plaza Iglesia 9, facing the church of Santa María, offers good, mid-priced meals, *tapas* and *raciones* and has a spectacular view over the town from its terrace. Slightly further out *El Duque*, Paseo Armada Española s/n, is a high class restaurant serving excellent meat dishes with superb views from its terrace.

Arcos de la Frontera

From whichever direction you approach it, your first view of **ARCOS DE LA FRON-TERA** – the westernmost of the White Towns – will certainly be fabulous. In full sun the town shimmers magnificently on its great double crag of limestone high above the Río Guadalete. This dramatic location, enhanced by low, white houses and fine sandstone churches, gives the town a similar feel and appearance to Ronda – except Arcos is rather poorer and, quite unjustifiably, far less visited.

Dating from Iberian times and known as *Arco Briga* to the Romans, Arcos came to prominence as a Moorish town within the Cordoban Caliphate. When Córdoba's rule collapsed in the eleventh century Arcos existed as a petty *taifa* state, until its annexation by al-Mu'tamid of Sevilla in 1103. The seizure of Arcos by Christian forces under Alfonso El Sabio (the Wise) in 1264 – over two centuries before Zahara fell – was a real feat against what must have been a wretchedly impregnable fortress.

Arrival, information and orientation

Most of Arcos's monuments are located in the higher old town – where you'll be spending much of your time. The new town has spilled out to the west and east of here at the foot of the crag. The **bus station** is in the new town on c/Corregidores (☎956 70 20 15), served by the *Comes* company, with regular buses to Cádiz and Jerez. Arcos de la Frontera has only recently improved tourist facilities; an underfunded **Turismo** on the Plaza del Cabildo (Mon–Fri 10am–2pm & 5.30–7.30pm, Sat 10am–2pm, Sun 10.30am–12.30pm) struggles to provide a service, but they do have a detailed **map** which you'll need to find your way around the new town. The Turismo also operates **guided tours** of the old town every day except Sunday, departing from their office at 10am, noon and 5pm (400ptas; not including admission to churches). A "Traditional Patios" tour (400ptas) starts from the same place and on the same days at 11am, 6pm and 7pm.

Accommodation

A number of **hostales** providing budget accommodation have recently opened up in the old town, formerly the exclusive preserve of well-heeled travellers able to afford to stay at a clutch of upmarket hotels. Lower down, the new town has many more options, including a renovated old *fonda* on the main street, c/Corredera. Staying a little out of town, at the **Lago de Arcos**, where there's a *hostal* and **campsite** (*Lago de Arcos*; ☎956 70 83 33), is another possibility – though you'll need insect repellent in summer. A bus to the lake leaves every half-hour from the bus station.

Hostal Andalucía, Carretera Nacional 342 (☎956 70 07 14). Motel-type hostal on the edge of town, a bit too close to the main Jerez road, offering decent rooms with bath, a restaurant and easy parking. ②.

Hotel Arcotur, c/Alta 1, in the new town (☎956 70 45 25, fax 956 45 25 24). Pleasant new small hotel with good value air-conditioned rooms with bath and TV; has a pleasant roof terrace café for breakfast. ④.

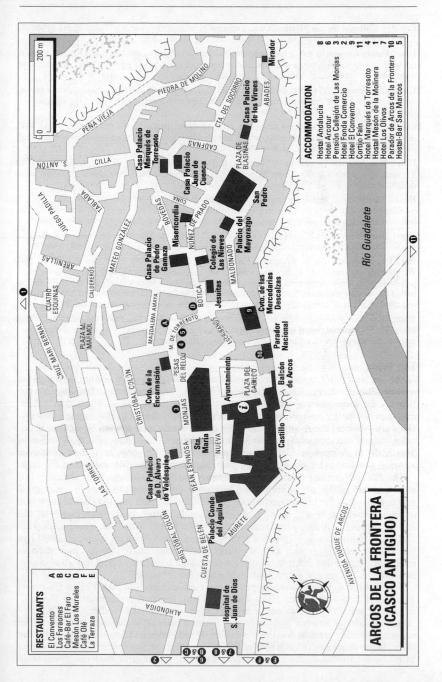

RESTAURANTS

El Convento — A
Los Faraones — B
Café-Bar El Faro — C
Mesón Los Murales — D
Café Olé — F
La Terraza — E

ACCOMMODATION

Hostal Andalucía — 8
Hotel Arcotur — 6
Pensión Callejón de Las Monjas — 3
Hotel Fonda Comercio — 2
Hotel El Convento — 9
Cortijo Faín — 11
Hotel Marqués de Torresoto — 4
Hostal Mesón de la Molinera — 1
Hotel Los Olivos — 7
Parador de Arcos de la Frontera — 10
Hostal-Bar San Marcos — 5

ARCOS DE LA FRONTERA (CASCO ANTIGUO)

Río Guadalete

Pensión Callejón de las Monjas, Dean Espinosa 4, behind the church of Santa María (☎956 70 23 02). Decent if cramped pensión right in the heart of the old town; some rooms with bath. ③.

Hotel Fonda Comercio, c/Corredera 83 (☎956 70 00 57). Atmospheric old fonda which has been taking in guests for well over a century; now rejuvenated as a friendly one-star hotel where rooms come with air conditioning, bath and TV. Pleasant bar-restaurant in the converted stables. ④.

Hotel El Convento, c/Maldonado 2 (☎956 70 23 33, fax 956 70 41 28). Upmarket hotel in a seventeenth-century former convent whose comfortable, air-conditioned rooms share the spectacular view over the *vega* with the *parador*. ⑥.

Cortijo Faín, 5km out of town along the road to Algar (☎956 23 13 96, fax 956 70 11 67). Sumptuously converted seventeenth-century pan-tiled farmhouse with pool, beautiful gardens and plenty of bougainvillea-draped, white-walled tranquillity. ⑦.

Hotel Marqués de Torresoto, c/Marqués de Torresoto 4 (☎956 70 07 17, fax 956 70 42 05). Pleasant, air-conditioned rooms in a converted mansion near the Plaza del Cabildo, complete with delightful colonnaded patio and Baroque chapel. ⑥.

Hostal Mesón de la Molinera, Lago de Arcos, lakeside (☎956 70 80 02, fax 956 70 80 07). Tranquil location on the waterfront with stunning views towards Arcos on its hill top. Chalet-style rooms with bath and terrace, great pool and easy parking. Also has its own bar and restaurant with *menú*. ⑤.

Hotel Los Olivos c/San Miguel 2 (☎956 70 08 11, fax 956 70 20 18). Near the Paseo de Andalucía gardens, in a superbly restored *casa antigua*. Some of the air-conditioned rooms have views. ⑥.

Parador de Arcos de la Frontera, Plaza del Cabildo (☎956 70 05 00, fax 956 70 11 16). Wonderfully situated close to the Santa María de la Asunción church, and perched on a rock pedestal – with reassuringly reinforced foundations to prevent it from sliding over the cliff – this is one of the smaller *paradores*. The delightful patio (open to the public for drinks and afternoon tea) and the "crow's nest" terrace gives the best views for miles. Also has own restaurant. ⑧.

Hostal-Bar San Marcos, c/Marqués de Torresoto 6 (☎956 70 07 21). Excellent *hostal* in the old town, offering pleasant rooms with bath. There's a roof terrace (for taking breakfast) with fine views and the friendly proprietors run a cosy bar-restaurant downstairs. ③.

The Town

By far the best thing to do in Arcos de la Frontera is take a stroll around the tangle of narrow Moorish streets, lined with a mix of Moorish and Renaissance buildings. At the heart of the **monumental quarter** is the Plaza del Cabildo, easily reached by following the signs for the *parador*, which occupies one whole side of it. Flanking another two sides are – behind the *Ayuntamiento* – the **castle walls and towers** (the castle is privately owned and shamefully off limits) and the large Gothic-Mudéjar church of **Santa María de la Asunción** (daily 10am–1pm & 4–7pm; 150ptas), built over an earlier mosque; one side is left open, offering plunging **views** to the river valley and the *vega*.

The fifteenth-century church's **Plateresque south facade** with later additions is a stunning work, although an unfinished bell tower unbalances the whole – the original was destroyed by the Lisbon earthquake of 1755 and the plan was to raise this new one to 58m, second in height only to Sevilla's Giralda. Three years later, however, the money ran out and the tower rested at a rather feeble 37m. The gloomy **interior** (Mon–Fri 10am–1pm & 4–7pm, Sat 10am–2.30pm, Sun 8.30am for Mass; 150ptas) has fine Gothic vaulting as well as a stunning *retablo*, exquisitely carved choir stalls in ebony, mahogany and cedar by Pedro Roldán, and a treasury with all the usual collection of church silver and some dubiously attributed art works.

East of here along c/Núñez de Prado, the Gothic church of **San Pedro** (Mon–Fri 10am–1pm & 4–6.30pm, Sat 10am–2pm; 150ptas), perched precariously on the cliff-edge, was rebuilt in the sixteenth century over an original Moorish fort. The later imposing Baroque exterior and tower are in strong contrast to the interior, where a fine sixteenth-century **retablo** documents the life of San Pedro and San Jerónimo and is the oldest in the province. To each side of this are paintings of *San Ignacio* and *La Dolorosa* by Pachecho, the tutor of Velásquez. There's also the rather grisly undecomposed body of *San Victor* (thankfully behind glass) and **image of the Virgin** attributed to La Roldana, the sculptor daughter of Pedro Roldán. You can climb the tower, but you'll need a good head for heights, as there are few guard rails on the top to prevent a nasty fall. Other monuments in this quarter include the **Palacio del Mayorazgo**, c/Maldonado, with a Renaissance facade, and further east still, the convent of **San Agustín** (daily except Tues 10.30am–2.30pm & 3.30–6.30pm), on the narrow neck of the spur, whose church contains a fine seventeenth-century carved wood *retablo* and the town's most venerated image of **Jesús Nazareno** (Christ bearing the Cross) carved in 1600 by Jácomi Velardi. Nearby, in c/Cuna, there's **Casa Cuna**, formerly the synagogue of the old Jewish ghetto, and further east again in the Plaza de la Caridad lies the **Iglesia de la Caridad** (daily 10.30am–12.30pm & 4.30–6pm; donations to the work of the nuns), an impressive sixteenth-century church and convent of the *Hermanitas de los Ancianos Desamparados* (nuns caring for the elderly) built in ornate colonial style with a beautiful patio and stunning carved wood *retablos*. Near the church of Santa María, the **Convento de la Encarnación**, c/de las Monjas, is worth a look, though only the church – with a sixteenth-century Plateresque facade – survives. Close by, and back in the Plaza del Cabildo, the **Ayuntamiento** boasts a superb Mudéjar coffered ceiling, while lower down along the Cuesta de Belén, the fourteenth-century ducal palace **Casa del Conde de Águila** has the town's oldest facade. At the end of this street, just before it joins the Paseo de Andalucía, the still functioning **Hospital de San Juan de Dios** (viewing daily at 9.45am – ring the bell) incorporates a charming early Baroque church with a sixteenth-century image of the crucified Christ.

Each September 29, Arcos's narrow streets echo to the screams of hundreds of children when they run the bulls in the **Feria de San Miguel** honouring the town's patron saint. To see these girls and boys leap up to grab a *reja*, or overhanging balcony, to lift themselves clear of the horns of the rampaging *toro* is a fantastic, truly nail-biting sight, and remarkably few seem to get injured.

East of town, the A372 road to Ronda leads down to a couple of sandy **beaches** on the riverbank, and to the north of here the **lake** (actually a reservoir) is a good spot for swimming. The Mississippi Paddle Boat (noon and 6pm; 250ptas) does trips around the lake in summer from the *Mesón de la Molinera hostal*. The lake is served by buses (July–Sept) leaving from the bus station roughly every half-hour.

Eating and drinking

There's little variety when it comes to **eating and drinking** in Arcos, but a couple of good restaurants are worth seeking out. In addition to the list below, many of the hotels and *hostales* (see "Accommodation") have restaurants of their own.

Mesón del Brigadier (aka Curro El Cojo), Lago de Arcos. Up a flight of steps close to the bridge leading back into town from the lake, this upmarket restaurant has been patronized by members of the Spanish royal family. House specials include *ajo molinera* (almond and garlic soup) and *cabrito al jerez* (kid in sherry). There's a mid-priced *menú* and terrace.

El Convento, c/Marqués de Torresoto 7. Mid-priced option in the old town, owned by the hotel of the same name, and renowned for its cooking; there's a *menú* here as well as specialities such as *perdiz en salsa de almendras* (partridge with almond sauce), and a tasty house soup, *sopa de clausura*, with pine nuts and cheese. *Crema de ángel* and *peras al vino* are two recommended desserts.

Café-Bar El Faro, c/Debajo del Corral 14, in the new town. Good *platos combinados* and an economical *menú*.

Los Faraones, c/Debajo del Corral 8. Arab restaurant in the new town, offering Spanish standards and *tapas* as well as some interesting North African dishes and an 800ptas *menú*.

Mesón Los Murales, Plaza de Boticas 1. One of the best low-priced options in the old town, close to the church of San Pedro, and serving an economical *menú* for about 900ptas. *Tapas* and *raciones* also available.

Café Olé, Cerro de la Reina 8, off Plaza de España. This is a new place serving well-prepared *platos combinados* on a terrace in a revamped plaza east of the old quarter and close to the place below.

La Terraza, c/Múñoz Vásquez. Below the monumental quarter, in the gardens of the Paseo de Andalucía, this is a pleasant place to sit out and serves a wide variety of economical *platos combinados*.

Nightlife

Arcos locals tend to gravitate to the bars and restaurants for **nightlife**. However, in summer there are quite a few free outdoor events, such as flamenco (and even rock) concerts and it's worth checking with the Turismo, or perusing the local paper, *Información Arcos*, to see what's coming up. On Thursdays at 10.30pm in July and August there are **flamenco** concerts in the Plaza del Cananeo close to the Palacio del Marques de Torresoto in the old town. The *Peña de Flamenco de Arcos* (☎956 70 12 51), Plaza de la Caridad 4, east of the old quarter, also stages regular – and authentic – flamenco. This is a very friendly *peña* (club) whose all-day bar is lined with photos of past greats, including El Camarón, who have appeared in its atmospheric theatre. There are *actuaciones* most weekends normally Saturdays after 10.30pm but ring first (Spanish only) to avoid a wasted journey. Alternatively, if you're raring to boogie, *Disco-Bar Porto Alegre* sets up an **open-air disco** at the lakeside in summer, which gets going after 11pm, and in July and August there are tented **music-bars** ("*Las Carpas*") below the Paseo de Andalucía, close to the restaurant *La Terraza*.

The Costa de la Luz

The villages along the **Costa de la Luz** – the stretch between Algeciras, over the bay from Gibraltar, and Cádiz – are in a totally different class from the resorts along the Costa del Sol. West from Algeciras the road climbs almost immediately into the rolling green hills of the **Sierra del Cabrito**, a region lashed for much of the year by the ferocious *levante* (east) and *poniente* (west) winds which vie continuously, it seems, for the upper hand. Now cluttered by an inevitable wind farm, from these heights there are fantastic views down to Gibraltar and across the straits to the just-discernible white houses and tapering mosques of Moroccan villages. Beyond, the Rif Mountains hover mysteriously in the background and on a clear day, as you approach **Tarifa**, you can distinguish Tangier on the edge of its crescent-shaped bay.

Tarifa

TARIFA, spilling out beyond its Moorish walls, was until the mid-1980s a quiet village, known in Spain, if at all, as the southernmost point on the European landmass and for its abnormally high suicide rate – attributed to the unremitting winds that blow across the town and its environs. Occupying the site of previous Carthaginian and Roman cities, Tarifa takes its name from Tarif Ibn Malik, leader of the first band of Moors to cross the straits in 710, a sortie that tested the waters for the following year's all-out assault on the peninsula. Today it's become a prosperous, popular and at times very crowded, resort, following its discovery as Europe's prime **wind-surfing** locale. Indeed, according to windsurfing aficionados, Tarifa now ranks alongside Diamond Head in Hawaii and Fuerteventura in the Canaries as one of the top three windsurfing beaches in the world. Equipment rental shops line the main street, and in peak season crowds of windsurfers pack out every available bar and *hostal*. Even in winter, there are windsurfers to be seen, drawn by regular competitions held year-round. Development continues at a rapid rate as a result of this new-found popularity, but for the time being Tarifa remains an attractive place for a stopover.

Arrival, information and orientation

On the main Algeciras–Cádiz road (c/Batalla del Salado) you'll find the **bus station**, a supermarket, fried fish and *churro* stalls and many of the largest hotels. Near here and south of the Avda. de Andalucía, the friendly **Turismo** (Mon–Fri 10am–2pm & 6–8pm; ☎956 68 09 93) is at the top of the Alameda, a tree-lined promenade flanking the old town's western wall. They can provide a useful map as well as a handy guide to the town's *tapas* haunts, *Guía de Tapear y Comer*. When the Turismo is closed, the kindly owner at the *Hostal Villanueva* (see "Accommodation") is not averse to lending you his window map to photocopy at the shop over the road.

The area around Tarifa is good **horse-riding** country and horses can be hired from Aky Oaky, c/Batalla del Salado 37 (☎956 68 53 56), for about 2500ptas an hour; they also rent out **mountain bikes** and run visits to local *ganadarías* to see *toros bravos* (fighting bulls). *Hotel San José del Valle* (☎956 68 71 22), on the N340 15km northwest of town at the junction with the turn off for Bolonia (see below), operates single or multiple-day excursions on horseback.

Accommodation

Tarifa has plenty of **places to stay**, though finding a bed in August – or whenever there are windsurfing tournaments – can be a struggle. The nearest **campsites**, *Río Jara* (☎956 68 05 70), and *Torre de la Peña* (☎956 68 49 03), lie 4km and 7km northwest of town on the Cádiz road respectively. Others nearby include *Tarifa* (☎956 68 47 78) and *Paloma* (☎956 68 42 03).

Hostal Alameda, Paseo de la Alameda 4 (☎956 68 11 81). Pleasant *hostal-restaurante* on the Alameda with sea views and rooms with bath. ⑤.

Hostal La Calzada, c/Justino Pertiñez 7 (☎956 68 03 66). Popular and friendly *hostal* in the centre of the old town, close by the church of San Mateo, offering rooms with bath. ④.

Pensión Correo, c/Coronel Moscardó 8 (☎956 68 02 06). Charming and reasonably tranquil *pensión* in the old post office offering en-suite rooms in the *casco antiguo*. ④.

Hurricane Hotel, Ctra. Cádiz s/n (☎956 68 49 19, fax 956 68 03 29). In dense gardens 7km west of Tarifa at the ocean's edge, this American-chic institution has a fully equipped gym, two pools, windsurfing school and its own restaurant. ⑧.

Hostal Tarik, c/San Sebastián 32–36 (☎956 68 52 40). Outside the walls in the northern part of town and overlooking the coast, this *hostal* is very clean and has helpful owners. ④.

Hostal Villanueva, Avda. Andalucía 11 (☎956 68 41 49). Excellent value at this *hostal-restaurante* built into the north wall of the old quarter; some rooms with bath. ③.

The Town

There's great appeal in wandering the crumbling ramparts of Tarifa's old walls, gazing out to sea or down into the network of lanes that surround the fifteenth-century church of **San Mateo** (daily 9am–1pm & 6–8.30pm). Don't be fooled by the crumbling Baroque exterior here, fine though it is; this was added in the eighteenth century and hides, inside, a beautiful late-Gothic church with elegant rib-vaulting in the nave and some interesting modern stained-glass windows. A very helpful leaflet in English will guide you around the church's many features, including delightful **reliefs** of Christ and the apostles, decorating the vaulting. A fine **crucified Christ** by the great eighteenth-century sculptor Pedro de Mena is situated along the right aisle. Nearby, a small **seventh-century tombstone** confirms that there was a Christian presence here before the Moorish invasion of 711. Further along, the **sagrario** is a stunning Baroque

---

ON TO MOROCCO

Tarifa offers the tempting opportunity of a quick approach **to Morocco** – Tangier is feasible as a day-trip on the once-daily seasonal ferry, which operates from May to September. Normally this leaves at 9.30am, returning at 4.30pm or 6pm (Spanish time – which is 1hr ahead of Moroccan); check current times with Tourafrica or the Turismo. The trip takes ninety minutes; tickets are available from the Tourafrica embarkation office on the quay (☎956 68 47 51) or in advance from travel agents along c/Batalla del Salado. If you're planning to do a day-trip you'd be wise to book a few days in advance – or you may find that a tour company has taken over the whole boat. A day-trip would also allow you time only for a brief look around, and an overnight stay might be a better way of justifying the 5600ptas round-trip ticket.

---

extravaganza in pink and violet, with an enchanting cupola. Further still, step through the chapel of San José into the sacristy where, hidden away, you'll find a modern **icon of the Virgin** by Tarifa's most famous son, modern artist Guillermo Pérez Villalta. The church's stirring finale is at the top of the left aisle, where a copy of the original (and now lost) *retablo* contains the **image of San Mateo by Montañes**, Spain's greatest exponent of wood sculpture.

The newly restored **Castillo de Guzmán** (Tues–Sun 10am–2pm & 6–8pm; 200ptas) has great **views** from its towers and battlements both over the town and across the straits towards the hazy Rif Mountains of Morocco. In origin the tenth-century Moorish Alcázar constructed by the great Abd ar-Rahman III, ruler of Córdoba, on the ruins of a Roman fort, this was the site of many a struggle for this strategic foothold into Spain. Known today as El Castillo de Guzmán, the appendage refers to Guzmán El Bueno (the Good), Tarifa's infamous commander during the Moorish siege of 1292, who earned his tag for his role in a superlative piece of tragic drama. Guzmán's nine-year-old son had been taken hostage by a Spanish traitor – surrender of the garrison was demanded as the price of the boy's life. Choosing "honour without a son, to a son with dishonour", Guzmán threw down his own dagger for the execution. The story, a famous piece of heroic resistance in Spain, had echoes in the Civil War siege of the Alcázar at Toledo, when the Nationalist commander refused similar threats; an echo much exploited for propaganda purposes.

Also worth a look is the charming Plaza de Santa María, behind the castle, where you'll find the *Ayuntamiento* and a small **museum** (Mon–Fri 11am–1pm; free) containing an interesting display of artefacts from the Neolithic, Roman and Moorish periods through to modern times. A **mirador** to the east of the square offers more views of the African coast. The daily covered **market** – close to the Puerta de Jerez and inside the walls – with Moorish-style arches is worth a visit; when in full swing the bars in the vicinity do a roaring trade.

A recent innovation in Tarifa are **dolphin- and whale-spotting boat trips** run by two non-profit-making organizations: Whale Watch, Café Continental, Paseo de la Alameda (☎956 68 47 76) and FIRMM (Foundation for Information and Research on Marine Mammals), c/Pedro Cortés 3, slightly east of the church of San Mateo (☎956 62 70 08). For trips with both groups you will need to book in advance (two days' notice is preferable) for which a donation of 4500ptas is required. The trips last about three hours and should you not see any dolphins or whales you may take a free trip on the next sailing.

Tarifa Beach

Heading northwest from Tarifa, you find what are perhaps the loveliest **beaches** along the whole Costa de la Luz – wide stretches of yellow or silvery-white sand, washed by some magical rollers. The same winds that have created such perfect conditions for windsurfing – the eastern *levante* and western *poniente* – can, however, be a problem for more casual enjoyment, sandblasting those attempting to relax on towels or mats and whipping the water into whitecaps. The beaches beckon immediately west of the town, and get better as you move past the tidal flats and the mosquito-ridden estuary of the Río de la Jara – until the dunes start, and the first campervans lurk among the bushes. At **TARIFA BEACH**, a little bay 9km from town, there are restaurants, campsites and a *hostal* at the base of a tree-tufted bluff. There is a windsurfing school here, which acts as the local centre for the sport. Nearby *Hotel Dos Mares* (☎956 68 40 35, fax 956 68 10 78; ⑦) is another windsurf centre which offers courses and rents out equipment. For more seclusion head for one of the numerous **beach-campsites** on either side (see "Accommodation" above), signposted from the main road or accessible by walking along the coast.

Eating, drinking and nightlife

Though Tarifa has some good places to **eat**, there's little in the way of entertainment except the bars. However, the *Peña de Flamenco de Tarifa* holds **flamenco** sessions most weekends in the neo-Moorish Miguel de Cervantes infants' school, alongside the *Ayuntamiento* in Plaza Santa María; visitors get a warm welcome and the bar serves *tapas* as well. In addition to the bars and clubs listed below is *Bar El Trato*, c/Sancho El Bravo 28, which is also Tarifa's **internet centre** where you can pick up your email over a beer (100ptas for ten minutes). Tarifa's best summer **disco** is the open-air *Balneario* fronting the Playa Grande, the larger of the town's twin beaches; on windier days there's *Tanakas*, Plaza de San Hiscio off c/San Francisco. In summer the local council also puts up *carpas* (disco tents) on the beach at the northern end of town.

Restaurante Alameda, Paseo Alameda 4. Popular restaurant outside the western wall, which does reasonable *platos combinados* and a tasty paella.

Café Central, c/Sancho El Bravo IV, 10. Good breakfast bar with the usual standards; serves more substantial dishes later in the day.

Mesón El Cortijo, c/General Copons. In the street alongside San Mateo's church in the old town, this vaguely upmarket restaurant serves a medium-priced *menú*.

Crèperie Santa Fé, c/Sancho El Bravo IV, 10, near San Mateo. Excellent French crèpes cooked by friendly Bretonne emigrés.

Casa Juan Luis, c/San Francisco 15 (evenings only). Despite its proximity to the sea this is a shrine to meat, in particular pork in all its Iberian variations. The restaurant, housed in a *casa antigua*, also has a beautiful patio and outdoor terrace. The eponymous owner is a big *toros* fan and the restaurant closes when there's a *corrida*. *Menú* for about 3000ptas.

Mandragora, c/Independencia 3, behind the Iglesia San Mateo. One of a number of restaurants and *tapas* bars in town offering dishes from both sides of the straits: in addition to Moroccan *couscous* and *berenjenas bereber* (aubergine), it does excellent *tapas* including *boquerones rellenos* (anchovies).

Bar Morilla, c/Sancho IV El Bravo 2. Central bar where *tarifeños* gather to munch early-evening *tapas* while contemplating the old stones of nearby San Mateo.

Rincon Guzman El Bueno, c/Cervantes 4 off c/San Francisco. Very good *tapas* and *raciones* bar and restaurant with a pleasant terrace and lots of choices including a *surtido de pescado frito* (fried fish platter).

Mesón de Sancho, Ctra. Cadíz–Málaga, 6km east of town. One of the top restaurants in this zone and not cheap. House specials include *urta al brandy* (sea bream). There's a *menú* for 2000ptas.

Restaurante Villanueva, Avda. Andalucía 11. Fine restaurant of the *hostal* of the same name; their *urta* (Cádiz sea bream) is prepared in five different ways and has a *menú*.

THE STRAITS OF DEATH

In Tarifa's cemetery above the town, lines of nameless headstones mark where the dead lie three deep. These are the remains of corpses – mostly unknown Africans – washed up on the beach. In recent years the trickle of "wetbacks" eager for a share of European prosperity has turned into a flood, as gangs operating in Tangier offer to get **illegal immigrants** into Spain by evading the Spanish helicopters and coastal patrols who are fully equipped with infra-red and satellite detection technology. The usual method of transport are *pateras*, flimsy, easily capsized, flat-bottomed fishing boats designed to carry six people. Often packed with as many as thirty – who pay the equivalent of up to £400 each to be dropped close to the Spanish shore – these fragile craft set out to cross one of the most treacherous straits of water in the world. Crooked gangster skippers often tip unfortunates into the water too far out from shore and many non-swimmers drown. More often though, the boats themselves don't make it and the toll of bodies washed up along Spanish beaches is rising to alarming levels. Of those that do get safely across the straits, many are picked up by the authorities and held in the detention centre on Tarifa's harbourside, pending extradition. The few that wriggle through the police net face a life as non-citizens without papers, drifting between illegal and low-paid jobs or street-selling. The high death toll seems to have no effect on the numbers willing to take their chances on the open seas and, as economic conditions in Africa worsen, the temptation to migrate becomes ever stronger. In the meantime, Tarifa's gravediggers are kept busy as more of these boat people perish on the way to their promised El Dorado.

Baelo Claudia

Around the coast from the Punta Paloma to the west of Tarifa and almost on the beach at Bolonia Cove, are the extensive ruins of the Roman town of **BAELO CLAUDIA**, (daily except Mon: July & Aug 10am–1.30pm & 4.30–8pm; rest of year 10am–2.30pm & 4–5.30pm; free with EU passport, otherwise 250ptas). Established in the second century BC, the town – rather like modern Zahara and Barbate nearby – became prosperous with the exploitation of tuna and mackerel fish to make a sauce or relish called *garum* of which the Romans were passionately fond. The town reached the peak of its prosperity during the first century AD when it was raised to the status of a *municipium* or self-governing township by Emperor Claudius, and the buildings you see today date from this period. Recently reorganized, there are now a series of information boards (sadly in Spanish only) which guide you around the site concluding at the fish factory on the beach.

Excavations began here in 1917 and have gradually revealed remains which confirm the importance of the ancient town. A **tour of the site** starts with a well-preserved rectangular forum best viewed from the platform at the northern end supporting a row of **three temples** to Jupiter, Juno and Minerva, the great gods of imperial Rome. Just west of here is a smaller temple dedicated to the Egyptian goddess, Isis, and directly ahead, occupying the whole south side of the forum are the remains of the **basilica**, or law court. At the eastern end of this building stood a colossal white marble statue of the second-century emperor Trajan, the head of which is now preserved in the museum at Cádiz. In conjunction with the new millennium a replica of the statue is being made to occupy the same site. On the forum's eastern flank stood a line of *tabernae* or shops, which seem to have been superseded by the later *macellum* or **market** built to the west of the basilica. Now included in the visit is the newly restored **theatre**, built into the hillside to take advantage of the slope. The **main street**, the *decumanus maximus*, runs east–west behind the basilica and is crossed to the east of the forum by the *cardo maximus* which cuts through the centre on a north–south axis. You will also see the remains of the public **baths** once supplied with water from the nearby Sierra de la Plata by three aqueducts. Excavations over the coming years are planned to reveal more of the town to the north and west of the forum.

Probably the most interesting series of buildings stand to the south of the site proper, actually on the beach. Here has been revealed a **fish factory** which produced the famous *garum*. You can clearly make out the great stone vats used to make this concoction; they were always located as near to the sea and as far away from the town as possible because of the putrid stench. This arose from a process whereby the heads, entrails, eggs, soft roes and blood of the fish were removed and then layered in the vats with salt and brine and left for weeks to "mature". The resulting mixture was then slopped into amphorae and shipped all over the empire, particularly to Rome, where the poet Martial droolingly described it as "made of the first blood of a mackerel breathing still, an expensive gift". The mackerel sauce was the Roman equivalent of beluga and they paid the earth for small quantities of it; the tuna-based sauce, however, was less of a luxury and much cheaper.

Practicalities

Baelo Claudia lies sheltered by the cape known as Punta Camarinal, and to get there from the Tarifa–Cádiz road you should turn off down a small side road (signed), on the left 15km beyond Tarifa, at a hotel-restaurant named *San José del Vallé* which, incidentally, serves a good *menú*. There's a great **beach** fronting the site, with a scattering of **bars** and **eating places** open in summer. You'll also find a very pleasant **place to stay**: *Hostal Baelo,* c/El Lentiscal 15 (☎956 68 85 62; ⑤), which has garden rooms with bath close to the beach, and a restaurant offering vegetarian dishes. It's located at the eastern end of the village next to the *Panadería Beatriz*, which is also where you'll find the proprietors. *Hostal Bellavista* (☎ & fax 956 68 85 53; ④), near the turn-off into the village, is another possibility for decent ensuite rooms. You can also **walk** to Bolonia along the coast from either the Punta Paloma west of Tarifa, or coming from the opposite direction, Zahara de los Atunes (3–4hr with a couple of natural obstacles en route).

Things, however, may be about to change dramatically here if the governments of Spain and Morocco get EU funding for a **vehicle-carrying train tunnel** connecting Andalucía with Tangier. Bolonia is regarded as the prime site for the entrance on the Spanish side and would tie up with a new rail link to be built between Cádiz and Algeciras. Enjoy the tranquillity while it lasts.

Zahara and Barbate

Eight kilometres north as the crow flies (but a hefty 28km dog-leg by road along the N340), **ZAHARA DE LOS ATUNES** is a small fishing village linked by an infrequent **bus** service with Barbate (see below). Beginning to show signs of development – with plans for the obligatory Paseo Marítimo well in hand – Zahara has a fabulous 8km-long **beach**. The best of the **places to stay** is *Hostal Monte Mar*, c/Peñón 12 (☎956 43 90 47; ④) bang on the shore, and reached by turning right immediately after crossing the bridge into the village and following the road to the end. Friendly owners Antonia and Antonio offer sea-view rooms with bath and balcony, and there are lots of terraces for lounging al fresco. Alternatives include a smallish, plush hotel, the *Gran Sol*, next to the beach at Avda. de la Playa 20 (☎956 43 93 01; ⑦). Of the handful of other places (all of which are usually full throughout August), *Hostal Castro* (☎956 43 93 58; ④), close to the *Gran Sol*, and the central *Hotel Nicolás*, c/María Luisa 13 (☎956 43 92 74; ⑤), are reasonable. **Sleeping on the beach** is also feasible, but don't forget the insect repellent.

Places to eat here include the central *Marisquería Porfirio*, Plaza Tamarón 5, for seafood *tapas* and *raciones*, and the nearby *Bar Ropiti*, c/María Luisa 6, for meat and fish *platos combinados*. One of the best *tapas* and *raciones* bars on this stretch of coast is *Casa Juanito* at c/Sagasta 7, serving up deliciously fresh seafood. The restaurants of the *Gran Sol* and *Nicolas* hotels are also good for more formal dining. The *Hotel Atlanterra* (☎956 43 90 00), 4km south along the beach road, rents out **horses** for exploring the surrounding *sierras*.

BARBATE DE FRANCO, next along the coast and linked by a frequent daily **bus** service with Vejer de la Frontera (p.171), is a featureless little town dominated by its harbour and canning industry which sometimes fills the air with a fishy pong. There is, however, **camping** on an extensive beach to the west of the town, which has the advantage of being shaded by pines.

Los Caños de Meca and El Palmar

From Barbate a rolling scenic road winds its way through the verdant pinewoods of the Parque Natural de Acantilado before descending after 11km into **LOS CAÑOS DE MECA** (served by sporadic buses from Barbate to Conil). A small village surrounded by pine groves and a favourite summer escape for *sevillanos*, Los Caños has a long, beautiful beach lined with rocky coves and freshwater springs, marred only by some unfortunate hotel developments on its southern flank. There used to be a hippy colony here and, although this crowd has now gone, some of the laid-back atmosphere lingers, especially among the groups of naturists who swim out to the more secluded coves along the coast. If you want to **stay** – and places tend to be pricey here – you'll find two mid-range *hostales* on Avda. Trafalgar; the *Hostal Villa Guadalupe* at no. 56 (☎956 43 72 29; ⑥), with pleasant gardens and rooftop solarium, and the cheaper *Mar y Sol* at no. 102 (☎956 43 72 55; ⑤), with rooms arranged around a patio. Another alternative is the *Hostal Fortuna*, Avda. Trafalgar 34 at the eastern end of the seafront (☎956 43 70 75; ⑤), for rooms with bath and TV. Just west of town, towards Cape Trafalgar, is a **campsite**, *Caños de Meca* (☎956 43 71 20), with plenty of shade, and just alongside it lies *Venta Zahora* (☎956 23 28 68; ⑤), a relaxed garden *hostal* with young owners, ensuite rooms and a youthful ambience. The central *Camping Camaleón* (☎956 43 71 54) on Avda. Trafalgar is less attractive and further from the beach.

The numerous **places to eat** close to the seafront include *El Caña* on c/Trafalgar, with a great balcony view of the beach. One place worth seeking out, though, if you're at the *Caños de Meca* campsite (or even if you're not) is *Venta Curro* (close to the *Venta Zahora hostal* above) where the food is excellent and there's a *menú* offering local specialities. Los Caños also has lots of **bars**, lively in season; *El Pirata* in the centre sometimes features live music, including jazz. Next door, *La Jaima*, a tented disco, attracts quite a crowd in summer. In the lighthouse zone, *Las Dunas* – a big log cabin with *copas* and music – and *Macondo*, another music bar, are two places worth trying.

The coast road west from Los Caños (taking a left after 5km and continuing for a further 3km) brings you to **EL PALMAR**, a sleepy and isolated seafront settlement, and about as peaceful a place as you could wish. Fronting an excellent, if narrow, Blue Flag strand you'll find a few seafood **restaurants** including the excellent *Hostal-Restaurant Francisco* (☎956 23 22 49, fax 956 23 27 88; ⑤) which also has delightful balcony **rooms**. At the north end of the beach *Hostal La Ilusión* (☎956 23 23 98; ⑤) has comfortable rooms beyond an extensive garden. To rent an **apartment** which sleeps two to six people, contact *La Chanca* (☎956 23 22 55; ⑥). Set one kilometre back from the beach there's a very good **campsite**, *El Palmar* (☎956 23 21 61) with a great pool, plenty of shade, restaurant, bar and supermarket. There are lots of activities on offer including trekking, tennis and scuba diving and they hire out horses, mountain bikes and even tents and mattresses.

Vejer de la Frontera

While you're on the Costa de la Luz, be sure to take time to head inland and visit **VEJER DE LA FRONTERA**, a classically white, Moorish-looking hill town set in a cleft between great protective hills that rear high above the road from Tarifa to Cádiz. Until a couple of decades ago, the women of Vejer wore long, dark cloaks that veiled their faces like nuns' habits; though trotted out in most guidebooks, this custom is now virtually extinct outside fiestas.

The bus usually makes a stop at two *hostal-restaurantes* on the major road at the foot of the hill – *La Barca de Vejer* (✆956 45 00 83, fax 956 45 10 83; ④) does superb *bocadillos de lomo* – before toiling up to the *pueblo* proper. The road winds upwards for another 4km but there's a donkey path from near the lower bus stop that allows you to approach the town along a traditional path, better attempted without excess baggage. This is a perfect approach, taking about twenty minutes – the drama of Vejer is in its isolation and its position, which gradually unfold before you.

"And the wind cries ¡Vejer!" proclaims a poem on a wall plaque in the square where the bus drops you, a testament to the town's elevated exposure to the elements. Maintaining a brooding detachment from the world below for most of its history, Vejer has a remoteness and a Moorish feel as potent as anywhere in Spain. Almost certainly a prehistoric hilltop Iberian citadel, Vejer was utilized as a fortress during the **Phoenician** and **Carthaginian** epochs of the first millennium BC to protect coastal factories and fishing grounds from the warlike Iberians of the interior. Dubbed *Besipo* by the later **Romans**, it was as the **Moorish** town of *Bekkeh* that Vejer rose to prominence as an important agricultural centre on the western frontier of the kingdom of Granada. Taken by Fernando III in 1250 during the *reconquista*, it was immediately handed over to Alonso Pérez de Guzmán, founder of the ducal house of Medina Sidonia and later hero of Tarifa (p.166). A hangover here from Moorish times was the agricultural practice of *"hazas de suerte"*, a rotating system of allocating farming land by lots to the peasantry which did much to temper the appearance of *latifundismo* in these parts, the curse of most of Andalucía ever since.

Vejer is best savoured by randomly exploring the brilliant white, labyrinthine alleyways, wandering past iron-grilled windows, balconies and patios, and slipping into the bars. Once you've visited the **Turismo**, c/Marqués de Tamarón 10, uphill from the central La Plazuela (Mon–Fri 8am–2pm & 6–9pm, Sat 8am–2pm; ✆956 45 01 91) and armed yourself with their excellent free **map** (also available from the *Hotel Convento* when the Turismo's closed), you'll be able to navigate your way around the maze of the walled old quarter – entered through its original Moorish gates – to reach the major sights. The **castillo** (daily 11am–2pm & 5–10pm; donations welcome), in the heart of the old quarter, is Moorish in origin but underwent substantial rebuilding in the fifteenth century when it was used by the dukes of Medina Sidonia as a summer retreat. Currently occupied by the Boy Scouts (one of whom will show you around and politely encourage you to buy something at their gift shop), the main things to see are a splendid **horseshoe arch** and some recently uncovered Moorish plasterwork, as well as great views from the terrace. A small **museum** houses finds ancient and not so old discovered in and around the town.

To the north of the castle, at the end of c/Ramón y Cajal, the church of **Divino Salvador** (daily 11am–1pm & 7–9pm) is a sixteenth-century rebuild of an earlier mosque whose minaret now serves as its tower. The interior is a curious mix of mainly Gothic and Mudéjar styles. From here c/Castrillón descends to the **Plaza de España**, the lovely main square, overlooked by a white-walled *Ayuntamiento*, and centring on a delightful fountain decorated with nineteenth-century Triana tiles from Sevilla. At the wrong end of town and needing a crowd to bring it to life, the plaza is not much favoured by locals and at night is often eerily still. North of here, the

Paseo de la Corredera offers spectacular views over the countryside to the near-by hill towns of Medina Sidonia and Alcalá de los Gazules. Incidentally, the **Torre de la Corredera** halfway along here was a watch tower used for communicating with those towns.

Practicalities

Limited **accommodation** can often make finding a room hard work in August, and all but impossible later on in the day. If you don't want to end up searching for equally hard-to-find *casas particulares*, try calling ahead. At other times of the year there's usually no great demand.

Budget options include *Casa de Huéspedes Doncel-Moriano*, c/Filmo 16 (☎956 45 02 46; ②) with a lovely patio, or, at no. 7 on the same street, *Casa Los Cántaros* (☎956 44 75 92; ②). At the other end of town on Plaza de España there are pleasant and good-value apartments (sleeping two to four; ④) and studios (sleeping one to two; ③) at the anonymous no. 17 (☎956 44 75 75; English spoken), facing the fountain. *Hostal La Posada*, c/Los Remedios 2 (☎956 45 02 58; ③) above a restaurant near the top of the hill as you enter the town, has rooms with bath, as does the excellent *Hostal La Janda*, Cerro Clarisas s/n (☎956 45 01 42; ③), signposted up a side road as you enter the town. Finally, the delightful and surprisingly reasonable *Hotel Convento San Francisco*, La Plazuela (☎956 64 35 70; ⑤), is housed in a converted seventeenth-century convent on the smaller of the old quarter's two main squares.

There are plenty of places for **eating** and **drinking**. In the old quarter, *Mesón Pepe Julián*, c/Juan Relinque 7 just off La Plazuela, serves up decent *tapas* and has an economical *menú*. Other good *tapas* places include *Café-Bar La Bodeguita*, c/Marqués de Tamarón 9, and *Bar Chirino* on La Plazuela next to the *Hotel Convento*, originally the earlier convent's choir, whose walls are covered with a fascinating photographic history of the town. The *Convento*'s **bar** next door is also a relaxing place for a quiet drink or leisurely breakfast. *La Posada* (see "Accommodation" above) is a more formal restaurant, with fine traditional dishes whilst the mid-priced *Mesón Judería* in an atmospheric Moorish alley, c/Arco de las Monjas, is also good and popular with locals. *Restaurante Trafalgar*, Plaza España 31, is another decent place at the northern end of town.

At the *Peña Flamenca Águilar de Vejer*, c/Rosario (near the castle), you can sample *manzanilla* from the barrel and take in occasional weekend **flamenco** performances; the Turismo keeps details of upcoming performances. *Bodegas Gallardo* (daily 10am–6pm), on the main Barbate road below the town, welcome visitors to sample and buy the wines and *finos* of the region. *Magnum*, Avda. Los Remedios 45 (☎956 44 75 75; *www.magnum.es*), leading into the town, is a good place to rent **mountain bikes** and **surf-boards** and its English-speaking proprietor is a mine of local information.

Conil

Back on the coast, a dozen or so kilometres further on, is the increasingly popular resort of **CONIL**. Outside August, when it's not too crowded, it's still a good place to relax, and in mid-season the only real drawback is trying to find a room. Though this former fishing village appears entirely modern when viewed from the beach, plenty of older buildings survive, and the majority of the tourists are Spanish, so there's an enjoyable, if rather family, atmosphere. If you're here in mid-season, you can also indulge in some very lively nightlife.

The **beach**, Conil's *raison d'être*, is a wide bay of brilliant yellow stretching for miles to either side of town and lapped by an amazingly, not to say disarmingly, gentle Atlantic – you have to walk halfway to Panama before it reaches waist height. The area immediately in front of town is the family beach: up to the northwest you can walk to some more sheltered coves; across the river to the southeast is a topless and nudist area. The beach here is virtually unbroken until it reaches the cape, the **Trafalgar**, off which Lord Nelson achieved victory and death on October 21, 1805. If the winds are blowing, this is one of the most sheltered beaches in the area. You can get there by road, save for the last 400m across the sands to the rock.

Practicalities

Most **buses** drop you off at the *Transportes Comes* station on c/Carretera; walk towards the sea and you'll soon pass Conil's helpful **Turismo** (Mon–Sat 9.30am–1.30pm & 6–9pm, Sun 9.30am–1.30pm; ☎956 44 05 01, fax 956 44 05 00), at the junction of Carretera and c/Menéndez Pidal. Make sure to pick up their useful booklet *Conil en su Bolsillo*, which details all the town's *tapas* bars, restaurants and much more. Conil has numerous **hotels and hostales** – August is the only time when you'll struggle to find a bed. Reasonable places include the central *Hostal La Villa*, Plaza de España 6 (☎956 44 10 53; ④), for rooms with bath, or nearby there's the simpler *Pensión Los Hermanos*, Conil's oldest *fonda*, at c/Virgen 2 (☎956 44 01 96; ②). Of the pricier seafront places you could try *Hostal Sonrisa del Mar* (☎956 44 27 18; ④) or *Hotel Oasis* (☎956 44 21 54; ⑤), both offering sea-view rooms with balconies. With transport, a pleasant alternative to staying in the town is to take the road north for 2km to the *Hostal Diufain* (☎956 44 25 51, fax 956 44 30 30; ④), a comfortable place in its own grounds on the road to the *urbanización* Fuente del Gallo; easy to find, it stands at the foot of a giant telephonic tower which dominates the skyline. In town there are also a multitude of *casas particulares*, details of which are available from the Turismo. Nearby **campsites** include *Fuente del Gallo* in the *urbanización* Fuente del Gallo, a three-kilometre walk despite all signs to the contrary (☎956 44 01 37; March–Oct).

Conil has lots of good **seafood restaurants** along the front; *ortiguillas* – deep fried sea anemones – are a delicious regional speciality. Either of Conil's two-star seafood restaurants, *Francisco* and *La Fontanilla*, side by side on the Playa de la Fontanilla, the northernmost beach, are worth a visit. The speciality of the house is *urta* (sea bream), and is equally excellent at both. **Nightlife** centres on the music and drinking **pubs** to the north of the centre around *calles* Cádiz and Baluarte, and **Las Carpas**, a remarkable municipal disco and entertainment complex on the beach which caters for all ages and tastes from techno to flamenco.

Sancti Petri and Chiclana

Heading north from Conil along the dirt road which hugs the coast brings you to the isolated fishing village of **SANCTI PETRI** surrounded by marshes and sand bars. This formerly wild stretch of coast has been developed into a dismal chain of overspill *urbanizaciones* for the growing population of sealocked Cádiz. Dubbed Novo Sancti Petri by the planners, it is a complex of hundreds of identical avenues lined with featureless tile-roofed dwellings, ugly lamp standards, over-manicured gardens and a golf course designed by Severiano Ballesteros. The old village – just about hanging on to its identity – is still worth a look, however, and harks back to a simpler, less materialistic age.

When you reach it, the village of Sancti Petri, 18km north of Conil at the end of a causeway across the surrounding *marismas* is a village under threat from the encroaching madness to the south and its future remains uncertain. The harbour now contains many more weekend yachts and launches than fishing vessels and, since the tuna canning factory closed down, there are few jobs. The focal point of the tiny cluster of dwellings is the *Club Náutico de Sancti Petri* where the few fishermen that are left meet up. On Sunday mornings they sell their catch outside the club and if old Manuel Ramírez is there he'll provide you with some of the freshest oysters and *cañaillas* (murex sea snails) you've ever had for ridiculously low prices. They're best washed down with a beer from the *Náutico*'s bar (they'll also lend you a plate) at a seat on the simple terrace overlooking the harbour. There's a small but nice enough **beach** to the south, where a friendly water sports centre *Sancti Petri Sport* (☎ & fax 956 49 20 22) hires out windsurf boards, kayaks and catamarans and offers guided canoe expeditions around the *marismas* and watercourses of the Natural Park to the north. They also make excursions to the **Castillo de Sancti Petri**, a ruined thirteenth-century castle on an offshore island, where the Phoenicians built an important first millennium BC temple to their god Melkaart which the Romans later turned into a shrine to Hercules. Hannibal was a visitor to the former and Julius Caesar to the latter, and major archeological finds have been discovered which are now on display in the museum at Cádiz.

There are no rooms to be had in Sancti Petri and the nearest place for an overnight stop is **CHICLANA DE LA FRONTERA**, 6km to the east, a pleasant enough place which also serves as a useful road junction, with sporadic buses to Medina Sidonia (see p.159). **Places to stay** include *Hostal Villa*, c/Virgen del Carmen 14 (☎956 40 05 12; ③), with simple rooms, and *Hotel Ideal*, c/Joaquín Santos 5 (☎956 40 05 12; ⑤), overlooking the river. Beyond Chiclana you emerge into a weird landscape of marshes, dotted with drying salt pyramids, in the midst of which lies the town of **San Fernando** – once an elegant place (and still so, at its centre) but quickly being swallowed up by industrial and commercial suburbs. These extend until you reach the long causeway that leads to Cádiz, an unromantic approach to what is one of the most extraordinarily sited and moody towns of the south.

Cádiz

Cádiz, from a distance, was a city of sharp incandescence, a scribble of white on a sheet of blue glass, lying curved on the bay like a scimitar and sparkling with African light.

Laurie Lee, As I Walked Out One Midsummer Morning

Once you've got through the tedious modern suburbs on its eastern flank, inner **CÁDIZ**, built on a peninsula-island entered via the **Puertas de Tierra** (Land Gates) – a substantial remnant of the eighteenth-century walls – looks much as it must have done in the great days of the empire, with grand open squares, sailors' alleyways and high, turreted houses. Literally crumbling from the effect of the sea air on its soft limestone, it has a tremendous atmosphere – slightly seedy, definitely in decline, but still full of mystique. Above all, Cádiz is a city that knows how to enjoy itself. It has always been noted for its vibrant fiestas: the ancient Roman poet Martial was among the many who commented on the sensuous and swirling dances of the townswomen ("they click their Tartessian castanets with a deft hand"), implying a pre-Moorish origin for flamenco. Although settled after the *reconquista* with immigrants from the northern city of Santander, Cádiz maintains its Roman reputation for joviality with an **annual carnival** in February, acknowledged to be the best – and wildest – in Spain.

Some history

Founded about 1100 BC by the Phoenicians as Gadir, a transit depot for minerals carried from the mining areas of the Río Tinto to the north, Cádiz has been one of Spain's principal ports ever since, and lays claim to being the oldest city in Europe. Sited on a tongue of land enclosing a bay and a perfect natural harbour, with some fine beaches besides, it has – you would think – all the elements that make for an appealing place to visit. But despite a charming old town, oddly enough the place seems unable to shake off a brooding lethargy when it comes to entertaining visitors, and the world of tourism has largely passed it by.

Historically Cádiz served as an important base for the navies of Carthage, Rome, and – following a long decline under the Moors – imperial Spain. Always prone to attack because of its strategic importance, the city's nose was bloodied on numerous occasions, especially by the English. Drake's "singeing of the king of Spain's beard" occurred here in 1587, followed not long after by Essex's ransacking of the port in 1596, and in 1797 Nelson's bombardment.

The city's greatest period, however, and the era from which much of **inner Cádiz** dates, was the eighteenth century. Then, with the silting up of the river to Sevilla, the port enjoyed a virtual monopoly on the Spanish-American trade in gold and silver: on its proceeds were built the golden-domed (in colour at least) **cathedral** – almost Oriental when seen from the sea – public halls and offices, broad streets and elegant

CARNIVAL!

Claiming to be saltier than the carnivals of Havana and Río de Janeiro rolled into one, each February Cádiz launches into its riotous **Carnaval**, the most important and wittiest in Spain. Largely a disorganized series of fiestas in origin, it was given its present shape in the late nineteeth century by Antonio Rodríguez Martínez, now known by his nickname *"El Tío de la Tiza"* ("Chalky"), who was improbably employed as a Customs official in the port. He organized the *murgas* or bands – a major feature of *Carnaval* – into four categories:

Coros: These are (recently mixed) groups of about thirty who tour the city on flamboyantly decorated floats singing to the accompaniment of guitars, lutes and mandolins.

Comparsas: Groups of around fifteen people who parade on foot with guitars and drums.

Chirigotas: Arguably the most popular with *gaditanos*, these are groups of around ten people accompanied on an impish reed whistle or *pito*, who tour the bars singing hilarious satirical songs about people and events in the public eye.

Trios, Cuartetos, Quintetos. These smaller groups not only sing, but also act out parodies and satirical sketches based upon current events as they tour the town in costume.

Illegales: Given the city's innate anarchy these bands do not compete officially (see below), but take to the streets for the sheer hell of it with whatever instruments they can lay their hands on. They include whole families, groups of friends and even collections of drunks, staggering about as they attempt to make music.

The above groups provide only the focus, however, for the real *Carnaval* which takes place on the streets with everyone dressed up in costume and apparently drunk for ten whole days. The "legal" groups compete before judges in the Teatro Falla in between sessions on the streets and are symbolically awarded *"un pelotazo"* (good shot) for a bitingly witty composition and *"un cajonazo"* (a box drum) for a bomb. The various groups work at their repertoire for months before, road-testing their compositions during the two weekends prior to *Carnaval*(but not in costume, which is regarded as bad form) at the warm-up shindigs of the *Erizada* (hedgehog party) or the *Ostionada* (oyster party), great street fiestas which feature sea-urchin and oyster tasting.

ATTENDING *CARNAVAL*
During *Carnaval* there are no **rooms** to be had in town at all unless you've made reservations well in advance. One way round this is to see it on **day-trips from Sevilla**, catching an evening train (a couple of hours' journey) and returning with the first train the next day, around 5.30am. These trains are a riotous party in themselves and, packed as they are with costumed carnival-goers from Sevilla, you'd be well advised to get dressed up yourself if you don't want to stand out like a sore thumb. The opening and final weekends are the high points of the whole show.

squares, as well as a clutch of smaller churches. This wealth spawned Spain's first modern middle class which, from early on, was free-thinking and liberal, demanding such novelties as a free press and open debate. One historian has claimed that political dialogue in Spain originated along the Calle Ancha, Cádiz's elegant central thoroughfare where politicians met informally.

In the early nineteenth century the city made arguably its greatest contribution to the development of modern Spain, when a group of radicals set up the short-lived Spanish Parliament or **Cortes** in 1812 during the Peninsular Wars. The Cortes drew up a constitution that upheld the sovereignty of the people against the throne and set down a blueprint for a liberal Spain that would take a further century and a half to emerge. Loyal to its traditions, the city relentlessly opposed General Franco during the **Civil War**, even though this was one of the first towns to fall to his forces, and was the port through which the Nationalist armies launched their invasion. Later, when Franco often referred in power to the forces of "Anti Spain" he had in mind the sentiments expressed in the Cádiz Constitution of 1812, ramming home his disapproval by renaming the city's major plazas after himself and other members of the Falangist pantheon. Left-wing Cádiz merely bided its time and now, in the new democracy, these landmarks have regained their original designations. The city's tradition of liberalism and tolerance is epitomized by the way *gaditanos* (as the inhabitants of the city are known) have always breezily accepted a substantial **gay** community here, who are much in evidence at the city's brilliant *Carnaval* festivities.

Arrival, information and city transport

Arriving by train you'll find yourself on the periphery of the old town, close to the Plaza San Juan de Dios, busiest of the many squares. By **bus** you'll be a few blocks to the north, along the water – either at the *Los Amarillos* terminal, Avda. Ramón de Carranza 31 (serving Rota, Chipiona and resorts west of Cádiz), or a few blocks north again at the *Estación de Comes*, Plaza de Independencia, near Plaza de España (serving Sevilla, Tarifa and other destinations toward Algeciras). *Los Amarillos* also runs a twice-daily service through Arcos to Ubrique, with a connection there to Ronda – by far the best route. Coming in **by car** you will soon discover Cadiz's acute lack of parking space, and if you don't want to spend an age searching you'd be best off taking accommodation with a garage or heading for a car park. Two of the most central are by the train station and along Paseo de Canalejas near the waterfront.

Timetables as well as general information, a detailed street **map** and a useful *Ruta de Tapas* leaflet are available from the **Turismo**, c/Calderón de la Barca 1 (Mon 9am–2pm, Tues–Fri 9am–7pm, Sat 10am–2pm; ☎956 21 13 13), which is effectively on Plaza de Mina close to the Museo de Bellas Artes. On Saturdays starting at 11am they offer a free guided walk around the city. There's also a useful **Turismo municipal** on the Plaza San Juan de Dios (Mon–Fri 9am–2pm & 5–8pm, Sat & Sun 10am–1.30pm & 5–7.30pm; ☎956 24 10 01), for maps and information. A nearby **kiosk** on the same square can also be helpful, and opens (in theory) the same hours. It's worth bearing mind that – in common with several other Andalucian towns – many of Cádiz's streets have multiple names; when in doubt, consult as many maps as possible. **City buses** are a handy way of getting around and a route map is available from the Turismo. A *Bonobus* travelcard (850ptas from any branch of *Banco Central Hispano*) allows you a saving on multiple journeys.

Accommodation

In tune with the city itself, much of Cádiz's budget **accommodation** has seen better days. Few places in the old town are either new or comfy, and for more sophisticated lodging you really need to head towards the beach. However, many of these crumbling old places are full of character, and efforts are now being made to retain this whilst upgrading the facilities. Except during the *Carnaval* and August, finding a place to stay shouldn't be a problem, and it's worth remembering that during slack periods many places will drop their prices to fill a room – an amiable haggle is always worth a try.

If you're not tempted by the excellent youth hostel, a good place to start hunting is Plaza San Juan de Dios and the surrounding network of alleyways, crammed with *hostales* and *fondas*. Calle Marqués de Cádiz also has several budget options, as does the pedestrianised c/Plocia, east of the plaza. More good *pensiones* and *hostales* are a couple of blocks away, towards the cathedral or Plaza de Candelaria and beyond.

Pensión La Argentina, c/Conde O'Reilly 1 (☎956 22 33 10). Simple, cheap and spotless rooms close to Plaza de España. ②.

Hotel Atlántico, Parque Genovés 9 (☎956 22 69 05, fax 956 21 45 82). Functional, modern *parador*, somewhat lacking in romance and not particularly welcoming, but with balcony rooms, Atlantic views and an outdoor pool. Garage. ⑦.

Hostal Bahía, c/Plocia 5 (☎956 25 90 61). By far the nicest *hostal* along this road, offering rooms with bath, TV and air conditioning; well worth the price. ⑤.

Pensión Cádiz, c/Feduchy 20 (☎956 28 58 01). Basic *pensión* with clean rooms, almost opposite one of the best *tabernas* in town, *Taberna La Manzanilla* (see p.186). ③.

Hostal Carlos I, Plaza de Sevilla s/n, next to the train station (☎956 28 66 00, fax 956 20 06 59). Excellent light and airy rooms with bath, air conditioning and TV. Don't let the location put you off. Parking nearby. ⑤.

Hostal Centro Sol, c/Manzanares 7 (☎ & fax 956 28 31 03). Slightly pricey for what you get, but the rooms are smart and arranged above a pleasant patio. Has its own café-bar. ⑤.

Hostal Colón, c/Marqués de Cádiz 6 (☎956 28 53 51). Good option for simple but spacious rooms. ③.

Las Cuatro Naciones, c/Plocia 3 (☎956 25 55 39). Clean, unpretentious place with low-priced rooms close to Plaza San Juan de Dios. ②.

Pensión del Duque, c/Ancha 13 (☎956 22 27 77). Decent rooms, some with bath and balcony, at this friendly old *pensión*. ③.

Quo Qádis Youth Hostel, c/Diego Arias 1 (☎ & fax 956 22 19 39). As eccentric as its name, this is a vibrant place and great if you want to meet people; has simple doubles, triples, a dorm and offers all kinds of activities including flamenco, language courses and mountain bike, snorkelling and walking excursions. Prices include breakfast, and there's a restaurant with vegetarian options. ①–③.

Hostal Fantoni, c/Flamenco 5 (☎956 28 27 04). Slightly north of Plaza San Juan de Dios, this hostal occupies a charming, renovated house filled with *azulejos* and cool marble. Rooms with and without bath. ④.

Hotel Francia y París, Plaza de San Francisco 2, close to Plaza de Mina (☎956 22 23 48, fax 956 22 24 31). Luxurious, quiet, Belle Époque hotel with some rooms overlooking an attractive square. ⑥.

Hostal La Isleña, Plaza San Juan de Dios 12 (☎956 28 70 64). Old and atmospheric *hostal* facing the *Ayuntamiento*, offering good-value and clean – if basic – rooms. ②.

Hostal Manolita, c/Benjumeda 2 (☎956 21 15 77). Simple rooms in this friendly, family-run *hostal*. ③.

Regio I, Avda. Ana de Viya 11 (☎956 27 93 31, fax 956 27 91 13). Older of the two Regio hotels behind the Playa de la Victoria; a good two-star place for rooms with bath, air conditioning and TV. Garage. ⑥.

Regio II, Avda. Andalucía 79 (☎956 25 30 08, fax 956 25 30 09). Upmarket version of the *Regio* hotel above, and worth the extra. Garage. ⑥.

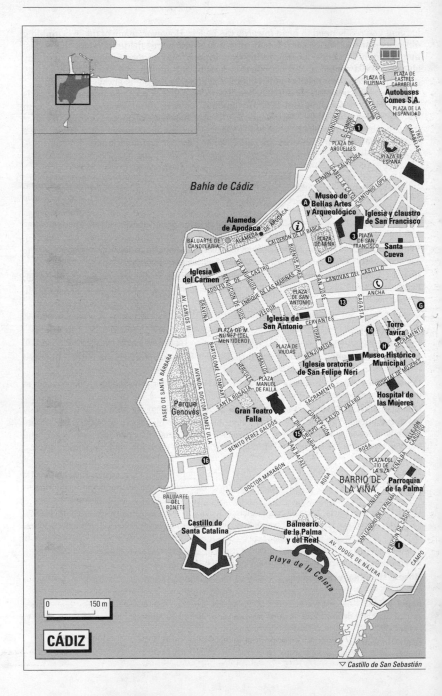

Bahía de Cádiz

PLAZA DE FILIPINAS
PLAZA DE LASTRES CARABELAS
Autobuses Comes S.A.
PLAZA DE LA HISPANIDAD
PLAZA DE ARGÜELLES
PLAZA DE ESPAÑA

Museo de Bellas Artes y Arqueológico
Alameda de Apodaca
Iglesia y claustro de San Francisco
PLAZA DE SAN FRANCISCO
PLAZA DE MINA
BALUARTE DE CANDELARIA
Santa Cueva

Iglesia del Carmen
PLAZA DE SAN ANTONIO
CÁNOVAS DEL CASTILLO
ANCHA

Iglesia de San Antonio
PLAZA DE VIUDAS
Torre Tavira

Iglesia oratorio de San Felipe Neri
Museo Histórico Municipal

PLAZA MANUEL DE FALLA
Parque Genovés
Gran Teatro Falla
Hospital de las Mujeres

BARRIO DE LA VIÑA
Parroquia de la Palma

BALUARTE DEL BONETE
Castillo de Santa Catalina
Balneario de la Palma y del Real
Playa de la Caleta

0   150 m

CÁDIZ

▽ *Castillo de San Sebastián*

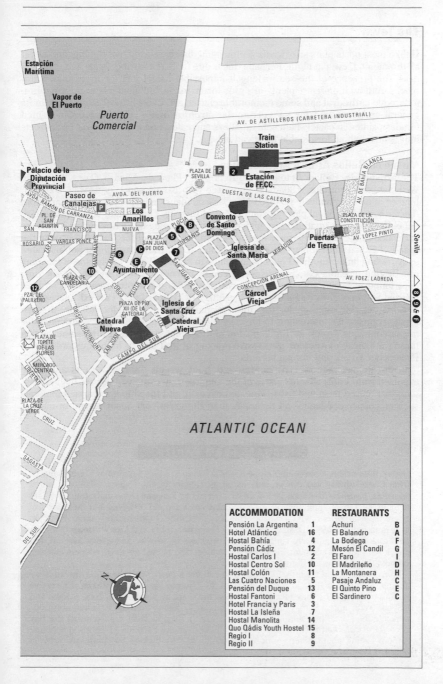

ACCOMMODATION

Pensión La Argentina	1
Hotel Atlántico	16
Hostal Bahía	4
Pensión Cádiz	12
Hostal Carlos I	2
Hostal Centro Sol	10
Hostal Colón	11
Las Cuatro Naciones	5
Pensión del Duque	13
Hostal Fantoni	6
Hotel Francia y Paris	3
Hostal La Isleña	7
Hostal Manolita	14
Quo Qádis Youth Hostel	15
Regio I	8
Regio II	9

RESTAURANTS

Achuri	B
El Balandro	A
La Bodega	F
Mesón El Candil	G
El Faro	I
El Madrileño	D
La Montanera	H
Pasaje Andaluz	C
El Quinto Pino	E
El Sardinero	C

The Town

Unlike most ports of its size, Cádiz seems immediately relaxed, easy-going, and not at all threatening, even at night. Perhaps this is due to its reassuring shape and compactness, the presence of the sea making it impossible to get lost for more than a few blocks. Although there are plenty of sights to aim for, including an excellent **museum**, a Baroque **cathedral** and some memorable church art, Cádiz is most interesting for its general ambience and for its **vernacular architecture** – elegant *mirador*-fronted facades painted in pastel shades, blind alleys and cafés, and ancient *barrio* backstreets imprisoned behind formidable fortifications.

Museo de Bellas Artes y Arqueológico

The **Museo de Bellas Artes y Arqueológico**, Plaza de Mina 5 (Tues 2.30–8pm, Wed–Sat 9am–8pm, Sun 9.30am–2.30pm; free with EU passport, otherwise 250ptas), housed in an imaginatively restored Neoclassical mansion just across the square from the Turismo, is an ideal place to start a tour of the city. The ground-floor **archeological collection** (information in Spanish only) includes some fine **Phoenician jewellery** excavated in the city and bronze figurines from the shrine of the god Melkaart on the island of Sancti Petri. Etruscan artefacts found at the same site hint at sophisticated early trading links. Another Phoenician temple to Astarte/Venus on the site of the modern Bastion of Santa Catalina yielded **incense burners** (*quemaperfumes* – the only ones found in Spain) with Egyptian decoration and a **terracotta head** with striking negroid features. Two remarkable fifth-century BC **Phoenician carved sarcophagi** in white marble (one male, the other female) are also unique to the western Mediterranean. It's interesting to observe the fusion of influences here: Egyptian for the sarcophagus, Greek for the depiction of the sculpted images. In the same section there's a display of **ancient glassware** – some of it of a very high standard – from Phoenician, Greek and Roman periods.

In the Roman section a **reconstructed boat wreck** displays various amphorae exported from Cádiz to other parts of the empire; they contained *garum* (fish sauce), *salazones* (cured meat and fish), wine and olive oil, and the ship also carried minerals such as copper and lead – all demonstrating the great part Spain played in making

---

BOATS FROM CÁDIZ

Before the decline of passenger ships it was possible to sail to London or South America from Cádiz – today you can go only as far as Tangier or the Canary Islands. Vapores Suardiaz, Estación Marítima (☎956 28 21 11) sails to **Tangier** twice daily (Sun–Fri 7am & 5pm; Sat 7am & 7pm; 3hr). A one-way ticket costs around 3000ptas, but there are frequent special offers which shave this considerably. Transmediterranea, Estación Marítima (☎956 22 74 21), have sailings to **Tenerife** (36hr) and **Las Palmas** (48hr). A ship makes this round-trip roughly every two days in season, and every five out, but check with the company for the latest timetables; tickets cost about 30,000ptas one-way (almost the same as for flights).

More locally – and for only 275ptas – you can get a boat (or *vapor* as it's known hereabouts, alluding to the old steamboats) to **El Puerto de Santa María**, a forty-five minute trip across the bay (see p.188). Departures are at 10am, noon, 2pm, 6.30pm and 8.30pm (returning at 9am, 11am, 1pm, 3.30pm and 7.30pm) from the Estación Marítima, opposite the *Comes* bus station near to the Plaza de España. Boat trips **around the bay** aboard the *Cabo Leiras* (with on-board bar) leave from the Estación Marítima at 8pm and 9.45pm lasting about ninety minutes (☎956 25 00 99). Tickets (800ptas) are sold on board.

Rome rich. Two enormous anchors nearby, found off Cádiz, attest to the size of vessels that were used. Notable among the Roman statuary is a giant marble sculpture of the second-century **Emperor Trajan**, which prior to excavation stood in the forum of Roman Bolonia, near Tarifa.

The second-floor **fine arts museum** is one of the best in Andalucía. The kernel of the collection is a group of twenty-one canvases by **Zurbarán** in Room 2, including a quite exceptional series of saints brought here from La Cartuja, the Carthusian monastery at Jerez, and one of only three such sets in the country preserved intact, or nearly so (the others are at Sevilla and Guadalupe). With their sharply defined shadows and intense, introspective air, Zurbarán's saints are powerful and very Spanish – even the English figures such as Hugh of Lincoln, or the Carthusian John Houghton, martyred by Henry VIII whom he refused to accept as head of the English Church. Perhaps this is not surprising, for the artist spent much of his life travelling round the Carthusian monasteries of Spain and many of his saints are in fact portraits of the monks he met. Highlights of the many other works on display include, in Room 3, Murillo's *Ecce Homo* and *San Pedro y San Paulo*, as well as his final work, the *Mystic Marriage of Santa Catalina* – during the painting of which he fell from a scaffold to his death – and a *Sagrada Familia* by **Rubens**. The same room also contains *The Vision of San Félix Cantalicio*, a canvas displaying tenebrist influences by seventeenth-century sculptor, painter and all-round genius *sevillano* Alonso Cano.

The museum's third floor has an interesting **ethnological collection** divided into two rooms; the first has examples of traditional *artesanía* including ceramics, basketwork, leatherwork and textiles. The second room contains some wonderful **antique marionettes**, part of a section covering the long tradition of *Tía Norica*, or satirical marionette theatre, in Cádiz. This art form has often been used to pillory the city's rulers and dignitaries, such as clergy and politicians, through the "mouths" of its characters taken from the streets – travelling salesmen, waiters, sailors, fishermen, *toreros*, drunks – often in times when overt political activity was dangerous. The city still holds an annual marionette theatre festival. Fascinating though the puppets are behind glass, they need to be brought to life in a show; an idea that awaits an enterprising museum director.

Oratorio de Santa Cueva

A short walk from the museum, on c/Rosario, the eighteenth-century **Oratorio de Santa Cueva** (Mon–Fri 10am–1pm; 50ptas), houses three fine **Goya frescoes**. The church is divided into two dramatically contrasting parts; in the elliptical **upper oratory** beneath an elegant dome decorated with plaster reliefs and flanked by lofty columns of red jasper, are the three frescoes representing the *Miracle of the Loaves and Fishes*, the *Bridal Feast* and the *Last Supper*, an unexpected depiction of Christ and the disciples dining sprawled on the floor, Roman style. In sharp contrast to the chapel above, steps lead down to a dimly lit **subterranean chapel** containing a sculpture of the crucifixion whose manifest pathos only adds to the gloom. An eighteenth-century work of the Genoa school, the image is said to have inspired visiting composer Joseph Haydn to write the score of his *Seven Last Words* (of Christ) oratorio.

The Catedral Nueva and around

The huge **Catedral Nueva** (church and museum: Tues–Sat 10am–1pm; 500ptas; church only: Mon–Sat noon–1pm; 100ptas; entry through the museum on west side when main doors are closed), so titled because it replaced the former cathedral, Santa Cruz, is one of the largest churches in Spain. Begun in 1722, it took 110 years to finish, and even then the towers – shortened when the money ran out – were completed only in 1853 in an unsympathetic white limestone whose patchwork effect jars with the original sandstone. The time lapse also led to a curious architectural potpourri, strikingly visible on the main facade, where an earlier and sober Neoclassical style was topped off with pure Baroque. What is more, on closer inspection you'll see that the distinctive "gilded" dome, which appears so impressive from afar, is in fact made from glazed yellow tiles.

Even if you don't normally go for High Baroque, it's hard to resist the attraction of the austere – and now seriously corroded – interior, which has more of the architect Vincente Acero's original design. From inside, the soaring 52m-high dome is illuminated by a powdery violet light, the whole, perfectly proportioned building decorated entirely in stone with no gold or white in sight. **Art works** include a sculpture of *San Bruno* by Montañes in the chapel of San Sebastián and some other polychromed sculptures including an *Ecce Homo* attributed to Luisa Roldán ("La Roldana"), the daughter of Pedro Roldán. Also worth a look are the wonderful **choir stalls** dating from 1702 which were originally in the Cartuja of Sevilla and moved here upon the latter's Disentailment in 1835. In the **crypt** (same hours) is buried Manuel de Falla, the great *gaditano* composer of such Andalucía-inspired works as *Nights in the Gardens of Spain* and *El amor brujo*. The cathedral's **museum** holds some dubiously attributed paintings as well as a rather tedious collection of ecclesiastical silver enlivened only by a monstrance – an eighteenth-century bejewelled custodia nicknamed the *Millón* (million), a reference to the number of precious gems and pearls set into the work.

Sadly, the building is now in an advanced state of decay underlined by the wire netting stretched across the nave to prevent crumbling masonry – caused by sea air calcifying the white stone – falling on the congregation below. Work has now begun, however, on restoring the interior and sealing the stone in a protective film. When the exterior has been similarly protected and an air-conditioning system fitted to the interior – all astronomically expensive – it is hoped that the problem will have been solved.

The best view of the cathedral is from the **waterfront** behind, where the golden dome is perfectly set off by the pastel-tinted facades of the adjacent houses along c/Campo del Sur. To the east of the Plaza de la Catedral fronting the cathedral lies the **Barrio del Pópulo**, a poor, run-down area of narrow alleyways and decaying tenements, a surviving remnant of the thirteenth-century medieval city. Many of its streets are graced by the odd crumbling *palacio*, formerly residences of merchants made wealthy by empire trade, and now split up into residential blocks. One of these, the **Casa del Almirante** on c/Posadilla is a superb Baroque pile with an ebullient facade featuring barley sugar and Tuscan columns in rose-tinted Italian marble. An ancient, though recently restored, seventeenth-century inn, the **Mesón del Pópulo**, c/Mesón Nuevo 11 – at the crook in the street – has the typical layout of these travellers' hostelries with stables below and living quarters above. Calles Sopranis and Santa María – where the Palacio Lasquetty (no. 11) and the church of Santa María are also worth a look – are other good places to sample the typical atmosphere of this quarter.

Iglesia de Santa Cruz and other churches

A little further east of the cathedral stands the "Old" Cathedral, the **Iglesia de Santa Cruz**. Originally a thirteenth-century church built on top of a mosque, it was almost destroyed by the Earl of Essex during the English assault on Cádiz in 1596, and is effectively a seventeenth-century rebuild with only odd vestiges such as the entrance arch surviving from the earlier Gothic structure. The sober grey stone interior contrasts with the magnificent seventeenth-century *retablo,* a beautiful work with sculptures by Martínez Montañes, as is the **Capilla de los Genoveses**, its stunning *retablo* of red, white and black Italian marble in dire need of restoration. Just behind the church is a recently discovered **Roman theatre** (Tues–Sun 11am–1pm; free) dating from the first century BC. Partly cut into by a corner of Santa Cruz and built over by a later Moorish *alcazaba*, the remaining banks of seats have been restored.

From here you could follow the waterfront west to the **Capilla de Santa Catalina** (presently closed), a shrine for Murillo fans. Located on the waterfront close to the c/Capuchinos, this seventeenth-century church was where – during the completion of a commission for the former Capuchin proprietors – the painter fell from a scaffold while finishing the *Mystic Marriage of Santa Catalina* on the high altar *retablo*. He was carried back to Sevilla where he died from his injuries a few days later, and the painting was completed by one of his pupils. Currently this work, together with an *Immaculada* and a stunning *Stigmata of San Francisco*, which also used to hang here, are displayed in the Museo de Bellas Artes.

Lastly, there are two churches of note for the paintings and sculptures they contain. Foremost of these is the chapel of the **Hospital de las Mujeres** (Mon–Fri 10am–1pm; 100ptas; ask the porter for admission) on the street of the same name, and one of the most impressive Baroque buildings in the city. Quite apart from its two elegant patios, the hospital's chapel has a brilliant El Greco of *San Francisco in Ecstasy*. The other church, the **Iglesia y claustro de San Francisco** just east of Plaza de Mina on a tiny square of the same name, has in its sacristy two sculptures of San Diego and San Francisco attributed to Martínez Montañes.

Oratorio de San Felipe Neri and the Museo Histórico Municipal

The eighteenth-century oratory of **San Felipe Neri**, c/San José, south of Plaza de Mina (Mon–Sat 10am–1.30pm; 150ptas) is one of the most important historical buildings in Spain, evidenced by the number of international plaques from countries as far apart as Chile and the Philippines attached to the exterior. It was here, on March 29, 1812, that a group of patriotic radicals defied the Napoleonic blockade and set up the Cortes, framing a liberal Constitution – the nation's first – which, although it was to be over a century and a half before Spain was ready to embrace its ideas, nevertheless had a major impact on the development of European liberal politics. The church itself, a charming oval structure, has a double tier of balconies which would once have rung with the roar of fierce debate, and above which eight *ventanillas* in the dome allow the brilliant light to illuminate the sky-blue decor and the central nave punctuated by seven chapels. The high altar's *retablo* is crowned by a fine *Immaculada* by Murillo.

Next door to the oratory in c/Santa Inés, the **Museo Histórico Municipal** (Tues–Fri 9am–1pm & 4–7pm, Sat & Sun 9am–1pm; free) was set up in 1912 to commemorate the first centenary of the 1812 Constitution. The highlights of the museum are a large Romantic-style **mural** depicting the events of 1812 together with a number of the original documents of the Cortes, and an enormous eighteenth-century **scale model** of the city – almost filling a room – made of mahogany and ivory at the behest of King Carlos III. Further north, Plaza de España is dominated by a rather pompous **monument to the 1812 Constitution**, also set up in 1912 and now crowned with the rather appropriate addition of a crane's nest. *Gaditanos* like to claim that it's the only monument in the world honouring and topped by a book – a representation of the 1812 Constitution.

Just south of the Museo Municipal and off c/Sacramento, the **Torre Tavira** (c/Marqués del Real Tesoro 10; daily 10am–8pm; 500ptas) is an eighteenth-century mansion with the tallest tower in the old city, which you can climb to get a great view over the white roofs below and the sea beyond. Many houses had these towers added sor that shipowners and merchants could see ships arriving in the port. The tower also holds a **camera obscura** which gives equally dramatic views, and the rooms below contain historical displays covering Cádiz and its past. A couple of blocks north, the **Calle Ancha** – the historic thoroughfare that is today an attractive pedestrianized street – has another impressive mansion, the nineteenth-century **Casa Mora** at no. 28 (Sat 10am–1pm; consult with the Turismo Municipal for other times; free) , which has an exquisite patio and is stuffed with porcelain, clocks and furnishings of the period spread over three floors.

Barrio de la Viña

Squeezed between c/Campo del Sur and the Playa de la Caleta to the west of the cathedral lies the **Barrio de la Viña**, the old fishermen's quarter, typically *gaditano* and traditionally renowned for the spirited and sarcastic humour of its inhabitants. Its main street is the c/Virgen de la Palma, close to the eastern end of which lies the tiny **Plaza Tío de la Tiza**, a charming square (filled with terraces for seafood *tapas* in summer) named after the man who, in the late nineteenth century gave the famous *carnaval* the form it has today (see p.175).

The beaches

The *barrio*'s southern flank faces the **Playa de la Caleta**, an over-popular – and often none too clean – **beach** in a small bay sandwiched between the most impressive of Cádiz's eighteenth-century sea fortifications, the **Castillo de Santa Catalina** and the **Castillo de San Sebastián**, the latter constructed on an islet and reached by a causeway. This is believed to be the site of the ancient Phoenician harbour where, tradition has it, there once stood an impressive temple to the Phoenician god Kronos. A walk along the seafront here can be wonderfully bracing day or night (when cooling breezes blow in off the Atlantic and many of the monuments are floodlit), with the possibility of a stroll through the Parque Genovés planted with palms and cypresses as far as the bastion of Candelaria, or onwards to the Alameda Apodeca, another waterfront garden, beyond. Across the road from the Parque Genovés near the bus stop there's a mammoth **dragon tree**, a centuries-old piece of natural sculpture.

An alternative **beach** to La Caleta is the **Playa de la Victoria**, longer, cleaner and usually less crowded. It's an easy thirty-minute walk from the old town – just find the seafront on the south side of the peninsula and head east – or there's a bus from Plaza de España (#1; direction Cortadura), which follows the interior route along the Avenida de Andalucía; ask for the "*Residencia*" stop (an enormous hospital that you can't miss), or get off anywhere after five or six stops as the beach is a long one.

Eating and drinking

Cádiz's best cafés, **tapas bars** and **restaurants** tend to be clustered around its many grand squares, especially Plaza San Juan de Dios, dominated by the delightful wedding-cake facade of the late eighteenth-century *Ayuntamiento* (whose bells sound the hour with notes from de Falla's *El amor brujo*) and the pleasant Plaza de Mina. Across the old town there are more places to hunt down in and around the adjoining Plaza de las Flores and Plaza de la Libertad, the latter containing the **market**. The *gaditanos*' summer playground, Paseo Marítimo – the long boulevard fronting the Playa de la Victoria – is lively and fun all season.

Fried fish is excellent everywhere, especially from stands around the beach; for sit-down dishes there are plenty of places to suit all wallets across the town where specialities include *almejas* (clams), *lubina* (sea bass) and *urta al horno*, a white member of the bream family that's a great favourite along the Cádiz coast. *Tapas* specialities include the tasty *caballa* (barbecued mackerel) and *tortilla de camarones*, a shrimp omelette.

Again, the major squares are the places to head for **breakfast** snacks, while the most tempting *heladerías* are dotted about the Paseo Marítimo. The *Heladerías Ibense Bornay* chain are renowned for their *batidos* (milk shakes), with *turrón* (nougat) and *pistacho* flavours among the most popular.

Restaurants

Restaurante Achuri, c/Plocia 15, near Plaza San Juan de Dios. One of the oldest places in the city and very popular with *gaditanos*, so it can be hard to find a table. Excellent Basque- and *andaluz-*

inspired dishes at reasonable prices. *Chipirones en su tinta* (squid in ink) and *bacalao al la andaluza* (cod) are recommended. Closed Sun–Wed eves.

El Balandro, c/Apodaca 22 (no nameplate outside). Highly popular venue with a view of the Bay of Cádiz. *Raciones* are served on the promenade terrace – a wonderful place to watch the sun set. House specials include *ensaladilla de gambas* (prawns) and *revueltos* (scrambled eggs).

La Bodega, Paseo Marítimo 23, on the Playa de la Victoria seafront and close to Cádiz's football stadium, Estadio Ramón de Carranza. Excellent mid-priced restaurant and *tapas* bar with a wide range of meat and fish dishes.

Mesón El Candil, Javier de Burgos 19. Solid *gaditano* fish and seafood restaurant with a pleasant ambience.

El Faro, c/San Félix 15. In the heart of the Barrio de la Viña, and one of the best fish restaurants in Andalucía. House specialities include *pulpo* (octopus), *merluza* (hake), *urta* (sea bream), and a delicious *arroz marinero* (Andalucían paella). There's also a reasonably priced *menú*.

Freiduría Las Flores, Plaza Las Flores. One of the best *freidurías* in town. You can get a take-away and eat it at the terrace tables of the nearby bar *La Marina* (facing the *correos*), who don't seem to mind – as long as you buy a drink. Another good one, *Freiduría Sopranis*, c/Sopranis 2, just off Plaza San Juan de Dios, at the other end of town, offers similar fare.

El Madrileño, Plaza de Mina. A diminutive place which puts out tables on this attractive square and serves up a budget *menú*.

La Montanera, c/Sacramento 39. Good place for carnivores in this fish-crazy city. The lamb dishes, especially, are excellent, and check out the dish of the day.

Pasaje Andaluz, Plaza San Juan de Dios. Friendly diner with outdoor terrace and a *menú* offering meat and fish dishes.

El Quinto Pino, c/San Fernando 2, just off Plaza San Juan de Dios. Friendly and buzzing little restaurant with good selection of *platos combinados*, a terrace and a 950ptas *menú*.

El Sardinero, Plaza San Juan de Dios 4. Ancient Cádiz institution with a wide range of Basque-*andaluz* dishes served on their terrace on this picturesque square. Specials include *callos* (stewed tripe) and *merluza vasco-andaluza* (hake). Also has a decent *tapas* bar.

Tapas bars

Mesón Las Americas, c/Ramón y Cajal. Good *tapas* and *raciones* bar near Plaza de España.

Cervecería-Marisquería Aurelio, c/Zorrilla 1, near Plaza Mina. Vibrant and outstanding seafood *tapas* bar with excellent *manzanilla*. The owners are the sons of roaming fish seller Aurelio, who sells shellfish outside the entrance most days. Specials include *merluza rebozada* (hake).

Bahía, Avda. Ramón Carranza 29. Wonderful old harbourfront bar with *fino* and delicious *guisos – tapas* in sauce; there's no frying here. Try the *costillas de cerdo* (pork ribs) or *papas aliñas* (potatoes in sauce).

Mesón de Churrasco, c/San Francisco (just off Plaza San Francisco, east of the Plaza de Mina). Excellent, atmospheric *tapas* bar.

Bar El Faro, c/San Félix 15. *Tapas* bar of the renowned restaurant (see above), and probably the best in town. A stand-up place where the *finos* are first rate, the service is so smooth it glides on wheels and the seafood *tapas* are mouthwateringly delicious. House specials include *tortillitas de camarones* (shrimp in batter) and *tostaditas de pan con bacalao* (cod).

Cervecería Gaditana, c/Zorrilla, near *Aurelio*. Fine *tapas* bar – the tasty *montaditos* (or titbits) are wonderful; try the salmon and Roquefort and their *Bombita* (baby bomb), a ball of potato with onion and tuna fish.

Marisquería Joselito, c/San Francisco 38. Venerable old haunt and one of a chain of *tapas* bars, but none the worse for that. There's a sister branch just around the corner, facing the port on Avda. Ramón Carranza. House specials include *salpicón de mariscos* (seafood cocktail) and *gambas al ajillo* (garlic prawns).

Casa Lucas, Plaza Cruz Verde, west of the market. Charming tiny bar in an ancient town house. Serves hearty *arroz* (paella) at lunchtimes and such house specials as *atún encebollado* (tuna) and *merluza* (hake).

Bar Manteca, Corrallón de los Carros 66, near c/San Félix. Great old place in the Barrio de la Viña run by a retired *torero* and decorated with bullfighting memorabilia. Excellent *fino* and *oloroso*. House specials include *chicharrones* (pork crackling) and *lomo* (cured pork loin).

Taberna La Manzanilla, c/Feduchy 18, north of Plaza Candelaria. Wonderful atmospheric eighteenth-century *bodega* serving the odd *tapa* in addition to excellent *manzanilla* served from huge butts. The elderly proprietor, Miguel García Gomez, will show you his cellar with some classic vintages if you ask.

Merodio, Plaza Libertad 4, fronting the market. One of the city's best-loved old bars which gets riotous during *Carnaval*. Specializes in *erizos de mar* (sea urchins) in season, as well as shellfish; including *coquinas* (clams).

La Rambla, c/Sopranis 11, near Plaza San Juan de Dios. Efficient little *tapas* and *raciones* place which also makes a good breakfast stop.

Bar Terraza, Plaza de la Catedral. Facing the cathedral, this is a superb *tapas* bar and restaurant with a pleasant terrace. The nearby *Bar La Catedral* also does tasty fish *tapas* and *raciones*.

Bar Zapata, Plaza Candelaria, at the corner with c/Zapata. Atmospheric new little bar with excellent selection of *jamón* and *chorizo tapas* and wines.

Cafés, bars and heladerías

Cafétería-Heladería Andalucía, Plaza de las Flores. Popular place for coffee and ice cream.

Bazar Inglés, c/San Pedro 18 near Plaza de San Francisco. Atmospheric bar in a converted nineteenth-century store (hence the name) for late-night carousing. Often has flamenco on Thursday night (after 10.30pm).

La Colonia, Alameda s/n, fronting the gardens near the sea slightly north of the Turismo. Wonderful little bar, with garden terrace, done out in surrealist style by noted local painter Luís Quintero. Friendly proprietors serve up potent cocktails; in summer try the *horchata* (tiger nut milk) laced with rum.

Café-Bar La Marina, Plaza de las Flores. With a terrace on this delightful square facing a fountain ringed by flower-sellers' stalls, this makes an excellent breakfast stop or, later in the day, a place for a quiet coffee or *aperitivo*.

Pastelería Orion, Plaza de San Francisco. Fine place for tasty breakfast pastries or afternoon tea and coffee on a tranquil square.

Tinte, c/Tinte, just east of Plaza de la Mina. Great old institution with period features and clientele to match – somewhat spoiled by the addition of a blaring TV. Will serve up *tapas* if asked.

Nightlife

Outside carnival and fiesta times, **nightlife** in Cádiz can be a bit of a damp squib. In summer much of the *marcha nocturna* migrates to the Paseo Marítimo, behind the beaches to the east of the centre, where you'll find most of the music bars and discos, though the laid-back *gaditanos* are not that keen on the latter. Revellers also flock to the **Punta de San Felipe**, the peninsula beyond the harbour to the north of Plaza de España (the best way to reach it is by taxi). Here, there are numerous bars and discos with plenty of frenetic activity in season.

In town, the area around the Plaza de España has a few lively **music bars**, especially along *calles* Antonio López, Rafael Viesca and Dr Zuria Zurita. **Flamenco** is an irregular feature at private *peñas* or clubs, and isn't that easy to find. We've listed a couple of places below, but check with the Turismo for more, as well as for details of special concerts and festivals.

Anfiteatro, c/Punta de San Felipe. Late-night *copas* and frenetic music venue in a zone with lots of similar places nearby.

Baluarte Candelaria, on the northern tip of the peninsula. This sea bastion is the venue for some wonderfully authentic flamenco staged every Thurs night by the *Peña Flamenca Enrique el Mellizo*; entry costs 1000ptas, it gets going around 10.30pm and there's food and drink.

El Café del Correo, c/Cardenal Zapata 6. Pleasant night spot close to Plaza Candelaria, with music and a relaxed atmosphere, although it tends to fill up at weekends.

Crash, c/R. Viesca, near Plaza de España. Loud music and a young crowd.

Café de Levante, c/Rosario near Plaza de San Agustín. Relaxed mixed gay/straight bar.

La Luna, c/Dr Zuria Zurita s/n, off the southwest corner of Plaza de España. Good late-night music bar open till early morning.

Bar Manteca, Corrallón de los Carros 66 (see "Tapas bars" above). Flamenco often takes place at this atmospheric bar in the heart of the Barrio de la Viña.

Persígueme, c/Tinte, near Plaza de Mina. Good music bar which gets very lively.

El Poniente, c/R. Viesca, near Plaza de España. Busy and upbeat gay scene rendezvous.

Listings

Banks Several banks around Plaza San Juan de Dios and Avda. Ramón de Carranza (facing the port) have ATMs/cash machines. The *Hotel Atlántico* will change travellers' cheques and currency outside business hours.

Books/newspapers Quorum, c/Ancha 27, is the best Spanish bookshop and stocks a decent selection of books in English. *El Diario de Cádiz* is the city's daily paper – good for local information, upcoming flamenco concerts and entertainment details.

Car and bike rental Atesa, c/Plocia 2, just off Plaza San Juan de Dios (☎956 25 82 07), is a national and reliable car rental company. Gesatur, c/Antonio López, 5 near Plaza de Mina (☎956 22 41 56), also rent out cars in addition to mopeds and mountain bikes.

Food market Daily market, from 7am to noon, inside the elegant market building on Plaza de la Libertad. This is a good place to pick up fresh produce, and quite a spectacle in its own right during the mid-morning bustle.

Football C.F. Cádiz is the town team based at the Estadio Ramón Carranza, Plaza Madrid, behind the Playa de la Victoria (☎956 21 22 19). Currently languishing in *Segunda B*, they have been pushing for promotion in the last few seasons, so far without success. Tickets can be purchased at the ground.

Hiking maps 1:25,000 and 1:50,000 IGN maps are available from CNIG, Edificio Nereida, Avda. Ana de Viya 5, behind the Playa de la Victoria. A detailed city map is published by Everest and is available from bookshops.

Internet, *Cybercafé Glorieta Ingeniero la Cierva*, Cádiz's solitary internet café, is some way from the centre on a plaza behind the Playa de la Victoria (250ptas for 15min).

Hospital For urgent medical treatment go the Urgencias (emergency) department of the Residencia Sanitaria Hospital, Avda. Ana de Viya 21, near the Hotel Playa Victoria (☎956 24 21 00).

Police The police station is at Campo del Sur s/n, near the central market (☎956 22 81 06). In emergencies dial ☎092.

Post office Plaza de las Flores, near the market (Mon–Fri 8.30am–8.30pm; Sat 9am–2pm). For poste restante, the Lista de Correos stays open Mon–Fri 9am–3pm, Sat 9am–2pm.

Wine Cádiz province is famed for its wines and you can buy and learn all about them at Magerit, c/Fermin Salvochea 2, west of Plaza de España (☎956 22 79 94, fax 956 62 21 94), whose engaging female proprietor is a Spanish Master of Wine and conducts tasting courses (5000ptas) in the *finos*, *manzanillas* and other great wines of the peninsula.

The Cádiz coast

If you fancy a change of beach – Cádiz's two beaches sometimes struggle to cope with the hordes during the summer months – a trip across the bay offers an attractive escape route. The resorts of **El Puerto de Santa María**, **Rota**, **Chipiona** and **Sanlúcar de Barrameda** have fine and spacious beaches and are all within easy distance by bus, boat or train as well as being in striking distance for a visit to the inland sherry capital, **Jerez**.

El Puerto de Santa María

Just 10km across the bay, **EL PUERTO DE SANTA MARÍA** is the obvious choice for a brief day-trip from Cádiz, a traditional family resort for both *gaditanos* and *sevillanos* – many of whom have built villas and chalets along the fine **Playa Puntilla** which you'll pass as the boat comes in to dock at the Muelle del Vapor in the estuary of the Río Guadalete. The town itself, some distance from the beach, has an easy-going air and, despite some ugly modern development on its periphery, is surprisingly picturesque with many narrow, white-walled streets and plant-filled balconies. An impressive medieval castle, a clutch of *señorial* mansions, some fine churches and Spain's third most prestigious bullring make the town well worth exploring before you head off to the beaches.

Today one of the three centres of **wine production** that make up the "sherry triangle" (along with Jerez and Sanlúcar), El Puerto de Santa María came to prominence in the eighteenth century as a botanical garden where plants brought from the New World were cultivated for seed. This and other trading enterprises increased prosperity, as demonstrated by the numerous mansions around the town, which was once known as the "*ciudad de los cien palacios*" or "city of a hundred palaces".

Arrival and information

Whether you arrive by bus (the "station" is little more than a couple of bus stops next to the Plaza de Toros), train or *vapor* (quicker, cheaper and more romantic than the bus, though marginally slower than the train – see p.180), the helpful **Turismo** at c/Luna 22 (daily 10am–2pm & 6–8pm; ☎956 54 24 13) is handily sited for picking up a free king-size **street map** as well as information. From here the heart of the town is within easy walking distance. Many of the main sights (including the Castillo San Marcos) are covered in a **free guided tour** by the Turismo on Tuesdays and Saturdays starting out from their office at 11am.

Accommodation

Most visitors come to El Puerto for the day, but should you be tempted to stay – and it makes a great break from Cádiz – there are plenty of **rooms** within easy walking distance of the ferry. Bear in mind that things tend to get tight during August, when you should fix something up as early as possible in the day. If you have problems, ask at the Turismo for assistance; they also keep a list of **apartments** for longer stays.

El Puerto has two **campsites**, both reasonably close to the beaches. *Camping Playa Las Dunas* (☎956 87 22 10), just behind the Playa Puntilla, has the advantage of plenty of shade. Take bus #2 from Plaza de Galeras, by the ferry dock. The other campsite, *Camping Guadalete* (☎956 56 17 49), is perhaps the better site but lies 1km inland from the Playa Valdelgrana and is reached by bus #35 from close to the ferry dock.

Hostal Chaikana, c/Javier de Burgos 17 (☎956 54 29 01, fax 956 54 29 22). Small but very comfortable *hostal* near the centre of the action. All rooms have bath, air conditioning and TV. ⑥.

Hostal Loreto, c/Ganado 17 (☎956 54 24 10). Clean and basic *hostal* with a nice patio, some rooms with bath. ④.

Pensión Manolo, c/Jesús de Milagros 18 (☎956 85 75 25). Pleasant doubles and singles, some with bath, above a charming patio. ③.

Monasterio San Miguel, c/Larga 27 (☎956 54 04 40, fax 956 54 26 04). The best in town, set in a sixteenth-century monastery converted into a luxurious hotel complete with pool. ⑨.

Pensión Piña, c/Larga 130 (☎956 85 35 32). Friendly, no-frills *pensión* near the centre. ②.

Hotel Santa María, Avda. Bajamar s/n (☎956 87 32 11, fax 956 87 36 52). Mid-range hotel in converted eighteenth-century *palacio* with air conditioning, restaurant, garage and rooftop pool. ⑦.

Pensión Santa María, c/Pedro Múñoz Seco 35 (☎956 85 36 31). Basic but reliable *pensión*, not to be confused with the hotel above. ②.

The Town

If you're arriving by ferry, as soon as you get off the boat you'll see a fine six-spouted eighteenth-century fountain, **El Fuente de las Galeras**, constructed, as the Latin inscription on it states, to provide galleys leaving for the Americas with water. West of here and a couple of blocks in – behind the elegant old fish market, now a bar – will bring you to the **Castillo de San Marcos** (Mon–Fri 10am, 11.30am & 1pm; Sat 11am–1.30pm; 300ptas) on Plaza de Alfonso El Sabio, a thirteenth-century fort built by Alfonso X on the site of a former Moorish watch-tower and mosque. The towers of the castle bear the stirring proclamations of devotion to the Virgin, a symbol of the victory over the vanquished Moors. So besotted was the king with her that he sang the Virgin's

praises in a surviving poetic work, *Las Cantigas*, and renamed El Puerto after her. Inside the fort – today owned by the Luis Caballero *bodega* – Alfonso also constructed a triple-naved **Mudéjar church**, in which the mosque's ancient *mihrab* can still be identified. The current proprietors have long used one of the castle's halls as a sherry *bodega*, stacked with butts. You can take a full tour of the castle, leaving via the *bodega* where they will invite you to taste (and buy) their *finos*.

Following the mostly pedestrianized c/Luna into town from the ferry quay will bring you to the convent of **Las Esclavas de la Sagrada Corazón de Jesús**, a seventeenth-century baroque church whose *retablo* has fine images of the Virgin and Christ. The church's *azulejo* **tile decoration** comes from the Triana factory of Charles Pickman at La Cartuja, Sevilla (see p.244), and was made in the early 1900s. Continuing along c/Luna brings you to El Puerto's **Plaza Mayor** (Plaza de España), fronted by the **Iglesia Mayor Prioral** (daily 10am–noon & 7–8.30pm). A thirteenth-century Gothic edifice, it has suffered much rebuilding and the shell is now largely Baroque, but don't miss its superb Plateresque south entrance. Inside, a richly gilded *retablo* in the *Capilla de la Virgen de los Milagros* holds **la Patrona**, a thirteenth-century image of the Virgin formerly housed in the castle of San Marcos and to which the town is devoted. The church's seventeenth-century images of Christ and San Juan are attributed to the *sevillano* sculptor Pedro Roldán. Note also some fine choir stalls richly carved in walnut and cedar.

A few blocks west lies the **Plaza de Toros** (Tues–Sun 11am–1.30pm & 6–7.30pm; free), one of the largest in Spain (second only to Madrid and Sevilla) and most celebrated by aficionados. Opened in 1880 with a capacity of 15,000, the bullring has hosted all the great names. A mosaic inside the entrance records the words of the legendary *sevillano* bullfighter Joselito, who fought here: "He who has not seen bulls in El Puerto does not know what bullfighting is."

THE PALACIOS AND OTHER SIGHTS

Scattered all over town are the **palacios** left behind by the great eighteenth-century families of El Puerto and decorated with their escutcheons. One block downstream of the ferry dock is the **Palacio Medinaceli**, on c/Amburu de Mora, formerly occupied by the powerful ducal family whose gardens once stretched to the river. Others worth seeing are the enormous eighteenth-century **Palacio Purullena**, c/F. Rubio 92, northwest of the bullring, a rare example of Spanish Rococo now in a tragic state of disrepair; **Casa de Vizarrón**, Plaza de Polvorista (slightly south of Palacio Medinaceli), with an elegant escutcheoned doorway; and **Palacio de Aranibar**, fronting the Castillo de San Marcos and now the law court. At c/Palacios 57, just east of Plaza España, a plaque marks the house where Washington Irving lived in 1828 whilst writing *The Conquest of Granada*.

The **Museo Municipal**, c/Pagador 1, just off the Plaza Mayor (Mon–Sat 10am–2pm; free), is housed in another mansion, the Casa de la Marquesa de Candia, and contains archeological finds from the surrounding area and a selection of fairly awful art works. Among other sights worth a look if you've got the time are the Baroque **Covento de Concepcionistas** (c/Federico Rubio, two blocks west of the Castillo de San Marcos) with a spectacular gilded *retablo*; the beautiful patio and chapel of the early eighteenth-century **Hospital de San Juan de Dios** (opposite the Palacio Medinaceli above); and the Jesuit college of **San Luís Gonzaga** (two blocks west of the bullring) which conserves the earlier sixteenth-century church of San Francisco where another soaring gilded *retablo* holds two magnificent early seventeenth-century sculptures of San Francisco and San Ignacio by Juan de Mesa.

Finally, another monument tucked away upstream and behind the train station is the poignant **Monasterio de la Victoria** (easily reached via a gate on the train station forecourt), a beautiful sixteenth-century monastery founded by the Medinaceli family for the Mínimos order of friars, which fell into a ruinous state after having been sacked by the French during the Napoleonic wars. Only the exterior – with an exquisite ogival portal – may currently be seen, but when restoration is completed, an equally fine Gothic church and cloister will be on view too.

THE BEACHES

The closest **beaches**, Playa La Puntilla and Playa Valdelgrana, are some distance from the town (15min walk or local buses from the ferry dock: #2 for La Puntilla or #35 for Valdelgrana) and are pleasant places to while away an afternoon with lots of lively *marisquerías* and beach bars. Another way to reach the beaches is to rent a **scooter**, which also offers the chance to escape the crowds; Autos Santo Domingo (c/Micaela Aramburu 8, near the ferry dock; ☎956 87 50 01) rent them by the day or week.

Eating and drinking

The best areas in town for **places to eat** are the Ribera del Marisco, a street upstream from the ferry dock lined with a variety of seafood restaurants and bars serving *tapas* and *raciones,* and the nearby Plaza de la Herrería. You should also try the beaches of La Puntilla and Valdelgrana for a cluster of friendly bars.

BARS AND RESTAURANTS

Las Capuchinas, *Monasterio de San Miguel*, c/Larga 27. The *Monasterio* hotel's swish cafetería, serving up a good-value *menú*.

El Faro de El Puerto, half a kilometre out, along the Rota road (take a taxi). Outstanding seafood and meat dishes produced under the direction of top chef Fernando Córdoba in this stylish twin establishment of the restaurant of the same name in Cádiz. They also have their own *tapas* bar, a pleasant garden terrace and a *menú de degustación* for about 4500ptas.

Bodega Jerezana, Avda. de la Paz, Valdelgrana seafront. Sea-salty *tapas* bar and restaurant with a wide range of well-prepared seafood dishes.

THE SHERRY BODEGAS OF EL PUERTO DE SANTA MARÍA

The long, whitewashed warehouses flanking the streets and the banks of the Río Guadalete belong to the big **sherry bodegas**: Luís Caballero, Terry, Osborne and Duff Gordon, the last three founded in the eighteenth and nineteenth centuries by Irish and English families. Osborne (pronounced "Osbornay" in Spanish) and Duff Gordon are now co-owned after a takeover by Osborne, although separate production is maintained. Osborne is also the largest producer of Spanish brandy, and its black-bull logo – long used as a billboard perched on hills throughout Spain – has become a familiar part of the country's landscape.

In sherry, El Puerto is noted for a lighter, more aromatic *fino* with more *flor* aroma imparted due to its humid geographical location, close to the sea (see box on p.203 for details of sherry styles). It's easy enough to visit the *bodegas*; Osborne and Duff Gordon, c/Fernán Caballero 3 (Mon–Fri; visits at 10.30am in English, 11am & noon in Spanish; ☎956 85 52 11; 300ptas); Fernando de Terry, c/Santísima Trinidad 2 (Mon–Fri; visits at 9.30am, 11am & 12.30pm; ☎956 85 77 00; 350ptas) with a museum and situated in a beautiful, converted, seventeenth-century convent along with the smaller Gutierrez Colosia (Sat 1.30pm; 350ptas). All welcome visitors for tours and tastings, although you'll need to **call in advance** to the first two *bodegas* to book a place (the afternoon before is usually enough notice). As English is very much the second language of the sherry world, you should have no problems in being understood.

Nuevo Portuense, c/Luna 31. Good and busy central bar with a *menú* for 1200ptas.

Pasta Gansa, c/Puerto Escondido 1, near the Ribera del Marisco. This is a stylish Italian restaurant serving pizzas and risottos in an attractive patio.

Romerijo, Ribera del Marisco. This enormous and justifiably popular seafood bar dominates the strip. You can get a take-away of *mariscos* in a *cartucho* (paper funnel) from their shop and eat it at outdoor tables where buckets are provided for debris and waiters serve beer; the *cóctel de mariscos* (seafood cocktail) or any of the six types of *langostinos* are delicious. The same firm's *freiduría* restaurant over the road is equally excellent, and a generous *frito variado* (assorted fried fish) easily serves two.

Tortillería La Misma, c/Palacios 4, one block south of the ferry dock. Loads of different *tortillas* to try at this cheap and cheerful diner.

TAPAS BARS

El Brillante, c/Dr Múñoz Seca 2 (aka c/Vicario). Slightly north of the Plaza de España, this venerable old *tapas* bar faces the market and is packed to the gunwales on market day when crowds flock in to feast themselves on the house special, *caracoles* (sea snails). *Caballa* (mackerel) is also delicious.

Las Cinco Farolas, c/Jesus Nazareno s/n, east of the Plaza de Toros and close to the Osborne Bodega. Another excellent *tapas* haunt in the *bodega* zone.

La Galera, Plaza de las Galeras, close to the *vapor* quay. Good bar for beer and seafood *tapas* and *raciones* if you're just off, or waiting for, the boat.

Bar Jamón, c/Capillera 5, a couple of blocks west of Plaza de España. Atmospheric bar specializing in *tapas* to accompany its specially made house bread: *jamón* (ham) and *anchoas* (anchovies) are favourites here. They also do excellent *croquetas* (fish-filled croquettes).

Sol y Sombra, Plaza de Ahuja, facing the bullring. Taking its name from the nearby bullring's seating arrangements, this is often a lively venue – especially on fight days – and prepares good and cheap *tapas*. House specials include *fideos con almejas* (vermicelli with clams) and *arroz marinero* (paella).

Bar Tapia, c/Ribera del Río 30. Good *tapas* and *raciones* bar with restaurant attached.

Nightlife

Nightlife in El Puerto centres around the bars in the areas mentioned above. The town's most bizarre night spot is *El Convento*, Avda. Bajamar 30 (fronting the river 500m downstream of the ferry dock), a ruined monastery transformed into a complex of bars and discos, with two patio dance floors in the former cloisters and incense wafting throughout(free entry). Disco bars worth checking out are *La Kama* and *El Rey de Copas*, just two of a cluster flanking c/Aramburu de Mora, downriver from the ferry dock. *Karaoke El Estanque*, Ribera del Río s/n (100m upstream from the Ribera del Marisco) is where locals bellow the night away, and the nearby *La Resaca* often puts on live flamenco after 10.30pm. *Taberna Gambribus* at c/La Palma 22 near the Castillo San Marcos, stages occasional **live bands** and sometimes jazz.

Rota

Much of the 15km between El Puerto and the town of **ROTA** is taken up by a massive tract of territory occupied by one of the three major **US military bases** in Spain. Installed in the 1950s as part of a deal in which Franco exchanged strips of Spanish sovereign territory for economic aid and international "respectability", the base is surrounded by a seemingly endless barbed-wire fence and bristles with the technological gadgetry of war. Behind the wire it's possible to glimpse farms and whole villages linked by their own bus service along a road system where signs are in English. Huge Ford trucks trundle to and from Rota's harbour from where the base is serviced and supplied by the US Sixth Fleet. Long-standing local resentment at this "occupation" occasionally surfaces. Not long ago Bronze Age cave dwellings were found on the territory of the base, but Spanish archeologists were refused permission to carry out investigations. The caves have since been looted by treasure-hunters.

That said, however, the US military population tends to keep to itself, and Rota exudes an affable character very much its own. In season the resort fairly bounces with life, its excellent EU blue-flagged **beach**, the Playa de la Costilla, being the main attraction for the crowds of *gaditanos* and *sevillanos* who flock here in August.

The town's sights can be seen in under an hour. Highlights include a thirteenth-century castle close to the Turismo – the frequently remodelled and much-restored **Castillo Luna** (Sat & Sun 10.30am–1.30pm & 5–8.30pm; free). Also worth a look is the sixteenth-century Gothic church, **Nuestra Señora de la Expectación** (known locally as Nuestra Señora de la O; daily 9am–1pm and service times), which hides, behind a box-like exterior, a fine single-naved church with elegant vaulting. If churches are your thing you may also want to take in the **Capilla de San Juan Bautista** (open service times only), Plaza Andalucía near the Turismo, with a spectacular Baroque altar mayor by Diego Roldán, one of the finest in the province.

Practicalities

Arriving **by car** you'll need to thread your way through a fiendishly convoluted one-way system to get to the helpful **Turismo**, Plaza de España (Mon–Fri 10am–1.30pm & 6–9pm, Sat & Sun 10am–2pm & 6–9pm; ☎956 82 91 05), in the old quarter on the town's southern flank. The Turismo has useful **maps** and can help you find a room during the summer scramble. Rota's **bus station** lies off Plaza del Triunfo, which is a ten-minute walk or an easy bus ride to the centre along c/Calvario.

Decent **places to stay** include *Hostal La Española*, c/García Sánchez 9 (☎956 81 00 98; ④), in a restored ancient mansion, and the simple but excellent *Hostal Macavi*, c/Écija 11, off the main Avda. Sevilla, and a mere fifty metres from the beach (☎956 81 33 36; ③). The town's stylish new flagship hotel, *Duque de Najera*, c/Gravina 2 (☎956 84 60 20, fax 956 81 24 72; ⑧) occupies a renovated mansion near the harbour. The nearest **campsite**, *Camping Punta Candor* (☎956 81 33 03), lies just outside the town on the same road and has a good restaurant.

The modern town fans out from the central **Plaza Jesús Nazareno** fronting the beach; around here you'll find most of the nightlife as well as **bars** and **restaurants**. Look out for the town's very own speciality, the outstandingly tasty *urta a la roteña* (sea bream in a caramelized onion and tomato sauce). Rota's *tapas* bars tend to be better value than the restaurants, many of which are overpriced and bland. Decent restaurants include *Mesón Alcantino*, Avda. Sevilla 39 (near *Hostal Macavi*) for fish and seafood and *Restaurante La Fería*, c/Higuerta 47 not far from the Turismo, which despite calling itself a pizzeria also knows a thing or two about cooking fish – it has won the *Fiesta de la Urta* competition (see below) five times over the last decade. For *tapas* head down the atmospheric c/La Mina, slightly north of the Turismo where a number of bars line the pedestrianised street, including the excellent *Emilio* and *El Fresquito*. **Nightlife** centres around the zone to the south and east of Plaza de Jesús Nazareno. Rota's big **festival** is the mid-August *Fiesta de la Urta*, when all the restaurants in town compete to win the prize for the best *urta*-based dish.

Chipiona

From Rota the road north winds inland behind a coast lined with more golden sand beaches to **CHIPIONA**, 18km away, on a point at the edge of the estuary of the Guadalquivir.

When you arrive, Chipiona presents itself as a modest, straightforward seaside resort crammed with family *pensiones*. In high summer, the town's many charms are all but submerged beneath an annual onslaught of mainly Spanish visitors. Older tourists come here for the spa waters, channelled into a fountain at the fourteenth-century church of **Nuestra Señora de Regla**, which incorporates a delightful Gothic cloister (daily 7–9pm) adorned with seventeenth-century Triana *azulejos*; often they don't open it so try and find a priest or church warden to do this for you. The town has a charming **old quarter** on its northern flank, cut through by sinuous, white-walled alleyways. The major thoroughfare here is the pedestrianized c/Isaac Peral, lined with shops, bars and some elegant buildings and hotels. But for most it's the twelve kilometres of beaches that are the lure; south of the town and lighthouse is the long **Playa de Regla**, best avoided in August but where for much of the year it's possible to leave the crowds behind. Northeast, towards Sanlúcar, are sand bars and rocks with fine views towards the Marismas de Doñana and the Guadalquivir estuary.

Practicalities

Maps, information and help with accommodation plus a list of *tapas* bars can be picked up from the *Casa de Cultura*, Plaza de Andalucía 2 (Mon–Fri 10am–1.30pm & 7–9pm; ☎956 37 28 28), in the old quarter at the northern end of town. **Buses** to and from Sevilla, Cádiz and Sanlúcar operate out of the *Amarillos* bus station on Avda. Nuestra Señora de Regla.

Accommodation can be expensive, and in August without an advance reservation you'll struggle to find anything. Most of the *hostales* are within a few minutes' walk of the beach; good options include *Hostal San Miguel*, Avda. de la Regla 79 (☎956 37 29 76; ④), in a charming 1930s mansion close to the church of Nuestra Señora de Regla. The friendly *Hostal Andalucía*, c/Larga 14 (☎956 37 07 05; ④), and *Hostal Gran Capitán*, c/Fray Baldomero González 3 (☎956 37 09 29; ④), both have ensuite rooms in the old quarter, and the simple and cheaper *Hostal Belén*, Avda. del Ejército 5 (☎956 37 26 80; ③) just to the south of them, is also worth a try. For a seafront possibility, head for the good value *La Española*, c/Isaac Peral 4 (☎956 37 37 71, fax 956 37 21 44; ⑤), a superbly renovated old hotel whose front door is a mere 20m from the Atlantic breakers. Best of the more upmarket places is *Hotel Al Sur de Chipiona*, facing the church of Nuestra Señora de Regla (☎956 37 03 00, fax 956 37 08 59; ⑦), which comprises an older, elegant hotel with a new wing – complete with pool – tacked on. During August you may have to fall back on rooms in *casas particulares* (which also go fast) offered by the troop of women who meet new arrivals at the bus station. The **campsite and youth hostal** *Pinar de Chipiona* (☎956 37 14 80), lies 3km out of town towards Rota; it rents out air-conditioned bungalows with bath (④ for up to four persons) and has a cheap self-service restaurant and pool. Get the Rota-bound bus to drop you off.

Chipiona has a gratifying range of **restaurants**, all excelling in seafood. For a good-value *menú*, try *La Pañoleta* (the restaurant of the *Hotel La Española*, near the beach) which is excellent. Equally tasty seafood is on offer at *Restaurante Peña*, Avda. Sevilla 43, near the lighthouse, a beautiful whitewashed building with a shaded terrace. If you want a break from fish, head for *Bar Playa*, c/Fray Baldomero González 4 off the north end of c/Isaac Peral, a fine little atmospheric restaurant with a decent terrace. Not far away from here *Bar-Restaurante Repostaero*, c/Dr Tolosa Latour 7, is a boisterous seafood *chiringuito* with a great atmosphere late at night when impromptu **flamenco** sometimes gets going. In the somewhat lifeless Puerto Deportivo, *Bar-Restaurante Paco* is an outstanding seafood restaurant and *tapas* bar with a waterfront terrace. For **tapas** and **drinking bars** – some with music – take a stroll along the pedestrianised c/Isaac Peral, where among many others *Bar Peña Betica* at the junction with c/Larga is good value. **Flamenco** often takes place at *Al Compa*, Avenida de Jerez s/n close to the sea, a cheap restaurant and bar with a good terrace.

Sanlúcar de Barrameda

Like El Puerto de Santa María, **SANLÚCAR DE BARRAMEDA**, 8km beyond Chipiona, is a major sherry town. A substantial place with an attractive old quarter set at the mouth of the Guadalquivir, it is the main depot for **manzanilla** wine (see box below) – a pale dry *fino* variety with a salty tang – highly regarded by connoisseurs and much in evidence in the bars round here. Sanlúcar is also one of the best places in Andalucía for **seafood**, for which *manzanilla* is the perfect accompaniment.

Although there was a small settlement here in Roman times and the Moors built a fort to guard the vital Guadalquivir estuary from sea raiders, it was after the recapture of the town in 1264 by Alfonso X that Sanlúcar grew to become one of sixteenth-century Spain's leading ports. **Columbus** sailed from here on his third voyage to the Americas and it was also from here in 1519 that Magellan set out to circumnavigate the globe. Decline in the eighteenth century, however, was exacerbated by the War of Independence and the town revived only in the mid-nineteenth century when the Duke of Montpensier built a summer palace here. Since then Sanlúcar has grown into the popular resort it is today. During the last week of May Sanlúcar stages a riotous **fiesta**, the *Feria de la Manzanilla*, to celebrate its great wine, which is copiously consumed throughout. In early and late August, the beach is the setting for some exciting **horse races**, a tradition dating from 1845, accompanied by riotous partying which goes on until dawn.

Arrival, information and orientation

Sanlúcar's two **bus stations** are close to each other in the Barrio Bajo; *Los Amarillos*, serving Chipiona, Cádiz and Sevilla, is on Plaza de la Salle (Plaza el Pradillo on some maps), while *Linesur*, leaving from c/Hermano Fermín near the Turismo, has buses from and to Jerez.

Sanlúcar is split into three distinct quarters, the older and formerly walled **Barrio Alto** on the hill, the **Barrio Bajo** below and the town's former port – the **Bajo de**

SANLUCAR'S MANZANILLA BODEGAS

The delicate taste of Sanlúcar's distinctive **manzanilla** is created by the seaside environment where the wine is matured, and by not being fortified with alcohol (as happens in Jerez and El Puerto). The humid microclimate necessary for the growth of the dense *flor* inside the wine butts is added to by the moist *poniente* wind which blows across the Coto de Doñana, imparting the characteristic saltiness to this driest of all sherries. Sanlúcar is less aggressive than Jerez in its public relations (despite *manzanilla* recently overtaking *fino* sales on the peninsula for the first time), and only a few of Sanlúcar's *bodegas* are open for **visits and tastings**. The town's major producer, Antonio Barbadillo, c/Sevilla 25, near the castle (Wed & Thurs 12.30pm; 300ptas; ☎956 36 08 94), which produces seventy percent of all *manzanilla*, also makes *manzanilla pasada*, an exceptional fifteen-year-old wine (as against the normal four for standard *fino*), besides one of Andalucía's best white table wines (Castillo de San Diego) from the same Palomino grape. The only other *bodegas* who welcome visitors are Pedro Romero c/Trasbolsa 84, east of the Plaza del Cabildo (Fri & Sat 12.30pm; 300ptas), and the tiny Bodega de Velasco, c/Truco s/n opposite the *Museo del Mar Las Caracolas* (Mon–Fri 8am–3pm), which is a friendly and intimate family-run place where they'll serve you their La Cigarrera brand *manzanilla* to try (and buy) straight from the butt. A tiny *despacho de vinos* (wineseller) Cruz de Los Caídos, on c/Ancha hard by the church of Santo Domingo, is piled with butts and will also allow you to try – and buy – the great wines of the region direct from the wood.

Guía – 1km away on the river. Many of the monuments are in the higher town, and as you ascend the long, tree-lined Alameda (Calzada del Ejército) leading from the river to the Plaza del Cabildo, the effective centre of the town, there's a pleasant hint of sherry in the air. Just before the plaza on the right you'll pass the **Turismo**, Calzada del Ejército s/n (Mon–Fri 9am–2pm & 6–9pm, Sat 10am–2pm, Sun 10am–1pm; ☎956 36 61 10), who can provide you with a detailed street map. They also offer a guided walking **tour of the town** (Wed 10.30am, in English and Spanish; 500ptas) which includes a *bodega* visit.

Accommodation

There's a shortage of budget **accommodation** in Sanlúcar, and in high season you'll be pushed to find anything at all. The Turismo can supply more addresses if you need them, and for longer stays they have information on apartments for rent (minimum three nights).

Pensión Blanca Paloma, Plaza de San Roque (☎956 36 36 44). Good-value *pensión* with simple rooms in a central position on this small plaza. ③.

Pensión Bohemia, c/Don Claudio 1 (☎956 36 95 99). Comfortable ensuite rooms in a quiet street near the church of Santo Domingo. ④.

Hotel Los Helechos, Plaza Madre de Dios 9 (☎956 36 13 49, fax 956 36 71 41). Smart, central hotel in converted former *bodega* with rooms around two charming patios and lots of traditional features. ⑤.

Posada de Palacio c/Caballeros 11 (☎956 36 48 40, fax 956 36 50 60). This elegant converted eighteenth-century monastery in the Barrio Alto has a delightful patio, rooms with character, and restaurant. Personal and friendly service from proprietors Antonio and Renata. ⑤.

Fonda Román, c/Barrameda 17 (☎956 36 60 01). The charming Señora Román takes in guests during high season and the rooms – overlooking a stunning, plant-filled patio which has attracted TV cameras – are spotless. July & Aug only. ②.

Hotel Tartaneros, c/Tartaneros 8 (☎956 36 20 44, fax 956 36 00 45). Pleasant, old-fashioned hotel with a dubious collection of negro dolls and effigies dotted around the staid interior. ⑥.

The Town

The **Plaza del Cabildo**, a charming, palm-fringed square with plenty of bars is as good a place as any to start your explorations. Directly north of the square, Plaza de San Roque adjoins the morning **market**, one of the town's great sights when it's in full swing. Just off this square, the interior of the fifteenth-century **Iglesia de la Trinidad** (Mon–Sat 10am–1.30pm) has a fine Mudéjar ceiling. Following c/Bretones uphill from the plaza, passing the seventeenth-century Convento de la Merced, will eventually lead you to the neo-Mudéjar **Palacio de Orleáns y Borbón** (guided visits daily except Wed 10am–2pm; 100ptas) a flamboyantly decorated nineteenth-century palace of the dukes of Montpensier, now occupied by the *Ayuntamiento* with the public library in the gardens. Taking a left at the top of this hill will bring you to – on the right – **Plaza de la Paz**, another delightful small square, and, almost opposite, the church of **Nuestra Señora de la O** (Mon–Fri 7.30–9pm, Sun 9–9.45am, 11.30am–1.15pm & 7.30–8.30pm), Sanlúcar's oldest church founded in the thirteenth century but much altered since and recently restored. The exterior has a fine Gothic-Mudéjar **portal** depicting lions bearing coats of arms and, inside, there is an impressive *artesonado* ceiling.

The church is connected to the *palacio* of the **Duques de Medina Sidonia** (guided tours on Sun & Mon, call ahead to book a place; ☎956 36 01 61; closed Aug), whose sixteenth- to eighteenth-century interior, which also houses the family's important historical archive, offers wonderful views over the Coto de Doñana. The Duchess of Medina Sidonia – a descendant of Guzman El Bueno of Tarifa – still lives here and is one of Sanlúcar's most controversial characters. Known as *la duquesa roja* ("the Red

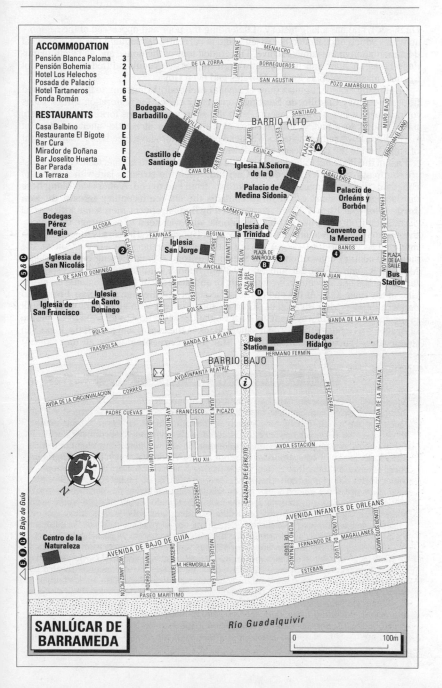

ACCOMMODATION

Pensión Blanca Paloma	3
Pensión Bohemia	2
Hotel Los Helechos	4
Posada de Palacio	1
Hotel Tartaneros	6
Fonda Román	5

RESTAURANTS

Casa Balbino	D
Restaurante El Bigote	E
Bar Cura	B
Mirador de Doñana	F
Bar Joselito Huerta	G
Bar Parada	A
La Terraza	C

SANLÚCAR DE BARRAMEDA

Río Guadalquivir

0   100m

Duchess"), she has a long history of defending the poor and oppressed of the region – activities which once landed her in jail – and is currently cataloguing the mass of ducal documentation in the family archive. The guided tour of the house and its beautiful gardens takes an hour and proceeds through impressive rooms stuffed with works of Spanish masters such as Roelas, Morales and even Goya.

Continuing along c/Eguilaz (now c/Sevilla) eventually brings you to the semi-ruined fifteenth-century **Castillo de Santiago**, currently closed for restoration works. Plans to transform it into a wine museum, with the sherry companies forking out the cash, have ground to a halt. A little further along the same street the sherry *bodega* of Barbadillo allows public visits on Wednesdays and Thursdays (see box p.195). A flight of steps beside the castle leads back down to the Barrio Bajo.

East of the Plaza del Cabildo, c/Ancha is the site of a colourful spectacle each August 15, the **fiesta of the Virgen de la Caridad**, when the street is laid with a carpet of colourful "flowers" – actually tinted sawdust – from end to end. A short way along here on the right, the short c/San Jorge contains the sixteenth-century **Iglesia de San Jorge** (Mon–Sat 10am–1.30pm), constructed by English sherry merchants with special permission from the Duke of Medina Sidonia, who was keen to encourage their lucrative trade. Inside, a magnificent *retablo* by Juan González de Herrera is topped off by a mounted San Jorge (St George) slaying the dragon. Further east along c/Ancha, the sixteenth-century convent church of **Santo Domingo** (30min viewing before services Mon–Fri 9.30am & 8pm, Sat 8pm, Sun 10.30am, noon & 8pm) is worth a look, especially for the tombs of a seventeenth-century duke and duchess of Medina Sidonia on either side of the main altar. At the end of the same street lies the church of **San Francisco** (service times or ring ☎956 36 01 26 for an appointment) with an elegant facade, built in the sixteenth century by Henry VIII of England – while he was married to Catherine of Aragón – as a hospital for British sailors. Back in the centre and just off the Plaza San Roque at c/Truco 4, the **Museo del Mar Las Caracolas** (daily all day; 50ptas)

THE COTO DOÑANA NATIONAL PARK

Access to the vast, marshy expanse of the **Coto Doñana National Park** (see p.291), on the opposite shore from Sanlúcar, is strictly controlled to protect Europe's largest wildlife sanctuary and a vital wetland for a variety of migrating birds. However, a **boat cruise** aboard the *Real Fernando* has been inaugurated to allow visitors to see the park; while it doesn't allow you to get into serious exploration, it is a wonderful introduction to this remarkable area and lasts approximately four hours. The boat – which has a *cafetería* on board – leaves from the Bajo de Guía daily (spring & summer 9.30am & 5pm; autumn & winter 10am; 2200ptas; advance booking essential; ☎956 36 38 13, fax 956 36 21 96). The trips allow two short guided walks led by wildlife experts inside the park where you'll visit a village of *chozas* (traditional Doñana huts) and should see *jabalí* (wild boars), wild horses, flamingos and a profusion of birdlife including buzzards, herons, kites, cranes, eagles as well as stunning wild flowers, depending on your luck and season. In summer it's best to book as early as you can, since the trips are limited to 94 passengers; binoculars (essential) can be hired on board for 200ptas. Collect your tickets from the Fábrica de Hielo, Bajo de Guía s/n (daily 9am–8pm) virtually opposite the *Real Fernando*'s jetty. This extravagant exhibition centre in Sanlúcar's old ice factory was recently created by the National Park and contains stunningly unimaginative displays of the park's flora and fauna. The Centro Interpretación de la Naturaleza, almost next door, Avda. Bajo de Guía s/n (Mon–Fri 9am–3pm) is the Junta de Andalucía's effort which has a slightly more interesting exhibition devoted to Doñana and its wildlife. Tourafrica, c/San Juan 20 (☎956 36 25 40), also do **Land Rover-based trips** into the park (May–Sept Tues & Thurs; pre-booking essential; 4700ptas) starting from the Bajo de Guía at 8.30am and 4.30pm and covering about 70km in four hours with an expert guide.

exhibits a bizarre lifetime collection of objects retrieved from the sea by eccentric proprietor Garrido García, who resembles a latterday Long John Silver and conducts tours around his house/museum with a feral pigeon perched on one shoulder.

Late afternoon is a good time to wander along to the small port of **BONANZA**, 4km upstream, the site of a raucous **fish auction** when the fishing fleet returns at around 5pm (Mon–Fri). This is also the very spot from where Columbus and Magellan set sail on their epic voyages. Fishermans' tales are exchanged at the earthy *Bar Morales* at the harbour entrance or in the more salubrious *Bar de la Campana*, slightly back along the road to Sanlúcar, which serves decent *tapas* and has a terrace; there's an excellent restaurant here too, *La Terraza* (see "Eating and drinking", below).

A good kilometre walk from the centre, Sanlúcar's shell-encrusted **river beach** – unfortunately marred by a lengthy and rather ugly concrete esplanade – is nevertheless a nice place to while away some time, and is usually quite deserted. The beach is also the setting for some exciting **horse races** in summer, when jockeys, clad in racing silks, pound thoroughbreds across the firm sand in the wake of the ebb tide. Races are usually held at the beginning and end of August; the Turismo can supply the precise dates.

In summer, private motor boats from the Bajo de Guía, near the *Real Fernando* jetty, will ferry you to the opposite bank for about 1000ptas (make sure to arrange a pick-up time with the boatman if you don't want to be stranded), where the **Coto de Doñana's beaches**, unfortunately not always the cleanest due to pollution from the Guadalquivir estuary currents, provide a change of scene and some bird-spotting possibilities. There are absolutely no facilities, so be sure to take along liquid refreshment and food. The Turismo have details of a number of companies who explore this area by guided tours on **horseback** (charging around 2000ptas per hour).

Eating and drinking

Sanlúcar is known the length of Andalucía for the quality of its **seafood**, and the place to head for is the Bajo de Guía, the old fishing district upstream from where the Alameda meets the river. Numerous **bars** and **restaurants** lining the waterfront have terrace views towards the Coto de Doñana and serve excellent seafood which demands to be washed down with your favourite brand of *manzanilla*, tasting sensational here in its own backyard. In the Barrio Bajo, the Plaza del Cabildo has a number of good tapas and breakfast bars, and higher still, Plaza de la Paz is a tranquil little square with various bars serving *tapas*. *El Rengue*, Avda. V Centenario s/n (near the Amarillos bus station) is a late night *rociero* bar (see also p.295) with a great atmosphere that often stages impromptu **flamenco**.

Casa Balbino, Plaza del Cabildo 11. Behind an unassuming facade lies one of the best *tapas* bars in Andalucía. Long established, its walls are hung with faded photos and the obligatory bulls' heads, and the smoothly efficient bar staff will guide you through a daunting *tapas* menu. The *manzanillas* are outstanding and everything served is straight from the sea. Their *tortillita de camarones* (shrimp in batter) is justly famous, while *ortiguillas* (sea anemones) and *patatas rellenas* (stuffed potatoes with tuna) are other house specials.

Bar-Restaurante El Bigote, Bajo de Guía. Celebrated establishment and one of the "big two" on the waterfront. You can eat great *tapas* in the lively bar next door or more formally in the restaurant, where the house *arroz de marisco* (seafood paella) and, in season, *urta* are outstanding. Don't miss the succulent *langostinos* (prawns).

Bar El Cura, c/Amargura 2 off Plaza del Cabildo. Relatively cheap and cheerful *platos combinados* at this recently renovated bar/restaurant. They also do decent *tapas*.

Mirador de Doñana, Bajo de Guía s/n. Outstanding restaurant, equal to *El Bigote*, with a terrace overlooking the river. Try their *mi barca Doñana*, white fish in a tomato sauce, or *sopa de Galeras*, a special *marisco* soup of which they're deservedly proud. When not busy, the waiters in the *tapas* bar will be happy to give you a master class in the thirty-plus brands of *manzanilla* on offer.

Bar Parada "El Gallego", Plaza de la Paz 6. Galician bar on this pleasant square in the Barrio Alto which serves excellent *tapas* at economical prices. *Bacalao con tomate* (cod) and *pulpo* (octopus) are good.

Bar Joselito Huerta, Bajo de Guía s/n, at the upstream end of the strip. Friendly seafood restaurant with a river terrace that is popular with locals in the know. *Almejas* (clams), *cazón con tomate* (shark) and *acedias* (baby sole) are things to try. They also serve good *tapas*.

La Terraza, Edificio Cofradía de Pescadores in Bonanza, 4km upstream. On the main road near the port in Bonanza (but easy to miss), a wonderful seafood restaurant and *tapas* bar, with views from its glassed-in terrace to the Coto de Doñana.

Jerez de la Frontera

Encircled by vines planted in the chalky, *albariza* soil, **JEREZ DE LA FRONTERA**, 22km inland from Sanlúcar, and 35km from Cádiz, is the home and heartland of **sherry** (itself an English corruption of the town's Moorish name, *Xerez*) and also, less known but equally important, of Spanish brandy. Once you've penetrated some architecturally bleak suburbs, the town centre possesses a charming *casco antiguo* and a number of elegant, palm-fringed squares, as well as a handful of notable Renaissance and Baroque churches and palaces.

The **Barrio de Santiago**, a fascinating and authentic white-walled *gitano* quarter to the north of the cathedral, contrasts sharply with the great *bodegas* of the sherry houses located, rather surprisingly, in the heart of the town. The sherry dynasties that own these companies (or used to own them, as many have been taken over by international conglomerates) are renowned as some of the biggest snobs in Spain, and take a haughty pride in apeing the traits and customs of the English upper-middle classes, strutting around on polo horses, wearing tweeds and speaking Spanish with an affected accent. This has earned them the derisive nickname among their compatriots of *señoritos* or "toffs". Jerez's innate sobriety is thrown to the wind, however, during one of the two big **festivals** – the May Horse Fair (perhaps the most refined – or snooty depending on your viewpoint – of Andalucian *ferias*), and the celebration of the vintage towards the end of September. The town's equine passion has led to its being awarded the World Equestrian Games in 2002.

Arrival and information

The **train** and **bus stations** are more or less next door to each other, eight blocks east of the Alcázar and the town's central square, the **Plaza del Arenal**. Urban buses, painted an eye-straining lurid lilac, pass the top of the rise outside the station from where Line 10 (which also calls at the bus station) will take you to the centre. RENFE (☎956 33 48 13) has an office at c/Larga 34, near the Turismo, for buying train tickets in advance. Coming in **by car** you will meet the familiar problem of finding a place to park; to avoid being clamped or towed, use the pay car-parks signed in the centre or park further out and walk in. There is no bus service from Jerez **airport** (7km out of town on the NIV; ☎956 15 00 00) so you will need to take a taxi (about 1500ptas) to the centre. The town's pedestrianized main street, **c/Larga**, heads north from the Plaza del Arenal, and half-way along here you'll find the well-stocked **Turismo** (Mon–Fri 8am–2pm & 5–8pm, Sat 10am–2pm; ☎956 33 11 50, fax 956 33 17 31), c/Larga 39, with maps and information.

Accommodation

Most of the budget **accommodation** in Jerez is conveniently located within a few minutes' walk of the bus and train terminals. More possibilities are to be found in the

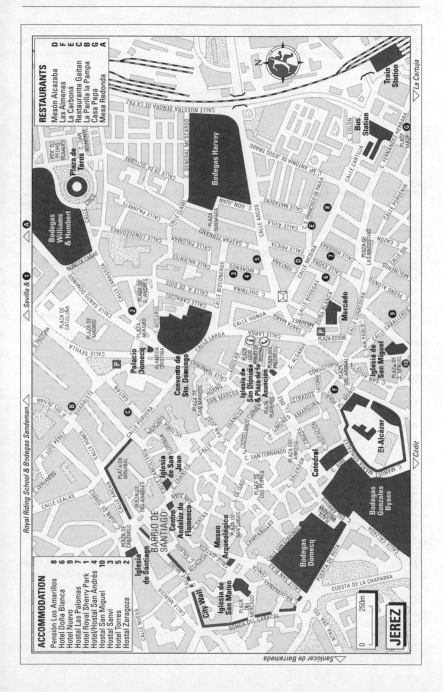

streets surrounding the church of San Miguel. Jerez's modern **Albergue Juvenil**, Avda. Carrero Blanco 30 (☎956 14 39 01; ①), has a fine pool but lies out in the suburbs; bus #9 from outside the bus station will take you there, with a stop close to the bus station on Plaza de las Angustias.

Pensión Los Amarillos, c/Medina 30 (☎956 34 22 96). Lowest prices in town for rooms without bath. To get there, turn left from the bus station and walk three blocks. ②.

Hotel Doña Blanca c/Bodegas 11 (☎956 34 87 61, fax 956 34 85 86). The most central and intimate of the upper range places with all facilities you'd expect for the price, except a pool. Garage. ⑥.

Hotel Nuevo, c/Caballeros 23 (☎956 33 16 00, fax 956 33 16 04). Attractive hotel set in a lovely old mansion. ⑤.

Hostal Las Palomas, c/Higueras 17 (☎956 34 37 73). Clean, simple and ensuite rooms in a quiet street. ②.

Hotel Royal Sherry Park, Avda. Alvaro Domecq 11 (☎956 30 30 11, fax 956 31 13 00). The nearest of the luxury hotels to the centre, this is a rather bland and modern affair despite an attractive pool and gardens. Car park. ⑧.

Hotel/Hostal San Andrés, c/Morenos 12 & 14 (☎956 34 09 83, fax 956 34 31 96). Excellent-value hotel and *hostal* side by side. Charming and friendly, there are rooms with and without bath, and a pleasant, plant-filled patio. Parking places nearby. ③–④.

Hostal San Miguel, Plaza de San Miguel 4 (☎956 34 85 62). Nicely located *hostal*, facing the church of San Miguel, and offering good-value rooms, some with bath. ④.

Hostal Sanvi, c/Morenos 10 (☎956 34 56 24). Lots of *azulejos* and some economical simple rooms with bath, near the *Hostal San Andrés*. ③.

Hotel Torres, c/Arcos 29 (☎956 32 34 00, fax 956 32 18 16). Comfortable hotel with two pretty patios. Garage. ⑤.

Hostal Zaragoza, c/Zaragoza 2 (☎956 33 44 27). Basic but clean accommodation in a family-run place with friendly proprietors. Close to the Palacio Domecq. ②.

The Town

Quite apart from the **sherry bodegas**, indisputably Jerez's biggest draw, the town has many sights which warrant a look, not least the gypsy quarter, **Barrio de Santiago**, which is a fascinating place to stroll around. Conveniently, all the major sights and most of the *bodegas* are within just a few minutes' walk of the central Plaza del Arenal.

The Alcázar

The substantial **Alcázar** (May–Sept daily 10am–8pm; Oct–April daily 10am–6pm; 250ptas) lies just to the south of the Plaza del Arenal. To reach the entrance to the complex, take a right off the southern end of the Plaza del Arenal into Plaza Monti, at the end of which you turn left into c/M. María González. The entrance lies uphill on the left. Constructed in the twelfth century by the Almohads, though much altered since, the Alcázar has been extensively excavated and restored in recent years. The **gardens** have received particular attention: the plants and arrangements have been modelled as closely as possible – using historical research – on the original. The interior contains a well-preserved **mosque** complete with *mihrab* from the original structure, now sensitively restored to its original state after having been used as a church for many centuries. There is also a **bath house** modelled, by the Almohads, on those of the earlier Romans with cold and hot plunges, as well as impressive walls and towers on the site's outer perimeter. The eighteenth-century **Palacio de Villavicencio** constructed on the west side of the Alcázar's Patio de las Armas (parade ground) houses an entertaining **camera obscura** (same hours; 500ptas extra) offering views of the major landmarks of the town as well as the sherry vineyards and the sea beyond.

The Cathedral and Plaza de la Asunción

West of Plaza del Arenal, the eighteenth-century **Cathedral of San Salvador** (daily 5.30–8pm or ring ☎956 34 84 82 for an appointment to view) was rather harshly dismissed by Richard Ford as "vile Churrigueresque" because of its mixture of Gothic and Renaissance styles. Inside, over-obvious pointing gives the building an unfinished, breeze-block aspect, while, in the sacristy, there's a fine, little-known painting by Zurbarán – *The Sleeping Girl*. The most exciting time to be here is September, when on the broad steps of the cathedral, below the free-standing bell tower – actually part of an

---

SHERRY – JEREZ'S LIQUID GOLD

It's believed that the Phoenicians brought the vine to this area early in the first millennium BC. The Romans shipped wine from here to all parts of their empire, and the Roman *Asido Caesaris* may well be the town from which Jerez derives its name, later corrupted to *Xerez* (pronounced "Sherrish") by the Moors.

British merchants were attracted here in the fourteenth century and, following the expulsions of Moors and Jews in the wake of the *reconquista*, they established firms that first traded, and later produced, Falstaff's "sack" (probably derived from the Spanish *sacar* – to draw out – referring to the *solera* system). Some of the *bodegas*, or cellars, were founded by British Catholic refugees, barred from careers at home by the sixteenth-century Supremacy Act. The names of the great sherry firms today testify to the continuing love affair of the British with this wine: Britain, along with the Netherlands, still consumes up to seventy percent of all exports.

It's a particular combination of climate, soil and grape variety that gives the distinctive style of **sherry wine**. The chalky, white *albarizo* soil of the region is the natural habitat for the Palomino sherry grape, and though the wine that results from this grape is ordinary stuff, it is what happens inside the *bodegas* that transforms it into sherry. Here the wine is transferred to oak butts with loose stoppers to let in air. Then the *flor* – a puffy layer of scum (actually yeast) – magically appears on the surface of the wine not only preventing oxidization, but feeding on it too, in the process adding a special flavour and bouquet. It is the subtle nature of the *flor*, the ingredient that cannot be duplicated by competitors, that imparts a different flavour to the sherries of Jerez, El Puerto de Santa Maria and especially Sanlúcar where it absorbs the salty breezes off the sea, producing the most delicate *fino* of all, *manzanilla*. The *bodegas* of Jerez, unlike in other wine producing areas, are situated above ground in order to maintain the humid conditions necessary for the growth of this *flor* – helped by sprinkling the sand-covered floors with water.

The final stage in the creation of sherry – but not *manzanilla* – is the fortification of the wine with alcohol (up to fifteen percent in the case of *fino* sherry) before it enters the *solera* system. Because sherry is not a vintage, or yearly, wine it is always blended with older wines through the *soleras* and *criaderas*, as many as six rows of butts placed on top of each other from which the wine is gradually transferred from the topmost to the bottommost over a period of time. This process, mixing the new, younger, wine with the greater quantity of mature, older, wine "educates" it to assume its character. The wine drawn off at the end for bottling has an even consistency year after year, conveniently with none of the problems of "good" and "bad" years. The classic sherry is the bone dry *fino*, but variations on the theme include *amontillado* (where the *flor* is allowed to "die" in the butt, imparting a nutty flavour), *oloroso* (produced as *fino* but minus the *flor*) and *cream* – pronounced "cray-am" in Andalucía – a purely British concoction where sweet grapes are blended with *oloroso*.

earlier, fifteenth-century Mudéjar castle – the wine harvest celebrations begin with the crushing of grapes.

Slightly northeast of here on the corner of c/Salvador is an elegant early eighteenth-century **mansion**, the former home of the Bertemati family and now a convent. The nun on duty in the office at the entrance will allow you inside to view the delightful patio. A little way east, along c/J. Luís Diez, lies the town's most charming square, the **Plaza de la Asunción** (known as Plaza San Dionisio to *jerezanos*), where a sixteenth-century former *Ayuntamiento* features ornamental statues of Hercules and Julius Caesar on its facade. It's flanked by the fifteenth-century Mudéjar **Iglesia de San Dionisio** with a graceful bell tower and an interior which underwent some later Baroque alterations.

Barrio de Santiago

Jerez's ancient *gitano* quarter, the Barrio de Santiago, stretches uphill from the cathedral in a maze of narrow lanes and alleys to the church of Santiago on its northern boundary. Part of the attraction of visiting the *barrio* is its many fascinating churches. The sixteenth-century Gothic **Iglesia de San Mateo** (St Matthew), with a fine *retablo* and superb vaulting over the chapels, is one of a quartet of churches dotted around the *barrio* dedicated to the four Evangelists (saints Marcos, Lucas and Juan are also worth seeking out). Facing the church, the Plaza del Mercado centres on the excellent Museo Arqueológico.

Museo Arqueológico

Located inside a renovated eighteenth-century mansion, the **Museo Arqueológico**, in Plaza del Mercado (June–Aug daily except Mon 10am–2.30pm; Sept–May Tues–Fri 10am–2pm & 4–7pm, Sat & Sun 10am–2.30pm; 250ptas), is a delight to visit. A plant-filled patio leads to the early rooms dealing with prehistory; upstairs, Room 3 has some curious **Chalcolithic** (early second millennium BC) cylinder-shaped idols with starburst eyes from Cerro de las Vacas, 20km to the north of the town. Room 4 has a wonderfully preserved **Greek** military helmet dating from the seventh-century BC, and found on the banks of the nearby Río Guadalete. This was a time when the early Greeks were colonizing sites all around the Mediterranean, and they evidently expected to meet resistance from the Iberian tribes. Also in Room 4 are finds from the ancient town of **Hasta Regia**, as Pliny, Strabo and Ptolemy referred to Jerez in Roman times. A wide range of amphorae, funerary stones and sculptures evidence Hasta's importance. Here also are **Iberian** works including an interesting sculpture of a ram's head from the third century BC, and at the end of this room, some fine Roman sculptures including a first-century AD head of Hermes.

More **Roman amphorae** – some stamped with the maker's name – appear in Room 5, once used for the shipping of *garum* (a fish sauce renowned for its quality in these parts; see p.169), olive oil and other products around the Mediterranean. Room 6 has items from the hazy **Visigothic** period and in Room 7 there's an interesting chronological display of **coins** found around Jerez; a good image of the Roman Emperor Tiberius (no. 44) is followed by dihrams of rulers Al-Hakam and Abd Ar-Rahman (no. 84) from the period of the Córdoban Emirate. Upstairs again, you'll find a **cafetería** with roof terrace, and Rooms 8 and 9, both holding the Moorish and medieval collections. Here are some fine **Moorish** ceramics, especially a tenth-century Caliphal bottle vase with Kufic script, found near Jerez. Before leaving, take a look at the striking works placed around the ground-floor patio. Among them, there's a powerful third- to first-century BC Iberian sculpture of a lion mauling a ram, found nearby, and an intriguing seventh-century Visigothic sarcophagus from La Peñuela carved with curious vegetal, animal and human symbols – a fascinating conclusion to an outstanding museum.

The Church of Santiago and the Flamenco Foundation

Just west of the museum, along c/Muro, is a bit of the original **Moorish city wall**, which you can follow north to another Gothic church, the fifteenth-century **Parroquia de Santiago**, with wonderfully florid Plateresque portals. Inside, a celebrated six-teenth-century sculpture of the *Prendimiento* – or arrest of Christ – attributed to La Roldana, is the centrepiece of Jerez's *Semana Santa* processions when it is carried through the streets. On the small square opposite the church stands a bronze bust dedicated to **Fernando Terremoto**, one of many legendary flamenco artists the *barrio* has produced. You'll come across others dotted around this quarter (there's one of Tío José de Paula behind the church), all testifying to the *barrio*'s great pride in its contribution to Andalucía's musical heritage.

Fronting the Plaza de San Juan, the **Centro Andaluz de Flamenco** (Mon–Fri 9am–2pm & Tues 5–7pm; free) is housed in an elegant eighteenth-century mansion, the Palacio de Pemartín. As one of the founding centres of flamenco song and dance, Jerez has created this library of *flamencología* as well as a sound and vision archive, to preserve the works and performances of past greats in the art; on the top floor, a dance room is used to teach students from all over the world. The staff are welcoming and anyone is free to use the video archive to see performances by flamenco masters past and present – just give them a name and they'll do the rest. There's also a good audio-visual presentation in Spanish, *El Arte Flamenco* (hourly, on the half-hour), which – if you know little about flamenco – will give you a grasp of the basics and an understanding of why it is so important to Andalucians.

The bodegas

The **tours of the sherry and brandy processes** in Jerez can be a fascinating insight into the mysteries of sherry production, although sampling – nowadays restricted to a couple of tots at the end of a tour – is hardly as much fun as when Richard Ford was here in the last century and saw visitors emerging "stupefied by drink".

There are a great many *bodegas* to choose from and, with the exception of August when all but a few firms close down, most welcome visitors throughout the year. Some houses insist that you book a place a day in advance; if your Spanish isn't too hot, don't worry, as English is very much the second language in Jerez's sherry fraternities. Below are a selection of *bodegas* offering tours throughout the whole or part of August; should you wish to visit some of the smaller establishments, get hold of a complete list from the Turismo or town centre travel agents. You should be aware in any case that visiting hours frequently change and it is worth confirming these in advance with the *bodega* or get an updated list from the Turismo.

The most central *bodega* and one of the two giants of Jerez – whose establishments are almost small towns in their own right – is **González Byass**, c/Manuel González s/n, behind the Alcázar (March–Sept Mon, Wed & Fri 9.30am–4.30pm & 5–7pm, Tues & Thurs 9.30am–7pm, Sat 10am–2pm & 5–7pm, Sun 10am–2pm; call for winter hours; 900ptas, which also includes a visit to their brandy *bodega*; book in advance ☎956 35 70 16). The González cellars are perhaps the oldest in Jerez and, though no longer used, preserve an old circular chamber, La Concha, designed by Eiffel (of Tower fame). Each *bodega* has its celebrity barrels signed by famous visitors: Martin Luther King, Orson Welles, Queen Victoria, Cole Porter and Franco (protected by a glass screen) are some of the big names in the González collection. A transparent butt (most *bodegas* have one) allows you to see the action of the magical flor on the sherry. The other major firm is **Domecq**, c/San Ildefonso 3 (Mon–Fri 9am–1pm, Sat & Sun 10am–1pm; Aug 3–16 Mon–Fri 10am–noon; 600ptas; book in advance ☎956 15 15 00); while **Sandeman**, c/Pizarro 10 (Mon–Fri

10am–2pm & 5.30–7.30pm, Sat & Sun 10am–2pm; 400ptas; book in advance ☎956 30 11 00) and **Williams and Humbert**, c/Nuño de Cañas s/n (Mon–Fri 10am–2pm; 400ptas; book in advance ☎956 32 40 51) near the bullring, have gardens and (at the latter) horse stables on their visits. **Harveys**, c/Arcos 53 (Mon–Fri 9.30am–1.30pm & 3–9pm; 350ptas & 500ptas; Sat 10am–1pm; 500ptas; ☎956 15 10 30), is another you may want to try.

Most of the *bodegas* have their own shop where you can buy the house brands. In town, the Sherry Shop, not far away at c/Divina Pastora 1 (top centre of our city map; ☎956 33 51 84) is a friendly and informative place that stocks them all and where you can sample as well. Bodega San Rafael, c/Arcos 4 near the *correos*, is a similar place.

The Convento de Santo Domingo, Palacio Domecq and Iglesia de San Miguel

The northern end of the pedestrianized c/Larga – which passes, at the junction with c/Santa María, the old Café Cena Cirullo, a fine turn-of-the-century building (now the *El Gallo Azul* bar-*heladería*) which used to be the great meeting place of Jerez's salon society – is dominated by the august frontage of the **Convento de Santo Domingo** (open service times). Although badly damaged by fire in the Civil War, it has since been diligently restored and, in common with many of the town's other religious buildings, has a curious mixture of styles: in this case Mudéjar, Romanesque and Gothic. The church's seventeenth-century *retablo mayor* is an orgy of gilded wood, with the *Virgen de la Consolación* – the patron of the city, carved in Italian marble – as its centrepiece. At the far end of this square stands the eighteenth-century **Palacio Domecq**, a grand pile erected by the sherry family. Behind an entrance flanked by barley-sugar pillars, an exquisite marble-floored **Baroque patio** is occasionally open to view. One final church worth a visit is the fifteenth-century Gothic **Iglesia de San Miguel**, just to the south of the Plaza del Arenal. An ornate classical facade added in the eighteenth-century climbs dizzily to a pretty bell tower adorned with blue and white *azulejos*, whilst the interior (Mon–Fri 8.15–9.45pm) has a fine *retablo* by Montañés.

The Museo de Relojes and the Riding School

At the northern end of town, the **Museo de Relojes**, c/Cervantes 3 (Mon–Sat 10am–2pm; 400ptas) claims to have the largest collection of fully-functioning antique clocks and watches in Europe, all chiming on the hour while nearby, north of the Alameda Cristina, at the **Real Escuela Andaluz del Arte Ecuestre** (Royal Andalucian School of Equestrian Art), Avda. Duque de Abrantes s/n, you can see teams of horses performing to music (Thurs noon; March–Oct also Tues noon; 1500–2500ptas;.☎956 31 96 35). Training, rehearsal and visits to the stables take place on other weekdays between 11am and 1pm, when admission is a more affordable 500ptas.

La Cartuja and around

The remarkable Carthusian monastery of **LA CARTUJA** (gardens daily 9.30am–6pm; free) lies 4km along the road out of town towards Medina Sidonia (see p.159) in the midst of lush countryside and surrounded in summer by a sea of sunflowers. The monastery was founded in 1477 and, following great destruction by billeted French troops in 1810, was abolished in 1835 during the Liberal backlash against the church and male religious orders.

After serving as a military barracks for almost a century, La Cartuja was restored to the Carthusians in 1949, since when the handful of monks here have dedicated themselves to restoring and maintaining this beautiful building. The **Baroque facade** you see today – added in the 1660s – is one of the most spectacular in the whole of Spain. Unfortunately, access is restricted to the building's exterior (with a magnificent main doorway), gardens and cloister; the church and other parts of the monastery and its art works may be seen by prior arrangement (Wed & Sat 5–6pm; ☎956 15 64 65), and then only by "respectably dressed" men wearing *pantalones largos* (long trousers). The monks may bow to pressure, however, and allow women to visit in the near future; check with the Turismo.

The Laguna de Medina

If you have transport, you could make another excursion from Jerez to the **LAGUNA DE MEDINA**, a small freshwater lake which – from late August on – attracts a great number of migrating birds returning from northern Europe to Africa. Under the care of ICONA (*Instituto para Conservación de la Naturaleza*), two paths skirt the lake from where, among a variety of waders, it's possible to spot white-headed duck, spoonbills and the greater flamingo in season. Fringed with reeds and tamarisk trees, the shallow lagoon is also home to numerous frogs, snakes and lizards. Because of its close proximity to the Coto Doñana across the Guadalquivir, many birds – particularly flamingos – use this as an alternative food source, especially if the Doñana's *marismas* are drier than normal towards the end of the summer.

To get there take the C440 out of Jerez for about 11km towards Medina Sidonia; the entrance to the lake area is signposted immediately opposite a cement factory, and there's a small car park.

Eating and drinking

Jerez's booming sherry trade – whose visiting clients need to be wined and dined – sees to it that the town's **restaurants** are kept busy, and a few of these are very good indeed. Befitting the capital of sherry production, however, Jerez has a range of great **bars** where *fino* – the perfect partner for *tapas* – can be sampled on its own turf. You can also do as the locals do: buy some take-away fried fish from a *freiduria* and carry it to a nearby bar. For breakfast and afternoon tea, head for *Cafetería San Francisco*, Plaza Estebe 2 near the market, or its twin *Mesón Reina de León*, c/Latorre 8, slightly north-east of Plaza Arenal. For ices and tasty *pasteles, Jerezanos* visit *El Gallo Azul* in a landmark building at the junction of c/Larga and c/Santa María.

Restaurants

Mesón Alcazaba, c/Medina 19, east of c/Larga. Low-priced *menú* fills you up and there's an attractive patio.

Las Almenas, c/Pescadería Vieja 7, opposite *Bar juanito* (see below). Popular restaurant with a budget *menú* and *tapas* served at outdoor tables in this shady alley.

La Carboná, c/San Francisco de Paula 2, slightly northwest of the bus station. Cavernous place inside an old *bodega*, specializing in charcoal-grilled fish and meat. There's tango here on Thursdays and often other entertainments, including flamenco.

Restaurante Gaitan, c/Gaitán 3, slightly northwest of the Covento de Santo Domingo. Pleasant upmarket restaurant specialising in Basque and *andaluz* dishes. Has a reasonably priced *menú de degustación*.

La Parilla la Pampa, c/Guadalete 24. Great Argentine restaurant with an excellent value five-course meal of Argentine specialities – the meat is flown in from South America. Expect 5000ptas for two.

Casa Pepa, Plaza Madre de Dios, near the train and bus stations. Good, inexpensive restaurant with a *menú del dia* for around 650ptas.

Mesa Redonda, c/Manuel de la Quintana 3, near the *Royal Sherry Park* hotel. One of the town's best places, this doesn't come cheap, but the food is truly memorable; as is their sherry trifle dessert.

Bars and marisquerías

El Arriate, c/Francos 43, in the Barrio de Santiago. Flamenco and jazz bar whose amiable proprietor is an aficionado of both traditions; live performances in winter.

El Boquerón de Plata, Plaza de Santiago, next to the church of the same name in the old *barrio*. One of the best *freidurías* in town.

Mesón Chinini, Plaza del Asunción. Fine little *tapas* bar on this beautiful square. There's a terrace for al fresco eating, and house specials include *jamón* and – typically – *riñones al jerez* (kidneys).

Marisquería Cruz Blanca, c/Consistorio 16, close to Plaza Asunción. Bustling place with outdoor seating beneath the jacarandas. You buy your seafood by weight and then get drinks from the bar; try their *cañadillas*, or *murex*, a spiky shellfish whose purple dye was used to stain the clothes of Mediterranean aristocrats two thousand years ago.

La Española, c/Larga s/n. Excellent *andaluz* bar/restaurant with a good value *menú* for about 1200ptas.

Bar Juanito, c/Pescadería Vieja 4. In a small passage off the east side of Plaza del Arenal, this is the best *tapas* bar in town, with a menu as endless as the number of excellent *finos* on offer. Specials include *alcauciles* (artichokes), *costillas* (spare ribs) and *fideos* (vermicelli) *con gambas*. Closed Sun.

Bar La Manzanilla, c/Veracruz 2, near the market. Atmospheric spit-and-sawdust haunt serving, as its name suggests, *finos* and *manzanillas*. *La Reja*, next door, is another popular place on market days. Closed Sat & Sun eves.

La Parra Vieja, c/San Miguel 9. One of Jerez's oldest *tapas* bars, in an alleyway downhill from the Iglesia de San Miguel. Specials include *croquetas de jamón* and *mollejas de cordero* (sweetbreads). The nearby *La Marea* at no. 3 in the same street is also worth a call for its excellent fried-fish *tapas*. Closed Mon.

Nightlife

Much of Jerez's **nightlife** centres around the bars and discos near the bullring and the zone around calles Divina Pastora and Cádiz (top centre of our map). One place which is very popular with young *jerezanos* is Plaza Canterbury, c/Nuño de Cañas s/n, almost opposite the Williams & Humbert *bodega*; a renovated plaza pulsing with numerous bars and discos. The local paper *El Diario de Jerez* is a good place to find out about upcoming concerts and festivals.

Cairo, c/José Cádiz Salvatierra. Stylish night-spot north of the bullring frequented by Jerez's young bloods and *chicas guapas*.

FLAMENCO IN JEREZ

Given Jerez's great **flamenco** traditions, it's worth trying to hear some of the real thing at one of the many *peñas* or clubs concentrated in the old gypsy quarter of Santiago, north of the cathedral (be watchful in this area after dark). The following are some of the best; turning up at around 10pm at weekends (although they're open at other times, too) should provide an opportunity to hear some authentic performances. Otherwise consult the Turismo, who publish a monthly listings sheet; the Centro Andaluz de Flamenco, who also have details of the special flamenco festivals held in town over the summer; or *El Diario de Jerez* who have a special flamenco listings page on Fridays.

Centro Andaluza de Flamenco, Plaza San Juan 1, Santiago (☎956 34 92 65).

Peña Los Cernicalos, c/Sancho Vizcaino 23, south of the church of San Miguel (☎956 33 84 82).

Peña Antonio Chacón, c/Salas 2, Santiago (☎956 34 74 72).

Peña La Buena Gente, Plaza San Lucas 9, Santiago (☎956 33 84 04).

Peña Tío José de Paula, c/La Merced 11, Santiago (☎956 30 22 24).

El Camino del Rocío, c/Cádiz s/n, north of Plaza Mamelón. Curious bar which commemorates the memory of the famous pilgrimage to El Rocío – every night. Rocío memorabilia covers the walls, and at midnight the lights go down, candles are lit and the singing of the *gitano Ave María* begins another night of frenzied flamenco dancing.

La Habana, c/Cádiz 181, near the riding school. Popular music bar; one of several along this street.

Bar El Laga, Plaza del Mercado, next to the Archeological Museum. Authentic flamenco bar with recitals and dancing on Monday to Saturday evenings starting around 10.30pm (admission free) with another show at 12.30am. There's also a highly entertaining *niños* flamenco on Sundays at 1pm when the *barrio*'s tiny tots (and future big names) put on a remarkably professional show.

Moët Moët, Avda. Méjico, north of the bullring. One of several lively music bars along this avenida – this particular one is popular with the over-30s.

La Taberna Flamenca, Angostillo de Santiago 3. Tucked down the west side of the Iglesia de Santiago. Slightly touristy flamenco on Tuesday and Thursday at 2pm and Friday nights at 8pm. Serves food.

travel details

TRAINS

Algeciras to: Córdoba (2 daily; 4hr 30min); Granada (3 daily; 4hr–4hr 30min); Madrid (3 daily; 12hr 30min–15hr; or 6hr 30min with AVE from Sevilla); Málaga (3 daily; 3hr 30min); Ronda (3 daily; 2hr); Sevilla (2 daily; 3hr 30min).

Cádiz to: Córdoba (6 daily; 3hr); Granada (3 daily; 4hr 30min–5hr); Jerez de la Frontera (12 daily; 40min); El Puerto de Santa María (12 daily; 25min); Sevilla (12 daily; 2hr).

Málaga to: Algeciras (3 daily; 2hr 30min, via Ronda); Antequera (2 daily; 45min); Córdoba (9 daily; 3hr 30min, via Bobadilla); El Chorro (2 daily; 30min); Fuengirola (every 30min; 14min, via Málaga airport); Granada (1 daily; 2hr 30min, via Bobadilla); Madrid (5 daily; 5–6hr); Ronda (3 daily; 1hr, via Bobadilla); Sevilla (6 daily; 2hr 15min–3hr 30min, via Bobadilla); Torremolinos (every 30min; 28min, via Málaga airport).

BUSES

Algeciras to: Cádiz (9 daily; 2hr 30min); Jerez (6 daily; 2hr 15min); La Línea (for Gibraltar: hourly; 30min); Madrid (1 daily; 10hr); Málaga (11 daily; 3hr 30min); Sevilla (5 daily; 3hr 30min); Tarifa (11 daily; 30min).

Cádiz to: Alcalá de los Gazules (2 daily; 1hr 15min); Algeciras (8 daily; 2hr 45min); Arcos de la Frontera (5 daily; 2hr); Chipiona (7 daily; 1hr 30min); Conil (13 daily; 1hr); Granada (2 daily; 8hr); Jerez de la Frontera (14 daily; 45min); Málaga (3 daily; 5hr); El Puerto de Santa María (15 daily; 40min); Sanlúcar de Barrameda (8 daily; 1hr 15min); Sevilla (12 daily; 1hr 30min); Tarifa (1 daily; 2hr); Vejer de la Frontera (10 daily; 1hr 15min); Zahara de los Atunes (2 daily; 1hr 40min).

Jerez to: Algeciras (3 daily; 2hr); Arcos de la Frontera (17 daily; 30min); Cádiz (21 daily; 1hr); Chipiona (8 daily; 40min); Córdoba (1 daily; 3hr 30min); El Puerto de Santa María (6 daily; 30min) ; Ronda (3 daily; 2hr 30min); Sanlúcar de Barrameda (16 daily; 30min); Sevilla (7 daily; 1hr 30min); Vejer de la Frontera (2 daily; 1hr 30min).

Málaga to: Algeciras (12 daily; 2hr 30min); Almería (8 daily; 4hr); Antequera (14 daily; 1hr); Cádiz (3 daily; 2hr 30min); Córdoba (5 daily; 3hr 30min); Estepona (12 daily; 1hr 30min); Granada (15 daily; 1hr 30min); Jerez (1 daily; 3hr); La Línea (4 daily; 2hr 30min); Madrid (6 daily; 6hr); Marbella (every 45min; 30min); Motril-Lanjarón (2 daily; 1hr); Nerja (11 daily; 45min); Río Gordo (4 daily; 1hr); Osuna (2 daily; 1hr 30min); Ronda (11 daily; 45min); Sevilla (9 daily; 2hr); Torremolinos (every 15min; 20min).

Ronda to: Arcos de la Frontera (5 daily; 1hr 30min); Cádiz (3 daily; 3hr 30min); Grazalema (2 daily; 20min); Jerez (5 daily; 2hr 30min); Málaga

(4 daily; 2hr); Marbella (5 daily; 1hr 30min); Olvera (2 daily; 30min); San Pedro de Alcántara (4 daily; 1hr 30min); Setenil (2 daily; 20min); Sevilla (5 daily; 2hr 45min); Ubrique (2 daily; 45min); Zahara (2 daily; 20min).

Rota to: El Puerto de Santa María (9 daily; 20min); Cádiz (9 daily; 45min); Sevilla (3 daily; 1hr 30min); Chipiona (1 daily; 15 min).

Sanlúcar de Barrameda to: Cádiz (9 daily; 1hr 15min); Chipiona (9 daily; 15min); El Puerto de Santa María (9 daily; 40min); Jerez (15 daily; 40min); Sevilla (9 daily; 2hr).

FERRIES

Algeciras to: Ceuta (18 daily; 1hr 30min; seasonal hydrofoil, 1 daily; 30min); Tangier (18 daily; 2hr; seasonal hydrofoil, 1 daily; 1hr).

Cádiz to: Las Palmas (every 2 days in season, every 5 out; 48hr); Tenerife (every 2 days in season, every 5 out; 36hr); El Puerto de Santa María (5 daily; 45min); Tangier (2 daily; 3hr).

Gibraltar to: Tangier (Mon, Wed & Fri; 2hr; 1 daily catamaran, 2 daily on Mon & Fri; 1hr 15min).

Málaga to: Melilla (daily except Sun; 7hr).

Tarifa to: Tangier (seasonal ferry boat 1 daily; 1hr 30min).

CHAPTER TWO

SEVILLA AND HUELVA

With the major exception of the irresistible city of Sevilla, the central and western regions of Andalucía are not much visited. This is a great pity, as these areas – consisting of the city's province and the neighbouring province of Huelva – are capable of springing a variety of surprises, both scenic and cultural, on those visitors prepared to wander off the beaten track to find them.

Sevilla, Andalucía's capital, has many of the region's most beautiful monuments: the **Giralda** tower, a magnificent Gothic **Cathedral** and a rambling Mudéjar **Alcázar** with fabulous ornamentation are only the highlights of a marvellous architectural feast. Add to these a stunning and revamped **Museo de Bellas Artes**, the Roman site of **Itálica** and a number of remarkable Renaissance mansions such as the **Casa de Pilatos**, and you're looking at a stay of at least two days. The most exciting parts of Sevilla, however, are its various **barrios**, each with its own strong character and traditions. These are atmospheric places to explore, warrens of delightful vernacular buildings and churches, plant-filled patios and welcoming *tapas* bars.

East of Sevilla, rewards include a clutch of smaller towns on the way to Córdoba; in particular Moorish **Carmona**, which possesses a remarkable Roman cemetery, and Baroque **Écija**, with its striking churches and mansions. Also in Sevilla's **Campiña** – the name given to this broad and fertile agricultural plain watered by the Guadalquivir – are the towns of **Osuna** and **Estepa**, both with their own Renaissance architectural gems. To the north, the wooded hills of the **Sierra Morena** offer welcome respite from the intense summer heat, with charming small towns making excellent base-camps for hikes into the surrounding oak- and pine-covered slopes and river valleys.

The **province of Huelva** stretches from Sevilla to the Portuguese border, and hardly deserves its reputation as the least-visited province of Andalucía. Although lacking the spectacular sights that you associate with Sevilla or Granada, this area boasts the huge nature reserve of the **Coto Doñana National Park**, spreading back from the Guadalquivir estuary in vast expanses of *marismas* – sand dunes, salt flats and marshes. The largest roadless area in western Europe, the park is vital to scores

---

ACCOMMODATION PRICE CODES

Throughout this guide, accommodation is graded on a scale from ① to ⑨. These show the cost per night of the cheapest double room in each establishment in high season, though remember that many of the cheap places will have more expensive rooms with en-suite facilities. See p.39 for more details. Approximate Euro rates (operative from January 2002) are given for each category:

① Under 2000ptas/
   Under €12
② 2000–3000ptas/
   €12–18
③ 3000–4500ptas/
   €18–27

④ 4500–6000ptas/
   €27–37
⑤ 6000–8000ptas/
   €37–49
⑥ 8000–10,000ptas/
   €49–60

⑦ 10,000–15,000ptas/
   €60–90
⑧ 15,000–20,000ptas/
   €90–120
⑨ Over 20,000ptas/
   Over €120

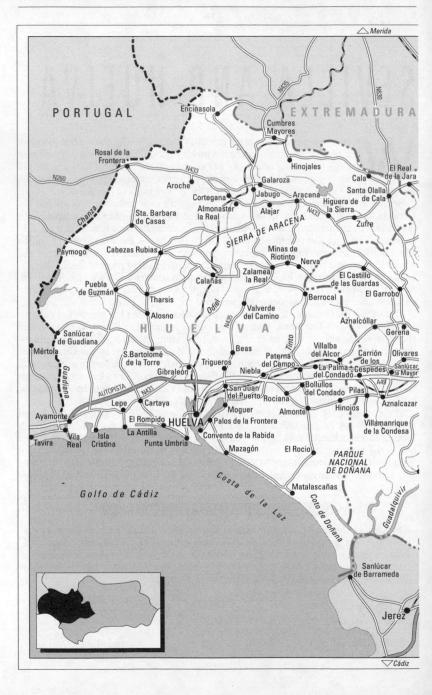

△ Merida

PORTUGAL

EXTREMADURA

N530

N435

Encinasola

Cumbres
Mayores

Rosal de la
Frontera

Hinojales

Cala

El Real
de la Jara

N260

N433

Galaroza

Santa Olalla
de Cala

Chanza

Aroche

Cortegana

Jabugo

Aracena

Higuera de
la Sierra

Almonaster
la Real

Alajar

N433

Zufre

Sta. Barbara
de Casas

SIERRA DE ARACENA

Paymogo

Cabezas Rubias

Minas de
Riotinto

Nerva

Puebla
de Guzmán

Calañas

Zalamea
la Real

El Castillo
de las Guardas

El Garrobo

Odiel

Berrocal

Tharsis

Alosno

Valverde
del Camino

Aznalcóllar

Gerena

Sanlúcar
de Guadiana

H U E L V A

N435

Tinto

Villalba
del Alcor

Olivares

Mértola

S.Bartolomé
de la Torre

Beas

Paterna
del Campo

Carrión
de los
Cespedes

Sanlúcar,
la Mayor

Guadiana

Trigueros

Niebla

La·Palma
del·Condado

A49

Gibraleón

San Juan
del·Puerto

Rociana

Bollullos
del Condado

Pilas

AUTOPISTA

N431

Lepe

Cartaya

Moguer

Almonte

Hinojos

Aznalcazar

Ayamonte

El Rompido

HUELVA

Palos de la Frontera

Villamanrique
de la Condesa

Vila
Real

Isla
Cristina

La Antilla

Punta Umbria

Convento de la Rabida

Tavira

Mazagón

El Rocio

PARQUE
NACIONAL
DE DOÑANA

Golfo de Cádiz

Costa de la Luz

Matalascañas

Coto de Doñana

Guadalquivir

Sanlúcar
de Barrameda

Jerez

▽ Cádiz

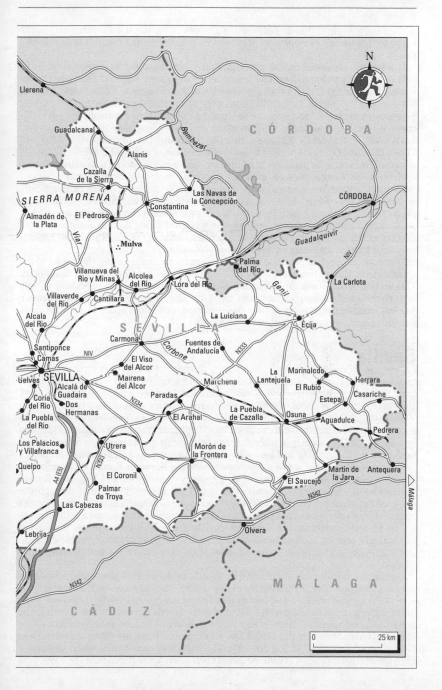

of migratory birds and to endangered mammals including the Iberian lynx, and is home to Andalucía's rumbustious Whitsuntide pilgrimage and fair, the **Romerío del Rocío**.

Huelva, the provincial capital, although scarred by its industrial surrounds, tries its best to be welcoming and does have a number of interesting sights; it also makes a convenient base for trips to local sites associated with the **voyages of Columbus** which set out from here. It was at the nearby monastery of **La Rábida** that the explorer's 1492 expedition was planned and from the tiny port of **Palos** that he eventually set sail to discover a new route to India. The province of Huelva was also the site of ancient **Tartessus**, a legendary kingdom rich in minerals that attracted the Minoans, Phoenicians and Greeks in ancient times and is mentioned in the Bible. Minerals are still extracted from the hills to the north of the city – the awesome **Río Tinto Mines** display evidence of the human quest for minerals stretching back over five thousand years.

Among the most beautiful and neglected parts of this region are even further north, in the dark, ilex-covered hills and sturdy rural villages of the **Sierra de Aracena**. Perfect walking country, with its network of streams and reservoirs between modest peaks, this is a botanist's dream, brilliant with a mass of spring flowers. Here also, along a sierra rich in cork oaks, chestnuts and poplars, some of the finest *jamón* in Spain is produced from acorn-eating *cerdos ibericos* (black pigs).

While the landlocked province of Sevilla takes its relaxation along the banks of the Guadalquivir, Huelva has a sea coast that harks back to pre-Costa del Sol tranquillity. This section of the **Costa de la Luz** has some of the finest **beaches** in Andalucía, with long stretches of luminous white sand and little sign of development. Here, between low-key coastal resorts all noted for their seafood, you'll find space to breathe along expansive beaches backed by shady pine woods.

Sevilla

"Seville," wrote Byron, "is a pleasant city, famous for oranges and women." And for its heat, he might perhaps have added, since summers here are intense and start in April. But the spirit of the quote, for all its nineteenth-century chauvinism, is about right. What is captivating about the city, as much as the monuments and works of art, is its essential romantic quality – the greatest city of the Spanish south, of Carmen, Don Juan and Figaro, and the archetype of Andalucian promise. It has a reputation for gaiety and brilliance, for theatricality and intensity of life, which seems well deserved. *Sevillanos* are world leaders in the art of street theatre. During **Semana Santa**, for example, in the grey dawn of Good Friday morning, a century of sandalled and helmeted Roman soldiers sombrely escorts the *paso*, or effigy, of the condemned Christ through the crowded but silent streets. Typically, the mood changes dramatically a couple of weeks later when the rags of mourning are cast off for flamenco costumes, and the city launches into the wild exuberance of the **Feria de Abril** which also inaugurates the start of the bullfight season, another *sevillano* passion. Either is worth considerable effort to get to. Sevilla is also Spain's second most important centre for **bullfighting**, after Madrid.

Despite its considerable charm, and its wealth, based on food processing, shipbuilding, construction and a thriving tourist industry, the city lies at the centre of a depressed agricultural area and has an unemployment rate of over forty percent – one of the highest in Spain, along with Cádiz and Jaén. You do not need to travel far into the suburbs to find slums of a developing world standard. The total refurbishment of the infrastructure boosted by the 1992 Expo – held to celebrate the 500th anniversary of Columbus's "discovery" of the New World – including new roads, seven bridges, a high-speed train link and a revamped airport was intended to regenerate the city's (and the region's) economic fortunes but has hardly turned out to be the catalyst for growth and prosperity promised at the time.

Petty crime is a notorious problem, with bag-snatching often carried out Italian-style, from passing *motos*. Non-*sevillanos* make much of the city's special breed of thief – *semaforazos*, who break the windows of cars stopped at traffic lights and grab what they can. Avoid leaving anything at all in a car parked on the street overnight; the guarded underground car parks are a possible alternative. Be careful in Sevilla, but don't be put off. Despite a worrying rise in the number of muggings in recent years, when compared with cities of similar size in northern Europe, violent crime is still relatively rare.

Sevilla's most famous present-day native son is socialist leader and ex-Prime Minister **Felipe González** who, until defeated in the 1996 election, led the country for fourteen years. Another, more bizarre *sevillano* is one **Gregorio XVII**, who calls himself the true Pope, in defiance of his excommunication by the Vatican. "Pope Greg" is leader of a large ultra-reactionary order which has made the dead Franco a saint and has constructed a mammoth "Vatican II" 40km south of the city (see p.273). Despite being blinded in a road accident, Gregorio conspicuously enjoys the good life and stalks the city's bars dressed in silken regalia, along with his "papal" entourage.

Some history

Sevilla began when ancient Iberian tribes settled on the banks of the Guadalquivir perhaps early in the first millennium BC. The settlement grew into the town now known as **El Carámbalo**, whose great wealth derived from the minerals from the mountains to the north. The demand for copper, silver and gold lured in the Greeks and Phoenicians, who traded their own ceramics, jewellery and ivory goods. It was the same Phoenicians, or perhaps their successors the Carthaginians, who attacked and then conquered the settlement around 500 BC, subsequently renaming it **Hispalis**, meaning "flat land".

When the **Romans** finally wrested Spain from Carthage the Roman general Scipio founded **Itálica** in 206 on a hill overlooking the river. The final conquest of the peninsula cost the Romans two hundred years of dogged campaigning against the ferocious Iberian peoples, and in the latter stages of this struggle **Julius Caesar** captured Hispalis in 45 BC and renamed it Julia Romula ("little Rome"). As a leading centre of the Roman province of Baetica (roughly corresponding to modern Andalucía) the city flourished and nearby Itálica provided Rome with two of its greatest second-century emperors, **Trajan** and **Hadrian**. The city later fell to the Visigoths, whose Christian archbishop **San Isidro** made sixth-century Sevilla into a European centre of learning.

Conquered by the **Moors** in 712, Sevilla briefly became **the capital of al-Andalus**. The Moors left an indelible imprint on the city, not only in its architecture, but also in the Arabic-influenced local dialect, renaming the River Baetis *Wadi El Kabir* ("great river"), a title it still keeps as the Guadalquivir. The **Almohad** dynasty of the twelfth and thirteenth centuries brought great prosperity, and when Sevilla was captured during the *reconquista* by **Fernando III** in 1258 the city became a favoured residence of the Spanish monarchy, in particular Pedro the Cruel who was responsible for the construction of the outstanding Mudéjar Alcázar. Religious intolerance racked the city in the wake of the Reconquest, however, and in 1391 the Jewish quarter in the Barrio Santa Cruz was sacked – a harbinger of the banishment of all Jews from Spain, to be proclaimed by Fernando and Isabel a century later.

The fifteenth century also saw, as well as the construction of the **Cathedral**, an event that would catapult the city to the forefront of Spanish affairs – the **discovery of the New World**. Sevilla's navigable river, with access to the Atlantic, made it a natural choice for the main port of commerce with the Americas. In the 1500s, as fabulous wealth poured in from the empire, Sevilla was transformed into one of the great cities of Europe and, with a population of over 150,000, one of the largest. The cultural renaissance that accompanied this prosperity attracted artists and writers from far and wide, including Cervantes, who spent some time here.

The **silting up of the Guadalquivir** in the 1680s deprived Sevilla of its port and with it the monopoly of trade with the Americas. The merchant fleet was transferred to Cádiz and the city went into a decline exacerbated by the great **earthquake** of 1755 which, although centred on Lisbon, caused much destruction. The city was further ravaged by the **Napoleonic occupation** of 1810–12 and was largely by-passed by the industrial revolution which permeated slowly from the north. It was only in the later nineteenth century that Sevilla was rediscovered by travellers such as Richard Ford who declared it to be "the marvel of Andalucía".

Arrival, orientation and information

Bisected from north to south by the Río Guadalquivir, Sevilla is easy and delightful to negotiate on foot or by bicycle, but can be hell if you're driving. For anything longer than a fleeting visit, the *Guía Verde Callejero* street guide (available from bookshops) is invaluable for unravelling the city's more convoluted corners.

The **old city** – where you'll spend most of your time – takes up the east bank. At its heart, side by side, stand the three great monuments: the **Giralda tower**, the **Cathedral** and the **Alcázar**, with the cramped alleyways of the **Barrio Santa Cruz**, the medieval Jewish quarter and now the heart of tourist life, extending east of them. North and west of the barrio is the main shopping and commercial district, its most obvious landmarks the **Plaza Nueva** and **Plaza Duque de la Victoria**, and the smart pedestrianized **Calle Sierpes** which runs between them. To the north of the area enclosed by the medieval walls lies the gritty **Macarena quarter** from whose church the *paso* of the bejewelled Virgin of Macarena – the most revered in Sevilla – sails forth on the Maundy Thursday of *Semana Santa* to enormous popular acclaim. Just beyond the walls here in the converted sixteenth-century Hospital de las Cinco Llagas ("five wounds of Christ") is the new permanent seat of the **Andalucían Parliament**.

Across the river is the very much earthier, traditionally working-class district of **Triana**, flanked to the south by **Los Remedios**, now transformed into the city's business zone. Adjoining this to the south lie the grounds where Sevilla's *Feria de Abril* is held and also on this bank, to the north of Triana, lie the remains of the *Expo 92* exhibition ground, at Isla de la Cartuja.

Points of arrival and information

Sevilla's **airport** (☎95 444 90 00) is 12km northeast of town along the NIV towards Córdoba. From here the *Amarillos* airport bus (hourly; 750ptas) runs down Avda. Kansas City and drops you at the Puerta de Jerez, close to the cathedral, stopping at the train station en route. You can get a **taxi** from the airport into the centre for around 2500ptas. The city's **train station**, Santa Justa (☎902 24 02 02), is some way northeast of the centre, on Avda. Kansas City. Bus #32 will get you from here to the central Plaza de la Encarnación, while bus #70, C1 or C2 takes you to the main bus station. A central point for train information and tickets is the RENFE office (Mon–Fri 9am–1.15pm & 4–7pm; ☎95 422 26 93), off Plaza Nueva at c/Zaragoza 29. Sevilla is linked to Córdoba and Madrid via a high-speed AVE train.

Most buses operate from the main bus station at the Prado de San Sebastián (%95 441 71 11), on the eastern edge of the Barrio Santa Cruz and a short bus-ride from the train station on line #70, C1 or C2, or from the Torre del Oro on C4. However, services from and to northern Sevilla, Extremadura (provinces of Cáceres and Badajoz), Huelva, Madrid, and international destinations arrive and depart from the station at Plaza de Armas (%95 490 80 40) by the Puente del Cachorro, on the river; from here, bus C3 will get you to Puerta de Jerez or the Prado de San Sebastián bus station.

NO 8 DO

On every manhole cover, bus and public building in Sevilla you will see the curious cipher **NO 8 DO**. What looks like a figure 8 is actually the symbol of a twisted skein of wool (*madeja* in Spanish). During the eleventh-century *reconquista*, Alfonso the Wise, King of Castile, tired of the endless war, made a truce with the Moors. This so angered his excitable son Sancho, that he rebelled against his father and launched a civil war. When the people of Sevilla stayed loyal to Alfonso, the king lauded them with the royal testimonial "**No me ha dejado**" (you have not deserted me). In medieval Spanish this came out as "*no ma dejado*" from which the *sevillanos* – long aficionados of word riddles – came up with NO MADEJA DO, soon encrypted as NO 8 DO and swiftly adopted as the city's crest.

Coming in **by car** you'll soon find that driving can be a nightmare here, especially when negotiating the inner-city barrios such as Santa Cruz. Finding a parking space can also be hell and your best bet is to find a paying car park (see the city map), or to choose a hotel with a garage (see the Accommodation section). Timing your arrival to coincide with the siesta (2–5pm) gives you the best chance of finding somewhere to park, and spaces are often to be found in the streets to the north and east of the Prado de San Sebastián bus station. Also never leave your car parked on the street with anything visible that looks remotely valuable (see p.32).

Sevilla's **Turismo**, just south of the cathedral at Avda. de la Constitución 21 (Mon–Sat 9am–7pm, Sun 10am–2pm; ☎95 422 14 04), can provide good city maps and an excellent free monthly listings guide, *El Giraldillo* (also available from newstands for 150ptas and posted on the internet at *www.elgiraldillo.es*), but is often over-whelmed in high season. There's a quieter and very helpful **municipal tourist office** (Mon–Sat 8.15am–8.45pm, Sun 8.30am–2.15pm; ☎95 450 56 00) at c/Arjona s/n, next to the Puente de Triana bridge on the east bank of the river, which gives information on the province as well as Sevilla itself. A smaller municipal office near the Parque de María Luisa, at Paseo de Delicias 9 (Mon–Fri 8.30am–6.30pm; ☎95 423 44 65) is another possibility.

The best – and most enjoyable – way to get around Sevilla is by **bike**; see "Listings" for rental information. If you're planning on getting around by **bus**, it might be wise to invest in a **bonobus** *carnet* ticket: the *sin transbordo* one (585ptas), gives you ten bus rides for half the price; the *transbordo* (650ptas) version allows you to change lines on the same journey – both passes are available from Tussam street kiosks, newstands or *estancos*. The current single fare journey throughout the city is 125ptas. A Tussam (bus company) route map is available from tourist offices or the company office at c/Diego de Riaño 2. Useful buses are the C1, C3 (clockwise), C2 and C4 (anti-clockwise) lines, which are circular around the city centre.

One way to get to grips with the city is on an **open-top bus tour** – especially good if you're pressed for time. This hop-on hop-off service is operated by Sevirama (☎95 456 06 93) and the buses leave half hourly from the Torre del Oro, stopping at or near the main sites (all-day tickets cost 1500ptas).

Accommodation

Rooms in Sevilla are relatively expensive and during the big festivals you can find yourself paying ridiculous amounts for what is little more than a cell. Out of high season (early summer, *Semana Santa* and *Feria de Abril*), however, prices can drop dramatically, and with owners competing for trade, it's worth haggling. During *Semana Santa* and the April *feria*, booking ahead is advised.

By far the most attractive (and priciest) area to stay is the **Barrio Santa Cruz**. You'll find lower-priced options around its periphery (especially immediately north, and southeast towards the bus station). More central possibilities are around the churches of **Santa Catalina** and **San Pedro**, and to the south of the **Alameda de Hercules** – areas possessing the charm of the older barrios without the high prices. Also promising is the area north of the **Plaza Nueva** and the **Maestranza bullring**, especially the streets beyond c/Reyes Católicos towards the Museo de Bellas Artes. Further out still, but walkable from the centre, the solidly working-class barrio of **La Macarena** can be a wonderful introduction to the real Sevilla, and there's now a *hostal* over the river in the equally atmospheric **Triana** barrio.

Sevilla's **youth hostel** is out in the university district to the south of the centre, and the nearest **campsite** lies some 6km outside the city.

Barrio Santa Cruz and Cathedral area

Hostal Águilas, c/Águilas 15 (☎95 421 31 77). Small, quiet *hostal* near the Casa de Pilatos. Some rooms with bath. Easy parking. ③.

Pensión Alcázar, c/Deán Miranda 12 (☎95 422 84 57, fax 95 442 16 59). Cosy *pensión* with air-conditioned rooms with bath in a tiny street off the Plaza de la Contratación. ④.

Hostal Atenas, c/Caballerizas 1 (☎95 421 80 47, fax 95 422 76 90). A pretty, plant-festooned passage leads to a charming *pensión* decorated with *azulejos*; all rooms with bath and air conditioning. ④.

Hostal Bienvenido, c/Archeros 17, east of c/Santa María la Blanca (☎95 441 36 55). Small simple rooms, and a nice roof terrace. ③.

Hotel Las Casas de la Judería, c/Callejón de Dos Hermanas 7, off Plaza Sta. María La Blanca (☎95 441 51 50, fax 95 442 21 70). Stunningly beautiful old ducal mansion transformed into a delightful hotel with exquisite patios, and a restaurant. Good value for this category. Garage. ⑧.

Hotel Las Casas de los Mercaderes c/Álvarez Quintero 12 (☎95 422 58 58, fax 95 422 98 84). Converted former *bodega* with delightful patio, roof terrace and great views from some rooms (especially no. 201–6). Just north of the cathedral and excellent value for this category. Garage. ⑦.

Hostal Córdoba, c/Farnesio 12 (☎95 422 74 98). Pleasant if overpriced *hostal* offering some rooms with bath, close to the church of Santa Cruz. ⑤.

Hostal Fabiola, c/Fabiola 16 (☎95 421 83 46). Small *hostal* with attractive patio and comfortable – although expensive for what you get – rooms with fans, some with bath, near the Plaza Santa Cruz. ⑤.

Hostal Goya, c/Mateos Gago 31 (☎95 421 11 70, fax 95 456 29 88). Good range of simple rooms with bath and fans, in a street with several other possibilities. ④.

Hostería del Laurel, Plaza de los Venerables 5 (☎95 422 02 95, fax 95 421 04 50). Pleasant en-suite rooms above a very good restaurant and *tapas* bar. Superb location which can get a bit overrun with visitors in high season. ⑥.

Hotel Murillo, c/Lope de Rueda 7 (☎95 421 60 95, fax 95 421 96 16). Traditional hotel in restored mansion with all facilities, plus amusingly kitsch features such as suits of armour, heavy leather chairs and paint-palette key rings. ⑥.

Hostal Pérez Montilla, Plaza Curtidores 13 (☎95 442 18 54). Spotless *hostal* on a tranquil square on the eastern edge of Santa Cruz. Quoted prices can drop dramatically. All rooms with bath and air conditioning. ⑤.

Hotel La Rábida, c/Castelar 24 (☎95 422 09 60, fax 95 422 43 75). Refurbished, traditional hotel with nice patio and good facilities. Between the Plaza de Toros and Plaza Nueva. ⑥.

Hostal San Pancracio, c/Cruces 9 (☎95 441 31 04). Decent range of room options here, some with bath, so check what's available. Close to Plaza Santa Cruz. ③.

Hostal Santa Cruz, c/Lope de Rueda 12 (☎95 421 76 95). Tiny *hostal* with some en-suite rooms, close to the Plaza Santa Cruz; curfew but owner lets you in after midnight. ④.

Hostal Santa María, c/Hernando Colón 19 (☎95 422 85 05). Small, simple place on a busy street in the Giralda's shadow. Has some en-suite rooms, and a good price. ④.

Hostal Sierpes, Corral del Rey 22, northeast of the cathedral (☎95 422 49 48, fax 95 421 21 07). Tricky to reach by car (ring them if lost and they'll come and get you), but one of the better- value places for rooms with bath in this area. Garage. ⑤.

Hotel Simón, c/García de Vinuesa 19 (☎95 422 66 60, fax 95 456 22 41). Eighteenth-century mansion with attractive patio and excellent position near the cathedral. All rooms are en-suite with air conditioning. ⑥.

Hostal Toledo, c/Santa Teresa 15 (☎95 421 53 35). Atmospheric and recently refurbished *pensión* in the heart of Santa Cruz. All rooms with bath. ⑤.

Plaza Nueva, Reyes Católicos, Museo de Bellas Artes, Triana

Hotel Bécquer, c/Reyes Católicos 4 (☎95 422 89 00, fax 95 421 44 00). Modern, comfortable and central hotel with air conditioning. Garage. ⑦.

Hostal Capitol, c/Zaragoza 66 (☎95 490 36 24). Pleasant en-suite air-conditioned rooms in an old Art-Deco house. ④.

Hostal La Gloria, c/San Eloy 58 (☎95 422 26 73). Good-value rooms, some with bath, in a wonderful neo-Moorish building above *Café Zafiro*. This street has other possibilities. ④.

Hostal Gravina, c/Gravina 46 (☎95 421 64 14, fax 95 421 96 45). Friendly, family-run *hostal* with simple rooms in a quiet street off c/Reyes Católicos. ②.

Hostal El Greco, c/San Vicente 14 (☎95 490 76 08). Close to the Museo de Bellas Artes, a pleasant *hostal* offering rooms with or without bath. ⑤.

Hostal Guadalquivir, c/Pagés del Corro 53 (☎95 433 21 00, fax 95 433 21 04). If you want to stay across the river in Triana, this is the only budget place you'll find. Pleasant and friendly; some rooms en-suite. ④.

Hostal Lis II, c/Olavide 5 (☎95 456 02 28). A couple of blocks east of the Museo de Bellas Artes, this is a clean and simple place offering rooms with and without bath. ③.

Hostal Paco's, c/Pedro del Toro 7, off c/Gravina (☎95 421 71 83 fax 95 421 96 45). Friendly offshoot of the *Hostal Gravina*, this has small rooms, including some en-suite. ③.

Hostal Paris, c/ San Pedro Mártir 14 (☎95 422 98 61, fax 95 421 96 45). Good-value *hostal* with lots of facilities, including air conditioning, in a tiny street near the Museo de Bellas Artes. All rooms with bath. ④.

Hotel Plaza-Sevilla, c/Canalejas 2, to the north of c/Reyes Católicos (☎95 421 71 49, fax 95 421 07 73). It's almost worth staying at this comfortable hotel for the stunning Neoclassical facade alone – the work of Anibal González, architect of the Plaza de España. ⑤.

Hostal Rivero, c/Bailén 67 (☎95 421 62 31). Eighteenth-century former bishop's residence with attractive, plant-filled patio, and run by two sprightly sisters. Situated in a quiet street, it's on the doorstep of the Museo de Bellas Artes. Some rooms with bath. ③.

Hostal Romero, c/Gravina 21 (☎95 421 13 53). Basic but efficient *hostal* with another plant-bedecked patio. Some rooms en-suite. ③.

Pensión Zahira, c/San Eloy 43 (☎95 422 10 61 fax 95 421 30 48). Comfortable air-conditioned rooms with bath. ⑤.

Hotel Zaida, c/San Roque 26, just south of Museo de Bellas Artes (☎95 421 11 38). Charming and intimate hotel with a fine exterior and an interior replete with Moorish-inspired decor. All rooms with bath. ④.

Santa Catalina, San Pedro, Alameda de Hércules

Hostal Alameda, Alameda de Hércules 31 (☎95 490 01 91, fax 490 22 48). Modern but pleasant *hostal* overlooking the tree-lined Alameda. Rooms with bath and air conditioning. ④.

Patio de la Alameda, Alameda de Hércules 56, northern end (☎95 490 49 99, fax 95 490 20 56). Old *señorial* house revamped into an elegant and fair-priced apart-hotel with three patios and easy parking. Rooms have kitchen and lounge. ⑥.

Patio de la Cartuja, c/Lumbreras 8, off the west side of the Alameda's northern end (☎95 490 02 00, fax 95 490 20 56). Unique, stylish and excellent-value apart-hotel created from an old *sevillano corral*, with balconies around a tiled patio. All rooms have kitchen and lounge. Garage. ⑥.

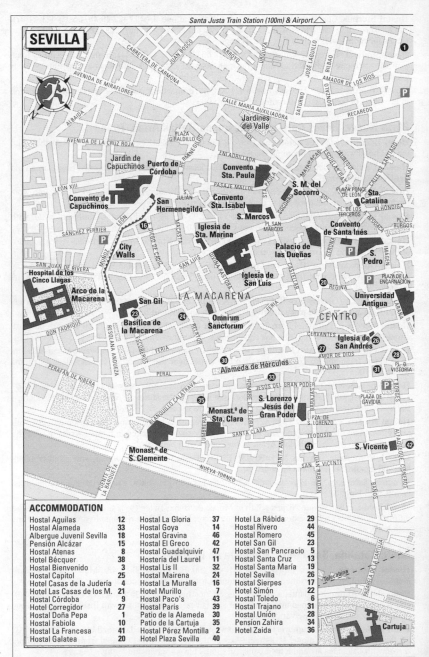

Santa Justa Train Station (100m) & Airport △

SEVILLA

ACCOMMODATION

Hostal Aguilas	12	Hostal La Gloria	37	Hotel La Rábida	29
Hostal Alameda	33	Hostal Goya	14	Hostal Rivero	44
Albergue Juvenil Sevilla	18	Hostal Gravina	46	Hostal Romero	45
Pensión Alcázar	15	Hostal El Greco	42	Hotel San Gil	23
Hostal Atenas	8	Hostal Guadalquivir	47	Hostal San Pancracio	5
Hotel Bécquer	38	Hostería del Laurel	11	Hostal Santa Cruz	13
Hostal Bienvenido	3	Hostal Lis II	32	Hostal Santa María	19
Hostal Capitol	25	Hostal Mairena	24	Hotel Sevilla	26
Hotel Casas de la Judería	4	Hostal La Muralla	16	Hostal Sierpes	17
Hotel Las Casas de los M.	21	Hotel Murillo	7	Hotel Simón	22
Hostal Córdoba	9	Hostal Paco's	43	Hostal Toledo	6
Hotel Corregidor	27	Hostal Paris	39	Hostal Trajano	31
Hostal Doña Pepa	1	Patio de la Alameda	30	Hostal Unión	28
Hostal Fabiola	10	Patio de la Cartuja	35	Pensión Zahira	34
Hostal La Francesa	41	Hostal Pérez Montilla	2	Hotel Zaida	36
Hostal Galatea	20	Hotel Plaza Sevilla	40		

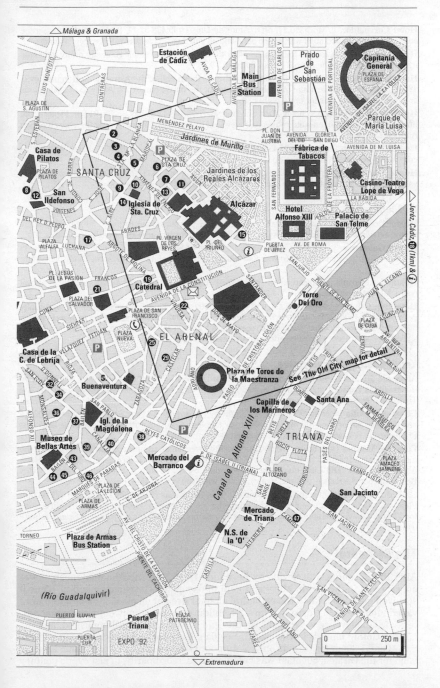

△ Málaga & Granada

Estación
de Cádiz

Prado
de
San
Sebastián

Capitanía
General

PLAZA DE
ESPAÑA

Main
Bus
Station

Parque de
María Luisa

MENÉNDEZ PELAYO

Jardines de Murillo

PLAZA DE
S. AGUSTÍN

Casa de
Pilatos

2
3
4
5

SANTA CRUZ

6
7

PLAZA DE
STA CRUZ

Jardines de los
Reales Alcázares

Fábrica de
Tabacos

PLAZA DE
PILATOS

San
Ildefonso

8   12

9   10

11

13

Casino-Teatro
Lope de Vega

LA RÁBIDA

14   Iglesia de
Sta. Cruz

Alcázar

Hotel
Alfonso XIII

Palacio de
San Telmo

15

17

PLAZA
ALFALFA

PL. VIRGEN
DE LOS
REYES

PL. DEL
TRIUNFO

PUERTA
DE JEREZ

AV. DE ROMA

PL. JESÚS
DE LA PASIÓN

21

19   Catedral

AVENIDA DE LA CONSTITUCIÓN

PLAZA DEL
SALVADOR

22

Torre
Del Oro

PLAZA DE SAN
FRANCISCO

EL ARENAL

25

PLAZA
NUEVA

PLAZA
DE CUBA

Casa de la
C. de Lebrija

29

Plaza de Toros do
la Maestranza

See 'The Old City' map for detail

5
Buenaventura

32

34

36

Capilla de
los Marineros

Santa Ana

37   Igl. de la
Magdalena

TRIANA

Museo de
Bellas Artes

39   40

38

Mercado del
Barranco

43

44   45   46

Canal de Alfonso XIII

San Jacinto

Mercado
de Triana

47

PLAZA DE
ARMAS

Plaza de Armas
Bus Station

N.S. de
la 'O'

TORNEO

(Río Guadalquivir)

PUERTO FLUVIAL

Puerta
Triana

PLAZA
PATROCINIO

0   250 m

EXPO '92

△ Jeréz, Cádiz, 18 (1km) & ⓘ

▽ Extremadura

Hotel Corregidor, c/Morgado 17, off c/Amor de Dios (☎95 438 51 11, fax 95 438 42 38). Serene and recently renovated hotel with a nice patio and all you'd expect for the price, except a garage. ⑦.

Hostal La Francesa, c/Juan Rabadán 28 (☎95 438 31 07). Quiet, simple rooms in pretty little family-run *hostal* close to the church of San Lorenzo. ③.

Hostal Mairena, c/Relator 49, to the east of the northern end of the Alameda de Hércules (☎95 490 80 98). Small, simple *hostal* in a vibrant corner of the barrio run by a friendly *dueña*. All rooms en suite, plus reductions for more nights. ③.

Hotel Sevilla, c/Daóiz 5, actually Plaza San Andrés (☎95 438 41 61, fax 95 490 21 60). Pleasant old hotel with a nice patio, en-suite rooms and views on to a pleasant *plazuela* near the church of San Andrés. ④.

Hostal Trajano, c/Trajano 3 (☎95 438 24 21). Good-value rooms with bath (but shared WC) at this cosy *hostal* near the Plaza Duque de la Victoria. ③.

Hostal Unión, c/Tarifa 4, near Plaza Duque de la Victoria (☎95 422 92 94). One of this zone's best value *hostales* with en-suite rooms and pleasant management. ④.

La Macarena

Hostal Doña Pepa, c/Juan de Vera 20, near Santa Justa train station (☎95 441 36 28). Completely renovated *hostal* with good rooms, some with bath. Ideal for late arrivals or early departures. ④.

Hostal Galatea, c/San Juan de la Palma 4, northwest of San Pedro (☎95 456 35 64, fax 95 456 35 17). Friendly place in a restored town house situated on a peaceful *plazuela*; some rooms with bath. ④.

Hostal La Muralla, c/Macarena 52 (☎95 437 10 49). Cosy, residential *hostal* near the medieval walls. All rooms with bath. ④.

Hotel San Gil, c/Parras 28 (☎95 490 68 11, fax 95 490 69 39). Luxurious apart-hotel in a beautifully restored early 1900s *palacio*. There's a garden with palms and cypresses, rooftop pool and interior decorated with mosaics and *azulejos*; all rooms have a lounge and kitchenette. Call in at their bar for a peek. Special offers can reduce prices dramatically. Garage. ⑦.

Youth hostel and campsites

Albergue Juvenil Sevilla, c/Isaac Peral 2 (☎95 461 31 50; they tend not to answer). Sevilla's leafy if sometimes crowded youth hostel is some way out; take bus #34 from Puerta de Jerez by the Turismo or from Plaza Nueva. ①.

Camping Sevilla (☎ & fax 95 451 43 79). Right by the airport, so very noisy but otherwise not a bad site. The airport bus will take you there, or take bus #70 from outside the main bus station at Prado de San Sebastián and ask to be dropped at "Parque Alcosa".

Camping Villsom (☎ & fax 95 472 08 28). Recently overhauled campsite 10km out of town on the main Cádiz road, with a pool. Half-hourly buses from c/Palos de la Frontera next to the Hotel Alfonso XIII (see "Old City" map) take twenty minutes. Make sure to take the bus signed "Dos Hermanas por Barriadas" (indirect route), which will drop you outside the campsite.

Club de Campo, 12km south of the centre in Dos Hermanas (☎95 472 02 50, fax 95 472 63 08). Pleasant, shady site with pool which has the edge on the nearby *Villsom*. Follow the directions for *Villsom* (above) but take bus signed "Dos Hermanas Directo" (direct route), a twenty-minute trip.

The Cathedral

After the Reconquest of Sevilla by Fernando III (1248), the Almohad mosque was consecrated to the Virgin Mary and kept in use as the Christian cathedral. Thus it survived until 1402, when the cathedral chapter dreamt up plans for a new and unrivalled monument to Christian glory: "a building on so magnificent a scale that posterity will believe we were mad." To this end the mosque was demolished, and the largest Gothic church in the world, Sevilla's **Catedral**, (Mon–Sat 10.30am–5pm; Sun 10am–1.30pm for Giralda only, 2–4pm for **Giralda** and cathedral; same ticket is valid for the Giralda; 600ptas) was completed, extraordinarily, in just over a century

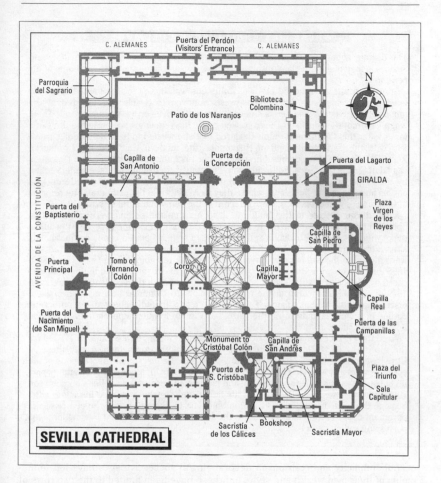

C. ALEMANES

Puerta del Perdón
(Visitors' Entrance)

C. ALEMANES

N

Parroquia
del Sagrario

Biblioteca
Colombina

Patio de los Naranjos

Puerta del Lagarto

GIRALDA

Capílla de
San Antonio

Puerta de
la Concepción

Plaza
Virgen
de los
Reyes

Puerta del
Baptisterio

Capilla de
San Pedro

AVENIDA DE LA CONSTITUCION

Puerta
Principal

Tomb of
Hernando
Colón

Coro

Capilla
Mayor

Capilla
Real

Puerta del
Nacimiento
(de San Miguel)

Puerta de las
Campanillas

Monument to
Cristóbal Colón

Capilla de
San Andrés

Plaza del
Triunfo

Puorta de
S. Cristóbal

Sala
Capitular

Sacristía
de los Cálices

Bookshop

Sacristía Mayor

SEVILLA CATHEDRAL

(1402–1506). As Norman Lewis said, "it expresses conquest and domination in architectural terms of sheer mass." Built upon the huge, rectangular base-plan of the old mosque, it was given the extra dimension of height by the Christian architects, probably under the direction of the French master architect of Rouen Cathedral. Its central nave rises to 42 metres, and even the side chapels appear tall enough to contain an ordinary church. The total area covers 11,520 square metres and was previously reckoned to be the third largest church in the world after St Paul's in London and St Peter's in Rome. However, new calculations based on cubic measurements have now placed it in the number one position, a claim upheld by the *Guinness Book of Records*, a copy of whose certificate is proudly displayed in the church.

Sheer size and grandeur are, inevitably, the chief characteristics of the cathedral. But as you grow accustomed to the gloom, two other qualities stand out with equal force: the rhythmic balance and interplay between the parts, and an impressive

WHERE LIES CHRISTOPHER COLUMBUS?

The dispute about **Christopher Columbus**'s birthplace – claimed by both Italy and Spain – is matched by the labyrinthine controversy surrounding the whereabouts of his **remains**.

After his death in Valladolid in 1506, Columbus was buried in that town, but not for long. Three years later the remains were removed to Sevilla and interred at the monastery of Santa María de las Cuevas, across the river on La Cartuja island. Then, when Columbus's eldest son Diego passed away, his remains were buried in the same tomb. After this Columbus's widow declared that she wished to have both bodies transferred to the Caribbean island of Hispaniola (the modern Haiti and the Dominican Republic), the site of Columbus's first landfall in 1492, for interment in Santo Domingo, capital of Spanish America. Following some bureaucratic resistance and an intervention by the emperor, Carlos V, in 1544 the remains of both bodies were packed into lead coffins and shipped to the island, where they were placed in the cathedral. The remains of Columbus's grandson, Luís, were interred in the same cathedral in 1783.

Later, during repairs to this building, it seems that the coffins were mislaid, then opened, and the names mixed up. It did not take the authorities long to resolve the dilemma of which was which, by having all three sets of remains placed in one coffin. Shortly after 1795, when Spain was forced to cede Santo Domingo to the French, the remains were moved to the cathedral in Havana, still Spanish territory. When Cuba was lost in 1898 the remains were transported back across the Atlantic and placed in the tomb prepared by Mélida in Sevilla. The lingering uncertainty lies in the accidental discovery in 1879 of another lead coffin in the cathedral in Santo Domingo bearing a silver plate inscribed with Columbus's name. This box of remains then disappeared, but numerous coffins of bones claiming to be the same have made frequent appearances at auction houses ever since.

Were the correct remains despatched from Santo Domingo to Havana in 1795? Was the discovery of 1879 a fraud? Are the remains in the tomb today really those of Christopher, Diego and Luís? We can only gaze into the inscrutable expressions of the coffin bearers and wonder. However, it is certain that one member of the Columbus family, at least, was buried in the cathedral and has stayed here – Christopher's bookish son Hernando, who wrote a biography of his father and donated his large library to what became the cathedral's Biblioteca Colombina. His tombstone lies in the centre of the pavement towards the main west door, the Puerta Principal, flanked by smaller slabs portraying sailing vessels.

overall simplicity and restraint in decoration. All successive ages have left monuments of their own wealth and style, but these have been limited to the two rows of side chapels. In the main body of the cathedral only the great box-like structure of the *coro* (choir) stands out, filling the central portion of the nave.

Entry to the cathedral – as it was to the earlier mosque – is through the **Puerta del Perdón** and it is worth taking a look at this magnificent gateway. Although sadly marred by Renaissance embellishments, there remains some exquisite Almohad plaster work and the original great doors made from larchwood faced with bronze. Minute Kufic script inside the lozenges proclaims that "the empire is Allah's". The pierced bronze door-knockers are copies of the beautiful hand-crafted twelfth-century originals now preserved inside the church. The main entrance leads into the **Patio de los Naranjos**, taking its name from the orange trees which now shade the former mosque's entrance courtyard where ritual ablutions were performed prior to worship. In the centre of the patio a **Moorish fountain** incorporates a sixth-century carved marble font, a surviving remnant of the earlier Visigothic cathedral which was itself levelled to make way for the mosque.

The Giralda

Unquestionably Sevilla's most beautiful building, the Moorish **Giralda** (entry through the cathedral - go through Puerta de la Concepcion and turn left), named after the sixteenth-century *giraldillo* or weather vane on its summit, dominates the skyline. In character with the city below, whose much-loved symbol it has become, and despite all its contradictions the Giralda remains, in its perfect synthesis of form and decoration, one of the most important examples of Islamic architecture in the world.

The **minaret** – according to Ford built on a foundation of destroyed Roman statuary – was the culmination of Almohad architecture, and served as a model for those at the imperial capitals of Rabat and Marrakesh. It was designed by the architect of the original mosque, Ahmed ibn Baso, and was used by the Moors both for calling the faithful to prayer and as an observatory. They so worshipped the building that they planned to destroy it before the Christian conquest of Sevilla, but were prevented from doing so by the threat of Alfonso (later King Alfonso X) that "if they removed a single stone, they would all be put to the sword." Instead the Giralda went on to become the bell-tower of the Christian cathedral. The **Patio de los Naranjos**, the old entrance to the mosque also survives intact.

From inside the cathedral you can ascend to the **bell chamber** for a remarkable view of the city – and, equally remarkable, a glimpse of the Gothic details of the cathedral's buttresses and statuary. Keep an eye out, too, for the colony of kestrels which has long nested in the tower – the descendants no doubt of the "twittering, careering hawks" seen by Ford when he climbed up here in the 1830s. Most impressive is the tower's inner construction, a series of 35 gently inclined ramps wide enough for two mounted guards to pass. The Moorish structure took twelve years to build (1184–96) and derives its firm, simple beauty from the shadows formed by blocks of brick trellis work or *ajaracas*, different on each side, and relieved by a succession of arched niches and windows. The original harmony has been somewhat blemished by the Renaissance-era addition of balconies and, to a still greater extent, by the four diminishing storeys of the belfry – added, along with the Italian-sculpted bronze figure of "Faith" which surmounts them, in 1560–68, following the demolition by an earthquake of the original copper spheres. The fact that a weathervane blown by the four winds should epitomize the ideal of constant faith, or that this female figure should possess a masculine name ("Giraldillo"), has never seemed to trouble whimsical *sevillanos*.

The interior

Beyond the Giralda the route around the cathedral then continues to the right, but should you be interested in studying the abundant artworks dotted around the various gloomy chapels en route – including important canvases by Zurbarán, Murillo, Ribera and Valdes Léal which are not identified – you should cross the nave to the bookshop (see plan) to obtain a copy of the official *Guide to the Cathedral of Seville* which deals with them in detail.

Dominating the central nave, the **choir** extends and opens on to the **Capilla Mayor**, dominated by a vast and fabulous Gothic *retablo* composed of 45 carved scenes from the life of Christ. Begun in 1482 and the lifetime's work of a single craftsman, Fleming Pieter Dancart, this is the supreme masterpiece of the cathedral – the largest and richest altarpiece in the world and one of the finest examples of Gothic woodcarving. The guides provide staggering statistics on the amount of gold involved. Above the central tabernacle, the **Virgen de la Sede** (Virgin of the Chair) is a stunning thirteenth-century Gothic figure of silver-plated cedar. Just to the right, a panel depicts an **image of the Giralda** as it appeared prior to any Renaissance additions.

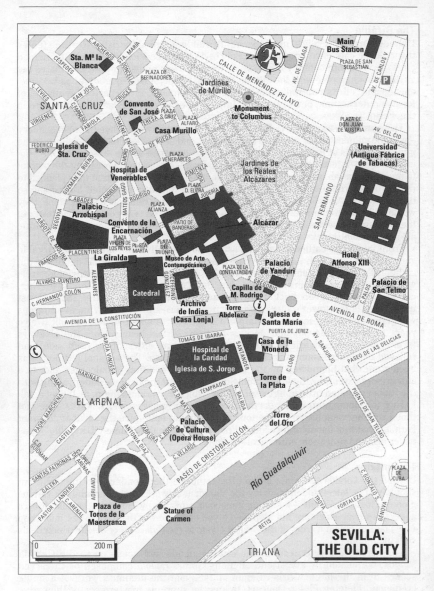

SEVILLA:
THE OLD CITY

Continuing along the north side of the nave the **Capilla de San Antonio** in the cathedral's northwest corner contains the *Vision of St Anthony*, a magnificent work by Murillo, depicting the saint in ecstatic pose before an infant Christ emerging from a luminous golden cloud. Try and spot where the restorers joined San Antonio back into place after he had been crudely hacked out of the picture by thieves in the nineteenth

MOORISH SEVILLA

Sevilla was one of the earliest **Moorish conquests** (in 712) and, as part of the Caliphate of Córdoba, became the second city of al-Andalus. When the Caliphate broke up in the early eleventh century it was by far the most powerful of the independent states (or *taifas*) to emerge, extending its power over the Algarve and eventually over Jaén, Murcia and Córdoba itself. This period, under a series of three Arabic rulers from the Abbadid dynasty (1023–91), was something of a golden age. The city's court was unrivalled in wealth, luxury and sophistication, developing a strong chivalric element and a flair for poetry – one of the most skilled exponents was the last ruler, al Mu'tamid, the "poet-king". But with sophistication came decadence, and in 1091 Abbadid rule was usurped by a new force, the **Almoravids**, a tribe of fanatical Berber Muslims from North Africa, to whom the Andalucíans had appealed for help against the threat from the northern Christian kingdoms.

Despite initial military successes, the Almoravids failed to consolidate their gains in al-Andalus and attempted to rule through military governors from Marrakesh. In the middle of the twelfth century they were in turn supplanted by a new Berber incursion, the **Almohads**, who by about 1170 had recaptured virtually all the former territories. Sevilla accepted Almohad rule in 1147 and became the capital of this last real empire of the Moors in Spain. Almohad power was sustained until their disastrous defeat in 1212 by the combined Christian armies of the north, at Las Navas de Tolosa in Jaén. Within this brief and precarious period Sevilla underwent a renaissance of public building, characterized by a new vigour and fluidity of style. The Almohads rebuilt the Alcázar, enlarged the principal **mosque** and erected a new and brilliant minaret, a tower over 100m tall, topped with four copper spheres that could be seen from miles round: the Giralda.

century. He was eventually discovered in New York – where art dealers recognized the work they were being asked to buy – and returned to the cathedral. The *Baptism of Jesus* here is another fine work by the same artist.

Crossing to the south side of the nave takes you past the **Puerta Principal** followed by the **Puerta del Nacimiento**, the gate through which pass all the *pasos* and penitents who take part in the *Semana Santa* processions. More chapels line the south side, and roughly half-way along, facing the Puerta de San Cristobál, is an enormous late nineteenth-century **Monument to Christopher Columbus** (Cristóbal Colón in Spanish), by Sevillian sculptor Arturo Mélida, which may or may not be the navigator's tomb (see box p.224). It was originally intended to be erected in the Cuban cathedral of Havana, Spain's colony, where it would become a sepulchre for Columbus's remains, but the Spanish-American War – and Cuba's subsequent independence – intervened. As a result the plans were changed and the work was placed here in Sevilla's cathedral. The mariner's coffin is held aloft by four huge allegorical figures, representing the kingdoms of León, Castile, Aragón and Navarra; the lance of Castile should be piercing a pomegranate (now inexplicably missing), the symbol of Granada, which was the last Moorish kingdom to be reconquered.

Beyond here to the right lies the **Sacristía de los Cálices** where many of the cathedral's main art treasures are displayed. Among some outstanding works are a masterly *Santas Justa y Rufina* by Goya, depicting Sevilla's patron saints who were put to death in 287 during the Roman emperor Diocletian's persecution of the Christians. Here also are canvases by Zurbarán, Roelas, Valdes Leál and Jordaens. Behind the **Capilla de San Andres**, which has an exceptional polychromed image of the crucified Christ by Martinez Montañes, lies the grandiose sixteenth-century **Sacristía Mayor** designed in 1528 by Diego de Riaño. It is a prime example of the rich Plateresque style, and Riaño was one of the foremost exponents of this predominantly decorative architecture of the late Spanish Renaissance. Forming a veritable church-within-a-church it induced Philip

II to remark to the members of the chapter: "Your sacristy is finer than my Chapel Royal". The sacristy houses more paintings, including a poignant *Santa Teresa* by Zurbarán, and the treasury, a collection of silver reliquaries and monstrances – dull and prodigious wealth. Here also are the **keys** presented to Fernando by the Jewish and Moorish communities on the surrender of the city; sculpted into the Moor's key in stylized Arabic script are the words "May Allah render eternal the dominion of Islam in this city." Nearby is a polychromed image of Fernando – *El Santo* – by Pedro Roldán, one of Andalucía's great eighteenth-century sculptors.

Through a small antechamber here you enter the remarkable oval-shaped **Sala Capitular** (Chapter House), whose elaborate domed ceiling is mirrored in the outstanding geometric marble decoration of the floor. The stone benches provide seats for the members of the chapter. It contains a number of paintings by Murillo, a native of Sevilla, the finest of which, a flowing *Concepción Inmaculada*, occupies a place of honour high above the bishop's throne. The nearby **exit from the cathedral** through the Puerta de las Campanillas brings you out into the Plaza del Triunfo.

The new routing in the cathedral means that a number of chapels at the eastern end of the nave may not be open to the public during visits (but may be open during or after services) including the domed Renaissance **Capilla Real**, built on the site of the original royal burial chapel and containing the body of Fernando III (*El Santo*) in a suitably rich, Baroque silver sepulchre before the altar. The large tombs on either side of the chapel are those of Fernando's wife, Beatrice of Swabia, and his son, Alfonso the Wise. To the left of here, the **Capilla de San Pedro** in the cathedral's northeast corner has a fine seventeenth-century *retablo* by Diego López Bueno with nine Zurbarán scenes depicting the life of Saint Peter (except for the image of God which is a later replacement). Also here is the Puerto del Lagarto ("door of the alligator"), so named in commemoration of a stuffed reptile given to Alfonso X by the Sultan of Egypt in 1260. A wooden replica now hangs in place of the perished original.

La Casa Lonja – Archive of the Indies

Should you be inspired by the Columbus saga, visit **La Lonja** (Mon–Fri 10am–1pm; free), opposite the cathedral. Built in the severe and uncompromisimg style of the Escorial near Madrid, and designed by the same architect, Juan de Herrera, it was the former merchants' commodity exchange (*lonja*), adapted in the eighteenth century to house the remarkable **Archivo de las Indias**, a monumental storehouse of the archives of the Spanish empire. The archive holds over 38,000 documents and files – all in the process of being computerized – from the four centuries of Spanish rule. Only bona fide researchers can get their hands on the dusty files containing letters signed by Columbus or other luminaries, however, and casual visitors must make do with an audio-visual presentation (in Spanish) and exhibition. Among the selection of objects on show in a changing display are Columbus's log and occasionally a letter from Cervantes (pre-*Don Quijote*) petitioning the king for a position in the Americas – fortunately for world literature, he was turned down.

VISITING THE ALCÁZAR

The pressure of visitors to the **Alcázar** has resulted in the introduction of a flow-control system whereby every twenty to thirty minutes 750 people are allowed in. This seems to be working and while it has reduced the unholy scrums which used to take place in the past, you would still be advised to visit during early morning or late afternoon to savour the experience in relative calm. An official guide to the complex on sale at the entrance has detailed maps of the palaces and information on the gardens beyond.

The Alcázar

Rulers of Sevilla occupied the site of the **Alcázar** (Tues–Sat 9.30am–7pm, Sun 9.30am–5pm; 700ptas) from the time of the Romans. The fortified palace was probably founded in the eighth century on the ruins of a Roman barracks, with the surrounding walls being added in the ninth.

In the eleventh century it was expanded to become the great court of the Abbadid dynasty, who turned the wealth gained from the production of olive oil, sugar cane and dyes into a palace worthy of their hubris. This regime reached a peak of sophistication and decadence under the ruthless al-Mu'tadid – a ruler who further enlarged the Alcázar in order to house a harem of eight hundred women and decorated the terraces with flowers planted in the skulls of his decapitated enemies. Later, in the twelfth and thirteenth centuries under the **Almohads**, the complex was turned into a citadel, forming the heart of the town's fortifications. Its extent was enormous, stretching to the Torre del Oro on the bank of the Guadalquivir. Parts of the Almohad walls survive, but the present structure of the palace dates almost entirely from the Christian period following the fall of the city in 1248.

Sevilla was a favoured residence of the Spanish kings for some four centuries after the Reconquest – most particularly of **Pedro the Cruel** (Pedro I; 1350–69) who, with his mistress María de Padilla, lived in and ruled from the Alcázar. Pedro embarked upon a complete rebuilding of the palace, utilizing fragments of earlier Moorish buildings in Sevilla, Córdoba and Valencia. Pedro's works form the nucleus of the Alcázar as it is today and, despite numerous restorations necessitated by fires and earth tremors, offer some of the best surviving examples of **Mudéjar architecture** – the style developed by Moors working under Christian rule. Later monarchs have also left many traces and additions. Isabel

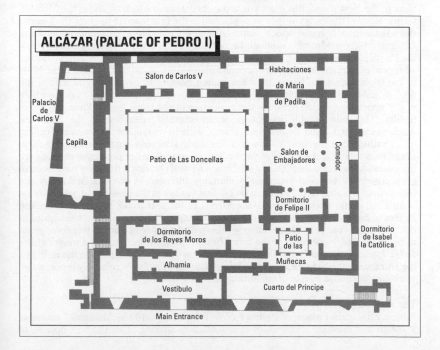

ALCÁZAR (PALACE OF PEDRO I)

Salon de Carlos V

Habitaciones de Maria de Padilla

Palacio de Carlos V

Capilla

Patio de Las Doncellas

Salon de Embajadores

Comedor

Dormitorio de Felipe II

Dormitorio de los Reyes Moros

Patio de las Muñecas

Dormitorio de Isabel la Católica

Alhamia

Vestibulo

Cuarto del Principe

Main Entrance

built a new wing in which to organize expeditions to the Americas and control the new territories; Carlos V married a Portuguese princess in the palace, adding huge apartments for the occasion; and under Felipe IV (c.1624) extensive renovations were carried out to the existing rooms. On a more mundane level, kitchens were installed to provide for General Franco, who stayed in the royal apartments whenever he visited Sevilla.

Entry – the Salón del Almirante

The Alcázar is entered from the Plaza del Triunfo, adjacent to the cathedral, through the **Puerta del León**, which bears an heraldic image of a lion in fourteenth-century glazed tiles above the lintel. The gateway, flanked by original Almohad walls, opens onto a courtyard where Pedro (who was known as "the Just" as well as "the Cruel", depending on one's fortunes) used to give judgement; to the left is the **Sala de Justicia** built by Alfonso XI in the 1340s with exquisite *yesería* (plasterwork) in the Grenadine style. Beyond, the restored **Patio del Yeso** has more fine plasterwork and the whole patio is the only visible surviving remnant of the Almohads' Alcázar. The main facade of Pedro's palace stands at the end of an inner court, the **Patio de la Montería**, or "hunting patio", where the royal hunt gathered; on either side are galleried buildings erected by Isabel. This principal facade is pure fourteenth-century Mudéjar and, with its delicate, marble-columned windows, stalactite frieze and overhanging roof, is one of the finest features of the whole Alcázar. The castles, lions and other heraldic devices were intended to emphasise the king's power over both Christians and Muslims, but Kufic lettering still proclaims that "There is no God but Allah".

It's a good idea to look round the **Salón del Almirante** (or Casa de la Contración de Indias), the sixteenth-century building on the right, before entering the main palace. Founded by Isabel in 1503 as an office where personnel could be hired to man expeditions to the New World, this gives you a standard against which to assess the Moorish forms. Many of the early voyages were planned in the first room to be seen, the **Cuarto del Almirante**, a name which commemorates Columbus's appointment as Gran Almirante (senior admiral), although he probably never used it. Balboa, discoverer of the Pacific, Vincente Pinzón, discoverer of the Amazon, and many other *conquistadores* all spread their maps across tables here and planned the plunder of the Americas. Most of the rooms seem too heavy, their decoration ceasing to be an integral part of the design, and much of the time many of them are closed to public view – as is the whole of the upper floor which provides the residence of the royal family when staying in Sevilla. The only notable exception, architecturally speaking, is the **Sala de Audiencias** (or Capilla de los Navigantes), with its magnificent *artesonado* ceiling inlaid with golden rosettes. Within is a fine early sixteenth-century *retablo* by Alejo Fernández depicting the *Virgin of the Navigators* spreading her protective mantle over the *conquistadores* and their ships – which are so well portrayed that they have been of great assistance to naval historians. Columbus (dressed in gold) is flanked by the Pinzón brothers who sailed with him on his first voyage to the New World, while Carlos V (in a red cloak) shelters beneath the Virgin. In the rear to the left are the kneeling figures of the Indians to whom the dubious blessings of Christianity had been brought by the Spanish conquest. The painting synthesizes the sense of a divine mission – given to Spain by God – prevalent at the time. Beside the altarpiece stands a model of the *Santa María*, Columbus's first flagship. Slightly further along the patio to the right lies the entrance to the **Sala de los Azulejos** containing a display of relatively modern tilework and, beyond, a couple of delightfully serene patios.

The Palace of Pedro I

Entering the main **Palace of Pedro I** (detailed on our map) the "domestic" nature of Moorish and Mudéjar architecture is immediately striking. This involves no loss of grandeur but simply a shift in scale: the apartments are remarkably small, shaped to human needs, and take their beauty from the exuberance of the decoration and the imaginative use of space and light. There is, too, a deliberate disorientation in the layout of the rooms which makes the palace seem infinitely larger and more open than it really is. From the entrance court a narrow passage leads beyond the **Vestibulo**, where visitors removed their outer clothing, straight into the central courtyard, the **Patio de las Doncellas** (Patio of the Maidens), its name recalling the Christians' tribute of one hundred virgins presented annually to the Moorish kings. The court's plaster frieze and dado composed of polychrome *azulejos* (tiles) and doors are all of the highest Granada craftsmanship, and are the finest in the palace. Interestingly, it's also the one location where Renaissance restorations are successfully fused – the double columns and upper storey were added by Carlos V, whose *Plus Ultra* ("Yet still further") motto recurs in the decorations here and elsewhere.

Past the **Salón de Carlos V**, distinguished by a truly magnificent *artesonado* ceiling, are three rooms from the original fourteenth-century design built for María de Padilla (who was popularly thought to use magic in order to maintain her hold over Pedro – and perhaps over other gallants at court, too, who used to drink her bath water). These open on to the **Salón de Embajadores** (Salon of the Ambassadors), the most brilliant room of the Alcázar, with a stupendous wooden dome of red, green and gold cells, and horseshoe arcades inspired by the great palace of Medina Azahara outside Córdoba. An inscription in Arabic states that it was constructed by craftsmen from Toledo and completed in 1366. Although restored, for the worse, by Carlos V – who added balconies and an incongruous frieze of royal portraits to commemorate his marriage to Isabel of Portugal here – the salon stands comparison with the great rooms of Granada's Alhambra. Note also the **original Mudéjar tiles**, with their Moorish geometric patterns expressing artistically the fundamental Islamic tenet of the harmony of creation. Adjoining are a long dining hall (*comedor*) and a small apartment installed in the late sixteenth century for Felipe II.

Beyond is the last great room of the palace, the **Patio de las Muñecas** (Patio of the Dolls), which takes its curious name from two tiny faces decorating the inner and outer surfaces of one of the smaller arches. The elegant columns in the tenth-century Caliphate style are believed to have come from the ruins of Medina Azahara near Córdoba. Thought to be the site of the harem in the original palace, it was here that Pedro is reputed to have murdered his brother Don Fadrique in 1358; another of his royal guests, Abu Said of Granada, was murdered here for his jewels, one of which, an immense ruby which Pedro later gave to Edward, the "Black Prince", now figures in the British Crown Jewels). The upper storey of the court is a much later, nineteenth-century restoration. On the other sides of the patio are the **bedrooms** of Isabel and of her son Don Juan, and the arbitrarily named *Dormitorio del los Reyes Moros* (Bedroom of the Moorish Kings).

Palacio de Carlos V and the gardens

To the east of the main palace (and reached via a stairway out of the southeast corner of the *Patio de las Doncellas*) loom the large and soulless apartments of the **Palacio de Carlos V**. Something of an endurance test, with endless tapestries (eighteenth-century copies of the sixteenth-century originals that are now in Madrid) and pink-orange or yellow paintwork, the apartments' classical style asserts a different and inferior mood. It's best to hurry through to the beautiful and relaxing **Alcázar gardens**, the rambling but enticing product of several eras. Here are the vaulted baths in which María de Padilla was supposed to have bathed (actually an auxiliary water supply for the palace), and the **Estanque del Mercurio**, a pool with a bronze figure of the messenger of the gods at its centre, specially built for Felipe V (1733), who whiled away two solitary years at the Alcázar fishing here and preparing himself for death through religious flagellation. In the gardens proper – and close to an unusual **maze** of myrtle bushes – lies the **pavilion of Carlos V**, the only survivor of several he built in the gardens. This one, designed by Juan Hernández, was completed in 1543 and has the king's motto *Plus Ultra* displayed on the tiles of the steps leading to the pavilion's entrance.

The gardens are a spacious and tranquil haven to escape the crowds – particularly the Jardín Inglés on the west side – and make an ideal place for a discreet picnic. A **cafetería** can be reached via the Puerta de Marchena, to the left of the Estanque del Mercurio, which has a pleasant terrace overlooking the gardens. The way out is via the **Apeadero**, a large coach hall built for Philip V in the eighteenth century which not only housed the coaches used by the royals, but also legions of servants who slept on the floor. Beyond lies the impressive **Patio de las Banderas** (Patio of the Flags) edged with orange trees and until fairly recently the parade ground of the military barracks surrounding it, now luxury apartments. The flags of the various regiments were assembled here and reviewed by the king prior to battle. Exit from this square by an arch to the street, where you emerge on the edge of the Barrio Santa Cruz.

The Barrio Santa Cruz

The **Barrio Santa Cruz** is very much in character with Sevilla's romantic image, its streets narrow and tortuous to keep out the sun, the houses brilliantly whitewashed and festooned with flowering plants. Many of the windows are barricaded with *rejas* (iron grilles) behind which girls once kept chaste evening rendezvous with their *novios* who were forced to *comer hierro* ("eat iron") as passion mounted. Almost all of the houses have patios, often surprisingly large, and in summer these become the principal family living room. Most of the time they can be admired from the street beyond the wrought-iron screen inside the doorway, something the residents don't appear to mind. One of the most beautiful is within the Baroque **Hospicio de los Venerables Sacerdotes** (guided tours only; daily 10am–2pm & 4–8pm; 500ptas), near the centre in a plaza of the same name. Built around the patio and originally a home for infirm clerics, the hospice and church now form a gallery of outstanding art works. These include **sculptures** by Montañés, Pedro and Luisa Roldán, a painting of the *Last Supper* by Roelas, plus some wonderfully restored **frescoes** by Lucás Valdés and Valdés Leal.

A walk around the Barrio Santa Cruz

The barrio is a great place for a stroll and you'll soon discover your own favourite nooks and crannies along the tangle of narrow streets with their beautiful patios and tiny squares. There's no set route around this fascinating area; the following **walk** highlights just a few of the barrio's many features.

Starting out from Plaza Virgen de los Reyes, behind the cathedral, the **Palacio Arzobispal** (free access to its patio if open) conceals behind a Baroque facade a remarkable staircase made entirely of jasper. Along c/Mateos Gago, *Bar Giralda*, at no. 2, incorporates part of a Moorish *hammam* or steam baths, while over the road and up a bit, at no. 20, is one of Sevilla's institutions, the hole-in-the-wall **bodega of Juan García Aviles** with its prized gleaming bar counter of Spanish mahogany, over a century old and one of the few remaining in the city.

When you've downed a *manzanilla*, continue east and turn right into c/Mesón del Moro, where the slightly incongruous *San Marco Pizzeria*, at no. 4, is another establishment operating inside a splendid **Moorish bathhouse**. Further up c/Mateos Gago, a left turn will bring you into c/Guzmán El Bueno where, at no. 10, the charming sisters at the **Convento de San José** will allow you to view some remarkable Mudéjar plaster decoration (its ornate appearance is on a par with the Alcázar) in what was the salon, and is now the chapel, of this former fourteenth-century palace. This street is an especially good one for patio hunting – no. 4, with its plants, *azulejos*, wall-mounted bulls' heads and Roman statuary, is a picture.

Retracing your steps and following the c/Mesón del Moro will bring you – via c/Ximénez de Enciso (a left and then a right) – to c/Santa Teresa where, at no. 8, you'll find the **Museo de Murillo** (Tues–Sat 10am–2pm & 5–8pm, Sun 10am–2pm; free). Located in the artist's seventeenth-century home, this house-museum is furnished with contemporaneous art works, craftsmanship and furniture, but, somewhat disappointingly, none of Murillo's original paintings. (See also p.237.)

Continuing along this street – note the old grindstones sunk into the wall on the left – will bring you to the delightful **Plaza Santa Cruz** where, until the French burned it down in 1810, stood the church which gave the square (and the barrio) its name and in which Murillo was buried. The attractive seventeenth-century cross, circled by rose bushes, marks the centre of the original church and was placed here when the plaza was created in 1918. Of three possible directions from here a route east (along *calles* Mezquita and Doncellas) would bring you to the ancient Gothic-Baroque church of **Santa María La Blanca**, on the street of the same name, which has, built into its south wall in c/de los Archeros, the entrance to the original synagogue, the only surviving architectural remnant of the *Jewish quarter*. The church's main portal is flanked by Visigothic columns probably from a church pre-dating both the synagogue and the Moorish period, while the interior has lots of *azulejos* from Triana as well as an extravagant filigree stucco ceiling and two artistic gems: a moving *Piedad* (pietà) by the sixteenth-century artist Luís de Vargas and a stunning *Last Supper* by Murillo, the latter a rare tenebrist work.

In the next street along from the church on the right heading north, the tiny c/Dos Hermanas has at no. 7 the *Casas de la Judería* hotel – a restored *casa señorial* formerly the residence of the dukes of Bejar – whose beautiful patio is worth a look, perhaps over a drink from the bar. Directly south from Plaza de Santa Cruz are the **Jardines de Murillo**, another peaceful oasis and a place to get your breath back in the midst of shady arbours decorated with Triana tiles. Alternatively, the Callejón del Agua will take you west back towards the town centre where, at no. 6, the **Corral del Agua** restaurant has yet another fine patio quickly followed by the sweet, plant-bedecked c/Pimienta (Pepper Street), thought to take its name from a Jewish spice merchant who once lived here. Turn right along here, at the end turning right again to reach the Plaza de los Venerables where, if you didn't want see the art works inside the *Hospicio de los Venerables* (see above), you could visit the celebrated *tapás* bars on the plaza, the *Hostería del Laurel* and the *Casa Román*. Otherwise, heading north and then west along c/Jamerdana and the Pasaje Vila returns you to the c/Mateos Gago, just before which (on the tiny c/Rodrigo Caro) there's the *Bar Santa Cruz*, another – and cheaper – Sevilla *tapas* institution.

The Plaza de España and María Luisa Park

Laid out in 1929 for an abortive "Fair of the Americas", the **Plaza de España** and adjoining **María Luisa Park** are among the most impressive public spaces in Spain. They are an ideal place to spend the middle part of the day, just ten minutes' walk to the south of the cathedral. En route you pass a number of buildings of note: the **Hotel Alfonso XIII**, the **Palacio de San Telmo** and the **Fábrica de Tabacos**, the city's old tobacco factory that was also the setting for Bizet's *Carmen*.

Hotel Alfonso XIII and Palacio de San Telmo

The **Hotel Alfonso XIII**, Sevilla's grandest, is worth a look inside – no one minds as long as you aren't dressed too outrageously. Named after the ill-starred monarch Alfonso XIII who was forced to abdicate soon afterwards, it was built to house important guests attending the 1929 exhibition, and an elegant neo-Baroque facade conceals one of the city's most beautiful patios, best enjoyed over a beer (or afternoon tea) from the bar.

Slightly west of here, the **Palacio de San Telmo**, built as a marine training academy for the Indies fleet and completed in 1734, is another expression of Sevilla's full-tilt Baroque period. During the mid-nineteenth century, as the city's naval importance declined, it was purchased by the dukes of Montpensier, a member of whose family – the Dowager Duchess María Luisa – in 1893 presented part of the palace's vast grounds to the city, which became the park now named after her. The palace's main facade overlooks Avda. de Roma and has a marvellous Churrigueresque entrance arch topped – in a central niche – by San Telmo, patron saint of navigators (of "St Elmo's fire" fame). The building's interior is presently closed to the public.

Nearby, on the northeast side of the Puerto de Jerez traffic junction – a name referring to its former importance as one of the twenty gates in the city's ancient walls – on the corner of c/San Gregorio, lies the small former mosque and now chapel of **Santa María de Jesús**. Converted into a Christian church in 1248, it was frequently visited by Columbus on his trips to the city.

Antigua Fábrica de Tabacos

The old **Tobacco Factory**, just behind the *Hotel Alfonso XIII* along Avda. San Fernando, was where Carmen – in the nineteenth-century story by Mérimée made into an opera by Bizet – worked as a cigar maker. A beautiful and sensual *gitana,* she falls in love with Don José, a corporal. He deserts his regiment to join her band of smugglers but she tires of him and transfers her affections to the toreador Escamillo, and is finally stabbed to death by an insanely jealous Don José outside the bullring where a statue of "Carmen" now stands. Legions of foreign travellers have made pilgrimages to Sevilla in search of their own Carmen. The disillusion of the 1930s Irish traveller Walter Starkie is typical: he said that he had never seen "an uglier collection of women in my life", and was then hounded out of the workshops with a chorus of obscene abuse.

Now part of the university, this massive structure – 250m long by 180m wide – was built in the 1750s and still retains its position as the largest building in Spain after El Escorial. Above the main entrance – facing Avda. San Fernando – perches a marble angel, a trumpet to its lips, which malicious popular legend has it would only sound when a virgin entered the factory for the first time. The entrance arch below aptly incorporates medallion busts of Columbus (discoverer of the tobacco lands) and Cortés (reputedly Europe's first smoker) – in effect the factory's founding fathers.

The building was divided into residential quarters below with the work areas on the upper – and lighter – level. The entrance leads through a vestibule into the Clock Patio off which, to the right, a short passage will bring you to the university's **cafetería,** open to all and offering a wide range of food at budget prices – there's a 475ptas *menú* – during term time. At its peak in the nineteenth century the factory was also the country's largest single employer, with a workforce of some 10,000 women *cigarreras* – "a class in themselves" according to Richard Ford (see p.438), and forced to undergo "an ingeniously minute search on leaving their work, for they sometimes carry off the filthy weed in a manner her most Catholic majesty never dreamt of." Production of cigars, cigarettes and snuff – originally ground by 200 donkey-driven rolling mills – continued here until 1965 when its operations were moved to a new factory across the river close to the Puente del Generalísimo.

The Plaza de España

The **Plaza de España** lies beyond the Avenida del Cid – the latter, incidentally, the site of the Inquisition's *quemadero,* or burning platform, where for three hundred years convicted heretics were put to death; the last witch was burned here in 1781. The vast semicircular complex was designed as the centrepiece of the Spanish Americas Fair (which was somewhat scuppered by the Wall Street crash), with fountains, majestic stairways and a mass of tile work – its flamboyance would seem strange in most Spanish cities but here it looks entirely natural, carrying on the great tradition of civic display. At the fair, the Plaza de España was used for the Spanish exhibit of industry and crafts, and around the crescent are *azulejo* scenes and maps of each of the provinces: an interesting record of the country at the tail-end of a monied era.

Locals and tourists alike come out to the plaza – slightly shabby now – to potter about in the little boats rented out on its tiny strip of canal, or to hide from the sun and crowds amid the ornamental pools and walkways of the **Parque de María Luisa**. The park is designed, like the plaza, in a mix of 1920s Art Deco and mock-Mudéjar. Scattered about, and round its edge, are more buildings from the fair, some of them amazingly opulent, built in the last months before the Wall Street crash undercut the scheme's impetus – look out, in particular, for the stylish **Guatemala building**, off the Paseo de la Palmera.

The Museo Arquelógico and Museo de Costumbres Populares

Towards the end of the park, the grandest mansions from the fair have been adapted as museums, of which the **Museo Arqueológico** (Tues 3–8pm, Wed–Sat 9am–8pm, Sun 9am–2pm; 250ptas; free with EU passport) is the most important of its kind in Andalucía. The collection's wide remit, divided between twenty-seven rooms on two floors, spans the period from prehistory to the end of the Moorish age.

Starting in the basement and following the prehistoric sections, Room 4 displays a collection of funerary stelae from the Iberian period, while a darkened Room 6 has a unique eighth-century BC bronze **statuette of Astarte-Tanit**, the Phoenician fertility goddess once worshipped throughout the Mediterranean. This room also contains the stunning **Carambalo Treasures** discovered in the Sevilla suburb of Camas in 1958. This remarkable hoard of gold jewellery further fuelled the debate surrounding the whereabouts and existence of the ancient land of Tartessus, known to the Greeks and mentioned in the Bible as Tarshish. The legendary mineral wealth of Tartessus probably indicates a location in the area between Sevilla and the mineral-rich hills of Huelva, but despite investigations by archeologists for most of the last century it has never been found.

Rooms 11 to 24 on the ground floor contain the substance of the **Roman** collection with an interesting display of kitchen equipment in Room 13, including what appears to be a modern-looking fork contradicting the theory that the implement was a medieval invention. The same room also has a fine third-century mosaic from Écija, depicting the god Bacchus being transported on a chariot drawn by tigers. In Room 17 there's a sensitive, second-century **sculpture of Venus** from Itálica, which was imported from Greece. There's yet more statuary in Rooms 19 and 20, as well as portrait busts of the emperors Augustus and Nero and local boys Trajan and Hadrian, the latter particularly striking. In a small room off Room 19 you'll find a number of remarkable **bronze plaques** inscribed with the "Lex Irnitana", a rare set of laws illustrating how the Romans – the inventors of jurisprudence – went about ruling their empire. The laws make a fascinating read but are sadly translated only into Spanish. Rubric 72 of the code deals with the freeing of public slaves whilst number 82 relates to the upkeep of roads, tracks, irrigation channels, drains and sewers, all vital to the Roman way of life. The laws are sanctioned by the despotic Emperor Domitian, whose name appears at the end of the document dated to April 10, 91 AD; a portrait bust of whom is displayed nearby. Finally, Rooms 26 and 27 display post-Roman finds including early Christian tombstones and Mudéjar ceramic works among which a fifteenth-century green-glazed **baptismal font** stands out.

Opposite is the fabulous-looking **Museo de Costumbres Populares** (Popular Arts Museum; Tues 3–8pm, Wed–Sat 9am–8pm, Sun 9am–2pm; 250ptas; free with EU passport)

BOAT TRIPS ON THE GUADALQUIVIR

A great way to get a different view of Sevilla is to take a **boat trip on the Guadalquivir**. Cruceros Turísticos (☎95 421 55 96) have a quayside office below the Torre del Oro and run an hour-long cruise (daily 11am–9pm, every 30min; 1000ptas) which takes in all the major riverside sights, including a view of the *Expo 92* site. On Saturdays they also run a scenic downriver cruise to **Sanlúcar de Barrameda** (see p.000), leaving the Torre del Oro at 8.30am (3300ptas round-trip). The cruise docks at 1pm at Sanlúcar's Bajo de Guía – with its outstanding fish restaurants – and leaves for Sevilla at 5.30pm, arriving back at the Torre del Oro at 10pm. Their **Crucero de Noche** (daily 10.15pm; 3500ptas) cruises the river by night with an on-board fiesta, including an orchestra, entertainers and as much free *sangría* as you can swallow.

---

which – despite displays of costumes, implements, furniture, photos and posters describing life in eighteenth- and nineteenth-century Andalucía – feels a bit lifeless. The basement ceramics displays are the highlight, illustrating the regional developments of this craft inherited from the Moors. In spring there are also special exhibitions devoted to *Semana Santa* and the April *feria*.

The River and the Museo de Bellas Artes

Down by the **Guadalquivir** – just below the Plaza de Toros – there are pedal-boats, convenient for idling away the afternoons, and at night a surprising density of local courting couples. The main riverside landmark here is the twelve-sided **Torre del Oro**, built by the Almohads in 1220 as part of the Alcázar fortifications. It was connected to another small fort across the river by a chain which had to be broken by the Castilian fleet before their conquest of the city in 1248. The tower later saw use as a repository for the gold brought back to Sevilla from the Americas; hence its name. It now houses a small, mildly interesting **naval museum** (Tues–Fri 10am–2pm; Sat & Sun 11am–2pm; 100ptas, free with EU passport), which exhibits charts and engravings of the port in its prime.

The Hospital de la Caridad

One block east of the Torre del Oro is the **Hospital de la Caridad** (Mon–Sat 9am–1.30pm & 3.30–6.30pm, Sun 9am–1pm; 400ptas; entry on c/Temprado), founded in 1676 by Don Miguel de Mañara, who may well have been the inspiration for Byron's Don Juan. According to the testimony of one of Don Miguel's friends, "there was no folly which he did not commit, no youthful indulgence into which he did not plunge ... (until) what occurred to him in the street of the coffin." What occurred was that Don Miguel, returning from a wild orgy, had a vision in which he was confronted by a funeral procession carrying his own corpse. He repented his past life, joined the Brotherhood of Charity (whose task was to bury the bodies of vagrants and criminals), and later set up this hospital for the relief of the dying and destitute, for which it is still used. Touchingly, whenever a patient dies here, the chapel is closed on the day of the funeral.

Between 1660 and 1674 Don Miguel commissioned a series of eleven paintings by **Murillo** for the chapel, seven of which remain after Marshal Soult looted four of them during the Napoleonic occupation; these were never returned. Murillo always created pictures "made to measure" for the available light, and it's a real treat to see the pictures in the place they were originally intended to hang. Among the surviving works are a colossal *Loaves and Fishes* depicting Christ feeding the Five Thousand, and "a *San*

MURILLO IN ALL HIS GLORY

Born in Sevilla in 1618 and orphaned ten years later, **Bartolomé Esteban Murillo** grew up in the home of his brother-in-law. After enrolling as a student under Juan de Castillo he came to the attention of another *sevillano*, Velázquez, who was by then established in Madrid. Murillo studied with Velázquez for three not very happy years in the capital, where he found the social scene oppressive, but was apparently much impressed by the works of the Flemish and Italian schools he saw in the royal collections there.

Once back in his native city Murillo started work in earnest, often using poor *sevillanos* from districts such as the Macarena as his models. In 1682, still at the height of his powers, he was painting an altarpiece for the Capuchin church in Cádiz when he fell from the scaffold, suffering serious injury. He was brought back to Sevilla where he died in the Convent of San José near to his home in the barrio Santa Cruz.

Downgraded by critics in the nineteenth century for his sentimentalism – a view largely based on the genre paintings of rosy-faced urchins that had found their way across Europe – Murillo's reputation has since been restored. A greater familiarity with the powerful works that remained in Sevilla, such as those in the Caridad, substantiates Ford's proclamation: "At Sevilla Murillo is to be seen in all his glory... a giant on his native soil".

Juan de Dios equal to Rembrandt" as Richard Ford, a fervent Murillo fan, described it. Mañara himself posed as the model for the saint. Alongside them hang two *Triumph of Death* pictures by Valdés Leal. One, portraying the fleeting nature of life, features a skeletal image of Death pointing to the message *in ictu oculi* ("in the blink of an eye"), while the other depicts a decomposing bishop being eaten by worms (beneath the scales of justice labelled *Ni más, Ni menos* – "No More, No Less"). Murillo found this so repulsive that he declared "you have to hold your nose to look at it." The mood of both works may owe a lot to the vivid memory of the 1649 plague which killed almost half the population of the city. The main altar's **retablo** features a superlative *Burial of Christ* carved by Pedro Roldán, and the steps to the left of this descend to a crypt where Mañara is buried.

As you're leaving the Caridad, look out for the **Torre de Plata**, a castellated Moorish watch-tower, at c/Santander 13. Now visible from just inside a car park, it probably got its name to correspond with the nearby Torre del Oro, although there is no evidence to suggest that it was once coated with silver tiles or was ever a silver store as local legends have it.

Plaza de Toros de la Maestranza and around

The **Maestranza bullring** (Tues–Sat 9.30am–2pm & on non-fight days 3–6pm; 400ptas) is the most famous and, for aficionados, the most beautiful bullring in the world. It was completed in the latter half of the eighteenth century to provide a home for the Real Maestranza de Caballería (Royal Equestrian Society). Altered subsequently, it is still one of the finest in Spain and has featured in numerous novels, poems and films – most enduringly in *Carmen*, the opera by Bizet. The ring is maintained in immaculate condition with never a blemish on the brilliant white and ochre paintwork. Once inside the arena, you will see a metal frame in the roof holding a furled canvas. On fight days this is unfurled - not to give spectators more shade but to temper the wind, which often whips up over the river causing the capes of the *matadores* to behave in unpredictable and possibly dangerous ways. The Maestranza's **museum** has the usual posters, prints, photographs and memorabilia. A monument to "Carmen" (see p.234) stands opposite the entrance to the bullring, across the road near the river.

Three blocks downriver – with a dome that's hard to miss – is the new **Teatro de la Maestranza** concert hall and opera house. Built as part of the *Expo 92* improvements, it incorporates the remains of the Artillería ammunition works which previously occupied the site. The rather dominating and uninspired design caused much controversy when it was unveiled because of its detrimental effect on the magnificent view of the city from across the river.

The Museo de Bellas Artes

To the north of c/Reyes Católicos on the Plaza del Museo and fronted by a formidable bronze statue of Murillo, the **Museo de Bellas Artes** (Tues–Sat 9am–8pm, Sun 9am–2pm; 250ptas, free with EU passport), housed in recently modernized galleries in a startlingly beautiful former convent, the Convento de la Merced, ranks second in Spain only to the Prado in Madrid. Founded in the thirteenth century by Ferdinand III after Sevilla had been taken from the Moors, the building was subsequently remodelled and reached its present form in the eighteenth century. The convent lost most of its own commissioned paintings during the nineteenth-century Disentailment when it was secularized, and it opened as a museum in 1838. You should be aware that the museum has a policy of rotating its artworks and not all the works mentioned here may be exhibited.

Among the highlights of an outstanding collection is a wonderful late fifteenth-century sculpture in painted terracotta in Room 1, *Lamentation over the Dead Christ*, by the Andalucian **Pedro Millán**, founding father of the Sevilla school of sculpture. A marriage of Gothic and expressive naturalism, this style was the starting point for the outstanding seventeenth-century period of religious iconography in Sevilla – a later example, in Room 2, is a magnificent *San Jerónimo* by the Italian **Pietro Torregiano**, who spent the latter years of his life in Sevilla. Ever his own man, Torregiano once broke the nose of his contemporary Michelangelo in a quarrel and eventually died at the hands of the Inquisition in Sevilla, condemned for impiety after he had smashed his own sculpture of a Virgin when the Duke of Arcos refused to pay the price asked. His *Virgen de Belén* here is another powerful work. This room also has **El Greco's** portrait of his son, *Jorge Manuel Theotokopoulos*.

Room 3 has a *retablo* of the Redemption, c.1562, with fine woodcarving by Juan Giralte. Originally made for the Convento de Santa Catalina in Aracena, tableaux 6 (the crowning with thorns) and 10 (Mark writing his gospel) are especially fine. There's also a **Velázquez** work here, a portrait of *Don Cristóbal Suarez de Ribera* produced in his teens, betraying sure signs of the master's touch as well as an unparalleled ability to illuminate his figures from within.

A monumental *Last Supper* by **Alonso Vásquez** painted for the monastery of La Cartuja covers an end wall of Room 4, while the grisly terracotta sculpture of the severed head of *John the Baptist* by **Núñez Delgado** may not be something you want to see too soon after lunch. Dated 1591, this work is a prototype of the Baroque images later to be carried on the *pasos* during *Semana Santa*. This room also has works by **Pachecho**, one of the protagonists of the Mannerist school and the father-in-law and tutor of Velázquez. His series of canvases for the Convento de la Merced (this building) is represented here by images of *San Pedro* and *San Ramón Nonato*.

Beyond a serene patio and cloister, Room 5 is located in the monastery's former church. The recently restored **paintings on the vault and dome** by the eighteenth-century *sevillano*, Domingo Martínez, are spectacular. Here also is the nucleus of the collection: **Zurbarán's** *Apotheosis of St Thomas Aquinas* as well as a clutch of **Murillos** in the apse crowned by the great *Immaculate Conception* – known as "*la colosal*" to distinguish it from the other work here with the same name. In an alcove nearby you'll see the same artist's *Virgin and Child*. Popularly known as **La Servilleta** because it was said to have been painted on a dinner napkin, the work is one of Murillo's greatest. In the same room are more Murillos and also works by the early seventeenth-century *sevillano* **Roelas**, including a magnificent *Martirio de San Andrés*. Upstairs, Room 6 (quadrated around the patio) displays works from the Baroque period, among which a moving *Santa Teresa* by **Ribera** – Spain's master of *tenebrismo* (darkness penetrated by light) – and a stark *Crucifixión* by **Zurbarán** stand out.

Room 7 is devoted to Murillo and his school and has a superb *San Agustín y la Trinidad* by the master. In Room 8, eighteenth-century *sevillano* **Valdés Leal** symbolizes the city's enduring fascination with agony and mortality: his depiction of *Fray Juan de Ledesma* wrestling with the devil disguised as a serpent has the brooding intensity of much of his work. There's more sculpture in Room 10, this time by **Montañes**, the sixteenth-century "Andalucian Lysippus", whose early *Saint Dominic in Penitence* and *San Bruno* from his mature period display mastery of technique. This room also contains works from the **European Baroque**, among which there's an outstanding *La Adoración de los Pastores* (Adoration of the Shepherds) by the Flemish painter Pieter Van Lint and an *Adoración de los Reyes* by his compatriot Cornelis de Vos, both connected with the school of Rubens. Also here are more imposing canvases by **Zurbarán**: *San Hugo visiting the Carthusian monks at supper, San Bruno's visit to Pope Urban II* and the *Virgen de las Cuevas* were all painted for the monastery of La Cartuja (see p.244) across the river. There's also another almost sculptural *Crucifixión* to compare with his earlier one in Room 6.

The collection ends with works from the Romantic and Modern eras where an austere late work by **Goya**, in Room 11, of the octogenarian *Don José Duaso* compensates for some not terribly inspiring works accompanying it. There's also a portrait of the incompetent and indolent ruler *Alfonso XIII* painted in 1929 by Gonzalo Bilbao which tells you all you need to know about this monarchical disaster. The same artist has more works in Room 12 – his *Las Cigarreras* is a vivid portrayal of the wretched life of women in the Tobacco Factory during the early years of the last century. Room 14 has an evocative image of *Sevilla en Fiestas* dated 1915 by Gustavo Bacarisas. Here also there's *Juan Centeno y su cuadrilla* by Huelvan artist Daniel Vásquez Díaz who worked in Paris and was a friend of Picasso. This monumental image of the *torero* and his team provides an appropriately *andaluz* conclusion to a memorable museum.

The Centro

The **Centro**, or central zone, lies north of the cathedral at the geographical heart of the city. It contains the main shopping areas, including **Calle Sierpes**, the city's most fashionable street. Here, too, you'll find many of Sevilla's finest churches, displaying a fascinating variety of architectural styles. Several•are converted mosques with belfries built over their minarets, others range through Mudéjar and Gothic (sometimes in combination), Renaissance and Baroque. Most are kept locked except early in the morning, or in the evenings from about 7 until 10pm – a promising time for a church crawl, especially as they're regularly interspersed with *tapas* bars.

The Casa de Pilatos

Of Sevilla's numerous mansions, by far the finest is the so-called **Casa de Pilatos** (daily 9am–6pm; 500ptas, both floors 1000ptas) in the Plaza de Pilatos, on the northwestern edge of Santa Cruz. Built by the Marqués de Tarifa of the Ribera family on his return from a pilgrimage to Jerusalem in 1519, the house was popularly – and erroneously – thought to have been an imitation of the house of Pontius Pilate, supposedly seen by the duke on his travels. In fact it's an harmonious mixture of Mudéjar, Gothic and Renaissance styles, featuring brilliant *azulejos*, a tremendous sixteenth-century stairway and the best domestic patios in the city. After the Civil War the Dukes of Medinaceli returned to live here and inaugurated a programme of restoration which has gradually brought the house back to its original splendour.

Entering by the Apeadero (refer to the plan on the back of your ticket), where the old carriages were boarded, and which for most of the year has a riot of magenta bougainvillea cascading over its arcade, brings you to a gateway leading into the wonderful **Patio Principal**. Here, Muslim elements such as the irregular arches, plaster work and glazed tiles combine with Gothic tracery on the upper balustrades and an Italian Renaissance fountain and columns below. The imposing statues in each corner of the patio are classical originals, of which the **Athene** (bearing a spear) is attributed to the fifth-century BC school of the Greek master, Phidias; the others are Roman. Antique Italian busts of Roman emperors and men of letters such as Trajan, Hadrian and Cicero occupy niches in the arcades.

The Salón Pretorio is notable for its coffered ceiling, incorporating the Ribera family's coat of arms. The Roman sculptures – collected in Italy by the sixteenth-century Duke of Alcalá – in the nearby Zaquizamí corridor are extremely fine, especially the **slumbering Venus** and a marble relief fragment, depicting weapons, above. Passing the Jardín Chico (Small Garden), the Chapel of the Flagellation (its central column is supposed to represent the one at which Christ was scourged) and Pilate's "study", you reach the **Jardín Grande**, a verdant oasis with palms, pavilions and a bower, not to mention a wonderful abundance of orange trees. A tradition associated with this garden relates that the first Duke of Alcalá obtained from Pope Pius V the ashes of the Emperor Trajan, which were then displayed in a vase in the library. Later, a servant is supposed to have dumped them in the garden thinking the urn to be full of dust. The legend grew that an orange tree sprouted up wherever the ashes had fallen.

The **upper floors** (still partly inhabited by the Medinaceli family) are reached from the Patio Principal via the fine, tiled staircase with a gilded, sixteenth-century semi-circular dome, but can be seen only by guided tour. The rooms are decorated with various frescoes, canvases by Goya (a tiny bullfighting scene), Ribera and Jordáns, and *objets d'art* collected by the family. Outstanding here is the **Salón de Pachecho** with the *Apotheosis of Hercules* painted on the cieling in 1603 by the *sevillano* artist after whom the room is named. A sixteenth-century **oak bench** carved in the Plateresque style is also worth closer inspection. As you leave the house, note a rather curious bust of **Julius Caesar** at the entrance to the toilets. It's a fine portrait and, given the wealth of artefacts the family have hauled back from classical parts, is probably a two-thousand-year-old original deserving a more seemly location.

Churches, convents and monuments in the Centro

Leaving the Casa de Pilatos, a circuit of the churches in the area will take you first via c/Caballerizas to **San Ildefonso**, a fourteenth-century church later rebuilt in the classical style. Inside, behind the altar on the north aisle, there's a **fresco of the Virgin** dating from the original building. The church also has some seventeenth-century wood sculptures by Roldán and a bas-relief, *The Trinity*, by Montañes dated 1609.

Not far away, and still heading in a more or less westerly direction, c/Boteros will bring you to **Plaza Alfalfa**, the forum of Roman Hispalis and a good place for *tapas* bars. A couple of blocks south of here, along c/Candilejos and c/Muñoz y Pavón, in c/Marmoles are the remains – three enormous columns known as **Los Monolitos Romanos** – once belonging to what must have been a gigantic Roman temple. Continuing north from Plaza Alfalfa, however, along *calles* Ferrer and Llop you'll reach the Plaza del Buen Suceso on which lies the **convent** of the same name. Inside, there's a marvellous sculpture of **Saint Anne with the Virgin** by Montañes. North again, c/Velilla leads to the Gothic **San Pedro** with a Mudéjar tower modelled on the Giralda, and where a marble tablet records Velázquez's baptism. Just behind the church on c/Dueñas, the **Palacio de los Dueñas** was the birthplace of another *andaluz* genius, the poet Antonio Machado.

A stroll west from San Pedro along c/Imagen passes the Renaissance chapel of the **Anunciación** on c/Larana, leading to c/Cuna on the left where, at no. 8, stands the eighteenth-century **Palacio Lebrija** (Mon–Fri 5–7pm; 500ptas) which has a collection of Iberian and Roman antiquities and some fine Roman mosaics from Itálica built into its three patios. A route directly north from here brings you to the tree-lined **Alameda de Hércules**, once a swamp and converted in the sixteenth century into a promenade. The southern end has two pillars taken from a Roman temple to Hercules, which give the promenade its name. Once fashionable, this area went to seed, and until recently was the city's red-light district. New bars and hotels have started to spring up here of late, the skin-trade has moved on, and the Alameda is re-emerging as a vibrant centre of *sevillano* nightlife.

West of the Alameda, on Plaza de San Lorenzo lies the church of San Lorenzo and, next to it, the modern church of **Jesús del Gran Poder**. In the latter's **retablo** is displayed the much venerated figure of *Jesús del Gran Poder* (Christ bearing his cross) by Juan de Mesa, carved in 1620. This image is borne in procession in the small hours of Good Friday morning. Continuing north along c/Eslava leads you into c/Santa Clara, making for the convent of the same name at no. 40. The convent's charming patio leads to the **Torre de Don Fadrique** (currently only visitable by appointment; ring ☎95 422 48 08) a medieval tower from the thirteenth century. Originally a defensive bastion protecting the palace of Don Fadrique, eldest son of Alfonso X, it is Romanesque-Gothic in style. As you climb to the top, note the slits in the walls through which arrows could be fired. The view from the top of the tower – reached via a perilous stepped wooden spar – is not to be missed. On your way out, should the convent's church be open, try to catch the splendid *retablo* by Montañes.

Plaza de San Francisco and Calle Sierpes

Because of the Muslim origin of its vernacular architecture – which was designed primarily to keep out the sun – Sevilla had no great squares on the European model until relatively recently. Most of the plazas it does possess are the result of palaces and convents being torn down to make way for them: some, such as the depressing Plaza del Duque de la Victoria, site of the *palacio* of the Guzmán family, were created as recently as the 1960s.

In the shadow of the Giralda, the **Plaza de San Francisco**, slightly north of the cathedral, takes its name from the great monastery that once covered much of this and the Plaza Nueva to the west. It was also the site of the Inquisition's first burning platform, or *quemadero*, where those convicted of crimes against the church were burned at the stake. During the *Semana Santa* processions, the whole square – filled wall-to-wall with specially constructed grandstands – is the prime site where Sevilla's great and good gather to see and be seen. On the plaza's eastern flank, elegant balconied nineteenth-century houses face the **Ayuntamiento**, constructed in the sixteenth century and noted for its richly ornamented Plateresque facade by Diego de Riaño. Interior features include a vaulted vestibule in the Gothic style and a decorated *sala capitular*.

To the north of the Plaza de San Francisco you'll find the true heart of Sevilla, **Calle Sierpes**, where, according to Cervantes – who spent some involuntary time here serving a sentence for his tax debts – "all the social classes of the city come together." This narrow pedestrianized street, lined with antique stores, *tapas* bars, private clubs and smart *pastelerías* is a wonderful place to stroll. It's particularly dramatic – though quite uncharacteristic – during *Semana Santa*, when the brotherhood of El Silencio passes through in total silence in the early hours of Good Friday, watched by an equally hushed crowd lining the route. Look out for Sevilla's most famous *pastelería*, La Campana, at no. 1 (the northern end). At no. 65 a wall plaque indicates the site of the Cárcel Real, or royal prison, where Cervantes was incarcerated. A short way down on the left, in c/Jovellanos, lies the small **Capillata de San José**, one of the best examples of full-blown Baroque in the city with, inside, a beautiful gilded *retablo*. Baroque enthusiasts will also want to detour three blocks west of here to take in the massive **Iglesia de la Magdalena**, an eighteenth-century extravaganza containing artworks by Zurbarán and Roldán, which also holds the font where Murillo was baptized. Otherwise, just behind c/Sierpes in the parallel c/Tetuan, a detour will lead you to a wonderful old tiled billboard advertising a 1924 Studebaker car. It's opposite the C&A department store.

Nearby, and to the east of c/Sierpes, the Plaza del Salvador contains the collegiate church of **San Salvador** (Mon–Sat 8.45am–10am & 6.30–9pm; free), built on the site of a ninth-century – and the city's first – Friday mosque. Most of what you see today dates from the seventeenth century, with remnants of the mosque preserved in its tower, formerly the minaret, and its patio, originally the ablutions courtyard. Inside, there's a magnificent Churrigueresque **retablo** as well as a number of sculptures, among them the renowned *Jesús del Pasión* by the great master of wood sculpture, Juan Martínez Montañes, who also embellished the church's exterior and whose bronze monument stands in the plaza outside.

The Barrio Triana

Over the river is the **Triana** barrio, scruffy, lively and not at all touristy. Generally believed to have taken its name from the Roman emperor **Trajan** who was born at nearby Itálica, this was once the heart of the city's gypsy community and, more specifically, home of the great flamenco dynasties of Sevilla. The gypsies lived in extended families in tiny, immaculate communal houses called *corrales* around courtyards glutted with flowers; today only a handful remain intact. Triana is still, however, the starting point for the annual pilgrimage to El Rocío (at the end of May), when myriad painted wagons leave town, drawn by elephantine oxen. And one of the great moments of *Semana Santa* occurs here in the early hours of Good Friday when the candlelit *paso* of the Virgin *Esperanza de Triana* is carried back over the Puente de Triana (Isabel II) to be given a rapturous welcome home by the whole barrio assembled on the other side. Triana has long been a centre of **glazed-tile production**, and you'll see plenty of examples of this fine ceramic work as you stroll around the streets.

A walk around the Barrio Triana

There are any number of ways to explore Triana, taking time to stop off in some of the scores of wonderful *tapas* bars on the way (for details see "Eating, drinking and nightlife"). This particular walk starts out from the Plaza de Cuba, reached by crossing the Puente de San Telmo to the river's western bank. From here head down c/Genova to the Plaza de la Virgen de la Milagrosa. In the centre of this square is a modern statue to **Roderigo de Triana**, a sailor on Columbus's initial voyage who was the first European to set eyes on the New World. In spite of his name, however, more recent research suggests that he hailed not from Triana, but Lepe, in the neighbouring province of Huelva. Determined not to be put off by this academic meddling with their history, the barrio erected the sculpture anyway with the laconic "*Tierra*" ("land") inscribed on its base, the word an unidentified Rodrigo is presumably yelling as he clings to the mast.

Turning right along c/Troya to c/Betis which fronts the river leads you into the **old docklands area** of Triana, before it was tarted up in the earlier part of the last century and planted with trees. To the right, in c/Gonzalo Segovia, was the location of the gunpowder factory which supplied the vessels of the Indies fleet. An enormous explosion here in 1579 not only destroyed half of Triana but also blew the stained-glass windows out of the cathedral across the river.

In Roman times, clay was collected from this riverbank to make the amphorae used to transport cereals, wine, oil and pickled fish to the imperial capital; much of the broken pottery piled up in ancient Rome's towering rubbish dump at Monte Testaccio has now been identified as coming from Triana. The same clay also made the bricks for the Giralda and many more of the city's houses and monuments. Behind the *Río Bravo* restaurant, which has great terrace views, there are **pedalos** and rowing boats for rent should you want to give the river a closer look.

Further along, a left turn at c/Duarte will bring you to Triana's main church of **Santa Ana**, the oldest parish church in Sevilla. Built for Alfonso X in the thirteenth century, it includes many later additions: note, for example, the Mudéjar tower with blocked lobed windows topped by a Renaissance belfry. Should you be able to gain entry – as ever, early evening is your best bet – look out for the fine sixteenth-century **retablo** of the *Virgen de la Rosa* by Alejo Fernández. The church's baptismal font – **Pila de los Gitanos** – is from where, according to tradition, the gifts of flamenco singing and dancing are bestowed on the newborn infants of the barrio. Take c/Pureza (at the church's eastern end) north to no. 53, the **Capilla de los Marineros**, an eighteenth-century chapel now famous as the seat of the *Cofradía de Jesús de las Tres Caídas y Nuestra Señora de la Esperanza* (Brotherhood of Jesus of the Three Falls and Our Lady of Hope), one of the major brotherhoods who march in the *Semana Santa* processions (see p.258). The chapel's Baroque *retablo* incorporates the figure of the Virgin known as the **Esperanza de Triana** to which the barrio is devoted and which is carried triumphantly through the streets of the city by the brotherhood during the same Easter processions.

Continue north, turning left along *calles* Rocío and Flota – streets which still have a few of the typical Triana dwellings – and then right along c/Rodrigo, crossing c/San Jacinto into c/Alfarería, where there are more *corrales*. A left turn a short way along here into c/Antillano Campos brings you to *Bar Anselma* (fronting c/Pages), a great old tiled place where you might be lucky enough to catch some impromptu flamenco. Still heading north along c/Alfarería, take a right along c/Procurador and right again to the sixteenth-century church of **Nuestra Señora de la "O"** at c/Castilla 30, with its splendid tiled tower. The interior, as well as holding more ceramics, contains a seventeenth-century sculpture of **Jesús Nazareno** by Pedro Roldán.

Heading south, with the river now on your left, and just before a twist in the street, a small alley bears the name Callejón de la Inquisición. This was the site of the former Castilla de Triana (or Triana Castle), the original **residence of the Inquisition** until it was forced out by a flood in 1626 or, as Ford colourfully puts it, until "the Guadalquivir, which blushed at the fires and curdled with the bloodshed, almost swept it away as if indignant at the crimes committed on its bank." Almost opposite, *Cervecería Casa Cuesta* is a welcoming old bar with tiled interior serving good *tapas*, and has a restaurant in the back. Continuing around the corner you'll come to the spectacular tiled facade of **Ceramica Santa Ana** at Plaza Callao 12. The city's oldest working ceramics factory, over a century old, this is a good place to buy hand-painted Triana pots and tiles, many depicting traditional geometric Moorish designs. Continuing south, you soon arrive in Plaza Altozano where there are monuments to the great 1920s *flamenco cantante* **Pastora Pavón** and Triana's famous *torero*, **Juan Belmonte**. The latter sculpture by Venancio Blanco nestles against the Puente de Triana – designed by Gustave Eiffel – just beside the celebrated *Kiosko de las Flores Freiduría*, which dishes up some of the best fried fish in town. Before crossing the bridge, which will take you back to the centre, look out over its north side at the **excavations of a Moorish castle** taking place near the river. The city is proceeding with an ambitious plan to put the exposed remains under a reinforced glass cover with a new and expanded market (replacing the old Mercado de Triana) on top.

La Cartuja and the Expo 92 site

Across the river and reached by the Pasarela de la Cartuja (or by buses C1 or C2, from the Prado de San Sebastián bus station or the Puente del Generalisimo), a pedestrian bridge constructed for *Expo 92,* is the fourteenth-century **La Cartuja** (Tues–Sat 10am–9pm, Sun 10am–3pm; 300ptas, free on Tues with EU passport), a former Carthusian monastery.

Founded in 1399 on the site where there had been an apparition of the Virgin in some pottery workshops (*cuevas*) installed here during the Almohad era, the monastery of **Santa María de las Cuevas** was expanded by the Carthusians in the fifteenth and sixteenth centuries with donations from Sevilla's leading families. This was where Columbus lodged on his visits to Sevilla, where he planned his second voyage to the New World, and where for a few years he was buried. The core of the monastery suffered eighteenth-century Baroque additions and was made the headquarters of the notorious Marshal Soult's garrison during the Napoleonic occupation of 1810–12, when the monks were driven out and fled to Portugal. A final indignity was visited on the place when, after Disentailment in 1836, it was purchased by a Liverpudlian, Charles Pickman, and turned into the ceramics factory it remained until 1982. The whole complex – including the towering brick kilns and chimney which can be glimpsed from outside the site, and which are now regarded as industrial history – was restored for *Expo 92* at enormous cost.

The following brief description follows the free plan handed out with your ticket. The visit begins at the **Capilla de Afuera** where the chapel's gilded Baroque *retablo* has lost its central effigy of the *Virgen de las Cuevas*, a carved work in cedar and once the monastery's most venerated image. In the chapels of **Santa Catalina** and **San Bruno** (the founder of the Carthusian order) there are fine Triana tiles, and Felipe II used the latter chapel as his oratory when he visited Sevilla in 1570. Apart from a few surviving architectural fragments, the monastery's church is now bare, but maintains a serene dignity after its use as a workshop in the ceramics factory. Off it, the chapel of Santa Ana contains the **tomb of Christopher Columbus** where the navigator's bones rested for 27 years prior to beginning their travels – the marble slab covering the subterranean vault is left evocatively open (see box, p.224). Also here in wall niches are the remains of some fine polychrome tile panels depicting San Juan Evangelista and San Mateo. The **Sacristía** has the mouldings made by Pedro Roldán where Zurbarán's three masterpieces, *Virgen de los Cartujos*, *San Hugo in the Refectory* and *The Visit of San Bruno to Pope Urban II* (all now in the Museo de Bellas Artes), were originally displayed. Here also are some impressive choir stalls by Valencia and Perea dating from the early eighteenth century.

Also off the church are the elegant **Mudéjar cloister**, the centre of Carthusian community life and where there is more tile work, and the **Capítulo de Monjes** (Chapter House) with the sixteenth-century tombs of the Ribeira family and finely sculpted *retablos* made in Italy. Finally, the **refectory**, with more partially tiled walls and a tiled pulpit, retains a beautiful *artesonado* ceiling which was used by the French for target practice. The visit ends with a chance to view Pickman's enormous bottle-shaped kilns close up en route to the *huerta* (market garden) of the former monastery, which will no doubt become a tranquil oasis once again when the newly planted trees have matured. Along the garden's northwest wall you can see the pumps which once drew water from the river to irrigate the garden, and from a *mirador* in the reconstructed **Casilla de Santa Justa y Rufina** there is a great **view** over the whole complex to the west, the river and city to the east and, to the north, the rather forlorn and weed-festooned site of *Expo 92*.

A separate building within the same complex now houses the **Centro Andaluz de Arte Contemporáneo** (Tues–Sat 10am–9pm, Sun 10am–3pm; 300ptas, free Tues with EU passport), which stages permanent exhibitions of work by modern *andaluz* artists as well as frequent shows by international big names.

Expo 92

The staging of **Expo 92** secured a year of publicity and prosperity for Sevilla during which the sybaritic *sevillanos* started to believe their own hype, billing it as the "event of the century". After the fuss died down and the visitors departed, the city was left with a staggering debt of 60 billion pesetas, financial scandals, endless recriminations, and a dilapidated site which no one knew what to do with. Plans to turn it into a science park came to nothing and the aftermath of this multi-billion peseta extravaganza may outstrip even the 1929 debacle in terms of folly. It has now been decided to split the western side of the complex between the University of Sevilla and a technological/industrial park. Expo's artificial lake on the east side of the site has been revamped as the focus of the **Isla Magica** amusement and theme park (April–Sept daily 11am–11pm; 3400ptas; *Tarde* or evening-only tickets 2300ptas) with rides and attractions (included in ticket price) based on the theme of the sixteenth-century Spanish empire.

The remains of the Expo site lying to the south of La Cartuja are mostly a hotchpotch of dilapidated buildings, including the Navigation Pavilion celebrating Columbus's voyages, the soaring Torre Mirador (which offers the best view in the city) plus gimmicks such as the monorail and the Omnimax giant cine screen. Currently closed to the public after the company which took them over closed down, they may be open to visitors again if the site finds a new buyer. Should you decide to walk back to the city via the Pasarela de la Cartuja footbridge across the river, look out upstream for the spectacular **Puente de la Barqueta**, another hugely extravagant Expo innovation connecting the city to La Cartuja. Designed by renowned architect Santiago Calatrava, its taut suspension cables resemble the strings of an elongated lyre.

The Barrio Macarena

"The **Macarena**, now as it always was, is the abode of ragged poverty, which never could or can for a certainty reckon on one or any meal a day." Things have changed considerably for the better since Ford was here in the middle of the nineteenth century, and since Murillo used the barrio's beggars and urchins as models for his paintings. Northwest of the Centro and enclosed by the best surviving stretch of the city's ancient walls, Macarena's very unfashionability, along with its solid working-class traditions, have helped prevent its wholesale dismemberment at the hands of speculators and builders. The result today is an area full of character, with many cobbled streets, its very own local dialect, and quite a few jewels to show off in the way of **churches** and **convents**. The Macarena's pride was further enhanced when it was decided that the barrio would become the home of the newly autonomous **Andalucian Parliament** in the converted Renaissance hospital of the Cinco Llagas.

A walk around the Barrio Macarena

A good place to start a **tour of the barrio** would be at **Plaza Terceros**, slightly to the northwest of the Casa de Pilatos. Here you'll find the fourteenth-century Mudéjar church of **Santa Catalina** with a tower modelled on the Giralda and topped off with Renaissance embellishments. The interior (access is difficult but try between 6.30–7.30pm) has some interesting Mudéjar features including an elegant panelled ceiling as well as a fine sculpture of Christ by Roldán. Within spitting distance of the church (on the corner of c/Gerona) lies another of Sevilla's great institutions, the bar **El Rinconcillo**, founded in 1670 and believed to be the oldest in the city – just the place for a *fino* and a *tapa*.

Follow c/Sol out of the Plaza Terceros to Plaza San Román where another fourteenth-century Gothic-Mudéjar church, **San Román**, has a fine coffered ceiling. Taking c/Enladrillada along the north side of the church will bring you to the fifteenth-century **Convento de Santa Paula** (Tues–Sun 10.30am–12.30pm & 4.30–6.30pm; donations welcome), renowned for its beautiful belfry and church. The church is entered through an imposing fifteenth-century **Gothic doorway** built with Mudéjar brickwork and decorated with Renaissance *azulejos* by Pedro Millán, with ceramic decoration by Niculoso Pisano. Inside there's a sumptuously gilded *San Juan Evangelista* **retablo** by Alonso Cano with a magnificent central figure of **St John** by Montañes dated 1637. The convent **museum**, crammed with treasures, is entered through a small patio to the left of the church entrance. Guided tours (in Spanish) are led by one of the convent's 48 nuns who has been given a special dispensation to break the order's vow of silence. The first room has a painting of *San Jerónimo* by Ribera, and, almost as beautiful, a view out on to a seventeenth-century patio cloister. In Room 2 there's a fascinating **maquette** made by Torregiano before starting on his full-size masterpiece of *San Jerónimo Penitente*, which is now in the Museo de Bellas Artes. Room 3 holds two outstanding, though damaged, painted **sculptures by Pedro de Mena**, a *Virgin* and an *Ecce Homo*. The damage to both works was caused by visits from unruly schoolchildren who pulled off Christ's fingers and knocked both works to the floor. Immediately before the exit there is also a *Crucifixión* by **Zurbarán**. The hard-working sisters are famous for their *dulces* and *mermaladas* (including a tomato jam), which you can buy from their small shop. Facing the convent's entrance a wall plaque marks a house described in *La Española Inglesa* by Cervantes.

From Santa Paula, head north along Pasaje Mallol to **San Julián**, yet another four-teenth-century church, with a Gothic-Mudéjar portal. Calle Madre Dolores Márquez will then take you the short distance to the **Puerto de Córdoba** (the Córdoba Gate) with its horseshoe arch and the best surviving section of the **city wall**. The Almoravids constructed the wall in the early twelfth century, possibly on Roman foun-dations, and it was further strengthened by the later Almohads as wars against the Christians intensified. This stretch of the fortification – which once spanned twelve gates and 166 towers – owes its survival to the poverty and unfashionability of the bar-rio during the nineteenth century when, elsewhere in the city, it was pulled down to allow expansion.

Follow the wall west until you reach the **Puerta de la Macarena**, the only one of the city's gates to retain its pre-Christian name and reconstructed in the eigh-teenth century. Just beyond it stands the **Macarena Basilica** (daily 9am–1pm & 5–9pm; museum 400ptas) which, despite an apparently Baroque facade, dates from the 1940s. The basilica's importance, however, derives from the revered image of the *Virgen de la Esperanza Macarena* it was constructed to house. Inside the church, to the left, is the solid silver *paso* used to carry the image around the city during the *Semana Santa* processions. To the right is a second *paso* (the brother-hoods normally carry them in pairs), *Jesús de la Sentencia*, depicting Pilate washing his hands with a fine, but now modestly cloaked, **Christ** by the seventeenth-centu-ry sculptor, Felipe Morales. The *retablo* of the main altar is dominated by a seven-teenth-century image of **La Macarena**, as the Virgin is popularly called by this city of fanatical devotees. Depicted in the trauma of the Passion when her son has been condemned, the work is attributed to La Roldana – largely based on the *sevillano* sentiment that only a woman could have portrayed the suffering of a mother with such intensity. La Macarena's elaborate costume is often decorated with five dia-mond and emerald brooches bestowed on her by Joselito el Gallo, a famous *gitano torero* of the early part of the last century, and on which he spent a considerable for-tune. She didn't show him many favours though; he died in the ring in 1920. Despite this mishap, the Virgin is still regarded as the patron of the profession and all *mata-dores* offer prayers to her before stepping out to do business in the Maestranza. The basilica's **treasury museum** features a rather gaudy display of the Virgin's other jewels and regalia.

Over the ring road and beyond a small garden lies the sixteenth-century **Hospital de las Cinco Llagas** (aptly, of the five wounds of Christ), one of the first true hospitals of its time and the largest in Europe. Sited outside the walls because hospitals then were places of pestilence and contagion, the restored building is now the seat of **Andalucía's autonomous government**. (Many *sevillano* wags drily comment that nothing's changed.) The enormous edifice, once capable of holding a thousand beds, is noted for a fine Mannerist **facade** with a Baroque central doorway of white marble. The **interior** – including the hospital's impressive former church, now the debating chamber – is open infrequently for public view (Mon only; guided tours 5pm & 6pm; must be booked in advance ☎95 459 21 00; free).

Crossing back to the Puerta de la Macarena, follow c/San Luís to the church of **San Gil** just behind the Macarena Basilica. Badly damaged in the Civil War, the church nevertheless still has a Mudéjar tower and, inside, a timber Mudéjar ceiling. Continuing south along the same street you'll come to the Gothic-Mudéjar church of **Santa Marina**, set back from the road in a *plazuela*. Founded in the thirteenth century, the oldest feature here must be the **doorway**, dating from around 1300, which has Gothic archivolts, or arch mouldings, with Mudéjar star decoration on the outer band. Another church badly damaged in the Civil War, Santa Marina was in ruins for decades, only spruced up for *Expo 92* when the interior was entirely restored. It is now home to the *Cofradía del Resucitado* (Brotherhood of the Resurrection – see box).

Back on c/San Luis, the eponymous church of **San Luís** (Wed & Thurs 9am–3pm, Fri & Sat 9am–2pm & 5–8pm) is a glorious eighteenth-century structure, recently preserved from the demolition hammer after the city government had said they couldn't afford to save it. Public outcry forced a change of heart and the riot of a **Churrigueresque facade**, topped by glazed-tile domes, has now been restored along with the interior which features a fine fresco by Lucas Valdés on the central dome. San Luís is **floodlit at night**, a spectacular sight.

Further along you'll come to the fourteenth-century **San Marcos** in the plaza of the same name. Another fine Macarena church built on the site of an earlier mosque, it has

---

THE FORGOTTEN BROTHERHOOD

The Macarena church of Santa Marina is home to the **Cofradía del Resucitado** (Brotherhood of the Resurrection), the newest of all the brotherhoods who march in the *Semana Santa* processions. Founded in 1969, it has never been taken to its heart by a citizenry whose apparent lack of interest in this celebration of the Redeemer's return is in marked contrast with the grisly enthusiasm they evidence for each act in the Passion leading up to his death. However, this apathy is the visitor's opportunity for when *El Resucitado* leaves Santa Marina at four-thirty in the early dawn of Easter Sunday you'll get a perfect view of the intricate manoeuvres performed by the *costaleros* (porters) to negotiate the two *pasos* – the *Risen Christ* and the aptly titled *Vírgen de la Aurora* (Virgin of the Dawn) – through the church's doors, which are normally obscured by vast crowds. And as there are no seats lining the atmospheric c/Sierpes, which is almost impossible to get near during the other processions, you will be able to accompany the *pasos*, the band and the masked, candle-bearing *nazarenos* (penitents) in their all-white tunics along here as the dawn breaks – calling in at nearby bars for a *café* and maybe a *churro* or two.

The procession then passes through a sombre Plaza de San Francisco where the normally packed grandstands are eerily empty. Security is also lax at the cathedral, and with a bit of nimble footwork you should be able to follow the *pasos* through the church and past the enormous monstrance inside to emerge in a sunlit Plaza Vírgen de los Reyes beneath the Giralda tower, where a few *sevillanos* have usually gathered to pay their respects. If you wanted to follow *El Resucitado* back to Santa Marina it's a great (if slow) meander until they arrive home at about two in the afternoon.

a Mudéjar tower – note the Giralda-style *sebka* brickwork – and a superb **Gothic-Mudéjar entrance**. Although gutted by fire during the Civil War and since restored, its interior uniquely preserves the original Mudéjar horseshoe arches dividing nave and aisles. At the head of the north aisle there's a seventeeth-century sculpture in painted wood of *San Marcos*, by Juan de Mesa. Cervantes used to climb San Marcos's tower to view the plant-filled and peaceful patio of the convent of **Santa Isabel** just behind the church. You can see why.

Outside the city: Itálica

The Roman ruins and remarkable mosaics of ITÁLICA (Tues–Sat 9am–8pm, Sun 9am–3pm; 250ptas, free with EU passport) lie some 9km to the north of Sevilla, just outside the village of **SANTIPONCE**. They're easily reached by bus; departures, every half-hour, are from the Plaza de Armas bus station (Bay 33) taking the Empresa Casal service to Santiponce, a journey of about twenty minutes, and the bus drops you outside the site office. A free site map from the ticket office will enable identification of the main features.

As you survey the dusty, featureless landscape of the site today it's hard to believe that this was once the third largest city of the Roman world, surpassed only by Alexandria and Rome itself. Itálica was the birthplace of two emperors (Trajan and Hadrian) and was one of the earliest Roman settlements in Spain. Founded in 206 BC by Scipio Africanus after his decisive victory over the Carthaginians at nearby Alcalá del Río, it became a settlement for many of his veterans, who called the place "Itálica" to remind them of home. With a thriving port – now beneath the village of Santiponce – the city rose to considerable military importance in the second and third centuries AD, when it was richly endowed during the reign of Hadrian (117–138). Grand buildings dripped with fine marble brought from Italy, Greece and places as far away as Turkey and Egypt, and the population swelled to half a million. Itálica declined as an urban centre only under the Visigoths, who preferred Sevilla, then known as Hispalis. Eventually the city was deserted by the Moors after the river changed its course, disrupting the surrounding terrain.

In the Middle Ages the ruins were used as a source of stone for Sevilla, and, from the eighteenth century onwards, lack of any regulation allowed enthusiastic amateurs to indulge their treasure-hunting whims and carry away or sell whatever they found. The Duke of Wellington spent some time excavating here during the Peninsular Wars and later the Countess of Lebrija conducted her own "digs" to fill her palace in Sevilla with mosaics and artefacts. Somehow, however, the shell of its enormous **amphitheatre** – the third largest in the Roman world – has survived. It is crumbling perilously, but you can clearly detect the rows of seats for an audience of 40,000, the corridors and the dens for wild beasts.

Beyond, within a rambling and unkempt grid of **streets** and **villas**, about twenty **mosaics** have been uncovered in what was originally the northern, richer sector of the city. Look for the outstanding **Neptune mosaic** in the house of the same name, as well as the colourful bird mosaic in the Casa de los Pájaros depicting 33 different species. Towards the baths, in the Casa del Planetario, there's a fascinating representation of the Roman planetary divinities who, in the Roman calendar, gave their names to the days of the week. Finally, the Hadrianic **baths** on the site's western edge are divided into those for men to the centre and right, and those for women to the left.

Itálica today is at the leading edge of archeological technology: advanced X-ray techniques, ground-penetrating radar and infra-red aerial photography are being used to gauge the scope of the subterranean remains. So far a large stretch of fourth-century wall has been identified along with what is believed to have been a great religious complex constructed by Hadrian and dedicated to the worship of his adoptive father Trajan.

There's also a well-preserved **Roman theatre** and **baths** in the village of Santiponce itself – beneath which lies another sizable chunk of the unexcavated town – a five-minute walk away from the site entrance and signposted from the main road. For a meal before or after your visit, the *Ventorrillo Canario* **restaurant** almost opposite the site entrance does good *platos combinados* and is famous for its charcoal grilled steaks served on wooden slabs with *papas arrugadas* – small baked potatoes in *mojo* spicy sauce.

A little over 1km to the south of Santiponce on the road back to Sevilla lies the former Cistercian **Monasterio Isidoro del Campo**. Founded by the thirteenth-century monarch Guzmán El Bueno, it is a masterpiece of Gothic architecture and its church contains – besides the tombs of Guzmán and his queen – a fine seventeenth-century *retablo* by Montañes. The monastery is currently only viewable by appointment (☎954 55 99 13), although it is hoped that it will soon have a regular *horario* (timetable); the ticket office at Itálica should be able to advise on this.

Eating

Sevilla is tremendously atmospheric in the evening, packed with lively and enjoyable bars and clubs. That the city has never been particularly noted for its **restaurants** may have a lot to do with its strong **tapas** tradition (see "Bars and tapas" p.251). Great though this is, even the most enthusiastic *tapeadores* eventually tire of "plate-pecking" to seek out a place to sit down for a more conventional meal.

Barrio Santa Cruz and Cathedral area

If you want to **eat** well without breaking the bank you'll generally have to steer clear of the restaurants concentrated around the major sights and in the **Barrio Santa Cruz**. However, as you're probably going to be spending quite a bit of your time here, it's worth listing some of the area's more reasonable options: the streets around the **barrio's** northern edge (framed by calles Menéndez Pelayo and Santa María la Blanca), make for a good hunting ground.

La Albahaca, Plaza Santa Cruz 9 (☎95 422 07 14). Charming traditional restaurant housed in a converted mansion where three intimate period rooms hung with paintings provide the ambience. Fairly expensive, but there's a *menú* for 3500ptas. Closed Sun.

Hotel Alfonso XIII, c/San Fernando 2. Sumptuous hotel near the Tobacco Factory, where dining in one of the city's most elegant patios has to be worth a lunchtime splurge. It can also be enjoyed for the price of a beer which comes with a generous ration of *tapas*.

Corral del Agua, Callejón del Agua 6 (☎95 422 07 14). Very good restaurant (owned by the same people who run the *Albahaca*), where you can eat in a lovely, plant-filled patio. Pricey, but well worth it. Closed Sun.

Doña Francisquita, c/Álvarez Quintero 58. Authentic pizzas near the cathedral.

La Judería, c/Cano y Cueto 13, near the Iglesia de Santa María la Blanca (☎95 441 20 52). Popular mid-price restaurant with a tempting *menú* for about 2000ptas. *Revueltos* are a speciality here.

Bodegón Pez Espada, c/Hernando Colón 8, near the cathedral. Bustling place which is the outstanding bargain in this area; excellent for cheap fried seafood.

Café Rayuela, c/Miguel de Mañara 9. Pleasant lunchtime venue which serves *raciones* and salads at outdoor tables in a pedestrianized street behind the Turismo.

The River and Triana

Across the river, **Triana** offers some excellent restaurants. Near the Puente San Telmo, a number of restaurants along c/Salado cater for workers from the Los Remedios business quarter, and along c/Betis close to the water's edge are a number of restaurants with terraces looking out over the city. Around c/García Vinuesa to the west of the cathedral there's an abundance of reasonable *bocadillo* bars and delis for picnic food.

Taberna El Alabardero, c/Zaragoza 20, just west of Plaza Nueva (☎95 456 06 37). Old *casa-pala-cio sevillana* with attractive decor and an upmarket clientele. Pricey – and excellent – restaurant upstairs but cheaper 1600ptas lunchtime *menú* in the patio bar below.

Restaurante Ancora, c/Virgen de las Huertas s/n, just off eastern end of c/Salado. Vibrant Triana fish restaurant with *tapas* bar attached. Closed Mon.

Restaurante Enrique Becerra c/Gamazo 2, east of the bullring (☎95 421 30 49). Mid-priced restaurant with a solid reputation for well-prepared *andaluz* dishes such as *cola de toro* (bull's tail) and *corvina al amontillado* (meagre fish). Closed Sun.

Casablanca, c/Zaragoza 50, east of the Maestranza bullring (☎95 422 46 98). Smart mid-price restaurant noted for its excellent fish dishes – including *mero con frambuesa* (grouper with raspberries) – but also does meat. Has a small *tapas* bar which, they insist, the king once visited incognito to sample their *papas aliñás*.

Horacio, c/Antonia Díaz 9. Moderately priced fish and *tapas* at this pleasant small restaurant near the bullring.

La Mandragora, c/Albuera 11 (☎95 422 01 84). One of Sevilla's two exclusively vegetarian restaurants, just to the north of the Maestranza bullring, across c/Reyes Católicos.

El Puerto, c/Betis, next door to the *Río Grande* (see below). Cut-price *platos combinados* on a terrace overlooking the river; the food may not be up to the *Río Grande*'s standards, but the view most certainly is.

Ox's Restaurante, c/Betis 61. Renowned for its pricey but authentic Basque fish dishes.

Río Grande, c/Betis 70 (☎95 427 39 56). One of the best places for a splurge. Whether you're seated behind panoramic windows or on the terrace, the view across the river to the Torre del Oro and Giralda, illuminated at night, is stunning. There's a 3000ptas lunchtime *menú*.

Mesón Serranito, Antonia Díaz 11, south side of the Plaza de Toros. Twin restaurant of the one mentioned below near El Corte Inglés with similar dishes and – due to location – a line of bulls' heads gazing down from the walls.

La Sopa Boba, c/Bailén 34. Mid-priced, modern and attractive place with a creative approach; specials include *manzana con bacalao y cabrales* (cod with apples and goat's cheese) and *gratinado de setas con alioli de miel* (mushrooms au gratin with garlic and honey); also has a *menú*.

Bodegón Torre del Oro, c/Santander 15, near the Hospital de la Caridad. Cavernous old *sevillano* institution with a popular 1500ptas *menú*. The excellent *tapas* bar specializes in *urta a la roteña* (bream in onion sauce).

Café-Bar Veracruz, opposite the Torre del Oro near the river. This simple roadside place, offering a 1000ptas *menú*, makes a good lunch stop.

Centro, La Macarena and Santa Justa

Many parts of the **Centro** still possess a seedy charm, especially in its southern reaches and the remoter bits of the Barrio **Macarena**. This is the real Sevilla and you'll have no trouble finding low-priced *comidas* in and around streets such as c/San Eloy which runs into Plaza Duque de la Victoria, as well as all the main arteries of La Macarena. The streets around the **Santa Justa** train station form another area with plenty of possibilities, and has some of the most economical places to eat in town.

El Ajo Blanco, c/Alhóndiga 19, east of Plaza Encarnacíon. Friendly little bar-restaurant with South American ambience. *Enchiladas* (tortillas) and a delicious *ajo blanco* (white gazpacho with floating grapes) are the things to try here. Also does South American *tapas*.

Bar Carlos Alberto, c/José Laguillo, highly illuminated and visible as you emerge from Santa Justa station. Lively diner with perhaps the cheapest *menú* in the city at just 600ptas.

Bar Dueñas, c/Dueñas 1, on corner of three streets. Ancient and attractive place to have lunch with delicious home cooking and a *menú* for 850ptas.

Entre dos Hermandades, c/Recaredo 13, near the Casa de Pilatos. Friendly restaurant and bar with perhaps the best value *menú* in town; 750ptas gets you three courses with wine and bread.

Restaurante Los Gallegos, c/Capataz Franco. Friendly Galician restaurant in a tiny alley off c/Martín Villa, serving *gallego* specialities (try their *tarta de Santiago* dessert). A recent refurbishment has pushed up prices, but it's still good value.

Hellas, c/Gonzalo Bilbao 26, one block south of, and in sight of Santa Justa train station. Rare Greek restaurant with well-prepared Balkan dishes at decent prices.

El Pucherito, c/Relator 37, off the north end of the Alameda de Hercules. Cheap, ecological and friendly restaurant serving up a long list of tasty traditional dishes at 300ptas per plate.

Rey Don Pedro, c/Cabeza del Rey Don Pedro 30. Fine looking mansion converted into less grand *tapas* bar and restaurant with a 1350ptas *menú*. Plenty of traditional *andaluz* dishes, but give their "special" *poleás* (polenta) dessert a miss.

Jalea Real, c/Sor Ángela de la Cruz 37 (☎95 421 61 03). Good vegetarian restaurant – with great salads – run by a friendly and enthusiastic *sevillana*. Closed Sun.

Lar Gallego, c/Gonzalo Bilbao, close to the Santa Justa train station. Excellent little mid-priced bar-restaurant serving *platos típicós gallegos* – try the octopus dishes – and equally good *tapas*.

Bar Los Niños del Flor, c/T. Borges 8, round the side of El Corte Inglés department store in the Plaza Duque de la Victoria. Popular good-value bar serves a 900ptas *menú*, but fills up quickly.

Bar Rincón San Eloy, c/San Eloy 24. Fairly ordinary and economical food and a colourful decor replete with *corrida* posters. Locally famed for its *pringá bocadillos* – tasty, if best unspecified, grilled meats. Has a *menú* for 900ptas.

Mesón Serranito, Alfonso XII 9, behind El Corte Inglés. Cosy little restaurant beyond the *tapas* bar out front, with good fish and meat dishes and a 1200ptas *menú*.

San Marco, c/Cuna 6, a few doors away from the Palacio de Lebrija (☎95 421 24 40). In an eighteenth-century mansion, this is one of the more affordable of Sevilla's upmarket restaurants, with an international menu and stylish service. Speciality is *pato con aceitunas* (duck with olives). The owners run similar restaurants at c/Mesón del Moro 6 (Santa Cruz), and c/Betis 68 (Triana).

La Yerbagüena, c/González Cuadrado 35. Hippy-style place cooking superb organic Latin American food at low prices; also with vegetarian options and a *menú*.

Bars and tapas

As the city which claims to have invented **tapas**, Sevilla knocks spots off the competition. There is simply nowhere else in Andalucía – or even Spain – with such a variety of places to indulge this culinary art. "**El tapeo**" means eating "on the go" and *sevillanos* do it on their feet, moving from bar to bar where they stand with a *manzanilla* or beer – leaving the seats to tourists – whilst wolfing back fistfuls of whatever *tapas* take their fancy. Many bars have barrelled sherries from nearby Jerez and Sanlúcar, the perfect accompaniment to the various plates. Locals drink the cold, dry *fino* with their *tapas*, especially *gambas* (prawns). A *tinto de verano* is the local version of *sangría* – wine with lemonade and ice, enjoyed in summer. Finally, don't think that because the servings are small they are always low-priced. Some seafood *tapas* can be pricey, as can the cured *jamón*, and the plates have a tendency to mount up. To avert a nasty shock, confirm prices before ordering. Making your way to some of the recommended bars listed below will lead you into areas where *tapas* outlets tend to congregate, enabling you to make discoveries of your own – an essential part of becoming a *tapeador*.

Barrio Santa Cruz and the Cathedral area

Bar Enrique Becerra, c/Gamazo 2. Outstanding bar and restaurant (see p.250) owned by the Becerra family. House specials: *cazón con patatas* (dogfish), *bocadito de mejillones* (mussels). Closed Sun.

Bodega Belmonte, c/Mateos Gago 24. New place with vibrant ambience and superb *tapas* – try their tasty *croquetas*.

Bodeguita Santa Justa, c/Hernando Colón 1. Prizewinning *tapas* outlet with a long list of mouthwatering possibilities including *pinchito de lomo con dátiles y miel* (pork with dates and honey). Also has a *menú del dia*.

Entrecárceles, c/Manuel Cortina s/n. Tiny century-old bar, on the site of the prison which once housed Cervantes, serving a magnificent, rare (and pricey) *Fino Imperial* sherry by the glass. Specials include *anchoas con queso* (anchovies with cheese) and *melva con pimientos* (tuna fish with peppers).

SEVILLA RESTAURANTS AND TAPAS BARS

RESTAURANTS

El Ajo Blanco	l
Taberna El Alabardero	e
La Albahaca	G
Hotel Alfonso XIII	K
Restaurante Ancora	d
Bar Carlos Alberto	A
Casablanca	a
Corral del Agua	H
Doña Francisquita	N
Bar Dueñas	M
Restaurante Enrique Becerra	X
Lar Gallego	C
Restaurante Los Gallegos	c
Hellas	B
Entre Dos Hermandades	D
Horacio	b
Jalea Real	O
La Judería	F
La Mandragora	i
Bar Modesto	E
Bar Los Niños Del Flor	f
Ox's Restaurante	Z
Bodegón Pez Espada	P
El Pucherito	W
El Puerto	V
Café Rayuela	L
Rey Don Pedro	J
Bar Rincón San Eloy	h
Río Grande	T
San Marco	U
Méson Serranito	Y
Méson Serranito	g
La Sopa Boba	j
Bodegón Torre del Oro	Q
Café-bar Veracruz	R
La Yerbagüena	S

BARS AND TAPAS

La Albariza	50
Bar Alicantina	22
Bar Anselma	55
Bar Antonio Romero	36
El Bacalao	6
Bodega Belmonte	9
Biemmesabe	25
Bar Bistec	43
Bar Enrique Becerra	32
Calle Larga	42
Casa Los Caracoles	16
Taberna Coloniales	12
Bar Emperador Trajano	39
Entrecárceles	26
Colmado Los Escolapios	8
Bar Eslava	49
Bar Europa	17
Bodega Extremeña	13
La Fabrica	53
Bar Giralda	14
Las Golondrinas	54
La Ilustre Victima	35
Jabugo 1	33
Jamón Real	40
Jamón Real II	46
Bar Jerusalem	37
Bar José Luis	31
Bodega de Juan García Aviles	11
Bar Kika	52
Kiosko de las Flores	51
Bar Laredo	27
Hostaría del Laurel	4
Mariscos Emilio (aka Cervecería La Mar)	34
La Moneda	21
Casa Morales	24
Las Nuevas Columnas	30
Casa Paco	1
Patio San Eloy	41
Puerta Grande	38
Bar Quita Pesares	2
El Refugio	18
El Retablo	48
El Rinconcillo	10
El Rincón Gallego	29
Casa Robles	20
Casa Román	5
Bar Casa Ruperto	56
Bodega Santa Cruz	7
Bodeguita Santa Justa	23
El Señorío	28
Mesón Serranito	44
Bodega Siglo XVIII	47
Bar Sol y Sombra	57
Sopa de Ganso	15
Las Teresas	3
Bar de la Torre	45
Café Universal	19

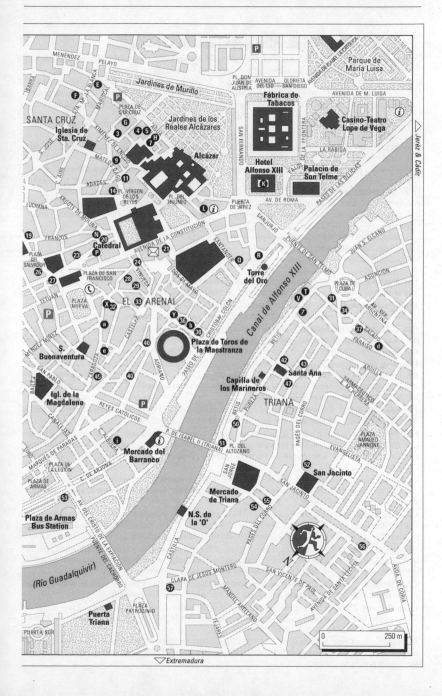

SEVILLA'S TOP TEN TAPAS

The origin of the *tapa* (literally "cover" or "lid") is generally believed to have come from the bartender's generous custom of placing a slice of ham or cheese over the top of a glass of *fino* before serving it to a customer. Many bars in remoter areas still continue this tradition, but most city establishments now charge for the much more elaborate *tapas* provided. Below is a selection of some of the outstanding taste-treats on offer:

Caracoles – snails.

Chanquetes – tiny fish similar to whitebait; dunked in flour, deep fried and eaten whole.

Cola de toro – bull's tail in a winey sauce.

Espinacas con garbanzos – spinach with chick peas.

Frito variado de pescado – all kinds of different fried fish. A *tapa* gets you a piece but most people order the better-value *ración*.

Jamón – slices of cured ham on bread; simple but traditional and delicious.

Pincho moruno – mini meat kebab usually grilled over charcoal.

Puntillitas fritas – tiny baby squid, deep fried.

Revueltos – scrambled egg with a variety of fillings ranging from asparagus to mushrooms and garlic or even all three.

Solomillo al whisky – small pork or beef steak in a Highland sauce probably made with Spanish grog.

Bar Europa, junction c/Alcaicería de Loza & c/Siete Revueltas. Fine old watering hole with excellent *manzanilla* and a variety of *tapas* served on marble-topped tables.

Bodega de Juan García Aviles, c/Mateos Gago 20. Ancient spit-and-sawdust place where the venerable owner serves *manzanilla* and, if pushed, beer. *Tapas* are limited to *jamón* and olives.

Bar Giralda, c/Mateos Gago 1. One of the city's leading bars, in a Moorish bathhouse with arched doorways and lots of *azulejos*, and serving a wide selection of *tapas*. House specials include *calabazín al horno* (baked courgette) and *cazuela Tío Pepe* (stewed meat with *fino*).

Hostaría del Laurel, Plaza de los Venerables 5. Historic and popular bar which is mentioned in nineteenth-century dramatist Zorilla's *Don Juan*. Superb decor with Triana tiles is complemented by hanging *jamónes* and mouthwatering *tapas*. House specials are *riñones al jerez* (kidneys in *fino*) and *zarzuelita de mariscos* (shellfish cocktail).

Jabugo 1, c/Arfe 5. Fans of the famed *jamón iberico* from the Sierra de Aracena have a bar all to themselves. Watch out though – the king of hams doesn't come cheap.

Bar Modesto, c/Cano y Cueto 5. Just about every imaginable *tapa* and, although more a restaurant these days, it still leaves the opposition trailing. House specials include *punta de solomillo* (pork tenderloin), *coquinas* (clams) and *cañaillas* (murex shellfish); and it also serves a good-value 2000ptas *menú*.

La Moneda, c/Almirantazgo 4. Lively haunt owned by a *sanluqueño* (from Sanlúcar de Barrameda), serving up *tapas* and excellent *manzanilla*. Specials include *langostinos* (king prawns) and *calamares rellenos* (stuffed squid).

Casa Morales, c/García de Vinuesa 11. Pleasant old bar, founded in 1850, serving barrelled Valdepeñas wine stored in great butts behind the counter. A few simple *tapas* served, but those in search of a snack tend to hop to the nearby *freiduría El Arenal*, and bring back a fried fish take-away.

El Rincón Gallego, c/Harinas 21. Tiny outpost of Galicia serving only *tapas* (which change daily) from this northwest province. House specials include *pulpo a la feira* (octopus with paprika), *empanada* (Galician pie) and a tasty *torta de Santiago* (almond cake).

Casa Robles, c/Álvarez Quintero 58. Fronting the cathedral, a first rate *tapas* venue, with an equally fine restaurant. House specials are *paella* and *pez espada al ajillo* (swordfish).

Casa Román, Plaza de los Venerables 1. Ancient and renowned *tapas* haunt specializing in *jamón*. *Tapas* at the bar, or has tables outside. House specials: *jamón de Jabugo*, *caña de lomo* (pork stew), and *morcón* (blood sausage). Closed Sun eves.

Bodega Santa Cruz, c/Justino de Neve 2. Close to the Hospital de Venerables, serving up generous *tapas* portions. House specials include *rabo de toro* (stewed bull's tail) and *montaditos* (toasted buns with *jamón* or cheese).

El Señorío, c/Jimios 14, near Plaza Nueva. New bar in traditional *sevillano* style with a wide *tapas* range and a shop section where you can buy the products of the region.

Las Teresas, c/Santa Teresa. L-shaped bar with cured hams hanging above tiled walls lined with photos of *toreros* and bottles of vintage sherry. Also a nice place to relax over breakfast. Specials include *queso viejo* (mature cheese) and *emparedados calientes* (fried sandwiches).

The River and Triana

The streets near the **river** surrounding the Maestranza bullring have always been a fertile breeding ground for *tapas* bars, no doubt to serve the gargantuan appetites of fight fans pouring in from all over the city who love nothing better than to *tapear* whilst debating the finer points of a matador's *faena* or *estocada*. Owing perhaps to its *gitano* traditions, **Triana** is another excellent hunting ground for *tapas*, both on the riverfront along c/Betis, and further into the barrio.

La Albariza, c/Betis 6. Triana bar fitted out like a Jerez *bodega* with butts used as tables. House specials include *tortilla de camarones* (shrimps in batter) and *caña de lomo* (cured pork).

Bar Anselma, c/Pagés del Corro 49. Fine old place with neo-Moorish facade owned by a *dueña* with many Rocío connections (every night at midnight the lights are dimmed and the Rocío hymn is sung). If you're lucky you may just catch some of the best impromptu flamenco in town. Opens after 11pm till dawn. House specials include *caldareta* (lamb stewed in *fino*), and *pisto* (stewed vegetables). Closed Sun.

Bar Antonio Romero, c/Antonia Díaz 19. A real *tapeador*'s bar, with tables to stand at, that is much visited by the Maestranza crowd before and after *corridas*. Specials are *muslo de pato* (duck) and *salmón ahumado con alcaparras* (smoked salmon with capers).

Bar Bistec, c/Pelay y Correa 34. Ancient and hearty Triana hostelry opposite the church of Santa Ana, with outdoor tables in summer. Specials include *cabrillas* (spicy snails), *codorniz en salsa* (quail) and *pan di mi pueblo* (cod *gazpacho*). Closed Wed.

Calle Larga, c/Pureza 72. Some of the best *tapas* in Triana at a neat little bar with a pavement terrace. Try their *flamenquines* (pork croquettes).

La Fabrica, Centro Comercial Plaza de Armas. New bar with the added feature of its own micro-brewery on the premises. Its terrace is popular with a young crowd and they have a variety of *tapas* as well as offerring a *menú*.

Las Golondrinas, Antillano Campos 26. Charming bar on two floors filled with Triana *azulejos* and serving quality *tapas*. Specials include *caballito de jamón* (ham with fried bread), *punta de solomillo* (sirloin steak) and *alcachofas aliñados* (artichokes). Closed Wed.

Bar José Luís, Plaza de Cuba 3. Lively *tapas* haunt with English-pub-style decor on this gateway plaza to Triana. Try their *revuelto de setas* (mushroom scrambled eggs).

Jamón Real, c/López de Arenas 5. On the Maestranza's doorstep, a "foreign" *tapas* bar offering delicacies from Sevilla's neighbouring province, including delicious Extremaduran *jamón serrano*.

Jamón Real II, c/Pastor y Landero 20. Twin *extremeño* establishment to the one mentioned above serving all the same delicacies. House specials are *jamón de Montánchez* (Spain's other top ham), *torta del casar* (delicious Extremaduran ewes'-milk cheese). Closed Mon.

Bar Jerusalem, c/Salado 5. Sevilla's only Jewish eating place is tiny and serves up *tapas* and *bocadillos*.

Kiosko de las Flores, Plaza del Altozano s/n. Old *freiduría*, tucked into the side of the Puente Triana, with views over the river. In season you can eat *raciones* at outdoor tables. *Tapas* served at the bar only. Specials include *coquinas* (clams).

Bar Kika, c/Pagés del Corro 76. Friendly, no-frills workers' bar with its own Triana clientele and a few *tapas*. Try their special, *solomillo* (beef in garlic).

Mariscos Emilio (aka **Cervecería La Mar**), c/Génova 1. Excellent bar specializing in seafood *tapas*. House specials include *almejas* (clams), *ostras* (oysters) and *cañaíllas* (murex shellfish). Equally good Triana offshoots of the same bar are to be found at c/López de Gomara 18 (with a terrace) and c/San Jacinto 39 (corner with c/San Romero).

Puerta Grande, c/Antonia Díaz 33. Within a stone's throw of the bullring, this bar takes its name from the gate through which successful *matadores* get carried shoulder high. Serves great *fino* along with house specials including *acelgas con pasas* (chard with raisins). There's also a stylish restaurant with *ambiente taurino* and a good-value *menú* for 2500ptas.

Bar Casa Ruperto, Avda. de Santa Cecilia 2, off c/San Jacinto. Awarded a bouquet by food writer Penelope Casas; it's worth the hike to get to this modest Triana outpost. Try their *cabrillas* (snails) and *pinchos morunos* (marinated kebabs). Closed Thurs.

Bodega Siglo XVIII, c/Pelay y Correa 32. Next to *Bar Bistec* (see above), this solid Triana establishment has pretty tiles, plenty of *corrida* posters and good *tapas*.

Bar Sol y Sombra, c/Castilla 151. At the northern end of Triana, this is another favourite with bullfight fans as well as an atmospheric bar in its own right. House specials include *cola de toro* (oxtail) *almejas* (clams) and *cazuela Tío Pepe* (stew with *fino*).

Bar de la Torre, c/Zaragoza 10. Excellent *tapas* – specialities are *gambas con bacón* (prawns with bacon) and *cordero con miel* (lamb with honey), although it's maybe best not to bother with the brains in garlic sauce (*sesos en ajilla*). Small diner also has a *menú*.

Centro, Alameda and La Macarena

The **Centro** is the bustling heart of Sevilla in a culinary as well as geographical sense. The zones surrounding four of the barrio's focal landmarks – the Museo de las Bellas Artes, the vibrant artery c/Sierpes, Plaza Alfalfa and the Iglesia de Santa Catalina – provide rewarding hunting grounds for the *tapeador*. The **Alameda de Hercules** used to be the town's red light district but all that has gone, and it's now become a new focus for *tapas* bars and nightlife.

Bodega Extremeña, Plaza de Alfalfa (on the square at the corner of c/Candilejo). Low-key bar specialising in *jamón* from Extremadura.

Bar Alicantina, Plaza del Salvador 2. Famous bar with outdoor tables on a pleasant pedestrianized square, offering excellent, though pricey, seafood *tapas* and a celebrated *ensalada rusa*. House specials are *gambas rebozadas* (prawns fried in breadcrumbs) and *huevas de atún* (tuna roe).

El Bacalao, Plaza Ponce de León 15. This venue is devoted to *bacalao* (cod) in all its manifestations, but they do have other dishes, too. Specials to try are their *tortillas*, *croquetas* and *taquitos* (all cod). Their other branch is near the Casa de Lebrija at the corner of calles Laraña and Cuna and both places have restaurants attached. Closed Sun.

Bienmesabe, c/Macarena 8. Close to the Basilica Macarena and named after the house special: *bienmesabe en adobo* (shark in vinegar). Closed Mon.

Casa Los Caracoles, c/Pérez Galdós, off Plaza Alfalfa. Long-established and friendly bar serving most *tapas*. House specials include *caracoles* (snails), *espinacas con garbanzos* (spinach with chickpeas) and *navajas* (razorshell clams).

Colmado Los Escolapios, Plaza Ponce de León 5. Busy and unusual little place specializing in mouthwatering cheeses as well as fine wines and game. House specials include *cinta de lomo a la salsa de manzana* (pork in apple sauce) and *alcachofas con jamoncítos* (artichokes with *jamón*); also has a terrace.

Bar Emperador Trajano, c/Trajano 10. This tribute to Sevilla's great Roman emperor has lots of brick and beams and offers some outstanding *tapas*; house special is *brocheta emperador* (chicken with plums).

Bar Eslava, c/Eslava 3. Excellent and popular *tapas* place with low prices and great atmosphere. House specials include *cordero con miel* (lamb with honey). Also has restaurant next door.

La Ilustre Victima, c/Dr Letamendi 35. Great *tapas* and drinking bar with original decor, music and house specials such as *couscous* and *shoarmas* (kebabs). Opens till late.

Bar Laredo, c/Sierpes 110. Half-century-old bar that is emblematic of this zone – a good place for a cheese or *tortilla tapa*, or even a coffee.

Mesón Serranito, Alfonso XII 9, behind El Corte Inglés. The bar adjoined to the restaurant (see p.251) is also worth a mention for great-value *tapas*. The house special, *serranito* (*bocadillo* with pork loin and *jamón*) uses the diminutive ironically – it's a meal in itself.

Casa Paco, c/Juzgado 21. Tiny Macarena place near San Julián, serving excellent *tapas*. Try their specials: *gambas* (prawns), *morcón* (blood sausage), and *cigalas* (small crayfish).

Patio San Eloy, c/San Eloy 9. Youthful bar on a busy pedestrianized street, specializing in *salmón ahumado* (smoked salmon) and *montaditos* (titbits on bread).

Bar Quita Pesares, Plaza Jerónimo de Córdoba 3. Lively bar, run by flamenco *cantaor* Peregil, and serving up decent *tapas*. Specials include *caña de lomo* (cured pork). Closed Sun.

El Refugio, c/Huelva 5, close to Plaza del Salvador. Good-value *tapas* bar with a wide variety of goodies, including vegetarian *tapas*.

El Retablo, c/Eslava 3, near the church of San Lorenzo. Friendly, family-run place, serving a great special – *espinacas con garbanzos* (spinach with chickpeas).

El Rinconcillo, c/Gerona 32. Sevilla's oldest bar (founded 1670), just off Plaza Los Terceros, and full of atmosphere. A meeting place for the city's literati, excellent *tapas* with a *coronel* ("colonel"), an ample *copa* of Valdepeñas red. Specials include *espinacos con garbanzos* (spinach with chickpeas) and *pavías de bacalao* (fish fingers). Closed Wed.

Sopa de Ganso, c/Pérez Galdós 8, close to Plaza Alfalfa. Young, lively bar in one of the city's main nightlife zones. House specials are *tagarninas* (a pastie) and *pudín de verduras* (vegetable bake).

Las Nuevas Columnas, c/Arguijo 5, off c/Laraña. Lively establishment with *tapas* served at tables in the small street outside.

Taberna Coloniales, Plaza Cristo de Burgos 19. Typical ancient *sevillano* tavern decorated with photos of the town's bygone days; house special is *salmorejo*. Has a pleasant terrace.

Café Universal, c/Cuesta Rosario, just east of Plaza del Salvador. Quality *tapas* in pleasant surroundings; house special is *patatones* (potatoes with various dips).

Breakfast, coffee bars, cakes and convent dulces

Sevilla's **breakfast bars** bustle with life on working days, and in the early morning rush hour (8–9am) they're usually packed with standing clients munching *pan tostadas* (toast with butter or oil) or a few *churros* (fritters) washed down with coffee or *chocolate*. The best are concentrated around the **centro** and **Macarena**; some to look out for are *Bar Santa Marta*, c/Angostillo 2, in a *plazuela* planted with orange trees next to the church of San Andrés, and the nearby *Café Zafiro*, c/San Eloy 58. A recent arrival is the *Jamaica Coffee Shop*, c/Sagasta 7 just west of Plaza del Salvador, which serves good coffee and a range of teas and confectionery in stylish surroundings. If you're visiting El Corte Inglés, *Cafetería Rioja La Esquina*, just off the Plaza Duque de la Victoria at c/Gran Poder 4, makes a good breakfast or lunch stop, with *platos combinados* listed above the bar. A place that turns out great *churros* – an essential part of the streetwise *sevillano*'s breakfast – is *Esperanza* at c/Feria 108, east of the Alameda de Hércules.

Bars for relaxing later in the day, perhaps with a coffee and a snack, include *Café Picalagartos*, c/Hernando Colón 7 by the cathedral, an attractive split-level place with newpapers to read; *Bulebar*, Alameda de Hércules 83, with good cakes and often theatre in the evening; *Alhucema*, c/Carlos Cañal 20 (off c/Zaragoza), a cute little café in the *planta baja* of an old house; and *Café de la Prensa*, c/Betis 8 in Triana, an expansive laid-back haven with classical music and a pavement terrace.

For the best **cakes** and **pastries** in town, head for the *pastelerías* along c/Sierpes. *La Campana*, at no. 1, is the most celebrated, although many of the others, such as *Ochoa* at no. 45, are just as good. *Horno de San Buenaventura*, at c/García de Vinuesa 10 on the cathedral's doorstep, has two floors where *sevillanos* love to indulge themselves.

Many of Sevilla's *conventos de clausura*, or enclosed orders of nuns, are today a small industry in themselves turning out a spectacular assortment of **dulces**. This took off in a big way in the 1950s, when the Pope gave permission for the struggling convents to earn money to support themselves. Some convents take in laundry, others perform tasks such as bookbinding, but most of them turn out the *dulces* which the city's population consumes with a passion equalled only by its contempt for calorie-counting and cholesterol. So skilled have the nuns become in this trade that today they supply many of the city's leading restaurants with their desserts. Among convents only too willing to lead you into temptation are the Convento de San Leandro, Plaza Ildefonso 1, renowned for its *yemas*, a sugar, syrup and egg-yolk concoction that defies description, or the Convento de Santa Inés, c/Doña María Coronel 5, near the church of San Pedro, whose speciality is *bollitos* (sweet buns) and *tortas almendradas* (almond cakes). The Convento de Santa Clara, c/Santa Clara 40, west of the Alameda de Hércules, has a shop where you can buy *pasteles de cidra* (cider cakes). In the heart of Macarena, Santa Paula – more famous for its nineteen varieties of jams and marmalades – also gets into the *dulces* business with another mouth-watering egg-yolk confection, *tocino de cielo* (translated, very inadequately, as "heavenly lard").

SEMANA SANTA AND THE FERIA DE ABRIL

Sevilla boasts two of the largest festival celebrations in Spain. The first, **Semana Santa** (Holy Week), always spectacular in Andalucía, is here at its peak with extraordinary processions of masked penitents and lavish floats carried bodily by young men. The second, the **Feria de Abril**, is unique to the city – a one-time market festival, long converted to a week-long party of drink, food and flamenco. The *feria* follows hard on the heels of *Semana Santa*. If you have the energy, experience both.

SEMANA SANTA

Semana Santa may be a religious festival, but for most of the week solemnity isn't the keynote – there's lots of carousing and frivolity, and bars are full day and night. In essence, it involves the marching in procession of brotherhoods of the church (*cofradías*) and penitents, followed by *pasos*, elaborate platforms or floats on which sit seventeenth-century images of the Virgin or of Christ depicted in eerily lifelike scenes from the Passion. For weeks beforehand, the city's fifty-plus *cofradías* painstakingly adorn the hundred or so *pasos* (each brotherhood normally carries two; Christ and a Virgin), spending as much as six million pesetas on flowers, costumes, candles, bands and precious stones. The bearers (*costaleros*, from the padded *costal* or bag protecting their shoulders) walk in time to stirring traditional dirges and drumbeats from the bands, which are often punctuated by impromptu street-corner *saetas* – short, fervent, flamenco-style hymns about the Passion and the Virgin's sorrows.

Each procession leaves its district of the city on a different day and time during Holy Week and finally ends up joining the official route at La Campana (off Plaza Duque de la Victoria) to proceed along c/Sierpes, through the cathedral and around the Giralda and the Bishop's Palace. **Good Friday** morning is the climax, when the *pasos* leave the churches at midnight and move through the town for much of the night. The highlights then are the procession of *El Silencio* – the oldest *cofradía* of all, established in 1340 – in total silence, and the arrival at the cathedral of **La Esperanza Macarena**, an image of the patron Virgin of bullfighters, and by extension of Sevilla itself.

The pattern of events changes every day, and while newsstands stock the official programme – *Programa de la Semana Santa* – they quickly sell out. A daily detailed **timetable** is issued with local papers (*El Correo* and *Diario de Sevilla* both do coloured route maps) and is essential if you want to know which processions are where. The ultra-Catholic *ABC* paper has the best background information, and the Turismo's *El Giraldillo* listings magazine prints a brief programme, whilst the banks and bigger hotels tend to produce their own guides. The national *El Mundo* newspaper also puts out an

Nightlife

Sevilla has plenty to offer in the way of **nightlife**, from expensive, touristy flamenco shows to atmospheric, tucked-out-of-the-way drinking holes. Major **concerts**, whether touring international bands or big Spanish acts such as Alejandro Sáenz, Ketama or Enrique Iglesias often take place in one or other of the football stadiums (see "Listings", p.262) but more frequently these days in the Auditorio de La Cartuja across the river. The local press and *El Giraldillo* list possibilities. La Teatral, c/Velasquez 12 near Plaza Duque de la Victoria (☎95 422 82 29), are the official ticket agents for many concerts. Through the summer the Plaza San Francisco (by Plaza Nueva) and other squares host occasional **free concerts**.

Flamenco

Flamenco music and dance is on offer at dozens of places around the city, some of them extremely tacky and over-priced. Finding *flamenco puro*, the real thing, isn't

---

excellent pocket guide with all the routes and *cofradías* tunics listed in colour, and is available from newsstands.

On **Maundy Thursday** women dress in black and it's considered respectful for tourists not to dress in shorts or T-shirts. Triana is a good place to be on this day when, in the early afternoon, **Las Cigarreras** (the *cofradía* attached to the chapel of the new tobacco factory) starts out for the cathedral with much *gitano* enthusiasm, its band playing marches in flamenco rhythm.

To see the climax of all the processions, save that of the Resurrection on **Easter Sunday** (see box, p.247), there's always a crush of spectators outside the cathedral and along c/Sierpes, the most awe-inspiring venue. However, without a seat (the best of which are rented by the hour and booked up weeks in advance) or an invitation to share someone's balcony, viewing spots near the cathedral arc almost impossible to find. As most of the crowd want to see the processions *enter* the cathedral, a good place to stand is at the rear, beneath the Giralda, where they exit into Plaza de la Virgen de los Reyes, but even here it gets chaotic. The best way of all to see the processions is to pick them up on the way from and to their barrios. And here you'll see the true *teatro de la calle* – theatre of the streets.

THE FERIA DE ABRIL

The non-stop, week-long **Feria de Abril** takes place in the second half of the month. For its duration a vast area on the west bank of the river in the barrio of Los Remedios, the *Real de la Feria*, is totally covered in rows of *casetas*, canvas pavilions or tents of varying sizes. Some of these belong to eminent *sevillano* families, some to groups of friends, others to clubs, trade associations or political parties. Each one resounds with flamenco singing and dancing from around 9pm until perhaps 6am or 7am the following morning. Many of the men and virtually all the women wear traditional costume, the latter in an astonishing array of brilliantly coloured, flounced gypsy dresses.

The sheer size of this spectacle makes it extraordinary, and the dancing, with its intense and knowing sexuality, is a revelation. But most infectious of all is the universal spontaneity of enjoyment; after wandering around staring you wind up a part of it, drinking and dancing in one of the "open" *casetas* which have commercial bars. Among these you'll usually find lively *casetas* erected by the anarchist trade union CNT and various leftist groups.

Earlier in the day, from 1pm until 5pm, *sevillana* society **parades** around the fairground in carriages or on horseback. An incredible extravaganza of display and voyeurism, this has subtle but distinct gradations of dress and style; catch it at least once. Each day, too, there are **bullfights** (at around 5.30pm; very expensive tickets in advance from the ring), generally reckoned to be the best of the season.

easy, possibly because – like good blues or improvized modern jazz with which flamenco shares an affinity – its spontaneous nature is almost impossible to timetable. Visitor demand for this romantic Spanish art form has resulted in a form of "theatre flamenco", where you can pay to see two shows a night – a far cry from the time when the *gitanos* sang in their *juergas* or shindigs for as long and as often as the mood took them.

The agents of every flamenco "show" or *tablao* will leap to assure you that you're lucky to have alighted on them before rubbishing the competition. Unless you've heard otherwise, avoid these fixed "shows", many of which are a travesty, even using recorded music. If you're here only for a while, however, and are determined to catch something of the flavour of this wonderful art form, we've listed a few of the better places below – where you'll have a fair chance of hitting upon a performance that you won't forget. Don't forget also that, again like jazz, flamenco is the music of the night and rarely takes off before 11pm.

El Arenal, c/Rodo 7, one block south of the Plaza de Toros (☎95 421 64 92). Most palatable of the pricey "bus 'em in" tourist flamenco spots, and run by a former dancer who sees to it that the spectacle doesn't veer too far into burlesque. Shows at 9.30 and 11.30pm with optional dinner at the earlier show for 3800ptas (on top of the steep 4100ptas entry). If they're not busy, after the first show you can stay to see the second for free.

Las Brujas, c/Gonzalo Bilbao 10, near Santa Justa station. Flamenco bar with a small theatre at the back; entertaining when there's a crowd. Two shows nightly at 10pm & midnight costing a pricey 4100ptas (for one show only), including one drink.

La Carbonería, c/Levíes 18. Excellent bar which often has spontaneous flamenco – Thursday is the best night, but not before 10pm. Once a coal merchant's building (hence the name), this is a large, welcoming place, run by flamenco expert Paco Lira, with its own patio at the back. Tricky to find, it's slightly to the northeast of the church of Santa Cruz, but well worth the effort.

Casa Juan Vila, c/Divina Pastora s/n. A little way down this street, almost opposite the church of Santa Marina in Macarena, you'll find this atmospheric barrio flamenco bar. Authentic performances are staged here most weekend evenings (after 10pm) outside July and Aug.

La Farándula, c/Cruz de la Tinaja 5, off east side of the Alameda de Hércules. This *Asociación Cultural* meets in a tiny and slightly subversive bar where they stage flamenco performances on Wednesdays from 10.30pm onwards; free entry.

Los Gallos, Plaza de Santa Cruz (☎95 421 69 81). Reputable flamenco show using a professional group of singers and dancers who sometimes get close to the real thing although a nagging feeling persists that the performers are going through the motions in an atmosphere not helped by the inevitable flashbulbs and chattering over attempts at *cante jondo*, the emotional and unaccompanied "deep song". Entry is 3500ptas and includes one drink.

Café Lisboa, c/Alhondiga 43, near the church of Santa Catalina. Music bar staging flamenco on Thursday nights; entry is free.

Bar El Mundo, c/Siete Revueltas s/n (off c/Pérez Galdós), just north of the church of El Salvador. Lively, offbeat bar which stages flamenco guitar, song and dance on Tuesdays. Don't turn up before 11pm or, for that matter, on any other day, unless you want to hit their striptease night. 300ptas including one drink.

Bar Quita Pesares, Plaza Jerónimo de Córdoba, near the church of Santa Catalina. Run by the flamenco singer Peregil, this is a chaotic venue where there's often spontaneous music, especially at weekends. Things get lively around midnight and, more importantly, when the owner is on song. If he isn't, he'll sell you a cassette of an occasion when he was – almost as good, but not quite.

Salamandra, c/Torneo 49 (☎95 490 14 30). A venue staging flamenco on Saturday nights after 10pm for about 1200ptas including one drink. This place puts on lots of other events too, including jazz and Latin nights so its worth getting hold of their programme.

El Simpecao, Paseo de la O s/n. Triana flamenco bar with a youthful crowd that often erupts into impromptu flamenco – especially at weekends after 10.30pm. To get there, follow a passage to the river just before the Iglesia de O on c/Castilla, then turn left along the riverbank for 100m.

Café Bar La Sonanta, c/San Jacinto 31, near the church of San Jacinto in Triana. Good local flamenco bar in this atmospheric barrio. Flamenco on Thursdays from 10pm (free).

La Taberna, c/Duarte 3, near the Iglesia de Santa Ana, Triana. Long established bar staging flamenco performances on Fridays from midnight on.

El Tamboril, Plaza de Santa Cruz s/n. Tucked into the northeast corner of the plaza, this is another place with a great *ambiente flamenco* where singers often drop in, guitars are strummed, hands start to clap and the magic takes over.

El Tejar, c/San Jacinto 68, in Triana. Attractive, new little place with exhibitions and flamenco on Friday nights with *actuaciones* from local artists. From 10pm until midnight; free.

Teatro Central, Isla de Cartuja (☎95 446 06 00). Worth checking on this venue in the local press or with the Turismo as they often stage festivals featuring up and coming flamenco talents as well as established performers.

Discos and live music

Earlier on in the evening, Sevilla's **discos** attract a very young crowd; the serious action starts after midnight and often lasts till well beyond dawn. Fashions in music change rapidly – the current rage is *bakalao* (literally "codfish"), furious synthesized techno which generates frenzied gyrating. For **live music** the bars around Plaza Alfalfa and Alameda de Hércules have the best of the action, and you'll find more music bars in c/Tarifa (at the end of c/Sierpes).

Alcaicería, c/Alcaicería s/n, off Plaza del Salvador. Very loud music bar, imaginatively decorated with antiques and old photos.

Antigua, c/Marqués de Paradas 30, near the Puente de Triana. Small gay disco-bar inside an attractive old building with free entry and reasonable drink prices.

Antigüedades, c/Argote de Molina 10. Arty music bar with paintings and sculptures hanging from roof, many the work of the owner.

El Barón Rampante, just off the west side of the Alameda de Hércules. New bar which often puts on live concerts.

Bestiario, Plaza Nueva end of c/Zaragoza. Disco-bar throbbing with manic *bakalao*.

Blue moon, c/J.A. Cavestany s/n, near the Santa Justa train station. Run by affable jazz guitarist Pitito Maqueda, with live jazz at weekends. Closed Aug.

Catedral, c/Cuesta del Rosario, near the Iglesia del Salvador. Upmarket disco with high prices to match.

Fun Club, Alameda de Hércules 86. Popular weekends-only music and dance bar with live bands. Open Thursday to Saturday from 11.30pm.

La Imperdible, Plaza San Antonio de Padua 9, between the Alameda de Hércules and the river. Vibrant café-bar which puts on fringe theatre, live jazz, exhibitions, flamenco on Wednesdays, and much more. Opens at 9pm. Closed on Mondays.

Itaca, c/Amor de Dios 25, south of the Alameda de Hércules. Gay and mixed disco, often featuring live bands and performers.

Jazz Bar Naima, c/Trajano 47, close to the Alameda. Down to earth and cheaper than *Blue Moon* (above) this a popular bar which often stages live gigs.

Maracabú, c/Jesus del Gran Poder 71, near the Alameda de Hercules. Popular disco attracting a slightly older clientele.

La Reja, c/Vargas Campos, just off c/Sierpes. Centre of town dance place which has occasional "American Party Nights".

Sopa de Ganso, c/Pérez Galdós 8. Music bar which serves *tapas* till late, and has a good selection of vegetarian goodies.

El Sur, c/Siete Revueltas, opposite *Bar El Mundo* (see "Flamenco" section). Seventies disco atmosphere with a small dance floor.

Urbano Comix, c/Matahacas, near the Convento de Santa Paula in Macarena. Popular student bar which stays open late and often has live bands.

Drinking

Sevilla is crammed full of bars for *tapas* and *finos* – nearly 3000 of them at the last count. For a long night of drinking, however, leisurely places to sit outside with a river view are the bars near the Plaza de Toros overlooking the Guadalquivir. *El Capote* (beside the Puente de Triana), a lively summer bar which spills over into the surrounding streets, is an interesting new arrival here.

In summer as the town heats up, much of the *movida* (action) switches to the bars along the river's eastern bank to the north of the Puente de Triana (aka Punte del Cachorro) as far as the Puente de la Barqueta. Many of these bars stay only for a season and open up the next under different names and owners. One that has stayed around is *La Barqueta*, just south of the spectacular bridge after which it's named, and here you'll find music, concerts, theatre and shows throughout the summer. A similar *copas terraza* in Triana is *La Otra Orilla*, Paseo de Nuestra Señora de la O, near c/Castilla. Two more possibilities in this vein – both with terraces – are Alfonso and *El Líbano* in the gardens of the Parque de Maria Luisa. *El Paseo*, Paseo Colón 2, near the Puente de Triana, is one of a clutch of gay bars here with terraces facing the river.

An excellent bar which serves as a vibrant cultural centre is the charming tiled *Taberna Anima*, c/Miguel Cid 80, north of the Museo Bellas Artes, frequently staging art and photo shows (try their *vino caliente*). For those with a penchant for Guinness the *Trinity Irish Pub*, c/Madrid s/n, just off Plaza Nueva, is Sevilla's nearest approximation to a Dublin hostelry. The city's most eccentric bar has got to be *Bar Carlochi*, c/Boteros 4, one block north of Plaza Alfafa, which has been converted into a wonderfully kitsch "religious shrine", complete with incense, candles and flying angels. Their sacrilegious "Sangre de Christo" cocktail is a must.

Listings

Airport information ☎95 444 90 00 for airport flight information. For international and domestic flights run by Iberia, contact their office at c/Almirante Lobo 2 (☎95 422 89 01).

American Express Plaza Nueva 7(Mon–Fri 9.30am–1.30pm & 4.30–8pm, Sat 9.30am–1pm; ☎95 421 16 17). Commission-free banknotes and travellers' cheques exchanged.

Banks and currency exchange Numerous places around the centre, specifically on the Avda. de la Constitución and around Plaza Duque de la Victoria, have ATMs/cash machines. Bureaux de change can be found on Plaza Nueva but banks – which no longer charge commission – are a cheaper option. Banking hours are Mon–Fri 8.30am–2pm. American Express (see above) and the department store El Corte Inglés on Plaza Duque de la Victoria (Mon–Sat 10am–9.30pm) offer good exchange rates. Most large hotels change notes.

Bike and scooter rental Sevilla Magica, c/Miguel Mañara 11 (☎ & fax 95 456 38 38), through the arch behind the Turismo, rents bikes by the hour or day (2000ptas per day, 1500ptas per half day); they also run escorted tours. El Ciclismo, Paseo Catalina de Ribera 2, at the north end of the Jardines de Murillo (☎95 456 38 38) is another possibility. Motorbikes and scooters can be rented from Alkimoto, at c/Fernando Tirado 5, slightly south of the Santa Justa train station (☎95 458 49 27); prices start at 3500ptas per day for a 50cc scooter.

Books and newspapers A wide range of books in English (and other languages) is stocked by Vértice, c/San Fernando 33 near the Alcázar, and the Beta chain is also good for guides and maps: central branches include Avda. Constitución 9 & 27 and Plaza de Gavidia 7. There's also a reasonable selection – mainly on Spain – at El Boto, c/Sagasta 5, just west of Plaza El Salvador. El Corte Inglés, Plaza Duque de la Victoria, stocks English titles and international press. A more comprehensive range of international newspapers is stocked by Esteban, c/Alemanes 15, right next to the cathedral. Sevilla's best all-round daily paper is currently *El Diario de Sevilla*, although the older *El Correo* and *Sevilla Información* also sell well; all are good for entertainment listings and local news.

Bullfights Tickets from the Plaza de Toros or (with commission) from a *taquilla* (ticket window) at c/Adriano 36.

Car removal If your car disappears off the street it will most likely have been removed from an illegal parking place. Ring the *Grua* (tow crane) office on ☎95 461 24 11.

Car rental Avis (☎95 453 78 61) and Europcar (☎95 453 39 14) are located at Santa Justa train station. Good local deals are to be had from Atlantic, c/Almirante Lobo 2 (☎95 422 78 93), off the Puerto de Jerez, and Alquile un Coche, Avda. Constitución 15 (☎95 421 65 49).

Consulates Australia, c/Federico Rubio 14 (☎95 422 09 71); Britain, Plaza Nueva 8B (☎95 422 88 75); Canada (in Madrid: ☎91 423 32 50); Ireland, Plaza Santa Cruz 6, Bajo A (☎95 421 63 61); Netherlands, c/Placentines 1 (☎95 422 87 50); USA, Paseo de las Delicias 7 (☎95 423 18 85).

Football Sevilla has two major teams. Sevilla CF – recently back in the top flight after an ignominious spell in Division 2 – play at the Sánchez Pizjuan stadium, Avda. Eduardo Dato s/n (☎95 448 94 00), on the east side of town. Real Betis – the better of the two over recent seasons – play at Estadio Benito Villamarín, Avda. Heliópolis s/n (☎95 461 03 40), in the southern suburbs. Pick up schedules from local or national press; you can usually buy tickets at the ground.

Hospital English-speaking doctors are available at Hospital Universitario Virgen Macarena, c/Dr Marañon s/n (☎95 455 74 00), behind the Andalucía parliament building to the north of the centre. For emergencies, dial ☎061.

Internet *Alfalfa 10*, Plaza de Alfalfa 10 (daily noon–1am; 600ptas per hr; ☎95 421 38 41) is probably the city's most attractive internet café. Other options include *Ciber-Café Undernet* (300ptas per hr; ☎95 499 14 19), which has branches at c/O'Donnell 19 (10am–10pm), near Plaza Duque de la Victoria, and Pages del Corro 182 in Triana.(11am–3am)

Laundry Tintorería Vera, c/Arjona 1 next to the Plaza de Armas bus station, cleans clothes in an hour (Mon–Fri 9.30am–1.30pm & 5–8pm, Sat 10am–1.30pm). Tintorería Roma, c/Castelar 4 east of the bullring (Mon–Fri 9.30am–1.30pm & 5–8.30pm, Sat 10am–2pm), is another place which will wash, dry and fold clothes the same day.

Lost property The *Oficina de Objetos Perdidos*, c/Manuel V. Sagastizabál 3 next to the Prado de San Sebastián bus station (9.30am–1pm; ☎95 442 04 03) deals with lost property.

Maps and hiking 1:50,000, 1:100,000 and 1:200,000 maps can be purchased from Cartolap, Edificio Sevilla, c/San Francisco Javier 9 (☎95 465 66 12), south of Santa Justa train station. A "made to measure map service" will make up maps in the above scales for a defined area; ring Francisco Marquez, c/Las Cruzadas 7, immediately behind the Plaza de España (☎95 442 30 63). Risko, Avda. Kansas City 26, close to Santa Justa train station (☎95 457 08 49), also stock maps and a wide range of outdoor equipment.

Police For emergencies dial ☎092 (local police) or ☎091(national). Central local police stations are at c/Arenal 1 (☎95 459 05 58) and c/Credito 11 (☎95 437 84 96), off the north end of the Alameda de Hércules. You can get any theft documented at the Plaza de la Gavidia station, near Plaza Duque de la Victoria (☎95 428 93 00).

Post office Avda. de la Constitución 32, by the cathedral; also for poste restante (*Lista de Correos*); open Mon–Fri 8.30am–8.30pm, Sat 9.30am–2pm.

Shopping Ceramica Santa Ana, c/San Jorge 31 near the Puente de Triana, has a wide selection of Triana pots and tiles. Flamenco dresses (10,000–20,000ptas each) to sport during the *feria* or simply to take home are available from Bordados Foronda, c/Francos 10, just south of Plaza El Salvador. Cutting-edge women's designer fashions are sold by Purificación García, c/Rioja 13 (off c/Sierpes), while Daniela, c/San Eloy 25, does imaginative women's shoes. Attractive modern porcelain can be seen at Sargadelos, c/Albareda 17 (off Plaza Nueva) and glassware and candles at Mercedes Marquez, c/Méndez Núñez 7, nearby. Casa Damas, c/Sierpes 61, has a wide range of flamenco CDs and books.

Taxis The main central taxi ranks are in Plaza Nueva, the Alameda de Hércules, and the Plaza de Armas and Prado de San Sebastián bus stations. A reliable taxi service is Radio Taxi, ☎95 441 71 18.

Telephones *Locutorio* in c/Sierpes 11 *pasaje* (down a small passage just off the street; Mon–Fri 10am–2pm & 5–8.30pm, Sat 10am–2pm) with phone cabins and phone directories.

East from Sevilla

The direct route east by train or bus along the valley of the Guadalquivir is a flat and largely unexciting journey. There's far more to see following the route just from Sevilla to Córdoba (see p.326), a distance of some 135km, to the south of this, via **Carmona** and **Écija**, both interesting towns. Plenty of buses run along these roads so there's no real need to stay – Carmona in particular is an easy 30km day-trip from Sevilla.

Leaving Sevilla the NIV crosses **La Campiña**, a rich and undulating lowland framed between the Guadalquivir to the north and the hills of Penibetic Cordillera to the south. It's a sparsely populated area, its towns thinly spread and far apart – a legacy of post-*reconquista* days when large landed estates were doled out to the nobility by the crown. The feudal nature of this system of *latifundia* (great estates where the nobles owned not only the towns but also the inhabitants and the serfs on the land) has wrought much bitterness in Andalucía, vividly described in Ronald Fraser's book, *Pueblo*.

Carmona

Sited on a low hill overlooking a fertile plain planted with fields of barley, wheat and sunflowers, **CARMONA** is a small, picturesque town which has burst beyond its ancient walls. Founded by the Carthaginians in the third century BC probably on the site of a Turditani Iberian settlement, they named it *Kar-Hammon* ("City of Baal-Hammon") after their great deity – the origin, via the Roman *Carmo,* of its present name. A major Roman town (from which era it preserves a fascinating subterranean necropolis), it was also an important *taifa* state in Moorish times. Following the *reconquista*, Pedro the Cruel built a palace within its walls, which he used as a "provincial" royal residence; it's now the modern *parador*.

Arrival, information and accommodation

The **bus** from Sevilla will drop you on the Paseo del Estatuto in sight of the Moorish **Puerta de Sevilla**, a grand and ancient fortified gateway to the old town. Located inside the gateway is the **Turismo** (Mon–Sat 10am–6pm, Sun 10am–3pm; ☎95 419 09 55). There is also an interactive **computerized information point** outside the Casa del Cabildo in Plaza de San Fernando (see below) with plenty of useful information on sights and transport times. Arriving by **car** can be a nightmare when traffic is heavy (which is the norm outside siesta time) but a convenient parking place is just to the right of the Puerta de Sevilla, on a patch of waste ground, and parking places become free along the main c/San Pedro after 7pm. This is also the halt for buses from Córdoba and Éjica.

Carmona has a shortage of **places to stay**, especially in the budget category; if you arrive late in the day during high season you'd be advised to grab what you can. The cheaper places lie outside the walls, whilst a clutch of more upmarket options all occupy scenic locations in the old town and have their own restaurants and garages.

Alcázar de la Reina, Plaza de Lasso 2 (☎95 414 01 13, fax 95 414 01 14). The latest, rather bland addition to Carmona's luxury hotel list. ⑧.

Hostal Carmelo, c/San Pedro 15 (☎95 414 05 72). Entered through an antiques emporium, there are some en-suite rooms here, with the lighter, front rooms being the better value ones. ④.

Casa de Carmona, Plaza de Lasso 1 (☎95 419 10 00, fax 95 419 01 89). Stylish transformation of a seventeenth-century *casa-palacio* into a serene hotel where rooms are decorated with genuine antiques and artworks. ⑨.

Pensión Comercio, c/Torre del Oro 56 (☎95 414 00 18). Built into the Puerta de Sevilla gateway, this is a charming small *hostal* with compact en-suite rooms around a pretty patio. The terrace overlooks the gate and a good restaurant offers an economical *menú*. ④.

Parador Nacional, Alcázar Rey Don Pedro (☎95 414 10 10, fax 95 414 17 12) Despite more recent competition at this end of the market, a superb location, patios and swimming pool ensure that this is still by far the nicest place in town. It's worth calling in for a drink at the bar, to enjoy the fabulous views from the terrace. ⑧.

Casa Huespedes El Potro, c/Sevilla 78 (☎95 414 14 65). The cheapest (and most spartan) option in town which has very basic rooms above a restaurant. ②.

Hostal San Pedro, c/San Pedro 3 (☎95 414 16 06). A new arrival, this pleasant budget place offers air-conditioned rooms with bath and TV. ④.

The Town

The fifteenth-century church of **San Pedro** (Tues–Sat 9.30am–2.30pm; 200ptas), near the bus stop, is a good place to start exploring Carmona. With its soaring tower built in imitation of the Giralda and added a century later, San Pedro evokes a feeling of Sevilla – entirely appropriate since the two towns share a similar history, and under the Moors Carmona was often governed by a brother of the Sevillian ruler. Inside, the church has a superb Baroque **sagrario chapel** by Figueroa.

The **old town** – circled by 4km of ancient walls containing substantial Carthaginian, Roman and Moorish elements – is entered by the **Puerta de Sevilla**, an impressive double gateway (tours organised by the Turismo Mon–Sat 10am–6pm, Sun 10am–3pm; 300ptas). Although most of what you see now is of Roman origin there has been a gate of some form here since Iberian times: remains dating back to the late second millennium BC have been found in recent excavations. Through this gate passed the great Vía Augusta on its way from Hispalis (Sevilla) to Corduba (Córdoba). During the Moorish period a fortified *alcázar* was added creating the great bastion that still dominates the town's western flank today.

Inside the walls, narrow streets wind upwards past Mudéjar churches and Renaissance mansions. Follow c/Prim uphill to the **Plaza San Fernando** (or Plaza Mayor), modest in size but overlooked by splendid Moorish-style buildings, including the **Casa del Cabildo** (the old *Ayuntamiento*). A striking Renaissance facade fronts the town's present **Ayuntamiento** (Mon–Fri 8am–3pm) in the square's southeast corner, which is worth a visit to view in its patio a striking geometric-patterned **Roman mosaic** with a head of Medusa. Behind the plaza (reached by taking c/Sacramento and turning right along c/Dominguez de Aposanto) there's a bustling fruit and vegetable market in an elegant porticoed square.

Moving east from the *Ayuntamiento* – along c/El Salvador, then left into c/Barrera and right along c/Ildefonso – you'll reach **Santa María la Mayor** (Tues–Sat 9.30am–2.30pm; 200ptas; Sun & Mon service times 9am–noon & 6–9pm; free), a fine fifteenth-century Gothic church built over the former Almohad Friday (or main) mosque, whose elegant patio it retains, complete with orange trees and horseshoe arches. Like many of Carmona's churches it is capped by a Mudéjar tower, possibly utilizing part of the old minaret. One of the patio's pillars is inscribed with a Visigothic liturgical calendar, said to be the oldest in Spain. The church's high altar has a splendid Renaissance *retablo* which can be illuminated by means of a slot machine and, in the third chapel to the right, a fifteenth-century triptych by Alejandro Fernández. Slightly east of here and housed in the elegant eighteenth-century Casa del Marqués de las Torres is the **Museo de la Ciudad** (daily 10am–2pm & 6.30–9.30pm; closed Tues afternoon; 300ptas) documenting the history of the town with displays of artefacts from the prehistoric, Iberian, Carthaginian, Roman, Moorish and Christian epochs. There is little in the way of bars in this area so the museum's caféteria provides a useful refreshment stop.

Looming above the town's southeastern ridge are the massive ruins of Pedro's **Alcázar**, an Almohad fortress transformed into a lavish residence by the fourteenth-century king – employing the same Mudéjar craftsmen who worked on the Alcázar at Sevilla – but which was destroyed by an earthquake in 1504. It received further architectural attentions from Fernando (after Isabel's death) but later fell into ruin, until it was recently renovated to become a remarkably tasteful *parador*, entered through an imposing Moorish gate. Just west of here along c/Puerta Marchena, the Mudéjar church of **San Felipe** (open service times 6–9pm) is worth a look, if you can gain entry, as it has a fine *artesonado* ceiling inside. Even if you don't get in, an elegant tower and facade are still worth the walk.

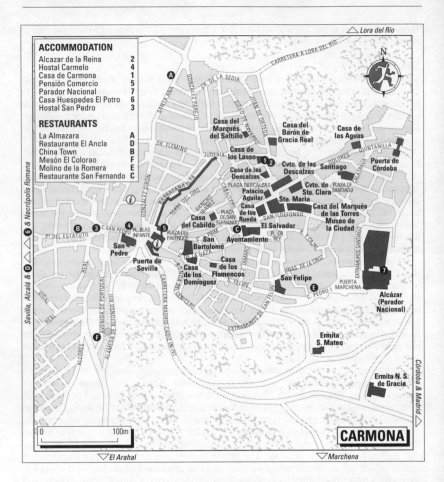

To the northwest, beyond and below Pedro's palace, the town comes to an abrupt and romantic halt at the Roman **Puerta de Córdoba**, a second-century gateway with later Moorish and Renaissance additions, from where the old Córdoba road (now a dirt track) drops down to a vast and fertile plain. Following this ancient route for a few kilometres will lead you to a five-arched **Roman bridge** just visible on the plain below. The nearby church of **Santiago**, at the end of c/Calatrava, is another impressive fourteenth-century Mudéjar building with an elegant brick tower decorated with *azulejos*. Following c/Dolores Quintanilla (and its continuation, c/López) from the Puerta de Córdoba back to the centre, you'll pass by more *palacios* and churches, among them the fifteenth-century **Convento de Santa Clara** (Sat & Sun 10am–1pm), with a *mirador* tower on the left and paintings by Valdés Leal in its church, and beyond the eighteenth-century **Convento de las Descalzas**, the Baroque **Palacio de los Águilar** on the right with a fine facade.

The Roman necropolis

Lying on a low hill outside the walls, as was the Roman custom, Carmona's remarkable **Necrópolis Romana** (guided tours: June–Sept Tues–Sat 9am–2pm; Oct–May Tues–Fri 9am–5pm, Sat & Sun 10am–2pm; 250ptas, free with EU passport) is one of the most important in Spain. To get there, walk out of town from San Pedro and take c/Enmedio, parallel to the main Sevilla road, for about 450m. Here amid the cypress trees, more than nine hundred family tombs dating from the second century BC to the fourth century AD were excavated between 1881 and 1915. Enclosed in subterranean *columbaria* – chambers hewn from the rock – the tombs are often frescoed in the Pompeian style with images of garlands, birds and fruit, and contain a series of niches in which many of the funeral urns remain intact.

Some of the larger tombs, such as the **Tumba del Elefante** (complete with a stone elephant, perhaps symbolic of long life) are enormously elaborate, in preparation for the ceremonies that went with burial and after, when the tomb became a focus for family ritual centred on the dead. Alongside its burial chamber, a bath, pantry kitchen with chimney as well as stone benches and tables for funeral banquets are wonderfully preserved. Most spectacular is the **Tumba de Servilia**, a huge colonnaded temple with vaulted side chambers and separate *columbaria* for the servants of the family. Tours (English spoken) lead you in gratifying detail round this extraordinary site, pointing out the various types of tombs, together with the **cremation pits** where the corpse would have been burned while members of the family (and hired mourners if they were rich) threw clothes and food into the flames for use in the afterlife. The paths between the tombs were also used in Roman times, and it doesn't take a lot of imagination to visualize a slow procession of grieving relatives and mourners preceded by flute players or trumpeters making their way to the family vault.

The site also has a small **museum**, whose finds from the tombs include gravestones, mosaics and vases. Opposite is a partly excavated **amphitheatre**, though as yet you can't see this on the tour.

Eating and drinking

There are plenty of places to eat both in the old and new town and you don't need to spend a fortune to eat well. However, a step up in price will allow you to sample some of the best food in the province. In addition to the places below, all the upmarket hotels have their own **restaurants**, often with a reasonably priced *menú*.

Carmona has its fair share of **tapas bars** too, and the Turismo have made it easy to do a *tapeadores* tour by producing a free *tapas* guide and map, called *Des Tapa Carmona*. In the old town it's worth seeking out *Mingalarío*, c/Salvador 1, near the church of El Salvador, which is a fine old bar with excellent *tapas*. *Bar Goya* c/Prim 42, off the west side of Plaza de San Fernando, *El Tapeo*, almost opposite, and *Bar Plaza*, on the square itself, are also well worth a try.

La Almazara, c/Santa Ana 33. Slightly out of the centre, this excellent, stylish restaurant and *tapas* bar also offers a *menú* for 2000ptas, and is definitely worth the walk.

Restaurante El Ancla, c/Bonifacio IV, about 500m along the Alcala road out of town on the right. Out of the centre but well worth the effort, this is a great fish restaurant; there's also an outstanding *tapas* bar (with a tempting *menú* for 950ptas).

China Town, Paseo del Estatuto 4. Friendly Asian restaurant which makes a change from the usual Spanish standards and has a *menú* for under 700ptas.

Mesón El Colorao, Avda. de Portugal 16. On the tree-lined promenade behind the church of San Pedro and beyond the famous fifteen-spouted fountain, this *cocina andaluza mesón* puts tables outside and has a *menú* for 900ptas. Specials include *revueltos* (scrambled eggs) and *churrascos* (barbecued meat).

Molino de la Romera, c/Pedro s/n, close to the Alcázar. With a great terrace view across the *Campiña* and housed in a former Moorish oil mill, this pleasant restaurant serves up the dishes of the region, a budget *menú* and *dulces* prepared by the nuns of the nearby Convento de Santa Clara.

Parador Nacional, Alcázar Rey Don Pedro (☎95 414 10 10). The restaurant of the *parador* is a model of baronial splendour which can be experienced on a *menú del día* for under 4000ptas; à la carte is another matter. Although competent, the fare is not on a par with the *Fernando* (below).

El Potro, *Casa Huéspedes El Potro*, c/Sevilla 78. The restaurant of the *hostal* is a reliable and cheap place to eat and the food is reasonable for the price.

Restaurante San Fernando, c/Sacramento 3. Carmona's top restaurant is situated in an ancient *casa señorial* and serves fish, game and meat dishes to a high standard; *menú de degustación* for around 4000ptas.

Écija

One of the most distinctive and individual towns of Andalucía, **ÉCIJA** lies almost midway between Sevilla and Córdoba, in a basin of low sandy hills. The town is known, with no hint of exaggeration, as *la sartenilla de Andalucía* (the frying-pan of Andalucía) and once registered an alarming 52°C on the thermometer. In mid-August the only way to avoid this heat is to slink from one tiny shaded plaza to another, putting off sightseeing until late in the day or early evening, or, if you have a burst of energy, to make for the riverbank. It's worth the effort, since Écija has eleven superb, decaying **church towers**, each glistening with brilliantly coloured tiles. The town also has a unique domestic architecture – a flamboyant style of twisted or florid forms, displayed in a number of fine mansions close to the centre.

The Romans knew Écija as *Astigi* (the modern inhabitants are known as *astigitanos*), probably the name of an earlier Iberian settlement. It was an important and prosperous olive-growing town, trading the prized Baetican oil all over the empire during the first and second centuries. In the early Christian era Écija became a bishopric, and in Moorish times (now named *Estadja*) sunk into relative obscurity as part of the Caliphate of Córdoba. Conquered by Fernando III in 1240, it was only in the seventeenth and eighteenth centuries that it staged a recovery, when the prosperity brought by the new *latifundia* – harking back to the great slave-worked Roman estates – encouraged the nobility to build impressive mansions in the town. Following the devastation wrought by the Lisbon earthquake of 1755, Écija's ruined churches were restored at great cost; hence the magnificent collection of the late **Baroque towers** that are the glory of the place today.

The Town

Écija's most important churches and palaces are all within a few minutes' stroll of the delightful arcaded and palm-shaded **Plaza Mayor** (Plaza de España), currently a building site due to the construction of a subterranean car park. At the western end of the plaza the *Ayuntamiento* (9am–1pm & 5–8pm) contains a fine second-century **Roman mosaic** depicting the mythological Dirce being dragged by a bull as a punishment meted out by the two sons of Antiope, Zethus and Amphion – whose mother she had mistreated.

To the west of the Plaza Mayor and just behind the *Ayuntamiento*, the lyrically beautiful tower of **Santa María** – one of the eighteenth-century rebuilds – overlooks the square. Inside, a cloister displays archeological finds from the surrounding area. Behind this church, on c/Castillo, the eighteenth-century **Palacio de Benamejí**, with a fine portal in contrasting tints of marble, has been relieved of its former role as an army barracks in order to house the Turismo (see below) and **Museo Historico Municipal** (Tues–Fri 9.30am–1.30pm & 4.30–6.30pm; Sat & Sun 9am–2pm; free). A visit to the museum also provides an opportunity to view this magnificent mansion and its patio, now declared a national monument. The museum's collection of artefacts illustrate the town's history, stretching from neolithic hunters and gatherers, through the

Romans – there's a particularly good section on Astigi's role in the olive-oil trade – to the Moorish and medieval epochs. South of here the fifteenth-century church of **Santiago** has a Mudéjar side facade and, inside, a fine *retablo* and stunning *Cristo de la Expiration* (crucifixion sculpture) by Roldán.

Backtracking to the quarter northwest of the Plaza Mayor, along c/El Conde behind the *Ayuntamiento*, will bring you to the **Convento de las Teresas**, a fourteenth-century Mudéjar palace which, although not open to the public, has been described as a miniature of the Alcázar in Sevilla with fine Mudéjar stucco work, *azulejos* and doors. Continuing ahead and then right along c/La Marquesa leads you to the church of **Los**

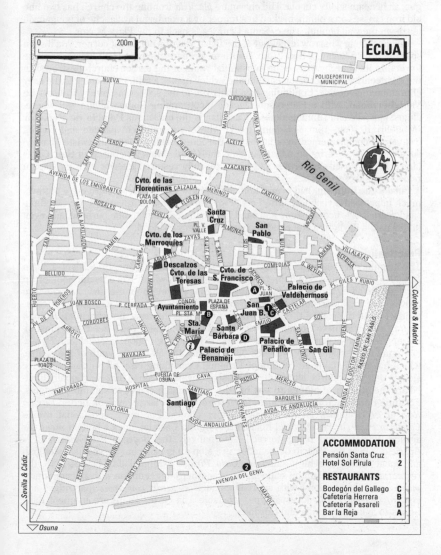

ÉCIJA

ACCOMMODATION

Pensión Santa Cruz	1
Hotel Sol Pirula	2

RESTAURANTS

Bodegón del Gallego	C
Cafetería Herrera	B
Cafetería Pasareli	D
Bar la Reja	A

Descalzos with its ornate Churrigueresque facade and fine woodcarvings within, followed just around the corner on c/Saltaderoto by another exquisite belfry belonging to the **Convento de los Marroquíes**. The nuns here are noted for their *bizcochos marroquíes* (almond cookies) sold through a *turno* and in local shops. Zigzagging north along *calles* Parda and Bizco allows you to take in the **Convento de las Florentinas**, whose church has a beautiful *retablo* by Roldán. Heading east along c/Pardo and then c/Santa Catalina leads to the church of **Santa Cruz**, whose brick tower was once a minaret and carries tenth-century Arabic inscriptions recording the setting up of public fountains. Inside, there are more superb *retablos* and an early Christian sarcophagus, all beneath a lofty cupola. The charming *plazuela* fronting the church has two fine old iron crosses on a plinth, backed in summer by a wonderful avalanche of bougainvillea down the wall behind. The c/Santa Cruz leads back to the Plaza Mayor.

Heading along a narrow street out of the Plaza Mayor's northeast corner, you'll soon spot the ornate belfry of **San Juan Bautista**, perhaps the best of all Écija's Baroque towers. In its churchyard are the substantial ruins of the earlier church destroyed in the eighteenth-century Lisbon earthquake, which makes a rather odd entry to the later church built alongside. Continuing east leads you to the sixteenth-century **Palacio de Valdehermoso**, with a Plateresque facade incorporating Roman pillars and where, almost opposite and running along c/Castellar, is the enormous **Palacio de Peñaflor** (Mon–Fri 10.30am–1pm & 5–8pm; free), where a magnificent painted and curved frontage is complemented by a full-blown Baroque portal topped with twisted barley-sugar columns. Nearby on c/San Antonio the Gothic-Mudéjar church of **San Gil** is famed for its pencil-slim tower, and has a recently restored interior with an elegant *retablo* in its *sagrario*.

Finally, the **bullring**, laid over a Roman amphitheatre on the western edge of town, much impressed a visiting Laurie Lee: "Big, empty, harsh and haunted, for two thousand years this saucer of stone and sand has been dedicated to one purpose, and even in this naked daylight it still exuded a sharp mystery of blood."

Practicalities

The magnificent Palacio de Benamejí houses the **Turismo** (Mon–Fri 9.30am–1.30pm & 4.30–6.30pm; Sat & Sun 9am–2pm; ☎95 590 29 33), which has a useful booklet (in Spanish) detailing the thirty-plus notable buildings throughout the town and can also provide opening hours for the privately owned historic mansions. As regards **accommodation**, to the east of the Plaza Mayor you'll find the basic but charming *Pensión Santa Cruz*, c/Romero Gordillo 8 (☎95 483 02 22; ③), where you'll need your mosquito repellent for a stay in summer. A more luxurious option is *Hotel Sol Pirula*, c/Miguel de Cervantes 50 (☎95 483 03 00, fax 95 483 58 79; ⑤) south of the centre, which has comfortable air-conditioned rooms. Everything else, all on the expensive side, is on the outskirts, along the depressing Sevilla–Cordoba *autovía*. Equally limited are the number of **places to eat** but there is enough choice to suit most budgets. For **tapas and raciones** try *Cafetería Herrera* on the Plaza Mayor or, better, *Bar La Reja* at c/Garcilopez 1, which has a wider choice. For more substantial **meals** *Cafetería Pasareli,* Pasaje V del Rocío, off c/Emilio Castelar, does a budget *menú* for around 1000ptas and has a terrace. Alternatively the *Bodegón del Gallego,* c/A. Aparicio 3, near the Palacio de Peñaflor, is a step up in price but serves fish, shellfish and meat dishes to a high standard. *Casa Pirula*, c/Miguel de Cervantes 48, the restaurant of the hotel of the same name, is another budget option with an economical *menú* for 1100ptas, along with specialities such as *perdiz con arroz* (partridge) and *espárragos trigueros* (wild asparagus) available à la carte. There are frequent daily **buses** to and from Sevilla and Córdoba.

THE NUEVAS POBLACIONES OF CARLOS III

A modern monument on the NIV at **La Carlota** commemorates one of the more curious episodes in Andalucía's history, when thousands of settlers were attracted from Germany, France, Switzerland and the Low Countries to resettle this corner of Andalucía after disastrous **depopulation** due to the eviction of the Jews and Moors and a plague around 1600. The government also believed that increasing the population would reduce banditry in an area through which passed the *camino real* (or royal road) transporting the wealth and bullion of the empire from the port of Cádiz to Sevilla and Madrid. But when **Carlos III** – urged on by a radical administrator named **Pablo de Olavide** – added a Utopian wish that these colonies should be egalitarian settlements untrammelled by rank, privilege or parasitic religious orders, he ran into opposition from the landed class of *señoritos* who were utterly opposed to parting with even the smallest plots of land.

The scheme was eventually set in train nevertheless, and twelve **colonies** were founded, stretching from La Carolina in Jaén to La Luisiana, 160km away near Écija. The foreigners – an application received from Casanova was turned down – soon came, attracted by grants of free land and cattle. But the scheme ran into trouble when many of the Germans were found to be Protestants; this greatly disturbed the Inquisition, who had them expelled. Others, unable to settle in one of the hottest areas of Europe, packed up and left of their own accord. Within two generations most of the foreign colonists had either been assimilated into Spanish stock or had died out. All that remains of this early attempt at social engineering today are place-names on the map, the geometrical layouts of their streets, the odd German, French or Flemish name listed in the phone books – and now the modern **monument** depicting the king and de Olavide bestowing the document of settlement on another colony.

Around Écija: La Carlota

Leaving Écija, the NIV towards Córdoba climbs slightly to give you a clear view back towards the town and its basin-shaped depression, which catches the heat. In early summer this road is flanked by fields of waving sunflowers, not quite so beautiful after the harvest when they are transformed into endless kilometres of stubble.

Some 20km on from Écija – you'll need to leave the *autovía* to see it – the village of **LA CARLOTA**, as its name indicates, was one of twelve colonies set up by Carlos III in the 1760s (see box). It's a tidy, anonymous place today, but its eighteenth-century **Ayuntamiento** on the main road is worth a look, as is the **coaching inn**, the *Real Casa de las Postas*, opposite, dating from the same period.

From Sevilla to Osuna and Estepa

The A92 *autovía* that leaves Sevilla to cut across the Campiña's southern flank bypasses, after 15km, **ALCALÁ DE GUADAIRA**, a large suburb of Sevilla, whose only interesting feature is a twelfth-century **Almohad fortress**, its well-preserved towers and battlements dominating the hilltop above an unkempt park. Some 16km further on, a turn-off right along a minor road provides a possible detour to **Utrera** with a couple of striking churches, and 14km on, **El Palmar de Troya,** the bizarre "new Vatican" of Andalucía's heretic "pope", the self-proclaimed Gregory XVII. The ducal village of **Osuna**, 40km beyond **El Arahal**, and its smaller neighbour **Estepa**, just 20km or so further east again, are architectural delights not to be missed.

Utrera

UTRERA, surrounded by olive groves – said to produce the finest green olives in Spain – is a dull, industrial place which is transformed each June during its famous flamenco festival known as the *Potaje gitano*, held in the park alongside a ruined Moorish fort. Nearby, the fifteenth-century church of **Santiago** has a fine, if worn, Plateresque west doorway. As you enter the town, on its northeastern outskirts there's also the seventeenth-century pilgrimage church of **Nuestra Señora de la Consolación** with a fine *artesonado* ceiling and glittering gold *retablo*. Should you need a room, *Hostal Las Delicias*, c/Abate Marchena 2 (☎95 486 10 12; ②) is basic, clean and central.

El Arahal

It's hard to believe today, but the pleasant agricultural town of **EL ARAHAL**, 20km northeast of Utrera, has long been one of the revolutionary hot spots of the region. Along with Marinaleda (see p.276), it has led the fight against the abuses and injustices of the great landed estates against the *braceros* or day labourers – one of Andalucía's most enduring social problems. The centre is a pleasant place to stop for a drink, and you could also take a look at the fifteenth-century **Hospital de la Caridad** and the Baroque churches of La Victoria and Santa María. For **rooms**, head for *Hostal Alfaro*, c/Madre de Dios 33 (☎95 484 01 59; ③).

Morón de la Frontera

Nine kilometres beyond El Arahal, a turn-off left to the north brings you, after 7km, to **Marchena**, a small town with a fifteenth-century Mudéjar church and some elegant mansions. Taking the southern turn at the same crossroads here allows you to visit **MORÓN DE LA FRONTERA**, 17km to the south. Standing on a hill at the southern edge of the Campiña, this is a charming small town with a couple of impressive churches, as well as a ruined castle. Just below the castle you'll see the Gothic and Renaissance church of **San Miguel**, an impressive pile of honey-coloured stone with a Giralda-style tower and ornate west doorway.

Following the street which descends from here to the Plaza de Ayuntamiento (the town's main road junction) takes you close to (down a street on the left) **San Ignacio**, with another fine Baroque portal. For **accommodation**, *Hostal Pasqual*, Plaza Ayuntamiento 10 almost on the junction (☎95 585 40 40; ②), is a simple place, with a few rooms with bath. *Hostal Morón*, c/Suárez Trasierra 6 near the hospital (☎95 485 23 66; ④), is a more comfortable option, offering rooms with bath and TV.

Osuna

A further 34km along the A92 (or easily reached by the back roads from Morón), little-visited **OSUNA** is one of those small Andalucian towns which are great to explore in the early evening: slow and quietly enjoyable, with elegant streets of tiled, whitewashed houses and some of the finest **Renaissance mansions** in the province.

Another settlement of obscure Iberian origin, Osuna first came to prominence as the Roman *Urso*, and ten bronze tablets from this period recording the town's statutes are preserved in Madrid's Archeological Museum. In Moorish times the town was of little note and it was during the post-*reconquista* period, when it became the seat of the dukes of Osuna with enormous territories, that it was embellished with most of the outstanding buildings that make it so attractive today.

THE MOUNT OF CHRIST THE KING

South of Utrera along the N333 lies one of the strangest sights in the whole of Andalucía. Across the parched, white fields the amazing towers and domes of the **Palmarian Church** of **EL PALMAR DE TROYA** dominate the horizon. The story goes that in 1968 the Virgin appeared on this spot to a *sevillano*, Clemente Domínguez, whose faith, the Palmarian church's literature states, was "wavering at the time". She apparently instructed him that he must deal with the "heresy and progressivism" which were destroying the church of Rome. Miraculous cures, stigmata and numerous conversions were the means chosen by the Virgin to establish her bona fides. Thus convinced, Clemente began his investigations and found that "freemasonry and communism were actually governing the church" and that Pope Paul VI "was kept under drugs, a prisoner within the walls of the Vatican".

Building work soon started at the "Mount of Christ the King" to create Vatican II, while Clemente headed off to Rome to see if he could persuade the erring church back on to the straight and narrow. It proved a hopeless task and upon his return the Roman Pope (and later the "two villains" that succeeded him) was excommunicated and the Holy See of St Peter transferred to Palmar. During the midst of all these adventures General Franco was posthumously canonized as a saint of the new church, and Clemente's "battles with Satan" – more realistically a road accident – left him blinded. This disability has not, however, impeded a racy lifestyle in which he and his bishops are seen touring the bars of Sevilla, often the worse for wear, and he confidently awaits a miraculous recovery of his sight.

It only remained for the leader of the new faith to have himself crowned Pope Gregorio XVII, since when there has hardly been a dull moment at the Mount of Christ the King. After it was attacked by riotous crowds of "true believers" – bussed in by local bishops, claim the Palmarians – walls had to be erected to protect the growing community inside from crimson-faced and belligerent Christians, irate at the frequent ordinations of new priests (from all parts of the globe) and the daily arrival from their convent in Sevilla of the Carmelites of the Holy Face, the new church's order of nuns.

To **visit the complex** (daily 6pm), you'll need to cover all parts of your body – women will be subjected to an obsessive examination by the guards to make sure they are wearing *medias* (tights/pantyhose), without which there is no chance of entry. The impressive building turns out up close to be a hideous mass of concrete and plastered brick. Inside the church the scene is incredible, too, with at least fifty altars – including the main one, often featuring Gregorio himself – simultaneously churning through "Masses", day and night.

The Town

From the elegant **Plaza Mayor** in the heart of the town it's a short walk to most of the major sights and monuments. Before heading off, take a look at the eighteenth-century **Ayuntamiento** here (which now houses the **Turismo**) and, nearby, the seventeenth-century **Convento de la Concepción**. The best of the **mansions** erected by the aristocrats and wealthy landowners are off c/Carrera, running north from the Plaza Mayor, particularly c/San Pedro which intersects it on the left. Here the **Cilla del Cabildo** (at no. 16) has a superb geometric relief round a carving of the Giralda. Further along, the eighteenth-century **Palacio de los Marqueses de Gomera** is another Baroque extravaganza with undulating ornamentation, balcony and solomonic columns beneath the family crest; it has now been converted into a restaurant and hotel (see "Practicalities"). Calle de la Huerta, off the Plaza Mayor, has more interesting buildings, including the **Palacio de los Cepadas** (now the palace of justice) with an elegant patio and staircase, and nearby slightly north, on c/Sevilla, the **Palacio de Puente Hermoso**.

Two huge stone buildings stand on the hilltop overlooking the town: the **old university**, founded in 1548 by one of the predecessors of the dukes of Osuna (later suppressed by the reactionary Fernando VII in 1820), and the lavish sixteenth-century **Colegiata**, which should be visited first. This latter (guided tours Mon–Sat 10am–1.30pm & 4–7pm; Sun 10am–1.30pm; 300ptas) is a fine Renaissance building with a damaged Plateresque west doorway caused, so the story goes, by French soldiers in the War of Independence who used it for target practice. Inside, an eccentric female guide (who often lights up as she conducts you around the church) will point out a sumptuous gilded *retablo* and the remarkable seventeenth-century *Expiración de Cristo* (crucifixion) by Ribera – one of the artist's greatest works. Also in the church some exquisite sculptures include a superb *Crucified Christ* by Juan de Mesa, from the same period. More Riberas are to be seen in the **sacristía**, which now holds the church's impressive art collection. His *San Jerónimo*, *San Pedro* and a moving *Martirio de San Bartolomé* are all of the best quality. The high-point of any visit is the descent to the subterranean depths to view the gloomy **pantheon and chapel of the dukes of Osuna**, where these descendants of the kings of Leon and once "Lords of Andalucía" are buried in niches in the walls. Some of the Renaissance ornamentation is extremely fine, especially the polychromed wooden *Santo Entierro* (burial of Christ), as well as panels from the Flemish school and a fine relief of *San Jerónimo*. The tour ends with the guide demonstrating her skills (often at length) on an antique portable **sixteenth-century organ** – one of few to survive from the period.

Downhill, opposite the entrance of the Colegiata, is the Baroque convent of **La Encarnación** (same hours; 300ptas), founded in the seventeenth century by a Duchess of Osuna, and where the highlight of the nun-led guided tour is a fine plinth of eighteenth-century Sevillian *azulejos* (from Triana) round its cloister and gallery depicting curiously secular scenes. After filling up on the tasty *convent dulces* sold here, you could take a walk north, passing the former convent church of **La Merced** with its stupendously carved late **Baroque tower**, and the ruins of Las Canteras, once a hermitage, on c/Camino de las Cuevas. Further along here you'll find the **excavations of Roman Ursa**, including a necropolis with tombs quarried from the sandstone, as well as the vague remains of a theatre and fort. Otherwise, the more direct descent to the town takes you past the Torre del Agua, a twelfth-century Almohad tower which houses a small **archeological museum** (daily 11am–1.30pm & 5–7pm; 250ptas) containing finds – and unfortunately many copies of the best items, the originals of which are in Madrid – discovered in the town and the nearby tombs.

Other churches around the town worth seeking out are the sixteenth-century **Santo Domingo** (at the northern end of c/Carrera), another fine Renaissance church; **Nuestra Señora de la Victoria** nearby, with an impressive Baroque *retablo* by José Mora; and, to the west, the **Convento del Carmen** on the street of the same name, whose church has a beautiful sixteenth-century *retablo* in carved wood.

Practicalities

Osuna's **Turismo**, in the *Ayuntamiento* on the Plaza Mayor (Mon–Sat 9.30am–2.30pm & 5–7.30pm; Sun 10am–2.30pm; ☎95 582 14 00), can provide a map which is useful for locating the town's monuments; a town map is also displayed on a board in the square. **Accommodation** is plentiful, but can be pricey for what you get. The best budget option is *Hostal Cinco Puertas*, c/Carrera 79 (☎ & fax 95 481 12 43; ③), at the northern end of the main street which offers some rooms with bath; opposite, the old coaching inn, *Hostal Caballo Blanco*, c/Granada 1 (☎95 481 01 84; ④), has better rooms, all en-suite. Both places serve decent meals in their restaurants. *Hostal Esmeralda*, c/Tesorero 7 (☎95 582 11 78; ③), through the double arch off the Plaza Mayor, then straight ahead turning right and left, is another budget option for rooms with bath.

Slightly further away from the centre and south-west of the Plaza Mayor, *Hostal Granadino*, Plaza Salitre 1 (☎95 481 00 00; ④), has rooms with bath above a restaurant.

For **food and drink** a good place to start is the marvellous **Casino** on the Plaza Mayor with 1920s Mudéjar-style decor and a grandly bizarre ceiling; open to all visitors, it is an excellent place for a drink while lounging in the chairs overlooking the square. One of the most pleasant restaurants in town is the *Mesón del Duque*, Plaza de la Duquesa 2, with meals and *tapas* served on its attractive, jasmine-fringed terrace; it's above the same square, and close to the Torre del Agua archeological museum. The most grandiose restaurant frontage in Andalucía, however, has to be that of *La Casa del Marqués*, c/San Pedro 20, an ancient *casa señorial*, transformed into a smart restaurant, and soon to be a hotel also. Sadly, the overpriced food isn't up to the standard of the architecture and to see a stunning patio (complete with chapel) you'd be better off calling in for a drink at the bar. The town's best food is served at *Doña Guadalupe*, Plaza Guadalupe 6, off c/Quijada, which is off c/Carrera, north of the Plaza Mayor. It has a tempting *menú* for around 1500ptas and *rabo de toro* (stewed bull's tail) is one of a number of specialities; its only drawback is the lack of a terrace on sultry summer evenings. Osuna's premier **tapas bar**, *Casa Curro*, lies southwest of the Plaza Mayor at Plaza Salitre 5, and is worth finding. *Bar Canaletas* on c/Carrera just beyond the *Hostal Cinco Puertas* (see above), also serves *tapas* and *raciones* and has a reasonably priced *menú*.

Estepa

Another delightful Baroque town, **ESTEPA**, 24km east of Osuna, resembles a miniature version of its larger neighbour. Originally a Carthaginian settlement, it took the side of the North African state during the Punic Wars with Rome, and when the victorious Romans finally took the city in 208 BC they found that the citizens had burned their possessions and killed themselves rather than surrender. Repopulated, it eventually became the Roman *Ostipo* and, later, the Moorish *Istabba*.

Close by the central Plaza del Carmen, the eighteenth-century **Iglesia del Carmen** has an exuberant Baroque facade in black and white stone and a stunningly ornate interior, recently restored. Above, in the *ciudad alta*, the **Iglesia de Santa María** is another impressive church, dating from the twelfth century, with a fine *retablo*. Alongside this church on the same hill, the sixteenth-century **Iglesia de la Santa María de la Asunción**, one of Estepa's oldest churches, is currently undergoing restoration as part of a youth employment venture. The Gothic interior has decaying treasures, many rescued from other churches and monasteries. Look out for a fine sculpture of *San Juan Evangelista* by Martínez Montañes. If you can get up to the roof there are great **views** over the town and beyond. Lower down in the *ciudad baja*, you'll notice the elegant **Torre de la Victoria** – all that remains of the convent of the same name. Taking c/Mesones (and its continuation, c/Castillejos) from the Plaza del Carmen back through the town, you'll pass another fine church, the **Iglesia de la Asunción** known locally as "Estepa's Sistine chapel" due to a splendid painted ceiling depicting scenes from the life of the Virgin. The church was originally the chapel of one of Estepa's best mansions, the **Palacio de los Marqueses de Cerverales** next door, a superb eighteenth-century palace with barley-sugar columns supporting its balcony. One block south, c/Nueva has some of the town's oldest mansions; among them nos. 14 and 16 are good examples, and at no. 2 take a look at a pair of ancient Visigothic columns built into the doorway of this much later house, a practice all too common in modern Spain where there is a thriving, no questions-asked, black market in these antiquities. Finally, at the western end of c/Mesones the sixteenth-century **Iglesia de San Sebastián** has a sculpture of *San Juan Bautista* by Martínez Montañes.

Estepa's small **Turismo**, Plaza del Carmen 1 (☎95 591 27 17), can supply a bedsheet-sized map of the town. **Rooms** are not plentiful but what there is you'll find along the main Avda. de Andalucía. The best deal is *Hostal Balcón de Andalucía* at no. 11 (☎ & fax 95 591 26 80; ④), where comfortable air-conditioned rooms come with TV and there's an excellent pool at the back. **Places to eat** are also along the Avda. de Andalucía, where *Hostal Balcón* (see above), *Hostal Rico* at no. 98 and *La Ponderosa* at no. 105 all serve decent meals and *menús*. For late-evening **drinks** many of the locals visit *El Jardín*, a charming bar in a garden in c/Los Vitos near the Plaza del Carmen in the old town.

Marinaleda

Sited 14km north of Estepa, the unassuming agricultural village of **MARINALEDA** seems to have inherited the do-or-die qualities of the early inhabitants of Estepa who resisted the might of Rome. Along with El Arahal to the east, "Red" Marinaleda has become the standard-bearer in the struggle of the *braceros*, or day labourers, against their exploitation by the great landowners. The leader in this struggle is Marinaleda's mayor of twenty years standing, Sánchez Gordillo, the village schoolteacher and – like the rest of the village almost to a man and woman – a committed communist. He came to prominence as the organiser of a "hunger strike against hunger", but since then has moved on to taking over large estates in the area, by force if necessary. A few years back he occupied a nearby estate belonging to of one of Andalucía's major landowners, the Duke of Infantado. The scene was vividly described by Michael Jacobs in his book *Andalusia* when he visited the "occupation".

> *Attached to the post at the entrance of the estate were the words "ESTA TIERRA ES NUESTRA MARINALEDA" (This land is our Marinaleda). On the long drive up to the cortijo I passed a group of villagers carrying hoes and rakes, the women dressed in black. They could have been straight out of a communist poster of the 1930s and this impression was reinforced by the political badges they were all wearing. In the middle of all this prowled the leonine and instantly recognisable figure of Sánchez Gordillo wearing a Tolstoyan suit and a red sash. He addressed me in a slow solemn voice with no trace of a smile. I could not help feeling, confronted by such a manner and appearance, that I was in the presence of one of the Messianic figures who toured the Andalusian countryside in the nineteenth century. He talked of the inadequacy of the present agrarian reforms, of the great extent of the Duke of Infantado's properties and of how the land in Andalusia continued to be in the hands of the very few.*

The romantic *cortijos* to be seen dotted across the Andalucian landscape – brilliant white pantiled farm buildings surrounded by walls and often shaded by a cluster of elegant palms – have for generations been the focus of the misery of the landless poor, for these are the homes of the landowners, or more often their overseers on whom the day labourers are dependent for what little seasonal work they can get. From the *Casa de Cultura* at Marinaleda – in reality a workers' club, on the main Plaza de la Libertad – the *Sindicato de Obreros del Campo*, led by Gordillo, continues to fight for change. The small **Ayuntamiento** – just off the main square and decorated with a mural owing much to Picasso's *Guernica* that denounces militarism and conscription – is a remarkable sight, and inside, pictures of Che Guevara, Marx and other left-wing icons line the walls, contrasting with the laid-back and unsanctimonious attitude of Gordillo and his officials. Despite the ever-present blight of chronic unemployment Marinaleda marches on and now has its own low-power TV station and communally owned crèche, and is constructing an impressive new town hall, a *Casa de Cultura* complete with theatre, and a secondary school.

One of the village's most established and successful customs is *Domingos Rojos* (Red Sundays) a number of days throughout the year when the council requests that the population – young and old – turn out to do voluntary work (street cleaning, painting, gardening, etc) in public places. Crime is so low that the village has only one police officer, in comparison with the norm of five or six, for its 2500 population. And, despite an ambivalent attitude towards Marinaleda by the previous socialist government and complete indifference from the current rightist *Partido Popular* administration, significant tracts of land have been transferred into the ownership of the village cooperative which now controls over 865 acres of land. Banners hanging from house balconies proclaim opposition to nuclear testing and landowner exploitation, and each street sign bears the legend "A Utopia building peace". In harmony with these sentiments, in the old *Casa de Cultura*'s lively **bar** you'll be served up the cheapest *tapas*, beer and *fino* in the whole of Andalucía. The nearest **accommodation** is in Estepa (see above), some 14km away.

West from Sevilla

With your own transport available, the fastest – but dullest – way from Sevilla west to Huelva is via the A49 *autovía*. More tranquil and interesting is the A472 which cuts through the area to the west of the city called El Aljarafe by the Moors (the "high lands," actually rather flat), planted with olives, vines and orange trees, and arrives after 8km at **CASTILLEJA LA CUESTA**. This village is famous as the place where Hernan Cortés, explorer and conqueror of Mexico, died, but is probably more familiar to most Andalucians, however, as the centre for some of the best pastries in the region – Castilleja's delicious cinnamon-coated *tortas* are exported all over Spain.

Ten kilometres beyond Castilleja, between Umbrete and Sanlúcar La Mayor, is *Restaurante Las Tejas* where at weekends after they've eaten (and drunk) a fair deal, *sevillanos* try out their skill in a bullring behind. Although the *toros* are only calves, some of them can still prove too much for most of these amateur *toreros*. **SANLÚCAR LA MAYOR** itself is a sturdy, rather unexciting place but does nevertheless retain parts of its Roman and Moorish walls and has three Mudéjar churches, the most notable of which is the thirteenth-century **Santa María** – in origin an Almohad mosque – with horseshoe arches, an *artesonado* ceiling and the former mosque's minaret, now the church tower. The olive-planted valley of the Guadiamar comes next, and 14km further on there's a turn-off to the ancient Moorish village of **CARRIÓN DE LOS CÉSPEDES**, also a stop on the train line from Sevilla to Huelva. Once a fief of the Knights of Calatrava, a twelfth-century military order formed to defend the southern frontier of Castile against the Moors, this is still an atmospheric place, retaining many of its Moorish narrow streets. Further west still on the A472, the village of **Manzanilla** looms into view beneath its church tower followed, 20km beyond Carrión, by the wine-producing town of **LA PALMA DEL CONDADO** off the road to the left. It's highly probable that this terrain, an area first planted with vines by the Greeks, produced the local wine taken on the voyage to the New World by Columbus when he sailed from nearby Palos. The wine produced here today is the Condado de Huelva, which hardly ranks with Spain's top-drawer vintages, but the dry whites are an excellent partner for seafood. With its impressive eighteenth-century Baroque church of **San Juan Bautista** towering over a palm-fringed central plaza, this slow-moving, white-walled country town makes a good stopping point for a drink of the local brew at one of the central bars. If you're tempted to **stay**, the *Hostal La Viña* (☎959 40 02 73; ④), on the junction of the A472, with a pool, is better value than *Hostal Morenos* nearer the centre. Over the road from *La Viña* the *venta* is a good and economical place **to eat**.

Heading south for 6km, **BOLLULLOS DEL CONDADO** is a pleasant little town filled with *bodegas* and *ventas*. As well as trying out the local wine, make sure to see some splendid eighteenth- and nineteenth-century **casas señoriales** around the Plaza Mayor (Plaza del Sagrado Corazón) and along c/Cervantes, just off it. On the same square stands the eighteenth-century **church of Santiago** with a snow-white colonial-style facade and wonderful tower, and an **Ayuntamiento** of the same period with an elegant red stone portal. A good **place to eat** is *Restaurante El Reñiero*, c/Cruz de Monteñina 6 (ask for a traffic junction named "La Piña"), which does excellent local dishes and has a *menú* and terrace. *Mesón Rociero* opposite is also good. The A483 continues south from here to El Rocío and the Coto de Doñana (see p.291).

Niebla and around

Twelve kilometres west from La Palma along the A472, the salmon-pink ancient walls and towers of **NIEBLA** make a spectacular sight. The approach is wonderful, almost a medieval fairytale come true, for this is a real walled town and looks the part. The **Roman bridge** you cross to reach it – probably built in the second century during the reign of Trajan – is remarkably well preserved and carried traffic for two thousand years until it was blown up during the Civil War. It has since been meticulously restored.

Little is known about Phoenician settlement here or the possible Iberian village of the Turditanian tribe which may have preceded it. However, coins found dating from the Roman period gave the town's name as *Ilipla,* which is probably derived from the Iberian name. Described by the Roman writer Pliny as a fortified city of strategic importance, it was a crucial link in the massive Roman mining operations carried out upriver at the Río Tinto mines. The metals – mostly silver – were moved down the river by barge and then transferred to galleys here for the voyage to Rome and other parts of the empire. A bishopric under the Visigoths, after the Moorish conquest it became successively part of the Almoravid and then Almohad domains until, as an independent *taifa* state it experienced its greatest period of prosperity during the twelfth century, trading in saffron and raisins. After falling to the Christian forces under Alfonso X in 1262, Niebla was passed around as a fief of various rulers, until in 1369 it came into the hands of the Guzmán dynasty, following which it entered a long period of decline.

The Town

Once inside the two-kilometre long encirclement of the walls, Niebla's tidy streets of whitewashed houses and small squares are a delight to explore. The Puerta del Socorro leads from the Sevilla–Huelva road to the Plaza Santa María in the heart of the town, dominated by the church of **Santa María de Granada**. The key is available from Sr. Juan de Dios, the genial custodian of the *Casa de Cultura* next to the church (the former fifteenth-century Hospital de Nuestra Señora de los Ángeles; bar hours 8am–3pm & 5.30pm–midnight). Entered through a splendid Mozarabic eleven-lobed portal, the original tenth-century church is believed to have been constructed over a Visigothic cathedral, and was used by Christians during the Almoravid period. It was converted into a mosque by the Almohads in the thirteenth century: the *mihrab* now to be seen in the side wall, as well as the elegant tower – its minaret – date from this period. The pillars in the second-floor windows of the tower, incidentally, are believed to have come from the original Visigothic church. Among the artefacts dotted around the austere and much restored Mudéjar-Gothic interior are a couple of Roman altars and the remarkable, stone-carved **Silla Episcopal**, the throne of the Visigothic bishops. Outside the entrance, a **patio** is dotted with remnants of the building's chequered history – various Visigothic, Christian and Moorish stones and pillars.

Of the ruined church of **San Martín** near the town's main gate and sliced through by a road, only the apse, bell tower and a chapel survive. It was built in the fifteenth century on the site of a former synagogue donated in more tolerant times by Alfonso X as a concession to the Jews of Niebla, and before the Inquisition began its grisly work. The locked chapel contains a fifteenth-century sculpture of Christ being scourged.

The town's **four gates** are also worth seeking out, each with its Moorish horseshoe arch and features, as is the **Castillo de Guzmán**, in origin the Moorish Alcázar, but much added to by Enrique de Guzmán in the fifteenth century. It later fell into decay and was ruined after Marshal Soult used it as a barracks for French troops during the War of Independence. Today it stages concerts and theatrical productions over the summer months as part of Niebla's annual festival of theatre and dance.

Practicalities

Niebla's **train station**, on the Sevilla–Huelva line, is served by two trains daily in each direction. You can pick up a map and visitor information at the town's small **Turismo** (Mon–Fri 9am–2pm & 4–6pm, Sat 11am–2pm & 4–6pm; ☎959 36 20 80) inside the Castillo. There's a **fonda**, *Los Hidalgos*, c/Moro 3 (☎959 36 20 80; ②), with some en-suite rooms, outside the walls near the Sevilla–Huelva **bus stop**, and nearby you'll find bars and cafés and, surprisingly, a couple of **disco bars**. For **tapas**, head for the bars around the Plaza Santa María; *Café-Bar Doylo* is recommended. Decent **restaurants** include *Brasería Las Almenas* (specialising in *carnes de la sierra*) at c/Padre Marchena 2, whilst the bigger *Restaurante Ramos*, Avda. de Andalucía 1, also has a *tapas* bar.

Dolmen de Soto

Five kilometres beyond Niebla the road crosses the A49 *autovía* and shortly after this a sign on the right indicates a sealed road leading to the prehistoric **Dolmen de Soto** (Mon–Fri 9am–2pm, Sat 10am–2pm). Follow the track for about 1km – in one section it fords a stream and can be tricky after heavy rain – until it winds around to a parking area with a curious canopy. To the south of this you'll see a mound (containing the dolmen); the gate should be open. Discovered in 1923, it dates back to about 2000 BC and consists of a long passage leading to a burial chamber topped by a headstone estimated to weigh some 21 tonnes. Parts of the walls are engraved with schematic symbols. Seven kilometres further towards Huelva a turn-off on the left leads to Moguer, one town on the Columbus trail (see p.286).

Huelva

Large, sprawling and industrialized, the city of **HUELVA** struggles to present an attractive face to its visitors. Still, once you've got past the messy suburbs with their fish canneries, cement factories and petrochemical refineries, the tidy city centre – perched on a peninsula between the confluence of the Odiel and Tinto river estuaries – comes as a pleasant surprise.

Huelva was born as *Onuba*, a trading settlement founded by the Phoenicians early in the first millennium BC (modern inhabitants still call themselves *onubenses*). These early merchant traders were attracted by the minerals yielded from the mountainous areas to the north, and by the time the Carthaginians came to dominate the area in the third century BC Onuba was an established port, conveying these minerals throughout the Mediterranean world. When Spain fell into Roman hands the mining operations at Río Tinto were dramatically expanded to satisfy the empire's insatiable demand for metals such as silver and copper and the city prospered even more. Following Rome's demise the Visigoths and Moors displayed little interest in mineral extraction; the latter concentrated on dominating the seaborne trade with North Africa.

Huelva's maritime prowess gained for the city its crowning glory when **Columbus** set out from across the Río Tinto to find a new sea passage to India in ships manned by hardy Huelvan sailors. The city enjoyed a boom when the Extremadurans to the north of Huelva – the men who conquered the Americas – used the port as a base for their trade with the new territories overseas, but eventually Sevilla, and later Cádiz, came to dominate the silver and gold routes from the Americas and Huelva was squeezed out. Largely flattened by the Lisbon earthquake of 1755, it is only in the last century that the place has begun to regenerate itself: first as the base for mineral exports from Río Tinto in the early 1900s, and later when Franco established a petrochemical industry here in the 1950s.

Huelva's biggest annual **fiesta**, the *Fiestas Colombinas*, begins on August 3 and lasts for a week, with processions, events, concerts, *corridas* and competitions.

Arrival and information

Huelva's **bus station** is at Avda. de Portugal 9 (☎959 25 69 00), and has frequent services to Sevilla, Ayamonte and Portugal, with connections to many other destinations. The *Autobuses Damas* timetable lists all services throughout the province – handy if you're going to be using the town as a base. Frequent trains to Sevilla and three through-trains a day to Madrid leave from the splendid neo-Moorish **train station** (☎959 24 56 14), a short distance south of the centre on Avda. Italia. Completed in 1880 the station is a perfect expression of the self-confidence of that period, and is well worth stopping by for a look even if you're not travelling by train.

If you're coming in **by car**, you'll find parking to be difficult. Take special care where you park, or there's a fair chance your car will be towed away by the *Grua* (crane); if it is, call ☎959 24 93 50. A pay car park (see town map) may be your best bet. Huelva has a drugs problem and theft from cars to support this is rife; be particularly cautious when using car parks outside supermarkets.

The **Turismo**, near the waterfront at Avda. de Alemania 14 (Mon–Fri 9am–7pm, Sat 9am–2pm; ☎ & fax 959 25 74 03), has stacks of brochures and timetables, and hands out full accommodation lists and details on current events.

In summer, frequent **boat trips** to Punta Umbría (see p.000) leave from the harbour, as do **cruises** around the **Río Odiel Marismas Natural Park** – a fine place to spot flamingos, spoonbills and great colonies of herons. For details and bookings contact Naval Punta Umbria (☎959 31 13 92; trips last 1hr 45min; 300ptas) or enquire at the Turismo.

Accommodation

Finding a **place to stay** is usually not a problem this far off the tourist trail, although it must be said that Huelva's choice at the budget end is none too sparkling. Most places are concentrated around **Avda. Martín Alonzo Pinzón** – the town's main artery – and the pedestrianized shopping street, c/Berdigón, to the south of it. For a touch of luxury you may wish to head further out and join Columbus's ghost at **La Rábida monastery** (see p.287).

Huelva's **youth hostel** (%959 25 37 93; a) is at Avda. Marchena Colombo 14 in the northern suburbs (bus #6 from the bus station, or #4 from Plaza de las Monjas) and has en-suite rooms; and the nearest **campsite**, at Punta Umbría, is a fifteen-minute bus ride away.

Hostal Andalucía, c/Vásquez López 22, near the pedestrianized shopping street c/Berdigón (☎959 24 56 67). A friendly *hostal*, although some of the en-suite rooms can be rather airless. ③.

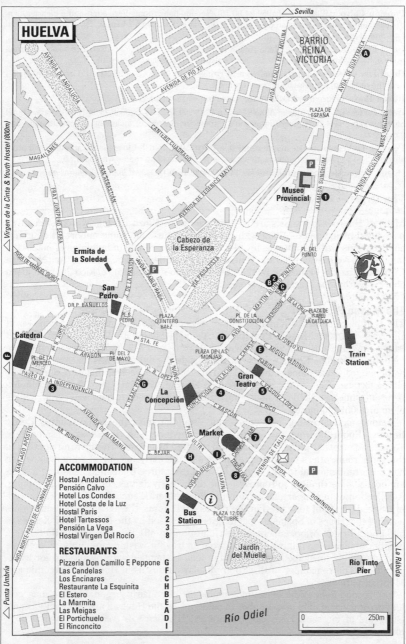

HUELVA

△ Sevilla

BARRIO REINA VICTORIA

AVENIDA DE ANDALUCÍA

AVENIDA DE PIO XII

AVDA. ALCALDE FED. MOLINA

AVDA. DE GUATEMALA

MAGALLANES

CANTERO CUADRADO

AVENIDA DE FEDERICO MAYO

PLAZA DE ESPAÑA

FRAY JUNÍPERO SERRA

SAN SEBASTIÁN

AVENIDA ESCULTORA MISS WHITNEY

P

Museo Provincial ●1

AVDA DE MANUEL SIURAT

Ermita de la Soledad

Cabezo de la Esperanza

PL. DEL PUNTO

AVDA DE LA PASIÓN

AVDA PABLO RADA

P

VÍA PAISAJISTA

●2 B

C. MARTIN ALONSO PINZÓN

PLAZA DE ISABEL LA CATÓLICA

San Pedro

DR. P. BAÑUELOS

PL. S. PEDRO

PLAZA QUINTERO BAÉZ

PL. DE LA CONSTITUCIÓN

C. BERDIGÓN

AVGDA DE LA CRUZ

C. ARAGÓN

Pº STA. FE

PL. DE LA MONJAS

AVDA.

C. ALFONSO XII

Catedral ●F

C. AIRES

PL. DEL 2 DE MAYO

PLAZA DE LAS MONJAS

C. CARASA

C. MIGUEL REDONDO

Train Station

PL. DE LA MERCED

M. NÚÑEZ

●D

C. PALACIOS

E ●

C. RÁBIDA

PASEO DE LA INDEPENDENCIA

●3

C. B. LÓPEZ

Gran Teatro

C. VÁSQUEZ LÓPEZ

C. CONCEPCIÓN

G ● C

La Concepción

●4

●5

C. GRACEFERAL

AVENIDA DE ALEMANIA

C. RASCÓN

C. RICO

DR. RUBIO

●6

SANTIAGO APÓSTOL

PLUS ULTRA

Market

C. CARDENAL CISNEROS

●7

H ●

C. BÉJAR

● I

●8

C. TENDALERAS

AVENIDA DE ITALIA

AVDA. TOMÁS DOMÍNGUEZ

P

AVDA NORTE–PASEO DE CIRCUNVALACIÓN

AVDA PORTUGAL

MARINA

Bus Station

ℹ

PLAZA 12 DE OCTUBRE

Jardín del Muelle

Punta Umbría △

Río Tinto Pier

△ La Rábida

Río Odiel

0   250m

△ Virgen de la Cinta & Youth Hostel (800m)

N

ACCOMMODATION

Hostal Andalucía	5
Pensión Calvo	6
Hotel Los Condes	1
Hotel Costa de la Luz	7
Hostal Paris	4
Hotel Tartessos	2
Pensión La Vega	3
Hostal Virgen Del Rocío	8

RESTAURANTS

Pizzeria Don Camillo E Peppone	G
Las Candelas	F
Los Encinares	C
Restaurante La Esquinita	H
El Estero	B
La Marmita	E
Las Meigas	A
El Portichuelo	D
El Rinconcito	I

Pensión Calvo, c/Rascón 33 (☎959 24 90 16). Second-floor rooms here surround a pleasant central patio unfortunately dominated for much of the day by the owner's blaring TV. The nearby *Hostal La Cinta* at no. 29 is similar. ②.

Hotel Costa de la Luz, José María Amo 8 (☎959 25 32 14, fax 959 25 64 22). The best of the mid-price options where the higher rooms have balcony terraces and come with TV. ⑤.

Hotel Los Condes, Alameda Sundheim 14 (☎959 28 24 00, fax 959 28 50 41). Comfortable hotel near the museum, with air-conditioned rooms. Garage. ⑤.

Hostal París, c/Rico 6 (☎959 24 88 16). Basic but clean *hostal*. ②.

Hotel Tartessus, Avda. Martín Alonso Pinzón 13 (☎959 28 27 11, fax 959 25 06 17). Upmarket hotel on the main street, with everything you'd expect for the price, including air conditioning and garage. ⑦.

Pensión La Vega, Paseo de la Independencia 15 (☎959 24 15 63). Close to the cathedral, and probably the best of the budget options, this *pensión* has immaculate rooms with bath. ③.

Hostal Virgen de Rocío, c/Tendaleras 14 (☎959 28 17 16). Decent *hostal*, all rooms en-suite. ③.

The City

Many of Huelva's key sights are a short walk from **Plaza de las Monjas**, the city's palm-lined main square. Along with a wonderful museum, some important churches and a curious British-built quarter, Huelva also has a couple of buildings of note – the impressive Neoclassical **Gran Teatro**, on c/Vásquez López, and the Art Nouveau **Clínica Sanz de Frutos** (now the Conservatorio de Música), c/Rico 26, both just a short way from the Plaza de las Monjas.

The Museo Provincial

The best place to start a tour of the city – especially if you're pressed for time – is at Huelva's excellent **Museo Provincial**, Alameda Sundheim 17 (summer Tues–Sat 9am–8pm, Sun 9am–3pm; winter Tues–Sat 9.30am–2pm & 4.30–7pm; free). Setting the tone, the enormous **Roman water wheel** inside the entrance was discovered during archeological excavations at the Río Tinto mines. Wheels such as this were operated by slaves to raise water to the surface and so prevent the mines from flooding. Often a series of wheels stacked one above the other would be used to haul water from depths of up to 100m and more.

Among an interesting collection, you shouldn't miss the reconstructed **Celtic house** (Room 1) from the north of the province, and, in Room 2, some rare Tartessian artefacts include a wonderfully crafted bronze jar. The **mining section** in the same room offers fascinating examples of the early history of an activity which has been fundamental to this region for well over three millennia, including a striking bronze boar thought to represent one of the early deities connected with mining. A collection of mining artefacts from the Roman period includes a remarkably well-preserved length of rope used in the mines. Herodotus, the ancient Greek historian, claimed that ropes of Spanish esparto grass were used by the Persian king Xerxes in building a bridge of boats across the Hellespont in 481 BC. In addition there are a number of terracotta miners' lamps, a wooden tray for washing minerals, as well as a lead pig – a prism-shaped cast of molten lead – stamped with ownership for transportation. The remainder of this room displays items from Huelva's Visigothic and Moorish periods.

The second floor of the museum contains the city's fairly forgettable **fine arts collection**, enlivened only by a number of paintings by the Huelvan artist Daniel Vásquez Díaz, one of Picasso's Paris contemporaries. His *Chico de Nerva* is a typical post-Impressionist work.

The Barrio Reina Victoria

One of Huelva's more bizarre features is a whole quarter designed by English archi-tects. The **Barrio Reina Victoria** (or Queen Victoria housing estate), east of the muse-um alongside the Avda. de Guatemala, was constructed by the Río Tinto Mining Company in the early years of the twentieth century to house its British workers. It's a truly weird experience to stroll along the tree-lined avenues flanked by bungalows with rose gardens and semis with dormer windows and mock-Tudor gables – more like Acacia Avenue, Essex, than an Andalucían town. Even the street names have a colonial symmetry about them: Calle A, Calle B and so on. Given the drab uniformity it's little wonder that the present native occupants have attempted to relieve these humdrum northern exteriors with a few primary colours.

Río Tinto pier

The **Río Tinto pier** (Muelle Río Tinto), on the east side of the harbour, is a huge nine-teenth-century ironwork structure formerly used to ship out the minerals which arrived by train from the mines to the north. Designed by the British engineer George Barclay Bruce and finished in 1874, the redundant pier's decaying ironwork curves gracefully out into the estuary, and today serves as a boardwalk for loungers and court-ing couples.

The British workers employed in the mines were also responsible for the importa-tion of **football** into Spain, helping set up Huelva's league club Recreativo in 1889, which is the oldest in the country. It's a pedigree hardly matched by their record, how-ever, which has been to languish for most of the last century in the lower leagues, although the club has recently been enjoying a purple patch in the Second Division.

Huelva's churches

The **Catedral de la Merced** (open service times at 7pm), just to the north of Plaza de las Monjas off Paseo de Buenos Aires, was one of the few buildings to survive the eigh-teenth-century earthquake, resulting in its upgrading to cathedral status which – apart from a brilliant white Baroque interior and an interesting salmon-pink colonial facade with elegant belfries – it hardly merits. It's worth looking inside at an image of Virgen de la Cinta (the city's patron) attributed to Montañes.

A more interesting church and one with Columbus connections lies 3km further out off the coast road heading west towards Portugal. This is the restored fifteenth-centu-ry **Virgen de la Cinta** (open daily), a simple white walled sanctuary set on a low hill overlooking the sea where Columbus is said to have prayed before setting out on his voyage. Inside, beneath the Mudéjar roof, you can see a medieval fresco of the Virgin, a fine altar grille, and a series of 1920s faience tiles by the painter Daniel Zuloaga depict-ing scenes from the explorer's life. To get there, take the #6 bus from Plaza de las Monjas, and ask for the "Parada de Santa Marta" stop.

Eating and drinking

Most **bars and restaurants** are to be found in the streets around the Plaza de las Monjas, particularly the pedestrianized c/Concepción through c/Berdigón. Huelva's best *heladería*, *Ibense Bornay*, c/Concepción 7, near Plaza de las Monjas, does great ices, *horchatas* and *granizados*.

Las Candelas, 7km from town at the Aljaraque crossroads on the road to Punta Umbría. An old *venta*, a step up in class and price from anywhere else in town, and recommended for its seafood. There's a good value *menú* for about 2000ptas. Without your own transport you'll need to get the Punta Umbría bus to drop you, otherwise take a taxi. Closed Sun.

Pizzeria Don Camillo e Peppone, c/Isaac Peral s/n. Genuine and delicious Italian pizzas, served up east of the Plaza de las Monjas. Closed Wed.

El Estero, Gran Via, Avda. Martín Alonso Pinzón 14, next to the *Hotel Tartessus*. Mid-priced restaurant specializing in Andalucian and international dishes. The cavernous interior can feel a bit lifeless if the place is quiet.

Los Encinares, junction of c/Pinzón & c/Sor Ángela de la Cruz. Wonderful and typical *andaluz* taverna serving *raciones* of *carnes a la parrilla* (grilled meat). Not cheap but very authentic.

Restaurante La Esquinita, c/Bejar 21, near the bus station. Soft lighting and romantic music at this tasteful restaurant, serving tasty local dishes with prices slightly above the average.

La Marmita, Miguel Redondo 12, Very pleasant restaurant with a wide range of well-prepared meat and fish dishes; *menú* for 950ptas.

Las Meigas, Avda. de Guatemala 48. Excellent restaurant offering Basque, Galician and *andaluz* dishes (especially seafood) and distinctive desserts – try the *tarta de Santiago*.

El Portichuelo, Avda. Martín Alonso Pinzón 1, just off Plaza de las Monjas. Pricey but good restaurant, with a 2000ptas *menú*.

La Prensa, Avda. Martín Alonso Pinzón 15. Old, stylish and central bar, good for coffee, too; its terrace and walls are lined with newsprint.

El Rinconcito, c/Marina 2. Decent tapas and a reasonably priced *menú* – often including paella. Flamenco is staged here (not during July or August though) in an atmospheric room at the back.

Nightlife

When it comes to **drinking and dancing**, during the summer most Huelvans make their way to Punta Umbría (see below) and the coast. However, c/Concepción through to c/Berdigón has numerous bars, *cafeterías*, ice-cream parlours and fast-food joints to cater to those left behind. In term time the university students create their own *marcha nocturna* in the numerous bars and music places along Avda. Pablo Rada, to the north of Plaza de las Monjas. Plaza de la Merced, near the cathedral, and the streets around the Plaza Dos de Mayo slightly southeast, provide another focus for their carousals; as a consequence the bars here can get quite lively.

For **tapas**, good seafood specialities are on offer at *Marisquería Huelva*, c/Cisneros alongside the impressive *Ayuntamiento* in Plaza de la Constitución. Off the western end of Plaza de las Monjas, *La Estrella*, c/Rafael López 1, has the lowest priced *tapas* in town at 175ptas a plate, and to the south of the same square *Bar Nueva Abundancía*, c/Vasquez López 45, has another varied selection, plus a 1000ptas *menú*. East of Plaza de las Monjas *Bar Agmanir*, c/Carasa 9, is great local bar with outdoor tables and a wide *tapas* range. Nearby, in the same direction, along c/Berdigón, more *tapas* are to be had at the friendly *Bar Berdigón* at no. 9 as well as at the atmospheric *Taberna El Condado*, nearby at c/Sor Angela de la Cruz 3, which specializes in Huelva's celebrated *jamón serrano*, and at *Bar Parral* opposite where the *fritos variados* (fried fish) is excellent. Another popular place to drink, with a decidedly Anglo-Saxon ambience, is *Bar Ottawa*, c/Berdigón 1.

The **drinking and music bars** between Plaza Merced and Plaza Dos de Mayo become lively after eleven and *Jard Rock* and *Bar Acme* are popular places in c/Amado de Lazaro. Other bars line the nearby *calles* Acabo del Barco and Ginés Martín where *Docklands* is a typical Irish-style bar. Should you feel the urge to visit a **disco**, *Alameda 9*, Alameda Sundheim 9, just below the museum, and *Coche Bamba* nearby at no. 26 are currently Huelva's only venues. Although Huelva bills itself as a **"flamenco capital"**, you'll be lucky to locate any flamenco at all in high summer. At other times the *Peña Flamenca de Huelva*, c/Nicolás 90 (☎959 23 09 61), or another nameless *peña* (☎959 25 87 52) on Avda. Andalucía, are the places to try, though ring to check first. The Turismo should also have details of any forthcoming performances.

Listings

Banks The major banks, most with ATM cash dispensers, are located along Gran Vía (Avda. Martín Alonso Pinzón), c/Vásquez López and at the bus station. The *Hotel Luz*, c/Alameda Sundheim 26, will change cash and travellers' cheques.

Car rental Try the reliable Auto Alquilar Huelva, in the bus station (☎959 28 31 38) or the pricier Avis at the *Hotel Luz*, Alameda Sundheim 26 (☎959 28 38 36).

Hospital Cruz Roja at Paseo Buenos Aires s/n, fronting the cathedral (☎959 26 20 20) offers emergency treatment. Huelva's Hospital General Juan Ramón Jiménez is on Ctra. Huelva–Sevilla (☎959 20 10 00).

Football Recreativo Huelva is the town team, currently holding its own in Division 2 after gaining promotion. Tickets and match details are available from the stadium, Colombino Municipal (☎959 27 02 08), Ctra. de Sevilla s/n, just to the north of the Barrio Reina Victoria housing estate.

Laundry A useful *lavandería-tintoría*, Odiel, c/Bejar 6, northeast of the bus station, will wash, dry and fold your clothes on the same day.

Markets The more-than-a-century old Mercado del Carmen to the east of the bus station is a beehive on weekdays (8am–noon), stacked with fresh landed fish and all the vegetables of the province. There's also a major weekly market on Fridays at the Recinto Colombino, east of the Río Tinto Pier.

Newspapers The local daily *Huelva Información* is good for listings of current events and forthcoming attractions.

Police The police station (☎959 21 02 21) is in Avda. Italia, near the post office. For emergencies dial ☎092 (local police) or ☎091 (national).

Post office The main *Correos* is on Avda. Italia s/n, which runs west from the train station (Mon–Fri 9am–1pm & 5–8pm, Sat 9am–1pm).

Telephones International calls can be made from street phone booths in the centre, or the *locutorio* office at c/Moras Claros 4, a couple of blocks west of Plaza de las Monjas.

The beaches: Punta Umbría and El Rompido

PUNTA UMBRÍA, 20km away (hourly buses) and sitting astride a finger of land between the Atlantic and the Tinto-Odiel river estuary, is Huelva's nearest – and biggest – seaside resort. English managerial staff from the Río Tinto Mining Company (see p.301) discovered the resort in the 1880s by seeking a place to sojourn by the sea. They constructed the first dwellings here in the British colonial style, quite a few of which survived until the 1970s; these buildings have now gone and the only vestige from this era is the barrio's name, Los Ingleses. Later growth into a seaside town has produced a tidy if uninspiring resort which does, however, have magnificent blue-flag **beaches** flanking the north and south sides of its *punta* (point). It makes a reasonable place to stopover if you don't want to stay in the city; be warned, though, that for the latter part of July and most of August every room will be taken. Once served only by ferries (which still run in the summer months), it is now reached by a long road bridge spanning the water and marshlands of the Río Odiel estuary.

Practicalities

The long and sandy beach – lined with some tasteless private villas – leads down to the *punta* where, following the road into town from Huelva (Avda. de Huelva) you'll come to a very helpful **Turismo**, located at the junction with Avda. de Andalucía (daily 9am–2pm & 5–9pm; July & Aug until midnight; ☎959 31 46 19), who stock copious amounts of information and a useful town **map**. You can't miss the place as it lies just beyond one of the most peculiar *Ayuntamientos* in Spain – a bizarre glass and wood structure perched on an artificial mudbank floating in a bath of green water and fronted by a clock tower resembling an oil rig. **Bikes and mopeds** can be rented from Moto Bonares (☎959 31 04 71), in an alley behind the Turismo. Turismar (☎959 31 55 26) run **boat trips** around the estuary and nature reserve of Marismas del Odiel from the Muelle Viajeros quay near the fishing harbour.

Beyond the Turismo you'll find most of the **places to stay**. At the very tip of the *punta* and close to the beach, *Hostal la Canaleta*, Punta de la Canaleta Bloque 3 (☎959 31 00 21; ④) has pleasant rooms with bath, or, near the harbour on the *punta*'s river flank, there's the pleasant and airy *Hostal Manuela*, c/Carmen 8 (☎959 31 07 60; ④), also with en-suite rooms. Places with a sea view are not a great step up in price: at Avda. del Océano 95 there's the comfortable *Hostal Playa* (☎959 31 01 12; ⑥). The *Hotel Emilio*, c/Ancha 21 (☎959 31 18 00, fax 959 31 03 16; ⑥) and *Pensión El Ancla*, Avda. Océano 29 (☎959 31 48 10; ⑤) are similar choices located nearby. High-season pressure on rooms could mean that the pleasant **youth hostel**, Avda. del Océano 13 (☎959 31 16 50; ①), with some double en-suite rooms is the only alternative, but here again it can be tight. The nearest **campsite**, *Camping La Bota* (☎959 31 45 37) lies 6km west, near the hamlet of La Bota, which – coming south along the A497 from Huelva – you will pass just after the road meets the ocean; it claims to be Andalucía's first "ecological" campsite, disposing of rubbish in an environmentally friendly way.

For **food and drink**, *chiringuitos* – open-air bars on the seafront serving snacks – are popular, and the resort is full of the usual *freidurías* and *marisquerías*. The central *La Esperanza*, Plaza Pérez Pastor 7, near the river harbour, is a good fish restaurant with an economical *menú*, and, on the same square, the even cheaper *Las Tinajas* is one of Punta Umbría's most celebrated *marisquerías*. On the seaward side, Plaza de la Atlantico, off Avda. del Océano, has the *Restaurante Tiburón* which is a good choice for seafood with a 950ptas *menú*, and, close to the youth hostel, *Miramar*, c/Miramar 3, is a welcoming place for *platos combinados* and *fritados variados* with a seafront terrace. On summer evenings the place throbs to a dozen **discos and bars** strung out along and around the pleasant pedestrianised c/Ancha which cuts through the town on the riverside. On the river itself and downstream from the fishing harbour, *Bar Chimbito*, housed in a old ferry boat, is a popular drinks bar and *chiringuito*.

El Rompido

For a more peaceful seaside retreat you might want to move further west along the coast – lined with fine beaches and backed by dunes, pinewoods and a unique juniper grove – to **EL ROMPIDO** (served by frequent buses from Huelva). Famous in the past for its oyster beds, it is now transformed into a small resort. There's another **campsite** here, *Catapum* (☎959 39 01 65), just outside the village as you approach, which in high summer can be a bit grim due to overcrowding.

The Columbus trail

Huelva's greatest source of pride lies with the momentous expeditions of **Christopher Columbus** to the New World, the first of which sailed from Palos de la Frontera (or simply Palos), across the Tinto estuary from the city. When he was unable to get the backing for the voyages he wished to make in order to discover a shorter route to the Indies, Columbus cooled his heels for many years in and around Huelva and the La Rábida monastery until he finally managed to obtain a commission from the king and queen in the spring of 1492. The main sites connected with Columbus – **La Rábida**, **Palos** and **Moguer** – are all within a 30km round-trip from Huelva. Buses running between Huelva and Moguer call at all three locations.

La Rábida

The monastery of **LA RÁBIDA**, 8km from Huelva, can be reached by bus (roughly hourly from Huelva) or, with your own transport, by taking the Mazagón road southeast

---

THE VOYAGES OF COLUMBUS

Probably born in Genoa around 1451 to the son of a weaving merchant, **Christopher Columbus** (in Spanish, Cristóbal Colón) went to sea in his early teens. After years of sailing around the Mediterranean, in 1476 he was shipwrecked off the coast of Portugal and it was in Lisbon – then the world leader in navigation – that Columbus learned the skills of mapmaking. In 1479 he married into a high-ranking Portuguese family and spent the following years on trading voyages to the British Isles and elsewhere, including in 1482 a journey down the coast of West Africa to **Ghana**, a major source of spices, ivory and slaves. During this time the idea germinated in his mind of attempting to sail west to reach the **Indies** and the Far East, thus shortening the route that Portugal was then exploring around the coast of Africa. He built up an enormous library of ancient and contemporary geographical writings now preserved in Sevilla, all heavily annotated in his own hand. By some optimistic interpretations of these works and a misreading of an Arab geographer, Alfraganus, Columbus seriously undercalculated the earth's circumference, believing that Marco Polo's fabulous island of **Cipangu** (Japan) lay a mere 2400 miles west of the Canaries instead of an actual 10,600. Even so, and had he been correct, this crossing was still further than any ship had sailed before across open sea.

Trying to find backers, when the Portuguese monarch, still more interested in the African route, demurred, Columbus turned to Spain. In 1486 at Córdoba he presented his plan to reach the gold-rich Orient to Ferdinand and Isabel, still involved in the protracted and costly war of *reconquista* against the Moors. Desirous of the gold to boost their fortunes but wary, after consultations with advisers, of Columbus's calculations, they both refused support. Now desperate, Columbus turned to France and then to Henry VIII of England, with no success. During his earlier journey from Portugal to Córdoba, Columbus had stayed at the **La Rábida** Franciscan monastery. It was to here that he returned frustrated and depressed in the autumn of 1491. The explorer's luck turned when Juan Pérez, the abbot of La Rábida and a former confessor to Isabel, was moved to write to the queen on Columbus's behalf. It was a timely moment. In January of 1492 Granada had fallen, the treasury was empty, and the promise of gold and glory for a resurgent Spain attracted the monarchs.

Columbus set out from Palos on August 3, 1492, with three small vessels, the *Santa María*, the *Niña* and the *Pinta*, carrying a total of 120 men recruited from Palos and Moguer by the Pinzón brothers. Columbus's discovery of the Atlantic wind patterns ranks alongside his other feats; he sailed via the Canaries to take advantage of the trade winds, but the incredible voyage almost ended in mutiny by crews who believed that they would never find a wind to bring them home. This was avoided when, on October 12, Columbus made landfall on Watling Island (now San Salvador) in the **Bahamas**. Watched by naked and silent natives he took the island in the name of Spain and gave thanks to God. After leaving a colony of men on **Hispaniola** (modern Haiti) he returned to Palos on March 15, 1493, to enormous acclaim.

Successful as a mariner, Columbus was disastrous as a colonizer, epitomized by his forcing of the native population of Hispaniola into the gold mines in a brutal process that reduced their numbers from a quarter of a million in 1492 to 60,000 fifteen years later. In 1500 Columbus was removed from office as governor and sent back to Spain in chains and disgrace. He eventually obtained release and made his final voyage in 1502 – a last desperate attempt to find a strait leading to India – but ended up stranded in Jamaica for a whole year after losing his ships to sea worms. Columbus died at Valladolid in 1506 still believing that he had reached the East Indies.

across the Río Tinto road bridge. At the Punta del Sebo – the tip of land where the Tinto and Odiel rivers meet – there's a **monument to Columbus** donated by the USA. This monster cubist-inspired statue, sculpted by Gertrude Vanderbilt Whitney in 1929, has the navigator looking a bit like a cowled boxer on his way to the ring.

Situated amid a forest of umbrella pines (which serve to mask the petrochemical refineries across the polluted river estuary), the small whitewashed Franciscan **monastery** is a surprisingly pleasant oasis once you reach it. Lying at the end of the Avda. de la América, a road linking it with Palos (see below) and lined with ceramic pavement tiles marking all the countries of the New World, the monastery may be visited only by guided tour (Tues–Sun hourly 10am–1pm & 4–6.15pm; donations). Dating from the fourteenth century, the buildings suffered structural damage during the Lisbon earthquake of 1755 and have been extensively restored.

The tour begins with the room containing stylized modern frescoes of the explorer's life by distinguished Huelvan artist Daniel Vásquez Díaz. At the building's heart is a tranquil fifteenth-century Mudéjar cloister filled with pot-plants, opening off the monks' refectory where Columbus would have dined during his many sojourns here. You will also see the cell where the abbot, Juan Pérez, and Columbus discussed the explorer's ideas. Beyond the cloister, a fourteenth-century church contains an alabaster statue of the **Virgin and Child** to which the mariner and his men prayed before setting sail. Upstairs, above the refectory, lies the **Sala Capitular** (Chapter House) an impressive beamed room with heavy period furniture where Fray Pérez, Columbus and the Pinzón brothers discussed the final plans before the first voyage set sail. On August 3, 1992, the king and the whole Spanish government gathered in this room to mark the 500th anniversary of the event. In other rooms on the same floor you can see models of the three caravels, as well as navigation charts, cases containing various artefacts brought back from the expedition and "team pictures" of the crew. Don't miss the curious **Sala de Banderas**, or Flag Room, where, beneath flags of the various South American nations of the New World, is a casket of earth donated by each. If some of these caskets look a bit roughed-up it's probably due to visiting South Americans who, after reverentially handling the soil of their fatherland, often treat the caskets of their neighbours with some disrespect.

The new **Harbour of the Caravels** (April–Sept Tues–Fri 10am–2pm & 5–9pm, Sat & Sun 11am–8pm; 430ptas), on the nearby Río Tinto estuary, has impressive full-size replicas of the three caravels which made the epic voyage to the New World. Realistic displays on board reconstruct the grim realities of life at sea, while the surrounding quays are lined with re-creations of fifteenth-century quayside bars and market stalls. In the adjoining museum are displays illustrating Columbus's life (including one of his geographical books annotated in a suprisingly delicate hand), video presentations on a giant screen and a *cafetería*.

The monastery's gardens contain an **information office** as well as a pleasant **bar-restaurant** with terrace tables. You can stay here too, at the *Hostería La Rábida* (☎959 35 03 12; ⑤), although the five luxurious rooms are booked well in advance during July and August.

Palos de la Frontera

Four kilometres north along the Río Tinto estuary lies **PALOS DE LA FRONTERA**, a rather featureless village but an important site in the Columbus story. It was from the silted-up bay below the church of San Jorge – then a major sea-port – that the three caravels, the *Niña*, the *Pinta* and the *Santa María* set out to reach Asia by crossing the western ocean.

O Palos, no one can equal your glory.
Not Memphis, nor Thebes nor eternal Rome.
Not Athens nor London.
No city can dispute your historical fame!

This modern poem fixed to the exterior wall of the fifteenth-century parish **church of San Jorge** leaves you in no doubt of how Palos views its role in world history. It was here that Columbus and his crewmen attended Mass before taking on water for their voyage from the nearby **La Fontanilla**, a medieval well recently tarted up as the centrepiece of a dismal park to mark the quincentenary. The harbour lay to the west of the fountain in an area now marshland, and it was due to the river's silting up that the decline of Palos set in. The church (daily 10.30am–1pm & 7–8pm, or ring ☎959 35 08 90 for appointment to view) has a simple, bare brick interior containing some mural fragments as well as a distinctive wrought-iron pulpit, – from which the edict was read ordering an initially reluctant Palos to provide ships, crew and provisions for the voyage, and some thirteenth- and sixteenth-century alabaster sculptures of *Santa Ana* and the *Crucifixion*.

On that August morning in 1492 Columbus is supposed to have left the church through its southern **Mudéjar portal** flanked by his captains Martín Alonzo Pinzón and his younger brother Vincente, both from Palos. And it is these native sons that Palos today celebrates, even more than its Columbus connection, claiming that their contribution to the epic voyage has been eclipsed. Indeed at the time the Pinzón family insisted that Martín – a mariner of great local repute – had planned such a voyage long before Columbus. South of San Jorge on the main street, the **house of Martín Alonzo Pinzón** at c/Colón 24 survives, now converted into a **museum** (Mon–Fri 10am–2pm; free). Here you'll see a model of the Spanish plane *Plus Ultra* – the first to fly across the Atlantic in 1927, two years before Lindbergh, who made it to the record books only because the Spanish flight made refuelling stops in the Canaries and Ascension Island before reaching Brazil. It was piloted by Ramón Franco, the dictator's brother.

The road north to Moguer runs through **strawberry fields** owned by one of the largest cooperatives in Europe, which has brought welcome prosperity to the area. By playing the market, which entails close scrutiny of weather forecasts for northern European customers such as Germany and Britain – sunshine there means high strawberry profits – they decide when is the best moment for picking. Then, loaded with 10,000 kilos of *fresones* apiece, the great refrigerated trucks roll north through the night.

Practicalities

The **Ayuntamiento**, facing the Plaza Mayor on c/Rábida 3, the main street, can provide tourist information and a town map. You'll find **places to stay and eat** close by: *Cafetería Pensión Rábida*, c/Rábida 9 (☎959 35 01 63; ②), is a good bet and serves *platos combinados*; nearby there are pricier rooms with bath at *Hotel La Pinta*, c/Rábida 75 (☎959 35 05 11, fax 959 53 01 64; ⑥), which also has a decent restaurant with an economical *menú*. With your own transport, a good-value alternative is *Pensión La Niña*, c/Juan de la Cosa 37 (☎959 53 03 60; ③), on the Mazagón road out of town, which has rooms with bath, air-conditioning and TV.

Moguer

The compact and beautiful whitewashed town of **MOGUER**, 8km north of Palos, also takes pride in its Columbus connection: many of the crew members were recruited here. Quite apart from this, it is a place with plenty to see, and achieved worldwide fame in 1956 as the birthplace of the Nobel prize-winning poet Juan Ramón Jiménez.

Starting from the **Plaza del Cabildo** in the centre – where there's a bronze statue of Jiménez – it's easy to find your way around. First take a look at the elegant eighteenth-century **Ayuntamiento** (free access to patio in mornings when open) on the same square, a quintessentially Andalucian edifice in cream and brown paint described by one art historian as "the finest Neoclassical building in the whole of Huelva Province". It also appears on the 2000-peseta banknote.

Close to here in c/Monjas lies the Gothic-Mudéjar **Convento de Santa Clara**. Founded in the fourteenth century, this housed nuns from the order of St Clare until 1898, but is now a **museum** (guided tours every half-hour Tues–Sat 11am–1pm & 5–7pm, Sun & Mon 11am–1pm; 250ptas). Inside, a Mudéjar cloister leads into the nuns' former quarters which include kitchen and refectory and a large sixteenth-century dormitory. The church possesses some notable alabaster tombs of the Portocarrero family, the convent's founders, as well as – at the entry to the choir – a seventeenth-century diptych of the Sienese school portraying the Immaculate Conception. Look out for an inscription in the right aisle, which tells of Columbus's visit to offer thanksgiving for his safe return. He is reputed to have spent the whole night in prayer here upon returning from his first voyage in March 1493, in fulfilment of a vow he made in the middle of a terrifying storm.

Other sights in town include the fifteenth-century monastery of **San Francisco**, behind Santa Clara (Mon–Fri 11am–2.30pm; free) with its stunning ochre-tinted Mudéjar brick church and from where legions of missionaries were sent out to the New World; and **Nuestra Señora de la Granada** (interior open at service times; try 7.30pm) which boasts a scaled-down, whiter version of Sevilla's Giralda tower "which from close-up looks like Sevilla's from far away," wrote Jiménez. The house where Jiménez was born, c/Jiménez 5, has been restored as an interesting **museum** (Mon–Sat hourly visits 10.15am–1.15pm & 5.15–7.15pm, Sun 10am–2pm; 250ptas) displaying various mementoes from the poet's life. On the road leading towards the Sevilla–Huelva highway, the **cemetery** has the grave of the poet and his wife, Zenobia. His body was returned to the town he loved for burial in 1958 after twenty years spent in exile in Puerto Rico, to where he had emigrated after Franco came to power. The work that most Andalucians remember him for today is *Platero y yo* ("Platero and I"), the story of a little donkey who is a "friend of the poet and children" based on his own donkey, Platero, in whose company he often toured Moguer's streets. Glazed plaques on walls around town mark streets or buildings that occur in the story. To the south of the centre in the grounds of the **Casa de Fuentepiña** – where Jiménez wrote most of the book – Platero's grave, beneath a great pine, has become a shrine for generations of children.

Practicalities

Moguer's small **Turismo** (Mon–Fri 10am–2pm & 6–8pm; ☎959 37 23 77) lies just off the main square, inside the *Casa de Cultura* at c/Andalucía 5, and can provide a basic map and information. **Buses** drop off and leave from c/Coronación to the north of Plaza Cabildo. If you're tempted to **stay**, close to the Convento de Santa Clara at the end of c/Monjas there's the delightful and excellent-value *Hostal Pedro Alonso Niño*, c/Pedro Alonso Niño 13 (☎959 37 23 92; ②), where all rooms come with shower and TV; get a room overlooking the patio at the back if you can. Around the corner, the slightly more expensive *Hostal Platero*, c/Aceña 4 (☎959 37 21 59; ③), has rooms with bath.

For **food**, *Mesón Restaurante Paralla*, Plaza de Monjas 22, opposite the entrance to Santa Clara, is the best restaurant in town, and serves up excellent regional fish and meat dishes, does *tapas* and has an economical *menú*. Opposite is a good breakfast café, *Azahar*. Moguer has some interesting nightime places to eat and drink, including one of the most bizarre bar/restaurants in Andalucía. This is *Mesón El Lobito* on c/La Rábida 31, which includes among its eccentric decor vast numbers of unidentified objects hanging from the ceiling, chickens in cages in a patio, walls completely covered in graffiti (which you're welcome to add to) and a labyrinth of enormous darkened rooms at the back. Wine is sold at crazy prices (25ptas a glass) and fish and meat dishes are served *a la brasa*. There's usually a good atmosphere if you turn up after 10pm. The rest of the venues pale by comparison, but *Cafetería Los Leones*, c/Andalucía 2, with a terrace and patio, serves *tapas* with background music and *Sanwichería Don Bocata*, c/Acena 14, also opens late and is often lively. **Disco bars** are located along c/San Rafael, three blocks south of Plaza del Cabildo.

Moguer holds an annual **Festival de Flamenco** at the beginning of September.

Coto de Doñana National Park

Sited at the estuary of the Guadalquivir, the vast roadless area of the **COTO DE DOÑANA** is Spain's largest wildlife reserve, a world-class wetland site for migrating birds and one of Europe's greatest areas of wilderness. The seasonal pattern of its delta waters, which flood in winter and then drop in the spring, leaving rich deposits of silt, raised sandbanks and islands, give the Coto de Doñana its special interest. Conditions are perfect in winter for ducks and geese, but spring is most exciting: the exposed mud draws hundreds of flocks of breeding birds. In the marshes and amid the cork oak forests behind you've a good chance of seeing squacco heron, black-winged stilt, whiskered tern, pratincole and sand grouse, as well as flamingos, egrets and vultures. There are, too, occasional sightings of the Spanish imperial eagle, now reduced to just fourteen breeding pairs. In late summer and early autumn, the swamps – or *marismas* – dry out and then support far less birdlife. The park is also home to 25 pairs of lynx.

Inevitably, it seems, the park is under threat from development and several lynx have been killed by traffic on the road to the beach resort at **Matalascañas**. Even at current levels the drain on the water supply is severe, and made worse by pollution of the Guadalquivir by farming pesticides, Sevilla's industry and Huelva's mines. The seemingly inevitable disaster finally occurred in April 1998 when an upriver mining dam used for storing toxic waste burst, unleashing millions of litres of pollutants into the Guadiamar river which flows through the park. The noxious tide was stopped just 2km from the park's boundary, but catastrophic damage was done to the surrounding farmland, with nesting birds decimated and fish poisoned. One expert has predicted that it will take 25 years for the area to recover. The proposals for a huge new tourist centre – to be known as the Costa Doñana – on the fringes of the park have now been shelved, but worryingly two smaller tourist *urbanizaciones* just to the north of Sanlúcar and near **Mazagón** on the park's western flank have been given the go-ahead, vividly demonstrating that the pressure for development remains. Bitter demonstrations organized by locals who saw the prospect of much-needed jobs in the Costa Doñana development – accompanied by mysterious outbreaks of vandalism against park property – have abated into an uneasy truce. Some experts have proposed that "green tourism", allowing a greater but controlled public access to the park, and thereby providing an income for the local community, is the only way to bring both sides together.

This area was known to the **Romans** as *Ligur*, and archeologists were recently surprised to discover a Roman quayside three kilometres into the *marismas*, showing just how much the area has expanded in the ensuing two millennia. It was Alfonso X, however, who claimed the territory of Las Rocinas as a hunting reserve for the Spanish crown in 1262 during the *reconquista*. In 1294 his heir, Sancho IV (the Brave), rewarded the "hero" of the siege of Tarifa, Guzmán El Bueno, with the territories of Doñana. The area, still a hunting reserve, remained part of the lands of the dukes of Medina Sidonia – as the Guzmán line became – for the next five centuries, and the park's hunting lodge was named the palace of Dona Aña in honour of the wife of the seventh duke in 1595. The reserve hit a bad patch when it was sold by the Medina Sidonias in 1897 to sherry baron William Garvey, whose company is still operating in Jerez (see p.200). Garvey turned it into a hunting club and sold off much of the woodland for profit, but saner times followed upon his death in 1909, when people began to realise the unique importance of the area.

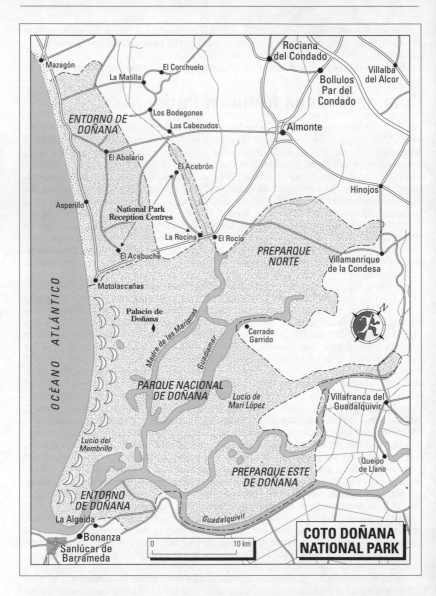

In 1957 scientific interest in the park began in earnest and, as a result of concern expressed about proposals to carve a highway across the zone and build tourist developments along its coastline, the **World Wildlife Fund** was set up in 1964. Five years later the Fund persuaded the Spanish government to set up the National Park. Since then the Coto de Doñana, now under the management of the National Institute for the Conservation of Nature (ICONA), has expanded to 190,000 acres. Recently the park's

TOURING THE COTO DE DOÑANA

The starting point for **tours of the park** in all-terrain 24-seater buses, and the place to book them, is at the Centro de Recepción de Acebuche, 4km north of Matalascañas towards El Rocío and Almonte (then 1.5km up a signed road on the left). For details of the tours (daily April–Sept 8.30am & 5pm; Oct–April 8.30am & 3pm; 2750ptas) call in at the centre or phone ahead (daily 9am–8pm; ☎959 44 87 11, English spoken; *donana@mma.es*). The tour operator, Cooperativa Marismas del Rocío, Plaza del Acebuchal 16, El Rocío (☎959 43 04 32, fax 959 43 04 51), can also provide information and take bookings. Although the Centro has some binoculars available for rent, you'd be well advised to bring your own as they are essential. Outside July, August and holiday periods you should be able to get on to the next day's trip, otherwise you'll need to book at least a week in advance. Tours consist of an eighty kilometre, 4hr trip sampling the park's various ecosystems: dunes, beach, *marismas* and woodland, with the guide pointing out only spectacular species such as flamingo, imperial eagle, deer and wild boar.

If you're a serious ornithologist and just as interested in variations on little brown birds, the tour isn't for you and you should consider a **group booking**, which costs a little more than the daily excursion and lets you create your own itinerary (details from the Centro). The best **map** for the national park is the IGN Parque Nacional de Doñana (1:50,000) sold at the Acebuche centre.

administrators enlisted divine assistance in safeguarding its future when they petitioned the brotherhoods to allow the Virgin of Rocío (see p.295) to become the National Park's patron. The brotherhoods gracefully agreed and the park's future now seems assured.

Doñana practicalities

Visiting the Coto de Donaña still involves – understandably – a certain amount of frustration. At present the heart of the reserve is still open only to brief, organised bus **tours** (see box above). You can also take a boat cruise into the park from Sanlúcar de Barrameda (see p.198).

Day visitors are currently restricted to the **hides** at three access and information centres open to the public. The first of these (moving north from Matalascañas) is the **Centro Recepción del Acebuche** (daily 8am–9pm), where there's also an information office, bookshop, natural history exhibition, a rather tedious audio-visual presentation and a **cafetería.** The five hides adjacent to the Centro overlook a lagoon where marbled teal, purple gallinule, various grebes and – around the trees – azure-winged magpies have all been spotted and where with luck, you may even glimpse the extremely rare Audouin's gull. You'll need to bring your own binoculars or they can be hired from the centre (200ptas per hr). At the eastern end of the lagoon you are allowed to view the **aviary** where rescued and recuperating birds enjoy intensive care – another good place for sighting some rare species.

Nine kilometres north, the other two centres are sited off the road close to the El Rocío bridge. **La Rocina** (daily 9am–3pm & 4–9pm) has a car park, information centre (get a map here) and a small open-air **museum** with historical reconstructions of life in the *marismas*. Beyond here a 2km route called the "Charco de la Boca" leads to five well-concealed hides in marshland, pine woods and along the riverbank where you might see Cetti's warbler, the spectacular hoopoe, red-crested pochard and herons as well as – in summer – flamingos and a plethora of singing nightingales. A minor road leads 5km west from here to **El Palacio de Acebrón** (same hours) – an impressive former hunting lodge – where there is another car park and information centre housing an exhibition called "Man and Donaña". A 1.5km marked route threads from the centre, circling a lake mainly through woodland, and offering possibilities to sight the rare hawfinch.

Back on the main road, the **El Rocío bridge** on the village's southern edge has been described by one naturalist as "the best free bird-watching site in Europe". From this spot, red kite – a common sight here – soaring flocks of whiskered terns, disturbed by the ominous approach of a majestic booted eagle, and migrating greenshank, ruff and sandpiper are all to be seen in season. In high summer, though, the marshes dry out and are grazed by horses while the birdlife is restricted to coot and avocets breeding by the river. The view across the marshes towards the village of El Rocío from here is superb.

El Rocío

Set on the northwestern tip of the marshes, **EL ROCÍO** – a tiny cluster of white cottages, sandy streets and a church stockade where the most famous pilgrimage-fair of the south occurs annually at Pentecost – is one of the most atmospheric places in Andalucía. As the cowboy-hatted farmers nonchalantly ride horses along the wide sandy streets and tie up at Wild West-style hitching rails in front of their timber cabins, you half expect Clint Eastwood to emerge from a nearby saloon chewing on a cheroot. And this frontier-like feeling isn't altogether accidental, as it was from this area that many of the colonizers of the New World set out, exporting their vernacular architectural preferences with them. In the evening the new street lights do little to undermine the time-warp quality of an area unchanged for centuries.

Centre of the town's Pentecost celebrations, the church of **Nuestra Señora del Rocío** (8.30am–2.30pm & 4.30–7.30pm) was, despite its Baroque appearance, built in the 1960s on the site of a church which collapsed in the eighteenth-century Lisbon earthquake. It holds the venerated image of the **Virgen del Rocío**, a thirteenth-century work in carved wood.

In the spring, El Rocío is probably the best **bird-watching** base in the area. The *marismas* and pine woods adjacent to the town itself are teeming with birds, and following tracks east and southeast along the edge of the reserve you'll see many species from white stork, herons and egrets to masked great grey shrike and honking wild geese. The Boca del Lobo ("wolf-breath") sewage treatment plant is an unlikely sounding bird-spotting location, but vultures and storks are frequent patrons here, and the village has now installed a hide.

With your own transport another great bird-watching location is the **Cerrado Garrido** (aka Centro José Antonio Valverde; 10.30am–7.30pm) on the park's northern fringes. To get there from El Rocío follow the signs from the centre of the village. One signed route (15km) is for *todo terreno* (four-wheel-drive vehicles) only; the second signed route for normal cars is a longer 30km trip via Villamanrique de la Condesa. The route traverses the *Preparque* along unmade tracks and is quite feasible in summer; after heavy rains access may not be possible and you should check with the El Acebuche visitors' centre (☎959 44 87 11; English spoken) who will advise on conditions. Cerrado's visitors' centre serves snacks, and also has telescopes and hides. You'll have plenty of other bird-watching and wildlife-spotting opportunities en route – keep an eye out for purple gallinules in the ditches between the paddy fields. The sunrises and sunsets over the *marismas* at Cerrado Garrido are quite spectacular, too.

Practicalities

A small **Turismo** (☎959 44 26 84) is located in the *Ayuntamiento*, c/Muñoz y Pavon s/n almost opposite the *Hotel Puente del Rey*, where staff can supply a town **map**. Both they and the *Hotel Puente del Rey* can also advise on **horse riding** treks in the park. El Rocío

THE ROMERÍO DEL ROCÍO

The **Romerío del Rocío**, a Whitsun pilgrimage to the sanctuary of the Virgen del Rocío, is one of the most extraordinary spectacles in Europe, with whole village communities and some eighty local "brotherhoods" from Huelva, Sevilla, Málaga and even one from Gibraltar, converging on the village on horseback and in lavishly decorated ox-carts. The event is part-pilgrimage and part-jamboree as the intense emotions awakened by the two-to four-day journey (not to mention the drinking) often spill over uncontrollably.

The brotherhoods coming from **Sanlúcar de Barrameda** have a special dispensation to follow their ancient route across the heart of the Parque de Donaña which takes them three nights and four days with all the attendant fire risks en route. The army is employed to get them and their carts over the Guadalquivir safely, and the park's rangers set up campsites for them and provide firewood for their great feasts in the woods. Sadly, the rubbish left behind by these large crowds is the cause of many wildlife fatalities as species such as boar choke on the plastic containers they attempt to devour. Throughout the *romerío*, which climaxes on the Saturday evening, everyone parties in fiesta costume, while by the time the carts arrive at El Rocío they've been joined by hundreds of bus-loads of pilgrims.

What they have all come for – apart from the spectacle itself – is the commemoration of the miracle of **Nuestra Señora del Rocío** (Our Lady of the Dew). This is a statue believed to have been found on this spot by a shepherd in the thirteenth century – conveniently after the eviction of the Moors – which, so it is said, resisted all attempts to move it elsewhere. A shrine was built, miraculous healings and events were reported, and El Rocío was suddenly on the map. In the early hours of Pentecost Sunday when many of the revellers are gripped either by religious frenzy or lie prostrate in an alcoholic stupor, the image of the Virgin, credited with all kinds of magic and fertility powers, is paraded before the faithful as she visits each one of the brotherhoods' houses (which lie empty for the rest of the year).

In recent years the sheer size of the Romerío has begun to worry the authorities as it has exploded from a few thousand pilgrims in the 1970s to an incredible half-a-million in the late 1990s. Despite the whole affair having become a spectacular TV event with arc lamps, amplified music and fireworks, popular enthusiasm is undiminished. The brotherhoods wrestle with each other to carry the Blanca Paloma ("the White Dove" as the Virgin is fondly known) one more time in procession before she's returned to her shrine for another year, and the weary homeward trek begins.

Accompanying one of the brotherhoods on their pilgrimage to El Rocío is a memorable and exhilarating experience. Anyone is entitled to be a pilgrim: just turn up when the processions leave the major villages in the provinces of Sevilla and Huelva in the days leading up to Pentecost, taking with you a sleeping bag and some food and water. The walking is easy with plenty of stops for dancing and liquid refreshment, and the nightly encampments, when folk songs are sung around campfires, are magical.

---

makes a nice **place to stay** – except during the *romerío* when rooms (costing a whopping 30–50,000ptas per night) are booked months and years in advance. Economical options at other times of the year include the basic *Hostal Vélez*, c/Algaida 2 (☎959 44 21 17; ③) slightly north of the church, and *Hostal Cristina*, c/Real 32 behind the church (☎959 40 65 13; ④), with en-suite rooms behind a decent restaurant. *Hostal Isidro*, Avda. Los Ansares 59 (☎959 44 22 42; ⑤), on the east side of the village has more facilities again. Upmarket options are the elegant and enormous *Hotel Puente del Rey*, Avda. del Canaliega s/n (☎959 44 25 75, fax 959 44 20 70; ⑦), close to the main road at the edge of the village; and *Hotel Toruño*, Plaza del Acebuchal 22 (☎959 44 23 23, fax 959 44 23 38; ⑥) around the corner from the *Cristina*, with comfortable rooms overlooking the *marismas*.

For **eating and drinking** all the hotels and *hostales* (except the *Vélez*) have restaurants but the upmarket places tend to be overpriced. *Tapas* and *raciones* are served at most of the bars along the main street – but to eat out on their terraces after sundown you'll need plenty of mosquito protection.

Matalascañas and Mazagón

Birds and other wildlife apart, **MATALASCAÑAS**, a fast-growing beach resort just outside the reserve, is unlikely to excite; with five large hotel complexes, a grim concrete shopping centre and tasteless beach front developments along a featureless promenade, it looks as if it's just been thrown together (as indeed it has), and it would be difficult to imagine a more complete lack of character. The **beach**, it must be said though, is attractive and you are allowed to use the strand inside the national park, too. You enter by a gate at the eastern end of the village and can walk along the sand (but not into the park proper) with plenty of opportunities for bird-watching; no vehicles or camping are allowed.

Outside high summer comfortable **rooms** with bath should be available at *Hostal Rocío*, c/Pintor El Greco 60 (☎959 43 01 41; ④), or *Hostal Romero*, Sector M, Parcela 98 (☎959 44 03 45; ④). From late July to the end of August all accommodation is generally booked solid and unless you plan in advance (any Sevilla travel agent will try to reserve you a room) you'll probably end up **camping** – either unofficially at the resort itself which is increasingly frowned upon, or at the *Camping Rocío Playa* (☎959 43 02 38), 1.5km down the A494 towards Huelva. This site lacks shade and is a little inconvenient without your own transport if you're planning to take regular trips into the fringes of the national park; if you just want a beach, though, it's not a bad option. Playa Doñana and its continuation Playa Mazagón – with two more campsites, *Fontanilla Playa* (☎959 53 60 52; just beyond the *parador*, see below) and the vast, densely wooded *Doñana Playa* (☎959 53 62 81; also has bungalows, ⑤) – stretch the whole distance to Huelva, with fine beaches backed by dunes and hardly another visitor in sight. With your own transport there are a number of access points (with car parks) to tranquil beaches such as the signed Playa Questa Maneli between the two campsites. This route is covered at present by three daily buses in both directions.

The small resort of **MAZAGÓN**, 23km west of Matalascañas, makes a preferable stopover with another fine sandy beach and ample restaurants and bars. The village is well served by **buses** from Huelva, Palos and Moguer, and from the centre – where the bus drops you – it's but a short walk to the beach. Outside August, **rooms** are easy to come by; *Hostal Álvarez Quintero*, c/Hernández de Soto 74 (☎959 37 61 69; ③), just off the beach road, is a good-value place to try first where en-suite rooms come with air-conditioning. In the village proper other choices include the pricier *Hostal Hilaria*, c/Hilaria 20 s/n (☎ & fax 959 37 62 06; ④), which has rooms with bath above a bar, and the basic *Pensión Acuario*, Avda. Fuentepiña 29 (☎959 37 72 86; ②), on a busy central avenue lined with bars and **places to eat**. *Hotel Albaida* (☎959 37 60 29, fax 955 37 61 08; ⑤) east of the centre is the best of the three-star places and has a restaurant. For five-star comfort, head for the modern *Parador Cristóbal Colón* (☎959 53 63 00, fax 959 53 62 28; ⑧), 6km east of Mazagón and set among pine woods; with its own restaurant this is a modern addition to the upmarket chain with average rooms, sometimes chilly service and attractive gardens (with pool) leading down to a superb beach.

The N442 road continues west from Mazagón running behind more inviting beaches for 10km before skirting an industrial zone filled with unsightly petrol refineries, beyond which lies the monastery of La Rábida (see p.287) and the city of Huelva (see p.279).

Along the coast to Portugal

This stretch of coast between the Guadiana – which marks the border with Portugal – and Tinto rivers is lined with some of the finest **beaches** in Andalucía and a scattering of low-key resorts that rarely see a foreign tourist. There's no train service, but plenty of buses run along this main route to the frontier, easily crossed by a spectacular road bridge over the Guadiana estuary.

From Huelva the **coast road to Portugal** loops around the Marisma de San Miguel, passing through the dull towns of Cartaya and **LEPE**. The latter glories in a mention by Chaucer (whose father was a vintner) in his *Pardoner's Tale* saying that the potent white wine of Lepe "creepeth subtilly… that whan a man hath dronken draughtes three, and weneth he be at hoom in Chepe, He is in Spaigne, right at the toune of Lepe" – an out-of-body experience no doubt familiar to many modern inebriates. Lepe's main claim to fame today however, is as the butt of hundreds of "did you hear about the man from Lepe…?" jokes, in which the town's supposedly gormless inhabitants are mercilessly pilloried by the rest of the nation. Taking this notoriety in its stride, Lepe capitalized on its fame by inaugurating an annual Jokes Festival that takes place during the last week in May.

Some 5km south of Lepe on the *marismas* of the Río Piedras, the tiny fishing port of **EL TERRÓN** boasts one of the best **fish restaurants** on the coast. Located on the harbour, *El Ancla* (which specializes in mouthwatering fried and marinated prawns) doesn't come cheap but also has an affordable *menú*. If you want to know a bit more about what you've just eaten the nearby Aula Marina **aquarium** (daily 5.30–9.30pm; 400ptas) has examples of most species to be found in this corner of the Mediterranean. About 2km down the road from here a **campsite**, *La Antilla* (☎959 48 08 29), may be your best bet if rooms are tight.

The road hits the coast at the **PLAYA DE LA ANTILLA**, a low-key beach resort invitingly peaceful outside high season, if that's what you're seeking. The blue-flag **beach** is good if slightly gravelly, and there's a scattering of *marisquerías* and restaurants to choose from. Many of these line the main street, Avda. de Castilla, a couple of blocks in from the sea. Locals pack the popular *Cervecería Estoril* about half way down on the right but more formal dining takes place at *Lino*, Avda. de Castilla 2, *Casa Rodri* (c/Adelfa s/n just off the same street and well signed) with a good-value *menú*, or the slightly pricier *Rodri La Langosta*, the last two run by the same family. The best of the bunch is, perhaps, *Feria*, Avda. Castilla 16, at the very far end, another excellent place for fish which also serves *tapas*.

You won't find a room here in August without pre-booking but at other times **places to stay** cluster around the junction of Avda. Castilla and c/La Parada, which is also where the bus drops you. *Hostal La Parada*, c/La Parada s/n (☎959 48 14 62; ③) has en-suite rooms and is owned by *Bar Parada* on the square opposite, which is a pleasant place for breakfast and snacks. *Hostal Playa*, Plaza La Parada s/n (☎959 48 15 66; ③) and the nearby *Hostal Sol y Mar*, (☎959 48 11 11; ④) offer rooms with bath and all three have attractive off-peak price deals. The cheapest room option is the pleasant *Hostal El Álamo*, Avda. Castilla 82 (☎959 48 10 18; ③), which has some rooms with bath and a decent restaurant, too. Otherwise there's a **campsite**, *Luz* (☎959 34 11 42), with a pool, 5km west towards Isla Cristina.

Isla Cristina

The road passes some pretty awful new beach development on the western edge of La Antilla as well as, a couple of kilometres further, the newly created coastal nightmare of **La Islantilla** where a clutch of fairly tasteless upmarket hotels and *urbanizaciones* are flanked to the right of the road by a sprawling 25-hole golf course. A misguided joint venture by Lepe and Isla Cristina to attract the seriously rich, the complex has a conveniently located **Turismo** (daily 10am–2pm & 5–9pm; ☎959 64 60 13), on the left of the through road, with stacks of information on the whole Costa de la Luz. Beyond the **campsites** *Luz* (see above) and *Taray* (☎959 34 11 02), the vista clears to provide a pleasant few kilometres of pine woods and, beyond the dunes, more good beaches.

ISLA CRISTINA, 8km further on, was, as its name implies, once an island but infilling has transformed it into a pleasant resort surrounded by *marismas* and tidal estuaries. For most of the year the town's prevailing atmosphere is one of nonchalant tranquillity, punctuated only in August by the annual invasion of *sevillanos*, who fill its holiday apartment blocks and beaches to bursting point. The commercial centre is concentrated around the **port** which is the second most important in the province and from where shellfish and wet fish are transported overnight on ice to the markets, bars and restaurants of Sevilla, Córdoba and Madrid. The fish that stays behind is processed in the local canning and salting plants. At the end of Carretera de la Playa, an avenue shaded by giant eucalyptus trees, the town's fine EU blue-flagged sandy **beach** somewhat makes up for a drab seafront. Back in town, life revolves around the central **Plaza de las Flores** (officially Plaza del Caudillo, one of several street names from the Franco period tellingly still much in use). The beach is an easy ten-minute walk from here or there's a half-hourly bus (except during the siesta) from the same square.

Practicalities

Southeast of Plaza de las Flores (go south along Gran Via Perez and left along c/Madrid) there's a **Turismo** (Tues–Sat 10am–2pm & 6–8pm; ☎959 33 26 94) on the unnamed square at the eastern end of c/Madrid, which can provide a town map and accommodation list. It frequently fails to open, however, in which case you should go to the reception desk in the nearby *Ayuntamiento*, c/Madrid, who also have maps. The **bus station** lies on Avda. de Huelva, a couple of blocks north of Plaza de las Flores and is served by frequent daily buses from Huelva and Sevilla and buses to the beach.

Due to the severe shortage of **accommodation**, if you want to stay – in August especially – you'll have to book ahead. The only budget option is the central *Hostal Gran Vía*, c/Gran Vía 10 (☎959 33 07 97; ④), which has rooms with bath or, further east, there's the very pleasant new *Hotel Brisamar*, c/29 de Julio 87 (☎959 33 11 30; ⑤). Plusher seafront options – all near the Playa Central beach at the eastern end of the town where you come in from La Antilla – include the friendly *Hotel Sol y Mar* (☎959 33 20 50; ⑥) right on the beach, and *Hotel Paraíso Playa*, Carretera de la Playa s/n (☎959 33 18 73, fax 959 34 37 45; ⑥), which also has a pool. The nearest **campsite**, *La Giralda* (☎959 34 33 18) lies 2km out of town on the La Antilla road, and makes the most of its waterside location with all kinds of canoeing and sailing activities.

For **eating** *Restaurante Acosta* on Plaza de las Flores is noted for its fish and *mariscos*, and the nearby *Restaurante Reyes* is another good bet for seafood specialities. Along Carretera de la Playa, the avenue leading to the beach, you'll find *Casa Rufino*, a superb fish restaurant which does a great *arroz negro de marisco*, a good-value *menú* and a house special called a *tonteo* – eight different kinds of fish, each with its appropriate sauce. **Drinks** and *tapas* are on offer at *Bar Casino*, the town's atmospheric turn-of-the-century casino on Plaza de las Flores, or *Hermanos Moreno*, Avda. Padre Mirabent 39, off the west end of c/Diego Perez, which also has a restaurant. *Puerta del Sol*, on c/Conde del Vallellano south of Plaza de las Flores, serves up good *raciones* and has a terrace. For **music bars** – which is about as near to nightlife as Isla Cristina gets – you need to head for the northwest point of the town's peninsula between Plaza de las Flores and the harbour. Here along the narrow, white-walled and cobbled streets of the old fishing quarter is where most of the bars are congregated. You could try *Almadrabera*, c/General Mola 17, or *Pipirigaña*, c/Diego Pérez Pascual 198, with inside and outdoor patios. There's often **flamenco** staged at *Las Cañas* and *La Resaca*, two bars on c/San Antonio, and also at *Bar Gonzalo*, c/Romeu 18, a fine old drinking den with a flamenco room at the back; all are close to Plaza de las Flores. The big event in Isla Cristina is its annual **Carnaval** held in February.

Ayamonte

Although the sprawling, slighty scruffy border town of ΛYAMONTE lies only 8km from Isla Cristina, the road has to dogleg 16km around the *marismas* to get there. With Portugal now only a few hundred metres away on the opposite bank of the Río Guadiana – and easily visitable – there's a pronounced Portuguese feel to the town, and in the *horario comercial* the streets hum with the conversations of cross-border visitors who come over to do their shopping.

The warren of narrow streets behind the main square, Plaza de Ribera (aka Plaza de la Coronación) overlooking the harbour, leads up to the old town, with a couple of churches to see. The mildly interesting fourteenth-century **Iglesia de San Francisco**, with a beautiful Mudéjar *artesonado* ceiling comes first, and, following the same street, c/San Francisco, even further north will bring you to the fifteenth-century **Iglesia de San Salvador** with a striking tower which you can climb, when open, for fine views across the river to Portugal. The town's EU blue-flagged **beach** at Isla Canela, 7km to the south, though nice enough, is almost impossible to reach without transport, although there's an half-hourly bus there (summer only) from Plaza de Ribera.

Practicalities

Frequent daily buses from Huelva and Sevilla arrive at the **bus station** on Avda. de Andalucía east of the centre. Ayamonte's sleepy **Turismo**, Avda. Ramón y Cajal s/n (Mon–Sat 9am–2pm; ☎959 47 09 87), can provide a town map and information, along with details of *casas particulares*. Should you fancy cycling to the beach Autos-Golf, c/Cervantes 15 close to Plaza Ribera (☎959 47 01 25), **rent bikes** as well as cars.

Places to stay can be hard to find, especially in summer. Behind the Turismo there's the friendly but basic *Pensión Guadiana*, c/Benavente 3 (☎959 32 05 23; ③), while the *Hotel Marqués de Ayamonte*, c/Trajano 12 off Plaza de Ribera (☎959 32 01 26; ④), offers comfortable rooms with bath. East of the main square, *Hostal-Restaurante Robles*, Avda. Andalucía 121 (☎959 47 09 59), also has some pleasant en-suite rooms. Almost opposite the Turismo *Hotel Diego* (☎959 47 02 50; ⑦) is a step up in price and quality, whereas *Hostal Europa*, Avda. de la Playa 45 (☎959 47 12 39; ④), 1km south from the Turismo along the road to the beaches, is the only other budget option. The town's *parador*, at El Castillita overlooking the Río Guadiana (☎ & fax 959 32 07 00; ⑧), is modern and rather bland. Should you want to splash out, Isla Canela, Ayamonte's beach resort, has a luxury hotel which leaves the *parador* standing; the 350-room *Hotel Riu Canela* (☎959 47 71 24, fax 959 47 71 70; ⑨) is an extravagant, neo-Moorish parody surrounded by Alhambra-style gardens, fountains and swimming pools.

Ayamonte scores well in terms of **eating and drinking**, with many options clustered around the central Plaza de Ribera. A very good economical restaurant in the old town, northwest from the plaza, is the *Méson La Vitola*, c/José Pérez Barroso s/n, which serves high-standard fish and meat dishes. *La Casona*, nearby at c/Lusitania 2, offers an inexpensive *menú*, and has a terrace. *Cafetería Restaurante Barberi*, next to where the bus stops, serves up economical *platos combinados*. For a pricey blowout, the town's best place – especially for fish – is *Casa Luciano*, c/Palma 2 near the Turismo, which, despite a drab exterior, does excellent food and has a *menú*. For meals at the beach, *Restaurante Andalucía* is a worthy choice and offers a variety of seafood options.

On to Portugal

For a change of scene you can cross over the expansive Río Guadiana to **Portugal** by boat, or by the impressive new road bridge (see below). A ferry (half-hourly until 9pm) plies across the estuary and border to **VILA REAL DE SANTO ANTONIO** which, although it has a dearth of overnight accommodation, has a riverside promenade packed with popular bars and restaurants. The ferry leaves from the Muelle de Portugal dock in Ayamonte – easily reached by taking the main pedestianized thoroughfare, c/Lusitania, from the west side of Plaza de Ribera. **By car** you simply head north out of town along c/Galdames following signs for Portugal and fairly soon you'll be flying effortlessly – and without any border checks whatsoever – high above the river via the magnificent Puente del Guadiana.

Inland to Río Tinto

Of the potential routes to the mountainous north of the province, the westernmost, from near Ayamonte, is the least interesting. Here the road ploughs on endlessly through a dreary landscape dominated by stands of voracious alien eucalyptus which have sucked the lifeblood from the soil. Far more attractive is the N435 route heading northeast from Huelva city towards Extremadura which offers – with your own transport – an interesting detour to the **mines of Río Tinto**. The **bus** uses the same route to reach Aracena or you could take a **train** which will drop you at Almonaster La Real at the Sierra de Aracena's western end.

THE MINES OF RÍO TINTO

The **Río Tinto** (or Red River) takes its name from the oxidised iron minerals which flow down from the fissured crags of this strange, forbidding landscape turning the river blood-red. Evidence of mineral exploitation here goes back at least five millennia – popular tradition asserts that these were the legendary mines of King Solomon, as seen in place names such as Cerro (or hill) de Saloman and Zalamea La Real. More secure historical evidence shows it was the **Phoenicians** who encouraged exploitation here early in the first millennium BC, during the age of the fabled kingdom of Tartessus from where they aquired the copper to smelt with the tin of Cornwall to make bronze. It was not copper but silver, however, which attracted the **Romans** in the second century BC. Production was dramatically stepped up during the late Republic and early Empire using remarkable – if brutal – systems to combat flooding, the perennial hazard in deep mining. This they overcame by means of slave-operated *norias*, or water wheels; in some workings as many as eight pairs of these wheels were used in relays to raise water from depths of 100 metres and more (see p.000). For the shackled slave miners working with primitive tools by the light of small clay lamps in warrens of cramped, dark galleries, life must have been wretched. The scale of the Roman operations can be judged from the fifty million tons of visible slag left behind.

After the Romans had gone, the **Visigoths** worked out the Roman shafts but the mines were then run down during the Moorish period – although Niebla built part of its prosperity on its rights of ownership by granting permits. The *conquista* brought further decline in its wake as cheap mineral wealth flooded into Spain from the New World. Loss of empire and hard times induced efforts to restart the industry which, in 1873, resulted in the Spanish government selling the mines to a consortium of British and German bankers. Out of this the **Río Tinto Mining Company** was born, bringing numerous northern Europeans to work here; in 1954 control of the company returned into Spanish hands.

Once clear of Huelva the N435 climbs steadily towards **TRIGUEROS**, a pleasant agricultural village which claims proprietorship over the Neolithic Dolmen de Soto 8km to the southwest (see p.279). **Valverde del Camino**, 24km north, is a market town noted more for its leather footwear than its charm, and the road continues a further 10km to where a turn on the right towards the hamlet of **EL POZUELO** allows you to see **three dolmens** from the third millennium BC. Following this road for about 2km brings you to a dirt track marked "dolmens", just before the cemetery on the outskirts of the village. A further 2km along, the road forks, with a gate on the left. Leave any transport here and follow the track on the right which ascends the hill through trees for about 100m to the first dolmen, from where the other two can be seen on hills nearby. The first dolmen has three burial chambers, two with their capstones still in place. The second has four burial chambers, and the last is in ruins.

The N435 winds into the wooded hill country of the Sierra Morena until – just beyond Zalamea La Real – a right turn along the C421 leads you into the area of the Río Tinto mines.

Minas de Riotinto and around

Set in an area dramatically scarred by open-cast mineworkings, where the exposed faces of mineral-rich rock are streaked with glinting rivulets of ochre, rust and cadmium, the village of **MINAS DE RIOTINTO** (served by daily buses from Huelva), 6km east of the N435, was created by the Río Tinto mining company in the early twentieth century after they had dynamited its predecessor – complete with Baroque church – which had stood in the way of mining operations.

As you approach it, watch out on the left for the **Barrio de Bella Vista**, or what the locals refer to as the "English colony". This estate of Victorian villas, complete with neo-Gothic Presbyterian church and village green, was constructed to house the largely British management and engineering staff when the mines passed into Anglo-German hands in the nineteenth century. The attitude of this elite to the surrounding village – where the mineworkers lived – is indicated by the estate's high perimeter wall and once-guarded entry gates intended rigorously to exclude "the natives" as they were disdainfully described. In a company policy with racist overtones these "colonialists" were forbidden from living in Bella Vista if they dared to marry a Spanish woman, thus deterring any dangerous interbreeding. In the woods beyond the laurel hedgerows surrounding the church, a war memorial records the names of company staff (management only) who fell in the Great War. The estate now houses local people and can be visited as part of the guided tour from the visitor centre at Nerva (see p.303), or you can usually just wander in for a look around.

The mining museum

At the village's western edge on a hill above the Río Tinto company's offices lies the Río Tinto Foundation's **mining museum**, Plaza del Museo s/n (daily 10am–3pm; 300ptas). With transport, continue past the office building – normally flying flags – and at the roundabout take the road ascending to the right. At the next junction turn right and follow the road to the top of the hill where, on the right, you'll see one of the old mine steam trains outside the museum. Alternatively, on foot, you can take the path from opposite the company offices uphill through the pine woods.

Housed in the company's former hospital, the museum presents an interesting panorama of mining in the area from prehistoric to modern times. The **Roman period** is the best represented, with exhibits illustrating their mining methods, daily life and burial practices in addition to a variety of coins and statuary. Modern mining is also covered, as well as the geology, flora and fauna of the area. Don't miss the luxurious **wagon of the maharaja**, built in 1892 by the Birmingham Railway Carriage and Wagon

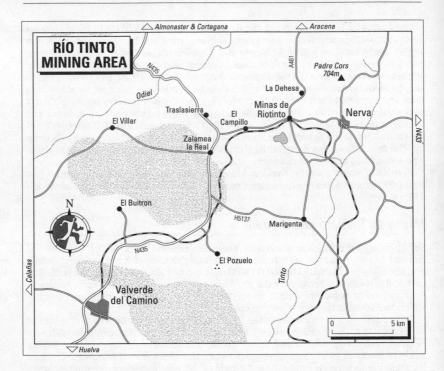

RÍO TINTO MINING AREA

Almonaster & Cortegana   Aracena

N435

Odiel

Padre Cors
704m▲

La Dehesa

Traslasierra   El
Campillo

Minas de
Riotinto   Nerva

El Villar

Zalamea
la Real

N

El Buitron

H5137   Marigenta

N435

El Pozuelo

Tinto

Valverde
del Camino

Calañas

0   5 km

Huelva

Company to be used by Queen Victoria on her proposed visit to India. When this didn't happen it was sold to the Río Tinto company and used for the visit of King Alfonso XIII to the mines. Though compact, the museum is ever-expanding, thanks to the energies of its enthusiastic director Pedro Lorenzo Gómez; recent additions include a wonderfully restored **steam train**. The museum can also provide information on a new visit to the old underground workings of Pozo Alfredo.

In addition, the Río Tinto Foundation's marketing arm, Aventura Minaparque runs **train trips**, lasting a couple of hours, through the mining area aboard century-old restored rolling stock – on the first Sunday of each month they use a 115-year-old steam locomotive (June–Sept Tues–Sun 1pm; ring ☎959 59 00 25 for winter/spring timetable; 1200ptas). The same organization also offers combined three-hour visits to the mining area taking in the Corta Atalaya and the Cerro Colorado mines, the Bella Vista Victorian housing estate, the Roman mineworkings and cemetery and the steam engine and mining museums (details from the museum).

To **stay** here *Hostal Galán,* c/Romero de Milla s/n (☎959 59 08 40; ③), around the corner from the museum, has rooms with bath and a good bar-restaurant below, or there's the *Hostal Los Cantos*, Bda. Los Cantos s/n (☎958 59 16 89; ④) a stone's throw away which has air-conditioned rooms above its own restaurant. On the hill above the village the good-value *Hotel Santa Barbara*, c/Cerro de los Embusteros s/n (☎959 59 18 52, fax 959 59 06 27; ⑤) is a more luxurious affair with great views and a pool, and the price includes breakfast. Downhill from the *Hostal Galán, Restaurante Epoca,* Paseo de los Caracoles 6, is another decent place for *platos combinados* and has a *menú*.

La Dehesa and Nerva

Two kilometres north of the village you pass two spectacular open-cast mines, the **Corta Atalaya** and – with 5000 years of exploitation behind it – the **Cerro Colorado**, set in an awesome landscape of rock cliffs glittering with iron pyrites, copper, silver and gold. From a **viewing platform** by the roadside you can see into the giant elliptical basin of the Corta Atalaya, which at 1200 metres long and 330 metres deep is one of the biggest open-cast mines in the world – far below, enormous trucks are dwarfed by the immense walls of rock. Another 2km further on, at **LA DEHESA**, the Río Tinto Company headquarters are backed by a recently discovered **Roman graveyard** featuring a number of interesting tombstones. Alarmingly close to the present mining operations which rumble on in the background, the graveyard is open to the public only on guided tours (see above).

NERVA, 4km west of Minas de Riotinto, is a pleasant little place, its pedestrianized main street fringed with orange trees and overlooked by a splendid redbrick *Ayuntamiento* with a wonderful minaret-inspired octagonal tower. Just opposite this there's an extravagant new **Centro de Arte Contemporáneo** (Tues–Fri 10am–2pm & 4–8pm) honouring Daniel Vásquez Díaz, a Paris contemporary of Picasso, who was born here. In addition to a handful of canvases by Díaz the museum also displays an indifferent collection of works by other *nerveuses* to fill the rather cavernous interior. Nerva's **Turismo**, Ctra. Sevilla s/n, by the Sevilla exit from the town under a huge pit wheel (daily 10am–2pm & 5–8pm; ☎959 58 00 73) also runs visits to the mines and offers guided walks and mountain bike tours of the mining zone. There are two daily **buses** (except Sun) to Aracena at 6am and 6.20pm.

Nerva also has a pleasant **place to stay**, the friendly, family-run *Hostal El Goro*, c/Reina Victoria s/n (☎ & fax 959 58 04 37; ②), close to the centre, with some en-suite rooms and its own bar. A good **place to eat** is the central *Bodegón El Sótano*, Avda. de Andalucía 40, serving *tapas* and a 900ptas *menú*.

Leaving the mining area by the A461, beyond Campofrío the landscape softens as the road progresses through verdant forests of cork and holm oaks, chestnut and walnut trees towards Aracena.

The Sierra Morena

The longest of Spain's mountain ranges, the **Sierra Morena** extends almost the whole way across Andalucía from Rosal on the Portuguese frontier to the dramatic pass of Despeñaperros, north of Linares. Its hill towns once marked the northern boundary of the old Moorish Caliphate of Córdoba and in many ways the region still signals a break today, with a shift from the climate and mentality of the south to the bleak plains and villages of Extremadura and New Castile. The range is not widely known – with its highest point a mere 1110m, it is not a dramatic sierra – and even Andalucians can have trouble placing it. All of which, of course, is to your advantage if you like to be alone.

Visiting the Sierra Morena

The Morena's **climate** is mild – sunny in spring, hot but fresh in summer – but it can get very cold in the evenings and mornings. A good time to visit is between March and June, when the flowers, perhaps the most varied in the country, are at their best. You may get caught in the odd thunderstorm but it's usually bright and hot enough to swim in the reservoirs or splash in the springs and streams, most of which are good to drink. This is an area rich in **wildlife**; if your way takes you along a river, you'll be entertained by armies of frogs and turtles plopping into the water as you approach, by lizards, dragonflies, bees, hares and foxes peering discreetly from their holes – and usually no humans for miles around. Bird fanciers should keep an eye out for imperial and booted eagles, as well as goshawks and the rare black vulture. The sierra is also home to one of two surviving populations of Spanish lynx on the peninsula, although, with only thirty or so pairs eking out an existence as their forest habitat is gnawed away, you're unlikely to spot one.

Locals maintain that while the last bears disappeared only a short time ago, there are still a few wolves in remoter parts. Of more concern to anyone hiking in the Sierra Morena, however, are the **toros bravos** (fighting bulls), always in fenced-off pastures. Observe signs by roads and tracks depicting a bull and sometimes labelled "*toros bravos*". Apparently, a group of bulls is less to be feared than a single one, and a single one only if he directly bars your way and looks mean. The thing to do, according to expert advice, is to stay calm, and without attracting the bull's attention, go round. If you even get a whiff of a fighting bull, though, it might well be best simply to drop everything and run.

East–west **transport** in the Sierra (see "Travel Details" on p.321) is limited but with a little planning most places mentioned below can be reached on public transport. For the zone east of Aracena, specifically the terrain beyond the main N630 in Sevilla Province, bus services are radial and north–south, with Sevilla as the hub. Tracks are still more common in these hills than roads, and rural tourism, which the government of Andalucía is keen to encourage, has so far led to little more than a handful of signs pointing out areas of special interest. The wealth of good **walking country** invites organizing your routes round hikes – if you want to spend any amount of time here. Hitching lifts between villages isn't too difficult as although cars are few, they're bound to be making for the same place as you, so drivers are often willing to stop. **Cycling**, too, is an option, though you'll need a sturdy bike with plenty of gears, especially on the winding and muscle-taxing hill roads.

Aracena

Clustered beneath its hill-top medieval castle, the attractive town of **ARACENA** is the highest conurbation in the Sierra Morena as well as the gateway to its own **Sierra de Aracena** to the south and west. Sheltered by this offshoot of the larger Morena range, Aracena is blessed by remarkably sharp, clear air – all the more noticeable, and gratifying, if you've arrived from the heat of Sevilla.

Although traces of Paleolithic occupation of this area have been found, it was only in the Middle Ages that more concrete historical events happened here, namely the passing of this territory into the kingdom of Castile by a treaty of 1267 following a long struggle with Portugal. Once inside the domains of Castile, Alfonso X ceded the zone around Aracena to the Knights Templars to maintain and protect the Sierra. They constructed the castle, one of many erected in this frontier zone, and ruled the roost here until 1312 (see box opposite). Today, the town's main role is as a centre of agriculture and cattle breeding, assisted by the tourist magnet of the Gruta de las Maravillas (Cave of Wonders).

The Town

Aracena itself is a sturdy but pretty Sierra town, its southern flank rambling up the side of a hill topped by the **Iglesia del Castillo** – or, more correctly, Nuestra Señora de los Dolores – a fine thirteenth-century Gothic-Mudéjar church built by the Knights Templar around the remains of a Moorish castle. The track up to the church begins from the **Plaza Alta**, where there's the unfinished church of **Nuestra Señora de la Asunción** with remnants of Renaissance craftsmanship, flanked by a sixteenth-century **Ayuntamiento**, the oldest in the province which now houses the natural park information centre (see below). The building's imposing main portal is by Hernán Ruíz II and dates to 1563. Slightly northeast of here, the interior of the **Convento de Santa**

THE KNIGHTS TEMPLARS

A military religious order founded in the twelfth century to protect pilgrims bound for the Holy Land, the **Knights Templars** derived their name from the Temple of Solomon in Jerusalem. An army of fighting monks in reality, their *raison d'être* became a permanent crusade against the Saracen infidel from their "commanderies" in the Holy Land and western Europe.

For over a century the Templars fought the Muslims for control of Jerusalem and its surrounding territories. A series of defeats culminated in the loss of Acre in 1291, their last Latin outpost in Palestine, and heralded the order's demise. They were also mistrusted by the European monarchs, such as Philip IV of France, who saw the order as a threat to their power. Long accused of being involved in witchcraft due to their interest in the occult, magic and the supernatural as paths to ultimate knowledge, the Templars were persecuted, condemned and executed for heresy by an alliance of monarchs and clerics across Europe. The order was finally dissolved by a bull of Pope Clement V in 1312. In the light of the above it's rather ironic that Aracena's Templar outpost was built on top of one of the most magical and mysterious places in Spain: the Gruta de las Maravillas, of which they must have been completely unaware.

Catalina, with its fine fifteenth-century Gothic panels, is also worth a look. It was for this convent that the stunning carved wood *retablo* by Juan Giralte, now in Sevilla's Museo de Bellas Artes, was made. The climb to the castle offers good views over the town from an imposing sixteenth-century brick gate complete with belfry, which allows access to the castle area. The church's elegant **Mudéjar tower** was formerly the minaret of the twelfth-century Almohad mosque prior to its destruction by the Templars, and its *sebka* brickwork ornamentation echoes the Giralda tower in Sevilla. Inside there's an unusual and finely made glazed clay tomb of the sixteenth-century prior, Pedro Vásquez de Miguel.

Aracena's principal attraction is the **Gruta de las Maravillas** (daily 10.30am–1.30pm & 3–6pm; guided hourly visits, half-hourly at weekends; 900ptas), the largest and arguably the most impressive cave in Spain. The Gruta lies at the western end of c/Rosal which you can pick up just south of the Plaza Mayor (Plaza Marqués de Aracena). Discovered, so they say, by a local boy in search of a lost pig, the cave is now illuminated and open for guided tours of up to fifty people; you may need a sweater. A guide takes you round the cave and the "marvels" are explained in Spanish only (leaflet in English). Although the garish coloured lighting is more Santa's Grotto than geological marvel, the cave is still astonishingly beautiful, and quite a laugh, too – the last chamber of the tour is known simply as the Sala de los Culos (Room of the Buttocks), its walls and ceiling an outrageous, naturally sculpted exhibition, tinged in a pinkish orange light. You might care to ponder why this section of the caves did not appear in the film *Journey to the Centre of the Earth*, much of which was shot here. In the plaza outside there's a permanent **outdoor museum of contemporary sculpture**. Sniffily dismissed by many of its critics, despite the vapid nature of some of the works on show it seems an interesting idea – make up your own mind.

Practicalities

For information and a town map, you'll find Aracena's **Turismo** beneath the Gruta de las Maravillas ticket office (daily 10am–2.30pm & 4–6.30pm; ☎959 12 82 06). Information on the surrounding Parque Natural Sierra de Aracena is obtainable from an **information centre** in the ancient *cabildo*, Plaza Alta 5 (see above).

Places to stay are limited: the budget option, the simple and friendly *Casa Manolo*, c/Barberos 6 (☎959 12 80 14; ③), lies below the main square, Plaza Marqués de

Aracena, but outside summer make sure to get an exterior room as the inside ones (which get no sun) can be freezing. Upmarket possibilities include the *Hotel Sierra de Aracena*, Gran Vía 21 (☎959 12 61 75, fax 959 12 62 18; ⑤), and the pleasant *Hotel de los Castaños*, Avda. de Huelva 5, off Gran Vía (☎959 12 63 00, fax 959 12 62 87; ⑤), both with heating, garage and many facilities. With your own transport, you could try the *Finca Valbono* (☎959 12 77 11, fax 959 12 76 79; ⑥), a new rural hotel with pool and restaurant set in thirty acres of scenic woodland, 1km north of town on the road to Carboneras. Beside hotel rooms there are also *casita* stone houses equipped with kitchens, and in addition all kinds of activities including hiking and horse-riding excursions are on offer. The nearest **campsite**, *Camping Aracena Sierra* (☎959 50 10 05) which has a pool, lies 3km along the Sevilla road, then left for 500m towards Corteconcepción.

EATING, DRINKING AND NIGHTLIFE

As Aracena is at the heart of a prestigious *jamón*-producing area, anything with pork is highly recommended – you should also try the delicious wild asparagus, mushrooms (Sepember onwards) and local snails (June to August). **Places to eat** in town are clustered around the main square, Plaza Marqués de Aracena. *Café-Bar Manzano*, at the southern end, serves great *tapas* and *platos combinados* and has a terrace, but for a splurge, head for *Restaurante José Vicente* Avda. Andalucía 51, where patrons gather to savour the five grades of Jabugo *jamón ibérico* (black pig ham) under the approving gaze of owner/chef Vicente Sierra. The *menú*, which often includes a mouthwatering *solomillo* (pork loin), is recommended and there is now a new *tapas* bar as well, *Despensa de José Vicente* that also sells natural products from the sierra. Vicente is also an expert on the sierra's *setas* (mushrooms), many remarkable examples of which he keeps in his freezer for use in the kitchen. You can find the restaurant by taking the first right uphill from the *Casino* (see below); after a couple of hundred metres it's on the left opposite the park. At lunchtime (that is, until 4pm) decent alternatives are provided by two restaurants near the entrance to the Gruta de las Maravillas: the outstanding *Casas*, Pozo La Nieve 39, and the nearby *La Serrana,* both slightly extravagant, with *menús* for around 2000ptas. More reasonable are the nearby *Mesón Rural Pepe Limón*, c/Pozo de la Nieve s/n, with an economical *menú*, and *Rábida*, in c/Chopos, on the right as you approach the *Gruta* from the centre, which has a 1000ptas *menú*.

For **breakfast** or **evening drinks**, sit with the locals at the outdoor tables of the Casino bar above the main square, from where you get a wonderful view towards the castle. Finally, for superb dulces, the century-old Confitería Casa Rufino, off the main square at c/Constitución 3, is a must; their tocino de cielo, vitorías (liqueur-soaked, iced cakes) and sultanas (filled coconut cakes) are truly memorable – in the afternoon do what everyone else does, and take your cakes to Café Manzano's terrace (see above).

Nightlife is low-key, but turning left at the end of Gran Vía along c/Juan del Cid will bring you to numerous **bars** and **discos** frequented by Aracena's younger set. *D'Acuña*, at Gran Vía 20 and the nearby *Cafetería Bronze* are other good *copas* bars with a lively atmosphere.

The Sierra de Aracena

With a few days to spare, the string of rugged villages perched on the hills to the **west of Aracena** make a fine walking tour. Along the route you'll find a number of good places to stay and plenty of tracks to follow through this rich landscape of orange and lemon orchards and forests of cork oaks, chestnut and gum trees. In spring the profusion of flowers is extraordinary: rosemary, French lavender, peonies, and Spanish irises are most common, and you may also be lucky enough to see the rare brown bluebell and members of the orchid family. You probably won't glimpse the Spanish lynx in its

last native habitat (outside the Coto de Doñana), but the skies are the place for sightings of black vultures on patrol, and even the occasional imperial eagle, a stirring image as they glide regally above their domain.

The **bus service** between Aracena and the villages of Alájar, Almonaster, Cortegana and Aroche currently runs twice daily at 1pm and 5.30pm (not Sun), the latter terminating at Cortegana. There are also four daily buses (Mon–Sat) between Aracena and Galaroza, Jabugo, Cortegana and Aroche at 7.30am, 10.30am (also Sun), 1.15am (terminates at Cortegana) and 5.30pm (this service is two buses with one calling at Linares, Alájar and Cortegana, the other passing all the rest along the main N432). Similar services return in the reverse direction. All leave from the Aracena bus station on Avda. Andalucía (near the Convento de Santa Catalina), but things change so check there or with the Turismo for the latest timetable.

Alájar

Leaving Aracena by the minor A470, after about 7km a turn-off left leads to the tiny village of **Linares de la Sierra**, a fairly simple and impoverished place huddled around its eighteenth-century Baroque church, a typical example of the sierra style, and curious unpaved bullring plaza. Its sandy surface and *barreras*, behind which the toreros dodge the fearsome fighting bulls, seem a somewhat eccentric aberration considering that the ring is put to use only a couple of times a year in the village's fiestas. There's no accommodation in the village, but the bars in the centre serve food and there's also a good **restaurant**, *El Arrieros*, c/Arrieros s/n. A further 4km along the A470, lined with chestnut orchards and great clumps of oregano, a turning on the left descends to **ALÁJAR**, a delightful, cobble-streeted hamlet at the foot of the Peña de Arias Montano. There's another eighteenth-century Baroque church here with the typical spire, besides plenty of places to eat or have a beer, all clustered around the main square.

Each September 7 and 8, the village holds a *romerío* or pilgrimage to the hermitage of the **Virgen de los Ángeles** – an isolated church or *ermita* – on the Peña de Arias Montano hill, 1km above the village. This involves the young men of the village in the *polleo,* a rite of passage in which these young bloods race horses along the narrow cobbled streets and then up the steep slope to the shrine high above. The horses are mercilessly spurred and arrive foaming and bleeding at the top of the climb.

For overnight **accommodation** there's the pleasant *Hotel La Posada,* c/Emilio González 2, off the west side of Plaza Constitución (☎959 12 57 12; ④), which has rooms with bath and heating and also serves **food**. An excellent place for more elaborate but equally inexpensive meals is the *Mesón El Molino,* in a converted old mill with all its original features just up from the main square at c/Alta 9.

Peña de Arias Montano

On quieter days the **Peña De Arias Montano**, the rock cliff which towers above the village, is a beautiful leafy spot set among woods of cork oaks, with cold springs surrounding its **shrine**. The Sierra Morena is liberally dotted with these buildings, almost always in isolated spots and dedicated to the Virgin. The site has been hallowed since prehistoric times, and Iberian shamans or priests are reputed to have gained their "second sight" from the hallucinogenic *amanita muscaria* mushroom which grows in the woods here – you are advised against experimenting as some species found in these hills can kill in thirty minutes. The sixteenth-century **hermitage of the Virgen de los Ángeles**, filled with ex-votos from pilgrims and distinguished more by the beauty of its setting than for any architectural qualities, is the former retreat of the humanist Benito Arias Montano, confessor and librarian to Philip II, who was born nearby in 1527 and gave his name to the site. The *espadaña,* or belfry, to the side of the church dates from the same period and offers glorious views over Alájar beneath, and the Sierra beyond. A **cavern** below the car park is said to be where magical and religious ceremonies were carried out in ancient times and where Philip II is supposed to have meditated during a visit here – giving it the name *Sillita del Rey* (the king's chair), a reference to the huge boulder at the cave's mouth. You reach it by steps from the car park, taking the path to the right at the bottom.

The true peace of the place is best appreciated by leaving the visitors' area with its car park, toilets, café and stalls selling honey, garish pots and religious tack, and heading along the track into the woods of cork oaks where there are plenty of likely picnic spots, and more fine views over the Sierra.

Santa Ana La Real and Almonaster La Real

Six kilometres west of Alájar the modest but pretty village of **SANTA ANA LA REAL** is worth a detour. *Bar Garrafa* is a handy place for refreshment, and a couple of kilo-

A WALK FROM ALÁJAR TO LINARES DE LA SIERRA

A fine 6km **walk** from Alájar to Linares de la Sierra takes in the delightful isolated hamlet of **Los Madroñeros** whose grassy streets can only otherwise be reached by tractors and off-road vehicles. To find the start of the walk take the street left along the north side of Alájar's church to a *plazuela* (small square) and follow the street downhill to an open area. The path follows the old road, climbing beyond an indicator board (detailing the walk) on the far side. Should you lose the way ask for the *camino antiguo a Los Madroñeros*. Once on the track it soon leads away from the village running between dry stone walls behind which are cork oaks sheltering *pata negra* black pigs, soon to be turned into the region's prized *jamón*. The settlement of Los Madroñeros is a tranquil haven: a huddle of traditional white-walled dwellings topped by distinctive chimney-pots with green grass all around. You'll be lucky to see any inhabitants as they seem to keep a low profile, unlike their numerous cats who will eye you curiously as they sun themselves on rooftops or any convenient flat stone.

The *camino* leads on eastwards away from the village, gently climbing and falling with only one place which may confuse. Just after crossing a stream, about half-way between Los Madroñeros and Linares, you'll come to a deserted semi-ruined farmhouse; the path here isn't immediately clear but you need to go through the gateway of this place to pick up the track on the other side. Soon after you reach **Linares**. To return to Alájar you can retrace your route or follow the road back (the A470). Alternatively you could time your arrival to meet up with Alájar-bound buses (see above) passing through about 1.15 or 5.45pm.

metres beyond it is a convenient **place to stay**, at the junction of the A470 and the N435 – is the modern *Hostal El Cruce* (☎959 12 23 33; ④), set in fine scenery with a lively *tapas* bar. A couple of kilometres north of here, along the N435, there's a charming Sierra restaurant, *La Abuela*, in the village of Aguafría. Specialities here include the great *jamones* of the region as well as tasty oven-baked (*horno*) and barbecued-pork dishes. Continuing east for another 6km brings you to the main village of this corner of the Sierra, the picturesque **ALMONASTER LA REAL** huddled in a river valley below the peak of the same name, which at 912m is the sierra's highest summit. A sturdy agricultural centre today, Almonaster has an impressive Moorish past and an important tenth-century **mosque** on a hill to the south of the town. The mosque may have Roman and Visigothic antecedents, and after it became Christianized in the thirteenth century was little altered, thus preserving its square minaret, the *mihrab* (said to be the oldest in Spain) and beautiful interior of five naves with brick horseshoe arches supported by what are probably recycled Roman columns. It should be open, but if not, ask at the *Ayuntamiento*, Plaza de la Constitución, for the key. Tacked on to the mosque/church is the village **bullring** where each August a *corrida* is staged during Almonaster's annual fiesta (see box p.310). The mosque's tower is a favourite with the kids of the village at this time, as it provides a free view of the ring.

The village's other main sight is the fourteenth-century Mudéjar-style church of **San Martín** (open service times 7–9pm), whose most notable feature is a superb sixteenth-century Manueline portal, probably Portuguese in inspiration. Also worth a look is the **hermitage of Santa Eulalia**, built over a Roman funerary monument and boasting late-Gothic frescoes depicting the exploits of Santiago the *matamoros* or "Moorslayer".

A popular event here in early summer is the **Cruz de Mayo** – a flamenco festival held over the last weekend in May – at which the celebrated *fandangos* of Almonaster are sung and the local women parade in the magnificent costume of the *Serrana* (highlands): colourful flounced dresses and tasselled shoes and shawls, complemented by

COUNTRY CORRIDAS

Like many other country rings, the **bullring** at Almonaster does not see much action. In fact, the prohibitive cost of mounting a **corrida** with six bulls, three *matadores* and their retinues often restricts a small village to one *corrida* each year, usually in the middle of its annual fiesta. To see a bullfight at places like Almonaster, however, is to get a fascinating insight into many of the secrets of the *corrida* hidden from view in the large city rings. Because the ring itself is barely large enough to hold the arena and a few hundred spectators, just squeezing in a room for the *matadores* and a pen for the bulls, many of the preparations have to take place outside.

First of all, while the arena is doused from a water tanker, the **picadores** select their 2.5m-long lances from a couple of dozen leaning against the wall of the ring. When they've chosen, a blacksmith attaches one of three lethal-looking steel points, again selected by the *picador*. Meanwhile, below the walls of the mosque, the grooms prepare the **horses** – whose vocal chords are severed so as not to alarm the crowd with their terrified shrieks – by fastening on the *peto* or heavy padding, protection against the bull's ferocious horns. Next the horses' ears are stuffed with oil-soaked rags and securely tied to block out the sound of the crowd and the bull. Finally, they are blindfolded over the right eye, the side from which the bull will attack. Fifteen minutes before the *corrida* is due to start the **village band** marches up the hill playing a lively tune – with frequent wrong notes – before disappearing inside the arena.

Inside, the band strikes up a *paso doble* for the pre-fight parade before the grotesque figure of the helmeted and armoured *picador* is pushed through the small doorway into the ring and a great cheer goes up from the crowd inside. They are soon yelling *"fuera!"* (away!), however, because they don't want the bull too weakened by the lance to be able to put up a decent fight. A few minutes later the trumpets sound and the door opens to allow the *picador* astride the strutting, snorting horse to exit from the arena. With fresh blood dripping from his lance, the image of this warrior is almost medieval. Big-name *toreros* appear in these village *corridas* because the pay is good, but equally the risks are high. The primitive nature of rings such as the one at Almonaster means a long journey to reach a hospital with adequate facilities should the *matador* be seriously gored, a factor which has, in the past, proved fatal.

bouquets of wild flowers. The whole affair provides the participants with an excuse to soak up prodigious quantities of the local *aguardiente* firewater, which is misleadingly described as brandy. If you can't make this one, similar festivals take place in the surrounding villages all through May.

Almonaster's **train** station – with infrequent services to Huelva – lies 3km north of the village and is, in fact, nearer to Cortegana (see below). Outside the festival period, finding a **place to stay** is usually no problem. At the entrance to the village *Hostal Casa García* (☎959 14 31 09; ③) is comfortable, and has a good restaurant downstairs – try their *tortilla de jamón y espárragos*. Further in, the village's other possibility, *Hostal La Cruz*, Plaza El Llano 8 (☎959 14 31 35; ③), nicely located on a tranquil square, is slightly less expensive and has its own restaurant and *tapas* bar. Perhaps the best place of all for **food** is the plant-bedecked *Las Palmeras* on the road into the village before *Casa García*. Voluble proprietor Alejandro produces everything on the economical *menú* himself from the tasty *caña de lomo* (cured *jámon* from his own pigs) to the salads from his *huerta*. *Mesón La Bodega*, c/Cervantes, off the Plaza de la Constitución, is an offshoot of *Casa García* in a large *casa antigua* with terrace and bar.

Cortegana

Roughly 2km out of Almonaster the road forks left to **CORTEGANA**, a pleasant and populous *pueblo* spreading along the valley of the Río Carabaña below a heavily

WALKS AROUND ALMONASTER

There are some superb **walks around Almonaster**, following the old cobbled mule paths and village tracks (*senderos*). The paths are well preserved, on the whole – though at times you are forced on to the tarmac road – and are waymarked with paint-splashes on trees and rocks. You need sharp eyes to spot the beginning of the paths, below the road, and if you can, you should try to get hold of the *Senderos de la Sierra de Aracena y Picos de Aroche* walks pamphlet from the *Ayuntamientos* in Almonaster, Cortegana or Jabugo. This is easy to follow with minimal Spanish and has route descriptions and an excellent fold-out survey map. Cortegana also produces its own leaflet, *Senderos de Pequeño Recorrido en el Entorno de Cortegana*, with a good map and covering much of the same ground, which is available from the *Ayuntamiento* (see below). You'd be advised to take along as well a decent 1:100,000 or 1:50,000 map (CNIG sheets 895 & 916 for the latter), just in case you lose the way.

One of the most enjoyable walks, starting from Almonaster, is the **PRA-5** which leads off to the left of the Cortegana road, around 1km out of Almonaster. This takes you through woodland peppered with streams to the hamlets of **Arroyo** and **Varedas** (2hr), where there are bars with food, and on to Cortegana (3hr). Alternatively, if it's just a brief country ramble you're after, follow the sign to Acebuches along the **PRA-5-2** path, under an hour from Almonaster, and again endowed with a small bar.

Another fine walk from Almonaster is to head straight up the hillside northeast of the village along the **PRA-5-1**. This is actually a paved Roman track, presumably built for some kind of quarrying. It takes a couple of hours' strenuous walking to get up to the summit, and, if you're making a day of it, you could continue on to Cortegana or Jabugo.

restored castle. Built in the thirteenth century during the frontier disputes with the Portuguese, the **Castillo** (officially open Mon–Fri 10am–1.30pm; otherwise enquire at the *Ayuntamiento*, c/Maura 1, just off the Plaza de la Constitución) provided a necessary observation post and today gives fine views from its battlements.

Two churches here are also worth visiting. The **Iglesia del Divino Salvador** (open service times; try 7–9pm) was started in the late sixteenth century but has elements added from much later, such as its bell tower, when the original collapsed in the Lisbon earthquake of 1755. The interior has a finely worked Baroque pulpit. Built in Gothic Mudéjar style, the church of **San Sebastián** (open service times; try 7–9pm) nearby has interesting Renaissance doors.

If you want to **stay** in Cortegana, you could try the *Hostal Cervantes*, c/Cervantes 27 (☎959 13 15 92; ②), which is clean and comfortable with some rooms en-suite. A more tempting option may be *Los Gallos* (☎959 50 11 67; apartments sleeping four for 12,000ptas) on the main road near to Almonaster train station. Here you can rent one of three apartments in a restored farmhouse, set in spectacular countryside with gardens and a pool. They have special mid-week and off peak deals which can reduce prices by half. At the start of the road out towards Aroche (no. 61 – there's no sign) the friendly *Villa Cinta* (☎959 13 15 22; ④ including breakfast) is another possibility where rooms are en suite and have stunning views.

For **eating and drinking** a number of bars around the centre serve **tapas**: the *Casino*, a turn-of-the-century institution, on Plaza Constitución, is one that also makes a pleasant morning-coffee stop as it has all the newspapers. The attractive *Meca Café* and *El Trueco* next door on the central Plaza del Divino Salvador serve *tapas* and act as hangouts for the local *juventud*, which is why they give out information on local events and concerts. The best (but not the cheapest) places for **meals** are *Restaurante Tito* on the main N433 road (a fifteen-minute walk from the centre) and *El Fogón* opposite the train station with a *tapas* bar. Less pricey alternatives include the rather chic *El Aceiton*,

A WALK FROM CORTEGANA TO LA POSADA

A scenic 10km **walk** north from Cortegana follows the valleys of the Arroyo Carabaña and Río Caliente to *La Posada de Cortegana*, a unique rural hotel and restaurant serving an excellent lunch. Leave Cortegana by c/Sevilla, located behind the church on the southeast side of the village. This soon leads into Callejón Carabaña – a rough track which descends to an *arroyo* or stream. When you meet the main N433 road keep ahead and follow a track to the left heading downhill. Cross a stream (the Arroyo Carabaña) in the valley and follow the path as it heads north along the right bank soon passing a *finca* (house) to the left named Los Molinos. Not far beyond this you'll reach a house at a crossing over the stream run by some friendly New Agers. Once over the stream continue north for about 3km.

The path zig-zags back and forth over the stream always heading north and it isn't always obvious where you should and shouldn't cross. However, if you're lucky one of the New Agers' friendly dogs may accompany you for the exercise and will guide you unerringly along the correct path which they know instinctively. You will eventually reach *La Posada* (☎959 50 33 01; ⑤) comprised of log cabins set in woodland with a great terrace **restaurant** making it the high point of the hike. Any of the pork dishes are recommended. Your only problem will be crossing the river to reach it which, if the river is high, may mean a barefoot wade. Should you decide to stop over they have **rooms** in woodland cabins, and offer horse riding, mountain biking and a pool. The path, which is signed back to Cortegana, continues behind the restaurant. Follow it for 3km until you reach a road (N433). Turn left along here to return to Cortegana, half a kilometre ahead.

Los Perales and the humble *Sierra de Cortegana* where you can contemplate fine views of the *pueblo* and sierra from your plastic chair. All three are near to c/Éritas in the town's northeast corner, and are worth the effort to find; they lie in an area where the streets have no names, so you'll need to ask.

Cortegana's big annual knees-up is the *Jornadas Medievales* **fería** held in the first or second week in August with archery contests, falconry, various tournaments and re-enactments of the storming of the castle walls – accompanied by much music, drinking and dancing. Its other main fería, *Fiestas Patronales,* occurs in early September with *corridas*, processions and concerts.

Aroche

Heading west for 14km along the N433 brings you to **AROCHE**, in sight of the border with Portugal. Perched on a hill dominated by its castle with a fertile plain below, it's a neat little place, with white-walled, cobbled streets where – because it gets so few visitors – you can be sure of a hearty reception. Aroche was originally the Roman town of *Arruci Vetus*, but many more ancient vestiges of habitation have been discovered here, including giant prehistoric single standing stones, or **menhirs**. (These **Piedras del Diablo** are on private land, so if you're interested in seeing them, enquire at the *Ayuntamiento*, Plaza de Juan Carlos I.)

Once you have made it up the hill to the village, the obvious place to aim for is the **Castillo** (Sat, Sun & public holidays 10am–2pm & 4–7pm). Constructed by the Almoravids in the twelfth century, the fort was remodelled after the *reconquista*, but the most bizarre alteration of all was to make the interior into a full-scale **bullring**. A curiosity here are the sallyports – narrow openings in the arena's stone wall – used by the *toreros* to dodge the bull, instead of the normal *barrera* or fence. Despite the primitive facilities, many big names have fought here, though it's unlikely that they stayed around long after the "kill" to use the ramshackle shower and leaking toilets in their room. If you arrive here outside the opening hours, call at the nearby *Cafetería Lalo* opposite the *Ayuntamiento*, from where local guide Manuel Amigo will open it up for you. Incidentally this bar also sells copies of *Guía de la Sierra de Aracena y Picos de Aroche*, a useful book with information about all the villages of the sierra. The *Ayuntamiento* (or Sr. Amigo) will also be able to advise on the new location of the castle's **archeological museum** – housing a collection of finds from prehistoric, Roman and Moorish periods – which, at the time of writing, is being moved. Just below the castle, the parish church of **Nuestra Señora de la Asunción** (same hours and procedure as castle above) was started in 1483 but added a mixture of Mudéjar, Gothic and Renaissance styles before its completion 150 years later. Behind a dour, buttressed exterior, the triple-naved church has a fine *retablo*, with a Baroque image of the Virgin, the patron of the town. The church's other treasures include the fifteenth-century crucifix of Cardenal Mendoza of Sevilla, the supporter of Isabel, as well as a seventeenth-century **Russian icon** from St Petersburg.

There are some pretty strange museums in Andalucía, but Aroche's **Museo del Santo Rosario** (Museum of the Holy Rosary) has to be one of the most eccentric. Located in a square at the entrance to the village off the N433 road, the exhibits consist of well over a thousand rosaries donated by such leading religious luminaries as Pope John XXIII and Mother Teresa, in addition to others from *toreros* and soccer players and one each from John F. Kennedy and King Juan Carlos. Those sent in by Richard Nixon and General Franco betray suspiciously little sign of wear.

PRACTICALITIES

Tourist information is provided by Aroche's *Ayuntamiento* in the central Plaza de Juan Carlos I (Mon–Fri 9am–1pm & 5–8pm; ☎959 14 02 01). For **accommodation**, the *Restaurante Pensión Romero*, near the entrance to the town from the N433, at c/Ordóñez Váldez s/n (☎959 14 00 22; ②) has comfortable en-suite rooms, with views and a bar. There's also *Hostal Picos de Aroche* further back down the same road, Carretera de Aracena 12 (☎959 14 04 75; ④), with more frills (literally everywhere) and TVs. When it comes to **eating and drinking** you could try *Pensión Romero*, which serves up decent *platos combinados*; alternatively, the *Centro Cultural Las Peñas*, c/Real 8, has a relaxing bar serving up a great selection of *tapas* – try the *chocos* (cuttlefish). There's also the spit and sawdust *El Chino*, c/Bellido 2, near the *Ayuntamiento*, which, despite the name, specializes in local pork dishes. The nearby and more refined *Cafetería La Peñas*, on the square, specialises in seafood *tapas* and *raciones* and has a terrace. *El Canario*, on the main road at the entrance to the village, is another decent restaurant whose specialities include a wide range of Sierra pork-based dishes. **Walks**

A WALK FROM REPILADO TO LOS ROMEROS

Returning to Aracena from Aroche by the N433 takes you through the village of **El Repilado** from where you could make a picturesque five-kilometre **walk** south along the Río Caliente to the charming village of Los Romeros. Leave Repilado by the N433 road towards Cortegana and after crossing the bridge over the river, turn left along the H111 going to Los Romeros. Where the road traverses to the east bank of the river, follow the track along the west bank which leads through woods of chestnut and black poplar, and where in spring you'll see a profusion of wild flowers. When the road recrosses the river, use the bridge to gain access to the tiny and picturesque village of **Los Romeros**, a place devoted to *jamón* production (it takes its name from a major ham family). There is no official **accommodation** but the *Hermanos Marquez* supermarket (☎959 12 44 50; ⑤) lets out houses in the village – minimum two nights, sleeping two to four people. *Bodegón Los Romeros* in Plaza del Valle Florido (by the church) does good *tapas* and *raciones* and has a terrace.

around Aroche are covered in the free map, *Senderos de la Sierra de Aracena y Picos de Aroche* (see p.311), available from the *Ayuntamiento*.

Jabugo

The mere mention of the name of **JABUGO** is enough to make any Spaniard's mouth water, and once you have tasted what all the fuss is about it's easy to understand why. As roadside billboards depicting smiling pigs proclaim for miles around, ham – or rather *jamón* – is king in Jabugo. To get stuck into *jamón* sampling, when you approach the village from the N433, ignore the sign directing you to the *centro urbano* and continue straight on. You'll pass half a dozen **bars** and **restaurants** all eager to sell you a *bocadillo* stuffed with *jamón de Jabugo* – or even a whole ham should you feel like splashing out. *Bodega Restaurante Jabugo* and *Mesón Sánchez Romero Carvajal* (the "company bar" of the major *jamón* producer) are probably the best. There are *tapas*, too, but keep an eye on the prices as the *pata negra* doesn't come cheap.

Ham apart, the village of Jabugo is a sleepy place for most of the year, gathered around a charming leafy square with a central dribbling fountain overlooked by the *Casino* and the crumbling Baroque **Iglesia de San Miguel**. If you can find a key (try the *Ayuntamiento*), the church is worth a look inside for its splendid *retablo* and original eighteenth-century organ. Otherwise, it's back to the *Casino* – a relaxing place for a beer. For full **meals**, *Restaurante Saúco* (with a *menú*), on the main road at the entrance to Jabugo, is a good bet and, for more elaborate fare, *Venta Yutera*, also at the entrance to the village coming from El Repilado, serves tasty local dishes with flair. Should you want to **stay**, head for the hospitable *Hostal Aurora*, c/ Barco 9 (☎959 12 11 46; ②–③), which has some rooms with bath.

The **villages around Jabugo** – Aguafría, Castaño del Robledo (with decaying mansions, huge Baroque church and the wonderfully rustic *Bar La Bodeguita*), and Fuenteheridos (see below) – all make rewarding destinations for walks amid splendid wooded hills, though all are equally ill-served by public transport and you may well find yourself in for a walk both ways.

Galaroza and Valdelarco

The N433 continues east from Jabugo through country filled with dense oak woods surrounded by dry stone walls, where you may catch a fleeting glimpse of a herd of *cerdos ibéricos*, the celebrated black pigs of the Sierra. **GALAROZA**, encircled by chestnut and fruit orchards, seems awash with water which for much of the year splashes and bubbles in its fountains and along the culverts lining the narrow streets. This may explain its annual *Fiesta de los Jarritos* during which everyone – including visitors – gets soaked with water when the town goes *agua* mad. September 6 is the date to avoid if you want to stay dry. The village has a striking **Baroque church**, which contains a unique seventeenth-century image of a pregnant Virgin by the sculptress La Roldana. Good **places to stay** include *Hostal Toribio*, c/Primo de Rivera 2 (☎959 12 30 73; ②) with rooms overlooking the main square, and *Hostal Venecia* (☎959 12 30 98; ②), on the main road – both have rooms with bath. More opulent lodgings are at the bucolic *Hotel Galaroza Sierra* (☎959 12 32 37, fax 959 12 32 36; ⑤), an attractive hotel with pool in its own grounds just outside the village on the Jabugo road. For **eating and drinking** your only options are the bars, but with transport there's an excellent restaurant at nearby Valdelarco (see below). *Bar La Fuente*, Plaza Alcalde Luis Navarro opposite *Hostal Venecia*, is a humble place with an eccentric proprietor and good economical *tapas* – try the *jamón con tomate*. *Bar Alonso* on the right as you come in from Aracena also does good *tapas*.

A long and winding 6km road leads north from just beyond Galaroza to the village of **VALDELARCO**. Set amongst cork oaks, chestnut and almond trees it's an attractive

THE KING OF HAMS

Surrounding Jabugo is a scattering of attractive but economically depressed villages mainly dependent on the **jamón industry** and its curing factory which is the major local employer. Things were little different when Richard Ford passed through here a century and a half ago, describing these mountain villages as "coalitions of pigsties", adding that it was the duty of every good pig to "get fat as soon as he can and then to die for the good of his country".

Sought out by classical writers such as Strabo for its distinctive flavour, and produced since long before by the peoples of the Iberian peninsula, *jamón serrano* (mountain ham from white pigs) is a *bocadillo* standard throughout Spain – the English words "ham" and "gammon" are both derived from the Spanish. Some of the best ham of all, *jamón ibérico* or *pata negra* (both acorn-fed ham) comes from the Sierra Morena, where herds of sleek pigs grazing beneath the trees are a constant feature. In October the acorns drop or are beaten down by their keepers and the pigs, waiting patiently below, gorge themselves, become fat and are promptly whisked off to the factory to be slaughtered and then cured in the dry mountain air. The meat of these black pigs is exceptionally fatty when eaten as pork but the same fat that marbles the meat adds to the tenderness during the curing process. This entails first of all covering the hams in coarse rock or sea salt to "sweat", after which they are removed to cool cellars to mature for up to two years. *Jamón serrano* from mass-produced white pigs is matured for only a few weeks, hence the incomparable difference in taste. At Jabugo the best of the best is then further graded from one to five *jotas* (the letter "J" for Jabugo) depending on its quality – *cinco jotas jamón* comes close to the price of gold.

The king of hams also demands an etiquette all of its own: in bars and restaurants everywhere it has its own apparatus (*la jamonera*) to hold it steady, and carving is performed religiously with a long, thin-bladed knife. The slices must not be wafer-thin nor bacon rashers and once on the plate *jamón ibérico* becomes the classic partner for a glass of *fino*.

place with a charming main square, Plaza Domínguez. The main reason for a trip here is, however, *Restaurante La Maja*, right at the entrance to the village (down the first street on the right) run by two emigrants from northern Spain. There are many adventurous dishes made with the region's outstanding pork, a 1000ptas *menú*, as well as a *tapas* bar and pleasant garden. You can **walk** here from Galaroza along the GR42.1 footpath.

Fuenteheridos

About 5km further east from Galaroza, a turn on the right brings you almost immediately to **FUENTEHERIDOS**, one of the most picturesque of these Sierra *pueblos* – a huddle of whitewashed dwellings with contrasting red pantiled roofs. The typical tiled Sierra spire of its fine eighteenth-century Neoclassical **Iglesia del Espíritu Santo** hovers above the rooftops. Fuenteheridos also has good possibilities for rooms and **food**. On the main road at the edge of the village, the *Restaurante La Capellanía* serves up a succulent *solomillo de cerdo ibérico* (pork loin) and has a *menú*. Nearer the centre *Bar Restaurante Biarritz*, c/Virgen de Fuente s/n just off the main square, is a cheap and cheerful alternative with tasty sierra *tapas* and great soups, stews and pork dishes. Tranquil **accommodation** is available at the monastery of the Hermanos Maristas, in their guesthouse *Villa Onuba* (☎959 12 50 24; ⑤), on the edge of the village and signed. More conventional rooms (some with bath) are to be had at *Hostal Carballo*, c/La Fuente 16 (☎ & fax 959 12 51 08; ②). There's also a new *Villa Turística* here (☎959 12 51 89; ⑦), a rather soulless artificial village with restaurant and pool, and reached by taking the Carretera Nacional 433 for 1km northwest. A good **campsite**, *El Madroñal* (☎959 50 12 01), lies half a kilometre out of the village towards Castaño Robledo and has plenty of shade.

Los Marines, Cortelazor and Cumbres Mayores

Beyond the turn-off for Fuenteheridos and 8km east of Galaroza, **LOS MARINES** is the last village before Aracena, and its prosperity depends on the dense chestnut orchards which encircle it. Some 4km to the north – should your feet be up to it – **CORTELAZOR** is a charming hamlet with a fifteenth-century church, that also registers the province's highest rainfall. Specializing in honey production, it was settled with emigrants from Galicia in the fourteenth century, after the expulsion of the Moors from the Sierra. With transport, you could do a 29-kilometre detour for a superb drive north to **CUMBRES MAYORES**, another fine Sierra village with a couple of ancient churches and a magnificent crenellated thirteenth-century **castillo** which dominates the skyline as you approach. Upon closer investigation you'll discover that inside the castle walls there's the ground of the local football team – on match days spectators get a great view of the action from the fort's battlements. Cumbres is another place to sample the region's pork – this time in the *salchichas* (sausages) for which it is renowned. Good-value **rooms** with bath are available at *Pensión Togahilo*, c/A. Machado 47 (☎959 71 00 06; ②).

Zufre and east towards Cazalla

East of Aracena there's more good hiking country – if slightly less wooded – along the northern frontier of Sevilla Province, which traverses the **Parque Natural de Sierra Norte**. From Aracena one daily bus (except Sun) currently at 5.30pm, connecting with the bus from Sevilla, covers the 25km southeast to Zufre. If you miss it, you'll have to walk, which takes the best part of a day but can be good in itself.

From Aracena you're looking to pick up the start of the waymarked PRA-44 *sendero* which heads roughly north for 8km to meet the waymarked GR-41. Turn east along this and you'll soon come upon the **Embalse de Aracena**, one of the huge reservoirs that supply Sevilla, dammed by a massive construction across the southern end of the valley. From here a lovely but circuitous 17-kilometre route (still following the GR-41) will take you down towards Zufre along the **Rivera de Huelva**. The free **map** (available from the Turismo in Aracena), *Senderos de la Sierra de Aracena y Picos de Aroche*, details the above routes plus others should you want to work out a shorter alternative.

Zufre

ZUFRE, about 25km southeast of Aracena, must be one of the most spectacular villages in Spain, hanging like a miniature Ronda on a high palisade at the edge of a ridge. Below the crumbling Moorish walls, the cliff falls away hundreds of feet, terraced into deep green gardens of orange trees and vegetables. In town, and sharing a charming and leafy *plazuela*, the arcaded **Ayuntamiento** and parish **church** – built of brick and pink stone – are both interesting sixteenth-century examples of the Mudéjar style, the latter built on the foundations of a mosque. In the basement of the *Ayuntamiento*, too, is a gloomy line of stone seats, said to have been used by the Inquisition. A friendly priest at the house on the other side of the square from the church will usually open it to let you see inside. The focus of town, however, is the **Paseo**, a little park with rose gardens, balcony and a bar at one end and a *Casino* at the other. The villagers gather round here for much of the day – there's little work either in Zufre or the surrounding countryside, and even the local **bullring**, cleverly squeezed on to a rock ledge, only sees use twice a year; at the beginning of the season in March, and at the town's September *feria*.

Finding **food and drink** shouldn't be a problem, as plenty of bars in the warren of Moorish streets above the park serve *tapas* – seek out *Aleman* and *Benito* on the main Plaza La Quebrada – and there's a decent provisions shop at c/Nuestra Señora del Puerto 3. Zufre now has a **hostal**, *La Posá*, c/Cibarranco 5 (☎959 19 81 10; ③), with decent en-suite rooms.

Santa Olalla del Cala and El Real de la Jara

There's no bus link between Zufre and **SANTA OLALLA DEL CALA**, 16km to the east, but it's not hard to arrange a lift with one of the many locals who drive the route daily on the way to school and work. If you do choose **to walk**, there's the road or the slightly longer, but infinitely preferable, country route via the waymarked *senderos* PRA-42 and GR-48; pick up the PRA-42 at Calleja del Cementerio, on the edge of Zufre. The latter hike is a memorable experience: a mostly flat route through open country with pigs and fields of wheat and barley, and then a sudden view of the impressive **castillo** – a thirteenth-century Christian construction but incorporating Moorish features – above the town. Below the walls, the fifteenth-century parish **church** has a fine Baroque interior and an image of the *Virgen de los Dolores* by Juan de Mesa.

Coming from Zufre it's a surprise to find several **hostales** in Santa Olalla, but the town is actually on the main Sevilla–Badajoz road and sees a fair amount of traffic (which somewhat dents its charm), including regular buses between both cities. These stop outside the basic but clean *Bar Primitivo*, at c/Marina 3, on the main thoroughfare. Nearby there's the equally friendly *Casa Carmelo*, c/Marina 23 (☎959 19 01 69; ③) which has rooms with bath. Both places serve **food** and offer economical *menús del día*, with the latter specialising in the region's excellent *jamones* and *salchichas* from the pig farms hereabouts.

Still heading east, **EL REAL DE LA JARA**, the next village you reach, has two ruined but impressive **Moorish castillos**. The friendly *casa de huéspedes* at c/Real 70 (②) has **rooms**. There are places **to eat**, a welcome public swimming pool in summer, but no buses.

Cazalla and the Central Sierra

The next village of any size, **CAZALLA DE LA SIERRA**, is some 45km further east along a mountainous and lonely route, stunning to look at if you're driving, but a real test on foot. When you finally reach it, Cazalla de la Sierra feels like a veritable metropolis, especially if you arrive on foot, and makes an ideal base for exploring the surrounding Sierra Norte Natural Park. This is a charming country town with a number of sights, and is one of the few places on the Sierra served by regular **buses** (daily between here and Sevilla).

An ancient Iberian settlement, Cazalla became the Roman *Callentum* and later the Moorish *Kazalla* ("fortified city") from which the modern name derives. Its importance in post-*reconquista* days was as a staging post along the route to Extremadura and the north. The place was noted in Roman times for its vines and wines, a tradition which survives today in the production of *aguardiente* (eau de vie), sold in *bodegas* around the town.

Cazalla's main attraction is the huge church of **Nuestra Señora de la Consolación** at the southern end of town, an outstanding example of *andaluz* "mix and match" architecture begun in the fourteenth century in Gothic-Mudéjar style, with some later Renaissance touches, and finally completed in the eighteenth century. The interior has a fine sixteenth-century *retablo* and an image of San Bruno by Juan Hernández. Fronting the church's northern door, c/Virgen del Monte – lined with some elegant **casas señoriales** – leads to the market area, a colourful and bustling place on weekdays. Just by here, along c/Carmelo Meclana, the former monastery church of **San**

Francisco has been converted into the sales depot of an *aguardiente* producer, *Miura*, and you can taste the local firewater while contemplating the church's beautiful – if dilapidated – Baroque interior and cloister.

A little out of town, Cazalla's fifteenth-century **Cartuja**, or Carthusian monastery (daily 10am–2pm & 5–8pm; 500ptas), was until recently a near ruin; it's now being gradually and privately restored as an upmarket hotel (see below) and arts centre. What remains, particularly a beautiful portal and a cupola of the church with Mudéjar frescoes, is set in picturesque surroundings. To reach it, take the C342 for 3km towards Constantina, turning off along a signposted side road.

From Cazalla you can take a **bus** (at 7am or 11.45am) as far as the Estación de Cazalla y Constantina, 7km east. A short walk south from this station there's some excellent **rural accommodation** at the restored *Molino del Corcho* (☎95 595 42 49; ③; see also below) which would make a good base to explore this stretch of the Sierra Norte natural park. The station can be reached by train direct from Santa Justa in Sevilla, via Villanueva Río Minas and El Pedroso; two trains a day (currently running at 6.29pm & 9.40pm) also run northwest to **GUADALCANAL**, a pleasant sierra town with three fine Mudéjar churches and rooms at a very comfortable Turismo Rural *hostal, Los Diezmos*, at c/Antonio Machado 11 (☎ & fax 95 488 61 90, *diezmos@zoom.es*; ⑤) with a pool and terrace.

Cazalla practicalities

You'll find the town's rather sleepy **Turismo** at Paseo del Moro 2, just south of the centre (Mon–Fri 9.30am–2pm & 5–7pm; ☎95 488 35 62), which can provide information on the area but not a map of the town; this is available from the *Ayuntamiento*, a five-minute-walk away at Plaza Dr. Narcea 1.

For **accommodation** there is a wide range of options, with some really attractive possibilities at the upper end of the scale. The town's only budget *hostal, La Milagrosa*, c/Llana 29 (☎95 488 42 60; ③), is a decent place for rooms with bath. For more com-

---

WALKS AROUND CAZALLA

There are some fine spots within easy wandering distance of Cazalla and some of these are listed in a useful booklet (in Spanish) available from the tourist office titled *La Sierra Morena de Sevilla*. A walk of just 5km, for example, will take you southeast to the **Ermita del Monte**, a little eighteenth-century church on a wooded hill above the Ribera del Huéznar.

If you're making southwards for **El Pedroso**, however, you might as well walk from the Cazalla train station, a lovely five-hour route along the banks of the Huéznar, flowing through woods of alder, elm and ash with the occasional weeping willow and a fabulous variety of valley flora and fauna. It's an excellent trout river and a wonderful place to swim, and it can get very crowded with locals during holidays and summer weekends. **To start the trail** from Cazalla station take the road towards Constantina, crossing the rail line. Just after this you'll come to a forest track on the right signed for the "Molino de Corcho", an old water mill. A short way downstream, cross the first bridge, and carry on along the prettier east bank of the river. Cross back at the third bridge and continue past the Molino del Corcho (which has been restored as a guesthouse by a cooperative; see p.000) and on to the Fábrica de Pedroso (an old factory which also has a train station). From here you can follow the road to El Pedroso, or continuing along the river, at a bridge 4km on you should climb up to the road, and follow the SE190 from where the village lies 3km east. With planning you could take a northbound train back from El Pedroso (currently running at 5pm, 6.11pm & 9.20pm).

fort, head for the *Posada del Moro*, c/Paseo del Moro s/n (☎95 488 43 26; ⑤) where stylish tiled rooms overlook a patio garden and pool. Out of town the La Cartuja monastery (see above) has its own atmospheric *hospedería* (☎95 488 45 16; ⑥), an inn with eight rooms in what was formerly the monastery's gatehouse. Perhaps the most attractive of Cazalla's accommodation is *La Navezuelas* (☎ & fax 95 488 47 64; ⑤), a white-walled sixteenth-century *cortijo* and olive mill in a superb setting among woods and olive groves; it also has its own reasonably priced restaurant and the owners can arrange horse-riding excursions and advise on trekking routes. The farm is signed on the left, 3km out of town along the road to El Pedroso.

For **eating and drinking** there are numerous bars dotted around the town where *tapas* are on offer. *Bar Torero*, c/Virgen del Monte near the former church of San Francisco, serves up substantial *raciones*; and *Bar Gonzalo*, c/Caridad 3 in the centre, has a good *menú*. A traditional bar and restaurant with fountain and terrace is *La Boleras* in c/Cervantes, close to the *Ayuntamiento*. For light refreshment and simple but hearty meals make for the *Casino* in La Plazuela. More formal dining takes place at the *Restaurante del Moro*, the restaurant of the hotel of the same name (see above) which may also offer a medium-priced *menú* if asked. The nearby *Mesón del Moro* in the same street offers a more economical selection of game and meat dishes of the region.

El Pedroso and Constantina

EL PEDROSO is a pleasant enough little place, with a notable Mudéjar church. If you fancy **staying the night**, you could enquire at the train station for a room in a *casa particular*, or there's a rather swish new hotel in a restored *casa señorial*, *Casa Montehuéznar*, Avda. de la Estación 15 (☎95 488 90 00; ⑤ including breakfast). There's also a good restaurant here serving up regional dishes including *solomillo* (pork loin) and wild boar. Across the road from the station, an excellent **tapas bar**, the *Serranía*, offers more local specialities such as venison, hare, pheasant and partridge and has a *menú*.

Eighteen kilometres further to the east – and as good a place as any to cut back to Sevilla if you're not counting on hiking the whole length of the range – leads you to **CONSTANTINA**, an important and beautiful mountain town with a population of almost fifteen thousand. Founded in the fourth century by the Romans during the reign of the Emperor Constantine, and named after his son, this was an important wine-producing centre along with nearby Cazalla and sent a wine named *cocolubis* to the imperial capital. The town is a delightful place to wander around, particularly the old quarter, which is dotted with a number of notable eighteenth-century mansions. High above the streets below, the **Castillo de la Armada** is an impressive medieval fortress surrounded by shady gardens descending in terraces to the old quarter. At the base you'll find the sixteenth-century parish church of **La Encarnación**, once again with a Mudéjar tower – Moorish influence having died hard in these parts – and a splendid, if crumbling, Plateresque portal by Hernán Ruíz, the architect of the cathedral inside the Mezquita at Córdoba and the belfry added to the Giralda in Sevilla. The church's *altar mayor*, a magnificent gilded work by Juan de Oviedo, is also worth a look. Constantina has a public **swimming pool** sited below the *castillo*, very welcome to beat the intense summer heat. With transport you can make a trip to **La Pantalla** – a lake for swimming and fishing – east along the road to El Pedroso. Constantina's **feria**, a rumbustious Sierra affair with horse-riding contests plus drinking, dancing and singing galore, takes place during the last week in August.

There's an **information office** (Mon–Fri 8am–3pm; ☎95 488 00 00) inside the *Ayuntamiento*, c/Eduardo Dato 7, near the Encarnación church, who will also provide a useful town **map**. The cheapest of the **places to stay** is the modern *Albergue Juvenil*, c/Cuesta Blanca s/n which lies slightly out of the centre, uphill behind a petrol station at the southern end of the town (☎95 588 15 89; ①) with double rooms and shared showers. Otherwise, there's a dearth of budget accommodation. The only *hostal* is the central *Casa Mari Pepa* at c/José de la Bastida 25 (☎95 588 01 58; ⑤), where a *casa señorial* mansion has been lovingly transformed into a delightful series of distinctively decorated rooms with bath, making it well worth the price. There's also a new three-star hotel, *San Blas* (☎95 588 00 77, fax 95 588 19 00; ⑥), with an elevated location at the northern end of town and a pool. As regards **eating and drinking**, there are numerous places along and around c/Mesones, the main street, including *Las Farolas* (no. 14), which serves up decent *tapas* and a wide range of *platos combinados*. The town's best eatery is *Cambio de Tercio*, Virgen del Robledo 53 near the Plaza de Toros, where King Juan Carlos dines when relaxing after sessions gunning down the local wildlife (this is one of his favourite hunting zones). There's a medium-priced *menú* and the *solomillo de cerdo* (pork loin) is excellent. **Nightlife** centres around the clutch of music bars in the centre, and there are three **discos** of which *Bonny Dog* is the most central.

Las Navas de la Concepción

With your own transport a worthwhile excursion from Constantina is the trip 22km northeast through rolling hill country, densely covered with woods of *alcornoques* (cork oaks), to **LAS NAVAS DE LA CONCEPCIÓN**, a charming sierra village with an eighteenth-century Baroque church containing sculptures attributed to La Roldana. There's a satisfying end-of-the-world feel about Navas but it's a surprisingly prosperous place too, with a thriving economy based on the cork industry, olives and pig breeding. For **rooms** there's a superb and friendly *hostal* on the edge of town, *Hostal Los Montaneros* (☎95 588 50 62 fax 95 588 53 93; ④) where rooms come with balcony views (ask for no. 14) and there's a good **restaurant** with an excellent-value *menú*. Near the church in the centre *Corte Navas*, c/García Lorca 7, is another place to eat serving good *platos combinados*. The **Ayuntamiento** on the Plaza Mayor produces a leaflet on the organized rural activities in which visitors can take part, ranging from collecting your own honey from a beehive, cheesemaking, gathering wild mushrooms or taking part in a *matanza* (killing and butchering of the prized *cerdo ibérico* black pig) to trekking, donkey safaris and caving. More information on all this is also available from the *Hostal Montaneros*. Las Navas is served by **buses** (weekdays only) from Sevilla (currently running at 2.30pm) with the return from Navas at 7.30am and 5.45pm.

Lora del Río and Villanueva del Río y Minas

South of Constantina the road descends for 28km through the Sierra de La Cruz until, at the rather dull agricultural town of **LORA DEL RÍO**, it joins the fertile valley of the Guadalquivir. The southern banks of the river from Lora are famous for rearing *toros de lidia*, the fighting bulls of the *corrida* who greedily graze on the rich river pastures; the Miura family, long renowned among aficionados as supplying the biggest, meanest beasts, has its *ganadería*, or ranch, here.

Heading west towards Sevilla along the C431, the flat and monotonous landscape of the river valley is overlooked 10km further on by the **Roman ruins** of Arva. Not much is visible yet of the first-century town which lies beneath the olive groves, but if you keep your eyes peeled, on the right you'll see the substantial remains of a bath house and – if you climb the fence – an impressive restored stone font.

Some 5km beyond Alcolea del Río a road on the right leads – after 3km – to the old coal-mining town of **VILLANUEVA DEL RÍO Y MINAS**, a starting point for a fine **walk** to the remarkable Roman ruins of Mulva, buried deep in verdant countryside. A fairly humdrum place, Villanueva is a casualty of the Europe-wide depression in the mining industry, and its abandoned pit makes a sad sight on the landscape. You can get **rooms** at the pleasant *Bar-Pensión Reche*, Avda. de la Constitución 179 (☎95 474 78 23;

A WALK FROM VILLANUEVA DEL RÍO Y MINAS TO MULVA

To **start out** on the 7km trek to Mulva (and in summer make sure you carry water), take the road opposite Villanueva's *pensión* and cross the railway line. Then follow a track which twists around the old colliery – with evocative pitwheel, chimneys and a curiously turreted administration building – down to the river. Head north along the river's east bank and then cross at a low footbridge, known locally as the *puente chico*. Now on the west bank, continue north and pass under the large bridge (*puente grande*) ignoring the sign for *Munigua* (Mulva) pointing left – this is a longer road route. Once under the big bridge follow the track into the hills until you come to a farmhouse, *La Palmilla*, with green gates. They will give you water. The next part of the walk is important, for in the woods beyond here you must take the **left fork** when the track divides ahead. This will eventually lead you – 3km on – to another gate, beyond which the ruins of **Mulva** will eventually appear through the woods, dominating the skyline.

③); take the balcony room, if it's available. You'll be a source of much hilarity over breakfast – the homemade *churros* are recommended – if you announce your plan to walk to Mulva as no one here seems to have walked further than the main street in their lives. However, they will clarify any queries regarding the route, if asked.

Mulva

The Roman ruins of **MULVA** (ancient *Munigua*) sit in a dramatic position atop a hill, just to one side of which sits the guardian, protecting the site from plunderers all year round; he will give you a ticket (free) and, if you're lucky, some cool water.

A prosperous city founded by the Romans on top of an earlier Iberian settlement, Munigua's wealth came from iron mining, backed, to judge from the numerous stone olive presses found here, by a flourishing oil industry. Recent excavations have uncovered a suite of **baths** together with some fresco fragments. You can climb the hill to the ruins and explore the **sanctuary** with its phenomenal bulwarking – the heart of ancient Munigua and believed to have been a copy of the great temple of Fortuna at Praeneste near Rome – as well as the forum, dwellings, a mausoleum and walls of this impressive "lost" city.

A two-kilometre track from Mulva leads to the train station of **Arenillas**, which is on the Sevilla–Zafra line. Villanueva is also on this line, but check with the site guardian as to whether a train is due. Heading east from Villanueva, the C431 road arcs south along the Guadalquivir, passing after 13km **Cantillana**, a pleasant town with a couple of Baroque churches, followed by the farming settlements of Villaverde del Río and **Alcalá del Río** – the latter's Renaissance church of Santa María has a stunning *retablo* – before entering Sevilla (see p.214).

travel details

TRAINS

Huelva to: Almonaster La Real (2 daily; 1hr 45min); Sevilla (3 daily; 1hr 30min); Zafra (1 daily; 3hr 45min).

Sevilla to: Algeciras (2 daily; 5hr); Cádiz (12 daily; 1hr 30min–2hr); Córdoba (AVE 17 daily 45min; 6 daily; 1–2hr); Granada (3 daily; 2hr 45min–3hr 30min); Huelva (3 daily; 1hr 30min); Jaén (1 daily; 3hr); Madrid (12 daily; AVE 2hr 15min or 6–9hr); Málaga (3 daily; 2hr 30min); Osuna (3 daily; 1hr).

BUSES

Aracena to: Alájar (3 daily; 30min); Aroche (4 daily; 1hr); Cortegana/Almonaster (6 daily;

50min); Huelva (2 daily; 2hr 30min); Jabugo (4 daily; 35min); Nerva/Río Tinto (1 daily; 1hr); Zufre (1 daily; 45min).

Huelva to: Aracena (2 daily; 1hr 30min); Ayamonte/Portuguese frontier (9 daily; 1hr); Granada (1 daily; 4hr); Isla Cristina (3 daily; 1hr); La Antilla (3 daily; 45min); Málaga (1 daily; 4hr); Matalascañas (6 daily; 1hr 15min); Punta Umbria (15 daily; 30min); Sevilla (16 daily; 1hr 15min).

Osuna to: Antequera (6 daily; 1hr); Granada (3 daily; 3hr 30min); Málaga (7 daily; 2hr); Sevilla (12 daily; 1hr 30min).

Sevilla to: Algeciras (5 daily; 3hr 30min); Almería (3 daily; 6hr); Aracena (2 daily; 2hr); Arcos de la Frontera (2 daily; 2hr); Ayamonte (access to Portugal's Algarve – 4 daily; 2hr 30min); Constantina (5 daily; 1hr); Cádiz (8 daily; 1hr 30min–2hr 30min); Carmona (34 daily; 45min); Córdoba (11 daily; 1hr 45min–3hr 15min); Écija (11 daily; 2hr); El Rocío (5 daily; 2hr 30min); Granada (7 daily; 4–5hr); Huelva (11 daily; 1hr 30min); Jerez (6 daily; 1hr); Málaga (6 daily; 2hr); Madrid (12 daily; 5–8hr); Marbella (2 daily; 3hr); Matalascañas (3 daily; 3hr); Ronda (5 daily; 3hr).

CHAPTER THREE

CÓRDOBA AND JAÉN

A ndalucía's most northerly province, **Córdoba**, is horizontally bisected by the Río Guadalquivir. Sited on the river's northern bank, the provincial capital is a handsome city whose outstanding attraction is its twelve-hundred-year-old Moorish **Mezquita**, one of the world's great buildings. In the tangled lanes of the Judería, the old Jewish quarter, that partially surrounds it, the sense of Córdoba's history as the centre of a vast and powerful empire is overwhelming. After the brilliance of the Mezquita the rest of the city, particularly the northern sector of modern Córdoba, can seem like an anticlimax; but persist and you'll discover a host of striking post-*reconquista* **churches** in addition to a number of elegant **convents and mansions**. Despite a reputation for aloofness and sobriety among its neighbours, Córdoba has some of the most distinctive old **bars** in Andalucía, where taking a drink and a *tapa* is a particularly unique experience. A few kilometres away there's more lingering Moorish splendour at the ruins of **Medina Azahara**, a once fabulous palace of the caliphs which is being painstakingly restored.

To the south of the river lies Córdoba's **Campiña**, a rolling landscape of grainfields, olive groves and vineyards, where *montilla*, the province's rival to the wines of Jerez, is made. Little visited, the more elevated southern reaches of this area are particularly delightful, with a number of towns and villages such as **Baena**, **Cabra** and **Zuheros** ringed by excellent hiking country. The equally unsung town of **Priego de Córdoba**, further south still, has a clutch of spectacular Baroque churches that are worth a trip in themselves. To the north of the capital, the hardy mining towns in the foothills of the **Sierra Morena** attract even fewer visitors, but there's a rich variety of birdlife here, and the higher slopes are home to deer and wild boar zealously stalked by the hunting fraternity in winter.

The **province of Jaén** has been regarded since Moorish times as Andalucía's gateway – through the **Despeñaperros Pass** – to Castile and the cities of Toledo and Madrid to the north. Although often used as this gateway's doormat and something of a forgotten entity, the region's poorest province has some surprisingly worthy sights to

---

ACCOMMODATION PRICE CODES

Throughout this guide, accommodation is graded on a scale from ① to ⑨. These show the cost per night of the cheapest double room in each establishment in high season, though remember that many of the cheap places will have more expensive rooms with en-suite facilities. See p.39 for more details. Approximate Euro rates (operative from January 2002) are given for each category:

① Under 2000ptas/ Under €12

② 2000–3000ptas/ €12–18

③ 3000–4500ptas/ €18–27

④ 4500–6000ptas/ €27–37

⑤ 6000–8000ptas/ €37–49

⑥ 8000–10,000ptas/ €49–60

⑦ 10,000–15,000ptas/ €60–90

⑧ 15,000–20,000ptas/ €90–120

⑨ Over 20,000ptas/ Over €120

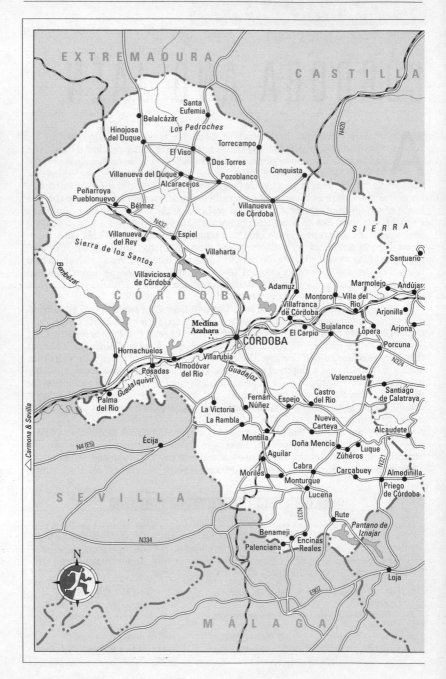

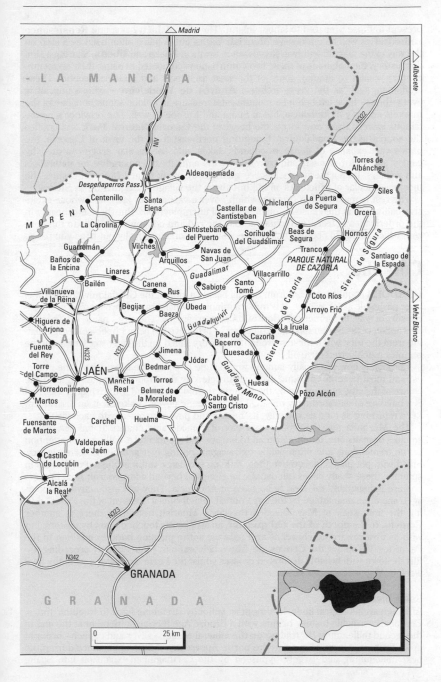

present to those prepared to labour inland. The **city of Jaén** has a fine **Renaissance cathedral** as well as impressive **Moorish baths** but is more often used as a stop on the way to the magnificent twin Renaissance towns of **Baeza** and **Úbeda**. Sharing a similar history, the nobilities of these two conurbations competed in using their sixteenth-century wealth to employ some of the best architects and builders around. These craftsmen, such as the great architect **Andrés de Vandelvira** – whose imprint is everywhere – have left behind a monumental treasure in golden sandstone, one of the marvels not only of Andalucía, but of Spain and Europe as well. The province's mountainous eastern flank now forms the heart of the **Cazorla Natural Park** and cradles the source of the Guadalquivir. Extending northeast from the town of **Cazorla**, the park's vast expanse of dense woodlands, lakes, and spectacular crags crowned by eagles' and vultures' nests and patrolled by the agile ibex is a paradise for naturalists and walkers. Its northerly reaches are guarded by many ruined Moorish castles, the most spectacular of which sits on the hill above the village of **Segura de la Sierra**.

The rest is mainly **olive groves**, which cover a vast area of Jaén, and whose exclusive cultivation is the cause of much seasonal unemployment. But there is a beauty in the orderly files of trees, stretching across the red and creamy white hills to the horizon, which seem "to open and close like a fan," as Lorca poetically put it, as you pass.

Córdoba

CÓRDOBA stands upstream from Sevilla beside a loop of the Guadalquivir, which was once navigable as far as here. It is today a minor provincial capital, prosperous in a modest sort of way, but a mere shadow of its past greatness. The city's name – a possible corruption of the Syrian *coteba* or "oil press" – is believed to be of Phoenician origin dating from the time when these merchant venturers sailed up the river to carry away the region's much-prized olive oil.

Córdoba is now principally famous for a single building, the **Mezquita** – the grandest and most beautiful mosque ever constructed by the Moors. It stands right in the centre of the city, surrounded by the Judería, the old Jewish and Moorish quarters, and is a building of extraordinary mystical and aesthetic power. Make for it on arrival and keep returning as long as you stay; its beauty and power increase with each visit.

The Mezquita apart, Córdoba is a city of considerable charm. It has few grand squares or mansions, tending instead to introverted architecture, calling your attention to the tremendous and often wildly extravagant **patios**, yet another Moorish legacy. Filled with pot plants, decorative tiles, tinkling fountains and a profusion of flowers in summer, these shady oases can usually be glimpsed beyond a forged iron *verja* or gate, and are indisputably the best to be seen in Andalucía. They are also actively encouraged and often maintained by the city council, which runs a "Festival of the Patios" during the first week in May. Besides the city's Moorish treasures, there is another Córdoba, to the **north of the old quarter**, an area rarely touched upon by visitors, but with its own rewarding churches and palaces, not to mention bars. In addition to the Patios festival above, the **Cruces de Mayo** celebrations – immediately preceding it – fills the town with lavishly decorated crosses whilst the **Feria de Mayo** during the final week in May is the major fiesta.

Some history

Although archeological finds document an antiquity stretching back to Neolithic times, Córdoba's verifiable history begins with a Bronze Age Iberian settlement at the end of the second millennium BC trading on the mineral wealth – silver and copper – brought down from the Sierra Morena to the north. Apparently of little importance during the next millennium, and largely bypassed by the Carthaginian expansion into Spain,

Córdoba rose to prominence under **Rome** in the years following the crushing victories against her North African enemy at the end of the third century BC.

Founded as the Roman city of *Corduba* in 152 BC, Córdoba flourished as the capital of Hispania Ulterior and, foreshadowing its later brilliance, became famous for its poetry as well as its olive oil. Cicero once cracked that Cordoban poetry sounded as if it had got mixed up with the oil due to its guttural style of delivery. Later, after Córdoba had backed the wrong horse in the wars between Caesar and Pompey at the end of the Republic, Caesar sacked the city and an estimated thirty thousand died. When Augustus reorganized Spain in 27 BC, Córdoba's fortunes improved as the capital city of the new province of Baetica, roughly corresponding to modern Andalucía. A brilliant period followed during which the city produced the poets **Lucan** and **Seneca** whilst prosperity – based upon oil, wool and minerals – increased.

As Roman power waned in the fifth century the area was overrun first by **Vandals** and then **Visigoths**. Leovigild took the city in 572 but it was inevitable that the unstable Visigothic territories, riven by civil wars, would not survive.

Córdoba fell to the Moors early in the eighth century, and in 756 became the **capital of Moorish Spain**. The succeeding three centuries – when Córdoba formed the heart of the Western Islamic Empire – were the city's golden age, as it grew to rival Cairo and Baghdad as a centre of Muslim art and learning. Though later its political power declined, Córdoba remained a centre of culture and scholarship and was the birthplace of the twelfth-century thinkers Averroës, the great Muslim commentator on Aristotle, and Maimónides the Jewish philosopher.

After **conquest by Fernando III** in 1236, Córdoba's glory vanished as the city sank into a long and steady **decline**. Such aspects of civilized life as the elaborate Moorish systems of water supply and sewerage disposal fell into ruin as the mosques were turned into churches. Little of the wealth of imperial Spain found its way here, although the city's leatherworkers, silversmiths and *parfumeurs* (all continuing Moorish traditions) achieved some renown in the sixteenth century. Plagues in the next century decimated the population and when Ford arrived in the 1830s he found "a poor and servile city". The city suffered terrible repression in the wars against the French as it was to do again in this century when, during the Civil War, it was captured by the Nationalists who carried out brutal atrocities.

Córdoba's voters took belated revenge for this in the first post-Franco elections of 1979 when it elected a **communist council** – the only major city in Spain to do so. Currently in opposition, the *Izquierda Unida* (United Left), as the communists now style themselves, are no longer led by the immensely popular mayor Julio Anguita who until recently was leader of the *IU*'s national party and a key player on Spain's political stage. Befitting its past, Córdoba is now a city of learning once again (the university was re-established in 1971) and its latest faculty is a centre devoted to the study of Muslim history and culture. The town today boasts a progressive air, and has built up a modestly successful economy based upon its agricultural wealth, light industry and tourism.

Arrival, information and orientation

Córdoba's magnificent new **train station** (☎957 40 02 02) and **bus station** (☎957 40 40 40; information on all routes and companies) complex is located on Plaza de las Tres Culturas, off the Avda. de America to the northwest of the old town. On the train station concourse Hostecor **information point** will book you into any hotel or *hostal* in the city without charge and tell you how to get there. In the adjacent bus station each bus company has its own *ventanilla* (sales window) and beneath the central concourse (and in the subterranean car park) impressive Roman and Moorish excavated remains from the city's distinguished past have been imaginatively incorporated into the new

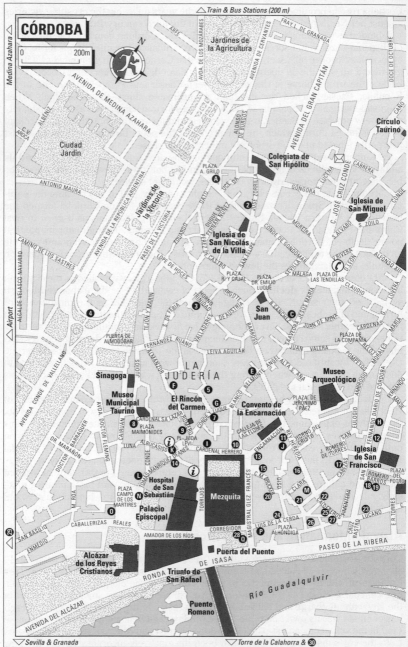

△ Train & Bus Stations (200 m)

CÓRDOBA

0 _____ 200m

Medina Azahara ◁

Airport ◁

AVENIDA DE MEDINA AZAHARA

Ciudad
Jardín

ANTONIO MAURA

Jardines de
la Victoria

Jardines de
la Agricultura

Círculo
Taurino

Colegiata de
San Hipólito

Iglesia de
San Miguel

PLAZA
A. GRILO
Ⓐ

Iglesia de
San Nicolás
de la Villa

Ⓑ

San
Juan

Ⓒ

Ⓓ

LA
JUDERÍA

Sinagoga

Museo
Municipal
Taurino

El Rincón
del Carmen

PLAZA
MAIMÓNIDES

Ⓔ

Ⓕ

Ⓖ

Ⓗ

Museo
Arqueológico

Convento de
la Encarnación

Iglesia
de San
Francisco

Ⓘ

Ⓙ

Ⓚ

Ⓛ

Ⓜ

Ⓝ

Ⓞ

Hospital
de San
Sebastián

Palacio
Episcopal

Mezquita

Ⓟ

Alcázar
de los Reyes
Cristianos

Puerta del Puente

Triunfo de
San Rafael

Puente
Romano

Río Guadalquivir

PASEO DE LA RIBERA

DE ISASA

▽ Sevilla & Granada

▽ Torre de la Calahorra & ㉚

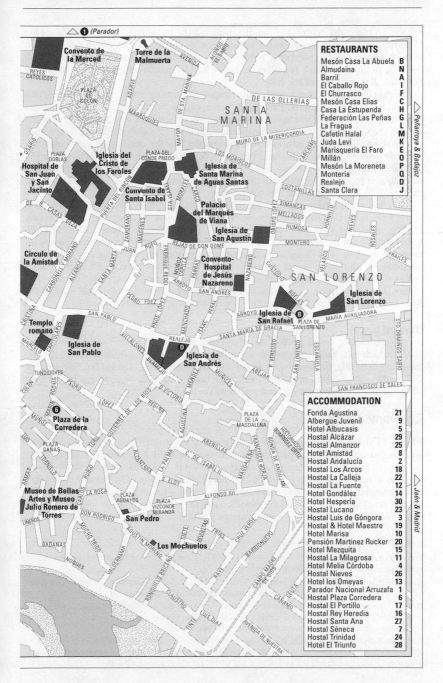

△ **①** (Parador)

Convento de la Merced
Torre de la Malmuerta
REYES CATÓLICOS
PLAZA DE COLÓN
AVENIDA
ALONSO EL SABIO
DE STA. MARINA
DE LAS OLLERÍAS
SANTA MARINA
MARROQUÍES
MAYOR
MURO DE LA MISERICORDIA
PLAZA DOBLAS
PLAZA DEL CONDE PRIEGO
Iglesia del Cristo de los Faroles
LOS MORISCOS
CARCAMO
Hospital de San Juan y San Jacinto
Convento de Santa Isabel
Iglesia de Santa Marína de Aguas Santas
COSTANILLAS
DE R. CASAS DEZA
PUERTA DEL RINCÓN
ZAMORANO
IMÁGENES
STA. MARTA
MORALES
ZARCO
Palacio del Marqués de Viana
OBISPO LÓPEZ
SIMANCAS
MELLADOS
HUMOSA
Círculo de la Amistad
CARBONELL
SANTA MARÍA
JUAN RUFO
REJAS DE DON GOME
Iglesia de San Agustín
MONTERO
VELASCO
ROSALES
FRAILES
ALFAROS
ENRIQUE REDEL
MUÑOZ CAPILLA
FABRIS
Convento-Hospital de Jesús Nazareno
NAZARENO
CUSTODIO
SAN LORENZO
Templo romano
CRISTINA
SAN PABLO
PEDRO FDEZ.
ROSAL
MANCHADO
SAN ANDRÉS
ARROYO
ROELAS
Iglesia de San Rafael **B**
PLAZA DE SAN LORENZO
MARÍA AUXILIADORA
Iglesia de San Lorenzo
STO. DOMINGO SABIO
MARCELO
CAPITULARES
Iglesia de San Pablo
VILLALONES
REALEJO
BLERMEO
ISAAC PERAL
SANTA MARÍA DE GRACIA
P. VERDUGO
SAN LORENZO
ESCANUELA
SAN FRANCISCO DE SALES
TUNDIDORES
Iglesia de San Andrés
D. VICTORIA
D. MONROY
MUNICES
ABEJAR
COLÓN
SAN RODRIG
PEDRO
LÓPEZ
GUTIÉRREZ DE LOS RÍOS
REGINA
D. AGUSTINA
PLAZA DE LA MAGDALENA
HISTORIADOR DOMÍNGUEZ ORTIZ
Plaza de la Corredera **⑥**
P. MUÑOZ
PLAZA CAÑAS
ALCÁNTARA
LA PALMA
C. DE ISABEL II
ARENILLAS
MAGDALENA
FRANCISCO BORJA
RONDA DE ANDUJAR
PLAZA DE LA MADALENA
ARMAS
TORNILLO
RUBIO
LA ROSA
S. ELOY
ALFONSO XII
Museo de Bellas Artes y Museo Julio Romero de Torres
DON RODRIGO
PLAZA AGUAYOS
PLAZA VIZCONDE MIRANDA
San Pedro
CRUZ VERDE
LINEROS
MUCHO TRIGO
AGUSTÍN MORENO
SIETE REVUELTAS
FRÍAS
BARRIONUEVO
BADANAS
NOQUES
VALDERRAMA
RONQUILLO BRICEÑO
Los Mochuelos
RAVE
CAMPO MADRE DE DIOS
CLAUSTRO
TINTE
LUIS DÍAZ
AVENIDA DE NUESTRA
CREUA
CARAMO

△ Peñarroya & Badajoz
△ Jaén & Madrid

RESTAURANTS

Mesón Casa La Abuela	B
Almudaina	N
Barril	A
El Caballo Rojo	I
El Churrasco	F
Mesón Casa Elias	C
Casa La Estupenda	H
Federación Las Peñas	G
La Fragua	L
Cafetín Halal	M
Juda Levi	K
Marisquería El Faro	E
Millán	O
Mesón La Moreneta	P
Montería	Q
Realejo	D
Santa Clara	J

ACCOMMODATION

Fonda Agustina	21
Albergue Juvenil	9
Hotel Albucasis	5
Hostal Alcázar	29
Hostal Almanzor	25
Hotel Amistad	8
Hostal Andalucía	2
Hostal Los Arcos	18
Hostal La Calleja	22
Hostal La Fuente	12
Hotel Gondález	14
Hotel Hesperia	30
Hostal Lucano	23
Hostal Luis de Góngora	3
Hostal & Hotel Maestre	19
Hotel Marisa	10
Pensión Martinez Rucker	20
Hotel Mezquita	15
Hostal La Milagrosa	11
Hotel Melia Córdoba	4
Hostal Nieves	26
Hotel los Omeyas	13
Parador Nacional Arruzafa	1
Hostal Plaza Corredera	6
Hostal El Portillo	17
Hostal Rey Heredia	16
Hostal Santa Ana	27
Hostal Séneca	7
Hostal Trinidad	24
Hotel El Triunfo	28

edifice. To reach the centre and old quarter from the station, pick up the Avda. de los Mozarabes, then veer east on to the broad Avda. del Gran Capitán which will lead you to the old town and the Mezquita, a mile to the south. Bus #3 from the bus station will take you to the focal Plaza Tendillas, and c/de San Fernando on the old quarter's eastern flank, if you can't face the hike.

Arriving **by car** can be a nightmare, especially during rush hour in the narrow streets around the Mezquita. Parking in this area and the whole city centre is also a major headache, and it's worth considering staying somewhere that doesn't require traversing the old quarter (see "Accommodation", below). Probably the best solution of all is to park up your vehicle (stripped of any valuables) for the duration of your stay – the Avda. de la República Argentina and the Paseo de la Victoria on the western edge of the old quarter are possible places – and get around the city on foot which is both easy and enjoyable. If you park illegally your car may well be towed, in which case you'll have to ring ☎957 25 72 97 and prepare to pay.

The city's main **Turismo** (Mon–Sat 9.30am–7pm, Sun 10am–2pm; ☎957 47 12 35) is at the Palacio de Congresos y Exposiciones at c/Torrijos 10 alongside the Mezquita, and has a detailed town plan. There's also a small **municipal tourist office** in Plaza Judá Leví, west of the Mezquita (Mon–Sat 8.30am–2.30pm; ☎957 20 05 22). You should be aware that Córdoba changes its **monument timetables** more than any other town in Andalucía and these ought to be confirmed with either tourist office. Both keep copies of the monthly *¿Que Hacer en Córdoba?*, a free listings mag detailing the main events. For information on cultural performances and music, make your way to the *Ayuntamiento's Casa de Cultura* at the Posada de Potro, Plaza del Potro 10.

Onward travel

If you're travelling on to **Sevilla** and **Granada**, you have a choice of using trains or buses, which cost more or less the same but the trains generally take longer. When travelling to Sevilla, however, you can use the AVE super-train (45min) but this will cost you double the price of an ordinary ticket. Going to Granada, be sure you take a train via Bobadilla (5hr) and *not* via Linares-Baeza (7–11hr).

Accommodation

Places to stay can be found all over Córdoba, but the majority (as well as the priciest) are concentrated in the narrow maze of streets around the Mezquita. If you can resist the urge to lodge on the Mezquita's doorstep, a five-minute walk away in all directions leads to a substantial drop in prices and some real bargains. On balance Córdoba's *hostales* tend to be better value – and more interesting – than the pricier hotels. Finding a room at any time of the year isn't usually a problem, but if you really want to be sure, ring ahead. All places listed below in category ④ and above have rooms with bath.

Budget options

Fonda Agustina, c/Zapatería Vieja 5 (☎957 47 08 72). Charming and spotlessly clean little *fonda*, with basic rooms in a tranquil location. ②.

Hostal Alcázar, c/San Basilio 2, near the Alcázar (☎957 20 25 61). Comfortable, family-run *hostal* with a nice patio, and a few slightly pricier rooms with bath. Parking space nearby. ③.

Hostal Almanzor, c/Corregidor Luís de la Cerda 10 (☎ & fax 957 48 54 00). Attractive newish place with charming proprietors and a delightful roof terrace; rooms come with bath, TV and air-conditioning. Some cheaper rooms without bath. A bargain. ③.

Hotel Andalucía, c/José Zorrilla 3, near the church of San Hipolito (☎957 47 60 00, fax 957 47 81 43). Handy hotel for drivers wanting to avoid the Mezquita maze, offering pleasant rooms with bath. Give them a ring and they'll tell you how to get there. Easy parking nearby. ④.

Hostal Los Arcos, c/Romeros Barros 14 (☎957 48 56 43, fax 957 48 60 11). Simple rooms in a quiet street behind the Plaza del Potro; this is a gem with a superb patio. ③.

Hostal La Calleja, Calleja de Rufino Blanco y Sanchez 6 (☎957 48 66 06). New, clean and comfortable place in tranquil location; some en-suite rooms. ③.

Hostal La Fuente, c/San Fernando 51, near the Plaza del Potro (☎957 48 14 78, fax 957 48 78 27). Sparkling *hostal* in refurbished town house with enthusiastic proprietor, delightful patio and pristine rooms with bath, TV and air conditioning. Parking nearby. ③–④.

Hostal Lucano, c/Lucano 1 (☎ & fax 957 47 60 98). Fairly good rooms with and without bath, and there's a pleasant bar below, also serving breakfast. ③.

Hostal Luís de Góngora, c/Horno de la Trinidad 7 (☎957 29 55 99). Decent rooms with bath. ④.

Hostal & Hotel Maestre, c/Romero Barros 4 & 16, behind the Plaza del Potro (*hostal* ☎957 47 53 95; hotel ☎957 47 24 10, fax 957 47 53 95). Friendly *hostal* with fine patio and charming rooms with bath; rooms at the nearby hotel have air-conditioning and TV. *Rough Guide* readers with this guide get free underground parking. ④–⑤.

Pensión Martínez Rucker, c/Martínez Rucker 14, immediately east of the Mezquita (☎957 47 25 62). Nice patio and rather spartan rooms lacking hot water. ③.

Hostal La Milagrosa, c/Rey Heredia 12, northeast of the Mezquita (☎957 47 33 17). Somewhat overpriced *hostal* offering clean and pleasant rooms, some en suite. ③.

Hostal Nieves, c/La Cara 12, a tiny street off c/Corregidor de la Cerda (aka c/González) near the southeast corner of the Mezquita (☎957 47 51 39). Very basic but clean *hostal*. ③.

Hostal Plaza Corredera, c/Rodríguez Marín 15 (☎957 48 45 70), on the Plaza Corredera but entry on c/Rodríguez Marín. Refurbished *pensión* on a wonderful old square, with spruce new rooms without bath, and some with great views over the plaza. Easy parking nearby. ③.

Hostal El Portillo, c/Cabezas 2, east of the Mezquita (☎ & fax 957 47 20 91). Beautiful old *hostal* with an elegant patio and friendly management. Simple rooms include a few singles, and many have balconies. ②.

Hostal Rey Heredia, c/Rey Heredia 26, slightly east of the Mezquita (☎957 47 41 82). Clean, airy whitewalled rooms with plenty of light at the front. Nice patio and modern communal bathrooms. ②.

Hostal Santa Ana, c/Cardenal González 25, near the Plaza del Potro (☎957 48 58 37). Air-conditioned rooms with and without bath and most with TV. There's a nice roof terrace. Garage. ③–④.

Hostal Séneca, c/Conde y Luque 7, just north of the Mezquita (☎ & fax 957 47 32 34). Delightful *hostal* with a stunning patio complete with original Moorish pavement. Breakfast is available. In summer you'll have to book ahead. One room with bath. ③.

Hostal Trinidad, c/Corregidor de la Cerda 58 (aka c/González; ☎957 48 79 05). Basic, no-frills accommodation – but not bad for the price. ②.

Hotels

Hotel Albucasis, c/Buen Pastor 11, slightly north of the Mezquita (☎ & fax 957 47 86 25). Ivy-clad courtyard, spotless en-suite bedrooms and pistols on the walls. Garage. ⑥.

Hotel Amistad Córdoba, Plaza de Maimónides 3 (☎957 42 03 35, fax 957 42 03 65). Stylish new hotel near the old wall in the Judería incorporating two eighteenth-century mansions with Mudéjar patio and staircase. They put a number of rooms on weekend discount which reduces the price by a third. Car park available. ⑧.

Hotel González, c/Manríquez 3, just northwest of the Mezquita (☎957 47 98 19, fax 957 48 61 87). Converted Moorish palace with rooms overlooking a brilliant white-walled, geranium-filled patio – entered through the hotel's rather tacky souvenir shop. Garage. ⑥.

Hotel Hesperia Córdoba, Avda. de la Confederación s/n (☎957 42 10 42, fax 957 29 99 97). New luxury hotel across the river with views, pool and garage. ⑦.

Hotel Marisa, c/Cardenal Herrero 6 (☎957 47 31 42, fax 957 47 41 44). You won't get closer to the Mezquita than this. Some find it stylish and functional, others soulless. Garage. ⑥.

Hotel Mezquita, Plaza Santa Catalina 1, by the Mezquita's east wall (☎957 47 55 85, fax 957 47 62 19). Charming and central new hotel in a converted sixteenth-century mansion with excellent air-conditioned rooms. ⑤.

Hotel Meliá Córdoba, Jardines de la Victoria s/n (☎957 29 80 66, fax 957 29 81 47). Easy to reach by car along the Avda. de la Republica, this is the Córdoba outpost of the *Meliá* chain of luxury hotels. There's a pool, restaurant, all mod cons and you're a one-minute walk from the Judería. Garage. ⑧.

Hotel Los Omeyas, c/Encarnación 17, near the Mezquita's northeast corner (☎957 49 22 67, fax 957 49 16 59). Pleasant and airy hotel built around a nice patio but with a severe kitsch problem; air-conditioned rooms come with TV, wall safe and more kitsch. Garage. ⑥.

Parador Nacional Arruzafa, Avda. de la Arruzafa s/n, 5km north of town in the El Brillante suburb (☎957 27 59 00, fax 957 28 04 09). Attractive, modern *parador* with pool, tennis courts, shooting range and views over the city. Worth a trip out for a drink in its gardens. ⑧.

Hotel El Triunfo, c/Corregidor Luís de la Cerda 79 (☎957 47 55 00, fax 957 48 68 50). Friendly, traditional hotel on the Mezquita's east face. Some of the pleasant air-conditioned rooms (on the front) have a Mezquita view, and there's a lively bar and restaurant. Garage. ⑤.

Youth hostels and campsites

Albergue Juvenil, Plaza Judá Leví s/n, in the heart of the Judería, off c/Albucasis (☎957 29 01 66). Eighty-one double, triple and 4-person rooms with en-suite bath/shower at this relaxed and superbly located hostel. Why can't they all be like this? ②.

Campamento Municipal, Avda. Brillante s/n, 2km north on the road to Villaviciosa (☎957 27 84 81). Good site with pool, reached by taking bus #12 from the Puente Romano.

The Mezquita

As in Moorish times, the **Mezquita** (April–Sept Mon–Sat 10am–7pm, Sun 3.30–7pm; Oct–March Mon–Sat closes 5pm; 800ptas) is approached through the **Patio de los Naranjos**, a classic Islamic ablutions court with fountains for ritual purification before prayer, which still preserves its orange trees. None of the original ablutions fountains survives, the present ones being purely decorative later additions. Originally, when in use for the Friday prayer, all nineteen naves of the mosque were open to this court, allowing the rows of interior columns to appear an extension of the trees. Today, with all but one of the entrance gates locked and sealed, the image is still there, though subdued and stifled by the loss of those brilliant shafts of sunlight filtering through. The mood of the building has been distorted a little, from the open and vigorous simplicity of the mosque, to the mysterious half-light of a cathedral.

Nonetheless, a first glimpse inside the Mezquita is immensely exciting. "So near the desert in its tentlike forest of supporting pillars," Jan Morris found it, "so faithful to Mahomet's tenets of cleanliness, abstinence and regularity." The mass of supporting pillars was, in fact, an early and sophisticated improvisation to gain height. The original architect, Sidi ben Ayub, working under the instruction of Abd ar-Rahman I, had at his disposal columns in marble, porphyry and jasper from the old Visigothic cathedral and from numerous Roman buildings, as well as many more shipped in from all parts of the former Roman empire. This ready-made building material could bear great weight, but the architect was faced with the problem of the pillars' varying sizes: many were much too tall but the vast majority would not be tall enough, even when arched, to reach the intended height of the ceiling. The long pillars he sunk in the floor, whilst his solution for the short pillars (which may have been inspired by Roman aqueduct designs) was to place a second row of square columns on the apex, serving as a base for the semicircular arches that support the roof. For extra strength and stability (and perhaps also deliberately to echo the shape of a date palm, much revered by the early Spanish Arabs), he introduced another, horseshoe-shaped arch above the lower pillars. A second and purely aesthetic innovation was to alternate brick and stone in the arches, creating the red-and-white striped pattern which gives a unity and distinctive character to the whole design. This architectural *tour de force* was unprecedented in the Arab world and set the tone for all future enlargements – excepting the

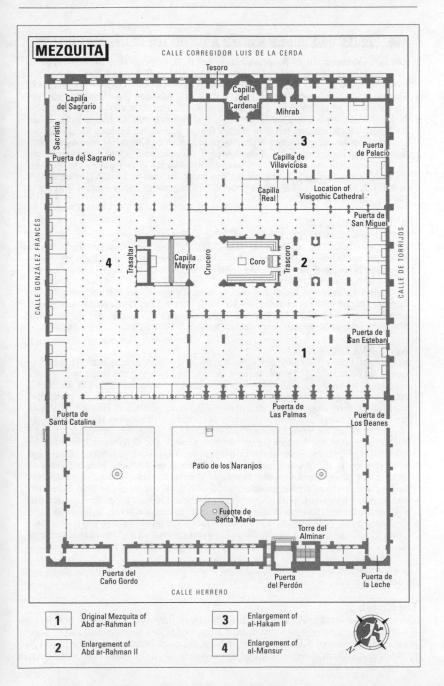

MEZQUITA

CALLE CORREGIDOR LUIS DE LA CERDA

Tesoro

Capilla del Sagrario

Capilla del Cardenal

Mihrab

Sacristia

3

Puerta del Sagrario

Capilla de Villaviciosa

Puerta de Palacio

Capilla Real

Location of Visigothic Cathedral

CALLE GONZÁLEZ FRANCÉS

4

Trasaltar

Capilla Mayor

Crucero

Coro

Trascoro

2

Puerta de San Miguel

CALLE DE TORRIJOS

Puerta de San Esteban

1

Puerta de Santa Catalina

Puerta de Las Palmas

Puerta de Los Deanes

Patio de los Naranjos

Fuente de Santa Maria

Torre del Alminar

Puerta del Caño Gordo

Puerta del Perdón

Puerta de la Leche

CALLE HERRERO

1 Original Mezquita of Abd ar-Rahman I	**3** Enlargement of al-Hakam II	
2 Enlargement of Abd ar-Rahman II	**4** Enlargement of al-Mansur	

MOORISH CÓRDOBA AND THE BUILDING OF THE MEZQUITA

Córdoba's **domination of Moorish Spain** began thirty years after the conquest – in 756, when the city was placed under the control of **Abd ar-Rahman I**, the sole survivor of the Umayyad dynasty which had been bloodily expelled from the eastern Caliphate of Damascus. He commenced the building of the **Great Mosque** (*La Mezquita*), purchasing the site of the former Visigothic Cathedral of Saint Vincent from the Christians. This building which, divided by a partition wall, had previously served both communities, had itself been constructed on top of an earlier Roman temple dedicated to the god Janus. Demolishing the church as they built, Abd ar-Rahman's architects, for reasons of speed and economy, incorporated one of the cathedral's original walls – that facing west – into the new structure and this is the reason why the *mihrab*'s prayer wall is not precisely aligned towards Mecca. This original mosque was completed by his son **Hisham** in 786 and comprises about one-fifth of the present building, the first dozen aisles adjacent to the Patio de los Naranjos.

ABD AR-RAHMAN II

The Cordoban Emirate soon began to rival Damascus both in power and in the brilliance of its civilization. **Abd ar-Rahman II** (822–52) initiated sophisticated irrigation programmes, minted his own coinage and received embassies from Byzantium. He in turn substantially enlarged the mosque. A focal point within the culture of *al-Andalus*, this was by now being consciously directed and enriched as an alternative to Mecca; it possessed an original script of the Koran and a bone from the arm of Muhammad, and, for the Spanish Muslim who could not go to Mecca, it became the most sacred place of **pilgrimage**. In the broader Islamic world it ranked fourth in sanctity after the Kaaba of Mecca, the city of Medina in Saudi Arabia, and the Al Aksa mosque of Jerusalem.

ABD AR-RAHMAN III

In the tenth century Córdoba reached its zenith under **Abd ar-Rahman III** (912–61), one of the great rulers of Islamic history. He assumed power at the age of twenty-three after his grandfather had killed his father during a period of internal strife and in his reign, according to a contemporary historian, "subdued rebels, built palaces, gave impetus to agriculture, immortalised ancient deeds and monuments, and inflicted great damage on infidels to a point where no opponent or contender remained in *al-Andalus*. People obeyed en masse and wished to live with him in peace." In 929, with Muslim Spain and a substantial part of North Africa firmly under his control, Abd ar-Rahman III adopted the title of "Caliph", or successor of the Prophet. It was a supremely confident gesture and was reflected in the growing splendour of Córdoba itself which, with a population approaching (if we take the not always reliable Moorish historians at face value) 500,000, had become the largest, most prosperous city of Europe, and outshone both Byzantium and Baghdad (the new capital of the eastern Caliphate) in science, culture and scholarship. At the turn of the tenth century it could boast some 27 schools, 50 hospitals (with the first separate clinics for the leprous and insane), 900 public baths, 60,300 noble mansions, 213,077 houses and 80,455 shops. The construction of a glorious new palace at

Christian cathedral – of the building. And it was completed within a year of its commencement in 785.

The Mihrab

The mosque's overall uniformity was broken only by the culminating point of al-Hakam II's tenth-century extension – the domed cluster of pillars surrounding the mosque's great jewel, the sacred **Mihrab**. And even here, although he lengthened the prayer hall by a third, al-Hakam carefully aligned the new *mihrab* at the end of the same central

Medina Azahara in the 930s as well as further **development of the Great Mosque** paralleled these new heights of confidence and splendour. Abd ar-Rahman III provided the Mezquita with a new minaret (which has not survived), 80m high, topped by three pomegranate-shaped spheres, two of silver and one of gold and each weighing a ton.

AL-HAKAM II

The Caliph's successor **al-Hakam II** (961–76) was a man from another mould than that of his warrior father, best epitomized by his advice to his own son:

> *Do not make wars unnecessarily. Keep the peace, for your own wellbeing and that of your people. Never unsheathe your sword except against those who commit injustice. What pleasure is there in invading and destroying nations, in taking pillage and destruction to the ends of the earth? Do not let yourself be dazzled by vanity; let your justice always be like a tranquil lake.*

In tune with these sentiments, al-Hakam was a poet, historian and the builder of one of the great libraries of the Middle Ages. This cultured ruler was also responsible for the mosque's most **brilliant expansion**, virtually doubling its extent. After demolishing the south wall to add fourteen extra rows of columns, he employed Byzantine craftsmen to construct a new **mihrab** or prayer niche; this remains complete and is perhaps the most beautiful example of all Moorish religious architecture.

AL-MANSUR

Under the vizier-usurper **al-Mansur** (977–1002), who used his position as regent to push al-Hakam's child successor, Hisham II, into the background (see p.000), repeated attacks were carried out on the Christians in the north, including the daring expedition to Santiago de Compostela in 997, when the pilgrimage cathedral's bells were seized. This **military might** was built on the incorporation of thousands of Berbers from North Africa into al-Mansur's army – a policy that was to have devastating implications for the future when the same Berbers turned on their paymasters and sacked and plundered the city, destroying al-Hakam's treasured library in the process. Within less than thirty years the brilliant Caliphate of Córdoba had collapsed in a bloody turmoil as short-lived puppet caliphs attempted to stave off the inevitable.

When he was not away on his military campaigns, al-Mansur gave his attention to further embellishing the great mosque. As al-Hakam had extended the building as far to the south as was possible, he completed the final enlargement by adding seven rows of columns to the whole east side. This spoiled the symmetry of the mosque, depriving the *mihrab* of its central position, but Arab historians observed that it meant there were now "as many bays as there are days of the year". They also delighted in describing the rich interior, with its 1293 marble columns, 280 chandeliers and 1445 lamps. Hanging inverted among the lamps were the bells of the cathedral of Santiago de Compostela. Al-Mansur had made his Christian captives carry them on their shoulders from Galicia – a process which was to be observed in reverse after Córdoba was captured by Fernando el Santo (the Saint) in 1236.

---

aisle which had led to the previous two. The *mihrab* had two functions in Islamic worship: it indicated the direction of Mecca (and hence of prayer) and it amplified the words of the *imam*, or prayer leader. At Córdoba it was also of supreme beauty. As Titus Burckhardt wrote, in *Moorish Art in Spain*:

> *The design of the prayer niche in Córdoba was used as a model for countless prayer niches in Spain and North Africa. The niche is crowned by a horseshoe-shaped arch, enclosed by a rectangular frame. The arch derives a peculiar strength from the fact*

that its central point shifts up from below. The wedge-shaped arch stones or voussoirs fan outwards from a point at the foot of the arch and centres of the inner and outer circumferences of the arch lie one above the other. The entire arch seems to radiate, like the sun or the moon gradually rising over the edge of the horizon. It is not rigid; it breathes as if expanding with a surfeit of inner beatitude, while the rectangular frame enclosing it acts as a counterbalance. The radiating energy and the perfect still-ness form an unsurpassable equilibrium. Herein lies the basic formula of Moorish architecture.

The paired pillars which flank the *mihrab* and support its arch were taken from the earlier *mihrab* of Abd ar-Rahman I, their prominent position no doubt a mark of respect by al-Hakam to his great predecessor. The inner vestibule of the niche (which is roped off – forcing you to risk the wrath of the attendants in getting a glimpse) is quite simple in comparison, with a shell-shaped ceiling carved from a single block of marble. The chambers to either side, as well as the dome above the *mihrab*, are decorated with exquisite **mosaics** of gold, rust-red, turquoise and green, the work of Byzantine crafts-men supplied by the emperor Nicephorus II at al-Hakam's request. These constitute the *maksura*, where the caliph and his retinue would pray, a fitting monument to this scholarly and sensitive ruler.

The Cathedral and other additions
Originally the whole design of the mosque would have directed worshippers naturally towards the *mihrab*. Today, though, you almost stumble upon it, for in the centre of the mosque squats a Renaissance **cathedral coro**. This was built in 1523, nearly three cen-turies of enlightened restraint after the Christian conquest, and in spite of fierce oppo-sition from the town council. The erection of a *coro* and *capilla mayor*, however, had long been the "Christianizing" dream of the cathedral chapter and at last they had found a monarch, predictably Carlos V, who was willing to sanction the work. Carlos, to his credit, realized the mistake (though it did not stop him from destroying parts of the Alhambra and Sevilla's Alcázar); on seeing the work completed he told the chapter, "You have built what you or others might have built anywhere, but you have destroyed something that was unique in the world." Some details are worth noting, though, par-ticularly the beautifully carved Churrigueresque **choir stalls** by Pedro Duque Cornejo, created with mahogany brought from the New World. To the left of the *coro* stands an earlier and happier Christian addition, the Mudéjar **Capilla de Villaviciosa**, built by Moorish craftsmen in 1371 (and now partly sealed up). Beside it are the dome and pil-lars of the **earlier mihrab**, constructed under Abd ar-Rahman II. The mosque's original and finely decorated timber-coffered ceiling was replaced in the eighteenth century by the present Baroque cupolas. Further post-Reconquest additions include the **Capilla Real**, installed by Alfonso X in the thirteenth century, with *azulejo* panels and lobed niches in Mudéjar style, and the early eighteenth-century **Capilla del Cardinal** (Chapter House), the *tesoro* (treasury) and *sacristía*, none of which detracts from the building's imposing majesty.

The evocative belfry, the **Torre del Alminar** at the corner of the Patio de los Naranjos, is built on the site of the original minaret and contemporary with the cathe-dral addition. The belfry was designed by Hernán Ruíz, who used the earlier tower as a core to support two additional sections more than doubling its height. The climb to the top is a dizzying experience and the **views** over the town and Mezquita itself tremendous. Close by, the **Puerta del Perdón**, the main entrance to the patio, was rebuilt in Moorish style in 1377. It's worth making a tour of the Mezquita's **outer walls** before leaving; parts of the original "caliphal" decoration (in particular some exquisite lattice-work) surrounding the portals are stunning. The west wall along c/Torrijos is the most striking where the **Puerta de San Esteban** was an important side entrance into the original mosque and is the oldest of the doorways, dated by an inscription above it to 855. The **Puerta de San Miguel** is sited in the oldest stretch of wall, and dates from the earlier Visigothic cathedral.

The Alcázar and river area

Dating from the time of the *reconquista*, the **Alcázar de Los Reyes Cristianos** (Tues–Sat 8.30am–2.30pm; Sun 9.30am–3pm; gardens only Tues–Sun 8pm–midnight; 450ptas; free on Fri), a Palace Fortress, was completed in the fourteenth century and now houses a small municipal museum. The original Moorish alcázar stood beside the Mezquita, on the site presently occupied by the Palacio Episcopal. After the Christian conquest it was rebuilt a little to the west and used by monarchs – including Fernando and Isabel who were visited here by Columbus in 1486 – when staying in the city, hence its name. That the buildings retain little of their original opulence today is due to their use as the residence of the **Inquisition** for three centuries prior to 1821, and later as a prison until as recently as 1951. The palace underwent extensive Mudéjar rebuilding during the fifteenth century, when the attractive **Moorish-style gardens** were added. From the tower's belvedere there are great **views** over the town and river where, to the west of the **Puente Romano**, it's possible to see one of the ancient **Moorish water wheels**, the Albolafia. This is the reconstructed sole survivor of a number of mills which crossed the river here and which, besides grinding flour, pumped water to the Alcázar's gardens. So noisy were this wheel's rumblings that Queen Isabel had it dismantled when it disturbed her sleep.

The **interior** of the Alcázar has some mildly interesting fifteenth-century royal baths and some fine **Roman mosaics** discovered in the city. The second-century depiction of *Polyphemus and Galatea* is outstanding and the monochrome mosaic beside it is one of the largest complete mosaics in existence. A third-century carved sarcophagus is also worth a look, with its portal ajar indicating that access is open to the person within.

In the gardens across the plaza to the north of the Alcázar are the remains of a **Moorish hammam** or bath house, now sadly neglected, filled up with rubbish and scrawled with graffiti. The city – somewhat belatedly – intends to protect and restore the baths and they were fenced off in 1999 prior to work commencing.

Palacio Episcopal

Opposite the Mezquita's west wall on the site of the former Moorish alcázar lies the **Palacio Episcopal** (Mon–Sat 9.30am–3pm; 150ptas or free with a Mezquita ticket). This elegant seventeenth-century building with a fine patio and fountain is now a **museum of religious art**, mainly sculpture. The highlights are in the early rooms where there are some outstanding examples of medieval wood sculpture – a great Spanish tradition. The anonymous thirteenth-century *Virgen de las Huertas* in Room 1 is finely worked, as is a striking fifteenth-century *Calvario Villaviciosá* or crucifixion. In Room 3, an anonymous early sixteenth-century *pietà* is another remarkable work with the agonized expressions of the onlookers beautifully portrayed. The remainder of the museum comprises more wood sculpture from later periods, as well as tapestries and furniture. On the ground floor, there's a beautiful **baroque chapel** dedicated to the Virgin and a room containing works by modern Cordoban artists (which may be closed).

Across the river, the **Torre de la Calahorra** (daily: April–Sept 10am–2pm & 4.30–8.30pm; Oct–March 10am–6pm; 500ptas), a medieval tower built to guard the Puente Romano, now houses another museum full of hi-tech gimmicks (you tour wearing headphones) including weird tableaux, a lit-up Alhambra as well as a model of the Mezquita prior to its Christian alterations and, improbably, a multimedia presentation on the history of man. From the tower you get a wonderful panoramic **view** towards the city.

The Judería and synagogue

Between the Mezquita and the beginning of the Avenida del Gran Capitán lies the **Judería**, Córdoba's old Jewish quarter. A fascinating network of lanes, it's more atmospheric and less commercialized than Sevilla's, though tacky souvenir shops are beginning to gain ground. Near the heart of the quarter, at c/Maimónides 18, is the **synagogue** (Tues–Sat 10am–1.30pm & 3.30–5.30pm; Sun 10am–1.30pm; free with EU passport, otherwise 50ptas), one of only three in Spain – the other two are in Toledo – that survived the Jewish expulsion of 1492. This one, built in 1315, is minute, particularly in comparison to the great Santa María in Toledo, but it has some fine stucco work elaborating on a Solomon's-seal motif together with Hebrew texts in the Mudéjar style, and it also retains its women's gallery. Just south of the synagogue in the *plazuela* named after him, is a statue of Maimónides, the Jewish philospher, physician and Talmudic jurist born in Córdoba in 1135.

Nearby is a rather bogus **Zoco** – an Arab *souk* turned into a crafts arcade – on the site of an old mule market. If you're not too impressed by the trinkets on offer, there's a bar and and a pleasant patio to enjoy a drink in. Adjoining this, the small **Museo Taurino** (Bullfighting Museum; Tues–Sat 8.30am–2.30pm, Sun 9.30am–3pm; 450ptas, free on Fri) warrants a look, if only for the kitschy nature of its exhibits: row upon row of bulls' heads, two of them given this "honour" for having killed matadors. Beside a copy of the tomb of Manolete, most famous of the city's fighters, is exhibited the hide of his taurine nemesis, Islero.

Finally, close to the Mezquita's northeast corner, you shouldn't miss Córdoba's most famous street, the **Callejón de los Flores**. This is a white-walled alley from whose balconies and hanging pots cascades a riot of geraniums in summer and which, when viewed from its northern end, neatly frames the Mezquita's belfry – the picture that decorates every postcard rack in town.

Plaza del Potro

A short walk east from the Mezquita along c/Corregidor de la Cerda is the **Plaza del Potro**, one of Córdoba's more historic landmarks. This fine old square is named after the colt (*potro*) which adorns its sixteenth-century fountain. Originally a livestock market dealing in horses and mules, the area once had a villainous reputation, as did the remarkable inn opposite, the **Posada del Potro**, which Cervantes mentions in *Don Quixote*, and where he almost certainly stayed. Sensitively restored, the building, with an atmospheric cattle yard, now houses the *Casa de Cultura*, municipal education and cultural offices, part of which is used for *artesanía* displays and art and photographic exhibitions, often worth a look.

Museo de Bellas Artes

On the other side of the Plaza del Potro, the former Hospital de la Caridad, founded in the sixteenth century, now contains the **Museo de Bellas Artes** (Tues 3–8pm, Wed–Sat 9am–8pm, Sun 9am–3pm; free with EU passport, otherwise 250ptas). Among a fairly unremarkable collection (rendered even more threadbare by the inexplicable disappearance of the Goyas and the best Riberas to Madrid) is an *Immaculate Conception* by Murillo as well as works by Valdés Leal and some dubious Zurbaráns. A couple of interesting drawings near the entrance by the British artist David Roberts depict the Mezquita's Patio de los Naranjos and the Puerta del Puente as they were in the last century. The ground floor has a small archeological collection which includes a fine second-century BC **Iberian sculpture** of a she-wolf despatching its victim, as well as a collection of rather humdrum modern sculpture and paintings.

Across the courtyard is a small museum (Tues–Sat 8.30am–2.30pm, Sun 9.30am–3pm; 450ptas, free on Fri) devoted to the Córdoban artist **Julio Romero de Torres** (1885–1930), painter of some sublimely dreadful canvases, most of which depict reclining female nudes with furtive male guitar players. Attacked by feminists and dubbed "the king of kitsch" by critics, the *cordobeses*, however, won't have a word said against him. If you wish to decide for yourself, the nightmarish *Cante Jondo* or the raunchy *Naranjas y Limones* (Oranges and Lemons) should be enough to give you the measure of Romero's oeuvre; alternatively, just flick through a catalogue in the foyer.

Probably more rewarding would be a visit to *Bodegas Campos*, just east of here at c/Lineros 32, a wonderful rambling old place where they will allow you to see the cellars – stacked with giant oak *botas* (barrels) – in which the company matures its wine through the *solera* system of blending. They'll be only to delighted to offer you a sample in the **bar**, but don't commit the ultimate *faux-pas* by asking for anything from Jerez. Montilla is the brew here, and very good it is, too.

North of the Plaza del Potro

To the north, in an area which was once the *plateros* or silversmiths' quarter you'll find **Plaza de la Corredera**. A wonderfully ramshackle colonnaded square, rather like a decayed version of Madrid's or Salamanca's Plaza Mayor, it is unique in Andalucía. The square's complete enclosure occurred in the seventeenth century and presented the city with a suitable space for all kinds of spectacles. These have included burnings by the Inquisition as well as bullfights, from which event the tiny *Callejón Toril* (bull pen) on the square's eastern side takes its name. Any other city, you feel, would make this into a monument to civic pride, but sadly the place has been a neglected for decades. Now belatedly undergoing a controversial and painfully slow programme of restoration, only when this is completed will the small daily and spectacularly colourful Saturday **markets** return.

Museo Arqueológico

To the northwest of the Plaza del Potro, on Plaza de Jerónimo Páez, lies the excellent **Museo Arqueológico** (Tues 3–8pm, Wed–Sat 9am–8pm, Sun 9am–3pm; free with EU passport, otherwise 250ptas), essential to gaining an understanding of Córdoba's importance as a Roman city in particular, as so little from this period survives above ground today. During the original conversion of the Casa Páez, this small sixteenth-century Renaissance mansion was revealed as the unlikely site of a genuine Roman patio. As a result, it is one of the most imaginative and enjoyable small museums in the country, with good local collections from the Iberian, Roman and Moorish periods.

Starting in Room 3 – where you can see evidence of the previous Roman building on this site – highlights include a large number of finds from the excavation of Córdoba's western necropolis, among which are a number of inscribed first-century gladiatorial tombstones, whilst Room 5 has a remarkably well-preserved set of **bronze horse bridles** from a Roman *quadriga*, or four-horse chariot. Some of the mosaic fragments here, with their geometrical designs, appear to anticipate the later Moorish patterns. Among other cases in this room displaying lamps, pottery and glassware is a fascinating carved stone relief depicting the **olive harvest** – then, as now, Córdoba was renowned for its oil. The stairs leading to Room 7 are flanked by fine mosaics including an outstanding one depicting a *quadriga* in action. The intricate **wooden Mudéjar ceiling** here is worth a look and apparently predates the mansion which was built to incorporate it.

Room 7 contains exhibits from the Moorish period among which is a fine inlaid tenth-century **bronze stag** – a gift of the Byzantine emperor Constantine VII to Abd ar-Rahman III – and found at the Moorish palace of Medina Azahara (see p.346) where it was used as the spout of a fountain. On the balcony a collection of wells attests to the Moorish attraction to water – a tradition continued by fountains throughout Andalucía today. The museum's beautiful double patio contains miscellaneous Roman statuary, mosaics and a superb fourth-century Christian marble **sarcophagus**. Also here is a fine second-century **sculpture of Mithras** slaying the bull from a mithraeum excavated at Cabra in the south of the province. This conventional image, which was placed in the *retablo* position in the small mithraic cult temples, shows Mithras plunging his dagger into the bull whose blood, initiates believed, gave birth to all living things, hence the dog and the snake trying to get their share. The ever-present problem of evil is portrayed by the symbolic scorpion attacking the bull's vitals.

The rest of the city

Many visitors to Córdoba make a stopover at the Mezquita and then leave without ever discovering the other Córdoba, to the north of the monumental quarter and the Judería, where the city's everyday life is carried on. Here, interspersed among the modern streets – many still built on the ancient grid – are any number of **Gothic churches**, **convents** and **Renaissance palaces** that are little visited but which are well worth an hour or two. Note that churches are usually locked outside service times, and early mornings or evenings (about 7–9pm) are the most promising times to catch them open, perhaps visiting a few *tapas* bars en route.

Plaza Tendillas and around
Plaza Tendillas is the vibrant centre of modern Córdoba, as it was in Roman times. Dominated by the bronze equestrian statue of El Gran Capitán, a Cordoban general whose Italian campaigns in the late fifteenth century helped to project post-*reconquista* Spain on to the world stage, the previously traffic-clogged square has recently received a makeover, and its fountains – spurting two metres into the air from the pedestrianized pavement – are a big hit with tourists, children and dogs.

Off the east side of the plaza, along c/Claudio Marcelo, lies the **Templo Romano**, the tortuously reconstructed remains (mostly pillars) of a first-century Roman temple thought to have been of a similar form to the Maison Carrée at Nîmes. Turning left along c/Capitulares from here brings you to the **Iglesia de San Pablo** fronting the street of the same name, a fine Romanesque-Gothic church. Dating from the period following the *reconquista* – as do many of Córdoba's churches in this part of town – it has undergone numerous later modifications including a Baroque facade. Its interior retains a fine Mudéjar dome and coffered ceiling as well as a seventeenth-century **sculpture of the Virgin**, *Nuestra Señora de las Angustias* (sorrows), a masterpiece by Juan de Mesa, himself a native of Córdoba.

Northwest from here, on c/Alfonso XIII, is the striking **Circulo de la Amistad**, a *Casino* or social club, founded in 1842, and set inside a former convent. Ask the porter to let you see the marvellous Renaissance **patio**, originally the convent's cloister. Continuing east again, beyond San Pablo lies **San Andrés**, another post-*reconquista* church and, further on, at the end of c/Santa María de la Gracia, is the Gothic **San Lorenzo**, whose converted Moorish minaret tower, outstanding **rose window**, and triple-arched portico combine to make it the best-looking church in the city. Inside, the apse has fifteenth-century **frescoes** depicting scenes from the Passion.

Turning north along c/Roelas, passing the nineteenth-century Neoclassical Iglesia de San Rafael, you'll come to another *reconquista* church, **San Agustín**, in the plaza of the same name. Originally a Gothic church, it was substantially altered in the sixteenth century; inside it has frescoes and another sculpture of the Virgin by Juan de Mesa.

Palacio de Viana

Slightly west of San Agustín in Plaza de Gome you'll find the **Palacio-Museo de Viana** (guided tours daily: June–Sept 9am–2pm; Oct–May 10am–1pm & 4–6pm; 500ptas), one of Córdoba's finest palaces and seat of the Marquises of Viana until the family sold up to a bank in 1981, after which it was opened – apparently just as the family left it – to the public. Started in the fourteenth century, the building has had numerous later additions tacked on, including most of the **twelve outstanding patios**, filled with flowers, the main attraction for many visitors today.

The compulsory guided tour shunts you around a bewildering number of drawing rooms, gaudy bedrooms (one with a telling Franco portrait), kitchens and galleries, linked by creaking staircases, whilst a commentary delivered in machine-gun Spanish (foreign-language room descriptions available) points out a wealth of furniture, paintings, weapons and top-drawer junk the family amassed over the centuries, giving you little time to take anything in.

More churches, convents and tabernas

North of the Palacio de Viana, the fortress-like **Iglesia de Santa Marina** dates from the thirteenth century (with Baroque modifications) and shares the charming plaza of the same name with a monument to the celebrated Cordoban *torero* **Manolete**, who was born in the Santa Marina *barrio* and died in the ring in 1947. At the square's eastern end, strictly speaking the Plaza del Conde Priego, the fifteenth-century Franciscan **convent of Santa Isabel** has a delightful patio with an imposing cypress. The *capilla mayor* inside the convent's church has sculptures by Pedro Roldán. The nuns here also sell their home-made *dulces*: the ebullient Hermana Isabel – given a special dispensation from the order's rule of silence to run the shop – will serve you.

Calle Conde de Priego leads east again to the Plaza Ruíz de Alda, beyond which, in the simple white-walled Plaza de Capuchinos lies **El Cristo de los Faroles** (Christ of the Lanterns), an eighteenth-century sculpture of the crucifixion which is the centre of much religious fervour. At night, when the lanterns flanking the cross are illuminated, the place has an uneasily, mystical ambience.

North from here are two features – on either side of the Plaza de Colón – worthy of a detour. Close to the northeast corner of this garden-square, the **Torre de la Malmuerta** ("bad death") is an early fifteenth-century battlemented tower, once part of the city walls. It takes its name from a crime of passion when a guard posted here is supposed to have killed his adulterous spouse. At the foot of the tower is one of the city's best loved *tabernas*, the *Casa de Paco Acedo* (see p.344), housed in part of a former barracks. The west side of the Plaza de Colón is dominated by the lavishly ornate facade of the eighteenth-century former **Convento de la Merced**, now the seat of the provincial government, and the biggest and best example of full-blown Baroque in town. The porter will allow you inside to view an exquisite Renaissance **patio** with paired columns, elegant staircases and a central fountain. The church, restored after a fire in 1978, has a fine **retablo** by Gómez de Sandoval. Unfortunately, the building is not often open; try service times in the early evening.

Picking up the route south towards the centre, follow c/del Osario until, just before Plaza Tendillas, a left turn brings you into Plaza San Miguel with its charming **Iglesia de San Miguel**, yet another *reconquista* church founded in the thirteenth century by Fernando III. Above the early Gothic entrance there's a magnificent **rose window** and, inside, a remarkable eighteenth-century **retablo** in red marble depicting the archangels Gabriel, Rafael and Miguel. Tucked behind the church lies one of Córdoba's most atmospheric taverns, the **Taberna San Miguel** (see p.344), a century-old place hung with faded *corrida* posters, the odd guitar and tiled *bon mots*.

Heading back to the Judería you pass another couple of churches: the fourteenth-century **San Nicolás**, at the end of c/Conde de Gondomar, east of Plaza Tendillas, with a spectacular **octagonal bell tower**, and the rather sad **Iglesia de San Juan** in a small square of the same name to the south, where the crumbling minaret of a former ninth-century mosque, complete with elegant horseshoe arches resting on Corinthian pillars, sits precariously beside its later rival.

Eating, drinking and nightlife

Coming from Sevilla or the coast, the nightlife in Córdoba will seem rather tame by comparison. Places start closing at around 11pm; by midnight, the empty streets around the Mezquita, lit by black lanterns, have a melancholy air. When they are open, however, many of the city's **bars and restaurants** are among the best in Andalucía and are well worth seeking out.

Restaurants

Córdoba's restaurants are on the whole reasonably priced – and quite a few of the upmarket establishments are really excellent; you need only to avoid some of the dismal touristy places surrounding the Mezquita. Whilst here be sure to try Córdoba's two most celebrated dishes, *rabo de toro* (slow-stewed bull's tail) and *salmorejo* (a hunky *gazpacho* with chunks of ham and egg), available all over town.

Mesón Casa La Abuela, Plaza San Rafael 8, near the church of San Lorenzo. A delightful little restaurant in the north of town with *salones* around a leafy central patio; there's a good-value *menú* for 900ptas.

Almudaina, Plaza Campo Santo de los Martires 1 (☎957 47 43 42). Top-notch restaurant with four stylish rooms in an atmospheric sixteenth-century mansion facing the walls of the Alcázar. Among many fine dishes *pechuga de corniz en salsa* (partridge breasts) is a house special. Expensive, but there's a *menú* for about 3000ptas. Closed Sun eve.

Bar-Restaurante Barril, c/Concepción 16. Super efficient *tapas* and breakfast bar with a small terrace and all day *platos combinados*.

El Caballo Rojo, c/Cardenal Herrero 28 (☎957 47 53 75). Beneath the Mezquita's belfry, this is one of Córdoba's choicest restaurants, although a café-style interior lacks intimacy. It prides itself on a Moorish-influenced menu offering such specialities as *cordero a la miel* (lamb in honey) and tasty desserts like *canutillo de almendra* (almond pastry). Expensive but offers a *menú*.

El Churrasco, c/Romero 16 (*not* c/Romero Barros) (☎957 29 08 19). The third – and probably the best – of Córdoba's top-drawer restaurants, with sumptuously decorated dining rooms and patio, has a long-standing reputation for its *churrasco* (a kind of grilled pork dish, served with pepper sauces). When booking mention that you wish to visit their *Museo del Vino Bodega* (diners only) where you may also choose the wine for your meal. Prices match its reputation, although there's set *menú* at 3500ptas. Closed Aug.

Círculo Taurino, Manuel María de Arjona 1, slightly south of Plaza de Colón. Excellent, mid-range, *cordobés* family-run restaurant offering a wide range of local dishes.

Mesón Casa Elias, c/Rodríguez Sánchez 5. This big, cheap and cheerful place with a patio makes a good lunch stop for *raciones* or a 950ptas *menú*.

Casa La Estupenda, c/San Fernando 39. Solid *casa de comidas* place with a good-value *menú* featuring some vegetarian dishes; pleasant atmosphere with classical music.

Marisquería El Faro, c/Ricardo de Montís 1 off c/Blanco del Monte. Good seafood *raciones* and a decent paella.

Bar-Restaurante Federación de Peñas, c/Conde y Luque 8. Moorish-style patio dining room offers a variety of economical *menús*.

Restaurante La Fragua, Calleja del Arco just off c/Tomás Conde, near Plaza Judá Leví. Tiny, economical restaurant with patio and a *menú* for about 900ptas.

Restaurante Cafetín Halal, c/Rey Heredia 28. Located in the Islamic cultural centre and serving excellent, inexpensive dishes with many vegetarian options, but no alcohol – however, their range of fruit cocktails is recommended.

Café-Bar Juda Levi, Plaza Juda Levi. Economical *platos combinados* from around 700ptas plus ice-creams with a pavement terrace.

Bar-Restarante Millán, Avda. Dr Fleming 14, just northwest of the Alcázar. Tranquil, economical bar-restaurant with a charming *azulejo*-lined room. *Rabo de toro, salmorejo* and *flamenquin de lomo* (breaded pork with *jamón*) are all good.

Los Mochuelos, c/Agustín Moreno 51, near the church of Santiago. Traditional patio restaurant with large variety of *raciones* dishes including *revuelto de setas con salmón* and *mochuelitos* (spicy meat); plenty of atmosphere, stacked butts, bullfight posters and a pleasant patio.

Restaurante Monteria, c/Corregidor Luís de la Cerda 75, facing the Mezquita. Good-value restaurant of the *Hotel El Triunfo*, serving a wide range of meat and fish dishes, with a pleasant room featuring lots of cool marble.

Mesón La Moreneta, c/González 63 (aka Corregidor de la Cerda) facing the Mezquita. One of the few worthwhile places to eat near the Mezquita with a nice patio and a variety of economical *menús*.

Cafe-Bar Realejo, c/Realejo 89 east of the church of San Andrés. Popular with locals and a good budget option if you happen to be up this end of town; there's a *menú* for 850ptas.

El Rincón del Carmen, c/Romero 4. Pleasant small cafetería-restaurant with an outdoor patio and restaurant upstairs. Has an economical *menú*.

Taberna Santa Clara, c/Osio 2. Friendly and good-value *taberna* (also serving *tapas*) run by Carmen and chef Julián, with a delightful patio terrace and tempting *menú* including some Moorish-inspired dishes such as *pollo a la miel* (chicken with honey). Their own house *Montilla* from the wood is also excellent. At the time of writing there is a rumoured move to a new location nearby; details should be posted outside.

Tabernas and tapas bars

In 1987 Córdoba held a *homenaje*, or tribute, to its treasured **tabernas** – and with good reason, for few places anywhere can match them for sheer character and variety, not to mention **tapas**. The municipal tourist office gives out copies of *La Ruta de las Tabernas de Córdoba* – a route map of the town's best *tapas* bars. Remember, too, when ordering *fino* that the equivalent brew here is *montilla* and the best way to get up a barman's nose is to ask for any of the wines of Jerez, the product of the upstart province downriver. If you're new to *montilla-moriles* to give it its full title, named after the villages further south where it's made (see p.351), or have been unimpressed with the insipid concoctions sold abroad under the *montilla* name, prepare for a pleasant surprise. *Montilla*, which vaguely resembles a mellow, dry sherry, is a giant on its native soil, and is considered a healthier tipple by the *cordobeses*; whereas Jerez sherry is fortified with alcohol, here the process is totally natural, leading (they insist) to fewer hangovers.

AROUND THE MEZQUITA

Bar Caballo Rojo, Cardenal Herrero 28, facing the Mezquita. The smoothly efficient – and slightly pricier – bar of the famous restaurant has excellent *tapas* and *raciones* including *boquerones en vinagre* (anchovies in vinegar).

Bodega Guzmán, c/Judíos 7, close to the synagogue. Cavernous old bar frequented by bullfight aficionados, with a small *taurino* "museum" in its inner sanctum and outstanding *amargoso montilla* served from a butt behind the bar.

Bar Miguelito, Acera Pintada 8, across the river near the Torre de la Calahorra. *Barrio* bar slightly off the tourist beat which is locally reputed for its *tapas* range.

Casa Pepe de la Judería, c/Romero 1. Sparkling *tapas* bar which has expanded into the restaurant business and has a fine terrace. The whole place exudes an air of quality. In their stand-up bar, house specials include *salmorejo* and *solomillo de venado* (venison).

Bar La Plazuela, Plaza Jerónimo Páez, near the archeological museum. Pleasant little bar with great terrace where you can knock back a *jarrón* of beer with some excellent *tapas* – try their *ensaladilla*. Slightly north of here in c/Ambrosio de Morales there's another branch of the *Sociedad Plateros* chain (see below) with more good *tapas*.

Bar-Mesón Rafaé, c/Deanes 4. North of the Mezquita in the Judería, this pleasant old bar offers a broad *tapas* range, well-kept *montilla* and a reasonably priced *menú*.

Casa Rubio, Puerta de Almodóvar 5, in the city wall. Atmospheric local bar with a good *tapas* range and excellent *montilla*. *Casa Bravo*, a few steps away and serving equally good *tapas*, is also worth a visit.

Casa Salinas, Puerto de Almodóvar s/n close to the one above. Stacked with butts holding its celebrated *montillas*, house *media raciones* include *boquerones en vinagre* and *pescaito frito*. The bar has longstanding flamenco traditions; well known practitioners often meet up here and impromptu *juergas* can result.

Bar Sociedad Plateros c/Deanes 5. Dusty old bar with a good *tapas* range – try *chorizo al vino* – and is part of the Plateros chain (see below).

AROUND THE PLAZA DEL POTRO

Bodegas Campos, c/Lineros 32. Full-scale *bodega* with great oak barrels (many signed by celebrities) stacked up in the *sacristía* cellar at the rear. A bar at the entrance sells their own excellent *montilla* by the *copita* or the bottle, and *tapas* are on offer. There's also a mid-priced restaurant behind.

Taberna El Potro, c/Lineros 2, slightly north of the square. Somewhat over-adorned with reproductions of Julio Romero de Torres's "art works", serving *tapas*, *platos combinados* and a *menú*.

Taberna San Pedro, Plaza San Pedro, three blocks east of the Plaza del Potro. Old *taberna* founded in 1868, lined with *azulejos* and serving decent *tapas* and *montilla*.

Bodega Sociedad Plateros, c/San Francisco 6. Headquarters of the *Plateros* chain, and in a converted former convent. What started out in 1868 as a mutual benefit society for the workers in Córdoba's silversmith trade eventually branched out into the *bodega* business, presently owning a chain of nine excellent bars around the city (ask for a free map detailing where they are). The bar – now over a century old and serving a wide range of *tapas* – is light and airy with a glass-covered patio complemented by hanging plants and *azulejos*.

AROUND AND NORTH OF PLAZA TENDILLAS

Casa del Abuelo, Plaza de San Miguel s/n, close to the church of San Miguel. Good and ancient *tapas* tavern popular with students. The house special is *berenjenas fritas* (fried aubergine); *lomo al abuelo* (pork) and *patatas a lo pobre* are also tasty.

La Canoa, c/Ronda de los Tejares 18, Pasaje Cajasur. On the west side of the Ronda between Avda. Gran Capitan & c/Doce de Octubre, this picturesque bar has its own *bodega* supplying excellent house *montilla*. Noted for its *jamón* and sheep's cheese *tapas*.

Bar Gaudí, Avda. Gran Capitán 22, near El Corte Inglés. In the commercial district, named after Catalunya's great architect and aptly decorated in Art Nouveau style; serves *tapas* and wide range of European beers.

Taberna Góngora, c/Torres Cabrera 4, close to the *Rinconcito* (below). Welcoming modern bar carrying on the *tapas* tradition and much favoured by *tapeadores*. Specials include *carne de monte* (cured meats) and *boquerones al limón* (anchovies).

Casa Paco Acedo, beneath the ancient Torre de Malmuerta. Fine old bar serving up a superb range of *tapas* and *raciones*, including *salmorejo* and all kinds of fried fish. The house speciality is a memorable *rabo de toro*, the perfect complement to the *montilla de la casa,* and best eaten at the tables outside beneath the tower, after sundown.

Taberna San Miguel, Plaza San Miguel 1, behind the church. Known to all as *El Pisto* (the barrel), this is one of the city's legendary bars and not to be missed. Wonderful *montilla* and *tapas*; *rabo de toro* and *callos en salsa picante* (tripe in a spicy sauce) are big favourites here.

AROUND PLAZA CORREDERA AND BEYOND

Casa Castillo, c/El Realejo 10. Friendly *barrio* bar built around an airy patio, and serving fine *montilla* and a hearty *salmorejo* (Córdoba's *gazpacho* with guts).

El Gallo, c/María Cristina 6, close to the Roman temple. Fine old *cordobés* drinking hole which has changed little since it opened at the turn of the twentieth century. Good *tapas* selection includes *cangrejo* (crab), *calamares*, *croquetas* and *gambas rebozadas* (fried prawns). The excellent *amargoso montilla* comes from their own *bodega* and is reckoned by experts to be the finest there is. They'll sell you a three-bottle pack to take home for a ridiculous price – almost an affront to such a great wine.

Casa El Juramento, c/Juramento 6, on east side of Plaza Corredera. Atmospheric bar with a charming patio a good *tapas* selection. House specials include *calamares en salsa* and *revuelto*.

Bar Regina, Plaza de Regina, slightly northeast of Plaza Corredera. Century-old bar with plenty of bullfight memorabilia, a nice patio and good *tapas*, including their noted *patatas bravas*.

Taberna Salinas, c/Tundidores 3. Century old *taberna* with dining rooms around a charming patio and an outstanding range of *raciones*; try their delicious *bacalao* with orange and olive oil or *setas en salsa* (mushrooms).

Sociedad Plateros, María Auxiliadora 25, close to the old city wall on the northeast side of town. Aficionados of the *Plateros* empire will enjoy this cavernous and attractive far-flung outpost, with more quality *tapas*. It's worth the walk, with a couple of nice churches to see along the way.

Flamenco, nightlife and discos

Outside Easter's *Semana Santa* and the annual fiesta at the end of May, the city's nightlife centres around bars and restaurants. The only **late-night drinking** you are likely to find is in the north of the city, where the bars in the El Brillante district and around Avda. Tejares, Avda. Gran Capitán and those near the provincial government building in c/Reyes Católicos tend to stay open after midnight. Córdoba's best non-membership **flamenco** *tablao* is *Tablao Cardenal*, c/Torrijos 10, next door to the Turismo (performances daily at 10.30pm except Sun; 2850ptas, includes first drink), where you can catch performances by established artists in a pleasant open-air patio, and reserve a table in advance (☎957 48 33 20). Also good is *La Bulería*, c/Pedro López 3, near Plaza de la Corredera, open from 10pm every night (performance starts 10.30pm; 1500ptas, includes first drink; they also serve food). The singer El Calli and his family are the core of the show, and get near enough to the real thing, although corners are sometimes cut when trade is slack. Free flamenco performances are also mounted by the local council in summer and various other concerts are staged at the Gran Teatro, Avda. Gran Capitan 3, and in the Alcázar gardens (details from the Turismo).

In summer the *marcha nocturna* moves out of town to the **El Brillante** suburb (just off our map and to the northwest of the Plaza de Colón). Here a whole *barrio* of **disco-bars** and music venues line the main road and are jammed to capacity with a heaving mass of bodies at weekends. For the heart of the action, head for **El Tablero**, a lively plaza surrounded by bars, restaurants and disco-bars. Conventional **discos** are in the centre of town around c/Cruz Conde, north of Plaza Tendillas. *QU*, c/Góngora 10, is Córdoba's entertaining attempt at an acid-house venue, while *Zahira*, c/Conde de Robledo 3, plays latin and rock until the early hours. A more spacious disco is *Kachao*, on the Carretera de Trassiera – the continuation of Avda. Mozárabes at the top of our city map.

Listings

Banks Numerous places (with ATM cash machines) are located along Ronda de los Tejares and the street that crosses this, Avda. del Gran Capitán.

Books & newspapers Librería Luque, c/Cruz Conde 19, off Plaza Tendillas, stocks walking maps and a selection of books in English. Córdoba's daily paper, *El Diario Córdoba*, is good for local events and entertainment. English and foreign press is available from Kiosko Fidela, c/Blanco Belmonte 10.

Bullfights Details and tickets (the May *feria* has the best *corridas*) from the Plaza de Toros, Avda. Gran Vía Parque (in the northwestern suburb). If bullfighting is your thing, it's possible to go on a guided tour of the city's bullring (☎957 23 25 07). Ask at the Turismo for further details.

Bus and train information *Alsina Graells*, Estación de Autobuses, Plaza de las Tres Culturas (☎957 27 81 00), for buses to Sevilla, Granada, Málaga, Almería, Cádiz, Jaén and the Costa del Sol. Details of services to all other destinations from the bus station information desk (☎957 40 40 40). Train information from RENFE, Plaza de las Tres Culturas (☎957 40 02 02).

Car rental Good deals are to be had from Europcar on the train station concourse (☎957 23 34 60) or Avis, Plaza de Colón 35 (☎957 47 68 62).

Football C.F. Córdoba won promotion to the Second Division in 1999 and are currently holding their own in the higher league. Details and tickets for matches are obtainable from the stadium, El Nuevo Arcángel (☎957 75 19 34), east of the river.

Hospital Cruz Roja, Avda. del Dr Fleming s/n (☎957 22 22 22); for emergencies dial ☎061.

Hiking maps 1:50,000, 1:100,000 and 1:200,000 maps are available from CNIG (National Geographic Service) branch office: c/Santo Tomás de Aquino 1–6º (☎957 23 35 46). The Turismo also sells a *Guía de Senderismo* hiking map for 600ptas.

Internet *Wildnet*, c/Vázquez Aroca 9 (☎957 76 13 49; Mon–Sat 9.30am–2pm & 5.30pm–midnight; closes Sat at 9pm) at the top left corner of our city map. Internet access 395ptas per hour.

Laundry Seco y Agua, c/Dr Marañon 3 slightly northwest of the Alcazár (☎957 20 35 51), is an efficient *tintorería* who will wash and dry 6kg of clothes the same day for 2000ptas.

Markets Plaza de la Corredera has a clothes and crafts market every morning, with the biggest on Saturday. There's also a market at El Jardín, Avda. Gran Vía Parque southwest of the old quarter, on Friday mornings.

Police Avda. del Dr Fleming 25, just beyond the walls to the west of the Mezquita (☎957 20 30 33). For emergencies dial ☎091.

Post office The main office is at c/Cruz Conde 15 (just north of Plaza Tendillas) and is also the place for poste restante (*lista de correos*). Mon–Fri 8.30am–8.30pm; Sat 9am–2pm.

Travel agent Viajes Halcon, Ronda de los Tejares 8 (☎957 47 10 69) or Viajes Intercontinental, Avda. del Gran Capitán 16 (☎957 47 06 94) are useful for all kinds of tickets and information.

Medina Azahara and beyond

Just a few kilometres from the city is the historic site of Medina Azahara, a must for those on the Moorish trail, and with a fascinating eighteenth-century hermitage nearby. Continuing west, along the southern fringes of the Sierra Morena, following the Río Guadalquivir, there's a remarkable castle to visit and a string of charming rural towns.

Medina Azahara

Some 7km to the northwest of Córdoba lie the vast and rambling ruins of **Medina Azahara**, a palace and administrative complex built on a dream scale by **Caliph Abd ar-Rahman III**. Naming it after a favourite wife, az-Zahra (the Radiant), he spent one-third of the annual state budget on its construction each year from 936 until his death in 961. Since the first archeological excavations were carried out in 1911, work has been going on continuously to piece together the fragments of this once fabulous creation, which is the reason it is currently only possible to visit a fraction of the excavated site.

The **site** (April–Sept Tues–Sat 10am–1.30pm & 6–8.30pm, Sun 10am–1.30pm; Oct–March Tues–Sat 10am–2pm & 5–6.30pm, Sun 10am–1.30pm; check winter hours with site; ☎957 32 91 30; free with EU passport, otherwise 250ptas) is entered by the **Puerta Norte**, the typically Moorish "twisted gate" which forced would-be invaders to double back on themselves, thus making them easy targets. Behind you at this point lies the Dar al-Mulk or royal palace (currently not open to visitors) which is thought to have been the residence of Abd ar-Rahman III. The signed route leads to **Dar al-Wuzara** (House of the Viziers), believed to have been the bureaucratic heart of the complex with administrative rooms, archives and a grand salon (with reconstructed horseshoe arches), originally fronted by a patio, now a garden. To the east of here, the route leads to the elegant arched **portico** and the **Plaza de Armas** – formerly a grand parade ground – beyond, still awaiting excavation. The portico is thought to have sup-

THE RISE AND FALL OF MEDINA AZAHARA

Ten thousand workers and 1500 mules and camels were employed in the construction of **Medina Azahara**, and the site, almost 2000m long by 900m wide, stretched over three descending terraces above the Guadalquivir valley. Roman masonry was taken from sites throughout Andalucía and re-used, whilst vast quantities of marble were shipped in from North Africa. In addition to the palace buildings, the complex contained a zoo, an aviary, four huge fish ponds, 300 baths, 400 houses, weapons factories, two barracks for the royal guard as well as numerous baths, markets, workshops and mosques. Visitors, so the chronicles record, were stunned by its wealth and brilliance: one conference room was provided with pure crystals, creating a rainbow when lit by the sun; another was built round a huge shallow bowl of mercury which, when the sun's rays fell on it, would be rocked by a slave, sending sunbeams reflected from its surface flashing and whizzing around the room, apparently alarming guests but greatly amusing the caliph.

Medina Azahara was a perfect symbol of the Western Caliphate's dominance and greatness, but it was to last for less than a century. **Al-Hakam II**, who succeeded Abd ar-Rahman, lived in the palace, continued to endow it, and enjoyed a stable reign. However, distanced from the city, he delegated more and more authority, particularly to his vizier Ibn Abi Amir, later known as **al-Mansur** (the Victor). In 976 al-Hakam was succeeded by his eleven-year-old son Hisham II and after a series of sharp moves al-Mansur assumed the full powers of government, keeping Hisham virtually imprisoned at Medina Azahara, to the extent of blocking up connecting passageways between the palace buildings.

Al-Mansur was equally skilful and manipulative in his wider dealings as a dictator, and Córdoba rose to new heights of prosperity, retaking large tracts of central Spain and raiding as far afield as Galicia and Catalunya. But with his death in 1002 came swift decline as his role and function were assumed in turn by his two sons. The first died in 1008; the second, Sanchol, showed open disrespect for the caliphate by forcing Hisham to appoint him as his successor. At this a popular revolt broke out and the caliphate disintegrated into civil war and a series of feudal kingdoms. Medina Azahara was looted by a mob at the outset and in 1010 was plundered and burned by retreating Berber mercenaries.

ported a terrace from where the caliph reviewed his troops. Turning south, you can see the **great mosque** below, one of the first buildings to be constructed on the site, oriented towards the southeast and Mecca. Its groundplan allows you to make out the main entrance, flanked by the base of a minaret (*alminar*), with patio, prayer hall – the floor of which was covered with esparto mats found in the excavations – and *mihrab*. The route now veers west passing the princely baths to the right, presently being painstakingly restored by archeologists repairing washing fountains and marble surfaces, beyond which lay the royal apartments.

For centuries, the site was looted for building materials; parts, for instance, were used in the Sevilla Alcázar and much of the surrounding town served as a quarry for the fifteenth-century construction of the monastery of San Jerónimo (now privately owned) at the end of the track which climbs above the ruins. In 1944, however, excavations unearthed the buried materials from a crucial part of the palace, the **Royal House**, where guests were received and meetings of ministers held. This has been meticulously reconstructed and, though still fragmentary, its main hall, the **Salón Rico de Abd al-Rahman III**, decorated with exquisite marble carvings, must rank among the greatest of all Moorish rooms. Modelled on the Roman basilica, it has a different kind of artistic representation from that found in the palaces at Granada or Sevilla – closer to natural and animal forms in its intricate Syrian *Hom* (Tree of Life) motifs. Unlike the later Spanish Arab dynasties, the Berber Almoravids and the Almohads of Sevilla, the caliphal Andalucians were little worried by Islamic strictures on the portrayal of nature, animals or even men – the beautiful hind in the

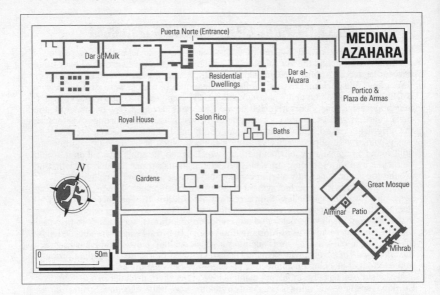

Córdoba museum is a good example (see p.339) – and it may well have been this aspect of the palace's artistic decor that led to such zealous destruction during the civil war.

The reconstructed palace gives a scale and focus to the site. Elsewhere there are little more than foundations, gardens and the odd horseshoe arch to fuel your imaginings, amid an awesome area of ruins, hidden beneath bougainvillea and rustling with cicadas. Biologists from Córdoba University have recently finished a study of soil samples from the site which has enabled them to determine exactly which plants and flowers were planted in the extensive gardens; plans are now being drawn up to reconstruct these as accurately as possible.

To reach Medina Azahara, follow the Avenida de Medina Azahara out of town, and on to the road to Villarubia and Posadas. About 4km out of town, make a right turn, after which it's another two or three kilometres to the site. Alternatively, the #01 city **bus** from the stop on the Paseo de la Victoria (almost opposite the *Melia* hotel) will drop you off at the intersection for the final three-kilometre walk. Ask the driver for the "Cruz de Medina Azahara". A **taxi** will cost you about 2500ptas one-way or there's a special round-trip fare of 4000ptas which includes a one-hour wait at the site while you visit – the Turismo can help with arranging this. Córdoba Vision (☎957 23 17 34) runs guided trips to the site daily (except Mon) at 10.30am (plus 4pm Oct–April; 2500ptas); buses leave from the Triunfo de San Rafael monument near the Turismo. With your own transport an atmospheric **place to eat** near the site is *Bar-Restaurante El Cruce* – with a leafy terrace and often serving *jabalí* (wild boar) – a 3km climb from the signed junction on the way to the entrance.

A scenic signed road climbs for 4km beyond this restaurant to **Las Ermitas** (Tues–Sun 10am–1.30pm & 4.30–7.45pm; 200ptas), a beautiful jasmine-scented hermitage filled with cypresses, olives and cacti. Here you can see twelve cells dating from the eighteenth century – spaced out around a central shrine – where hermit monks once flagellated themselves in splendid isolation. Solitaries lived here until as recently as 1957 and there are dramatic **views** over the valley of the Guadalquivir from the *mirador* of the giant cross, La Cruz del Humilladero.

Almodóvar del Río and Palma del Río

If you have your own transport, it's possible to continue a further 17km west along the C431 to **ALMODÓVAR DEL RÍO**, where an impressive **castle** sits on a hill high above the town dominating the landscape. Dating originally from the eighth century, but with many later additions and restorations, it is today privately owned by the Marqués de Motilla, but can be visited (outside siesta hours of 2–4pm) up to 8.30pm; a voluntary contribution of 250ptas per person is expected. Find your way up to the castle from the town – a pleasant walk – or, with transport, negotiate the unpaved track and park by the castle walls. Ring the bell and eventually the guardian, Eulogio Navarro, will open up and show you around. There are fine **views** from the battlements but watch your step as there are no handrails.

At **PALMA DEL RÍO**, a small farming town 10km further east, you can spend the night in a converted **fifteenth-century monastery**. *Hospedería de San Francisco*, Avda. Pío XII 35 (☎957 71 01 83, fax 957 71 07 32; ⑦), preserves much of the former monastic tranquillity with a charming cloister, now a patio. The excellent Basque-inspired **restaurant** has a *menú*, or you could have a drink in the monastic bar furnished with stone benches and antique paintings.

South of Córdoba – the Campiña

To the south of Córdoba, and stretching to the mountains of the province's southern border, lies the **Campiña Cordobesa**, a fertile, undulating region of wheatfields, olive groves and productive vineyards renowned since Roman times. Indeed, the fine relief in Cordóba's archeological museum depicting the olive harvest came from here, and the eminent Roman writers Pliny and Martial praised its artichokes, fruit, wool and the excellence of its olive oil. The town of **Baena** keeps up the tradition with an oil so good that it carries an official *denominación de origen* label. Each of the villages of the Campiña has its own interesting castle, church or palace and sometimes a *bodega* – and there are towns such as **Priego de Córdoba**, a Baroque architectural feast and well off the tourist trail, that are undiscovered jewels. The two itineraries described here roughly follow the **bus routes** from Córdoba to Málaga and Granada respectively, making it easy to stop off along the way, as even the smallest villages usually have a *fonda* or *hostal* to provide a **bed** for the night. This opens up the possibility of **walks** exploring some of the Campiña's delightful countryside, replete with wooded hills and river valleys. Obviously, your own transport – and a little zigzagging and backtracking – would allow you to combine both routes.

The Ruta del Vino

This itinerary, heading **south** towards **Montilla** and **Iznájar**, leaves Córdoba by the NIV and, after 14km, forks left along the N331 towards Fernan Nunez, a pleasant hill village a further 14km down the road. Among a number of interesting places along this route are **Montilla**, the centre of Córdoba's wine production, and **Rute** where *anís*, a far stronger brew, is concocted. The itinerary ends at the beautiful lakeside village of **Iznájar** in the midst of some good trekking country.

Montemayor

Just beyond Fernan Nunez is **MONTEMAYOR**, a charming and typical *campiña* village with a fourteenth-century **castle**. In the centre of its neat little plaza, there's an amusing copy of the Alhambra's fountain of the lions in Granada. More interesting is the sixteenth-century church of **Nuestra Señora de la Asunción** with a beautifully painted stucco *sagrario* and a sixteenth-century carved baptismal font, still used to initiate the newborn of the parish. You'll need to find the priest, Padre Pablo Moyano, to open the church and he may well be in the *Casino*, a fine old institution across the square. If you ask, Padre Pablo will also let you see his personal **archeological collection**, kept in a vault beneath the church and for which he is famous for miles around. This enormous accumulation of artefacts includes coins, agricultural implements, grindstones and jewellery – most of it from Roman *Ulia*, as Montemayor then was – and has been collected on his walks over the years in the surrounding fields. Close to the village, there are **rooms** at *Hostal El Artista*, Carretera Córdoba–Málaga s/n (☎957 38 42 36, fax 957 37 50 69; ⑤), which despite a main-road location is friendly, efficient and has a good-value **restaurant**.

La Rambla

With your own transport, a detour to the right off the N331 on Montemayor's southern edge climbs 4km to the hill-top **pottery centre** of **LA RAMBLA**. Famed for the production of spouted drinking jars called *botijos* which, due to their method of fabrication, keep water ice-cold in furnace temperatures, these can be bought in numerous workshops around the village. The church of the **Colegio de Espíritu Santo** is worth a visit for its fine sculpture of Christ in pine and cedar by the eighteenth-century maestro, Juan de Mesa.

Montilla

The main N331 presses on into the Sierra de Montilla and endless rows of vines begin to creep across the landscape as you near the heart of Córdoba's **wine-producing region**. The tough Pedro-Ximénez vines planted here have to withstand searing summer temperatures, and send their roots deep down into the whitish-grey *albariza* soil searching for moisture. Eleven kilometres beyond Montemayor, **MONTILLA**, the capital of Córdoba's wine country, comes into view. Hardly the region's prettiest town, you may want to call in, however, to visit one of the leading **bodegas**, *Alvear SA*, Avda. María Auxiliadora 1 (visits and tastings Mon–Fri 10am–2pm; ☎957 65 01 35), a picturesque place founded in the eighteenth century.

Almost opposite the *bodega*, the *Barril del Oro*, Avda. de Andalucía 22, makes a good place to stop for **tapas**; try their *flamenquines* (stuffed rolls of veal and *jamón serrano*). Surprisingly, the excellent *montilla* served here comes not from the *bodega* over the road, but is bought in by the *patrón* from his own favourite growers. The medium-priced *Restaurante Camachas*, on the main road at the entrance to the town, is recommended for more substantial meals – specialities include the delicious *pez espada a la montillana* (swordfish with a montilla sauce) – and a good-value *menú* for about 1400ptas. If you want **to stay**, the simple *Hostal Nuestra Señora del Carmen*, c/Escuelas 3 (☎957 65 07 34; ②), should be able to provide a room; alternatively, *Hotel Don Gonzalo*, Ctra. Córdoba–Málaga km-47 (☎957 65 06 58; ⑥), is a smarter option with pool on the N331, to the south of the town.

Aguilar and the Laguna de Zónar

AGUILAR, 7km further south, perched on top of a hill, is worth a visit to see its wonderful eighteenth-century **octagonal plaza of San José**, probably inspired by the better-maintained one at Archidona in Málaga. The rest of the town is charming, its

MONTILLA-MORILES: NO HANGOVER GUARANTEED

The Romans and later the Moors (in spite of the Prophet's prohibition) developed the Campiña as a **wine region**. The great wine of Córdoba, **montilla** (often called *Montilla-Moriles*, the latter village being its partner in production to the south) has suffered over the years from comparison with the wines of Jerez, with which it shares similar characteristics. The reasons for this are largely historical as, prior to the 1940s, much of Córdoba's vintage was sold to the great *fino* houses of Jerez and eventually marketed as sherry. In 1944 this was made illegal, since when *montilla* has been granted its own *denominación* and the producers have had to stand on their own feet. But the notion that the wines of this region are merely a less expensive alternative to sherry has been a tag that the industry here has found hard to shake off.

The most visual difference in the production of *montilla* are the great **tinajas** – huge, earthenware urns in which the wine undergoes its fermentation. These Ali-Baba jars, the direct descendants of the Roman *dolium*, have pointed ends which are buried in the earth inside the *bodegas* and are believed to impart a unique character to the wine. As in Jerez the wine in these great vats also develops a *flor* (a thick layer of yeast) which covers the narrow neck of the urns. Later, the *solera* system (see p.000) during which the wine is aged and blended in oak butts for two years, is used to finish the process. The response you get around these parts should you bring up the subject of comparisons with the *finos* of Jerez is the assertion that *montilla* is a natural product, whilst the wines of Jerez need to have their alcohol added. The Pedro-Ximénez grape used for *montilla* is baked in the furnace heat of the Campiña sun and produces wines of 16 percent proof which, the *bodegas* here like to claim – unlike that synthetic *jerezano* – never give you a hangover.

sloping streets lined with white-walled houses, their windows protected by *rejas*, or iron grilles. From the **Torre del Reloj** there are excellent views over the Campiña. The sixteenth-century **Santa María del Soterraño**, with an *artesonado* Mudéjar ceiling and a Plateresque doorway, is Aguilar's best church.

There's also a *montilla* **bodega** here, *Carbonell SA*, on the Puente Genil road (visits Mon–Fri 8am–1pm; ring first ☎957 66 06 43). Owned by one of Spain's major olive oil producers, this is a beautiful *cortijo* with an ageing hall modelled on Córdoba's Mezquita. If you're looking for **accommodation**, *Hostal San José*, c/Pescadería 6 (☎957 66 02 22; ②), with simple rooms, is clean and central.

Some 4km southwest of Aguilar along the A309 and easily walkable, the **Laguna de Zóñar** is the largest of a group of little-known inland salt lakes. Visited in winter by large numbers of **migrating waterfowl**, this time of the year is best for spotting white-headed duck, a species that once almost disappeared but is now on the increase. Other species which can be seen here include red-crested pochard, mallard, great-crested grebe, tufted duck and marsh harrier. In summer there is less to see, although sometimes flamingos fly in from the Fuente de Piedra in nearby Málaga, for a change of scene. There's an observation **hide** here as well as an **information centre** (☎957 66 11 52). Other lakes in this group include the Laguna del Rincón north of Moriles, and the Laguna de Tiscar, north of Puente Genil, both of which, unlike this one, tend to dry up in summer.

Cabra

At Monturque, 9km south of Aguilar, there's a turn-off to Moriles, the other great *montilla* name but in truth a dull village, and only to be sought out if you're a wine aficionado. Much more rewarding is the A342 road which heads 12km east from Monturque to **CABRA**, another pleasant Campiña town. Possessing an old quarter with steep, winding streets lined with *rejas* – many holding pots sprouting colourful geraniums in summer – and a number of Baroque mansions, it's a lovely place to wander for an hour or so, or even stopover. At the end of the town, near the castle, the Baroque **Iglesia de la Asuncíon** (☎957 52 01 10 for an appointment to view), built over a mosque, is surrounded by palms and cypresses. It has a fine portal with twisted marble Solomonic pillars, and inside, an altar of red and black jasper together with fine **choir stalls**. The church of **San Juan Bautista** in the old quarter – Visigothic in origin but much altered since – is reckoned to be one of Spain's oldest, with Moorish and Baroque features added. The *Casa de Cultura*, c/Martín Belda 27, has a small **tourist office** (Mon–Fri 10.30am–1pm & 6–8.30pm, Sat 11am–1pm; ☎957 52 01 10) who can supply a town map, and in the same building there's a modest **archeological museum** with local finds from the prehistoric, Visigothic, Roman and Moorish periods.

On the road leading east out of town towards Priego de Córdoba, there's a wooded picnic and swimming area, **La Fuente del Río**, centred around a natural spring which is the source of the Río Cabra. Seven kilometres beyond this, a road on the left climbs 6km to the **Ermita de la Virgen de la Sierra**, a hermitage sited at an altitude of over 1200m from where there are stupendous **views** west towards the valley of the Guadalquivir, and east to the mountains of the Sierra Nevada. This is also the start point for a hike to Zuheros (see p.357).

Places to stay in Cabra are usually easy to come by; try *Pensión Guerrero*, c/Pepita Jiménez 7 (☎957 52 05 07; ③), close to the Parque Alcantara Romero (a tree-lined garden in the centre) or the good value *Hostal San José*, Avda. Fuente del Río 12 (☎957 52 03 68; ②), if you fancy being near the swimming pool. Both places have rooms with bath. There are numerous bars and **places to eat** around the town; the best is *Mesón El Vizconde*, c/Martín Belda 16, where the *fritura de pescado* and *merluza con salsa de puerros* (hake in leek sauce) are outstanding; there's also a less expensive *menú*. If you're a **beer** fan you should on no account miss Cabra's remarkable *Cervecería Botinero*, Avda. Fernando Pallares 3 off the south end of Parque Alcantara Romero, which stocks an amazing 500 of the world's beers. There is nowhere else like it in Andalucía and proprietor Antonio Mesa Jurado serves some pretty good meals to go with them, too. The nearby c/Vado del Moro has quite a few **discos** (all free) which contribute to the town's surprisingly lively nightlife scene.

Lucena

Surrounded by hills covered with vines and olives, **LUCENA**, 11km down the N331 from Monturque, is a large, unsightly industrial town which makes its money from furniture production, and manufacture of the great *tinajas*, or earthenware urns, used in the making of *montilla*. One reason to close your eyes to all of this and stop off is the church of **San Mateo**, on the central Plaza Nueva, which houses one of the Baroque glories of the province. The church was started in the fifteenth century over a mosque and has a superb *retablo* and a breathtakingly beautiful eighteenth-century Baroque **sagrario**, with exquisitely painted stucco cherubs and a feast of decorative detail topped off by a remarkable **cupola**, all the work of local artist Antonio de Castro. Nearby, the **Torre del Moral** is the surviving tower of the castle where Boabadil, the last sultan of Granada, was briefly imprisoned by Isabel la Católica in 1483.

Should you need a **place to stay** – although once you've seen the church, there's not much to hang around for – *Hostal Muloz*, c/Cabrillana 88 (☎957 50 10 52; ②), is central, clean and has its own **tapas** bar.

Rute

The scenic N331 Málaga road continues to **Benameji**, 20km away, a pleasant agricultural village with a couple of *fondas,* close to the provincial border. However, the more interesting route lies along the road (CP167) which turns off left 8km south of

Lucena, heading towards the small town of **RUTE**. Twelve kilometres from the turn, the whitewashed town, sited picturesquely on a hill overlooked by the hazy Sierra de Rute behind, comes into view. Beyond a ruined Moorish castle and a Baroque church, it has few monuments to attract visitors and Rute's fame throughout Andalucía is based on a far more potent allure: the manufacture of a lethal **anís**, the local eau-de-vie made with springwater from the Sierra and, at its most potent, an undiluted (and illegal) 96 percent proof. The milder *anís seco* at 55 percent is still fierce enough, and the syrupy *anís dulce* (a mere 35 percent) is probably the safest bet. Different variations on the *anis* theme can be tasted at the twenty or so small *bodegas* scattered around the town; *Bodega Machaquita*, Paseo del Fresno 7, is regarded as one of the best. Perhaps the easiest way is to try it is at either of the two bars on the upper square, the Paseo del Fresno. A guided tour at the **Anís Museum** (daily 9am–2pm & 5–8pm, but ring the bell if closed; free) nearby on the same square will tell you all you need to know about the making of *anís* and its history, with a chance to taste and buy at the end. There's a **tourist office** in the Parque Nuestra Señora del Carmen (Mon–Fri 10am–2pm; ☎957 53 29 29), close to the landmark Anís monument (complete with copper still) on the road through, who can provide a town map.

If you need a **place to stay**, the central and friendly *Hostal Rosales*, c/Toledo 9 (☎957 53 85 57; ②) has good value rooms with bath and a charming patio, or there's the plusher *Hotel María Luisa*, Ctra. Lucena–Loja 22 (☎957 53 80 96; ⑤), at the southern end of the town on the C334 with a pool. Rute's **campsite** (☎957 53 29 29) lies above the town,

---

SAVE THE DONKEY

One of Rute's more surprising features is a sanctuary for ill-treated donkeys. Founded by local draper Pasqual Rovira in 1989, ADEBO (Association for the Defence of the Donkey) is Spain's first-ever donkey refuge, and well worth a visit. Spain's donkey population has shrunk dramatically from over one million fifty years ago to a current 100,000 – most of which are crossbreeds. Only a few hundred remain of the five breeds of pure Spanish burro which have existed on the peninsula since pre-Roman times. One of these, the *raza córdobes*, was so renowned in the eighteenth century for its strength that George Washington asked the Spanish king, Carlos III, to send him some for his farm. Used for centuries as beasts of burden, the donkeys often receive brutal treatment at the hands of uncaring owners. Working with scarce resources, and using the meagre profits from the family drapery business, Pasqual and his wife Kika have devoted their lives to ending this cruelty and saving the Spanish breeds – including the *córdobes* – from extinction. They were greatly helped in this when Queen Sofía rang Pasqual in 1999 after reading about his work and offered her support, expressing a wish to visit the sanctuary. This changed everything, and previously sceptical politicians in Córdoba and Madrid became suddenly enthusiastic. For the queen's visit the *Guardia Civil* built an asphalt road up to the sanctuary plus helicopter pad in three days and the central, regional and local governments are currently underwriting the construction of a state-of-the-art complex (named the *Casa del Burro*) to include an expanded sanctuary, donkey history museum and environmental education centre.

A charming and voluble *cordobés*, Pasqual has a fund of horror stories concerning the animals he's rescued: one poor beast spent five years locked up in a small shed (after arriving at the sanctuary he was christened Mandela) whilst another, a jenny named Alondra, was found abandoned halfway down a ravine with a washing machine tied around her neck. The sanctuary is open daily (9am–noon). To get there, continue uphill from the Museo de Anís in the Paseo del Fresno, following the road for the campsite. The sanctuary (☎957 53 20 32) will provide directions, or enquire at the Turismo (☎957 53 29 29) who will supply a map.

4km beyond the Paseo del Fresno and near the donkey sanctuary (see box p.353). The best **place to eat** is *Restaurante Casa Paco*, c/Blas Infante s/n near the Anis monument on the main road through, where there's a *menú* for 800ptas. Another good possibility is *Restaurante El Vado*, 6km out along the A331 to Lucena. When you've eaten it's worth paying a visit to Rute's superb and friendly flamenco venue, *Repostería Peña Flamenca*, c/Blas Infante 42 (the main road through), which is a great place to have a drink with *tapas* and has a stunning state of the art open-air flamenco terrace and stage at the back.

Iznájar

Reached by following the attractive road A331 from Rute, **IZNÁJAR** is a charming, whitewashed farming village, with a spectacular location overlooking a reservoir. Despite the beauty, this is a place of long-standing poverty; it was here in 1861 that peasants, or *braceros*, revolted against the injustices of the landowning class – an uprising that was viciously suppressed.

Of Moorish origin, Iznájar's ruined **Alcazaba** was constructed in the eighth century, and the church of **Santiago** was added to its interior in the sixteenth. Almost alongside the church, the public library (Mon–Sat 9am–2pm & 5–8pm) can provide **information** and just downhill there's a small **museum** with a display of antique farm implements. From the plaza next to the church there are stunning **views** over the Embalse and village below. Iznájar has no official places to stay, but **camping** is allowed on the nearby Valdearenas beach on the Embalse. Here also the *Club Nautico* (☎957 53 43 04) hires out **sailing dinghies**, canoes and offers courses from its beachfront yacht club. For **food**, try *Restaurante Rosi* on the road towards Loja; alternatives are *El Montecillo* near the *gasolinera*, or *El Charcon*, a good bar-restaurant 2km along the Rute road on the left.

Twenty kilometres south of Iznájar close to the junction with the A92 *autovía*, a signed entrance on the left indicates a long drive at the end of which lies the grandiose *Finca La Bobadilla* (☎958 32 18 61, fax 958 32 18 10; ⑨), one of the most exclusive hotels in Spain. Surrounded by acres of woodland and built on the model of a typical Andalucian village it has appealed to guests as diverse as Tom Cruise and King Juan Carlos. To stay at this Iberian Xanadu will cost you a king's ransom too, and dinner at the à la carte restaurant – supplied by its own farm on the estate – doesn't come cheap either. Call in for a drink if you're curious.

A WALK TO IZNÁJAR

From Rute it's possible to make an eighteen-kilometre **walk** around the **Embalse de Iznájar** (reservoir) to the village of the same name, a beautiful white-walled hamlet perched on a promontory below an impressive castle, surrounded by water. There are plenty of opportunities for bird-watching and in spring the flora is delightful. The walk should take about three to four hours, depending on how many stops you make and you should be aware that there's no official accommodation at Iznájar (you may be able to hitch the 14km back to Rute), though there are a number of places to eat.

Start by leaving Rute along the road south (the A331) towards Iznájar, veering left at the fork and then taking a track on the right about half a kilometre further on. This slowly descends to the reservoir edge with a pleasant view over the lake. Turn right along the bank following the dirt track in and out of the creeks and coves until you arrive at a rocky promontory where there's a disused mine and from where you can get fine views over the Embalse towards Iznájar. After ascending a hill, the Camorro de la Isla, you arrive at an asphalted road which will bring you around the south side of the Embalse and, across the bridge, to the village of Iznájar, on its scenic peninsula.

The Ruta del Aceite

This itinerary towards Priego de Córdoba, known as the *Ruta del Aceite* (oil route), follows the N432 **southeast** out of Córdoba. It takes in the olive-oil producing region centred on **Baena** before visiting some of the province's most picturesque villages, including Luque and Zuheros. The route concludes at the town of **Priego de Córdoba** which has one of the most remarkable collections of Baroque churches in Andalucía.

Espejo

At **ESPEJO**, 41km to the south of Córdoba, an impressive Moorish castle looms above the white-walled village, vineyards and olive groves spread out below. The fourteenth-century Gothic-Mudéjar **castillo** is the property of the dukes of Osuna, the great ruling family based in Osuna to the southwest (see p.273), which once owned an enormous tract of Andalucía. The Gothic-Renaissance church of **San Bartolomé**, dating from the fifteenth and sixteenth centuries, is also worth seeking out for its fine **retablo mayor** by Pedro Romana and its *artesonado* ceiling.

Castro del Río

Sited on a low hill on the north bank of the Río Guadajoz, **CASTRO DEL RÍO**, 9km down the road, has a **Roman bridge** spanning the river and a ruined **Moorish castle** built on the foundations of a Roman fort. The village also claims a footnote in Roman history as this is believed to be the place where Pompey's troops rested up prior to their showdown battle with Caesar in 45 BC at nearby Montilla (Munda) which ended the Roman civil war and, briefly, gave Caesar control of the whole empire. The **Iglesia de la Asunción**, founded in the thirteenth century with later additions, has a fine if somewhat eroded Plateresque portal, and the **Ayuntamiento** preserves the prison in which Cervantes was locked up for a week in 1568 when, then working as a tax collector, he was falsely accused of fiddling the books.

Baena

The road continues south into the area geographically known as the **Sierra Subbética Cordobesa**, a rugged, rambling spur of the Cordillera Betica range in the province's southeastern corner, and now officially a **natural park**. Beyond Castro del Río the N432 climbs gently through hills covered with olive groves until it reaches Andalucía's most celebrated oil production centre, **BAENA**. Famous for centuries for the high quality of its olive oil, the huge metal tanks for storing the oil can be seen on the outskirts of town. Baena was an important place in the Moorish period, but has declined as a result of emigration in more recent times. A pleasant and busy place today, on arrival you should aim for the **Turismo** on the focal Plaza de España (Mon–Fri 11.30am–1.30pm; ☎957 66 50 15) who can supply a town map; when closed the *Ayuntamiento* on the Plaza de la Constitución (see below) can provide the same.

Most of Baena's sights lie in the upper town reached by following c/Juan Rabadan from Plaza de España to the **Plaza de la Constitución**. The eighteenth-century **arcaded almacén**, or warehouse, is now a cultural centre and another part of the same building houses *Mesón Casa del Monte*, a good *tapas* bar and restaurant.

From the same square, c/Henares leads to the eighteenth-century **Casa de la Tercia** (Mon–Fri 10am–1pm & 6–8pm, Sat 10am–1pm; free) an elegant *casa señorial* now converted into an interesting **archeological museum** (with much about ancient olive oil production) and **Museo de Semana Santa** on the history of Baena's Holy Week and its drums (see below). Continuing along c/Henares and veering left brings you to the early sixteenth-century Gothic church of **Santa María** with a fine portal and a Moorish tower, probably the minaret of a former mosque. The church is a sad

BAENA'S OIL FOR CONNOISSEURS

Spain produces, and probably consumes, more **olive oil** than any other country in the world. However, this wasn't always so, and when the Greeks introduced the olive to the peninsula in the first millennium BC, it was regarded with suspicion by the native Iberians who went on using their traditional lard. Only with the arrival of the Roman legions did they begin to acquire a taste for it, and under Roman supervision Hispanic oil became the finest and most expensive in the empire. Later, sophisticated Moorish invaders taught the Iberians better cultivation techniques, as well as culinary and medicinal possibilities. The Moorish, and now Spanish, names for oil and the olive, *aceite*, and *aceituna*, are a legacy of this time.

Today, Spaniards are great connoisseurs of quality oil and **Baena** has its own official **denominación de origen**, backed by an official regulatory body, the *Consejo Regulador*, guaranteeing the standards attained by strict methods of production. Baena's finest oil stands comparison with the best in Europe, and *almazaras* (oil mills) such as that operated for several generations by the Núñez de Prado family in the town, take a great amount of care at every stage in the production process. The olives cultivated on the estate are all harvested by hand prior to being ground to a paste on ancient granite stone mills. The "free run" oil – with no further pressure applied – that results from this process is regarded as the *grand cru* of the oil trade and it takes eleven kilos of olives to yield just one litre of such oil. With a markedly low acid content and an unfatty, concentrated flavour, this oil is far too good (and expensive) for cooking and is sparingly used to flavour *gazpacho* – in Córdoba province, *salmorejo* – or tasted on a morsel of bread as a *tapa*.

The *Núñez de Prado* mill, Avda. de Cervantes 15 (☎957 67 01 41; Mon–Fri 9am–2pm & 4–6.30pm, Sat 9am–1pm) with parts dating from the eighteenth century, is close to Plaza de España and can be visited, although most of the action takes place between November and February when the harvested olives are pressed. Their shop sells a range of oils.

testament to the ferocity of the Civil War, during which this beautiful building was put to the torch. It has only recently aquired a temporary roof over its burnt-out interior, of which a wonderful *reja* (altar screen) survives as a reminder of former days. The image of what was lost, including a precious *retablo*, is preserved in a faded photograph hanging in the sacristy. The church is currently undergoing a substantial restoration. Nearby is the sixteenth-century Mudéjar convent of **Madre de Dios**, with fine late Gothic porch, *retablo*, *coro* and *artesonados*. The nuns here also sell convent *dulces*, and are noted for their *magdalenas*. Besides oil, Baena is also famous for its *Semana Santa* rituals which include a **drum-rolling contest** when the streets are filled with the ear-splitting sound of up to 2000 drums being struck simultaneously. From Wednesday to Friday during Holy Week is the time to avoid, unless you have ear plugs.

Finding **places to stay** outside this period is not a problem; *Hostal Rincón*, c/Llano del Rincón 13 off Plaza de España (☎957 67 02 23; ③), has en-suite rooms with a restaurant below. The nearby *Pensión Claveles*, c/Juan Valera 15 (☎957 67 01 74; ②) has simpler, but perfectly adequate, rooms while the equally close *Hotel Iponuba*, c/Nicolas Alcalá 9 (☎957 67 00 75; ⑤) is the upmarket option. There are plenty of places for **eating and drinking** around the centre; one restaurant a cut above the rest is *Mesón Casa del Monte*, on Plaza de la Constitución.

Luque

Seven kilometres beyond Baena, a right turn leads to the attractive village of **LUQUE**, spread over a rocky outcrop topped by the almost obligatory castle. Dating from the thirteenth century, the ruins of the **Moorish castillo** are worth a look, and beside them is the golden limestone facade of the Gothic-Renaissance church of **La Asunción** with a *retablo* whose central image of San Juan is attributed to Martínez Montañés. There is no accommodation, but the *Villa de Luque*, on the central Plaza de España, is a **restaurant** converted from a fine old refurbished *casa andaluza* serving good food and an economical *menú*. For **tapas** and *raciones* there's *Bar La Plancha*, across from the church, which is a lively local meeting place.

Zuheros

Nestling in a gorge backed by steep rock cliffs some 5km west of Luque, **ZUHEROS** is another stunningly beautiful *Subbética* village. A cluster of white houses tumbles down the hill below a romantic Moorish **castle** built on and into the rock. Later Christian additions were made after it fell to Fernando III in 1240 and became a frontier bastion against the kingdom of Granada. The nearby early seventeenth-century **Iglesia de los Remedios** has a fine *retablo* as well as a tower built on the remains of a minaret from an earlier mosque and on the small square nearby a **mirador** gives a great view over the surrounding countryside. On the edge of the square facing *Bar Plaza* is the village's new **museum** (Sat & Sun 12.30–2.30pm & 4.30–6.30pm; other times ring ☎957 69 45 45; 215ptas including guided castle visit) displaying fascinating finds from the Cueva de los Murciélagos (see below) as well as others from the Roman and Moorish periods. A new **tourist office** (Mon–Fri 9am–2pm & 5–8pm, Sat & Sun 10am–3pm & 5–8pm; ☎957 69 47 75) at the entrance to the village on the Baena road has lots of information on the village and the *Subbética* and sells the products of the region, particularly Zuheros's noted cheeses and olive oil. They also have information about a number of *casas rurales* (sleeping up to five persons) for rent in the area. Downhill from the castle there's a charming **place to stay**, the *Hotel Zuhayra*, c/Mirador 10 (☎957 69 46 93, fax 957 69 47 02, *zuhayra@siapi.es*; ④), which uses the village's ancient Moorish name and makes a perfect base to explore the surrounding country; guests get free use of the village **swimming pool**, located near the tourist office. For **food** the *Zuhayra* has a good restaurant with a *menú*, and there are a couple of lively bars for **tapas** and **raciones** – *Bar Plaza*, facing the castle, and *Mesón Atalaya*, c/Santo 58, at the eastern end of the village, next to the turn-off to the Cueva de los Murciélagos.

In the hills behind the village, reached by a paved, 4km road the **Cueva de los Murciélagos** (guided visits April–Sept Tues–Thurs, Sat & Sun, hourly 11am–1pm & 4–6pm; 525ptas; ring ☎957 69 45 45 for winter hours) is spectacular and well worth

---

WALKS AROUND ZUHEROS

With the aid of a good map (1:50,000 CNIG sheet 967, or the 1:50,000 *Parque Natural Sierras Subbéticas* published by the Junta de Andalucía), you can follow the Bailón river valley south from Zuheros to the Ermita de Nuestra Virgen de la Sierra near Cabra (see p.000), a splendid **walk** through rugged hill country. The distance is about 14km, with a stiff climb at the end to the Ermita. From here, you could continue 13km to Cabra, taking a taxi back to Zuheros (about 2000ptas), if you don't want to stay overnight in Cabra itself. An alternative way of doing this walk (and conveniently avoiding the climb to the Ermita) is to do it in reverse, taking a taxi from Zuheros to the Ermita, then following the valley of the Bailón back to Zuheros.

For readers of Spanish, Zuheros's tourist office can provide a **pack of walks** in this zone titled *Rutas Senderistas de la Subbética Cordobesa* which details ten waymarked walks on handy cards with a sketch map on the reverse (however, you'd still be advised to take a good map along). Walk no. 3 describes an easy and picturesque 4km walk from Zuheros following the Cañon (gorge) de Bailón, passing caves where Neolithic cave paintings were discovered, to the Fuente de la Mora, returning to the village on the river's eastern bank. Any queries regarding the walks can be directed to the manager of the *Hotel Zuhayra*, Juan Carlos Ábalos, who speaks English (see above).

a visit. First explored in 1938, its name means "cave of the bats" and the hour-long tour (bring a sweater) takes in impressive stalagmites, stalactites, and awesome rock formations while the guide relates the fascinating story (revealed by recent excavations) of the remarkable **Neolithic cave paintings** and human remains found here.

Doña Mencía

Not quite as pretty as other villages in the area, **DOÑA MENCÍA**, 5km to the west of Zuheros, is a sizeable oil and wine centre lying at the foot of a slope that's covered with silver-leaved olives, interrupted by the occasional vineyard. There's a fifteenth-century ruined **castle** and, nearby at the end of c/Juan Valera, a small **museum**, c/Juan Ramón Jiménez 8, in the former house of the nineteenth-century novelist Juan Valera, whose best-known work, *Pepita Jiménez*, was set in Cabra. There are a surprising number of *bodegas* here, and a clutch of **places to eat** around the pleasant Plaza Mayor. For simple **rooms**, try the village **fonda**, *Casa Morejón*, c/Obispo Cubero 1 (☎957 67 61 69; ②).

Priego de Córdoba

PRIEGO DE CÓRDOBA, 20km southeast of Luque and capital of the *Subbética*, is one of Andalucía's little-known Baroque wonders which offers a feast of superb churches and a remarkable fountain, making it an inviting place to stopover. Situated beneath the province's highest mountain, the 1600m La Tiñosa, the northern approach to the town presents a dramatic view of the whitewashed buildings of its old quarter, laid out along the edge of a picturesque escarpment known as the Adarve. The centre of this tranquil town is the Plaza de la Constitución, an elegant square fronted by the **Ayuntamiento**, from where all the monuments are within easy walking distance.

Despite evidence of long prehistoric habitation in nearby caves and a later Roman settlement, it was under the Moors that *Medina Bahiga*, as Priego was then known, flourished as part of the kingdom of Granada. Following a tug of war between the Moors and Christians during the fourteenth century, in which the town changed hands three times, it finally fell to the Christians in 1341. Recovery from the aftermath of this turbulent era came only in the eighteenth century when, in 1711, Priego became a dependency of the dukes of Medinaceli. An economic resurgence based on the production of silk and textiles poured great wealth into the town and it was during this time that most of the **Baroque churches**, Priego's outstanding attraction today, were constructed or remodelled. In the nineteenth century, though, the industry found it hard to compete with cheap cotton textiles produced in Catalunya and Britain, and a slow decline set in. The European slump in textiles in the 1950s and 1960s caused by imports from Asia accelerated the problems and, as factories closed, many people emigrated to seek work elsewhere. Today the remnants of the textile industry, along with farming, are the town's main employers.

Arrival, information and accommodation

Buses arriving in Priego will drop you in the central Plaza de la Constitución although the actual bus station is a five-minute walk to the east of the centre on c/Nuestra Señora de los Remedios. There are easy connections with Córdoba, Granada and Málaga.

The town's helpful **Turismo**, c/Río 33 (Tues–Sun 9am–1pm; ☎957 70 06 25), just south of the Plaza de la Constitución, can provide a good **map**. It's run by an ebullient human dynamo named José Mateo Aguilera, who encourages visitors to call at his home (not during the siesta), c/Real 46, in the old quarter near the church of the Asunción, when the office is closed. The building housing the Turismo is itself historic, the birthplace of (and now shrine to) **Niceto Alcalá Zamora**, first president of the ill-fated Spanish Republic from 1931 to 1936. Much of the furniture of this middle-class nineteenth-century family mansion survives intact, and you are free to look around.

Places to stay are short in supply, but there's usually no great demand. The best deal in town is *Hostal Rafi*, c/Isabel la Católica 4 (☎957 54 07 49; ③), a tiny street east of the main square offering air-conditioned en-suite rooms, with a good restaurant. Slightly further out, *Río Piscina* (☎957 70 01 86, fax 957 70 06 38; ④) lies on the eastern edge of town with a pool, restaurant, tennis court and gardens. Back in the centre, near the Turismo, there's the very basic *Hostal Andalucía*, c/Río 13 (☎957 54 01 74; ②). Priego also has a **Villa Turística** (☎957 70 35 03, fax 957 70 35 73; ⑥) built on traditional lines with lots of Moorish-inspired decor, water features and gardens where 52 chalets – all with kitchen and four-star hotel facilities – are built around a stylish neo-Moorish central patio. Among the activities on offer are horse riding, mountain biking and guided walking excursions. It's located 7km northeast of town (and signed) along the CO230 to Zagrilla.

The Town

All Priego's **churches** are open daily for visits between 11am and 1pm, which allows you just enough time to see them all in a day. The Turismo will advise on opening times

PRIEGO DE CÓRDOBA

ACCOMMODATION
Hostal Andalucía	3
Hostal Rafi	2
Río Piscina Hotel	1

RESTAURANTS
El Aljibe	A
El Virrey	B

outside these hours and (if convenient) will open them up on request. It also offers free guided tours of the town.

Iglesia de la Asunción

From the Plaza de la Constitución head northeast towards the **Barrio de la Villa**, the old quarter, which contains most of Priego's principal monuments. A good place to begin is with the austere Moorish **castillo**, whose impressive keep dominates the small Plaza de Abad Palomino. Altered in the thirteenth and fourteenth centuries, the interior is now privately owned. In the square's southeast corner lies the first of the Baroque churches, the **Iglesia de la Asunción**, its modest whitewashed exterior dating from the sixteenth century. The original Gothic building was remodelled in the Baroque style in the eighteenth century by Jerónimo Sánchez de Rueda, an architect who did a similar job on many of Priego's other churches.

It is inside, however, that the surprises begin: an ornate white stucco Baroque interior leads towards a stunningly beautiful carved Mannerist **retablo** with images attibuted to Juan Bautista Vázquez. The greatest surprise of all, though, lies through a portal on the left aisle where you enter the breathtaking **sagrario**, one of the masterpieces of Spanish Baroque. Here, a dazzling symphony of wedding-cake white stucco work and statuary, punctuated by scrolls and cornices, climbs upwards beyond a balcony into a fabulous cupola illuminated by eight windows. The frothy depth of the stucco plaster was achieved by the use of esparto grass to lend it additional strength – a material which has played a remarkable part in the craft history of Andalucía, even found in hats, baskets and sandals discovered in the Neolithic caves of Granada. This recently restored octagonal chapel is the work of Francisco Javier Pedrajas, a native of Priego and one of a number of leading sculptors, carvers and gilders working in the town at this time. The *altar mayor* and the *sagrario* have been declared national monuments.

Barrio de la Villa and Paseo del Adarve

Before taking in more Baroque mastery, the nearby and delightful **Barrio de la Villa** provides a welcome opportunity for a stroll. The ancient Moorish part of the town, a maze of sinuous whitewashed alleys with balconies and walls loaded with pot plants, leads to a number of typical *plazuelas*. You should eventually stumble on one of the most charming, the **Plazuela de San Antonio**, replete with palms and wrought-iron *rejas*; if you don't, just ask any of the passing locals who will be only too pleased to show you around their pride and joy. Behind the church of the Asunción, c/Bajondillo leads to the **Paseo de Adarve**, a superb, and originally Moorish, promenade with a spectacular **view** over the valley of the Río Salado and undulating groves of olives stretching to the distant hills.

San Pedro and San Juan de Dios

Just to the west of the *castillo*, the **Iglesia de San Pedro** is another Baroque treat with more stucco and a wonderful **altar mayor** in painted wood and stucco with a delightful domed *camarín* (side room) behind, which holds a stirring image of the *Immaculada* attributed to *granadino* sculptor Diego de Mora. The side chapel of the **Virgen de la Soledad**, with another *camarín*, has an image of the Virgin at the centre of its *retablo* by Pablo de Rojas. To the north of the *castillo*, and close to the **Carnicerías Reales**, a sixteenth-century abattoir and meat market with a fine cobbled patio, the church of **San Juan de Dios**, with a finely crafted cupola, is an early example of Priego Baroque, completed in 1717.

La Aurora and San Francisco

Moving south along c/Argentina and its continuation c/Álvares will lead you to the church of **La Aurora**, yet another Baroque gem remodelled from a former *ermita*, whose exuberant facade, with Corinthian and Solomonic pillars topped by a Virgin and flanked by exquisite stone and marble decoration, is only a prelude to the interior. This, now restored to its full glory, is a single-naved Baroque explosion in painted wood and stucco descending from the grey and white cornices, with polychromed figures on its ceiling, dome and walls, to an animated and sumptuously theatrical **retablo**. This *retablo* is a glittering amalgam of vegetal and geometrical forms, and the crowning achievement of Juan de Dios Santaella, another native Priego talent, born here in 1716. The church is also home to the **Cofradía de la Aurora**, a brotherhood whose sixteenth-century articles of foundation stipulate that they must proceed through the streets in musical procession every Saturday at midnight. Thus, whatever the weather, this band of men, hatted and cloaked, gather behind their banner and a huge lantern to proceed through the streets singing hymns to *La Aurora* (Our Lady of the Dawn) accompanied by guitars, accordions and tambourines.

Just south of here along c/Buen Suceso, the **Iglesia de San Francisco**, on an elegant old square, is another late Gothic church that Santaella had a hand in remodelling and which has recently been restored to its former splendour. Once you've admired the **facade and portal** (both by Santaella), employing contrasting tones of marble, look inside; the *retablo mayor* is a splendid gilded work by Santaella again. The **chapel of Jesús Nazareno** has a sumptuous gilded and polychromed wood and stucco **retablo** by Pedrajas, the creator of the *sagrario* in the Asunción, and is topped off by another extravagant cupola by Santaella. The altarpiece's central image of **Jesús Nazareno** (Christ bearing the cross) is a fine work, attributed to Pedro de Mena.

The Fuente del Rey

At the southern end of the town, and easily reached by following c/Río – a street dotted with many fine Baroque portals – to its end, lies the **Fuente del Rey**, a spectacular sixteenth-century 180-jet fountain (with many later additions) which pours water into a number of basins. The highest of these has a sculpture of a lion struggling with a serpent, whilst the second contains a larger late eighteenth-century depiction of Neptune and Amphitrite, the king and queen of the sea. Amphitrite is clutching the dolphin that returned her to Neptune after her attempted escape, incidentally emphasizing the power of the king, the work's intended ideological message, given that over the border in France, monarchs were losing their heads. There are in fact two fountains here, the second being the **Fuente de la Salud**, to the rear of the plaza, a sixteenth-century Italianate work built on the spot, according to legend, where the conquering Alfonso XI pitched his camp in 1341. One of the most tranquil squares in Andalucía, this leafy area is a wonderful place to relax and get away from it all, which is why there are so many seats.

From just beyond the square you can **walk** to the Ermita del Calvario from where there are fine **views** over the town. Take the steps to the left of the Fuente de la Salud.

The rest of the churches and museums

When you've seen the main churches, there are many more almost as good. Just off the Plaza de la Constitución at the start of c/Río, the **Iglesia de las Angustias** is a charming small church and another work by Santaella. The interior has a fine cupola with more typically exuberant polychromed stucco decoration. Further along c/Río beyond the Turismo, the **Iglesia del Carmen** has a *retablo* by Santaella, probably an early work. Finally, to the west on Carrera de las Monjas, the **Iglesia del Mercedes** was an ancient hermitage prior to its remodelling in the latter part of the eighteenth century when it was decorated in Rococo style by Pedrajas, highlighted by the four winged archangels at the scalloped corners. Another stunningly ornate snow-white cupola (which is almost Pedrajas's trademark), is balanced by an elegant *retablo* below. The exterior is an incomplete later addition.

It's encouraging to know that all this splendour, and its maintenance, has brought into being a **crafts academy**, *La Escuela Taller Juan de Dios Santaella*, appropriately named after Priego's Baroque genius. Here the myriad skills and crafts necessary to restore and care for these buildings, as well as others throughout Andalucía, Spain and beyond, will be nurtured and passed on.

Almost opposite the Iglesia de Mercedes, Priego's **Museo Histórico Municipal** (Tues–Fri 10am–2pm, Sat & Sun 11am–2pm; free), c/Monjas 9 off Plaza Constitución, is housed in an elegant *señorial* mansion with a fine patio. An interesting collection displays finds from the surrounding area dating from the Paleolithic down to the Roman and Moorish periods.

Eating, drinking and nightlife

For **eating and drinking** the bars around the main square are good for breakfast and *tapas*, and the restaurant attached to the *Hostal Rafi* is especially good. More good **tapas bars** are *Bar Río* at the start of c/Río, *Los Pinos*, c/República Argentina 12, near the *castillo*, *Los Pinchos* on c/Real, behind the church of the Asunción and *El Telar*, c/Buen Suceso 2, close to the Iglesia de San Francisco. Other **restaurants** are few, but *El Aljibe*, c/Abad Palomino 7, opposite the Iglesia de la Asuncion, is built over a Moorish bathhouse (which you can glimpse through a glass floor), has some apt Moorish inspired dishes and a 1000ptas *menú*; there's also an outdoor terrace. Another good place is *El Virrey*, c/Solana 16, off Plaza San Pedro, preparing a wide range of local dishes and again with a 1000ptas *menú*. Outside the first week in September when Priego celebrates its annual *Feria Real*, **nightlife** is generally confined to sipping drinks at tables on the Plaza Mayor. However, one interesting diversion is the *Peña Flamenca Fuente del Rey*, c/Río 50, a friendly **flamenco** club where you'll get a warm welcome and, after ten, just maybe some good flamenco. Those wanting to check out what passes for Priego's **club scene** could take in the interesting decor at *Pub Gaudi*, c/Paseo de Colombia 5, south of the Barrio de la Villa or *Pub Hollywood*, with a movie theme on Avenida España, near the bus station.

Around Priego

With your own transport you could take in a few of the surrounding towns and villages which, although often lacking anything compelling in the way of sights, are situated in wonderful *Subbética* countryside (see p.355). A little further afield, however, the picturesque town of **Montefrío**, and its nearby prehistoric site to the southeast, is well worth a visit.

Carcabuey, Amedinilla, Alcaudete and Alcalá La Real

CARCABUEY, 7km east of Priego and reachable by bus, is a charming place laid out on a hill topped by a ruined castle. The Gothic-Renaissance church of **La Asunción** lower down has a good portal flanked with Solomonic marble pillars, and inside a superb **retablo** with the central figure of Christ attributed to Pedro de Mena and Alonso Cano. It is usually locked, so you'll need to enquire at the nearby houses for the key.

ALMEDINILLA, 9km west on the Jaén border, is another characteristic *Subbética* village squatting along the valley of the Río Caicena. There are important Roman remains being excavated here including the substantial Roman villa of El Ruedo (information from the archeological workshop at c/Franco 5) and the church has a sculpture attributed to Martínez Montañes.

ALCALÁ LA REAL, 27km east of Priego, is a pleasant country town at the foot of a hill dominated by an impressive Moorish fort later reconstructed as the **Castillo de la**

Mota (Tues–Sat 10am–1pm & 5–9pm), which preserves among its earlier gates the Moorish **Puerta de la Imagen**. After the fort had been taken during the *reconquista*, Alfonso XI built – and this became the custom – the Renaissance church of **Santa María la Mayor** inside the walls; now in semi-ruined state and lacking a roof, the building was designed by the leading architect of the sixteenth century, Diego de Siloé.

ALCAUDETE, 25km northeast of Priego in Jaén province, tumbles down a hill below yet another impressive Moorish castle, this one dating from the tenth century and with a massive keep. There are a few sixteenth-century churches to see here, too.

Montefrío and the Peña de los Gitanos

One of the more spectacularly sited towns in this part of the country is **MONTEFRÍO**, 42km southeast of Priego, and just over the Granada border. Cradled between two rocky outcrops, each topped by a church which can be visited, the town has the even bigger Neoclassical **Iglesia de la Encarnación** at its heart, with an enormous dome and some bizarre acoustics. The most interesting of the hill-top churches is the sixteenth-century **Iglesia de la Villa** (daily 10am–1.30pm & 4–6pm), a superb building designed by Diego de Siloé, but no longer used because of its congregation's reluctance to climb the hill. The interior has some exquisite **vaulting** and is surrounded by the ruins of the Moorish alcazaba; there are fine **views** over the town and beyond from its tower. The church is reached by a bracing climb along the road which ascends beyond the Turismo (see "Practicalities" below).

Nearby, 8km east along the GR222 towards Illora and signposted, is the remarkable Neolithic site of **Las Peñas de los Gitanos**. Six kilometres long and demarcated by limestone outcrops, the site was occupied by stone-age people in the third millennium BC. The overhanging rocks and caves were used as shelters by bulls, goats, sheep and other ancient beasts and this food source attracted early humans who would have hunted these animals in groups. These ancient hunters left behind paintings inside the caves (currently not on view), various **stone tombs** – some with carvings of animals and horns – and the remains of later stone and clay dwellings when they became Chalcolithic (copper age) village dwellers. A detailed leaflet (in Spanish) is available from the Turismo in Montefrío.

To reach the site, follow the signed turn-off from the GR222 on the left; this soon becomes a dirt track proceeding uphill through a stone quarry. Beyond this you'll reach a wide expanse of grassland with a clump of trees at its centre where you should leave any vehicle. A guard on duty here will indicate the path leading to the tombs. To see the two best preserved dolmens, keep ahead along the path until you come to an open area encircled by a low mound. From here a group of **dolmens** is visible straight ahead; the most impressive of all lies off to the right and up a rise into trees about a hundred metres away, marked by a green sign.

PRACTICALITIES

Montefrío's **Turismo** (Tues–Fri 9am–2pm & 4–7pm; ☎957 33 60 04) lies just uphill on the left from the Encarnación church and can supply a map and information. A number of **casas rurales** are available for rent in and around the town – one is sited on the outcrop just below La Villa church; information is available from the Turismo or by ringing ☎957 31 01 24 (English spoken).

When it comes to **eating and drinking** Montefrío is acclaimed for its *morcilla* (black pudding) and *chorizo*, both excellent at the *Café Bar La Fonda*, c/Amat 7, close to the Encarnación church, which also has simple **rooms** (☎957 33 61 27; ②). Another good place to try these delicacies is *Bar Uno Más* ("one more") facing the same church. More elaborate meals are to be had at *Mesón Coronichi*, Avda. de la Paz 23, and *Restaurante Los Arcos*, c/Juan Ramón Jiménez 3, both near the centre.

North of Córdoba

To the north of Córdoba lies the province's stretch of the Sierra Morena, an area rich in scenery and wildlife but poor in sights. Many of the hardy granite villages are casualties of the Europe-wide depression in mining, and the sad air pervading them is possibly why they see few visitors. Persevere into the region's higher reaches, however, and you enter a landscape most frequented by hunters and anglers; outside the winter hunting season, it's ideal rambling territory as well – Santa Eufemia is located in richly scenic hill country. This is also another region of the Sierra Morena famed for its *jamón ibérico* or cured ham, and a chance to sample this in the bars and *ventas* along the way shouldn't be missed. For a tour of the area you're at a definite advantage with your own transport and although there are frequent daily buses run by *Alsina Graells*, *López* and *Ureña*, from Córdoba to Peñarroya and Pozoblanco, public transport off the beaten track is minimal.

The main **N432** snaking and climbing north out of Córdoba takes the traffic heading for the towns of Badajoz and Cáceres in Extremadura, to the north. Although this road follows a rail line, there are no longer passenger services. After 44km the road forks just before **Espiel**, a small coal-mining town, and you can follow the **N502 route** towards Hiñojosa del Duque and the valley of Los Pedroches (see below).

Belmez and Peñarroya

From Espiel, the N432 trails the wooded valley of the Río Guadiato until, 21km further on, it passes the dour village of **BELMEZ** with a spectacular thirteenth-century **castle** crowning a rocky outcrop, from which there are fine views. Seven kilometres further, **PEÑARROYA-PUEBLANUEVO** is the main town of the area, and another sturdy mining centre that would be more at home in northern England than Andalucía. If you're looking for sights, there's an eighteenth-century brick church, but little else to detain you.

Fuente Obejuna

FUENTE OBEJUNA, 16km west of Peñarroya, is famous for its insurrection of 1476 when the population rose against their tyrranical lord, Fernán Gómez de Guzmán, and hacked him to death in the main square. The event was immortalized by the great seventeenth-century playwright, Lope de Vega, in his play *Fuenteovejuna* and this was performed in the village square in 1933 by the *Barraca* theatre company under the direction of Federico García Lorca. The poet was only too aware that the fundamental injustices portrayed in the work were still true for most of modern Andalucía; the play's Republican-populist theme, and its ecstatic reception in the villages, contributed to making him a marked man by the Right.

Despite its history, the small town is hardly an inspiring place today, and in the Plaza Mayor – named after Lope de Vega – a plaque commemorates the playwright for celebrating "the civic virtues" of its citizenry. The fifteenth-century church of the **Virgen del Castillo** was erected on the site of murdered Guzmán's palace, which was pulled down shortly after his death. It's an impressive Gothic building with a fine **retablo** in polychromed wood. The village also has a few Renaissance mansions to seek out in the streets surrounding the square and a fine Art Nouveau mansion, the **Casa Cardona** which should not be missed. Sadly fallen into a terrible state of disrepair it is still one of the finest houses of its kind in Andalucía with a flamboyant facade adorned with vegetal reliefs, *rejas* and tinted windows. Should you need a **place to stay**, close to the Casa Cardona the dapper *Hotel El Comendador*, c/Luís Rodríguez (☎ & fax 957 58 52 22; ④) with its own exuberantly painted frontage is very pleasant. They also have a **restaurant** with an excellent value *menú*.

Towards Hinojosa del Duque and Santa Eufemia

Just before it reaches Espiel, the N502 forks right and crosses a number of wooded valleys and watercourses to **Alcaracejos**, where it joins up with the A420. A detour 11km to the east of here allows you to take in **POZOBLANCO**, the sizeable capital of the area known as Los Pedroches. A fairly humdrum place with a couple of sixteenth-century churches, and noted for its *salchichón*, it hasn't changed very much since Gerald Brenan was here in the 1940s gathering material for his book, the *Face of Spain*:

> Although Pozoblanco belongs to the province of Córdoba, it cannot be said to lie in Andalusia. That low step up from the Guadalquivir valley to the meseta lands one in an altogether different geographic and ethnic region. Take architecture. The houses with their deep windows and granite lintels look cold and severe. . . The people too are quite different from the Andalusians. They are hard and dour, with a look of purpose and determination which one certainly does not see south of the Sierra Morena.

Most Andalucians remember the town today as the place where **Francisco Rivera**, or *Paquirri* as he was known, came to a sticky end in the town's bullring during the annual fiesta in 1984. This celebrated *torero's* nemesis appeared in the form of a bull named *Avispado* (Wide-awake) which gored him badly. The town's new hospital, long behind schedule, had not yet opened and the 85km journey to Córdoba was the main reason he died. The *matador's* son, also named *Paquirri*, has since fought a number of times in the ring where his father was mortally wounded.

Hinojosa del Duque

Turning left at Alcaracejos, the road passes the village of Villanueva del Duque to arrive, 21km further on, at **HINOJOSA DEL DUQUE**, another sombre town with an outsize church. Popularly known as the "Catedral de la Sierra", the granite Gothic-Renaissance church of **San Juan Bautista** has a fine **entrance portal** by Hernán Ruíz who designed the belfry for the Mezquita at Córdoba, as well as a superb Gothic interior with beautiful *retablos* and *rejas*. If you want to **stay**, there's the serviceable *Hostal Ruda*, c/Padre Manjón 2 (☎957 14 07 78; ③). **Food** is on offer at the central *Mesón Condesito*, c/Brigadier Romero 3, just behind the "catedral", which also stocks the region's prized *jamones*.

Belalcázar and Santa Eufemia

BELALCÁZAR, 9km north and close to the border with Extremadura, has the ruins of a fifteenth-century **castle** with an impressive keep and a sixteenth-century church of **Santiago** with a fine Plateresque *retablo*. Should you need a **place to stay** there are rooms with bath at *Hostal La Bolera* (☎957 14 63 00; ③) which also has a restaurant. However, the best place for **food** is a friendly *tapas* and *raciones* bar on the main square, *Donde Va La Gente*, Plaza Constitución 8.

Some 28km to the east, **SANTA EUFEMIA** is a picturesque hill village which more than makes up for the journey getting here. Occupying a striking location on a low ridge backed by spectacular crags topped by a ruined eleventh century Moorish fort, this typical north Sierra *pueblo* has an ancient heart where the twelfth-century Gothic-Mudéjar church of **La Encarnación** was one of the south's first post-*reconquista* churches built in the wake of the victories of Alfonso XI over the Moors. There's some fine **walking country** in the hills surrounding the town and the *Ayuntamiento*, Plaza Mayor 1 (☎957 15 82 29), can provide an information leaflet and a map of the village and hands out a booklet of hiking routes (in Spanish), which details a walk taking in the Moorish castle with spectacular views over the Sierra. There's also an excellent value **place to stay**, *Hostal La Paloma*, c/El Calvario 6 (☎957 15 80 76; ②), where balcony rooms come with bath and the **restaurant** has a bargain *menú*.

Northeast from Córdoba

The NIV highway which heads northeast out of Córdoba along the valley of the Guadalquivir is the main road to Madrid and one of the great **historical highways** of Andalucía. Not only was this the bullion route between Madrid and its imperial seaports of Sevilla and later Cádiz, but over a millennium and a half earlier, as the Vía Augusta, it formed the vital overland link joining Roman Spain with Gaul, Italy and Rome itself. This route has a number of delightful stopovers including the handsome small town of Montoro, an outstanding Moorish castle at Baños de Encina and the historic Despeñaperros Pass. Transport is easy and **buses** link Córdoba with most places on the route. Montoro, Andújar and Bailén are served by **trains** on the Córdoba–Linares–Madrid line.

Montoro

MONTORO lies 43km from Córdoba, past the villages of El Carpio and Pedro Abad, and just off the NIV. Dramatically sited on an escarpment above a horseshoe-bend in the Guadalquivir, the town is a centre of olive-oil production obtained from extensive groves planted in the foothills of the Sierra Morena to the north. A labyrinth of narrow, white-walled streets surrounds the main square, the Plaza de España, dominated by the lofty tower of its Gothic-Mudéjar church, **San Bartolomé**. The interior, behind the red sandstone facade, has a fine *artesonado* ceiling inlaid with mother-of-pearl, recently recovered from under layers of whitewash. A small **tourist office** (Mon–Fri 8.30am–3pm, Sat 11am–1.30pm & 7.30–9.30pm; ☎957 16 00 89) at no. 8 on the same square can provide basic information. Also here is the sixteenth-century **Ayuntamiento**, an old ducal mansion with a fine Plateresque frontage, and a historic inn – now closed – at no. 19 whose kindly owner will let you in for a look around (avoid siesta time). A narrow street uphill out of the north side of the square leads into an atmospheric old quarter whose main feature is the thirteenth-century church of **Santa María de la Mota** with some interesting Romanesque capitals, now converted into a small **archeological museum** (Sat 6–8pm, Sun 11am–1pm; outside these times visits can be arranged through the Turismo). One other curiosity which also shouldn't be missed is the **Casa de las Conchas** in nearby c/Grajas (no. 17 and signed from the plaza) – this is the house of Señor Francisco del Río who has had its exterior and interior covered with millions of seashells; he or his wife will proudly show you around and relate the story behind their twenty-year obsession.

The narrow main street connects Plaza de España with **Plaza del Charco** (aka Plaza Caridad). Plaza del Charco also has the town's main **bars** and two casinos, the larger *Casino de los Ricos* (rich) and the *Casino de los Pobres* (poor), reflecting the bitter class divisions that once existed here and to some extent persist. The former is a fascinating time-warp of a place with an elegant interior patio and, upstairs, the dusty rooms, furnished with drapes, tarnished chandeliers and faded frescoes of flappers, where the town's *señoritos* once held court. Today the dwindling clientele are still the town's right-wingers, and can be overheard reminiscing over their *finos* about the good old (Francoist) days. Both places welcome visitors, but the plaza's liveliest bar is *Bar Yepez* where ebullient proprietor Paco Yepez will serve up *tapas* and *raciones* and fill you in on local information. Slightly uphill from the square lies the eighteenth-century Capilla de San Jacinto, now converted into the **Museo Antonio Rodríguez de Luna** (Sat & Sun 11am–1pm; or arrange a visit with the Turismo) housing some powerful abstract works by the Montoro-born artist who spent part of his life in Paris and Mexico and died in 1985.

Montoro's other notable monument is the elegant sixteenth-century **bridge of Las Donadas** over the Guadalquivir, paid for by local women who, tradition holds, sold their jewellery to place the town on a more direct, and lucrative, route to the north. Across the bridge, the Cardeña road leading up into the hills offers superb **views** back over the town.

Andújar

Flanked by the mountains of the Sierra Morena which are visible on the northern horizon, the NIV continues to Villa del Río and enters the province of Jaén. Lying some 32km beyond Montoro, **ANDÚJAR** is a sizeable if simple country town which claims to be the world's biggest centre of sunflower-oil bottling. There's also a thriving commercial ceramics industry, as well as a couple of churches worth a visit for their art works.

The road into the town crosses a fifteen-arched **Roman bridge** spanning the Guadalquivir, which has been considerably restored from Moorish times onwards. The central Plaza de España, a baking furnace in the heat of high summer, contains the impressive Gothic church of **San Miguel** with a fine stone tower and Plateresque features, flanked by an equally striking late-Baroque **Ayuntamiento** – recently restored to its full glory – with elegant portals. But the more important church for the visitor will be the **Iglesia de Santa María** on the plaza of the same name, reached by following c/Feria between the two squares. Built on the site of a former mosque, the free-standing bell tower probably replaced the mosque's minaret and now houses a small **tourist office** (Tues–Sun 8am–3pm). Inside (best to try in the early evening) a chapel on the left has a fine *Christ in the Garden of Olives* by **El Greco**, a startling surprise in a nondescript country church, highlighted by another painting, an *Inmaculada* by Pachecho, the teacher of Velázquez, in a chapel to the left of the *altar mayor*. The superb **reja** which stands before the El Greco is the work of Master Bartolomé of Jaén, who also created the more famous one in the Capilla Real at Granada.

Of Andújar's traditional **ceramics industry**, only one exponent survives: José Castillo sells his wares – including the blue and white pottery for which the town is known – from his *alfarería* at c/Alfarero Castillo 7, just north of the Plaza de España.

PRACTICALITIES

The *Ayuntamiento* on the Plaza Mayor (Plaza de España) or the tourist office (see above) can provide information and a **town map** and most of the hotels stock these as well. Central **places to stay** include the pleasant *Hostal La Española*, Corredera San Bartolomé 26 (☎953 50 01 50; ③), slightly west of the centre with a garden, and *El Turis*, Puerta de Madrid 23 (☎953 50 10 01; ②), with its own bar. The more upmarket *Hotel Logasasanti*, c/Dr Fleming s/n (☎953 50 05 00, fax 953 50 50 05; ⑤), is central, modern and comfortable but *Hospedería La Fuente* c/Vendederas 4 close to the main square (☎953 50 46 29, fax 953 50 19 00; ④), a charming small hotel in a period building with bar and restaurant, probably has the edge. There's also a **campsite**, *Camping Andújar* (☎953 50 07 00), surprisingly close to the centre of town at the junction of c/Corredera Capuchinos and c/Granados, with an on-site restaurant.

Plenty of **bars** in town offer **tapas** – *Bar La Tasca* on Plaza de España and *Cafetería Los Naranjos*, c/Guadalupe 4, are both good. One **place to eat** which is well worth seeking out is the family-run *Restaurante Madrid Sevilla*, Plaza del Sol 4, a little to the east of the Plaza de España. It's a homely little place and charming proprietor/chef Manuel Gómez Sotoca will not only guide you through his house specials – the *flamenquines* and *perdiz* (partridge) and all meat dishes are recommended – but can also provide a printed recipe for the dish should you want to try it at home.

Around Andújar

A wonderful thirty-kilometre drive into the **Parque Natural Sierra de Andújar** to the north of Andújar along the J5010 leads to the thirteenth-century hermitage of **Nuestra**

Virgen de la Cabeza, one of the most revered of Andalucía's shrines. There's not much left of the ancient building, which was destroyed in the Civil War when two hundred *Guardia Civil* officers seized the shrine, declaring their support for Franco's rebellion. Bombarded for eight months by Republican forces, the sanctuary was eventually set alight and the guards captured on May 1, 1937. (Pre-democracy Spanish guidebooks felt obligated to append an emphatic exclamation mark to the eight months the siege lasted and the more sycophantic compared it to Numancia and Sagunto, two of the great Spanish sieges of Roman times – thus turning the episode into a symbol of fascist heroism.) The distasteful rebuild flanked by equally bleak *Guardia Civil* monuments was carried out during the Franco period, but the famous *romería* – in which brotherhoods and pilgrims converge on the shrine from all over Andalucía and Spain on the last Sunday in April – carries on undaunted. There's a decent **hostal** here which would provide a base for exploring the surrounding countryside of the natural park; *Hostal Virgen de la Cabeza* (☎957 10 21 65; ④) has rooms with bath and an economical **restaurant**. There is also a **campsite** nearby.

Just beyond Andújar the NIV turns away from the Guadalquivir valley to head northeast to **Bailén**, a dull farming town where Napoleon's troops suffered a crushing defeat in 1808, but with little to stop for. From here it pushes on for another 45km to Andalucía's border with La Mancha at the Despeñaperros Pass (see below) and Madrid. Other **possible routes** from this junction lead south to the city of Jaén (see p.370), or east to Baeza and Úbeda (see p.383) via Linares.

Baños de la Encina

Some 6km after Bailén a left turn leads to the village of **BAÑOS DE LA ENCINA**, which has one of the most impressive Moorish castles in Andalucía. Crowning a low hill above the village, the tenth-century **Alcázar** is a magnificent sight with its fourteen square towers and enormous keep spaced out along a crenellated curtain wall. Built at the behest of al-Hakam II of Córdoba, the fort was completed in 967, no doubt to control the rugged and mountainous territory to the north, the domain of various unruly Iberian clans. Entered through a double-horseshoe arch, where a plaque in Arabic script dates the edifice to year 357 of the *hegira* (967 AD), the fort has an oval ground plan and from the battlements (take care as there are no handrails) there are **fine views** over the village and towards the Sierra de Cazorla to the east and the less impressive reservoir behind. Before visting the Alcázar you should collect the **key** from the **tourist office** (Mon–Fri 8.30am–2pm), just off the main square. They can also provide information on walking in the area, a number of caves with prehistoric paintings nearby, a Bronze Age site at **Peñalosa** where an important Iberian mining settlement is being excavated, and the opening times for the nearby **Ermita de Cristo del Llano**, an eighteenth-century hermitage with stunning stucco stellar decoration inspired by the Alhambra at Granada. When the tourist office is closed the *Bar Restaurant Mirasierra* – further along the same street to the right – should be able to advise on castle visiting. The village's splendid red stone Gothic-Renaissance church of **San Mateo**, with an elegant octagonal tower, is also worth a look, as are its narrow, whitewashed streets dotted with a clutch of *señorial* mansions. There's no accommodation here, but you can get **tapas** at **bars** on the main square and, behind the castle, at *Restaurante La Encina*, c/Ambulatorio 1, which serves hearty Sierra dishes and a good-value *menú*.

La Carolina

LA CAROLINA, 20km further to the northeast, is the most important of the new towns set up by Carlos III in the eighteenth century (see p.271) to protect the bullion route from Cádiz to Madrid. As with the other settlements it was named after a member of the royal family – in this case the king himself – settled with foreign immigrants and laid out on a regular grid-pattern street plan which survives today. The town's central square, the Plaza del Ayuntamiento, has the imposing, honey-coloured sandstone **Palacio de Pablo de Olavide**, built for Carlos III's radical minister, the force behind the *Nuevas Poblaciones* idea. De Olavide did not long enjoy the fruits of his labours however, for the clergy, who were denied access to these new towns, wreaked their vengeance by denouncing him to the Inquisition. Arrested in 1776, he was divested of his property and confined to a covent in La Mancha subject to whatever penances the monks thought appropriate. He subsequently escaped to France. Flanking the *palacio*, the parish church of **La Concepción** contains a fine Baroque image of the *Virgen de las Angustias* in alabaster. The square is linked by a thoroughfare to an impressive tree lined avenue entered via a gateway bearing images of Carlos III, at the far end of which lies the municipal **swimming pool**. The town also has a small **archeological museum** (c/Alfredo Calderón s/n; ☎953 68 00 36); ring or check with the *Ayuntamiento* on the main square regarding opening times.

There are a number of **places to stay**: the basic *El Retorno*, c/Sanjurjo 5 (☎953 66 16 13; ②), would do for a night, or you could try the more luxurious *La Perdiz* (☎953 66 03 00; ⑦) – not be confused with the uninviting *Orellana Perdiz* nearby – on the main NIV road (km-269) at the edge of town. Even if you're not staying, it's worth knowing about their pleasant garden **swimming pool** which you are welcome to use for the price of a drink in the bar.

El Centanillo

A minor road out of La Carolina winds northwest into the hills and ends up at the tiny mountain hamlet of **EL CENTANILLO**, about as far off the tourist trail as it's possible to get in Andalucía. Situated in densely wooded hunting country, *Bar La Entrada* (③) on the edge of the village, used by the shooting fraternity in winter, should have a **room**, although this establishment does have an eccentric streak; their good restaurant always seems to have fresh *venado* (venison) on the menu even outside the legal hunting season. There's plenty of good **walking country** around El Centanillo; you could try tracing the Río Grande to its source (about 8km) or, more ambitiously, and with a map (CNIG sheet 862), trekking west along the Sierra de los Calderones to the valley of the Río Jándula bordering the province of Ciudad Real.

The Despeñaperros Pass

Two kilometres beyond La Carolina, slightly before the village of Navas de Tolosa, a huge **roadside monument** marks the site of the important battle which took place in 1212 between the Christian armies under Alfonso VIII and the Almohad forces. The Moors suffered a crippling defeat, opening the way for the Reconquest of Andalucía. The monument depicts the Christian monarchs as well as the shepherd, an apparition of St Isidore in disguise, who, according to Christian belief, guided them through the well-defended Sierra Morena, thus enabling a surprise attack on the Moorish army who fled after defeat through the Despeñaperros Pass. This event, in fact, gave the pass its name – meaning the "overthrow of the dogs" (or Moors).

The **Despeñaperros Pass**, 14km further on, is the dramatic gateway between Andalucía and La Mancha and the only natural breach in the 500-kilometre length of the Sierra Morena. This narrow defile, flanked by daunting crags and slopes covered with dense pine woods, was for centuries the main point of entry into Andalucía from the north and many travellers have left vivid accounts of arriving in the lush promised land of the south after traversing the dry and arid plains of La Mancha (from the Moorish *manxa*, or parched earth). George Borrow, however, also related the sense of foreboding due to the pass's evil reputation "on account of the robberies which are continually being perpetrated in its recesses". Ford, when going the other

DON QUIJOTE AND THE DESPEÑAPERROS PASS

Cervantes would have been familiar with the route through the pass, connecting La Mancha with Sevilla and Córdoba, where he lived both as a child and in later life. The brooding and threatening nature of the pass – probably greater before it was blasted to make room for road widening and the rail line – appealed to him, for he used it in two of the most memorable scenes in the adventures of **Don Quijote** and Sancho Panza. The centre of the pass is where Don Quijote ran mad and played "the desperate, the raving, the furious lover", in order that Sancho could convey news of this penance to his fantasized Lady Dulcinea del Toboso, in reality a slatternly country lass named Alonza Lorenzo:

"Observe the landmarks, and I will try to remain near this spot," said Don Quijote. "And I will even take the precaution of climbing the highest of these crags to look out for you on your return. But your surest way of not missing me, and not getting lost yourself, will be for you to scatter some of the broom that is so plentiful around here. Scatter it at intervals as you go till you get out to open country. The sprigs will serve as landmarks and signs for you to find me by when you come back, just like the thread in Theseus's labyrinth."

This botanical link with the world of Quijote is still strong when, in early summer, the clumps of brilliant yellow flowers are everywhere. About 1km further on, the **Venta de Cardenas** was the inn which the deluded knight errant imagined to be a castle. When the morning after a night's hospitality the innkeeper demanded payment, Quijote refused with the explanation that knights never paid for their accommodation and made his exit. Sancho, however, was not so lucky and was given a violent tossing in a blanket to teach him a lesson. The old *venta* apparently survived until the last century, when it was seen by Borrow. However, it was subsequently demolished and a characterless hotel now stands on the site. But it's still a stopover on this major transportation route and the lines of articulated lorries parked outside belong to the truck drivers who use this inn today, the successors of the muleteers, drovers and carriers of Cervantes's time.

way, described the land beyond the pass as where "commences the *paño pardo*, the brown cloth, and the *alpargata*, or the hempen sandal of the poverty-stricken Manchegos".

Jaén

Surrounded by olive groves and huddled beneath the fortress of Santa Catalina on the heights above, **JAÉN**, the provincial capital and by far the largest town in the province, is an uneventful sort of place. Derived from the Arabic *Geen*, meaning a stop on the caravan route, the modern town is more northerly than Andalucian in its appearance and character, doubtless stemming from its resettlement with emigrants from the north following the *reconquista,* and the subsequent long centuries spent as the front-line bulwark of Christian Spain against Moorish Granada. At the centre of an area impoverished by lack of economic development and chronic unemployment, while you would hardly want to go out of your way to get here, the city makes an easy place to stopover en route to destinations such as Baeza, Úbeda and Cazorla to the northeast. And, given a chance, it has a surprising number of worthwhile sights, including a fine cathedral, the largest Moorish baths in Spain, some elegant old churches and mansions and an important museum.

Some history

Although the area around the city is liberally dotted with Iberian settlements, it was probably as the Roman settlement of *Auringis* that Jaén was born. A centre noted for its **silver mines** and settled by the Moors shortly after the conquest of 711, to judge by the number of mosques it must have been a thriving place. The Moors also made use of the **hot springs** that had been known to the Romans and utilized them in the construction of several baths. Fernando III's Christian forces captured the city – then part of the newly founded Nasrid kingdom of Granada – in 1246 and made its ruler Ibn al-Ahmar (aka Muhammad ibn Yusuf ibn Nasr) into a vassal, obliged to pay annual tribute. It was from Jaén, two and a half centuries later, that the final assault on Boabdil's Granada was launched. The city then entered into a slow decline which gathered pace in the seventeenth and eighteenth centuries and led many of its citizens to emigrate to the imperial colonies, evidenced by towns with the same name in countries as far apart as Peru and the Philippines. Although Jaén's strategic importance played a part in the War of Independence, the economic disruption caused brought further decline in its wake, from which the city never really recovered. The situation is not much improved today and in a survey carried out by the *Junta de Andalucía*, the city and province registered the largest percentage of Andalucía's population describing themselves as living in poverty (61 percent). The survey also showed that a quarter of all the province's citizens live on an income of less than 17,000 pesetas a month.

Arrival, information and accommodation

Jaén's **bus station** is on Plaza Coca de la Pinera, just off the Paseo de la Estación. There are frequent daily services to and from Úbeda and Baeza and, less often, Cazorla. The **train station** (☎953 27 02 02) is a bit further out, at the end of Paseo de la Estación, and a good ten-minute walk (or an easier ride on bus #10) from the centre. There are train connections to Córdoba and Madrid. Arriving **by car** you will encounter the parking problems that plague all Andalucía's provincial capitals, and if you don't want to use the signed pay car parks around the centre then consult where you're staying; even if they don't have a garage they should be able to advise. The streets around the bullring to the east of the centre usually have parking spaces. The **Turismo**, c/Arquitecto Bergés 1 (Mon–Fri 8.30am–2.30pm, Sat 10am–12.30pm; ☎953 22 27 37), is just off the Paseo de la Estación, on the opposite side to the bus station. The more friendly **municipal tourist office**, c/Maestra 18 slightly north of the cathedral (Mon–Fri 8am–3pm; ☎953 21 91 16), has lots of information on the town, while inside the striking nineteenth-century Diputación Provincial building fronting Plaza de San Francisco the **provincial tourist office** (Mon–Fri 8am–3pm; ☎953 24 80 00) has information on the province.

It's worth noting (and applauding) that admission to all Jaén's monuments is **free**.

Accommodation

Places to stay in town are limited and relatively expensive. The few budget-priced places in the centre are around the cathedral and Plaza de la Constitución. Just a short way north of the cathedral, *Hostal La Española*, c/Bernardo López 9 (☎953 23 02 54; ④), is friendly and clean and has some rooms with bath; note that mosquitos can be a real problem both here and elsewhere in the town during the high summer season. Off the south side of Plaza de la Constitución, *Hostal Martín*, c/Cuatro Torres 5 (☎953 22 06 33; ②), is a less expensive, but more spartan alternative. Just off the west side of the Plaza de la Constitución, *Hotel Xuen*, Plaza Deán Mazas 3 (☎953 24 07 89, fax 953 19 03 12; ⑤), is probably the best of the pricier options with air-conditioned rooms. A couple of blocks down from here, *Hotel Europa*, Plaza de Belén 1 (☎953 22 27 00, fax 953 22 26 92; ⑤) has

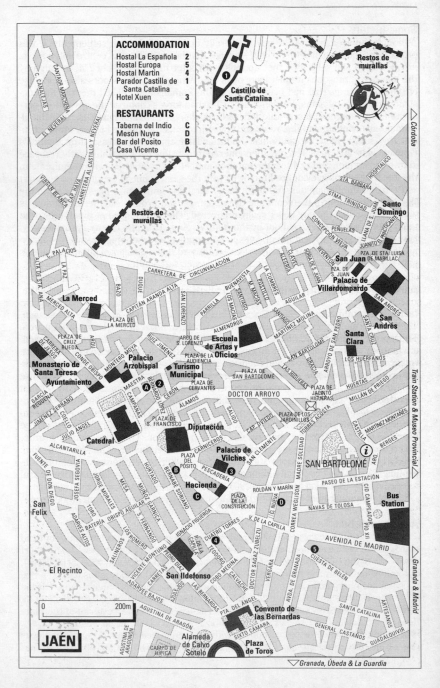

ACCOMMODATION

Hostal La Española	2
Hostal Europa	5
Hostal Martin	4
Parador Castilla de Santa Catalina	1
Hotel Xuen	3

RESTAURANTS

Taberna del Indio	C
Mesón Nuyra	D
Bar del Posito	B
Casa Vicente	A

JAÉN

Granada, Úbeda & La Guardia

air conditioning and a garage. For a truly memorable experience you could stay in the *Parador Castillo de Santa Catalina* (☎953 23 00 00, fax 953 23 09 30; ⑨), one of the most spectacularly sited hotels in Spain. The rooms all have fine balcony views with a sheer drop to the valley below, and there's a pool as well.

The Town

Most of Jaén's sights lie within a few minutes' walk of the rather characterless main thoroughfare, the **Paseo de la Estación**. This cuts through the heart of the city from north to south linking the train station with the Plaza de la Constitución, the major hub of activity. The *paseo* is interrupted only by the Plaza de las Batalles, a square dominated by a grotesque sculpture commemorating the battles of Nava de Tolosa (against the Moors) and Bailén (against the French).

The Cathedral and around

Jaén's massive and magnificent **Catedral** (daily 8.30am–1pm & 5–8pm; museum Sat & Sun 11am–1pm), lying to the west of the Plaza de la Constitución, dwarfs the city. Begun in 1492 after the demolition of the great mosque which had previously occupied the site, the cathedral was not completed until 1802. A number of architects turned their hand to the project during this period, including the great Andrés de Vandelvira whose imprint is on most of the building as it looks today. The spectacular **west facade**, flanked by twin sixty-metre-high towers framing Corinthian pillars and statuary by the seventeenth-century master, Pedro Roldán, is one of the masterpieces of Andalucian Renaissance architecture. Inside, the overall mood of the building is more sombre, with bundles of great Corinthian columns surging towards the roof of the nave. Fine sixteenth-century **choir stalls** have richly carved images from the Old Testament as well as a number of grisly martyrdoms. The dim side chapels also have some interesting art works, among them an eighteenth-century *Virgen de las Angustias* (Our Lady of the Sorrows) by José de Mora in the fifth side chapel to the right. The church fills up on Fridays (11.30am–1pm) when the **lienzo del Santo Rostro** is ritually removed from its coffer behind the high altar. This Byzantine cloth icon bearing a likeness of Christ is believed locally to be the napkin with which St Veronica wiped his face en route to Calvary. Long queues form to kiss the icon (preserved behind glass) and the attending priest wipes it with a handkerchief after each devotee.

The **sacristy museum** displays works by artists of the region as well as the **Tenebrario**, a fifteen-armed candlestick by Master Bartolomé de Jaén who also made the magnificent *reja* in the Capilla Real at Granada. Two fine seventeenth-century **sculptures by Montañes**, *San Lorenzo* and *Christ Nazareno*, are also on display.

Near the cathedral are a number of **palaces** that are a feature of most of the larger Andalucian towns. The fifteenth-century **Palacio del Condestable**, c/Martínez Molina 24, has a beautiful patio and interior decoration by Moorish craftsmen from the kingdom of Granada. The elegant portico of the seventeenth-century **Palacio de los Vilches**, c/Pescadería (and now occupied by a bank), once fronted Jaén's central Plaza Mayor before the present, featureless Plaza de la Constitución replaced it. A short distance east of the cathedral the fifteenth-century (in origin) church of **San Ildefonso** (daily 8.30am–noon & 6–9pm) – an impressive amalgam of Gothic, Mannerist and Neoclassical styles – is worth a look, as is the striking facade and exquisite cloister of the beautiful seventeenth-century convent and church of the **Convento de las Bernardas**.

The Baños Árabes

The main cluster of the city's other sights lies to the north of the cathedral, along c/Martínez Molina in what was formerly the old Moorish town. The most interesting of these is the **Baños Árabes** (Tues–Fri 9am–8pm, Sat & Sun 9.30am–2.30pm), a remarkable Moorish *hammam* or baths, and the largest to survive in Spain. Originally part of an eleventh-century Moorish palace, the baths fell into disuse after the *reconquista* and were used as a tannery. In the sixteenth century the Palacio de Villadompardo (now a museum of popular arts and crafts) was built over them. They were rediscovered early this century and in the 1980s were painstakingly restored. Recent modifications now lead you into the baths over a glass floor allowing views of the Roman and Moorish remains which surround the complex. The various rooms (cold, tepid and hot) have wonderful brickwork ceilings with typical star-shaped windows, and pillars supporting elegant horseshoe arches. An underground passage (now closed) connected the baths with the centre of the Moorish palace, on top of which was built the Monastery of Santo Domingo (see below). The **museum of arts and crafts** (same hours as the baths) contains a fascinating and well-presented folk history of the province on three floors using artefacts, clothing, toys, ceramics, photos and audiovisual aids. A new addition here is the **Museo Internacional de Arte Naif** (same hours) with works by (mainly) Spanish and some international artists.

The baths are flanked by the **Palacio de los Uribes**, a sixteenth-century mansion, on the northern side, whilst the church of **San Andrés**, which contains a fabulous **reja** (altar screen) depicting the *Holy Family* and the *Tree of Jesse* by Maestro Bartolomé of Jaén, here working on his home patch, lies just to the south. Slightly west of here, the ancient post-*reconquista* church of **San Juan**, in the Plaza de San Juan, has an elegant Romanesque tower and, inside, a fine sixteenth-century sculpture of the crucifixion by by Sebastián de Solís. A couple of streets north, the c/Santísima Trinidad leads to a **path** which climbs, ruggedly in parts, to the castle of Santa Catalina (see below), a much shorter route than the 3km-plus road. The path starts from the *Bar Sobrino Bigotes*.

Santo Domingo, La Magdalena and other churches

Standing on c/Santo Domingo, north of San Juan, the **Monastery of Santo Domingo**, erected over a Moorish palace, was originally a fourteenth-century Dominican monastery and later became Jaén's university; later still it was a seat of the Inquisition, before being transformed in more recent times into the office of the provincial historical archive (Archivo Historico). From its earlier incarnations a fine sixteenth-century **portal** by Vandelvira and a beautiful **patio** with elegant twinned Tuscan columns survive. The building is closed to visitors, but you can gain access to view the patio by ringing the intercom outside.

A little further north still, the church of **La Magdalena** (daily 6–8pm), the oldest in Jaén, was built over a mosque, the minaret of which is now its bell tower, and a patio at the rear preserves a pool used in Moorish times for ritual ablutions. In the cloister you can still see a few Roman tombstones used in the construction of the original Moorish building; this quarter was also the centre of the ancient Roman town. Inside, the church has a superb **retablo** by Jacobo Florentino depicting scenes from the Passion.

Two more churches nearby are the sixteenth-century **San Bartolomé** (daily 6.30–8pm), with a fine Mudéjar *artesonado* ceiling, Gothic ceramic font and an outstanding *Expiration of Christ* by José de Medina, and the **Convento de Santa Clara** (open service times) with a fine choir and sixteenth-century Ecuadorian sculpture of *Cristo de bambú*.

The Museo Provincial

The **Museo Provincial** at Paseo de la Estación 27 (Tues 3–8pm, Wed–Sat 9am–8pm, Sun 9am–3pm) is worth a visit if only for its remarkable collection of **Iberian stone sculptures**, among the most important in Spain. Recently housed in a separate building to the side of the museum (ask at the admission desk for directions) these remarkable sculptures were found near the town of Porcuna, close to the province's western border, and date from the fifth century BC. One is of a magnificent bull, whilst another is a strange fragment – titled *grifomaquia* – depicting a struggle between a man and a griffon. All the works betray the artistic influence of the classical Greek world on the fertile Iberian imagination. The strange fact revealed by the archeological excavations when these works came to light is that they had been deliberately broken a short time after their execution and then laid in a long trench. No satisfactory explanation for this has yet been put forward. More sculptures are being put on show each year as they are uncovered by archeologists, and it is intended that this will eventually become the major museum for Iberian art in Spain.

Items on display in the main building include Phoenician jewellery and ointment phials, Greek vases (demonstrating how widepread trading links were in the Mediterranean world), as well as Roman mosaics and sculpture, including an outstanding fourth-century **sarcophagus** found near Martós depicting seven miracles of Christ including the transformation of water into wine. Room 7 deals with Jaén's significant **Moorish period** and has lamps and stoneware as well as a whole jugful of money – dirhams and califalas – that someone buried and never got back to collect. This room also has some fine **ceramics** which verify the Moorish origin of the green glazed plates and vases, still the hallmark of the pottery of Jaén province.

Upstairs, the **Museo de Bellas Artes** starts out with some interesting medieval wood-sculpture before quickly degenerating into a hotchpotch of fairly awful stuff from the nineteenth and twentieth centuries, although there are a few laughs, not to mention a large number of steamy nudes.

Castillo de Santa Catalina

The **Castillo de Santa Catalina**, dominating the crag which rises behind the city, was in origin a Moorish fortress constructed in the thirteenth century by Ibn al-Ahmar. After the Reconquest, the castle was much altered. Part of it has been stylishly converted into a modern *parador*, and little of the Moorish edifice now survives. A number of secret passageways connected the Moorish fortress with the town below and a few of these have been discovered. A path from the *parador* car park leads to the older and ruined part of the edifice at the castle's southern end where a *mirador* beneath a huge, whitewashed cross gives a **spectacular view** of the city laid out below your feet and dominated by the massive cathedral. Beyond, Jaén's wealth and misery, the endless lines of olive groves, disappear over the hills into the haze. Non-residents are welcome to use the *parador*'s bar and restaurant. If you don't fancy the three-kilometre, near-vertical hike to reach the castle, you can take a taxi from Plaza Coca de la Piñera by the bus station.

Eating, drinking and nightlife

Jaén tends to die after dark and in the absence of much nightlife you'll probably compensate by **eating and drinking**. In the centre, the best place to find food is around the east side of the Plaza de la Constitución. Here, the tiny c/Nueva has a whole crowd of *tapas* bars and places to eat; *Mesón Río Chico*, *La Gamba de Oro* and *Bodegón de Pepe* are all good. Above the west side of the Plaza de la Constitución, you'll find two popular *tapas* and *raciones* bars, both with outdoor tables on shady squares; *Taberna del Indio* on Plaza Deán Mazas, and *Bar del Posito*, on the plaza of the same name. Jaén's best restaurant is *Casa Vicente*, c/Maestra 8, just north of the cathedral, and housed in a superbly restored old mansion with a delightful patio; specialities include *pastel de carne de caza* (game pie) and *cordero mozárabe* (spiced lamb) and there's also a medium-priced *menú*. Another possibility in the same price bracket is *Mesón Nuyra*, Pasaje Nuyra s/n off c/Nueva (see above) with good fish and meat dishes. To feast in baronial splendour you'll need to climb – or take a taxi – to the *Castillo de Santa Catalina parador* whose recreated medieval dining room, with stone vaulted roofs, tapestries and suits of armour, can't help but feed your fantasies, although the service can be a bit fussy. A good-value *menú*, around 3500ptas, usually includes several local specialities such as *morcilla* and *pipirrana* (cucumber and tomato salad). Finally, a popular haunt with *jiennenses* – especially on Sundays – is *El Mirador*, a great family-run restaurant 7km along the road to Jabalcuz to the south of the town. The local dishes served up are excellent, there's an economical *menú* and – as its name implies – fine views from its terraces (closed Mon). Back in town, a good **breakfast** stop is *Cafetería Yucatán*, up a flight of steps off the Plaza del Posito, with a terrace; later in the day it also serves economical *platos combinados*.

Bars for **tapas** around the centre include *Manila*, c/Maestra 4, north of the cathedral or, a couple of streets away, the cosy *Tasca Los Amigos*, c/Bernardo López, where there's good *jamón* and *morcilla* (blood pudding); the nearby *Bar 82* is also worth a visit. One street south, on c/Arcos del Consuelo, *El Gorrión* serves cheese *tapas* and *La Catedral* is popular with a younger crowd. Around the corner and slightly north, the curiously named *Bar Nueva Delhi*, c/Cerón 19 (whose owner has no Asian connections), is another decent *tapas* and *raciones* option. The nightime *movida* takes place in the **drinking bars** of the Barrio de San Ildefonso to the east of the cathedral centering on c/Hurtado, where the friendly *Bar Azulejo* at no. 8 is located inside a *casa señorial* and gives a free *tapa* with every drink. *Santuario* and *77* on the same street are also worth a try. *Ramirez* in the adjacent Plaza de San Ildefonso, and *Iroquai* along c/Las Bernadas slightly east, are other good places nearby.

What serious **nightlife** there is takes place along the lower end of the Paseo de la Estación towards the train station, where a couple of tame discos and some music bars cater for the city's teenage set. A couple of places offering a slightly maturer alternative in the same area are *Chubby Cheek*, c/San Francisco Javier 7, which often stages live **jazz**, and *Café Latino*, c/Santa Alicia 3, which puts on live **salsa**.

Listings

Banks Numerous places with ATM/cash machines are located along the town's two main thoroughfares, the Paseo de la Estación and the Avda. de Madrid.

Car rental Viajes Sacramonte, Pasaje Maza, Paseo de la Estación 12 (☎953 22 22 12) and Autos del Pino, c/La Luna 6 (☎953 25 09 01), slightly east of the Avda. de Madrid, are both reliable and undercut the majors.

Football Real Jaén have been having a good spell in recent seasons in Section B of Division 2. They play at the Estadio de la Victoria (☎953 26 39 38), near the train station.

Hospital The city's main hospital is Hospital Ciudad de Jaén, Avda. Ejército Español s/n, west of the Monumento a las Batallas (☎953 29 90 00). In emergencies dial ☎061.

Hiking maps 1:50,000, 1:100,000 and 1:200,000 maps are available from CNIG (National Geographic Service) branch office: Plaza de la Constitución 10 (☎953 22 18 32).

Markets A vibrant weekly market takes place on Thursdays on the *recinto ferial* between Avda. de Granada and the bullring.

Newspapers Jaén's daily paper, *Jaén*, is a good source of information on both the town and province, and has details of entertainment, plus updated train and bus timetables.

Police Plaza Santa María, in the *Ayuntamiento* building fronting the cathedral (☎953 21 91 05). For emergencies dial ☎091.

Post office Plaza Jardinillos, near the Convento de Santa Clara (Mon–Fri 8.30am–8pm, Sat 9.30am–2pm).

Taxis These congregate outside the bus station on Plaza Coca de la Piñera.

Around Jaén

Two good **day trips** from Jaén are to La Guardia de Jaén, 10km southeast, and Martos, 24km to the west, both with impressive hill top forts. La Guardia isn't too difficult a journey without your own transport, with three daily buses on weekdays, whilst Martos has hourly buses with a skeleton service on Sundays. Also worth a visit if you are likely to be travelling to Baeza with your own transport is the **Museo de la Cultura del Olivo** (Tues–Sun 11am–2pm & 5–8pm; free) – a museum in an old oil factory dedicated to the history and development of Jaén's great wealth earner. The museum is located down a signed left turn off the A316 just before the village of Puente del Obispo, 8km short of Baeza.

La Guardia

Reached along a minor road which branches off the main N323 to Granada, **LA GUARDIA** is a charming white-walled village gathered beneath its ruined eighth-century **castillo** (collect key from the *Ayuntamiento* in the village) which contains elements of previous Iberian, Roman and Visigothic fortifications. The village also has the ruined church of **Santo Domingo**, originally part of a Dominican monastery founded in 1530, and a major work by Andrés de Vandelvira, who was also responsible for the cathedral at Jaén. The arcades around the patio (or cloister) and a central fountain are all that remains of the monastery, whilst the sanctuary, nave and transept crossing give some idea of what a fine construction the church must once have been. At the edge of the village on Monte Salido, a small hill, are some rock-cut **Visigothic graves** where numerous artefacts were found, now on display in the museum at Jaén.

Martos

Along the A316 to the west of Jaén, and surrounded by an ocean of olive groves, it doesn't take long to realize why **MARTOS** is Spain's number one producer of **olives**. The ruins of a Moorish fortress *La Peña*, on a great rock outcrop that towers over the small town, are a vivid reminder of the great struggles of the *reconquista* when the Moorish forts of Jaén became the front line against hostile Christian incursions, and the scene of bitter battles and sieges. This one fell to Fernando III on St Marta's Day in 1225, thus giving the town its present name. In the old quarter with its narrow, winding streets the church of **Santa María de la Villa** is thirteenth-century, constructed soon after the victory, although it underwent substantial rebuilding in the fifteenth and later centuries. The interior has an outstanding Baroque **retablo** as well as a fine **early Christian sarcophagus** dating from the fourth century. The fifteenth-century church of **Santa Marta** with its Isabelline entrance and the former sixteenth-century prison, now the **Ayuntamiento**, graced by another fine portal, are also worth a look.

If you want **to stay**, *Hostal Fernando IV*, c/Lope de Vega 19 (☎953 55 15 75; ③), is central, pleasant and has rooms with bath. For **eating and drinking** there are numerous *tapas* bars around the centre and a surprisingly good restaurant is to be found at the bus station, Avda. Moris 3, with a terrace which, on summer nights, becomes a lively social hub.

Baeza

Campo de Baeza, soñaré contigo cuando no te vea.

Fields of Baeza, I will dream of you when I can no longer see you.

Antonio Machado (1875–1939)

Fifty kilometres from Jaén along the winding N321, **BAEZA** is a tiny, compact and provincial country town with a perpetual Sunday air about it. Sited on the escarpment

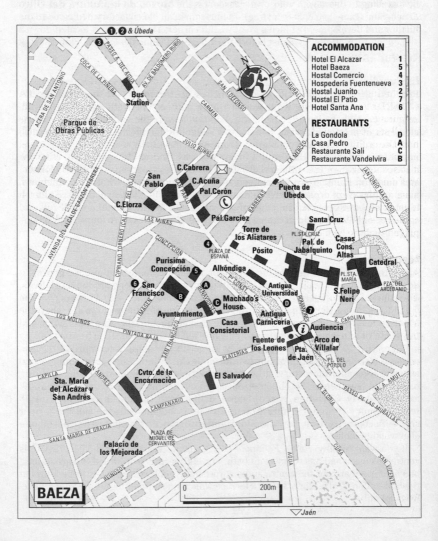

△ **❶**, **❷** & Úbeda

ACCOMMODATION

Hotel El Alcazar	1
Hotel Baeza	5
Hostal Comercio	4
Hospedería Fuentenueva	3
Hostal Juanito	2
Hostal El Patio	7
Hotel Santa Ana	6

RESTAURANTS

La Gondola	D
Casa Pedro	A
Restaurante Sali	C
Restaurante Vandelvira	B

BAEZA

0   200m

▽ Jaén

of the Loma de Úbeda, both Baeza, and the neighbouring town of Úbeda (see p.383), have an extraordinary density of exuberant **Renaissance palaces**, richly endowed churches and magnificent public squares which are among the finest in Spain.

Important in Roman times as *Beatia*, Baeza was later a Visigothic bishopric and then a prosperous commercial and agricultural centre under the Moors. After a prolonged and bitter struggle the town fell to the Christian forces in 1227, and *hidalgos* or nobles were granted estates in the surrounding countryside with orders to defend this frontier zone. The power of these noble houses was so untrammelled that they were soon warring among themselves for control of the town (a favoured place of battle being Baeza's Alcázar – until Isabel had it demolished). It was later, in the sixteenth century, however, that Baeza embarked on its most prosperous period. The nobility, made rich by farming and textile production, endowed the town with numerous striking Renaissance buildings as the population expanded.

Arrival, information and accommodation

The nearest **train station** to Baeza is **Linares-Baeza**, 14km away and served by frequent trains from Sevilla, Córdoba and Granada (buses connect with most trains, or it's a 2000ptas taxi ride), where you'll find fronting the station a good-value hotel and restaurant, *Las Palmeras* (☎953 69 89 79; ④). Otherwise, you're dependent on buses, and all services (around fourteen daily) between Jaén and Úbeda, 9km further east, call in at Baeza. If you're coming from Granada, there's currently a 4pm departure, stopping at Jaén and arriving in Baeza at 6.30pm. The **bus station** (☎953 74 04 68), officially at Paseo de Elorza Garat 1, is actually at the end of c/San Pablo and along the Paseo Arca del Agua. Baeza's **Turismo** in the sixteenth-century former **Audiencia**, or appeal court, on the Plaza de los Leones (Mon–Fri 9am–2.30pm, Sat 10am–1pm; ☎953 74 04 44), can supply maps and information. The account below deals with only the major sights out of Baeza's fifty-plus monuments and the Turismo can supply an English-language brochure detailing them all.

Accommodation

Baeza has a decent range of **places to stay**, some of which are architectural gems.

Hotel El Alcázar, Paseo Arca del Agua s/n, north of the bus station (☎953 74 00 28). Decent rooms with bath above a restaurant. ④.

Hotel Baeza, c/Concepción 3, near the Plaza de España (☎953 74 81 30, fax 953 74 25 19). Housed in a stylishly converted Renaissance monastery with a glassed-in patio and its own restaurant. ⑦ includes breakfast.

Hostal Comercio, c/San Pablo 21, slightly north of the Plaza de España (☎953 74 01 00). Old-fashioned and friendly budget *hostal*, with en-suite rooms. Room 215 is marked with a plaque; it was once occupied by the famous poet Antonio Machado when he lodged here in 1911. ③.

Hospedería Fuentenueva, Paseo Arca del Agua s/n, just north of the bus station (☎953 74 31 00, fax 953 74 31 00). Delightful small hotel housed in an ancient but tastefully refurbished former women's prison, with friendly proprietors, well-appointed rooms, restaurant and pool. ⑥.

Hostal El Patio, c/Conde Romanones 13, behind the Plaza de los Leones (☎953 74 02 00). Wonderfully seedy Renaissance mansion set around a courtyard (now enclosed), decorated with mangy mounted bulls' heads and a central fountain. Some slightly pricier rooms have bath. ②–③.

Hostal Juanito, Paseo Arca del Agua s/n (☎953 74 00 40, fax 953 74 23 24). The service can be a bit sniffy, but there's a top-notch restaurant downstairs. Insist on a west-facing room at the back or a high room on the front to avoid the odour of a *gasolinera* forecourt right next door. ⑤.

Hotel Santa Ana, c/Santa Ana Vieja 9 (☎953 74 07 65, fax 953 74 16 57). Charming new hotel with stylish rooms in a striking stone-built sixteenth-century *casa señorial*. ⑥.

The Town

Most of Baeza's main attractions lie within a few minutes' walk of the pleasant central joined squares of **Plaza de España** and the larger **Paseo de la Constitución**. These are flanked by cafés and are very much the hub of the town's limited animation. There are no charges to enter any of the monuments but you may offer the guardian a small *propina* (tip).

Paseo de la Constitución

On the eastern side of the bar-lined *paseo* is **La Alhóndiga**, an elegant porticoed six-teenth-century corn-exchange and, almost opposite across the gardens, the arcaded eighteenth-century **Casa Consistorial**, or old town hall, which once fronted the old market square. At the southern end of the *paseo*, you'll find the **Plaza de los Leones** (also called the Plaza del Populo), a delightful cobbled square enclosed by Renaissance buildings. A central **fountain** incorporates Roman lions and a statue – which locals believe is Imilce, the Iberian wife of the Carthaginian general, Hannibal. The fountain is overlooked by some remarkable buildings including the old **slaughterhouse**, bear-ing the arms of Carlos V, and beside the arch at the far end, the *Audiencia* housing the Turismo (see above). Also here, on a rounded balcony flanking the **double arch** of the Arco de Villalar and the Puerta de Jaén, the first Mass of the Reconquest is reputed to have been celebrated. The **Puerta de Jaén** was a memento (or rebuke) left by Carlos V to the town which had opposed him, and commemorated the Germanic ruler's pro-cession through here in 1526 en route to marry Isabel of Portugal.

Palacio de Jabalquinto and the Antigua Universidad

The stepped street behind the Plaza de los Leones ascends (via c/Romanones and c/Juan de Ávila) to another cluster of monuments including the finest of Baeza's palaces, the **Palacio de Jabalquinto** (patio open Tues–Sun 10am–1pm & 4–6pm), now a seminary, with an elaborate "Isabelline" front (showing marked Moorish influence in its stalactite decoration). Built in the fifteenth century by the Benavides family, the tran-quil interior patio has a double tier of arcades around a central fountain and a superb **Baroque staircase** with fine carving. Next to this palace, the **Antigua Universidad** or old university (patio open Tues–Sun 10am–1pm & 4–6pm) was founded in 1538 and, after functioning for nearly three centuries as a centre of study and debate, its charter was revoked in 1824 during the tyrannical reign of Fernando VII. From 1875 the build-ings were used as a school until, in 1979, the building once again became a centre of higher learning albeit as a summer school for the University of Granada. The interior has an elegant patio and, next to a sixteenth-century lecture hall, the preserved **class-room** (ask the guardian to open it up) used by the great *sevillano* poet and writer Antonio Machado when he served as a teacher here from 1912 to 1919. This experience must have provided much of the material for his most famous prose work *Juan de Mairena*, the observations on life and culture of a fictional schoolmaster.

A little to the north of here in Plaza Santa Cruz, the remarkable church of **Santa Cruz** (Mon–Sat 11am–1pm & 4–6pm) is Baeza's oldest, built shortly after the Reconquest in the thirteenth century, although later much restored. Converted from an earlier mosque, the church betrays a combination of late Romanesque and early Gothic architectural styles. The austere, white-walled interior has slender stone columns as well as some four-teenth- and fifteenth-century **frescoes**. Also preserved is the **arch of the mihrab** which would have directed the worshippers in the pre-Christian building towards Mecca.

At c/Arcos de las Escuelas 2, near the north end of c/Romanones, stands one of Baeza's more eccentric attractions – a **shop** (Mon–Sat 8.30am–10pm), run by Diego Lozano Jiménez, ostensibly selling local ceramics. Once you've penetrated the shelves of pots and a bottling plant for mineral water behind, you'll enter the studio of self-taught sculptor Diego where he has fashioned a series of remarkable **marble replicas** of Baeza's famous buildings, including the *Ayuntamiento* and the Palacio Jabalquinto. Created in eye-straining detail by Diego, when not behind the counter of his shop or looking after his six children, the replicas are well worth a look.

The Cathedral

To the east of Santa Cruz along the Cuesta de San Felipe, the **Plaza de Santa María** is another of Baeza's glorious squares, with a few welcome and shady trees, fronted by a nucleus of fine Renaissance buildings. The rather squat sixteenth-century **Catedral de Santa María** (daily 10.30am–1pm & 4.15–6pm) dominates the square and inside has a fine nave by Andrés de Vandelvira which is, in many ways, a scaled-down version of his cathedral at Jaén. Like many of Baeza's and Úbeda's churches, the cathedral also has painted **rejas** by Maestro Bartolomé, a local craftsman who was responsible for some of the finest examples of this uniquely Spanish contribution to Renaissance art. His work enclosing the choir, with its depictions of a Virgin and child accompanied by angels and cherubs, is stunning. In the Gothic **cloister**, part of the old mosque – which the church replaced – has been uncovered, but the cathedral's real novelty is a huge silver *custodia* cunningly hidden behind a painting of Saint Peter which whirls aside for a 100ptas coin. To the east of the cathedral, and beyond Plaza de Arcediano, a narrow street leads to a *mirador* with a fine **view** over the olive groves in the valley of the Guadalquivir towards the distant Cazorla mountain range beyond.

Adjoining the cathedral on the north side is the old Renaissance **town hall** with Plateresque features, formerly the palace of the Cabrera family who have another mansion in the town. In the centre of the Plaza de Santa María is a sixteenth-century **fountain** erected by the same family, with pilasters and crude caryatids supporting the arms of Felipe II. Beyond this are the graffiti-covered walls of the sixteenth-century seminary of **San Felipe Neri** where students record their names and dates in bull's blood – a traditional way of celebrating graduation. The building now houses the International University of Andalucía.

The Ayuntamiento and more churches

West of the Paseo de la Constitución, in c/Benavides, the magnificent **Ayuntamiento** was originally the Palace of Justice and prison. Completed in 1559, its richly ornamented facade is exuberantly Plateresque with elegant balconies, coats of arms and, above, a phalanx of gargoyles decorating the cornice. Inside, the main hall upstairs (viewing Mon–Fri 9am–2pm) has a fine **coffered ceiling**. At the end of the street and facing the same edifice is the sweet (privately owned) little **house of Antonio Machado**, marked with a plaque, where the poet lived for most of his time in Baeza.

The nearby c/San Francisco passes the exterior of the **Hospital of the Purísima Concepción** with an elegant Renaissance facade. Adjoining it is the ruined convent of **San Francisco**, designed by Vandelvira and badly damaged during the War of Independence. Sections of both buildings have now been converted into a hotel, banqueting hall and restaurant (see p.382). At the end of this street and then right along c/San Andrés – lined with ancient *casas señoriales* – lies the early sixteenth-century church of **San Andrés** with a Plateresque facade and **sagrario** off the left aisle by Vandelvira.

Renaissance palaces

Heading north from the Plaza de España, the recently and pleasantly pedestrianised c/San Pablo has a number of interesting Renaissance palaces, many with impressive facades, dating from the sixteenth century. You'll pass the Gothic **Palacio Garcíez**, with a fine patio, the **Palacio Cerón** and the **Casa Acuña**. The best of all is the **Casa Cabrera**, with an elegant Plateresque facade incorporating a double window and frieze

---

WALKS AROUND BAEZA

There are some nice **wandering routes** in town: up through the Puerta de Jaén on the Plaza de los Leones and along the Paseo Murallas/Paseo de Don Antonio Machado takes you round the edge of Baeza and gives good views over the surrounding plains. **El Abuelo**, a house on the Paseo de Don Antonio Machado, is noteworthy for its garden sculpture and towering wrought-iron work. It's the first house past the modern bronze bust of the poet Antonio Machado – who was a frequent walker here – looking out over the olive groves. You can cut back to the Plaza Mayor via the network of narrow, stone-walled alleys – with the occasional arch – that lies behind the cathedral.

Going further afield, near El Abuelo, some tracks lead down to the plain. Take the right-hand fork and after about 45 minutes you'll come to the right of way of a former rail line, now used as a road for farm vehicles. This offers scope for easy walks across country.

---

over the entrance. In a street to the west of here, the fifteenth-century Gothic church of **San Pablo** has an image of **Christ** by Roldán, and in c/Biedma, behind the church, you'll find the **Casa de los Elorza**, which is also worth a look.

Eating, drinking and nightlife

For **tapas** and **raciones** you're best sticking in and around Paseo de la Constitución and the adjacent Plaza de España. The atmospheric *Bar Cafetería Mercantil* overlooking the Plaza de España is the town's most popular haunt, well over a century old and once patronized by Antonio Machado; the terrace is a great place for **breakfast** and eavesdropping on local gossip – in winter there's a dining room upstairs. Nearby, *Casa Lucas*, Plaza de España 13, is a good place for *tapas* and *platos combinados*. You'll find low-priced *tapas*, *raciones* and *platos combinados*, too, at *Bar Puerta de Úbeda*, facing the Úbeda gate at the junction of c/Narvaez and c/Julio Burell.

For **restaurant** eating, *La Gondola*, Portales Carbonería 7, serve up local dishes on their portico terrace and has a lunchtime *menú del dia*. Opposite the *Ayuntamiento* in c/Benavides, *Restaurante Sali* has a *menú* for around 1600ptas and tables outside so you can feast your eyes on this beautiful building. On the same street at no. 3, *Casa Pedro* is a solid newcomer offering a varied *carta* and a *menú* for around 2000ptas. Nearby, on c/Concepción, the restaurant of the elegant *Hotel Baeza* (see "Accommodation") is popular with *baezanos* and offers a good-value *menú* incorporating local dishes such as *pipirrana* (*jamón* and vegetable salad). Slightly west of here on c/San Francisco, the expensive *Restaurante Andrés de Vandelvira* at no. 14 is installed in the restored ruin of Vandelvira's once-magnificent sixteenth-century convent, and is worth a look, even if you don't intend dining(*menú* for about 2000ptas). The patio has been fitted with a temporary roof to create a banqueting hall, and the restaurant lies beyond this – specialities here include *trucha escabechada* (pickled trout). Baeza's other celebrated restaurant is *Casa Juanito*, attached to the hotel of the same name (see "Accommodation"); the walls are covered with photos of Spain's great, good and glitterati who have dined here, but note that for lesser mortals the service can be brusque. You could probably eat just as well for half the price at the restaurant of the nearby *Hospedería Fuentenueva*, which has a good-value *menú* offering a variety of fish and meat dishes.

For picnickers, the *Palacio de Pollo*, c/San Pablo 33 (actually a passage on the left off it), serves good **take-away** roast chicken. Alternatively, all kinds of local provisions are on offer at *Alimentación Cantos*, c/San Pablo 10 just off Plaza de España; delicacies include local *jamón*, *ciervo* (cured venison), *jabalito* (wild boar) as well as Jaen's top olive oils. Teatime treats are to be had nearby at *Pastelería Martínez*, c/San

Pablo next to the Palacio Cabrera, a pleasant **café** serving pastries made on the premises.

Nightlife

There's occasional **flamenco** at the *Peña Flamenca*, Conde Romanones 6, just behind the Plaza de los Leones; ask the Turismo for details of imminent performances. Baeza's solitary **disco** is *Al-Bacara* with a pleasant terrace, 100m down the Jaén road out of town. En route you'll pass *Bar Harley 95*, an improbable US-influenced country music bar. Baeza's lively annual **feria** takes place during the second and third weeks in August and is a wonderfully rural affair with processions of *gigantones* (carnival giants), fireworks, and an enormous funfair on the edge of town.

Úbeda

Little is known of **ÚBEDA**'s previous incarnation as the Roman town of *Betula*, and it's only in the Moorish period that *Obdah*, as it became, grew into a prosperous and important centre endowed with walls and a castle. Following the Christian victory over the Moors at Navas de Tolosa in 1212, the Moors from Baeza moved into the city, feeling it provided a more secure refuge against the Christian forces. Despite this, Úbeda was taken a week later and, although an interlude of further freedom for the Muslim occupants was purchased from the Christian armies with massive donations, the town fell conclusively to Fernando El Santo in 1234. As happened in Baeza, numerous noble families were then established by the king and built their mansions in the town. These haughty "lions of Úbeda", as they styled themselves, were soon warring amongst each other, the Arandas fighting the Traperas, and the Molinas against the Cuevas. The fighting got so bad at one point that in 1503 Fernando and Isabel ordered the destruction of the town's walls and towers, to enable the unruly aristocrats to be kept in check. Twelve of these noble families are represented by the twelve lions on the town's coat of arms.

In common with Baeza, it was in the sixteenth century, as a producer of textiles traded across Europe, that Úbeda's fortunes reached their zenith and members of the same noble families came to hold prominent positions in the imperial Spanish court. This was the age of the houses of **Cobos** and **Molinos**, two families who, linked by marriage, dominated the town's affairs. They were also responsible for employing **Andrés de Vandelvira** as their principal architect, whose buildings are the glory of Úbeda today. This prosperity, however, was shortlived and the town declined in the seventeenth century as sharply as it had flourished in the sixteenth, which explains its architectural unity and lack of any significant Baroque edifices. Úbeda is a moderately prosperous provincial town today, its main source of income coming from the manufacture of farm machinery and sodium sulphates, as well as the more traditional olives and ceramics, and carpets and baskets made from esparto grass.

Arrival, information and accommodation

The main **bus station**, c/San José s/n, lies to the west of the centre beyond the Hospital de Santiago; there are currently 14 buses a day from Jaén (all stopping en route at Baeza). **Linares-Baeza** is the nearest **train station**, about 15km from Úbeda (see p.379; connecting buses for most trains, except Sun, or a taxi costing 2700ptas).

Úbeda's **Turismo** (Mon–Fri 9am–3pm, Sat 9am–2pm; ☎953 75 08 97) is located in the Palacio del Marqués del Contadero, c/Baja del Marqués s/n in the old quarter, an elegant Renaissance palace. They can provide a detailed map and, if you are visiting in the May–June period, a leaflet on Úbeda's annual International Festival of Music and Dance which attracts big names from the fields of flamenco, rock, opera, jazz, blues and ballet.

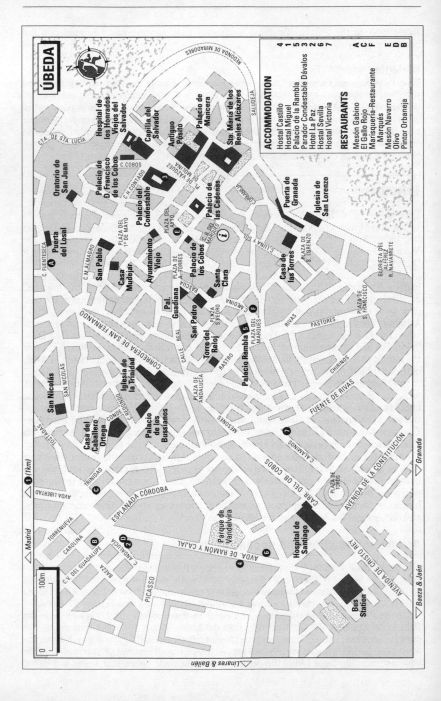

ÚBEDA

Madrid
Linares & Bailén
Baeza & Jaén
Granada

ACCOMMODATION
Hostal Castillo   4
Hostal Miguel   1
Palacio de la Rambla   5
Parador Condestable Dávalos 3
Hotel La Paz   2
Hostal Sevilla   6
Hostal Victoria   7

RESTAURANTS
Mesón Gabino   A
El Gallo Rojo   C
Marisquería-Restaurante F
 Marqués
Mesón Navarro   E
Olivo   D
Pintor Orbaneja   B

Hospital de
 los Honrados
 Viejos del
 Salvador

Capilla del
 Salvador

Antiguo
 Pósito

Palacio de
 Mancera

Sta. María de los
 Reales Alcázares

Oratorio de
 San Juan

Palacio de
 D. Francisco
 de los Cobos

Palacio del
 Condestable

Palacio de
 las Cadenas

Puerta de
 Granada

Iglesia de
 San Lorenzo

Puerta
 del Losal

San Pablo

Casa
 Mudéjar

Ayuntamiento
 Viejo

Palacio de
 los Cobos

Santa
 Clara

Casa de
 las Torres

San Nicolás

Iglesia de
 la Trinidad

Pal.
 Guadiana

San Pedro

Torre del
 Reloj

Palacio Rambla

Casa del
 Caballero
 Ortega

Palacio
 de los
 Bussianos

Parque de
 Vandelvira

Hospital de
 Santiago

Plaza de
 Toros

Bus
 Station

100m
0

Accommodation

You'll find plenty of budget **places to stay** within walking distance of the bus station, in the modern part of town. The *casco antiguo* (old quarter) has only two options, both of which are expensive.

Hostal Castillo, Avda. Ramón y Cajal 16 (☎953 75 04 30). Friendly, clean and comfortable *hostal*, with a good restaurant. Some rooms have bath. ③.

Hostal Miguel, Avda. Libertad 69 (☎953 75 20 49). Úbeda's cheapest *hostal* is some distance away in the north of town, offering a few en-suite rooms and an economical restaurant. ③.

Palacio de la Rambla, Plaza del Marqués 1 (☎953 75 01 96, fax 953 75 02 67). In the old quarter, this upmarket Renaissance palace is owned by the Marquesa de la Rambla who has decided to raise some extra cash by taking in lodgers. The lavish interior – with palatial rooms set around a Renaissance patio – contains valuable furnishings and art works, which is why you have to use an entryphone to get in. ⑦.

Parador Condestable Dávalos, Plaza de Vázquez de Molina 1 (☎953 75 03 45, fax 953 75 12 59). Housed in a fabulous sixteenth-century Renaissance mansion in the old quarter, on what is arguably the most beautiful square in Andalucía. Some of the well-appointed rooms overlook the square. Call in for a drink. ⑧.

Hotel La Paz, c/Andalucía 1 (☎953 75 21 40, fax 953 75 08 48). This decent mid-range hotel has air-conditioned balcony rooms with TV. ⑤.

Hostal Sevilla, Avda. Ramón y Cajal 9 (☎953 75 06 12). Good-value place with comfortable, ensuite and air-conditioned rooms. ③.

Hostal Victoria, c/Alaminos 5, just east of the bullring (☎953 75 29 52). Recently refurbished *hostal* offering pleasant, air-conditioned rooms with bath. ④.

The Town

Some 9km east of Baeza and built on the same escarpment overlooking the valley of the Guadalquivir, Úbeda looks less promising when you reach it. Don't be put off, though, for hidden away in the old quarter is one of the finest Renaissance architectural jewels in the whole of Spain, and perhaps even in Europe.

The Plaza de Vázquez de Molina

Follow the signs to the *Zona Monumental* and you'll eventually reach the **Plaza Vázquez de Molina**, a magnificent Renaissance square at the heart of the old town which immediately overshadows anything in Baeza.

Most of the buildings around this square were the late-sixteenth-century work of Andrés de Vandelvira, the architect of Baeza's cathedral and of numerous churches in both towns. At the western end he built the **Palacio de las Cadenas** (or "chains", which once decorated the facade), for the secretary of Felipe II, Juan Vázquez de Molina, whose family arms crown the doorway of a beautiful classical facade. The interior, these days occupied by the *Ayuntamiento*, features a superb double-tier arcaded patio. (To see this you'll need to go to the back of the building and the *Ayuntamiento* entrance where the security guard will allow you a peep.) Part of the same building also houses the **Museo de Alfarería** (daily 10.30am–2pm & 5–7pm; free) a ceramic museum dedicated to Úbeda's history in this field dating back to Moorish times (see p.387). Opposite, and between the lions marking the edge of the mansion's domain, lies the church of **Santa María de los Reales Alcázares**, built on the site of a former mosque. Behind the facade, topped by a double belfry, an elegant Gothic cloister encloses what was once the patio of the mosque. The church contains another fine **reja** by Maestro Bartolomé of Jaén depicting the tree of Jesse. At the side of the church, as you move east, is the entrance to the sixteenth-century **Cárcel del Obispo** or bishop's prison, which was formerly a convent and is now used as the court house. Opposite this is the **Palacio de Marqués de Mancera**, another stately Renaissance edifice with an elegant tower. Adjoining this building and fronting the plaza is the **Antiguo Pósito** or old granary, which later served as a prison and now houses the police station. Close to the two buildings above is a **statue honouring Vandelvira**, the architectural genius who made it all possible. Across the square again, the **Condestable Dávalos**, which Vandelvira had a hand in designing, is the former dwelling of the chaplain of the church of El Salvador. This elegant building now houses what must be the most impressive *parador* in Andalucía. Above the door two angels support the arms of the first chaplain, Déan (Dean) Fernando Ortega Salido, who was also responsible for its construction. A stunning **arcaded interior patio** now serves as the hotel's bar, and is perhaps best contemplated over a cool drink.

Chapel of El Salvador

At the eastern end of the Plaza Vázquez de Molina, Vandelvira erected the **Capilla del Salvador**, Úbeda's finest church and one of the masterpieces of Spanish Renaissance architecture. Although executed by Vandelvira, he was in fact working to a design created in 1536 by Diego de Siloé (architect of the Málaga and Granada cathedrals) but typically added his own flourishes. The church was originally the chapel of the mansion – which later burned down – of Francisco de Cobos y Molina, secretary of state to Carlos V and one of the most powerful men of his time. This remarkable building is almost unique in Spain for being built within a very short period (1540–1556) with hardly any later alterations. It also preserves many of its interior furnishings. The exterior **facade** has a carving of the Transfiguration of Christ flanked by statues of San Pedro and San Andrés with a wealth of Plateresque detail. Above the north door around the corner, Vandelvira has placed an image in the tympanum which is almost his trademark – Santiago the Moor slayer, used in Baeza and on the hospital of Santiago in the north of the town.

Entry to the church (daily 10am–2pm & 5–7.30pm; 350ptas) is via the doorway on the south side. The single naved interior with a beautiful cupola has a brilliantly animated **retablo** on the high altar representing the Transfiguration with a sensitively rendered image of Christ by Alonso de Berruguete who studied under Michelangelo; this is the only part of the altarpiece completely to survive damage during the Civil War. The **reja** fronting the altar is yet another fine work by Maestro Bartolomé de Jaén. In the **sacristy** (all Vandelvira's work) there's a photograph of a statue by Michelangelo given to Francisco de Cobos by the state of Venice, which alas was another Civil War casualty.

Behind El Salvador, and beyond the sixteenth-century **Hospital de los Honorados Viejos del Salvador** (another Vandelvira work), Úbeda comes to a sudden halt at a **mirador** with fine views over a sea of olive groves backed by the Sierra de Cazorla.

The Casa de las Torres and Palacio Vela de los Cobos

To the west of the Plaza Vázquez de Molina along *calles* Orbaneja and Luna y Sol lies the **Casa de las Torres** (daily 4–9pm), a sombre building with two enormous keeps, framing an ornate Plateresque facade. Now an art school, when it is open you can view the building's elegant double-tiered patio.

Just behind Plaza Vázquez de Molina, the Plaza del Ayuntamiento has **Palacio Vela de los Cobos**, another impressive building by Vandelvira dating from the middle of the sixteenth century, with an interesting corner balcony and an elegant facade topped off by a delightful arcaded gallery. This is one of the few palaces that can be visited but prior application must be made to the Turismo.

Oratorio de San Juan de la Cruz and the Church of San Pablo

To the north of Plaza Vázquez de Molina (easily reached along c/Francisco de los Cobos), the **Oratorio de San Juan de La Cruz** is where San Juan (Saint John of the

Cross), an accomplished poet and mystic, died of gangrene in 1591. The original monastery was damaged in the Civil War and little of it survives, although a small **museum** (Tues–Sun 11am–12.45pm & 5–6.30pm) preserves memorabilia from the saint's lifetime as well as his writing desk and the cell in which he died. At the end of c/San Juan de la Cruz facing the monastery, the **Plaza del Primero de Mayo** (formerly the Plaza del Mercado) is a charming acacia-lined square with a bandstand at its centre marking the site of the fires of the *autos-da-fé* which were once carried out here on the orders of the Inquisition. The Town Council presided over these grisly events from the superb arcaded sixteenth-century **ayuntamiento viejo** on the square's western side. Dominating its northern flank is the idiosyncratic **Iglesia de San Pablo** (daily 7–9pm), incorporating various Romanesque, Gothic and Renaissance additions and crowned by a Plateresque tower. It boasts a thirteenth-century balcony (a popular feature in Úbeda), and a superb **portal**. The interior has a fine **capilla** by Vandelvira (chapel of Camarero Vago) as well some intricate carving in the Capilla de la Mercedes and more superb *rejas*.

Around the Plaza del Primero de Mayo

Calle Horno Contado, which leaves Plaza del Primero de Mayo at the southeast corner, has two more palaces you might want to see: a short way down on the right, the **Casa de los Manueles** has a fine facade and, a little further down on the left, the fifteenth-century **Casa de los Salvajes** (savages) is named after the two figures clothed in animal skins supporting the arms of its founder, Francisco de Vago. In reality they are probably natives of the imperial colonies, from whose exploitation much of this conspicuous wealth was derived. Off the north side of the square in c/Cervantes the **Casa Mudéjar** at no. 6 is a fine fourteenth-century building whose elegant Mudéjar **patio** has pointed horseshoe arches. It houses a small **archeological museum** (Tues 3–8pm, Wed–Sat 9am–8pm, Sun 9am–3pm; free).

Calle Melchor Almagro, leaving the square on the north side of San Pablo, has another mansion, the wonderful Plateresque **Casa Montiel** and, further along, a sixteenth-century Carmelite convent.

The Potters' Quarter

Leaving the Plaza del Primero de Mayo by the c/Losal in its northeast corner leads to the **Puerta del Losal**, a magnificent thirteenth-century Mudéjar gate with a double-horseshoe arch which was formerly one of the main entrances to the old walled town. At the end of c/de la Merced, facing the arch and beyond the Plaza Olleros (Potters' Square) marked by an enormous pot on a plinth, c/Valencia is the old **potters' street** where the workshops of Úbeda's main ceramic craftsmen are located. Alfarería Tito, c/Valencia 22, is one of the friendliest, where the renowned ceramic artist Paco Tito has his workshop and museum. A diffident and engaging man, after showing you around the workshop Paco will usually will give you a demonstration on the potter's wheel. Nearby in the yard is the kiln, where the system used to fire the pots – many glazed and tinted with Úbeda's traditional deep green – is one inherited from the Moors; once the wood is burning, olive stones are introduced into the fire which builds up a more intense heat giving superior results in both colour and strength. There are only six of these traditional kilns left in the whole of Spain and three are in this street. The museum/gallery upstairs is devoted to Paco's more ambitious works including statuary, huge amphoras and a completely ceramic (and fully functioning) bathroom. Nearby are the workshops of other potters – including Juan and Antonio Almarza, and Góngora – all famous throughout Spain. Paco Tito's brother, Juan, also has a workshop on the Plaza del Ayuntamiento, near the Turismo.

Plaza San Pedro and Calle Real

Starting out from Plaza San Pedro (to the west of the Plaza del Ayuntamiento) there are a number of other important sights to see in the north of the town. On the Plaza San Pedro itself, the thirteenth-century **Convento de Santa Clara** contains a patio with a fine Gothic-Mudéjar multi-lobed portal. The convent also sells its home-made *dulces* – tasty cakes, biscuits and pastries. Another mansion, the **Palacio de la Rambla**, lies at the end of c/Medina off the west side of the square. The facade is another graceful work by Vandelvira, and the interior is now an upmarket hotel (see "Accommodation" p.385). Otherwise, across the square, the church of **San Pedro** with a noteworthy portal leads into c/Pascua where, on the junction with c/Real, stands the impressive tower of the **Palacio del Conde de Guadiana**, one of the most striking of all Úbeda's palaces. The tower is, in fact, a seventeenth-century work and the richly ornamented balconies are a delight.

Turning into **Calle Real** brings you to the heart of the old town and its former main shopping street. Many establishments are now deserting this for new premises in the modern town but a few of the more traditional traders are still here. Pedro Blanco at no. 47 is still making and selling goods made from traditional esparto grass, a versatile material used in the area since ancient times. Although much of the business is devoted to supplying the olive oil industry with collecting and extracting baskets, the firm also makes carpets, bags and all kinds of accessories. Heading north along here brings you eventually to the **Plaza de Andalucía**, an unremarkable square with a monument to General Saro, a Civil War general with Fascist affiliations. The general's bullet-hole riddled metal skull demonstrates how local disapproval of his ideas was expressed. Just off the plaza, the **Torre del Reloj** is a remnant of the thirteenth-century ramparts, crowned with a later sixteenth-century temple.

San Nicolás and the Hospital de Santiago

Just to the north of the Plaza de Andalucía at the start of c/Trinidad is the **Iglesia de la Trinidad** (daily 7.20–8.30pm), an eighteenth-century – and unusually for Úbeda – Baroque building. Further along c/Trinidad, it's back to the Renaissance with the **Palacio de los Bussianos**, attributed to Vandelvira. Taking the next right after this, c/Redondo, and then first left into c/Condesa you pass the **Casa de Caballerizo Ortega**, a sixteenth-century Plateresque mansion. Calle Condesa continues to the church of **San Nicolás** (daily 8.30–9.30am), which, although fourteenth-century, has a fine Renaissance west portal by Vandelvira. The sober interior is relieved by a profusely decorated but incredibly sinister, "sculpted" **chapel of Déan Ortega** by Vandelvira whose effect is only partially offset by a life-size, plastic choirboy. The **reja** (iron screen) fronting it by Álvarez de Molina is another fine example of the art.

Five minutes west of the Iglesia de la Trinidad along c/Cobos, and worth every bead of sweat getting there, is Vandelvira's huge **Hospital de Santiago**. Perhaps the scale put him off, for the exterior decoration is untypically restrained, and its austere dignity has led to the building being described as "Andalucía's Escorial". Commissioned by Bishop Cobos y Molina and begun in 1562, the flight of steps at the entrance is flanked by more "lions of Úbeda", beyond which Vandelvira has inserted his trademark – Santiago the Moor slayer – above the arch. The equally restrained interior has a patio with columns of Genoa marble and a staircase with stunning vaulting, in addition to a striking chapel – all further evidence of Vandelvira's mastery.

Eating, drinking and nightlife

Most reasonably priced **restaurants** are in the modern part of town, along the Avenida Ramón y Cajal. The restaurant of the *Hostal Castillo* at no. 16 is good value for basic fare, and further along, at no. 6, *Restaurante El Olivo* serves economical *platos combinados*. At the end of this street and close to the junction with the Avenida de la Libertad, *El Gallo Rojo*, c/Torrenueva 3, set back from the road, is one of the town's best restaurants, with local specialities, a medium-priced *menú* and outdoor tables in the evening. Just north from here along c/Virgen de Guadalupe, *Pintor Orbaneja* at no. 5 does *platos combinados* and excellent *tapas* and *raciones*. On the northern edge of the old quarter, in c/Fuente Seca near the Puerto del Losal, *Mesón Gabino* is a good place for *tapas* and *raciones*, in a converted old cellar.

In the old quarter, *Mesón Navarro*, Plaza del Ayuntamiento, behind the Palacio de las Cadenas, is one of only three restaurants, but most people stick to *tapas* here – especially as one comes free with every *fino*. Nearby, *Marisquería-Restaurante Marqués*, Plaza Marqués de la Rambla 2, has a mid-priced *menú*, *zarzuela de pescado* (fish in saffron broth) as a speciality, and a terrace on this square which allows you to contemplate the *Palacio de la Rambla*'s elegant exterior, even if you can't afford to stay there. Otherwise, if you want to dine in the old quarter and in style it has to be the expensive *Parador Condestable Dávalos*, although superbly prepared regional dishes are available on a great-value lunch *menú* (about 2500ptas), which includes wine and one of their delicious *postres*.

Nightlife is limited but does exist. There's a **disco**, *El Califa*, Avda. Cristo Rey s/n, near the bus station; **drinking bars** can be found north and west of c/San Pedro – try the atmospheric *Siglo XV* on the nearby c/Prior Blanca; and there's occasional **flamenco** at the *Peña Flamenca El Quejío*, Alfareros 5, in the northern suburbs – check their programme at the Turismo before setting out. Úbeda's big **fiesta** is the *Día de San Miguel* on September 29, when carnival giants, fireworks and a *flamenco* festival honour the town's patron saint.

Towards Cazorla

From Úbeda, the next destination for most travellers is the spectacular **Cazorla Natural Park**, a wilderness area filled with deep ravines, wooded valleys and which, in its mountains, gives birth to the mighty Río Guadalquivir. The park's towering rock cliffs are the preserve of the acrobatic ibex, whilst the valleys and gorges swarm with birdlife and are home to unique pre-Ice Age plants. From Úbeda there are **two routes into the park**. The more conventional one, taken by the bus, is via the small town of Cazorla, located on the park's southern edge and the main gateway to it. Another route, however, skirts the park's western flank and allows visits to a number of interesting sights – including the picturesque hill villages of **Sabiote**, with a castle and Renaissance mansions, and **Iznatoraf**, with its distinctive Moorish feel – before turning into the park close to the small town of Villanueva.

Into the Park via Sabiote, Villacarillo and Iznatoraf

Leaving Úbeda by the N322 brings you first to Torreperogil, 8km east and – unusually for Jaén – a centre of wine rather then olive production. A turning here leads to the pretty hill village of **SABIOTE**, 4km distant, a cobble-streeted hamlet still girdled by much of its medieval walls, with a pedigree dating back to Roman times. The church of **San Pedro Apostól** at its heart has a fine, if worn, Plateresque facade. At the foot of c/Castillo, which has a couple of striking Renaissance mansions, the ruined **castillo** dates back to Roman times, although the Moors made subsequent alterations. More modifications were added during the Renaissance period by Francisco Cobos of the noble house based at Úbeda, and it's thought that he drafted in his architect Andrés de Vandelvira to carry them out. The elegant **cloister** of the sixteenth-century Carmelite convent is also worth a look.

Villacarillo and Iznatoraf

VILLACARILLO, 20km further along the N322, is a fairly featureless town surrounded by olive groves but with an impressive Renaissance **Church of the Asunción** by
Vandelvira (Aug & Sept daily 10.30am–1.30pm), whose major interior features are some
finely painted domes. About 6km after this, a road on the left snakes dizzily upwards to
the spectacularly sited hill top village of **IZNATORAF**. At the end of the climb, the village is clustered around a pleasant Plaza Mayor with a Renaissance arch and the great
stone church of **Santo Cristo** dominating its eastern end. After you've wandered
around the narrow Moorish streets, many decorated with colourful geraniums in summer, and had a look over the ruins of its walls and castle, don't miss the spectacular
views over the valley of the Río Guadalimar towards the bordering province of Albacete
from a *mirador* perched above the cliff at the village's northern edge.

Not quite 2km beyond the turn-off for Iznatoraf and before Villanueva del Arzobispo,
a road leaves the N322 on the right for Tranco and the Cazorla Natural Park. Take note
of the signs warning you that there is **limited petrol to be had in the park** – a full
tank would be a wise precaution. Some 7km from the turn-off the road joins the densely wooded valley of the newly born Guadalquivir, a mere stream compared to the
mighty torrent which flows through Sevilla over 200km downstream. After a further
14km the road arrives at Tranco on the banks of the Embalse del Tranco (reservoir)
which is described in the main account of the park below.

Into the Park via Peal de Becerro and Cazorla

The bus route to Cazorla heads southeast from Úbeda, passing through olive country
and crossing the Guadalquivir before turning off the main road to the village of **PEAL
DE BECERRO**. The village spreads over a low hill beneath the crumbling towers of
its medieval fort. With your own transport, you can take a minor road out of the village
4km southeast to **Toya**, where there's an important Iberian underground tomb. Should
you want to **eat** or **stay**, the *Hostal-Restaurante Juanito* (☎953 73 07 16; ③), Carretera
de Quisada 20, has en-suite rooms and a decent restaurant.

Toya Iberian necropolis

In 1909 a large rectangular underground stone tomb was discovered by a farmer near
the hamlet of **Toya**, the former Iberian settlement of *Tugia*. Unfortunately, the family
cleared the tomb – used from the fifth to the second century BC – of a whole treasure
house of artefacts which they then sold. Some fine Greek vases were later recovered,
and testified to this remote tribe's sophistication and trading contacts with the
Mediterranean world. The stone-built **necropolis** is impressive and the largest of its
kind in Spain. The tomb is located a few kilometres outside Toya, but you'll need to visit
the *Ayuntamiento* there first to get the key; they will also provide directions.

Cazorla

The village of **CAZORLA**, 15km beyond Peal at an elevation of 900m, huddles towards
the top of a valley which runs from the rugged limestone cliffs of the Peña de los
Halcones. This rocky bluff, with its wheeling buzzards and occasional eagle, marks the
southwestern edge of a vast, protected area, the **Cazorla Natural Park**, containing the
sierras of Cazorla and Segura and the headwaters of the Río Guadalquivir.

Little about the attractive small town today would lead you to believe that Cazorla
had been around for over two thousand years, but not only were there significant
Iberian and Roman settlements here, this was also the see of one of the first bishoprics
of early Christian Spain. Under the Moors it was a strategic stronghold and one of

dozens of fortresses and watch towers guarding the Sierra. Taken after a bitter struggle in 1235, during the *reconquista*, the town then acted as an outpost for Christian troops. Nowadays, the two castles which dominate the village testify to its turbulent past; both were originally Moorish but later altered and restored by their Christian conquerors.

Arrival, information and accommodation

The main road climbs between concrete blocks of flats, disgorging you into the busy Plaza de la Constitución. Arriving **by car**, you should take a right here downhill to the **car park** as trying to find a place to park anywhere else can be a nightmare. Three **buses** a day (10am, 1.30pm & 6pm) go from Úbeda to Cazorla. The same buses leave Baeza half-an-hour earlier and there are also buses from Jaén and Granada. *Alsina Graells*, the main bus operator, has a ticket office next to the fountain on the Plaza de la Constitución, where the bus drops you.

In the Plaza de la Constitución, you'll also find a privately run **Turismo**, *Quercus* (Mon–Fri 9am–2pm, Sat & Sun 9am–2pm & 6–9pm; ☎953 72 01 15, fax 953 71 00 68). The staff are friendly but their information, especially that pertaining to independent ramblings, is none too reliable; the office exists to promote Land Rover excursions, photo safaris and the like. Their horse-riding treks into the park are popular – horses can be rented hourly, or by the day or half-day. The town's official **Turismo** (April–Sept Mon–Fri 10am–2pm; ☎953 71 01 02) on Paseo del Santo Cristo 17, 100m north of Plaza de la Constitución, can provide a useful town map; they also have a **roadside kiosk** on the way into town at c/Hilario Marco s/n near the bullring, which opens the same hours, and weekends as well. The official *Junta de Andalucía* **Natural Park Information Centre** (Mon–Wed & Fri–Sun 11am–2pm & 4–7pm; ☎953 72 01 25) is at c/Martínez Falero 11, off the Plaza de la Constitución. Each of the above can provide details on all aspects of the park and activities. Information on guided **horse treks** in the park is also available from Señor Marcos Ruíz (☎953 72 19 10).

Accommodation

Outside August, finding a **place to stay** is usually no problem, as most visitors are either en route to, or are leaving, the park. Cazorla's **campsite**, *Camping Cortijo* (☎953 72 12 80), is located beyond the Castillo de la Yedra, 1km from the centre; to get there, follow the Camino San Isicio from the Plaza de Santa María.

Albergue de la Juventud, Plaza Mauricio Martínez 6 (☎953 71 03 29). Cazorla's tidy youth hostel has some double rooms and a pool, and is reached by following c/Juan Domingo from Plaza de la Constitución. ①–②.

Hotel Andalucía, c/Martínez Falero 42 (☎953 72 12 68). Fairly central, near the Natural Park Information Office, and offering comfortable en-suite rooms. ④.

Hostal Betis, Plaza Corredera 19 (☎953 72 05 40). Friendly proprietor and good-value accommodation, with many rooms overlooking the square; some with shower. ②.

Hotel Ciudad de Cazorla, Plaza de la Corredera 8 (☎953 72 17 00, fax 953 71 04 20). The exterior of Cazorla's newest hotel caused a ruckus when it was unveiled (see below). Inside, functional rooms come with heating and air-conditioning and there's a pool. ⑦includes breakfast.

Mesón La Cueva de Juan Pedro, Plaza Santa María (☎953 72 12 25). Rustic restaurant (see "Eating, drinking and nightlife") which also offers rooms with bath (②) and excellent studio apartments with kitchen and TV (④) for longer stays.

Hotel Guadalquivir, c/Nueva 6 (☎ & fax 953 72 02 68). Charming and friendly small hotel offering en-suite air-conditioned rooms in a central location. ④.

Hotel de Montaña Riogazas, 7km south of Cazorla along the road to El Chorro and Nacimiento (source) del Río Guadalquivir (☎953 12 40 35, fax 953 71 00 68). Another attractive country option in the Sierra de Cazorla with rooms inside a *casa forestal* with pool and restaurant. ⑤.

Parador El Adelantado, 25km away in the park (☎953 72 70 75, fax 953 72 70 77). Somewhat featureless modern building made attractive by its wonderful setting and a swimming pool. ⑦.

Pensión Taxi, Travesía de San Antón 7 (☎953 72 05 25). Up the steps opposite the bus stop in Plaza de la Constitución, this is the town's least expensive place to stay, and has a good-value *comedor*. ②.

Hotel Sierra de Cazorla, 2km outside Cazorla, in the village of La Iruela (☎953 72 00 15, fax 953 72 00 17). Modern and good value luxury hotel set in scenic surroundings, with restaurant, bar and pool. ⑤.

Villa Turística de Cazorla, Ladera de San Isicio s/n (☎953 71 01 00, fax 953 71 01 52). Most attractive of the upmarket in-town places, with a series of self-contained chalets with kitchen plus communal pool and restaurant, all a five-minute walk from the Plaza de Santa María, along c/Fuente de la Peña. ⑦.

The Town and around

A few minutes' walk along the main c/Dr Muñoz leads to the **Plaza de la Corredera** (or *del Huevo*, "of the Egg", because of its shape). This is the traditional meeting place for the *señoritos*, the class of landowners and their descendants who, through influence and privilege, still lay claim to the most important jobs and mould local destiny. The seat of the administration, the *Ayuntamiento*, is here too – a fine Moorish-style palace off the far end of the plaza. The arrival of the new *Hotel Ciudad de Cazorla* on the square's east side has caused a controversy in the town because of its jarring architectural style.

Beyond Plaza de la Corredera, c/Gómez Calderón (passing the *Ayuntamiento*) is one of a labyrinth of narrow, twisting streets, which descend to Cazorla's liveliest square, the **Plaza de Santa María**. This takes its name from the sixteenth-century cathedral church of **Santa María**, designed by Andrés de Vandelvira which, although damaged by floods in the seventeenth century, was later torched by Napoleonic troops. Its impressive ruins, now preserved, and the fine open square with a Renaissance fountain form a natural amphitheatre for concerts and local events as well as being a popular meeting place. The square is dominated by **La Yedra**, the austere, reconstructed tower of the lower of two Moorish castles. It also houses the **Museo de Artes y Costumbres** (Mon–Sat 9am–2.30pm; free), a notable folklore museum. There's a fine **view** from just above the plaza of the castle perched on its rock.

Some 2km up the road heading into the park from Cazorla, the village of **LA IRUELA** has the other ruined Moorish **fortress** perched on a daunting but picturesque rock peak which must have been a wretched struggle for the Christian troops to subdue. It was later rebuilt by the Templars. There's also another ruined church here, Santo Domingo, attributed to Vandelvira. The village has a number of upmarket hotels (see "Accommodation").

Eating, drinking and nightlife

You'll find several bars serving up good *tapas* (see below) around the Plaza Santa María, where for more substantial **eating** there's also the rustic *Mesón La Cueva de Juan Pedro* which has been in the same family (the Muñoz) for over a century and offers authentic local food – *conejo* (rabbit) is recommended – cooked on a wood-fired range. On Plaza de la Corredera *Bar Las Vegas* does good sit-down *tapas* and *raciones* including tasty *revueltos*; between here and Plaza de la Constitución left off c/Muñoz – and down some steps – *Mesón Don Chema* is a good *platos combinados* possibility, with many local specialities. Continuing down the same steps to the market square leads to the rather swish *La Sarga*, Cazorla's top restaurant preparing regional dishes with flair;

lomos de venado con miel (venison with honey) is one of a number of game options prepared here, and there's also a *menú* for around 1700ptas. Almost next door, *Juan Carlos* is similar but slightly cheaper, serving up delicious trout and also has a *menú* for around 1200ptas.

It's worth mentioning a few of Cazorla's excellent **tapas bars** which provide the route for an entertaining bar crawl between the town's three squares. On Plaza de la Constitución you'll find *Bar Sola* and the bustling *Bar Rojas*, whilst Plaza Corredera has the popular *Bar La Montería* (try its famous *plato olimpico* for 800ptas which gets you a selection of all their *tapas*) and earthier *Bar Nino*, offering fresh *mariscos*. On the same square and near the *Ayuntamiento*, *Bar Rincón Serrano* has a pleasant terrace with oleander tree, and specializes in *jamón*. Plaza de Santa María has *Bar Julián* where the delicious *callos* (tripe) is only one of many dishes popular with locals who fill its lively terrace in summer. The daily **market** in Plaza del Mercado (below c/Dr Muñoz) is a good place to gather ingredients for picnics in the park.

Cazorla has a low key **nightlife** scene with one **disco**, *Layston's* on the Úbeda road on the edge of town; **music bars** include *Pub El Barco*, c/Escuelas 2 and *Liberty*, c/Hilario Marco 4, both a little way north of Plaza de la Constitución, or *Pub Yedra* on the plaza itself. On May 14 Cazorla honours its patron, San Isicio, with a vibrant **romería** preceded the night before by **La Hoguera** (bonfires) and in mid-September there's the **fiesta de Cristo del Consuelo**, with fairgrounds, fireworks and religious processions.

Day trips from Cazorla

Wild and relatively unspoiled country, with grand panoramas west over the olive plains of Jaén, begins at the edge of Cazorla, and if you choose to base yourself here, you can make a number of good **day trips**.

Just over an hour's walk away (head up behind the fountain on Plaza Santa María, then pick up the mule track which skirts the hill topped by the ruined upper castle of *Cinco Esquinas*) is the intriguing sixteenth-century **Monasterio de Monte Sion**. One of the brothers who worked on its reconstruction remains there (summer only), and will proudly show you round his isolated domain. Be prepared to step back into the Middle Ages – as exemplified by the scourges hanging over the beds in the cells used for retreat. Another hour's walk beyond the cloister to the south will bring you to the base of **Gilillo**, highest point in the southwest of the park, with a yawning gorge to the right.

You can follow the main path over a pass from here to a dilapidated *casa forestal* and then down to **Cañada de las Fuentes**, source of the Guadalquivir, within another two hours. Alternatively – and a more feasible day walk – you might bear left at the saddle on to a trail descending towards Cazorla town through the **canyon of Riogazas**. This path ends in a jumble of tractor tracks after an hour, after which you must pick your way down through the various water courses for another hour and a half. This five-hour walking day allows ample time for dawdling, but unfortunately many of the pools in the stream on the descent are either difficult to get to or on private property. A good **map** (see below) would be a useful aid to staying on the right track on all the above hikes.

A popular trip by car is to the **source of the Guadalquivir** river, in the mountains to the south of Cazorla. When you reach the source you'll find the infant river innocently bubbling from beneath a rock as it begins its 700-kilometre journey to the Atlantic. To get there, take the road out to La Iruela and then follow the signs for La Cañada de los Fuentes, around a 25-kilometre journey.

The Cazorla Natural Park

The **Cazorla Natural Park** – or Parque Natural de Cazorla, Segura y Las Villas to give its official name – is not as lofty as the Sierra Nevada (the highest peaks are 2000m), but outdoes it for beauty, slashed as it is by river gorges and largely covered in forest. The **best times to visit** are late spring and early autumn. The winters can be uncomfortably wet and cold, and roads are often closed due to snow. In summer, although walking is pleasant before noon, the climate tends to be hot and dry.

Judging from the number of *cabra hispanica* (Spanish mountain goat), deer, *jabalí* (wild pig), birds and butterflies that even the casual visitor is likely to spot, the Cazorla reserve is fulfilling its role handsomely. Ironically, though, much of the best wildlife viewing will be at the periphery, or even outside the park, since the wildlife is most successfully stalked on foot and walking opportunities within the park itself are somewhat limited.

Inside the park **public transport** is limited and currently there are just two daily buses running between Cazorla and Coto Ríos 39km into the park (see below). Distances between points are enormous, so to explore it well you'll need a car or be prepared for long hikes; otherwise day trips to the outskirts of the park are possible. However, a number of **campsites** – both *camping libre* (free camping) and official sites – dotted around the park make walking tours possible. The official **Natural Park Information Centre** at Cazorla (see p.391) will provide a complete list and map of campsites within the park.

There are in fact only three **signposted tracks**, all pitifully short. One leads from the Empalme de Valle to the Puente de las Herrerías via the Fuente del Oso (2km one-way), another of about 1700m curls round the Cerrada (Narrows) del Utrero near Vadillo-Castril village; the best-marked segment, through the lower Borosa gorge (see below), is also a mere 1700m long.

Before heading into the park, it is worth stopping at the private cooperative **Turismo**, *Quercus*, in Cazorla (see p.391). Both they and the Torre del Vinagre Centro de Interpretación (visitors' centre – see below) should have copies of the new 1:40,000 **map and guide packs** titled *Mapa y Guía Excursionista* (Editorial Alpina). They split the park in two parts: *Sierra de Cazorla* (covering the southern zone) and *Sierra de Segura* (the central and northern sectors). These are now the most accurate maps available on the park and detail *senderos* (footpaths), mountain bike routes, refuges, campsites and hotels. The accompanying booklet (in Spanish) has useful background information on the park's flora and fauna as well as villages, and includes half a dozen described walks.

Torre del Vinagre and Coto Ríos

Two daily (except Sun) **buses** link Cazorla town with **Coto Ríos** – where there's a campsite and accommodation – near the middle of the park via Torre del Vinagre: one at 6.45am, the other at 2.30pm; there's also a 6.30pm bus on Saturday. Return buses from Coto leave at 8am and 4.15pm. Taking the early departure allows you to do the classic **walk along the Río Borosa** as a day trek (but it would be wise to confirm all the above times in Cazorla to avoid being stranded). The road into the park passes Burunchel and climbs over the Puerto de las Palomas with spectacular views before descending into the valley of the Guadalquivir. A little further on there's a turning for the scenically sited **parador** (see p.392) which, with your own transport, would allow you to stop off for a drink; they also offer a good-value set *menú* for lunch and dinner which sometimes includes the excellent local river trout served *a la cazuleña* (with *jamón serrano* and almonds). The road into the park soon passes the hamlet of **ARROYO FRIO** where the tourist complex of *Los Enebros* (☎953 72 71 33, fax 953 72

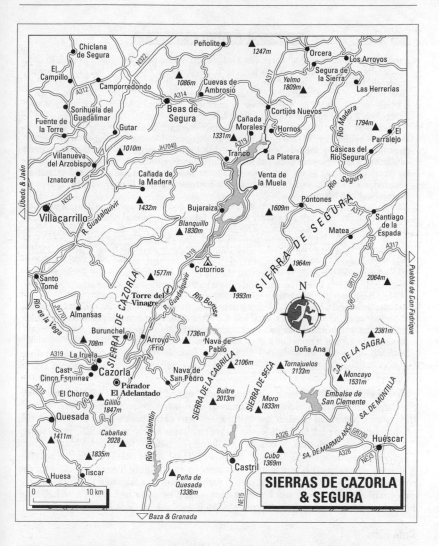

SIERRAS DE CAZORLA & SEGURA

71 34; ⑤) has a campsite, hotel and rents out freestanding wood cabins. A little further east the *Monte Piedra Aparthotel* (☎ & fax 953 71 31 45) has great views, a pool, restaurant and good value apartments (⑤) and rooms (④) which are available for day-lets outside the high summer peak, when you're looking at a one-week minimum.

The Río Borosa walk begins at **TORRE DEL VINAGRE**, 9km from Arroyo and 34km from Cazorla, where there is a visitors' centre, the **Centro de Interpretación Torre del Vinagre** (daily 11am–2pm & 5–8pm; ☎953 71 30 40). Packed to the gunwales with motoring tourists in high summer, this has informative exhibits on the park's ecology as well as a disturbing number of stuffed animals and mounted ibex and deer heads in a

THE RÍO BOROSA WALK

From the visitors' centre at Torre del Vinagre, cross the road and take the path to the side of the Jardín Botánico. When you reach an electricity pylon turn left on to a down-hill track. After passing a campsite and sportsfield on the left cross a footbridge over the river and turn right, aiming for a white building peeping above the trees. Soon you'll pass a small campsite (with an open-air bar in summer) and about a kilometre from the foot-bridge you'll come to a car park at a trout hatchery.

From here follow the track along the northwest (right) bank of the Borosa, swift and cold even in summer. Within a few minutes a signposted footpath diverges to the right; this also marks the beginning of the Cerrada de Elías **gorge**. Two or three wooden bridges now take the path back and forth across the river, which is increasingly confined by sheer rock walls. At the narrowest points the path is routed along planked catwalks secured to the limestone cliff. The walk from Torre del Vinagre to the end of the narrows takes about two hours.

Here the footpath rejoins the track; after another half-hour's walk you'll see a turbine and a long metal pipe bringing water from **two lakes** – one natural, one a small dam – up the mountain. The road crosses one last bridge over the Borosa and stops at the turbine house. When you get to the gate, beyond which there's a steeply rising gully, count on another full hour up to the lakes. Cross a footbridge and start the steep climb up a nar-row track over the rocks below the cliff (at one point the path passes close to the base of the palisade – beware falling stones). At the top of the path is a cavernous amphitheatre, with a waterfall in winter. The path ends about halfway up the cliff, where an artificial tun-nel has been bored through the rock; walk through it to get to the lake.

Allow three and a half hours' walking time from Torre del Vinagre for the whole route, slightly less going down. It's a very full day's excursion but you should have plenty of time to catch the afternoon bus back, which currently passes the visitors' centre at around 4.30pm, but it would be a good idea to confirm this before starting out. This walk is clearly detailed on the **Editorial Alpina map** (see above).

rather dismal hunting museum – including one bagged by General Franco (from which the nameplate has mysteriously disappeared) who was a frequent visitor here. Next to the centre a **botanical garden** has living specimens of the park's flora. The centre also offers tours of the park by Land Rover, as well as horse and mountain bike excursions.

For **accommmodation**, a couple of kilometres before Torre del Vinagre, *Hotel Noguera de la Sierpe* (☎953 71 30 21, fax 953 71 31 09; ⑥) is one of a string of relative-ly upmarket hotels – this one is used in winter by the hunting fraternity – close to the road and is housed in a converted *cortijo* with views over a lake and the Guadalquivir valley. There's also a pool and horse stables – each booking includes a free half-hour horse hire. More economical accommodation is available at Coto Ríos (see below).

Coto Ríos

Some 5km on from Torre del Vinagre, **COTO RÍOS** is a pleasant village with a river beach on the Guadalquivir. There's a **campsite** here, the shady *Camping Chopera de Coto-Ríos* (☎953 71 30 05), plus two others – *Fuente de Pascala* (☎953 72 12 28) and *Llanos de Arance* (on the opposite bank; ☎953 71 31 39) – just to the north. A couple of kilometres back towards Torre del Vinagre you'll find good-value **accommodation** at the *Hotel La Hortizuela* (☎ & fax 953 71 31 50; ④), a delightfully serene hideaway down a signed track on the left with garden pool and restaurant. Slightly closer to Coto Ríos, the cheaper *Hostal Mirasierra* (☎ & fax 953 71 30 44; ④), has suffered from "refur-bishment" but still serves excellent trout in its restaurant. Just north of Coto Ríos is the economical *Pensión Casa Maximo* (☎953 71 31 10; ②), which has simple rooms and a restaurant with a *menú*. One *hostal* worth avoiding on this stretch is *La Golondrina*, which is a clip joint; it's also worth noting that there are no further campsites or places to stay until Tranco.

Six kilometres beyond Coto Ríos, keeping to the river's west bank, at the southern end of the Embalse del Tranco reservoir, is the Parque Cinegético, a **wildlife park** which eventually hopes to include specimens of all the park's fauna, although at present you'll be lucky to see some rather bewildered deer from the viewing balcony. To reach the viewing areas, park at the entrance and walk a good kilometre through the woods (many Spaniards head back to their cars when they realize this) to get to the first viewing hide. The early morning and evening are the best times to see the animals not struck down by midday torpor.

Tranco and the north of the Park

The road continues along the west bank of the river, passing more picnic spots and *ventas* along the way, en route to **TRANCO**, 21km north, where the Guadalquivir is dammed to create a reservoir, the Embalse de Tranco. The island in the centre of the lake contains the ruined castle of **Bujaraiza**, all that remains of the village of the same name which disappeared beneath the waters when the dam was created. Apart from a few holiday villas, a lakeside bar, and **campsite** at *Montillana* (☎953 12 61 94), 4km north of the village, Tranco has little to detain you. A couple of places **to stay** beyond here are, after 3km down a turning on the right, the lakeside *Hotel Los Parrales* (☎953 12 61 70; ④) and, 4km further, *Hotel Losam* (☎953 49 50 88; ④) with a restaurant.

Hornos

From Tranco, the road circles around the northern end of the reservoir before turning into the valley of the Río Hornos from where you can glimpse the village of **HORNOS**, perched on a daunting rock pinnacle beneath the tower of its Moorish castle. When you reach it, the village has an isolated air with plenty of Moorish atmosphere. Its narrow, white-walled streets are perfect for meandering, and the castle is worth a look, although once you've got up close there isn't much to it apart from the tower. The pleasant Plaza Mayor is overlooked by a solid fifteenth-century church, the **Iglesia de la Asunción**, the interior of which is bare of features, but a *mirador* through a door at the back has wonderful **views** over the reservoir, flanked by the heights of the Sierra de Segura. The waters, which lapped the foot of the outcrop below, have receded dramatically in recent years – a symptom of Andalucía's chronic and continuing drought. A stretch of the village's ancient walls is still intact, complete with a horseshoe-arched Moorish gateway.

A pleasant **walk** can be made from Hornos along the reservoir's eastern banks to the hamlet of **La Platera** and the hill of Montero, with views along the reservoir, 4km beyond. The rock faces above the pine-covered slopes are home to a variety of plants, including yellow-flowered flax and throatwart. Common bird species in this area include azure-winged magpies, kestrels and sparrowhawks, but you will be extremely lucky to see the **Lammergeier** or bearded vulture in this, its only breeding habitat in Spain outside the Pyrenees; the species is now down to a mere handful of breeding pairs as the carrion these scavengers rely on has diminished. The vultures are known as *quebrantahuesos* (bone-breakers) in Spanish, after their habit of hoisting the leg bones of victims high into the air and dropping them on to a rock below (nearly always the same one) – once the leg is broken, the birds extract the marrow with their specially suited tongue.

Places to stay in Hornos include the *Hostal El Cruce* (☎953 49 50 35; ③), with en-suite rooms and decent **restaurant** whose gable mural is hard to miss as you enter the village. More rooms with bath are available at the *Hostal Mirador* (☎953 49 50 19; ③) towards the centre of the village, with fine balcony **views** over the Embalse de Tranco; the proprietor also rents out **apartments** for longer stays. The nearby grocer, Comestibles El Rapido, is getting into the tourist business by renting out **mountain bikes**.

Segura de la Sierra

Scenic though Hornos is, it is overshadowed in every sense by the Cazorla park's most spectacularly sited village, **SEGURA DE LA SIERRA**, 20km to the northeast. With a romantic castle crowning an almost conical 1100m-high hill top, beneath which the tiered village streets seem in danger of collapsing into the olive groves far below, it's a landmark for miles around.

Once you've managed to climb the road which snakes up to it and passed through the medieval gate, Segura is a warren of narrow streets left behind by its former Moorish occupants. But its history goes back much further, perhaps as far as the Phoenicians who, local historians claim, called it *Tavara*. Greeks, Carthaginians, Romans and Visigoths came in their wake, until the last of these were prised out of this mountain eyrie by the invading Moors who constructed the castle they called *Saqura*. When it fell to the Christian forces under Alfonso VIII during the thirteenth century *reconquista*, the fort became a vital strategic outpost on the frontiers of the kingdom of Granada, whose borders were framed by the Guadalquivir and Segura river valleys.

The **castle** – now somewhat over-restored after being torched by French troops during the War of Independence – can be visited from dawn to dusk. On your way up to it you can take in views over the country for miles around, including an amusingly primitive rectangular **bullring** below. Once inside the walls, you can climb the tower from which there are more magnificent **views**. The village's other major monument is the **Baños Arabes** (open daily as castle above), a splendid Moorish bath house off the central Plaza Mayor. Inside, three well-preserved chambers are illuminated by overhead light vents and contain elegant horseshoe arches. To reach the baths follow a descending street to the side of the parish church of Nuestra Señora Collado which brings you to a superb **Moorish double arch** in a preserved tower of the ancient walls. The baths are facing this. Near the church there's also a fine Renaissance **fountain** which bears the arms of Carlos V.

Practicalities

There are no bus services to Segura. The village's **tourist office** (daily 10am–2pm & 4–8pm; ☎953 48 02 80) lies to the right before the arch at the top of the street leading into the village.

You'll find pleasant en-suite **rooms** at *Casa Mesón Jorge Manríque* (☎953 48 03 80; ③), up a small street facing the church, with a good little **restaurant** attached. Another good place to eat is *El Mirador Messia de Leiva*, c/Postigo 2 in the upper village, with a *menú* for 1500ptas; they also rent out fully equipped **apartments** for stays of at least two days (☎953 48 21 01; ⑥). The nearest **campsite** is *Camping El Robledo* (☎953 12 61 56), 4km east of Cortijos Nuevos, passed on the road from Hornos. Segura's top notch **olive oil** (including an organic variety) is famed throughout Spain for which it has a coveted *Denominación de Origen* label (one of only four in the whole country); not always easy to get hold of, the *almacen* near the church should have a few bottles, or enquire at the tourist office. If you need to cool down, there's a pleasant **swimming pool** on the road leading to the castle.

Leaving the park

With your own transport, you can avoid backtracking to Cazorla and take an alternative and attractive route out of the park heading south from Hornos along the A317 through the **Sierra de Segura** to **Pontones** and **Santiago de Espada**, on the border with Granada. There are plenty more campsites signed along this route and Santiago has *hostales*. The same road continues to Puebla de Don Fadrique where you have a choice between the routes to Granada and Almería. The Granada route via Huéscar, following the A330, takes in the interesting towns of Baza (see p.463) and Guadix (see p.462) and provides an opportunity en route to see the remarkable prehistoric discoveries at Orce (p.489); otherwise the A317 heads across the deserted but picturesque wheatfields of Granada Province's eastern panhandle towards Vélez Blanco (see p.487) with its prehistoric caves, and eventually hits the coast near the Almerian resort of Mojácar (see p.483).

travel details

TRAINS

Córdoba to: Algeciras (2 daily; 4hr 30min); Granada (2 daily; 4hr); Jaén (1 daily; 1hr 30min); Madrid (13 daily; 4–6hr; AVE 14 daily; 1hr 45min); Málaga (2 daily; 3hr); Ronda (2 daily; 3hr); Sevilla (6 daily; 1–2hr; AVE 16 daily; 45min).

Jaén to: Córdoba (1 daily; 1hr 30min); Madrid (2 daily; 4hr 30min–6hr); Sevilla (1 daily; 2hr 50min).

BUSES

Baeza to: Granada (8 daily; 2hr 30min); Jaén (10 daily; 1hr); Úbeda (10 daily; 15min).

Córdoba to: Almería (1 daily; 5hr 15min); Algeciras (2 daily; 5hr 45min); Cádiz (1 daily; 4hr); Écija (5 daily; 1hr 15min); Granada (5 daily; 2–4hr 15min); Jaén (7 daily; 2hr); Madrid (6 daily; 4hr 30min); Málaga (7 daily; 3hr 30min); Sevilla (11 daily; 45min–2hr 30min).

Jaén to: Almería (2 daily; 4hr 30min); Baeza/Úbeda (14 daily; 1hr/1hr 30min); Cazorla (2 daily; 2hr); Córdoba (8 daily; 2hr); Granada (14 daily; 2hr); La Guardia (3 daily; 20min); Madrid (6 daily; 6hr); Málaga (4 daily; 4hr); Martos (13 daily; 30min); Sevilla (3 daily; 5hr).

Úbeda to: Baeza (12 daily; 15min); Córdoba (3 daily; 2hr 30min); Granada (8 daily all calling at Baeza; 2 direct, 6 via Jaén; 2–3hr). Jaén (14 daily; 1hr 30min); Sevilla (3 daily; 5hr).

CHAPTER FOUR

GRANADA AND ALMERÍA

T here is no more convincing proof of the diversity of Andalucía than its eastern provinces: **Granada**, dominated by the Spanish peninsula's highest mountains, the snowcapped Mulhacén and Veleta peaks of the Sierra Nevada; and **Almería**, a waterless and, in part, semi-desert landscape.

For most visitors, the city of **Granada** is not only the highlight of its province but one of the great destinations of Spain, as the home of Andalucía's most precious monument, the exquisite Moorish **Alhambra** palace and gardens. The city preserves, too, the old Moorish quarter of Albaicín and gypsy *barrio* of Sacromonte – places filled with the lingering atmosphere of this last outpost of Muslim Spain – as well as a host of Christian monuments, including the beautiful Capilla Real, with the tombs of Fernando and Isabel, *Los Reyes Católicos*, who finally wrested the kingdom from Moorish rule. Granada is also a good place to be during **Semana Santa** (the Easter week of floats and processions), and a place of literary pilgrimage through its associations with Spain's greatest modern poet, Federico García Lorca.

South from Granada rear the peaks of the **Sierra Nevada** and its lower slopes, **Las Alpujarras**, a series of wooded valleys sprinkled with whitewashed villages. This is wonderful country for walks and wildlife, with ancient cobbled paths connecting many of the villages, among them **Yegen**, one-time base of author Gerald Brenan, and **Trevélez**, Spain's highest village, famed for its snow-cured *jamón serrano*. The province makes the boast that you can ski in the Sierra Nevada's snowcapped peaks in the morning and swim on the coast in the afternoon. And so you

---

ACCOMMODATION PRICE SYMBOLS

Throughout this guide, accommodation is graded on a scale from ① to ⑨. These show the cost per night of the cheapest double room in each establishment in high season, though remember that many of the cheap places will have more expensive rooms with en-suite facilities. See p.39 for more details. Approximate Euro rates (operative from January 2002) are given for each category:

① Under 2000ptas/
   Under €12
② 2000–3000ptas/
   €12–18
③ 3000–4500ptas/
   €18–27

④ 4500–6000ptas/
   €27–37
⑤ 6000–8000ptas/
   €37–49
⑥ 8000–10,000ptas/
   €49–60

⑦ 10,000–15,000ptas/
   €60–90
⑧ 15,000–20,000ptas/
   €90–120
⑨ Over 20,000ptas/
   Over €120

could, if you really wanted to: the resorts of **Almuñecar**, **Salobreña** and **Castell de Ferro**, along the **Costa Tropical**, all have fine beaches and less development than the Costa del Sol.

There's less of interest west and east of Granada. To the west, **Alhama de Granada** is a delightful spa on a scenic backroad to Málaga. To the east, amid a landscape of dusty hills covered with clumps of esparto grass, lies **Guadix**, famous for its cave dwellings hacked out of the soft tufa rock, and the red stone Renaissance castle of **La Calahorra**. Beyond here, Granada's panhandle extends past the ancient country town of **Baza** to a lonely landscape of rolling *sierras* where small farms and isolated villages watch over fields of wheat, fruit orchards and pasture.

The **province of Almería** is a strange corner of Spain. Inland it has an almost lunar landscape of desert, sandstone cones and dried-up riverbeds; on the coast, with a few exceptions, it is relatively unspoilt, with development thwarted by sparse water supplies. As Spain's hottest province, the beach resorts are worth considering during what would be "off-season" elsewhere, since Almería's summers start well before Easter and last into November. In midsummer it's incredibly hot, frequently touching 35°C in the shade – while all year round there's an intense, almost luminous, sunlight.

The provincial capital and port, **Almería**, enjoyed a brief period of prosperity under the Moors and has been a bit of a backwater ever since – a workaday place with a life very much its own. It is overlooked by the largest castle the Moors built in Andalucía, the **Alcazaba**, below whose walls is a cave quarter, still populated by gypsies.

Almería's best **beaches and resorts**, the least developed of the Spanish Mediterranean, lie to the east of the capital. One of the nicest, the small resort of **San José**, lies inside the **Cabo de Gata Natural Park**, a wildlife and wetland area that is home to some interesting desert plants as well as a breeding ground for enormous flocks of **flamingos** in summer. Further north, **Las Negras**, **Agua Amarga** and **Carboneras** are all attractively low-key places fronting a crystal-clear blue sea where, if it's isolation you're after, there are strands within walking distance that scarcely see visitors. North again, things liven up at **Mojácar**, Almería's most fashionable resort, an ancient hill-top village that has spawned an enjoyable seafront quarter. To the west of Almería city a dismal sea of plastic tents – *invernaderos* – covers the **plain of Dalías** from the hills to the coast: a bonanza of drip-irrigation agriculture where exotic vegetables are force-grown to supply northern European markets all year round.

Inland, to the northeast of Almería, begins the most remarkable **desert landscape** in Europe: badlands of twisted gulches, dry river beds and eroded hills that have long attracted film producers. Much of *Lawrence of Arabia* was shot here, along with scores of spaghetti westerns, whose sets have been preserved at **Mini Hollywood**, near Tabernas: a fun visit, especially if you have kids to entertain. This weird scenery also shelters some interesting villages such as **Níjar**, a long-established ceramics centre, and the cliff-top **Sorbas**.

The province of Almería also maintains relics of a rich prehistoric past, when the rains were regular and the landscape verdant. In the northeast, near the village of **Vélez Rubio**, is the **Cueva de los Letreros**, whose prehistoric cave paintings are among the most important in Spain and where the famous *Indalo* symbol was found. Over to the west, in the Almerian reaches of Las Alpujarras, is the exceptional archeological site of **Los Millares** where nearly five thousand years ago people hunted, mined and farmed.

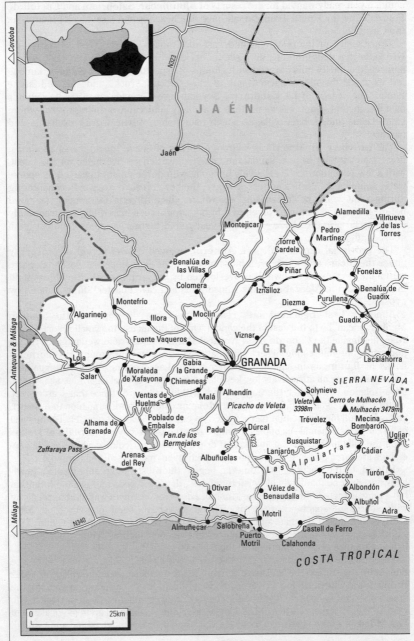

△ Cordoba

J A É N

Jaén

△ Antequera & Málaga

N323

Alamedilla

Villnueva
de las
Torres

Montejicar

Torre
Cardela

Pedro
Martínez

Benalúa de
las Villas

Piñar

Fonelas

Colomera

Iznalloz

Benalúa de
Guadix

Montefrío

Diezma

Purullena

Algarinejo

Illora

Moclin

Guadix

Fuente Vaqueros

Viznar

G R A N A D A

Lacaláhorra

Loja

Gabia
la Grande

GRANADA

Salar

Moraleda
de Xafayona

Chimeneas

SIERRA NEVADA

Ventas de
Huelma

Malá

Alhendín

Solynieve

Veleta
3398m

Cerro de Mulhacén

Picacho de Veleta

Mulhacén 3479m

Alhama de
Granada

Poblado de
Embalse

Padul

Dúrcal

Trévelez

Mecina
Bombarón

*Pan. de los
Bermejales*

N323

Busquistar

Ugíjar

Zaffaraya Pass

Albuñuelas

Lanjarón

L a s   A l p u j a r r a s

Cádiar

Arenas
del Rey

Torviscón

Turón

Otivar

Vélez de
Benaudalla

Albondón

△ Málaga

N340

Motril

Albuñol

Adra

Almuñecar

Salobreña

Castell de Ferro

Puerto
Motril

Calahonda

C O S T A   T R O P I C A L

0 _____ 25km

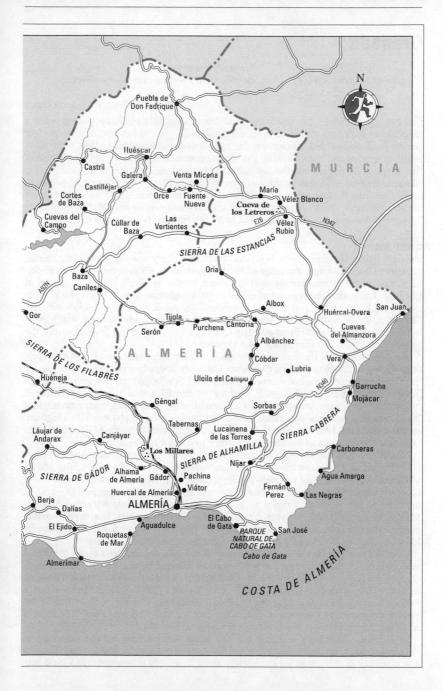

Granada

| Los dos ríos de Granada | Granada's twin rivers |
| bajan de la nieve al trigo ... | tumble down from the snow to the wheat ... |

Federico García Lorca

The city of **GRANADA** has one of the most dramatic locations in Spain, poised below a magnificent backdrop of the snowcapped peaks of the Sierra Nevada. It is the perfect setting for a near-perfect monument, the extraordinary **Alhambra palace** – the most exciting, sensual and romantic of all European monuments. It was the palace-fortress of the Nasrid Sultans, rulers of the last Spanish Muslim kingdom, and in its construction Moorish art reached a spectacular and serene climax. The building, however, seems to go further than this, revealing something of the whole brilliance and spirit of Moorish life and culture. It should on no account be missed – and neither should the city, with its network of Moorish streets, panoply of Christian monuments and gypsy quarter.

Some history

Before the arrival of the Moors, Granada's mark on history was slight. An early Iberian settlement here, *Elibyrge*, was adapted by the **Romans** as *Illiberis*, but although its fertility was prized, it was greatly overshadowed by the empire's provincial capital at Córdoba. Later, after the region had come under **Visigothic** control in the sixth century, the old Roman town, centred on the modern-day Albaicín, grew a **Jewish suburb**, *Garnatha,* on the south slope of the Alhambra hill. Popular tradition has it that friction between this Jewish settlement and the Christian town led to the Jews assisting the **Moors** to take the city shortly after the invasion of 711.

The Moors adapted the name to *Karnattah,* and for three centuries it was an important city under the control of the Cordoban Caliphate and, when this fell in 1031, under the Almoravid and Almohad Berber dynasties of Sevilla. When, however, Almohad power crumbled in the thirteenth century as the Christian *reconquista* gathered momentum, an astute Arab prince of the **Nasrid** tribe, which had been driven south from Zaragoza, saw his opportunity to create an independent state. The kingdom, established in the 1240s by **Ibn al-Ahmar** (aka Muhammad ibn Yusuf ibn Nasr), was to outlast the vanished *al-Andalus* by a further two and a half centuries.

Nasrid Granada was always a precarious state. Ibn al-Ahmar proved a just and capable ruler but all over Spain the Christian kingdoms were in the ascendant. The Moors of Granada survived only through paying tribute and allegiance to Fernando III of Castile – whom they were forced to assist in the conquest of Muslim Sevilla – and by the time of Ibn al-Ahmar's death in 1273 Granada was the only surviving Spanish Muslim kingdom. It had, however, consolidated its territory, which stretched from just north of the city down to a coastal strip between Tarifa and Almería, and, stimulated by Muslim refugees, developed a flourishing commerce, industry and culture.

Over the next two centuries, Granada maintained its autonomy by a series of shrewd manoeuvres, its rulers turning for protection, as it suited them, to the Christian kingdoms of Aragón and Castile and the Merinid sultans of Morocco. The city-state enjoyed its most confident and prosperous period under **Yusuf I** (1334–54) and **Muhammad V** (1354–91), the rulers responsible for much of the existing Alhambra palace. But by the mid-fifteenth century a pattern of coups and internal strife became established and a rapid succession of rulers did little to stem Christian inroads.

In 1479 the kingdoms of Aragón and Castile were united by the marriage of Fernando and Isabel and within ten years had conquered Ronda, Málaga and Almería. The city of Granada now stood completely alone, tragically preoccupied in a **civil war** between supporters of the sultan's two favourite wives. The *Reyes Católicos* made escalating and finally untenable demands upon it, and in 1490 war broke out. **Boabdil**, the last Moorish king, appealed in vain for help from his fellow Muslims in Morocco, Egypt and Ottoman Turkey, and in the following year Fernando and Isabel marched on Granada with an army said to total 150,000 troops. For seven months, through the winter of 1491, they laid siege to the city. On January 2, 1492, Boabdil formally surrendered its keys. The Christian Reconquest of Spain was complete.

There followed a century of repression for Granada, during which Jews and then Muslims were treated harshly and finally expelled by the Christian state and church, both of which grew rich on the confiscated property. The loss of Muslim and Jewish artesans and traders led to gradual economic decline, which was reversed only temporarily in the seventeenth century, the period when the city's Baroque monuments – La Cartuja monastery and San Juan de Dios hospital – were built. The city suffered heavily under **Napoleonic occupation**, when even the Alhambra was used as a barracks, causing much damage, and, although the nineteenth-century Romantic movement saw to it that the Alhambra suffered few more such violations, the sober *granadino* middle class have been accused repeatedly since of caring little for the rest of their city's artistic legacy. Over the last century and a half, they have covered over the River Darro – which now flows beneath the town centre – and demolished an untold number of historic buildings to build avenues through the centre of the city. Things have hardly changed and in recent years the Andalucian Parliament has had to block a preposterous plan by the city council to cover much of the Alhambra hill with a luxury housing estate – the bulldozers had actually begun digging.

Lorca described the *granadinos* as "the worst bourgeoisie in Spain", and they are regarded by many other Andalucians as conservative, arrogant and cool, like a colony somehow transplanted from northern Spain. A strong small-shopkeeper economy – which discouraged industrial development – and a society where military and clerics were dominant discouraged innovation and liberal ideas through the early part of the twentieth century. This introverted outlook perhaps contributed also to the events of the **Civil War**, one of the greatest stains on the city's name. In 1936, following Franco's coup, a fascist bloodbath was unleashed during which an estimated seven thousand of the city's liberals and Republicans were assassinated, among them poet and playwright **Federico García Lorca**. The poet deserved better from his native city, of which he had written, "The hours are longer and sweeter here than in any other Spanish town... Granada has any amount of good ideas but is incapable of acting on them. Only in such a town, with its inertia and tranquillity, can there exist those exquisite contemplators of water, temperatures and sunsets."

Orientation and arrival

Like many other towns and cities in Spain where the historical past and commercial present are locked in permanent conflict, the area of central Granada is often choked with more traffic than its streets are able to bear, and parking is a nightmare. If you do arrive by car, you're best off leaving it in a car park or garage for the duration of your stay (see below). Practically everything of interest in Granada, including the hills of **Alhambra** (to the east) and **Sacromonte** (to the north), is within easy walking distance of the centre. The only times you'll need a local bus or taxi are if you're arriving or leaving on public transport, since both the bus and train stations are some way out.

Gran Vía is the city's main street, cutting its way through the centre along a roughly north–south axis between the Jardines del Triunfo and **Plaza Isabel la Católica**. It forms a T-junction at its southern end with c/Reyes Católicos, which runs east to the **Plaza Nueva** and west to the **Puerta Real**, Granada's two main squares.

The city's **Turismo** is located in the Corral de Carbón on c/Mariana Pineda, just east of the cathedral (Mon–Sat 9am–7pm, Sun 10am–2pm; ☎958 22 10 22). There's also a good and less frenetic **Turismo municipal** at Plaza Mariana Pineda 10 (Mon–Fri

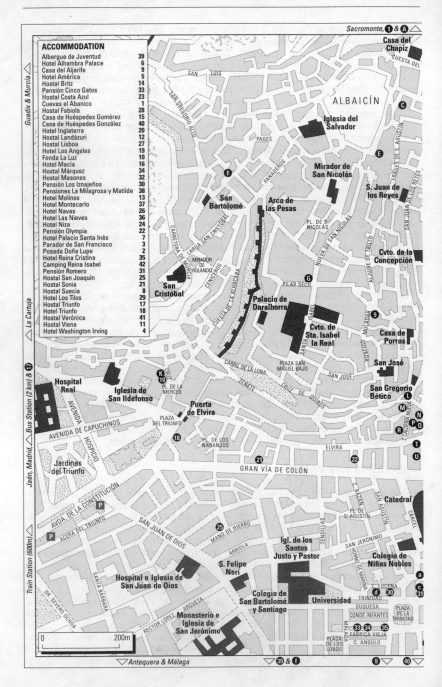

ACCOMMODATION

Albergue de Juventud	39
Hotel Alhambra Palace	6
Casa del Aljarife	9
Hotel América	5
Hostal Britz	14
Pensión Cinco Gatos	33
Hostal Costa Azul	23
Cuevas el Abanico	1
Hostal Fabiola	28
Casa de Huéspedes Gomérez	15
Casa de Huéspedes González	40
Hotel Inglaterra	20
Hostal Landázuri	12
Hostal Lisboa	27
Hotel Los Angeles	19
Fonda La Luz	10
Hotel Macía	16
Hostal Márquez	34
Hostal Mesones	32
Pensión Los Iznajeños	30
Pensiones La Milagrosa y Matilde	38
Hotel Molinos	13
Hotel Montecarlo	37
Hotel Navas	26
Hotel Las Nieves	36
Hotel Niza	24
Pensión Olympia	22
Hotel Palacio Santa Inés	7
Parador de San Francisco	3
Posada Doña Lupe	2
Hotel Reina Cristina	35
Camping Reina Isabel	42
Pensión Romero	31
Hostal San Joaquin	25
Hostal Sonia	21
Hostal Suecia	8
Hotel Los Tilos	29
Hostal Triunfo	17
Hotel Triunfo	18
Hostal Verónica	41
Hostal Viena	11
Hotel Washington Irving	4

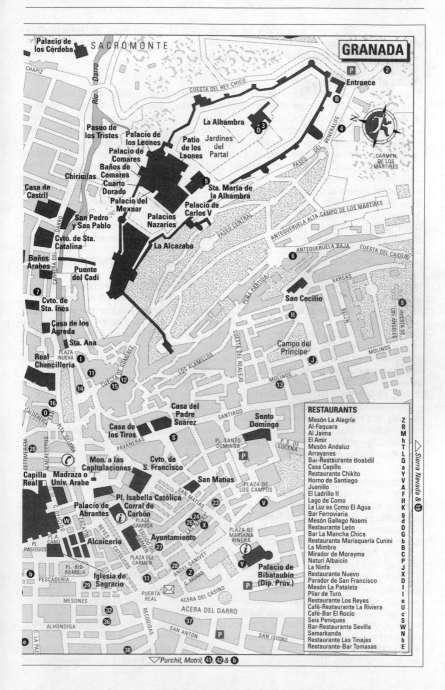

GRANADA

SACROMONTE

Palacio de los Córdoba

CHAPIZ

Río Darro

CUESTA DEL REY CHICO

P

Entrance

2

B

La Alhambra

D 3

4

Paseo de los Tristes

Palacio de los Leones

Patio de los Leones

Jardines del Partal

JARDINES DEL PENERALIFE

N

CARMEN DE LOS MARTIRES

Palacio de Comares

Baños de Comares

Chirimías

Cuarto Dorado

5

PASEO DEL

Casa de Castril

Palacio del Mexuar

Palacios Nazaríes

Sta. María de la Alhambra

Palacio de Carlos V

ANTEQUERUELA ALTA CAMPO DE LOS MARTIRES

San Pedro y San Pablo

Cvto. de Sta. Catalina

La Alcazaba

PASEO CENTRAL

Baños Árabes

7

Puente del Cadí

ANTEQUERUELA BAJA

CUESTA DEL CAIDERO

6

PEÑA PARTIDA

VARGAS

Cvto. de Sta. Inés

San Cecilio

BILEN

8

HUERTA DE LOS ANGELES

Casa de los Agreda

Sta. Ana

II

MOLINOS

Real Chancillería

PLAZA NUEVA

I

Campo del Príncipe

CUESTA DEL REALEJO

MOLINOS

LOS ALAMILLOS

11

12

15

CUESTA DE GOMEREZ

14

MOLINOC

13

16

O

CALDERERIA

Casa del Padre Suárez

SANTIAGO

Santo Domingo

P S DE LUCENA

CÉTTIMEHEM

PLTA SILLERIA

Casa de los Tiros

PAVANERAS

PL. SANTO DOMINGO

20

ALMIREROS

C

Mon. a las Capitulaciones

Cvto. de S. Francisco

San Matías

PLAZA DE LOS CAMPOS

Capilla Real

Madraza o Univ. Árabe

S

Palacio de Abrantes

Pl. Isabella Católica

Corral de Carbón

i

PLAZA GAMBOA

SAN MATIAS

23

PLAZA DE MARIANA PINEDA

V

Alcaicería

REYES CATÓLICOS

PLAZA DEL CARMEN

24 25

26

X

PL PASIEGOS

PLA CANO

OFICIOS

Ayuntamiento

27

i

Y

Palacio de Bibataubín (Dip. Prov.)

PL. BIB-RAMBLA

b

PESCADERIA

Iglesia de Sagrario

29

II

ÁNGEL GANIVET

28

C. MORAS

PUERTA REAL

P

MESONES

RECOGIDAS

ACERA DEL CASINO

ACERA DEL DARRO

32

36

SAN ANTÓN

37

SAN ISIDRO

ALHÓNDIGA

C LA PAZ

e

38

▽ Purchil, Motril, 41, 42 & h

△ Sierra Nevada & 19

RESTAURANTS

Mesón La Alegría	Z
Al-Faquara	R
Al Jaima	M
El Amir	h
Mesón Andaluz	T
Arrayanes	L
Bar-Restaurante Boabdil	Q
Casa Cepillo	a
Restaurante Chikito	y
Horno de Santiago	V
Juanillo	A
El Ladrillo II	F
Lago de Como	H
La Luz es Como El Agua	K
Bar Ferroviaria	g
Mesón Gallego Noemi	d
Restaurante León	O
Bar La Mancha Chica	G
Restaurante Marisquería Cunini	b
La Mimbre	B
Mirador de Morayma	C
Naturi Albaicín	P
La Ninfa	J
Restaurante Nuevo	X
Parador de San Francisco	D
Mesón La Palateta	f
Pilar de Turo	l
Restaurante Los Reyes	e
Café-Restaurante La Riviera	U
Café-Bar El Rocío	c
Seis Peniques	S
Bar-Restaurante Sevilla	W
Samarkanda	N
Restaurante Las Tinajas	h
Restaurante-Bar Tomasas	E

9.30am–7pm, Sat 10am–2pm; ☎958 22 66 88), east of Puerta Real. An **information office** (Mon–Fri 10am–2pm & 4.30–8pm) inside the *Ayuntamiento* on Plaza del Carmen is another source of city maps and transport information.

Points of arrival

The **train station** lies a kilometre or so out on the Avda. de Andaluces, off Avda. de la Constitución; to get in or out of town take bus #11 which runs a circular route: inbound on the Gran Vía de Colón and back out via the Puerta Real and Camino de Ronda; a convenient stop is by the cathedral on the Gran Vía (leaving, take the bus from across the road). Buses #3, #4, #6, and #9 also run between the station and Gran Vía.

The city's new **main bus station**, Carretera de Jaén s/n (☎958 18 50 10), is some way out of the centre in the northern suburbs, and now handles all services, except those to Viznar (see p.427) and the Sierra Nevada (see p.440). The bus station is next to the well-known Hipermercado Alcampo and is served by the #3 bus which leaves from outside and will drop you in the centre on Gran Vía Colón near the cathedral (a fifteen-minute journey). If you're heading for the Albergue de Juventud (youth hostel) you should take bus #11 from the Hipermercado. The return journey from the centre is on the same #3 bus (every fifteen minutes) which can be picked from a stop opposite the cathedral (ask for the "*estación de autobuses*").

Coming in **by car** with an out-of-town number plate, you may well be buttonholed by one of the **orejas** ("ears"), a bunch of friendly uniformed men on motor scooters (paid for by the hotels) who can provide city maps, hotel and parking information as well as guidance on how to reach your destination – often taking you there. It's a free service and there's no obligation to use any of their hotels. Underground **car parks** (*parking subterráneo*) are located at Puerta Real (down the right-hand side of the post office), La Caleta near the train station, and on c/San Agustín beneath the new municipal market off the west side of Gran Vía near the cathedral. Long-term free street parking places are often to be found along Carrera del Genil and the Paseo del Salón slightly southwest of the centre, but you should strip your car of any contents. If your vehicle disappears it's probably been hauled away from an illegal parking spot by the *Grúa* (tow-truck). Phone ☎958 20 94 61 and prepare to pay.

Domestic flights into Granada's **airport**, 17km to the west of the city on the A92 *autovia*, are served by seven daily buses (425ptas one-way) into town; six daily buses (four on Sat & Sun) also run out to the airport from a stop on the east side of Gran Vía opposite the cathedral. Check with the bus operator (Gonzalez S.L.; ☎958 13 13 09) for the latest timetable. A taxi will cost about 2500ptas.

Accommodation

Finding **a place to stay** in Granada usually isn't a problem, except at the very height of season and during *Semana Santa* (Easter week). However, if you want to be certain of finding somewhere to stay it would be wise to ring ahead. There are plenty of *pensiones* and *hostales*, a frequent turnaround of visitors, and prices are no higher than elsewhere in Andalucía. It is also worth remembering for winter or early spring visits that many of the cheaper accommodation options will not provide heating in their rooms.

Most visitors want to put up as close to the Alhambra's doorstep as they can – and there are a couple of pricey options (one very pricey) up inside the walls. Unless you book ahead, however, you'll have to content yourself with streets such as the Cuesta de Gomérez, which ascends towards the Alhambra from the Plaza Nueva; once one of the noisiest streets in town, it is now tranquil thanks to traffic restrictions and a new ring road carrying cars and buses to the Alhambra. Attractive options are also to be found in the streets between the picturesque Plaza de Bib-Rambla and Plaza de la Trinidad in the university area. Don't bother trying to find interesting budget accommodation in the Albaicín area – there are only two upmarket places to stay which are listed below. All places listed in category ④ and above have rooms with en suite bath or shower, and toilet.

If you plan a longer stay, check the notice boards in the university, especially the translation faculty at c/Puentezuelas 55.

Around Plaza Nueva and towards the Alhambra

Hostal Britz, Cuesta de Gomérez 1 (☎958 22 36 52). Small, very comfortable and well-placed *hostal* near the Plaza Nueva. Some rooms with bath. ③.

Casa de Huéspedes Gomérez, Cuesta de Gomérez 2–3º (☎958 22 63 98). Simple but convenient guesthouse; basic rooms with extra charges for showers. ②.

Hostal Landázuri, Cuesta de Gomérez 24 (☎958 22 14 06). Pleasant, good-value rooms, some en suite, plus its own restaurant, bar and a roof terrace with a view of the Alhambra. ③.

Hotel Macía, Plaza Nueva 4 (☎958 22 75 36, fax 958 22 75 35). Centrally located, offering comfortable, air-conditioned rooms with TV overlooking the square. ⑥.

Hostal Viena, c/Hospital de Sta. Ana 2, first left off Cuesta de Gomérez (☎958 22 18 59). Excellent, friendly, Austrian-run *hostal* in a quiet street, with a car park. Some rooms with bath. The owners run several places around here and if this is full should be able to fit you in at the nearby *Hostal Austria* or *Hostal Venecia* (same phone number). ③.

Cathedral area

Hostal Costa Azul, c/Rosario 5, close to Plaza María De Mariana (☎958 22 22 98). Decent, central, small *hostal* for rooms with bath. ③.

Hostal Fabiola, c/Ángel Gavinet 5–5º, close to the Puerta Real (☎958 22 35 72). Good-value for such a central location and not too noisy; all rooms with bath and many have sit-out balconies. ③.

Hotel Inglaterra, c/Cetti Meriem 4, just north of the cathedral (☎958 22 15 59, fax 958 22 71 00). Newish hotel with comfortable air-conditioned rooms in a stylishly modernized building in the old part of town. Car park. ⑦.

Pensión Los Iznajeños, c/Lucena 1 (☎958 27 82 55). Very friendly and good value family *pensión* with spotless rooms in a tiny street just off Plaza de la Trinidad. ②.

Hostal Lisboa, Plaza del Carmen 27 (☎958 22 14 13, fax 958 22 14 87). Modern, clean and comfortable *hostal* bang in the centre. Many rooms with bath. ④.

Hostal Mesones, c/Mesones 44, southwest of the cathedral (☎958 26 32 44). Simple but cosy, family-run place. ②.

Hotel Montecarlo, c/Acera del Darro 44, off the Puerta Real (☎958 25 79 00, fax 958 25 55 96). Comfortable, modern hotel with in-room TV & video and air conditioning. ⑥.

Hotel Navas, c/Las Navas 24 (☎958 22 59 59, fax 958 22 75 23). Elegant and central small hotel on a quiet street with air-conditioned rooms, which have a safe and satellite TV. ⑦.

Hotel Niza, c/Las Navas 16, off Plaza del Carmen (☎958 22 54 30, fax 958 22 54 27). Small, traditional one-star hotel in quiet pedestrianized street. ④.

Pensión Olympia, c/Álvaro de Bazán 6 – off Gran Vía opposite the Banco de Jerez building (☎958 27 82 38). Central, basic but clean *pensión* run by pleasant people. ②.

Hostal Sonia, Gran Vía de Colón 38 (☎958 20 61 46). Recently refurbished *hostal* offering rooms with bath, air-conditioning and TV. Garage. ④.

Hotel Los Tilos, Plaza de Bib-Rambla 4 (☎958 26 67 12, fax 958 26 68 01). Plain, two-star hotel on this charming square near the cathedral. Decent rooms with TV, but make sure to request one on the exterior. ⑤.

Hostal Verónica, c/Ángel 17, off c/Recogidas (☎958 25 81 45). Friendly *hostal* with pleasant rooms, most with bath. ③.

Plaza de la Trinidad and around the university

Pensión Cinco Gatos, c/Fábrica Vieja 4 (☎958 20 36 80). Homely *pensión* with clean, good-value rooms – some with bath – and an ebullient *dueña*. ③.

Casa de Huéspedes González, c/Buensuceso 52, between Plaza de la Trinidad and Plaza de Gracia west of the cathedral (☎958 26 03 51). Good-value basic rooms and welcoming proprietors. ②.

Hostal Márquez, c/Fábrica Vieja 8, off northwest side of Plaza de la Trinidad (☎958 27 50 13). Cheerful, simple *hostal* with lobby dominated by a snarling boar's head bagged by the *patrón*. Parking spaces. ③.

Pensiones La Milagrosa y Matilde, c/Puentezuelas 46, slightly southwest of Plaza de la Trinidad (☎958 26 34 29). Two serviceable *pensiones* under the same ownership; their cheaper rooms (which you need to ask for) are good value. Some rooms with bath. ③.

Hotel Reina Cristina, c/Tablas 4, close to Plaza de la Trinidad (☎958 25 32 11, fax 958 25 57 28). Modern and friendly hotel inside an older building where Lorca spent his last days before being seized by the fascists. Also with its own (good) restaurant and garage. ⑦.

Pensión Romero, c/Sillería 1, on corner of Plaza de la Trinidad (☎958 26 60 79). Charming family-run *pensión* with spotless if basic rooms, many with balconies overlooking this delightful square. ②.

Hostal San Joaquin, c/Mano de Hierro 14 – near the church of San Juan (☎958 28 28 79). A great, rambling old place with simple rooms and charming patios; probably the best deal in this area. ③.

Hotel Las Nieves, c/Alhóndiga 8 (☎958 26 53 11, fax 958 52 31 95). Comfortable and central mid-range hotel west of Plaza Bib-Rambla. ⑤.

Albaicín, Sacromonte and north of the centre

Casa del Aljarife, Plazeta de la Cruz Verde 2 (☎ & fax 958 22 24 25). Charming small upmarket *hostal* in a restored sixteenth-century house, near the heart of the Albaicín; beautiful en-suite rooms and patio, plus use of email and fax. ⑥.

Cuevas el Abanico, Verea de Enmedio near the Casa del Chapiz (☎ & fax 958 22 61 99). Fully equipped and stylishly renovated en-suite cave-dwellings – with kitchen – are available for a minimum stay of two nights. ⑤.

Fonda La Luz, c/Cruz de Arqueros 3 (☎958 20 13 68). Attractive rooms (one en-suite) on the western periphery of the Albaicín, run by English-speaking Belgians and decorated with old Belgian furniture. Also has a charming restaurant. ③.

Hotel Palacio Santa Iné, Cuesta de Santa Inés 9 (☎958 22 23 62, fax 958 22 24 65). Sumptuous eleven-room hotel – air-conditioned – in a beautiful, restored sixteenth-century Mudéjar mansion on the south side of the Albaicín with Alhambra views. The nearby *Carmen de Santa Inés*, Placeta de Porras 7 off c/San Juan de los Reyes (☎958 22 63 80, fax 958 22 44 04) is owned by the same proprietors and occupies an equally attractive restored Moorish *palacio*. ⑦.

Hostal Triunfo, Ancha de Capuchinos 5-1º slightly north of the Jardines del Triunfo (☎958 27 19 29). Basic but clean rooms not far from the train station. ②.

Hotel Triunfo, Plaza del Triunfo 19 (☎958 20 74 44, fax 958 20 76 73). Not to be confused with the above. Well-appointed upmarket hotel on the edge of the Albaicín with comfortable rooms and flanked by an imposing Moorish arch, the Puerta de Elvira. Garage. ⑧.

Inside and around the Alhambra

Hotel Alhambra Palace, Peña Partida 2–4 (☎958 22 14 68, fax 958 22 64 04). On the Alhambra hill and a 5-minute walk from the palace entrance, this opulent *Belle Époque* hotel in neo-Moorish style offers every service you could wish for the price, except a pool. The bar's terrace (open to the public) has dramatic views over the city. Car park. ⑨.

Hotel América, Real de la Alhambra 53 (☎958 22 74 71, fax 958 22 74 70). Charming, small hotel in the Alhambra grounds, bang opposite the *parador*, so you can get an early march on the queues and take a siesta midday. You pay for the location – and prices have risen steeply here – rather than creature comforts, and for a one-star hotel it's now doubtful whether it's worth it. ⑦.

Hotel Los Angeles, Cuesta Escoriaza 17 (☎958 22 14 23, fax 958 22 21 25). Pleasant upmarket hotel on a leafy, quiet avenue in walking distance of the Alhambra. All rooms come with balcony, and there's a garden pool and car park. ⑦.

Hotel Molinos, c/Molinos 12 (☎ & fax 958 22 73 67). Little over four metres wide, this place is listed in the *Guinness Book of Records* as the narrowest hotel in the world. Pleasant air-conditioned en-suite balcony rooms, and a friendly owner. ⑥.

Parador de San Francisco, Real de la Alhambra (☎958 22 14 40, fax 958 22 22 64). Without doubt the best hotel in Granada – a converted monastery in the Alhambra grounds. Alas, this top-of-the-range *parador* is also the most expensive in the city; rooms to go for are those in the 200s, with views of the Alhambra and Generalife. Booking is advised at least three months ahead in summer or over Easter. Call in for a drink at the terrace bar. Car park. ⑨.

Posada Doña Lupe, Alhambra/Avda. Generalife s/n (☎958 22 14 73, fax 958 22 14 74). Rambling place on the Alhambra hill with a rigid student hostel atmosphere; there are numerous permutations of prices, some exceptionally cheap. Has its own *cafetería* and small swimming pool. All rooms with bath. Easily reached by the *Alhambrabus* from Plaza Nueva. ③.

Hostal Suecia, Huerta de los Ángeles 8, a cul-de-sac off c/de Molinos (☎958 22 50 44, fax 958 22 77 81). Charming, good-value small *hostal* – with some rooms en suite – in a quiet, leafy area below the Alhambra with garden terrace to eat breakfast. Easy parking. ④.

Hotel Washington Irving, Paseo del Generalife 2, in the woods just below the Alhambra (☎958 22 75 50, fax 958 22 75 59). Described in the nineteenth century as "the most comfortable hotel in Spain", this offers faded grandeur today, and is one of the city's institutions, with loads of historical associations. ⑦.

Youth hostel

Albergue de Juventud, c/Ramón y Cajal 2, off the Camino de Ronda (☎958 27 26 38). If you arrive late, this is handy for the train station (from the train station, turn left on to Avda. de la Constitución, left again on to Camino de Ronda – it's the large white building by the stadium); from the bus station take bus #3 to the cathedral and then bus #11, which will drop you outside. Recently renovated with lots of facilities, all rooms are en-suite doubles, the staff are friendly but the food is institutional. There is also an excellent new hostel at Viznar, in the hills above the city (see p.427). ①.

Campsites

Camping Sierra Nevada, Avda. de Madrid 107, northwest of the centre and 200m south of the bus station (☎958 15 00 62; March–Oct only). Easiest reached from the centre on bus #3, this is the most convenient city site, and – with a pleasant pool – probably the best too.

Camping Reina Isabel, 4km along the Zubia road to the southwest of the city (☎958 59 00 41). With a pool, less noisy and with more shade than the above, this makes a pleasant rural alternative and – with your own transport – the city is within easy reach.

The Alhambra and Generalife

The Sabika hill sits like a garland on Granada's brow,
In which the stars would be entwined
And the Alhambra (Allah preserve it)
Is the ruby set above that garland.

Ibn Zamrak, vizier to Muhammad V (1362–91)

There are three distinct groups of buildings on the Alhambra hill (known as Sabika to the Moors): the **Casa Real** (Royal Palace), the palace gardens of the **Generalife**, and the **Alcazaba**. This last, the fortress of the eleventh-century Ziridian rulers, was all that existed when the Nasrids made Granada their capital, but from its reddish walls the hill-top had already taken its name: *Al Qal'a al-Hamra* in Arabic means literally "the red fort".

The first Nasrid king, Ibn al-Ahmar, rebuilt the Alcazaba and added to it the huge circuit of walls and towers which forms your first view of the castle. Within the walls he began a palace, which was supplied with running water by diverting the Río Darro nearly 8km to the foot of the hill; water is an integral part of the Alhambra and this engineering feat was Ibn al-Ahmar's greatest contribution. The Casa Real was essentially the product of his fourteenth-century successors, particularly **Muhammad V**, who built and decorated many of its rooms in celebration of his accession to the throne (in 1354) and conquest of Algeciras (in 1369).

TICKETS AND ADMISSION TO THE ALHAMBRA

The overwhelming number of visitors to the Alhambra has made it imperative to turn up as early in the day as possible during high season to be sure of getting in. To protect the monument only 8800 daily admissions are allowed, 75 per cent of which are sold through the new Banco de Bilbao Vizcaya arrangement (see below). The remaining **tickets to visit the complex** (March–Oct daily 8.30am–8pm; Nov–Feb daily 8.30am–6pm; the ticket office opens at 8am; 1000ptas, EU senior citizens 600ptas, under 8s and disabled free) can be purchased at the entrance but be prepared for lengthy queues in high season; tickets may also be purchased on the day and during business hours from the main Granada office of the Banco Bilbao Vizcaya (BBV), Plaza Isabel la Católica 1, in the centre.

One way to **avoid the queues** is to use a new reservation system also operated by the BBV which enables you to **book your tickets in advance** from abroad or anywhere in Spain (ring ☎902 22 44 60) a minimum of one day, or maximum of one year, ahead. You can usually choose your time slot for the Palacios Nazaríes (see below), but at peak periods a time will be allocated to you. You are required to pay for the tickets with a **credit card** (Visa or Mastercard only) and a commission of 125ptas is levied for each ticket. The same service is also available on the **internet** at *decompras.bbv.es/*. Once your booking is confirmed you are given a code number which allows you to collect your tickets from any of the 2800 BBV branches in Spain (at least one day before the visit takes place) or the Alhambra ticket office (at least two hours before your allotted visit time). To check any changes to opening times, admission charges or booking procedures visit the **Alhambra's Web site** (*www.alhambra-patronato.es*) where the latest information is posted.

Tickets have **sections** for each part of the complex – Alcazaba, Palacios Nazaríes (Royal Palace), Generalife – which must be used on the same day. Note that you won't be permitted to enter the complex (even with pre-booked tickets) less than an hour before closing time. To alleviate the overcrowding of recent years, tickets are stamped with a **half-hour time slot** during which you **must** enter the Palacios Nazaríes. You will not be allowed to enter before or after this time, but once inside you can stay as long as you like. When you've got your ticket, any waiting time can be spent in the Alcazaba or at one of the cafés. The Alhambra is also open for floodlit **night visits** (March–Oct Tues–Sat 10–11.30pm, ticket office open 9.45–10.15pm only; Nov–Feb Fri & Sat 8–9.30pm, ticket office open 7.45–8.15pm only; 1000ptas), limited to the Palacios Nazaríes.

The **new entrance** to the Alhambra brings you into the complex at the eastern end, near to the Generalife gardens. However, as you will have a time slot for entering the Royal Palace (usually up to an hour ahead) it makes sense chronologically and practically to start your visit with the Alcazaba at the Alhambra's opposite, or western, end. To get there from the entrance walk up the short avenue lined with cypresses to a three-way fork, taking the signed path to the Alhambra. Cross the bridge over the "moat" following signs to the Alcazaba and Palacios Nazaríes. You will eventually pass the gates of the *Parador de San Francisco* (right) and the *Hotel América* to enter the Calle Real. Continue alongside the Palace of Carlos V to pass through the **Puerto del Vino** where our account begins (see page opposite).

After their conquest of the city, **Fernando and Isabel** lived for a while in the Alhambra. They restored some rooms and converted the mosque but left the palace structure unaltered. As at Córdoba and Sevilla, it was their grandson **Emperor Carlos V** who wreaked the most insensitive destruction. He demolished a whole wing of rooms in order to build yet another grandiose Renaissance palace. This and the Alhambra itself were simply ignored by his successors and by the eighteenth century the Royal Palace was in use as a prison. In 1812 it was taken and occupied by **Napoleon's forces**, who looted and damaged whole sections of the palace, and on their retreat from the city tried to blow up the entire complex. Their attempt was thwarted only by the action of a crippled soldier who remained behind and removed the fuses.

Two decades later the Alhambra's "rediscovery" began, given impetus by the American writer **Washington Irving**, who set up his study in the empty palace rooms and began to write his marvellously romantic *Tales of the Alhambra* (on sale all over Granada – and good reading amid the gardens and courts). Shortly after its publication the Spaniards made the Alhambra a **national monument** and set aside funds for its restoration. This continues to the present day and is now a highly sophisticated project, scientifically removing the accretions of later ages in order to expose and restore meticulously the Moorish creations.

Approaches to the Alhambra

The standard **approach** to the Alhambra is along the Cuesta de Gomérez, a narrow, semi-pedestrianized road which climbs uphill from Plaza Nueva. Aside from taxis the only vehicle allowed to use this road in daytime is the **Alhambrabus**, a dedicated minibus service linking the Plaza Nueva with the Alhambra palace. Buses run every ten minutes between 7am and 10pm and tickets are 120ptas. This service also has a continuation into the Albaicín and Sacromonte from the same terminus. To approach the Alhambra **by car** you'll need to head south from the Puerta Real along the Paseo del Salón and the Paseo de la Bomba; the route is well signed and will eventually bring you to the new **car park** on the Alhambra's eastern edge. The entrance lies at the western end of the car parking area.

Should you decide to **walk** up the hill (a pleasant twenty-minute stroll from Plaza Nueva), after a few hundred metres you reach the **Puerta de las Granadas**, a massive Renaissance gateway erected by Carlos V and topped by three open pomegranates which became the city's symbol (*granada* is the fruit's Spanish name). Here two paths diverge to either side of the road: the one on the right climbs up towards a group of fortified towers, the **Torres Bermejas**, parts of which may date from as early as the eighth century (see p.420 for other sights on this route). Take the left-hand path through the woods of closely planted elms, past a huge terrace-fountain (again courtesy of Carlos V), and you reach the main gateway of the Alhambra.

This gate is the **Puerta de la Justicia**, a magnificent tower which forced three changes of direction, making intruders hopelessly vulnerable. It was built by Yusuf I in 1348 and preserves above its inner arch the Koranic symbol of a key (for Allah, the opener of the gates of Paradise) and, over the outer arch, an outstretched hand whose five fingers represent the five Islamic precepts: prayer, fasting, alms-giving, pilgrimage to Mecca and the oneness of God. A Moorish legend stated that the gate would never be breached by the Christians until the hand reached down to grasp the key.

Within the citadel stood a complete "government city" of mansions, smaller houses, baths, schools, mosques, barracks and gardens. Of this only the **Alcazaba fortress** and the **Palacios Nazaríes** (Royal Palace) remain; they face each other across a broad terrace constructed in the sixteenth century over a dividing gully, flanked by the majestic though incongruous **Palace of Carlos V**.

Within the walls of the citadel, too, are a handful of overpriced **restaurants** and the beautiful **Parador de San Francisco**, whose terrace-bar (and restaurant) are open to everyone. There are a handful of **drinks stalls**, too, including one, very welcome, in the Plaza de los Aljibes just beyond the Puerta del Vino, and another in the Portal gardens (towards the Carlos V Palace after you leave the Casa Real).

Leaving the Alhambra, a lovely route down to the city is the **Cuesta de los Chinos**, which winds past the walls, just below the entrance to the Generalife, towards the Río Darro and the old Arab quarter of the Albaicín.

The Alcazaba

Having made your way from the entrance (see box opposite), go through the **Puerta del Vino** – named from its use in the sixteenth century as a wine cellar – and across

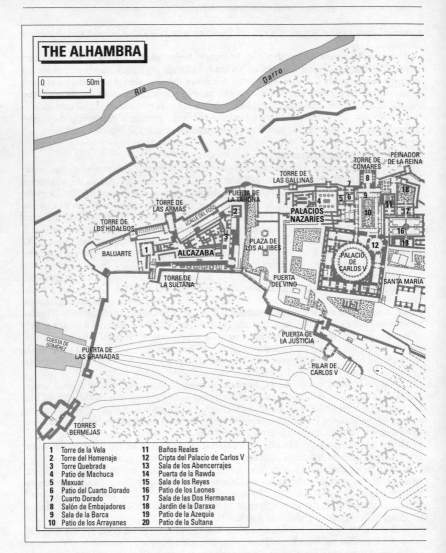

THE ALHAMBRA

0 — 50m

1 Torre de la Vela
2 Torre del Homenaje
3 Torre Quebrada
4 Patio de Machuca
5 Mexuar
6 Patio del Cuarto Dorado
7 Cuarto Dorado
8 Salón de Embajadores
9 Sala de la Barca
10 Patio de los Arrayanes

11 Baños Reales
12 Cripta del Palacio de Carlos V
13 Sala de los Abencerrajes
14 Puerta de la Rawda
15 Sala de los Reyes
16 Patio de los Leones
17 Sala de las Dos Hermanas
18 Jardín de la Daraxa
19 Patio de la Azequia
20 Patio de la Sultana

the Plaza de los Aljibes you are confronted by the walls of the **Alcazaba**, the earliest, though most ruined, part of the fortress. Quite apart from filling in time before your ticket admits you to the Palacios Nazaríes, this is an interesting part of the complex and one where you can get a grip on the whole site.

Once inside, thread your way to the left, through remnants of the barracks, to take a look at the **Jardín de los Ardaves**, a delightful seventeenth-century garden laid out along the fort's southern parapets with creepers, fountains and sweet-scented bushes. There is access from here to the Alcazaba's summit, the **Torre de la Vela**, named after

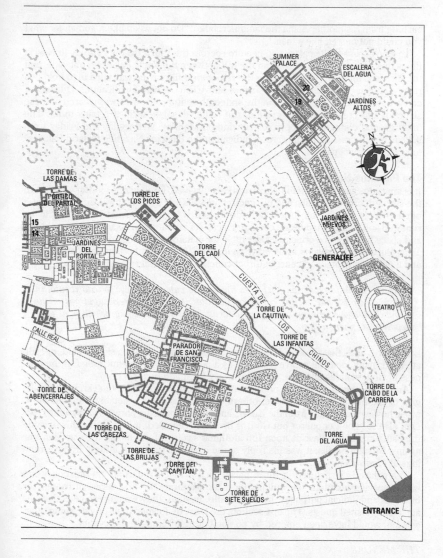

a huge bell on its turret which until recent years was rung to mark the irrigation hours for workers on the *Vega*, Granada's vast and fertile plain. The views from here are spectacular: west over the plunging ravine of the Darro with the city and the *Vega* beyond, and north towards the Albaicín and Sacromonte hills, with the Alhambra itself behind and the snowcapped peaks of the Sierra Nevada forming a backdrop. It was on this same parapet at 3pm on January 2, 1492, that the Cross was first displayed above the city, alongside the royal standards of Aragón and Castile and the banner of Saint James. Boabdil, leaving Granada for exile in the Alpujarras, turned and wept at the sight, earning from his mother Aisha the famous rebuke: "Do not weep like a woman for what you could not defend like a man."

To gain access to the palace you need to recross the **Plaza de los Aljibes**. In Nasrid times this area was a ravine dividing the hill between the Royal Palace on one side, and the Alcazaba on the other. Following the *reconquista* the ravine was filled in to hold two rainwater cisterns (*aljibes*) and the surface above laid out with fortifications. During the construction of Carlos V's palace in the sixteenth century, the area was cleared of these structures to create a parade ground, the rather desolate form it retains today. The underground **cisterns** are open for viewing on Monday, Wednesday and Friday from 9.30am to 1.30pm. Follow the arrows indicating the Palacios Nazaríes (Nasrid Palaces) to reach the royal palace.

The Palacios Nazaríes

It is amazing that the **Palacios Nazaríes** has survived, for it stands in utter contrast to the strength of the Alcazaba and the encircling walls and towers. It was built lightly and often crudely from wood, brick and adobe, and was designed not to last but to be renewed and redecorated by succeeding rulers. Its buildings show a superb use of light and space but they are principally a vehicle for ornamental stucco decoration. This, as Titus Burckhardt explains in *Moorish Culture in Spain*, was both an intricate science and a philosophy of abstract art in direct contrast to pictorial representation:

> *With its rhythmic repetition, [it] does not seek to capture the eye to lead it into an imagined world, but, on the contrary, liberates it from all pre-occupations of the mind. It does not transmit any specific ideas, but a state of being, which is at once repose and inner rhythm.*

Burckhardt adds that the way in which patterns are woven from a single band, or radiate from many identical centres, served as a pure simile for Islamic belief in the oneness of God, manifested at the centre of every form and being.

Arabic inscriptions feature prominently in the ornamentation. Some are poetic eulogies of the buildings and builders, others of various sultans – notably Muhammad V. Most, however, are taken from the Koran, and among them the phrase *Wa-la ghaliba illa-Llah* (There is no Conqueror but God) is tirelessly repeated. It is said that this became the battle cry of the Nasrids upon Ibn al-Ahmar's return from aiding the Castilian war against Muslim Sevilla; it was his reply to the customary, though bitterly ironic, greetings of *Mansur* (Victor).

The palace is structured in three parts, each arrayed round an interior court and with a specific function. The sultans used the **Mexuar**, the first series of rooms, for business and judicial purposes. In the **Serallo**, beyond, they would receive embassies and distinguished guests. The last section, the **Harem**, formed their private living quarters and would have been entered by no one but their family and servants.

THE MEXUAR

The council chamber, the main reception hall of the **Mexuar**, is the first room you enter. It was completed in 1365 and hailed (perhaps formulaically) by the court poet and vizier Ibn Zamrak as a "haven of counsel, mercy and favour". Here the sultan heard the pleas and petitions of the people and held meetings with his ministers. At the room's far end is a small **oratory**, one of a number of prayer niches scattered round the palace and immediately identifiable by their angular alignment to face Mecca.

This "public" section of the palace, beyond which few would have penetrated, is completed by the Mudéjar **Cuarto Dorado** (Golden Room), redecorated under Carlos V, whose *Plus Ultra* motif appears throughout the palace, and the **Patio del Cuarto**

Wa-la ghaliba illa-Llah
"There is no Conqueror but God"
(stylized inscription from the
Alhambra)

Dorado. This latter has perhaps the grandest facade of the whole palace, for it admits you to the formal splendour of the Serallo.

THE SERALLO

The **Serallo** was built largely to the design of Yusuf I (1333–54), a romantic and enlightened sultan who was stabbed to death by a madman while worshipping in the Alhambra mosque. Its rooms open out from delicate marble-columned arcades at each end of the long **Patio de los Arrayanes** (Myrtles) with its serene fountain and pool flanked by clipped myrtle bushes. At the court's northern end is the **Sala de la Barca**, with a fine copy of its original cedar ceiling (destroyed by fire in the last century), and the fortified **Torre de Comares**, two floors of which are occupied by the royal throne room.

This, the **Salón de Embajadores** (Hall of the Ambassadors), is the palace's largest and most majestic chamber. It was where the delicate diplomacy with the Christian emissaries would have been transacted – the means by which the Nasrid dynasty preserved itself – and as the sultan could only be approached indirectly it stands at an angle to the entrance from the Mexuar. It is perfectly square, with a stunning wooden dome, a superb example of *lacería*, the rigidly geometric "carpentry of knots" domed roof, and with a complex symbolism representing the seven heavens of the Muslim cosmos. The walls are completely covered in tile and stucco decoration and inscriptions, one of which states simply "I am the Heart of the Palace". It was here, symbolically, that Boabdil signed the terms of his city's surrender to the *Reyes Católicos*, whose motifs (the arms of Aragón and Castile) were later worked into the dome. Here, too, so it is said, Fernando met with Columbus to discuss his planned voyage to find a new sea route to India – the trip which led to the discovery of the Americas.

Carlos V tore down the rooms at the southern end of the Patio de los Arrayanes. From the arcade there is access to the gloomy **chapel crypt** (*cripta*) of his palace; it has a curious "whispering gallery" effect.

THE HAREM

The **Patio de los Leones** (Court of the Lions), which has become the archetypal image of Granada, constitutes the heart of the harem section of the palace. It was this area that moved Washington Irving to write in his *Tales of the Alhambra*:

It is impossible to contemplate this scene, so perfectly Oriental, without feeling the early associations of Arabian romance, and almost expecting to see the white arm of some mysterious princess beckoning from the gallery, or some dark eye sparkling through the lattice. The abode of beauty is here as if it had been inhabited but yesterday.

The stylized and archaic-looking lions beneath its fountain probably date, like the court itself, from the reign of Muhammad V, Yusuf's successor; a poem inscribed on the bowl tells how much fiercer the beasts would look if they weren't so restrained by respect for the sultan. The court was designed as an interior garden and planted with shrubs and aromatic herbs; it opens on to three of the finest rooms in the palace, each of which looks directly on to the fountain.

The most sophisticated rooms in this part of the complex, apparently designed to give a sense of the rotary movement of the stars, are the two facing each other across the court. The largest of these, the **Sala de los Abencerrajes**, has the most fabulous ceiling in the whole Alhambra complex: sixteen-sided, supported by niches of astonishing stalactite vaulting and lit by windows in the dome. Based on Pythagoras's theorem, the whole stupendous design – with a final and deft artistic flourish – is reflected in a fountain on the floor. Its light and airy quality stands at odds with its name and history, for it was here that Abu al-Hassan, Boabdil's father, murdered sixteen princes of the Abencerraj family, whose chief had fallen in love with his favourite, Zoraya. The stains in the fountain – popularly supposed to be indelible traces of blood from the severed heads thrown into it – are more likely to be from rust.

At the far end of the court is the **Sala de los Reyes** (Hall of the Kings), whose dormitory alcoves preserve a series of unique paintings on leather. These, in defiance of Koranic law, represent human scenes. They were probably painted by a Christian artist in the last decades of Moorish rule and were once thought to portray images of the Nasrid rulers – hence the room's name.

The second of the two facing chambers on the court's north side, the **Sala de las dos Hermanas** (Hall of the Two Sisters), is more mundanely named – from two huge slabs of white marble in its floor – but just as spectacularly decorated, with a dome of over 5000 "honeycomb cells". It was the principal room of the sultan's favourite, opening on to an inner apartment and balcony, the **Mirador de la Daraxa** ("Eyes of the Sultana"); the romantic garden patio below was added after the Reconquest.

Beyond, you are directed along a circuitous route through **apartments** redecorated by Carlos V (as at Sevilla, the northern-reared emperor installed fireplaces) and later used by Washington Irving. Eventually you emerge at the **Peinador de la Reina** (Queen's pavilion), which served as an oratory for the sultanas and as a dressing room for the wife of Carlos V; perfumes were burned beneath its floor and wafted up through a marble slab in one corner.

From there, passing the **Patio de la Reja** (Patio of the Grille) added in the seventeenth century, you pass the **Baños Reales** (Royal Baths). These are tremendous, decorated in rich tile mosaics and lit by pierced stars and rosettes once covered by coloured glass. The central chamber was used for reclining and retains the balconies where singers and musicians – reputedly blind to keep the royal women from being seen – would entertain the bathers. At present, entry is not permitted to the baths, though you can make out most of the features through the doorways.

Towers and the Palacio de Carlos V

Before leaving the palace compound a number of the **towers** are worth a look. Most are richly decorated – particularly the first, the **Torre de las Damas** (Ladies' Tower), which stands in front of its own patio, well restored to the original design.

The usual exit from the Palacios Nazaríes is through the courtyard of the **Palacio de Carlos V**, where bullfights were once held. The palace itself was begun in 1526 but never finished. It seems totally out of place here but is a distinguished piece of Renaissance design in its own right – the only surviving work of Pedro Machuca, a former pupil of Michelangelo.

The palace's lower floor houses a **Museo Hispano-Musulman** (Tues–Sat 9am–2.30pm; free entry with EU passport, otherwise 250ptas), a wonderful collection of artefacts which visitors are often too jaded to take in after the marvels of the Moorish palace outside. As well as fragments of sculptured plaster arabesques saved from the Alhambra and a splendid ceramic collection, look out for some outstanding fourteenth- and fifteenth-century Nasrid paintings and equally stunning carved wood panels and screens. The rare and beautiful fifteenth-century **Alhambra Vase** (Jarrón de las Gacelas) is the museum's centrepiece. Almost a metre and a half in height, and made

Puente de la Barqueta, Sevilla

Semana Santa, Sevilla

Alcázar, Sevilla

Giralda Tower, Sevilla

Feria de Abril, Sevilla

Mezquita, Córdoba

Mezquita, Córdoba

Palacio de las Cadenas, Úbeda, Jaén

Patio de los Leones, Alhambra

Alhambra, Granada

Olive groves, La Iruela, Cazorla, Jaén

Carmen de los Mártires

Sierra Nevada

for the Nasrid palace from local red clay enamelled in blue and gold with leaping *gacelas* (gazelles), it is the ceramic equal of the artistic splendours in the palace.

On the upper floors of the palace is a **Museo de Bellas Artes** (Tues 2.30–8pm, Wed–Sat 9am–8pm, Sun 9am–2.30pm; entry conditions as for the museum above), a cavernous gallery whose paintings and sculpture might command more attention elsewhere. At the time of writing the room numbers here had been removed, but this account follows the room sequence. In Room 1 there's a fine sixteenth-century wood-carving of the *Virgin and Child* by Diego de Siloé. Room 4 is dedicated to the works of Alonso Cano the seventeenth-century *granadino* painter and sculptor. His *Virgin and Child* and *San Bernadino de Siena* panels are outstanding, as are the sculptures of *San Antonio* and the head of *San Juan de Dios*, the latter executed with some assistance from Granada's other great sculptor, Pedro de Mena. Room 5 has more examples of the Andalucian sculptural tradition, with a brace of *Dolorosas* matched by a pair of *Ecce Homos*, a fervent theme of the region's artists reflected in the *pasos* carried during the *Semana Santa* processions; the *Ecce Homo* by Diego de Mora is the better of the two, whilst his more famous brother José de Mora has the finer *Dolorosa*. The later rooms, devoted to paintings from the nineteenth and twentieth centuries are fairly forgettable, but look out for a small watercolour by nineteenth-century artist David Roberts depicting the *Puerto del Vino*.

It's worth noting that both the above museums are known to remove items into storage to free up space for exhibits on loan from other museums.

The Convento de San Francisco

Behind Carlos V's palace are the remnants of the town (with a population of 40,000 during the Nasrid period) which once existed within the Alhambra's walls. On the main street is a cluster of overpriced restaurants and tatty tourist shops, which you'd do well to pass by.

However, before proceeding to the Generalife, it is worth looking into the fifteenth-century **Convento de San Francisco**. Built by Fernando and Isabel on the site of another Moorish palace, this is now a *parador* whose marvellous plant-filled patio, dominated by a soaring cypress projecting above the roof, preserves part of the chapel where the Catholic monarchs were buried – commemorated by a marble slab – before being removed to the cathedral. It's tricky to find, and you'll need to ask for directions at the hotel's reception. At the rear of the building, there's a restaurant and a very pleasant terrace bar.

The Generalife

Paradise is described in the Koran as a shaded, leafy garden refreshed by running water where the "fortunate ones" may take their rest under tall canopies. It is an image which perfectly describes the **Generalife**, the gardens and summer palace of the sultans. Its name means literally "garden of the architect" and the grounds consist of a luxuriantly imaginative series of patios, enclosed gardens and walkways.

By chance an account of the gardens during Moorish times, written rather fancifully by fourteenth-century Moorish historian, poet and palace vizier Ibn Zamrak, survives. The descriptions that he gives aren't all entirely believable but they are a wonderful basis for musing as you lie around by the patios and fountains. There were, he wrote, celebrations with horses darting about in the dusk at speeds that made the spectators rub their eyes (a form of festival still indulged in at Moroccan *fantasías*); rockets shot into the air to be attacked by the stars for their audacity; tightrope walkers flying through the air like birds; men bowled along in a great wooden hoop, shaped like an astronomical sphere…

Today, even devoid of such amusements, the gardens remain deeply evocative, above all, perhaps, the **Patio de los Cipreses**, a dark and secretive walled garden of sculpted junipers where the Sultana Zoraya was suspected of meeting her lover Hamet, chief of the unfortunate Abencerrajes. The trunk of the seven-hundred-year-old **cypress tree** (marked by a plaque) is where legend says their trysts took place and where the grisly fate of the Abencerraj clan was sealed.

Nearby is the inspired flight of fantasy of the **Camino de las Cascadas**, a staircase with water flowing down its stone balustrades. At its base is a wonderful little **Summer Palace**, with various decorated belvederes.

If you're looking for a lunchtime **place to eat** or a refreshing drink between palaces and museums, the shady terrace of *Restaurante La Mimbre* is one of the best-value places on the hill (see "Eating and Drinking" p.431).

Other sights on the Alhambra hill

From the Puerta de las Granadas, taking the right hand path uphill leads, in its higher reaches, to the **Casa Museo Manuel de Falla**, c/Antequerela s/n (Tues–Sat 9am–3pm; 250ptas), the former home of, and now a museum devoted to, the great Cádiz composer. The house is laid out just as he left it in 1939 – with domestic clutter, medicine bottles by his bed, and stacks of books – before quitting fascist Spain for an exile spent in Argentina where he died in 1946. Occasional concerts of his works are performed in the nearby **Centro Cultural de Manuel de Falla**, Paseo de los Mártires s/n, on Saturday evenings and Sunday mornings throughout the year (details from the Turismo). Beyond the Centro Cultural at the end of an avenue is the **Carmen de los Mártires** (Mon–Fri 10am–2pm & 5–7pm; Sat & Sun 10am–7pm; free), a turn-of-the-century house set in a charming garden filled with grottos, statues, follies and peacocks.

Just opposite the de Falla Museum, the terrace of the exclusive neo-Moorish **Alhambra Palace Hotel** (open to the public providing you're not dressed too outrageously) with fine **views** over the city is a great place for a drink. Ask at the reception desk to see the hotel's charming **theatre**, also in pseudo-Moorish style and where on June 7, 1922, an evening of poetry and song launched the career of a youthful Federico García Lorca (the guitarist Segovia appeared on the same bill). Just to the north of here on the Paseo del Generalife, the nineteenth-century **Hotel Washington Irving** is another of Granada's hotels with many historical associations. In 1928, *New York Times* journalist Mildred Adams met García Lorca here for the first time and fell under his spell. Lorca sat down at the hotel's battered, out-of-tune piano in the lobby and sang her a ballad about the arrest and death of a local flamenco singer. "In gesture, tone of voice, expression of face and body, Lorca himself was the ballad," she wrote later.

Granada's other sights

If you're spending just a couple of days in Granada it's hard to resist spending both of them in the Alhambra. It takes a distinct readjustment and effort of will to appreciate the city's later Christian monuments – although the **Capilla Real**, at least, demands a visit, and Baroque enthusiasts are in for a treat at the Cartuja. There are, too, a handful of minor Moorish sites in and around the run-down medieval streets of the **Albaicín**, the largest and most characteristic Moorish quarter that survives in Spain, and the quarter also has an excellent **archeology museum**.

The Albaicín

The **Albaicín** stretches across a fist-shaped area bordered by the Río Darro, Sacromonte hill, the old town walls and the winding Calle de Elvira (which runs parallel to the Gran Vía). From the centre, the best approach is from the Plaza Nueva and along the Carrera del Darro, beside the river. Coming from the Alhambra or

PERSONAL SECURITY IN THE ALBAICÍN

There has been an increasing number of **thefts from tourists in the Albaicín** in recent years, often by drug addicts to fund their addiction. The preferred method is bag snatching, and is rarely accompanied by violence. However, don't let the threat put you off visiting one of the city's most atmospheric quarters; applying a few common-sense measures should ensure that you come to no harm.

Firstly, do not take any valuables (including airline tickets and passports) or large amounts of cash with you when visiting the Albaicín and keep what you have on your person, not in a bag. Leave your valuables and cash in the room safe of your hotel or *hostal* or ask the proprietor to place them in the hotel safe. If your bag is snatched don't offer resistance – the thief will be concerned only with making a speedy getaway. Some people use their bag as a "decoy", even stuffing it with rubbish. Finally, and especially at night, keep to well-lit streets where there are other people around.

Generalife, you can make your way down the Cuesta de los Chinos – a beautiful path and a short cut.

PLAZA NUEVA AND CUESTA DE GOMÉREZ

Before starting out from the **Plaza Nueva**, take a look at the square itself. It was constructed just after the *reconquista* as a new focus for the city, and soon served as the site of an act of stunning Christian barbarity: a bonfire of 80,000 books from the former Muslim university.

Flanking the plaza's north side is the austerely impressive **Real Chancillería** (Royal Chancery), built at the same time as the square, and now the law courts. Beyond its monumental entrance lies an elegant two-storeyed **patio** designed by Diego de Siloé with marble Doric columns and a staircase with stalactite ceiling.

On the opposite side of the square, the **Cuesta de Gomérez** leads up to the Alhambra. It is here that most of Granada's renowned guitar manufacturers are gathered. Behind the windows of these places you may catch sight of a major concert or flamenco musician trying out a new instrument. On a recent visit I encountered the noted *granadino* classical guitarist José-Carlo Gutierrez purchasing a new guitar from *Casa Morales* at number 9; he treated the shop to a virtuoso display whilst the jovial Señor Morales beamed approvingly.

SANTA ANA AND THE ARAB BATHS

Perched over the Darro at the Plaza Nueva's eastern end is the sixteenth-century church of **Santa Ana**, whose bell tower is the converted minaret of the mosque it replaced. Following the river's northern bank along the **Carrera del Darro**, glance back to where the river disappears from sight under the city and "moans as it loses itself in the absurd tunnel" as the young Lorca put it.

A little way up at no. 31 are the remains of the **Baños Árabes** (Tues–Sat 10am–2pm; free), a marvellous and little-visited Moorish public bath complex. Built in the eleventh century, the sensitively restored building consists of a series of brick-vaulted rooms with typical star-shaped skylights (originally glazed) and columns incorporating Roman and Visigothic capitals. When Richard Ford was here in the 1830s he found it being used as a wash-house by the local women because "one of the first laws after the conquest of the Catholic sovereigns was to prohibit bathing by fine and punishment." To get an idea of what a **Moorish bathhouse** was like when functioning, one has been recreated just behind the church of Santa Ana. At *Baños Arabes Al Andalus*, c/Santa Ana 16 (reservation required ☎958 22 99 78; bath 1400ptas) you can wallow in the graded temperatures (cold, tepid and hot) of the traditional bath surrounded by marble pavements, mosaic wall decor and plaster arabesques. There's also a pleasant *tetería* (tearoom) upstairs.

CASA DE CASTRIL: THE ARCHEOLOGICAL MUSEUM

At Corredera del Darro no. 43 is the **Casa de Castril**, a Renaissance mansion with a fine Plateresque facade and doorway, which houses the city's **Museo Arqueológico** (Tues 3–8pm, Wed–Sat 9.30am–8pm, Sun 9am–3pm; free with EU passport or 250ptas), with its interesting exhibits of finds from throughout the province. Rooms 1 and 2 cover the Paleolithic and Neolithic periods, among which are some remarkable artefacts from the **Cueva de los Murciélagos** near Albuñol. In this fourth-millennium BC Neolithic cave, alongside a dozen cadavers arranged in a semi-circle around that of a woman, were found some modern-looking esparto grass sandals and baskets, as well as a golden diadem. Room 4 contains the Iberian and pre-Roman collection with some fine examples of early lapidary work, including a hefty carved stone bull, stone vases and outstanding alabaster vessels. The finds from the necropolis at **Punté Noye** near Almuñecar (the Phoenician *Sexi*) suggest a large colony here trading as far afield as Egypt and Greece from where the vases (some bearing pharaonic titles) were imported. The Roman section in Room 5 has a striking third-century bronze statue as well as some interesting **early Christian lamps** from the fourth century; exhibit 4420 bears the Chi-Rho symbol, the first two letters of Christ's name in Greek. Among some Visigothic artefacts in Room 6 is a carved stone plaque with another Chi-Rho symbol.

Pride of place in the **Moorish section** (Room 7) is a fourteenth-century **bronze astrolabe**, demonstrating the superior scientific competence of the Arabic world at this time. The instrument was adopted by the Arabs from ancient Greece and used for charting the position of the stars in astrology, precisely orienting the *mihrab* of the mosques towards Mecca, determining geographical coordinates as well as trigonometry and converting Muslim dates into Christian ones. Its transmission from the Arab to the Christian world made possible the voyages of discovery to both east and west. More Moorish symmetry is evident in the designs on the vases, wooden chests and amphoras also displayed here.

FURTHER ALONG THE DARRO AND THE CASA DEL CHAPIZ

Alongside the Casa de Castril, c/Zafra has a Moorish house, the **Casa Zafra**, with a pleasant patio and pool, whilst close by again is the convent of **Santa Catalina de Zafra**, housed in a sixteenth-century Mudéjar palace. The nuns here are renowned for their convent *dulces* and will gladly supply you (through a *turno*) with their speciality, *glorias* (almond cakes); they're open daily except in August. At the top of the same street, **San Juan de los Reyes** is another church – the first established in Granada after the *reconquista* – built around the courtyard of a former mosque whose minaret, with characteristically Moorish *sebka* decoration, now serves as a belfry.

Continuing along the Darro you'll eventually come to **Paseo de los Tristes** (aka Paseo del Padre Manjón), a delightful esplanade beside the river overlooked by the battlements of the Alhambra high on the hill above, a great spot for a drink and especially so at night when the Alhambra is floodlit. There are several attractive bars fronting on to the river.

Two streets off here also contain **Moorish houses**: c/del Horno de Oro (no. 14) and, two streets further along, Cuesta de la Victoria (no. 9). The street after this, the **Cuesta del Chapiz**, climbs left into the heart of the Albaicín, passing first, on the right, the **Casa del Chapiz**, in origin a sixteenth-century Moorish mansion – with a charming patio – and today reclaimed as a school of Arabic studies. The **Camino del Sacromonte**, just beyond it, heads east towards the *gitano* caves where, after sundown, the *gitanos* will attempt to entice you in for some raucous but often dubious flamenco (see box opposite).

SACROMONTE: GRANADA'S GITANO QUARTER

Granada has an ancient and still considerable **gitano** (gypsy) population, from whose clans many of Spain's best flamenco guitarists, dancers and singers have emerged. Traditionally the gypsies inhabited cave homes on the **Sacromonte hill**, and many still do, giving lively displays of dancing and music in their *zambras* (shindigs). These were once spontaneous but are now blatantly contrived for tourists, and are often shameless rip-offs: you're hauled into a cave, leered at if you're female, and systematically extorted of all the money you've brought along (for dance, the music, the castanets, the watered-down sherry…). Which is not to say that you shouldn't visit – just to take only as much money as you want to part with. Turn up mid-evening; the lines of caves begin off the Camino de Sacromonte, just above the Casa del Chapiz (centre top on our map). When the university is in session, the cave dwellings are turned into **discos** and are packed with students at weekends.

For revelations of a different kind wander up to Sacromonte a little earlier in the day and take a look at the old **caves** on the far side of the old Moorish wall – most of them deserted after severe floods in 1962. There are fantastic views from the top. In this area and Sacromonte generally it would also be wise to heed the warnings on personal security mentioned above (see box on p.421).

The Cuesta del Chapiz eventually loops around to the Plaza del Salvador where the church of **San Salvador** (daily 10am–1pm & 4–7.30pm; 100ptas) is built on the site of a mosque of which the courtyard with whitewashed arches and Moorish cisterns is beautifully preserved. Diego de Siloé, the architect of the sixteenth-century church, which was badly damaged in the Civil War, converted the mosque's original **minaret** into its tower.

PLAZA LARGA AND THE MIRADOR DE SAN NICOLÁS
From San Salvador, c/Panaderos leads into **Plaza Larga**, the busy heart of the Albaicín, with a concentration of restaurants and bars. The nearby c/Agua has more **Moorish dwellings**: try numbers 1, 37, 28, and 19. A busy little **market** is held in Plaza Larga on Saturday mornings selling the usual fruit and vegetables as well as potted plants and bootleg cassettes.

From here the obvious route is to the **Mirador de San Nicolás** with its justly famous panoramic **view** of the Sierra Nevada, the Alhambra and Granada spread out below. To get there from Plaza Larga, go through the Arco de las Pasas, an old arch in the west corner, and turn sharply left up Callejón de San Cecilio. On the square, the fifteenth-century church is of little note but the nearby **aljibe** (fountain) is a Moorish original, one of many in the Albaicín to survive from the time when every mosque – there were more than thirty of them – had its own.

Below the *mirador*, c/Nuevo de San Nicolás descends into c/Santa Isabel la Real, passing, on the right, the early sixteenth-century convent of **Santa Isabel**, partly constructed within a Nasrid palace – La Daralhorra – of which only the patios and some arches survive. To see the **patio** you'll need to go to a door (marked with a metal plaque and currently open Monday only 10am–1pm) in c/Callejón de las Monjas at the back of the convent, and reachable from Plaza San Miguel Bajo (see below). The **convent church** (open 10am–6pm) has a superb Plateresque doorway and, inside, a Mudéjar ceiling.

PLAZA DE SAN MIGUEL BAJO AND SAN JOSÉ
Alternatively, c/Santa Isabel drops into one of the Albaicín's most delightful squares, **Plaza de San Miguel Bajo**, lined with acacia and chestnut trees. The church of **San**

Miguel on its eastern side is another sixteenth-century work by Diego de Siloé, built over yet another mosque, and preserves its original **thirteenth-century** *aljibe* (fountain) where the ritual ablutions would have been performed before entering. The square also has a clutch of good bars, whose terraces are extremely popular at night; *Bar Lara* serves the potent barrelled *costa* wine brewed in the Alpujarras. The opposite end of the plaza leads to the **Mirador del Carril de la Lona** with its views over the western side of the city. You could also detour north from here – climbing uphill beyond the walls – to the church of **San Cristóbal**, which has another fine **view** of the Alhambra from its own *mirador*.

One final church worth taking in on the way back to the centre is **San José**, reached by following *Calles* San Miguel and San José from Plaza San Miguel. This is another sixteenth-century conversion from a ninth-century mosque, whose minaret forms its belfry, and its interior has a superb gilded Mudéjar coffered ceiling and octagonal dome.

Slightly south of the church on the Cuesta de San Gregorio, you could take a look at the **Casa de Porras** with its Plateresque facade and, opposite, the **Carmen de Cipreses**, one of the most picturesque garden-villas in the Albaicín. At the bottom of here, Placeta San Gregorio gives access, along c/Cárcel Alta, to Plaza Nueva. Alternatively, you could head west to the nearby *Calles* Calderería Nueva and Calderería Vieja which have been transformed into a vibrant and delightful "Little Morocco" with food shops, restaurants and excellent tea-houses serving a wide variety of refreshing teas, infusions and pastries – *As Sirat* and *Al-Faquara* on c/Calderería Nueva are recommended – (see "Eating, drinking and nightlife" on p.434).

Other Moorish remains

A further group of Moorish buildings are located just outside the Albaicín. The most interesting of them, and oddly one of the least known, is the so-called **Palacio Madraza** (Mon–Fri 8am–10pm; closed August; free), a strangely painted building opposite the Capilla Real. Built in the early fourteenth century at the behest of Yusuf I, though much altered since, this is a former Islamic college (*medressa* in Arabic) and retains part of its old prayer hall, including a magnificently decorated **mihrab**. Note that the hours change here when it is used for exhibitions.

Slightly south of here, and housing the city's tourist office, is the **Corral del Carbón**, a fourteenth-century *caravanserai* (an inn where merchants would lodge and, on the upper floors, store their goods) which is unique in Spain. A wonderful horseshoe arch leads into a courtyard with a marble water trough. Remarkably, it survived intact through a stint as a sixteenth-century theatre – with the spectators watching from the upper galleries – and later as a charcoal burners' factory, the origin of its present name. The building is a little tricky to find: it lies down an alleyway off the c/de los Reyes Católicos, opposite the **Alcaicería**, the old Arab silk bazaar, burned down in the nineteenth century and poorly restored as an arcade of souvenir shops.

Another impressive Moorish mansion, the **Casa de los Tiros** stands on c/Pavaneras, just behind Plaza de Isabel Católica. This was actually built just after the *reconquista* and has a curious facade adorned with various Greek deities and heroes as well as a number of *tiros* (muskets) projecting from the upper windows. Above the door is a representation of the sword of Boabdil which the family who lived here claimed they held in custody. The interior has a couple of elaborately decorated rooms and a fine Moorish courtyard, often used to stage art exhibitions – which is also the only time it's open to the public.

Capilla Real

The **Capilla Real** (Royal Chapel; daily: April–Sept 10.30am–1pm & 4–7pm; Oct–March 10.30am–1pm & 3.30–6.30pm; 300ptas) is Granada's most impressive Christian building, flamboyant late Gothic in style and built ad hoc in the first decades of Christian rule as a mausoleum for *Los Reyes Católicos*, the city's "liberators". Before entering, note the stone frieze above the entrance which romantically alternates the initials of the two monarchs. Isabel, in accordance with her will, was originally buried on the Alhambra hill (in the church of the San Francisco convent, now part of the *parador*) but her wealth and power proved no safeguard of her wishes; both her remains and those of her spouse Fernando, who died eleven years later in 1516, were removed here in 1522. Isabel's final indignity occurred in the 1980s, when the candle that she asked should perpetually illuminate her tomb was replaced by an electric bulb – after many protests the candle has been recently restored. But, as with Columbus's tomb in Sevilla, there is considerable doubt as to whether any of the remains in these lead coffins – so reverentially regarded by visiting Spaniards – are those of the monarchs at all. The chapel and tombs were desecrated by Napoleon's troops in 1812 and the coffins opened and defiled.

The monarchs' **tombs** in a plain underground crypt below are as simple as could be imagined: Fernando and Isabel, flanked by their daughter Joana ("the Mad") and her husband Felipe ("the Handsome"), rest in lead coffins placed in a plain crypt (a not easily spotted "F" marking that of the king on the left of the central pair). The smaller coffin to the right is that of the infant Príncipe de Asturias who died before reaching the age of two. Above them, however, is an elaborate Renaissance monument, with sculpted effigies of all four monarchs – the response of their grandson Carlos V to what he found "too small a room for so great a glory". The figures of Fernando and Isabel are easily identified by the rather puny-looking lion and lioness at their feet. Popular legend has it that Isabel's head sinks deeper into the pillow due to the weight of her intelligence compared with that of her husband; this is not without some truth as Fernando was never much more than a consort. Carved in Carrera marble by the Florentine Domenico Fancelli in 1517, the tomb's **side panels** depict the Apostles and scenes from the life of Christ and are especially fine. The Latin inscription at the monarchs' feet is brutally triumphalist in tone: "Overthrowers of the Mahometan sect and repressors of heretical stubbornness." The tomb of Joana and Felipe, a much inferior work, is by Ordóñez.

In front, dating from the same period, is an equally magnificent **reja**, or gilded grille, the work of Maestro Bartolomé of Jaén, and considered one of the finest in Spain. Its outstanding upper tier has scenes from the life of Christ and a crucifixion. The altar's striking **retablo** is by Felipe Vigarny dated 1522, depicting in one scene San Juan being boiled in oil; beneath the kneeling figures of Fernando and Isabel – sculptures possibly by Diego de Siloé – are images depicting events close to both their hearts, Boabdil surrendering the keys of Granada for him, the enforced baptism of the defeated Moors for her.

In the capilla's **Sacristy** are displayed the sword of Fernando, the crown of Isabel, and the banners used at the conquest of Granada. Also here is Isabel's outstanding personal collection of **medieval Flemish paintings** – including important works by Memling, Bouts and van der Weyden – and various Italian paintings, including panels by Botticelli and Pedro Berruguete.

The Cathedral

For all its stark Renaissance bulk, Granada's **Catedral**, adjoining the Capilla Real and entered from the door beside it (same hours and another 300ptas), is a disappointment. It was raised on the site of the Great Mosque which was demolished to accommodate it, and work commenced in 1521, just as the royal chapel was finished, but it was then left uncompleted until well into the eighteenth century – like Málaga's *La Manquita* (the one-armed lady) it still lacks a tower. The main west facade by Diego de Siloé and Alonso Cano is worth a look, however. It still carries a provocative inscription honouring Primo

LORCA'S GRANADA

One of the ghosts that walks Granada's streets and plazas is that of Andalucía's greatest poet and dramatist **Federico García Lorca**. He was born in 1898 at Fuente Vaqueros, a village in the *Vega*, the fertile plain to the west of the city, and moved to Granada eleven years later. This childhood spent growing up on the family farm, where he soaked up both the countryside and the folklore of its people, was to have an enduring influence on his work.

Lorca published his first book of essays and poems while still at university in Granada, in 1918. It was in 1928, however, aged thirty, that he came to national prominence with *El Romancero Gitano*, an anthology of gypsy ballads. This success led to a trip to New York in 1929 where he spent a year ostensibly at Columbia University learning English, but actually gathering material for the collection of poems, *Poeta in Nueva York*, published after his death.

He returned to Spain in 1931 at the advent of the Spanish Republic. It was a time of great optimism and Lorca was given a government grant to run a travelling theatre group, *La Barraca* (the cabin), taking drama to the people. From this period the poet's major works for the stage – *Bodas de Sangre* (Blood Wedding) and *Yerma* – emerged.

In July 1936, on the eve of the Civil War, Lorca went back to Granada for the summer. This visit coincided with Franco's coup and control of the city was wrested by the Falangists, who initiated a reign of terror. Lorca, as a Republican sympathizer and declared homosexual, was hunted down by fascist thugs at the house of a friend, now the *Hotel Reina Cristina*. Two days later he was brutally murdered in an olive grove near the village of Viznar, in the hills to the east of the city. His body was never found.

It has taken the city a long time to accord Lorca the recognition he deserves, partly because of his sexual inclinations, and mainly through guilt concerning the way he died. Should you have an interest in tracing the locations of his life, both in Granada and around, the most important are detailed below. More avid followers will want to get hold of the excellent *Lorca's Granada* by Ian Gibson, his biographer.

Huerta de San Vicente

West of the centre is the **Huerta de San Vicente** (Tues–Sun 10am–1pm & 5–8pm; 300ptas, Wed free; guided tours every 45min), an orchard where the poet's family used to spend the summer months. It spreads back from c/de la Virgen Blanca, behind *Los Jardines Neptuno Flamenco* nightclub; to get there take the southbound bus #4 from Gran Via or Plaza del Carmen near the Turismo (direction Palacio de Deportes), or a taxi.

The **house** – now restored and opened as a museum – has been set in the centre of what is planned to become the largest rose garden in Europe, the **Parque Federico García Lorca**, the city's belated tribute. When the Lorcas had it, the five-acre holding was planted with vegetables and fruit trees. Then a tranquil rural plot on the city's edge, it has since been enveloped by ugly urban sprawl and it's hard to square the scene today with the poet's description of a "paradise of trees and water and so much jasmine and nightshade in the garden that we all wake up with lyrical headaches". The light and airy rooms contain some of their original furniture including, in Lorca's bedroom, his work desk, bed, a poster of the *Barraca* theatre company and the balcony (from outside the furthest left of the three) looking towards the Sierra Nevada, which inspired one of his best-known poems, *Despedida* (Farewell):

Si muero, dejad el balcón abierto.
El niño come naranjas. (Desde mi balcón lo veo.)
El segador siega el trigo. (Desde mi balcón lo siento.)
Si muero, dejad el balcón abierto!

If I die, leave the balcony open.
The child eats oranges. (From my balcony I see him.)
The harvester scythes the corn. (From my balcony I hear him.)
If I die leave the balcony open!

In a *hornacina* or wall niche outside is the tiny image of San Vicente placed there by Lorca's father – and where it has remained ever since – when he bought the house in 1925 and changed its name to that of the saint.

Fuente Vaqueros

In this village I dreamt my first ambitious dreams. In this village one day I will merge with the earth and flowers . . .

Lorca's birthplace in the solid farming village of **FUENTE VAQUEROS**, 17km west of Granada, is the site of the **Lorca Museum** (Tues–Sun 10am–1pm & 6–8pm; guided visits on the hour; 200ptas; ☎958 51 64 53). The house lies just off the village's main square on c/Poeta García Lorca. Now a charming shrine to Lorca's memory and watched over by the amiable director Juan de Loxa (a poet himself), the museum is stuffed with Lorca memorabilia, manuscripts and personal effects. It also has a fleeting video fragment of Lorca on tour with the *Teatro Barraca* – the only piece of cinema film to capture the poet and his engaging smile.

After you have seen the house, pay a visit to the parish church at the end of the street opposite, where Lorca's mother took him regularly as a child. Although the church has been heavily reconstructed since, the old stone font can still be seen where Lorca – or "Federico" as he is known to all the world here – was baptized.

From Granada, **buses** operated by *Ureña* run to the village from the Avda. de Andaluces fronting the train station; the weekday outward service leaves on the hour (except 10am) from eight in the morning, with the return also hourly (except 11am) from Fuente Vaqueros; it's a twenty-minute trip and the last bus returns to Granada at 8pm. Should you want **to stay**, there are simple rooms at the friendly *Hostal-Restaurante Moli-Lorc* at c/Ancha Escuelas 11 (☎958 51 63 48; ②) next to the church, and a decent place **to eat**, *Restaurante Genil*, 2km out of the village on the Chauchina road with a good-value *menú*. On Saturday mornings a lively **market** fills the street fronting the church.

Viznar and Lorca's death

The village of **VIZNAR**, 10km northeast of Granada, in the foothills of the Sierra Nevada, will always be linked with the assassination of Lorca in August 1936. After his arrest in Granada by the Fascist insurgents, Lorca was taken to Viznar – along with hundreds of others during the reign of terror – and held for two days at a farmhouse called La Colonia before being taken to a *barranco*, a bleak gully nearby, where he was shot. A poem of Lorca's seemed eerily prescient about his own end:

. . . I realized I had been murdered.
They searched cafés and cemeteries and churches,
they opened barrels and cupboards,
they plundered three skeletons to remove their gold teeth.
They did not find me.
They never found me?
No. They never found me.

From the centre of the village – the Falangist headquarters were in the eighteenth-century archbishop's palace behind the fountain – take the road out towards La Fuente Grande. You will pass the site of **La Colonia** (later demolished), which stood on a bend, near to a white-walled cottage. From here, the road curves around the valley to the **Parque Federico García Lorca**, a sombre monumental garden marking the *barranco* and honouring all the Civil War dead. Climb the steps to the garden and veer left up more steps: the site of Lorca's murder was here, beneath a solitary olive tree. After the killing – he was shot with three others – a young gravedigger threw the bodies into a narrow trench. The supposed site is marked by a granite memorial.

Viznar is served by **bus** from Granada's Arco de Elvira terminal (on the Plaza del Triunfo at the northern end of Gran Via) at 7.30am, 2.15pm and 8pm, with the return buses at 8am and 4pm (no service Sun). The village also has a superb **youth hostel** (☎958 54 33 07 ①), complete with swimming pool which is open to all.

de Rivera, founder of the fascist Falange Party, added in the Franco period, and, significantly for Granada today, never removed.

Inside, the church is pleasantly light and airy due to its painted stonework and twenty giant pillars which push the central dome to a height of over thirty metres. The Capilla Mayor has figures by Pedro de Mena of Fernando and Isabel at prayer, with, above them, oversized busts of Adam and Eve by Alonso Cano, who also left quite a bit of work in the other chapels.

In the eighteenth-century **sagrario** there are more works by Cano as well as a fine *Crucifixión* by Montañés. If you have a fistful of coins, you can light up some of the chapels, too, revealing a triumphant sculpture of *Santiago* (St James) in the saddle, by Pedro de Mena (Capilla de Santiago) and an El Greco *Saint Francis* (Capilla de Jesús Nazareno).

The University quarter: San Juan and San Jerónimo

Other of Granada's churches have, perhaps, rather more to offer than the cathedral and with sufficient interest you could easily fill a day of visits. The university quarter contains a couple of outstanding examples.

North of the cathedral, ten minutes' walk along c/San Jerónimo, the Renaissance **Hospital de San Juan de Dios** is well worth a visit. It was founded in 1552 by Juan de Robles (Juan de Dios) as a hospital for the sick and a refuge for foundlings, and its elaborate facade has a statue by Mora depicting the saint on his knees and holding a cross, which popular legend says is how he died. The hospital itself is still a going concern and you'll have to get by a sometimes grumpy porter who will allow you *"cinco minutos"* to view two marvellous **patios**. The outer and larger one is a beautiful double-tiered Renaissance work with a palm at each of its four corners and a fountain in the centre; the inner patio – with orange trees in the corners here – has delightful but deteriorating frescoes depicting the saint's miracles. Next door, the church, a Baroque addition, has a Churrigueresque *retablo* – a glittering, gold extravaganza by Guerrero.

Close by lies a little-known jewel: the sixteenth-century **Convento de San Jerónimo** (daily 10am–1pm; April–Sept also 4–7pm ; 300ptas), founded by the Catholic monarchs, though built after their death. This has a further exquisite pair of Renaissance **patios** (or cloisters in this context), the largest an elegant work by Diego de Siloé with two tiers of 36 arches. The **church**, also by Siloé, has been wonderfully restored after use as cavalry barracks. It has fabulous eighteenth-century frescoes, another monumental carved and painted *retablo*, and, on either side of the altar, monuments to "El Gran Capitán" Gonzalo de Córdoba and his wife Doña María. The remains of this general, responsible for many of the Catholic monarchs' victories, may lie in the vault beneath, but the Napoleonic French were here too and, as Ford noted not much later, had "insulted the dead lion's ashes before whom, when alive, their ancestors had always fled." The church is little visited, and in late afternoon you may hear the nuns singing their offices in the railed-off choir loft above; if it's a feast day, the altar will be filled with lilies, their fragrant perfume wafting through the church. A small shop at the entrance sells the convent's marmalade and *dulces*.

A short walk away along c/de la Duquesa and left into Plaza Universidad lies the **old University building** – now the Law faculty – founded by Carlos V with a Baroque portal flanked by twin barley-sugar pillars; no one minds if you step inside to view the patio. In the same square the eighteenth-century **Iglesia de Santos Justo y Pastor** has an impressive facade and, inside, an elaborately decorated cupola and gilded *retablo*.

Just behind this church, with its entrance on c/San Jerónimo, the **Colegio de San Bartolomé y Santiago** is a sixteenth-century university college with an elegant patio, off which is a students' *cafetería* which they don't mind sharing with visitors. Slightly further out, to the north along the Ancha de Capuchinos, the **Hospital Real** (Mon–Fri 9am–1pm), a magnificent Renaissance building designed by Enrique Egas and formerly known as the Hospital de los Locos, was founded by the Catholic monarchs and finished by Carlos V. As its former name implies, it was one of the first lunatic asylums in Europe, though it now houses the main library of the University of Granada. Inside, a beautiful arcaded patio and some fine *artesonado* ceilings are worth a look.

La Cartuja

Granada's **Cartuja** (Mon–Sat 10am–1pm & 4–8pm, Sun 10am–noon & 4–8pm; 300ptas), on the northern outskirts of town, is the grandest and most outrageously decorated of all the country's lavish Carthusian monasteries. On foot, it is a ten- to fifteen-minute walk beyond San Juan de Dios; alternatively, bus lines #8 or "C" (Línea C) going north along Gran Vía pass by.

The monastery was founded in 1516 on land provided by "El Gran Capitán", Gonzalo de Córdoba (see above), though the building is noted today for its heights of Churrigueresque-inspired Baroque extravagance – added, some say, to rival the Alhambra. The **church** is of staggering wealth, surmounted by an altar of twisted and coloured marble described by one Spanish writer as "a motionless architectural earthquake". There are Bocanegra paintings and a seventeenth-century sculpture of the *Assumption* by José de Mora.

The **sagrario** drips with more marble, jasper and porphyry and has a breathtakingly beautiful gilded and frescoed **cupola** by Antonio Palomino, while the **sacristía** pulls out yet more stops with another stunning painted cupola and fascinating sculptural features influenced by the art of the Aztec and Maya civilizations encountered in the New World. Here also are fine sculptures of *San Bruno* by José de Mora in a side niche, and an *Inmaculada* by Alonso Cano.

Eating, drinking and nightlife

Granada is quite a sedate place, at least compared to Sevilla or Málaga, and if it weren't for the university, you sense the city would go unnaturally early to bed. However, on a brief stay, there's more than enough to entertain you, with some decent restaurants and plenty of animated bars, especially in the zone between **Plaza Nueva** and **Grand Vía**, the plazas of the **Albaicín** quarter, whose streets make for enjoyable (if confusing) evening wanderings, around the **Campo del Príncipe**, a spacious square with outdoor eating and drinking, at the foot of the west slopes of the Alhambra hill, and along the **Carrera del Darro**. Granada's discos – mostly dismal teeny hangouts – are concentrated along the **c/Pedro Antonio** to the west of the centre, which turns into one big disco at weekends. For serious drinking into the early hours head out to the bars along calles Gran Capitán, San Juan de Dios and Pedro Antonio de Alarcón in the university zone.

Restaurants

Granada is not noted for the quality of its **restaurants**, and service and standards even at the best places often leave a lot to be desired. That said, good-value food is to be found all over town, and there are a number of places worth paying a bit more for, too. Beware, of course, the inevitable tourist traps, particularly around the Plaza Nueva and on the Alhambra hill. It's worth remembering that you can also get substantial meals at many of the bars listed in the following section.

PLAZA NUEVA AND CATHEDRAL AREA

Al-Faquara, c/Calderería Nueva, just off c/Elvira. Juices and *crêpes* to the accompaniment of classical music. They also do a wide range of teas – try their *"té Pakistani"* or *"té Al-Faquara"*.

Al Jaima, c/Calderería Nueva 15. Friendly little place serving take-away *couscous* and *felafel* on the door or in their cosy diner upstairs.

Mesón Andaluz, c/Elvira 10. Pleasant, slightly pricey restaurant with a renowned *fritura mixta* (fried fish platter).

Arrayanes, Cuesta Marañas 4 (off c/Calderería Nueva). Excellent North African restaurant with many vegetarian offerings and great flat breads and pastries.

Bar-Restaurante Boabdil, c/Corpus Cristi s/n (a small alley between c/Elvira and c/Calderería Vieja). Good and friendly neighbourhood restaurant with a small terrace outside and a cheap and filling *menú* for 850ptas.

Restaurante León, c/Pan 3. Long-established economical *cordobés* restaurant serving many *carne de monte* (game) dishes and *migas* (fried breadcrumbs); offers a cheap *menú* and also has a good *tapas* bar on the other side of the street.

Naturi Albaicín, c/Calderería Nueva 10. Imaginative veggie cooking – fine salads, spinach-stuffed mushrooms and the like – served up with New Age music and green magazines; quality makes up for often slow service. Take tea or coffee after at the nearby tea-houses.

Pilar de Toro, c/Hospital de Santa Ana 12 on Plaza Nueva, near the church of Santa Ana (☎958 22 38 47). Stylish, medium-priced bar-restaurant inside a former seventeenth-century *casa señorial* with exterior *terraza*, elegant "palm court" patio bar (serving *tapas*) and, upstairs, a mid-priced restaurant with its own leafy and secluded patio.

Cafetería-Restaurante La Riviera, c/Cetti Meriem 5, off Gran Vía. Features a decent *menú económico*, including a vegetarian option.

Samarkanda, c/Calderería Vieja, about halfway up. Excellent Lebanese restaurant (with quite a few vegetarian options) and the best of the few places in "Little Morocco", where it's worth having a full meal.

Bar-Restaurante Sevilla, c/Oficios 12 – opposite the entrance to the Capilla Real (☎958 22 12 23). One of the few surviving pre-war restaurants from the old Granada. It's steeped in literary history and Lorca spent many happy hours here. There's a 2500ptas *menú* and, in the evenings, tables outside with a view of the *capilla*. Closed Mon.

ALBAICÍN

Juanillo, Camino del Monte 81. Well-known low-priced restaurant in Sacromonte serving typical no-nonsense but well prepared dishes with great views of the Alhambra. Take the bus from Plaza Nueva if you can't face the hike.

El Ladrillo II, Placeta de Fatima – close to El Salvador church. This place specializes in *barcos* (boats) of fried fish, served at economical prices on tables beneath the stars – all of which make the climb worthwhile.

La Luz es como el Agua, c/Cruz de Arqueros 3 – slightly northeast of the Plaza del Triunfo. Charming little Belgian-run restaurant serving up tasty dishes, including good pasta and salads. Closed Mon.

Bar La Mancha Chica, c/Nueva de San Nicolás 1 – a little way down from the *mirador*. Simple place with an outdoor terrace serving *platos combinados*.

Mirador de Morayma, c/Pianista García Carrillo 2 – east of El Salvador (☎958 22 82 90). Situated in a delightful Albaicín *carmen* (villa and garden) with a fine view of the Alhambra, *granadino* specialities here include *tortilla de Sacromonte*, and the desserts are made by the sisters at the Convento de Santa Catalina de Zafra below. Expensive but there is a good-value *menú*. Closed Sun.

Restaurante-Bar Tomasas, Callejón de las Tomasas, just below the Mirador de San Nicolás. Mid-priced summer restaurant in a huge and beautiful *carmen* with a stunning terrace view of the floodlit Alhambra at night. *Ajo blanco* (white *gazpacho*) is a speciality. You can also nurse a *tinto de verano* here if you don't want to eat. *El Agua*, nearby to the south at c/Aljibe de Trillo 7, is a similar place – with terrace view – specializing in fondues.

PLAZAS BIB-RAMBLA AND TRINIDAD

El Amir, c/General Narváez 3 – west along c/Recogidas from Puerta Real and off to the right. On the southwest edge of this zone, this is a fairly pricey Arab restaurant with delicious *hummus* and *felafel*, and dishes made of rice and ground meat with pine nuts and cinnamon.

Casa Cepillo, Plaza Pescadería 8 – a marketplace linking the two squares. Cheap *comedor* with an excellent *menú*; the soups are especially good here.

Restaurante-Marisquería Cunini, Plaza Pescadería 14 (☎958 25 07 77). A gleaming, marble-topped bar serves standing customers with high-quality fish *tapas* and *raciones* and there's a pricier and equally excellent small seafood restaurant behind.

Bar Ferroviaria, c/Lavadero Tablas 1, off c/Tablas. This is in fact a Railway Pensioners' club but don't let that put you off, for behind the anonymous exterior you'll find an amazingly cheap *menú* which attracts workers and students for miles around; if the paella is on, it's your lucky day. Open daily 2–4.30pm & 8–10pm.

Mesón Gallego Noemi, c/Trinidad 8, off Plaza de la Trinidad. Tiny, economical Galician restaurant which specializes in *pulpo a la gallega* and paella, and has a *menú*.

Mesón La Pataleta, Plaza Gran Capitan 1. Very good mid-priced restaurant renowned for its barbecued meat dishes.

Restaurante Los Reyes, c/Buensuceso 9 – southwest side of Plaza de la Trinidad. Wonderful neighbourhood restaurant serving *granadino* specialities; excellent value with an economical *menú* and great seafood *tapas* at the bar.

Café-Bar El Rocío, c/Sillería 4, off Plaza de la Trinidad. Bustling, friendly and inexpensive place specializing in *pollo asado con patatas* (chicken and chips).

Restaurante Las Tinajas, c/Martínez Campos 17, close to the *El Amir* (see above) (☎958 25 43 93). One of Granada's top-notch restaurants offering a range of *granadino* dishes as well as some northern Spanish specialities. Recommended here are *berenjenas rellenas de setas* (aubergine stuffed with wild mushrooms) and *rape mozárabe* (monkfish). There's also a *menú* for around 3000ptas.

PLAZA MARIANA PINEDA AND THE SOUTH CENTRAL AREA

Mesón La Alegría, c/Moras 4, south of the Puerta Real. Atmospheric local *mesón* noted for its meat dishes *a la parrilla* – fried by yourself on a table hotplate. Has a terrace and serves good *tapas* and *finos*.

Restaurante Chikito, Plaza del Campillo 9, south of Puerta Real (☎958 22 33 64). Fronted by four towering plane trees, and formerly the *Café Alameda* where Lorca, Falla and the *Rinconcillo* group met to debate and discuss. Literary lights from abroad such as Kipling and H.G. Wells all visited the bar's corner table (*rincón*). Today's restaurant is one of Granada's better ones for à la carte, but the medium-priced *menú* is unexciting. The nearby Plaza Mariana Pineda has a statue of Mariana Pineda, a *granadina* heroine who was executed in the reign of Fernando VII for embroidering a Liberal flag, and about whose life Lorca wrote a play. Closed Wed.

Horno de Santiago, Plaza de los Campos 8 (☎958 22 34 76). Probably the best restaurant in town, offering classic regional fish, meat and game dishes cooked with finesse. There's a *menú* for about 3000ptas. Closed Sun eve.

Restaurante Nuevo, c/Navas 25. Good budget restaurant with an economical *menú*.

Seis Peniques, Plaza de Padre Suárez. Quite a good little bar-restaurant with a small terrace facing the Casa de los Tiros; serves a decent *menú* for around 1100ptas.

ALHAMBRA AND CAMPO DEL PRÍNCIPE

Parador de San Francisco, Alhambra (☎958 22 14 40). The *parador's* restaurant has fine views and offers a varied and not-too-bank-breaking *menú* for around 3700ptas; à la carte, though, is another story.

La Mimbre, Paseo del Generalife s/n, near the Alhambra's entrance. With a delightful terrace shaded by willows (*mimbres*) this is one of the best restaurants on the Alhambra hill. The food is good but they are sometimes overwhelmed in high season. Good-value *menú* for around 1500ptas, which you may need to ask for.

La Ninfa, Campo del Príncipe. Popular Italian restaurant which puts out tables on this pleasant plaza, and is often full to bursting at weekends. The *ensalada primavera* is a must for your first course and the desserts are diet-bustingly delicious.

Lago de Como, Campo de Príncipe 8. Slightly cheaper than the one above, this two-storeyed Italian restaurant at the top end of the square is more routine but is more likely to have a table.

Tapas and drinking bars

Granada's proximity to the Sierra Nevada brings a coolness to the city which carries over into its imbibing and its nightlife. In the **bars** here you're just as likely to find locals ordering a glass of *rioja* as soon as the beloved *fino* of the rest of Andalucía. One local wine which the *granadinos* do cherish, though (and which you shouldn't miss), is *vino de la costa* (coast wine – ironically made in the mountains of the Alpujarras); amber in colour, fairly potent, but relatively easy on hangovers, it's the ideal partner for a *tapa*.

The **bars** recommended below are mainly for drinking, though most serve *tapas* and *raciones* and you could happily fill up and forget about going to a restaurant. The city has quite a reputation for its **tapas**, which are more elaborate than is usual in Andalucía and in most bars one comes free with each drink – a laudable trait in a city generally regarded as penny-pinching by most *andaluzes*. It's worth noting that the Turismo produces a glossy free **Rutas de Tapas pamphlet** which has maps and recommendations for places in both Granada and its province.

PLAZA NUEVA AND CATHEDRAL AREA

Aljibe, c/Animas 7, up the steps behind *Trastienda* (see below). Modern minimalist decor and loud music cater for a younger crowd; this bar does some *tapas* but most people turn up for its (often live) music. Improbably, on Monday nights there's a live classical set.

Al Pie de la Torre, c/Pie de la Torre s/n. Close to the foot of the cathedral's tower this is an atmospheric little bar for simple *tapas*.

Bodegas Castañeda, c/Almireceros 1, at the corner of c/Elvira – across Gran Vía from the cathedral. One of the city's oldest bars, alas much refurbished and prettified. Still, it makes an attractive first stop of an evening. Good *tapas* include generous paté and cheese boards (*tablas*), *montaditos* (small open sandwiches), baked potatoes and *gazpacho*. A lethal house special is the notorious *Calicasas* cocktail which seems to include just about everything behind the bar – downing two may mean a hands-and-knees crawl home.

Las Cuevas, c/Calderería Nueva, top end, next to Iglesia de San Gregorio. Good *tapas* guarantee that this place is always packed; they have a terrace fronting the church and do great pizzas cooked in a wood-burning oven.

Casa Enrique, Acera de Darro 8, near the Puerta Real. Good daytime or early-evening haunt with a wide *tapas* selection. Specializes in *jamón iberico* and *lomo* (pork loin) and *chorizo* from Salamanca. Wide-ranging wine list.

Hannigan and Sons, c/Cetti Merriem s/n, near the *Taberna del Irlandés* below. Independent Irish house whose owner *is* named Hannigan. The place has an airy bar-room feel to it and there's a snug, decorative stained glass and the only wooden floor in town. If you throw your cigarette ends on it Tony Hannigan will chuck you out; confusingly for locals every other bar in town encourages you to do just that.

Casa Julio, c/Hermosa, off Plaza Nueva. A pocket-sized boozers' bar lined with fine old *azulejos* that nonetheless turns out some excellent fried seafood *tapas*.

Bodegas La Mancha, c/Joaquín Costa 10 – around the corner from *Bodegas Castañeda*. Monumental spit-and-sawdust establishment (slightly more refined after refurbishment) hung with hams, and with great wine vats stationed behind the bar like rockets on a launch pad. Tasty *tapas* on offer include *jamón serrano*; they also sell excellent hot and cold *bocadillos* to eat in or take away.

Nueva Bodega, c/Cetti Meriem 3, off Gran Vía. Good-value local *bodega* which serves up basic *tapas* and *bocadillos* downstairs and a *menú* in an upstairs *comedor*.

Café-Bar Oliver, Plaza Pescadería 12, slightly north-west of the Plaza de la Trinidad. Another good *tapas* bar with a popular outdoor terrace.

Bar Reca, Plaza de la Trinidad, corner with c/Infantes. Lively *tapas* venue on a leafy square which fairly hums at lunchtime and in the early evening.

Bar Ricardo, Plaza Nueva (western end). One of several *terraza* bars on this popular plaza. A place to while away warmer evenings munching *tapas* and people-watching.

El Rinconcillo, Plaza Nueva, next to Pilar de Toro restaurant (above). Friendly Lilliputian bar with *terraza* serving good *tapas* and *raciones*.

Bar Sabanilla, c/San Sebastián 14 – not easy to find, just off the southeast corner of Plaza Bib-Rambla, down a passageway behind an unmarked door. This bar claims to be the oldest in Granada (it certainly looks it) and stays open till late. It's a basic, poky place, run by two friendly women who offer a free *tapa* with every drink. The barrelled *costa* wine here (from the Alpujarra village of Albondón) is recommended.

Taberna del Irlandés, c/Almireceros 7 just north of the cathedral. Vibrant and popular little "Irish" bar – with well-kept stout – run by ebullient hibernophile Manolo. A good deal more authentic than most of the dismally synthetic Irish theme pubs being set up across the south by the Cruz Campo group.

La Trastienda, c/Cuchilleros 11, on a small plaza just off c/Reyes Católicos. Plush little drinking den hidden behind a shop selling wine, cheese and *jamón serrano*. Once you've negotiated your way around the counter it's surprisingly cosy in the back.

ALBAICÍN

Bar Aixa, Plaza Larga. Welcoming bar with terrace tables serving up well-prepared *tapas* and *raciones*. Try their *migas* (fried breadcrumbs) stir-fried with crispy pork fat and green peppers or fresh anchovies.

Bar Aliatar, Plaza Aliatar, slightly northeast of the Iglesia del Salvador. Popular and atmospheric *tapas* place, famous for its *caracoles* (snails).

Bar El Berrios, c/Panaderos 20, off Plaza Larga. *Tapas* on offer here include *setas con gambas* (mushrooms and prawns) and *cazón al alioli* (shark) and *longaniza* (sausage).

Bar Lara, Plaza San Miguel Bajo. A fine bar which puts out tables on this picturesque Albaicín square, and serves *tapas*, *platos combinados* and an excellent *costa* wine.

Rincón del Aurora, Plaza San Miguel Bajo 7. Another good bar with outdoor tables on the same square. Try the *fritura* (fried fish) or *carne al la Rondeña*.

El Yunque, Plaza San Miguel Bajo 3. Probably the best of this square's bars owned and run by a noted *flamenco cantaor*, Antonio, and his wife – who was a well-known dancer in her time. House specials include *pollo en salsa de almendras* (chicken in almond sauce) and *lomo alpujarreño* (pork loin). They have inside seating on the adjacent corner if it's chilly or wet.

CAMPO DEL PRÍNCIPE AND CARRERA DEL DARRO

Bar Amparo, Campo del Príncipe 18. One of the best bars on this ever-popular square, with fine *tapas* to wash down with *manzanilla* and *fino*.

En un lugar del Alhambra, Carrera del Darro 51. Highly attractive bar, which follows the river gorge dividing the Alhambra hill from the Albaicín. *Puerta del Vino*, further along, is another good stopover, as is *Fondo Reservado* up the nearby Cuesta Santa Inés, both catering for a trendier crowd, while further along still is *Pie de la Vela*, which has some striking decor.

Café-Bar Ocaña, Plaza del Realejo 1, north of Campo del Príncipe. Bustling neighbourhood bar serving up great *bocadillos* with a very spicy *tomate* relish.

Rabo de Nube, Paseo de los Tristes (aka Paseo del Padre Manjón). One of many bars on this plaza – at the far end of the Carrera del Darro – and a wonderful place to sit out at night with a drink whilst gazing up at the Alhambra's illuminated battlements. This place serves *tablas* (paté and cheese boards) and pizza. The city council often puts on concerts here during the summer.

Tasca de la Pie de la Vela, Carrera del Darro 35. Offshoot of the bar with the same name mentioned above, this is another pleasant haunt offering *tapas* and simple meals.

UNIVERSITY ZONE

Café Laguna, c/Martinez de la Rosa 6, close to Plaza del Gran Capitán. Good *tapas* and *raciones* at this relaxed neighbourhood bar with a serious wine cellar.

Bar Lax, c/Veronica de la Magdalena 31, a couple of blocks west of Plaza de la Trinidad. Pleasant Swedish bar serving – amongst others – salmon *tapas* and smorgasbord; has a small courtyard terrace.

La Tertulia, c/Pintor López Mezquita 3, slightly northeast of the bus station. Argentinian bar with some *tapas* and live tango on Tuesday nights. They also do tango classes here.

Breakfast bars, tea rooms and ice cream

Granada's **breakfast bars** set the city up for work in the mornings and to watch the best of them dishing up *pan tostada*, *chocolate* and *cafés exprés* with production-line efficiency is an entertainment in itself. The show begins all over town around 8am and lasts about an hour. You'll soon spot the best places – they're packed – but a typical one is *Café Bib-Rambla* on the plaza of the same name which also serves up delicious *churros*. More leisurely breakfasts are to be had in the beautiful patio of *Pilar de Toro* on Plaza Nueva (see restaurant listings) where toast and coffee come surprisingly cheap considering the location. Late or early travellers might appreciate *Café Bar Ochando*, by the train station on Avda. de los Andaluces, open 24 hours and serving a good breakfast. For sit-down **cakes and pastries** later in the day, in the Albaicín you could try *Casa de los Pasteles* in Plaza Larga, or in the centre *Cafetería Lisboa*, at the corner of c/Elvira and c/Reyes Católicos, which turns out its own range of mouthwatering confections.

In the "Little Morocco" district in and around the Calles Calderería Nueva and Calderería Vieja a large number of **teterías** or **tea-houses** have sprung up to become a colourful part of the city's social scene. However, so many have climbed on the bandwagon in recent times that service and standards in some leave a lot to be desired. The friendly, Moroccan-run *As-Sirat* ("bridge between earth and paradise"), c/Calderería Nueva 5, is one of the oldest and offers eighty-plus teas in its Moorish-inspired interior. At the top of the hill, the multi-storeyed *Pervane*, Calderería Nueva 24, is popular with a younger crowd. Also worth a try are *Kasbah* at the foot of Calderería Nueva, and *Tetería Tuareg*, c/Corpus Cristi 5 just off the foot of c/Calderería Vieja, where a cave-like interior recesses into candlelit gloom and teas are served along with *crêpes* in summer and *pasteles* in winter. An interesting newcomer here is *Repostería Morisca*, c/Calderería Vieja 12, a bakery selling Moroccan cakes, pastries and pies – try their *pastela*, a delicious spicy chicken- and egg-filled filo pastry.

The undisputed queen of Granada's **ice-cream** parlours is the popular *Los Italianos*, opposite the cathedral at Gran Vía 4, with excellent home-made ices: their *cassata* is recommended. The *helados* at *La Perla* (Plaza Nueva 16) are just as good, and they certainly have the better location; try their refreshing *horchata* in summer. Both places also serve up the refreshing summertime *blanco y negro* – iced coffee with cinnamon-flavoured ice-cream. The *Café Football Heladería*, Plaza María Pineda (near Puerta Real), is another pleasant place, with tables on this leafy square; they also do good breakfast *churros* here.

Discobares and discotecas

Conventional **discotecas** aren't too popular with the restrained *granadinos*, though the university guarantees a bit of action during term time and particularly at weekends; **c/Pedro Antonio**, to the west of the centre, is where the action is. There are, as everywhere in Spain, a fair scattering of **discobares** – drinking bars with loud sound systems, trendy decor and a fashion-conscious clientele.

Babylon, c/Silleria (between Plaza Nueva and Gran Via). Reggae club much favoured by US students in Granada.

Berlín and **Espacio Abierto**, c/Obispo Hurtado – west of Plaza de la Trinidad. Two *discobares* with *moda* sounds and decor.

Camborio, Sacromonte. Fashionable *discobar* which is especially lively at weekends.

Entresuelo, c/Azacayas, off Gran Vía. Popular *discobar* frequented by many of the city's English-language teachers – also has twice weekly transvestite show.

La Estrella, c/Cuchilleros near Plaza Nueva. A central *discobar*.

Granada 10, c/Carcél Baja 10, off Gran Vía near the cathedral. Small but central disco inside a beautifully restored retro cinema – which is what it still is before the disco gets going. Worth seeing a film first just to wallow around in its marvellously decadent gold lamé sofas.

Lo Lamento, c/del Buen Suceso at junction with c/Puentzuelas west of Puerta Real. Popular lesbian bar. Slightly north, *Tic Tac* on c/Horno de Haza is similar and also good.

Morgan, c/Obispo Hurtado 15, to the west of Plaza de la Trinidad. Lively disco-bar with DJs; Thurs–Sat.

Oh! Granada, c/Dr Guirao (no number – it's at the near end of this street leading to the Plaza de Toros). The city's largest disco has three dance floors and plenty of strobes.

Patapalo, c/Naranjos 2 behind Plaza del Carmen. Stylish *discobar*.

Planta Baja, Horno de Abad, off Carril del Picón and slightly northwest of Plaza de la Trinidad. Long-established *discobar* now in a new home.

Sacromonte caves. When the university is in session, the line of caves just above the Casa del Chapiz are turned into discos. They're always packed out at weekends and generally fun. After dark be alert for bag snatchers in this zone and carry as few valuables as possible.

Live music, theatre and dance

Like many cities of Andalucía, Granada lays claim to the roots of **flamenco**, though you'd hardly believe it from the travesties dished up these days in the gypsy quarter of Sacromonte (see box on p.423). The "flamenco shows" on offer in the city aren't much better, either, being geared firmly to tourism. However, up in the Albaicín there is one genuine club (see below), with consistently good artists and an audience of aficionados. Generally more rewarding are the **festivals** held throughout the year, such as the city's Theatre Festival at the end of May, or the International Music and Dance Festival at the end of June, during which you may just be lucky enough to see a performance under the stars in the Alhambra. Tickets for these events are sold at a *kiosko* on Acero del Casino, close to the post office on Puerta Real. Other concerts by folk, rock and flamenco artistes are staged throughout the year in locations such as the **Corral del Carbón** or Moorish patios in the Albaicín. Watch out for street posters, check listings in the local daily paper *Ideal* or the monthly *Guía del Ocio* (see "Listings"). There's also an annual **jazz festival** in October or November – the Turismo will have details.

FLAMENCO

Los Faroles, Sacromonte, almost at the very end of the line of "caves" – ask anyone for directions as it's well known. A good place for a lunchtime or evening drink with a view of the Alhambra from its terrace. The genial owner, Quiqui, is a fount of information on flamenco and the impromptu real thing often happens here after dark, but not always.

Los Jardines Neptuno, junction of c/Arabial and c/Virgen Blanca, 2km southeast of the centre. Long-established flamenco theatre run by a noted dancer which in summer is a tourist trap; during the winter months it is more like the real McCoy.

El Niño de los Almendras, signless in c/Muladar de Doña Sancha at the junction with c/La Tiña and southeast of Plaza San Miguel Bajo, Albaicín. This tiny bar – done up inside to resemble a cave – is owned by the flamenco singer of the same name. Only open Friday nights (starts around midnight) but *inolvidable* flamenco when it happens.

Peña Platería, Patio de los Aljives 13, Albaicín. Private club devoted to the celebration of Andalucía's great folk art. Flamenco is performed most nights, particularly at weekends, and visitors are generally welcomed, so long as they show a genuine interest and aren't in too large a group. You'll need to speak some Spanish and use a bit of charm. Closed August.

JAZZ

Club de Música, c/de las Moras 2, just above the Puerta Real (☎958 22 41 26). Live jazz is often performed here, but ring ahead before turning up.

Echevaria, c/Postigo de la Cuna 2, a tiny alley off c/Azacayas which is off the east side of Gran Vía. Jazz/flamenco bar which gets quite lively. Wed, Thurs and Sun nights only.

Listings

Airport Granada airport (☎958 24 52 23) handles domestic flights to Madrid and Barcelona; details from Iberia (☎958 22 99 71), Air Aviaco (☎958 22 75 92) or Air Europa (☎902 24 00 42).

Banks Numerous banks and ATM cash points are available along c/Reyes Católicos and Gran Vía.

Books/newspapers Metro, c/Gracia 31, off c/Alhóndiga, to the southwest of Plaza de la Trinidad, is the best international bookshop with wide selection of books on Granada, Lorca and walking maps. Librería Atlantida, Gran Vía 9, has a wide selection of books, including a good array on aspects of Granada, and Librería Urbano, c/San Juan de Dios 33, is another shop with a broad range and many books in English. Foreign press is sold by the *kioskos* in Plaza Nueva and Puerta Real. The monthly *Guía del Ocio* (available from newspaper *kioskos*) lists most of what's happening on the cultural and entertainment front though it tends to be less up-to-date than the city's rather staid daily paper, *Ideal*, which has a more reliable entertainment guide, particularly in its weekend editions.

Bullfights are held in season at the Plaza de Toros, Avda. Dr Olóriz in the northern suburbs.

Bus departures See "Arrival" for details and addresses of the train station and bus terminal. For information on bus services and current timetables check with the companies, which are all (except for services to the Sierra Nevada) based at the new bus station. *Alsina Graells* (☎958 18 50 10) for Almería, Alpujarras (high and low), Córdoba, Jaén, Málaga, Motril, Úbeda, Sevilla and the coast. *Empresa Autedia* (☎958 15 36 36) for Baza and Guadix. *Autocares Bonal* (☎958 27 31 00) for Veleta and the north side of Sierra Nevada (see p.440).

Camping/hiking equipment Armería, c/Mesones 53 (near Plaza de la Trinidad), stocks a range of camping and hiking gear.

Car rental Autos Fortuna, c/Infanta Beatriz 2 (☎958 26 02 54), are a reliable local outfit who undercut the big boys. Atesa, c/Rector Marín Ocete 8 (☎958 28 87 55), has reasonable deals with national back-up.

Football C.F. Granada are yet another of Andalucía's clubs plodding along in Group IV of *Segunda División "B"*. In recent seasons they've been regular top six finishers, but so far promotion has eluded them. The stadium, Nuevo los Cármenes (☎958 25 33 00), lies northwest of the Hospital Real.

Hiking maps for the Sierra Nevada and Las Alpujarras can be obtained from the Turismo, though for a more specialist selection try Cartografica del Sur, c/Valle Inclán 2 southwest of the train station in the university zone (☎ & fax 958 20 49 01), which sells a wide range, including military maps. The CNIG (National Geographic Institute), c/Divina Pastora 7, by the Jardines del Triunfo (☎958 29 04 11), also sells 1:50,000 and 1:25,000 maps.

Hospital Cruz Roja (Red Cross), c/Escoriaza 8 (☎958 22 22 22) or Hospital Clinico San Cecilio, Avda. Dr Olóriz, near the Plaza de Toros; (☎958 27 02 00). For advice on emergency treatment phone ☎061.

Internet *Internet*, Plaza de los Girones 3 near the Casa de Los Tiros (Mon–Sat 9am–11pm, Sun 4–11pm; ☎958 28 92 69), is Granada's most efficient online operation; screens cost 400ptas per hr and readers with this guide receive 25 per cent discount. Other central internet cafés open daily are *Madar Internet*, c/Calderería Nueva 12 (mobile ☎656486993) and *Freememory*, c/San Jerónimo 14 (☎958 80 60 80).

Laundry Lavandería La Paz, c/La Paz 19 just west of Plaza de la Trinidad, is Granada's last remaining laundrette, and will wash, dry and fold 6kg of washing the same day for 1200ptas.

Left luggage There are lockers at both train and bus stations as well as a *consigna* at the latter.

Markets The main – and ultra modern – *mercado* is in Plaza San Agustín, just north of the cathedral (Mon–Fri early until 1.30pm). For natural/Moroccan/traditional Spanish groceries try c/Calderería Nueva and neighbouring c/Calderería Vieja. Encarni II is a recommended general store in the latter and La Tienda is a excellent health food store (at no. 8) in the former.

Police For emergencies dial ☎091 (national) or ☎092 (local). The Policía Nacional are located at c/Duquesa 15 off Plaza de la Trinidad (☎958 27 83 00). The Policía Local station is in the *Ayuntamiento* building on Plaza del Carmen (☎958 20 94 61). There is also a property lost-and-found section in the same building (☎958 24 81 03).

Post office Puerta Real: Mon–Fri 9am–8.30pm, Sat 9am–2pm.

Shopping Granada and its province are noted for ceramics, and Artesanía El Suspiro, Plaza Santa Ana 1 at the northeast end of Plaza Nueva, has a selection from surrounding *granadino* villages, as well as Moroccan pottery and jewellery; its charming Scottish *dueña* is a fund of local information. Castellano, c/Almireceros 6, between c/Elvira and Gran Vía, is the best place to buy *jamón serrano* and also stocks regional wines and brandies. La Casa de Los Tés, c/Calderería Vieja s/n, sells herbs and spices, incenses and exotic teas plus foreign imports like peanut butter and veggie patés. Traditional perfumes are made by Aromas de Al-Andalus, c/Almireceros 5 (near Castellano above), using ancient Moorish formulas. La Alcena, c/San Jerónimo 3 on the cathedral's north side, is a great place to find the special products of Andalucía including olive oil, wines, cheeses (try the *queso de almendras*), *embutidos* and lots more; the friendly proprietor speaks good English.

Swimming pool Piscina Miami (☎958 25 00 31), junction c/Arabial and c/Virgen Blanca (west of the centre), makes an ideal break from the city heat in summer and has an Olympic-size pool, kids' pool, sunbeds and a good restaurant.

West towards Málaga: Alhama de Granada

Travelling from Granada to Málaga by bus will take you along the fast but dull A92 *autovía*, which crosses the *Vega* to the west of the city. With your own transport and time to spare, a more interesting and scenic route passes through the delightful but little-visited town of **Alhama de Granada** and traverses the spectacular **Zaffaraya Pass**, descending into Málaga by way of the ruggedly beautiful **Axarquía** region.

Leave Granada by the route for Motril and the coast, the N323 – but avoid the *autovía*. The road branches right at Armilla, 4km southwest of the city, where you should take the A338, towards the village of **Malá** (which has a fine roadside *venta*), and, 10km beyond, **Ventas de Huelma**. From here the road twists and climbs into the Sierra de la Pera and, after descending to the lakeside village of **Poblado del Embalse** – where there is a good **campsite** *Los Bermejales* (☎958 35 93 36) with pool and restaurant – continues through a rich landscape of bubbling streams and rocky gulches overlooked by hills planted with olives, to Alhama de Granada, 14km further.

Alhama de Granada

Scenically sited along along a ledge overlooking a broad gorge or *tajo* created by the Río Alhama, the spa town of **ALHAMA DE GRANADA** is one of the unsung gems of Granada province and makes a wonderful overnight stop. It has a couple of striking churches in a well-preserved old quarter, and its baths, dating back to Roman and Moorish times (*Al Hamma* in Arabic means "hot springs") still draw in numerous visitors during the season to take the waters. They were greatly treasured during Moorish times, and the Spanish expression of regret *"¡Ay de mi Alhama!"* was the cry of sorrow attributed to Abu al-Hacen (the Mulhacen after whom the Sierra Nevada peak is named) when he lost the town in a crucial battle here against the Christian forces in 1482. It was this loss that severed the vital link between Granada and Málaga (and hence North Africa), foreshadowing the end of eight centuries of Moorish rule. Settlement started here much earlier, however, and the ancient Iberian town on the site was referred to by the Romans as *Artigi*.

The Town

Most of Alhama's sights are within a short walk of Plaza de la Constitución, the main square fronted by bars and restaurants. At the square's northern end there's a ruined and now privately owned **Moorish castle** with the unfortunate addition of nineteenth-century crenellated battlements. To the right of this, the sixteenth-to-eighteenth-century **Iglesia del Carmen** (open evenings at 8pm) is Alhama's

RICHARD FORD AND THE *HANDBOOK FOR SPAIN*

Very few books have been written about Spain that do not draw on **Richard Ford** and his 1845 *Murray's Handbook for Spain* – arguably the best, the funniest and the most encyclopedic guidebook ever written on any country.

Born in 1796 into a family of means, Ford studied law but never practised and in 1824 married Harriet Capel, the attractive daughter of the Earl of Essex. When she received medical advice to seek a warmer climate for her health, Ford – inspired by Irving's recent publication of the *Conquest of Granada* – took his family off to Spain where they lived for three years, wintering in Sevilla and spending the summers living in part of the Alhambra in Granada.

Ford spent most of his time traversing the length and breadth of the country – but particularly Andalucía – on horseback, making notes and sketches (his mother had been a skilled amateur artist). It's hard to believe that all this was not meant for some literary purpose, but it was only back in England – and six years after his return – when publisher John Murray asked him to recommend someone to write a Spanish travel guide, that Ford suggested himself.

His marriage now broken, he settled down in a Devon village in a house to which he added many Spanish features (including some souvenirs from the Alhambra) to work solidly for nearly five years on what became the *Handbook for Spain*. When Murray and others took exception to the final manuscript's often caustic invective, he was advised to tone it down and a revised – but still gloriously outspoken – edition finally appeared in 1845 to great acclaim. Curiously, although he became *the* resident expert on Spain, he never returned to the country which had put him on the literary map.

Ford's blind spots, such as British prejudice against Baroque architecture (the more extravagant styles of which he dismissed as "vile Churrigueresque"), are often irritating, and High Tory attitudes sometimes verging on jingoism, added to a splenetic francophobia, often threaten to tip over into the worst kind of churlishness. However, the author's enduring fascination with Spain and all things Spanish – he personally introduced *amontillado* sherry and Extremaduran *jamón serrano* into England – allied to a crisp writing style and a dry wit, invariably save him, and some of his passages are still hilariously funny and related with a wry irony.

His description of the hostelry at Alhama is typical:

"The *Posada* at Alhama, albeit called *La Grande*, is truly iniquitous; diminutive indeed are the accommodations, colossal the inconveniences; but this is a common misnomer, *en las cosas de España*. Thus Philip IV was called El Grande, under whose fatal rule Spain crumbled into nothing; like a ditch he became greater in proportion as more land was taken away. All who are wise will bring from Málaga a good hamper of eatables, a bota of wine, and some cigars, for however devoid of creature comforts this grand hotel, there is a grand supply of creeping creatures, and the traveller runs risk of bidding adieu to sleep, and passing the night exclaiming, *Ay! de mi Alhama*."

prettiest church, overlooking the **Tajo** and fronted by an old fountain where the farmers water their donkeys on sultry summer evenings. Just off to the right here, with its back to the *tajo*, is *Artesanía Los Tajos*, c/Peñas 34, selling local ceramics as well as some remarkable traditional clay water-whistles called *canarios*. Once used by local shepherds and goatherds, they make an ear-splitting racket, as the proprietor will eagerly demonstrate.

To reach the other monuments you'll need to backtrack slightly to c/Baja Iglesia which leads up to Plaza los Presos, passing en route (up a ramp to the left) the **Casa de la Inquisición**, which may have nothing to do with the Inquisition at all, but is noted for a fine Plateresque facade. The town's main church, **La Encarnación**, dominates the Plaza de los Presos, a pleasant little square with a central fountain. Donated by Fernando and Isabel after the conquest of the town from the Moors, it was completed in the first half of the sixteenth century by some of the major architects of the time – among them Enrique Egas and Diego de Siloé, the designers of the Capilla Real and cathedral at Granada. Siloé was responsible for the striking and massive Renaissance belfry which towers above the town. The restrained interior has an impressive *artesonado* ceiling and the *sacristía* has fifteenth-century vestments with embroidery attributed to Isabel herself.

Opposite the church, on the same square, there's an ancient **posito** (granary) dating from the thirteenth century but incorporating parts of an earlier synagogue. Just downhill from here the sixteenth-century **Hospital de la Reina**, c/Vendederas s/n, houses a lethargic **Turismo** (Mon–Fri 10am–1pm & 4–7pm; ☎957 36 06 86) which, when open (and this often doesn't happen) can provide maps and information on walking in the area. Leaving the square to the right of the church along c/Alta Iglesia takes you past the misleadingly named **Casa Romana** on the right, an eighteenth-century mansion believed to have been constructed on the site of a Roman villa. The same street returns to the Plaza Mayor.

Alhama's only other site of note is a well-preserved **Roman bridge** at the edge of the town, close to the C340 to Granada, a short distance along the road to the *balneario* (baths). Beyond here, a signed and twisting road leads 1km to the **baths** which give the town its name. Although little remains of the Roman baths seen by Ford in the nineteenth century, elements of the Moorish *hammam* survive and can be seen by enquiring at the *Hotel Balneario* (daily 12.30–1.30pm; 100ptas) whose staff will conduct you into the depths to see some astonishing Moorish arches and the odd stone inscribed in Latin.

Practicalities

On the **accommodation** front things have improved immeasurably since Ford was here (see box opposite) and the dreaded *La Grande* is no more. If you want to stay, outside August there's usually no problem fixing up a room at *Hostal San José*, Plaza de la Constitución 27 (☎958 35 01 56; ③), right on the main square with en-suite rooms. A more attractive rural alternative is the new *Hotel El Ventorro* 2km out of town on the Málaga road, fronting a lake (☎958 35 04 38; includes breakfast; ④). They offer walking, *burro*, horse and mountain bike excursions and have a good restaurant. A more upmarket option is the spa hotel *Balneario de Granada* (☎958 35 00 11; ⑤), at the baths 1km off the road into town from Granada which, although situated in dense pine woods, has the ambience of a sanitorium. **Meals** are available from restaurants on the main square, Plaza de la Constitución, the best of which is *El Sitio de Paco Moyano* – run by a retired flamenco *cantante* – and the nearby *Bar Ochoa* (slightly uphill from *Hostal San José*) serves up tasty **tapas**. There's also a **swimming pool** with shade just out of town along the Málaga road.

Towards the Zaffaraya Pass

South of Alhama, the A335 climbs out towards Ventas de Zaffaraya – passing a great value *venta*, *Los Caños de Alcaiceria*, 10km out – cutting through a rich agricultural area where tomatoes, cereals and other vegetables are planted in deep brown soil. The spectacular **Zaffaraya Pass**, which slips through a cleft in the Sierra de Tejeda and was part of the old coach route, provides a dramatic entrance into the Axarquía region of Málaga Province, with superb **views** to the distant Mediterranean. Roughly 6km beyond the pass lies the deserted medieval village of **Zalía** (see p.102), after which the road continues to **Vélez-Málaga** (see p.99) and the coast.

The Sierra Nevada

South from Granada rise the mountains of the **SIERRA NEVADA** (soon to be awarded the status of a National Park), a startling backdrop to the city, snowcapped for most of the year and offering skiing from November until late May. The ski slopes are at **Solynieve**, an unimaginative, developed resort just 28km away (40min by bus). Here, the direct car route across the range stops, but from this point walkers can make the relatively easy two- to three-hour trek up to **Veleta** (3470m), the second highest peak of the range (see p.441) and the second-highest summit on the Spanish peninsula.

Before the road was constructed in the 1920s few *granadinos* ever came up to the Sierra, but one group who had worn out a trail since the times of the Moors were the *neveros* or icemen, who used mules to bring down blocks of ice from the mountains, which they then sold in the streets. Their route to Veleta can still be followed beyond the village of **Monachil**, to the southeast of the city, which has, incidentally, a good little mid-priced restaurant, the *Casa Bienvenido* (closed Mon). The A395 road, though, has been a mixed blessing for the delicate ecosystem of the Sierra, and the expanding horrors of the Solynieve ski centre, which was chosen to hold the 1995 World Ski Championships (subsequently cancelled due to lack of snow and then held in 1996), has only made things worse.

The best general **map** of the Sierra Nevada and of the lower slopes of the Alpujarras is the one co-produced by the Instituto Geográfico Nacional and the Federación Española de Montañismo (1:50,000). The CNIG's 1:25,000 sheets are more detailed for trekking purposes, and both can be obtained in Granada (see "Listings" p.436).

Solynieve and the Veleta/Mulhacén ascent

Throughout the year *Autocares Bonal* runs a **daily bus** from Granada to the Solynieve resort and, just above this, to the *Parador de Sierra Nevada*. The bus leaves from the Palacio de Congresos (Paseo del Violon) across the Río Genil, southwest of the city centre, at 9am, returning from the *parador* at 5pm (and passing Solynieve 10 minutes later). For the winter service (Oct–March) ring the bus company (see Granada "Listings"). If you don't want to walk from the centre, bus #1 going east along Gran Vía will drop you off very near the Palacio de Congressos stop; tickets to Solynieve (800ptas round-trip) can be bought in advance from *Bar El Ventorrillo* next door.

The route leaves Granada via the Paseo del Salón where two wagons stand as a memory to the tram-service which, from the 1920s until 1970, used to ascend as far as

---

THE SIERRA NEVADA FLORA AND FAUNA

The Sierra Nevada is particularly rich in **wild flowers**. Some fifty varieties are unique to these mountains, among them five gentians, including *Gentiana bory*, the pansy *Viola nevadensis*, a shrubby mallow *Lavatera oblongifolia*, and a spectacular honeysuckle, the seven- to ten-metre high *Lonicera arborea*.

Wildlife, too, abounds away from the roads. One of the most exciting sights is the *Cabra hispanica*, a wild horned goat which you'll see standing on pinnacles, silhouetted against the sky. They roam the mountains in flocks and jump up the steepest slopes with amazing agility when they catch the scent of the walker on the wind. The higher slopes are also home to a rich assortment of **butterflies**, among them the rare Nevada Blue as well as varieties of Fritillary. **Bird-watching** is also superb, with the colourful hoopoe – a bird with a stark, haunting cry – a common sight.

Güejar Sierra. Beyond Pinos de Genil the road begins to climb seriously and, after 28km the ski resort of **Solynieve** appears.

With **your own transport** take the Acera del Darro east from the Puerta Real and follow the signs for the Sierra Nevada. Once on the ascent to the mountains the road is dotted with alpine-style **eating places** which do good business in season. After some 17km you could make a stop at the **Balcón de Canales** with fine views over the Río Genil and its dam. At the 22km mark and signposted just off the road is the **Sierra Nevada Natural Park Information Centre** (daily 10.30am–2.30pm & 4.30–7pm; ☎958 34 06 25), which sells guidebooks, maps and hats (sun protection is vital; see below), and has a permanent exhibition on the park's flora and fauna. There's also a pleasant **cafetería** with a stunning terrace view.

Solynieve

SOLYNIEVE ("Sun and Snow", aka Pradollano) is a hideous-looking ski resort – worse than usual – and regarded by serious Alpine skiers as something of a joke. But with snow lingering so late in the year (Granada's Turismo should be able to advise on the state of this, or contact Sierra Nevada Club's interactive phone line on ☎958 24 91 19) it has obvious attractions for *granadinos* and others determined to ski in southern Spain. From the middle of the resort a lift takes you straight up to the main ski lifts, which provides access to most of the higher **slopes**, and when the snow is right you can ski a few kilometres back down to the *zona hotelera* (the lifts run only when there's skiing). There are plenty of places to rent gear. If you intend to ski (or walk) here be sure to double your **skin protection** as this is the most southerly ski centre in Europe with intense sun at high altitudes. Visiting Solynieve in high summer is a surreal experience as it's almost a ghost town with only the odd shop or bar open and a vast, central plaza – teeming with crowds of multicoloured skiers in winter – eerily empty.

The Turismo at Granada can advise on **places to stay** at the resort (many hotels open only during the ski season) or contact the Sierra Nevada Club (☎958 24 91 11). The cheapest accommodation is the modern and comfortable *Albergue Juvenil*, c/Peñones 22 (☎958 48 03 05, fax 958 48 13 77; open all year), on the edge of the ski resort, where you can get great value double (②) and four-bed rooms, all en suite. They also rent out skis and equipment in season. Other places in the resort proper are incredibly **expensive** in season, with even the cheapest doubles priced at the lower end of our ⑦ category. Higher still, and 3km away in isolated Peñones de San Francisco are a couple more options: the *Albergue Universitario* (☎958 48 10 03; ③ half-board), just off the main road towards the *parador*, has bunk rooms, doubles and a restaurant, while the bleakly modern *Parador Sierra Nevada* (☎958 48 06 61, fax 958 48 02 12; ⑤), no longer part of the state *parador* chain, opens only in the ski season. Without transport both places are extremely isolated, which may, of course, be just what you are looking for. The bus turns around at the *parador* and this marks the start of the Veleta ascent (see below).

The Capileira road, Veleta and Mulhacén

In summer the bleak, cluttered landscape of the ski resort is good to leave behind. The **ascent of Veleta** is a none-too-challenging hike rather than a climb but should only be attempted between May and September – unless you're properly geared up – but even then you'll need warm and waterproof clothing. From the *parador* the **Capileira-bound road** – now permanently closed to traffic to protect the sierra's delicate environment – actually runs past the peak of Veleta. Recently asphalted – somewhat removing the sense of adventure from the trek – it is perfectly, and tediously, walkable (cycles are allowed but it's a fierce climb). However, most hikers follow the well-worn shortcuts between the snakes the road is forced to make. With your own transport it's possible to shave a couple of kilometres off the total by ignoring the no-entry signs at the car park near to the *Albergue Universitario* and continuing on to a second car park further up the mountain from which point the road is then barred. Although the peak of the mountain looks deceptively close from here you should allow two to three hours to reach the summit and one-and-a-half hours down. Make sure to bring **food and water** along as you will not be able to find either en-route – although on summer weekends, an enterprising roadside vendor often dispenses gin and tonic midway from a bucket of snow – and a picnic at the summit is one of the best meals to be had in Spain, weather permitting (don't leave rubbish behind).

With a great deal of energy you could conceivably walk to Capileira (see p.451), though it's a good 30km, there's nothing along the way and temperatures drop pretty low by late afternoon. En route, an hour beyond Veleta, you pass just under **Mulhacén** – the tallest peak on the Iberian peninsula at 3479m. The climb is two hours of exposed and windy ridge-crawling from the road, and with a sudden, sheer drop on its northwest face. There is a gentler slope down to the Siete Lagunas valley to the east.

Ruta de los Tres Mil (High Peaks Traverse)

The classic *Ruta Integral de los Tres Mil*, a complete traverse of all the Sierra's peaks over 3000m high, starts in Jeres del Marquesado on the north side of the Sierra Nevada (due south of Guadix) and finishes in Lanjarón, in the Alpujarras. It's an exhausting **three- to four-day itinerary** – four unless you're an active and experienced climber. Taking four days entails overnight stays near Puntal de Vacares, in the Siete Lagunas valley noted above, at the *Refugio de la Caldera*, and at the Cerro de Caballo hut. Slightly shorter and more practicable variations involve a start from the Vadillo refuge in the Estrella valley (northwest of Vacares), or from Trevélez in the Alpujarras, and a first overnight at Siete Lagunas.

Whichever way you choose, be aware that the section between Veleta and Elorrieta calls for rope, an ice axe (and crampons before June) and good scrambling skills. (There is another difficult section between Peñón Colorado and Cerro de Caballo.) If you're not up to this, it is possible to **detour** round the Veleta–Elorrieta section, but you will end up on the ridge flanking the Lanjarón river valley on the east rather than on the west; here there is a single cement hut, the *Refugio Forestal*, well-placed for the final day's walk to Lanjarón.

For **any exploration of the Sierra Nevada**, it is essential to take a tent, proper gear and ample food. It's a serious mountain and you should be prepared for the eventuality of not being able to reach or find the huts (which are marked correctly on the 1:50,000 map), or the weather turning nasty.

An approach from Trevélez

The full *Ruta de los Tres Mil* is probably more than most walkers – even hardy trekkers – would want to attempt. A modified version, starting in Trevélez (see "Las Alpujarras" section) and ending in Lanjarón, with the detour noted above, is a bit easier – though still strenuous.

Ascending Mulhacén from Trevélez is going to take a full six hours up, four hours down – assuming that you do not get lost or rest (both unlikely) and that there is no snowpack on Mulhacén's east face (equally unlikely until July). If you decide to try, be prepared for an overnight stop. Heading out of Trevélez, make sure that you begin on the higher track over the Crestón de Posteros, to link up with *acequias* (irrigation channels) coming down from the top of the Río Culo Perro (Dog's Arse River) valley; if you take the main, tempting trail which goes toward Jeres del Marquesado, and then turn into the mouth of the Río Culo Perro, you face quagmires and thorn patches that beggar belief. The standard place to camp is in the Siete Lagunas valley below the peak, allowing an early-morning ascent to the summit before the mists come up.

Continuing the traverse, you can drop down the west side of Mulhacén (take care on this awkward descent) to the road coming from Veleta. Follow this toward Veleta, and you can spend a second night at the very basic *Refugio Pillavientos*. Moving on, to the west, plan on a third night spent at either the *Refugio Elorrieta*, Cerro de Caballo or the *Refugio Forestal*, depending on your capabilities.

Las Alpujarras

The road south from Granada to Motril crosses the fertile *Vega* after leaving the city and then climbs steeply until at 850m above sea level it reaches the **Puerto del Suspiro del Moro** – the Pass of the Sigh of the Moor. Boabdil, last Moorish king of Granada, came this way, having just handed over the keys of his city to the *Reyes Católicos* in exchange for a fiefdom over the Alpujarras. From the pass you catch your last glimpse of the city and the Alhambra. The road then descends and beyond Padul crosses the valley of Lecrín planted with groves of orange, lemon and almond trees, the latter a riot of pink and white blossom in late winter. To the east, through a narrow defile close to Béznar, lie the great **valleys of the Alpujarras** – "the Switzerland of Spain" as Ford described them – first settled in the twelfth century by Berber refugees from Sevilla, and later the Moors' last stronghold in Spain.

Some Alpujarran history – and developments

The valleys are bounded to the north by the Sierra Nevada, and to the south by the lesser *sierras* of Lujar, La Contraviesa and Gador. The eternal snows of the high *sierras* keep the valleys and their seventy or so villages well watered all summer long. Rivers have cut deep gorges in the soft mica and shale of the upper mountains, and over the centuries have deposited silt and fertile soil on the lower hills and in the valleys; here the villages have grown, for the soil is rich and easily worked. The intricate terracing that today preserves these deposits was begun perhaps as long as two thousand years ago by Visigoths or Ibero-Celts, whose remains have been found at Capileira.

The Moors carried on the tradition, and modified the terracing and irrigation in their inimitable way. They transformed the Alpujarras into an earthly paradise, and there they retired to bewail the loss of their beloved lands in *al-Andalus*. After the fall of Granada, many of the city's Muslim population settled in the villages, and there resisted a series of royal edicts demanding their forced conversion to Christianity. In 1568 they rose up in a final, short-lived revolt, which led to the expulsion of all Spanish Moors. Even then, however, two Moorish families were required to stay in each village to show the new Christian peasants, who had been marched down from Galicia and Asturias to repopulate the valleys, how to operate the intricate irrigation systems.

Through the following centuries, the villages fell into impoverished existence, with the land owned by a few wealthy families, and worked by peasants. It was one of the most remote parts of Spain in the 1920s, when the author Gerald Brenan settled in one of the eastern villages, Yegen, and described the life in his book *South from Granada*, and things changed little over the next forty-odd years. During the Civil War, the occasional truckload of Nationalist youth trundled in from Granada, rounded up a few bewildered locals, and shot them for "crimes" of which they were wholly ignorant; Republican youths came up in their trucks from Almería and did the same thing. Towards the end, there was a front here of sorts, though it remained out of the mainstream. In the aftermath, under Franco, there was real hardship and suffering, and in the 1980s the region had one of the lowest per capita incomes in Spain, with – as an official report put it – "a level of literacy bordering on that of the Third

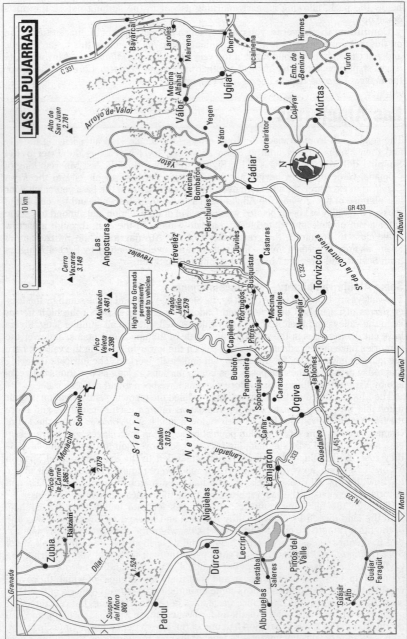

LAS ALPUJARRAS

World, alarming problems of desertification, poor communications and high under-employment".

Ironically, the land itself is still very fertile – oranges, chestnuts, bananas, apples and avocados grow here, while the southern villages produce a well-known dry rosé wine, *costa*. However, it is largely the recent influx of **tourism** and **foreign purchase of houses and farms** that has turned the area's fortunes around, bringing pockets of wealth and a bit of new life to the region.

The so-called "**High Alpujarras**" – the villages of **Pampaneira**, **Bubión** and **Capileira** – have all been scrubbed and whitewashed and are now firmly on the tourist circuit, as popular with Spanish as foreign visitors. Lower down, in the **Órgiva area**, are the main concentration of expatriates – mainly British, Dutch and Germans, seeking new Mediterranean lives. Most seem to have moved here permanently, rather than establishing second homes (though there are houses for rent in abundance), and there's a vaguely alternative aspect to the new community, which sets it apart from the coastal expats. In addition to property owners, the area has also attracted groups of British new-age travellers – the youthful hippies of the 1990s. The locals, to their credit, seem remarkably tolerant of the whole scene.

Approaches and buses

From Granada, the most straightforward **approach to the Alpujarras** is to take the Lanjarón turning – the A348 – off the Motril road. Coming from the south, you can bear right from the road at Vélez Benaudalla and continue straight along the A346 to Órgiva, the market town of the western Alpujarras. There are several **buses** a day from both Granada and Motril, and one a day from Almería, to **Lanjarón** and **Órgiva**.

A **bus** operated by *Alsina Graells* (☎958 18 54 80) direct to the "**High Alpujarras**", via Trevélez as far as Bérchules, currently leaves the main Granada bus station at noon and 5.15pm daily: in the other direction it leaves Bérchules at 5am or 5pm, passing Trevélez half an hour later, to arrive in Granada at 8.45am or 8.45pm respectively. There's also a bus from Granada to Ugíjar in the "Low Alpujarras", via Lanjarón, Órgiva, Torvizcón, Cádiar, Yegen and Valor, currently departing at 8.30am and 6pm; this takes a little over four hours to the end of the line. There are also nine buses daily between Granada and Órgiva (three via Lanjarón) and vice-versa, and three daily buses link with Pampaneira, Bubión, Capileira and Pitres.

Lanjarón and around

LANJARÓN has known tourism and the influence of the outside world for longer than anywhere else in the Alpujarras due to the curative powers of its **spa waters**. These gush from seven natural springs and are sold in bottled form as mineral water through-out Spain. Between March and December, when the spa baths are open, the town fills with the aged and infirm and the streets are lined with racks of herbal remedies, all of which imparts a rather melancholy air. This might seem good reason for passing straight on to the higher villages, though to do so would be to miss out on some beautiful local walks. Should you wish to try a cure at the **Balneario**, a basic soak will cost about 1500ptas with add-ons for massage, mud baths, pressure showers and all kinds of other alarming-sounding *tracciónes* and *inyecciónes*.

Like so many spa towns Lanjarón is Roman in origin, though today the place is large-ly modern, with a ribbon of buildings flanking its pleasant, tree-lined main thorough-fare, the Avenida de Andalucía (aka Avda. de La Alpujarra). Below this, marking Lanjarón's medieval status as gateway to the Alpujarras, is a **Moorish castle**, now dilapidated and barely visible. It was here on March 8, 1500, that the Moorish popula-tion made its final heroic stand against the Christian troops under the command of Fernando. Pounded by artillery, hundreds died as the town was taken. A ten-minute stroll reveals its dramatic setting – follow the signs downhill from the main street and out onto the terraces and meadows below the town.

Lanjarón puts on a stirring **Semana Santa** – one of the best in the province, and worth going out of your way to see if you're in this area.

Information and accommodation

Lanjarón has no tourist office but *Union Travel*, Avda. de Andalucía s/n operates a semi-official **information kiosk** (Mon–Fri 9.30am–1.30pm & 5.30–8.30pm; ☎958 77 02 82), opposite the *Balneario* on the right coming in from Granada, which can provide basic information. Midway along the main street is the *Alsina Graells* **bus terminal**.

Due to the Balneario, there's no shortage of **places to stay** in town, though in high summer it's almost essential to book ahead – as indeed it is worth doing throughout the Alpujarras – and in winter many places close in January and February. Also note that evening temperatures stay low here well into late spring; the hotels listed below in category ③ and above have central heating.

Apartamentos Castillo Alcadima, c/General Rodrigo 3, down a signed turnoff from the main street (☎ & fax 958 77 08 09). Excellent studio apartments with kitchenette and stunning balcony views over the castle below the town; also has a pool. Friendly proprietor hires out mountain bikes and offers horse riding treks and rock climbing courses. ⑤.

Hostal El Dólar, Avda. de Andalucía 5 (☎958 77 01 83). Pleasant, simple and inexpensive *hostal* with mountain-view rooms. ③.

Hotel España, Avda. de La Alpujarra 42 (☎ & fax 958 77 01 87). Grand-looking, good-value hotel near the Balneario which is very friendly and offers en-suite rooms and a pool. ④.

Hostal Florida, c/Pérez Chaves 4 (☎958 77 00 80). Central *hostal* which has rooms with and without bath. ②.

Bar Galvez, c/Real 95, the eastern continuation of Avda. de Andalucía (☎958 77 07 02). Cheapest rooms in town and excellent meals. ②.

Pensión El Mirador, 1km east of town on the Órjiva road (☎958 77 03 50). Peaceful en-suite rooms, good restaurant, hearty breakfasts and excellent *tapas* in their bar. ②.

Hotel Miramar, Avda. de Andalucía 10 (☎ & fax 958 77 01 61). For a step up in price you can enjoy the relative luxury of the town's top hotel with pool, garden and garage. ⑥.

Hotel El Sol, Avda. de Andalucía 22 (☎ & fax 958 77 01 30). Good-value main street choice if you're here in winter or early spring as there is reliable heating in their en-suite rooms. ④.

Eating and drinking

Plenty of **bars and restaurants** line the Avenida de Andalucía and many of the hotels and *hostales* have good-value meals and *tapas*, too – especially the hotels *España* and *El Sol*, *Bar Galvez* and the *Pensión El Mirador*. *Bar-Restaurante Manolete*, c/San Sebastián 3, is a good *tapas* bar and restaurant too, while the more expensive *El Club* at Avda. de Andalucía 18 specializes in Alpujarran dishes and is reckoned to serve the best food in town. For seafood, try *Los Mariscos*, Avda. de La Alpujarra 6, or the cheaper *tapas* and *raciones* bar, *Los Briscos*, in a small square off the east end of the main street – the *cazon* (shark) is recommended. The restaurant of *Apartamentos Castillo Alcadima* (see above) has a superb terrace view. On the main "square", Plaza de La Constitución, beyond the church, lies Lanjarón's celebrated *churrería*, claimed by some to sell the best home-made potato crisps in Andalucía, opposite which are a couple of good ice-cream parlours. Almost next door to the *churrería*, *Noche Azul*, is a popular **nightclub** for late-night dancing and drinking.

Walks from Lanjarón

The countryside and mountains around Lanjarón are beyond compare. Wander up through the backstreets behind the town and you'll come across a track that takes you steeply up to the vast spaces of the **Reserva Nacional de la Sierra Nevada**.

For a somewhat easier **day's walk**, go to the bridge over the river just east of town and take the sharply climbing, cobbled track which parallels the river. After two to two-and-a-half hours' walk through small farms, with magnificent views and scenery, a downturn to a small stone bridge lets you return to Lanjarón on the opposite bank. Allow a minimum of six hours for a leisurely day's expedition. The town produces a leaflet – *Turismo Activo in Lanjaron* – detailing more walks, which should be available from the information kiosk.

Las Barreras

Heading east from Lanjarón towards Órgiva or the High Alpujarras, you pass through the village of **LAS BARRERAS**. If you're not in a hurry, stop for a **meal** at the *Venta María* on the roadside – a somewhat quirky establishment that can, with luck, come up with a magnificent meal. Next door is a tiny **tile factory**, started recently by local women, using traditional techniques and designs.

Órgiva (Órjiva)

ÓRGIVA, 11km east of Lanjarón, is the market centre of the western Alpujarras. It's a lively little town, with a number of good bars and hotels, and an animated **Thursday market**, when everyone from miles around – Spanish and foreign – turns up with something to sell or buy, a drum to beat, a pipe to finger, a guitar to strum and a bowl to fill with *duros*. The contrast between the timeworn *campesinos* and their pack-mules, and some of the foreign new-age travellers who seek their indulgence and charity is as bizarre as anything this side of Madrid.

The everyday covered **mercado**, just north of the "Plaza Mayor" (actually a junction in front of the church), is quite a sight, too. With its juggling and health food stalls, and its posters for the local personal development centre, *Cortijo Romero*, offering programmes of shiatsu and other activities – it could as easily be in Amsterdam or Bristol. The foreign input, however, is probably crucial to the market's survival. The *mercado* was once the most important institution in most Spanish villages, but these days most struggle to keep their head above water in competition with the local supermarkets. Many of the New Agers here inhabit a **tepee village**, *El Beneficio*, on the edge of town where a polyglot community of mainly northern Europeans and their offspring endure freezing winters under canvas.

Órgiva's other sights line the main street: the sixteenth-century **Baroque church** of Nuestra Señora de la Expectación, whose towers add a touch of fancy to the townscape, and a crumbling **Moorish palacio** which today houses various shops.

Practicalities

Órgiva has a fair choice of **accommodation**. Just beyond the traffic lights at the town's main intersection, the pretty and economical *Pensión Alma Alpujarreña* (☎958 78 40 85; ③), has some en-suite rooms and a restaurant under a vine trellis. Even cheaper basic rooms are to be had above the nearby *Bar El Semáforo* (②) set a little back from the traffic lights along Avda. Gonzalez Robles. Good rooms with bath are also on offer at *Hostal Mirasol*, Avda. González Robles 3, on the way in from Lanjarón (☎958 78 51 59; ③); they also have a more upmarket hotel (⑤) next door. Perhaps the most attractive place to stay with transport is the rural *Hotel Taray* a bit over a kilometre along the A348 south of the town (☎958 78 45 31; ⑥), with a good restaurant and pool. The town's **campsite**, *Camping Órgiva* (☎958 78 43 07) 2km south of the centre past the *Hotel Taray*, has a pool and restaurant and can advise on **walking routes** nearby.

The best **tapas and raciones** in town are the *calamares* at *Bar Semáforo*, by the traffic lights. Other good *tapas* places include *Quini* and *Agustín*, opposite one another at the top of the town in c/Alcalde Jesús Moreno, near the health centre, and *Nemesis I* and *II* and *Paraíso* near the church. The *Hostal Mirasol* (see above) also does good *tapas* and offers a restaurant *menú* inside or on their terrace. For coffee and cakes there's *Café Galindo Plaza* on the square, and the town *churrería* is just round the corner.

Órgiva comes to life with its **annual fiesta** on September 24 and 25 when the population doubles as prodigal sons and daughters all return to join in the fun. A more eccentric festival is the **Dia del Señor** on the second Thursday before Easter. Opening with a terrifying salvo of rockets, this fiesta went disastrously wrong a few years back when the bank's windows were blown in. On the Friday morning all the town's womenfolk attack the church until they are able to make off with the effigy of *El Señor* (Christ), which is then paraded around town accompanied by great displays of emotion – not to mention more rocketry.

Daily **buses** from the Alsina Graells stop on Avda. González Robles, run east across the Alpujarras to Ugíjar, and up to all the High Alpujarran villages; the latter service is the Granada bus, which passes through Lanjarón at 11.30am, 1pm and 6.15pm and Órgiva thirty minutes later. If you're **driving**, note that Órgiva is the last stop for filling up before Cádiar or Ugíjar.

The High Alpujarras: Órgiva to Capileira

From Órgiva, you can reach the High Alpujarran villages by car or bus, or you could walk – the best way to experience the region. There is a network of paths in this zone, though to avoid getting lost it's wise to equip yourself with a compass and the *Instituto Geográfico Nacional/Federación Española de Montañismo* 1:50,000 map, which covers all the territory from Órgiva up to Berja. A reasonable knowledge of Spanish is also invaluable.

At their best, **Alpujarran footpaths** are remnants of the old Camino Real, the mule-routes which crossed Spain, and are engineered with cobblestones, and beautifully contoured, alongside mountain streams, through woods of oak, chestnut and poplar, or across flower-spangled meadows. In their bad moments they deteriorate to incredibly dusty firebreaks, forestry roads or tractor tracks, or (worse) dead-end in impenetrable thickets of bramble and nettle. Progress is slow, gradients are sharp and the heat (between mid-June and Sept) is taxing. Over the past few years part of the path network through the High Alpujarras has been upgraded as the final section of the **European long-distance footpath** which begins in Athens and ends in Algeciras. Designated as footpaths E4 or GR7 in Spain, the full route is now waymarked (in theory – you'll still need a good map where the posts are missing or misplaced) with red and white ringed posts and each village along the route – 23 of them between Lanjarón and Bayárcal – should carry a special symbol on its nameplate. Maps detailing the footpath should be available from tourist offices and *Ayuntamientos* along the route.

HIGH ALPUJARRAS HIKES: THE HIGHLIGHTS

Rewarding **hikes** in the High Alpujarras include:

Pitres to Mecina Fondales: Twenty minutes' hike, and then a good hour-plus from neighbouring Ferreirola to Busquistar.

Busquistar toward Trevélez: One hour's hike, and then two-plus hours of road walking.

Pórtugos toward Trevélez: Two hours' hike, meeting the tarmac a little beyond the end of the Busquistar route.

Trevélez to Berchules: Four hours' hike, but the middle two hours is dirt track.

Trevélez to Juviles: Three hours' hike, including some sections of firebreak.

Cañar, Soportújar and Carataunas

Following the high road from Órgiva, the first settlements you reach, almost directly above the town, are the isolated but pretty **CAÑAR** – at the end of a sinuous 5km drive off the main road – and **SOPORTÚJAR**, a maze of picturesque white-walled alleys bridged by numerous *tinaos* (see p.450). Like many of the High Alpujarran villages, they congregate on the neatly terraced mountainside, planted with poplars and laced with irrigation channels. Both have **bars** where you can get a meal, and Soportújar can provide excellent value en-suite **rooms** for the night; ask at *Bar Correillo* (☎958 78 75 78; ②) on c/Real (behind the church). Perched precariously on the steep hillside, both villages share a rather sombre view of Órgiva in the valley below, and on a clear day the mountains of North Africa over the ranges to the south. Each village has a sixteenth-century church in a terrible state of disrepair, although Soportújar's is currently undergoing a slow restoration.

Just below the two villages, the tiny hamlet of **CARATAUNAS** is particularly attractive. Above the village on the main road is the small *Hotel El Montañero* (☎ & fax 958 78 75 28; ⑤), a pleasant **place to stay**, with restaurant, small pool and the possibility of activities including horse riding, mountain biking and guided walks. Carataunas puts on a lively start to its *Semana Santa* on Palm Sunday, when an effigy of Judas is tossed on a bonfire.

The Poqueira Gorge and up to Capileira

Shortly beyond Carataunas the road swings to the north after passing the turnoff to the Buddhist monastery of Oscl Ling (see below), and you have your first view of the **Gorge of the Poqueira**, a huge gash into the heights of the Sierra Nevada. Trickling deep in the cleft is the Río Poqueira, which has its source near the peak of Mulhacén. The steep walls of the gorge are terraced and wooded from top to bottom, and dotted with little stone farmhouses. Much of the surrounding country looks barren from a distance, but close up you'll find that it's rich with flowers, woods, springs and streams. A trio of spectacular villages – Pampaneira, Bubión and Capileira – teeter on the steep edge of the gorge among their terraces. They are, justifiably, the most touristy villages in the region and a bit over-prettified, with craft shops and the like, but nonetheless well worth a visit and, even if you have a car, some walking on the local mule paths. A number of fine **walking routes** in this zone are detailed with maps in *Landscapes of Andalucía* (see Books in *Contexts*).

Pampaneira and the Tibetan monastery

PAMPANEIRA, the first of the Poqueira villages, is a neat, prosperous place, and a bit less developed and spoilt than its neighbours. Around its main square are a number of bars, restaurants, *hostales* and craft shops, one of which, just down the hill, is a weaving workshop that specializes in traditional *Alpujarreño* designs. For **rooms** there's the homely *Hostal Pampaneira* (☎958 76 30 02; ②) at c/José Antonio 1, with some en-suite rooms and, for a bit more comfort, the *Hostal Ruta del Mulhacén*, Avda. de Alpujarra 6 (☎958 76 30 10; ③), which has balcony rooms with bath and central heating. On the main square, the leafy Plaza de la Libertad, *Casa Diego* (☎958 76 30 15; ②) is another budget option for basic rooms. All three places have **restaurants**, of which *Casa Diego* and *Hostal Pampaneira* are the best value; and also worth considering is *Casa Julio*, up the steps from the latter *hostal*.

Also on Plaza de la Libertad you'll also find *Nevadensis* (☎958 76 31 27; English spoken), an **information centre** for the Natural Park of the Sierra Nevada. As well as providing information they sell large-scale topographical maps of the zone, walking guidebooks and a leaflet in English (200ptas) detailing a trekking route through the Poquiera valley. They also organize themed guided walks (botanical, ornithological,

ALPUJARRAN ARCHITECTURE

Alpujarran village houses are unlike any others in Spain – though they are almost identical to Berber houses across the straits in the Rif mountains of Morocco, where many of the Moorish refugees settled. They are built of grey stone, flat-roofed and low; traditionally they are unpainted, though these days *cal* (whitewash) – a luxury until recent times – is increasingly common. The coarse walls are about 75cm thick, for summer coolness and protection from winter storms. Stout beams of chestnut, or ash in the lower valleys, are laid from wall to wall; on top of these is a mat of canes, ilex or split chestnut; upon this flat stones are piled, and on the stones is spread a layer of *launa*, the crumbly grey mica clay found throughout the area, which is made waterproof when pressed down.

The *launa* must – and this maxim is still observed today – be laid during the waning of the moon (though not, of course, on a Friday) in order for it to settle properly and thus keep rain out. Gerald Brenan wrote in *South from Granada* of a particularly ferocious storm: "As I peered through the darkness of the stormy night, I could make out a dark figure on every roof in the village, dimly lit by an esparto torch, stamping clay into the holes in the roof."

Another feature peculiar to the Alpujarras are the *tinaos*, a kind of portico or bridge that enables access from a dwelling in one row to another in an upper or lower row. In summer, time is passed on the roof terrace or *terrao*, especially once the sun has cooled in early evening. Bubión, Capileira and Pitres all have good examples of the traditional architectural style.

etc) and rent out bikes, horses, hang-gliders, and cross-country skis. If you're thinking of a longer stay, this is where you can pick up a list of hostels, village houses, and farmhouses for rent throughout the Alpujarras.

Above Pampaneira, on the very peak of the western flank of the Poqueira gorge in a stunning location, is the small **Tibetan Buddhist Monastery of Osel Ling** ("Place of Clear Light"). Founded in 1982 by a Tibetan monk, the monastery welcomes visitors between 3–6pm. A baby boy born to Spanish parents in Granada in 1985 was recognised by the Dalai Lama as the reincarnation of the former head lama – one Yeshé – and is currently undergoing training in the Himalayas. Lectures and courses on Buddhism are held regularly and facilities exist for those who want to visit the monastery for periods of retreat; overnight visits in simple accommodation are also possible but you need to ring first (☎958 34 31 34; ③). The monastery is reached by a track on the left – signed "camino forestal" – 1km east of the turning to Soportujar (see above). Should you encounter difficulty locating it, enquire at *Nevadensis* (see above) or *Rustic Blue* (see Bubión account below) who will set you right.

Bubión

BUBIÓN is next up the hill, backed for much of the year by snowcapped peaks. Lacking the focus of a main square, it's probably the least attractive of these high villages but – perhaps because of this – it certainly seems the most peaceful. The tranquillity may not last long, though, if the property developers have their way and already there is quite a bit of development taking place on the lower slopes. Plentiful **accommodation** includes a fancy apart-hotel built along traditional lines, the *Villa Turística de Bubión*, Barrio Alto s/n (☎958 76 31 11, fax 958 76 31 36; ⑦), where detached dwellings come with a kitchen and four-star facilities. Less ostentatiously, there's a comfortable *pensión*, *Las Terrazas*, Plaza del Sol 7 (☎958 76 30 34, fax 958 76 32 52; ③), who also have some excellent apartments downhill at c/Parras s/n (☎958 76 32 17; ④), which come with terrace, kitchen, satellite TV and fine views. Signs around the village will lead you to cheaper rooms in private houses. The information office (see below) also have a register of some two hundred fully equipped houses for rent in Bubión and the Alpujarras (minimum two nights stay; from £200/$125 per week). For **food** a couple of bars serve up *tapas* and *raciones*, and a very good restaurant, *La Artesa*, at c/Carretera 2, turns out *alpujarreño* specialities with a *menú*.

A private **information office**, *Rustic Blue* (☎958 76 33 81; *www.rusticblue.com*; English spoken) at the entrance to the village on the right, is a useful source of local knowledge and stocks maps and walking guides to the area as well as organizing week-long guided treks (led by resident Irish Alpujarras expert Conor Clifford) and horse-riding tours. The village has two ranches for **horseback riding** in the Alpujarras, offering a couple of hours or one- to five-day trips in groups with a guide; the friendly *Rancho Rafael Belmonte* (☎958 76 31 35) at the bottom of the village near *Rustic Blue*, or the English-run *Dallas Ranch* (☎958 76 30 38) are the places to contact.

Towards the end of August, Bubión celebrates its **Fiestas Patronales** with music, dance, fireworks and copious imbibing.

Capileira

CAPILEIRA is the highest of the three villages and the terminus of the road – Europe's highest, but now closed to traffic – across the heart of the Sierra Nevada from Granada (see p.442). A picturesque and tranquil place, somewhat less frenetic and commercialized than its neighbours, Capileira makes a fine walking base from which to explore the Poqueira Gorge, or you could even strike out for Trevélez (see below) about five hours to the northeast. The **kiosko** at the centre of the village near where the bus drops you sells newspapers, large scale walking maps, hands out a free **village map** and acts as an **information office**. Just downhill from here lies the village's **museum** (Tues–Sun 11.30am–2.30pm), containing displays of regional dress and handicrafts as well as various bits and pieces belonging to, or produced by, Pedro Alarcón, the nineteenth-century Spanish writer, born in Guadix, who made a trip through the Alpujarras and wrote a (not very good) book about it.

Among several **places to stay**, the *Mesón-Hostal Poqueira*, c/Dr Castilla 1, where the bus drops you (☎ & fax 958 76 30 48; ③), has good-value en-suite heated rooms, plus one of the best value set *menús* in the mountains. The *Fonda Restaurante El Tilo* (☎958 76 31 81; ②), on Plaza Calvario, has quiet rooms, away from the main road, and *Hostal Paco Lopez* (☎958 76 30 11; ②) near the bus halt, and *Ruta de Las Sierra Nieves* (☎958 71 31 06; ③) higher up the same road both have rooms with bath and heating. All the above have **restaurants** or *tapas* and *raciones* bars attached, and *Paco Lopez*'s restaurant offers quite a few vegetarian options, too. One place with an interesting **flamenco** ambience is the nearby *Panjuila*, Barranco de Poqueira 24, where in addition to a *menú* filled with *alpujarreña* dishes, there's often the possibility of flamenco performances, especially at weekends. The restaurant of the *Finca Los Llanos*, uphill beyond the *Ruta de Las Sierra Nieves*, is another decent place, famed for its *berenjenas con miel* (aubergine with honey).

There are daily **buses** to Capileira from Granada (see "Travel Details" on p.493). Buses out of Capileira to Órgiva and Granada leave at 6.20am, 3.50pm and 6.20pm.

On the Sunday prior to August 5, Capileira embarks on its annual **romería** to the summit of Mulhacén and the *ermita* of the Virgen de las Nieves.

The Poqueira gorge

Capileira is a handy base for easy day walks in the **Poqueira gorge**. For a not-too-strenuous ramble, take the northernmost of the three paths below the village, each of which spans bridges across the river. This one sets off from alongside the *Pueblo Alpujarreño* villa complex and winds through the huts and terraced fields of the river valley above Capileira, ending after about an hour-and-a-half at a dirt track within sight of a power plant at the head of the valley. From here, you can either retrace your steps or cross the stream over a bridge to follow a dirt track back to the village. In May and June, the fields are tended laboriously by hand, as the steep slopes dictate.

A number of reasonably clear paths or tracks also lead to **Pampaneira** (2–3hr; follow the lower path to the bridge below Capileira), continuing to **Carataunas** (a further 1hr, mostly road) and **Órgiva** (another 45min on an easy path) from where you can get a bus back.

In the other direction, taking the Sierra Nevada road and then the first major track to the right, by a ruined stone house, you can reach **Pitres** (2hr), **Pórtugos** (30min more) and **Busquistar** (45min more). Going in the same direction but taking the second decent-sized track (by a sign encouraging you to "conserve and respect nature"), **Trevélez** is some five hours away. More skilled, equipped and ambitious climbers may wish to attempt the **summit of Mulhacén**, the peninsula's highest peak at 3479m, achievable in a day from Capileira, but perhaps more sensibly done over two days with an overnight stop at the *Refugio Poqueira* (☎958 34 33 49; open all year but book ahead) at the head of the Poqueira valley.

Further along the High Route to Trevélez and Cádiar

The "High Route" continues east from Pampaneira through **Pitres** and **Pórtugos** before making a great loop to Trevélez, Spain's highest permanent settlement. From there, the road drops down to a junction, with a crossing to **Torvizcón**, on the south side of the Alpujarras, and east to the valley and village of **Cádiar**.

Pitres

PITRES is less picturesque and less developed than the trio of high villages to its west and, like its equally unpolished neighbour, Pórtugos, offers more chance of rooms during high season. All around, too, spreads some of the best Alpujarran **walking country**.

Possible **accommodation** options include the *Fonda Sierra Nevada*, on the main square (☎958 76 60 17; ②), which is flanked by a couple of bar-restaurants – *Bar La Tahá* is friendly – or *Posada La Tahá* (☎958 34 30 41; ⑤) with comfortable apartments in a traditional stone built house, for longer stays. For **food**, on the village's eastern edge *El Jardín* is a British-run restaurant with garden terrace, great views and an eclectic **vegetarian** *menú*. Nearby, the *Refugio Los Albergues* (☎958 76 60 04; ①), is an old Civil War hostel rustically refurbished to provide dormitory beds (there's one double room; ②), but outside toilets. It's signposted from the main road, but if you get lost ask for *Casa Barbara* (Hauck), the name of the friendly German who runs it. There's use of a library and kitchen to cook organic veg from an extensive garden. A very pleasant upmarket alternative is to be found in the nearby village of Mecina Fondales (see below) where the *Hotel San Marcos* (☎958 76 61 36, fax 958 76 60 16; ⑥) is a delightful hideaway – and passed on the Tahá walk below – where you can also hire horses and mountain bikes.

Alternatively, there's a **campsite**, the *Balcón de Pitres* (☎958 76 61 11; March–Oct), in a stunning position just out of town to the west, with a swimming pool; it also has a charming little **restaurant** serving Alpujarran specialities such as *solomillo de cerdo* (sirloin of pork) and *cordero rellena* (stuffed shoulder of lamb). You may also be lucky enough on Saturday or Sunday nights here to stumble on an authentic and memorable mountain flamenco session.

Pórtugos and its neighbours

PÓRTUGOS is equally rustic and its centre has a couple of **places to stay**, including *Hostal Mirador* (☎958 76 60 14; ③), on the main square with en-suite rooms. A kilometre east, at Los Castaños, there's a delightful *fonda* (②), with excellent food. Don't bother with the *Hotel Nuevo Malagueño* on the main road, whose rooms and restaurant are overpriced.

Down below the main road are a trio of villages – **MECINA FONDALES, FER-REIROLA** and **BUSQUISTAR** – which along with Pitres and Pórtugos and a couple

---

A WALK AROUND THE TAHÁ

A circuit of the Tahá villages – with many fine stopping places for a picnic – is a good introduction to the Alpujarras, offering opportunities to appreciate both typical architecture and landscape within a compact area. The following **walk around the Southern Tahá** is an easy two-hour hike, although you'll probably want to take the diversion down to the picturesque Trevélez gorge which adds another half-hour or so; allow three hours for the full circuit. There is little shade on parts of the route, so avoid the afternoon sun in summer. Remember that the second (uphill) part of the walk is the most strenuous.

The route starts in **Pitres**. Follow the narrow path, which begins as a concrete driveway curving behind *Restaurante La Carretera* (on the main road to the right as you enter the village) and descends southwards – veering left – to **Mecinilla**, which is soon visible below; you should be aiming for the left of the church tower. Ignoring turnings, after 15 minutes or so, you emerge in the upper part of the village (Mecilla). Cross the main Pitres–Ferreirola road into the lower village (Mecinilla), following the road past the upmarket *Hotel San Marcos* and the church on the left. Just after the *Bar El Aljibe* (on the left), go through a gap and take an immediate right. After a drinking fountain (marked 1964), turn left; continue downwards through the narrow streets, eventually leaving the village beneath a *tinao* (see box p.450). Initially following the edge of a ravine, the path continues downwards through orchards (crossing the road once but continuing clearly a little to the right) until reaching the maze of narrow, white streets which make up **Mecina–Fondales** – this should take another half-hour or so. Take your time here, partly as it's one of the most peaceful and least spoilt villages, but also as the maze of streets makes it easy to get lost and the vociferous dogs zealously guarding their patches can be off-putting; ask for directions if you can.

From here, **for the shorter route**, take the *Camino Real* towards Ferreirola, a well-maintained mule track leaving the centre of the village heading east. **For the longer route**, head to the wash place (known locally as "La Fuente") in the village's southeast corner – veer downhill to the left from the road to pass beneath an elaborate *tinao* topped by a vine trellis – to reach the **five-basined fuente** or wash place. From here take the track descending towards the river, bearing left where there's any confusion. After a while the gushing waters become audible below, and the path emerges high above the gorge with the Trevélez bridge visible ahead. Immediately before the bridge, turn left up a small path which crosses the Río Bermejo, before climbing steeply over rocks (ignore the right-hand fork) and continuing uphill to **Ferreirola**.

In Ferreirola, head for the church square; close by is another wash place. Take the path rising north alongside it which, after another steepish climb, leads to **Atalbéitar**. The path actually emerges on the road below the village from where you turn left to continue the walk, but first you should visit Atalbéitar as this is another unspoilt hamlet, well off the usual tourist trail. Leaving the village, passing a lifeless oak tree and rubbish container on the right, turn left as the road bends to the right and follow this track in the direction of Pitres (now visible above) past a few houses. The path twice briefly joins the "road" (more of a dirt track); each time, take the path to the left where the road bends right. Leaving the track the second time, just before it joins the "main road", the path first skirts the Bermejo gorge but then drops sharply to cross the river – some welcome greenery here hides the bridge until you're close to it. Across the river, the path climbs to an *acequia* (irrigation channel); turn right here and continue along the wooded path, past the *Albergue*, till emerging on the main road slightly to the east of **Pitres**.

of smaller settlements formed a league of seven villages known as the *Tahá* (from the Arabic "Tá" meaning obedience) under the Moors. These are among the most unspoilt of the Alpujarra *pueblos* where you can find plenty of examples of typical regional architecture (see box p.450). Ferreirola and Busquistar – the latter a huddle of grey *launa* roofs – are especially attractive, as is the path between the two, clinging to the north side of the valley of the Río Trevélez. You're out of tourist country here and the villages display their genuine characteristics to better effect.

For **accommodation**, Mecina Fondales has a friendly new *hostal, L'Atelier*, located in the old village bakery at c/Alberca s/n (☎ & fax 958 85 75 01; ④ including breakfast) specialising in **vegetarian/vegan** cuisine and also offers cookery courses. Another option is the recently refurbished inn, the *Hostal Mirador de la Alpujarra* (☎ & fax 958 85 74 70; ④), which is just uphill from the church in Busquistar, which has one of the best views in the Alpujarras, a good **restaurant**, and is well sited for a hike up to Trevélez and beyond. Ferreirola also has the delightful Scandinavian-run *Sierra y Mar*, c/Albaycin 16 (☎958 76 61 71; fax 958 85 73 67; ④ including breakfast), with more views and where the owners – enthusiastic walkers – will advise on routes in the area and guests have use of a kitchen to prepare their own food. To get there, take the road to the right of the fountain out of the main plaza. A circuit of the Tahá villages starting out from either Pitres (see box) need take no more than two hours' walking, though you'll probably want to linger along the way.

Trevélez

The cut into the mountain made by the Río Trevélez – sadly, rather polluted on its lower reaches – is similar to the Poqueira, but grander and more austere. **TREVÉLEZ** village stands on a flank at the end of the ravine and its altitude – this is Spain's highest conurbation – makes it a cool place even in summer when many of the inhabitants continue to don sweaters and coats. It's built in traditional Alpujarran style, with a lower and two upper *barrios* overlooking a grassy, poplar-lined valley where the river starts its long descent. The upper *barrios* (*alto* and *medio*) are probably the most pleasant places to stay as the lower (*barrio bajo*) is the more touristy and filled with stalls selling crystals, earrings and herbal remedies, especially at weekends. There are fine walks in the valley and you can swim, too, in a makeshift pool by the bridge.

The village is well provided with **places to stay**, in both the lower and upper squares, and with *camas* advertised over a few bars; if you are susceptible to low temperatures, outside July and August you may want a place with efficent **heating**. In the *barrio medio* the pleasant *Hostal Fernando*, c/Pista del Barrio Medio s/n (☎958 85 85 65; ③), offers rooms with bath and great views, while beside the *Ayuntamiento* in the *barrio alto*, the centrally-heated *Hotel La Fragua*, c/San Antonio 4 (☎958 85 86 26, fax 958 85 86 14; ④), is probably the nicest of the village places with en-suite rooms and more fine views plus an excellent and good-value restaurant. *Pensión Regina* in Plaza Francisco Abellán (☎958 85 85 64; with heating; ③) in the *barrio bajo* has some rooms with bath and views from the rear rooms, and the *Hostal Mulhacén*, Ctra. Ugíjar s/n (☎ & fax 958 85 85 87; with heating; ③–④), also in the lower *barrio*, is another possibility for rooms with or without bath, with more great views down the valley. Perhaps the most attractive place of all to stay in this zone is at the *Alcazaba de Busquistar* (☎958 85 86 87, fax 958 85 86 93; ⑤), a tranquil hideaway some 5km south along the GR421 road which descends along the east side of the ravine to meet the A348; this apart-hotel has traditional-style Alpujarran dwellings (no. 411 is recommended) with launa roofs and fine views, plus a restaurant and pool. Trevélez's **campsite** (☎958 85 87 35) has again opened after closure; it lies 1km out along the Órgiva road and is officially open all year, although you can expect arctic conditions in midwinter.

Among **restaurants**, besides the *Hotel La Fragua* (see above) the *Río Grande*, down near the bridge, serves up good, solid mountain food. Other good places are: *Casa*

Julio, Plaza de la Iglesia in the *barrio medio*; the excellent value *Mesón Haraicel*, c/Real in the *barrio bajo*, which also offers *tapas* and *raciones* in its bar; the nearby *Restaurante Bar Alvarez* on Plaza Abellán Gómez; and *Piedra Ventana*, a little way out along the Ugjiar road. Trevélez's celebrated **jamón serrano** is justifiably a local passion and can be tried along with many other specialities at *Mesón del Jamón*, which has an attractive terrace above the Plaza de la Iglesia in the *barrio medio*. Another *jamón* specialist is *Mesón Joaquín*, at the entrance to the village in the *barrio bajo*, where beneath a ceiling hung with hams, regional specialities are served including *habas con jamón* (beans with ham), *plato alpujarreño* (mixed fry with blood pudding, ham and egg) and *trucha* (river trout) with *jamón*; there's also a 900ptas *menú*. These famous *jamones dulces* sent Ford into raptures when he passed through Trevélez on horseback in the 1830s: "No gastronome should neglect these sweet hams. Very little salt is used; the ham is placed eight days in a weak pickle, and then hung up in the snow."

Trevélez is traditionally the jump-off point for the **high Sierra Nevada peaks** (to which there is a bona fide path) and for treks across the range (on a lower, more conspicuous track). The latter begins down by the bridge on the eastern side of the village. After skirting the bleak Horcajo de Trevélez (3182m), and negotiating the Puerto de Trevélez (2800m), up to which it's a very distinct route, it drops down along the north flank of the Sierra Nevada to Jeres del Marquesado. (For more details, see the section on the *Ruta de los Tres Mil*, p.442.)

South to Torvizcón

South from Trevélez, you can head by road or by footpath to **Almegijar** and **Torvizcón**. On foot, it is around 15km: a very pleasant walk, lined with masses of wild flowers and fragrant herbs in spring and early summer.

Start by following the road down the valley from Trevélez in the direction of Juviles. At the junction after 7km, ignore the road going east to Juviles and take the turn on the right signed to Castaras. Two kilometres along this you'll meet another junction; ignore the route east to Castaras and veer right towards Almegijar, then down another left turning after 2km. You could call in at Almegijar which you'll pass on the left or carry on, descending through olive groves and orchards to Torvizcón.

TORVIZCÓN is another sturdy Alpujarran village with cobbled streets and whitewashed houses stacked up the northern slopes of the Sierra de Contraviesa. **Rooms** are available at *Pensión Moreno*, Plaza del Arroyo 4 (☎958 76 30 06; ②), a friendly, family-run place on the main square which serves food accompanied by the local *costa* wine. For en-suite rooms, try *Hotel Sahyl*, Carretera s/n (☎958 85 20 06; ③) which also has a decent **restaurant** and *menú*.

East to Juviles, Bérchules and Cádiar

Heading east from Trevélez, either by vehicle or on foot, you come to **JUVILES**, a great centre of silk production in Moorish times, and today an attractive village straddling the road. At its centre is an unwhitewashed, peanut-brittle-finish church with a clock that's slightly slow (like most things round here). The villagers don't appear to have taken to their newly renovated plaza with jarring ornamental fountains, lamp-standards and trees in brick boxes, and in the evening people still promenade in the road, knowing that there will be no traffic. A single all-in-one *fonda-restaurante*-bar-store, *Bar Fernández* (☎958 76 91 68; ②), has rooms with great views east over the valley from the second floor, and will cook meals on demand. There are a couple of other basic *restaurante-hostales* along the main road through the village, one of which, *Pensión Tino* (☎958 76 91 74; ②), has more views and a pretty, flower-filled terrace.

BÉRCHULES, a high village of grassy streams and chestnut woods, lies just 6km beyond Juviles, but a greater contrast can hardly be imagined. It is a large, abruptly demarcated settlement, three streets wide, on a sharp slope overlooking yet another canyon. There's a handful of **places to stay** including *Fonda-Restaurante Carayol* (☎958 76 90 92; ②) with basic rooms, and *La Posada* (☎ & fax 958 85 25 41; ③), both on the central Plaza Victoria, or the friendly *Alojamiento Rural La Tahoma*, c/Baja de la Iglesia s/n, which (as the street name tells you) is just below the church (☎958 76 90 51; ③); here, excellent value apartments come with kitchen, *salon* and TV and single night stays are possible. Rooms with bath are also available at the pleasant but pricier *Hotel Bérchules*, Carretera s/n (☎ & fax 958 85 25 30; ⑤) with a restaurant. Good **tapas** and **raciones** are to be had at *Bar Vaqueras*, on Plaza Victoria. On the same square there's also an excellent grocery – a godsend if you're planning on doing any walking out of here, since most village shops in the Alpujarras are primitive.

CADIAR, just below Bérchules and the central town – or "navel" as Gerald Brenan termed it – of the Alpujarras, is more attractive than it seems from a distance. Most of the life is around its main square, fronted by a sixteenth-century stone church. There are a few *hostales* and *camas* if you're **staying**, among them the inexpensive *Hostal Montoro*, c/San Isidro 20 (☎958 76 80 68; ②), near the central plaza, with heated rooms. For **food**, the *Bar-Restaurante La Pará de la Suerte* is owned by the same people, sited near the gas station as you come in from Bérchules, and is very good. The more upmarket apartment-hotel *Alquería de Morayma* (☎958 34 33 03, fax 958 34 32 21; ⑤), 2km out of town along the A348 towards Torvizcón, is a typical Alpujarran *cortijo* in 86 acres of farmland with a lovely setting and friendly proprietors; a good restaurant, pool and activities such as trekking, cycling and horse riding are on offer. Various events in Cádiar are worth keeping in mind, too. A colourful **produce market** takes place on the 3rd and 18th of every month, sometimes including livestock, and from October 5 to 10 the **Fuente del Vino** wine and cattle fair takes place, turning the waters of the fountain literally to wine.

The eastern and southern Alpujarras

Cádiar and Bérchules mark the end of the western Alpujarras, and a striking change in the landscape; the dramatic, severe, but relatively green terrain of the Guadalfeo and Cádiar valleys gives way to open, rolling and much more arid land. The villages of the **eastern Alpujarras** display many of the characteristics of those to the west but as a rule they are poorer and less visited by tourists. There are attractive places nonetheless, among them **Yegen**, which Brenan wrote about, the market centre of **Ugíjar** and, down on the southern slopes, the *costa* wine-producing villages of **Albuñol** and **Albondón**.

Yegen and Mecina Bombarón

YEGEN, some 7km northeast of Cádiar, is where **Gerald Brenan** lived during his ten or so years of Alpujarran residence (see box). Brenan connections aside, Yegen is one of the most characteristic of the central Alpujarran villages, with its two distinct quarters, cobbled paths and cold-water springs. It has a couple of **places to stay**, the *Bar La Fuente*, opposite the fountain in the square (☎958 85 10 67; ②), which also has some apartments to let (⑤) and serves **tapas** and **raciones**; there are rooms with bath at *El Tinao* (☎958 85 12 12; ③) on the main road. Heading east out of the village, the more luxurious *El Rincón de Yegen* (☎958 85 12 70; ④) has heated rooms with TV, apartments (⑥) for longer stays, a pool and a good **restaurant** – try the *bacalao con pimientas* (cod with peppers) – with a lunchtime *menú*.

From Yegen there's an easy 4km **walk** up to the hamlet of **MECINA BOMBARÓN**, along one of the old cobbled mule paths. This starts out from the old bridge across the gorge and is easy to follow from there, with Mecina clearly visible on the hill above. In

SOUTH FROM GRANADA

Gerald Brenan's autobiography of his years in the Alpujarras, *South from Granada*, is the best account of rural life in Spain between the wars, and also describes the visits made here by Bloomsburyites Virginia Woolf, Bertrand Russell and the arch-complainer Lytton Strachey who attributed his Iberian ailments to "crude olive oil, greasy tortillas and a surfeit of *bacalao*" and proclaimed when he got home that "Spain is absolute death". Disillusioned with the strictures of middle-class life in England after World War I, Brenan rented a house in Yegen and shipped out a library of 2000 books, from which he was to spend the next eight years educating himself. Since only a handful of the inhabitants of Yegen were literate, the reserved, lanky stranger was regarded as an exotic curiosity by the villagers. With glazed windows in only two dwellings, no doctor, electricity or telephone and no road to the outside world, Yegen's rustic isolation together with its characters, traditions, superstitions and celebrations provided the raw material for his great work. Towards the end of his stay he became involved in a number of scandals and, after getting a young teenage girl pregnant, moved to the hills of Churriana behind Torremolinos, with his wife, US writer Gamel Woolsey. Here he died in 1987, a writer better known and respected in Spain (he made an important study of Saint John of the Cross) than in his native England. The contribution he made to informing the world about the Alpujarras, its history and culture, is recorded on a plaque fixed to his former home, now the **Casa de Brenan**, just along from the fountain in Yegen's main square.

the village (also reachable by road) the *Casas Blancas* rural **hotel** (☎ & fax 958 85 11 51, *barnes@mundivia.es*; ③) is a pleasant place to stay, where studio rooms come with TV, kitchen and sun balcony. For **food** there's *Casa Joaquín*, just below the church.

Válor and Ugíjar

Six kilometres beyond Yegen, and sited between deep ravines, **VÁLOR** is a charming and sleepy hamlet, a fact which belies its history as a centre of stubborn resistance in the sixteenth-century revolt by the Moors against the "insults and outrages" of the Christian ascendancy. These events are "celebrated" in the annual *Fiestas Patronales* in mid-September when the whole story – including battles between Moors and Christians – is colourfully re-enacted in the main square. Should you wish to stay, **rooms** with bath are to be had at the comfortable *Hostal Las Perdices* on the road through (☎958 85 18 21; ③) with – as its name implies – a **restaurant** noted for its partridge dishes and a 1600ptas *menú*. The nearby *Fonda "El Suizo"* (☎958 85 18 36; ③) has slightly cheaper rooms, some en suite. The tranquillity here doesn't seem to have been disturbed by the arrival of the *Aben Humeya* disco-pub which also puts on weekend karaoke sessions.

UGÍJAR, 6km on from Valor, is the largest community of this eastern sector, and an unassuming, quiet market town. There are easy and enjoyable walks to the nearest villages – up the valley to Mecina-al-Fahar, for example – and plenty of **places to stay**. Try the comfortable *Pensión Pedro*, c/Fábrica de Sedes s/n (☎958 76 71 49; ③), which has en-suite rooms, heating and serves midday meals; *Hostal Vidaña* (☎958 76 70 10, fax 958 85 40 04; ③) nearby on the Almería road has rooms with bath, plus a restaurant with outdoor terrace and a cheap *menú*. With your own transport you may wish to take in the impressive **Museo Historico de las Alpujarras** (daily 1–8pm; free; ☎958 85 30 74) 10km to the southwest along the GR471 in the village of Jorairátar, where rooms stuffed with artefacts and reconstructions document a centuries-old way of life here, gradually being left behind.

Buses, which stop in the central plaza, run onward to Almería (3hr). Slightly west of Ugíjar a road heads north to Laroles to join the A337, which climbs over Puerto de la Ragua pass (p.465), descending beyond to the spectacular castle of La Calahorra (p.465) on the northern slopes of the Sierra Nevada.

The southern ranges

The tiny hamlets of the **southern Alpujarras** have an unrivalled view of the Mediterranean, the convexity of the hills obscuring the developments and acres of growers' plastic that mar the coast. There are few villages of any size, as there is little water, but the hills host the principal **wine-growing district** of the Alpujarras. For a taste of the best of this *costa* wine, try the *venta* at **HAZA DEL LINO** (Plain of Linen) on the western edge of the Sierra de la Contraviesa; the house brew is a full-bodied rosé. Also worth a look on the village's northern edge is an enormous **chestnut tree**, reputedly the oldest in Andalucía.

ALBUÑOL and **ALBONDÓN** to the east are other scenic centres of wine production. The local wines can be **tasted** only at Albondón, however, where various *bodegas* are located along the main street. Much of the *costa* wine drunk in Granada comes from Albondón and excellent stuff it is, too. If you want to buy, take your own container, or be prepared to have it served to you in a rinsed Pepsi bottle. Just outside Albuñol, along the Rambla de Angusturas (and signposted), is the Neolithic **Cueva de Los Murciélagos** which produced the remarkable esparto baskets, sandals and jewellery now exhibited in the museum at Granada. The cave can be visited but there's not an awful lot to see.

The Almerian Alpujarras

From Ugíjar the A348 toils eastwards and, once across the Río de Alcolea, enters the province of Almería where the starker – but no less impressive terrain – gradually takes on the harsh and desiccated character of the deserts that lie ahead. There are still the odd oases to be found, however, in **Láujar de Andarax** and the spa of **Alhama de Almería**, and a remarkable prehistoric site, **Los Millares**.

Láujar de Andarax

It was at **LÁUJAR DE ANDARAX**, 16km east of Ugíjar, at the source of the Río Andarax, that Boabdil, the deposed Moorish king of Granada, settled in 1492 and from where he intended to rule the Alpujarras fiefdom granted to him by the Catholic monarchs. But Christian paranoia about a Moorish resurgence led them to tear up the treaty and within a year Boabdil had been shipped off to Africa, an event which set in train a series of uprisings by the Alpujarran Moors, ending in their suppression and eventual deportation, to be replaced by Christian settlers from the north.

The **Río Andarax's source** is at the town's eastern edge; it is signposted (*nacimiento*) and is a pleasant and shady spot, with a restaurant, the *Mesón El Nacimiento*, serving hearty *platos combinados* at lunchtime, beside the falls. In the centre, the **Plaza Mayor** has a seventeenth-century four-spouted fountain – one of many dotted around the town – and an elegant late eighteenth-century **Ayuntamiento**, where you can pick up a street map. This will enable you to find four crumbling seventeenth-century **palacios** as well as an impressive Mudéjar-style seventeenth-century church of **La Encarnación**, which contains a sculpture of the Virgin by Alonso Cano.

Should you decide **to stay**, Láujar offers two good-value *hostales*; the friendly *Hostal Fernández* on c/General Mola 4 (☎950 51 31 28; ③) has rooms with and without bath, plus a lovely salon and terrace with views over the valley, in addition to a superb **restaurant** with a low-priced *menú* washed down with local wine. West along the main street, *Hostal Nuevo Andarax*, c/Canalejas 27 (☎950 51 31 13; ③) is also good with en-suite rooms above a bar-restaurant. Alternatively, the *Hotel Almírez*, on the main road at the western edge of town (☎ & fax 950 51 35 14; ④), has immaculate rooms with bath and TV plus a restaurant. This has recently been upstaged by the arrival of a spanking new, if somewhat soulless, *Villa Turistica* (☎950 51 30 27, fax 950 51 35 54; includes breakfast; ⑤–⑧) on a low hill at the eastern end of town with mock-Alpujarran style bungalows, pool and gardens.

Láujar is the centre of a burgeoning **wine industry**, and although smoother and slightly less potent than the *costa* wines further west, the brew is just as palatable. The *Cooperativo Valle de Láujar*, on the main road 2km west of town, was founded in 1992 and is just beginning to commercialize these wines both within Spain and abroad. At their small shop (Mon–Sat 8.30am–noon & 3.30–6.30pm) you can taste and buy their two good reds as well as whites and a rosé, and their *digestif* made from grape juice, coffee and *anís*, plus cheeses and other local produce.

For a good **walk** in this area, follow the road forking right on the western edge of the town which climbs into the wooded slopes of the Sierra Nevada, where there are forest tracks east towards the abandoned lead mines, and west to the mountain villages of **Paterna del Río**, a spa with a sulphur spring, and **Bayarcal**, higher still. On these lower slopes of the Sierra Nevada covered with ilex and pine, you may be lucky enough to spot the *cabra hispanica*, or wild Spanish goat, as well as eagles and a variety of other birdlife, plus the odd wild boar.

East to Alhama de Almería

The road east of Láujar de Andarax passes a series of unremarkable villages, surrounded by slopes covered with vine-trellises, little changed since Moorish times and little visited today. Among them is **FONDÓN**, with a **campsite** (☎950 51 42 90) and whose church tower was the minaret of the former mosque, and **PADULES**, 11km beyond Láujar, where the municipal swimming pool might prove a greater lure in the baking heat of high summer. The prettier village of **CANJÁYAR**, 4km further on, also has a swimming pool, and becomes a centre of frenetic activity during the autumn *vendimia*, when the grapes are gathered in. At other times it reverts to a sleepy hamlet beneath its small church.

The road then trails the course of the Andarax river valley through an arid and eroded landscape, skirting the Sierra de Gádor before climbing slightly to **ALHAMA DE ALMERÍA**, 16km further on. This is a pleasant spa town, dating back to Moorish times, and most of its visitors are here to take the waters – hence the rather incongruous three-star *Hotel San Nicolás*, c/Baños s/n (☎951 64 13 61; ④), sited on the location of the original baths. If you want a slightly cheaper **place to stay** – and Los Millares (see below) is a reason why you might – *Pensión Chiquito*, c/Pablo Picasso 5 near the church (☎950 64 02 31; ④) has very pleasant air-conditioned en-suite rooms with TV. Alhama also has a delightful municipal **swimming pool** with plenty of shade, at the western end of the town.

Los Millares: the Chalcolithic settlement

Leaving Alhama by the Almería road, after 4km the road passes the remarkable pre-Bronze Age settlement of **LOS MILLARES**, one of the most important of its kind in Europe. Situated on a low triangular spur between two dried-up river beds, this was exposed in 1891 during the construction of the Almería-to-Linares railway line that passes below the site today. Two Belgian mining engineers, Henri and Louis Siret, who were also enthusiastic amateur archeologists, took on the excavations at the turn of the century, funding them from their modest salaries. What they revealed is a Chalcolithic or Copper Age (the period between the Neolithic and the Bronze Age) **fortified settlement**. It dates from c.2700 BC and was occupied until c.1800 BC, when both stone and copper but not bronze were used for weapons and tools. Whilst it is not entirely

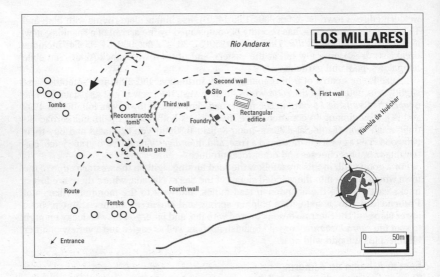

clear who the occupants were – possibly emigrants from the eastern Mediterranean or perhaps an indigenous group – the settlement they left behind is exceptional. Spread over twelve acres it consists of four sets of defensive walls, with a number of advanced fortlets beyond these, as well as an extraordinary cemetery with over one hundred **tombs** which are without equal in Europe.

Looking over the barren landscape that surrounds the site today, it is hard to believe that five thousand years ago this was a fertile area of pine and ilex forests, inhabited by deer and wild boar. The nearby Río Andarax was then navigable and the inhabitants used it to bring copper down from mines in the Sierra de Gádor to the west. The population – perhaps as many as two thousand – not only hunted for their food but bred sheep, goats and pigs, grew vegetables and cereals, made cheese and were highly skilled in the manufacture of pottery, basketwork and jewellery, as is evidenced by the finds now in museums at Almería and Madrid.

THE SITE

A tour of the **site** (April–Sept Wed–Sat 9.30am–2pm & 4–6pm, Sun 9am–2.30pm; check winter timetable with Almería Turismo or the site guardian on ☎608 95 70 65; free) begins with the outermost of **four exterior walls** which were built successively further west as the settlement expanded across the escarpment in the latter part of the third millennium BC. An impressive structure 4m high when built, the **fourth** (and last) **wall** was lined with outward-facing bastions or towers, and at 310m is the longest wall known in Europe from this period. Its layout bears a striking similarity to a wall of the same epoch at the early Cycladic site of Halandriani on the island of Síros in Greece, suggesting a possible link with the Aegean. The **main gate**, towards the centre, is flanked by barbicans or watch towers, beyond which a walled passage gave access to the settlement.

A little way north of here are the remains of a primitive **aqueduct** which cut through the wall to carry water from a spring near to the village of Alhama into the populated area. Fifty metres east of the main gate remains can be seen from the **third wall**. Close to here also are the remains of a number of **circular huts** – one of which has been partially reconstructed – in which the inhabitants of the site lived. Six to seven metres in diameter with pounded earth floors, they consisted of cavity stone walls filled with mud and pebbles, with a roof probably made from straw. Inside the huts the excavators found remains of hearths as well as grindstones, pottery and a variety of utensils.

Moving east again, beyond the **second wall** lies a **primitive foundry** where the copper ore was crudely smelted by means of fire and bellows before being hammered into the required form. Moulds arrived only in the later Bronze Age. Further north, on the line of the wall, lies a **silo** used for storing grain. Behind this wall are the foundations of a **rectangular edifice**, 32m in length, whose function is as yet unknown. The settlement at first appeared to lack a hierarchical social structure due to the overall similarity of the huts, but after the discovery of this building – much larger than the rest – some have speculated that it could have served as a form of council chamber or even a royal palace.

The remains of the **first wall**, enclosing what may have been the citadel, lie further back still and excavations here recovered many of the patterned, bell-shaped vases to be seen in the museum at Almería.

THE NECROPOLIS

Retracing your steps to the outer (or fourth) wall will bring you to one of the reconstructed tombs, part of the **ancient necropolis**. This "beehive" **tomb**, originally sited outside the third wall, was encompassed by the later fourth wall. It is one of more than a hundred tombs (the rest lie west of this wall), and the typical structure of a low corridor punctuated by perforated slate slabs leading to a domed burial chamber bears a striking resemblance to tholos tombs of a similar date from the Aegean, particularly southern Crete. It has been suggested that early Cretans (for whom the bull was religiously significant) may have found their way here and that the importance of bulls and bullfighting on the Iberian peninsula may owe something to this link. Present academic thinking, however, tends towards the idea that the civilization here was of local origin.

More tombs, most in a collapsed state, in which clan members were buried together with their possessions such as arms, tools and what appear to be ceramic idols (suggesting the existence of a cult) lie beyond the outer wall. Originally, and again as in the Aegean, the tombs were covered with an earth mound or tumulus. Try to resist climbing over them as many are in a fragile condition and the importance of this site for posterity is hard to overstate.

Inland towards Almería: Guadix and Baza

An alternative **route from Granada to Almería** – via the N342 and covered by *Empresa Autodía* buses from the main bus station – runs close to **Viznar** (where Lorca was assassinated – see p.427) and **Purullena** 30km further, a centre of ceramic production. The town's pottery output is on show at colourful roadside stalls, where there's also a good-value **pensión** with restaurant, *El Caminero*, Avda. Andalucía 30 (☎958 69 01 54; ②). The road drives on to **Guadix**, a crumbling old Moorish town with a vast and extraordinary cave district. For those with transport, the route also offers the opportunity for a detour to the impressive Renaissance castle of **La Calahorra**.

To the north, the A92N *autovía* speeds traffic from Guadix towards Lorca and Murcia, and there is a possible stop at the pleasant market town of **Baza** beyond which the road pushes on through a sparsely populated landscape for the 70km between here and the towns of Vélez Rubio and Vélez Blanco (p.487).

Guadix

Sited on the banks of the Río Guadix, in the midst of a fertile plain, **GUADIX** is a ramshackle, windblown sort of town, often coated in the red dust which gusts in from the surrounding hills. It is not a particularly attractive place and if it were not for its remarkable cave district there would be little reason to stop.

It is in fact an ancient settlement dating back to Paleolithic times, and the later Roman town of *Julia Gemella Acci* was established by Julius Caesar in 45 BC as a base for exploiting seams of silver in the surrounding hills. Following on a period of decline during the Visigothic era, the conquering Moors revived its fortunes and renamed the town *Guadh-Haix* ("River of Life") which rapidly grew in size and was soon a rival for Granada. It was renowned for its poetry, and bards such as Ibn Tofayl sang the praises of Guadix's beauty and its valley. It was also during the Moorish period that the town developed an important silk industry, whose mulberry trees can still be seen along the river. More recently, industrial development was based upon the production of esparto products and cutlery. Guadix endured terrifying atrocities during the Civil War, which Gerald Brenan vividly described in *South from Granada*.

The Town

Guadix's old quarter is still largely walled, and the circuit includes an imposing Moorish gateway, the Puerta San Turcuato. Within, it is dominated by the red sandstone towers of its sixteenth-century **Catedral** (Mon–Sat 10am–1pm & 4–6pm; 200ptas) – circled on Saturdays by a lively **market** – built on the site of a former mosque. This has been much hacked around and embellished over the years and the exterior is eighteenth-century Corinthian, the work of Vincente Acero; it still bears a commemorative plaque to Primo de Rivera, founder of the Falangist Party. The sombre, late Gothic interior was designed by Diego de Siloé, based on that of the cathedral at Málaga. Its best feature is the superb Churrigueresque **choir stalls** by Ruíz del Peral. Civil War reminders from both sides of the conflict include the defaced and destroyed heads of the saints on the carved marble pulpit and, near to the entrance, two plaques recording the names of local priests "killed by Marxism".

Just across from the cathedral entrance, beneath an arch, stands the elegant **Plaza Mayor**, an arcaded Renaissance square which was reconstructed after severe damage in the Civil War. A right turn in the stepped street (c/Ancha) at the far end of the square leads up to the Renaissance **Palacio de Peñaflor**. Nearby in the Placeta de Santiago the whitewashed church of **Santiago** (daily 6.15–8pm), another work by de Siloé, has an imposing Plateresque entrance and, inside, a fine *artesonado* ceiling.

Next to the Peñaflor mansion a theological seminary alongside the sixteenth-century church of **San Agustín** gives access to the conclusively ruined ninth-century Moorish **Alcazaba** (Mon–Fri 9am–2pm & 4–7pm, Sat 9am–2pm; 100ptas). From the restored battlements there are **views** over the cave district of Santiago (see below) and beyond towards the Sierra Nevada.

The cave district

Close to the Alcazaba and sited in a weird landscape of pyramidal red hills, the cave district of the **Barrio Santiago** still houses some 10,000 people (most of whom, incidentally, are not *gitanos* or gypsies), and to take a look round it is the main reason for most visitors stopping off.

The quarter extends over a square mile or so in area, and the lower caves, on the outskirts, are really proper cottages sprouting television aerials, with upper storeys, electricity, and running water. But as you walk deeper into the suburb, the design quickly becomes simpler – just a whitewashed front, a door, a tiny window and a chimney – and the experience increasingly voyeuristic. Penetrating right to the back you'll come upon a few caves which are no longer used: too squalid, too unhealthy, their long-unrepainted whitewash a dull brown. Yet right next door there may be a similar, occupied hovel, with a family sitting outside, and other figures following dirt tracks still deeper into the hills.

Beware that offers to show you around the interior of a cave will often be followed by a demand for substantial sums of money when you emerge. A newly opened **Cueva Museo** (Cave Museum; Mon–Sat 10am–2pm & 5–7pm, Sun 10am–2pm; 200ptas), Plaza Padre Poveda, opposite the church of San Miguel – and signed from the centre – is the easiest way to get an understanding of cave culture. Sited in a series of rehabilitated cave dwellings, it documents the history and reality of cave living with audiovisual aids and reconstructed rooms. On the way to the museum you will pass a private cave museum on your left which – although friendly and mildly interesting – is not worth the entry fee and is mainly a front for selling the wares of the *alfarería* (pottery) opposite.

Practicalities

Guadix is not a large place and, if you arrive at the **bus station**, it's easy enough to set your sights on the walls and cathedral – around five minutes' walk. A small and helpful **Turismo** (Mon–Fri 8am–3pm; ☎958 66 26 65) along the Ctra. de Granada, not far from the cathedral, will provide a town map. **Horses** can be hired to explore the surrounding country by contacting Manuel Ruiz Navarro on ☎958 66 22 01.

Should you want to **stay** overnight, there's little in the way of budget accommodation. The *Hotel Mulhacén*, Avda. Buenos Aires 41 (☎958 66 07 50; ④), is near the centre and functional, but the slightly higher priced *Hotel Comercio*, c/Mira de Amezcua 3 (☎958 66 05 00, fax 958 66 50 72; ⑤), an elegant and refurbished turn-of-the-century hotel, is easily the best place in town; it has an excellent **restaurant** as well – the *perdiz* (partridge) dishes are recommended – with a good-value *menú*.

For cheaper **meals** head for the Plaza de Naranjos, a stone's throw east of the cathedral. Here among a bunch of popular eating places *Cafetería Hawai* does **tapas**, **raciones**, hamburgers and a cheap *menú*, whilst the nearby *El Nido*, c/Duque de Gor 5, beyond the Puerto de Torcato, is a more conventional place serving up excellent fish and meat *tapas* and *raciones*. *Restaurante El Albergue* at Avda. Medina Olmos 48, next to the bus station, is reasonable, too.

If you've been smitten with the idea of cave life there's a chance to experience it for a night at the **cave hotel** *Pedro Antonio Alarcón* (☎ & fax 958 66 49 86; ⑤), a luxurious complex of nineteen apart-caves with pool, gardens and restaurant just over a kilometre from the centre along Avda. de Buenos Aires.

Baza

BAZA, 44km northeast of Guadix along the A92N, is another old Moorish town, well worth a detour if you have time and transport. Approached through an ochre landscape dotted with weird conical hillocks covered with esparto grass, the town is slightly smaller than Guadix, with a web of streets encircling its ancient central plaza. As with many towns in these parts, it has a history dating back well into prehistoric times. A prosperous Iberian settlement here named *Basti* produced the remarkable *Dama de Baza* sculpture (see below) and the town remained a considerable centre under the Romans and later, like Guadix, a focus of silk production under the Moors; it was especially renowned for its silk prayer mats. Taken by Christian forces in 1489 after a long siege, the town has had a less-than-glorious past few centuries, in part due to trouble from earthquakes, which have crumbled away most of the old Moorish Alcazaba.

Like Guadix, Baza also has a **cave quarter**, on the eastern side of town, beyond the railway tracks and close to the bullring.

Arrival, information and accommodation

The **bus station** (with frequent connections to Guadix) is located on Avda. Reyes Católicos to the west of the centre, and an easy five-minute walk from the Plaza Mayor. Along a narrow street to the north of the church of Santa María, c/Arco de la Magdalena, is a small and friendly **information office** (Mon–Fri 10am–3pm & 6–10pm; ☎958 70 06 91), which will provide you with a good map for further explorations. When this office is closed, maps are also available from the reception of the *Ayuntamiento* on the nearby Plaza Mayor.

Due to recent closures there are limited budget **places to stay** in Baza. The only central options now are the very comfortable *Hostal Anabel* (☎958 86 09 98; ⑤), about four blocks east of the Plaza Mayor on c/María de Luna. In the same area *Hostal Avenida*, Avda. José Mora 3 (☎958 70 03 77; ③), is a cheaper alternative. *Hostal Baza*, Virgen de las Angustias s/n, to the west of the Plaza Mayor and close to the bus station (☎958 70 07 50; ④), with balcony and en-suite rooms is another reasonable possibility.

The Town

The impressive Renaissance collegiate church of **Santa María** – and its eighteenth-century brick tower – leads you to the pedestrianised Plaza Mayor. Built over an earlier mosque, the church's elegant **Plateresque main door** – attributed to Diego de Siloé – is worth a look and inside there's an interesting marble pulpit and elegant vaulting. On the corner of c/Arco de la Magdalena and fronting the Plaza Mayor is *Confitería Emilio Castellaño*, which opened its doors in 1857 and has been in the same family for five generations – the sixth has just been born. The shop maintains much of its period interior and is still turning out delicious *pasteles* made to the same recipes as a century ago. On the opposite side of the Plaza Mayor a small **Museo Arqueológico** (Mon–Fri 10am–1pm & 6–8pm; free) preserves finds from the town's ancient past, including a copy of the *Dama de Baza*, a magnificent life-size fourth-century BC Iberian painted sculpture unearthed in 1971 in a necropolis on the outskirts of the town. The original is now in Madrid, where it is exhibited alongside the century later *Dama de Elche*, another iconic work of Spain's early artistic tradition.

A few minutes' walk to the east of Plaza Mayor, following c/Cabeza then turning left along c/del Agua, are the **Baños Árabes**, a tenth-century Moorish bath complex – one of the oldest surviving in Spain. The building is still privately owned (the local council is negotiating to take it over) so you'll need to visit the owners' home at c/Caniles 19, close by, to get someone to show you around. Either Manuela or Mateo will produce a key and provide you with an entertaining commentary – in Spanish – as they show you around their remarkable family heirloom.

The other sight of note is the **Palacio de los Enriquez**, Carrera de Palacio, to the south of the Plaza Mayor (enquire at the information office for visiting times), an early sixteenth-century Mudéjar mansion. Built by Don Enrique Enriquez, uncle of King Fernando, it served as a country residence and has many outstanding Moorish features including stunning *artesonado* ceilings and ornamentation.

Heading on from Guadix, possible destinations include the Cazorla Natural Park, to the north (see p.394), or the Almería coast via the A92N *autovía* with the option of a detour to Orce, the site of recent sensational finds concerning early humans in Spain (see p.489), and Vélez Rubio (see p.486).

Eating and drinking

There are plenty of places for **eating and drinking** in Baza led by the excellent *La Curva*, Carretera de Granada, a few blocks northwest of the Plaza Mayor, a mid-priced restaurant renowned for its *jamón iberico* and *mariscos*. *Mesón Siglo XX*, c/Solares 5, north of the Plaza Mayor, is the kind of splendid local restaurant that Andalucía excels in; an all-female kitchen cooks up a range of local delicacies including great soups, stews and a tasty paella, and the *menú* is a gift at 900ptas. A cluster of pleasant **tapas bars** – some with terraces – lie slightly east of the Plaza Mayor at the end of c/Serrano, with *Bar El Yoyo*, *Bar Perdiz* and *La Solana* all good possibilities. *La Bodega*, beneath two lofty plane trees and next to the fountain and church in the charming Plaza Santo Domingo, to the north of the Plaza Mayor, also has tables to sit out and serves a free *tapa* with every drink. Incidentally, the town's old theatre on this square, the turn-of-the-century *Teatro Dengra*, despite being converted into a cinema retains many of the antique fittings from its earlier incarnation, including boxes and scarlet velvet seats, and is worth a peep. The terrace of the *Casino* on the east side of the Plaza Mayor is a great place for a leisurely **breakfast** and they also serve up *tapas* later in the day.

Guadix to Almería: La Calahorra

Continuing southeast of Guadix along the A92 to Almería, the spectacular domed **Renaissance castle** of **LA CALAHORRA** heaves into view at the 16km point. A turn-off to the right takes you the 4km to the village of the same name, where, brooding on its hill above, this red stone monster was constructed in 1510. Its architect was Italian and its owner, one Rodrigo de Mendoza, was the bastard son of the powerful Cardinal Mendoza, who did much to establish Isabel on the throne. Rodrigo, created Marquis of Zenete by Isabel, acquired a taste for the Renaissance during an Italian sojourn, and ordered the castle as a wedding gift for his wife María de Fonseca. The bleak situation proved unattractive both to them and their descendants, however, and it was rarely used.

The castle is open to the public on Wednesdays only (10am–1pm & 4–6pm); outside these times access is possible by visiting c/de los Claveles 2 in the village (avoid siesta time), where the guardian Antonino Tribáldoz will open it up for a consideration (he'll also tell you of how he came to be born in the castle if you ask him). Once inside you'll be able to view an exquisite **Renaissance patio** – the last thing you'd expect behind such a dour exterior. The doorways, arches and stairway of this two-storey courtyard are beautifully carved from Carrara marble. Some of the palace's rooms have finely crafted *artesonado* ceilings and there's also a curious women's prison.

Should you wish **to stay** in the village, en-suite rooms are available at the comfortable *Hostal Manjón*, c/Los Caños 20 (☎958 67 70 81; ③). The *Bar Labella* also does *tapas* and simple **meals**.

From La Calahorra, a lonely but scenic road – the A337 – toils south to the **Puerto de la Ragua**, at 1993m Andalucía's highest all-weather pass. The hairpin climb offers spectacular views back over the plain of the Hoya de Guadix and the rose-tinted La Calahorra castle. When you reach the pass – where it's inclined to be chilly even in high summer – you'll find a new **refuge** with comfortable bunk accommodation and a restaurant. To be certain of a bed, ring ahead (☎958 34 51 62; English spoken; ①) the friendly warden, Antonio Mesa, will provide details of fine **walks** in the vicinity, horse riding and (in winter) cross-country skiing, both available at the refuge. Beyond the pass the road forks, offering alternative descents to the Alpujarras villages of Válor or Ugíjar to the west (see p.457), and Láujar de Andarax (see p.458) in the east.

Towards Almería

Beyond La Calahorra, the N324 crosses the border into Almería and passes by **FIÑANA**, with another castle, this time Moorish and in a more ruinous state. Five kilometres beyond Fiñana a turn on the right leads 2km to the village of **Abrucena**, perched on the foothills of the Sierra Nevada, with a delightful isolated rural hotel a little beyond, *Hostería Tautila* (☎950 52 10 05; ④) with restaurant, sited in rugged rambling country. Some 20km further along the N324 there's a turn-off for **GERGAL**, with another well-preserved fortress and, on the highest summit of the Sierra de los Filabres behind, an observatory housing one of the largest telescopes in Europe, sited here by a German–Spanish venture to take advantage of the almost constantly clear skies (see p.490). The N324 gradually descends into the valley of the Río Andarax – where you could detour to the prehistoric site of Los Millares (see p.459) – which it follows for the final 15km to Almería.

Almería

Cuando Almería era Almería, Granada era su alquería.
When Almería was Almería, Granada was but its farm.

A traditional Almerian couplet

ALMERÍA is a pleasant and largely modern city, spread at the foot of a stark grey hill dominated by a magnificent Moorish fort. Founded by the Phoenicians and developed by the Romans, who named it *Portus Magnus*, it was as a Moorish city – renamed *al-Mariyat* ("the mirror of the sea") – that Almería grew to prominence. The sultan Abd ar-Rahman I began the building programme soon after the conquest, in 713, with an arsenal beside the port, and the great **Alcazaba**, still the town's dominant feature, was added, in the tenth century by Abd ar-Rahman III, when the city formed part of the Cordoban Caliphate.

The splendours created here by the Moors – most of which have been lost – inspired the popular rhyme at the beginning of this section, contrasting this early prosperity with the much later glories of Nasrid Granada. After the collapse of Moorish Córdoba, Almería's prosperity was hardly affected and, as a principality or *taifa* state, it became the country's major port famed for its exports of silk, as well as a pirates' nest feared around the adjacent coasts. This period ended when the city fell to the forces of Fernando in 1490 and the Moors were expelled. Their possessions and lands were doled out to the officers of the conquering army, forming the basis for the *señoritismo* which has plagued Almería and Andalucía throughout modern times. Predictably, there followed a prolonged decline over the next three hundred years, reversed only by the introduction of the railway and the building of a new harbour in the last century, as well as the opening up to exploitation of the province's vast mineral wealth, particularly iron, lead and gold.

The Civil War interrupted this progress. The city's communist dockworkers gave staunch backing to the Republic, at one point in 1937 causing Hitler to order that the city be shelled from offshore by the German fleet. It was one of the last cities to fall to Franco's forces in 1939, after which many suicides took place to avoid the fate planned for the most bitter enemies of the new order.

Although still the centre of one of the poorest zones in Europe, Almería today is seeking a more prosperous future based upon intensive vegetable production in the surrounding *Vega*, in tandem with gaining a greater share of Spain's tourist economy. Whilst even its most devoted admirers wouldn't describe it as a beautiful place, the city deserves more visitors than it gets. There are areas with considerable charm; a handful of fascinating sights; and a friendly welcome in some great bars and restaurants, which may well make you want to give it a bit longer than the customary one-night transit.

Orientation and accommodation

The **Avenida de Federico García Lorca** (aka Rambla de Belén), formerly an unsightly dry river bed but now dramatically transformed into a stately avenue with palms, fountains and newsstands, bisects the city from north to south. Most of the action takes place to the west of this artery, where you'll find the **old town** and, to the north, the **Puerta de Purchena**, a busy traffic junction where six thoroughfares meet, which effectively marks the centre of the modern city.

Arrival and departure

Almería's **bus station** is on Plaza Barcelona, a couple of blocks east of the Avda. de Federico García Lorca, and a couple of minutes' walk north from the splendid stone, brick and steel nineteenth-century neo-Moorish **train station**, with direct services to Guadix, Granada and Baeza as well as longer-haul destinations such as Madrid (via Linares).

Train tickets and schedules are also available from the RENFE office at c/Alcalde Muñoz 7, behind the church of San Sebastián near the Puerta de Purchena. For bus schedules, it's easiest to consult the **Turismo** (Mon–Fri 9am–7pm, Sat 10am–2pm; ☎950 27 43 55, fax 950 27 43 60) at Parque Nicolás Salmarón (junction with c/Martínez Campos) fronting the harbour. They also have a good city map (100ptas). The friendly **Oficina Turística Municipal**, Avda. Federico García Lorca s/n (Mon–Fri 10am–1pm & 6–8pm, Sat 10am–noon; ☎950 28 07 48) is, if anything, even better and has lots of information on the town including a good map and free *tapas* bar guide.

Almería's sparkling new **airport** (☎950 22 41 14) lies 8km east from the city, along the coast. Local buses make the journey from the centre every half-hour between 7am and 9pm; take line #14 labelled "El Alquián" from the junction of the Avda. Federico García Lorca and c/Gregorio Marañón (one block above the top right corner of our map).

There is a **daily boat to Melilla** on the Moroccan coast throughout the summer (less often out of season), a six-hour journey, but one which cuts out the haul to Málaga or the usual port for Morocco, Algeciras. For information and tickets contact the *Compañía Transmediterránea* (☎950 26 37 14), Parque Nicolás Salmerón 19, near the port. The daily six-hour route to Nador (south of Melilla) is operated by *Ferrimaroc* (☎950 27 48 00) who have an office in the port.

Accommodation

Rooms are generally easy to come by at any time of the year and there are concentrations of *hostales* particularly around the Puerta de Purchena.

Hostal Americano, Avda. de la Estación 6, near the bus and train stations (☎950 25 80 11). Nothing special, but offers rooms with bath and is convenient if you arrive late or plan to leave early. ④.

Hostal Bristol, Plaza San Sebastián 8, near the Puerta de Purchena (☎950 23 15 95). Central and reliable two-star place with en suite rooms. ⑤.

Casa Francesca, c/Narvaez 18 (☎950 23 75 54). Friendly *fonda* a couple of blocks west of the cathedral which has some rooms with bath. ③.

Hotel Costasol, Paseo de Almería 58, near the Rambla end (☎ & fax 950 23 40 11). Best value of the more upmarket hotels; comfortable and central. ⑦.

Hostal Nixar, c/Antonio Vico 24, uphill from the Puerta de Purchena (☎ & fax 950 23 72 55). Good-value rooms with bath and air-conditioning in a quiet street; ask for the higher floors, which are airier. ④.

Hotel La Perla, Plaza del Carmen 7, off the Puerta de Purchena (☎950 23 88 77, fax 950 27 58 16). The city's oldest hotel (recently refurbished) has pleasant air-conditioned rooms with TV. ⑥.

Hostal Sevilla, c/Granada 23, near the Puerta de Purchena (☎950 23 00 09). Pleasant, modern *hostal* with en-suite bath, air-conditioning and TV in each room. ④.

Fonda Universal, Puerta de Purchena 3 (☎950 23 55 57). Atmospheric old *fonda* with a fabulous foyer staircase; very basic but clean. ②.

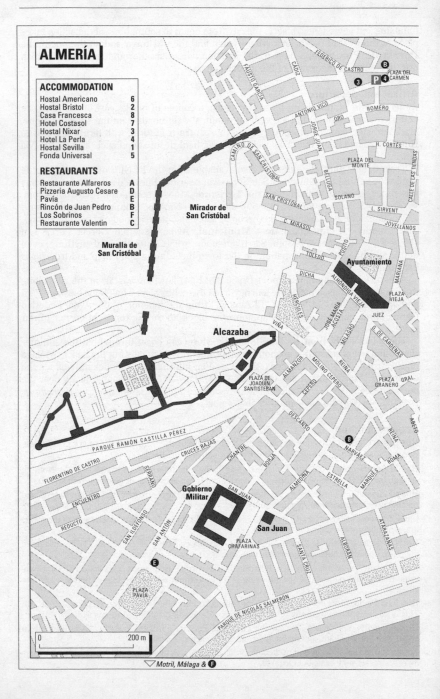

ALMERÍA

ACCOMMODATION

Hostal Americano	6
Hostal Bristol	2
Casa Francesca	8
Hotel Costasol	7
Hostal Nixar	3
Hotel La Perla	4
Hostal Sevilla	1
Fonda Universal	5

RESTAURANTS

Restaurante Alfareros	A
Pizzeria Augusto Cesare	D
Pavía	E
Rincón de Juan Pedro	B
Los Sobrinos	F
Restaurante Valentín	C

Mirador de
San Cristóbal

Muralla de
San Cristóbal

Alcazaba

Ayuntamiento

PARQUE RAMÓN CASTILLA PÉREZ

Gobierno
Militar

San Juan

PLAZA
PAVÍA

PARQUE DE NICOLÁS SALMERÓN

0   200 m

▽ *Motril, Málaga &* **F**

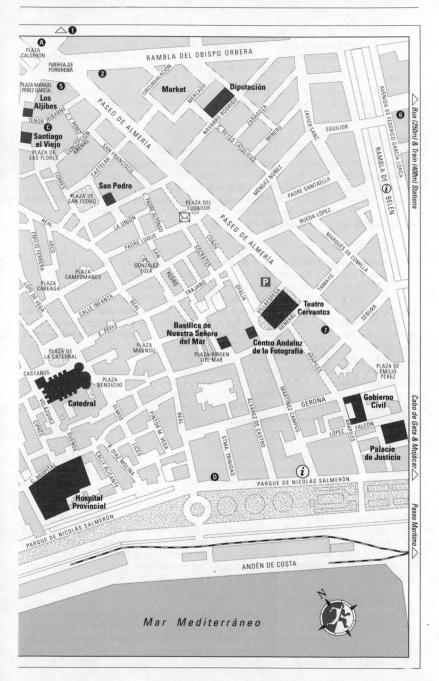

YOUTH HOSTEL & CAMPING

Albergue Juvenil Almería, c/Isla de Fuerteventura s/n (☎950 26 97 88). Almería's swish new 150 double-roomed (all ensuite) youth hostel lies on the east side of town next to the *Estadio Juventud* sports arena. Take bus #1 from the junction of Rambla del Obispo Orberá and Avda. F. García Lorca (top right corner of our map). ②.

Camping La Garrofa (☎950 23 57 70). The nearest campsite to town – 5km west, on the coast at La Garrofa, and easily reached by the buses to Aguadulce and Roquetas de Mar (where there's another, giant site).

The Town

Almería's most impressive monument, the formidable **Alcazaba**, is probably the best surviving example of a Moorish military fortification. It can be reached by following any of the narrow streets which climb the hill west of the cathedral, aiming for the entrance below the walls in the Plaza Joaquín Santisteban, at the end of c/Almanzor. The city's other sights pale by comparison, though it is worth taking time to look over the **cathedral** and the **Puerta de Purchena** area.

The Alcazaba

The **Alcazaba** (daily 9.30am–1.30pm & 3.30–7.30pm; free with EU passport, otherwise 250ptas) was begun by Abd ar-Rahman III of Córdoba in 955 and was just one part of a massive building programme which included a great mosque and city walls. During the eleventh century when the city enjoyed a period of prosperous independence, between the fall of the Cordoban Caliphate and its capture by the Almoravids, the medina (walled city) here contained immense gardens and palaces and housed some 20,000 people. It was adapted after the *reconquista* by the Catholic monarchs but severely damaged during a great earthquake in 1522. A programme of restoration in recent years has begun to reverse the centuries of crumbling decay.

Through the **Puerta Exterior**, a zig-zagged entrance ramp – a traditional Moorish architectural feature to make attack precarious – leads to the **Puerta de la Justicia**, the gateway to the first of the Alcazaba's three great compounds. Halfway up the ramp to the right is the **Tower of Mirrors**, a fifteenth-century addition, where mirrors were employed to communicate with ships approaching the port below.

THE FIRST COMPOUND

The first compound is the largest of the three. It is laid out today as a garden but was designed as a military camp and an area in which the populace could seek protection when under siege. A **well** in the centre of this area raised water from a depth of 70m to supply the site. At the eastern end of the enclosure, the **Saliente Bastión** was a lookout point over the town below, and the sea beyond.

Below the north side of the compound, the **eleventh-century wall** descends the hill; it originally formed part of a great complex of walls, not only surrounding the city but also dividing it internally. Above the wall, which divides the first and second compounds, is the **Campana de Vela**, a bell erected during the eighteenth century to announce ships sighted nearing the port, or to summon soldiers to their battle stations.

THE SECOND COMPOUND

The second compound accommodated the Moorish kings, when resident in the city, and at other times served as the governor's quarters. In the eleventh century, when Almería was the wealthiest, most commercially active city of Spain, the buildings here were of unparalleled brilliance. Their grandeur was even reputed to rival the later court of Granada, but the ruins that remain today make a valid comparison impossible.

What you can see, however, are the remains of **cisterns**, the old **mosque** – converted into a chapel by the *Reyes Católicos* – and once palatial dwellings, but sadly no sign of the magnificent stucco work said to equal that of the Alhambra, the last remnants of which were sold off by the locals in the eighteenth century. The **Ventana de Odalisca**, a *mirador* window in the compound's northern wall, is a poignant reminder of lost glory. A legend attached to this concerns an eleventh-century Moorish slave-girl, Galiana, the king's favourite, who fell in love with a prisoner and arranged to help him to escape. But the guards discovered them in the attempt and the prisoner threw himself from this window into the valley below, whilst Galiana died of a broken heart a few days later.

THE THIRD COMPOUND

The third and highest compound demonstrates the starkly contrasting style of the conquering Christians. When they took the city, the Catholic monarchs found the fortress substantially damaged due to an earthquake a couple of years before. They thererefore built walls much stronger than the original Moorish structure, to cope both with potential future earthquakes and the recent innovation of artillery. Triangular in form, this upper fort is guarded by three semi-circular towers built of ashlar masonry, both features at odds with the earlier Moorish design.

To the right, the **Torre del Homenaje** (Tower of Homage) bears the crumbling escutcheon of the Catholic monarchs and looks out over the **Patio de Armas** (Courtyard of Arms) where the guard would be assembled. From the **Torre de Pólvora** (Gunpowder Tower) and the battlements (take care as there are few handrails) fine views are to be had of the coast and of Almería's *gitano* cave quarter – the Barrio La Chanca – on a low hill to the west.

The Mirador de San Cristóbal and Wildlife Centre

The hill-top **Mirador de San Cristóbal**, which can be seen from the Alcazaba, has more fine views over the town and the coast, and can be visited by following c/Antonio Vico west from the Puerta de Purchena. Adjoining the *mirador* is a chapel with a huge figure of Christ, erected in 1928 over the site of an earlier chapel founded by the Templars after the Christians, under Alfonso VI, took the city, briefly, in 1147. The open-air chapel's altar at the rear of Christ's statue has been completely hacked apart and the walls covered with graffiti – a telling comment on Spain's rapid transition to a secular state. The **sunsets** to be seen both from here and the Alcazaba are legendary.

North of the *mirador* and Alcazaba – and visible from both – is a curious-looking farm, where you can often see gazelles sprinting around. This is the **Sahara Wildlife Rescue Centre**, a research organization studying and breeding animals in danger of disappearing from their natural habitat. The centre can be visited only by prior application (the day before is usually okay) to their office at c/General Segura 1 (☎950 27 64 00), off the south end of the Paseo de Almería, who will give you an *autorización*.

The Cathedral

Located in the heart of the old quarter, the **Catedral** (Mon–Fri 10am–5pm, Sat 10am–1pm; 300ptas) is another building with a fortress look about it. Begun in 1524 on the site of the great mosque – conveniently destroyed by the 1522 earthquake – it was designed in the late Gothic style by Diego de Siloé, the architect of the cathedral at Granada. Because of the danger of attack in this period from Barbarossa and other Turkish and North African pirate forces, the corner towers once held cannons. The threat was real and not long after its construction the cathedral chapter is recorded purchasing guns, muskets and gunpowder.

Like many of Andalucía's cathedrals, it was never completely finished and it may be that the city's inhabitants had no great affection for this austere giant, preferring instead their more intimate parish churches. The exterior is of little interest apart from a curious, pagan-looking relief of a garlanded **radiant sun** on the eastern wall – that is, facing the rising sun. Echoing the Roman *Sol Invictus*, or unconquerable sun, its appearance on the church has been put down to a sixteenth-century bishop with masonic leanings, but its true significance will probably never be known. Appropriately, as the province with the highest sun-hours statistic in Spain, Almería now uses the image as its official logo.

The cathedral is entered through the Puerta Principal, an elegant Renaissance doorway flanked by buttresses. Within, the sober Gothic **interior** is distinguished by some superb sixteenth-century **choir stalls** carved in walnut by Juan de Orea. Just behind this, the **retrochoir** is a stunning eighteenth-century altar in contrasting red and black jasper. Behind the Capilla Mayor (or high altar) with some elegant and sinuous vaulting, the Capilla de la Piedad has a painting of the *Annunciation* by Alonso Cano and *Immaculate Conception* by Murillo, whilst the Capilla de Santo Cristo – next door to the right – contains the sixteenth-century sculptured tomb of Bishop Villalán, the cathedral's founder, complete with faithful hound at his feet. Further along again, a door (often closed) leads to the sacristy and a rather uninspiring Renaissance cloister – relieved by a small garden with palms and orange trees. The church also contains a number of fine **pasos** of the Passion carried in the *Semana Santa* processions at Easter; among these, *El Prendimiento* (the Arrest of Christ) is outstanding.

Around the old town

To the west of the cathedral stands the seventeenth-century church of **San Juan** (open service times only), built over a tenth-century mosque. Inside, the church's southern wall preserves the *mihrab* (or prayer niche) of the original building. Next to this, there's another niche that would have contained the wooden pulpit used for readings from the Koran.

West of here lies the **Barrio de Chanca**, an area of grinding poverty occupied by *gitanos* and hard-pressed fisherfolk which has hardly changed since Brenan vividly described it in his *South from Granada*; there are some occupied cave dwellings here, too, but it's not a place to visit alone at night. East towards the port, on c/Hospital, the eighteenth-century **Hospital Real** has an elegant Neoclassical facade and, inside, a beautiful marble-tiled patio usually containing a few prostrate patients on hospital trolleys. Like many others in Spain, this is a still fully-functioning infirmary two-and-a-half centuries after it was built.

A couple of blocks east of the cathedral, and housed in an eighteenth-century former Dominican convent with a stunning patio, the **Centro Andaluz de la Fotografía**, c/Conde Ofalía 30 (Mon–Fri 9am–2pm & 4–9pm; free), is Andalucía's first photo museum, often staging interesting exhibitions. To the north of the cathedral the **Plaza Vieja** (officially Plaza de la Constitución) is a wonderful pedestrian square which – because of its restricted entrance – you would hardly know was there. It contains the **Ayuntamiento**, a flamboyant early twentieth-century building with a pink and cream facade, and a monument to citizens put to the firing squad in 1824 for opposing the tyrannical reign of Fernando VII. This square has bags of potential and elsewhere would be full of restaurants and nightlife; at present, though, it's a rather melancholy place after dark. Near to the train station an impressive new **Centro de Arte** (Mon–Fri 11am–2pm & 6–8pm, Sat 6–8pm, Sun 11am–2pm; free), Plaza Barcelona s/n, has a collection of modern art (mainly paintings) and often stages special exhibitions by famous names.

Around the Puerta de Purchena

Further sights are located within a couple of minutes' walk of the **Puerta de Purchena**, which takes its name from a Moorish gate – long gone – where al-Zagal, the city's last Moorish ruler, surrendered to the Catholic monarchs in 1490.

On the west side of the junction, at the end of c/Tenor Iribarne at c/de los Aljibes 20, are some well-preserved eleventh-century Moorish water cisterns – known as **Los Aljibes** (Mon–Fri 11am–2pm & 5.30–7.30pm; free). The **Calle de las Tiendas** (the continuation of c/de los Aljibes) – the oldest street in the city – was formerly called Calle Lencerías (drapers' street) and in the last century was Almería's most fashionable shopping thoroughfare. Some of the street lamps survive from this period, although the place has now become rather seedy.

A little further down you'll arrive at the church of **Santiago**, dating from the same period as the cathedral, and built with stone from the same quarry. A fine Plateresque portal incorporates a statue of Santiago slaying the Moors as well as the coat of arms of the all-powerful Bishop Villalán, the cathedral's founder.

Finally, across the Alameda (Paseo de Almería), the main street which leaves the Puerta de Purchena from its southern side, a colourful **daily market** at the end of c/Aguilar de Campo is also worth a look.

The Archeological Museum

Almería's **Museo Arqueológico** has been closed since the building developed dangerous structural faults in 1993. The Turismo should be able to advise on developments. When it re-opens (almost certainly on a new site), its important collection of artefacts from the prehistoric site of Los Millares (see p.459) will be on view again. The museum also has interesting Roman and Moorish sections. As a temporary measure some of the artefacts from Los Millares are currently on display in the *Biblioteca Pública* (public library; Tues–Fri 9am–2pm, Sat 9.30am–1.30pm) at c/Hermanos Machado s/n, off the southern end of the Avda. Federico García Lorca. A selection of items from the Roman and Moorish sections can similarly be seen at the *Archivo Historico Provincial* (Mon–Fri 9am–2.30pm) c/Infanta s/n, slightly northeast of the cathedral.

Eating, drinking and entertainment

Almería has a surprising number of interesting and good-value places to **eat and drink**. Most of the best eating options are to be found around the Puerta de Purchena and in the web of narrow streets lying between the Paseo de Almería and the cathedral. For seafood there are a number of places in the Barrio de los Pescadores, the old fishing quarter at the western end of the commercial port. On the **nightlife** front, the city's music bars can be lively and in summer there are late-night marquees on the beach.

In August the city holds its annual **music and arts festival**, the *Fiesta de los Pueblos Ibéricos y del Mediterráneo*, with concerts and dance events, many of them free, taking place in the squares and various other locations throughout the city (details from the Turismo). During the last week of the month, the city's main **annual fiesta**, the *Romería de Augusto*, also takes place with lots of street parties and spectacular processions with carnival giants.

Restaurants and tapas bars

The best place for early-evening **tapas** is around the Puerta de Purchena, where the whole town turns out during the evening *paseo* to see and be seen. Places around the cathedral and old town are more lively at lunchtime.

AROUND PUERTA DE PURCHENA

Bar El Alcázar, Paseo de Almería 4. Popular *marisquería* and *freiduría* with plenty of *tapas* possibilities and tables to sit out at to watch the early-evening *paseo*.

Restaurante Alfareros, c/Marcos 6, slightly northeast of the Puerta de Purchena. Wonderful cheap place to eat, packed at lunchtime with people in town for the market, with an excellent-value *menú* for 950ptas.

Bodega Las Botas, c/Fructuoso Pérez 3, just south of the Puerta de Purchena. Great *tapas* place with hanging *jamón serrano* shanks and upturned sherry butt tables; excellent *fino* and *manzanilla* (served with a free *tapa*) goes well with the house special, *merluza en escabeche* (marinated hake).

Rincón de Juan Pedro, Plaza del Carmen. One of the town's pricier restaurants, serving top-quality Almerian specialities. On a budget, stick to the medium-priced *menú*.

El Quinto Toro, c/Reyes Católicos 6, just south of the market. Top notch atmospheric *tapas* bar taking its name from the fifth bull in the corrida (reputed always to be the best). Friendly service and mouthwatering *patata a lo pobre*. The same people also run the good beer bar *Cervecería La Estrella*, Plaza del Carmen 12, off the Puerta de Purchena.

Peña Taurina Almiriente, c/Regocijos 23, north of the Puerta de Purchena. Great old bar where *corrida* aficionados gather to talk about the fights, looked down on by photos and paraphernalia from the past.

Restaurante Valentin, c/Tenor Iribarne 19. Owned by the same people as *Bodega Las Botas*, this is a mid-priced stylish restaurant and *tapas* bar noted for its seafood; has a small terrace. In fact, this whole street is full of good *tapas* bars.

AROUND THE CATHEDRAL

Pizzeria Augusto Cesare, Parque Nicolás Salmerón 17, on the seafront. Authentic Italian pizzas, plus an improbably impressive wine list with stratospherically costly vintage bottles (cheap house wine, too) and outdoor tables.

Bar Bahía de la Palma, c/Mariana, next to Plaza de la Constitución (aka Plaza Vieja). Good lunchtime *tapas* stop. Recorded flamenco music is the accompaniment to the drinking here and some evenings they even put on live sessions.

Casa Joaquín, c/Real 113, near the port. Fine and popular *tapas* bar which buzzes with contented imbibers most evenings. All *tapas* and *raciones* are excellent, especially the seafood.

Bodega Montenegro, Plaza Granero, just west of the cathedral. Delightful neighbourhood bar, stacked with barrels. Once they've got over the initial novelty of seeing a foreigner walk through the door, they will serve up great local wines and seafood *tapas*.

Bodega del Patio, c/Real 84. Another wonderful old Almerian *bodega*, little changed for decades.

Casa Puga, corner of c/Lope de Vega and c/Jovellanos. With marble-topped tables and walls covered with *azulejos*, this is another *tapas* bar with a great atmosphere and loyal clientele; try their *pescado frito*.

Bodega Ramón and **Bodega El Ajoli**, c/Padre Alfonso, slightly south of the Iglesia de San Pedro. Two good *tapas* bars on a pleasant street, both with tables to sit out at. *El Ajoli* specializes in pork products – ordering their *surtido* gets you a bit of everything.

BARRIO DE LOS PESCADORES

Pavía, Plaza Pavía 10. Fine fish and seafood served on tables in the square in summer.

Los Sobrinos, Cuesta de Muelle 32, slightly east of Plaza Pavía and Plaza San Roque, facing the port. Serves up fish dishes and is a slightly cheaper place than the one above.

Breakfast

For breakfast, there are plenty of bars and **pastelerías** along the Paseo de Almería, and more still along the newly revamped Avda. Federico García Lorca, but a good and cheap option is *El Oasis*, a self-service kiosk bar on the western side of the Puerta de Purchena. There are tables to sit out at and – because it's self-service – you avoid the normal terrace surcharge.

Nightlife and flamenco

Most of Almería's **nightlife** takes place in the beach resorts to the west of the town. However, if you're determined to party, head for the bars in the streets around the Plaza Masnou near the cathedral, and c/San Pedro south of the Puerta de Purchena, which attract big night-time crowds, especially at weekends. The *Irish Tavern*, Plaza González Egea just west of c/San Pedro is the best of the town's twin Hibernian bars and has tables outside on a pleasant terrace.

To move the nightime *marcha*, or scene, away from the residential area in summer, the city council erects a line of **disco marquees** at the start of the Paseo Marítimo, near the beach. At around 3am these places start to get quite wild. At other times of the year the focus moves back into town and the streets around c/Trajano off the Paseo de Almería where indie bars *Vértice* and *Vhada* and dance clubs *Subway*, *Velvet* and *Chamakas* are popular. Further east, across the Avda. Federico García Lorca, the *Lord Nelson* **disco**, c/Canónigo Molina Alonso, is sometimes lively.

For **flamenco**, the only genuine establishment is *Peña El Taranto,* taking its name from the *taranto*, Almería's dramatic and clamorous contribution to the flamenco canon. In temporary premises in the Plaza de las Flores, slightly south of the Puerta de Purchena and opposite the *Hotel Torreluz*, this club holds regular concerts (except in August) and their good-value *tapas* bar is always worth a visit.

Listings

Banks The major banks, most with ATM cash dispensers, are located along the Paseo de Almería and close at 2pm; there is also an ATM at the airport.

Beaches The city beach, southeast of the centre beyond the rail lines, is long but crammed with day-trippers for most of the summer. For a day trip, the best options are Cabo de Gata or San José, both easily accessible by bus.

Books and newspapers Papelería Goya, Paseo de Almería 8, has a good book selection on the town and province. Almería's main daily paper is *Voz de Almería*, a useful source for local and provincial news as well as entertainment listings at weekends.

Car rental Europcar, c/Rueda López 23, off the east side of the Paseo de Almería (☎950 23 49 66), or Alva, Rambla Alfareros 11, north of Puerta de Purchena (☎950 23 56 88) for a cheaper local alternative.

Football Almería supports two teams, both founded in the 1980s. Polideportivo Almería (☎950 22 91 83), are currently performing in *Segunda Division B*, whilst their fierce rivals C.F. Almería (☎950 22 87 06), are toiling in the third division. Both play matches at the Estadio Municipal, Avda. Torrecardenas s/n, in the northern suburbs.

Hiking maps Librería Cajal, c/Navarro Rodrigo 14, just south of the market, stocks walking guides and maps.

Hospital Hospital Provincial, c/Hospital s/n, near the cathedral (☎950 22 75 01).

Police Contact the *Policia Municipal* c/Santos Zárate 11, off the north end of the Avda. Federico García Lorca, to report thefts or lost property (☎950 21 00 29). In case of emergency dial ☎092 (local police) or ☎092 (national).

Post office The main *Correos* is at Plaza Cassinello 1, near Plaza del Ecuador, off Paseo de Almería.

West of Almería: the Costa Tropical

Almería's best beach resorts lie on its eastern coast, the Costa de Almería, between the city and Mojácar. On the so-called **Costa Tropical**, west of the city, the nearest beaches such as **Aguadulce**, **Roquetas de Mar** and **Almerimar** are overdeveloped and the landscape is dismal, backed by an ever-expanding plastic sea of *invernaderos*, hothouses for cultivation of fruit and vegetables for the export market (see box below). Beyond Adra things improve, and smaller resorts such as **La Rábita**, **Castell de Ferro** and **Calahonda** make tolerable places to stop.

Almería to Adra

This section of coast is described here for little reason other than completeness – it's certainly not an unspoilt paradise; indeed, no one comes here for the beaches. The one half-decent reason for a stop in these parts is if you're a **bird-watcher**, in which case the inland salt lakes may well appeal.

PLASTICULTURA: EL EJIDO'S ELDORADO

West of Almería, and stretching from beneath the hills of the Sierra de Gador to the sea, lies the **Campo de Dalías**, a vast plain of salt flats and sand dunes which has become a shining sea of *plasticultura* – the forced production of millions of tons of tomatoes, peppers, cucumbers, strawberries and exotic flowers. This industry has wrought quite a revolution in impoverished Almería, covering a once-barren wilderness with a shimmering sea of 64,000 acres of polythene canopies (producing 20,000 tons of plastic waste annually) propped up by eucalyptus supports.

The boom is all due to the invention of drip-feed irrigation and it has led to phenomenal increases in the year-round production of crops, allowing cheap tropical fruit and flowers to fill the supermarket shelves of northern Europe throughout the year. The appliance of biological engineering now means that El Ejido's farmers can produce vegetables to almost any specification – "name your size" tomatoes, red peppers with large cavities for stuffing or lettuces without coarse outer leaves which look green even under fluorescent supermarket lights. The miracle, however, may be precarious. Scientists have serious worries about the draining of the province's meagre water resources through the tapping of countless artesian wells – many as deep as 100m.

The centre of this area is **El Ejido**, which appears on most maps as an inconspicuous dot and on others not at all, despite being a conurbation getting on for city status. Indeed, it has multiplied from a modest population of two thousand, twenty years ago, to some fifty thousand today, making it second in the province only to the capital itself. Like some Wild West town, El Ejido has grown up for a dozen kilometres along the main highway with little or no planning restraints and with the free market in almost total control. The bonanza has lured in peasants from all over Spain and beyond, and many *andaluzes* who formerly worked in the factories of Barcelona and Germany have come home with their savings and bought plots. Recently, the high demand for workers willing to toil in the terrible conditions has led to the arrival of 10,000 immigrants (mostly illegal) from Morocco and other African countries, who have built squalid shanty villages on the edges of town.

The lack of facilities for this enormous population growth – now belatedly to be investigated by the authorities – has led to serious problems and the social cost of this boom has been high: the suicide rate has risen sharply as those who don't make the easy money anticipated get deep into debt, and the twelve- to fifteen-hour days worked in jungle humidity all year long inside the *invernaderos* (plastic tents) often lead to breakdowns. Besides illness and alcoholism, gambling and drug addiction are also taking their toll. Early in 2000 simmering local resentment at this invasion erupted into violence when a two-day riot followed the lethal stabbing of a local women who had resisted an immigrant (and mentally unstable) thief intent on taking her bag. The furious townspeople attacked the shops, bars and support centres of the immigrant population, setting some hostels ablaze and covering others with racist slogans. It took six hundred Guardia Civil to quell the disorder and the government's Interior Minister described it as "a disgrace for Spanish society".

Aguadulce, Roquetas de Mar – and some birdwatching

AGUADULCE, 13km west of Almería, is the oldest of the city's local resorts, with a palm-lined promenade that does its best to offset the miserable concrete boxes flanking it. There's a reasonable beach, the usual *costa* nightlife, and some fairly expensive accommodation, full all summer.

The next place along, **ROQUETAS DE MAR**, used to be another old fishing port, though its remaining whitewashed core is now submerged by an ugly conglomeration of hotels and beach emporia. On the plain behind the resort, plastic greenhouses compete fiercely with developers for land and this must be the only place in Spain where agricultural land is more profitable than tourist development – a couple of acres sells for millions of pesetas. The centre of the cultivation is the boom town of **EL EJIDO** (see box), 30km inland from Roquetas de Mar along the arrow-straight N340.

Some relief from the tedium can be found 5km to the south of Roquetas, where **Las Marinas** is a good place for spotting birdlife. A saline marsh fringed by tamarisks, it attracts greater flamingos, little egrets and avocets, and, in winter, the white wagtail. The lake is reached by turning left beyond the *Urbanización Roquetas de Mar*. A road joins this to a second area at **Punta Sabinar**, 1km south, consisting of beach, sand dunes and salt-marsh with possible sightings of crested larks, great grey shrikes and fantailed warblers.

Almerimar and Adra

ALMERIMAR is a long 18km from Roquetas, through the plastic-covered desert – and not much relief when you eventually arrive. A rather tasteless conglomeration of *urbanizaciones* – with more being assembled by cranes dominating the skyline – crowd around a dismal yacht harbour where the local *plasticultura* billionaires park their floating assets alongside craft from the four corners of the Mediterranean. Less interested in attracting foreign package tours, this is the "glitz" resort for the nouveau riche of El Ejido, and the place where these agricultural tycoons can indulge in conspicuous consumption. Tacky shopping arcades with neo-Moorish facades, overpriced restaurants and three golf courses – one designed by Gary Player – complete the picture.

It's a relief to join the main N340 heading west, although not for long because you soon arrive in **ADRA**, another place with non-existent charms. "The last king of the Moors, the unfortunate Boabdil, stayed in Adra immediately before leaving Spain for good. If he sighed when leaving Granada, he would have sighed even more had Adra in the fifteenth century been anything like it is today." Few would argue with Michael Jacobs's comments on this seedy industrial port in his book *Andalusia*. The best that can be said for it is that the planners have considerately sited the **bus station** on the seafront near the harbour, thus allowing for a speedy and relatively painless getaway.

Some 16km inland from Adra is the solid farming town of **BERJA**, the capital of *Alpujarra Baja*, surrounded by vineyards and fruit orchards, with a considerable Roman and Moorish past (there's an impressive ruined alcazaba in the suburb of Villavieja) and a lively daily market. Its eastern suburb, Alcaudique, has the remains of a Moorish bath. Nearby **DALÍAS**, another pleasant farming village, is founded upon the ruins of Roman *Murgis*.

Adra to Motril

Things start to look up along the coast to the west of Adra, and there are attractions inland, too. From La Rábita a scenic secondary road, the A345, heads up into Las Alpujarras, passing by the *costa* wine villages of **Albuñol** and **Albondón** (see p.458).

Güainos Bajos and Castillo de Baños

Around 5km west of Adra, **GÜAINOS BAJOS** fronts a pleasant and small beach. A further 10km along – and over the provincial border in Granada – you reach **LA RÁBITA**, another place that might invite a stop. Enclosed in a rocky creek, it has a reasonable beach (though it is often litter-strewn after the weekend onslaught), as well as a clutch of bars and restaurants. The central *Hostal Las Olas*, Avda. Generalísimo s/n (☎958 82 90 89; ②), has decent and inexpensive **rooms** with bath.

CASTILLO DE BAÑOS, 13km west of La Rábita, takes its name from a nearby *atalaya* or watch tower and is another possibility for a stopover with a decent beach and a good **campsite**, *Camping Castillo de Baños* (☎958 82 95 28), with plenty of shade but surrounded by plastic tents.

Castell de Ferro and beyond

CASTELL DE FERRO, 6km on from Castillo de Baños, is by far the best of the resorts along this stretch of coast and even preserves remnants of its former existence as a fishing village. Dominated by another hill-top *atalaya*, it's quite sheltered and has a couple of wide, if pebbly, beaches to the west and especially east, although the town beach fronting the small assemblage of bars, restaurants, and *hostales* is a filthy disgrace. Among the **places to stay** (all on the seafront Plaza de España), the friendly *Pensión Bahia* (☎958 65 60 60; ③) is the best value and has seaview rooms with terrace, with the *Costa del Sol* (☎958 65 60 54; ④) a good second choice. Of Castell's four **campsites**, *Camping Las Palmeras* (☎958 65 61 30) to the east is the one to go for, with shade, plenty of space and access to the beach. For **meals**, *Restaurante La Brisa* does a good and inexpensive *menú*, as do most of the places along the seafront.

The coast road east again from here skirts the foothills of the Sierra de Carchuna where **CALAHONDA** is another small resort with a good beach, the Playa de Carchuna, often full to the gunwales in summer. In the centre, *El Ancla* is the best of the eating places and a pleasant beach bar, *El Farillo*, is to be found by an old watchtower at the western end of the strand. Next comes the unremarkable **TORRENUEVA**, where there's a reasonable beach but little else to stop for, before the road crosses a dreary plain planted with sugar-cane, to the north of which lies the large and ugly chemical and industrial town of **MOTRIL**, and to the south its equally unappealing port-resort. The beaches to the west of Motril are described in Chapter One.

The Costa de Almería

The **Costa de Almería**, east of Almería, has a somewhat wild air, with developments constrained by lack of water and roads and by the confines of the **Parque Natural de Cabo de Gata** – a protected zone since 1987. If you have transport, it's still possible to find deserted beaches without too much difficulty, while small inlets shelter relatively low-key resorts such as **San José**, **Los Escullos**, **Las Negras** and **Agua Amarga**.

Further north is **Mojácar**, a picturesque hill village, which has grown a beach resort of quite some size over the past decade. It is easiest – and most speedily – approached on the inland routes via Níjar (the N344) or the "desert" road (A370) through Tabernas (see p.491) and Sorbas (p.492).

Almería to Mojácar

The coast between Almería and Mojácar is backed by the **Sierra del Cabo de Gata**, which gives it a bit of character and wilderness. **Buses** run from Almería to all the main resorts, though to do much exploring, or seek out deserted strands, transport of your

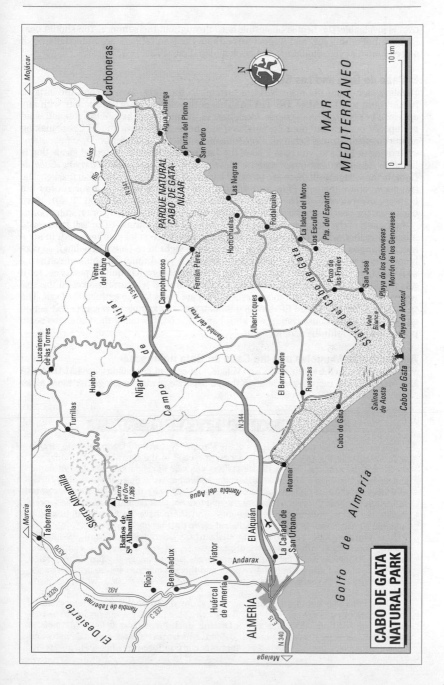

CABO DE GATA
NATURAL PARK

own is invaluable; the heat is blistering here throughout the summer. You should bear in mind that during July and August throughout the Natural Park accommodation is at a premium, and you should try and book ahead if possible.

El Cabo de Gata and Las Salinas

Heading east along the main N344, a turn-off to the right, 4km beyond the airport, heads south to **EL CABO DE GATA**. This is the closest resort to the city with any appeal: a lovely expanse of coarse sand, best in the mornings before the sun and wind get up. Six buses a day (four on Sundays) run between Almería and El Cabo, making an intermediate stop at Retamar, a retirement/holiday development.

Arriving at El Cabo, you pass a lake, the **Laguna de Rosa**, a protected locale that is home to flamingos and other waders. Nearby there's a **campsite**, *Camping Cabo de Gata*. In the village itself there are plentiful bars, cafés and shops, plus a fish market. The two *fondas* above the bars *Playa* and *Mediterráneo* on the beach have basic **rooms** but both are overpriced (③). The brand-new *Hostal Las Dunas* (☎950 37 00 72; ⑤), 100m back from the beach at c/Barrionuevo 58, is a more expensive option for en-suite rooms.

Just south of the village is another area known as **Las Salinas** – The Salt Pans – and it is exactly that, with a commercial salt-drying enterprise at its southern end. In summer **flamingos** and other migrants are a common sight here (see box below), so take binoculars if you have them – just before dusk is a good time. The hills of salt are a striking sight in the bright sun, too, and the industry here has quite a pedigree, for it was the Phoenicians way back in the first millennium BC who first controlled the seawater which entered through the marshes to create pools for the extraction of salt. The park authorities like to cite the modern industry as an example of resource extraction and environmental conservation working hand-in-hand. Certainly the flamingos seem perfectly happy with the arrangement.

Almadraba de Montelva and the Cabo de Gata lighthouse

Four kilometres to the south of El Cabo village, just beyond Las Salinas, is **ALMADRABA DE MONTELVA**, more a continuation than a separate place, but altogether more pleas-

---

PARQUE NATURAL DE CABO DE GATA

Protected since 1987, the 71,500 acres of the **Parque Natural de Cabo de Gata** stretch from Retamar to the east of Almería across the cape to the Barranco del Honda, just north of Agua Amarga. The Sierra de Gata is volcanic in origin and its adjacent dunes and saltings are some of the most important wetland areas in Spain for **breeding birds and migrants**. At Las Salinas saltings alone (see text) more than eighty species can be sighted throughout the year, including the magnificent pink flamingos as well as avocet, storks and egrets during their migrations. And there have been rarer sightings of Andouin's gull, as well as Bonelli's eagle and eagle owls around the crags.

Other **fauna** include the rare Italian wall lizard (its only habitat in Spain), with its distinctive green back with three rows of black spots, as well as the more common fox (sporting its Iberian white tail tip), hare and grass snake. Among the **flora**, the stunted dwarf fan palm is Europe's only native palm and the salt marshes are home to a strange parasitic plant – the striking yellow-flowering *Cistanche phelypaea* – which feeds on goosefoot.

The best times for sighting the fauna here are at **dawn and dusk** for, with temperatures among the highest in Europe, and rainfall at 10cm a year the lowest, energy has to be conserved. Cabo de Gata village has a park **Oficina de Información** at Avda. Miramar 88 (☎950 38 02 99; daily 10am–2.30pm & 5.30–9pm) which also rents out mountain bikes and has information on walking; there's another office in San José (see opposite).

ant for hanging around. You'll find a few bars and a couple of **restaurants** here: *La Almadraba* is the friendlier and more down-to-earth, whilst the nearby *Hotel Restaurante Morales* (☎950 37 01 03; ⑦) has a terrace and prices to reflect it; its kitschy hotel also has some pricey rooms.

Another 4km south, past a hill known as the Pico de San Miguel, the **Faro de Cabo de Gata** (lighthouse) marks the cape's southern tip. There's a friendly *tapas* bar here, *Bar José y María*, serving up tasty locally caught fried fish, as well as a *mirador* from where you can get a great view of the rock cliffs and – on clearer days – a sight of Morocco's Rif mountains.

Beyond the lighthouse a track leads to two of the finest **beaches** in the province, and to the resort of San José beyond. This track is closed to cars, which is all to your advantage for it makes for a fine walk through the Natural Park. Starting out as a paved road, climbing up from the lighthouse, this soon degenerates into a dirt track, passing prickly pear cactus plantations grown for their fruit, and access tracks to the wonderful fine sand beaches of **Monsul** – with fresh water springs and a track west to the even more secluded Media Luna cove – and further east, **Los Genoveses**. A couple of kilometres ahead, and beyond another spur, you'll sight the sea and the resort of San José.

To reach San José **by car**, you'll need to double back to El Cabo de Gata and follow the signed road further inland.

San José

The attractive little resort of **SAN JOSÉ** (served by bus from Almería) has a sandy beach in a small cove, with shallow water, while more fine beaches (see above) lie within walking distance. Only a few years ago it was almost completely undeveloped, though things are changing, with a rash of apartments and a new yacht harbour. Hopefully, it won't go the way of the resorts to the west of Almería. On the plaza near the centre of the village you'll find the official **Centro de Información** for the Natural Park (daily 10.30am–10.30pm; ☎950 38 02 99) who have lots of information, do guided walking and horse treks and hire out mountain bikes; they also have a complete list of accommodation and information on apartments to rent which may be a cheaper option for a longer stay.

Rooms can be hard to come by even outside high season, when without a reservation you can forget it, whilst prices and standards vary greatly – and you'll struggle to find anything really cheap; oddly, the *fondas* tend to be pricier than the *hostales*. *Casa de Huéspedes Costa Rica* (☎950 38 01 03; ③), above the restaurant of the same name in the centre of town, is one of the cheapest and also serves a reasonable *menú*. Nearby, *Hostal Bahia*, c/Correos 5 (☎950 38 01 14; ⑤), is one of the best of the pricier places with bath, especially if you get a balcony/sea view room. The swishest place though is the tiny *Hotel San Jose* (☎950 38 01 16; ⑦), around the western end of the bay. On the main road into town, the larger *Las Gaviotas*, c/Córdoba s/n (☎950 38 00 10, fax 950 38 00 13; ⑥), is another en-suite rooms possibility, but a fair walk from the centre. There's also a good **campsite**, *Camping Tau* (☎950 38 01 66; April–Oct), close to the beach and on the same road as the **Albergue Juvenil** (☎950 26 97 88; ②) whose 150 double rooms are usually booked solid in high summer.

For **food and drink** there are numerous bars and restaurants facing the beach on c/del Puerto Deportivo, offering everything from fast food and pizzas to excellent fresh local fish. Try the *salmonetes* (red mullet fried with garlic) at *La Cueva*. Next door to the latter, the equally good *El Tempranillo* does a tasty *besugo* (red bream with parsley and garlic) and treats its clientele to some excellent – and cheap – Láujar wines from the Almerian Alpujarras. The beachfront restaurants can be pricey, unless you opt for a pizza; slightly back from the beach and more reasonable, *El Ancla* does decent paellas and good fresh fish. For a splurge, the zone's only place with any pretensions is *La Gallineta*, 4km back along the entry road at El Pozo de Frailes; it offers sophisticated meat and fish dishes in a restored traditional house beside a restored Moorish water-wheel. Back in the centre, there are a couple of well-stocked **supermarkets** for picnic supplies.

If you've followed the walk from the lighthouse to San José (described above) and want to continue along the coast there's another **track**, running 12km north to Los Escullos and La Isleta. To start the walk take the road north out of San José, along which you'll shortly come to a turn-off along a dirt track on the right that heads around a hill – Cerro del Enmedio – towards the coast. The track branches at various points and you'll have to decide whether to follow the coastal tracks (which can be impass-able) or the surer inland route. The first track off to the coast provides access to a beau-tiful and secluded cove.

Further on, the route skirts the 500m high Cerro de los Frailes, beyond which lie the inlets of Los Escullos and La Isleta.

Los Escullos, La Isleta and Las Negras

Next along this rugged coastline is the isolated but developing **LOS ESCULLOS**, 8km north by road, with a good if rather pebbly beach and a formidable ruined fort, the eigh-teenth-century **Castillo de San Felipe**. The pleasant if slightly overpriced beachfront hotel-restaurant, *Casa Emilio* (☎950 38 97 61; ⑤) has now been joined by the new *Hotel Los Escullos* (☎950 38 97 33; ⑥) which has air-conditioned rooms with TV. There's also a **campsite**, *Camping Los Escullos* (☎950 38 98 11), set back from the sea with very lim-ited shade. **LA ISLETA**, 2km beyond, is another fishing village which is slowly expand-ing, but it still manages to retain a sleepy atmosphere and has a rather scruffy pebble beach – although there's a better one to the east backed by a car park. A **hostal**, *Isleta del Moro* (☎950 38 97 13; ④), overlooks the harbour, is reasonably priced and for **meals** has a bar–restaurant serving *tapas* and a good value *menú* for 1200ptas. The nearby *Restaurante La Ola* is another decent alternative for *tapas* and *raciones*.

The road north of here climbs over the cliffs above Isleta before descending to a pleasant valley, passing after 4km the hamlet of **Rodalquilar**, where the good-value *Restaurante Ajillo* does an excellent *fideuá* – vermicelli paella; it's on the eastern edge of the village, down a signed track on the right.

LAS NEGRAS, 5km further, is situated in the folds of a beautiful cove, with an *ata-laya*, or watch tower, sited on the edge of the village as you approach. There's a pebbly beach, a few **bars** – including the pleasant *La Manteca* on the seafront which stays open all year – and a decent **restaurant**, *La Palma*, which overlooks the beach. A **campsite**, *La Caleta* (☎950 52 52 37), set in a tranquil location with its own bay, is reached via a bumpy 1km track just outside the village on the way in. For **rooms**, the brand-new *Hostal Arrecife* (☎950 38 81 40; ④), close to the *estanco* (see below), has sea-view bal-cony rooms with bath. More possibilities aren't difficult to spot in summer as many shops and bars post signs offering accommodation to let. Another option for longer stays (2 nights plus) is the collection of **apartments and chalets** (④–⑥) in coastal and country locations rented by out *Estanco García* (☎ & fax 950 38 80 75), the main street tobacconist and information office whose proprietors speak English. For a change of beach the *Estanco* should be able to arrange for someone to row you up the coast to the ruined village of San Pedro (see below).

If you can't find an oarsman, you'll have to walk – no bad hike when it's cool – to the deserted coastal village of **SAN PEDRO** with its caves and a ruined castle; it lies 4km north on a poor track. The place used to be inhabited until a few years ago when the mainly elderly residents upped sticks to Las Negras, which had acquired a road, leav-ing their houses to crumble. If you are feeling really energetic, you could walk 7km on from here along the coast to Agua Amarga, via another pleasant beach at **Cala del Plomo**.

Agua Amarga

Officially there's no road from Las Negras to Agua Amarga (10km north as the crow flies) but a dusty track – not on the maps and passable by car – heads east from the inland village of **Fernan Pérez**. As you come into the village, pick up the track just before an aqueduct on the right where there should be an improvised sign marked "Agua Amarga". This leads through a no-man's-land, eventually bringing you to an asphalt road where you need to turn right to reach Agua Amarga, a couple of kilometres further. For an all-asphalt alternative, keep ahead through Fernan Pérez to reach the N344, then head east turning off at Venta del Pobre. This longer route would also allow a visit to Níjar (see p.491), 4km beyond the main road. There is no public transport on either route.

AGUA AMARGA, when you reach it, is the last stop before the Natural Park's northern boundary and a delightful little fishing village cut off from the surrounding world by a long road and a lack of accommodation. Most of the summer visitors here are Italians who rent a tasteful crop of villas. The fine sand EU blue-flagged beach is excellent, and there are a number of bars and restaurants backing it. Should you wish **to stay**, there's the friendly French-run *Pensión Family* on c/La Lomilla (☎950 13 80 14, fax 950 13 80 70; ⑤ including breakfast) set back from the south end of the beach, where en-suite rooms are complemented by a small pool, garden, and **restaurant** offering an excellent value 2000ptas *menú*. For **tapas** the *Restaurant El Pozo* is recommended, and does a tasty *ensalada de verano* – just what you need during a break from the beach. Alternative accommodations are *Hostal-Restaurante La Palmera* (☎950 13 82 08; ⑤) with en-suite rooms behind the beach or – for longer stays – **renting an apartment** from *Casas Requeña*, c/Aguada s/n (☎950 13 82 46).

Towards Mojácar

Leaving the Natural Park behind, the road north from Agua Amarga soon lands you in Carboneras, a fishing port with an average beach, and scarred by a massive cement factory dominating its bay. North of Carboneras lies a succession of small, isolated coves, backed by a characteristically arid Almerian landscape of scrub-covered hills and dried up *arroyos*, or watercourses. The **Carboneras–Mojácar road** itself winds perilously – and scenically – through the hills and offers access to some deserted grey-sand beaches before ascending to the Punta del Santo with fine views along the coast. The descent from here brings you to the **Playa de Macenas**, another pleasant beach with wild-camping possibilities. There are a couple more beaches – **Costa del Pirulico** is a good one with a beach *chiringuito* – before the urban sprawl of Mojácar takes over.

Mojácar

MOJÁCAR, Almería's main and growing resort, is split between the ancient hill top village – **Mojácar Pueblo** – sited a couple of kilometres back from the sea, a striking town of white cubist houses wrapped round a harsh outcrop of rock, and the resort area of **Mojácar Playa** which ribbons for a couple of miles along the seafront.

In the 1960s, when the main Spanish *costas* were being developed, this was virtually a ghost town, its inhabitants having long since taken the only logical step, and emigrated. The town's fortunes revived, however, when the local mayor, using the popularity of other equally barren spots on the Spanish islands and mainland as an example, offered free land to anyone willing to build within a year. The bid was a modest success, attracting one of the decade's multifarious "artist colonies", now long supplanted by package holiday companies and second-homers. A plush new 280-room hotel has opened in the village as well as a *parador* on the beach, and there's a burgeoning foreign jet-set which lives here for half the year and migrates in summer, all of which has rapidly downgraded Mojácar's obvious charms.

Mojácar Pueblo

Mojácar's hill-top settlement goes back to prehistoric Iberian times, and probably earlier, and became prominent during the Roman period when Pliny described it as one of the most important towns of *Baetica* – as the Roman province was called. Coins found from this era give the Roman name as *Murgis*, which the later Moors adapted to *Muxacra*. Near the village's **main fountain** – signed to the right off the road climbing towards the centre – now newly restored with lots of marble and loads of geraniums, and where thirty years ago veiled women used to do the family washing, a plaque relates how keen the Moors were to hang on to their hill-top eyrie when challenged by the *reconquista*. First declaring loyalty to the *Reyes Católicos* the Moorish mayor, Alabez, then stated that if the Catholic monarchs wouldn't accede to the request to be left in peace, "rather than live like a coward I shall die like a Spaniard. May Allah protect you!" The monarchs were impressed and, for a time at least, prudently granted Alabez's wish.

An ancient custom, no longer practised but parodied on every bangle and trinket sold in the tourist shops, was to paint an **indalo** on the doorways of the village to ward off evil. This symbol – a match-stick figure with arms outstretched, holding an arc – comes from the six-thousand year old Neolithic drawings in the caves at Vélez Blanco to the north (see p.487), and anthropologists believe that it is a unique case of a prehistoric symbol being passed down in one location for numerous millennia.

Indalos apart, sights in the upper village are limited to strolling around the sinuous, white-walled streets, looking over the heavily restored fifteenth-century church of **Santa María**, and savouring the view over the strangely formed surrounding hills and coast to the north from the **mirador** in the main square. After which it's either a tour of the boutiques and souvenir shops, a seat on the terraces of drinking dens with names like *Gordon's Bar* and *Time and Place*, or a crawl around noisier disco pubs such as *Budu*, *Lapu Lapu* or *La Muralla*.

The **Turismo** (Mon–Fri 10am–2pm & 5–8pm; Sat 10am–1pm ☎950 47 51 62) is located just below the main square – you'll need their free **map** to negotiate the maze of narrow streets – with the **post office** in the same building and a bank **cash machine** next door. If you want **to stay**, there are a handful of small *hostales*, all with some en-suite rooms, including the good-value *Casa Justa* at c/Morote 5 (☎950 47 83 72; ④), behind the church. Alternatives include *La Esquinica* on nearby c/Cano (☎950 47 50 09; ③), or, slightly east, the friendly *Pensión El Torreón*, c/Jazmín 4 (☎ & fax 950 47 52 59; ④). On the way into town, the more upmarket but good-value *Mamabel's* at c/Embajadores 3 (☎ & fax 950 47 24 48; ⑤) has beautiful, individually styled en-suite rooms (no. 1 is a dream), some with stunning view, and a restaurant. The grand new *Hotel El Moresco* (☎950 47 80 25, fax 950 47 82 62; ⑥) despite its pool, comes second best. Mojácar's **campsite** *El Quinto* (☎950 47 87 04), lies 2km below the village along the Turre road.

Places to **eat and drink** tend to be a bit pretentious and most of the overpriced restaurants are best avoided. Stick with the *tapas* bars around the square: *Bar Indalo* and *Bar Elizabeth* (both just above it) which are decent value, or for cheap eats, *Rincón de Embrujo*, with a terrace on the plazuela fronting the church does a decent *menú* for 950ptas. For a more memorable meal the excellent-value *menú* (1800ptas including wine) at *Mamabel's* (see above) is a must, with spectacular views from their terrace. A couple of interesting drinking places to seek out are *Nora's Bar*, c/Enmedio 24, which often stages art and photo exhibitions, and the oddball *El Loro Azul*, c/de la Iglesia s/n, both near the church.

Mojácar Playa

Down below on the seafront, **Mojácar Playa** is refreshingly brash: an excellent beach with warm and brilliantly clear waters, flanked by lots of fine beach bars and discos,

rooms for rent, several hotels and hostales, and a good campsite, *El Cantal de Mojácar* (☎950 47 82 04). The beach resort's focal point is an ugly Centro Comercial, at the intersection – known locally as "El Cruce" – of the seafront highway with the road leading inland to Mojácar Pueblo.

Among the **places to stay**, the seafront *Hotel El Puntazo* on the Paseo del Mediterráneo s/n 1km south from *El Cruce* (☎950 47 82 29; ⑤) with a pool is good-value, or next door there's *Hostal Nuevo Puntazo* (☎950 47 82 65, fax 950 47 82 85; ⑦), an ultra-modern expansion where rooms have TV, wall safe, and sea-view terrace. Nearby, the simpler *Hostal Bahía* (☎951 47 80 10; ④) has en-suite rooms ranged around a charming patio. Next door, *Hotel Marazul* (☎950 47 83 36, fax 950 47 22 30; ⑦) rents out fully equipped seaview apartments. Another reasonable option is *Rancho del Mar*, Playa del Desgargador 700m north of El Cruce (☎950 47 86 15; ⑥). Mojácar's nonde-script *parador*, the modern *Reyes Católicos* (☎950 47 82 50, fax 950 47 81 83; ⑧), with pleasant gardens and pool, also fronts the beach. **Food** along the seafront is fairly dis-mal and standards fall markedly in high season; the sterile *parador* restaurant has a 3500ptas *menú*, or there's the no-frills *Cafetería Rosa*, facing the south side of the Centro Comercial, for *platos combinados*. **Vegetarians** are catered for at the paradoxi-cally named *Bar El Toro* in the Centro Comercial, which also does veggie *tapas*.

Nightlife happens all along the beach strip and it's fun just to cruise and see what's on offer. The sassiest of the discos is *Pascha*, easily tracked down at the foot of the strobe-light it beams high into the sky every night, and the beachfront *Goa*, near El Cruce is similar. *Tuareg*, 5km south towards Carboneras, is another raucously exotic dance palace set in expansive gardens beneath palm and eucalyptus trees.

Hourly **buses** from the beach up to Mojácar Pueblo run from a stop outside the Centro Comercial at El Cruce, or you can pick them up at various stops along the seafront.

North from Mojácar

North from Mojácar, there's a clutch of resorts – none of them much to write home about – and a few last sights of interest, before the road crosses the border into Murcia. Inland, two small towns are worth an excursion: at **Vélez Rubio**, there is a cave with important **prehistoric paintings** depicting the *indalo* whilst at neighbouring **Vélez Blanco**, there's a fine **Renaissance castle**. Although both are served by a single daily **bus** from Almería, transport of your own will make these detours much more reward-ing.

Garrucha and Vera

North from Mojácar, and served by occasional buses, **GARRUCHA** is a lively, if un-attractive, town and fishing harbour with a sizeable fleet. When this comes home to port with its catch in mid-afternoon the ensuing auction at the port-side market is won-derfully entertaining. The fleet also lands a good supply of the seafood – the *gambas* (prawns) are renowned – served at the numerous **fish restaurants** lining the seafront harbour promenade, El Malecón. The most celebrated place in town is *El Almejero*, with its terrace actually fronting the Puerto Pesquero harbourside, where the fish is landed – if what's caught doesn't meet their exacting standards they don't open. There's a good *tapas* bar attached, too.

From Garrucha, the road heads 9km inland, skirting the estuary of the Río Almanzora, to **VERA**, a small farming town with a fortified sixteenth-century church, **La Encarnación** with four huge towers, and a Renaissance **Ayuntamiento**, as well as a couple of **hostales** of which *Hostal Regio* on c/Ancha 4–6 (☎950 39 09 89; ③) with en-suite rooms is reasonable; their restaurant also does a decent *menú*.

PALOMARES AND SOME BOMBS

Just for the record – and as a chilling reminder of nuclear madness – it should be noted that the village of **Palomares**, by the mouth of the Río Almanzora, was once at the centre of one of the world's biggest nuclear scares. Here, on January 17, 1966, an American B-52 bomber collided with a tanker aircraft during a mid-air refuelling operation. Following the collision, three ten-megaton **H-bombs** fell on land and a fourth into the sea, just off the village.

Those that fell in the fields were recovered quickly, though one had been damaged, causing radioactive contamination nearby. Fifteen US warships and two submarines searched for many weeks before the fourth bomb was recovered. On March 19, thousands of barrels of plutonium-contaminated soil were transported by the USAF for disposal in South Carolina. Nobody has ever convincingly explained how the incident happened, nor is it known why the bombs didn't explode, for the damaged bomb had actually lost its safety catch.

North along the coast

The town of **CUEVAS DE ALMANZORA**, 6km north of Vera, has a well-preserved sixteenth-century Gothic castle built to defend the settlement from piracy, and a handful of Guadix-style cave dwellings where evidence of habitation by Neanderthal and Cromagnon man was found nearby, but not a lot more. Slightly back from here, there's a road which returns you to the coast and the village of **PALOMARES**, of nuclear notoriety (see box above). The rather curious feature of this otherwise dull hamlet is a church tower which resembles – with its rounded cone – an atom bomb. Near to where you rejoin the coast Vera's *Parque Aquatico* (daily 10am–7pm) is a fun place to kill a couple of hours, especially if you're towing kids; it's got all the usual water features, and they allow you to take your own picnic inside.

Three kilometres on from Palomares, **Villaricos** is a humdrum resort with an uncomfortable black pebble beach. North again from here, the road cuts between the sea and the **Sierra Almagrera**, riddled with mine workings. The mining settlements beyond these hills, in a landscape of scrub and desert cactuses, are eerie, godforsaken places where any strangers are regarded with suspicion. Back on the coast, **POZO DEL ESPARTO**, 12km from Villaricos, has a reasonable pebble beach with plenty of shade, and quite a few places where wild-campers can pitch their tents. Another 4km on, **SAN JUAN DE LOS TERREROS** straddles the seafront behind a narrow beach flanked by characterless *hostales* and holiday apartments. Just to the north of here, however, the coast road passes a number of temptingly isolated coves and inlets with small beaches, before Andalucía's border with Murcia is reached.

Vélez Rubio and the Letreros cave

Inland from Vera, a rambling 60km detour along the N340 and A327 will bring you out at the town of **VÉLEZ RUBIO**, surrounded by *sierras*, olive groves and fields of cereals. It is no great shakes as towns go (Vélez Blanco is a better proposition for an overnight stop), but the **Turismo** (Mon–Fri 10am–2pm & 5–8pm; ☎950 41 01 48), housed in the town **museum**, c/Carrera del Carmen 29 (Mon–Fri 10am–2pm & 5–8pm), can provide information and a town map. The museum, itself located inside the eighteenth-century Hospital Real contains an interesting collection of artefacts and ceramics from prehistoric to Moorish times and includes a section on the ancient cave paintings in this area.

The main monument of note here is the magnificent Baroque church (Almería province's biggest) of **La Encarnación** on the plaza of the same name. Constructed in the eighteenth century, this has an imposing carved facade which includes, above the entrance, the arms of the Marquises of Villafranca y Vélez, who built it. Inside, the main altar has a superbly detailed, 20-metre-high carved wood **retablo**.

What makes a trip here really worthwhile, however, is to see the prehistoric cave paintings of the **Cueva de los Letreros**, 4km out of town. To get there take the A317 north until you reach a *gasolinera* (petrol station) on the left, next to which is a signed turning to the cave. You will first need to obtain the key (see below) to gain entry to the site. With the key, follow a newly made path leading behind the filling station as it swings left before ascending steeply to a stairway which climbs halfway up a cliff to the fenced-off *abrigo* (rock shelter); a good kilometre's walk. Once through the gate of the compound (don't forget to lock it when leaving) you will be able to see remarkably fresh-looking red and brown sketches of human figures, birds, animals, astronomical signs and not very well-preserved *indalos* (see p.484) which have been dated to around 4000 BC and are amongst the oldest representations of people and animals together. Unfortunately the local practice of touching the *indalos* and throwing water on the paintings in order to make them clearer has not helped their preservation, but what remains is still stunning. Without your own transport (it's 2km each way), **obtaining the key** to open the site is now somewhat onerous. You need to go to the Almacen del Trigo **information office** (see below) in Vélez Blanco, at the far end of the town (follow the signs), where in return for depositing your passport, you will be given the key.

Further paintings at **La Cueva del Gabar**, another *abrigo* to the north of Vélez Blanco, are in a much better state of preservation but only visitable with a guide. However, if you're interested, the Turismo at Vélez Rubio or the *Ayuntamiento* at Vélez Blanco (see below) can advise on a guide who will produce a rope and ladder to get you up the sheer rock face – one of the reasons, of course, why they have survived more or less intact.

Vélez Blanco

Nestling at the foot of a rocky outcrop, the whitewashed village of **VÉLEZ BLANCO**, 6km north of its neighbour, is a smaller and more attractive conurbation. Atop the hill is an outstanding **Renaissance castle** (see below for opening times; 150ptas) – an extension of the original Moorish alcazaba – built by the Marquises of Vélez Blanco in the early years of the sixteenth century. It is today something of a trompe l'oeil, with an empty shell behind the crenellated battlements: a gutting that took place as recently as 1904, after the castle was sold off by the impecunious Marquis (for 80,000ptas) to an American millionaire, George Blumenthal, who tore out the whole interior including the **Patio de Honor** – a fabulous courtyard carved in white marble by Italian craftsmen – and shipped it off to the United States. After service as this plutocrat's Xanadu, it has since been reconstructed inside the Metropolitan Museum of Art in New York. The castle's interior, much of it now supported by steel girders, has fragments of the original decoration and, given the Met's reluctance to return its dubiously acquired prize exhibit, there are now plans to carry out a complete reconstruction of the original using marble from the nearby quarries of Macael. A book on sale in the small shop at the entrance – *El Castillo de Vélez Blanco* by Alfonso Ruiz García – has an image of the reconstituted patio in the New York Met plus a watercolour of what it looked like *in situ*. Make sure to take in the fine **views** from the tower, the Torre del Homenaje. The fort is normally open daily in summer (Mon–Fri 10.30am–1pm & 4–8pm, Sat & Sun 11am–8pm; ☎950 41 50 27). At other times, ask at the *Ayuntamiento* (☎950 61 48 00) on c/La Corredera or *Bar La Sociedad* (when that's closed) for Julio El Pata, the guardian and a bit of a local character who will be happy to open it up for you. At the opposite end of the town, the sixteenth-century **Convento de San Luís**, also built by the Vélez family, has a fine chapel (currently closed to visitors) which was damaged during the Civil War.

The Almacen del Trigo **information office** (daily 10am–2pm; ☎950 41 56 51) has information on the town and the surrounding Parque Natural de la Sierra de María (see below). Should you need a **place to stay** in Vélez Blanco, the *Hostal La Sociedad*, c/Corredera 14 (☎950 41 50 27; ③) is central and friendly for en-suite rooms, or moving upmarket there's the elegant and good-value *Casa de los Arcos*, c/San Francisco 2, near the information office (☎950 61 48 05, fax 950 61 49 47; ⑥), a beautifully restored eighteenth-century *señorial* mansion overlooking a gorge. A **campsite**, *Pinar del Rey* (☎950 41 56 51), lies on the edge of town towards Vélez Rubio, close to the Letreros cave. For **meals** the *Hostal Sociedad*'s owners, *Bar Sociedad* over the road, serve decent *tapas* and *raciones* on their lively terrace. More formal meals and good local cooking are on offer at *Restaurante El Molino*, up some steps opposite a tiled fountain at the west end of the main street, with a charming patio terrace (the fresh trout is good here). *Mesón Antonia* near the castle entrance with a *menú* for 900ptas, and the nearby *Barbacoa María Fernández*, c/Al'qua-sid 10, are other good little local places to eat.

West of Vélez Blanco

The A317 continues west of Vélez Blanco traversing the wooded **Sierra de María** with possibilities for walking before reaching **Orce**, site of recent sensational discoveries regarding the arrival of Stone Age people in Europe. At villages nearby you can try a night in your very own **cave dwelling**. Beyond Orce, Baza (p.463), Guadix (p.462) and Granada (p.404) lie within easy distance along the A92N *autovía*. Although the daily **bus** from Almería also calls at María, this area is not well served by public transport and is really practicable only with your own vehicle.

Sierra de María

Walkers – and those in need of greenery after endless desert landscapes – may be tempted to continue northwest from Vélez Blanco along the C321 to María, a small town set among pine woods and, incidentally, the highest settlement in Almería, which is also the jumping-off point for the **Sierra de María**, a newly declared Natural Park. This little-known area is visited mainly by Almerían and Murcian weekenders seeking cooler air, trees and (in winter) a rare glimpse of snow. **MARÍA** itself is unremarkable, but its setting beneath rocky crags is quite dramatic and there's a pleasant central plaza where simple **rooms** are available at *Hostal Sevilla* (☎950 41 74 10; ②) opposite the church; for rooms with bath, head for *Hostal-Restaurante Torrente*, c/Camino Real 10 (☎950 41 73 26; ③) on the main road, which also serves **meals**. Just outside the town towards Orce and then off the road to the left, a scenic hour's **walk** leads to the Ermita de la Virgen de la Cabeza. To do more serious walking – and you're in largely virgin territory here – good maps will be required, although a number of waymarked routes ranging from eight to fifteen kilometres have already been completed inside the park, such as the *Ruta de Gabar*, a scenic 8km circular hike around the 1500m peak of Gabor, the park's highest. While in the park keep an eye out for **griffon vultures** which have been recently reintroduced after disappearing in the 1940s and are now breeding successfully. Information on walking trails, the park's *refugios* (mountain huts) and on the park in general is available from a new **visitors' centre** (daily 9am–1pm & 3–5pm; ☎950 41 74 53), 2.5km beyond María on the Orce road. Although it seems to have been designed mainly for kids, the centre's interactive displays will appeal to those with an interest in flora and fauna. Three kilometres beyond the centre there's a new **campsite** – down a turn on the right – managed by the Junta de Andalucía.

Orce

Beyond María the SE35 soon enters an extensive plain covered with wheatfields and stretches arrow-straight and apparently endlessly to the distant mountains. In high summer this plain is a cauldron beneath vast cloudless skies and you'll be lucky to meet another vehicle. Apart from a couple of godforsaken hamlets and the occasional wheeling eagle overhead hunting for prey, there are few features to punctuate this desolate but beautiful panorama. The landscape takes on a doubly dramatic aspect when you realise that one-and-a-half million years ago this plain was a great lake visited by elephants, hippos, rhinos, water buffaloes, musk oxen, giant bears and ferocious hyenas as well as lions, leopards and lynxes. Early humans were known to have been in the area as early as 500,000 years ago but recent finds seem to have pushed this back by an astonishing additional one million years which, if scientifically confirmed, would make it the earliest appearance of primitive humans on the continent of Europe by a long way. These Stone Age arrivals probably came from Africa and lived on a diet of wild plants and carrion supplemented by fracturing the craniums and bones of the dead beasts to extract the brains and marrow – they had not yet developed the technology to take on and hunt big game.

When you finally reach it, the dusty and impoverished little settlement of **ORCE** hardly lives up to the self-styled billing – now proclaimed on all its literature – as *Cuna de la Humanidad Europea* (Cradle of European Man). The heart of the village is a tree-lined main square, Plaza Nueva, fronted by the *Ayuntamiento* and in one corner the village's main bar, *Bar Molina*. This ramshackle institution is a hangout for the largely unemployed male population, and on searing summer afternoons it draws its curtains and turns on the fans, while the whiskery clientele get down to serious games of dominós.

Just off the square lies an impressive eleventh-century Moorish alcazaba, the tower of which – **Torre del Homenaje** – has been converted into the **Museo de la Prehistoria** (daily 11am–2pm & 6–8pm; 200ptas) to exhibit the finds. As well as impressive animal remains from the periods of the finds there are displays (in Spanish) reconstructing the lifestyle of these early humans. The third floor has the small million-and-a-half year old **fragment of human skull** which has brought worldwide celebrity to Orce. Whilst not accepted conclusively by many experts (see below), its discoverers claim it belonged to a child of unknown sex which is thought to have been devoured by a great hyena. Various free leaflets on the finds in Spanish and an informative book, *El Hombre de Orce*, are available from the curator. Archeologists and paleontologists working in the area are now fairly sure that the skull fragment is not human but local politicians – who have turned the whole issue into a matter of civic pride and tourist income – have made it heresy to say so. However, the same experts are convinced that the dating *will* eventually be confirmed due to crucial evidence turned up in 1998–99 of human artefacts 1.4 million years old; finding genuine human remains, they believe, is only a matter of time.

Orce's only other sights of note are the impressive eighteenth-century **Iglesia de Santa María** and the **Casa Palacio de los Segura**, a sixteenth-century *señorial* mansion with an elegant tower; this now houses a **tourist office** (daily 9am–1pm & 6–8pm; ☎958 74 61 71) which will also provide a tour of the house. There is no **accommodation** in Orce although in the hamlet of **FUENTE NUEVA** – 7km back towards María – *Habitaciones Laveranda* (☎ & fax 958 34 43 80; ⑤) has some wonderful all-mod-cons refurbished **cave dwellings**. At **GALERA**, a pleasant well ordered little town 7km west of Orce, there are more delightful cave houses for rent from *Casas Cueva*, c/Cervantes 11 (☎ & fax 958 73 90 68; ④); their nearby **restaurant** *La Zalona*, is also recommended. Along the Galera road, 1km out of Orce, the green valley of the Río Galera contains the Manantial de Fuen Caliente, a beautiful natural pond filled with fish which has become the local **swimming pool**, complete with *cafetería*.

At Cúllar Baza, 23km southwest of Orce along routes SE33 and A330, you can pick up the A92N *autovía* heading towards Granada, 130km distant.

Inland Almería: Movieland and Níjar

An alternative way of reaching the coast to the east of Almería is to take a trip through the weird lunar landscape of Almería's distinctive **desert scenery**. There are two possible routes: via **Níjar** along the N344 *autovía* to Carboneras, or via the more interesting **Tabernas** and **Sorbas** route to Mojácar. The latter more northerly route, described below, passes by Almería's old western film set, "Mini Hollywood", and a detour off this road can also be made to the pottery centre of **Níjar**. A visit to the underground **caves of Sorbas** is also a great adventure. This route also avoids the N344, the main route for the Costa del Sol-bound holiday traffic and heavy trucks which thunder down from the north.

Mini Hollywood and Tabernas

The main road to Tabernas heads north out of Almería along the valley of the Río Andarax and forks right at Benhadux – along the A370 – passing the village of **Rioja** before it enters a dramatic brown-tinged-with-purple eroded landscape which looks as if it should be the backdrop for a Hollywood western. Some 10km past Rioja, in a particularly gulch-riven landscape, at **Mini Hollywood** you discover that someone else had the same idea first.

Mini Hollywood and Texas Hollywood

A visit to **MINI HOLLYWOOD** (July–Sept daily 10am–9pm; Oct–June 10am–7pm; 1500ptas, 2200ptas including zoo) is hard to resist – especially if you're travelling with kids – although better value if timed with one of the daily *espectaculos* (see below). The pay booth sets the scene straight out with an endless tape-loop of this old film set's most famous production, *A Fistful of Dollars*. Beyond lies a main street overlooked by a water tower, which you may just recognize from the 1960s classic, or from *The Good, the Bad and the Ugly*, both of which were filmed here along with countless spaghetti and paella westerns. You can wander into the *Tombstone Gulch* saloon for a drink, and in summer there are daily "shows" (noon & 5pm), when actors in full cowboy rig blasting off six-guns stage such epics as the capture, escape and final shooting of Jesse James. The complex has now added a somewhat incongruous **zoo** with birds, reptiles and big cats prowling depressingly small cages.

Further along the road towards Tabernas, on the left, is **Texas Hollywood** (same hours; shows at 2.30 & 5.30pm; 950ptas), where a couple of less commercialized film sets in a much more spectacular setting have an Indian village complete with wigwams, a Mexican town and a US cavalry frontier fort as well as camels and buffaloes. Recently a third site **Western Leone** (same hours and prices as above) has opened.

As well as the landscape and cheap labour costs, the film-makers were also drawn to the same unpolluted crystalline air which has lured astronomers here, and to the north of Tabernas, at Calar Alto in the Sierra de Filabres, a series of high-powered telescopes to study the heavens have been installed. The **Hispano–German observatory**, an 18km climb into the mountains north of Tabernas, and accurately marked on the *Michelin Andalucía* map, is open for free guided visits (in Spanish and with a slide show) on Wednesdays at 3pm. Ring ahead to book a place on the visit (☎950 23 09 88).

Tabernas

Surrounded by torrid scrubland, **TABERNAS** lies at the foot of a hill dominated by an impressive-looking **Moorish castle** where Fernando and Isabel ensconced themselves during the siege of Almería. Unfortunately, closer inspection reveals it to be mainly ruined and there's little to hang around for, except a drink, in the searing summer heat. Just beyond the village a road on the left – followed after 1km by a right turn towards the hamlet of Senés – leads to the **Centro Solar**, one of Europe's biggest solar energy fields, where row upon row of mirrors reflect the powerful sunlight and generate heat energy. Still at the development stage, it's hoped that when the system is commercially viable it could power massive desalination plants to regenerate the desert. If you have your own transport and are looking for **food** the *Venta Compadre* on the N340, just beyond Tabernas, is an excellent stop for a hearty *menú*.

A detour to Níjar and Sorbas

Beyond Tabernas there are more dramatic landscapes – badlands with naked ridges of pitted sandstone, cut through by twisted and dried-up riverbeds, all of which vary in colour from yellow to red and from green to lavender-blue depending on the time of day and the nature of the stone. After 9km a road on the right opens up the possibility of a wonderfully scenic trip south to Níjar across the **Sierra Alhamilla**.

This road climbs through more Arizona-type landscape, first to the hamlet of **Turrillas** and then turns east to **LUCAINENA DE LAS TORRES**, a cluster of white boxes surrounding its red-roofed church. Here, a narrow main street leads up to the church, fronted by a tiny square where old men sit around in the shade staring at nothing in particular as the sun beats down remorselessly. The road beyond snakes over the rugged Sierra Alhamilla to descend into Níjar, 16km to the south.

Níjar

NÍJAR is a neat, white and typically Almerian little town, with narrow streets in its upper Moorish quarter designed to give maximum shade. Now firmly on the tourist trail due to the inexpensive **handmade pottery** manufactured in workshops around the town and sold in the shops along the broad main street – Avda. García Lorca – and c/Real to the west, it still retains a relaxed and tranquil air. Little remains of the Moorish fort here but the pottery tradition – dating back to when the Moors held sway and including attractive traditional patterns created with mineral dyes – lives on, as exhibits in the museum at Almería clearly demonstrate. The more authentic potters are located in the **barrio alfarero**, along c/Real running parallel to the main street, where the *talleres* (workshops) of Gongora, Granados, El Oficio and the very friendly and cheaper Angel y Loli (at no. 54) are located. The town is also known for its *jarapas*: bed-covers, curtains and rugs made from rags. An English ceramic artist, Matthew Weir (married to an *almeriense*), has recently settled in Níjar; his *taller*, the bullishly named La Tienda de los Milagros at c/Lavadero 2, is reached by continuing uphill to the town proper and veering left beyond the church. His wife is a skilled producer of *jarapas* and textiles in her own right. Just before the church on c/Maestros, a small **information office** (daily 10am–1pm & 5–8pm) has pottery samples and information on the town and region.

There are a number of small **hostales** for staying over, of which the best for en-suite rooms is *Montes* (☎950 36 01 57; ②) at Avda. García Lorca 26; they also have a *comedor* serving a *menú*. Other places along the main street serving **meals** include the very good *Casa Pedro* and there are a couple of decent **tapas** and **raciones** bars on Plaza La Glorieta, the upper square beyond the church.

LORCA'S 'BLOOD WEDDING'

An event that happened at Níjar in 1928 inspired one of Lorca's most powerful plays, *Bodas de Sangre* (Blood Wedding). A young woman named Francisca was about to marry a man named Casimiro at a farmhouse near Níjar. She was an heiress with a modest dowry and a reluctant bride, he a labourer pressured by his scheming brother and sister-in-law to make this match and thus bring money into the family. A few hours prior to the wedding taking place, Francisca eloped with her cousin, with whom she had been in love since childhood, but who had only realized his feelings when confronted with the reality of losing her. They were swiftly intercepted by Casimiro's brother, who shot her cousin dead. His brother was convicted of the murder, whilst Casimiro, the groom, was unable to overcome his humiliation and, it is said, never looked upon Francisca or even her photograph again. Francisca never married and lived as a recluse until her death in 1978.

Lorca avidly followed the story in the newspapers and had a knowledge of the area from time spent in Almería as a child. An interesting afterword is told by the writer Nina Epton, who, on a visit to San José in the 1960s, was dining at the house of a wealthy Spanish *señoron*, or landowner, while a group of farm labourers waited outside on a long bench, no doubt for payment. In her book *Andalusia* she describes what happened when eventually she accompanied Don José, her host, to speak to the men:

> *Among them was a wizened old man called Casimiro whom I would not have looked at twice before I was told that a dramatic incident in his youth had inspired Federico García Lorca to take Casimiro for his model of the novio in "Blood Wedding".*

In the hills just above Níjar, the village of **HUEBRO** is another place with Moorish roots and is known locally for its staging of a Moors-against-Christians mock battle during the first week in October. It has a great country **restaurant** *Aldea El Riqueta* (☎950 16 50 71) which cooks up some tasty dishes and you'll need to give advance notice for the house specials *patatas a lo pobre* and *conejo al ajillo* (rabbit).

Sorbas

This corner of Almería has one last dramatic sight in **SORBAS**, an extraordinary place, surrounded by more moonscapes, whose houses overhang an ashen gorge, best seen from the main road. Like Níjar, it is reputed for its pottery – although the designs are less original – which is sold at a trio of inconspicuous *alfarerías* (workshops, one of which still has its original Moorish oven) in the lower part of the village, near a white-walled church. This tidy little place is also on the tourist trail, especially on Thursdays when trippers flock in from Mojácar for the weekly **market** in the central plaza. There's a small **Turismo** on c/Terraplén, just off the A370 (Thurs–Sun 10.30am–2.30pm; ☎950 36 44 76), whose town map will guide you around a number of faded **señorial mansions**, including the seventeenth-century erstwhile summer retreat of the Duques de Alba.

But the main pull for visitors to these parts is the astonishing scenery in the surrounding **Parque Natural de Karst en Yesos** (just south of town and signed from the main A370), where around six million years ago water erosion carved out subterranean chasms full of stalagmites and stalactites. Guided visits to the caves are a two-hour adventure – with helmets and lights and not a little scrambling and squeezing – organized by the Turismo (daily on the hour from 10am–8pm in summer; 1100ptas). Above ground, the water's action has created flat-topped, volcano-like protrusions and deep gorges. These are visible from the main A370, but for a closer look take the minor AL140 towards Los Molinos de Agua east of Sorbas. At the crest of a hill, a track to the left leads to a peak above the gorge, where sweeping circular views extend over the lunar landscape as far as the snowcapped peaks of the Sierra Nevada; it's a great place to watch the sunset. Alternatively, and if it's too hot, you could follow the track descending through the tumbledown but picturesque hamlet of **Los Molinos** to follow the course of the dried-up river gorge.

For a **place to stay** *Hostal Sorbas* (☎950 36 41 60; ③), on the A370 outside the town, has rooms with bath, whilst **food** is available at bars on the main square. On the main road to the east of town – where you'll get the best view of the cliff-top houses – the *Café-Bar Chacho* does *platos combinados*.

To reach Sorbas from Níjar you could retrace your path back over the **Sierra Alhamilla** (there's a 4km short cut to the A370 from Lucainena) or, for a bit of variety, follow the N344 east for about 18km, turning off along a minor road (the AL140) for the final 10km to Sorbas.

If you find this surreal landscape to your taste – and it's surprising how it begins to grow on you – with transport you might like to try a trip starting 16km west of Sorbas, where a turn-off on the right heads into relatively uncharted territory, north along the C3325 to **Cobdar** and the surrounding mountain villages in the **Sierra de los Filabres**. For 35km the scenic road winds upwards past abandoned *fincas* and pastures of wild thyme, with occasional splashes of green and plenty of opportunities for bird and butterfly spotting. When you get there, **COBDAR** turns out to be a surprisingly neat little village of parallel white streets perched on a towering outcrop of reddish rock, where the friendly locals will be bemused, but pleased, to see you. Extraction of marble from this rock – the main source of income for the surrounding towns and villages – mars parts of the landscape further north where man-made, volcano-like craters and umber-tinted landslides dominate the views.

travel details

TRAINS

Almería to: Granada (4 daily; 2hr 10min); Guadix (4 daily; 1hr 15min); Madrid (2 daily; 6hr 40min–8hr 40min); Sevilla (3 daily; 5hr 10min).

Granada to: Algeciras (2 daily; 4hr 30min); Almería (4 daily; 2hr 10min); Córdoba (1 daily; 3hr 20min); Guadix (4 daily; 1hr 10min); Madrid (2 daily; 6–8hr, via Linares–Baeza 6hr 30min); Málaga (1 daily; 2hr 35min); Ronda (3 daily; 3hr–3hr 30min); Sevilla (4 daily; 2hr 50min–3hr 30min).

BUSES

Almería to: Agua Amarga (1 daily; 1hr 15min); Almerimar (3 daily; 45min); Cabo de Gata (via Retamar; 6 daily; 30min); Carboneras (3 daily; 1hr 15min); Córdoba (2 daily; 5–6hr); Granada (5 daily; 2hr 15min); Guadix (9 daily; 2hr); Jaén (1 daily; 4hr); Láujar de Andarax (5 daily; 1hr 15min); Málaga (3hr 15min–4hr); Mojácar (3 daily; 2hr); Las Negras (2 daily; 1hr 15min); Madrid (2 daily; 7hr 30min); Níjar (1 daily; 45min); Roquetas de Mar (18 daily; 25min); Sevilla (3 daily; 5–6hr); San José (3 daily; 1hr); Santa Fe de Mondújar/Los Millares (2 daily; 30min); Tabernas (6 daily; 1hr).

Granada to: Almería (8 daily; 2hr 15min); Almuñecar (6 daily; 1hr 30min); Baeza/Úbeda (7 daily; 2hr, or 3hr via Jaén); Cazorla (2 daily; 1hr 30min); Baza (8 daily; 2hr 15min); Cádiz (2 daily; 5hr); Córdoba (7 daily; 2hr 30min); Guadix (12 daily; 1hr 15min); Jaén (12 daily; 2hr); Madrid (9 daily; 5–6hr); Málaga (15 daily; 2hr); Montefrío (2 daily; 1hr 30min); Mojácar (2 daily; 3hr 30min); Motril (9 daily; 2hr); Nerja (2 daily; 2hr); Salobreña (6 daily; 1hr 15min); Sevilla (9 daily; 4–5hr); Sierra Nevada/Alpujarras: the following all pass Lanjarón and Órgiva, a 1hr trip from the city; current departure times from Granada to other villages are: 8.30am & 6pm to Ugíjar (also passing Albondón, Cádiar & Yegen); 10.30am, noon & 5.15pm to Berchules (also passing Pampaneira, Bubión, Capileira, Pitres, Busquistar & Trevélez); 1pm to Berja.

FERRIES

Almería to: Melilla, seasonal boat (1 daily April–Sept; 6hr); Nador (1 daily April–Sept; 6hr).

PART THREE

THE
CONTEXTS

THE HISTORICAL FRAMEWORK

As the southernmost region of the Iberian peninsula, Andalucía has manifested throughout its history a character essentially different from the rest of Spain. Due to the variety of peoples who came and settled here, the region has always had an enriching influence on the territories further north. This meeting place of seas and cultures, with Africa only nine miles off the coast of its southern tip, brought Andalucía into early contact with the sophisticated civilizations of the eastern Mediterranean and a long period as part of the North African Moorish empire. The situation was later reversed when Andalucía sent out explorers to the New World and became the gateway to the Spanish American Empire.

PREHISTORY

The first Europeans of whom we have knowledge lived in Andalucía. A recent series of spectacular discoveries at **Orce** (p.489), seventy miles east of Granada, rocked the archeological world as the date for the **arrival of early humans in Europe** was pushed back from c.700,000 years ago to perhaps a million years before this, making Orce – if the findings are scientifically confirmed – the earliest known site of human occupation in

Europe by a long way. Arriving from Africa and crossing the straits by swimming or on rafts these Stone Age people colonized an area of now vanished lakeland near Orce. Here they hunted hippos, hyenas, mammoths and vultures and made tools from flint. Evidence of occupation by Stone Age societies stretching back some 400,000 years was already known about from discoveries at nearby **Venta Micena** where early inhabitants hunted elephant and rhino and left behind tools and camp fires. Archeologists will now get to work on filling in the gaping prehistorical record between these two sites. Some of the earliest **human fossils** found on the Iberian peninsula were unearthed inside the **Gibraltar** caves with evidence of **Neanderthals** dating from around 100,000 BC. In the Paleolithic period, the first **homo sapiens** arrived on the Iberian peninsula from southern France, settling around the Bay of Biscay as well as in the south. They were cave dwellers and hunter-gatherers and at the Pileta and Nerja caves in Málaga have left behind remarkable **cave paintings** depicting the animals that they hunted. During the later Neolithic phase, a sophisticated material culture developed in southern Spain attested to by the finds of esparto sandals and baskets as well as jewellery in the **Cueva de los Murciélagos** in Granada.

Subsequent prehistory is more complex and confused. There does not appear to have been any great development in the cave cultures of the north. Instead the focus shifts south – where **Neolithic colonists** had arrived from North Africa – to Valencia and **Almería**. Cave paintings have been found in rock shelters such as those at **Vélez Blanco** dating from around 4000 BC. Here also, not long afterwards, **metalworking** began and the debate continues as to the cause of this dramatic leap forward: a development by the indigenous inhabitants or the arrival of "technicians" – evidenced by many trading artefacts such as ivory and turquoise – from the eastern Mediterranean. The fortified site of **Los Millares** (c.2700 BC), in the centre of a rich mining area in Almería, with its Aegean-style "beehive" tombs is one of the most important remains from this era. In the same period, **dolmens** were being built such as those at **Antequera**, a building style which spread from here throughout the peninsula and into Europe. This dolmenic culture also influenced a ceramic style, typified by bell-shaped artefacts and giving rise to the name **Beaker folk**. More developments occurred in the same area of Almería about 1700 BC when the **El Argar** civilization started to produce bronze and worked silver and gold, trading across the Mediterranean. This culture fanned out across the south between 1700 and 1000 BC and, during the first millennium BC, the **Iberian civilization** fully established itself.

TARTESSUS AND THE IBERIANS

The **kingdom of Tartessus** appeared early in the first millennium BC and typifies the great strides forward being made by the Iberians of the south. Both the Bible (which names it Tarshish) and Greek and Latin texts refer to this important kingdom and trading centre. It was probably sited on the estuary of Río Guadalquivir on the border of Huelva and Sevilla provinces; its precise location has yet to be identified, although its prowess as a producer and exporter of bronze, gold and silver as well as a creator of sophisticated **jewellery** is apparent from the finds displayed in Sevilla's archeological museum. The Tartessians were also a literate people but nothing of their literature survives apart from scattered inscriptions which have yet to be translated. In the mid-sixth century BC Tartessus incurred the wrath of the rising power of Carthage through its friendship with the Greeks and not long after this appears to have been destroyed by them.

The Iberians at other centres in the south also developed sophisticated cultures based upon agriculture, stock breeding, fishing, mining and iron production. When the Romans came into contact with them in the third century BC they found a literate people with written laws, and a vibrant culture which included music and dance. Their skills in the plastic arts – an enduring flair throughout the peninsula's history – are displayed in artefacts such as the splendid **Dama de Baza**, a dramatic fourth-century BC painted terracotta statue of a woman, discovered at Baza in Granada. The Iberian skill with masonry and stone sculpture can be seen at the necropolis at **Toya** in Jaén province, and other remarkable works from the fifth century BC are in the museum at Jaén itself.

THE FIRST COLONISTS

The southern coast attracted colonists from different regions of the Mediterranean. The **Phoenicians** – founders of a powerful trading empire based in modern Lebanon – established the port of Gadir (Cádiz) about 1100 BC. This was obviously connected with their intensive **trading operations** in the metals of the Guadalquivir valley carried from Tartessus where they may even have had a factory. Their wealth and success gave rise to a Spanish "Atlantis" myth, based around Huelva. Besides metals, the Phoenicians also came for the rich fishing along the southern coast which stimulated industries for salting and preserving the catch. The salt itself was gained from beds such as those at the **Cabo de Gata** – still in commercial operation – in Almería. Other operations, such as the **purple dyeing industry**, for which the Phoenicians were famous, exploited the large stocks of murex shellfish in coastal waters. The coastline of Andalucía is dotted with Phoenician **settlements** from this time such as those at Malaka (Málaga), Sexi (Almuñecar) and Abdera (Adra). Market rivalry also brought the **Greeks**, who established their trading colonies along the northeastern coast – the modern Costa Brava – before penetrating southwards into the Phoenician zone. They were encouraged by the Tartessians, no doubt in an attempt to break the Phoenician economic stranglehold on the region.

When the Phoenicians were incorporated into the Persian empire in the sixth century BC, however, a former colony, **Carthage**, moved into the power vacuum, destroyed Tartessus and ejected the Greeks from the south. Carthage then turned the western Mediterranean into a jealously guarded trading monopoly, sinking ships of other states who attempted to trade there. This she tenaciously held on to, as the rising power of Rome forced her out of the central Mediterranean. In the course of the third century BC, Carthage built up Spain into a new base for her empire, from which to regain strength and strike back at her great rival. Although making little impact inland, the Carthaginians occupied most of Andalucía and expanded along the Mediterranean seaboard to establish a new capital at Cartagena ("New Carthage") in Murcia. The mineral wealth of Andalucía, particularly **silver**, was used to finance the military build-up as well as to recruit an enormous army of Iberian mercenaries. Under Hannibal they prepared to invade Italy and in 219 BC attacked

Saguntum (modern Sagunto), a strategic ally of the growing Roman Empire. This precipitated the **Second Punic War** bringing Roman legions to the Spanish peninsula for the first time. Heading south from modern Catalunya, the coastal towns were successively conquered and the **end of Carthaginian domination** of Spain was sealed in 206 BC at the battle of Ilipa (Alcalá del Río), just north of Sevilla. When Cádiz fell the following year, Rome became master of the southern peninsula and **Itálica** (near Sevilla) was founded as the first Roman city in Spain. A new and very different age had begun.

ROMANS AND VISIGOTHS

The **Roman colonization** of the peninsula was far more intense than anything previously experienced and met with great resistance from the Celtiberian tribes of the north and centre, although much less so in Andalucía where the Turditanian people, tired of Carthaginian oppression, welcomed the invaders. In the final years of the Roman republic many of the crucial battles for control of the Roman state were fought out in Spain, ending with Julius Caesar's victory at Munda, south of Córdoba, in 45 BC. After Caesar's assassination, his successor Augustus reorganized Spain into three provinces, the southernmost of which became **Hispania Baetica**, roughly modern Andalucía, with **Corduba** (Córdoba) as its capital.

In this period Spain became one of the most important and wealthiest centres of the Roman Empire and Andalucía was its most urbane heartland. Unlike the rugged and fractious Celtiberians further north, the sophisticated Iberians of the south had their own municipal traditions and took easily to Roman ideas of government. Indeed, their native languages and dialects had disappeared early in the first century AD as Latinization became complete. For four centuries Andalucía enjoyed a **"Golden Age"** with unprecedented prosperity based on the production of olive oil, wool, grain, wine and the highly prized garum fish sauce made at centres such as **Baelo Claudia** near Tarifa. Another important development was a massive expansion of mining at **Río Tinto** in Huelva. During this period, Baetica supplied **two Roman emperors**, Trajan (one of the greatest) as well as his adopted son Hadrian, along with the outstanding writers Seneca and Lucan. The

finest monuments of the period were built in the provincial capital at Córdoba, and cities such as Cádiz, Itálica, Málaga and Carmona, linked by a network of superb roads and adorned with temples, baths, amphitheatres and aqueducts, were the equal of any in the empire.

In the fourth and fifth centuries, however, the Roman political framework began to show signs of **decadence and corruption**. Although the actual structure didn't totally collapse until the Muslim invasions of the early eighth century, it became increasingly vulnerable to **barbarian invasions** from northern Europe. Early in the fourth century AD, the Suevi (Swabians), Alans and Vandals swept across the Pyrenees leaving much devastation in their wake. The Romans, preoccupied with attempts to stave off Gothic attacks on Italy bought off the invaders by allowing them to settle within the imperial borders. The Suevi settled in Galicia, the Alans in Portugal and Murcia, whilst the **Vandals** put down roots in Baetica, providing the origin of Andalucía's name. The resulting wars between the invaders only served to weaken further Rome's grip on the peninsula as a burgeoning Christian Church – its first Spanish council was held at Iliberis (Granada) – gained more influence over the population.

Internal strife was heightened by the arrival of the **Visigoths** from Gaul, allies of Rome and already Romanized to a large degree. The triumph of Visigothic strength in the fifth century resulted in a period of spurious unity, based upon an exclusive military rule from their capital at Toledo, but their numbers were never great and their order was often fragmentary and nominal, with the bulk of the subject people kept in a state of disconsolate servility and held ransom for their services in times of war. Above them in the ranks of the military elite there were constant plots and factions – exacerbated by the Visigothic system of elected monarchy and by their adherence to the heretical Arian philosophy. When **King Leovigild** attempted ito impose this creed on Andalucía in the mid-sixth century the region revolted with the king's son Hermenegild at its head, but the insurrection was brutally crushed. In 589 **King Recared** converted to Catholicism which for a time stiffened Visigothic control, but religious strife was only multiplied: forced conversions, especially within the Jewish enclaves, maintained a constant simmering of discontent. The Visigoths precariously held on to their domain for a further century as plots and counterplots surrounded the throne. This infighting led indirectly to the Moorish invasions of Andalucía when **King Witiza**, who died in 710, was thwarted by a usurper, Roderic, Duke of Baetica, from handing over the throne to his son, Achila. Once **King Roderic** had installed himself on the throne the embittered family of Witiza appealed to the Muslims in North Africa for assistance to overthrow him. The North Africans, who had long eyed the riches of Andalucía with envy, now saw their opportunity.

THE MOORISH CONQUEST

In contrast to the long-drawn-out Roman campaigns, **Moorish conquest** of the peninsula was effected with extraordinary speed. This was a characteristic phenomenon of the spread of Islam – Muhammad left Mecca in 622 and by 705 his followers had established control over all of North Africa. Spain, with its political instability, its wealth and fertile climate, was an inevitable extension of their aims. In 711 **Tariq**, governor of Tangier, led a force of 7000 Berbers across the straits and routed the Visigoth army of King Roderic on the banks of the Río Guadalete close to Jerez. Two years later the Visigoths made a last desperate stand at Mérida and within a decade the Moors had conquered all but the wild mountains of Asturias. The land under their authority was dubbed "**al-Andalus**", a fluid term which expanded and shrunk with the intermittent gains and losses of the Reconquest. It was Andalucía, however, which was destined to become the heartland of the Moorish ascendancy and where the Moors were to remain in control for most of the next eight centuries.

The Moorish incursion was not simply a military conquest. The Moors (a collective term for the numerous waves of Arab, Syrian and Berber settlers from North Africa) were often content to grant a limited autonomy in exchange for payment of tribute; their administrative system was tolerant and easily absorbed by both Spanish Jews and Christians, those who retained their religion being known as "Mozarabs". This **tolerant attitude** was illustrated when the Moorish army reached Córdoba where they found the large Visigothic church of St Vincent, now the fabulous Mezquita. Unlike previous invaders, they did not sack or burn the

heathen temple but purchased half of it to use as a mosque whilst the Christians continued to use the other half for their own services.

Al-Andalus was a distinctly Spanish state of Islam. Though at first politically subject to the Eastern Caliphate (or empire) of Baghdad, it was soon virtually independent. In the tenth century, at the peak of its power and expansion, Abd ar-Rahman III asserted total independence, proclaiming himself Caliph of a new **Western Islamic Empire**. Its capital was **Córdoba** – the largest, most prosperous and most civilized city in Europe. This was the great age of Muslim Spain: its scholarship, philosophy, architecture and craftsmanship were without rival and there was an unparalleled growth in urban life, trade and agriculture, aided by magnificent irrigation projects. These and other engineering feats were not, on the whole, instigated by the Moors who instead took the basic Roman models and adapted them to a new level of sophistication. In **architecture** and the **decorative arts**, however, their contribution was original and unique – as may be seen in the astonishingly beautiful monuments of Sevilla, Córdoba and Granada.

The Cordoban Caliphate created a remarkable degree of unity, despite a serious challenge to its authority by the rebel leader **Ibn Hafsun** from his Bobastro fortress (north of Málaga) in the latter years of the ninth century. But its rulers were to become decadent and out of touch, prompting the brilliant but dictatorial **al-Mansur** to usurp control. Under this extraordinary ruler Moorish power reached new heights, using a professional Berber army to push the Christian kingdom of Asturias-León back into the Cantabrian mountains and sacking its most holy shrine, Santiago de Compostela in 997. However, after al-Mansur's death the Caliphate quickly lost its authority and in 1031 disintegrated into a series of small independent kingdoms or *taifas*, the strongest of which was Sevilla.

Internal divisions amongst the taifas offered less resistance to the Christian kingdoms which were rallying in the north, and twice North Africa had to be called upon for reinforcement. This resulted in two distinct new waves of Moorish invasion – first by the fanatically Islamic **Almoravids** (1086) and later by the **Almohads** (1147), who restored effective Muslim authority and left behind one of Moorish Spain's most elegant monuments, the

Giralda tower in Sevilla. However, their crushing defeat by the Christian forces under Alfonso VIII in 1212, at the battle of **Las Navas de Tolosa** in Jaén, marked the beginning of the end for Moorish Spain.

THE CHRISTIAN RECONQUEST

The **reconquest** of land and influence from the Moors was a slow and intermittent process. It began with a symbolic victory by a small force of Christians at Covadonga in the region of Asturias (727) in northern Spain and was not completed until 1492 with the conquest of Granada by Fernando and Isabel.

Covadonga resulted in the formation of the tiny Christian **Kingdom of the Asturias**. Initially just 40 by 30 miles in area, it had by 914 reclaimed León and most of Galicia and northern Portugal. At this point, progress was temporarily halted by the devastating campaigns of al-Mansur. However, with the fall of the Cordoban Caliphate and the divine aid of Spain's Moor-slaying patron saint, the avenging Santiago (Saint James the Apostle), the Reconquest moved into a new and powerful phase.

The frontier castles built against Arab attack gave name to **Castile**, founded in the tenth century as a county of León-Asturias. Under Fernando I (1037–65) it achieved the status of a kingdom and became the main thrust and focus of the Reconquest. In 1085 this period of confident Christian expansion reached its zenith with the capture of the great Moorish city of Toledo. The following year, however, the Almoravids arrived by invitation from Sevilla, and military activity was effectively frozen – except, that is, for the exploits of the legendary **El Cid**, a Castilian nobleman who won considerable lands around Valencia in 1095, thus checking Muslim expansion up the eastern coast.

The next concerted phase of the Reconquest began as a response to the threat imposed by the Almohads. The kings of León, Castile, Aragón and Navarra united in a crusade which resulted in the great victory at Las Navas de Tolosa. Thereafter Muslim power was paralyzed and the **Christian armies** moved on to take most of al-Andalus. Fernando III ("El Santo", the saint) led Castilian soldiers into Córdoba in 1236 and twelve years later into Sevilla. By the end of the thirteenth century only the Nasrid **Kingdom of Granada** remained under Muslim

authority and this was to provide a brilliant sunset to Moorish rule in Andalucía. Its survival for a further two centuries whilst surrounded by its Christian enemies was due as much to skilful diplomacy as to payment of tribute to the monarchs of Castile.

Two factors should be stressed regarding the Reconquest. First, its unifying religious nature – the **spirit of crusade**, intensified by the religious zeal of the Almoravids and Almohads, and by the wider European climate (which in 1085 gave rise to the First Crusade). At the same time the Reconquest was a movement of **re-colonization**. The fact that the country had been under arms for so long meant that the nobility had a major and clearly visible social role, a trend perpetuated by the redistribution of captured land in huge packages, or "**latifundia**". Heirs to this tradition still remain as landlords of the great estates, most conspicuously in Andalucía where it has produced wretched conditions for the workers on the land ever since. Men from the ranks were also awarded land, forming a lower, larger stratum of nobility, the **hidalgos**. It was their particular social code that provided the material for Cervantes in Don Quixote.

Any spirit of mutual cooperation that had temporarily united the Christian kingdoms disintegrated during the fourteenth century, and independent lines of development were once again pursued. **Castile** emerged as the strongest over this period: self-sufficiency in agriculture and a flourishing wool trade with the Netherlands enabled the state to build upon the prominent military role under Fernando III.

LOS REYES CATÓLICOS

Los Reyes Católicos – **the Catholic Monarchs** – was the joint title given to **Fernando V of Aragón** and **Isabel I of Castile**, whose marriage in 1479 united the two largest kingdoms in Spain. Unity was in practice more symbolic than real: Castile had underlined its rights in the marriage vows and Aragón retained its old administrative structure. So, in the beginning at least, the growth of any national unity or Spanish – as opposed to local – sentiment was very much dependent on the head of state. Nevertheless, from this time on it begins to be realistic to consider Spain as a single political entity.

At the heart of Fernando and Isabel's popular appeal lay a **religious bigotry** that they shared with most of their Christian subjects. The **Inquisition** was instituted in Castile in 1480 and in Aragón seven years later. Aiming to establish the purity of the Catholic faith by rooting out heresy, it was directed mainly at Jews (despite Fernando's half-Jewish parentage) – resented for their enterprise in commerce and influence in high places, as well as for their faith. Expression had already been given to these feelings in a pogrom in 1391; it was reinforced by an edict issued in 1492 which forced up to 400,000 Jews to flee the country. A similar spirit was embodied in the reconquest of the Nasrid **Kingdom of Granada**, also in 1492. During this long campaign Gonzalo Fernández de Córdoba, "El Gran Capitán," developed the Spanish army into a formidable force that was set to dominate the battlefields of Europe for the next century and a half. As Granada was the last stronghold of Muslim authority, the religious rights of its citizens were guaranteed under the treaty of surrender. Then the policy was reversed and forced mass conversions were introduced. The subsequent and predictable rebellions – particularly violent in **Las Alpujarras** – were brutally put down and within a decade those Muslims under Christian rule had been given the choice between conversion or expulsion.

The year 1492 was symbolic of a fresh start in another way: it was in this year that **Columbus** sailed from Huelva to make the **discovery of America**, and the Papal Bull that followed, entrusting Spain with the conversion of the American Indians, further entrenched Spain's sense of a mission to bring the world to the "True Faith". The next ten years saw the systematic conquest, colonization and exploitation of the **New World**, with new territory stretching from Labrador to Brazil, and newfound wealth pouring into the royal coffers. The control of trade with the New World was carried on through **Sevilla** where the Casa de Contración (House of Trade) was established in 1503. The city rapidly grew into one of the great cities of Europe during which it enjoyed two centuries of commercial monopoly. Paradoxically, Andalucía as a whole benefited little from this wealth which was appropriated by the crown for its foreign campaigns and by absentee landlords. Over the succeeding two centuries the region languished as a backwater and the poverty of the peasants led many to emigrate to the New World in order to better themselves, at the same time turning much of the region into a vast, unpopulated desert.

THE HABSBURG AGE

Carlos I, a Habsburg, came to the throne in 1516 as a beneficiary of the marriage alliances of the Catholic monarchs. Five years later, he was elected Emperor of the Holy Roman Empire as Carlos V (**Charles V**), inheriting not only Castile and Aragón, but Flanders, the Netherlands, Artois, the Franche-Comté and all the American colonies to boot. With such responsibilities it was inevitable that attention would be diverted from Spain, whose chief function became to sustain the Holy Roman Empire with gold and silver from the Americas. It was only with the accession of **Felipe II** in 1556 that Spanish politics became more centralized and that the notion of an absentee king was reversed.

This was a period of unusual religious intensity: the **Inquisition** was enforced with renewed vigour, and a "final solution" to the problem of the Moriscos (subject Moors), who continued to adhere to their ancient traditions and practised Muslim worship in secret, resulted in a decree banning Arabic dress, books and speech. The result was another rising of Moriscos in Las Alpujarras which was fiercely suppressed with Muslims being forcibly deported to other parts of the country. Felipe III later ordered the expulsion of half the total number of Moriscos in Spain – allowing only two families to remain in each village in order to maintain irrigation techniques. The **exodus** of both Muslim and Jew created a large gulf in the labour force and in the higher echelons of commercial life – and in trying to uphold the Catholic cause, an enormous strain was put upon resources without any clearcut victory. Despite being a golden literary and artistic age, politically and economically the seventeenth century was a disaster for Spain. Lurching progressively deeper into debt, she suffered heavy defeats on the battlefield as her possessions in the Netherlands and France were lost, and recurring financial crises and economic stagnation engendered a deepening mood of disillusionment. **Andalucía** shared in this decline, exacerbated by the tendency of the mercantile classes to involve themselves only in entrepôt trade which left most of the profits in the hands of other countries. There was also no stimulus given to industrial production by the custom of merchants retiring from commerce and investing their profits in land, which created a landed gentry weighed down by honours and titles whose lifestyle came to be looked upon as being incompatible with commerce.

THE BOURBONS

The **Bourbon dynasty** succeeded to the Spanish throne in the person of Felipe V (1700); with him began the **War of Spanish Succession** against the rival claim of Archduke Charles of Austria, assisted by British forces. As a result of the Treaty of Utrecht which ended the war (1713), Spain was stripped of all territory in Belgium, Luxembourg, Italy and Sardinia, but Felipe V was recognized as king. **Gibraltar** was seized by the British in the course of the war. For the rest of the century Spain fell very much under the French sphere of influence, an influence that was given political definition by an alliance with the French Bourbons in 1762. This Gallic connection brought the ideas of Enlightenment Europe into the peninsula and during the reign of Carlos III (1759–88) a number of radically-minded ministers attempted to deal with the nation's chronic problems. Along with a more tolerant attitude towards the **gypsies**, who had become victims of racial abuse and hostility, the king's minister, Pablo de Olavide, began an imaginative, if ultimately unsuccessful, scheme to **repopulate the Sierra Morena** in Andalucía with foreign immigrants.

Contact with France also made involvement in the **Napoleonic Wars** inevitable and led eventually to the defeat of the Spanish fleet at the **Battle of Trafalgar** off the coast of Cádiz in 1805. Popular outrage was such that the powerful prime minister, Godoy, was overthrown and King Carlos IV forced to abdicate (1808). Napoleon seized the opportunity to instal his brother, Joseph, on the throne, whilst French armies and generals ransacked and stole much of the country's artistic heritage.

Fierce local resistance in the form of guerrilla warfare was accompanied by armies raised by the various local administrations. Thus it was that a militia put in the field by the junta of Sevilla inflicted a resounding defeat on a French army at **Bailén** in Jaén in 1808, which forced Joseph, the "intruder king", to flee back across the border. This resistance was eventually backed by the muscle of a British army, first under Sir John Moore, later under the Duke of Wellington, and the French were at last driven out in the course of the **War of Independence** (Peninsular War). Meanwhile, the **American colonies** had been successfully asserting their independence from a preoccupied centre and with them went Spain's last real claim of significance on the world stage. The entire nineteenth century was dominated by the struggle between an often reactionary monarchy and the aspirations of liberal constitutional reformers.

SEEDS OF CIVIL WAR

Between 1810 and 1813, whilst the war raged on across the peninsula, an ad hoc Cortes (parliament) meeting in **Cádiz** had set up a **liberal constitution** which stipulated a strict curtailment of the powers of the crown with ministers responsible to a democratically elected chamber. The first act of the despotic Fernando VII on being returned to the throne was to abolish this, and until his death in 1033 he continued to stamp out the least hint of liberalism. But the Constitution of 1812 was to remain a "sacred text" for a future democratic Spain, besides introducing the word "liberal" to Europe's political vocabulary. On Fernando's death, the right of succession was contested between his brother, Don Carlos, backed by the Church, conservatives and Basques, and his infant daughter, Isabel, who looked to the Liberals and the army for support.

So began the **First Carlist War**, a civil war that divided Spanish emotions for six years. Isabel II was eventually declared of age in 1843, her reign a long record of scandal, political crisis and constitutional compromise. Liberal army generals under the leadership of General Prim effected a coup in 1868 and the queen was forced to abdicate, but attempts to maintain a Republican government foundered. The Cortes was again dissolved and the throne returned to Isabel's son, Alfonso XII. The military began increasingly to move into the power vacuum left by the weakened monarchy. The **pronunciamiento** – whereby an officer backed by military force "pronounced" what was in the best interests of a city or region – was born in this period and was to plague the country into modern times.

The **nineteenth century in Andalucía** mirrored Spain's national decline. The loss of the

American colonies had badly hit the region's trade, and this was compounded by the phylloxera plague from the 1870s onwards which wiped out most of the vineyards, brought the sherry industry to its knees, and fuelled the growth of strikes in the cities and popular uprisings on the land as the economy deteriorated. Parodoxically, this century also did more than any other to bestow on Andalucía the image it has held ever since. Writers, artists and travellers of the **Romantic Age** saw in its bullfights, flamenco, bandits and beguiling women a world of gaiety and colour epitomized in the operas *Carmen* and *The Barber of Seville*, both works from this period.

The years preceding World War I merely heightened the discontent, which found expression in the growing **political movements** of the working class. The Socialist Workers' Party was founded in Madrid after the restoration of Alfonso XII, and spawned its own trade union, the UGT (1888). Its anarchist counterpart, the CNT (Confederación Nacional de Trabajo), was founded in 1911, gaining substantial support among the oppressed peasantry of Andalucía.

The loss of **Cuba** in 1898 emphasized the growing isolation of Spain in international affairs and added to economic problems with the return of soldiers seeking employment where there was none. In Andalucía a regionalist movement known as *Andalucismo* was born demanding land reform and greater Andalucian autonomy. A call-up for army reserves to fight in **Morocco** in 1909 provoked a general strike and the "Tragic Week" of rioting in Barcelona. Between 1914 and 1918, Spain was outwardly neutral but inwardly turbulent; inflated prices made the postwar recession harder to bear.

The general disillusionment with parliamentary government, together with the fears of employers and businessmen for their own security, gave **General Primo de Rivera** sufficient support for a military coup in 1923. Coming himself from Jerez de la Frontera, the paternalistic general backed the great **Ibero-American Exhibition of 1929** at Sevilla which was hoped would calm the agitation for radical change by promoting a "rose-coloured" image for the troubled region; its most immediate effect was to bankrupt the city. Dictatorship did result in an increase in material prosperity, heavily assisted by a massive public works policy, but serious

political misjudgments and the collapse of the peseta in 1929 made Rivera's voluntary resignation and departure into exile inevitable. The legacy of this dictatorship was to reinforce a belief on the Right that only a firm military hand would be capable of holding the society together, and many of those who served in Primo de Rivera's administration were to back the Franco regime in the next decade. The victory of anti-monarchist parties in the 1931 municipal elections forced the abdication of the hopelessly out of touch King Alfonso XIII, and the **Second Republic** was declared.

THE SECOND REPUBLIC

The Second Republic which lasted from 1931 to 1936 was ushered in on a wave of optimism that finally some of the nation's fundamental ills and injustices would be rectified. But the government – a coalition of radicals, socialists and leftist republicans – struggling to curb the power of vested interests such as the army, the church and the landowning class, was soon failing to satisfy even the least of the expectations which it had raised. Moreover it lost support when it got involved in activities identified with earlier repressive regimes when, as happened at the village of **Casa Viejas** (modern Benalup de Sidonia) in Cádiz, it ordered the troops to open fire on a group of starving workers who had been the victims of a lockout by the local landowner and who were attempting to raise the area in an Anarchist revolt.

Anarchism was gaining strength among the frustrated middle classes as well as among workers and peasantry. The **Communist Party** and left-wing **Socialists**, driven into alliance by their mutual distrust of the "moderate" Socialists in government, were also forming a growing bloc. There was little real unity of purpose on either left or right, but their fear of each other and their own exaggerated boasts made each seem an imminent threat. On the right the **Falangists**, basically a youth party founded in 1923 by **José Antonio Primo de Rivera** (son of the dictator), made uneasy bedfellows with conservative traditionalists and dissident elements in the army upset by modernizing reforms.

In an atmosphere of growing confusion, with mobs fighting on the streets and churches and monasteries being torched whilst landed estates were taken over by those impatient for agrarian reform, the left-wing Popular Front alliance won the general election of **February 1936** by a narrow margin. Normal life, though, became increasingly impossible: the economy was crippled by strikes, the universities became hotbeds for battles between Marxists and Falangists, and the government failed to exert its authority over anyone. Finally, on July 17, 1936, the military garrison in Morocco rebelled under **General Franco**'s leadership, to be followed by risings at military garrisons throughout the country. It was the culmination of years of scheming in the army, but in the event far from the overnight success its leaders almost certainly expected. Airlifting his troops into Sevilla by means of German transport planes, Franco ensured that the south and west quickly fell into Nationalist hands, but Madrid and the industrialized north and east remained loyal to the Republican government.

THE CIVIL WAR

The ensuing **Civil War** was undoubtedly one of the most bitter and bloody the world has seen. Violent reprisals were taken on their enemies by both sides – the Republicans shooting priests and local landowners wholesale, the Nationalists carrying out mass slaughter of the population of almost every town they took. Contradictions were legion in the way the Spanish populations found themselves divided from each other. Perhaps the greatest irony was that Franco's troops, on their "holy" mission against a godless "anti-Spain", comprised a core of Moroccan troops from Spain's North African colony.

It was, too, the first modern war – Franco's German allies demonstrated their ability to wipe out entire civilian populations with their bombing raids on Gernika and Durango in the Basque country, and radio proved an important weapon, as Nationalist propagandists offered the starving Republicans "the white bread of Franco".

Despite sporadic help from Russia and thousands of volunteers in the International Brigades, the Republic could never compete with the professional armies and the massive assistance from Fascist Italy and Nazi Germany enjoyed by the Nationalists. As hundreds of thousands of refugees flooded into France, General Francisco Franco, who had long before proclaimed himself Head of State, took up the reins of power.

FRANCO'S SPAIN

The early reprisals taken by the victors were on a massive and terrifying scale. Executions were commonplace in town and village, and upwards of two million people were put in concentration camps until "order" had been established by authoritarian means. Only one party was permitted and censorship was rigidly enforced. By the end of World War II, during which Spain was too weak to be anything but neutral, **Franco** was the only fascist head of state left in Europe, one responsible for sanctioning more deaths than any other in Spanish history. Spain was economically and politically isolated and, bereft of markets, suffering – almost half the population were still tilling the soil for little or no return. The misery of the peasantry was particularly acute in Andalucía and forced mass emigrations to Madrid and Barcelona and Europe beyond.

When General Eisenhower visited Madrid in 1953 with the offer of huge loans, it came as water to the desert, and the price, the **establishment of American nuclear bases** such as that at Rota near Cádiz, was one Franco was more than willing to pay. Once firmly in the US camp the Franco regime (administered by the so-called "tecnocratas" group of ministers) rapidly transformed Spain into a market economy and in the late Fifties the country joined the International Monetary Fund, the International Bank for Reconstruction and Development and the OECD in quick succession. However belated, economic development was incredibly rapid, with Spain enjoying a growth rate second only to that of Japan for much of the 1960s, a boom fuelled by the tourist industry, the remittances of Spanish workers abroad and the illegality of strikes and industrial action at home.

Increased **prosperity**, however, only underlined the political bankruptcy of Franco's regime and its inability to cope with popular demands. Higher incomes, the need for better education, and a creeping invasion of Western culture made the anachronism of Franco ever clearer. His only reaction was to attempt to withdraw what few signs of increased liberalism had crept through, and his last years mirrored the repression of the postwar period. Franco finally died in November 1975, nominating **King Juan Carlos** as his successor.

THE NEW SPAIN

On October 28, 1982, *sevillano* Felipe González's Socialist Workers' Party – the PSOE – was elected with massive support to rule a country that had been firmly in the hands of the right for 43 years. The **Socialists** captured the imagination and the votes of nearly ten million Spaniards with the simplest of appeals: "for change". It was a telling comment on just how far Spain had moved since Franco's death, for in the intervening years change seemed the one factor that could still threaten the new-found democracy.

Certainly, in the Spain of 1976 the thought of a freely elected left-wing government would have been incredible. **King Juan Carlos** was the hand-picked successor of Franco, groomed for the job and very much in with the army – of which he remains official Commander-in-Chief. His initial moves were cautious in the extreme, appointing a government dominated by loyal Francoists who had little sympathy for the growing opposition demands for "democracy without adjectives".

To his credit, however, Juan Carlos recognized that some real break with the past was now urgent and inevitable, and set in motion the process of **democratization**. He legitimized the Socialist Party and, controversially, the Communists. When elections were held in June 1977, the centre-right **UCD** Christian–Democrat party gained a 34 percent share of the vote, the **PSOE** (Spanish Socialist Workers' Party) coming in second with 28 percent, and the Communists and Francoist Alianza Popular both marginalized at 9 percent and 8 percent.

It was almost certainly a vote for democratic stability rather than for ideology. The king, perhaps recognizing that his own future depended on the maintenance of the new democracy, lent it his support – most notably in February 1981 when a tragi-comic Civil Guard colonel named Tejero stormed the Cortes brandishing a revolver and, with other officers loyal to Franco's memory, attempted to institute an **army coup**. But the crisis, for a while, was real. Tanks were brought out on to the streets of Valencia, and only three of the army's ten regional commanders remained unreservedly loyal to the government. But as it became clear that the king would not support the plotters, most of the rest affirmed their support.

Tejero, now released from prison, remains a fading icon for the extreme right but for most Spaniards his attempted coup is now a distant irrelevance. Spanish democracy – even in army circles where most of the old guard have been pensioned off – is now firmly institutionalized. And in the fourteen-year rule of the charismatic **Felipe González** (always known as "Felipe") and the PSOE the system found, at least until the Nineties' slide into the political mire and defeat, a party of enduring **stability** and to the left of exasperating **moderation**.

The nation's progressive disillusion with González's government in the Nineties as it became enveloped in sleaze and scandals saw the rise to prominence of **José-María Aznar** as leader of the **Partido Popular** conservatives (a merger of the UCD and Alianza Popular). A former tax inspector utterly devoid of charisma, Aznar's dogged criticism of the PSOE government's incompetence and corruption finally won the PP a narrow **victory** in the 1996 elections, following on an equally narrow defeat in 1993. Problems for both major parties ensued from this indecisive result, however, for Aznar had to stitch up a precarious deal with the Basque and Catalan nationalist parties (whom he had described as "greedy parasites" on the hustings) in order to have a workable parliamentary majority, whilst the PSOE's avoidance of the expected crushing defeat was proclaimed as a vindication by González – who hastily dismissed ideas of retirement. This merely delayed the inevitable and, unable to make any significant impact on changing public opinion and with his party still in turmoil, early in 1998 **González** finally **resigned** from the leadership of the party he had led for 23 years.

González was replaced as PSOE leader by his former transport minister, **José Borrell**. A Catalan, and not González's choice to succeed him. The former leader hovered constantly in the background making it impossible for Borrell to stamp his own mark on the party or the leadership. When a financial scandal was unearthed involving Borrell while he had been a minister he opted to resign to be replaced by the party's – and González's – original nominee **Joaquín Almunia**. Paunchy and balding, Almunia cut little ice with the Spanish electorate, not helped by his refusal to criticise the record of his mentor González. In an attempt to forestall a seemingly inevitable electoral defeat, early in 2000

Almunia stitched up a deal with the PSOE's bitter arch rival the ex-communist Izquierda Unida (United Left) party, thinking that their combined votes could overturn a likely Aznar victory. However, many of the rank and file on both sides were unhappy about this "shotgun marriage" (each has long blamed the other for Franco's victory in 1939) and the disorganisation on the ground (many local IU and PSOE politicians refused to share the same platform) was reflected in their leaders lack of a coherent policy.

The outcome of the March 2000 **general election** was a stunning **victory for Aznar** and the PP in which – for the first time since the death of Franco – the right were in power with an overall majority, and no longer dependent on the whims of nationalist coalition partners. It seems that the great majority of the electorate were not willing to risk the economic gains of Aznar's period in office, while many on the left didn't bother to turn out to support a leftist coalition which smacked more of political opportunism than a government in waiting. Joaquin Almunia, the architect of this crushing defeat for the left, **resigned** on election night. The PSOE will now begin the search for a political big gun able to revitalize a bewildered organisation which once dominated the Spanish political scene as the natural party of government. Potential leadership candidates include ex-NATO secretary general Javier Solana, the popular president of Castilla La Mancha José Bono, and possibly the charismatic PSOE leader in Andalucía, Manuel Chaves.

In hindsight, the left's defeat always appeared the most likely outcome if only because the lacklustre Aznar (when asked for the major achievement of his government he replied "normality") has nevertheless kept the **economy** on course with an economic growth rate among the highest in Europe causing a majority of Spaniards – according to a recent opinion poll – to feel extremely satisfied with life. He has also taken care not to endanger the delicate consensus which has maintained political stability in the post-Franco period. Declaring himself a supporter of the "third way" policies of Britain's Labour premier Tony Blair, with whom he has good relations, has further enabled him to soften his party's rightist image in a left-of-centre dominated EU.

The consensus across Spanish politics on Spain's role in **Europe** also means that while the nation is no longer as starry-eyed about the EU as it was a decade ago, Spaniards still identify strongly with European integration and see their participation at the launch of the **single currency** and the replacement of the peseta with the **euro** in 2002, as a landmark in the country's move into the European mainstream.

MODERN ANDALUCÍA

Andalucía shared in the progressive decentralization of power in Spain throughout the post-Franco period and in 1980 became an **Autonomous Region** with a regional government based in Sevilla exercising a large amount of control over its own destiny for the first time. Largely because of its enduring social problems, Andalucía remained a socialist bulwark for the PSOE throughout the eighties – the so-called *sartenilla* (frying pan) of the south which traditionally "fries" the right-wing votes further north. However, whilst the government's reluctance to grasp the nettle of fundamental change, especially in the area of land reform, lost it some support in the 1993 elections, the region's enduring, if increasingly sceptical, commitment to González ensured the PSOE's narrow election victory over the emergent Partido Popular. The **elections of 1996** followed a similar pattern and Andalucía confounded the polls to turn out once more for "Felipe" (himself a *sevillano*) which, whilst not enough to bring about another socialist victory, crucially denied Aznar an overall majority of seats in the Cortes (parliament). The *sartenilla* (Andalucía returns 62 members to the Madrid parliament, more than any other autonomous region) had cooked the northern votes yet again. But the tide was turning and in the **general election of 2000** there was a significant shift in voting patterns away from the left and towards Aznar and the PP which contributed significantly to the right's victory.

Apparently contradicting the national picture, the same poll also re-elected a new **Socialist Parliament** for Andalucía's autonomous government. However, while this result appeared to go against the prevailing mood, the voting figures showed that the PSOE's vote had remained static across the region whilst the PP had dramatically increased its support to come within six seats of unseating the PSOE dominated assembly. This PP surge deprived the leader of the regional government – canny PSOE secretary-general of

Andalucía Manuel Chaves – an overall majority and represented an ominous warning shot across the left's bows in this, its principal power base.

Despite the sunny image presented to most of its visitors, the chronic economic and social problems remain, and not for nothing is Andalucía known as the "workhouse of Spain". The **unemployment** level is among the European Union's highest at an alarming 30 percent (compared with 15 percent for Spain as a whole), and earnings per head are a third lower. Recently, efforts have been made to remove some of the serious obstacles to economic progress with radical improvements in the region's infrastructure and above all communications with the rest of the country and Europe. **Expo 92** brought new road and rail links aimed at providing faster connections with Madrid and Barcelona whilst a start was made on upgrading the internal links between the provinces of Andalucía as well. Additional funding from the EU – Spain receives the highest share of its regional aid budget – has upgraded airports and created industrial parks, and more investment is in the pipeline for the years opening the new century. However, serious structural problems remain and the task of training and retraining workers in new skills has hardly begun. Meanwhile, the Partido Popular government is placing its faith in Spanish access to a single European currency, with the promise of a stable economic environment as a magnet for investment into Andalucía, to provide future prosperity.

The **sovereignty of Gibraltar** continues to be an important issue in Spanish and Andalucian politics and whilst viewed less urgently in London, the British – at Spain's bidding – have begun to pressure the Gibraltar authorities into clamping down on the twin scourges of drug and tobacco smuggling and money laundering which have exploded in the colony over the last decade. A recent proposal by Spain to share sovereignty over Gibraltar for one hundred years, after which the colony would revert to Spain received a predictable blast of abuse from the inhabitants of the Rock and its political leaders, and an inscrutable silence from London. Gibraltar's current leadership remains uninterested in any deals with Spain except on its own narrowly defined terms – such as opening the Rock's airport to international flights – and there is currently no sign of the deadlock being broken.

The position of Andalucía's 200,000 **agricultural workers** on the land who face nine months' unemployment each year and depend on patronage from the great landowners for work during the other three remains unresolved, despite the PSOE government having introduced a minimal unemployment benefit scheme in the 1980s. Vastly increased land improvement grants from the European Union have further enriched the landowners, enabling them to mechanize their farms, whilst the *braceros* or landless day-labourers get nothing and have fewer job opportunities as a result.

All this has compelled a greater dependence on **tourism**, a sector which despite predictions of a downturn has remained buoyant providing much needed, if seasonal, jobs. This success has produced its own problems as many flock to the coast in search of work leaving a mere twenty per cent of the population in provinces such as Almería inhabiting the hinterland. The Junta de Andalucía regional government has now stepped up its campaign to attract visitors inland in order to channel some of the tourist income away from the coast. Another area now receiving long-overdue attention is the region's **education system**, which has so far largely failed to provide the vocational courses necessary to train the skilled workers essential to drive a modern economy. Although prospects look brighter than ever before as Andalucía enters the new millennium, the land which produced Picasso, Manuel de Falla, Federico García Lorca and Juan Ramón Jiménez will have to wait some time yet for all its people to enjoy, as well as to endure, their place in the sun.

CHRONOLOGY OF MONUMENTS

c.25,000 BC	Cave dwellers occupying caves in Málaga province.	**Cave paintings** at La Pileta and Nerja.
c.4000 BC	Neolithic colonists arrive from North Africa.	Esparto baskets, sandals and jewellery found in the Cueva de Murciélagos near Albuñol in Granada.
c.2500 BC	Los Millares Chalcolithic site flourishes in Almería.	Dolmens constructed at Antequera.
c.1100 BC	**Phoenicians** found Cádiz.	Remains of later Phoenician settlements at Málaga, Almuñecar and Adra.
C9th–4th BC	Celts settle in the north of Spain. Kingdom of **Tartessus** flourishes around Guadalquivir estuary. **Greeks** establish trading posts along east coast.	
C5th BC	**Carthage** colonizes southern Spain.	Celto-Iberian culture develops, with Greek influence: statue of La Dama de Baza, necropolis at Toya (Jaén), Iberian stone sculptures made at Porcuna (Jaén museum).
214 BC	Second Punic War with Rome.	
210 BC	**Roman colonization** begins.	Important Roman cities at Itálica, Córdoba, Cádiz, Carmona, Málaga.
27 BC	Octavian-Augustus becomes first Roman emperor and divides Spain into three parts: Andalucía is named **Baetica**.	**Golden Age** and Latinization of Baetica. Mining expanded at Río Tinto.
c.409	**Vandals** invade southern Spain.	
C5th–7th	**Visigoths** arrive and take control of most of Spain including Andalucía.	Visigothic cities founded at Mérida and Córdoba.
711	**Moors** under Tariq invade and defeat Visigothic King Roderic at Río Guadalete, near Jerez. Peninsula conquered in seven years.	
718	Pelayo defeats Moors in a battle at Covadonga in Asturias in northern Spain marking the start of the **Reconquest**.	
756	Abd ar-Rahman I proclaims **Emirate of Córdoba**.	Great Mosque (**Mezquita**) begun at Córdoba, climax of early Moorish architecture.
928	Abd ar-Rahman II establishes Cordoban Caliphate.	**Mozarabic churches** built by Arabized Christians. Construction of palace at **Medina Azahara** and extensions to Mezquita in **caliphal style**.
967	**Al-Mansur** usurps caliphal powers and forces Christians back into Asturias.	Final enlargement of the Mezquita at Córdoba.

1013	Caliphate disintegrates into **taifas**, petty kingdoms.	Medina Azahara palace destroyed by Berber mercenaries. Alcazabas built at Málaga, Sevilla, Carmona, Ronda, etc.
1086	**Almoravids** invade from North Africa.	Philosopher Averroës born at Córdoba (1126). Sevilla becomes new Moorish capital in Spain.
1146	Invasion by **Almohads** from Morocco; Muslim authority re-established.	Almohad minarets include La Giralda and Torre del Oro.
1212	Almohad advance halted by **Christian victory** at Las Navas de Tolosa (Jaén).	**Mudéjar** style emerges through Moorish craftsmen working on Christian buildings: good examples in Sevilla (Alcázar, Casa de Pilatos) and in Córdoba (Capilla Real inside Mezquita).
1236–48	Fernando III conquers Córdoba and then Sevilla.	
1238	Ibn al-Ahmar (aka Muhammad ibn-Yusuf ibn-Nasr) takes Granada and founds the Nasrid dynasty.	Granada's **Alhambra** palace constructed under Ibn al-Ahmar (1238–73) and his successors.
1262–92	Cádiz falls to Alfonso X, Sancho IV takes Tarifa.	
1479	Castile and Aragón united under **Fernando and Isabel**. Spanish Inquisition set up in Sevilla.	**Sevilla Cathedral** built (1402–1506).
1492	**Fall of Granada**, the last Moorish kingdom. Discovery of America by Columbus. Expulsion of Jews from Spain.	
1516	**Carlos V** succeeds to the throne and in 1520 becomes Holy Roman Emperor inaugurating the **Golden Age**.	**Renaissance** reaches Spain. Elaborate early style known as Plateresque, best represented by the *Ayuntamiento* at Sevilla and the Colegiata at Osuna. Later key figures include Diego de Siloé (1495–1563; Granada, etc) and Andres de Vandelvira (d. 1575; Jaén, Úbeda, Baeza).
1519	**Magellan** starts global voyage from Sanlúcar de Barrameda; Córtes lands in Mexico.	
1556	Accession of **Felipe II** (d. 1598).	Painters and sculptors include: El Greco (1540–1614), Ribera (1591–1652), Zurbarán (1598–1664), Alonso Cano (1601–67), Velázquez (1599–1660), Murillo (1618–82), Roldán (1624–1700), de Mena (1628–88), Martínez Montañés (1580–1649). All are represented in Museo de Bellas Artes, Sevilla.
1587	Drake carries out raid on Cádiz.	
1588	Sinking of the Armada.	
1609	Expulsion of Moriscos, last remaining Spanish Muslims.	
1649	Great plague in Sevilla wipes out one third of the population.	
1700	War of the Spanish Succession brings Felipe V (1713–45), a Bourbon, to the throne. British seize Gibraltar.	**Baroque** develops in reaction to the severity of the High Renaissance and reaches a flamboyant peak in the Churrigueresque style of the C18th: La Cartuja (Granada), Caridad (Sevilla), Écija, Lucena, Priego de Córdoba, etc.

1759–88	Reign of Carlos III.	**Enlightenment** ideas enter Spain. Colonies of Germans, French and Swiss settled in the Sierra Morena.
1808	French occupy Spain. Liberal constitution declared in Cádiz (1812). Andalucía divided into eight provinces (1834).	Romantic era brings travellers to Spain. English cemetery set up at Málaga (1830). Washington Irving publishes *Tales of the Alhambra* (1832).
1835	**First Carlist War**. Peasant risings begin throughout Andalucía (1855).	**Dissolution of monasteries** and confiscation of church lands.
1874	**Second Carlist War**.	Many of Andalucía's greatest creative artists born in last part of C19th: Antonio Machado (sevilla)1875; Manuel de Falla (Cádiz) 1876; Picasso (Málaga) and Juan Ramón Jiménez (Moguer) both 1881; guitarist Segovia (Andújar) 1893; Federico García Lorca (Granada) 1898.
1898	Loss of Cuba, Spain's last American colony.	
1923	Primo de Rivera dictatorship	Ibero-American Exhibition flops in Sevilla (1929). Site now Plaza de España.
1931	Second Republic.	
1936–9	**Spanish Civil War**. Franco dictatorship begins.	
1953	Franco secures economic aid from US in return for military bases	
		Costa del Sol opened up to tourist development (1962).
1975	Death of Franco; restoration of democracy.	
1980	Andalucía votes to become an **Autonomous Region**.	
1982	*Sevillano* and *PSOE* leader **Felipe González** elected prime minister. Elections for first Andalucian parliament.	
1985	Frontier between Spain and Gibraltar opens (1985). Spain joins European Community (1986).	
1992		Expo '92 in Sevilla celebrates the 500th anniversary of Columbus's discovery of America. Many striking buildings and bridges constructed in Sevilla and elsewhere to coincide with this event.
1993	Minority *PSOE* government returned to power with aid of Catalan Nationalist Party.	
1996	Election of minority *Partido Popular* (Conservative) government led by José María Aznar.	
1998	Felipe González **resigns** as leader of PSOE.	

1999   Spain joins ten other EU states to create the European Economic and Monetary Union (EMU) and a **single currency**, the **Euro**.

2000   Emphatic **victory** by Jose María Aznar's *Partido Popular* over a *PSOE/IU* electoral coalition in March general election giving the right an overall majority for the first time since the end of the Franco regime. *PSOE* hangs onto power in Andalucía's **regional elections** but loses its majority.

2001   New **Picasso Museum** opens in Málaga displaying major works by the **malagueño** painter.

FLAMENCO

Scratch a hot night in Andalucía, even on the much maligned Costa del Sol, and you'll find flamenco. "You carry it inside you," said a man in his sixties sitting in the local municipal stadium in downtown Marbella at 2am with not a tourist in sight; the sky was deep blue-black, patterned with stars, the stadium cluttered with families enjoying the most pleasant hours of the *andaluz* summer, flapping their fans until dawn, children asleep on laps.

Flamenco is undoubtedly the most important musical-cultural phenomenon in Spain, and over the past decade or so it has experienced a huge resurgence in popularity, and a profile that has reached out far beyond its Andalucian home land. The sanitized kitsch flamenco, all frills and castanets, exploited as an image of tourist Spain during the Franco period, has been left far behind by a new age expressing the vitality and attitudes of a younger generation of flamenco clans.

In the 1980s, the Spanish press hailed **Ketama** (named after a Moroccan village famed for its hashish) as creators of the music of the "New Spain", after their first album which fused flamenco with rock and Latin salsa. Since then they have pushed the frontiers of flamenco still further by recording *Songhai*, an album collaborating with Malian kora player Toumani Diabate and British bassist Danny Thompson. *Blues de la Frontera* (Frontier Blues), the first disc of **Pata Negra** ("black leg" – the

highest quality Andalucian leg of cured ham – and an everyday term used for anything good), caused an equal sensation.

This flamenco revival of the 1980s and 1990s is no longer confined to the purists who kept old-time flamenco alive in their *peñas* or clubs. On radio and on cassettes blaring from market stalls right across the country you hear the typical high-pitched treble tones of commercial flamenco singers such as **Tijeritas**. The European success of the flamenco-rumba of the **Gipsy Kings**, a high-profile gypsy group from southern France, has further opened and prepared the ear of European popular audiences for something more powerful. Rumba, a Latin form, has come back to Spain from Latin America, and so is known as a music of *ida y vuelta* ("go and return"), one of the many fusions of the Spanish music taken to the New World with the conquistadores and their descendants, where it has mixed with African and other elements, before making its way back again. The impetus began at the end of the 1970s, with the innovations of guitarist **Paco de Lucía** and, especially, the late great, singer, **El Camarón de la Isla**. These were musicians who had grown up learning from their flamenco families but whose own musical tastes have embraced international rock, jazz and blues. Paco de Lucía blended jazz and salsa on to the flamenco sound. Camarón, simply, was an inspiration – and one whose own idols (and fans) included Chick Corea and Miles Davis, as well as flamenco artists. Latterly flamenco musicians are to be found playing in many different contexts, including rock and folk genres – the result is an exciting and dynamic scene.

ORIGINS

The **roots of flamenco** evolved in southern Spain from many sources: Morocco, Egypt, India, Pakistan, Greece and other parts of the Near and Far East. How exactly they came together as flamenco is a source of great debate and obscurity, though most authorities believe the roots of the music were brought by **gypsies** arriving in the fifteenth century. In the following century, it fused with elements of Arab and Jewish music in the Andalucian mountains, where Jews, Muslims and "pagan" gypsies had taken refuge from the forced conversions and clearances effected by the

Catholic monarchs and the church. The main flamenco centres and families are to be found today in quarters and towns of gypsy and refugee origin, such as Alcalá del Río, Utrera, Jerez, Cádiz and the Triana barrio of Sevilla.

There are two theories about the origins of the name flamenco. One contends that Spanish Jews migrated through trade to Flanders, where they were allowed to sing their religious chants unmolested, and that these chants became referred to as flamenco by the Jews who stayed in Spain. The other is that the word is a mispronunciation of the Arabic words *felag* (fugitive) and *mengu* (peasant), a plausible idea, as Arabic was a common language in Spain at the time.

Flamenco aficionados enjoy heated debate about the purity of their art and whether it is more validly performed by a **gitano** (gypsy) or a **payo** (non-gypsy). Certainly, flamenco seems to have thrived enclosed, preserved and protected by the oral tradition of the gypsy clans. Its power, and the despair which its creation overcomes, has emerged from the precarious and vulnerable lives of a people surviving for centuries at the margins of society. Flamenco reflects a passionate need to preserve their self-esteem.

These days, there are as many acclaimed *payo* as *gitano* flamenco artists. However, the concept of an **active inheritance** is crucial. The veteran singer **Fernanda de Utrera**, one of the great voices of "pure flamenco", was born in 1923 into a gypsy family in Utrera, one of the *cantaora* centres. She was the grand-daughter of the legendary singer "Pinini", who had created her own individual flamenco forms, and with her younger sister Bernarda, also a notable singer, inherited their flamenco with their genes. Even the members of Ketama, the Madrid-based flamenco-rock group, come from two gypsy clans – the Sotos and Carmonas.

Although flamenco's exact origins are obscure, it is generally agreed that its "laws" were established in the nineteenth century. Indeed, from the mid-nineteenth century into the early twentieth, flamenco enjoyed a legendary "**Golden Age**", the tail-end of which is preserved on some of the earliest 1930s recordings. The original musicians found a home in the *café cantantes*, traditional taverns which had their own group of performers (*cuadros*). One of the most famous was the *Café de Chinitas* in Málaga, immortalized by the Granada-born poet García Lorca. In his poem *A las cinco de la tarde* (At five in the afternoon), Lorca claimed that flamenco is deeply related to bullfighting, not only sharing root emotions and passions, flashes of erratic genius, but because both are possible ways to break out of social and economic marginality.

Just such a transformation happened in 1922 when the composer Manuel de Falla, the guitarist Andrés Segovia and the poet García Lorca were present for a legendary *Concurso de Cante Jondo*. A gypsy boy singer, **Manolo Caracol**, reportedly walked all the way from Jerez and won the competition with the voice and flamboyant personality that were to make him a legend throughout Spain and South America. The other key figure of this period, who can be heard on a few recently re-mastered recordings, was **Pastora Pavón**, known as *La Niña de Los Peines*, and popularly acclaimed as the greatest woman flamenco voice of twentieth century.

In addition to *café cantantes*, flamenco surfaced – as it does today – at fiestas, in bars or *tablaos*, and at *juergas*, informal, private parties. The fact that the Andalucian public are so knowledgeable and demanding about flamenco means that musicians, singers and dancers found even at the most humble local club or festival are usually very good indeed.

THE ART OF FLAMENCO

It is essential for an artist to invoke a response, to know they are reaching deep into the emotional psyche of their audience. They may achieve the rare quality of ***duende*** – total emotional communication with their audience, and the mark of great flamenco of whatever style or generation. *Duende* is an ethereal quality: moving, profound even when expressing happiness, mysterious but nevertheless felt, a quality that stops listeners in their tracks. And many of those listeners are intensely involved, for flamenco is not just a music, for many it is a way of life, a **philosophy** that influences daily activities. A flamenco is not only a performer but anyone who is actively and emotionally involved in the unique philosophy.

For the musicians, this fullness of expression is integral to that art, which is why for as many famous names as one can list, there are many, many other lesser-known musicians whose work is startlingly good. Not every superb flamenco musician gets to be famous, or even to record, for flamenco thrives most in **live performance**. Exhilarating, challenging and physically stimulating, it is an art form which allows its exponents huge scope to improvize while obeying certain rules. Flamenco guitarist Juan Martín has remarked that "in microcosm it imitates Spanish society – traditional on the outside but, within, incredible anarchy".

There is a **classical repertoire** of more than sixty flamenco songs (*cantes*) and dances (*danzas*) – some solos, some group numbers, some with instrumental accompaniment, others a capella. These different forms of flamenco are grouped in "families" according to more or less common melodic themes. The most common beat cycle is twelve – like the blues. Each piece is executed by juxtaposing a number of complete musical units called *coplas*. Their number varies depending on the atmosphere the *cantaor* wishes to establish and the emotional tone they wish to convey. A song such as a *cante por solea* may take a familiar 3/4 rhythm, divide phrases into 4/8 measures, and then fragmentally sub-divide again with voice ornamentation on top of that. The resulting complexity and the variations between similar phrases constantly undermines repetition, contributing greatly to the climactic and cathartic structure of each song.

SONGS AND SINGER

Flamenco **songs** often express pain, and with a fierceness that turns that emotion inside out. Generally, the voice closely interacts with improvizing guitar (*toque*), the two inspiring each other, aided by the *jaleo*: the hand-clapping *palmas*, finger-snapping *palillos* and shouts from participants at certain points in the song. This *jaleo* sets the tone by creating the right atmosphere for the singer or dancer to begin, and bolsters and appreciates the talent of the artist as they develop the piece.

Aficionados will shout encouragement, most commonly "¡Olé!" – when an artist is getting deep into a song – but also a variety of stranger-sounding phrases. A stunning piece of dancing may, for example, may be greeted with "¡Viva la maquina escribir!" (long live the typewriter), as the heels of the dancer move so fast they sound like a machine; or the cry may be "¡Agua!" (water), for the scarcity of water in Andalucía has given the word a kind of glory.

It is an essential characteristic of flamenco that a singer or dancer takes certain risks, by putting into their performance feelings and emotions which arise directly from their own life experience, exposing their own **vulnerabilities**. Aficionados tend to acclaim more a voice that gains effect from surprise and startling moves than one governed by recognized musical logic. Vocal prowess or virtuosity can be deepened by sobs, gesticulation and an intensity of expression that can have a shattering effect on an audience. Thus pauses, breaths, body and facial gestures of anger and pain transform performance into **cathartic events**. *Siguiriyas* which date from the Golden Age, and whose theme is usually death, have been described as cries of despair in the form of a funeral psalm. In contrast there are many songs and dances such as *tangos*, *sevillanas* and *fandangos* which capture great **joy** for fiestas.

The *sevillana* originated in medieval Sevilla as a spring country dance, with verses improvized and sung to the accompaniment of guitar and castanets (which are rarely used in other forms of flamenco). **El Pali** (Francisco Palacios), who died in 1988, was the most well-known and prolific *sevillana* musician, his unusually gentle voice and accompanying strummed guitar combining an enviable musical pace with a talent for composing popular poetic lyrics. In the last few years dancing *sevillanas* has become popular in bars and clubs throughout Spain, but their great natural habitats are **Sevilla's April Feria** and the annual pilgrimage to **El Rocío**. It is during the Sevilla *feria* that most new recordings of *sevillanas* emerge.

Among the best contemporary singers are the aforementioned **Fernanda and Bernarda de Utrera**, **Enrique Morente**, **El Cabrero**, **Juan Peña El Lebrijano**, the **Sorderas**, **Fosforito**, **José Menese** and **Carmen Linares**. However, one of the most popular and commercially successful singers of modern flamenco was the extraordinary **El Camarón de la Isla**, (the "shrimp" of the "isle" de León near his Cádiz home), who died in 1992.

Collaborating with the guitarists Paco and Pepe de Lucía, and latterly, Tomatito, Camarón raised **cante jondo**, the virtuoso "deep song", to a new art. His high-toned voice had a corrosive, rough-timbred edge, cracking at certain points to release a ravaged core sound. His incisive sense of rhythm, coupled with almost violent emotional intensity, made him the quintessential singer of the times.

FLAMENCO GUITAR

The flamenco performance is filled with pauses. The singer is free to insert phrases seemingly on the spur of the moment. The **guitar accompaniment**, while spontaneous, is precise and serves one single purpose – to mark the *compas* (measures) of a song and organize rhythmical lines. Instrumental interludes which are arranged to meet the needs of the *cantaor* (as the creative singer is called) not only catch the mood and intention of the song and mirror it, but allow the guitarist to extemporize what are called *falsetas* (short variations) at will. When singer and guitarist are in true rapport the intensity of a song develops rapidly, the one charging the other, until the effect can be overwhelming.

The flamenco **guitar** is of lighter weight than most acoustic guitars and often has a pine table and pegs made of wood rather than machine heads. This is to produce the preferred bright responsive sound which does not sustain too long (as opposed to the mellow and longer sustaining sound of classical guitar). If the sound did sustain, particularly in fast pieces, chords would carry over into each other.

The guitar used to be simply an accompanying instrument – originally the singers themselves played – but at the end of last century and in the early decades of this it began developing as a **solo** form, absorbing influences from classical and Latin American traditions. The greatest of these early guitarists was **Ramón Montoya**, who revolutionized flamenco guitar with his harmonizations and introduced tremolo and a whole variety of arpeggios – techniques of right-hand playing. After him the revolution was continued by Sabicas and Niño Ricardo and Carlos Montoya. The classical guitarist **Andrés Segovia** was another influential figure; he began his career playing flamenco in Granada. Then in the 1960s came the two major guitarists of modern times, **Paco de Lucía**, of whom more later, and **Manolo Sanlucar**.

Solo guitarists, these days, have immediately identifiable sounds and rhythms: the highly emotive **Pepe Habichuela** and **Tomatito**, for example, or the unusual rhythms of younger players like **Ramón el Portugués**, **Enrique de Melchor** and **Rafael Riqueni**. Flamenco guitar has now consolidated its position on the world's great stages as one of the most successful forms of instrumental music.

NUEVO FLAMENCO

One of flamenco's great achievements has been to sustain itself while providing much of the foundation and inspiration for **new music** emerging in Spain today. In the 1950s and 1960s, rock'n'roll displaced traditional Spanish music, as it did indigenous music in many parts of the world. In the 1980s, however, flamenco re-invented itself, gaining new meaning and a new public through the music of Paco de Lucía, who mixed in jazz, blues and salsa, and, later, groups like Pata Negra and Ketama, who brought in more rock influences. Purists hated these innovations but, as José "El Sordo" (Deaf One) Soto, Ketama's main singer, explained, they were based on "the classic flamenco that we'd been singing and listening to since birth. We just found new forms in jazz and salsa: there are basic similarities in the rhythms, the constantly changing harmonies and improvizations. Blacks and gypsies have suffered similar segregation so our music has a lot in common."

Paco de Lucía, who made the first moves, is the best-known of all contemporary flamenco guitarists, and reached new audiences through his performance in Carlos Saura's films *Blood Wedding* and *Carmen*, along with the great flamenco dancers, Cristina Hoyos and Antonio Gades. Paco, who is a non-gypsy, won his first flamenco prize at the age of 14, and went on to accompany many of the great traditional singers, including a long partnership with Camarón de la Isla, one of the greatest collaborations of modern flamenco. He introduced new harmonies, chord structures, scales, open tunings and syncopation that initiated the most vital renaissance of *toque* since Ramón Montoya, a remarkable achievement considering the rigid and stylized nature of this most traditional of forms. He started forging new sounds and rhythms for flamenco following a trip to Brazil, where he fell in love with bossa nova, and in the 1970s he established a sextet with electric bass, Latin percussion, and, perhaps most shocking, flute and saxophone from Jorge Pardo. Paco has also introduced into Spanish flamenco the Peruvian **cajón**, a half-box resembling an empty drawer played by sitting straddled across the top; this reintroduced the sound of the foot of the dancer. Over the past twenty years he has

FLAMENCO DANCE

Most popular images of flamenco dance – twirling bodies in frilled dresses, rounded arms complete with castanets – are *sevillanas*, the folk dances performed at fiestas and, in recent years, on the disco and nightclub floor. "Real" flamenco dance is something rather different and, like the music, can reduce the onlooker to tears in an unexpected flash, a cathartic point after which the dance dissolves. What is so visually devastating about flamenco dance is the physical and emotional control the dancer has over the body: the way the head is held, the tension of the torso and the way it allows the shoulders to move, the shapes and angles of seemingly elongated arms, and the feet, which move from toe to heel, heel to toe, creating rhythms. These rhythms have a basic set of moves and timings but they are improvised as the piece develops and through interaction with the guitarist.

Flamenco dance dates back to about 1750 and, along with the music, moved from the streets and private parties into the *café cantantes* at the end of the nineteenth century. This was a great boost for the dancers' art, providing a home for professional performers, where they could inspire each other. It was here that legendary dancers like **El Raspao** and **El Estampio** began to develop the spellbinding footwork and extraordinary moves that characterizes modern flamenco dance, while women adopted for the first time the flamboyant *bata de cola* – the glorious long-trained dresses, cut high at the front to expose their fast moving ankles and feet.

Around 1910, flamenco dance had moved into Spanish theatres, and dancers like **La Niña de los Peines** and **La Argentina** were major stars. They mixed flamenco into programmes with other dances and also made dramatic appearances at the end of comic plays and silent movie programmes. **Flamenco opera** was soon established, interlinking singing, dancing and guitar solos in comedies with a local flamenco flavour. In 1915 the composer Manuel de Falla composed the first **flamenco ballet**, *El Amor Brujo* (Love, the Magician), for the dancer Pastora Imperio. **La Argentina**, who had established the first Spanish dance company, took her version of the ballet abroad in the 1920s, and with her choreographic innovations flamenco dance came of age, working as a narrative in its own right. Another key figure in flamenco history was **Carmen Amaya**, who from the 1930s to the 1960s took flamenco dance on tour around the world, and into the movies.

In the 1950s, dance found a new home in the *tablaos*, the aficionados' bars, which became enormously important as places to serve out a public apprenticeship. More recently the demanding audiences at local and national fiestas have played a part. Artistic developments were forged in the 1960s by **Matilde Coral**, who updated the classic dance style, and in the 1970s by **Manuela Carrasco**, who had such impact with her fiery feet movement, continuing a rhythm for an intense and seemingly impossible period, that this new style was named after her (*manuelas*).

Manuela Carrasco set the tone for the highly individual dancers of the 1980s and 1990s, such as **Mario Maya** and **Antonio Gades**. These two dancers and choreographers have provided a theatrically inspired staging for the dance, most significantly by extending the role of a dance dialogue and story – often reflecting on the potency of love and passion, their dangers and destructiveness.

Gades has led his own company on world tours but it is his influence on film which has been most important. He had appeared with Carmen Amaya in *Los Arañas* in 1963 but in the 1980s began his own trilogy with film-maker Carlos Saura: *Boda de Sangre* (Lorca's play, Blood Wedding), *Carmen* (a re-interpretation of the opera), and *El Amor Brujo*. The films featured Paco de Lucía and his band, and the dancers **Laura del Sol** and **Christina Hoyos** – one of the great contemporary dancers, who has herself created a superb ballet, *Sueños Flamencos* (Flamenco Dreams).

Aside from the great companies and personalities of flamenco dance, there are an enormous number of local dancers all over Andalucía, whose dancing brings flamenco to life, and whose moves can be sheer poetry.

worked with jazz-rock guitarists such as John McLaughlin and Chick Corea, while his own regular band, featuring singer Ramón de Algeciras, remains one of the most original and distinctive sounds on the flamenco scene.

Other artists experimented, too, throughout the 1980s. **Lolé y Manuel** updated the flamenco sound with original songs and huge success; **Jorge Pardo** followed Paco's jazz direction; **Salvador Tavora** and **Mario Maya** staged

DISCOGRAPHY

All recommendations below are available on CD.

CLASSIC FLAMENCO ANTHOLOGIES

Cante Flamenco live in Andalucía (Nimbus, UK).
Early Cante Flamenco – Classic Recordings from the 1930s (Arhoolie, USA).
Magna Antología del Cante Flamenco (Hispavox, Spain; 10 volumes).
Noches Gitanas (EPM, Spain; 4CDs).
Sevillanas: the soundtrack of Carlos Saura's film (Polydor, UK).
Various *Flamenco: The Rough Guide* (World Music Network).

INDIVIDUAL ARTISTS

Camarón de la Isla *Una leyenda flamenca, Vivire and Autorretrato* (Philips, Spain).
Agustín Carbonell Bola *Carmen* (Messidor, Spain).
Carmen Linares *La luna en el río* (Auvidis, Spain).
Duquende *Duquende y La Guitarra de Tomatito* (Nuevos Medios, Spain).
Federico García Lorca (piano) **y La Argentinita** (Hispavox, Spain).
El Indio Gitano *Nací gitano por la gracia de Dios* (Nuevos Medios, Spain).
Paco de Lucía y Paco Peña *Paco Doble* (Philips, Spain).
Enrique de Melchor *Cuchichi* (Fonodisc, Spain).
José Menese *El viente solano* (Nuevos Medios, Spain).
Moraíto *Morao y oro* (Auvidis, Spain).
Enrique Morente *Negra, si tú supieras* (Nuevos Medios, Spain).
Ramón el Portugués *Gitanos de la Plaza* (Nuevos Medios, Spain).
Tomatito *Barrio Negro* (Nuevos Medios, Spain).
Fernanda et Bernarda de Utrera *Cante Flamenco* (OCORA, France).

NUEVO FLAMENCO AND CROSSOVERS

Amalgama y Karnataka College of Percussion (Nuba, Spain).
Chano Domínguez *Chano* (Nuba, Spain).
Ray Heredia *Quien no corre, vuela* (Nuevos Medios, Spain).
Jazzpaña (Nuevos Medios, Spain).
Ketama *Canciones hondas* (Nuevos Medios, Spain) and *Ketama* (Hannibal, UK).
Lole . . . y Manuel (Gong Fonomusic, Spain).
Los Jóvenes Flamencos Vol I & II (Nuevos Medios, Spain/Rykodisc, UK).
Martirio *Estoy Mala* (Nuevos Medios, Spain).
Paco de Lucía Sextet *Solo Quiero Caminar* (Philips, Spain), *Live… One Summer Night* (Phonogram, UK), *Almoraima*, and *Siroco* (Polygram, Spain).
Juan Peña Lebrijano y Orquestra Andalusi de Tanger *Encuentros* (Ariola/Globestyle).
Paco Peña *Misa Flamenca* (Nimbus, UK).
Pata Negra *Blues de la Frontera* (Nuevos Medios, Spain/Hannibal, UK).
Radio Tarifa *Rumba argelina* (Música Sin Fin, Spain), *Temporal* (World Circuit).
Songhai: Ketama/Toumani Diabate/Danny Thompson (Nuevos Medios, Spain/Hannibal, UK).

GETTING STARTED

Juan Martín's Guitar Method (United Music Publishers). *Self-tuition flamenco guitar course with audio cassette of practice pieces.*
La Guitarra Flamenca (Flamenco Vision). *Self-tuition guitar course based on three videos.*

Many of the recordings recommended here can be obtained from El Mundo Flamenco, 62 Duke Street, London W1 (☎020/7493 0033; *www.btinternet.com/~londonguitarstudio*), who also stock flamenco guitars, videos, books, costumes and shoes and sell the quarterly *Flamenco International* magazine. Flamenco Connections, PO Box 76, Falls Church, VA 22046 (☎703/533-3215) does a similar job in the USA. A new online operation, Flamenco Store, also sells flamenco CDs, books, dancewear, shoes, guitars and lots more over the internet (*www.andalucia.com/flamenco*).

flamenco-based spectacles; and **Enrique Morente** and **Juan Peña El Lebrijano** both worked with Andalucian orchestras from Morocco, while **Amalgama** worked with south-ern Indian percussionists, revealing surprising stylistic unities. Another interesting crossover came with **Paco Peña**'s 1991 *Misa Flamenca* recording, a setting of the Catholic Mass to flamenco forms with the participation of established singers such as Rafael Montilla "El Chaparro" from Peña's native Córdoba, and a classical academy chorus.

The more commercially successful crossover with rock and blues, pioneered by **Ketama** and **Pata Negra**, has become known, in the 1990s, as **nuevo flamenco**. This "movement" is associated particularly with the label Nuevos Medios and in Andalucía, and also Madrid, where many of the bands are based, is a challenging, versatile and musically incestuous new scene, with musicians guesting at each others' gigs and on each others' records.

The music is now a regular sound at nightclubs, too, through the appeal of young singers like **Aurora**, whose salsa-rumba song "Besos de Caramelo", written by Antonio Carmona of Ketama, was the first 1980s number to crack the pop charts, and **Martirio** (Isabel Quinones Gutierrez), one of the most flamboyant personalities on the scene, who appears dressed in lace mantilla and shades, like a cameo from a Pedro Almodóvar film, and sings songs with ironical,

contemporary lyrics about life in the cities. In general, the new songs are more sensual and erotic than the traditional material, expressing a pain, suffering and love worth dying for.

Martirio's producer, **Kiko Veneno**, who wrote Camarón's most popular song, "Volando voy", is another artist who has brought a flamenco sensitivity to Spanish rock music, as has Rosario, one of Spain's top woman singers. Other contemporary bands and singers to look out for on the scene include **La Barbería del Sur** (who add a dash of salsa), **Wili Giménez** and **Raimundo Amador**, and **José El Francés**. In the mid-1990s **Radio Tarifa** emerged as an exciting group who started out as a trio, expanded to include African musicians, and whose output mixes Arabic and traditional sounds on to a flamenco base. Flamenco is one of the most powerful popular traditions of music to be found in Europe today, distinguished by its ability to renew itself constantly.

Jan Fairley

WILDLIFE

The incredible diversity of natural habitats, flora and fauna to be found in Andalucía makes it one of the most attractive destinations for wildlife enthusiasts in western Europe. With 82 protected areas, together accounting for almost 15,000 square kilometres – more than 17 percent of the region – the Junta de Andalucía has shown a dedication to environmental preservation unrivalled in Spain. It also produces a series of leaflets describing the wildlife of Andalucía's protected areas, which can be obtained from park offices and Turismos.

HABITATS

Andalucía lies at two major **geographical crossroads**: the meeting point of Africa and Europe, and the convergence of the Atlantic Ocean with the Mediterranean Sea at the Straits of Gibraltar. Andalucía also harbours a wide range of topographical and climatic conditions, with altitudes ranging from sea level to over 3700m, and precipitation from 170mm to over 2000mm (both the driest and the wettest places in Spain are found here).

In terms of habitats, Andalucía can be divided broadly speaking into coasts, arid lands, inland wetlands and mountains. West of Tarifa, the **Atlantic coast** is characterized by long, sandy beaches and extensive dune systems, while the relatively flat landscape means that the rivers have so little gradient in their lower

reaches that they are tidal for many kilometres upstream and generally form great marshes where they meet the sea. The mountains lying behind the **Mediterranean coast**, in contrast, give rise to long stretches of sea cliffs, while rivers here have steeper inclines, are faster-flowing and are thus less likely to form great estuarine marshes. The **arid lands** of Almería and eastern Granada, with as little as 170mm of precipitation per year and almost constant sunshine, are one of the driest regions in western Europe, with semi-desert landscapes more appropriate to Morocco.

Throughout Andalucía, a network of **inland wetlands** – permanent or seasonal, freshwater or saline, still or fast-flowing – provides oases for wildlife in a land where there is a pronounced summer drought. Many lie close to the **Straits of Gibraltar**, the primary bird migration route in the western Mediterranean, thus providing refuge for the millions of birds needing to rest and feed en route between Africa and Europe in spring and autumn.

Almost one-fifth of Andalucía is mountain; that is, lies above 1000m. Two great ranges dominate the landscape: the **Sierra Morena**, which separates Andalucía from the rest of Spain, and the **Cordillera Bética**, which runs in a northeasterly direction from Tarifa, continuing out under the Mediterranean to emerge later as the Balearic Islands. The **Sierra Nevada**, at the heart of the Cordillera Bética, possesses the Iberian peninsula's highest mountain – **Mulhacén**, at 3482m.

PLANTS

More than half of the **8000 species** of vascular plant known to occur in peninsular Spain and the Balearic Islands are found in Andalucía, including 152 species which are found nowhere else in the world; more than any European country except for Greece. Particular centres of endemism in Andalucía are the arid lands of Almería, the Sierras de Cazorla y Segura, the Serranía de Ronda and the Sierra Nevada.

Perhaps the most important botanical feature of Andalucía, however, is the **pinsapo forests** of the Serranía de Ronda. This tree, *Abies pinsapo*, is a species of fir which is thought to have arrived in Andalucía during the Quaternary, pushed south by the ice sheets, becoming isolated in a few mountain areas when the glaciers retreated. Although only six square kilometres of pinsapo forest remained in 1950, an intensive conservation programme has more than quadrupled this area today.

MAMMALS

Andalucía is home to 54 species of mammal, the most outstanding of which is the **pardel lynx**, unique to the Iberian peninsula. It is one of Europe's most endangered vertebrates, with a world population now estimated at only 600 individuals, 60 per cent of which live in Andalucía. However, in 1999 the Worldwide Fund for Nature severely censured the Spanish government for the inadequacy of its plans to protect the lynx. The primary enclaves for this magnificent feline are the Doñana National Park and the Sierra Morena. **Genets** and **Egyptian mongooses** are also widespread and abundant in Andalucía, although both are thought to have been introduced from North Africa in ancient times, with other common carnivores including wildcats, otters, polecats, beech martens, badgers and weasels. The main stronghold for the **wolf** in Andalucía is the Sierra Morena, which houses up to 75 individuals in small family groups; Sierra farmers angry at the wolf's protected status are now entitled to compensation if their livestock is attacked by wolves. The **Algerian hedgehog**, distinguished from its western European relative by its paler colouring, longer legs and larger ears, is another species of northwest African origin; it has tentatively established itself in a few places on the Iberian coast, particularly in eastern Andalucía. The most noteworthy large herbivore of Andalucía is the **Spanish ibex**, the most significant populations inhabiting the Sierras de Cazorla y Segura, the Sierra Nevada and the Serranía de Ronda, with satellite populations recently establishing themselves in some of the nearby ranges. **Mouflon**, originally from Corsica and Sardinia, have been introduced to several areas, notably the Sierras de Cazorla y Segura, as a game species.

BIRDS

Outstanding among the **wildfowl** of Andalucía is the **white-headed duck**, the western subspecies of which is confined to southern Spain and a small enclave in the Maghreb. Fifteen years ago the Spanish population was on the verge of extinction, but a phenomenal conservation effort

has resulted in a population of 545 birds today. Andalucía is also the European stronghold of the secretive **purple gallinule**, distinguished by its long red legs and metallic blue-purple plumage, while the Iberian population of the **collared pratincole** is practically the last one in Europe, a major breeding site being the Guadalquivir marshes.

Crested coots, marbled teal and ferruginous ducks are also virtually unknown as European breeding birds outside Andalucía, while the European stronghold of the greater **flamingo** is the salt-lake of Fuente de Piedra, in Málaga, where more than 14,000 pairs have gathered to breed in recent years, relegating the French Camargue to second place. The Spanish **imperial eagle**, Europe's most endangered raptor, is endemic to the Iberian peninsula. The world population of this bird is only 126 pairs, about a quarter of which are found in Andalucía, primarily in the Doñana National Park and the Sierra Morena. The Sierra Morena also contains the largest European enclave of **black vultures**, numbering over 70 breeding pairs.

REPTILES AND AMPHIBIANS

Some 25 species of **reptile** occur in Andalucía, with noteworthy species including the **chameleon**, confined to the coastal areas of Huelva, Cádiz and Málaga, and only found elsewhere in Iberia in the Portuguese Algarve. **Spur-thighed tortoises**, which are globally at risk from habitat loss and collecting, are found in northeastern Almería and Doñana; the only localities in the Iberian peninsula. **Spiny-footed lizards**, endemic to southern and central Iberia and northwest Africa, are extremely common in dry, sandy habitats, the young animals resplendent with bright red tails. By contrast, two much rarer Andalucian lizards are the Spanish algyroides, known only in a small area in the Sierras de Cazorla y Segura, and the Italian wall lizard, surprisingly present at Cabo de Gata, despite having a main area of distribution in Italy and the Balkans.

The peculiar **amphisbaenian**, like a fat pinkish earthworm, occupies an intermediate position between snakes and lizards. Although found throughout Andalucía, this subterranean creature is rarely seen, although it sometimes comes to the surface at night or after heavy rain. Confined to Iberia and northern Africa are the **false smooth snake**, identified by its dark hood, and **Lataste's viper**, distinguished from all other Iberian vipers by its distinct nose-horn, while the beautifully patterned **horseshoe whipsnake** has a similar distribution, but is also found in Sardinia.

Of the fifteen species of **amphibian** which occur in Andalucía, the most noteworthy are the sharp-ribbed salamander, a large warty creature up to 30cm long, which is found only in southern Iberia and Morocco; the tiny, orange-bellied Bosca's newt, confined to western Iberia and thus occurring only in Huelva and northern Sevilla in Andalucía; and the Iberian midwife toad, a southwest Iberian endemic, the males of which carry the egg-strings wound around their hind legs until they hatch.

BUTTERFLIES

Andalucía is home to many **butterflies** which occur only in the southern Iberian peninsula and North Africa, including the desert orange tip, Lorquin's and false baton blues, the Spanish fritillary and the Spanish marbled white. Yet others are true Spanish endemics, such as the Panoptes, Nevada and mother-of-pearl blues and the Nevada grayling. Several interesting butterflies are particularly associated with the Andalucian coast, including the extremely rare **Zeller's skipper**, recorded near Algeciras, as well as the more widespread pygmy and Mediterranean skippers. Several large and attractive vagrant species turn up sporadically from across the Atlantic, including the American painted lady, the milkweed, or monarch and the plain tiger.

WHEN AND WHERE TO GO

The Mediterranean habitats of Andalucía have a climate so mild that a visit at any time of year – even Christmas – will be rewarding for **wild flowers**. The arid lands of Almería are best seen in early spring, however, while the alpine flora of Sierra Nevada and other high mountain regions is not at its peak until summer.

Wetland birds are generally a spring and autumn proposition, although some of the rarer breeding species – purple gallinules, white-headed ducks, crested coots and spoonbills – are perhaps more obvious during the summer. Winter concentrations of wildfowl and waders sometimes number hundreds of thousands, especially in the larger wetlands, such as Doñana. **Raptors**

are best seen in late spring and early summer, when the adults must venture out continuously in search of food for their young. By this time too, the short-toed and booted eagles, Egyptian vultures and Montagu's harriers have arrived from Africa. Many of the smaller, colourful birds typically associated with Mediterranean scrub and forest are also summer visitors.

The **carnivores** are virtually impossible to see at any time of year, as most of them are secretive and nocturnal creatures, although the Egyptian mongoose is sometimes encountered trotting through the scrub in broad daylight. Ibex and mouflon are a different proposition altogether, being easily spotted at all times of year and often approached with relative ease.

Summer is best for the **snakes** and **lizards** of the region, although even in the depths of winter they will emerge on sunny days. Alpine **butterflies** generally appear only in late summer, but many species of the milder Mediterranean habitats have two broods a year and can be seen from early spring onwards.

MARISMAS DEL ODIEL

The **Marismas del Odiel** is an extensive wetland area consisting of a maze of islands, creeks, saltmarshes and salinas lying to the west of the Río Odiel where it flows into the Atlantic. Although immediately adjacent to the industrial port of Huelva, this *paraje natural* supports a rich and varied fauna.

More than 200 species of bird have been recorded here, with pride of place going to the 300-odd pairs of **spoonbills**, about 30 percent of the European population, which nest in the grassy marshes of the Isla del Enmedio; one of only three breeding sites in Europe. The Odiel marshes also support large colonies of purple and grey herons and little egrets, as well as hundreds of pairs of little terns and black-winged stilts. Concentrations of up to 2,000 **flamingos** are commonplace, particularly during the winter and on migration, when they are often accompanied by large numbers of common cranes, sanderling, avocets and curlews. To the west of the Odiel marshes, the coastal juniper forests of Punta Umbría are an important refuge for chameleons.

DOÑANA

One of the greatest of all European wetlands, the **Coto de Doñana** truly merits its reputation as a superb destination for wildlife enthusiasts. Spain's premier national park covers 500 square kilometres and is centred on the extensive marshes on the west bank of the Río Guadalquivir. It is almost completely surrounded by a *parque natural* known as the Entorno de Doñana, which acts primarily as a protective buffer zone against industrial pollution from the city of Sevilla and the mines of Huelva, but is also important for wildlife in its own right. A long-feared disaster finally occurred in 1998 when an upriver mining dam burst unleashing millions of tons of toxic waste, threatening the park and its wildlife (see p.291). At first sight a flat, monotonous landscape, the Doñana marshes are in fact highly diverse, consisting of **vetas**, raised areas which are rarely covered with water, **lucios**, great depressions, sometimes several kilometres long, which retain water until early summer, and **caños**, the reed-fringed channels which wind through the marshes, carrying water in all but the most extreme periods of drought. The coast of Doñana consists of a wide, sandy beach, backed by four parallel fronts of mobile **dunes** which are gradually advancing inland.

The park also contains large areas of *monte*: dense **Mediterranean scrublands**, dominated by species of Cistus, Halimium, thyme and rosemary. Spring-flowering bulbs include *Dipcadi serotinum*, looking rather like a dull brown bluebell, wild gladioli, irises and trident-shaped asphodels over a metre tall. The *monte* and dune chains also conceal numerous **lagoons**, whilst between the *monte* and the marshlands lies a unique transitional habitat known as the *vera*, its cork-oak studded pastures undoubtedly one of the most diverse ecosystems of the park.

The vertebrate populations of Doñana are almost without parallel in Spain, including eight species of fish, 31 reptiles and amphibians, 29 mammals and 125 breeding birds, with a further 125 species of bird utilizing the park during the winter and on migration. Among the **reptiles**, the most noteworthy species are the chameleon, spur-thighed tortoise, Montpellier and ladder snakes, Lataste's viper, ocellated and spiny-footed lizards, both European pond and stripe-necked terrapins and three-toed skinks, as well as the bizarre, wormlike amphisbaenian, while unusual **amphibians** include stripeless

tree-frogs, western spadefoots and sharp-ribbed salamanders.

The list of **mammals** is impressive indeed, topped by the pardel lynx, one of Europe's most endangered mammals, as well as other hunters such as badgers, otters, weasels, mongooses and genets. Wild boar, red deer and the introduced fallow deer are present in considerable numbers, particularly in the *monte*, but the most abundant herbivore is the rabbit, the main prey of the lynx.

Doñana harbours one of the largest populations of Spanish **imperial eagles** in the world (a recent census revealed a minimum of 16 pairs), as well as breeding populations of red and black kites, booted and short-toed eagles and hobbies. Azure-winged magpies, great grey and woodchat shrikes, nightingales, great spotted cuckoos and Scops owls breed in the monte, while the venerable cork oaks of the vera support mixed colonies of spoonbills, white storks, little and cattle egrets, and purple, grey, squacco and night herons.

The dunes, open grasslands and stunted halophytic vegetation of the dried-out marshes provide suitable nesting areas for lesser short-toed and Thekla larks, red-necked nightjars, stone curlews and pin-tailed sandgrouse, while the marshes support breeding black-winged stilts, avocets, slender-billed gulls, gull-billed, little and whiskered terns, purple gallinules and collared pratincoles, as well as many species of wildfowl, the most significant being large numbers of red-crested pochard, crested coot and marbled teal, with the rare ferruginous and white-headed ducks putting in a sporadic breeding appearance. Many other birds flock to the marshes in winter and on migration, including tens of thousands of greylag geese, pintails, teal, shovellers and black-tailed godwits, as well as lesser numbers of shelduck, wigeon, red-crested pochard, gadwall, common cranes, flamingos and waders.

BAHÍA DE CÁDIZ

The 100-square-kilometre *parque natural* of the **Bahía de Cádiz** encompasses a wide range of coastal habitats, including sand dunes, stone pine forests, sandy beaches, extensive intertidal saltmarshes, abandoned saltpans and small lagoons. Despite the proximity of the 400,000-plus inhabitants of Cádiz itself, the bay is a veritable paradise for **birds**, supporting one of the largest breeding colonies of little terns in Spain, as well as several hundred breeding pairs of black-winged stilts, avocets and Kentish plovers. Its proximity to the European-North African migration route is responsible for a number of more unexpected guests, including arctic skuas, red-breasted mergansers, razorbills and scoters.

The extensive stone pine forests, best preserved at La Algaida, close to Puerto Real, are renowned for their **chameleons**, many of which unfortunately meet their maker on the plethora of busy roads which ring the bay.

ACANTILADO Y PINAR DE BARBATE

With the exception of Gibraltar, the *parque natural* of the **Acantilado y Pinar de Barbate** is the only cliffed section on the Atlantic coast of Andalucía. The sheer walls of **Los Caños de Meca**, plunging over 80m into the sea, are topped by one of the most diverse and best conserved coastal plateau forests on the Andalucian shore, **El Pinar de la Breña**. Stone pines and junipers are interspersed with Mediterranean scrub, hosting barn owls, kestrels and buzzards, as well as a thriving population of chameleons. The isolation of the cliffs themselves has encouraged the establishment of a great colony of **cattle egrets**, numbering over 2500 pairs and unique on the Andalucian coast, as well as breeding peregrines, blue rock thrushes and rock doves.

SIERRAS DE LA PLATA Y RETÍN

These small sierras lie close to the coast between Barbate and Tarifa, close to the town of Zahara de los Atunes, where, in the 1960s, the first **white-rumped swifts** to breed in Europe were observed; curiously, this bird will only rear its young in the abandoned nests of red-rumped swallows.

The **vegetation** is primarily Mediterranean scrub, dominated by Kermes and cork oaks, lentisc, wild olives and dwarf fan palms, forming a mosaic with limestone grasslands that are a riot of colour in spring; some of the more eye-catching species are Spanish iris, Peruvian squill, wild tulip, palmate anemone and star of Bethlehem. Commonly seen **butterflies** include cleopatras, Moroccan orange tips, Spanish festoons and long-tailed blues plus the occasional monarch, a vagrant from North America.

The skies above the Sierras are rarely without the profile of **griffon vultures** riding the thermals – the precipitous cliffs, known locally as *lajas*, support dozens of pairs of nesting griffon vultures – but you can also expect to see Egyptian vultures, Montagu's harriers and peregrines. The Mediterranean scrub is home to a colourful array of smaller birds, including woodchat shrikes, hoopoes, Orphean warblers, rollers and golden orioles, while the drier areas support both great and little bustards, Calandra and crested larks, black-eared and black wheatears and Spanish sparrows.

PLAYA DE LOS LANCES

Close to Tarifa, on the Atlantic coast of Cádiz, lies the *paraje natural* of **Playa de los Lances**, a classic coastal site, comprising a long beach of fine white sands, a ridge of dunes and the marshlands of the Ríos Jara and Valle, both of which run parallel to the coast here for several kilometres.

The **beach flora** includes such gems as sea daffodil, cotton-weed, southern birdsfoot-trefoil and sea medick, while further inland, a mosaic of stone pine forests, dense Mediterranean scrub dominated by lentisc and dwarf-fan palms and dry grasslands covers the plains and hills of the Santuario valley.

Great flocks of **waders** visit the reserve in winter and on migration, the most commonplace being sanderling, dunlin, grey, ringed and Kentish plovers, turnstones, bar-tailed godwits and oystercatchers, as well as hundreds of the rare Audouin's gull. It is a particularly important migration stopover for thousands of white storks and black kites, particularly when bad weather prevents them from crossing the Straits, while ospreys too put in an occasional appearance. Little terns and Kentish plovers both breed in fair numbers on the beach and dunes, while the wealth of piscine life in the rivers and marshes attracts otters, the most characteristic mammal of the reserve.

PUNTA ENTINAS-SABINAR

The *paraje natural* of **Punta Entinas-Sabinar**, which extends along 15km of coast between the resorts of Almerimar and Roquetas in Almería, contains a wide range of habitats, including a sandy beach, littoral dunes clothed with Mediterranean scrub, the saltpan complex of Salinas Viejas and Salinas de Cerillos, and the lagoons of Punta Entinas, all of which are backed by the scarp of Los Alcores, itself a superb example of a raised beach.

Mammals recorded here include the garden dormouse and Mediterranean pine vole, the latter confined to the southern Iberian peninsula, while Lataste's viper is a noteworthy member of the reptilian fauna. But it is the birdlife of the reserve that is truly outstanding, the tally to date numbering almost 200 species.

Among the **breeding birds**, hundreds of pairs of stone curlews and lesser short-toed larks make use of the drier habitats, while the salinas attract post-nuptial concentrations of flamingos of up to 1000 birds, as well as red-crested pochard, cormorants, grey herons and avocets. May is a particularly good time to visit the reserve, affording the chance to see Montagu's harriers, collared pratincoles, Mediterranean and Audouin's gulls, sandwich and whiskered terns, fan-tailed and spectacled warblers and black-eared wheatears. Look out also for woodchat and great grey shrikes, red-necked nightjars, Thekla larks and Marmora's and Dartford warblers in the Mediterranean scrublands.

CABO DE GATA–NÍJAR

This *parque natural* in southern Almería extends over some 260 square kilometres of the volcanic headland known as **Cabo de Gata** and the steppes of the **Campo de Níjar**. Essentially an arid area with large expanses of semi-desert vegetation, it also includes a wide variety of coastal habitats, ranging from precipitous cliffs over 100m high to dunes, saltmarshes and salinas, as well as encompassing the marine ecosystem to a depth of 100m.

The sierra itself boasts important formations of **dwarf fan-palm**, Europe's only native species of palm, growing amid lentisc, holly oak, Mediterranean mezereon and wild olive, as well as extensive steppes dominated by drought-adapted shrubby thymes or the spiny, deciduous shrub Zizyphus lotus. Cabo de Gata–Níjar is home to many plants which occur nowhere else in the world, including the **snap-dragon** Antirrhinum charidemi, known locally as flor del dragon, which grows only on volcanic pinnacles in the sierra, as well as the **pink** Dianthus charidemi and the **toadflax** Linaria benitoi, which flowers only at the onset of the spring rains. Look out too for the short-stalked

clusters of mauve-striped white flowers of the endangered lily Androcymbium europaeum, also endemic to this part of Spain.

No fewer than 16 species of **reptiles** and **amphibian** are here, including Lataste's viper, Iberian wall lizards, confined to Iberia, northwest Africa and the western Mediterranean coast of France, and Italian wall lizards, a more easterly species which is found in only a handful of places in Spain. **Butterflies** of interest include desert orange tip and common tiger blue, both essentially African species whose only European populations are found in southern Spain.

Breeding **birds** of the saltmarshes include little terns, Kentish plovers, black-winged stilts and avocets, with Cetti's and great reed warblers in the reedbeds. Between June and September, 2000–3000 **flamingos** descend on the coastal areas to feed, particularly when other Andalucian sites have dried out, while wintering and passage birds on the coast include spoonbills, Audouin's gulls, shelduck and red-breasted mergansers. The sierra itself is renowned for its breeding **eagle owls**, **Bonelli's eagles** and **Montagu's harriers**, as well as rufous bushchats and red-necked nightjars, but it is the dry steppes of Níjar which are of supreme ornithological significance, supporting important nesting concentrations of little bustards, stone curlews, black-bellied sandgrouse, lesser short-toed larks and trumpeter finches. Perhaps the most noteworthy bird of Cabo de Gata–Níjar, however, is **Dupont's lark**, an essentially North African species which was only recently discovered as a breeding bird in Europe.

DESIERTO DE LAS TABERNAS

Immediately inland from Cabo de Gata, sandwiched between the Sierras Alhamilla and de los Filabres, lies one of the most spectacular landscapes in the Iberian peninsula: the arid lands of the **Desierto de las Tabernas**.

The vegetation of Tabernas consists mainly of **steppes**, dominated either by false esparto grass and Stipa tenacissima, or by stunted spiny bushes of Ziziphus lotus, the endemic crucifer Euzomodendron bourgaeanum, and aromatic thymes, or by salt-tolerant, often succulent, members of the goosefoot family, particularly Salsola genistoides and S. papillosa, both of which are endemic to southern Spain.

These arid lands are home to many plants which are found nowhere else in the world, including the **toadflax** Linaria nigricans, the **rockrose** Helianthemeum almeriense, and the **sea lavender** Limonium insignis, which flowers promptly in response to the first rains.

Reptiles are in their element here, the commonest species being ocellated and spiny-footed lizards and ladder snakes. Animals requiring greater humidity in order to survive, such as marsh frogs, natterjack toads, stripe-necked terrapins and viperine snakes, are found only in the seasonal creeks, or ramblas, which thread their way between the eroded hills and plateaux. The Desierto de las Tabernas is also one of the few places where both western and Algerian hedgehogs occur, the latter essentially a northwest African species, established in only a few places on the Spanish coast.

The **birdlife** of Tabernas is extremely diverse, with the soft, eroding cliffs formed by the meanders of the ramblas supporting breeding jackdaws, blue rock thrushes, crag martins, black wheatears, bee-eaters, rollers and alpine and pallid swifts. The steppes themselves support important populations of stone curlews, black-bellied sandgrouse, Thekla larks and black wheatears, as well as being one of the best places in Europe to see trumpeter finches.

AROUND TABERNAS

To the south of the Desierto de las Tabernas lies the 25km-long range of the **Sierra Alhamilla**, where, amid the dry, rocky outcrops, steep gullies and arid grasslands and scrub, you can hope to see little bustards, black-bellied sandgrouse, trumpeter finches, Thekla and Dupont's larks, the latter distinguished by their long, down-curved bills, as well as stone curlews and black wheatears galore.

To the west of Tabernas, in the eastern part of the province of Granada, two great semi-arid depressions also support important populations of steppe birds. The **Hoya de Baza** is largely dedicated to dry cereal croplands today, but nevertheless supports important breeding populations of little bustards, stone curlews, black-bellied sandgrouse and Dupont's and lesser short-toed larks, while the nearby **Hoya de Guadix** is formed predominantly of soft gypsum, carved by flash floods into steep-sided ravines.

Guadix is one of the best areas for observing dry grassland birds in Andalucía, its extensive steppes, cereal cultivations and patches of holm oak scrub providing the perfect habitat for hundreds of little bustards, stone curlews and black-bellied sandgrouse. Montagu's harriers, peregrines and hobbies hunt here by day, replaced by long-eared and eagle owls at dawn and dusk.

ZONAS HÚMEDAS DEL SUR DE CÓRDOBA

The **Zonas Húmedas del Sur de Córdoba** is a series of widely dispersed wetlands in the southern part of the province of Códoba. The six *reservas naturales* – three permanent and three seasonal **lagoons** – which make up the complex have a total area of over ten square kilometres; the reservoirs of Cordobilla and Malpasillo on the Río Genil, both *parajes naturales*, are also sometimes included.

The permanent lagoons are **Zóñar**, **Amarga** and **Rincón**, of which the largest and deepest is the Laguna de Zóñar, up to 8m deep. All are slightly brackish and contain abundant submerged vegetation as well as being surrounded by thick belts of peripheral vegetation – poplars, tamarisks, reeds and reedmace – up to 15m wide in places.

The abundance of submerged vegetable matter supports a wealth of breeding wildfowl, the most noteworthy of which is undoubtedly the **white-headed duck**; these wetlands are the main breeding area for this diminutive stifftail in Spain, with over 45 nesting pairs and winter concentrations of 100-plus birds. Red-crested pochard, pochard, little grebes, purple gallinules, little bitterns, great reed warblers and kingfishers also breed here. In winter and during migration periods, the resident birdlife of the permanent lagoons is swelled by the arrival of large numbers of tufted duck, shovellers, wigeon, teal and pintail, with greylag geese, scaup, shelduck and the rare ferruginous duck also putting in an occasional appearance.

All three permanent lagoons support interesting **reptiles and amphibians**, notably stripe-necked terrapins, grass and viperine snakes, painted frogs and sharp-ribbed salamanders. By contrast, the shallow seasonal lakes of **El Conde o Salobral**, **Los Jarales** and **Tíscar** contain notably saline waters and are surrounded by halophytic vegetation. During the summer these lagoons often dry out completely, such that their ornithological significance is largely concerned with wintering and passage birds. A visit after the autumn rains should turn up black-winged stilts, avocets, grey herons, red-crested pochard, shoveller and wigeon, as well as an occasional greylag goose, flamingo or shelduck. Great bustards are sometimes seen in the dry cereal croplands surrounding the Laguna del Conde o Salobral, while the Laguna de los Jarales, rather surprisingly, supports populations of apparently salt-tolerant natterjack toads, western spadefoots and painted and marsh frogs.

FUENTE DE PIEDRA

A little further south, in the north of Málaga, lies the *reserva natural* of **Fuente de Piedra**, a shallow, saline **lagoon** of endorreic origin; that is, it is the result of the accumulation of ground and surface water from the surrounding area and has no outlet. Some 6km long and 2.5km wide, Fuente de Piedra is the largest natural lake in Andalucía.

Salt-tolerant herbs and shrubs surround the lagoon and also thrive on the long banks which traverse the lake. It is these raised areas that support Fuente de Piedra's pride and joy: the largest breeding colony of **flamingos** in Europe, and the only regular nesting site on the continent, apart from the French Camargue. In 1991, more than 14,000 pairs of flamingos raised some 12,000 young at Fuente de Piedra. During the winter, when full, the lake covers an area of some 14 square kilometres, but during the summer it becomes little more than a glistening sheet of dried salts, although pumps installed in recent years ensure that sufficient water remains in the centre of the lake for the young flamingos to fledge. During times of low water, the adult flamingos disperse all over Andalucía in search of food, turning up hundreds of kilometres away at Doñana, the Odiel marshes and Cabo de Gata.

A freshwater channel surrounds the main lagoon, supporting a rich marsh vegetation and attracting **other wetland birds**: at least 20 pairs of marsh harriers, up to 200 pairs of the rare gull-billed tern, a few pairs of the equally rare slender-billed gull, black-winged stilts, avocets, red-crested pochard, gadwall, garganey and great crested and black-necked grebes all breed here. In the winter, look out for common cranes, as well as greylag geese and shelduck among the 50,000 wildfowl present, while in spring the lake becomes a focal point for thousands of black terns on migration.

The cereal fields and Mediterranean scrublands surrounding Fuente de Piedra are worth a look for crested larks, stone curlews, bee-eaters, great grey shrikes, hoopoes and pallid and alpine swifts in the summer.

LAGUNAS DE CÁDIZ

The **Lagunas de Cádiz**, which are scattered across the hinterland of the Bahía de Cádiz, are renowned for their important breeding populations of white-headed duck, crested coot and purple gallinules, all virtually unknown as European breeding birds outside Andalucía.

The most important lake in the complex is the **Laguna de Medina**, the largest in Cádiz. Like most of the lagoons it is surrounded by a thick belt of emergent vegetation, dominated by reeds, reedmace, rushes and stands of tamarisk, which grades into cereal cultivations interspersed with dense patches of Mediterranean scrub away from the shore. Here spring brings a flush of orchids into bloom, including the exotic sawfly, mirror, yellow bee and bumblebee orchids.

Other **breeding birds** of the Lagunas de Cádiz include black-necked grebes, red-crested pochard, black-winged stilts and Kentish plover, with the reedbeds attracting little bitterns, great reed and Cetti's warblers, marsh harriers and possibly spotted crakes.

The lagoons come into their own in the winter months and during migration periods, when thousands of ducks, coots and geese arrive, including greylag geese, wigeon, garganey, gadwall, pintail and such rarities as marbled teal and ferruginous duck. White storks, purple squacco and night herons, bitterns and little bitterns, spoonbills, flamingos and common cranes can be seen feeding here when the lagoons are full, as well as black and whiskered terns, collared pratincoles and an occasional osprey on migration.

SIERRA MORENA

The 500km-long ridge of the **Sierra Morena**, which virtually cuts Andalucía off from the rest of Spain, reaches a maximum altitude of only 1323m, comprising for the most part low, rounded hills, clothed with dense forests that are favoured by many animals not found elsewhere in the region.

Within Andalucía much of the Sierra Morena is protected by a series of *parques naturales*. At the western end, bordering Portugal and Extremadura, lie the **Sierra de Aracena y Picos de Aroche**, the **Sierra Norte** and the **Sierra de Hornachuelos**, while the eastern Sierra Morena holds the **Sierra de Cardeña–Montoro** and the adjacent **Sierra de Andúar**. In northern Jaén, the kilometre-deep river gorge of Despeñaperros – the only crossing point between Andalucía and the *meseta* in ancient times – is also a *parque natural*.

The vegetation of the Sierra Morena was originally composed of **Mediterranean forests** dominated by holm, Lusitanian and cork oaks, interspersed with wild olives, cistuses, lentisc, strawberry tree and myrtle; the best-preserved examples are found today in the Sierra de Andújar. Other woodland types are also present, however, such as the magnificent enclave of Spanish chestnuts which thrives around Galaroza and Fuenteheridos, in the Sierra de Aracena, and the rich gallery forests of alders, elms, ashes and willows which line many of the rivers of the Sierra. In the western Sierra Morena, extensive areas of the original Mediterranean forest have been converted to *dehesa* – the evergreen oak "parkland-and-pastures" which dominates much of southwestern Iberia – dedicated largely to cork and charcoal production and the rearing of black pigs, whose succulent, acorn-fed hams are famous worldwide. The *dehesa* grasslands are a riot of colour in spring, some of the more attractive species including Spanish bluebell, wild tulip, star-of-Bethlehem, tassel hyacinth, asphodels, Spanish iris, Barbary nut, peonies and palmate anemone.

The mammalian fauna of the Sierra Morena comprises good populations of **wild boar** and red and fallow **deer**, as well as all the Andalucian small carnivores: weasels, beech martens, polecats, badgers, mongooses, genets and wildcats, with otters particularly abundant along the Río de las Yeguas, which separates the Sierra de Cardeña-Montoro from Andújar. The Andalucian stronghold for the **wolf** is the eastern Sierra Morena, although it also strays westwards into the Sierra Norte, while the endangered **pardel lynx** is known to occur in the Sierras de Hornachuelos, Cardeña–Montoro and Andujar.

The Sierra Morena is also a superb locality for **birds of prey**, housing important populations of golden, Bonelli's, short-toed and booted eagles, griffon and Egyptian vultures and eagle owls, as well as a few pairs of Spanish imperial eagles. Here, too, you will find the most important population of **black vultures** in Andalucía, nesting in the tops of the ancient cork and holm oaks, with more than 30 pairs in the Sierra de Aracena and 20-plus pairs in the Sierra de Hornachuelos. The Sierra Morena is also the only place in Andalucía with breeding **black storks**.

SIERRA NEVADA

Almost 80km long and 15–30km wide, the **Sierra Nevada** is one of the best-known mountain ranges in Spain, not least for its highest peak, **Mulhacén**, which at 3482m is known colloquially as the "roof" of the peninsula. The southern foothills of the Sierra Nevada, the **Alpujarras**, have an almost tropical climate owing to their proximity to Africa, while the highest peaks – twelve of which are over 3000m – are snow-clad for up to nine months of the year. Composed mainly of mica schist, the Sierra Nevada is very different geologically from the nearby limestone ranges, which may account partly for the large number of endemic species found here.

A botanical enclave of supreme importance, the Sierra Nevada – soon to become Andalucía's second national park – houses almost **2000 species of vascular plant**, more than 70 of which are found nowhere else in the world. Most of the endemic species occur in the highest peaks, forming part of a unique snow-tolerant community whose members include the endangered daffodil *Narcissus nevadensis*, one of the first plants to flower in the spring, the white-flowered Nevada saxifrage (*Saxifraga nevadensis*), the wormwood *Artemisia granatensis*, found only above 3000m, glacier toadflax (*Linaria glacialis*), another endangered species which occurs at similar altitudes, the white-flowered buttercup *Ranunculus acetosellifolius*, distinguished by its arrow-shaped leaves and mauve sepals, and the cushion-forming, pinkish-flowered violet *Viola crassiuscula*.

The Sierra Nevada is also famed for its large number of endemic **butterflies**, including the subspecies of the Spanish brassy ringlet, found only above 2000m; *ssp. nevadensis* of the apollo, which can be seen in late summer at altitudes ranging from 700 to a phenomenal

3000m; and the Nevada blue, which flies between 2100 and 2400m, while the zullichi subspecies of the Glandon blue, perhaps **Iberia's rarest butterfly**, has only been found by a handful of specialists near Pico Veleta. The lower slopes of the Sierra Nevada have Lorquin's and zephyr blues, which also occur in the Sierra Morena.

Even among the larger animals, the diversity is incredible. Within the boundaries of the parque natural alone, you could find 35 mammals, 125 breeding birds and 29 reptiles and amphibians. The **Spanish ibex**, which almost became extinct here in the 1930s, now numbers more than 3000 individuals, but the largely treeless terrain is less favourable for other mammals; the pine plantations of the lower slopes support a few badgers, beech martens and wildcats. Breeding raptors include golden, Bonelli's, short-toed and booted eagles, goshawks and peregrines. Several hundred pairs of choughs nest around the high level cliffs, while the alpine grasslands are the only place where alpine accentors – undoubtedly the tamest high mountain birds – breed in the southern half of Spain. The approach into the Sierra Nevada via the Alpujarras will add some of the smaller and more colourful birds to your list, including hoopoes, bee-eaters, woodchat shrikes, black redstarts, black-eared wheatears and blue rock thrushes.

SIERRA DE MARÍA

At the eastern end of the **Cordillera Subbética** in Andalucía lies the *parque natural* of the **Sierra de María**, centred on the almost naked limestone outcrop of María (2045m). The lower slopes support extensive shady forests of aleppo and laricio pine, interspersed with relict Scots pines and small patches of junipers, maples and holm oak: home to wildcats, badgers and red squirrels, as well as eagle owls. Above the tree-line you should be able to spot golden, booted and short-toed **eagles** soaring on the thermals, as well as wallcreepers, peregrine falcons and alpine swifts. An interesting botanical locality, Sierra de María contains several endangered species, including the knapweeds Centaurea mariana and C. macrorrhiza, both of which are found only here and in the adjacent Sierra del Gigante in Murcia, and Sideritis stachydioides, a member of the mint family which is unique to María.

Sierra de Maria is also renowned for its **butterfly** fauna, particularly at high altitudes, including the Spanish argus, unique to Iberia, an endemic subspecies of apollo (*ssp. mariae*), and the Nevada grayling (also in the Sierra Nevada), represented in Spain by the subspecies *williamsi*; this species is otherwise found only in southern Russia, some 5000km distant.

SIERRAS DE CAZORLA, SEGURA Y LAS VILLAS

In the extreme northeast of Andalucía, in the province of Jaén, lies a series of deep valleys separated by parallel limestone ridges running in a northeast-southwesterly direction: the parque natural of the **Sierras de Cazorla, Segura y las Villas** (over 2000 square kilometres), the largest protected area in Andalucía. With average annual precipitation exceeding 2000mm, this is one of the rainiest places in Spain, and it is here that the headwaters of the great Río Guadalquivir rise. Originally one of Spain's foremost hunting reserves, the park has lost much of its native vegetation owing to extensive planting with aleppo, maritime and laricio pines, although the latter is a very ancient species which also occurs here naturally. Above the tree-line the vegetation is more or less still in a natural state, the predominant plants being stunted laricio pines and junipers and cushion-forming members of the pea family: purple-flowered hedgehog broom, yellow-flowered Echinospartium boissieri and white- or pink-flowered mountain tragacanth, as well as the spiny crucifer Ptilotrichum spinosum.

The **flora** of the Sierras de Cazorla, Segura y las Villas numbers some 1300 species, including more than 30 endemics, such as the pale blue columbine *Aquilegia cazorlensis* and the cranesbill *Geranium cazorlense*, neither of which was discovered until the 1950s. The stronghold for both species is the peak of Cabañas (2036m).

Other endemics are the insectivorous butterwort *Pinguicula vallisneriifolia*, an endangered species whose bluish-white flowers are only found on damp, shady limestone cliffs, and the smallest Iberian narcissus – a tiny hoop-petticoat daffodil which goes under the name of *Narcissus hedreanthus* – as well as the largest, the 1.5m *N. longispathus*. The carmine-flowered Cazorla violet (*Viola cazorlensis*), a rare species which flowers towards the end of May, also occurs in the nearby Sierra Mágina.

The park is also home to more than 140 species of bird and is an important refuge for **raptors**. Griffon vultures and booted eagles nest in large numbers (the lammergeier, or bearded vulture, is now believed to be extinct here as a breeding bird), as well as a few pairs of Egyptian vultures, golden, Bonelli's and short-toed eagles, peregrine falcons, hobbies and goshawks. At dusk look (or listen) out for eagle, Scops and tawny owls in the forests.

Red and fallow **deer** and **mouflon** were introduced as game species during the park's time as a game reserve, but the outstanding large herbivore is undoubtedly the **Spanish ibex**, which inhabits the rocky pastures above the tree-line. Unfortunately, in 1987 the Cazorla ibex became infected with mange, which wiped out almost 90 per cent of the population, but it is on the increase again today.

Mammalian **predators** include wildcats, genets, beech martens and polecats, with pardel lynx reputed to frequent the Segura forests, while otters occur on all the major rivers. Greater white-toothed shrews, an endemic subspecies of red squirrel (*ssp. segurae*) and garden dormice provide the main diet for the forest carnivores, since rabbits and hares are both uncommon here. The tiny Spanish algyroides, sometimes called Valverde's lizard, is endemic to the Sierras de Cazorla y Segura, where it inhabits damp rock-strewn habitats; it was only discovered in 1957 and can be distinguished by its coffee-coloured back, usually with a narrow black vertebral stripe, and distinct collar. Other **reptiles** of interest include Lataste's viper, horseshoe whipsnake, ladder snake, amphisbaenian, Bedriaga's skink, Iberian wall lizard and stripe-necked terrapin. The more notable **butterflies** of the park include the mother-of-pearl blue and Spanish argus, both of which are unique to Spain, but they are outshone by an endemic subspecies of the Spanish moon moth (*ssp. ceballosi*), a pale green and bronze beauty, a hand's span across, which occurs only in pine forests in Spain and parts of the French Alps.

SIERRA MÁGINA

At the heart of the Cordillera Subbética lies the *parque natural* of the **Sierra Mágina**, centred on the 2167m peak of Mágina itself. Above the tree-line is a landscape dominated by cushion-forming species such as hedgehog broom, junipers and the prickly crucifer *Ptilotrichum spinosum*, domain of Spanish ibex, blue rock thrush, choughs and alpine swifts, while golden and Bonelli's eagles soar overhead.

The middle zone is occupied by fairly humid deciduous **Mediterranean forest**, with Montpellier maple and Lusitanian oak, Spanish barberry and St Lucie's cherry, haunt of wild boar and small predators such as wildcats, beech martens and weasels, although you're more likely to see one of the recently introduced red deer. Short-toed treecreepers, crested tits and goshawks are the most typical birds to look for at this level.

The lowest levels are clothed with the typical **evergreen forests** and scrub of the region, characterized by holly and holm oaks, prickly juniper and Mediterranean mezereon. Although rarely seen, polecats, genets and badgers favour the dense vegetation, with Moorish geckoes, ocellated and Iberian wall lizards, and ladder and Montpellier snakes frequenting the more open areas. Some of the more interesting vascular plants of the Sierra Mágina limestone include the Iberian endemic *Lonicera arborea*, an unusual honeysuckle in that it takes the form of a small tree rather than a climber, the red-berried mistletoe *Viscum cruciatum*, and several southern Iberian endemics: the Cazorla violet *Viola cazorlensis*, the dwarf daffodil *Narcissus cuatrecasasii* and the yellow-flowered, shrubby kidney vetch *Anthyllis ramburii*. The gromwell *Lithodora nitida*, which grows between the cushions of hedgehog broom and *Echinospartium boissieri*, is an endangered species unique to Mágina.

EL TORCAL DE ANTEQUERA

In the centre of the province of Málaga, just a few kilometres south of Fuente de Piedra, lies **El Torcal de Antequera**, a remarkable landscape resembling a petrified city, and considered to be one of the best karstic phenomena in southern Europe.

The fluted and scalloped limestone turrets are dotted with **rock-plants** such as the endemic saxifrage *Saxifraga biternata*, Antequera toadflax, which is also found in the Serranía de Ronda, the yellow violet *Viola demetria*, with flowers often only millimetres across, and the glaucous-leaved *Rupicapnos africana*, a bizarre member of the poppy family. Grassy areas between the pillars are a paradise for spring-flowering **orchids**, including many members of the genus Ophrys: yellow bee, bumblebee, brown bee, mirror, sawfly and woodcock orchids, to mention but a few.

From the top of El Torcal, at 1369m, the view over the surrounding countryside is spectacular, as well as offering the possibility of spotting a passing griffon or Egyptian vulture, or short-toed or Bonelli's eagle.

SERRANÍA DE RONDA

The westernmost massif of the Cordillera Subbética is the **Serranía de Ronda**, which straddles the borders of Cádiz and Málaga. The eastern part of this huge limestone range coincides with the *parque natural* of the **Sierra de las Nieves**, a formidable landscape riddled with deep gorges and vertiginous cliffs, while the western massifs lie within the *parque natural* of the **Sierra de Grazalema** one of southern Spain's prime wildlife sites, also renowned for being the rainiest place in Iberia. The vegetation is predominantly Mediterranean evergreen and deciduous woodlands and low scrub, interspersed with extensive dry pastures, nibbled to the roots by wild and domestic herbivores alike, but studded with rocky outcrops where huge flowering clumps of saxifrages, catchflies and stonecrops thrive by virtue of their inaccessibility. More than **1300 species of vascular plant** have been recorded in the Serranía de Ronda, among the more eye-catching being six daffodils, including the endangered *Narcissus baeticus*, seven irises and 27 orchids. Several species are found nowhere else in the world, such as the delicate orange-red poppy *Papaver rupifragum*, the toadflax *Linaria platycalyx* and the endangered *Merendera androcymbioides*, a member of the lily family. The outstanding botanical feature of the Serranía de Ronda, however, is the **pinsapo**; a species of fir which is found nowhere else in the world. Although the largest forests lie in the Sierra de las Nieves, the more accessible examples occupy the northern slopes of Grazalema's Sierra del Pinar.

Over 200 species of vertebrates are known to occur in the Serranía de Ronda, 40 of which are mammals, including several thriving populations of Spanish ibex, roe and red deer and small carnivores such as genets, mongooses, wildcats, badgers and otters. The cave system of Hundidero-Gata houses more than 100,000 **Schreiber's bats** in winter: one of the largest concentrations of hibernating bats in Europe.

The birds of prey are outstanding here, the Serranía being one of the primary breeding areas for **griffon vultures** in Europe. Bonelli's, golden, short-toed and booted eagles are all common here, as well as Egyptian vultures, goshawks, peregrines and eagle owls. The rock-bird community includes choughs, alpine swifts, black wheatears and blue rock thrushes, as well as a colony of the rare white-rumped swift.

LOS ALCORNOCALES

Immediately south of the Sierra de Grazalema lies a range of low, forested sandstone hills that extends almost to Tarifa. Known as **Los Alcornocales**, it houses **one of the largest cork-oak forests** in the world. The vegetation here is a superb example of the original Iberian forests, comprising jungle-like, thick forests of massive Lusitanian and cork oaks and wild olives, some of which are thought to be over 1000 years old. Laurels and rhododendrons also thrive here, relics of the Tertiary semitropical flora that was once widespread in Europe but has virtually disappeared today as a result of climatic change. These forests are the haunt of the southern-most population of roe deer in Europe, as well as of red deer, genets, mongooses and wildcats. Golden eagles, griffon vultures and eagle owls are the commonest birds of prey, while a handful of black vultures nest in the ancient cork oaks and olives.

Teresa Farino

BOOKS

The listings below represent a highly selective reading list on Andalucía and matters Spanish, especially in the sections on history. Most titles are in print, although we've included a few older classics, many of them easy enough to find in second-hand bookshops and libraries.

Two reliable specialist sources in the UK for out-of-print books on all aspects of Spain are Keith Harris Books, PO Box 207, Twickenham TW2 5BQ (☎020/8898 7789, fax 8898 8812; *www.books-on-spain.com*), and Paul Orssich, 2 St Stephens Terrace, London SW8 1DH (☎020/7787 0030, fax 7735 9612; *www.orssich.com*). For all books in print, publishing details are in the form (UK publisher/US publisher), where both exist; if books are published in one country only, this follows the publisher's name (eg Serpent's Tail, UK). University Press is abbreviated as UP.

IMPRESSIONS, TRAVEL AND GENERAL ACCOUNTS

THE BEST INTRODUCTIONS

David Baird *Inside Andalusia* (Lookout, Málaga). A book that grew out of the author's series of articles published in *Lookout* magazine. Anecdotal yet perceptive overview of the region with plenty of interesting and offbeat observations and glossy illustrations. The same author's *Excursions in Southern Spain* (Ediciones Santana) is a drivers' guide to Andalucía displaying the same erudition.

Ian Gibson *Fire in the Blood: the New Spain* (Faber/BBC, UK). Gibson is a Madrid-based

writer, resident since 1978, and a Spanish national since 1984. He is a passionate enthusiast and critic of Spain and the Spanish, both of which he gets across brilliantly in this 1993 book – the accompaniment to a gripping TV series – in all their mass of contradictions, attitudes, obsessions, quirks and everything else. Hugely recommended with strong pieces on Andalucía, but did receive flak from outraged Spanish reviewers.

John Hooper *Spaniards: A Portrait of the New Spain* (Penguin, UK/US). Excellent, insightful portrait of post-Franco Spain and the new generation by *The Guardian's* former Spanish correspondent. Although it has only passing references to Andalucía, along with Ian Gibson's book (above), this is the best possible introduction to contemporary Spain.

Michael Jacobs *Andalusia* (Pallas Athene, UK/US). Well-crafted, opinionated and wide-ranging introduction to Andalucía. Covers everything from prehistory to the Civil War and manages to cram in perceptive pieces on flamenco, gypsies and food and drink. A gazeteer at the back details major sights. Revised and updated in 1998, this remains the best single-volume introduction to the region.

Allen Josephs *White Wall of Spain* (Iowa State UP, US). Intelligent series of essays on the mysteries of Andalucian folk culture from the origins of flamenco to the significance of Semana Santa and bullfights by the president of the Ernest Hemingway Foundation.

RECENT TRAVELS AND ACCOUNTS

Alastair Boyd *The Sierras of the South: Travels in the Mountains of Andalusia* (Collins, UK). A sensitively worked portrait of the Serranía de Ronda which describes one Englishman's continuing love affair with a region he knew as home for twenty years. His earlier *The Road from Ronda* (Collins, UK) is a Sixties' view of the same landscape – the peasants are still struggling.

Sarah Jane Evans *Seville* (Sinclair-Stevenson, UK). One of a number of books released to coincide with Sevilla's new-found popularity in the wake of Expo '92 exposure, this is more thorough than most and provides a useful, if sometimes rather jejune, introduction to the city.

David Gilmour *Cities of Spain* (John Murray/ Ivan R Dee). A modern cultural portrait of Spain which attempts to describe the country's history through portraits of selected cities. Very much in the old tradition, it is a little fogeyish at times but excellent, nonetheless, in its evocation of history, especially on the Moorish cities of Andalucía – though curiously not Granada.

Adam Hopkins *Spanish Journeys: A Portrait of Spain* (Penguin, UK). Published in 1993, this is an enjoyable and highly stimulating exploration of Spanish history and culture, weaving its considerable scholarship in an accessible and unforced travelogue form, and full of illuminating anecdotes.

Nicholas Luard *Andalucía – A Portrait of Southern Spain* (Century, UK). English writer and naturalist Luard went off to live in Andalucía with his cookery-writer wife and kids for a decade which spanned the end of dictatorship and the early post-Franco years. The result is a closely observed and well-written account of the passing of the seasons in an isolated valley in the Campo de Gibraltar.

Peter B. Meyer *A True Story About Doing Business in Spain* (Avon Books, UK). This quirkily written tale of a Dutch businessman's adventures setting up enterprises in Spain features encounters with corrupt bureaucracy, knavish builders, yacht and car thieves, shifty lawyers, crooked business partners and a parade of police and politicos straight out of central casting. A sometimes skewed, always fascinating and often hair-raising insider's view of Spanish business life.

Chris Stewart *Driving Over Lemons* (Sort Of Books, UK). A contributor to this guide ploughs the same furrow as Luard (above) only this time in Granada, where he describes – often with humour – his move with family to an Alpujarran farmhouse and the numerous adventures involved in setting up house there.

Ted Walker *In Spain* (out of print). The poet Ted Walker has lived and travelled in Spain on and off since the 1950s. This is a lyrical and absorbing account of the country and people, structured around his various sorties, a couple of them in Andalucía.

EARLIER 20TH-CENTURY WRITERS

Gerald Brenan *South From Granada* (Penguin/Cambridge UP) and *The Face of Spain* (Penguin, UK). *South From Granada* is an enduring classic. Brenan lived in a small village in Las Alpujarras in the 1920s, and records this and the visits of his Bloomsbury contemporaries Virginia Woolf, Lytton Strachey and Bertrand Russell. *The Face of Spain* is a later collection of highly readable travel writings gathered on a trip through Franco's Spain in 1949 with a substantial chunk devoted to Andalucía.

Penelope Chetwode *Two Middle-Aged Ladies in Andalucía* (Century, UK). Poet John Betjeman's wife took to the roads of Andalucía with another middle-aged lady – her horse. A paean to "picturesque poverty", this is Southern Spain seen from a quaintly English perspective.

Nina Epton *Andalusia* (Weidenfeld & Nicolson, UK). Sixties portrait of the region by a friend of Gerald Brenan. Contains interesting vignettes on people and places immediately prior to the arrival of mass tourism.

Laurie Lee *As I Walked Out One Midsummer Morning* (Penguin, UK/US), *A Rose For Winter* (Penguin, UK), *A Moment of War* (Penguin/New Press). *Midsummer Morning* is the irresistibly romantic account of Lee's walk through Spain – from Vigo to Málaga – and his gradual awareness of the forces moving the country towards Civil War. As an autobiographical account, of living rough and busking his way from the Cotswolds with a violin, it's a delight; as a piece of social observation, painfully sharp. In *A Rose For Winter* Lee describes his return, twenty years later, to Andalucía, while in *A Moment of War* he looks back again to describe a winter fighting with the International Brigade in the Civil War – an account by turns moving, comic and tragic.

Rose Macaulay *Fabled Shore* (out of print). The Spanish coast as it was in 1949 (read it and weep), travelled and described from Catalunya to the Portuguese Algarve. More focused on culture than people.

James A. Michener *Iberia* (Corgi/Crest). A bestselling, idiosyncratic and encyclopedic compendium of interviews and impressions of Spain on the brink – in 1968 – looking forward to the post-Franco years. Fascinating, still.

Jan Morris *Spain* (Penguin/Prentice-Hall). Morris wrote this in six months in 1960, on her (or, at the time, his) first visit to the country. It is an impressionistic account – good in its sweeping control of place and history, though prone to see everything as symbolic. The updated edition is plain bizarre in its ideas on Franco and dictatorship – a condition for which Morris seems to believe Spaniards were naturally inclined.

Walter Starkie *Don Gypsy* (out of print). The tales of a Dublin professor who set out to walk the roads of Spain and Andalucía in the 1930s with only a fiddle for company. The pre-Civil War world – good and bad – is astutely observed and his adventures are frequently amusing. Like Borrow earlier, he fell for the gypsies and became an expert on their culture.

J. B. Trend *Spain from the South* (Darf, UK). A classic look at the south in the 1920s by a well-travelled Hispanist who intermingles perceptive observations on the region's history, culture and landscape with shrewd and entertaining sketches of the contemporary scene.

OLDER CLASSICS

George Borrow *The Bible in Spain* and *The Zincali* (both out of print). On first publication in 1842, *The Bible in Spain* was subtitled by Borrow "Journeys, Adventures and Imprisonments of an English-man"; it is one of the most famous books on Spain – slow in places but with some very amusing stories. *Zincali* is an account of the Spanish gypsies, whom Borrow got to know pretty well and for whom he translated the Bible into *gitano*.

Richard Ford *A Handbook for Travellers in Spain and Readers at Home* (Centaur Press/Gordon Press); *Gatherings from Spain* (out of print). *The Handbook*, first published in 1845, must be the best guide ever written to any country and stayed in print as a Murray's Handbook (one of the earliest series of guides) well into this century. Massively opinionated, it is an extremely witty book and in its British, nineteenth-century manner, incredibly knowledgeable and worth flicking through for the proverbs alone. Copies of Murray's may be available in second-hand bookstores – the earlier the edition the purer the Ford. The *Gatherings* is a filleted – but no less entertaining – abridgement of the Handbook produced "for the ladies" who were not expected to be able to digest the original.

Washington Irving *Tales of the Alhambra* (originally published 1832; abridged editions are on sale in Granada). Half of Irving's book consists of oriental stories, set in the Alhambra; the rest of accounts of his own residence there and the local characters of his time. A perfect read in situ. Irving also wrote *The Conquest of Granada* (1829; out of print), a description of the fall of the Nasrids.

ANTHOLOGIES

Jimmy Burns (ed) *Spain: A Literary Companion* (John Murray, UK). A good anthology, including worthwhile nuggets of most authors recommended here, amid a whole host of others.

Lucy McCauley *Travellers' Tales: Spain* (Travellers' Tales Inc., US). A wide-ranging anthology slanted towards more recent writing on Spain; includes strong pieces on Andalucía by many of the authors mentioned in this section.

David Mitchell *Travellers in Spain: an Illustrated Anthology* (Cassell, UK). A well-told story of how four centuries of travellers – and most often travel-writers – saw Spain. It's interesting to see Ford, Brenan, Laurie Lee and the rest set in context. Also published as *Here in Spain* (Lookout, Málaga) and widely available at bookshops in tourist areas.

CUSTOMS AND CULTURE

Carrie B. Douglass *Bulls, Bullfighting and Spanish Indentities* (Arizona UP, US). Anthropologist Douglass enters the *corrida* debate by first delving into the symbolism of the bull in the Spanish national psyche, and then examining the bullfight's role in some of the thousands of countrywide fiestas that support it.

Timothy Mitchell *Flamenco Deep Song* (Yale, UK/US). Diametrically opposed to Woodall's work (below), the author sets out to debunk the mystagogy of flamenco purists by arguing that they are shackling the form's development and ends up with an improbable defence of the Gipsy Kings. A well-researched and entertaining read whether or not you accept its iconoclastic premise.

Eamonn O'Neill *Matadors* (Mainstream, UK). Subtitled "a journey into the heart of modern bullfighting" this is part autobiographical travelogue, part sociological study of the role of bullfighting in modern Spain, throwing light on a peculiarly Iberian industry worth a billion dollars annually and employing a quarter of a million people.

Sarah Pink *Women and Bullfighting* (Berg, UK, US). Based on a doctoral thesis carrying out field research in Córdoba, this analysis of women in the ring also examines the reaction – frequently negative – that this phenomenon attracts from Spanish male society.

Paul Richardson *Our Lady of the Sewers* (Little Brown, UK). Presents an articulate and kaleidoscopic series of insights into rural Spain's customs and cultures, fast disappearing.

James Woodall *In Search of the Firedance: Spain through Flamenco* (Sinclair-Stevenson, UK). This is a terrific history and exploration of flamenco, and as the subtitle suggests it is never satisfied with "just the music" in getting to the heart of the culture.

HISTORY

GENERAL

Juan Lalaguna *A Traveller's History of Spain* (Windrush, UK). A lucid – and pocketable – background history to the country which spans the Phoenicians to Franco, Felipe González and the emergence of democratic Spain.

M. Vincent & R.A. Stradling *Cultural Atlas of Spain and Portugal* (Andromeda, UK). A deceptive, coffee-table format belies a formidable historical, artistic and social survey of the Iberian peninsula from ancient times to the present; excellent colour maps and well-chosen photos amplify the text.

EARLY, MEDIEVAL AND BEYOND

Manuel Fernández Álvarez *Charles V* (out of print); **Peter Pierson** *Philip II of Spain* (Thames & Hudson, UK). Good studies in an illustrated biography series.

James M. Anderson *Spain: 1001 Archaeological Sites* (Hale/Calgary UP). A good guide and gazetteer to 95 percent of Spain's archeological sites with detailed instructions of how to get there.

Henri Breuil *Rock Paintings of Southern Andalucía* (Oxford UP, UK). Published in 1929, this is still the definitive guide to the subject.

J.M. Cohen *The Four Voyages of Christopher Columbus* (Cresset Library, UK) The man behind

the myth; one of the best books on Columbus in English.

Roger Collins *Spain: An Archeological Guide* (Oxford UP, UK). Covering around 130 sites, temples, mosques and palaces dating from pre-history to the twelfth century, this book devotes more space per entry to maps, plans and data making it a more useful vade mecum to the major sites than Anderson's work (above).

Roger Collins *The Arab Conquest of Spain 710–97* (Blackwell, UK). Cogently argued and controversial study which documents the Moorish invasion and the significant influence that the conquered Visigoths had on the formative phase of Muslim rule by a scholar uniquely expert in both fields. Collins's *Visigothic Spain* (Blackwell) is a significant new companion volume to the above and his earlier *Early Medieval Spain 400–1000* (Macmillan, UK) takes a broader overview of the same subject.

John A. Crow *Spain: the Root and the Flower* (California UP, US/UK). Cultural/social history from Roman Spain to the present.

J.H. Elliott *Imperial Spain 1469–1716* (Penguin, US/UK). Best introduction to "the Golden Age" – academically respected and a gripping tale.

Maria Cruz Fernández Castro *Iberia in Prehistory* (Blackwell, UK) A major study of the Iberian peninsula prior to the arrival of the Romans which includes extensive coverage of early Andalucían sites such as Los Millares as well as the later Iberian settlements encountered by the Phoenicians and Greeks. This is the first volume of this publisher's important new series on the history of Spain from the prehistoric era through to the Civil War.

Richard Fletcher *Moorish Spain* (Weidenfeld & Nicolson/California UP). A fascinating, provocative and highly readable narrative with a suitably iconoclastic conclusion to the history of Moorish Spain. The best introduction to the subject.

L.P. Harvey *Islamic Spain 1250–1500* (Chicago UP, US/UK). Comprehensive account of its period – both the Islamic kingdoms and the Muslims living beyond their protection.

Henry Kamen *The Spanish Inquisition* (Mentor, US). Highly respected examination of the causes and effects of this grisly institution and the long shadow it cast across Spanish history and development. The same author's masterly

Spanish Inquisition: An Historical Revision (Weidenfeld & Nicolson, UK) returns to the subject in the light of more recent evidence and attempts to place the phenomenon in the context of Spanish history while his *Philip of Spain* (Yale UP, US/UK) is the first fully researched biography of Felipe II, the ruler most associated with the Inquisition.

S.J. Keay *Roman Spain* (British Museum Publications/California UP). Definitive survey of a neglected subject, well illustrated and highly readable.

Elie Kedourie *Spain and the Jews: the Sephardi Experience, 1492 and after* (Thames & Hudson, UK/US). A collection of essays on the three-million-strong Spanish Jews of the Middle Ages and their expulsion by the Catholic Kings.

John Lynch *Spain 1516–1598* (Blackwell, UK). New interpretation of Spain's rise to Empire with plenty of interesting detail on Andalucía's trading role – especially the cities of Sevilla and Cádiz – in the exploitation of the Americas. The same author's *Hispanic World in Crisis and Change 1598–1700* and *Bourbon Spain 1700–1808* (both Blackwell, UK) carry the story forward to the critical crossroads which determined Spain's future for the ensuing century and a half.

Bernard F. Reilly *The Contest of Christian and Muslim Spain* (Blackwell). A fascinating and detailed study of the stresses and strains of the crucial tenth and eleventh centuries when Christians, Muslims and Jews were locked in a struggle for supremacy on one hand and survival on the other, by an acknowledged expert on the subject.

John S. Richardson *The Romans in Spain* (Blackwell, UK). A new look at how Spain came to be a part of the Roman world which also examines the influences that flowed from Spain to Rome as well as vice-versa.

Adrian Shubert *A Social History of Modern Spain* (Routledge, UK). This accomplished first social history of Spain in English documents the turbulent history of post-1800 Spain from a people's perspective. An essential read to understand the origins of modern Andalucía's structural and social problems – such as *latifundismo* – in their Spanish and European context.

Colin Smith, Charles Melville & Ahmad Ubaydli *Christians and Moors in Spain* (Aris & Phillips, UK; 3 vols). A fascinating collection of documents by Spanish and Arabic writers from the Muslim conquest to the Christian supremacy which are intended for the lay reader as well as the academic. The bilingual parallel text (including Arabic) allows you to read first hand not only the key historical, military and literary accounts but also the invariably fascinating views of Christians and Moors on each other. Recommended.

Chris Stringer & Robin McKie *African Exodus* (Jonathan Cape, UK). If you want to grasp Spain's part in the Neanderthal story, this lively and accessible account by an expert in the field aided by the London *Observer*'s Science editor is the book. The account of the last of the Neanderthals hanging on in a cave above the Zaffaraya Pass in northern Málaga only adds to the drama of the landscape on the ground.

THE 20TH CENTURY AND THE CIVIL WAR

Gerald Brenan *The Spanish Labyrinth* (Cambridge UP, US/UK). First published in 1943, Brenan's study of the social and political background to the Civil War is tinged by personal experience, yet still an impressively rounded account.

Raymond Carr *Modern Spain 1875–1980* (Oxford UP, US/UK) and *The Spanish Tragedy: the Civil War in Perspective* (Weidenfeld, UK). Two of the best books available on modern Spanish history – concise and well-told narratives.

Ronald Fraser *Blood of Spain* (Pantheon, US). Subtitled "The Experience of Civil War, 1936–39", this is an impressive piece of research, constructed entirely of oral accounts. *In Hiding* (Penguin, UK), by the same author, is a fascinating individual account of a Republican mayor of Mijas (in Málaga) hidden by his family for thirty years until the Civil War amnesty of 1969. *The Pueblo* (Allen Lane, UK) is a penetrating and compelling study of the trials and struggles of one Costa del Sol mountain village seen through the eyes of its inhabitants which speaks for much of Andalucía today.

Ian Gibson *Federico García Lorca* (Faber & Faber/Pantheon), *The Assassination of Federico García Lorca* (Penguin, UK) and *Lorca's Granada* (Faber & Faber, US/UK). The biography is a gripping book and *The Assassination* a brilliant reconstruction of the events at the end of his life, with an examination of fascist corruption and of the shaping influences on Lorca, twentieth-century Spain and the Civil War. Granada explores Lorca's city by way of a collection of fascinating walks around the town.

Gerald Howson *Arms for Spain: the Untold Story of the Spanish Civil War* (John Murray, UK). One of the most important books of recent times uses recently opened Russian and Polish archives to explain how the Republicans were duped, double-crossed and betrayed by almost every government (including the Nazis who used the profits to finance a clandestine drugs ring) they attempted to purchase arms from – with their avowed ally Moscow one of the major culprits.

Joe Monk *With the Reds in Andalucía* (out of print). One Irishman's account of the optimism, hell, and finally despair, of fighting with the Irish Brigade of the international volunteers during the Civil War.

Paul Preston *Concise History of the Spanish Civil War* (Fontana/HarperCollins), *Franco* (HarperCollins, UK/US), *The Triumph of Democracy in Spain* (Routledge, UK). A formidable expert on the period, Preston has succeeded in his attempt to provide a manageable guide to the Civil War labyrinth – with powerful illustrations. *Franco* is a penetrating – and monumental – biography of the dictator and his regime, which provides as clear a picture as any yet published of how he won the Civil War, survived in power so long, and what, twenty years on from his death, was his significance. *Triumph* presents the absorbing story of the unravelling of the Franco years and the ultimate burial of the past with the election of the 1982 Socialist government.

Hugh Thomas *The Spanish Civil War* (Penguin/Touchstone). This exhaustive 1000-page study is regarded (both in Spain and abroad) as the definitive history of the Civil War, but is not as accessible for the general reader as Preston's account (above).

ART AND ARCHITECTURE

Marianne Barrucand and Achim Bednoz *Moorish Architecture* (Taschen, Germany). A beautifully illustrated guide to the major Moorish monuments.

Bernard Bevan *History of Spanish Architecture* (Batsford UK; out of print). Classic study of Iberian and Ibero-American architecture which includes extensive coverage of the Mudéjar, Plateresque and Baroque periods.

Titus Burckhardt *Moorish Culture in Spain* (out of print). An outstanding book which opens up ways of looking at Spain's Islamic monuments, explaining their patterns and significance and the social environment in which, and for which, they were produced.

Jerrilyn D. Dodds *Al-Andalus* (Abrams, UK/US). An in-depth study of the arts and monuments of Moorish Andalucía, put together as a catalogue for a major exhibition at the Alhambra.

Godfrey Goodwin *Islamic Spain* (Viking, UK/Chronicle Books, US). Architectural guide with descriptions of virtually every significant Islamic building in Spain, and a fair amount of background. Portable enough to take along.

José Gudiol *The Arts of Spain* (Thames & Hudson, UK). Good general introduction to Spanish art covering prehistory to Picasso.

Michael Jacobs *Alhambra* (Frances Lincoln/ Rizzoli). If you've fallen under the Alhambra's spell then this sumptuously produced volume with outstanding photographs and expert commentary will rekindle the memory. Authoritatively guides you through the history and architecture of Andalucía's emblematic monument placing it in its Islamic context, and concludes with a fascinating essay on the hold that the palace has had on later artists, travellers and writers from Irving and Ford to de Falla and Lorca.

David Talbot Rice *Islamic Art* (Thames & Hudson, UK). A classic introduction to the whole subject.

Meyer Schapiro *Romanesque Art* (Thames & Hudson/Braziller). An excellent, illustrated survey of Romanesque art and architecture – and its Visigothic and Mozarabic precursors.

Sacheverell Sitwell *Spanish Baroque* (Ayer, US). First published in 1931, this is interesting mainly for the absence of anything better on the subject.

George Kubler and Martin Soria *Art and Architecture in Spain and Portugal 1500–1800* (Pelican, UK). Provides an alternative to, if not a vast improvement on, the work above.

Anatzu Zabalbeascoa *The New Spanish Architecture* (Rizzoli, UK/US). A superb, highly illustrated study of the new Spanish architecture of the 1980s and 1990s in Barcelona, Madrid, Sevilla, and elsewhere.

FICTION AND POETRY

SPANISH FICTION

Pedro de Alarcón *The Three-Cornered Hat and Other Stories* (out of print). Ironic nineteenth-century tales of the previous century's corruption, bureaucracy and absolutism by a writer born in Guadix. He also wrote *Alpujarra* (out of print), a not very well observed tour through the Sierra Nevada.

Miguel de Cervantes *Don Quixote* (Penguin/Signet). Quixote (or Quijote) is of course the classic of Spanish literature and remains an excellent and witty read, especially in J.M. Cohen's fine translation.

Juan Ramón Jiménez *Platero and I* (out of print). Andalucía's Nobel Prize-winning poet and writer from Moguer in Huelva paints a lyrically evocative picture of Andalucía and its people in conversations with his donkey, Platero.

Antonio Machado *Eighty Poems* and *Juan de Mairena* (out of print). The best-known works in English of this eminent *sevillano* poet and writer. The latter novel draws on his experience as a schoolteacher in Baeza.

MODERN FICTION

Arturo Barea *The Forging of a Rebel* (out of print). Superb autobiographical trilogy, taking in the Spanish war in Morocco in the 1920s, and Barea's own part in the Civil War in Andalucía and elsewhere. The books were published under the individual titles *The Forge*, *The Track* and *The Clash*.

Arturo Pérez Reverte, *The Seville Communion* (Harvill Press, UK). An entertaining crime yarn by one of Spain's leading writers involving a hacker in the Pope's computer, a stubborn old local priest up against rapacious bankers eager to bulldoze his church, a number of corpses, and an investigator dispatched by the Vatican. All is played out against the colourfully described backdrop of Sevilla.

PLAYS AND POETRY

A.J. Arberry (trans.) *Moorish Poetry* (Cambridge UP, UK). Excellent collection of Hispano-Arab verse.

Cola Franzen (trans.) *Poems of Arab Andalusia* (City Lights, US). Sensitively rendered collection of verse by some of the best poets of Moorish al-Andalus.

Federico García Lorca *Five Plays: Comedies and Tragicomedies* (Penguin/New Directions); *Selected Poems* (Bloodaxe Books, UK); *Poem of the Deep Song* (City Lights, US). Andalucía's great pre-Civil War playwright and poet. The first two volumes have his major theatrical works and poems, whilst the latter is a moving poetic paean to *cante jondo*, flamenco's blues, inspired by his contact with *gitano* culture. Arturo Barea's *Lorca: the Poet and His People* is also of interest.

San Juan de la Cruz *The Poetry of Saint John of the Cross* (Penguin, UK). Excellent translation by South African poet Roy Campbell of the poems of this mystical confessor to Teresa of Ávila who died at Úbeda.

FOREIGN FICTION

Tariq Ali *Shadows of the Pomegranate Tree* (Chatto & Windus, UK). Pakistani/British author digs into his Muslim roots to come up with a story about the end of Nasrid Granada seen through the eyes of a well-to-do family.

Douglas Day *Journey of the Wolf* (Penguin, UK). Outstanding first novel by an American writer, given the seal of approval by Graham Greene ("gripping and poignant"). The subject is a Civil War fighter, "El Lobo", who returns as a fugitive to Poqueira, his village in the Alpujarras, forty years on.

Ernest Hemingway *Fiesta/The Sun Also Rises* (Cape/Scribner) and *For Whom the Bell Tolls* (Cape/Scribner). Hemingway remains a big part of the American myth of Spain. *Fiesta* contains some lyrically beautiful writing while the latter – set in Civil War Andalucía – is a good deal more laboured. He also published an enthusiastic and not very good account of bullfighting, *Death in the Afternoon* (Cape/ Scribner).

David Hewson *Semana Santa* (Harper Collins UK/US). A well-crafted whodunnit set against the background of Sevilla's major religious event by a journo-turned-writer. Strong on detail.

Amin Maalouf *Leo the African* (Quartet, UK). A wonderful historical novel, recreating the life of Leo Africanus, the fifteenth-century Moorish geographer, in the last years of the kingdom of Granada, and on his subsequent exile in Morocco and world travels.

SPECIALIST GUIDEBOOKS

M.J. Gómez Lara & J. Jiménez Barrientos *Guía de la Semana Santa en Sevilla* (Taba Press, Spain). The best guide available to Semana Santa in Sevilla – and a book for which you don't need very much Spanish, all the processions and routes are detailed along with superb illustrations.

Charles Teetor *Strolling through Seville* (Iberica, UK/US). More anecdotal version of the below with rather wobbly references to the Civil War.

Christopher Turner *The Penguin Guide to Seville* (Penguin, UK/US). A set of interesting guided walks around Andalucía's capital city.

HIKING AND CYCLING

J.L. Barrenetxea & K. Muñoz *La Alpujarra en Bici* (Sua Edizioak, Spain). An excellent guide to getting your bike around the villages and landscape of this stunningly picturesque corner of Andalucía. It forms part of a superb range of regional guides for cyclists, functionally ringbound, with detailed maps and route contours.

David and Ros Brawn *Alpujarras: A Walking Guide to the Poqueira and Trevélez Valleys* (Discovery UK; ☎ & fax 01604/752576). Details seventeen walks with accompanying maps – graded according to time distance and difficulty – in the this outstandingly picturesque corner of the Alpujarras.

José Luís Clavero Toledo *Sendas y Caminos por los Campos de la Axarquía* (Editorial Clave, Málaga). Excellent Spanish guidebook to this scenic corner of Málaga Province with loads of background on the region, information on flora and fauna as well as seventeen clearly described walks.

Robin Collomb *Sierra Nevada* (West Col, UK). A detailed guide aimed primarily at serious hikers and climbers.

Chris Craggs *Andalusian Rock Climbs* (Cicerone Press, UK). Introductory guide to one of Andalucía's fastest-growing sports. Has descriptions of all the major climbs plus details of how to get there.

Marc S. Dubin *Trekking in Spain* (Lonely Planet, UK/US). A detailed and practical trekking guide (with maps) by a Rough Guide author moonlighting for the opposition. It has a section on Andalucía's Sierra Nevada.

John & Christine Oldfield *Andalucía and the Costa del Sol* (Sunflower Books). This new addition to the popular *Landscapes* walking guide series has twenty-three clearly described walks (with maps) ranging from 5km to 22km in Las Alpujarras, Sierra Nevada, Axarquía and Grazalema, as well as the areas bordering the Costa del Sol.

Guías Penthalon (Penthalon, Spain). Detailed and reliable series of walking guides to various regions of Andalucía including the Sierra de Aracena and Sierra Nevada.

Interguías Clave *50 Rutas por la Serranía de Ronda* (widely available in bookshops in Andalucía). Fifty walking routes between six and forty kilometres in the Serranía de Ronda are well described with sketch maps. Also has information on refuges and places to find food and accommodation.

Andy Walmsley *Walking in the Sierra Nevada* (Cicerone, UK). Forty five walks of varying distance and difficulty from three-hour strolls to the seriously arduous Tres Mils (3000m-plus) peaks.

WILDLIFE

Ernest García and Andrew Paterson *Where to Watch Birds in Southern Spain* (A&C Black, UK). A well-planned guide to bird-watching sites throughout Andalucía with location maps and reports detailing species to be seen according to season.

Frederic Grunfeld and Teresa Farino *Wild Spain* (Sheldrake Press/Sierra Club). A knowledgeable and practical guide to Spain's national parks, ecology and wildlife with a section on Andalucía. Highly recommended.

Heinzel, Fitter and Parslow *Collins Guide to the Birds of Britain and Europe* (Collins, UK). Alternative to the *Collins* below. Also includes North Africa and the Middle East.

John Measures *The Wildlife Travelling Companion: Spain* (Crowood Press, UK). Clearly laid-out field guide to specific wildlife areas complete with an illustrated index of the most common flora and fauna.

Peterson, Mountfort and Hollom *Collins Field Guide to the Birds of Britain and Europe* (Collins Reference/Houghton Mifflin). Standard reference book – covers most birds in Spain though you may find yourself confused by the bird-song descriptions.

Oleg Polunin and Anthony Huxley *Flowers of the Mediterranean* (Chatto, UK). Useful if by no means exhaustive field guide.

FOOD AND WINE

Nicholas Butcher *The Spanish Kitchen* (Macmillan, UK). A practical and knowledgeable guide to creating Spanish – and *andaluz* – dishes when you get back. Lots of informative detail on tapas, olive oil, jamón serrano and herbs.

Bob Carrick *Ventas Within a Short Drive of the Costa del Sol* (Santana, Málaga). Useful guide to some of the best *ventas* – Spain's bargain roadside restaurants – within easy reach of the Málaga coast. Widely available at bookshops in major resorts.

Penelope Casas *The Foods and Wines of Spain* (Penguin/Knopf) and *Tapas: the little dishes of Spain* (Pavilion). An excellent overview of classic Spanish and Andalucian cuisine, plus the same author's guide to the *tapas* labyrinth.

Alan Davidson *The Tio Pepe Guide to the Seafood of Spain and Portugal* (Anness, UK). An indispensible pocket book that details and illustrates every fish and crustacean you're likely to meet in Andalucía.

Julian Jeffs *Sherry* (Faber, UK). The story of sherry – history, production, blending and brands. Rightly a classic and the best introduction to Andalucía's great wine.

Elisabeth Luard *The La Ina Book of Tapas* (Martin/Simon & Schuster) and *Flavours of Andalucía* (Collins & Brown, UK). Once you're hooked on *tapas*, this is the bible for all classic recipes. The Andalucía volume parades the major dishes of the region province by province.

Maite Manjon *Gastronomy of Spain and Portugal* (Garamond, UK). Useful alphabetical guide to food and drink on the peninsula.

Mark and Kim Millon *Wine Roads of Spain* (HarperCollins, UK/US). Everything you ever wanted to know about Spanish wine and sherry: when it's made, how it's made and where to find it, with lots of useful maps.

John Radford, *The New Spain* (Mitchell Beazley, UK). Lavish coffee table format disguises this book's serious content: a detailed region-by-region guide to Spanish wine with colour maps, bodega and vintage evaluations and fine illustrations.

Jan Read *Guide to the Wines of Spain* (Mitchell Beazley, UK). Encyclopedic (yet pocketable) guide to the classic and emerging wines of Spain by a leading authority. Includes maps, vintages and vineyards.

Antonio Zapata *Guía Gastronomica de la Alpujarra* (Junta de Andalucía, Spain). Spanish guide to the eastern, as well as western Alpujarras detailing village restaurants and *ventas* and their specialities. The latter part of the book has numerous *alpujarreña* recipes.

LEARNING SPANISH/LIVING IN SPAIN

Breakthrough Spanish (Macmillan, UK). The best of the tape and book linked home study courses which aims to give you a reasonable fluency within three months. The same series has advanced and business courses.

Collins Spanish Dictionary (HarperCollins UK/US). Recognized as the best single volume bookshelf dictionary. Regularly revised and updated so make sure to get the latest edition.

Get by in Spanish (BBC Publications, UK; book and cassette). One of the BBC's excellent crash-course introductions which gets you to survival level (bars, restaurants, asking the way, etc) Spanish in a couple of weeks.

Jonathon Packer *Live and Work in Spain and Portugal* (Vacation Work, UK). Well researched handbook full of useful information on moving to the peninsula, buying property, seeking work, starting a business, finding schools and lots more.

Rough Guide Spanish Dictionary (Rough Guides). Good pocket-size dictionary which should help with most travel situations.

LANGUAGE

Once you get into it, Spanish is one of the easiest languages to learn – and you'll be helped everywhere by people who are eager to try and understand even the most faltering attempt. English is spoken, but only in the main tourist areas to any extent, and wherever you are you'll get a far better reception if you at least try communicating with Spaniards in their own tongue. Being understood, of course, is only half the problem – getting the gist of the reply, often rattled out at a furious pace, may prove far more difficult.

The rules of **pronunciation** are pretty straightforward and, once you get to know them, strictly observed. Unless there's an **accent**, words ending in d, l, r, and z are stressed on the last syllable, all others on the second last. All **vowels** are pure and short; combinations have predictable results.

A somewhere between the "A" sound of back and that of father

E as in get

I as in police

O as in hot

U as in rule

C in *castellano* (standard Spanish) is lisped before E and I, hard otherwise: *cerca* is pronounced "thairka". However, many parts of Andalucía pronounce this case as an "s" – "sairka" or even "Andalusia".

G works the same way, a guttural "H" sound (like the ch in loch) before E or I, a hard G elsewhere – *gigante* becomes "higante".

H is always silent

J the same sound as a guttural G: *jamón* is pronounced "hamon".

LL sounds like an English Y or LY: *tortilla* is pronounced torteeya/torteelya.

N is as in English unless it has a tilde (accent) over it, when it becomes NY: *mañana* sounds like "manyana".

QU is pronounced like an English K.

R is rolled, RR doubly so.

V sounds more like B, *vino* becoming "beano".

X has an S sound before consonants, normal X before vowels.

Z (in *castellano*) is the same as a soft C, so *cerveza* becomes "thairvaitha", but again much of Andalucía prefers the "s" sound – "sairvaisa".

A list of a few essential words and phrases follows which should be enough to get you started, though if you're travelling for any length of time, a dictionary or phrasebook is obviously a worthwhile investment. If you're using a dictionary, bear in mind that in Spanish CH, LL, and N count as separate letters and are listed after C, L, and N respectively. For recommended books and tapes on learning Spanish, see the "Books" section.

SPANISH WORDS AND PHRASES

BASICS

Yes, No, OK	*Sí, No, Vale*	With, Without	*Con, Sin*
Please, Thank you	*Por favor, Gracias*	Good, Bad	*Buen(o)/a, Mal(o)/a*
Where, When	*Dónde, Cuando*	Big, Small	*Gran(de), Pequeño/a*
What, How much	*Qué, Cuánto*	Cheap, Expensive	*Barato, Caro*
Here, There	*Aquí, Allí*	Hot, Cold	*Caliente, Frío*
This, That	*Esto, Eso*	More, Less	*Más, Menos*
Now, Later	*Ahora, Más tarde*	Today, Tomorrow	*Hoy, Mañana*
Open, Closed	*Abierto/a, Cerrado/a*	Yesterday	*Ayer*

GREETINGS AND RESPONSES

Hello, Goodbye	*Hola, Adiós*	Not at all/You're welcome	*De nada*
Good morning	*Buenos días*	Do you speak English?	*¿Habla (usted) inglés?*
Good afternoon/night	*Buenas tardes/noches*	I don't speak Spanish	*(No) Hablo español*
See you later	*Hasta luego*	My name is…	*Me llamo…*
Sorry	*Lo siento/disculpéme*	What's your name?	*¿Como se llama usted?*
Excuse me	*Con permiso/perdón*	I am English/	*Soy inglés(a)/australiano(a)/*
How are you?	*¿Como está (usted)?*	Australian/Canadian/	*canadiense(a)/*
I (don't) understand	*(No) Entiendo*	American/Irish/	*americano(a)/irlandés(a)*

NEEDS – HOTELS AND TRANSPORT

I want	*Quiero*	How do I get to…?	*¿Por dónde se va a…?*
I'd like	*Quisiera*	Left, right, straight on	*Izquierda, derecha,*
Do you know…?	*¿Sabe…?*		*todo recto*
I don't know	*No sé*	Where is…?	*¿Dónde está…?*
There is (is there)?	*(¿)Hay(?)*	…the bus station	*…la estación de*
Give me…	*Deme…*		*autobuses*
(one like that)	*(uno así)*	…the railway	
Do you have…?	*¿Tiene…?*	station	*…a estación de*
…the time	*…la hora*		*ferrocarril*
…a room	*…una habitación*	…the nearest bank	*…el banco mas cercano*
…with two beds/	*…con dos camas*	…the post office	*…el correos/la oficina*
double bed	*cama matrimonial*		*de correos*
…with shower/bath	*…con ducha/baño*	…the toilet	*…el baño/aseo/*
It's for one person	*Es para una persona*		*servicio*
(two people)	*(dos personas)*	Where does the bus	*¿De dónde sale el*
…for one night	*…para una noche*	to…leave from?	*autobús para…?*
(one week)	*(una semana)*	Is this the train for	*¿Es este el tren para*
It's fine, how much		Sevilla?	*Sevilla?*
is it?	*¿Está bien, cuánto es?*	I'd like a (return)	*Quisiera un billete*
It's too expensive	*Es demasiado caro*		*(de ida y vuelta)*
Don't you have any	*¿No tiene algo más*	ticket to…	*para…*
thing cheaper?	*barato?*	What time does it	*¿A qué hora sale*
Can one…?	*¿Se puede…?*	leave (arrive in…)?	*(llega a…)?*
camp (near) here?	*¿acampar aquí (cerca)?*	What is there to eat?	*¿Qué hay para comer?*
Is there a hostel		What's that?	*¿Qué es eso?*
nearby?	*¿Hay un hostal aquí*	What's this called in	*¿Como se llama este*
	cerca?	Spanish?	*en español?*

NUMBERS AND DAYS

1	*un/uno/una*	12	*doce*	70	*setenta*	second	*segundo/a*
2	*dos*	13	*trece*	80	*ochenta*	third	*tercero/a*
3	*tres*	14	*catorce*	90	*noventa*	fifth	*quinto/a*
4	*cuatro*	15	*quince*	100	*cien(to)*	tenth	*décimo/a*
5	*cinco*	16	*diez y seis*	101	*ciento uno*	Monday	*lunes*
6	*seis*	20	*veinte*	200	*doscientos*	Tuesday	*martes*
7	*siete*	21	*veintiuno*	201	*doscientos uno*	Wednesday	*miércoles*
8	*ocho*	30	*treinta*	500	*quinientos*	Thursday	*jueves*
9	*nueve*	40	*cuarenta*	1000	*mil*	Friday	*viernes*
10	*diez*	50	*cincuenta*	2000	*dos mil*	Saturday	*sábado*
11	*once*	60	*sesenta*	first	*primero/a*	Sunday	*domingo*

SPANISH TERMS: A GLOSSARY

ALAMEDA park or tree-lined promenade.

ALBARIZA type of soil in wine-growing zones with high chalk content enabling retention of moisture.

ALCAZABA Moorish castle.

ALCÁZAR Moorish fortified palace.

ALMOHADS Muslims originally of Berber stock, who toppled the Almoravids and ruled Spain in the late twelfth and early thirteenth centuries.

ALMORAVIDS fanatical Berber dynasty from the Sahara who ruled much of Spain in the eleventh and twelfth centuries.

ARTESONADO wooden coffered ceiling of Moorish origin or inspiration.

ATALAYA watch tower.

AUTOVÍA/AUTOPISTA Dual carriageway or highway/motorway or expressway.

AYUNTAMIENTO town hall (also CASA CONSISTORIAL).

AZULEJOS glazed ceramic tiles (originally blue – hence the name).

BARRIO suburb or quarter.

BODEGA cellar, wine bar, or warehouse.

BRACERO landless agricultural worker.

CALLE street.

CAMARÍN shrine (inside a church) with a venerated image.

CAMPIÑA flat stretch of farmland or countryside.

CANTE JONDO deeply-felt flamenco song.

CAPILLA MAYOR chapel containing the high altar.

CAPILLA REAL royal chapel.

CARMEN Granadan villa with garden.

CARRETERA main road

CARTUJA Carthusian monastery.

CASINO social and gaming club.

CASTILLO castle.

CHIRINGUITO beachfront restaurant.

CHURRIGUERESQUE extreme form of Baroque art named after José Churriguera (1665–1725) and his extended family, its main exponents.

CIUDAD town or city.

CIUDADELA citadel.

COLEGIATA collegiate (large parish) church.

COMUNIDAD AUTÓNOMA autonomous region with significant powers of self government. Andalucía is one of seventeen autonomous regions set up following the return to democracy in the 1970s.

CONVENTO monastery or convent.

CONVERSO Jew who converted to Christianity.

CORO central part of church built for the choir.

CORO ALTO raised choir, often above west door of a church.

CORREOS post office.

CORRIDA DE TOROS bullfight.

CORTIJO rural farmhouse in Andalucía.

COTO hunting reserve.

CUESTA slope/hill.

CUEVA cave.

CUSTODIA large receptacle or monstrance for Eucharist wafers.

DESAMORTIZACIÓN (disentailment) nineteenth-century expropriation of church buildings and lands.

DUENDE to have soul (in flamenco).

EMBALSE artificial lake, reservoir or dam.

ERMITA hermitage.

FERIA annual fair.

GITANO gypsy.

IGLESIA church.

ISABELLINE ornamental form of late Gothic developed during the reign of Isabel and Fernando.

JORNALERO landless agricultural day labourer.

JUDERÍA Jewish quarter.

JUERGA (gypsy) shindig.

JUNTA DE ANDALUCÍA government of the Autonomous Region of Andalucía.

LATIFUNDIO large estate.

LONJA stock exchange building.

MARISMAS marshes.

MEDINA Moorish town.

MERCADO market.

MEZQUITA mosque.

MIHRAB prayer niche of Moorish mosque facing towards Mecca.

MIRADOR viewing point (literally balcony).

MONASTERIO monastery or convent.

MORISCO Muslim Spaniard subject to medieval Christian rule – and nominally baptized.

MOZARABE Christian subject to medieval Moorish rule; normally allowed freedom of worship. Mozarabic is the architectural style evolved by Christians under Arab domination.

MUDÉJAR Muslim Spaniard subject to medieval Christian rule, but retaining Islamic worship; most commonly a term applied to architecture which includes buildings built by Moorish craftsmen for the Christian rulers and later designs influenced by the Moors. The 1890s–1930s saw a Mudéjar revival, blended with Art Nouveau and Art Deco forms.

PALACIO aristocratic mansion.

PANTANO reservoir held by a dam.

PARADOR luxury state-run hotel, often converted from minor monument.

PARROQUIA parish church.

PASEO promenade; also the evening stroll thereon.

PASO float bearing tableau carried in Semana Santa processions.

PATIO inner courtyard.

PISCINA swimming pool

PLATERESQUE elaborately decorative Renaissance style, the sixteenth-century successor of Isabelline forms. Named for its resemblance to silversmiths' work (*platería*).

PLAZA square.

PLAZA DE TOROS bullring.

PLAZA MAYOR a town or city's main square regardless of its name.

POSADA old name for an inn.

PUEBLO village or town.

PUERTA gateway, also mountain pass.

PUERTO port.

RAMBLA dry river bed.

RECONQUISTA the Christian reconquest of Moorish Spain between 718 and 1492.

REJA iron screen or grille, often fronting a window or guarding a chapel.

RETABLO carved or painted altarpiece.

RÍO river.

ROCOCO late Baroque style with a profusion of rock-like forms, scrolls and crimped shells. From the French *rocaille* – "rock-work".

ROMERÍA religious procession to a rural shrine.

SACRISTÍA, SAGRARIO sacristy or sanctuary of a church.

SAETA passionate flamenco song in praise of the Virgin and Christ.

SEBKA decorative brickwork developed by the Almohads (eg, Giralda).

SEMANA SANTA Holy Week, celebrated throughout Andalucía with elaborate processions.

SEVILLANA rythmic flamenco dance.

SIERRA mountain range.

SILLERÍA choir stall.

SOLAR aristocratic town mansion.

SOLERA blending system for sherry and brandy.

TABLAO flamenco show.

TAIFA small Moorish kingdom, many of which emerged after the disintegration of the Córdoba Caliphate.

TRASCORO end-wall of the choir.

TORNO dumbwaiter used by convents to sell their cakes and pastries.

VEGA cultivated fertile plain.

VENTA roadside inn.

POLITICAL PARTIES AND ACRONYMS

ETA Basque terrorist organization. Its political wing is Herri Batasuna.

FALANGE Franco's old fascist party; now officially defunct.

FUERZA NUEVA descendants of the above, also on the way out.

IR Izquierda Republicana, left-wing republican party.

IU Izquierda Unida, broad-left alliance of communists and others.

MC Movimiento Comunista (Communist Movement), small radical offshoot of the PCE.

MOC Movimiento de Objectores de Conciencia, peace group, concerned with NATO and conscription.

OTAN NATO.

PA Partido Andalucista, the Andalucian Nationalist Party

PASOC Partido de Acción Socialista, "traditional" socialist group to the left of the PSOE.

PCE Partido Comunista de España (Spanish Communist Party).

PP Partido Popular, the right-wing party formed by a union of Alianza Popular and the Christian Democrats, led by José María Aznar. Currently the government party.

PSOE Partido Socialista Obrero Español, the Spanish Socialist Workers' Party was in power for 14 years until defeated in 1996.

UGT Unión General de Trabajadores, Spain's most powerful trade union.

INDEX

Stay in touch with us!

ROUGH*NEWS* **is Rough Guides' free newsletter. In four issues a year we give you news, travel issues, music reviews, readers' letters and the latest dispatches from authors on the road.**

I would like to receive ROUGH*NEWS*: please put me on your free mailing list.

NAME . . . .

ADDRESS . . . .

Please clip or photocopy and send to: Rough Guides, 62–70 Shorts Gardens, London WC2H 9AH, England or Rough Guides, 375 Hudson Street, New York, NY 10014, USA.

ROUGH GUIDES: Travel

Amsterdam
Andalucia
Australia

Austria
Bali & Lombok
Barcelona
Belgium &
  Luxembourg
Belize
Berlin
Brazil
Britain
Brittany &
  Normandy
Bulgaria
California
Canada
Central America
Chile
China
Corfu & the
  Ionian Islands
Corsica
Costa Rica
Crete
Croatia
Cyprus
Czech & Slovak
  Republics
Dodecanese &
  the East Aegean

Dominican
  Republic
Ecuador
Egypt
England
Europe
Florida
France
French Hotels &
  Restaurants
  1999
Germany
Goa
Greece
Greek Islands
Guatemala
Hawaii
Holland
Hong Kong &
  Macau
Hungary
India
Indonesia
Ireland
Israel & the
  Palestinian
  Territories
Italy
Jamaica
Japan
Jordan

Kenya
Lake District
Laos
London
Los Angeles
Malaysia,
  Singapore &
  Brunei
Mallorca &
  Menorca
Maya World
Mexico
Morocco
Moscow
Nepal
New England
New York
New Zealand
Norway
Pacific
  Northwest
Paris
Peru
Poland
Portugal
Prague
Provence & the
  Côte d'Azur
The Pyrenees
Rhodes & the
  Dodecanese

Romania
St Petersburg
San Francisco
Sardinia
Scandinavia
Scotland
Scottish
  highlands and
  Islands
Sicily
Singapore
South Africa
South India
Southwest USA
Spain
Sweden
Syria

Thailand
Trinidad &
  Tobago
Tunisia
Turkey
Tuscany &
  Umbria
USA
Venice
Vienna
Vietnam
Wales
Washington DC
West Africa
Zimbabwe &
  Botswana

AVAILABLE AT ALL GOOD BOOKSHOPS

ROUGH GUIDES: Mini Guides, Travel Specials and Phrasebooks

MINI GUIDES

Antigua
Bangkok
Barbados
Big Island of
  Hawaii
Boston
Brussels
Budapest

Dublin
Edinburgh
Florence
Honolulu
Jerusalem
Lisbon
London
  Restaurants
Madrid
Maui
Melbourne
New Orleans
Rome
Seattle
St Lucia

Sydney
Tokyo
Toronto

TRAVEL SPECIALS

First-Time Asia
First-Time
  Europe
Women Travel

PHRASEBOOKS

Czech
Dutch

Egyptian Arabic
European
French
German
Greek
Hindi & Urdu
Hungarian
Indonesian
Italian
Japanese

Mandarin
  Chinese
Mexican
  Spanish
Polish
Portuguese
Russian
Spanish
Swahili
Thai
Turkish
Vietnamese

ROUGH GUIDES:
Reference and Music CDs

REFERENCE

Classical Music
Classical:
  100 Essential CDs
Drum'n'bass
House Music
Jazz
Music USA

Opera
Opera:
  100 Essential CDs
Reggae
Reggae:
  100 Essential CDs
Rock
Rock:
  100 Essential CDs
Techno
World Music
World Music:
  100 Essential CDs
English Football
European Football

Internet
Millennium

ROUGH GUIDE MUSIC CDs

Music of the
  Andes
Australian
  Aboriginal
Brazilian Music
Cajun & Zydeco

Classic Jazz
Music of
  Colombia
Cuban Music
Eastern Europe

Music of Egypt
English Roots
  Music
Flamenco
India & Pakistan
Irish Music
Music of Japan
Kenya & Tanzania
Native American
North African
Music of Portugal

Reggae
Salsa
Scottish Music
South African
  Music
Music of Spain
Tango
Tex-Mex
West African
  Music
World Music
World Music Vol 2
Music of
  Zimbabwe

AVAILABLE AT ALL GOOD BOOKSHOPS